D0926043

THE DOCTRINE AND COVENANTS

THE PEARL OF GREAT PRICE

Published by
The Church of Jesus Christ
of Latter-day Saints

Salt Lake City, Utah, USA

1994

Printed in the United States of America 4/2001

ABBREVIATIONS AND DESIGNATIONS
IN FOOTNOTES AND INDEX

Old Testament

Gen.	Genesis
Ex.	Exodus
Lev.	Leviticus
Num.	Numbers
Deut.	Deuteronomy
Josh.	Joshua
Judg.	Judges
Ruth	Ruth
1 Sam.	1 Samuel
2 Sam.	2 Samuel
1 Kgs.	1 Kings
2 Kgs.	2 Kings
1 Chr.	1 Chronicles
2 Chr.	2 Chronicles
Ezra	Ezra
Neh.	Nehemiah
Esth.	Esther
Job	Job
Ps.	Psalms
Prov.	Proverbs
Eccl.	Ecclesiastes
Song.	Song of Solomon
Isa.	Isaiah
Jer.	Jeremiah
Lam.	Lamentations
Ezek.	Ezekiel
Dan.	Daniel
Hosea	Hosea
Joel	Joel
Amos	Amos
Obad.	Obadiah
Jonah	Jonah
Micah	Micah
Nahum	Nahum
Hab.	Habakkuk
Zeph.	Zephaniah
Hag.	Haggai
Zech.	Zechariah
Mal.	Malachi

New Testament

Matt.	Matthew
Mark	Mark
Luke	Luke
John	John
Acts	Acts
Rom.	Romans
1 Cor.	1 Corinthians
2 Cor.	2 Corinthians
Gal.	Galatians
Eph.	Ephesians
Philip.	Philippians
Col.	Colossians
1 Thes.	1 Thessalonians
2 Thes.	2 Thessalonians
1 Tim.	1 Timothy
2 Tim.	2 Timothy
Titus	Titus
Philem.	Philemon
Heb.	Hebrews
James	James
1 Pet.	1 Peter
2 Pet.	2 Peter
1 Jn.	1 John
2 Jn.	2 John
3 Jn.	3 John
Jude	Jude
Rev.	Revelation

Book of Mormon

1 Ne.	1 Nephi
2 Ne.	2 Nephi
Jacob	Jacob
Enos	Enos
Jarom	Jarom
Omni	Omni
W of M	Words of Mormon
Mosiah	Mosiah
Alma	Alma
Hel.	Helaman
3 Ne.	3 Nephi
4 Ne.	4 Nephi
Morm.	Mormon
Ether	Ether
Moro.	Moroni

Doctrine and Covenants

D&C	Doctrine and Covenants
OD	Official Declaration

Pearl of Great Price

Moses	Moses
Abr.	Abraham
JS-M	Joseph Smith—Matthew
JS-H	Joseph Smith—History
A of F	Articles of Faith
BD	Bible Dictionary
HC	History of the Church
JST	Joseph Smith Translation
TG	Topical Guide

THE
DOCTRINE
AND
COVENANTS
OF
THE CHURCH OF JESUS CHRIST
OF LATTER-DAY SAINTS

CONTAINING REVELATIONS GIVEN TO
JOSEPH SMITH, THE PROPHET

WITH SOME ADDITIONS BY HIS SUCCESSORS
IN THE PRESIDENCY OF THE CHURCH

PUBLISHED BY
THE CHURCH OF JESUS CHRIST
OF LATTER-DAY SAINTS
SALT LAKE CITY, UTAH, U.S.A.

EXPLANATORY INTRODUCTION

The Doctrine and Covenants is a collection of divine revelations and inspired declarations given for the establishment and regulation of the kingdom of God on the earth in the last days. Although most of the sections are directed to members of The Church of Jesus Christ of Latter-day Saints, the messages, warnings, and exhortations are for the benefit of all mankind, and contain an invitation to all people everywhere to hear the voice of the Lord Jesus Christ, speaking to them for their temporal well-being and their everlasting salvation.

Most of the revelations in this compilation were received through Joseph Smith, Jun., the first prophet and president of The Church of Jesus Christ of Latter-day Saints. Others were issued through some of his successors in the Presidency. (See headings to Sections 135, 136, and 138, and Official Declarations 1 and 2.)

The book of Doctrine and Covenants is one of the standard works of the Church in company with the Holy Bible, the Book of Mormon, and the Pearl of Great Price. However, the Doctrine and Covenants is unique because it is not a translation of an ancient document, but is of modern origin and was given of God through his chosen prophets for the restoration of his holy work and the establishment of the kingdom of God on the earth in these days. In the revelations one hears the tender but firm voice of the Lord Jesus Christ, speaking anew in the dispensation of the fulness of times; and the work that is initiated herein is preparatory to his second coming, in fulfillment of and in concert with the words of all the holy prophets since the world began.

Joseph Smith, Jun., was born December 23, 1805, in Sharon, Windsor County, Vermont. During his early life he moved with his family to Manchester, in western New York. It was while he was living near Manchester in the spring of 1820, when he was fourteen years of age, that he experienced his first vision, in which he was visited in person by God, the Eternal Father, and his Son Jesus Christ. He was told in this vision that the true Church of Jesus Christ that had been established in New Testament times, and which had administered the fulness of the gospel, was no longer on the earth. Other divine manifestations followed in which he was taught by many angels; it was shown to him that God had a special work for him to do on the earth, and that through him the Church of Jesus Christ would be restored to the earth.

In the course of time Joseph Smith was enabled by divine assistance to translate and publish the Book of Mormon. In the meantime he and Oliver Cowdery were ordained to the Aaronic Priesthood by John the Baptist in May 1829 (D&C 13), and soon thereafter they were also ordained to the Melchizedek Priesthood by the ancient apostles Peter, James, and John (D&C 27: 12). Other ordinations followed in which priesthood keys were conferred upon them by Moses, Elijah, Elias, and many ancient prophets (D&C 110; 128: 18, 21). These ordinations were, in fact, a restoration of divine authority to man on the earth. On April 6, 1830, under heavenly direction, the Prophet Joseph Smith organized the Church, and thus the true Church of Jesus Christ is once again operative as an institution among men, with authority to teach the gospel and administer the ordinances of salvation. (See Pearl of Great Price, Joseph Smith—History 1: 1–75; D&C 20.)

These sacred revelations were received in answer to prayer, in times of need, and came out of real-life situations involving real people. The Prophet and his associates sought for divine guidance, and these revelations certify that they received it. In the revelations one sees the restoration and unfolding of the gospel of Jesus Christ and the ushering in of the dispensation of the fulness of times. The westward movement of the Church from New York and Pennsylvania, to Ohio, to Missouri, to Illinois, and finally to the Great Basin of western America, and the mighty struggles of the saints in attempting to build Zion on the earth in modern times, are also shown forth in these revelations.

Several of the earlier sections involve matters regarding the translation and publication of the Book of Mormon (see Sections 3, 5, 10, 17, 19). Some later sections reflect the work of the Prophet Joseph Smith in making an inspired translation of the Bible, during which many of the great doctrinal sections were received (see, for example, Sections 37, 45, 73, 76, 77, 86, 91, and 132, each of which has some direct relationship to the Bible translation).

In the revelations the doctrines of the gospel are set forth with explanations about such fundamental matters as the nature of the Godhead, the origin of man, the reality of Satan, the purpose of mortality, the necessity for obedience, the need for repentance, the workings of the Holy Spirit, the ordinances and performances that pertain to salvation, the destiny of the earth, the future conditions of man after the resurrection and the judgment, the eternity of the marriage relationship, and the eternal nature of the family. Likewise the gradual unfolding of the administrative structure of the Church is shown with the calling of bishops, the First Presidency, the Council of the Twelve, and the Seventy, and the establishment of other presiding offices and quorums. Finally, the testimony that is given of Jesus Christ—his divinity, his majesty, his perfection, his love, and his redeeming power—makes this book of great value to the human family and of more worth than the riches of the whole earth.

A number of the revelations were published in Zion (Independence), Missouri, in 1833, under the title *A Book of Commandments for the Government of the Church of Christ.* Concerning this publication the elders of the Church gave solemn testimony that the Lord had borne record to their souls that these revelations were true. As the Lord continued to communicate with his servants, an enlarged compilation was published two years later in Kirtland, Ohio, with the title *Doctrine and Covenants of the Church of the Latter Day Saints.* To this publication in 1835, the written testimony of the Twelve Apostles was attached as follows:

TESTIMONY OF THE
TWELVE APOSTLES TO THE TRUTH OF THE
BOOK OF DOCTRINE AND COVENANTS

The Testimony of the Witnesses to the Book of the Lord's Commandments, which commandments He gave to His Church through Joseph Smith Jun., who was appointed by the voice of the Church for this purpose:

We, therefore, feel willing to bear testimony to all the world of mankind, to every creature upon the face of the earth, that the Lord has borne record to our souls, through the Holy Ghost shed forth upon us, that these commandments were given by inspiration of God, and are profitable for all men and are verily true.

We give this testimony unto the world, the Lord being our helper; and it is through the grace of God the Father, and His Son, Jesus Christ, that we are permitted to have this privilege of bearing this testimony unto the world, in the which we rejoice exceedingly, praying the Lord always that the children of men may be profited thereby.

The names of the Twelve were:

Thomas B. Marsh	Orson Hyde	William Smith
David W. Patten	Wm. E. McLellin	Orson Pratt
Brigham Young	Parley P. Pratt	John F. Boynton
Heber C. Kimball	Luke S. Johnson	Lyman E. Johnson

In successive editions of the Doctrine and Covenants, additional revelations or other matters of record have been added, as received, and as accepted by competent assemblies or conferences of the Church.

Beginning with the 1835 edition a series of seven theological lessons was also included; these were titled the "Lectures on Faith." These had been prepared for use in the School of the Prophets in Kirtland, Ohio, in 1834–1835. Although profitable for doctrine and instruction, these lectures have been omitted from the Doctrine and Covenants since the 1921 edition because they were not given or presented as revelations to the whole Church.

In the current edition of the Doctrine and Covenants three documents have been included for the first time. These are Sections 137 and 138, setting forth the fundamentals of salvation for the dead; and Official Declaration 2, announcing that all worthy male members of the Church may be ordained to the priesthood without regard for race or color.

It is evident that some errors have been perpetuated in past editions, particularly in the historical portions of the section headings. Consequently this edition contains corrections of dates and place names and also a few other minor corrections when it seemed appropriate (such as discontinuing the unusual names beginning with Section 78). These changes have been made so as to bring the material into conformity with the historical documents. Other special features of this latest edition include maps showing the major geographical locations in which the revelations were received, plus improvements in cross references, section headings, and subject-matter summaries, all of which are designed to help readers to understand and rejoice in the message of the Lord as given in the Doctrine and Covenants.

CHRONOLOGICAL ORDER OF CONTENTS

	Time	Place					Sections
1823	September	Manchester, New York .	.	.	.	.	2
1828	July	Harmony, Pennsylvania .	.	.	.	.	3
	Summer	Harmony, Pennsylvania .	.	.	.	.	10
1829	February	Harmony, Pennsylvania .	.	.	.	.	4
	March	Harmony, Pennsylvania .	.	.	.	.	5
	April	Harmony, Pennsylvania .	.	.	.	6, 7, 8, 9
	May	Harmony, Pennsylvania .	.	.	.	11, 12, 13
	June	Fayette, New York	.	14, 15, 16, 17, 18
1830	March	Manchester, New York .	.	.	.	.	19
	April	Fayette, New York	.	.	.	.	20*, 21
	April	Manchester, New York .	.	.	.	22, 23
	July	Harmony, Pennsylvania .	.	.	.	24, 25, 26
	August	Harmony, Pennsylvania .	.	.	.	.	27
	September	Fayette, New York	.	28, 29, 30, 31
	October	Fayette, New York	.	.	.	32*, 33
	November	Fayette, New York	.	.	.	.	34
	December	Fayette, New York	.	.	.	35, 36, 37
1831	January	Fayette, New York	.	.	.	38, 39, 40
	February	Kirtland, Ohio	.	.	.	41, 42, 43, 44
	March	Kirtland, Ohio	.	.	45, 46, 47, 48, 49
	May	Kirtland, Ohio	.	.	.	.	.	50
	May	Thompson, Ohio	.	.	.	.	.	51
	June	Kirtland, Ohio	.	.	52, 53, 54, 55, 56
	July	Zion, Jackson County, Missouri	.	.	.	57
	August	Zion, Jackson County, Missouri	.	58, 59, 60
	August	By Missouri River, Missouri	.	.	.	61, 62
	August	Kirtland, Ohio	.	.	.	.	.	63
	September	Kirtland, Ohio	.	.	.	.	.	64
	October	Hiram, Ohio .	.	.	.	.	.	65
	October	Orange, Ohio .	.	.	.	.	.	66
	November	Hiram, Ohio .	.	.	1, 67, 68, 69, 133
	November	Kirtland, Ohio	.	.	.	.	.	70
	December	Hiram, Ohio .	.	.	.	.	.	71
	December	Kirtland, Ohio	.	.	.	.	.	72
1832	January	Hiram, Ohio .	.	.	.	.	73, 74
	January	Amherst, Ohio	.	.	.	.	.	75
	February	Hiram, Ohio .	.	.	.	.	.	76

* At or near place specified.

	Time	Place	Sections
1832	March	Hiram, Ohio . . .	77, 78, 79, 80, 81
	April	Jackson County, Missouri . . .	82, 83
	April	Independence, Missouri	83
	August	Hiram, Ohio	99
	September	Kirtland, Ohio	84
	November	Kirtland, Ohio	85
	December	Kirtland, Ohio . . .	86, 87*, 88
1833	February	Kirtland, Ohio	89
	March	Kirtland, Ohio	90, 91, 92
	May	Kirtland, Ohio	93, 94
	June	Kirtland, Ohio	95, 96
	August	Kirtland, Ohio	97, 98
	October	Perrysburg, New York	100
	December	Kirtland, Ohio	101
1834	February	Kirtland, Ohio . . .	102, 103
	April	Kirtland, Ohio	104*
	June	Fishing River, Missouri . . .	105
	November	Kirtland, Ohio	106
1835	March	Kirtland, Ohio	107
	August	Kirtland, Ohio	134
	December	Kirtland, Ohio	108
1836	January	Kirtland, Ohio	137
	March	Kirtland, Ohio	109
	April	Kirtland, Ohio	110
	August	Salem, Massachusetts	111
1837	July	Kirtland, Ohio	112
1838	March	Far West, Missouri	113*
	April	Far West, Missouri	114, 115
	May	Spring Hill, Daviess County, Missouri .	116
	July	Far West, Missouri . .	117, 118, 119, 120
1839	March	Liberty Jail, Clay County, Missouri	121, 122, 123
1841	January	Nauvoo, Illinois	124
	March	Nauvoo, Illinois	125
	July	Nauvoo, Illinois	126
1842	September	Nauvoo, Illinois	127, 128
1843	February	Nauvoo, Illinois	129
	April	Ramus, Illinois	130
	May	Ramus, Illinois	131
	July	Nauvoo, Illinois	132
1844	June	Nauvoo, Illinois	135
1847	January	Winter Quarters (now Nebraska) . .	136
1890	October	Salt Lake City, Utah . Official Declaration–1	
1918	October	Salt Lake City, Utah . . .	138
1978	June	Salt Lake City, Utah . Official Declaration–2	

* At or near place specified.

THE
DOCTRINE AND COVENANTS

SECTION 1

Revelation given through Joseph Smith the Prophet, during a special conference of elders of the Church, held at Hiram, Ohio, November 1, 1831. HC 1: 221–224. Many revelations had been received from the Lord prior to this time, and the compilation of these for publication in book form was one of the principal subjects passed upon at the conference. This section constitutes the Lord's Preface to the doctrines, covenants, and commandments given in this dispensation.

1–7, *The voice of warning is to all people;* 8–16, *Apostasy and wickedness precede the Second Coming;* 17–23, *Joseph Smith called to restore to earth the Lord's truths and powers;* 24–33, *The Book of Mormon brought forth and true Church established;* 34–36, *Peace shall be taken from the earth;* 37–39, *Search these commandments.*

HEARKEN, O ye people of my *b*church, saith the voice of him who dwells on high, and whose *c*eyes are upon all men; yea, verily I say: Hearken ye people from afar; and ye that are upon the islands of the sea, listen together.

2 For verily I say: The *a*voice of the Lord is unto all men, and there is none to *b*escape; and there is no eye that shall not see, neither *c*ear that shall not hear, neither *d*heart that shall not be penetrated.

3 And the *a*rebellious shall be *b*pierced with much *c*sorrow; for their iniquities shall be *d*spoken upon the housetops, and their secret acts shall be revealed.

4 And the *a*voice of warning shall be unto all people, by the mouths of my disciples, whom I have *b*chosen in these *c*last days.

5 And they shall *a*go forth and none shall stay them, for I the Lord have commanded them.

6 Behold, this is mine *a*authority, and the authority of my servants,

1 1*a* Deut. 32: 1; Isa. 1: 2; 49: 1.
 b 3 Ne. 27: 3 (1–8); D&C 20: 1; 21: 3. TG Jesus Christ, Head of the Church.
 c Ps. 33: 18; Amos 9: 8; D&C 38: 7 (7–8). TG God, Omniscience of.
 2*a* Ps. 65: 2; Micah 1: 2; D&C 1: 34 (34–35); 18: 28 (26–28); 39: 15; 42: 58; 68: 8; 138: 30. TG Israel, Mission of.

 b Job 34: 22; 1 Thes. 5: 3.
 c TG Conversion.
 d TG Heart.
 3*a* TG Rebellion.
 b TG Conscience.
 c Ps. 32: 10.
 d Prov. 28: 13; Isa. 57: 12 (11–12); 2 Ne. 27: 11; Morm. 5: 8; D&C 88: 108; 112: 25 (25–26).

 4*a* Ezek. 3: 21 (17–21); D&C 63: 37. TG Israel, Mission of; Mission of Latter-day Saints; Warn, Warnings.
 b TG Priesthood, Authority.
 c TG Last Days.
 5*a* TG Missionary Work.
 6*a* TG Jesus Christ, Authority of; Priesthood, Authority.

and my preface unto the book of my [b]commandments, which I have given them to [c]publish unto you, O [d]inhabitants of the earth.

7 Wherefore, [a]fear and [b]tremble, O ye people, for what the Lord have [c]decreed in them shall be [d]fulfilled.

8 And verily I say unto you, that they who go forth, bearing these tidings unto the inhabitants of the earth, to them is power given to [a]seal both on earth and in heaven, the unbelieving and [b]rebellious;

9 Yea, verily, to seal them up unto the [a]day when the [b]wrath of God shall be poured out upon the [c]wicked without measure—

10 Unto the [a]day when the Lord shall come to [b]recompense unto every man according to his [c]work, and [d]measure to every man according to the measure which he has measured to his fellow man.

11 Wherefore the voice of the Lord is unto the ends of the earth, that all that will hear may hear:

12 Prepare ye, [a]prepare ye for that

which is to come, for the Lord is [b]nigh;

13 And the [a]anger of the Lord is kindled, and his [b]sword is bathed in heaven, and it shall fall upon the inhabitants of the earth.

14 And the [a]arm of the Lord shall be revealed; and the [b]day cometh that they who will not [c]hear the voice of the Lord, neither the voice of his [d]servants, neither give [e]heed to the words of the prophets and [f]apostles, shall be [g]cut off from among the people;

15 For they have [a]strayed from mine [b]ordinances, and have [c]broken mine [d]everlasting covenant;

16 They [a]seek not the Lord to establish his righteousness, but every man [b]walketh in his own [c]way, and after the [d]image of his own god, whose image is in the likeness of the world, and whose substance is that of an idol, which waxeth [e]old and shall perish in Babylon, even [f]Babylon the great, which shall fall.

17 Wherefore, I the Lord, [a]know-

6b D&C 33: 14; 42: 13;
   51: 4.
 c Acts 13: 49; D&C 72:
   21.
 d Joel 1: 2; Micah 1: 2.
7a Deut. 5: 29; Eccl. 12:
   13.
 b Ezra 9: 4.
 c Isa. 10: 22 (21–34);
   Matt. 24: 34.
 d Isa. 34: 16 (16–17).
8a D&C 68: 12.
   TG Priesthood, Keys
   of; Sealing.
 b TG Rebellion.
9a 2 Cor. 1: 14.
 b Nahum 1: 3;
   Mosiah 16: 2; JS-M 1:
   55 (31, 55).
10a TG Day of the Lord.
 b Prov. 11: 31; Isa. 65:
   6 (6–7, 11); Ezek. 7: 4;
   Mosiah 12: 1; D&C 56:
   19.
   TG Jesus Christ, Judge.
 c Job 34: 11; Prov. 24:
   12; Isa. 59: 18; Alma 9:

28; 36: 15; 41: 3 (2–
5); 42: 27; D&C 6: 33.
 d Matt. 7: 2; Luke 6: 38.
12a TG Millennium, Pre-
   paring a People for.
 b D&C 2: 1; 49: 28; 58:
   65; 68: 11; 68: 35; 84:
   119.
   TG Jesus Christ,
   Second Coming.
13a D&C 63: 6. TG Anger;
   God, Indignation of.
 b Ezek. 21: 3; D&C 35:
   14; 84: 114; 85: 3.
14a Isa. 40: 10 (5–10);
   D&C 45: 47; 56: 1.
 b Zech. 14: 1.
 c Ezek. 33: 31 (30–33);
   Matt. 11: 15; Heb. 5:
   11 (11–14); 2 Ne. 9:
   31; Mosiah 26: 28;
   Moses 6: 27.
   TG Hardheartedness;
   Haughtiness.
 d TG Prophets, Rejection
   of.
 e D&C 11: 2.
   TG Disobedience.
 f TG Apostles.
 g Acts 3: 23 (22–23);
   Alma 50: 20; D&C 5:

15 a 5: 50; 8: 56; 3: 6 (3, 1, 3–4).
 a Josh. 23: 16 (15–16);
   Isa. 24: 5; D&C 3: 6
   (6–8); 104: 52.
 b TG Ordinance.
 c TG Apostasy of
   Individuals; Apostasy
   of Israel; Apostasy
   of Early Christian
   Church.
 d Ezek. 44: 7.
   TG New and Ever-
   lasting Covenant.
16a Matt. 6: 33.
 b TG Walking in Dark-
   ness.
 c Isa. 53: 6; Jer. 44: 17.
 d Gen. 6: 12; D&C 82: 6;
   Moses 8: 29.
 e Ex. 20: 4; Isa. 41: 24
   (24, 29); 3 Ne. 21: 17
   (17–19).
   TG Idolatry.
 f Isa. 50: 9.
 g Isa. 21: 9; 48: 14;
   D&C 64: 24; 133: 14.
   TG Babylon; Worldli-
   ness.
17a TG God, Foreknow-
   ledge of.

ing the calamity which should come upon the *b*inhabitants of the earth, *c*called upon my *d*servant Joseph Smith, Jun., and *e*spake unto him from heaven, and gave him *f*commandments;

18 And also gave commandments to others, that they should proclaim these things unto the world; and all this that it might be fulfilled, which was written by the prophets—

19 The *a*weak things of the world shall come forth and break down the mighty and strong ones, that man *b*should not counsel his fellow man, neither *c*trust in the arm of flesh—

20 But that every man might *a*speak in the name of God the Lord, even the Savior of the world;

21 That faith also might increase in the earth;

22 That mine everlasting *a*covenant might be established;

23 That the *a*fulness of my *b*gospel might be *c*proclaimed by the *d*weak and the simple unto the ends of the world, and before *e*kings and *f*rulers.

24 Behold, I am God and have spoken it; these *a*commandments are of me, and were given unto my servants in their weakness, after the manner of their *b*language, that they might come to *c*understanding.

25 And inasmuch as they *a*erred it might be made known;

26 And inasmuch as they sought *a*wisdom they might be *b*instructed;

27 And inasmuch as they sinned they might be *a*chastened, that they might *b*repent;

28 And inasmuch as they were *a*humble they might be made strong, and blessed from on high, and receive *b*knowledge from time to time.

29 And after having received the record of the Nephites, yea, even my servant Joseph Smith, Jun., might have power to *a*translate through the *b*mercy of God, by the power of God, the *c*Book of Mormon.

30 And also those to whom these commandments were given, might have *a*power to lay the foundation of this *b*church, and to bring it forth out of obscurity and out of *c*darkness, the only true and living *d*church upon the face of the whole earth, with which I, the Lord, am well *e*pleased, *f*speaking unto the church collectively and not individually—

31 For I the Lord cannot look upon *a*sin with the least degree of allowance;

32 Nevertheless, he that *a*repents and does the *b*commandments of the Lord shall be *c*forgiven;

17b Isa. 24: 6 (1–6).
 c TG Called of God.
 d TG Servant.
 e TG Revelation.
 f D&C 1: 30 (23–28, 30).
19a Isa. 54: 4; Acts 4: 13; 1 Cor. 1: 27; 1 Ne. 7: 8 (8–18); D&C 35: 13; 124: 1.
 b Isa. 8: 10.
 c Ps. 44: 6 (6–8); Jer. 9: 4; 17: 5; 2 Ne. 28: 31 (30–31).
  TG Trust Not in the Arm of Flesh.
20a TG Authority.
22a D&C 39: 11.
  TG Covenants; New and Everlasting Covenant.
23a Rom. 15: 29.
 b TG Gospel.

 c TG Missionary Work.
 d 1 Cor. 1: 27 (26–29).
  TG Strength.
 e TG Kings, Earthly.
 f Ps. 119: 46; Matt. 10: 18; Acts 9: 15; D&C 124: 3 (3, 16, 107).
24a Isa. 51: 16; 2 Ne. 33: 10 (10–11); Moro. 10: 27 (27–29).
 b 2 Ne. 31: 3; Ether 12: 39; D&C 67: 5.
  TG Language.
 c D&C 50: 12.
  TG Understanding.
25a Isa. 29: 24.
26a Eccl. 8: 16 (16–17); D&C 42: 68.
  TG Wisdom.
 b TG Teachable.
27a TG Chastening; Reproof.
 b TG Repentance.

28a TG Humility; Poor in Spirit.
 b TG Knowledge.
29a D&C 3: 12.
 b TG Mercy.
 c TG Book of Mormon.
30a D&C 1: 17 (4–5, 17–18).
 b TG Restoration of the Gospel.
 c TG Darkness, Spiritual.
 d 1 Cor. 14: 33; Eph. 4: 5 (3–13).
  TG Church.
 e D&C 38: 10.
 f D&C 50: 4.
31a Lev. 5: 17(17–19); D&C 24: 2.
  TG Sin.
32a TG Repentance.
 b Prov. 19: 16.
 c Ps. 65: 3; D&C 58: 42 (42–43).
  TG Forgiveness.

33 And he that ^arepents not, from him shall be ^btaken even the light which he has received; for my ^cSpirit shall not always ^dstrive with man, saith the Lord of Hosts.

34 And again, verily I say unto you, O inhabitants of the earth: I the Lord am willing to make these things ^aknown unto ^ball flesh;

35 For I am no ^arespecter of persons, and will that all men shall know that the ^bday speedily cometh; the hour is not yet, but is nigh at hand, when ^cpeace shall be taken from the earth, and the ^ddevil shall have power over his own dominion.

36 And also the Lord shall have ^apower over his ^bsaints, and shall ^creign in their ^dmidst, and shall come down in ^ejudgment upon ^fIdumea, or the world.

37 ^aSearch these ^bcommandments, for they are true and ^cfaithful, and the prophecies and ^dpromises which are in them shall all be fulfilled.

38 What I the Lord have spoken, I have spoken, and I excuse not myself; and though the heavens and the earth pass away, my ^aword shall not pass away, but shall all be ^bfulfilled, whether by mine own ^cvoice or by the ^dvoice of my ^eservants, it is the ^fsame.

39 For behold, and lo, the Lord is God, and the ^aSpirit beareth record, and the record is true, and the ^btruth abideth forever and ever. Amen.

SECTION 2

An extract from the words of the angel Moroni to Joseph Smith the Prophet, while in the house of the Prophet's father at Manchester, New York, on the evening of September 21, 1823. HC 1: 12. Moroni was the last of a long line of historians who had made the record that is now before the world as the Book of Mormon. Compare Malachi 4: 5–6; also Sections 27: 9; 110: 13–16; and 128: 18.

33a D&C 3: 11; 121: 37 (34–37).
  b Matt. 25: 29 (29–30); D&C 60: 3 (2–3).
  c TG God, Spirit of; Holy Ghost, Loss of.
  d Gen. 6: 3; 1 Sam. 28: 15; Isa. 57: 16; Moro. 9: 4.
34a Isa. 45: 19.
  TG Testimony.
  b D&C 1: 2; 18: 28 (26–28); 39: 15; 42: 58.
35a Deut. 1: 17; 10: 17; Prov. 24: 23; Acts 10: 34; Col. 3: 25; Alma 1: 30; 16: 14; D&C 38: 16; Moses 5: 21 (20–21).
  b TG Last Days.
  c Rev. 6:4.
  TG Peace; War.

d TG Devil.
36a TG Protection, Divine.
  b TG Saints.
  c Micah 4: 7.
  TG Jesus Christ, Millennial Reign.
  d Zech. 2: 11 (10–12); D&C 29: 11 (9–11); 45: 59; 84: 119 (118–119); 104: 59.
  e TG Judgment.
  f TG World, End of. See also "Idumea" in BD.
37a TG Priesthood, Magnifying Callings within; Scriptures, Study of; Study.
  b Rev. 21: 5.
  c TG Trustworthiness.
  d Rev. 17: 17; D&C 58: 31; 82: 10.
38a 2 Kgs. 10: 10; Ps. 33: 11; 119: 89; Matt. 5:

18; 24: 35; 2 Ne. 9: 16; 10: 17; D&C 5: 20; 101: 64; Moses 1:4; JS-M 1: 35.
  b TG Promise.
  c Deut. 18: 18; Jer. 1: 7; 23 (21–28); D&C 18: 35 (33–39); 21: 5.
  TG Obedience; Prophecy; Revelation.
  d Isa. 50: 10; 1 Jn. 4: 6 (1–6); D&C 25: 16.
  TG Priesthood, Authority.
  e 1 Thes. 4: 2.
  TG Prophets, Mission of; Servant.
  f TG Sustaining Church Leaders.
39a 1 Jn. 5: 6; D&C 20: 27; 42: 17.
  b TG Truth.

1, *Elijah is to reveal the priesthood;*
2–3, *Promises of fathers are planted in hearts of children.*

BEHOLD, I will reveal unto you the Priesthood, by the hand of [a]Elijah the prophet, before the coming of the great and [b]dreadful day of the Lord.

2 And [a]he shall plant in the hearts of the children the [b]promises made to the fathers, and the hearts of the children shall turn to their fathers.

3 If it were not so, the whole [a]earth would be utterly wasted at his coming.

SECTION 3

Revelation given to Joseph Smith the Prophet, at Harmony, Pennsylvania, July 1828, relating to the loss of 116 pages of manuscript translated from the first part of the Book of Mormon, which was called the "Book of Lehi." The Prophet had reluctantly allowed these pages to pass from his custody to that of Martin Harris, who had served for a brief period as scribe in the translation of the Book of Mormon. The revelation was given through the Urim and Thummim. HC 1: 21–23. See also Section 10.

1–4, *The Lord's course is one eternal round;* 5–15, *Joseph Smith must repent or lose the gift to translate;* 16–20, *The Book of Mormon comes forth to save the seed of Lehi.*

THE [a]works, and the designs, and the purposes of God cannot be [b]frustrated, neither can they come to naught.

2 For God doth not [a]walk in crooked paths, neither doth he [b]turn to the right hand nor to the left, neither doth he vary from that which he hath said, therefore his paths are straight, and his [c]course is one eternal round.

3 Remember, remember that it is not the [a]work of God that is frustrated, but the work of men;

4 For although a man may have many [a]revelations, and have [b]power to do many mighty works, yet if he [c]boasts in his own [d]strength, and sets at naught the [e]counsels of God, and follows after the dictates of his own will and [f]carnal desires, he must fall and incur the [g]vengeance of a [h]just God upon him.

5 Behold, you have been [a]entrusted with these things, but how strict were your commandments; and remember also the promises which were made to you, if you did not transgress them.

6 And behold, how [a]oft you have

---

2 1a Mal. 4: 5 (5–6);
    3 Ne. 25: 5 (5–6);
    D&C 35: 4; 110: 13
    (13–15); 128: 17;
    JS-H 1: 38 (38–39).
    TG Last Days; Priesthood, Keys of.
  b 1 Cor. 5: 5; D&C 1:
    12; 34: 8 (6–9); 43: 17
    (17–26).
  2a 2 Kgs. 2: 15; D&C 27:
    9; 98: 16 (16–17).
  b TG Family, Children,
    Duties of; Genealogy
    and Temple Work;
    Promise; Salvation for
    the Dead.

3a Luke 1: 17.
  TG Earth, Purpose of.
3 1a TG God, Works of.
  b Jer. 1: 8 (7–8).
  2a Neh. 9: 8; Isa. 45: 19;
    Alma 7: 20.
    TG God, Perfection of.
  b Josh. 1: 7; 3 Ne. 18: 13
    (12–14).
  c 1 Ne. 10: 19 (18–19);
    D&C 35: 1.
  3a Acts 5: 38; Morm. 8:
    22; D&C 10: 38
    (38–40).
  4a TG Revelation.

  b Alma 19: 4.
  c Amos 6: 13 (13–14);
    Mosiah 11: 19;
    D&C 84: 73.
    TG Boasting.
  d TG Strength.
  e Josh. 9: 14; Jacob 4:
    10; Alma 37: 37.
    TG Counsel.
  f TG Carnal Mind;
    Chastity; Lust.
  g TG Vengeance.
  h 2 Ne. 1: 22.
  5a Alma 37: 14.
  6a D&C 5: 21; 20: 5;
    JS-H 1: 28 (28–29).

*b*transgressed the commandments and the laws of God, and have gone on in the *c*persuasions of men.

7 For, behold, you should not have *a*feared man more than God. Although men set at naught the counsels of God, and *b*despise his words—

8 Yet you should have been faithful; and he would have extended his arm and *a*supported you against all the fiery *b*darts of the *c*adversary; and he would have been with you in every time of *d*trouble.

9 Behold, thou art Joseph, and thou wast chosen to do the work of the Lord, but because of transgression, if thou art not aware thou wilt *a*fall.

10 But remember, God is merciful; therefore, repent of that which thou hast done which is contrary to the commandment which I gave you, and thou art still chosen, and art *a*again called to the work;

11 Except thou *a*do this, thou shalt be delivered up and become as other men, and have no more gift.

12 And when thou deliveredst up that which God had given thee sight and power to *a*translate, thou deliveredst up that which was *b*sacred into the hands of a wicked *c*man,

13 Who has set at naught the counsels of God, and has broken the most sacred promises which were made before God, and has depended upon his own judgment and *a*boasted in his own wisdom.

14 And this is the reason that thou hast lost thy privileges for a season—

15 For thou hast suffered the counsel of thy *a*director to be trampled upon from the beginning.

16 Nevertheless, my *a*work shall go forth, for inasmuch as the knowledge of a Savior has come unto the world, through the *b*testimony of the Jews, even so shall the *c*knowledge of a *d*Savior come unto my people—

17 And to the *a*Nephites, and the Jacobites, and the Josephites, and the Zoramites, through the testimony of their fathers—

18 And this *a*testimony shall come to the knowledge of the *b*Lamanites, and the Lemuelites, and the Ishmaelites, who *c*dwindled in unbelief because of the *d*iniquity of their fathers, whom the Lord has suffered to destroy their *e*brethren the Nephites, because of their *f*iniquities and their abominations.

19 And for this very *a*purpose are these *b*plates *c*preserved, which contain these records—that the *d*promises of the Lord might be fulfilled, which he made to his *e*people;

6*b* Josh. 23:16 (15–16);
 Alma 12:31.
 TG Transgression.
c Titus 1:14; D&C 45:
 29; 46:7; JS–H 1:19.
 TG Motivations; Peer
 Influence.
7*a* Neh. 6:13; Ps. 27:1
 (1–14); Isa. 57:11;
 Luke 9:26; John 12:
 43 (42–43); Acts 4:19;
 D&C 122:9 (4–9).
 TG Courage; Fearful-
 ness.
b Num. 15:31 (30–31);
 2 Sam. 12:9 (7–9);
 1 Ne. 19:7; 2 Ne. 33:
 2; Jacob 4:14 (8–14).
 TG Hate.
8*a* TG God, Power of.
b Eph. 6:16; 1 Ne. 15:
 24; D&C 27:17.
c TG Devil.
d Ps. 81:7; Alma 9:17;

38:5.
9*a* Acts 1:25; 1 Cor. 10:
 12.
 TG Apostasy of
 Individuals.
10*a* D&C 10:3.
11*a* Luke 13:3; D&C 1:
 33; 121:37 (34–37).
12*a* D&C 1:29; 5:4 (4, 30–
 31).
b TG Sacred; Sacrilege.
c D&C 10:6 (6–8).
13*a* Jacob 4:10.
 TG Haughtiness; Pride.
15*a* IE the Lord; see v. 6.
16*a* TG Israel, Mission of.
b John 5:39; 1 Ne. 13:
 25 (23–25); 2 Ne. 29:4
 (4–6); D&C 20:26.
c Mosiah 3:20.
17*a* 1 Ne. 13:30; 2 Ne. 29:
 12 (12–13); Alma 45:
 14 (10–14).

18*a* TG Testimony.
b Jacob 1:13; Enos 1:
 13; D&C 10:48 (46–
 52); 109:65.
c 2 Ne. 26:15;
 Jacob 3:7.
 TG Doubt.
d TG Family, Children,
 Responsibilities
 toward; Sin.
f Morm. 8:2 (2–3).
f Mosiah 12:7.
19*a* 1 Ne. 9:3 (3, 5).
b TG Book of Mormon.
c TG Scriptures, Preservation of.
d Enos 1:16 (13–18);
 Mosiah 21:4; 3 Ne. 5:
 14 (13–15); D&C 10:
 47 (46–50).
e TG Israel, Joseph,
 People of; Israel,
 Restoration of.

20 And that the ^aLamanites might come to the knowledge of their fathers, and that they might know the ^bpromises of the Lord, and that they may ^cbelieve the gospel and ^drely upon the merits of Jesus Christ, and be ^eglorified through faith in his name, and that through their repentance they might be saved. Amen.

SECTION 4

Revelation given through Joseph Smith the Prophet to his father, Joseph Smith, Sen., at Harmony, Pennsylvania, February 1829. HC 1: 28.

1–4, Valiant service saves the Lord's ministers; 5–6, Godly attributes qualify them for the ministry; 7, Things of God must be sought after.

Now behold, a ^amarvelous work is about to come forth among the children of men.

2 Therefore, O ye that embark in the ^aservice of God, see that ye ^bserve him with all your heart, might, mind and strength, that ye may stand ^cblameless before God at the last day.

3 Therefore, if ye have desires to serve God ye are ^acalled to the work;

4 For behold the ^afield is white already to ^bharvest; and lo, he that thrusteth in his sickle with his might, the same layeth up in ^cstore that he perisheth not, but bringeth salvation to his soul;

5 And ^afaith, ^bhope, ^ccharity and ^dlove, with an ^eeye single to the ^fglory of God, ^gqualify him for the work.

6 Remember faith, ^avirtue, knowledge, ^btemperance, ^cpatience, ^dbrotherly ^ekindness, ^fgodliness, charity, ^ghumility, ^hdiligence.

7 ^aAsk, and ye shall receive; ^bknock, and it shall be opened unto you. Amen.

20a 2 Ne. 30: 5 (3–6); D&C 28: 8 (8–9, 14); 32: 2; 49: 24.
 b 2 Ne. 10: 9 (9, 21); Alma 9: 24.
 c Morm. 3: 21.
 d 2 Ne. 31: 19; Moro. 6: 4.
 e Moro. 7: 26 (26, 38).
4 1a 1sa. 29: 14; 1 Ne. 14: 7 (7–17); 22: 8; D&C 6: 1; 11: 1; 12: 1; 18: 44.
   TG Missionary Work; Restoration of the Gospel.
 2a Acts 20: 19.
   TG Children of Light; Service.
 b Josh. 22: 5; Judg. 6: 14; 1 Sam. 7: 3; D&C 20: 19; 76: 5.
   TG Commitment;

Dedication; Heart; Mind; Strength.
 c 1 Cor. 1: 8; Col. 1: 22; Jacob 1: 19; Mosiah 3: 21; 3 Ne. 27: 20; D&C 88: 85.
3a Matt. 8: 19 (19–22); D&C 11: 4, 15; 36: 5; 63: 57. TG Called of God; Service.
4a John 4: 35; Alma 26: 5; D&C 11: 3; 12: 3; 14: 3; 33: 3 (3, 7); 101: 64.
 b Joel 3: 13; D&C 31: 4. TG Harvest.
 c Gen. 41: 36 (33–57); 1 Tim. 6: 19; 3 Ne. 4: 18.
5a TG Faith.
 b TG Hope.
 c TG Charity.
 d TG Love.

 e Ps. 25: 15; 141: 8; Matt. 6: 22; Morm. 8: 15.
 f TG Glory; Motivations.
 g TG Priesthood, Qualifying for.
6a TG Chastity; Virtue.
 b TG Temperance.
 c TG Patience.
 d TG Brotherhood and Sisterhood.
 e TG Benevolence; Courtesy; Kindness.
 f TG Godliness.
 g TG Humility; Meekness; Poor in Spirit.
 h TG Diligence.
7a Matt. 7: 7 (7–8). TG Prayer.
 b TG Objectives.

SECTION 5

Revelation given through Joseph Smith the Prophet, at Harmony, Pennsylvania, March 1829, at the request of Martin Harris. HC 1: 28–31.

1–10, *This generation shall receive the Lord's word through Joseph Smith;* 11–18, *Three witnesses shall testify of the Book of Mormon;* 19–20, *The word of the Lord will be verified as in previous times;* 21–35, *Martin Harris may repent and be one of the witnesses.*

BEHOLD, I say unto you, that as my servant ^aMartin Harris has desired a witness at my hand, that you, my servant Joseph Smith, Jun., have got the plates of which you have testified and borne record that you have received of me;

2 And now, behold, this shall you say unto him—he who spake unto you, said unto you: I, the Lord, am God, and have given these things unto you, my servant Joseph Smith, Jun., and have commanded you that you should stand as a ^awitness of these things;

3 And I have caused that you should enter into a ^acovenant with me, that you should not ^bshow them except to those ^cpersons to whom I commanded you; and you have no ^dpower over them except I grant it unto you.

4 And you have a gift to ^atranslate the plates; and this is the first gift that I bestowed upon you; and I have commanded that you should pretend to no other gift until my purpose is fulfilled in this; for I will grant unto you no other gift until it is finished.

5 Verily, I say unto you, that ^awoe shall come unto the inhabitants of the earth if they will not ^bhearken unto my words;

6 For hereafter you shall be ^aordained and go forth and deliver my ^bwords unto the children of men.

7 Behold, if they will not ^abelieve my words, they would not believe you, my servant Joseph, if it were possible that you should show them all these things which I have committed unto you.

8 Oh, this ^aunbelieving and ^bstiffnecked generation—mine ^canger is kindled against them.

9 Behold, verily I say unto you, I have ^areserved those things which I have entrusted unto you, my servant Joseph, for a wise purpose in me, and it shall be made known unto future generations;

10 But this generation shall have my word ^athrough you;

11 And in addition to your testimony, the ^atestimony of three of my servants, whom I shall call and ordain, unto whom I will show these things, and they shall go forth with my words that are given through you.

12 Yea, they shall know of a ^asurety that these things are true, for from heaven will I declare it unto them.

---

5 1*a* D&C 5: 23 (23–24);
    JS-H 1: 61.
  2*a* TG Witnesses.
  3*a* TG Covenants.
    b 2 Ne. 27: 13. See also
       the Testimony of
       Three Witnesses and
       the Testimony of
       Eight Witnesses in the
       Book of Mormon, preliminary pages.
    c Prov. 25: 2.
    d 2 Ne. 3: 11.
  4*a* D&C 3: 12; 6: 25 (25, 28).
  5*a* Rev. 8: 13; Hel. 7: 22;
       D&C 1: 14.
    b Jer. 26: 4; Alma 5: 37 (37–38).
  6*a* D&C 20: 2 (2–3).
    b 2 Ne. 29: 7.
  7*a* Luke 16: 30 (27–31);
       D&C 63: 7–12.
  8*a* TG Unbelief, Unbelievers.
    b Morm. 8: 33.
       TG Haughtiness;
       Stiffneckedness.
    c TG Anger; God,
       Indignation of.
  9*a* Alma 37: 18.
  10*a* Mosiah 18: 19 (18–20);
       D&C 31: 4; 42: 12; 52: 36.
  11*a* 2 Ne. 27: 12; Ether 5: 3 (3–4); D&C 17: 3 (1–5); 20: 10.
  12*a* Ether 5: 3.

13 I will give them power that they may behold and view these things as they are;

14 And to ^anone else will I grant this power, to receive this same testimony among this generation, in this the beginning of the rising up and the coming forth of my ^bchurch out of the wilderness—clear as the ^cmoon, and fair as the sun, and terrible as an army with banners.

15 And the testimony of three ^awitnesses will I send forth of my word.

16 And behold, whosoever ^abelieveth on my words, them will I ^bvisit with the ^cmanifestation of my ^dSpirit; and they shall be ^eborn of me, even of water and of the Spirit—

17 And you must wait yet a little while, for ye are not yet ^aordained.

18 And their testimony shall also go forth unto the ^acondemnation of this generation if they ^bharden their hearts against them;

19 For a desolating ^ascourge shall go forth among the inhabitants of the earth, and shall continue to be poured out from time to time, if they ^brepent not, until the earth is ^cempty, and the inhabitants thereof are ^dconsumed away and utterly destroyed by the brightness of my ^ecoming.

20 Behold, I tell you these things, even as I also ^atold the people of the destruction of Jerusalem; and my ^bword shall be verified at this time as it hath hitherto been verified.

21 And now I command you, my servant Joseph, to ^arepent and ^bwalk more uprightly before me, and to yield to the ^cpersuasions of men no more;

22 And that you be ^afirm in ^bkeeping the commandments wherewith I have commanded you; and if you do this, behold I grant unto you ^ceternal life, even if you should be ^dslain.

23 And now, again, I speak unto you, my servant Joseph, concerning the ^aman that desires the witness—

24 Behold, I say unto him, he exalts himself and does not ^ahumble himself sufficiently before me; but if he will ^bbow down before me, and humble himself in mighty ^cprayer and faith, in the ^dsincerity of his heart, then will I grant unto him a ^eview of the things which he desires to see.

25 And then he shall say unto the people of this generation: Behold, I have seen the things which the Lord hath shown unto Joseph Smith, Jun., and I ^aknow of a surety that they are true, for I have seen them, for they have been shown unto me by the power of God and not of man.

14a 2 Ne. 27:13.
 b Rev. 12:1 (1–6).
   TG Church; Jesus
   Christ, Head of the
   Church.
 c Song. 6:10; D&C 105:
   31; 109:73.
15a D&C 17:1.
   TG Witnesses.
16a Ether 4:11.
 b Ps. 8:4; 1 Ne. 2:16;
   19:11; Alma 17:10.
 c D&C 8:1 (1–3); 70:
   13.
 d TG God, Spirit of.
 e TG Baptism; Holy
   Ghost, Baptism of;
   Man, New, Spiritually
   Reborn.
17a TG Priesthood,
   Authority; Priest-

hood, Ordination.
18a 1 Ne. 14:7; D&C 20:
   13 (13–15).
 b TG Hardheartedness.
19a Isa. 28:18 (15, 18),
   D&C 29:8; 35:11
   (11–16); 43:17 (17–
   27). TG Last Days.
 b TG Repentance.
 c Isa. 24:1 (1, 5–6).
 d Mal. 3:6 (6–7).
 e Isa. 66:15 (15–16);
   D&C 133:41.
   TG Jesus Christ,
   Prophecies about;
   Jesus Christ, Second
   Coming.
20a Lam. 1:8 (7–9); 1 Ne. 1:
   18; 2 Ne. 25:9.
 b D&C 1:38.

21a D&C 3:6; 20:5;
   JS-H 1:28 (28–29).
 b 1 Ne. 16:3.
 c TG Peer Influence.
22a Hel. 7:7.
 b TG Obedience.
 c D&C 132:49.
23a D&C 5:1.
24a Ether 9:35.
 b Alma 22:17.
   TG Reverence.
 c TG Prayer.
 d TG Sincerity.
 e D&C 17:1. See also
   the Testimony of
   Three Witnesses in the
   Book of Mormon,
   preliminary pages.
25a Ether 5:3.

26 And I the Lord command him, my servant Martin Harris, that he shall say no more unto them concerning these things, except he shall say: I have seen them, and they have been shown unto me by the power of God; and these are the words which he shall say.

27 But if he deny this he will break the *covenant which he has before covenanted with me, and behold, he is condemned.

28 And now, except he humble himself and acknowledge unto me the things that he has done which are wrong, and covenant with me that he will keep my commandments, and exercise *faith in me, behold, I say unto him, he shall have no such views, for I will grant unto him no views of the things of which I have spoken.

29 And if this be the case, I command you, my servant Joseph, that you shall say unto him, that he shall do no more, nor trouble me any more concerning this matter.

30 And if this be the case, behold, I say unto thee Joseph, when thou hast translated a few more pages thou shalt stop for a season, even until I command thee again; then thou mayest translate again.

31 And except thou do this, behold, thou shalt have no more gift, and I will take away the things which I have entrusted with thee.

32 And now, because I foresee the lying in wait to destroy thee, yea, I foresee that if my servant Martin Harris humbleth not himself and receive a witness from my hand, that he will fall into *transgression.

33 And there are many that lie in wait to *destroy thee from off the face of the earth; and for this cause, that thy days may be *prolonged, I have given unto thee these commandments.

34 Yea, for this cause I have said: Stop, and *stand still until I command thee, and I will *provide means whereby thou mayest accomplish the thing which I have commanded thee.

35 And if thou art *faithful in keeping my commandments, thou shalt be *lifted up at the last day. Amen.

SECTION 6

Revelation given to Joseph Smith the Prophet and Oliver Cowdery, at Harmony, Pennsylvania, April 1829. HC 1: 32-35. Oliver Cowdery began his labors as scribe in the translation of the Book of Mormon, April 7, 1829. He had already received a divine manifestation of the truth of the Prophet's testimony respecting the plates on which was engraved the Book of Mormon record. The Prophet inquired of the Lord through the Urim and Thummim and received this response.

1-6, Laborers in the Lord's field gain salvation; 7-13, There is no gift greater than the gift of salvation; 14-27, Witness of truth comes by the power of the Spirit; 28-37, Look unto Christ, and do good continually.

27a TG Covenants.
28a Ether 4: 7.
32a Enos 1: 13.
33a D&C 10: 6 (6, 25); 38:
  13 (13, 28); 42: 64.
  b Ex. 20: 12; Deut. 4: 40;

11: 9 (8-9); Prov. 3: 2
  (1-2); Hel. 7: 24; 15:
  11 (10-11).
34a 1 Sam. 9: 27; Isa. 30:
  15.
  b 1 Ne. 3: 7.

35a Ex. 15: 26; D&C 11:
  20.
  b John 6: 39; 1 Thes. 4:
  17; 3 Ne. 15: 1; D&C 9:
  14; 17: 8; 52: 44;
  75: 16, 22.

A GREAT and ^amarvelous work is about to come forth unto the children of men.

2 Behold, I am God; give heed unto my ^aword, which is quick and powerful, ^bsharper than a two-edged sword, to the dividing asunder of both joints and marrow; therefore give heed unto my words.

3 Behold, the ^afield is white already to harvest; therefore, whoso desireth to reap, let him thrust in his sickle with his might, and reap while the day ^blasts, that he may ^ctreasure up for his soul everlasting salvation in the kingdom of God.

4 Yea, whosoever will thrust in his sickle and reap, the same is ^acalled of God.

5 Therefore, if you will ^aask of me you shall receive; if you will knock it shall be opened unto you.

6 Now, as you have asked, behold, I say unto you, keep my commandments, and ^aseek to bring forth and establish the cause of ^bZion;

7 ^aSeek not for ^briches but for ^cwisdom, and behold, the ^dmysteries of God shall be unfolded unto you, and then shall you be made ^erich. Behold, he that hath ^feternal life is rich.

8 Verily, verily, I say unto you, even as you ^adesire of me so it shall be unto you; and if you desire, you shall be the means of doing much ^bgood in this generation.

9 Say nothing but ^arepentance unto this generation; keep my commandments, and assist to bring forth my work, according to my commandments, and you shall be blessed.

10 Behold thou hast a gift, and blessed art thou because of thy ^agift. Remember it is ^bsacred and cometh from above—

11 And if thou wilt ^ainquire, thou shalt know ^bmysteries which are great and marvelous; therefore thou shalt exercise thy ^cgift, that thou mayest find out mysteries, that thou mayest bring ^dmany to the knowledge of the truth, yea, ^econvince them of the error of their ways.

12 Make not thy gift known unto any save it be those who are of thy faith. Trifle not with ^asacred things.

13 If thou wilt do ^agood, yea, and ^bhold out ^cfaithful to the ^dend, thou shalt be saved in the ^ekingdom of God, which is the greatest of all the ^fgifts of God; for there is no gift greater than the gift of ^gsalvation.

14 Verily, verily, I say unto thee,

6 1a Isa. 29: 14; D&C 4: 1
    (1–7); 18: 44.
2a Heb. 4: 12; Rev. 1: 16;
    D&C 27: 1.
  b Hel. 3: 29 (29–30);
    D&C 15: 7; 33: 1; 85:
    6; 121: 43.
3a Joel 3:13; D&C 101:
    64.
  b TG Procrastination.
  c TG Treasure.
4a D&C 11: 4 (3–4, 27);
    12: 4 (3–4); 14: 4
    (3–4).
5a Matt. 7: 7.
6a Matt. 6: 33, fn. a;
    Luke 12: 31, fn. a.
  b D&C 35: 24.
    TG Mission of Latter-
    day Saints; Ob-
    jectives; Zion.
7a Alma 39: 14 (12–14);
    D&C 68: 31 (31–32).
    TG Study.
  b 1 Kgs. 3: 11 (10–13);

Matt. 19: 23 (23–26);
    Jacob 2: 18.
    TG Worldliness.
  c TG Education;
    Wisdom.
  d Rom. 16: 25; D&C 42:
    65 (61–65); 121:
    27 (25–27).
    TG Mysteries of Godli-
    ness.
  e ‡ Ne. 1: 3.
    TG Treasure.
  f Prov. 13: 7;
    Rev. 3: 18.
8a TG Motivations;
    Prayer.
  b TG Good Works.
9a D&C 15: 6; 18: 14;
    34: 6.
    TG Missionary Work;
    Prophets, Mission of;
    Repentance.
10a TG God, Gifts of.
  b D&C 63: 64.
11a D&C 46: 7; 102: 23;
    JS-H 1: 18 (18, 26).

TG Prayer.
  b Matt. 11: 25; 13: 11;
    Alma 12: 9.
  c TG Talents.
  d 1 Tim. 2: 4; Alma 36:
    26. TG Knowledge.
  e James 5: 20; Alma 12:
    1; 62: 45; D&C 18: 44.
12a Prov. 23: 9; Matt. 7:
    6; D&C 10: 37 (36–37).
    TG Sacred; Sacrilege.
13a TG Good Works.
  b 1 Tim. 1: 19; 1 Ne. 15:
    24.
  c Ps. 31: 23; Mosiah 2:
    41; Ether 4: 19;
    D&C 51: 19; 63: 47;
    138: 12.
    TG Perseverance;
    Steadfastness.
  d Rev. 2: 10.
  e TG Kingdom of God, in
    Heaven.
  f TG God, Gifts of.
  g TG Salvation.

blessed art thou for what thou hast done; for thou hast ᵃinquired of me, and behold, as often as thou hast inquired thou hast received instruction of my Spirit. If it had not been so, thou wouldst not have come to the place where thou art at this time.

15 Behold, thou knowest that thou hast inquired of me and I did enlighten thy ᵃmind; and now I tell thee these things that thou mayest know that thou hast been ᵇenlightened by the ᶜSpirit of truth;

16 Yea, I tell thee, that thou mayest know that there is none else save God that ᵃknowest thy thoughts and the ᵇintents of thy ᶜheart.

17 I tell thee these things as a witness unto thee—that the words or the work which thou hast been writing are ᵃtrue.

18 Therefore be diligent; ᵃstand by my ᵇservant Joseph, faithfully, in whatsoever difficult circumstances he may be for the word's sake.

19 Admonish him in his faults, and also ᵃreceive admonition of him. ᵇBe patient; be sober; be temperate; have patience, faith, hope and charity.

20 Behold, thou art Oliver, and I have spoken unto thee because of thy desires; therefore ᵃtreasure up these words in thy heart. Be faithful and ᵇdiligent in keeping the commandments of God, and I will encircle thee in the arms of my ᶜlove.

21 Behold, I am Jesus Christ, the ᵃSon of God. I am the same that came unto mine ᵇown, and mine own received me not. I am the ᶜlight which shineth in ᵈdarkness, and the darkness comprehendeth it not.

22 Verily, verily, I say unto you, if you desire a further witness, cast your mind upon the night that you cried unto me in your heart, that you might ᵃknow concerning the truth of these things.

23 Did I not speak ᵃpeace to your mind concerning the matter? What greater ᵇwitness can you have than from God?

24 And now, behold, you have received a ᵃwitness; for if I have ᵇtold you things which no man knoweth have you not received a witness?

25 And, behold, I grant unto you a gift, if you desire of me, to ᵃtranslate, even as my servant Joseph.

26 Verily, verily, I say unto you, that there are ᵃrecords which contain much of my gospel, which have been kept back because of the ᵇwickedness of the people;

27 And now I command you, that if you have good desires—a desire to lay up ᵃtreasures for yourself in

---

14a TG Guidance, Divine.
15a TG Mind.
   b Eph. 1: 18.
     TG Holy Ghost, Mission of.
   c TG God, Spirit of.
16a 2 Sam. 7: 20; 1 Chr. 28: 9; Ps. 139: 2; Matt. 12: 25; Heb. 4: 12; Morm. 6: 22; D&C 15: 3. TG God, Omniscience of.
   b TG Motivations; Sincerity.
   c 1 Kgs. 8: 39.
17a D&C 18: 2.
18a TG Diligence; Loyalty.
   b D&C 124: 95.
19a TG Teachable.

b See Topical Guide entry on each of the qualities listed here.
20a D&C 11: 26; 84: 85. TG Treasure.
   b TG Diligence.
   c John 15: 12 (12–15). TG God, Love of.
21a TG Jesus Christ, Divine Sonship.
   b John 1: 11; Acts 3: 17 (14–17); 3 Ne. 9: 16. TG Prophets, Rejection of.
   c John 1: 5; D&C 10: 58. TG Jesus Christ, Light of the World; Light; Light of Christ.
   d TG Darkness, Spiritual.
22a TG Discernment,

Spiritual; God, Access to.
23a Gen. 41: 16. TG Contentment; Peace; Peace of God.
   b Rom. 2: 15 (14–15); 1 Jn. 5: 9.
24a D&C 18: 2.
   b TG God, Omniscience of.
25a Mosiah 8: 13; D&C 5: 4 (4, 30–31); 9: 2 (1–3, 5, 10).
26a D&C 8: 1; 9: 2. TG Record Keeping; Scriptures, Writing of; Scriptures to Come Forth.
   b TG Wickedness.
27a TG Treasure.

heaven—then shall you assist in bringing to light, with your gift, those parts of my *b*scriptures which have been hidden because of iniquity.

28 And now, behold, I give unto you, and also unto my servant Joseph, the *a*keys of this gift, which shall bring to light this ministry; and in the mouth of two or three *b*witnesses shall every word be established.

29 Verily, verily, I say unto you, if they *a*reject my words, and this part of my gospel and ministry, blessed are ye, for they can do no more unto you than unto me.

30 And even if they *a*do unto you even as they have done unto me, blessed are ye, for you shall *b*dwell with me in *c*glory.

31 But if they *a*reject not my words, which shall be established by the *b*testimony which shall be given, blessed are they, and then shall ye have joy in the fruit of your labors.

32 Verily, verily, I say unto you,

as I said unto my disciples, where two or three are gathered together in my *a*name, as *a*touching *b*one thing, behold, there will I be in the *c*midst of them—even so am I in the *d*midst of you.

33 *a*Fear not to do *b*good, my sons, for whatsoever ye *c*sow, that shall ye also reap; therefore, if ye sow *d*good ye shall also reap good for your *e*reward.

34 Therefore, fear not, little *a*flock; do good; let earth and hell combine against you, for if ye are *b*built upon my rock, they cannot prevail.

35 Behold, I do not condemn you; go your ways and *a*sin no more; perform with soberness the work which I have commanded you.

36 *a*Look unto me in every *b*thought; *c*doubt not, fear not.

37 *a*Behold the wounds which pierced my side, and also the prints of the *b*nails in my hands and feet; be faithful, keep my commandments, and ye shall *c*inherit the *d*kingdom of heaven. Amen.

SECTION 7

Revelation given to Joseph Smith the Prophet and Oliver Cowdery, at Harmony, Pennsylvania, April 1829, when they inquired through the Urim and Thummim as to whether John, the beloved disciple, tarried in the flesh or had died. The revelation is a translated version of the record made on parchment by John and hidden up by himself. HC 1: 35-36.

27*b* D&C 35: 20.
28*a* D&C 7: 7.
  b Deut. 19: 15; 2 Cor. 13: 1.
29*a* John 15: 20.
30*a* D&C 5: 22; 135: 1 (1-7).
  TG Martyrdom.
  b Rev. 3: 21.
  c TG Glory.
31*a* 3 Ne. 16: 10 (10-14); D&C 20: 15 (8-15).
  b TG Testimony.
32*a* Matt. 18: 19 (19-20); D&C 29: 6; 84: 1.
  b TG Unity.

  c D&C 32: 3; 38: 7.
  d D&C 29: 5; 88: 63 (62-63).
33*a* TG Fearfulness.
  b TG Good Works.
  c Job 34: 11; Ps. 7: 16; Hosea 8: 7; Gal. 6: 7-8; Mosiah 7: 30; Alma 9: 28; D&C 1: 10.
  TG Harvest.
  d TG Benevolence.
  e TG Reward.
34*a* TG Church; Sheep.
  b Ps. 71: 3; Matt. 7: 24 (24-25); Hel. 5: 12; D&C 10: 69; 11: 16

(16, 24); 18: 4 (4, 17); 33: 13; Moses 7: 53.
  TG Rock.
35*a* John 8: 11.
36*a* Isa. 45: 22; D&C 43: 34.
  b TG Motivations.
  c TG Doubt.
37*a* TG Jesus Christ, Appearances, Postmortal.
  b TG Jesus Christ, Crucifixion of.
  c Matt. 5: 10 (3, 10).
  d TG Kingdom of God, in Heaven.

1–3, John the Beloved shall live until the Lord comes; 4–8, Peter, James, and John hold gospel keys.

AND the Lord said unto me: John, my ^abeloved, what ^bdesirest thou? For if you shall ask what you will, it shall be granted unto you.

2 And I said unto him: Lord, give unto me ^apower over ^bdeath, that I may live and bring souls unto thee.

3 And the Lord said unto me: Verily, verily, I say unto thee, because thou desirest this thou shalt ^atarry until I come in my ^bglory, and shalt ^cprophesy before nations, kindreds, tongues and people.

4 And for this cause the Lord said unto Peter: If I will that he tarry till I come, what is that to thee? For he desired of me that he might bring ^asouls unto me, but thou de-

siredst that thou mightest speedily come unto me in my ^bkingdom.

5 I say unto thee, Peter, this was a good desire; but my beloved has desired that he might do more, or a greater ^awork yet among men than what he has before done.

6 Yea, he has undertaken a greater work; therefore I will make him as flaming fire and a ^aministering angel; he shall minister for those who shall be ^bheirs of salvation who dwell on the earth.

7 And I will make thee to minister for him and for thy brother James; and unto you three I will ^agive this power and the ^bkeys of this ministry until I come.

8 Verily I say unto you, ye shall both have according to your desires, for ye both ^ajoy in that which ye have desired.

SECTION 8

Revelation given through Joseph Smith the Prophet to Oliver Cowdery, at Harmony, Pennsylvania, April 1829. HC 1: 36–37. In the course of the translation of the Book of Mormon, Oliver, who continued to serve as scribe, writing at the Prophet's dictation, desired to be endowed with the gift of translation. The Lord responded to his supplication by granting this revelation.

1–5, Revelation comes by the power of the Holy Ghost; 6–12, Mysteries of God and the power to translate ancient records come by faith.

^aOLIVER Cowdery, verily, verily, I say unto you, that assuredly as the Lord liveth, who is your God

and your Redeemer, even so surely shall you receive a ^bknowledge of whatsoever things you shall ^cask in faith, with an ^dhonest heart, believing that you shall receive a ^eknowledge concerning the engravings of old ^frecords, which are ancient, which contain those parts

---

7 1a John 19: 26 (26–27); 20: 2 (2–9).
  b 2 Chr. 1: 7 (7–12); 3 Ne. 28: 1 (1–12).
2a TG Death, Power over.
  b Luke 9: 27.
3a John 21: 22 (20–25).
  TG Translated Beings.
  b TG Glory; Jesus Christ, Glory of; Jesus Christ, Second Coming.

c Rev. 10: 11.
4a TG Conversion; Worth of Souls.
  b TG Kingdom of God, in Heaven.
5a Philip. 1: 24 (23–24); 3 Ne. 28: 9 (1–12).
6a Heb. 1: 14; D&C 43: 25; 130: 5.
  b D&C 76: 88.
7a Matt. 16: 19.
  b Acts 15: 7; D&C 6: 28; JS-H 1: 72.

TG Priesthood, Keys of.
8a TG Joy.
8 1a JS-H 1: 66.
  b Dan. 5: 16; Mosiah 8: 13 (13–18); D&C 6: 25; 9: 5 (1–5).
  c Isa. 58: 9 (8–9).
  d TG Prayer; Sincerity.
  e TG Knowledge.
  f D&C 6: 26; 9: 2.

of my scripture of which has been spoken by the *manifestation of my Spirit.

2 Yea, behold, I will *tell you in your mind and in your *heart, by the *Holy Ghost, which shall come upon you and which shall dwell in your heart.

3 Now, behold, this is the spirit of revelation; behold, this is the spirit by which Moses *brought the children of Israel through the Red Sea on dry ground.

4 Therefore *this is thy *gift; apply unto it, and blessed art thou, for it shall *deliver you out of the hands of your *enemies, when, if it were not so, they would slay you and bring your soul to destruction.

5 Oh, remember these *words, and keep my commandments. Remember, this is your gift.

6 Now this is not all thy *gift; for you have another gift, which is the gift of Aaron; behold, it has told you many things;

7 Behold, there is no other power, save the power of God, that can cause this gift of Aaron to be with you.

8 Therefore, *doubt not, for it is the gift of God; and you shall hold it in your hands, and do marvelous works; and no power shall be able to take it away out of your hands, for it is the *work of God.

9 And, therefore, whatsoever you shall ask me to tell you by that means, that will I grant unto you, and you shall have knowledge concerning it.

10 Remember that without *faith you can do nothing; therefore ask in faith. Trifle not with these things; do not *ask for that which you ought not.

11 Ask that you may know the mysteries of God, and that you may *translate and receive knowledge from all those ancient records which have been hid up, that are *sacred; and according to your faith shall it be done unto you.

12 Behold, it is I that have spoken it; and I am the same that spake unto you from the beginning. Amen.

SECTION 9

Revelation given through Joseph Smith the Prophet to Oliver Cowdery, at Harmony, Pennsylvania, April 1829. HC 1: 37–38. Oliver is admonished to be patient, and is urged to be content to write, for the time being, at the dictation of the translator, rather than to attempt to translate.

1–6, Other ancient records are yet to be translated; 7–14, The Book of Mormon is translated by study and by spiritual confirmation.

BEHOLD, I say unto you, my son, that because you did not *translate according to that which you desired of me, and did commence again to *write for my servant, Joseph Smith, Jun., even so I would that ye should continue until you have finished this record, which I have entrusted unto him.

1g D&C 5: 16.
2a D&C 9: 8 (7–9).
     TG Guidance, Divine.
   b Ezek. 40: 4.
     TG Heart; Inspiration.
   c Rom. 8: 9.
     TG Holy Ghost,
     Mission of.
3a Ex. 3: 10 (2–10); 13:
     14; 14: 16; Deut. 11:

4; Josh. 2: 10; Neh. 9:
     11; 1 Ne. 4: 2; 17:
     26; Mosiah 7: 19;
     Hel. 8: 11; D&C 17: 1.
     TG Israel, Deliverance
     of.
4a 2 Tim. 1: 6.
   b TG Deliverance.
   c Ex. 23: 22 (20–23);
     D&C 105: 15; 136: 40.

5a Deut. 11: 18.
6a D&C 6: 10.
8a TG Doubt.
   b TG God, Works of.
10a TG Faith.
   b D&C 88: 65 (63–65).
11a D&C 1: 29; 9: 1, 10.
   b TG Sacred.
9a D&C 8: 11 (1, 11).
   b JS-H 1: 67.

2 And then, behold, ^aother ^brecords have I, that I will give unto you power that you may assist to ^ctranslate.

3 Be patient, my son, for it is ^awisdom in me, and it is not expedient that you should translate at this present time.

4 Behold, the work which you are called to do is to ^awrite for my servant Joseph.

5 And, behold, it is because that you did not continue as you commenced, when you began to translate, that I have taken away this privilege from you.

6 Do not ^amurmur, my son, for it is wisdom in me that I have dealt with you after this manner.

7 Behold, you have not understood; you have supposed that I would give it unto you, when you took no thought save it was to ask me.

8 But, behold, I say unto you, that you must ^astudy it out in your ^bmind; then you must ^cask me if it be right, and if it is right I will cause that your ^dbosom shall ^eburn within you; therefore, you shall ^ffeel that it is right.

9 But if it be not right you shall have no such feelings, but you shall have a ^astupor of thought that shall cause you to forget the thing which is wrong; therefore, you cannot write that which is ^bsacred save it be given you from me.

10 Now, if you had known this you could have ^atranslated; nevertheless, it is not expedient that you should translate now.

11 Behold, it was expedient when you commenced; but you ^afeared, and the time is past, and it is not expedient now;

12 For, do you not behold that I have ^agiven unto my servant ^bJoseph sufficient strength, whereby it is made up? And neither of you have I condemned.

13 Do this thing which I have commanded you, and you shall ^aprosper. Be faithful, and yield to no ^btemptation.

14 Stand fast in the ^awork wherewith I have ^bcalled you, and a hair of your head shall not be lost, and you shall be ^clifted up at the last day. Amen.

SECTION 10

Revelation given to Joseph Smith the Prophet, at Harmony, Pennsylvania, in the summer of 1828. HC 1: 20–23. Herein the Lord informs Joseph of alterations made by wicked men in the 116 manuscript pages from the translation of the "Book of Lehi," in the Book of Mormon. These manuscript pages had been lost from the possession of Martin Harris, to whom the sheets had been

2a An allusion to additional translation activity, i.e., the Joseph Smith translation of the Bible and the Book of Abraham, in which Oliver Cowdery assisted as a scribe. See also BD, "Joseph Smith Translation."
  b D&C 6: 26; 8:1.
   TG Scriptures to Come Forth.
  c D&C 6: 25 (25, 28); 10: 3 (3, 18, 41, 45).

3a TG God, Wisdom of; Stewardship.
4a D&C 18: 2; 24: 1.
   TG Scribe; Scriptures, Writing of.
6a Acts 1: 24 (22–26).
   TG Murmuring.
8a Acts 1: 24 (22–26).
   TG Knowledge; Meditation; Problem-Solving; Study; Testimony.
  b TG Mind.
  c TG Communication; Prayer.
  d Luke 24: 32.
  e TG Inspiration; Revelation.

f D&C 8: 2 (2–3).
   TG Holy Ghost, Source of Testimony.
9a D&C 10: 2.
  b TG Sacred.
10a D&C 8: 11.
11a TG Fearfulness.
12a D&C 1: 29.
  b D&C 18: 8.
13a Deut. 29: 9; Ps. 1: 3 (2–3).
  b TG Temptation.
14a 1 Cor. 16: 13.
  b TG Called of God.
  c D&C 5: 35; 17: 8.

temporarily entrusted. See heading to Section 3. The evil design was to await the expected retranslation of the matter covered by the stolen pages, and then to discredit the translator by showing discrepancies created by the alterations. That this wicked purpose had been conceived by the evil one, and was known to the Lord even while Mormon, the ancient Nephite historian, was making his abridgment of the accumulated plates, is shown in the Book of Mormon (The Words of Mormon 1: 3-7).

1-26, Satan stirs up wicked men to oppose the Lord's work; 27-33, He seeketh to destroy the souls of men; 34-52, The gospel is to go to Lamanites and all nations through Book of Mormon; 53-63, The Lord will establish his Church and the truth among men; 64-70, He will gather the repentant into his Church and will save the obedient.

Now, behold, I say unto you, that because you ^adelivered up those writings which you had power given unto you to translate by the means of the ^bUrim and Thummim, into the hands of a wicked man, you have lost them.

2 And you also lost your gift at the same time, and your ^amind became ^bdarkened.

3 Nevertheless, it is now ^arestored unto you again; therefore see that you are faithful and continue on unto the finishing of the remainder of the work of ^btranslation as you have begun.

4 Do not run ^afaster or labor more than you have ^bstrength and means provided to enable you to translate; but be ^cdiligent unto the end.

5 ^aPray always, that you may come off ^bconqueror; yea, that you may conquer Satan, and that you may ^cescape the hands of the ser-

vants of Satan that do uphold his work.

6 Behold, they have sought to ^adestroy you; yea, even the ^bman in whom you have trusted has sought to destroy you.

7 And for this cause I said that he is a wicked man, for he has sought to take away the things wherewith you have been entrusted; and he has also sought to destroy your gift.

8 And because you have delivered the writings into his hands, behold, wicked men have taken them from you.

9 Therefore, you have delivered them up, yea, that which was ^asacred, unto wickedness.

10 And, behold, ^aSatan hath put it into their hearts to alter the words which you have caused to be ^bwritten, or which you have translated, which have gone out of your hands.

11 And behold, I say unto you, that because they have altered the words, they read contrary from that which you translated and caused to be written;

12 And, on this wise, the devil has sought to lay a cunning plan, that he may destroy this work;

13 For he hath put into their hearts to do this, that by lying they may say they have ^acaught you in

---

10 1a D&C 3: 12 (1-15).
   b TG Urim and Thummim.
 2a Eph. 4: 18.
   TG Mind.
   b D&C 9: 5.
 3a D&C 3: 10.
   b D&C 9: 2 (1-3, 5, 10);
    10: 18 (18, 41, 45);

    11: 19.
 4a Mosiah 4: 27;
    Alma 1: 26.
   b Ex. 18: 18 (13-26).
   TG Health; Strength.
   c Matt. 10: 22.
   TG Diligence.
 5a TG Prayer.
   b TG Self-mastery.
   c Ps. 59: 2 (1-5).

 6a D&C 5: 33 (32-33);
    38: 13 (13, 28);
    42: 64.
   b D&C 3: 12 (7-13); 5: 2
    (1-18).
 9a TG Sacrilege.
 10a TG Devil.
   b D&C 3: 12.
 13a Jer. 5: 26.

the words which you have pretended to translate.

14 Verily, I say unto you, that I will not suffer that Satan shall accomplish his ᵃevil design in this thing.

15 For behold, he has put it into their ᵃhearts to get thee to ᵇtempt the Lord thy God, in asking to translate it over again.

16 And then, behold, they say and think in their hearts—We will see if God has given him power to translate; if so, he will also give him power again;

17 And if God giveth him power again, or if he translates again, or, in other words, if he bringeth forth the same words, behold, we have the same with us, and we have altered them;

18 Therefore they will not agree, and we will say that he has lied in his words, and that he has no ᵃgift, and that he has no power;

19 Therefore we will destroy him, and also the work; and we will do this that we may not be ashamed in the end, and that we may get ᵃglory of the world.

20 And, verily, I say unto you, that ᵃSatan has great hold upon their hearts; he stirreth them up to ᵇiniquity against that which is good;

21 And their hearts are ᵃcorrupt, and ᵇfull of wickedness and abominations; and they ᶜlove ᵈdarkness rather than light, because their

ᵉdeeds are evil; therefore they will not ask of me.

22 ᵃSatan stirreth them up, that he may ᵇlead their souls to destruction.

23 And thus he has laid a cunning plan, thinking to ᵈdestroy the work of God; but I will ᵇrequire this at their hands, and it shall turn to their shame and condemnation in the day of ᶜjudgment.

24 Yea, he stirreth up their hearts to ᵃanger against this work.

25 Yea, he saith unto them: ᵃDeceive and lie in wait to catch, that ye may destroy; behold, this is no harm. And thus he flattereth them, and telleth them that it is no sin to ᵇlie that they may catch a man in a lie, that they may destroy him.

26 And thus he ᵃflattereth them, and leadeth them along until he draggeth their souls down to ᵇhell; and thus he causeth them to catch themselves in their own ᶜsnare.

27 And thus he goeth up and down, ᵃto and fro in the earth, seeking to ᵇdestroy the souls of men.

28 Verily, verily, I say unto you, wo be unto him that ᵃlieth to ᵇdeceive because he supposeth that another lieth to deceive, for such are not exempt from the ᶜjustice of God.

29 Now, behold, they have altered these words, because Satan saith unto them: He hath deceived you—and thus he ᵃflattereth them away

14a TG Evil.
15a John 13:2.
  b TG Test, Try, Prove.
18a D&C 10:3.
19a Matt. 4:8.
20a TG Devil.
  b 2 Ne. 28:20–22.
  c TG Sin.
21a Gen. 6:5 (5–6, 11);
    Ps. 14:1; 2 Tim. 3:8;
    D&C 112:23 (23–24);
    Moses 8:28 (28–30).
  b Rev. 17:4.
    TG Wickedness.
  c Moses 5:18 (13–18).
  d Job 24:13 (13, 16);
    Mosiah 15:26.

    TG Darkness, Spiritual.
  e John 3:19 (18–21);
    D&C 29:45.
    TG Evil.
22a Luke 22:31; 2 Ne. 2:
    18 (17–18, 27); 3 Ne.
    18:18; D&C 50:3.
  b TG Damnation.
23a Neh. 6:2 (1–14).
  b TG Accountability.
  c Hel. 8:25; D&C 121:
    24 (23–25).
24a TG Anger.
25a Prov. 26:19 (16–19);
    Luke 20:23; Alma 10:
    17. TG Lying.
  b 2 Ne. 2:18; 28:8
    (7–23); Moses 4:4.

    TG Gossip.
26a TG Apostasy of
    Individuals.
  b TG Hell.
  c Esth. 7:10; Ps. 69:22;
    Prov. 26:6 (3–8);
    Matt. 7:2 (1–2); 1 Ne.
    14:3.
27a Job 1:7; Prov. 7:12.
  b Rev. 13:7; 2 Ne. 2:
    18; 28:20 (19–23);
    D&C 76:29.
28a TG False Doctrine;
    Honesty.
  b TG Deceit.
  c Rom. 2:3.
29a TG Flattery.

to do iniquity, to get thee to [b]tempt the Lord thy God.

30 Behold, I say unto you, that you shall not translate again those words which have gone forth out of your hands;

31 For, behold, they shall not accomplish their evil designs in lying against those words. For, behold, if you should bring forth the same words they will say that you have lied and that you have pretended to translate, but that you have contradicted yourself.

32 And, behold, they will publish this, and Satan will [a]harden the hearts of the people to stir them up to anger against you, that they will not believe my words.

33 Thus [a]Satan thinketh to over-power your [b]testimony in this generation, that the work may not come forth in this generation.

34 But behold, here is wisdom, and because I show unto you wisdom, and give you commandments concerning these things, what you shall do, show it not unto the world until you have accomplished the work of translation.

35 Marvel not that I said unto you: Here is [a]wisdom, show it not unto the world—for I said, show it not unto the world, that you may be preserved.

36 Behold, I do not say that you shall not show it unto the righteous;

37 But as you cannot always judge the [a]righteous, or as you cannot always tell the wicked from the righteous, therefore I say unto you, hold your [b]peace until I shall see fit to make all things known unto the world concerning the matter.

38 And now, verily I say unto you, that an account of those things that you have written, which have gone out of your hands, is engraven upon the [a]plates of Nephi;

39 Yea, and you remember it was said in those writings that a more particular account was given of these things upon the plates of Nephi.

40 And now, because the account which is engraven upon the plates of Nephi is more particular concerning the things which, in my wisdom, I [a]would bring to the knowledge of the people in this account—

41 Therefore, you shall translate the engravings which are on the plates of Nephi, down even till you come to the reign of king Benjamin, or until you come to that which you have translated, which you have retained;

42 And behold, you shall publish it as the record of Nephi; and thus I will [a]confound those who have altered my words.

43 I will not suffer that they shall destroy my [a]work; yea, I will show unto them that my [b]wisdom is greater than the cunning of the devil.

44 Behold, they have only got a part, or an [a]abridgment of the account of Nephi.

45 Behold, there are many things engraven upon the [a]plates of Nephi which do throw greater views upon my gospel; therefore, it is wisdom in me that you should [b]translate this first part of the engravings of Nephi, and send forth in this work.

46 And, behold, all the remainder of this work does contain all those parts of my [a]gospel which my holy prophets, yea, and also my disciples,

---

29b Matt. 4: 7.
32a TG Hardheartedness.
33a TG Devil.
  b TG Testimony.
35a TG God, Wisdom of.
37a Prov. 23: 9; Matt. 7: 6; 15: 26 (26–28); 23: 28; D&C 6: 12 (10–12).
  b Ex. 14: 14.

38a 1 Ne. 9: 2 (2–6); W of M 1: 3.
40a W of M 1: 7(3–7).
42a TG Book of Mormon. In the Preface to the first edition of the Book of Mormon, the Prophet explained that the material in the 116 pages had been translated from a

portion of the plates called the "Book of Lehi."
43a TG God, Works of.
  b TG God, Wisdom of; Wisdom.
44a W of M 1: 3.
45a TG Book of Mormon.
  b D&C 10: 3.
46a TG Gospel.

[b]desired in their prayers should come forth unto this people.

47 And I said unto them, that it should be [a]granted unto them according to their [b]faith in their prayers;

48 Yea, and this was their faith—that my gospel, which I gave unto them that they might preach in their days, might come unto their brethren the [a]Lamanites, and also all that had become Lamanites because of their dissensions.

49 Now, this is not all—their faith in their prayers was that this gospel should be made known also, if it were possible that other nations should possess this land;

50 And thus they did leave a blessing upon this land in their prayers, that whosoever should believe in this [a]gospel in this land might have eternal life;

51 Yea, that it might be [a]free unto all of whatsoever nation, kindred, tongue, or people they may be.

52 And now, behold, according to their faith in their prayers will I bring this part of my gospel to the knowledge of my people. Behold, I do not bring it to [a]destroy that which they have received, but to build it up.

53 And for this cause have I said: If this generation [a]harden not their hearts, I will establish my [b]church among them.

54 Now I do not say this to destroy my church, but I say this to build up my church;

55 Therefore, whosoever belongeth to my church need not [a]fear, for

such shall [b]inherit the [c]kingdom of heaven.

56 But it is they who do not [a]fear me, neither keep my commandments but build up [b]churches unto themselves to get [c]gain, yea, and all those that do wickedly and build up the kingdom of the devil—yea, verily, verily, I say unto you, that it is they that I will disturb, and cause to tremble and shake to the center.

57 Behold, I am Jesus Christ, the [a]Son of God. I came unto mine own, and mine own [b]received me not.

58 I am the [a]light which shineth in darkness, and the darkness comprehendeth it not.

59 I am he who said—[a]Other [b]sheep have I which are not of this fold—unto my disciples, and many there were that [c]understood me not.

60 And I will show unto this people that I had other [a]sheep, and that they were a [b]branch of the house of [c]Jacob;

61 And I will bring to light their marvelous works, which they did in my name;

62 Yea, and I will also bring to light my gospel which was ministered unto them, and, behold, they shall not deny that which you have received, but they shall build it up, and shall bring to light the true points of my [a]doctrine, yea, and the only doctrine which is in me.

63 And this I do that I may establish my gospel, that there may not be so much [a]contention; yea,

---

46b Enos 1: 13 (12–18);
  Morm. 8: 24 (24–26);
  9: 36 (34–37).
47a Enos 1: 16 (13–18);
  3 Ne. 5: 14 (13–15);
  D&C 3: 19.
  b TG Faith.
48a Moro. 10: 1 (1–5);
  D&C 3: 18; 109: 65.
50a TG Gospel.
51a TG Mission of Latter-day Saints.
52a Matt. 5: 17.
53a TG Hardheartedness.

b TG Church.
55a TG Fearfulness.
  b Matt. 5: 10 (3, 10).
  c TG Kingdom of God, in Heaven.
56a Eccl. 8: 13 (12–13); 12:
  13–14; Jer. 44: 10
  (10–11); Rom. 3: 18;
  D&C 45: 39.
  b TG Devil, Church of.
  c 4 Ne. 1: 26.
57a Rom. 1: 4.
  b TG Prophets,

Rejection of.
58a D&C 6: 21.
59a John 10: 16.
  b TG Jesus Christ, Good Shepherd.
  c 3 Ne. 15: 16–18.
60a TG Sheep.
  b TG Israel, Joseph, People of; Vineyard of the Lord.
  c TG Israel, Origins of.
62a 1 Ne. 13: 34 (34–42).
63a TG Self-mastery; Strife.

[b]Satan doth [c]stir up the hearts of the people to [d]contention concerning the points of my doctrine; and in these things they do err, for they do [e]wrest the scriptures and do not understand them.

64 Therefore, I will unfold unto them this great mystery;

65 For, behold, I will [g]gather them as a hen gathereth her chickens under her wings, if they will not harden their hearts;

66 Yea, if they will come, they may, and partake of the [a]waters of life freely.

67 Behold, this is my doctrine—whosoever repenteth and [a]cometh unto me, the same is my [b]church.

68 Whosoever [a]declareth more or less than this, the same is not of me, but is [b]against me; therefore he is not of my church.

69 And now, behold, whosoever is of my church, and [a]endureth of my church to the end, him will I establish upon my [b]rock, and the [g]gates of hell shall not prevail against them.

70 And now, remember the words of him who is the life and [a]light of the [b]world, your Redeemer, your [c]Lord and your God. Amen.

SECTION 11

Revelation given through Joseph Smith the Prophet to his brother Hyrum Smith, at Harmony, Pennsylvania, May 1829. HC 1 : 39–46. This revelation was received through the Urim and Thummim in answer to Joseph's supplication and inquiry. "History of the Church" suggests that this revelation was received after the restoration of the Aaronic Priesthood.

1–6, Laborers in the vineyard will gain salvation; 7–14, Seek wisdom, cry repentance, trust in the Spirit; 15–22, Keep the commandments and study the Lord's word; 23–27, Deny not the spirit of revelation and of prophecy; 28–30, Those who receive Christ become the sons of God.

A GREAT and [a]marvelous work is about to come forth among the children of men.

2 Behold, I am God; give [a]heed to my [b]word, which is quick and [c]powerful, [d]sharper than a two-edged sword, to the dividing asunder of both joints and marrow; therefore give [a]heed unto my word.

3 Behold, the field is [a]white already to harvest; therefore, whoso desireth to reap let him thrust in his sickle with his [b]might, and reap while the day lasts, that he may [c]treasure up for his soul [d]everlasting salvation in the kingdom of God.

4 Yea, whosoever will thrust in his sickle and [a]reap, the same is [b]called of God.

63b TG Devil.
  c TG Provoking.
  d TG Contention; Disputations.
  e 2 Pet. 3: 16.
65a Luke 13: 34; D&C 39: 22.
  TG Israel, Gathering of; Last Days.
66a TG Living Water.
67a Matt. 11: 28.
  b TG Church; Jesus Christ, Head of the Church.
68a 1 Tim. 6: 3.

  b Luke 11: 23.
69a TG Perseverance.
  b D&C 6: 34; 11: 16 (16, 24); 18: 4 (4, 17); 33: 13. TG Rock.
  c Matt. 16: 18; D&C 17: 8; 18: 5; 21: 6; 33: 13; 98: 22; 109: 26.
70a TG Jesus Christ, Light of the World; Light of Christ.
  b TG World.
  c TG Jesus Christ, Lord.
11 1a Isa. 29: 14; D&C 4: 1 (1–7).

2a D&C 1: 14 (14, 37); 84: 43 (43–45).
  b Heb. 4: 12.
  c Alma 4: 19; 31: 5.
  d Hel. 3: 29; D&C 6: 2.
  e 1 Ne. 15: 25 (23–25).
3a D&C 4: 4.
  b TG Dedication.
  c TG Treasure.
  d 1 Tim. 6: 19.
4a TG Harvest.
  b Rev. 14: 15; D&C 4: 3; 6: 4; 12: 4 (3–4); 14: 4 (3–4).

5 Therefore, if you will ask of me you shall receive; if you will ^aknock it shall be opened unto you.

6 Now, as you have asked, behold, I say unto you, keep my commandments, and seek to bring forth and establish the cause of ^aZion.

7 Seek not for ^ariches but for ^bwisdom; and, behold, the mysteries of God shall be unfolded unto you, and then shall you be made ^crich. Behold, he that hath eternal life is rich.

8 Verily, verily, I say unto you, even as you desire of me so it shall be done unto you; and, if you desire, you shall be the means of doing much good in this generation.

9 ^aSay nothing but ^brepentance unto this generation. Keep my commandments, and assist to bring forth my ^cwork, ^daccording to my commandments, and you shall be blessed.

10 Behold, thou hast a ^agift, or thou shalt have a gift if thou wilt desire of me in faith, with an ^bhonest heart, believing in the power of Jesus Christ, or in my power which speaketh unto thee;

11 For, behold, it is I that speak; behold, I am the ^alight which shineth in darkness, and by my ^bpower I give these words unto thee.

12 And now, verily, verily, I say unto thee, put your ^atrust in that ^bSpirit which ^cleadeth to do ^dgood—yea, to do ^ejustly, to walk ^fhumbly, to ^gjudge righteously; and this is my Spirit.

13 Verily, verily, I say unto you, I will impart unto you of my Spirit, which shall ^aenlighten your ^bmind, which shall fill your soul with ^cjoy;

14 And then shall ye know, or by this shall you know, all things whatsoever you desire of me, which are pertaining unto things of ^arighteousness, in faith believing in me that you shall receive.

15 Behold, I command you that you need not suppose that you are ^acalled to ^bpreach ^cuntil you are called.

16 Wait a little longer, until you shall have my word, my ^arock, my ^bchurch, and my gospel, that you may know of a surety my doctrine.

17 And then, behold, according to your desires, yea, even according to your ^afaith shall it be done unto you.

18 Keep my commandments; hold your peace; appeal unto my Spirit;

19 Yea, ^acleave unto me with all your heart, that you may assist in bringing to light those things of which has been spoken—yea, the ^btranslation of my work; be patient until you shall accomplish it.

20 Behold, this is your work, to ^akeep my commandments, yea, with all your might, ^bmind and strength.

5a TG Objectives; Prayer.
6a Isa. 52: 8; D&C 66: 11.
  TG Zion.
7a 1 Kgs. 3: 11 (11–13);
  2 Ne. 26: 31; Jacob
  2: 18 (17–19); D&C
  38: 39.
  b TG Education;
  Wisdom.
  c TG Treasure.
9a D&C 19: 21 (21–22).
  b TG Repentance.
  c TG God, Works of.
  d D&C 105: 5.
10a D&C 46: 8.
  b Luke 8: 15.
  c TG Motivations.
11a TG Light of Christ.
  b TG Jesus Christ,
  Authority of.

12a Prov. 28: 25 (25–26);
  D&C 84: 116.
  TG Trust in God.
  b Rom. 8: 1 (1–9); 1 Jn.
  4: 1 (1–6). TG God,
  Spirit of.
  c TG Guidance, Divine.
  d TG Benevolence.
  e TG Justice.
  f TG Humility.
  g Matt. 7: 1 (1–5); Rom.
  14: 4 (4–6); Alma 41:
  14 (14–15).
13a Eph. 1: 18; D&C 76:
  12. TG Discernment;
  Spiritual; Inspiration;
  Light of Christ.
  b TG Mind.
  c TG Joy.

14a TG Righteousness.
15a TG Authority.
  b A of F 5.
  TG Preaching.
  c D&C 30: 5.
16a D&C 6: 34; 10: 69; 18:
  4 (4, 17); 33: 13.
  TG Rock.
  b TG Church; Jesus
  Christ, Head of the
  Church.
17a TG Faith.
19a Josh. 23: 8; Jacob 6:
  5; Hel. 4: 25.
  b D&C 10: 3.
20a Ex. 15: 26; D&C 5: 35.
  TG Commitment;
  Obedience.
  b TG Dedication.

21 Seek not to *declare my word, but first seek to *obtain my *word, and then shall your tongue be loosed; then, if you desire, you shall have my *Spirit and my word, yea, the power of God unto the *convincing of men.

22 But now hold your *peace; study my word which *hath gone forth among the children of men, and also *study my word which shall come forth among the children of men, or that which is *now translating, yea, until you have obtained all which I shall *grant unto the children of men in this generation, and then shall all things be added thereto.

23 Behold thou art *Hyrum, my son; *seek the kingdom of God, and all things shall be added according to that which is just.

24 *Build upon my *rock, which is my *gospel;

25 Deny not the spirit of *revelation, nor the spirit of *prophecy, for wo unto him that *denieth these things;

26 Therefore, *treasure up in your *heart until the time which is in my wisdom that you shall go forth.

27 Behold, I speak unto *all who have good desires, and have thrust in their sickle to reap.

28 Behold, I am Jesus Christ, the *Son of God. I am the life and the *light of the world.

29 I am the same who came unto mine own and mine own *received me not;

30 But verily, verily, I say unto you, that as many as receive me, to them will I give *power to become the *sons of God, even to them that *believe on my name. Amen.

SECTION 12

Revelation given through Joseph Smith the Prophet to Joseph Knight, Sen., at Harmony, Pennsylvania, May 1829. HC 1: 47–48. Joseph Knight believed the declarations of Joseph Smith concerning his possession of the Book of Mormon plates and the work of translation then in progress, and several times had given material assistance to Joseph Smith and his scribe, which enabled them to continue translating. At Joseph Knight's request the Prophet inquired of the Lord and received the revelation.

1–6, Laborers in the vineyard are to gain salvation; 7–9, All who desire and are qualified may assist in the Lord's work.

*A GREAT and *marvelous work is about to come forth among the children of men.

2 Behold, I am God; give heed to

21a TG Missionary Work; Preaching.
  b Alma 17: 2 (2–3); D&C 84: 85.
  c TG Learning; Scriptures, Value of.
  d TG Teaching with the Spirit.
  e TG Conversion.
22a Ex. 14: 14.
  b IE the Bible.
  c TG Education; Scriptures, Study of; Study.
  d IE the Book of Mormon.

  e Alma 29: 8; 3 Ne. 26: 8 (7–10).
23a JS-H 1: 4.
  b Matt. 6: 33.
24a Matt. 7: 24.
  b TG Rock.
  c TG Gospel.
25a TG Revelation.
  b Rev. 19: 10.
    TG Prophecy.
26a Deut. 11: 18; D&C 6: 20; 43: 34; 84: 85; JS-M 1: 37.
  b Prov. 20: 5.

27a TG Mission of Latter-day Saints.
28a Rom. 1: 4.
  b TG Light; Jesus Christ, Light of the World.
29a TG Prophets, Rejection of.
30a John 1: 12.
  b TG Sons and Daughters of God.
  c 1 Jn. 3: 23 (19–24).
12 1a See D&C 11: 1–6 for similar concepts and cross references.
  b Isa. 29: 14; D&C 4: 1 (1–4).

my ^aword, which is quick and powerful, sharper than a two-edged sword, to the dividing asunder of both joints and marrow; therefore, give heed unto my word.

3 Behold, the field is ^awhite already to harvest; therefore, whoso desireth to reap let him thrust in his sickle with his might, and reap while the day lasts, that he may treasure up for his soul everlasting salvation in the kingdom of God.

4 Yea, whosoever will thrust in his sickle and will ^areap, the same is ^bcalled of God.

5 Therefore, if you will ask of me you shall receive; if you will knock it shall be opened unto you.

6 Now, as you have asked, behold, I say unto you, keep my commandments, and seek to bring forth and establish the cause of ^aZion.

7 Behold, I speak unto you, and also to all those who have desires to bring forth and establish this work;

8 And no one can assist in this work except he shall be ^ahumble and full of ^blove, having faith, hope, and charity, being temperate in all things, whatsoever shall be ^centrusted to his care.

9 Behold, I am the light and the life of the world, that speak these words, therefore give heed with your might, and then you are called. Amen.

SECTION 13

Ordination of Joseph Smith and Oliver Cowdery to the Aaronic Priesthood along the bank of the Susquehanna River, near Harmony, Pennsylvania, May 15, 1829. HC 1: 39–42. The ordination was done by the hands of an angel, who announced himself as John, the same that is called John the Baptist in the New Testament. The angel explained that he was acting under the direction of Peter, James, and John, the ancient apostles, who held the keys of the higher priesthood, which was called the Priesthood of Melchizedek. The promise was given to Joseph and Oliver that in due time the Priesthood of Melchizedek would be conferred upon them. See also Section 27: 7, 8, 12.

Keys and powers of Aaronic Priesthood are set forth.

UPON you my fellow servants, in the name of Messiah I ^aconfer the ^bPriesthood of Aaron, which holds the ^ckeys of the ministering of ^dangels, and of the gospel of ^erepentance, and of ^fbaptism by immersion for the remission of sins; and this shall never be taken again from the earth, until the sons of ^gLevi do offer again an offering unto the Lord in ^hrighteousness.

2a Heb. 4: 12.
3a D&C 4: 4; 14: 3; 33: 3
  (3, 7); 101: 64.
4a Rev. 14: 15.
  b D&C 6: 4; 11: 4 (3–4,
  27); 14: 4 (3–4).
6a Isa. 52: 8.
8a TG Humility.
  b TG Charity; Faith;
  Hope; Love; Temperance.
  c 1 Thes. 2: 4; D&C 124:
  113.

13 1a JS-H 1: 69 (68–75).
  TG Delegation of Responsibility; Ordination; Priesthood, Authority; Restoration of the Gospel.
  b D&C 27: 8.
  TG Priesthood, Aaronic.
  c D&C 84: 26.
  TG Priesthood, Keys.
  d TG Angels.
  e D&C 84: 26 (26–28).
  TG Repentance.

  f TG Baptism; Remission of Sins.
  g See JS-H 1: 71, footnote by Oliver Cowdery on the restoration of the Aaronic Priesthood. Gen. 49: 5;
  Deut. 10: 8; 1 Chr. 6:
  48; 23: 24;
  D&C 84: 31 (18–34);
  124: 39; 128: 24;
  JS-H 1: 69.
  h TG Righteousness.

SECTION 14

Revelation given through Joseph Smith the Prophet to David Whitmer, at Fayette, New York, June 1829. HC 1: 48–50. The Whitmer family had become greatly interested in the translating of the Book of Mormon. The Prophet established his residence at the home of Peter Whitmer, Sen., where he dwelt until the work of translation was carried to completion and the copyright on the forthcoming book secured. Three of the Whitmer sons, each having received a testimony as to the genuineness of the work, became deeply concerned over the matter of their individual duty. This revelation and the two next following (Sections 15 and 16) were given in answer to an inquiry through the Urim and Thummim. David Whitmer later became one of the Three Witnesses to the Book of Mormon.

1–6, Laborers in the vineyard will gain salvation; 7–8, Eternal life is the greatest of God's gifts; 9–11, Christ created the heavens and the earth.

A GREAT and ^amarvelous work is about to come forth unto the children of men.

2 Behold, I am God; give heed to my word, which is quick and powerful, sharper than a two-edged sword, to the dividing asunder of both joints and marrow; therefore give heed unto my word.

3 Behold, the field is white already to harvest; therefore, whoso desireth to reap let him thrust in his sickle with his might, and reap while the day lasts, that he may treasure up for his soul everlasting salvation in the kingdom of God.

4 Yea, whosoever will thrust in his sickle and reap, the same is called of God.

5 Therefore, if you will ask of me you shall receive; if you will ^aknock it shall be opened unto you.

6 Seek to bring forth and establish my Zion. Keep my commandments in all things.

7 And, if you ^akeep my commandments and ^bendure to the end you shall have ^ceternal life, which gift is the greatest of all the gifts of God.

8 And it shall come to pass, that if you shall ask the Father in my name, in faith ^abelieving, you shall receive the ^bHoly Ghost, which ^cgiveth utterance, that you may stand as a ^dwitness of the things of which you shall both ^ehear and see, and also that you may declare ^frepentance unto this generation.

9 Behold, I am ^aJesus Christ, the ^bSon of the ^cliving God, who ^dcreated the heavens and the ^eearth, a ^flight which cannot be hid in ^gdarkness;

10 Wherefore, I must bring forth

---

14 1a See D&C 11: 1–6
    for similar concepts
    and cross references.
  5a TG Objectives.
  7a Ps. 19: 11 (9–11);
    Prov. 7: 2; Mosiah 2:
    22; D&C 58: 2.
   b TG Steadfastness.
   c D&C 6: 13; 88: 4.
    TG Eternal Life;
    Exaltation; God, Gifts
    of; Man, Potential to
    Become like Heavenly
    Father.

  8a 2 Cor. 4: 13.
    TG Trust in God.
   b Acts 2: 4.
   c TG Holy Ghost, Mission
    of.
   d Acts 26: 16; 2 Ne. 27:
    12 (12–14); Ether 5: 4
    (3–5). TG Witnesses.
   e See the Testimony of
    Three Witnesses, Book
    of Mormon, pre-
    liminary pages.
   f TG Repentance.
  9a Mosiah 4: 2; Morm. 9:

    11; D&C 76: 24 (20–24).
   b Rom. 1: 4.
   c Dan. 6: 26; Alma 7:
    6; D&C 20: 19.
   d Jer. 14: 22; Acts 4: 24
    (23–24); Mosiah 4: 2;
    3 Ne. 9: 15; D&C 45:
    1. TG Creation; Jesus
    Christ, Creator.
   e Abr. 4: 12 (12, 24–25).
   f 2 Sam. 22: 29.
    TG Light; Light of
    Christ.
   g TG Darkness, Spiritual.

the *a*fulness of my *b*gospel from the *c*Gentiles unto the house of Israel.

11 And behold, thou art David, and thou art called to assist; which

thing if ye do, and are faithful, ye shall be blessed both spiritually and temporally, and great shall be your reward. Amen.

SECTION 15

Revelation given through Joseph Smith the Prophet to John Whitmer, at Fayette, New York, June 1829. HC 1: 50; see also heading to Section 14. The message is intimately and impressively personal, in that the Lord tells of what was known only to John Whitmer and himself. John Whitmer later became one of the Eight Witnesses to the Book of Mormon.

1–2, The Lord's arm is over all the earth; 3–6, To preach the gospel and save souls is the thing of most worth.

HEARKEN, my servant John, and listen to the words of Jesus Christ, your Lord and your Redeemer.

2 For behold, I speak unto you with *a*sharpness and with power, for mine arm is over the *b*earth.

3 And I will *a*tell you that which no man *b*knoweth save me and thee alone—

4 For many times you have desired

of me to know that which would be of the most worth unto you.

5 Behold, blessed are you for this thing, and for speaking my words which I have given you according to my commandments.

6 And now, behold, I say unto you, that the thing which will be of the most worth unto you will be to *a*declare *b*repentance unto this people, that you may bring *c*souls unto me, that you may *d*rest with them in the *e*kingdom of my *f*Father. Amen.

SECTION 16

Revelation given through Joseph Smith the Prophet to Peter Whitmer, Jun., at Fayette, New York, June 1829. HC 1: 51; see also heading to Section 14. Peter Whitmer, Jun., later became one of the Eight Witnesses to the Book of Mormon.

1–2, The Lord's arm is over all the earth; 3–6, To preach the gospel and save souls is the thing of most worth.

*a*HEARKEN, my servant Peter, and listen to the words of Jesus Christ, your Lord and your Redeemer.

2 For behold, I speak unto you with sharpness and with power, for mine arm is over all the earth.

3 And I will tell you that which no man knoweth save me and thee alone—

4 For many times you have desired

10a Rom. 15: 29; D&C 20: 9 (8–9); JS–H 1: 34.
  b TG Israel, Restoration of.
  c 1 Ne. 10: 14; 13: 42; 15: 13 (13–20).
15 2a Hel. 3: 29 (29–30).
  TG God, Power of.
  b Ex. 9: 29; D&C 14: 9;

Abr. 4: 12 (12, 24–25).
3a TG God, Omniscience of.
  b D&C 6: 16.
6a D&C 6: 6; 18: 15 (15–16); 30: 9 (9–10).
  b TG Missionary Work; Repentance.
  c TG Conversion; Soul;

Worth of Souls.
  d TG Rest.
  e TG Kingdom of God, in Heaven.
  f TG God the Father—Elohim.
16 1a See D&C 15: 1–6 for similar concepts and cross references.

of me to know that which would be of the most worth unto you.

5 Behold, blessed are you for this thing, and for speaking my words which I have given unto you according to my commandments.

6 And now, behold, I say unto

you, that the thing which will be of the most worth unto you will be to declare repentance unto this people, that you may bring souls unto me, that you may rest with them in the kingdom of my Father. Amen.

SECTION 17

Revelation given through Joseph Smith the Prophet to Oliver Cowdery, David Whitmer, and Martin Harris, at Fayette, New York, June 1829, prior to their viewing the engraved plates that contained the Book of Mormon record. HC 1: 52–57. Joseph and his scribe, Oliver Cowdery, had learned from the translation of the Book of Mormon plates that three special witnesses would be designated. See Ether 5: 2–4; also 2 Nephi 11: 3 and 27: 12. Oliver Cowdery, David Whitmer, and Martin Harris were moved upon by an inspired desire to be the three special witnesses. The Prophet inquired of the Lord, and this revelation was given in answer, through the Urim and Thummim.

1–4, By faith the Three Witnesses shall see the plates and other sacred items; 5–9, Christ bears testimony to the divinity of the Book of Mormon.

BEHOLD, I say unto you, that you must rely upon my word, which if you do with full purpose of heart, you shall have a ᵃview of the ᵇplates, and also of the ᶜbreastplate, the ᵈsword of Laban, the ᵉUrim and Thummim, which were given to the ᶠbrother of Jared upon the mount, when he talked with the Lord ᵍface to face, and the ʰmiraculous directors which were given to Lehi while in the wilderness, on the borders of the ⁱRed Sea.

2 And it is by your faith that you

shall obtain a view of them, even by that faith which was had by the prophets of old.

3 And after that you have obtained faith, and have seen them with your eyes, you shall ᵃtestify of them, by the power of God;

4 And this you shall do that my servant Joseph Smith, Jun., may not be destroyed, that I may bring about my righteous purposes unto the children of men in this work.

5 And ye shall testify that you have seen them, even as my servant Joseph Smith, Jun., has seen them; for it is by my power that he has seen them, and it is because he had faith.

6 And he has translated the ᵃbook, even that ᵇpart which I have com-

17 1a 2 Ne. 27: 12; Ether
        5: 4 (2–4); D&C 5: 15
        (15, 24). See also the
        Testimony of Three
        Witnesses, Book of
        Mormon, preliminary
        pages.
     b Morm. 6: 6; Ether 4: 5
        (4–7); JS–H 1: 52.
     c Ex. 25: 7.

     d 1 Ne. 4: 9; 2 Ne. 5: 14;
        Jacob 1: 10; Mosiah 1:
        16.
     e TG Urim and Thum-
        mim. See also " Urim
        and Thummim" in BD.
     f Ether 3: 28 (1–28).
     g Gen. 32: 30; Num. 12:
        8; Moses 1: 2.
     h 1 Ne. 16: 16 (10, 16,
        26); 18: 12 (12, 21);

        2 Ne. 5: 12; Alma 37:
        38 (38–47).
     i 1 Ne. 2: 5.
    3a 2 Ne. 5: 3 (3–4);
        D&C 5: 11.
        TG Witnesses.
    6a TG Book of Mormon.
     b 2 Ne. 27: 8 (7–11, 21);
        3 Ne. 26: 9 (7–12, 18);
        Ether 4: 5 (4–7); 5: 1.

manded him, and as your Lord and your God liveth it is true.

7 Wherefore, you have received the same power, and the same faith, and the same gift like unto him;

8 And if you do these last *a*commandments of mine, which I have given you, the *b*gates of hell shall not prevail against you; for my *c*grace is sufficient for you, and you shall be *d*lifted up at the last day.

9 And I, Jesus Christ, your *a*Lord and your God, have spoken it unto you, that I might bring about my righteous purposes unto the children of men. Amen.

SECTION 18

Revelation to Joseph Smith the Prophet, Oliver Cowdery, and David Whitmer, given at Fayette, New York, June 1829. HC 1: 60–64. When the Aaronic Priesthood was conferred, the bestowal of the Melchizedek Priesthood was promised. See heading to Section 13. In response to supplication for knowledge on the matter, the Lord gave this revelation.

1–5, Scriptures show how to build up the Church; 6–8, The world is ripening in iniquity; 9–16, The worth of souls is great; 17–25, To gain salvation, men must take upon them the name of Christ; 26–36, The calling and mission of the Twelve are revealed; 37–39, Oliver Cowdery and David Whitmer are to search out the Twelve; 40–47, To gain salvation, men must repent, be baptized, and keep the commandments.

Now, behold, because of the thing which you, my servant Oliver Cowdery, have desired to know of me, I give unto you these words:

2 Behold, I have *a*manifested unto you, by my Spirit in many instances, that the *b*things which you have written are *c*true; wherefore you know that they are true.

3 And if you know that they are

true, behold, I give unto you a commandment, that you *a*rely upon the things which are *b*written;

4 For in them are all things *a*concerning the foundation of my church, my gospel, and my *b*rock.

5 Wherefore, if you shall build up my *a*church, upon the foundation of my gospel and my *b*rock, the *c*gates of hell shall not prevail against you.

6 Behold, the *a*world is ripening in iniquity; and it must needs be that the children of men are stirred up unto repentance, both the *b*Gentiles and also the house of Israel.

7 Wherefore, as thou hast been *a*baptized by the hands of my servant Joseph Smith, Jun., according to that which I have commanded him, he hath fulfilled the thing which I commanded him.

8 And now, marvel not that I have *a*called him unto mine own purpose,

---

8a D&C 19: 13.
  b Matt. 16: 18; 1 Ne. 22: 26; Alma 48: 17 (16–17); 3 Ne. 11: 39 (39–40); D&C 10: 69.
  c TG Grace.
  d 1 Ne. 13: 37; 3 Ne. 27: 14 (14–15, 22); D&C 5: 35; 9: 14; 27: 18.
9a TG Jesus Christ, Lord.
18 2a D&C 6: 24 (22–24).
  b D&C 9: 4.
  c D&C 6: 17 (15–17).

3a Prov. 22: 21; D&C 98: 11. TG Dependability; Guidance, Divine; Scriptures, Value of.
  b D&C 18: 30 (29–30).
4a D&C 20: 9 (8–11); 39: 11; 68: 1. TG Gospel.
  b D&C 6: 34; 10: 69; 11: 16 (16, 24); 33: 13.
5a TG Church; Jesus Christ, Head of the Church.

  b TG Rock.
  c Matt. 16: 18; D&C 10: 69.
6a TG World.
  b Rev. 14: 15.
  c 1 Ne. 13: 42; D&C 18: 26; 19: 27; 21: 12; 90: 9 (8–9); 107: 33; 112: 4. TG Gentiles; Israel, Restoration of; Missionary Work.
7a JS-H 1: 71 (70–71).
8a D&C 9: 12.

which purpose is known in me; wherefore, if he shall be *b*diligent in keeping my commandments he shall be *c*blessed unto eternal life; and his name is *d*Joseph.

9 And now, Oliver Cowdery, I speak unto you, and also unto David Whitmer, by the way of commandment; for, behold, I *a*command all men everywhere to repent, and I speak unto you, even as unto Paul mine *b*apostle, for you are called even with that same calling with which he was called.

10 Remember the *a*worth of *b*souls is great in the sight of God;

11 For, behold, the Lord your *a*Redeemer suffered *b*death in the flesh; wherefore he *c*suffered the *d*pain of all men, that all men might repent and *e*come unto him.

12 And he hath *a*risen again from the dead, that he might bring all men unto him, on conditions of *b*repentance.

13 And how great is his *a*joy in the *b*soul that *c*repenteth!

14 Wherefore, you are called to *a*cry repentance unto this people.

15 And if it so be that you should labor all your days in crying repentance unto this people, and bring, save it be one *a*soul unto me, how great shall be your joy with him in the kingdom of my Father!

16 And now, if your joy will be great with one soul that you have brought unto me into the *a*kingdom of my Father, how great will be your *b*joy if you should bring many *c*souls unto me!

17 Behold, you have my gospel before you, and my rock, and my *a*salvation.

18 *a*Ask the Father in my *b*name, in faith believing that you shall receive, and you shall have the Holy Ghost, which manifesteth all things which are *c*expedient unto the children of men.

19 And if you have not *a*faith, *b*hope, and *c*charity, you can do nothing.

20 *a*Contend against no church, save it be the *b*church of the devil.

21 Take upon you the *a*name of Christ, and *b*speak the truth in *c*soberness.

22 And as many as repent and are *a*baptized in my name, which is Jesus Christ, and *b*endure to the end, the same shall be saved.

23 Behold, Jesus Christ is the *a*name which is given of the Father, and there is none other name given whereby man can be *b*saved;

24 Wherefore, all men must take upon them the *a*name which is given of the Father, for in that name shall they be called at the last day;

8*b* TG Diligence.
  c TG Blessing.
  d 2 Ne. 3: 15 (14–15).
     TG Joseph Smith.
9*a* Acts 17:30.
  b Rom. 1: 1.
10*a* Isa. 43: 4.
     TG Life, Sanctity of; Worth of Souls.
  b TG Soul.
11*a* TG Jesus Christ, Redeemer.
  b TG Death; Jesus Christ, Death of.
  c TG Redemption; Self-sacrifice.
  d Isa. 53: 4 (4–5).
     TG Jesus Christ, Atonement through; Pain.
  e John 12: 32.
12*a* TG Jesus Christ, Resurrection.

  b D&C 19: 4 (4–18).
13*a* Luke 15: 7.
  b TG Worth of Souls.
  c TG Repentance.
14*a* D&C 6: 9; 34: 6; 63: 57.
15*a* TG Missionary Work; Worth of Souls.
16*a* TG Kingdom of God, in Heaven.
  b John 4: 36; 1 Thes. 3: 9; Alma 26: 11 (11–13); D&C 50: 22 (17–22). TG Joy.
  c TG Conversion.
17*a* TG Rock; Salvation.
18*a* TG Prayer.
  b John 15: 16.
  c D&C 88: 64 (63–65).
19*a* TG Faith.
  b TG Hope.

  c TG Charity.
20*a* 2 Tim. 2: 24 (23–24); 3 Ne. 11: 29 (29–30).
  b TG Devil, Church of.
21*a* TG Jesus Christ, Taking the Name of.
  b 2 Cor. 4: 13; D&C 100: 7 (5–8).
  c Rom. 12: 3; D&C 43: 35.
22*a* TG Baptism, Essential.
  b TG Perseverance; Steadfastness.
23*a* Mal. 1: 11; Acts 4: 12.
  b TG Jesus Christ, Atonement through; Jesus Christ, Savior; Salvation; Salvation, Plan of.
24*a* TG Jesus Christ, Taking the Name of.

25 Wherefore, if they ^aknow not the ^bname by which they are called, they cannot have place in the ^ckingdom of my Father.

26 And now, behold, there are others who are ^acalled to declare my gospel, both unto ^bGentile and unto Jew;

27 Yea, even twelve; and the ^aTwelve shall be my disciples, and they shall take upon them my name; and the Twelve are they who shall desire to take upon them my ^bname with full purpose of heart.

28 And if they desire to take upon them my name with full purpose of heart, they are called to go into all the ^aworld to preach my ^bgospel unto ^cevery creature.

29 And they are they who are ordained of me to ^abaptize in my name, according to that which is written;

30 And you have that which is written before you; wherefore, you must perform it ^aaccording to the words which are ^bwritten.

31 And now I speak unto you, the ^aTwelve—Behold, my grace is sufficient for you; you must walk uprightly before me and sin not.

32 And, behold, you are they who are ordained of me to ^aordain ^bpriests and teachers; to declare my gospel, ^caccording to the power of the Holy Ghost which is in you, and according to the ^dcallings and gifts of God unto men;

33 And I, Jesus Christ, your Lord and your God, have spoken it.

34 These ^awords are not of men nor of man, but of me; wherefore, you shall testify they are of me and not of man;

35 For it is my ^avoice which speaketh them unto you; for they are given by my Spirit unto you, and by my power you can read them one to another; and save it were by my power you could not have them;

36 Wherefore, you can ^atestify that you have ^bheard my voice, and know my words.

37 And now, behold, I give unto you, Oliver Cowdery, and also unto David Whitmer, that you shall search out the Twelve, who shall have the desires of which I have spoken;

38 And by their ^adesires and their ^bworks you shall know them.

39 And when you have found them you shall show these things unto them.

40 And you shall fall down and ^aworship the Father in my ^bname.

41 And you must preach unto the world, saying: You must ^arepent and be baptized, in the name of Jesus Christ;

42 For all men must repent and be baptized, and not only men, but women, and ^achildren who have arrived at the years of ^baccountability.

43 And now, after that you have received this, you must keep my ^acommandments in all things;

44 And by your hands I will work a ^amarvelous work among the child-

25a TG Ignorance.
  b Mosiah 5: 12 (9-14).
  c TG Kingdom of God, in Heaven.
26a TG Authority.
  b 1 Ne. 13: 42; D&C 18: 6; 19: 27; 21: 12; 90: 9 (8-9); 107: 33; 112: 4.
27a TG Apostles.
  b Jer. 15: 16; D&C 27: 12.
28a Mark 16: 15 (15-16).
  b Gospel.
  c D&C 1: 2 (2, 34-35); 39: 15; 42: 58.
29a John 4: 2 (1-2); 3 Ne. 11: 22 (21-22); 12: 1;

D&C 20: 38.
30a 3 Ne. 11: 22 (22-28); D&C 20: 72 (72-74).
  b D&C 18: 3 (3-4).
31a D&C 107: 23 (23-39).
32a Moro. 3: 4 (1-4); D&C 20: 39 (39, 60); 107: 58. TG Priesthood, Ordination.
  b TG Priest.
  c 2 Pet. 1: 21; D&C 68: 3 (3-4).
  d D&C 20: 27.
34a TG Scriptures, Value of.
35a D&C 1: 38. TG Revelation.

36a TG Testimony.
  b Ex. 19: 9 (7-13).
38a TG Motivations.
  b TG Good Works.
40a TG Worship.
  b 1 Kgs. 8: 29. TG Name.
41a TG Baptism, Essential; Repentance.
42a TG Children; Family, Children, Duties of.
  b D&C 20: 71; 29: 47; 68: 25 (25-27).
43a TG Commandments of God.
44a Isa. 29: 14; D&C 4: 1; 6: 1.

ren of men, unto the ᵇconvincing of many of their sins, that they may come unto their repentance, and that they may come unto the kingdom of my Father.

45 Wherefore, the blessings which I give unto you are ªabove all things.

46 And after that you have re-

ceived this, if you ªkeep not my commandments you cannot be saved in the kingdom of my Father.

47 Behold, I, Jesus Christ, your Lord and your God, and your ªRedeemer, by the ᵇpower of my Spirit have spoken it. Amen.

SECTION 19

Revelation given through Joseph Smith, at Manchester, New York, March 1830. HC 1: 72–74. In his history the Prophet introduced it as "a commandment of God and not of man, to Martin Harris, given by him who is Eternal."

1–3, Christ has all power; 4–5, All men must repent or suffer; 6–12, Eternal punishment is God's punishment; 13–20, Christ suffered for all, that they might not suffer if they would repent; 21–28, Preach the gospel of repentance; 29–41, Declare glad tidings.

I AM ªAlpha and Omega, ᵇChrist the Lord; yea, even I am he, the beginning and the end, the Redeemer of the ᶜworld.

2 I, having accomplished and ªfinished the will of him whose I am, even the Father, concerning me—having done this that I might ᵇsubdue all things unto myself—

3 Retaining all ªpower, even to the ᵇdestroying of Satan and his works at the ᶜend of the world, and the last great day of judgment, which I shall pass upon the inhabitants

thereof, ᵈjudging every man according to his ᵉworks and the deeds which he hath done.

4 And surely every man must ªrepent or ᵇsuffer, for I, God, am ᶜendless.

5 Wherefore, I ªrevoke not the judgments which I shall pass, but woes shall go forth, weeping, ᵇwailing and gnashing of teeth, yea, to those who are found on my ᶜleft hand.

6 Nevertheless, it is ªnot written that there shall be no end to this torment, but it is written ᵇendless ᶜtorment.

7 Again, it is written ªeternal damnation; wherefore it is more express than other scriptures, that it might work upon the hearts of the children of men, altogether for my name's glory.

8 Wherefore, I will explain unto

44b Job 13: 23 (23–28);
  Alma 12: 1; 36: 17
  (12–19); 62: 45;
  D&C 6: 11.
45a D&C 76: 92; 84: 38
  (35–38).
46a 1 Pet. 4: 17 (17–18);
  D&C 82: 3.
47a TG Jesus Christ,
  Redeemer.
  b TG Jesus Christ, Power
  of.
19 1a Rev. 1: 8 (8, 11);
  D&C 35: 1; 45: 7; 54:
  1; 61: 1; 68: 35; 75: 1.
  b TG Jesus Christ,

Messiah.
  c TG World.
2a John 17: 4; 3 Ne. 11:
  11.
  b Philip. 3: 21.
  TG Jesus Christ,
  Mission of.
3a TG Jesus Christ, Power
  of.
  b Gen. 3: 15; Rom. 16:
  20; 1 Jn. 3: 8; Rev. 20:
  10 (8, 10); D&C 29: 28
  (27–30, 44); 88: 114
  (111–115).
  c TG World, End of.
  d TG Jesus Christ,

Judge; Judgment,
  The Last; Justice.
  e TG Good Works.
4a TG Repentance.
  b Luke 13: 3.
  c Moses 1: 3.
5a D&C 56: 4; 58: 32.
  b Matt. 13: 42.
  c Matt. 25: 41.
6a D&C 76: 106 (105–
  106); 138: 59.
  b D&C 76: 44 (33, 44–
  45).
  c TG Punishment.
7a Hel. 12: 26 (25–26);
  D&C 29: 44.

you this ^amystery, for it is meet unto you to know even as mine apostles.

9 I speak unto you that are chosen in this thing, because ye are one, that you may enter into my ^arest.

10 For, behold, the ^amystery of godliness, how great is it! For, behold, I am ^bendless, and the punishment which is given from my hand is endless ^cpunishment, for ^dEndless is my name. Wherefore—

11 ^aEternal punishment is God's punishment.

12 Endless punishment is God's punishment.

13 Wherefore, I command you to repent, and keep the ^acommandments which you have received by the hand of my servant Joseph Smith, Jun., in my name;

14 And it is by my almighty power that you have received them;

15 Therefore I command you to repent—repent, lest I ^asmite you by the rod of my mouth, and by my wrath, and by my anger, and your ^bsufferings be sore—how sore you know not, how exquisite you know not, yea, how hard to bear you know not.

16 For behold, I, God, have ^asuffered these things for all, that they might not ^bsuffer if they would ^crepent;

17 But if they would not repent they must ^asuffer even as I;

18 Which ^asuffering caused myself, even God, the greatest of all, to tremble because of pain, and to bleed at every pore, and to suffer both body and spirit—and would that I might ^bnot drink the bitter cup, and shrink—

19 Nevertheless, glory be to the Father, and I partook and ^afinished my preparations unto the children of men.

20 Wherefore, I command you again to repent, lest I ^ahumble you with my almighty power; and that you ^bconfess your sins, lest you suffer these ^cpunishments of which I have spoken, of which in the smallest, yea, even in the least degree you have ^dtasted at the time I withdrew my Spirit.

21 And I command you that you ^apreach naught but repentance, and show ^bnot these things unto the world until it is wisdom in me.

22 For they cannot ^abear meat now, but ^bmilk they must receive; wherefore, they must not know these things, lest they perish.

23 ^aLearn of me, and listen to my words; ^bwalk in the ^cmeekness of my Spirit, and you shall have ^dpeace in me.

24 I am Jesus Christ; I ^acame by the ^bwill of the Father, and I do his will.

25 And again, I command thee that thou shalt not ^acovet thy

8a Matt. 13:11.
9a Heb. 4:3 (3, 5); 2 Ne. 21:10.
10a 1 Tim. 3:16; Jacob 4:8; D&C 76:114 (114–116).
b TG God, Eternal Nature of.
c TG Punishment.
d Ex. 3:15; Moses 1:3; 7:35.
11a Matt. 25:46. TG Punishment.
13a D&C 5:2 (1–18); 10:6 (6–7); 17:8 (1–9).
15a Ps. 2:9; Isa. 11:4 (1–4).
b Alma 36:12 (11–19).
16a 2 Cor. 5:14; Alma 11:40 (40–41). TG Jesus

Christ, Atonement through; Jesus Christ, Redeemer; Redemption.
b TG Mercy.
c TG Remission of Sins.
17a Mark 14:36; Alma 11:40 (40–41); D&C 29:17.
18a TG Suffering; Pain.
b Luke 22:42 (42–44).
19a John 17:4; 19:30; Heb. 12:2 (1–3).
20a TG God, Indignation of.
b Num. 5:7 (6–10); D&C 58:43; 64:7. TG Confession.
c TG Despair; Punishment.
d D&C 10:7 (1–7).

TG Holy Ghost, Loss of.
21a D&C 11:9.
b Moses 1:42; 4:32; JS-H 1:42.
22a D&C 78:18 (17–18).
b Isa. 28:9; 1 Cor. 3:2 (2–3); Heb. 5:12 (11–14); D&C 50:40.
23a TG Education; Learning.
b 1 Jn. 2:6; Moro. 7:4 (3–4).
c TG Meekness.
d Micah 5:5. TG Peace of God.
24a TG Jesus Christ, Birth of.
b TG God, Will of; Jesus Christ, Authority of.
25a TG Covetousness.

*b*neighbor's *c*wife; nor seek thy neighbor's life.

26 And again, I command thee that thou shalt not *a*covet thine own property, but impart it freely to the printing of the Book of Mormon, which contains the *b*truth and the word of God—

27 Which is my word to the *a*Gentile, that soon it may go to the *b*Jew, of whom the Lamanites are a *c*remnant, that they may believe the gospel, and look not for a *d*Messiah to come who has already come.

28 And again, I command thee that thou shalt *a*pray *b*vocally as well as in thy heart; yea, before the world as well as in secret, in public as well as in private.

29 And thou shalt *a*declare glad tidings, yea, *b*publish it upon the mountains, and upon every high place, and among every people that thou shalt be permitted to see.

30 And thou shalt do it with all humility, *a*trusting in me, *b*reviling not against revilers.

31 And of *a*tenets thou shalt not talk, but thou shalt declare repentance and *b*faith on the Savior, and *c*remission of sins by *d*baptism, and by *e*fire, yea, even the *f*Holy Ghost.

32 Behold, this is a great and the last *a*commandment which I shall give unto you concerning this mat-

ter; for this shall suffice for thy daily walk, even unto the end of thy life.

33 And misery thou shalt receive if thou wilt slight these *a*counsels, yea, even the destruction of thyself and property.

34 *a*Impart a portion of thy property, yea, even part of thy lands, and all save the support of thy *b*family.

35 Pay the *a*debt thou hast *b*contracted with the printer. Release thyself from *c*bondage.

36 *a*Leave thy house and home, except when thou shalt desire to see thy family;

37 And *a*speak freely to all; yea, preach, exhort, declare the *b*truth, even with a loud voice, with a sound of rejoicing, crying— Hosanna, hosanna, blessed be the name of the Lord God!

38 *a*Pray always, and I will *b*pour out my Spirit upon you, and great shall be your blessing—yea, even more than if you should obtain *c*treasures of earth and corruptibleness to the extent thereof.

39 Behold, canst thou read this without *a*rejoicing and lifting up thy heart for *b*gladness?

40 Or canst thou run about longer as a *a*blind guide?

41 Or canst thou be *a*humble and meek, and conduct thyself wisely before me? Yea, *b*come unto me thy Savior. Amen.

25*b* TG Neighbor.
　c Ex. 20: 17; 1 Cor. 7: 2 (2–4).
　TG Adultery; Lust; Marriage, Husbands; Marriage, Wives.
26*a* Acts 5: 1 (1–11).
27*a* 1 Ne. 13: 42; 3 Ne. 16: 7 (4–13); D&C 18: 6 (6, 26); 21: 12; 90: 9 (8–9); 107: 33; 112: 4.
　b 2 Ne. 26: 12; 30: 7 (7–8); Morm. 5: 14 (12–14).
　c Omni 1: 15 (14–19); Mosiah 25: 2 (2–4); Hel. 8: 21; D&C 52: 2; 109: 65.
　d Jesus Christ, Messiah.
28*a* 1 Tim. 2: 8. TG Prayer.

　b D&C 20: 47 (47, 51); 23: 6.
29*a* TG Preaching.
30*a* TG Trust in God.
　b TG Forbearance; Retribution; Reviling; Strife.
31*a* 2 Tim. 2: 23 (23–24).
　b TG Baptism, Qualifications for; Faith.
　c TG Remission of Sins.
　d TG Baptism.
　e Matt. 3: 11.
　f TG Holy Ghost, Baptism of.
32*a* D&C 58: 26 (26–29).
33*a* TG Counsel.
34*a* Acts 4: 37 (34–37).
　b TG Family.
35*a* TG Debt.

　b IE to pay for the publication of the first edition of the Book of Mormon.
　c Prov. 22: 7.
　TG Bondage, Physical.
36*a* Matt. 19: 29.
37*a* Ps. 105: 2; Heb. 13: 16; D&C 58: 47; 63: 37; 68: 8; 71: 7.
　b 2 Cor. 4: 2; D&C 75: 4.
38*a* TG Prayer.
　b Prov. 1: 23; Acts 2: 17; D&C 95: 4.
　c TG Treasure.
39*a* TG Joy.
　b TG Cheerfulness.
40*a* Matt. 23: 16 (16, 24).
41*a* TG Humility; Meekness.
　b Matt. 11: 28 (28–30).

SECTION 20

Revelation on Church Organization and Government, given through Joseph Smith the Prophet, April 1830. HC 1: 64–70. Preceding his record of this revelation the Prophet wrote: "We obtained of him [Jesus Christ] the following, by the spirit of prophecy and revelation; which not only gave us much information, but also pointed out to us the precise day upon which, according to his will and commandment, we should proceed to organize his Church once more here upon the earth."

1–16, The Book of Mormon proves the divinity of the latter-day work; 17–29, The doctrines of creation, fall, atonement, and baptism are affirmed; 29–37, Laws governing repentance, justification, sanctification, and baptism are set forth; 38–67, Duties of elders, priests, teachers, and deacons are summarized; 68–74, Duties of members, blessing of children, and mode of baptism are revealed; 75–84, Sacramental prayers and regulations governing church membership are given.

THE ᵃrise of the ᵇChurch of Christ in these last days, being one thousand eight hundred and thirty years since the ᶜcoming of our Lord and Savior Jesus Christ in the flesh, it being regularly ᵈorganized and established agreeable to the ᵉlaws of our country, by the will and commandments of God, in the fourth month, and on the sixth day of the month which is called April—

2 Which commandments were given to Joseph Smith, Jun., who was ᵃcalled of God, and ᵇordained an ᶜapostle of Jesus Christ, to be the ᵈfirst ᵉelder of this church;

3 And to Oliver Cowdery, who was also called of God, an apostle of Jesus Christ, to be the ᵃsecond elder of this church, and ordained under his hand;

4 And this according to the ᵃgrace of our Lord and Savior Jesus Christ, to whom be all glory, both now and forever. Amen.

5 After it was truly manifested unto this first elder that he had received a ᵃremission of his sins, he was ᵇentangled again in the ᶜvanities of the world;

6 But after ᵃrepenting, and humbling himself sincerely, through faith, God ministered unto him by an holy ᵇangel, whose ᶜcountenance was as lightning, and whose garments were pure and white above all other whiteness;

7 And gave unto him ᵃcommandments which inspired him;

8 And ᵃgave him power from on high, by the ᵇmeans which were before prepared, to translate the Book of Mormon;

9 Which contains a ᵃrecord of a fallen people, and the ᵇfulness of the ᶜgospel of Jesus Christ to the Gentiles and to the Jews also;

---

20 1a JS-H 1: 2.
  b 3 Ne. 27: 3 (1–8);
    D&C 1: 1. TG Church.
  c Matt. 1: 18.
    TG Jesus Christ, Birth of.
  d D&C 21: 3.
  e D&C 58: 21; 98: 4
    (4–5).
 2a TG Authority; Called of God.
  b D&C 5: 6.
  c TG Apostles.

  d D&C 21: 11; 30: 7.
  e TG Elder—Melchizedek Priesthood.
 3a D&C 28: 1.
 4a TG Grace.
 5a D&C 21: 8; 23: 5;
    JS-H 1: 73 (68–74).
    TG Remission of Sins.
  b 2 Pet. 2: 20; D&C 3: 6;
    5: 21; 20: 32 (31–34);
    JS-H 1: 28 (28–29).
  c Ps. 25: 7. TG Vanity.
 6a TG Priesthood, Quali-

fying for.
  b JS-H 1: 30 (29–35).
    TG Angels.
  c Matt. 28: 3.
 7a TG Guidance, Divine.
 8a Luke 24: 49.
  b TG Urim and Thummim.
 9a TG Record Keeping.
  b D&C 14: 10; 18: 4;
    JS-H 1: 34.
  c TG Book of Mormon;
    Gospel.

10 Which was given by inspiration, and is confirmed to *others by the ministering of angels, and is *declared unto the world by them—

11 Proving to the world that the holy scriptures are *true, and that God does *inspire men and call them to his *holy work in this age and generation, as well as in generations of old;

12 Thereby showing that he is the *same God yesterday, today, and *forever. Amen.

13 Therefore, having so great witnesses, by *them shall the world be judged, even as many as shall hereafter come to a knowledge of this work.

14 And those who receive it in faith, and work *righteousness, shall receive a *crown of eternal life;

15 But those who *harden their hearts in *unbelief, and *reject it, it shall turn to their own *condemnation—

16 For the Lord God has spoken it; and we, the elders of the church, have heard and bear *witness to the words of the glorious Majesty on high, to whom be glory forever and ever. Amen.

17 By these things we *know that there is a *God in heaven, who is infinite and *eternal, from everlasting to everlasting the same *unchangeable God, the framer of heaven and earth, and all things which are in them;

18 And that he *created man, male and female, after his own *image and in his own likeness, created he them;

19 And gave unto them commandments that they should *love and *serve him, the only *living and true *God, and that he should be the only being whom they should worship.

20 But by the *transgression of these holy laws man became *sensual and *devilish, and became *fallen man.

21 Wherefore, the Almighty God gave his *Only Begotten Son, as it is written in those scriptures which have been given of him.

22 He *suffered *temptations but gave no heed unto them.

23 He was *crucified, *died, and *rose again the third day;

24 And *ascended into heaven, to sit down on the right hand of the

10a Moro. 7: 31 (29–32); D&C 5: 11.
  b See Book of Mormon, preliminary pages, the testimonies of the three and the eight witnesses.
11a D&C 66: 11. TG Scriptures, Value of.
  b TG Inspiration.
  c TG Sacred.
12a Heb. 13: 8; 1 Ne. 10: 18 (18–19); Morm. 9: 9 (9–11); D&C 35: 1; 38: 1 (1–4); 39: 1 (1–3); 76: 4.
  b Ps. 48: 14.
13a Dan. 7: 22; Rev. 20: 4 (4–6); D&C 5: 18.
14a TG Righteousness.
  b Rev. 2: 10. TG Exaltation.
15a TG Hardheartedness.
  b TG Unbelief, Unbelievers.

c D&C 6: 31.
  d John 5: 24.
16a D&C 20: 36 (35–36); 109: 79.
17a 1 Sam. 17: 46; D&C 76: 22 (22–23).
  b Josh. 2: 11; 2 Ne. 10: 14.
  c TG Eternity; God, Eternal Nature of; Immortality.
  d TG God, Perfection of.
18a TG Creation; God, Creator; Man, Physical Creation of.
  b Gen. 1: 26 (26–28); Mosiah 7: 27; Ether 3: 15 (14–17). TG Man, Body of (Corporeal Nature).
19a Jacob 1: 1; Mosiah 2: 4; Moro. 10: 32; D&C 59: 5 (5–6); Moses 7: 33. TG God, Love of; Love.
  b Deut. 6: 13 (13–15).

D&C 4: 2. TG Duty; Obedience.
  c Ps. 42: 2; Dan. 6: 26; 1 Thes. 1: 9; Alma 5: 13; 7: 6; D&C 14: 9.
  d Deut. 6: 14.
TG Worship.
20a TG Transgression.
  b TG Sensuality.
  c TG Devil.
  d TG Man, Natural, Not Spiritually Reborn.
21a TG Jesus Christ, Divine Sonship.
22a Matt. 4: 6; 27: 43. TG Jesus Christ, Temptation of; Temptation.
23a TG Jesus Christ, Crucifixion of.
  b TG Jesus Christ, Death of.
  c TG Jesus Christ, Resurrection; Resurrection.
24a TG Jesus Christ, Ascension of.

[b]Father, to [c]reign with almighty power according to the will of the Father;

25 That as many as would [a]believe and be baptized in his holy name, and [b]endure in faith to the end, should be saved—

26 Not only those who believed after he came in the [a]meridian of time, in the [b]flesh, but also those from the beginning, who were even as were before he came, who believed in the words of the holy prophets, who [c]spake as they were inspired by the [d]gift of the Holy Ghost, who truly [e]testified of him in all things, should have eternal life,

27 As well as those who should come after, who should believe in the [a]gifts and callings of God by the Holy Ghost, which [b]beareth record of the Father and of the Son;

28 Which Father, Son, and Holy Ghost are [a]one God, infinite and eternal, without end. Amen.

29 And we know that all men must [a]repent and [b]believe on the name of Jesus Christ, and worship the Father in his name, and [c]endure in [d]faith on his name to the end, or they cannot be [e]saved in the kingdom of God.

30 And we know that [a]justification through the [b]grace of our Lord and Savior Jesus Christ is just and true;

31 And we know also, that [a]sanctification through the grace of our Lord and Savior Jesus Christ is just and true, to all those who [b]love and serve God with all their [c]mights, minds, and strength.

32 But there is a possibility that man may [a]fall from [b]grace and depart from the living God;

33 Therefore let the church take heed and pray always, lest they fall into [a]temptation;

34 Yea, and even let those who are [a]sanctified take heed also.

35 And we know that these things are true and according to the revelations of John, neither [a]adding to, nor diminishing from the prophecy of his book, the holy scriptures, or the revelations of God which shall come hereafter by the gift and power of the Holy Ghost, the [b]voice of God, or the ministering of angels.

36 And the Lord God has [a]spoken it; and honor, power and glory be rendered to his holy [b]name, both now and ever. Amen.

37 And again, by way of commandment to the church concerning the manner of baptism—All those who [a]humble themselves before God, and desire to be baptized, and come forth with broken hearts and [b]contrite spirits, and witness before the church that they have truly re-

---

24b TG God the Father—Elohim.

c TG Jesus Christ, Authority of.

25a D&C 35: 2; 38: 4; 45: 5 (5, 8); 68: 9; 76: 51.

b TG Baptism; Faith; Perseverance.

26a D&C 39: 3.

b TG Jesus Christ, Condescension of.

c 1 Pet. 1: 11; Jacob 4: 4; 7: 11 (11–12); Mosiah 13: 33 (33–35).

d Moses 5: 58 (57–58). TG Holy Ghost, Gift of.

e John 5: 39; D&C 3: 16. TG Jesus Christ, Prophecies about; Prophets, Mission of; Testimony.

27a D&C 18: 32.

b D&C 1: 39; 42: 17.

28a John 17: 20–22; Alma 11: 44; 3 Ne. 11: 27 (27–28, 36); 28: 10; Morm. 7: 7. TG God, Eternal Nature of; Godhead; Unity.

29a TG Repentance.

b 1 Jn. 3: 23 (19–24).

c TG Perseverance.

d TG Faith.

e TG Salvation.

30a Rom. 3: 24. TG Justification.

b Eph. 2: 8 (8–9). TG Salvation, Plan of.

31a TG Sanctification.

b Ps. 18: 1; Alma 13: 29; D&C 76: 116.

c Deut. 6: 5.

32a Gal. 5: 4; D&C 20: 5;

50: 4. TG Apostasy of Individuals.

b Rom. 6: 1 (1–2). TG Grace.

33a Mark 14: 38. TG Temptation.

34a TG Sanctification.

35a Rev. 22: 18 (18–19); D&C 68: 34; 93: 25 (24–25). TG Scriptures, Value of.

b 1 Kgs. 19: 12 (11–13).

36a Ezek. 5: 13; D&C 20: 16; 109: 79.

b 1 Kgs. 8: 29; D&C 18: 40 (21–41); 97: 15 (15–17); 109: 26 (16–26). TG Name.

37a TG Baptism, Qualifications for.

b TG Contrite Heart; Poor in Spirit.

pented of all their sins, and are willing to take upon them the *name of Jesus Christ, having a *d*determination to serve him to the end, and truly manifest by their *works that they have received of the *f*Spirit of Christ unto the *g*remission of their sins, shall be received by baptism into his church.

38 The *d*duty of the elders, priests, teachers, deacons, and members of the church of Christ—An *b*apostle is an *c*elder, and it is his calling to *d*baptize;

39 And to *ordain other elders, priests, teachers, and deacons;

40 And to administer *d*bread and wine—the *b*emblems of the flesh and blood of Christ—

41 And to *confirm those who are baptized into the church, by the laying on of *b*hands for the *baptism of fire and the Holy Ghost, according to the scriptures;

42 And to teach, expound, exhort, baptize, and watch over the church;

43 And to confirm the church by the laying on of the hands, and the giving of the Holy Ghost;

44 And to take the *d*lead of all meetings.

45 The elders are to *conduct the *b*meetings as they are *c*led by the Holy Ghost, according to the commandments and revelations of God.

46 The *priest's duty is to preach,

*b*teach, expound, exhort, and baptize, and administer the sacrament,

47 And visit the house of each member, and exhort them to *a*pray *b*vocally and in secret and attend to all *family duties.

48 And he may also *a*ordain other priests, teachers, and deacons.

49 And he is to take the *d*lead of meetings when there is no elder present;

50 But when there is an elder present, he is only to preach, teach, expound, exhort, and baptize,

51 And visit the house of each member, exhorting them to pray vocally and in secret and attend to all family duties.

52 In all these duties the priest is to *assist the elder if occasion requires.

53 The *a*teacher's duty is to *b*watch over the *church always, and be with and strengthen them;

54 And see that there is no iniquity in the church, neither *a*hardness with each other, neither lying, *b*backbiting, nor *c*evil *d*speaking;

55 And see that the church meet together often, and also see that all the members do their duty.

56 And he is to take the lead of meetings in the absence of the elder or priest—

57 And is to be assisted always, in all his duties in the church, by the *a*deacons, if occasion requires.

37c Mosiah 5:8 (2–14);
18:8 (8–10). TG Jesus
Christ, Taking the
Name of.
  d Prov. 24:16.
    TG Commitment.
  e James 2:18. TG Good
Works.
  f TG Light of Christ;
Spirituality.
  g TG Remission of Sins.
38a TG Church Organization; Duty; Priesthood, History of;
Priesthood, Magnifying Callings within.
  b TG Apostles.
  c TG Elder.
  d 3 Ne. 11:22 (21–22);
D&C 18:29.

39a Moro. 3:4 (1–4);
D&C 18:32; 107:58.
40a TG Sacrament.
  b TG Jesus Christ,
Types of, in Memory.
41a D&C 33:15 (11, 14–
15); 55:3.
  b TG Hands, Laying on
of; Holy Ghost,
Baptism of.
44a TG Leadership.
45a Moro. 6:9; D&C 46:2.
  b TG Meetings.
  c Gal. 5:18.
46a Ezra 6:18; D&C 84:
111; 107:61 (20, 61).
    TG Priest, Aaronic
Priesthood; Priesthood, Aaronic.
  b Lev. 10:11.

47a TG Teaching.
  a 1 Tim. 2:8.
  b D&C 19:28; 23:6.
  c TG Family; Family,
Children, Responsibilities toward.
48a TG Priesthood,
Ordination.
49a TG Leadership.
52a D&C 107:14 (5, 14).
53a TG Teachers.
  b D&C 84:111.
  c Prov. 27:23.
54a 1 Thes. 5:13.
    TG Backbiting;
Gossip.
  c TG Evil; Slander.
  d TG Profanity;
Reviling.
57a TG Deacon.

58 But neither teachers nor deacons have authority to baptize, administer the ^asacrament, or lay on ^bhands;

59 They are, however, to warn, expound, exhort, and teach, and invite all to come unto Christ.

60 Every ^aelder, ^bpriest, teacher, or deacon is to be ^cordained ^daccording to the gifts and callings of God unto him; and he is to be ^eordained by the power of the Holy Ghost, which is in the one who ordains him.

61 The several elders composing this church of Christ are to ^ameet in conference once in three months, or from time to time as said conferences shall direct or appoint;

62 And said conferences are to do whatever church business is necessary to be done at the time.

63 The elders are to receive their ^alicenses from other elders, by ^bvote of the church to which they belong, or from the conferences.

64 Each priest, teacher, or deacon, who is ordained by a priest, may take a certificate from him at the time, which ^acertificate, when presented to an elder, shall entitle him to a license, which shall authorize him to perform the duties of his calling, or he may receive it from a conference.

65 No person is to be ^aordained to any office in this church, where there is a regularly organized branch of the same, without the ^bvote of that church;

66 But the presiding elders, traveling bishops, high councilors, high priests, and elders, may have the privilege of ordaining, where there is no branch of the church that a vote may be called.

67 Every president of the high priesthood (or presiding elder), ^abishop, high councilor, and ^bhigh priest, is to be ordained by the direction of a ^chigh council or general conference.

68 *The ^aduty of the members after they are received by ^bbaptism.*— The elders or priests are to have a sufficient time to expound all things concerning the church of Christ to their ^cunderstanding, previous to their partaking of the ^dsacrament and being confirmed by the laying on of the ^ehands of the elders, so that all things may be done in ^forder.

69 And the members shall manifest before the church, and also before the elders, by a ^agodly walk and conversation, that they are worthy of it, that there may be works and ^bfaith agreeable to the holy scriptures—walking in ^choliness before the Lord.

70 Every member of the church of Christ having ^achildren is to bring them unto the elders before the church, who are to lay their ^bhands upon them in the name of Jesus Christ, and bless them in his name.

71 No one can be received into the church of Christ unless he has arrived unto the years of ^aaccountability before God, and is capable of ^brepentance.

58a TG Sacrament.
  b TG Hands, Laying on of.
60a TG Elder—Melchizedek Priesthood.
  b TG Priest, Aaronic Priesthood.
  c TG Called of God.
  d Moro. 3:4 (1–4).
  e TG Priesthood, Ordination.
61a TG Meetings.
63a D&C 73:2.
  b TG Sustaining Church Leaders.
64a D&C 20:84; 52:41; 72:17 (17, 19–26);

112:21.
65a TG Priesthood, Ordination.
  b D&C 26:2; 28:13. TG Common Consent.
67a TG Bishop.
  b TG Church Organization; High Priest—Melchizedek Priesthood.
  c D&C 102:2 (1–3).
68a TG Duty.
  b TG Baptism.
  c TG Understanding.
  d TG Sacrament.
  e TG Hands, Laying on of.

f TG Order.
69a TG Godliness.
  b James 2:14.
  c TG Holiness.
70a TG Blessing; Children; Family, Love within.
  b TG Hands, Laying on of.
71a D&C 18:42; 29:47; 68:25 (25–27). TG Accountability; Baptism, Qualifications for; Salvation of Little Children.
  b TG Repentance.

72 ^aBaptism is to be administered in the following manner unto all those who repent—

73 The person who is called of God and has authority from Jesus Christ to baptize, shall go down into the water with the person who has presented himself or herself for baptism, and shall say, calling him or her by name: Having been commissioned of Jesus Christ, I baptize you in the name of the Father, and of the Son, and of the Holy Ghost. Amen.

74 Then shall he ^aimmerse him or her in the water, and come forth again out of the water.

75 It is expedient that the church ^ameet together often to ^bpartake of ^cbread and wine in the ^dremembrance of the Lord Jesus;

76 And the elder or priest shall administer it; and after this ^amanner shall he administer it—he shall kneel with the church and call upon the Father in solemn prayer, saying:

77 O God, the Eternal Father, we ask thee in the name of thy Son, Jesus Christ, to bless and sanctify this ^abread to the souls of all those who partake of it, that they may eat in remembrance of the body of thy Son, and ^bwitness unto thee, O God, the Eternal Father, that they are willing to take upon them the name of thy Son, and always remember him and keep his ^ccommandments which he has given them; that they may always have his ^dSpirit to be with them. Amen.

78 The ^amanner of administering the wine—he shall take the ^bcup also, and say:

79 O God, the Eternal Father, we ask thee in the name of thy Son,

Jesus Christ, to bless and sanctify this ^awine to the souls of all those who drink of it, that they may do it in remembrance of the blood of thy Son, which was shed for them; that they may witness unto thee, O God, the Eternal Father, that they may have his Spirit to be with them. Amen.

80 Any member of the church of Christ ^atransgressing, or being ^bovertaken in a fault, shall be dealt with as the scriptures direct.

81 It shall be the duty of the several churches, composing the church of Christ, to send one or more of their teachers to attend the several conferences held by the elders of the church,

82 With a list of the ^anames of the several members uniting themselves with the church since the last conference; or send by the hand of some priest; so that a regular list of all the names of the whole church may be kept in a book by one of the elders, whomsoever the other elders shall appoint from time to time;

83 And also, if any have been ^aexpelled from the church, so that their names may be blotted out of the general church ^brecord of names.

84 All members removing from the church where they reside, if going to a church where they are not known, may take a letter ^acertifying that they are regular members and in good standing, which certificate may be signed by any elder or priest if the member receiving the letter is personally acquainted with the elder or priest, or it may be signed by the teachers or deacons of the church.

72a 3 Ne. 11:22 (22–28); D&C 18:30.
74a TG Baptism, Immersion; Jesus Christ, Types of, in Memory.
75a TG Assembly for Worship; Meetings.
   b Acts 2:7.
   c TG Bread.
   d TG Sacrament.
76a Moro. 4:1 (1–3).

77a Luke 22:19 (15–20).
   b Mosiah 5:8 (8–12); 18:8 (8–10); D&C 20:37. TG Commitment.
   c TG Obedience.
   d John 14:16.
78a Moro. 5:1 (1–2).
   b Luke 22:20.
79a D&C 27:2–4.
80a TG Offense.
   b Gal. 6:1.

82a Moro. 6:4; D&C 85:3 (3–5, 11–12).
83a Ex. 32:33; Deut. 9:14; Ps. 109:13; Alma 5:57; Moro. 6:7.
   TG Excommunication.
   b TG Record Keeping.
84a D&C 20:64; 52:41; 72:17 (17,19–26); 112:21.

SECTION 21

Revelation given to Joseph Smith the Prophet, at Fayette, New York, April 6, 1830. HC 1: 74–79. This revelation was given at the organization of the Church, on the date named, in the home of Peter Whitmer, Sen. Six men, who had previously been baptized, participated. By unanimous vote these persons expressed their desire and determination to organize, according to the commandment of God; see Section 20. They also voted to accept and sustain Joseph Smith, Jun., and Oliver Cowdery as the presiding officers of the Church. With the laying on of hands, Joseph then ordained Oliver an elder of the Church; and Oliver similarly ordained Joseph. After administration of the sacrament, Joseph and Oliver laid hands upon the participants individually, for the bestowal of the Holy Ghost and for the confirmation of each as a member of the Church.

1–3, Joseph Smith is called to be a seer, translator, prophet, apostle, and elder; 4–8, His word shall guide the cause of Zion; 9–12, The saints shall believe his words as he speaks by the Comforter.

BEHOLD, there shall be a *a*record kept among you; and in it thou shalt be called a *b*seer, a translator, a prophet, an *c*apostle of Jesus Christ, an elder of the church through the will of God the Father, and the grace of your Lord Jesus Christ,

2 Being *a*inspired of the Holy Ghost to lay the foundation thereof, and to *b*build it up unto the most holy faith.

3 Which *a*church was *b*organized and established in the year of your Lord eighteen hundred and thirty, in the fourth month, and on the sixth day of the month which is called April.

4 Wherefore, meaning the church, thou shalt give *a*heed unto all his words and *b*commandments which he shall give unto you as he receiveth them, walking in all *c*holiness before me;

5 For his *a*word ye shall receive, as if from mine own mouth, in all patience and faith.

6 For by doing these things the *a*gates of hell shall not prevail against you; yea, and the Lord God will disperse the powers of *b*darkness from before you, and cause the heavens to *c*shake for your *d*good, and his name's *e*glory.

7 For thus saith the Lord God: Him have I inspired to move the cause of *a*Zion in mighty power for good, and his diligence I know, and his prayers I have heard.

8 Yea, his weeping for Zion I have seen, and I will cause that he shall mourn for her no longer; for his days of rejoicing are come unto the *a*remission of his sins, and the mani-

21 1a D&C 47: 1; 69: 3
        (3–8); 85: 1.
      TG Record Keeping.
    b TG Seer.
    c 2 Cor. 1: 1.
      TG Apostles.
  2a TG Inspiration.
    b Jude 1: 20.
  3a D&C 1: 1. TG Church
        Organization
    b D&C 20: 1.

  4a Heb. 2: 1. TG Priest-
        hood, Magnifying
        Callings within.
    b TG Scriptures, Study
        of.
    c TG Holiness.
  5a D&C 1: 38.
      TG Sustaining Church
        Leaders; Prophets,
        Mission of.
  6a Matt. 16: 18; D&C

        10: 69.
    b Col. 1: 13.
    c Joel 3: 16; Hag. 2: 7;
        D&C 35: 24; 45: 48 (22,
        48); 49: 23; 84: 118.
    d Deut. 10: 13; D&C
        61: 13.
    e TG Glory.
  7a TG Zion.
  8a D&C 20: 5 (5–6);
        JS-H 1: 73 (68–74).

festations of my blessings upon his works.

9 For, behold, I will ^bbless all those who labor in my vineyard with a mighty blessing, and they shall believe on his words, which are given him through me by the ^bComforter, which ^cmanifesteth that Jesus was ^dcrucified by ^esinful men for the sins of the ^fworld, yea, for the remission of sins unto the ^gcontrite heart.

10 Wherefore it behooveth me that

he should be ^aordained by you, Oliver Cowdery mine apostle;

11 This being an ordinance unto you, that you are an elder under his hand, he being the ^afirst unto you, that you might be an elder unto this church of Christ, bearing my name—

12 And the first ^apreacher of this church unto the church, and before the world, yea, before the Gentiles; yea, and thus saith the Lord God, lo, lo! to the ^bJews also. Amen.

SECTION 22

Revelation given through Joseph Smith the Prophet, at Manchester, New York, April 1830. HC 1: 79–80. This revelation was given to the Church in consequence of some who had previously been baptized desiring to unite with the Church without rebaptism.

1, Baptism is a new and everlasting covenant; 2–4, Authoritative baptism is required.

BEHOLD, I say unto you that all ^aold covenants have I caused to be done away in this thing; and this is a new and an ^beverlasting ^ccovenant, even that which was from the beginning.

2 Wherefore, although a man should be baptized an hundred times it availeth him nothing, for you can-

not enter in at the strait gate by the ^alaw of Moses, neither by your ^bdead works.

3 For it is because of your dead works that I have caused this last covenant and this church to be built up unto me, even as in days of old.

4 Wherefore, enter ye in at the ^agate, as I have commanded, and ^bseek not to counsel your God. Amen.

SECTION 23

Revelation given through Joseph Smith the Prophet, at Manchester, New York, April 1830, to Oliver Cowdery, Hyrum Smith, Samuel H. Smith, Joseph Smith, Sen., and Joseph Knight, Sen. HC 1: 80. As

9a 1 Ne. 13: 37; Jacob 5: 75 (70–76).
  b TG Holy Ghost, Comforter.
  c TG Testimony.
  d Lev. 16: 9 (7–10). TG Jesus Christ, Crucifixion of.
  e TG Sin.
  f 1 Jn. 2: 2. TG World.
  g TG Contrite Heart.
10a TG Priesthood, Ordination.

11a D&C 20: 2 (2, 5).
12a TG Mission of Latter-day Saints; Missionary Work.
  b 1 Ne. 13: 42; D&C 18: 6, 26; 19: 27; 90: 9 (8–9); 107: 33; 112: 4.
22 1a Heb. 8: 13; 3 Ne. 9: 17; 12: 47 (46–47).
  b D&C 66: 2. TG New and Everlasting Covenant.

  c TG Covenants.
2a Gal. 2: 16. TG Law of Moses.
  b Moro. 8: 23 (23–26).
4a Matt. 7: 13 (13–14); Luke 13: 24; 2 Ne. 9: 41; 31: 9 (9, 17–18); 3 Ne. 14: 14 (13–14); 27: 33; D&C 43: 7. TG Baptism, Essential.
  b Rom. 11: 34; 1 Cor. 2: 16; Jacob 4: 10.

the result of earnest desire on the part of the five persons named to know of their respective duties, the Prophet inquired of the Lord, and received this revelation.

1–7, These early disciples are called to preach, exhort, and strengthen the Church.

BEHOLD, I speak unto you, Oliver, a few words. Behold, thou art blessed, and art under no condemnation. But beware of *a*pride, lest thou shouldst enter into *b*temptation.

2 Make known thy calling unto the church, and also before the *a*world, and thy heart shall be opened to preach the truth from henceforth and forever. Amen.

3 Behold, I speak unto you, Hyrum, a few words; for thou also art under no condemnation, and thy heart is opened, and thy tongue *a*loosed; and thy calling is to exhortation, and to *b*strengthen the church continually. Wherefore thy duty is unto the church forever, and this because of thy family. Amen.

4 Behold, I speak a few words unto you, *a*Samuel; for thou also art under

no condemnation, and thy calling is to exhortation, and to strengthen the church; and thou art not as yet called to preach before the world. Amen.

5 Behold, I speak a few words unto you, Joseph; for thou also art under no *a*condemnation, and thy calling also is to exhortation, and to strengthen the church; and this is thy duty from henceforth and forever. Amen.

6 Behold, I manifest unto you, Joseph Knight, by these words, that you must take up your *a*cross, in the which you must *b*pray *c*vocally before the world as well as in secret, and in your family, and among your friends, and in all places.

7 And, behold, it is your duty to unite with the true *a*church, and give your language to exhortation continually, that you may receive the reward of the *b*laborer. Amen.

SECTION 24

Revelation given to Joseph Smith the Prophet and Oliver Cowdery, at Harmony, Pennsylvania, July 1830. HC 1: 101–103. Though less than four months had elapsed since the Church was organized, persecution had become intense, and the leaders had to seek safety in partial seclusion. The following three revelations were given at this time to strengthen, encourage, and instruct them.

1–9, Joseph Smith is called to translate, preach, and expound scriptures; 10–12, Oliver Cowdery is called to preach the gospel; 13–19, Law is revealed relative to miracles, cursings, casting off the dust of one's feet, and going without purse or scrip.

BEHOLD, thou wast called and chosen to *a*write the Book of Mormon, and to my ministry; and I have *b*lifted thee up out of thine afflictions, and have counseled thee, that thou hast been delivered from all thine enemies, and thou hast been *c*de-

---

23 1a TG Pride.
    b Mark 14: 38.
      TG Temptation.
  2a Rom. 10: 18.
  3a 3 Ne. 26: 14 (14, 16).
    b D&C 81: 5 (4–5); 108: 7.
  4a JS-H 1: 4.

  5a D&C 20: 5.
  6a Matt. 10: 38; 3 Ne. 12: 30.
    b 1 Tim. 2: 8. TG Prayer.
    c D&C 19: 28; 20: 47 (47, 51).
  7a TG Baptism, Essential;

      Commitment.
    b TG Industry.
24 1a D&C 9: 4.
    TG Scribe; Scriptures, Writing of.
    b Acts 7: 10.
    c TG Deliverance.

livered from the powers of Satan and from ^ddarkness!

2 Nevertheless, thou art not excusable in thy ^atransgressions; nevertheless, go thy way and sin no more.

3 ^aMagnify thine office; and after thou hast ^bsowed thy fields and secured them, go speedily unto the church which is in ^cColesville, Fayette, and Manchester, and they shall ^dsupport thee; and I will bless them both spiritually and ^etemporally;

4 But if they receive thee not, I will send upon them a ^acursing instead of a blessing.

5 And thou shalt continue in calling upon God in my name, and writing the things which shall be given thee by the ^aComforter, and expounding all scriptures unto the church.

6 And it shall be given thee in the very moment what thou shalt ^aspeak and ^bwrite, and they shall hear it, or I will send unto them a cursing instead of a blessing.

7 For thou shalt devote all thy ^aservice in Zion; and in this thou shalt have strength.

8 Be ^apatient in ^bafflictions, for thou shalt have many; but ^cendure them, for, lo, I am with thee, even unto the ^dend of thy days.

9 And in temporal labors thou shalt not have strength, for this is not thy calling. Attend to thy ^acalling and thou shalt have wherewith to magnify thine office, and to expound all scriptures, and continue in laying on of the hands and ^bconfirming the churches.

10 And thy brother Oliver shall continue in bearing my name before the ^aworld, and also to the church. And he shall not suppose that he can say enough in my cause; and lo, I am with him to the end.

11 In me he shall have glory, and not of himself, whether in weakness or in strength, whether in ^abonds or free;

12 And at all times, and in all places, he shall open his mouth and ^adeclare my gospel as with the voice of a ^btrump, both day and night. And I will give unto him strength such as is not known among men.

13 Require not ^amiracles, except I shall ^bcommand you, except ^ccasting out ^ddevils, ^ehealing the sick, and against ^fdeadly serpents, and against deadly poisons;

14 And these things ye shall not do, except it be required of you by them who ^adesire it, that the scriptures might be ^bfulfilled; for ye shall do according to that which is written.

15 And in whatsoever place ye shall ^aenter, and they receive you not in my name, ye shall leave a cursing instead of a blessing, by casting off the ^bdust of your feet against them as a testimony, and cleansing your feet by the wayside.

16 And it shall come to pass that whosoever shall lay their hands upon you by violence, ye shall com-

---

1d TG Darkness, Spiritual.
2a D&C 1:31 (31–33).
3a Rom. 11:13; Jacob 1:19; 2:2.
  b TG Industry; Labor.
  c D&C 26:1; 37:2.
  d D&C 42:71 (70–73); 70:12.
  e Deut. 28:8; Luke 12:31.
4a TG Curse.
5a TG Holy Ghost, Comforter; Scriptures, Writing of.
6a Ex. 4:12 (12–16); Matt. 10:19 (19–20); Luke 12:12 (11–12); Hel. 5:18 (18–19); D&C 28:4; 84:85;

100:5 (5–8); Moses 6:8 (8, 32).
  TG Prophets, Mission of.
  b TG Scribes.
7a TG Service.
8a Rom. 12:12.
  TG Patience.
  b Job 2:13; Hel. 5:12.
  TG Affliction.
  c TG Steadfastness.
  d Matt. 28:20.
9a TG Stewardship.
  b Acts 15:41.
10a Rom. 10:18.
11a 1 Cor. 12:13.
12a TG Preaching.
  b D&C 34:6.
13a Matt. 7:5 (5–7).

TG Miracle; Sign Seekers.
  b 1 Ne. 7:12; 17:50.
  c Mark 16:17 (17–18).
  d TG Devil.
  e TG Healing.
  f Acts 28:3 (3–9); D&C 84:72 (71–72); 124:99 (98–100).
14a TG Administrations to the Sick.
  b Matt. 4:14.
15a Matt. 10:11 (11–15).
  b Mark 6:11; Luke 10:11 (11–12); Acts 13:51; 18:6 (5–6); D&C 60:15 (13–15); 75:20 (19–22); 99:4 (4–5).

mand to be smitten in my name; and, behold, I will [a]smite them according to your words, in mine own due time.

17 And whosoever shall go to law with thee shall be cursed by the law.

18 And thou shalt take no [a]purse nor scrip, neither staves, neither two coats, for the church shall give unto thee in the very hour what thou needest for food and for raiment, and for shoes and for money, and for scrip.

19 For thou art called to [a]prune my vineyard with a mighty pruning, yea, even for the last time; yea, and also all those whom thou hast [b]ordained, and they shall do even according to this pattern. Amen.

SECTION 25

Revelation given through Joseph Smith the Prophet, at Harmony, Pennsylvania, July 1830. See HC 1: 103–104; see also heading to Section 24. This revelation manifests the will of the Lord to Emma Smith, the Prophet's wife.

1–6, Emma Smith, an elect lady, is called to aid and comfort her husband; 7–11, She is also called to write, to expound scriptures, and to select hymns; 12–14, The song of the righteous is a prayer unto the Lord; 15–16, Principles of obedience in this revelation are applicable to all.

HEARKEN unto the voice of the Lord your God, while I speak unto you, Emma Smith, my daughter; for verily I say unto you, all those who [a]receive my gospel are sons and daughters in my [b]kingdom.

2 A revelation I give unto you concerning my will; and if thou art faithful and [a]walk in the paths of [b]virtue before me, I will preserve thy life, and thou shalt receive an [c]inheritance in Zion.

3 Behold, thy [a]sins are forgiven thee, and thou art an [b]elect [c]lady, whom I have [d]called.

4 [a]Murmur not because of the [b]things which thou hast not seen, for they are [c]withheld from thee and from the world, which is wisdom in me in a time to come.

5 And the office of thy calling shall be for a [a]comfort unto my servant, Joseph Smith, Jun., thy [b]husband, in his [c]afflictions, with consoling words, in the spirit of [d]meekness.

6 And thou shalt go with him at the time of his going, and be unto him for a scribe, while there is no one to be a scribe for him, that I may send my servant, Oliver Cowdery, whithersoever I will.

7 And thou shalt be [a]ordained under his hand to expound scriptures, and to exhort the church,

16a TG Retribution.
18a Matt. 10: 9 (9–10);
   Luke 10: 4; D&C 84:
   78 (78–80, 86).
19a Jacob 5: 61 (61–74);
   D&C 39: 17; 71: 4;
   95: 4. TG Millennium,
   Preparing a People
   for.
 b TG Priesthood,
   Ordination.
25 1a John 1: 12.
   TG Sons and Daughters
   of God.

 b TG Kingdom of God,
   on Earth.
2a Deut. 30: 16.
 b TG Virtue; Zion.
 c D&C 52: 42 (2, 5, 42);
   58: 51 (17, 28, 51);
   63: 48 (29, 31, 48); 64:
   30; 85: 7 (1–3, 7, 9);
   99: 7; 101: 18 (1, 6,
   18); 103: 14 (11, 14).
3a Matt. 9: 2.
 b IE one chosen or set
   apart. 2 Jn. 1: 1 (1, 13).
 c TG Woman.
 d TG Authority; Called

 of God.
4a TG Murmuring.
 b TG Knowledge.
 c Luke 24: 16 (10–24);
   Alma 40: 3; Ether 3:
   25. TG God, Wisdom
   of.
5a TG Comfort; Compassion; Family, Love
   within.
 b TG Marriage, Wives.
 c TG Affliction.
 d 2 Cor. 10: 1.
7a OR set apart.

according as it shall be given thee by my [b]Spirit.

8 For he shall lay his [a]hands upon thee, and thou shalt receive the Holy Ghost, and thy time shall be given to writing, and to learning much.

9 And thou needest not fear, for thy [a]husband shall support thee in the church; for unto them is his [b]calling, that all things might be [c]revealed unto them, whatsoever I will, according to their faith.

10 And verily I say unto thee that thou shalt lay aside the [a]things of this [b]world, and [c]seek for the things of a [d]better.

11 And it shall be given thee, also, to make a selection of [a]sacred [b]hymns, as it shall be given thee, which is pleasing unto me, to be had in my church.

12 For my soul [a]delighteth in the [b]song of the [c]heart; yea, the [d]song of the righteous is a prayer unto me, and it shall be answered with a blessing upon their heads.

13 Wherefore, [a]lift up thy heart and [b]rejoice, and cleave unto the covenants which thou hast made.

14 Continue in the spirit of meekness, and beware of [a]pride. Let thy soul delight in thy [b]husband, and the [c]glory which shall come upon him.

15 Keep my commandments continually, and a [a]crown of [b]righteousness thou shalt receive. And except thou do this, where I am you [c]cannot come.

16 And verily, verily, I say unto you, that this is my [a]voice unto all. Amen.

SECTION 26

Revelation given to Joseph Smith the Prophet, Oliver Cowdery, and John Whitmer, at Harmony, Pennsylvania, July 1830. See HC 1: 104; see also heading to Section 24.

1, They are instructed to study the scriptures and to preach; 2, The law of common consent is affirmed.

BEHOLD, I say unto you that you shall let your [a]time be devoted to the [b]studying of the scriptures, and to preaching, and to confirming the church at [c]Colesville, and to per-

forming your [d]labors on the land, such as is required, until after you shall go to the west to hold the next conference; and then it shall be made [e]known what you shall do.

2 And all things shall be done by [a]common consent in the [b]church, by much prayer and faith, for all things you shall receive by faith. Amen.

7b 1 Cor. 12: 8.
8a TG Hands, Laying on of.
9a TG Marriage, Husbands.
  b TG Called of God; Stewardship.
  c TG Prophets, Mission of; Revelation.
10a TG Covetousness.
  b 2 Cor. 6: 17; D&C 30: 2. TG Treasure; World.
  c Ether 12: 4.
  d TG Reward.
11a TG Sacred.
  b Eph. 5: 19 (19–20).
12a TG God, the Standard

  of Righteousness.
  b TG Communication.
  c TG Heart.
  d 1 Chr. 16: 9; Ps. 33: 3; 96: 1; D&C 25: 11; 136: 28. TG Prayer; Singing.
13a Lam. 3: 41.
  b TG Joy.
14a TG Meekness; Pride.
  b TG Family, Love within; Marriage, Continuing Courtship in.
  c TG Glory.
15a TG Exaltation.

  b TG Righteousness.
  c John 7: 34.
16a Jer. 42: 6; D&C 1: 38.
26 1a TG Time.
  b TG Scriptures, Study of; Study.
  c D&C 24: 3; 37: 2.
  d TG Industry.
  e TG Guidance, Divine.
2a 1 Sam. 8: 7; Mosiah 29: 21; Alma 29: 4. TG Common Consent; Sustaining Church Leaders.
  b 1 Cor. 13: 4. TG Church; Church Organization.

SECTION 27

Revelation given to Joseph Smith the Prophet, at Harmony, Pennsylvania, August 1830. HC 1: 106–108. In preparation for a religious service at which the sacrament of bread and wine was to be administered, Joseph set out to procure wine for the occasion. He was met by a heavenly messenger and received this revelation, a portion of which was written at the time, and the remainder in the September following. Water is now used instead of wine in the sacramental services of the Church.

1–4, The emblems to be used in partaking of the sacrament are set forth; 5–14, Christ and his servants from all dispensations are to partake of the sacrament; 15–18, Put on the whole armor of God.

LISTEN to the ᵃvoice of Jesus Christ, your Lord, your God, and your Redeemer, whose word is ᵇquick and powerful.

2 For, behold, I say unto you, that it mattereth not what ye ᵃeat or what ye shall drink when ye partake of the sacrament, if it so be that ye do it with an eye single to my ᵇglory —ᶜremembering unto the Father my ᵈbody which was laid down for you, and my ᵉblood which was shed for the ᶠremission of your sins.

3 Wherefore, a commandment I give unto you, that you shall not purchase ᵃwine neither strong drink of your enemies.

4 Wherefore, you shall partake of none except it is made ᵃnew among you; yea, in this my Father's kingdom which shall be built up on the earth.

5 Behold, this is wisdom in me; wherefore, marvel not, for the hour cometh that I will ᵃdrink of the fruit of the ᵇvine with you on the earth, and with ᶜMoroni, whom I have sent unto you to reveal the Book of Mormon, containing the fulness of my everlasting gospel, to whom I have committed the keys of the ᵈrecord of the ᵉstick of ᶠEphraim;

6 And also with ᵃElias, to whom I have committed the keys of bringing to pass the restoration of all things spoken by the mouth of all the holy prophets since the world began, concerning the last days;

7 And also John the son of Zacharias, which Zacharias he ᵃ(Elias) visited and gave promise that he should have a son, and his name should be ᵇJohn, and he should be filled with the spirit of Elias;

8 Which John I have sent unto you, my servants, Joseph Smith, Jun., and Oliver Cowdery, to ordain you unto the first ᵃpriesthood which you have received, that you might be called and ᵇordained even as ᶜAaron;

9 And also ᵃElijah, unto whom I

---

27 1a ᵀᴳ Revelation.
  b Hel. 3: 29; D&C 6: 2.
2a ᵀᴳ Sacrament.
  b ᵀᴳ Glory.
  c ᵀᴳ Jesus Christ, Types of, in Memory.
  d ᵀᴳ Sacrifice.
  e ᵀᴳ Blood, Symbolism of.
  f ᵀᴳ Remission of Sins.
3a D&C 89: 5 (4–7).
4a Isa. 65: 8; Joel 1: 5; 3: 18; Hag. 1: 11; Matt. 26: 29.

5a Mark 14: 25; Luke 22: 18.
  b Deut. 32: 14.
  c D&C 17: 16; 128: 20 (19–21).
  d ᵀᴳ Book of Mormon.
  e Ezek. 37: 16.
  f ᵀᴳ Israel, Joseph, People of.
6a See "Elias" in BD.
7a Luke 1: 19 (17–19).
  b Luke 1: 13 (13–19); D&C 84: 27 (27–28).

8a D&C 13: 1.
  ᵀᴳ Priesthood, Aaronic.
  b ᵀᴳ Authority; Priesthood, Ordination.
  c Ex. 28: 1 (1–3, 41); D&C 107: 13.
9a 1 Kgs. 17: 1 (1–22); 2 Kgs. 1: 1—2: 15. D&C 2: 2 (1–3); JS-H 1: 38 (38–39). ᵀᴳ Genealogy and Temple Work.

have committed the keys of the power of turning the hearts of the fathers to the children, and the hearts of the children to the *b*fathers, that the whole earth may not be smitten with a *c*curse;

10 And also with Joseph and *a*Jacob, and *b*Isaac, and Abraham, your *c*fathers, by whom the *d*promises remain;

11 And also with Michael, or *a*Adam, the father of all, the prince of all, the *b*ancient of days;

12 And also with Peter, and James, and John, whom I have sent unto you, by whom I have *a*ordained you and confirmed you to be *b*apostles, and especial *c*witnesses of my *d*name, and bear the keys of your ministry and of the same things which I revealed unto them;

13 Unto whom I have *a*committed the *b*keys of my kingdom, and a *c*dispensation of the *d*gospel for the *e*last times; and for the *f*fulness of times, in the which I will gather together in *g*one all things, both which are in heaven, and which are on earth;

14 And also with all those whom my Father hath *a*given me out of the world.

15 Wherefore, *a*lift up your hearts and *b*rejoice, and *c*gird up your loins, and take upon you my whole *d*armor, that ye may be able to withstand the evil day, having done all, that ye may be able to *e*stand.

16 Stand, therefore, having your loins *a*girt about with *b*truth, having on the *c*breastplate of *d*righteousness, and your feet shod with the preparation of the *e*gospel of *f*peace, which I have sent mine *g*angels to commit unto you;

17 Taking the shield of faith wherewith ye shall be able to quench all the *a*fiery darts of the wicked;

18 And take the helmet of salvation, and the sword of my *a*Spirit, which I will pour out upon you, and my word which I reveal unto you, and be agreed as touching all things whatsoever ye ask of me, and be faithful until I come, and ye shall be *b*caught up, that where I am ye shall be *c*also. Amen.

SECTION 28

Revelation given through Joseph Smith the Prophet to Oliver Cowdery, at Fayette, New York, September 1830. HC 1: 109-111. Hiram Page, a member of the Church, had a certain stone, and

9b TG Honoring Father and Mother.
  c TG Earth, Curse of.
10a Alma 7:25.
  b Gen. 21:12; Heb. 11:18 (17-18); 1 Ne. 17:40.
  c Deut. 11:9; D&C 98:32. TG Israel, Origins of.
  d Ex. 32:13 (11-13).
11a 1 Cor. 15:45 (45-48); 2 Ne. 2:20 (19-20); Moses 1:34. TG Adam.
  b Dan. 7:22 (13, 22).
12a JS-H 1:72.
    TG Priesthood, Authority; Priesthood, History of; Priesthood, Me chizedek; Priesthood, Ordination.
  b TG Apostles.
  c Luke 24:48; Acts 1:8.

  TG Witnesses.
  d D&C 18:27.
13a Matt. 16:19.
  b D&C 113:6.
  c TG Priesthood, Keys of.
  d TG Gospel.
  e Jacob 5:71 (71-75); D&C 43:28 (28-30).
  f Eph. 1:10 (9-10); D&C 76:106; 112:30; 124:41.
  g D&C 84:100.
14a John 6:37; 17:9 (9, 11, 14); 3 Ne. 15:24; D&C 50:41 (41-42); 84:63.
15a Lam. 3:41.
  b TG Joy.
  c Hag. 2:4; D&C 75:22.
  d Ex. 12:11; Rom. 13:12; Eph. 6:11.

  TG Children of Light; Protection, Divine; War.
  e Mal. 3:2; D&C 87:8 (1-8).
16a Isa. 11:5.
  b TG Truth.
  c Lev. 8:8 (7-9); Isa. 59:17; JS-H 1:35.
  d TG Righteousness.
  e Rev. 14:6 (6-7).
  f Micah 5:5; 2 Ne. 19:6; D&C 111:8.
  g D&C 27:5 (5-14); 128:20 (19-21).
17a 1 Ne. 15:24; D&C 3:8.
18a TG God, Spirit of.
  b 1 Ne. 13:37; 3 Ne. 27:14 (14-15, 22); D&C 17:8.
  c John 14:3.

professed to be receiving revelations by its aid concerning the up-building of Zion and the order of the Church. Several members had been deceived by these claims, and even Oliver Cowdery was wrongly influenced thereby. Just prior to an appointed conference, the Prophet inquired earnestly of the Lord concerning the matter, and this revelation followed.

1–7, Joseph Smith holds keys of the mysteries, and only he receives revelations for the Church; 8–10, Oliver Cowdery is to preach to the Lamanites; 11–16, Satan deceived Hiram Page and gave him false revelations.

BEHOLD, I say unto thee, [a]Oliver, that it shall be given unto thee that thou shalt be heard by the church in all things whatsoever thou shalt teach them by the [b]Comforter, concerning the revelations and commandments which I have given.

2 But, behold, verily, verily, I say unto thee, [a]no one shall be appointed to receive commandments and [b]revelations in this church excepting my servant [c]Joseph Smith, Jun., for he receiveth them even as [d]Moses.

3 And thou shalt be obedient unto the things which I shall give unto him, even as [a]Aaron, to [b]declare faithfully the commandments and the revelations, with power and [c]authority unto the church.

4 And if thou art [a]led at any time by the Comforter to [b]speak or teach, or at all times by the way of commandment unto the church, thou mayest do it.

5 But thou shalt not write by way of [a]commandment, but by wisdom;

6 And thou shalt not command him who is at thy head, and at the head of the church;

7 For I have given him the [a]keys of the [b]mysteries, and the revelations which are sealed, until I shall appoint unto them another in his stead.

8 And now, behold, I say unto you that you shall go unto the [a]Lamanites and preach my [b]gospel unto them; and inasmuch as they [c]receive thy teachings thou shalt cause my [d]church to be established among them; and thou shalt have revelations, but write them not by way of commandment.

9 And now, behold, I say unto you that it is not revealed, and no man knoweth where the [a]city [b]Zion shall be built, but it shall be given hereafter. Behold, I say unto you that it shall be on the borders by the Lamanites.

10 Thou shalt not leave this place until after the conference; and my servant Joseph shall be appointed to preside over the conference by the voice of it, and what he saith to thee thou shalt tell.

11 And again, thou shalt take thy brother, Hiram Page, [a]between him and thee alone, and tell him that those things which he hath written

28 1a D&C 20: 3 (3, 38).
  b TG Holy Ghost, Comforter; Teaching with the Spirit.
2a D&C 32: 4; 35: 17 (17–18); 43: 4.
  TG Church Organization; Order.
  b TG Revelation.
  c 2 Ne. 3: 15 (14–20).
  TG Joseph Smith.
  d Lev. 1: 1.
3a Ex. 4: 30 (14–16, 30); 28: 1 (1–5).
  b Jer. 26: 2.
  c TG Priesthood, Authority.
4a Gal. 5: 18.
  b Ex. 4: 12 (12–16); D&C 24: 6 (5–6); Moses 6: 8 (8, 32).
5a D&C 43: 5; 63: 22 (22–23).
7a D&C 35: 18; 64: 5; 84: 19. TG Priesthood, Keys of.
  b TG Mysteries of Godliness.
8a 2 Ne. 3: 19 (18–22); Alma 17: 1; D&C 30: 5; 32: 2 (1–3); 42: 24.
  b D&C 3: 20.
  c TG Teachable.
  d Ether 13: 6 (6–10).
9a D&C 57: 2; 103: 24 (22–24).
  b D&C 52: 42 (42–43).
  TG Zion.
11a Matt. 18: 15.

from that *b*stone are not of me and that *c*Satan *d*deceiveth him;

12 For, behold, these things have not been appointed unto him, neither shall anything be appointed unto any of this church contrary to the church covenants.

13 For all things must be done in *a*order, and by common *b*consent in the church, by the prayer of faith.

14 And thou shalt assist to settle all these things, according to the covenants of the church, before thou shalt take thy journey among the Lamanites.

15 And it shall be *a*given thee from the time thou shalt go, until the time thou shalt return, what thou shalt do.

16 And thou must open thy mouth at all times, declaring my gospel with the sound of rejoicing. Amen.

SECTION 29

Revelation given through Joseph Smith the Prophet, in the presence of six elders, at Fayette, New York, September 1830. HC 1 : 111–115. This revelation was given some days prior to the conference beginning September 26, 1830.

1–8, Christ gathers his elect; 9–11, His coming ushers in the Millennium; 12–13, The Twelve shall judge all Israel; 14–21, Signs, plagues, and desolations will precede the Second Coming; 22–28, The last resurrection and final judgment follow the Millennium; 29–35, All things are spiritual unto the Lord; 36–39, The devil and his hosts were cast out of heaven to tempt man; 40–45, Fall and atonement bring salvation; 46–50, Little children are redeemed through the atonement.

LISTEN to the voice of Jesus Christ, your Redeemer, the Great *a*I AM, whose arm of *b*mercy hath *c*atoned for your sins;

2 Who will *a*gather his people even as a hen gathereth her chickens under her wings, even as many as will hearken to my voice and *b*humble themselves before me, and call upon me in mighty prayer.

3 Behold, verily, verily, I say unto you, that at this time your *a*sins are *b*forgiven you, therefore ye receive these things; but remember to sin no more, lest perils shall come upon you.

4 Verily, I say unto you that ye are chosen out of the world to declare my gospel with the sound of rejoicing, as with the *a*voice of a trump.

5 Lift up your hearts and be *a*glad, for I am in your *b*midst, and am your *c*advocate with the Father; and it is his good will to give you the *d*kingdom.

6 And, as it is written—Whatsoever ye shall *a*ask in *b*faith, being *c*united in prayer according to my command, ye shall receive.

11b TG Sorcery; Superstitions.
  c Rev. 20: 10; D&C 50: 4.
  d D&C 43: 6 (5–7); 46: 7.
13a TG Order.
  b TG Common Consent.
15a 2 Ne. 32: 5 (3, 5).
29 1a TG Jesus Christ, Jehovah.
  b TG Mercy.
  c TG Jesus Christ, Atonement through.

2a Matt. 23: 37.
  b TG Israel, Gathering of.
3a 3 Ne. 8: 1; D&C 50: 29 (28–29).
  b TG Forgiveness.
4a Isa. 58: 1; Rev. 1:10; Alma 29: 1 (1–2); D&C 19: 37; 30: 9; 33: 2.
5a Rom. 8: 35 (35–39).
  b Matt. 18: 20; D&C 6: 32; 38: 7; 88: 63

(62–63).
  c TG Jesus Christ, Advocate; Jesus Christ, Relationships with the Father.
  d Luke 12: 31 (22–34); D&C 35: 27.
  TG Kingdom of God, on Earth.
6a Matt. 21: 22; John 14: 13.
  b Mark 11: 24.
  c 3 Ne. 27: 1 (1–2); D&C 84: 1.

7 And ye are called to bring to pass the *gathering of mine *elect; for mine elect *hear my voice and *harden not their *hearts;

8 Wherefore the decree hath gone forth from the Father that they shall be *gathered in unto one place upon the face of this land, to *prepare their hearts and be prepared in all things against the day when *tribulation and desolation are sent forth upon the wicked.

9 For the hour is nigh and the *day soon at hand when the earth is ripe; and all the *proud and they that do wickedly shall be as *stubble; and I will *burn them up, saith the Lord of Hosts, that wickedness shall not be upon the earth;

10 For the hour is nigh, and that which was *spoken by mine *apostles must be fulfilled; for as they spoke so shall it come to pass;

11 For I will reveal *myself from heaven with power and great glory, with all the *hosts thereof, and *dwell in *righteousness with men on earth a *thousand years, and the wicked shall not stand.

12 And again, verily, verily, I say unto you, and it hath gone forth in

a firm decree, by the will of the Father, that mine *apostles, the Twelve which were with me in my ministry at Jerusalem, shall stand at my right hand at the day of my coming in a pillar of *fire, being clothed with robes of righteousness, with crowns upon their heads, in *glory even as I am, to *judge the whole house of Israel, even as many as have loved me and kept my commandments, and none else.

13 For a *trump shall sound both long and loud, even as upon Mount Sinai, and all the *earth shall quake, and they shall *come forth—yea, even the *dead which died in me, to receive a *crown of righteousness, and to be clothed upon, *even as I am, to be with me, that we may be one.

14 But, behold, I say unto you that before this great *day shall come the *sun shall be *darkened, and the moon shall be turned into blood, and the stars shall fall from heaven, and there shall be greater *signs in heaven above and in the earth beneath;

15 And there shall be weeping and *wailing among the hosts of men;

7a TG Israel, Gathering of; Mission of Latter-day Saints.
b Matt. 24: 24; Mark 13: 20; 1 Ne. 6: 44 (44, 63–65); D&C 84: 34; JS-M 1: 23.
TG Election; Foreordination.
c 1 Jn. 4: 6 (1–6); Alma 5: 41 (37–41).
TG Missionary Work.
d TG Hardheartedness.
e TG Heart.
8a Matt. 24: 28; D&C 45: 66 (64–66); 52: 1 (2, 42); 57: 1; 101: 3, 24.
b 3 Ne. 17: 3; D&C 58: 6; 78: 7; 132: 3.
TG Millennium, Preparing a People for.
c Isa. 47: 11; 35: 11 (11–15); 43: 17 (17–27).
9a TG Day of the Lord.

TG Pride.
c Ex. 15: 7 (7–8); Ps. 37: 2; Nahum 1: 10; Mal. 4: 1; 1 Ne. 22: 23 (15, 23); 2 Ne. 26: 6 (4–6); JS-H 1: 37.
d Ps. 21: 9 (8–10); 1 Ne. 22: 15; D&C 45: 57; 63: 34 (34, 54); 64: 24; 88: 94; 101: 24 (23–25); 133: 64.
TG Earth, Cleansing of.
10a Matt. 16: 27. TG Jesus Christ, Prophecies about; Jesus Christ, Second Coming.
b D&C 45: 16 (15–16).
11a D&C 101: 23.
b JS-M 1: 37.
c D&C 1: 36 (35–36); 45: 59; 84: 119 (118–119); 104: 59.
d TG Righteousness.
e TG Jesus Christ, Millennial Reign; Millennium.

12a TG Apostles.
b Ex. 3: 2; Isa. 66: 15 (15–16); D&C 130: 7; 133: 41.
c TG Glory; Jesus Christ, Glory of.
d Matt. 19: 28; Luke 22: 30; 1 Ne. 12: 9 (9–10); Morm. 3: 18 (18–19).
13a Ex. 19: 13, 19; D&C 43: 18; 45: 45 (45–46).
b TG Earth, Destiny of.
c D&C 76: 50 (17, 50).
d Rev. 11: 18 (18–19); D&C 88: 97 (96–97); 133: 56.
e TG Exaltation.
f D&C 76: 95; 78: 5 (5–7); 84: 38 (35–39); 132: 20 (18–20).
14a TG Last Days.
b Joel 2: 10; JS-M 1: 33.
c TG Darkness, Physical.
d Gen. 1: 14. TG World, End of.
15a Matt. 13: 42.
TG Mourning.

16 And there shall be a great *hail-storm sent forth to destroy the *crops of the earth.

17 And it shall come to pass, because of the wickedness of the world, that I will take *vengeance upon the *wicked, for they will not repent; for the *cup of mine *indignation is full; for behold, my *blood shall not *cleanse them if they hear me not.

18 Wherefore, I the Lord God will send forth *flies upon the face of the earth, which shall take hold of the inhabitants thereof, and shall eat their flesh, and shall cause maggots to come in upon them;

19 And their tongues shall be stayed that they shall not *utter against me; and their flesh shall fall from off their bones, and their eyes from their sockets;

20 And it shall come to pass that the *beasts of the forest and the fowls of the air shall devour them up.

21 And the great and *abominable church, which is the *whore of all the earth, shall be cast down by *devouring fire, according as it is spoken by the mouth of Ezekiel the prophet, who spoke of these things, which have not come to pass but surely *must, as I live, for *abominations shall not reign.

22 And again, verily, verily, I say unto you that when the *thousand years are ended, and men again begin to deny their God, then will I spare the earth but for a *little season;

23 And the *end shall come, and the heaven and the earth shall be *consumed and *pass away, and there shall be a new heaven and a *new earth.

24 For all *old things shall *pass away, and all things shall become new, even the heaven and the earth, and all the fulness thereof, both men and *beasts, the fowls of the air, and the fishes of the sea;

25 And not one *hair, neither mote, shall be lost, for it is the *workmanship of mine hand.

26 But, behold, verily I say unto you, before the earth shall pass away, *Michael, mine archangel, shall sound his *trump, and then shall all the dead *awake, for their graves shall be opened, and they shall *come forth—yea, even all.

27 And the *righteous shall be gathered on my *right hand unto eternal life; and the wicked on my left hand will I be ashamed to own before the Father;

28 Wherefore I shall say unto them —*Depart from me, ye cursed, into

16a Ex. 9: 18 (13–35); Isa. 32: 19 (15–19); Ezek. 13: 13; 38: 22; Rev. 11: 19; 16: 21; Mosiah 12: 6; D&C 109: 30.
TG Last Days.
b TG Famine.
17a Ps. 73: 17 (3–17); Rev. 16: 9–11; 2 Ne. 30: 10; JS-M 1: 55. TG God, Justice of; Vengeance.
b TG Wickedness.
c Jer. 25: 15.
d TG God, Indignation of.
e 1 Jn. 1: 7; Alma 11: 40 (40–41); D&C 19: 17 (16–18).
f TG Purification.
18a TG Plagues.
19a Ex. 16: 8; Zech. 14: 12; Rev. 16: 9 (9, 11, 21); 1 Ne. 16: 22 (20–25).

20a Isa. 18: 6; Jer. 15: 3; Ezek. 39: 17 (17–20); Rev. 19: 17 (17–18).
21a TG Devil, Church of.
b Rev. 19: 2.
c Ezek. 38: 22; Joel 1: 19 (19–20); 2: 3; D&C 45: 41 (40–41); 97: 26 (25–26).
TG Earth, Cleansing of.
d Dan. 1: 38.
e Ezek. 5: 9 (9–11).
22a TG Millennium.
b Rev. 20: 3 (3–10); Jacob 5: 77 (76–77); D&C 43: 31 (30–31); 88: 111 (110–112).
23a Matt. 24: 14.
TG Earth, Destiny of; World, End of.
b Matt. 24: 35; JS-M 1: 35.

c TG Earth, Renewal of.
24a Rev. 20: 11 (11–15).
b 2 Cor. 5: 17.
c D&C 77: 3 (2–4); Moses 3: 19.
25a Luke 21: 18; Alma 40: 23.
b Eph. 2: 10.
26a TG Adam.
b 1 Cor. 15: 52.
c TG Immortality; Resurrection.
d John 5: 29 (28–29).
27a Ps. 5: 12.
TG Righteousness.
b Matt. 25: 33.
TG Judgment, The Last.
28a Matt. 25: 41; Luke 13: 27; Rom. 16: 20; 1 Jn. 3: 8; D&C 19: 3; 29: 41; 76: 37; 88: 114 (111–115).

everlasting [b]fire, prepared for the [c]devil and his angels.

29 And now, behold, I say unto you, never at any time have I declared from mine own mouth that they should return, for [a]where I am they cannot come, for they have no power.

30 But remember that all my judgments are not given unto men; and as the words have gone forth out of my mouth even so shall they be fulfilled, that the [a]first shall be last, and that the last shall be first in all things whatsoever I have created by the word of my power, which is the power of my [b]Spirit.

31 For by the power of my Spirit [a]created I them; yea, all things both [b]spiritual and temporal—

32 [a]First [b]spiritual, secondly temporal, which is the beginning of my work; and again, first temporal, and secondly spiritual, which is the last of my work—

33 [a]Speaking unto you that you may naturally understand; but unto myself my works have no [b]end, neither beginning; but it is given unto you that ye may understand, because ye have asked it of me and are agreed.

34 Wherefore, verily I say unto you that all things unto me are spiritual, and not at any time have I given unto you a [a]law which was [b]temporal; neither any man, nor the children of men; neither Adam, your father, whom I created.

35 Behold, I gave unto him that he should be an [a]agent unto himself; and I gave unto him commandment, but no temporal commandment gave I unto him, for my [b]commandments are [c]spiritual; they are not natural nor temporal, neither carnal nor sensual.

36 And it came to pass that Adam, being tempted of the [a]devil—for, behold, the [b]devil was before Adam, for he [c]rebelled against me, saying, Give me thine [d]honor, which is my [e]power; and also a [f]third part of the [g]hosts of heaven turned me away from me because of their [h]agency;

37 And they were thrust down, and thus came the [a]devil and his [b]angels;

38 And, behold, there is a place [a]prepared for them from the beginning, which place is [b]hell.

39 And it must needs be that the [a]devil should [b]tempt the children of men, or they could not be [c]agents unto themselves; for if they never should have [d]bitter they could not know the sweet—

40 Wherefore, it came to pass that the devil tempted Adam, and he partook of the forbidden [a]fruit and [b]transgressed the commandment, wherein he became [c]subject to the

28b Dan. 7: 11; D&C 43: 33.
  c TG Devil.
29a John 7: 34 (33–36);
     D&C 76: 112 (51–112).
30a Matt. 19: 30; Luke 13:
     30.
  b TG God, Spirit of.
31a TG Creation; Jesus
     Christ, Creator.
  b Moses 3: 5.
32a 1 Cor. 15: 46 (44–46);
     D&C 128: 14; Moses 3:
     5 (5–7).
  b TG Earth Creation;
     Resurrection.
33a TG Communication;
     Language.
  b Ps. 111: 8 (7–8);
     1 Ne. 14: 7; Moses 1: 4.
34a Rom. 7: 14.
  TG God, Law of.

  b TG God, Eternal
     Nature of.
35a TG Agency.
  b TG Commandments of
     God.
  c TG Spirituality.
36a TG Devil.
  b D&C 76: 25 (25–26);
     Moses 4: 1 (1–4).
  c TG Council in Heaven;
     Rashness.
  d TG Honor.
  e Isa. 14: 14; D&C 76:
     28 (25–29).
  f Luke 8: 30; Rev. 12: 4
     (3–4); Moses 4: 6.
  g Gen. 2: 1; D&C 38: 1;
     45: 1; Moses 3: 1; Abr.
     5: 1.
  TG Man, Antemortal
     Existence of.

  h TG Agency; Initiative.
37a TG Devil.
  b 2 Pet. 2: 4; Jude 1: 6;
     Moses 7: 26. TG Angels.
38a Moses 6: 29.
  b Prov. 9: 18; Alma 12:
     11; D&C 76: 84
     (84–86). TG Hell.
39a TG Devil.
  b 1 Thes. 3: 5; Moses 4:
     4 (3–4). TG Opposition;
     Temptation.
  c TG Agency.
  d Moses 6: 55.
40a Gen. 3: 6; Moses 4: 12
     (7–13).
  b John 8: 34. TG Trans-
     gression.
  c 2 Ne. 10: 24; Mosiah
     16: 3 (3–5); Alma 5: 41
     (41–42).

will of the devil, because he yielded unto temptation.

41 Wherefore, I, the Lord God, caused that he should be *a*cast out from the Garden of *b*Eden, from my presence, because of his transgression, wherein he became *c*spiritually *d*dead, which is the first death, even that same death which is the last *e*death, which is spiritual, which shall be pronounced upon the wicked when I shall say: Depart, ye *f*cursed.

42 But, behold, I say unto you that I, the Lord God, gave unto Adam and unto his seed, that they should not *a*die as to the temporal death, until I, the Lord God, should send forth *b*angels to declare unto them *c*repentance and *d*redemption, through faith on the name of mine *e*Only Begotten Son.

43 And thus did I, the Lord God, appoint unto man the days of his *a*probation—that by his *b*natural death he might be *c*raised in *d*immortality unto eternal life, even as many as would believe;

44 And they that believe not unto eternal *a*damnation; for they cannot

be redeemed from their spiritual *b*fall, because they repent not;

45 For they love darkness rather than light, and their *a*deeds are evil, and they receive their *b*wages of *c*whom they list to obey.

46 But behold, I say unto you, that little *a*children are *b*redeemed from the foundation of the world through mine Only Begotten;

47 Wherefore, they cannot *a*sin, for power is not given unto Satan to *b*tempt little children, until they *c*begin to become *d*accountable before me;

48 For it is given unto them even as I will, according to mine own *a*pleasure, that great things may be required at the hand of their *b*fathers.

49 And, again, I say unto you, that whoso having knowledge, have I not commanded to *a*repent?

50 And he that hath no *a*understanding, it remaineth in me to do according as it is written. And now I declare no more unto you at this time. Amen.

SECTION 30

Revelation given through Joseph Smith the Prophet to David Whitmer, Peter Whitmer, Jun., and John Whitmer, at Fayette, New York, September 1830, following the three-day conference at

---

41a TG Fall of Man.
  b TG Eden.
  c TG Man, Natural, Not Spiritually Reborn.
  d TG Death, Spiritual, First.
  e Alma 40: 26.
    TG Death, Spiritual, Second.
  f D&C 29: 28; 76: 37; Moses 5: 36.
42a 2 Ne. 2: 21. TG Death.
  b Alma 12: 29 (28–30).
  c TG Repentance.
  d TG Redemption.
  e TG Jesus Christ, Divine Sonship.
43a TG Earth, Purpose of; Mortality; Probation.
  b 1 Cor. 15: 44.

  c TG Resurrection.
  d Matt. 5: 48; Rom. 8: 17 (14–21), 2 Ne. 2: 15 (14–30), Alma 12: 26; Moses 1: 39.
    TG Immortality.
44a D&C 19: 7.
    TG Damnation; Hell.
  b TG Death, Spiritual, Second.
45a John 3: 19 (18–21); Jude 1: 4; D&C 10: 21; 84: 46–48; 93: 31–32.
  b Mosiah 2: 32 (32–33); Alma 3: 27 (26–27); 5: 42 (41–42); 30: 60.
    TG Wages.
46a Moro. 8: 12 (8, 12, 22); D&C 93: 38.

    TG Children; Conceived in Sin; Salvation of Little Children.
  b D&C 74: 7. TG Jesus Christ, Redeemer; Redemption.
47a TG Sin.
  b TG Temptation.
  c Moses 6: 55.
  d D&C 18: 42; 20: 71; 68: 25 (25–27).
    TG Accountability.
48a TG Pleasure.
  b D&C 68: 25.
    TG Family, Children, Responsibilities toward.
49a TG Repentance.
50a D&C 137: 7 (7–10).
    TG Understanding.

Fayette, but before the elders of the Church had separated. HC 1: 115–116. Originally this material was published as three revelations; it was combined into one section by the Prophet for the 1835 edition of the Doctrine and Covenants.

1–4, David Whitmer is chastened for failure to serve diligently; 5–8, Peter Whitmer, Jun., is to accompany Oliver Cowdery on a mission to the Lamanites; 9–11, John Whitmer is called to preach the gospel.

BEHOLD, I say unto you, David, that you have *a*feared man and have not *b*relied on me for strength as you ought.

2 But your mind has been on the things of the *a*earth more than on the things of me, your Maker, and the ministry whereunto you have been called; and you have not given heed unto my *b*Spirit, and to those who were set over you, but have been persuaded by those whom I have not commanded.

3 Wherefore, you are left to inquire for yourself at my hand, and *a*ponder upon the things which you have received.

4 And your home shall be at your *a*father's house, until I give unto you further commandments. And you shall attend to the *b*ministry in the church, and before the world, and in the regions round about. Amen.

5 Behold, I say unto you, Peter, that you shall take your *a*journey with your brother Oliver; for the *b*time has come that it is expedient in me that you shall open your mouth to declare my gospel; there-

fore, fear not, but give *c*heed unto to the words and advice of your brother, which he shall give you.

6 And be you afflicted in all his *a*afflictions, ever *b*lifting up your heart unto me in prayer and faith, for his and your *c*deliverance; for I have given unto him power to *d*build up my *e*church among the *f*Lamanites;

7 And none have I appointed to be his counselor *a*over him in the church, concerning church matters, except it is his brother, Joseph Smith, Jun.

8 Wherefore, give heed unto these things and be diligent in keeping my commandments, and you shall be blessed unto eternal life. Amen.

9 Behold, I say unto you, my servant John, that thou shalt commence from this time forth to *a*proclaim my gospel, as with the *b*voice of a trump.

10 And your labor shall be at your brother Philip Burroughs', and in that region round about, yea, wherever you can be heard, until I command you to go from hence.

11 And your whole labor shall be in Zion, with all your soul, from henceforth; yea, you shall ever open your mouth in my cause, not *a*fearing what *b*man can do, for I am *c*with you. Amen.

---

30 1a Acts 5:29. TG Peer
    Influence.
   b 2 Chr. 16:7.
  2a D&C 25:10.
   b TG God, Spirit of.
  3a TG Meditation.
  4a D&C 128:21.
   b TG Ministry; Service.
  5a D&C 28:8; 32:2
    (1–3).

   b D&C 11:15; 16:6.
   c TG Sustaining Church
    Leaders.
  6a TG Affliction.
   b Lam. 3:41.
   c TG Deliverance.
   d D&C 39:13; 42:8.
   e TG Jesus Christ,
    Head of the
    Church.

   f D&C 3:20; 49:24.
  7a D&C 20:3 (2–3).
  9a Jer. 3:12; D&C 15:6
    (1–6).
   b D&C 19:37; 29:4;
    33:2.
  11a TG Courage.
   b Isa. 51:7.
   c Matt. 28:20.

SECTION 31

Revelation given through Joseph Smith the Prophet to Thomas B. Marsh, September 1830. HC 1: 115–117. The occasion was immediately following a conference of the Church. See heading to Section 30. Thomas B. Marsh had been baptized earlier in the month, and had been ordained an elder in the Church before this revelation was given.

1–6, Thomas B. Marsh is called to preach the gospel and is assured of his family's well-being; 7–13, He is counseled to be patient, pray always, and follow the Comforter.

1 ^aTHOMAS, my son, blessed are you because of your faith in my work.

2 Behold, you have had many afflictions because of your family; nevertheless, I will bless you and your ^afamily, yea, your little ones; and the day cometh that they will believe and know the truth and be one with me in my church.

3 Lift up your heart and rejoice, for the hour of your mission is come; and your tongue shall be loosed, and you shall declare ^aglad tidings of great joy unto this generation.

4 You shall ^adeclare the things which have been revealed to my servant, Joseph Smith, Jun. You shall begin to preach from this time forth, yea, to reap in the field which is ^bwhite already to be burned.

5 Therefore, ^athrust in your sickle with all your soul, and your sins are ^bforgiven you, and you shall be laden with ^csheaves upon your back, for the ^dlaborer is worthy of his hire. Wherefore, your family shall live.

6 Behold, verily I say unto you, go from them only for a little ^atime, and declare my word, and I will prepare a place for them.

7 Yea, I will ^aopen the hearts of the people, and they will receive you. And I will establish a church by your hand;

8 And you shall ^astrengthen them and prepare them against the time when they shall be gathered.

9 Be ^apatient in ^bafflictions, ^crevile not against those that revile. Govern your ^dhouse in meekness, and be ^esteadfast.

10 Behold, I say unto you that you shall be a physician unto the church, but not unto the world, for they will not receive you.

11 Go your way whithersoever I will, and it shall be given you by the ^aComforter what you shall do and whither you shall go.

12 ^aPray always, lest you enter into ^btemptation and lose your ^creward.

13 Be ^afaithful unto the ^bend, and lo, I am ^cwith you. These words are not of man nor of men, but of me, even Jesus Christ, your Redeemer, by the ^dwill of the Father. Amen.

---

31 1a D&C 52: 22; 56: 5 (5–6); 75: 31.
  2a TG Family; Unity.
  3a TG Isa. 52: 7 (7–10); Luke 2: 10 (10–11); Rom. 10: 15; Mosiah 3: 3 (3–5).
  4a Mosiah 18: 19 (18–20); D&C 5: 10; 42: 12; 52: 36.
    b D&C 4: 4 (4–6).
  5a Rev. 14: 15.
    b TG Forgiveness.
    c Ps. 126: 6; D&C 79: 3.
    d Luke 10: 7 (3–11);

D&C 51: 14; 75: 24; 84: 79.
    TG Consecration; Wages.
  6a TG Family, Children, Responsibilities toward.
  7a TG Conversion.
  8a Zech. 10: 12; D&C 81: 5; 108: 7.
  9a Rom. 12: 12.
    TG Patience.
    b TG Affliction.
    c TG Forbearance; Malice; Retribution;

Reviling.
    d TG Family, Love within.
    e TG Steadfastness.
  11a TG Holy Ghost, Comforter.
  12a TG Prayer.
    b Mark 14: 38.
    TG Temptation.
    c TG Reward.
  13a TG Steadfastness.
    b Rev. 2: 10.
    c Matt. 28: 20.
    d TG Jesus Christ, Authority of.

SECTION 32

Revelation given through Joseph Smith the Prophet to Parley P. Pratt and Ziba Peterson, October 1830. HC 1: 118–120. Great interest and desires were felt by the elders respecting the Lamanites, of whose predicted blessings the Church had learned from the Book of Mormon. In consequence, supplication was made that the Lord would indicate his will as to whether elders should be sent at that time to the Indian tribes in the West. The revelation followed.

1–3, Parley P. Pratt and Ziba Peterson are called to preach to the Lamanites and to accompany Oliver Cowdery and Peter Whitmer, Jun.; 4–5, They are to pray for an understanding of the scriptures.

AND now concerning my servant "Parley P. Pratt, behold, I say unto him that as I live I will that he shall declare my gospel and [b]learn of me, and be meek and lowly of heart.

2 And that which I have appointed unto him is that he shall [a]go with my servants, Oliver Cowdery and Peter Whitmer, Jun., into the wilderness among the [b]Lamanites.

3 And "Ziba Peterson also shall go with them; and I myself will go with them and be in their [b]midst; and I am their [c]advocate with the Father, and nothing shall [d]prevail against them.

4 And they shall give "heed to that which is written, and pretend to no other [b]revelation; and they shall pray always that I may [c]unfold the same to their [d]understanding.

5 And they shall give heed unto these words and trifle not, and I will bless them. Amen.

SECTION 33

Revelation given through Joseph Smith the Prophet to Ezra Thayre and Northrop Sweet, at Fayette, New York, October 1830. HC 1: 126–127. In recording this revelation the Prophet affirmed that "the Lord is ever ready to instruct such as diligently seek in faith."

1–4, Laborers are called to declare the gospel in the eleventh hour; 5–6, The Church is established and the elect are to be gathered; 7–10, Repent, for the kingdom of heaven is at hand; 11–15, The Church is built upon the gospel rock; 16–18, Prepare for the coming of the Bridegroom.

BEHOLD, I say unto you, my servants "Ezra and Northrop, open ye your ears and hearken to the voice of the Lord your God, whose [b]word is quick and powerful, sharper than a two-edged sword, to the dividing asunder of the joints and marrow, soul and spirit; and is a discerner of

---

32 1a D&C 50: 37; 52: 26; 97: 3; 103: 30 (30–37).
  b Matt. 11: 29.
2a D&C 28: 8; 30: 5.
  b D&C 3: 20 (18–20).
3a D&C 58: 60.
  b Matt. 18: 20; D&C 6: 32; 38: 7.

c TG Jesus Christ, Advocate; Jesus Christ, Relationships with the Father.
  d Mosiah 28: 7 (6–7); Moses 8: 18 (18–19).
4a 1 Ne. 15: 25 (23–25); D&C 84: 43 (43–44).

b D&C 28: 2.
  c JS–H 1: 74.
  d TG Understanding.
33 1a D&C 52: 22; 56: 5 (5–8).
  b Heb. 4: 12; Hel. 3: 29 (29–30).

the thoughts and ᶜintents of the heart.

2 For verily, verily, I say unto you that ye are called to lift up your voices as with the ᵃsound of a trump, to declare my gospel unto a crooked and ᵇperverse generation.

3 For behold, the ᵃfield is ᵇwhite already to harvest; and it is the ᶜeleventh hour, and the last time that I shall call ᵈlaborers into my vineyard.

4 And my ᵃvineyard has become ᵇcorrupted every whit; and there is none which doeth ᶜgood save it be a few; and they ᵈerr in many instances because of ᵉpriestcrafts, all having corrupt minds.

5 And verily, verily, I say unto you, that this ᵃchurch have I ᵇestablished and called forth out of the ᶜwilderness.

6 And even so will I ᵃgather mine elect from the ᵇfour quarters of the earth, even as many as will believe in me, and hearken unto my voice.

7 Yea, verily, verily, I say unto you, that the field is ᵃwhite already to harvest; wherefore, thrust in your sickles, and reap with all your might, mind, and strength.

8 ᵃOpen your mouths and they shall be filled, and you shall become even as ᵇNephi of old, who journeyed from Jerusalem in the wilderness.

9 Yea, open your mouths and spare not, and you shall be laden with ᵃsheaves upon your backs, for lo, I am with you.

10 Yea, open your mouths and they shall be filled, saying: Repent, ᵃrepent, and prepare ye the way of the Lord, and make his paths straight; for the ᵇkingdom of heaven is at hand;

11 Yea, ᵃrepent and be baptized, every one of you, for a ᵇremission of your sins; yea, be baptized even by water, and then cometh the baptism of fire and of the Holy Ghost.

12 Behold, verily, verily, I say unto you, this is my ᵃgospel; and remember that they shall have faith in me or they can in nowise be saved;

13 And upon this ᵃrock I will build my church; yea, upon this rock ye are built, and if ye continue, the ᵇgates of hell shall not prevail against you.

14 And ye shall remember the church ᵃarticles and covenants to keep them.

15 And whoso having faith you shall ᵃconfirm in my church, by the laying on of the ᵇhands, and I will bestow the ᶜgift of the Holy Ghost upon them.

16 And the Book of Mormon and the holy scriptures are given of me for my ᵃinstruction; and the power of my ᵇSpirit ᶜquickeneth all things.

17 Wherefore, be faithful, pray-

1c Amos 4 : 13.
2a Isa. 58 : 1; D&C 19 : 37; 29 : 4; 30 : 9.
 b Deut. 32 : 5.
3a John 4 : 35.
 b D&C 4 : 4; 12 : 3; 14 : 3; 101 : 64.
 c Matt. 20 : 6 (1–16).
 d Jacob 5 : 71 (71–75); D&C 43 : 28.
4a TG Vineyard of the Lord.
 b 2 Ne. 28 : 11 (2–14); Morm. 8 : 28 (28–41); D&C 38 : 11.
 c Eccl. 7 : 20; Jer. 13 : 23; Rom. 3 : 12; D&C 35 : 12.
 d 2 Ne. 27 : 35 (34–35); 28 : 14.

 e TG Priestcraft.
5a TG Church; Jesus Christ, Head of the Church.
 b TG Mission of Latter-day Saints.
 c Rev. 12 : 6 (1–6).
6a Deut. 30 : 3. TG Israel, Gathering of.
 b Jer. 49 : 36; Rev. 20 : 8; D&C 45 : 46.
7a D&C 4 : 4 (2–4).
8a TG Missionary Work.
 b 2 Ne. 1 : 27 (27–28).
9a Ps. 126 : 6; Alma 26 : 5; D&C 75 : 5.
10a Matt. 3 : 2.
 b Mark 1 : 15.
11a TG Baptism, Qualifica-
    tions for; Repentance.

 b TG Remission of Sins.
12a TG Gospel; Salvation, Plan of.
13a TG Rock.
 b Matt. 16 : 18; D&C 10 : 69.
14a D&C 1 : 6 (6, 37); 42 : 13; 51 : 4.
15a D&C 20 : 41.
 b TG Hands, Laying on of.
 c TG Holy Ghost, Gift of.
16a TG Scriptures, Study of; Scriptures, Value of.
 b TG God, Spirit of.
 c Ps. 71 : 20; 1 Tim. 6 : 13.

ing always, having your ^alamps ^btrimmed and burning, and oil with you, that you may be ^cready at the coming of the ^dBridegroom—

18 For behold, verily, verily, I say unto you, that I ^acome quickly. Even so. Amen.

SECTION 34

Revelation given through Joseph Smith the Prophet to Orson Pratt, at Fayette, New York, November 4, 1830. HC 1: 127–128. Brother Pratt was nineteen years old at the time. He had been converted and baptized when he first heard the preaching of the restored gospel by his older brother, Parley P. Pratt, six weeks before. This revelation was received in the Peter Whitmer, Sen., home.

1–4, The faithful become the sons of God through the atonement; 5–9, Preaching of the gospel prepares the way for the Second Coming; 10–12, Prophecy comes by the power of the Holy Ghost.

MY son ^aOrson, hearken and hear and behold what I, the Lord God, shall say unto you, even Jesus Christ your Redeemer;

2 The ^alight and the life of the world, a light which shineth in darkness and the darkness comprehendeth it not;

3 Who so ^aloved the world that he ^bgave his own life, that as many as would believe might become the ^csons of God. Wherefore you are my son;

4 And ^ablessed are you because you have believed;

5 And more blessed are you because you are ^acalled of me to preach my gospel—

6 To lift up your voice as with the sound of a ^atrump, both long and loud, and ^bcry repentance unto a crooked and perverse generation, ^cpreparing the way of the Lord for his second ^dcoming.

7 For behold, verily, verily, I say unto you, the ^atime is soon at hand that I shall ^bcome in a ^ccloud with power and great glory.

8 And it shall be a ^agreat day at the time of my coming, for all nations shall ^btremble.

9 But before that great day shall come, the ^asun shall be darkened, and the moon be turned into blood; and the stars shall refuse their shining, and some shall fall, and great destructions await the wicked.

10 Wherefore, lift up your voice and ^aspare not, for the Lord God hath spoken; therefore ^bprophesy, and it shall be given by the ^cpower of the Holy Ghost.

17a D&C 88: 92; 133: 19 (10, 19).
  b Matt. 25: 7 (1–13).
  c TG Procrastination.
  d TG Jesus Christ, Prophecies about.
18a Rev. 22: 20; D&C 34: 12. TG Jesus Christ, Second Coming.
34 1a D&C 52: 26; 103: 40; 124: 129; 136: 13.
  2a John 1: 5.
  3a John 3: 16; 15: 13.
  b TG Jesus Christ, Redeemer.

c Luke 8: 21; John 1: 12 (9–13); Rom. 8: 17 (12–17); Moses 6: 68 (64–68). TG Sons and Daughters of God.
4a John 20: 29.
5a TG Called of God.
6a D&C 24: 12.
  b D&C 3: 20; 6: 9; 18: 14.
  c Matt. 3: 3.
  d TG Jesus Christ, Second Coming; Millennium, Preparing a People for.
7a Rev. 1: 3.

b TG Jesus Christ, Prophecies about.
  c Num. 11: 25; Luke 21: 27; Ether 2: 4 (4–5, 14); JS-H 1: 68 (68–71).
8a Joel 2: 11; Mal. 4: 5; D&C 2: 1; 43: 17 (17–26). TG Day of the Lord.
  b Isa. 64: 2.
9a TG Last Days.
10a Isa. 58: 1.
  b TG Prophets, Mission of.
  c 2 Pet. 1: 21; D&C 18: 32; 42: 16; 68: 3.

11 And if you are faithful, behold, I am with you until I come—

12 And verily, verily, I say unto you, I come "quickly. I am your *b*Lord and your Redeemer. Even so. Amen.

SECTION 35

Revelation given to Joseph Smith the Prophet and Sidney Rigdon, at or near Fayette, New York, December 1830. HC 1: 128–131. At this time the Prophet was engaged almost daily in making a translation of the Bible. The translation was begun as early as June 1830, and both Oliver Cowdery and John Whitmer had served as scribes. Since they had now been called to other duties, Sidney Rigdon was called by divine appointment to serve as the Prophet's scribe in this work (verse 20). As a preface to his record of this revelation the Prophet wrote: "In December Sidney Rigdon came [from Ohio] to inquire of the Lord, and with him came Edward Partridge. . . . Shortly after the arrival of these two brethren, thus spake the Lord."

1–2, *How men may become the sons of God;* 3–7, *Sidney Rigdon is called to baptize and confer the Holy Ghost;* 8–12, *Signs and miracles are wrought by faith;* 13–16, *The Lord's servants shall thrash the nations by the power of the Spirit;* 17–19, *Joseph Smith holds the keys of the mysteries;* 20–21, *The elect shall abide the day of the Lord's coming;* 22–27, *Israel shall be saved.*

LISTEN to the voice of the *a*Lord your God, even *b*Alpha and Omega, the beginning and the end, whose *c*course is one *d*eternal round, the *e*same today as yesterday, and forever.

2 I am Jesus Christ, the Son of God, who was *a*crucified for the sins of the world, even as many as will *b*believe on my name, that they may become the *c*sons of God, even *d*one in *e*me as I am *f*one in the Father, as the Father is one in me, that we may be one.

3 Behold, verily, verily, I say unto my servant Sidney, I have looked upon thee and thy works. I have *a*heard thy prayers, and prepared thee for a greater work.

4 Thou art blessed, for thou shalt do great things. Behold thou wast sent forth, even as *a*John, to prepare the way before me, and before *b*Elijah which should come, and thou knewest it not.

5 Thou didst baptize by water unto repentance, but they *a*received not the Holy Ghost;

6 But now I give unto thee a commandment, that thou shalt *a*baptize by water, and they shall receive the *b*Holy Ghost by the laying on

---

12a D&C 33:18.
  b TG Jesus Christ, Lord.
35 1a TG Jesus Christ, Lord.
  b Rev. 1:8; D&C 19:1.
  c 1 Ne. 10:19; D&C 3:2.
  d TG God, Eternal Nature of.
  e Heb. 13:8; D&C 20:12; 38:1 (1–4); 39:1 (1–3); 76:4.
2a TG Jesus Christ,

Crucifixion of.
  b D&C 20:25; 38:4; 45:5 (5, 8).
  c TG Sons and Daughters of God.
  d John 17:21; Moses 6:68. TG Unity.
  e TG Jesus Christ, Exemplar.
  f TG Godhead.
3a Ex. 2:24 (23–24); Mosiah 9:18 (17–18);

Abr. 1:15 (15–16).
4a Mal. 3:1; Matt. 11:10; John 5:33; 1 Ne. 11:27; D&C 84:27 (27–28).
  b 3 Ne. 25:5 (5–6); D&C 2:1; 110:13 (13–15); 128:17.
5a Acts 19:2 (1–6).
6a TG Baptism.
  b TG Holy Ghost, Gift of.

of the ᶜhands, even as the apostles of old.

7 And it shall come to pass that there shall be a great work in the land, even among the ᵃGentiles, for their ᵇfolly and their abominations shall be made manifest in the eyes of all people.

8 For I am God, and mine arm is not ᵃshortened; and I will show ᵇmiracles, ᶜsigns, and wonders, unto all those who ᵈbelieve on my name.

9 And whoso shall ask it in my name in ᵃfaith, they shall ᵇcast out ᶜdevils; they shall heal the ᵈsick; they shall cause the blind to receive their ᵉsight, and the deaf to hear, and the dumb to speak, and the lame to walk.

10 And the time ᵃspeedily cometh that great things are to be shown forth unto the children of men;

11 But ᵃwithout faith shall not anything be shown forth except ᵇdesolations upon ᶜBabylon, the same which has made ᵈall nations drink of the wine of the wrath of her ᵉfornication.

12 And there are ᵃnone that doeth good except those who are ready to ᵇreceive the fulness of my gospel, which I have sent forth unto this generation.

13 Wherefore, I call upon the ᵃweak

things of the world, those who are ᵇunlearned and despised, to thrash the ᶜnations by the power of my ᵈSpirit;

14 And their arm shall be my arm, and I will be their ᵃshield and their buckler; and I will gird up their loins, and they shall fight manfully for me; and their ᵇenemies shall be under their feet; and I will let ᶜfall the ᵈsword in their behalf, and by the ᵉfire of mine indignation will I preserve them.

15 And the ᵃpoor and the ᵇmeek shall have the gospel preached unto them, and they shall be ᶜlooking forth for the time of my coming, for it is ᵈnigh at hand—

16 And they shall learn the parable of the ᵃfig-tree, for even now already summer is nigh.

17 And I have sent forth the ᵃfulness of my gospel by the hand of my servant Joseph; and in weakness have I blessed him;

18 And I have given unto him the ᵃkeys of the mystery of those things which have been ᵇsealed, even things which were from the ᶜfoundation of the world, and the things which shall come from this time until the time of my coming, if he ᵈabide in me, and if not, ᵉanother will I plant in his stead.

19 Wherefore, watch over him that

6c TG Hands, Laying on of.
7a Isa. 66: 12.
    TG Gentiles.
  b Eccl. 10: 12 (1–3, 12); 2 Tim. 3: 9; 2 Ne. 9: 28 (28–29); 19: 17.
8a Isa. 50: 2 (2–4); 59: 1.
  b TG Miracle.
  c TG Signs.
  d TG Believe; Trust in God.
9a TG Faith.
  b Mark 16: 17.
  c Mark 1: 39 (21–45).
  d TG Healing; Sickness.
  e TG Sight.
10a JS-H 1: 41.
11a D&C 63: 11 (7–12).
  b Jer. 51: 62; D&C 5: 19 (19–20); 29: 8; 43: 17 (17–27).

  c TG Babylon.
  d 1 Ne. 14: 11 (10–13).
  e Rev. 18: 3.
12a Rom. 3: 12; Moro. 7: 13 (12–13); D&C 33: 4; 38: 11; 84: 47 (47–51).
  b TG Missionary Work; Teachable.
13a 1 Cor. 1: 27; D&C 1: 19 (19, 23); 124: 1.
  b Acts 4: 13.
  c TG Nations.
  d TG God, Spirit of.
14a 2 Sam. 22: 3; Ps. 33: 20; 91: 4.
  b D&C 98: 37 (34–38).
  c D&C 1: 14 (13–14); 45: 47.
  d D&C 1: 13.
  e Num. 11: 1 (1, 10); D&C 128: 24; Moses 7: 34.

15a Matt. 11: 5.
  b TG Meekness.
  c 2 Pet. 3: 12 (10–13); D&C 39: 23; 45: 39; Moses 7: 62.
  d D&C 63: 53.
16a Matt. 24: 32; Luke 21: 29 (29–30); D&C 45: 37 (36–38); JS-M 1: 38.
    TG Last Days.
17a Rom. 15: 29; D&C 42: 12; 135: 3.
18a D&C 28: 7; 84: 19.
  b Dan. 12: 9; Matt. 13: 35; 1 Ne. 14: 26; 2 Ne. 27: 10; Ether 4: 5 (4–7); JS-H 1: 65.
  c D&C 128: 18.
  d John 15: 4 (4, 7).
  e D&C 42: 10; 64: 40; 104: 77; 107: 99 (99–100).

his faith fail not, and it shall be given by the ^aComforter, the ^bHoly Ghost, that knoweth all things.

20 And a commandment I give unto thee—that thou shalt ^awrite for him; and the ^bscriptures shall be given, even as they are in mine own bosom, to the salvation of mine own ^celect;

21 For they will hear my ^avoice, and shall ^bsee me, and shall not be ^casleep, and shall ^dabide the day of my ^ecoming; for they shall be ^fpurified, even as I am pure.

22 And now I say unto you, ^atarry with him, and he shall journey with you; forsake him not, and surely these things shall be fulfilled.

23 And ^ainasmuch as ye do not write, behold, it shall be ^bgiven unto

him to prophesy; and thou shalt preach my gospel and call on ^cthe holy prophets to prove his words, as they shall be given him.

24 ^aKeep all the commandments and covenants by which ye are bound; and I will cause the heavens to ^bshake for your ^cgood, and ^dSatan shall tremble and ^eZion shall ^frejoice upon the hills and ^gflourish.

25 And ^aIsrael shall be ^bsaved in mine own due time; and by the ^ckeys which I have given shall they be led, and no more be confounded at all.

26 ^aLift up your hearts and be glad, your ^bredemption draweth nigh.

27 Fear not, little ^aflock, the ^bkingdom is yours until I come. Behold, I ^ccome quickly. Even so. Amen.

SECTION 36

Revelation given through Joseph Smith the Prophet to Edward Partridge, near Fayette, New York, December 1830. HC 1 : 131. See heading to Section 35. The Prophet said that Edward Partridge "was a pattern of piety, and one of the Lord's great men."

1–3, The Lord lays his hand upon Edward Partridge by the hand of Sidney Rigdon; 4–8, Every man who receives the gospel and the priesthood to be called to go forth and preach.

THUS saith the Lord God, the ^aMighty One of Israel: Behold, I say unto you, my servant ^bEdward, that you are blessed, and your sins are forgiven you, and you are called to

---

19a John 14: 16, 26; 15: 26; 1 Cor. 12: 8.
  b 1 Cor. 2: 10.
20a The Prophet was at this time engaged in a revelatory translation of the Bible, to which Sidney Rigdon was called as scribe.
  b D&C 6: 27; 37: 1; 42: 15 (15, 56–58).
  c TG Election.
21a Joel 2: 11; John 10: 3; D&C 43: 18 (17–25); 88: 90; 133: 50 (50–52).
  b John 16: 16.
    TG God, Privilege of Seeing.
  c Matt. 25: 5.
  d Mal. 3: 2.
  e TG Jesus Christ, Prophecies about; Jesus

Christ, Second Coming.
  f TG Purification.
22a D&C 90: 6; 100: 9 (9–11).
23a IE whenever you are not occupied with writing.
  b 1 Cor. 12: 8.
  c IE the scriptures.
24a D&C 66: 11; 103: 7.
  b D&C 21: 6.
  c TG Blessing.
  d 1 Ne. 22: 26; Alma 48: 17.
  e D&C 6: 6.
  f TG Joy.
  g D&C 39: 13; 49: 25; 117: 7 (7–8).
25a TG Israel, Blessings of; Israel, Restoration of; Israel, Tribes of, Ten Lost; Israel, Tribes of, Twelve.

  b Ps. 94: 14; Isa. 45: 17; 1 Ne. 19 (15–16); 22: 12. TG Israel, Deliverance of.
  c TG Priesthood, Keys of.
26a Lam. 3: 41.
  b Luke 21: 28; Rom. 13: 11.
27a Luke 12: 32.
    TG Church; Sheep.
  b D&C 29: 5; 38: 9.
    TG Kingdom of God, on Earth; Jesus Christ, Second Coming.
  c Rev. 22: 20.
36 1a TG Jesus Christ, Jehovah.
  b D&C 41: 9 (9–11).
    See also Partridge, Edward, in Index.

preach my gospel as with the voice of a trump;

2 And I will lay my ^ahand upon you by the hand of my servant Sidney Rigdon, and you shall receive my Spirit, the Holy Ghost, even the ^bComforter, which shall ^cteach you the peaceable things of the kingdom;

3 And you shall declare it with a loud voice, saying: Hosanna, ^ablessed be the name of the most high God.

4 And now this calling and commandment give I unto you concerning all men—

5 That as many as shall come before my servants Sidney Rigdon and Joseph Smith, Jun., embracing this calling and commandment, shall be

^aordained and sent forth to ^bpreach the everlasting gospel among the nations—

6 Crying repentance, saying: ^aSave yourselves from this untoward generation, and come forth out of the fire, hating even the ^bgarments spotted with the flesh.

7 And this commandment shall be given unto the elders of my church, that every man which will ^aembrace it with ^bsingleness of heart may be ordained and sent forth, even as I have spoken.

8 I am Jesus Christ, the Son of God; wherefore, gird up your loins and I will ^asuddenly ^bcome to my ^ctemple. Even so. Amen.

SECTION 37

Revelation given to Joseph Smith the Prophet and Sidney Rigdon, near Fayette, New York, December 1830. HC 1: 139. Herein is given the first commandment concerning a gathering in this dispensation.

1–4, The saints are called to gather at the Ohio.

BEHOLD, I say unto you that it is not expedient in me that ye should ^atranslate any more until ye shall go to the Ohio, and this because of the enemy and for your sakes.

2 And again, I say unto you that ye shall not go until ye have preached my gospel in those parts, and have ^astrengthened up the church whithersoever it is found,

and more especially in ^bColesville; for, behold, they pray unto me in much faith.

3 And again, a commandment I give unto the church, that it is expedient in me that they should assemble together at ^athe Ohio, against the time that my servant Oliver Cowdery shall return unto them.

4 Behold, here is wisdom, and let every man ^achoose for himself until I come. Even so. Amen.

2a TG Hands, Laying on of.
  b TG Holy Ghost, Comforter.
  c D&C 39: 6; 42: 61.
    TG Holy Ghost, Mission of.
3a Gen. 14: 20.
5a D&C 4: 3 (3–6); 63: 57. TG Priesthood, Ordination.
  b TG Mission of Latter-

day Saints; Missionary Work.
6a Acts 2: 40.
  b Jude 1: 23.
7a TG Commitment; Priesthood, Magnifying; Callings within; Priesthood, Qualifying for.
  b TG Sincerity.
8a D&C 42: 36.

  b TG Jesus Christ, Second Coming.
  c Mal. 3: 1.
37 1a IE the translation of the Bible already in process. D&C 1: 29; 35: 20.
2a Zech. 10: 12.
  b D&C 24: 3; 26: 1.
3a IE state of the Ohio. D&C 38: 32.
4a TG Agency.

SECTION 38

Revelation given through Joseph Smith the Prophet, at Fayette, New York, January 2, 1831. HC 1: 140–143. The occasion was a conference of the Church.

1–6, Christ created all things; 7–8, He is in the midst of his saints, who shall soon see him; 9–12, All flesh is corrupted before him; 13–22, He has reserved a land of promise for his saints in time and in eternity; 23–27, The saints are commanded to be one and esteem each other as brethren; 28–29, Wars are predicted; 30–33, The saints are to be given power from on high and go forth among all nations; 34–42, The Church is commanded to care for the poor and needy, and to seek the riches of eternity.

THUS saith the Lord your God, even Jesus Christ, the Great *a*I AM, Alpha and Omega, the *b*beginning and the end, the *c*same which looked upon the *d*wide expanse of eternity, and all the seraphic *e*hosts of heaven, *f*before the world was *g*made;

2 The same which *a*knoweth all things, for *b*all things are *c*present before mine eyes;

3 I am the same which *a*spake, and the world was made, and all things came by me.

4 I am the same which have taken the *a*Zion of *b*Enoch into mine own bosom; and verily, I say, even as many as have *c*believed in my name, for I am Christ, and in mine own name, by the virtue of the *d*blood which I have spilt, have I pleaded before the Father for them.

5 But behold, the residue of the *a*wicked have I kept in *b*chains of darkness until the *c*judgment of the great day, which shall come at the end of the earth;

6 And even so will I cause the wicked to be kept, that will not hear my voice but *a*harden their hearts, and wo, wo, wo, is their doom.

7 But behold, verily, verily, I say unto you that mine *a*eyes are upon you. I am in your *b*midst and ye cannot *c*see me;

8 But the day soon cometh that ye shall *a*see me, and know that I am; for the *b*veil of darkness shall soon be rent, and he that is not *c*purified shall not *d*abide the day.

9 Wherefore, gird up your loins and be prepared. Behold, the *a*kingdom is yours, and the enemy shall not overcome.

10 Verily I say unto you, ye are *a*clean, but not all; and there is none else with whom I am well *b*pleased;

38 1a TG Jesus Christ, Jehovah.
  b Rev. 1: 8.
  c Heb. 13: 8; D&C 20: 12; 35: 1; 39: 1 (1–3); 76: 4.
  d Isa. 57: 15.
  e Gen. 2: 1; D&C 45: 1.
  f TG Man, Antemortal Existence of.
  g Ps. 90: 2.
 2a D&C 88: 41; Moses 1: 35 (35–37); 7: 36. TG God, Omniscience of.
  b Prov. 5: 21; 2 Ne. 9: 20.
  c TG God, Foreknowledge of.
 3a Ps. 33: 9. TG Jesus Christ, Creator.
 4a See Bible, Appendix,

JST Gen. 14: 30–34.
  D&C 45: 11 (11–12); 76: 67; 84: 100 (99–100); 133: 54; Moses 7: 18 (18, 21).
  TG Zion.
  b Gen. 5: 23.
  c D&C 20: 25; 35: 2; 45: 3 (3–8).
  d TG Jesus Christ, Atonement through.
 5a TG Wickedness.
  b 2 Pet. 2: 4 (4–9); Jude 1: 6. TG Hell; Spirits in Prison.
  c TG Judgment, The Last.
 6a TG Hardheartedness.
  b Ps. 33: 18; Amos 9: 8;

D&C 1: 1.
  b Josh. 1: 9; D&C 6: 32; 29: 5; 32: 3; 88: 63 (62–63).
  c Isa. 45: 15.
 8a John 16: 16; Rev. 22: 4 (1–5). TG Jesus Christ, Second Coming.
  b TG Veil.
  c TG Purification; Worthiness.
  d Mal. 3: 2.
 9a Luke 6: 20; D&C 35: 27; 45: 1. TG Kingdom of God, on Earth.
 10a Dan. 3: 10.
  TG Cleanliness.
  b D&C 1: 30.

11 For all ᵃflesh is corrupted before me; and the powers of ᵇdarkness prevail upon the earth, among the children of men, in the presence of all the hosts of heaven—

12 Which causeth ᵃsilence to reign, and all eternity is ᵇpained, and the ᶜangels are waiting the great command to ᵈreap down the earth, to ᵉgather the ᶠtares that they may be ᵍburned; and, behold, the enemy is combined.

13 And now I show unto you a mystery, a thing which is had in secret chambers, to bring to pass even your ᵃdestruction in process of time, and ye knew it not;

14 But now I tell it unto you, and ye are blessed, not because of your iniquity, neither your hearts of unbelief; for verily some of you are ᵃguilty before me, but I will be merciful unto your ᵇweakness.

15 Therefore, be ye ᵃstrong from henceforth; ᵇfear not, for the kingdom is yours.

16 And for your salvation I give unto you a commandment, for I have heard your ᵃprayers, and the ᵇpoor have complained before me, and the ᶜrich have I made, and all flesh is mine, and I am no ᵈrespecter of persons.

17 And I have made the earth rich,

and behold it is my ᵃfootstool, wherefore, again I will stand upon it.

18 And I hold forth and deign to give unto you greater riches, even a land of ᵃpromise, a land ᵇflowing with milk and honey, upon which there shall be no ᶜcurse when the Lord cometh;

19 And I will give it unto you for the land of your inheritance, if you seek it with all your hearts.

20 And this shall be my covenant with you, ye shall have it for the land of your inheritance, and for the ᵃinheritance of your children forever, while the earth shall stand, and ye shall possess it again in eternity, no more to pass away.

21 But, verily I say unto you that in time ye shall have no ᵃking nor ruler, for I will be your king and watch over you.

22 Wherefore, hear my voice and ᵃfollow me, and you shall be a ᵇfree people, and ye shall have no laws but my laws when I come, for I am your ᶜlawgiver, and what can stay my hand?

23 But, verily I say unto you, ᵃteach one another according to the office wherewith I have appointed you;

24 And let every man ᵃesteem his brother as himself, and practise ᵇvirtue and holiness before me.

11a Gen. 6: 12; Ex. 32: 7; Isa. 1: 4 (3–4); Hosea 9: 9 (7–9); D&C 33: 4; 35: 12 (7, 12).
  TG Filthiness.
  b Micah 3: 6; Col. 1: 13; D&C 112: 23; Moses 7: 61 (61–62).
12a Lam. 2: 10; D&C 88: 95. TG Silence.
  b Moses 7: 41.
  c D&C 86: 5 (3–7).
  d TG Harvest.
  e TG Last Days.
  f D&C 86: 7; 88: 94; 101: 66.
  g Matt. 13: 30.
13a Ether 8: 21 (20–22); D&C 5: 33 (32–33); 10: 6 (6, 25); 38: 28; 42: 54.
14a TG Guilt.

b Heb. 8: 12.
15a Deut. 11: 8.
  TG Courage.
  b TG Fearfulness.
16a Ex. 3: 7.
  b Isa. 10: 2; Mosiah 4: 16 (16–18).
  c Gen. 14: 23; 1 Sam. 2: 7.
  TG Treasure.
  d Deut. 1: 17; Isa. 56: 7 (3–8); Acts 10: 34; Eph. 6: 9; Col. 3: 25; Alma 1: 30; Moro. 8: 12; D&C 1: 35 (34–35).
  TG Judgment.
17a Lam. 2: 1; 1 Ne. 17: 39; Abr. 2: 7.
18a Heb. 11: 9.
  b Ex. 3: 8; Lev. 20: 24.
  c TG Earth, Curse of.

20a Isa. 29: 19; Matt. 5: 5; D&C 45: 58.
21a 1 Sam. 8: 5 (4–22); 12: 12 (12–15); Ps. 44: 4; Zech. 14: 9; 2 Ne. 10: 14; Alma 5: 50.
  TG Kingdom of God, on Earth.
22a John 10: 27.
  b TG Liberty.
  c Gen. 49: 10; Isa. 33: 22; Micah 4: 2; D&C 45: 59.
23a Ex. 35: 34; Heb. 3: 13; Moro. 10: 9 (9–10); D&C 88: 77 (77–78, 118); 107: 85 (85–89).
  TG Teaching.
24a Deut. 17: 20; 1 Cor. 4: 6 (6–7). TG Brotherhood and Sisterhood.
  TG Holiness; Virtue.

25 And again I say unto you, let every man esteem his ^abrother as himself.

26 For what man among you having twelve sons, and is no respecter of them, and they serve him obediently, and he saith unto the one: Be thou clothed in robes and sit thou here; and to the other: Be thou clothed in rags and sit thou there—and looketh upon his sons and saith I am ^ajust?

27 Behold, this I have given unto you as a parable, and it is even as I am. I say unto you, be ^aone; and if ye are not one ye are not mine.

28 And again, I say unto you that the enemy in the secret chambers seeketh your ^alives.

29 Ye hear of ^awars in far countries, and you say that there will soon be great wars in far countries, but ye know not the hearts of men in your own land.

30 I tell you these things because of your prayers; wherefore, ^atreasure up ^bwisdom in your bosoms, lest the wickedness of men reveal these things unto you by their wickedness, in a manner which shall speak in your ears with a voice louder than that which shall shake the earth; but if ye are prepared ye shall not fear.

31 And that ye might escape the power of the ^aenemy, and be gathered unto me a righteous people, without ^bspot and blameless—

32 Wherefore, for this cause I gave unto you the ^acommandment that ye should go to the ^bOhio; and there I will give unto you my ^claw; and

there you shall be ^dendowed with power from on high;

33 And from thence, whosoever I will shall go forth among ^aall nations, and it shall be told them what they shall do; for I have a great work laid up in store, for Israel shall be ^bsaved, and I will ^clead them whithersoever I will, and no power shall ^dstay my hand.

34 And now, I give unto the church in these parts a commandment, that certain men among them shall be appointed, and they shall be ^aappointed by the ^bvoice of the church;

35 And they shall look to the poor and the needy, and administer to their ^arelief that they shall not suffer; and send them forth to the place which I have commanded them;

36 And this shall be their work, to govern the affairs of the property of this ^achurch.

37 And they that have farms that cannot be sold, let them be left or rented as seemeth them good.

38 See that all things are preserved; and when men are ^aendowed with power from on high and sent forth, all these things shall be gathered unto the bosom of the church.

39 And if ye seek the ^ariches which it is the will of the Father to give unto you, ye shall be the richest of all people, for ye shall have the riches of eternity; and it must needs be that the ^briches of the earth are mine to give; but beware of ^cpride, lest ye become as the ^dNephites of old.

40 And again, I say unto you,

25a Acts 17: 26 (26–34).
26a TG God, Justice of.
27a John 17: 21 (21–23);
    1 Cor. 1: 10; Eph. 4:
    13 (11–14); 3 Ne. 11:
    28 (28–30); Moses 7:
    18. TG Unity.
28a D&C 5: 33 (32–33);
    10: 6 (6, 25); 38: 13;
    42: 64.
29a D&C 42: 64; 45: 63
    (26, 63); 87: 2 (1–5);
    130: 12.
30a JS-M 1: 37.
    b TG Study; Wisdom.

31a TG Enemies.
    b 2 Pet. 3: 14.
32a D&C 42: 3.
    b D&C 37: 3.
    c D&C 42: 2 (1–93).
    d Luke 24: 49; D&C 39:
      15; 43: 16; 95: 8 (8–9);
      110: 9 (9–10).
33a TG Missionary Work.
    b Isa. 45: 17; Jer. 30: 10;
      31: 7 (6–7); Hosea 13:
      9; D&C 136: 22.
    c TG Guidance, Divine.
    d Dan. 4: 35.
34a TG Delegation of
      Responsibility.

    b TG Sustaining Church
      Leaders.
35a TG Welfare.
36a TG Church Organiza-
      tion.
38a TG Endowment,
      Endow; Genealogy
      and Temple Work.
39a 2 Ne. 26: 31; Jacob 2:
      18 (17–19); D&C 11: 7.
      TG Objectives.
    b Hag. 2: 8.
    c Prov. 11: 2; 2 Ne. 26:
      20 (20–22). TG Pride.
    d Moro. 8: 27.

I give unto you a commandment, that every man, both elder, priest, teacher, and also member, go to with his might, with the ^alabor of his ^bhands, to prepare and accomplish the things which I have commanded.

41 And let your ^apreaching be the ^bwarning voice, every man to his neighbor, in mildness and in ^cmeekness.

42 And go ye ^aout from among the ^bwicked. Save yourselves. Be ye ^cclean that bear the vessels of the Lord. Even so. Amen.

SECTION 39

Revelation given through Joseph Smith the Prophet to James Covill, at Fayette, New York, January 5, 1831. HC 1: 143–145. James Covill, who had been a Baptist minister for about forty years, covenanted with the Lord that he would obey any command that the Lord would give to him through Joseph the Prophet.

1–4, The saints have power to become the sons of God; 5–6, To receive the gospel is to receive Christ; 7–14, James Covill is commanded to be baptized and labor in the Lord's vineyard; 15–21, The Lord's servants are to preach the gospel before Second Coming; 22–24, Those who receive the gospel shall be gathered in time and in eternity.

HEARKEN and listen to the voice of him who is from all ^aeternity to all eternity, the Great ^bI AM, even Jesus Christ—

2 The ^alight and the life of the world; a light which shineth in darkness and the darkness comprehendeth it not;

3 The same which came in the ^ameridian of time unto mine own, and mine own ^breceived me not;

4 But to as many as received me, gave I power to become my ^asons;

and even so will I give unto as many as will receive me, power to become my sons.

5 And verily, verily, I say unto you, he that ^areceiveth my gospel ^areceiveth me; and he that ^breceiveth not my gospel receiveth not me.

6 And this is my ^agospel—repentance and baptism by water, and then cometh the ^bbaptism of fire and the Holy Ghost, even the Comforter, which showeth all things, and ^cteacheth the peaceable things of the kingdom.

7 And now, behold, I say unto you, my servant ^aJames, I have looked upon thy works and I ^bknow thee.

8 And verily I say unto thee, thine heart is now right before me at this time; and, behold, I have bestowed great ^ablessings upon thy head;

9 Nevertheless, thou hast seen great ^asorrow, for thou hast ^bre-

---

40*a* TG Industry.
  b 1 Cor. 4:12.
41*a* TG Preaching.
  b TG Warnings.
  c Titus 3:2.
42*a* Isa. 52:11.
  b Ps. 26:4; Rom. 12:9.
  c Lev. 21:6; Ether 12:37.
39 1*a* Heb. 13:8; D&C 20:12; 35:1; 38:1 (1–4); 76:4. TG Eternity.
  b Ex. 3:14; Isa. 44:6;

Rev. 1:8. TG Jesus Christ, Jehovah.
2*a* TG Jesus Christ, Light of the World.
3*a* D&C 20:26; Moses 5:57; 6:57 (57, 62); 7:46.
  b TG Prophets, Rejection of.
4*a* John 1:12. TG Sons and Daughters of God.
5*a* John 13:20.
  b TG Teachable.
6*a* TG Baptism; Gospel;

Repentance.
  b TG Holy Ghost, Baptism of; Holy Ghost, Comforter; Holy Ghost, Mission of.
  c D&C 36:2; 42:61.
7*a* D&C 40:1.
  b Gen. 18:19.
8*a* Prov. 10:6.
9*a* Mosiah 7:29.
  b John 12:48; Alma 10:6.

jected me many times because of pride and the cares of the ^cworld.

10 But, behold, the days of thy ^adeliverance are come, if thou wilt ^bhearken to my voice, which saith unto thee: Arise and be baptized, and ^cwash away your sins, calling on my name, and you shall receive my Spirit, and a blessing so great as you never have known.

11 And if thou do this, I have prepared thee for a greater work. Thou shalt preach the ^afulness of my gospel, which I have sent forth in these last days, the ^bcovenant which I have sent forth to ^crecover my people, which are of the house of Israel.

12 And it shall come to pass that power shall ^arest upon thee; thou shalt have great faith, and I will be with thee and go before thy face.

13 Thou art called to ^alabor in my vineyard, and to ^bbuild up my ^cchurch, and to bring forth ^dZion, that it may rejoice upon the hills and ^eflourish.

14 Behold, verily, I say unto thee, thou art not called to go into the eastern countries, but thou art called to go to the Ohio.

15 And inasmuch as my people shall assemble themselves at the Ohio, I have kept in store a ^ablessing such as is not known among the children of men, and it shall be poured forth upon their heads. And from thence men shall go forth into ^ball nations.

16 Behold, verily, verily, I say unto you, that the people in Ohio call upon me in much faith, thinking I will ^astay my hand in judgment upon the nations, but I cannot ^bdeny my word.

17 Wherefore lay to with your might and call faithful laborers into my vineyard, that it may be ^apruned for the last time.

18 And inasmuch as they do repent and receive the fulness of my gospel, and become sanctified, I will stay mine hand in ^ajudgment.

19 Wherefore, go forth, crying with a loud voice, saying: The kingdom of heaven is at ^ahand; crying: Hosanna! blessed be the name of the Most High God.

20 Go forth ^abaptizing with water, preparing the way before my face for the time of my ^bcoming;

21 For the time is at hand; the ^aday or the hour no man ^bknoweth; but it surely shall ^ccome.

22 And he that receiveth these things receiveth me; and they shall be ^agathered unto me in time and in eternity.

23 And again, it shall come to pass that on as many as ye shall baptize with water, ye shall lay your ^ahands, and they shall receive the ^bgift of the Holy Ghost, and shall be ^clooking forth for the signs of my ^dcoming, and shall know me.

24 Behold, I come quickly. Even so. Amen.

9c Matt. 13: 22; Hel. 7: 5.
10a TG Deliverance.
   b D&C 40: 3 (1–3).
   c TG Baptism, Essential; Purity; Repentance.
11a Rom. 15: 29; D&C 18: 4.
   b D&C 1: 22.
   c TG Israel, Restoration of.
12a 2 Cor. 12: 9. TG Deliverance; Guidance, Divine.
13a Matt. 20: 8 (1–16).
   b D&C 30: 6; 42: 8.
   c TG Jesus Christ, Head of the Church.

d Isa. 52: 8.
   e D&C 35: 24; 49: 25; 117: 7 (7–8).
15a D&C 38: 32; 43: 16; 95: 8 (8–9); 110: 9 (8–10).
   b D&C 1: 2, 34 (34–35); 18: 28 (26–28); 42: 58.
16a 2 Sam. 24: 16; Moses 7: 51.
   b 2 Tim. 2: 13.
17a Jacob 5: 61 (61–75); D&C 24: 19; 95: 4.
18a TG Jesus Christ, Judge.
19a Matt. 3: 2.

20a TG Baptism, Essential.
   b TG Jesus Christ, Prophecies about; Jesus Christ, Second Coming.
21a Matt. 24: 36; 1 Cor. 5: 5.
   b JS-M 1: 40.
   c Hab. 2: 3.
22a D&C 10: 65.
23a TG Hands, Laying on of.
   b TG Holy Ghost, Gift of.
   c Rev. 3: 3; D&C 35: 15; 45: 39.
   d 2 Pet. 3: 12.

SECTION 40

Revelation given to Joseph Smith the Prophet and Sidney Rigdon, at Fayette, New York, January 1831. HC 1: 145. Preceding the record of this revelation, the Prophet wrote: "As James Covill rejected the word of the Lord, and returned to his former principles and people, the Lord gave unto me and Sidney Rigdon the following revelation."

1–3, *Fear of persecution and cares of the world cause rejection of the gospel.*

BEHOLD, verily I say unto you, that the heart of my servant "James Covill was right before me, for he covenanted with me that he would obey my word.

2 And he "received the word with gladness, but straightway Satan "tempted him; and the fear of "persecution and the cares of the world caused him to "reject the word.

3 Wherefore he "broke my covenant, and it remaineth with me to do with him as seemeth me good. Amen.

SECTION 41

Revelation given through Joseph Smith the Prophet to the Church, at Kirtland, Ohio, February 4, 1831. HC 1: 146–147. The Kirtland Branch of the Church at this time was rapidly increasing in numbers. Prefacing this revelation the Prophet wrote: "The members were striving to do the will of God, so far as they knew it, though some strange notions and false spirits had crept in among them... [and] the Lord gave unto the Church the following."

1–3, *The elders shall govern the Church by the spirit of revelation;* 4–6, *True disciples will receive and keep the Lord's law;* 7–12, *Edward Partridge is named as a bishop unto the Church.*

HEARKEN and "hear, O ye my people, saith the Lord and your God, whom I delight to bless with the greatest of all "blessings, ye that hear me; and ye that hear me not will I "curse, that have "professed my "name, with the heaviest of all cursings.

2 Hearken, O ye elders of my church whom I have called, behold I give unto you a commandment, that ye shall assemble yourselves together to "agree upon my word;

3 And by the prayer of your faith ye shall receive my "law, that ye may know how to govern my "church and have all things right before me.

4 And I will be your "ruler when

---

40 1a D&C 39:7.
2a Mark 4:16.
  b TG Test, Try, Prove.
  c Matt. 13:21 (20–22).
    TG Persecution.
  d TG Apostasy of
    Individuals.
3a D&C 39:10 (7–24).

41 1a Deut. 32:1.
  b TG Blessings.
  c Deut. 11:28; 1 Ne. 2:
    23; D&C 50:8.
    TG Curse.
  d D&C 50:4; 56:1;
    112:26.
  e TG Jesus Christ,
    Taking the Name of.

2a TG Unity.
3a D&C 42:2 (1–93).
  b TG God, Law of.
  b TG Jesus Christ, Head
    of the Church.
4a Zech. 14:9; 1 Tim. 6:
    15 (14–15); D&C 45:
    59. TG Governments.

I ^bcome; and behold, I come quickly, and ye shall see that my law is kept.

5 He that ^areceiveth my ^blaw and ^cdoeth it, the same is my disciple; and he that saith he receiveth it and ^ddoeth it not, the same is not my disciple, and shall be ^ecast out from among you;

6 For it is not meet that the things which belong to the children of the kingdom should be given to them that are not worthy, or to ^adogs, or the ^bpearls to be cast before swine.

7 And again, it is meet that my servant Joseph Smith, Jun., should have a ^ahouse built, in which to live and ^btranslate.

8 And again, it is meet that my servant Sidney Rigdon should live as seemeth him good, inasmuch as he keepeth my commandments.

9 And again, I have called my servant ^aEdward Partridge; and I give a commandment, that he should be appointed by the voice of the church, and ordained a ^bbishop unto the church, to leave his merchandise and to ^cspend all his time in the labors of the church;

10 To see to all things as it shall be appointed unto him in my laws in the day that I shall give them.

11 And this because his heart is pure before me, for he is like unto ^aNathanael of old, in whom there is no ^bguile.

12 These words are given unto you, and they are pure before me; wherefore, beware how you hold them; for they are to be answered upon your ^asouls in the day of judgment. Even so, Amen.

SECTION 42

Revelation given through Joseph Smith the Prophet, at Kirtland, Ohio, February 9, 1831. HC 1: 148–154. It was received in the presence of twelve elders, and in fulfillment of the Lord's promise previously made that the "law" would be given in Ohio; see Section 38: 32. The Prophet specifies this revelation as "embracing the law of the Church."

1–10, The elders are called to preach the gospel, baptize converts, and build up the Church; 11–12, They must be called and ordained, and are to teach the principles of the gospel found in the scriptures; 13–17, They are to teach and prophesy by the power of the Spirit; 18–29, The saints are commanded not to kill, steal, lie, lust, commit adultery, or speak evil against others; 30–39, Laws governing the consecration of properties are set forth; 40–52, The sick are to be healed through administrations and by faith; 53–60, Scriptures govern the Church and are to be proclaimed to the world; 61–69, Site of the New Jerusalem and the mysteries of the kingdom shall be revealed; 70–73, Consecrated properties are to be used to support Church

---

4b TG Jesus Christ, Second Coming.
5a Matt. 7: 24.
b Josh. 1: 8; Jer. 26: 4; Mosiah 3: 14 (14–15); 13: 29 (29–32); Alma 25: 15 (15–16).
c Rom. 2: 13; James 1: 22 (22–25); D&C 42: 60.
d Matt. 21: 30.
TG Hypocrisy.

e D&C 42: 37; 50: 8 (8–9); 64: 35.
TG Excommunication.
6a Matt. 15: 26; Mark 7: 27 (25–30).
b Matt. 7: 6.
TG Holiness.
7a D&C 42: 71 (70–73).
b IE translate the Bible. D&C 37: 1; 45: 60–62; 73: 3; 76: 15; 93: 53.

9a D&C 36: 1; 42: 10.
b D&C 58: 24 (14–24); 68: 14; 72: 6 (6, 9–12); 107: 69 (69–75).
TG Bishop.
c D&C 51: 1 (1–20); 57: 7; 58: 17 (14–18).
11a John 1: 47.
b TG Guile.
12a TG Accountability; Responsibility.

officers; 74–93, *Laws governing fornication, adultery, killing, stealing, and
confession of sins are set forth.*

HEARKEN, O ye elders of my
"church, who have assembled yourselves together in my name, even
Jesus Christ the Son of the living
God, the Savior of the world; inasmuch as ye believe on my name and
keep my commandments.

2 Again I say unto you, hearken
and hear and obey the "law which
I shall give unto you.

3 For verily I say, as ye have
assembled yourselves together according to the "commandment
wherewith I commanded you, and
are agreed as "touching this one
thing, and have asked the Father
in my name, even so ye shall receive.

4 Behold, verily I say unto you, I
give unto you this first commandment, that ye shall "go forth in my
name, every one of you, excepting
my servants Joseph Smith, Jun.,
and Sidney Rigdon.

5 And I give unto them a commandment that they shall go forth
for a little season, and it shall be
"given by the power of the Spirit
when they shall return.

6 And ye shall go forth in the power
of my Spirit, preaching my gospel,
"two by two, in my name, lifting up
your voices as with the sound of a
"trump, declaring my word like unto
angels of God.

7 And ye shall go forth baptizing
with water, saying: Repent ye,
repent ye, for the kingdom of heaven
is at hand.

8 And from this place ye shall go
forth into the regions westward; and
inasmuch as ye shall find them that
will receive you ye shall "build up
my church in every region—

9 Until the time shall come when it
shall be revealed unto you from on
high, when the "city of the "New
Jerusalem shall be prepared, that
ye may be "gathered in one, that ye
may be my "people and I will be
your God.

10 And again, I say unto you, that
my servant "Edward Partridge shall
stand in the office whereunto I have
"appointed him. And it shall come
to pass, that if he transgress "another
shall be appointed in his stead.
Even so. Amen.

11 Again I say unto you, that it
shall not be given to any one to go
forth to "preach my gospel, or to
build up my church, except he be
"ordained by some one who has
"authority, and it is known to the
church that he has authority and
has been regularly ordained by the
heads of the church.

12 And again, the "elders, priests
and teachers of this church shall
"teach the principles of my gospel,
which are in the Bible and the "Book
of Mormon, in the which is the "fulness of the "gospel.

42 1a TG Jesus Christ,
Head of the Church.
  2a Jer. 26: 4; D&C 41: 3;
    43: 2; 58: 23. TG God,
    Law of.
  3a D&C 38: 32.
   b Matt. 18: 19.
  4a TG Mission of Latter-
    day Saints.
  5a TG Guidance, Divine;
    Holy Ghost, Mission
    of.
  6a Mark 6: 7; Rom. 10:
    14. TG Gospel; Mis-
    sionary Work.
   b Isa. 58: 1.
  8a D&C 30: 6; 39: 13.
  9a D&C 57: 2.
   b Ether 13: 6 (2–11);

D&C 45: 66 (66–71);
48: 4; 64: 30; 84: 2, 4
(2–5); Moses 7: 62;
A of F 10.
  TG Jerusalem, New.
 c TG Israel, Gathering of.
 d Zech. 8: 8.
10a D&C 41: 9 (9–11); 50:
    39; 124: 19.
  b TG Delegation of
    Responsibility.
  c D&C 35: 18 (17–18);
    64: 40; 104: 77;
    107: 99 (99–100).
11a TG Missionary Work;
    Preaching.
  b TG Called of God;
    Priesthood, Authority;
    Priesthood, Ordina-

tion; Priesthood,
Qualifying for.
 c Acts 18: 27.
  TG Authority;
    Leadership.
12a TG Elder–Melchizedek
    Priesthood.
  b Mosiah 18: 19 (19–20);
    D&C 5: 10; 31: 4; 52:
    9 (9, 36). TG Education;
    Mission of Latter-day
    Saints; Priesthood,
    Magnifying Callings
    within.
  c TG Book of Mormon.
  d Rom. 15: 29; D&C
    35: 17; 135: 3.
    TG Scriptures, Value of.
  e TG Gospel.

13 And they shall ^aobserve the ^bcovenants and church articles to ^cdo them, and these shall be their teachings, as they shall be ^ddirected by the Spirit.

14 And the Spirit shall be given unto you ^aby the prayer of faith; and if ye receive not the ^bSpirit ye shall not teach.

15 And all this ye shall observe to do as I have ^acommanded concerning your teaching, until the fulness of my ^bscriptures is given.

16 And as ye shall lift up your voices by the ^aComforter, ye shall speak and prophesy as seemeth me good;

17 For, behold, the ^aComforter knoweth all things, and ^bbeareth record of the Father and of the Son.

18 And now, behold, I speak unto the church. Thou shalt not ^akill; and he that ^bkills shall ^cnot have forgiveness in this world, nor in the world to come.

19 And again, I say, thou shalt not kill; but he that ^akilleth shall ^bdie.

20 Thou shalt not steal; and he that ^astealeth and will not repent shall be ^bcast out.

21 Thou shalt not ^alie; he that lieth and will not repent shall be cast out.

22 Thou shalt ^alove thy wife with all thy heart, and shalt ^bcleave unto her and none else.

23 And he that ^alooketh upon a woman to lust after her shall deny the faith, and shall not have the ^bSpirit; and if he repents not he shall be cast out.

24 Thou shalt not commit ^aadultery; and he that committeth ^badultery, and repenteth not, shall be ^ccast out.

25 But he that has committed adultery and repents with all his heart, and forsaketh it, and doeth it ^ano more, thou shalt forgive;

26 But if he doeth it ^aagain, he shall not be forgiven, but shall be cast out.

27 Thou shalt not ^aspeak evil of thy neighbor, nor do him any harm.

28 Thou knowest my laws concerning these things are given in my scriptures; he that sinneth and ^arepenteth not shall be ^bcast out.

29 If thou ^alovest me thou shalt ^bserve me and ^ckeep all my commandments.

30 And behold, thou wilt remember the ^apoor, and ^bconsecrate of thy properties for their ^csupport that which thou hast to impart unto

---

13a TG Commitment.
  b D&C 1: 6 (6, 37); 33:
    14; 51: 4; 68: 24.
  c D&C 84: 57.
  d Gal. 5: 18.
14a D&C 63: 64.
    TG Prayer.
  b Ex. 35: 34; 1 Cor. 4:
    20. TG Holy Ghost,
    Mission of; Missionary
    Work; Teacher;
    Teaching with the Spirit.
15a TG Commandments of
    God.
  b D&C 35: 20; 42: 56
    (56–58).
16a 2 Pet. 1: 21; D&C 18:
    32; 34: 10; 68: 3.
17a 1 Cor. 2: 10. TG Holy
    Ghost, Comforter.
  b D&C 1: 39; 20: 27.
    TG Holy Ghost, Source
    of Testimony.
18a Ex. 20: 13 (13–17);
    Deut. 5: 17 (17–21);
    Matt. 5: 21 (21–37);

Mosiah 13: 21 (21–24);
    3 Ne. 12: 21 (21–37).
  b TG Life, Sanctity of;
    Murder.
  c D&C 76: 34; 84: 41;
    132: 27.
19a TG Blood, Shedding of.
  b TG Capital Punish-
    ment.
20a TG Stealing.
  b Zech. 5: 3.
21a Luke 18: 20.
    TG Honesty; Lying.
22a TG Family, Love
    within; Love;
    Marriage, Continuing
    Courtship in;
    Marriage, Husbands;
    Marriage, Wives.
  b Gen. 2: 24 (23–24);
    D&C 49: 15 (15–16);
    Moses 3: 24 (23–24);
    Abr. 5: 18 (17–18).
    TG Divorce.
23a 2 Sam. 11: 2.
    TG Carnal Mind;
    Lust.

  b D&C 63: 16. TG Holy
    Ghost, Loss of.
24a Ezek. 18: 6; Luke 18:
    20; D&C 63: 14.
  b TG Adultery; Sexual
    Immorality.
  c Prov. 6: 33 (32–33).
25a John 8: 11.
    TG Forgiveness.
26a Ps. 85: 8; 2 Pet. 2: 20.
27a Prov. 3: 29. TG Gossip;
    Slander.
28a TG Repentance.
  b TG Excommunication;
    Punishment.
29a John 14: 15 (15, 21).
    TG Love.
  b TG Service.
  c TG Obedience.
30a Prov. 31: 20; Mosiah
    4: 26 (16–26); Alma 1:
    27; Hel. 4: 12. TG Poor.
  b Micah 4: 13; D&C 72:
    15; 85: 3.
    TG Consecration.
  c TG Welfare.

them, with a covenant and a deed which cannot be broken.

31 And inasmuch as ye *a*impart of your *b*substance unto the *c*poor, ye will do it unto me; and they shall be *d*laid before the *e*bishop of my church and his *f*counselors, two of the elders, or high priests, such as he shall appoint or has appointed or *g*set apart for that purpose.

32 And it shall come to pass, that after they are laid before the bishop of my church, and after that he has received these testimonies concerning the *a*consecration of the properties of my church, that they cannot be taken from the church, agreeable to my commandments, every man shall be made *b*accountable unto me, a *c*steward over his own property, or that which he has received by consecration, as much as is sufficient for himself and *d*family.

33 And again, if there shall be properties in the hands of the church, or any individuals of it, more than is necessary for their support after this first consecration, which is a *a*residue to be consecrated unto the bishop, it shall be kept to administer to those who have not, from time to time, that every man who has need may be amply supplied and receive according to his wants.

34 Therefore, the residue shall be kept in my *a*storehouse, to administer to the poor and the needy, as shall be appointed by the *b*high council of the church, and the bishop and his council;

35 And for the purpose of *a*purchasing lands for the public benefit of the church, and building houses of *b*worship, and building up of the *c*New Jerusalem which is hereafter to be revealed—

36 That my covenant people may be gathered in one in that day when I shall *a*come to my *b*temple. And this I do for the salvation of my people.

37 And it shall come to pass, that he that sinneth and repenteth not shall be *a*cast out of the church, and shall not receive again that which he has *b*consecrated unto the poor and the needy of my church, or in other words, unto me—

38 For inasmuch as ye *a*do it unto the least of these, ye do it unto me.

39 For it shall come to pass, that which I spake by the mouths of my prophets shall be fulfilled; for I will consecrate of the *a*riches of those who embrace my gospel among the Gentiles unto the *b*poor of my people who are of the house of Israel.

40 And again, thou shalt not be *a*proud in thy *b*heart; let all thy *c*garments be plain, and their *d*beauty the beauty of the *e*work of thine own hands;

41 And let all things be done in *a*cleanliness before me.

42 Thou shalt not be *a*idle; for he that is idle shall not eat the

---

31a Dan. 4: 27; Mosiah 2: 17.
  b Lev. 19: 9.
    TG Generosity.
  c Job 29: 12.
    TG Almsgiving; Poor.
  d D&C 58: 35.
  e TG Bishop.
  f TG Counselor.
  g TG Setting Apart.
32a D&C 51: 4; 64: 15.
  b D&C 72: 3 (3–11).
    TG Accountability;
    Judgment.
  c D&C 72: 17 (17, 22).
    TG Stewardship.
  d D&C 51: 3.

33a D&C 42: 55; 51: 13;
    82: 18 (17–19); 119:
    1 (1–3).
34a D&C 42: 55; 51: 13.
  b D&C 102: 1 (1–30).
35a D&C 57: 5 (5–7); 58:
    49 (49–51); 101: 70
    (68–74); 103: 23 (22–
    24).
  b TG Worship.
  c TG Zion.
36a D&C 36: 8.
  b Mal. 3: 1.
37a D&C 41: 5; 50: 8 (8–
    9); 64: 35.
    TG Excommunication.
  b D&C 51: 5.
38a Matt. 25: 40 (34–40).

39a TG Treasure.
  b TG Poor.
40a Prov. 16: 5.
    TG Haughtiness; Pride.
  b TG Hardheartedness.
  c TG Apparel;
    Clothing;
    Modesty.
  d TG Beauty.
  e TG Industry.
41a TG Cleanliness;
    Purification.
42a D&C 60: 13; 68: 30–
    32; 75: 29.
    TG Idleness;
    Laziness; Welfare.

*b*bread nor wear the garments of the *c*laborer.

43 And whosoever among you are *a*sick, and have not faith to be healed, but believe, shall be *b*nourished with all tenderness, with herbs and mild *c*food, and that not by the hand of an enemy.

44 And the elders of the church, two or more, shall be called, and shall pray for and *a*lay their *b*hands upon them in my name; and if they *c*die they shall *d*die unto me, and if they live they shall live unto me.

45 Thou shalt *a*live together in *b*love, insomuch that thou shalt *c*weep for the loss of them that die, and more especially for those that have not *d*hope of a glorious resurrection.

46 And it shall come to pass that those that die in me shall not *a*taste of *b*death, for it shall be *c*sweet unto them;

47 And they that die not in me, wo unto them, for their death is bitter.

48 And again, it shall come to pass that he that hath *a*faith in me to be *b*healed, and is not *c*appointed unto death, shall be *d*healed.

49 He who hath faith to see shall see.

50 He who hath faith to hear shall hear.

51 The lame who hath faith to leap shall leap.

52 And they who have not faith to do these things, but believe in me, have *a*power to become my *b*sons; and inasmuch as they break not my laws thou shalt *c*bear their infirmities.

53 Thou shalt *a*stand in the place of thy stewardship.

54 Thou shalt not take thy brother's *a*garment; thou shalt *b*pay for that which thou shalt receive of thy brother.

55 And if thou *a*obtainest more than that which would be for thy support, thou shalt give it into my *b*storehouse, that all things may be done according to that which I have said.

56 Thou shalt ask, and my *a*scriptures shall be given as I have appointed, and they shall be *b*preserved in safety;

57 And it is expedient that thou shouldst hold thy peace concerning them, and *a*not teach them until ye have received them in full.

58 And I give unto you a commandment that then ye shall teach them unto all men; for they shall be *a*taught unto *b*all *c*nations, kindreds, tongues and people.

59 Thou shalt take the things which thou hast received, which have been given unto thee in my scriptures for a law, to be my *a*law to govern my *b*church;

42b TG Bread.
  c TG Labor; Work, Value of.
43a TG Sickness.
  b TG Health.
  c TG Food.
44a TG Hands, Laying on of.
  b TG Administrations to the Sick.
  c Rom. 14: 8 (5–9); D&C 63: 49.
  d Rev. 14: 13.
45a 1 Jn. 4: 16.
  b John 11: 36 (35–36). TG Family, Love within; Love.
  c Gen. 50: 1; Alma 28: 11 (11–12); 48: 23.
  d 1 Cor. 15: 19 (19–22).

TG Hope.
46a John 8: 52 (51–52).
  b John 11: 26; 1 Cor. 15: 56. TG Death.
  c Job 13: 15 (15–16); Rev. 14: 13.
48a D&C 46: 19. TG Faith.
  b Luke 18: 42 (35–43). TG Healing.
  c 2 Kgs. 20: 1 (1–6); Job 7: 1; Isa. 38: 5; 1 Cor. 4: 9; Alma 12: 27 (26–28); D&C 121: 25.
  d TG Death, Power over.
52a TG Initiative.
  b TG Sons and Daughters of God.
  c Rom. 15: 1.
53a TG Stewardship;

Trustworthiness.
54a Ex. 22: 26.
  b D&C 51: 11.
55a D&C 82: 18 (17–19); 119: 1 (1–3).
  b D&C 42: 34; 51: 13.
56a An allusion to the translation of the Bible. D&C 42: 15; 45: 60 (60–61).
  b TG Scriptures, Preservation of.
57a Moses 1: 42; 4: 32.
58a D&C 124: 89.
  b D&C 1: 2, 34 (34–35); 18: 28 (26–28); 39: 15.
  c TG Nations.
59a Josh. 1: 8.
  b TG God, Law of; Jesus Christ, Head of the Church.

60 And he that ᵃdoeth according to these things shall be saved, and he that doeth them not shall be ᵇdamned if he so continue.

61 If thou shalt ask, thou shalt receive ᵃrevelation upon revelation, ᵇknowledge upon knowledge, that thou mayest know the ᶜmysteries and ᵈpeaceable things—that which bringeth ᵉjoy, that which bringeth life eternal.

62 Thou shalt ask, and it shall be revealed unto you in mine own due time where the ᵃNew Jerusalem shall be built.

63 And behold, it shall come to pass that my servants shall be sent forth to the east and to the west, to the north and to the south.

64 And even now, let him that goeth to the east teach them that shall be converted to flee to the ᵃwest, and this in consequence of ᵇthat which is coming on the earth, and of ᶜsecret combinations.

65 Behold, thou shalt observe all these things, and great shall be thy ᵃreward; for unto you it is given to know the ᵇmysteries of the kingdom, but unto the world it is not given to know them.

66 Ye shall observe the laws which ye have received and be faithful.

67 And ye shall hereafter receive church ᵃcovenants, such as shall be sufficient to establish you, both here and in the New Jerusalem.

68 Therefore, he that lacketh ᵃwisdom, let him ask of me, and I will give him liberally and upbraid him not.

69 Lift up your hearts and rejoice, for unto you the ᵃkingdom, or in other words, the ᵇkeys of the church have been given. Even so. Amen.

70 The priests and ᵃteachers shall have their ᵇstewardships, even as the members.

71 And the elders or high priests who are appointed to assist the bishop as counselors in all things, are to have their families ᵃsupported out of the property which is ᵇconsecrated to the bishop, for the good of the poor, and for other purposes, as before mentioned;

72 Or they are to receive a just remuneration for all their services, either a stewardship or otherwise, as may be thought best or decided by the counselors and bishop.

73 And the bishop, also, shall receive his support, or a just remuneration for all his services in the church.

74 Behold, verily I say unto you, that whatever persons among you, having put away their ᵃcompanions for the cause of ᵇfornication, or in other words, if they shall testify before you in all lowliness of heart that this is the case, ye shall not cast them out from among you;

75 But if ye shall find that any persons have left their companions for the sake of ᵃadultery, and they themselves are the offenders, and their companions are living, they shall be ᵇcast out from among you.

76 And again, I say unto you, that ye shall be ᵃwatchful and careful, with all inquiry, that ye receive none such among you if they are married;

60a D&C 41: 5.
  TG Salvation.
  b Moses 5: 15.
  TG Damnation.
61a D&C 59: 4; 76: 7; 98: 12; 101: 32; 121: 28 (26–33). TG Revelation.
  b Prov. 19: 2; Abr. 1: 2. TG Knowledge; Learning; Testimony.
  c D&C 63: 23; 71: 1. TG Mysteries of Godliness.
  d D&C 36: 2; 39: 6.
  e TG Joy.

62a D&C 57: 2 (1–5).
64a D&C 45: 64; 48: 2.
  b D&C 38: 29 (28–30).
  c Ether 8: 24 (22–25); D&C 5: 33 (32–33); 10: 6 (6, 25); 38: 13, 28.
65a TG Reward.
  b Rom. 16: 25; Alma 12: 9; D&C 6: 7 (7–11); 121: 27 (25–27).
67a D&C 82: 11 (11–15); 84: 39; 132: 4 (4–7).
68a James 1: 5; D&C 1: 26. TG God, Wisdom of.
69a TG Kingdom of God, on Earth.

  b Matt. 16: 19; D&C 65: 2. TG Priesthood, Keys of.
70a TG Priest, Aaronic Priesthood; Teacher, Aaronic Priesthood.
  b TG Stewardship.
71a D&C 41: 7.
  b TG Consecration.
74a Matt. 5: 32.
  b TG Fornication; Sexual Immorality.
75a TG Adultery.
  b TG Excommunication.
76a TG Watchfulness.

77 And if they are not married, they shall repent of all their sins or ye shall not receive them.

78 And again, every person who belongeth to this church of Christ, shall observe to keep all the commandments and covenants of the church.

79 And it shall come to pass, that if any persons among you shall ᵃkill they shall be delivered up and dealt with according to the laws of the land; for remember that he hath no forgiveness; and it shall be proved according to the laws of the land.

80 And if any man or woman shall commit ᵃadultery, he or she shall be tried before two elders of the church, or more, and every word shall be established against him or her by two ᵇwitnesses of the church, and not of the enemy; but if there are more than two witnesses it is better.

81 But he or she shall be condemned by the mouth of two witnesses; and the elders shall lay the case before the ᵃchurch, and the church shall lift up their hands against him or her, that they may be dealt with according to the ᵇlaw of God.

82 And if it can be, it is necessary that the ᵃbishop be present also.

83 And thus ye shall do in all cases which shall come before you.

84 And if a man or woman shall rob, he or she shall be delivered up unto the law of the land.

85 And if he or she shall ᵃsteal, he or she shall be delivered up unto the law of the land.

86 And if he or she shall ᵃlie, he or she shall be delivered up unto the law of the land.

87 And if he or she do any manner of ᵃiniquity, he or she shall be delivered up unto the law, even that of God.

88 And if thy ᵃbrother or sister ᵇoffend thee, thou shalt take him or her between him or her and thee alone; and if he or she ᶜconfess thou shalt be ᵈreconciled.

89 And if he or she confess not thou shalt deliver him or her up unto the church, not to the members, but to the elders. And it shall be done in a ᵃmeeting, and that not before the world.

90 And if thy brother or sister offend many, he or she shall be ᵃchastened before many.

91 And if any one offend ᵃopenly, he or she shall be rebuked openly, that he or she may be ᵇashamed. And if he or she confess not, he or she shall be delivered up unto the law of God.

92 If any shall offend in secret, he or she shall be rebuked in secret, that he or she may have opportunity to confess in secret to him or her whom he or she has offended, and to God, that the church may not speak reproachfully of him or her.

93 And thus shall ye conduct in all things.

SECTION 43

Revelation given through Joseph Smith the Prophet, at Kirtland, Ohio, in February 1831. HC 1: 154–156. At this time some members of the Church were disturbed by people making false claims as revelators. The Prophet inquired of the Lord and received this com-

---

79a Luke 18: 20. TG Blood, Shedding of; Murder.
80a TG Adultery.
  b TG Witnesses.
81a Matt. 18: 17 (16–17).
  b D&C 64: 12.
82a TG Bishop.

85a TG Stealing.
86a TG Honesty; Lying.
87a D&C 43: 11.
88a TG Brotherhood and Sisterhood.
  b Matt. 18: 15 (15–18). TG Offense.
  c TG Confession.

d TG Reconciliation.
89a TG Judgment; Justice.
90a TG Chastening; Reproof.
91a Ezek. 5: 8; 1 Tim. 5: 20 (19–21).
  b TG Shame.

munication addressed to the elders of the Church. The first part deals with matters of Church polity; the latter part contains a warning that the elders are to give to the nations of the earth.

1–7, Revelations and commandments come only through the one appointed; 8–14, The saints are sanctified by acting in all holiness before the Lord; 15–22, Elders are sent forth to cry repentance and prepare men for the great day of the Lord; 23–28, The Lord calls upon men by his own voice and through the forces of nature; 29–35, The Millennium and the binding of Satan shall come.

O HEARKEN, ye elders of my church, and give ear to the words which I shall speak unto you.

2 For behold, verily, verily, I say unto you, that ye have received a commandment for a ^alaw unto my church, through him whom I have appointed unto you to receive commandments and ^brevelations from my hand.

3 And this ye shall know assuredly —that there is ^anone other appointed unto you to receive ^bcommandments and revelations until he be taken, if he ^cabide in me.

4 But verily, verily, I say unto you, that ^anone else shall be appointed unto this gift except it be through him; for if it be taken from him he shall not have power except to appoint another in his stead.

5 And this shall be a law unto you, that ye ^areceive not the ^bteachings of any that shall come before you as revelations or commandments;

6 And this I give unto you that you may not be ^adeceived, that you may know they are not of me.

7 For verily I say unto you, that he that is ^aordained of me shall come in at the ^bgate and be ordained as I have told you before, to teach those ^crevelations which ye have received and shall receive through him whom I have appointed.

8 And now, behold, I give unto you a ^acommandment, that when ye are ^bassembled together ye shall ^cinstruct and ^dedify each other, that ye may know ^ehow to act and direct my church, how to act upon the points of my law and commandments, which I have given.

9 And thus ye shall become instructed in the law of my church, and be ^asanctified by that which ye have received, and ye shall bind yourselves to act in all holiness before me—

10 That inasmuch as ye do this, glory shall be ^aadded to the kingdom which ye have received. Inasmuch as ye do it not, it shall be ^btaken, even that which ye have received.

11 ^aPurge ye out the ^biniquity which is among you; sanctify yourselves before me;

12 And if ye desire the glories of the kingdom, ^aappoint ye my servant Joseph Smith, Jun., and uphold him before me by the prayer of faith.

13 And again, I say unto you, that if ye desire the ^amysteries of the kingdom, provide for him food and raiment, and whatsoever thing he needeth to accomplish the work wherewith I have commanded him;

14 And if ye do it not he shall re-

43 2a D&C 42: 1 (1–93).
b TG Commandments of God; God, Law of; Revelation.
3a TG False Prophets.
b TG Prophets, Mission of.
c John 15: 4.
4a D&C 28: 2 (1–3, 11–13).
5a D&C 28: 5 (3–8).
b TG False Doctrine.
6a D&C 28: 11; 46: 7.
TG Deceit.

7a TG Authority; Called of God.
b Matt. 7: 13; 2 Ne. 9: 41; 31: 9 (9, 17–18);
3 Ne. 14: 14 (13–14);
D&C 22: 4.
c TG Scriptures to Come Forth.
8a TG Commandments of God.
b TG Assembly for Worship; Meetings.

c D&C 88: 77 (77–79).
d TG Edification.
e D&C 82: 9; JS-H 1: 12.
9a TG Sanctification.
10a Alma 12: 10 (9–11).
b Mark 4: 25.
11a 1 Cor. 5: 7.
b D&C 42: 87. TG Sin.
12a TG Sustaining Church Leaders.
13a TG Mysteries of Godliness.

main unto them that have received him, that I may reserve unto myself a ªpure ᵇpeople before me.

15 Again I say, hearken ye elders of my ªchurch, whom I have appointed: Ye are not sent forth to be ᵇtaught, but to ᶜteach the children of men the things which I have put into your hands by the power of my ᵈSpirit;

16 And ye are to be ªtaught from on high. ᵇSanctify yourselves and ye shall be ᶜendowed with power, that ye may give even as I have spoken.

17 Hearken ye, for, behold, the ªgreat ᵇday of the Lord is nigh at hand.

18 For the day cometh that the Lord shall utter his ªvoice out of heaven; the heavens shall ᵇshake and the earth shall ᶜtremble, and the ᵈtrump of God shall sound both long and loud, and shall say to the sleeping nations: Ye saints ᵉarise and live; ye sinners ᶠstay and ᵍsleep until I shall call again.

19 Wherefore gird up your loins lest ye be found among the wicked.

20 Lift up your voices and spare not. Call upon the nations to repent, both old and young, both ªbond and free, saying: Prepare yourselves for the great day of the Lord;

21 For if I, who am a man, do lift up my voice and call upon you to

repent, and ye ªhate me, what will ye say when the ᵇday cometh when the ᶜthunders shall utter their voices from the ends of the earth, speaking to the ears of all that live, saying—Repent, and prepare for the great day of the Lord?

22 Yea, and again, when the ªlightnings shall streak forth from the east unto the west, and shall utter forth their voices unto all that live, and make the ears of all tingle that hear, saying these words—Repent ye, for the great day of the Lord is come?

23 And again, the Lord shall utter his voice out of heaven, saying: Hearken, O ye nations of the earth, and hear the words of that God who ªmade you.

24 O, ye nations of the earth, how often would I have ªgathered you together as a ᵇhen gathereth her chickens under her wings, but ye ᵇwould not!

25 How oft have I ªcalled upon you by the mouth of my ᵇservants, and by the ᶜministering of angels, and by mine own voice, and by the voice of ᵈthunderings, and by the voice of lightnings, and by the voice of tempests, and by the voice of earthquakes, and great hailstorms, and by the voice of ᶠfamines and pestilences of every kind, and by the

14a ᴛɢ Purity.
  b ᴛɢ Millennium, Preparing a People for.
15a ᴛɢ Jesus Christ, Head of the Church.
  b 1 Jn. 2: 27.
    ᴛɢ Teaching.
  c D&C 50: 13.
    ᴛɢ Mission of Latter-day Saints;
    Missionary Work;
    Priesthood, Ordination.
  d ᴛɢ Teaching with the Spirit.
16a ᴛɢ Inspiration; Teachable.
  b Josh. 3: 5.
    ᴛɢ Sanctification.
  c Luke 24: 49; D&C 38: 32; 39: 15; 95: 8 (8–9); 110: 9 (8–10).
17a Mal. 4: 5; D&C 2: 1;

34: 8 (6–9).
  b D&C 5: 19 (19–20); 29: 8; 35: 11 (11–16).
18a Joel 2: 11; D&C 35: 21; 88: 90; 133: 50 (50–52).
  b Joel 2: 10; 3: 16; D&C 45: 48. ᴛɢ Last Days.
  c D&C 45: 33 (33, 48); 84: 118; 88: 87 (87, 90).
  d D&C 29: 13; 45: 45.
  e ᴛɢ Resurrection.
  f Rev. 20: 13 (12–13); Alma 11: 41; D&C 76: 85; 88: 100 (100–101).
  g Dan. 12: 2; Morm. 9: 13 (13–14).
20a 1 Cor. 12: 13.
21a ᴛɢ Hate.
  b ᴛɢ Day of the Lord.
  c 2 Ne. 27: 2; D&C 88: 90.

22a Amos 4: 6 (6–10).
23a Deut. 32: 6; 1 Ne. 2: 12.
24a Matt. 23: 37; Luke 13: 34; 3 Ne 10: 6 (4–6).
  b ᴛɢ Rebellion.
25a Lev. 26: 16; Ezek. 26: 6; 1 Ne 21: 26 (25–26); Mosiah 7: 29;
    11: 22 (20–22);
    Hel. 12: 3 (2–4).
  b Matt. 23: 34.
    ᴛɢ Prophets, Mission of.
  c D&C 7: 6; 130: 5.
  d Rev. 16: 18; 2 Ne. 6: 15. ᴛɢ Nature.
  e Jer. 24: 10; Joel 1: 10; Amos 4: 6; D&C 87: 6 (1–8); JS-M 1: 29.
    ᴛɢ Drought; Famine.

great sound of a 'trump, and by the voice of judgment, and by the voice of *g*mercy all the day long, and by the voice of glory and honor and the *h*riches of eternal life, and would have saved you with an 'everlasting salvation, but ye would not!

26 Behold, the day has come, when the *a*cup of the *b*wrath of mine indignation is full.

27 Behold, verily I say unto you, that these are the words of the Lord your God.

28 Behold, labor ye, *a*labor ye in my vineyard for the last time— for the last time call upon the inhabitants of the earth.

29 For in mine own due time will I *a*come upon the earth in *b*judgment, and my people shall be *c*redeemed and shall *d*reign with me on earth.

30 For the great *a*Millennium, of

which I have spoken by the mouth of my servants, shall come.

31 For *a*Satan shall be *b*bound, and when he is loosed again he shall only reign for a *c*little season, and then cometh the *d*end of the earth.

32 And he that liveth in *a*righteousness shall be *b*changed in the twinkling of an eye, and the earth shall pass away so as by *c*fire.

33 And the wicked shall go away into unquenchable *a*fire, and their end no man knoweth on earth, nor ever shall know, until they come before me in *b*judgment.

34 Hearken ye to these words. Behold, I am Jesus Christ, the *a*Savior of the world. *b*Treasure these things up in your hearts, and let the *c*solemnities of *d*eternity *e*rest upon your *f*minds.

35 Be *a*sober. Keep all my commandments. Even so. Amen.

SECTION 44

Revelation given to Joseph Smith the Prophet and Sidney Rigdon, at Kirtland, Ohio, in the latter part of February 1831. HC 1: 157. In compliance with the requirement herein set forth, the Church appointed a conference to be held early in the month of June following.

1–3, Elders are to assemble in conference; 4–6, They are to organize according to the laws of the land and to care for the poor.

BEHOLD, thus saith the Lord unto you my servants, it is expedient in me that the elders of my church should be *a*called together, from the

25f Ex. 19: 19 (13, 16, 19).
  g TG Mercy.
  h TG Treasure.
  i TG Eternal Life; Immortality; Salvation.
26a Lam. 4: 21.
  b Ezek. 21: 31. TG God, Indignation of.
28a Jacob 5: 71 (71–75); D&C 27: 13; 33: 3. TG Vineyard of the Lord.
29a TG Jesus Christ, Second Coming.
  b TG Judgment, The Last.
  c Rev. 14: 4 (2–5).
  d TG Jesus Christ, Millennial Reign.

30a TG Millennium.
31a 1 Ne. 22: 26. TG Devil.
  b D&C 45: 55; 84: 100; 88: 110 (110–112); 101: 28.
  c Rev. 20: 3 (3–10); Jacob 5: 77 (76–77); D&C 29: 22; 88: 111 (110–112).
  d Matt. 24: 14. TG World, End of.
32a TG Righteousness.
  b 1 Cor. 15: 51 (51–52); D&C 63: 51; 88: 28 (20, 28); 101: 31. TG Resurrection.
  c Matt. 3: 12.

33a Dan. 7: 11; D&C 29: 28 (21, 26–30). TG Hell.
  b TG Jesus Christ, Judge.
34a TG Jesus Christ, Savior.
  b Isa. 45: 22; D&C 6: 36; 11: 26; JS-M 1: 37. TG Treasure.
  c D&C 84: 61; 88: 121; 100: 7.
  TG Levity.
  d TG Eternity.
  e TG Meditation.
  f TG Mind.
35a Rom. 12: 3; D&C 18: 21.
44 1a TG Assembly for Worship; Meetings.

east and from the west, and from the north and from the south, by letter or some other way.

2 And it shall come to pass, that inasmuch as they are faithful, and exercise faith in me, I will pour out my ᵃSpirit upon them in the day that they assemble themselves together.

3 And it shall come to pass that they shall go forth into the regions round about, and ᵃpreach repentance unto the people.

4 And many shall be ᵃconverted, insomuch that ye shall obtain ᵇpower to organize yourselves ᶜaccording to the laws of man;

5 That your ᵃenemies may not have power over you; that you may be preserved in all things; that you may be enabled to keep my laws; that every bond may be broken wherewith the enemy seeketh to destroy my people.

6 Behold, I say unto you, that ye must ᵃvisit the poor and the needy and administer to their relief, that they may be kept until all things may be done according to my law which ye have received. Amen.

SECTION 45

Revelation given through Joseph Smith the Prophet to the Church, at Kirtland, Ohio, March 7, 1831. HC 1: 158–163. Prefacing his record of his revelation, the Prophet states that "at this age of the Church many false reports and foolish stories were published and circulated, to prevent people from investigating the work or embracing the faith; but to the joy of the saints. . . I received the following."

1–5, *Christ is our Advocate with the Father;* 6–10, *The gospel is a messenger to prepare the way before the Lord;* 11–15, *Enoch and his brethren received by the Lord unto himself;* 16–23, *Christ revealed signs of his coming as given on the Mount of Olives;* 24–38, *The gospel shall be restored, the times of the Gentiles be fulfilled, and a desolating sickness cover the land;* 39–47, *Signs, wonders, and the resurrection are to attend the Second Coming;* 48–53, *Christ shall stand on Mount of Olives, and Jews shall see the wounds in his hands and feet;* 54–59, *The Lord shall reign during the Millennium;* 60–62, *The Prophet is instructed to begin the translation of the New Testament,* through which important information would be made known; 63–75, *The saints are commanded to gather and build the New Jerusalem, to which people from all nations will come.*

HEARKEN, O ye people of my ᵃchurch, to whom the ᵇkingdom has been given; hearken ye and give ear to him who laid the foundation of the earth, who ᶜmade the heavens and all the ᵈhosts thereof, and by whom all things were made which ᵉlive, and move, and have a being.

2 And again I say, hearken unto my voice, lest ᵃdeath shall overtake you; in an ᵇhour when ye think not the summer shall be past, and the

2a Acts 2: 17.
3a ᵀᴳ Preaching.
4a ᵀᴳ Conversion.
  b ᵀᴳ Authority; Church Organization.
  c 1 Pet. 2: 13 (13–14);
    D&C 51: 6; 98: 5 (5–7);
    109: 54.
5a Lev. 26: 7 (1–13).

2 Ne. 4: 33 (16–35).
6a James 1: 27.
  ᵀᴳ Compassion;
    Service; Welfare.
45 1a ᵀᴳ Jesus Christ,
    Head of the
    Church.
  b D&C 38: 9; 50: 35.
  c Jer. 14: 22; Mosiah 4:
    2; 3 Ne. 9: 15; D&C

14: 9. ᵀᴳ Jesus Christ,
    Creator.
  d Gen. 2: 1; D&C 38:
    1; Moses 3: 1;
    Abr. 5: 1.
  e Acts 17: 28.
2a Alma 34: 33 (33–
    35).
  b Matt. 24: 44.

ᶜharvest ended, and your souls not saved.

3 Listen to him who is the ᵃadvocate with the Father, who is pleading your cause before him—

4 Saying: Father, behold the ᵃsufferings and ᵇdeath of him who did no ᶜsin, in whom thou wast well pleased; behold the blood of thy Son which was shed, the blood of him whom thou gavest that thyself might be ᵈglorified;

5 Wherefore, Father, spare these my ᵃbrethren that ᵇbelieve on my name, that they may come unto me and have ᶜeverlasting life.

6 Hearken, O ye people of my church, and ye elders listen together, and hear my voice while it is called ᵃtoday, and harden not your hearts;

7 For verily I say unto you that I am ᵃAlpha and Omega, the beginning and the end, the light and the life of the world—a ᵇlight that shineth in darkness and the darkness comprehendeth it not.

8 I came unto mine own, and mine own ᵃreceived me not; but unto as many as received me gave I ᵇpower to do many ᶜmiracles, and to become the ᵈsons of God; and even unto them that ᵉbelieved on my name gave I power to obtain eternal ᶠlife.

9 And even so I have sent mine ᵃeverlasting ᵇcovenant into the world, to be a ᶜlight to the world, and to be a ᵈstandard for my people, and for the ᵉGentiles to seek to it; and to be a ᶠmessenger before my face to prepare the way before me.

10 Wherefore, come ye unto it, and with him that cometh I will ᵃreason as with men in days of old, and I will show unto you my strong reasoning.

11 Wherefore, hearken ye together and let me show unto you even my ᵃwisdom—the wisdom of him whom ye say is the God of ᵇEnoch, and his brethren,

12 Who were ᵃseparated from the earth, and were received unto myself—a ᵇcity reserved until a ᶜday of righteousness shall come—a day which was sought for by all holy men, and they found it not because of wickedness and abominations;

13 And confessed they were ᵃstrangers and pilgrims on the earth;

14 But obtained a ᵃpromise that they should find it and see it in their flesh.

15 Wherefore, hearken and I will reason with you, and I will ᵃspeak unto you and prophesy, as unto men in days of old.

16 And I will show it plainly as I showed it unto my ᵃdisciples as I stood before them in the flesh, and spake unto them, saying: As ye have

2c Jer. 8: 20; D&C 56: 16; 76: 79 (71–79).
    TG Harvest.
3a Isa. 59: 16; D&C 62: 1.
    TG Jesus Christ, Advocate.
4a TG Jesus Christ, Atonement through; Jesus Christ, Redeemer; Pain; Suffering.
  b TG Jesus Christ, Death of.
  c Heb. 4: 15; 7: 26.
  d John 12: 28.
5a 1 Jn. 3: 14 (10–18).
  b John 17: 20; D&C 20: 25; 35: 2; 38: 4.
  c John 3: 16.
6a John 9: 4; Heb. 3: 13; D&C 64: 23 (23–25).
7a Rev. 1: 8; 21: 6; D&C 19: 1.

b John 1: 5.
8a TG Prophets, Rejection of.
  b TG Priesthood, Power of.
  c TG Miracle.
  d TG Sons and Daughters of God.
  e TG Believe; Faith.
  f 2 Pet. 1: 3 (2–4).
9a TG New and Everlasting Covenant.
  b Jer. 31: 33 (31–34); Hosea 2: 19 (14–23); Morm. 5: 20.
    TG Covenants.
  c 2 Cor. 4: 6.
  d TG Ensign; Israel, Gathering of.
  e Isa. 42: 6; Matt. 8: 11 (11–12); Luke 13: 29 (28–30); Acts 10: 45; 2 Ne. 10: 18 (9–18).

f Mal. 3: 1; Matt. 11: 10; Luke 7: 27.
10a Isa. 41: 21; D&C 50: 10 (10–12).
11a TG God, Wisdom of.
  b D&C 38: 4; 76: 67; 84: 100 (99–100); 133: 54.
12a See Bible. Appendix, JST Gen. 14: 30–34; D&C 38: 4; Moses 7: 21.
  b Heb. 11: 16; D&C 84: 100; Moses 7: 63 (62–64). TG Translated Beings; Zion.
  c 1 Cor. 5: 5.
13a IE sojourners; see Gen. 15: 13, 1 Pet. 2: 11. TG Travelers.
14a Heb. 11: 13 (8–13); Moses 7: 63.
15a TG Scriptures to Come Forth.
16a D&C 29: 10.

asked of me concerning the ^bsigns of my coming, in the day when I shall come in my ^cglory in the clouds of heaven, to fulfil the promises that I have made unto your fathers,

17 For as ye have looked upon the long ^aabsence of your ^bspirits from your bodies to be a bondage, I will show unto you how the day of redemption shall come, and also the ^crestoration of the ^dscattered Israel.

18 And now ye ^abehold this temple which is in Jerusalem, which we call the house of God, and your enemies say that this house shall never fall.

19 But, verily I say unto you, that ^adesolation shall come upon this generation as a thief in the night, and this people shall be destroyed and ^bscattered among all nations.

20 And this ^atemple which ye now see shall be thrown down that there shall not be left one stone upon another.

21 And it shall come to pass, that this ^ageneration of Jews shall not pass away until every desolation which I have told you concerning them shall come ^bto pass.

22 Ye say that ye know that the ^aend of the world cometh; ye say also that ye know that the heavens and the earth shall pass away;

23 And in this ye say truly, for so it is; but these things which I have

told you shall not ^apass away until all shall be fulfilled.

24 And this I have told you concerning Jerusalem; and when that day shall come, shall a remnant be ^ascattered among all ^bnations;

25 But they shall be ^agathered again; but they shall remain until the times of the ^bGentiles be fulfilled.

26 And in ^athat day shall be heard of ^bwars and rumors of wars, and the whole earth shall be in commotion, and men's hearts shall ^cfail them, and they shall say that Christ ^ddelayeth his coming until the end of the earth.

27 And the ^alove of men shall wax cold, and ^biniquity shall abound.

28 And when the times of the ^aGentiles is come in, a ^blight shall break forth among them that sit in darkness, and it shall be the fulness of my ^cgospel;

29 But they ^areceive it not; for they perceive not the light, and they turn their ^bhearts from me because of the ^cprecepts of men.

30 And in that generation shall the ^atimes of the Gentiles be fulfilled.

31 And there shall be men standing in that ^ageneration, that shall not pass until they shall see an overflowing ^bscourge; for a desolating ^csickness shall cover the land.

32 But my disciples shall ^astand in

16b Matt. 24: 3 (3–46);
   Luke 21: 7 (7–36);
   JS-M 1: 4 (4–55).
   TG Last Days.
 c TG Jesus Christ, Glory
   of; Jesus Christ,
   Second Coming.
17a Luke 1: 79; D&C
   138: 50.
 b TG Spirit Body;
   Spirits, Disembodied.
 c TG Israel, Restoration
   of.
 d Dan. 12: 7; 1 Ne. 10:
   12 (12–14); 22: 3 (3–8).
18a Matt. 24: 2 (1–2).
19a Ps. 79: 3 (1–4);
   Luke 21: 20 (20–24).
 b TG Israel, Scattering of.
20a Matt. 24: 1 (1–3);
   Luke 21: 6 (5–6).
21a Mark 13: 30;

JS-M 1: 34.
 b Matt. 24: 34.
22a Matt. 24: 3. TG World,
   End of.
23a Matt. 24: 35.
24a Zech. 2: 6; 1 Ne. 10: 12
   (12–13); 22: 4 (3–8);
   2 Ne. 25: 15 (15–16).
 b Gen. 48: 19.
25a Neh. 1: 9; 1 Ne. 22:
   12 (10–12); 2 Ne. 21:
   12 (11–16). TG Israel,
   Gathering of.
 b Luke 21: 24; Rom. 11:
   25 (25–27).
26a TG Day of the Lord.
 b D&C 63: 33; 87: 1
   (1–8); 88: 91;
   JS-M 1: 23.
 c Luke 21: 26.
 d Matt. 24: 48;
   2 Pet. 3: 4 (3–10).

JS-M 1: 51.
27a JS-M 1: 10.
 b Matt. 24: 12.
28a TG Gentiles.
 b D&C 45: 36. TG Light.
 c TG Restoration of
   the Gospel.
29a John 1: 5.
 b Matt. 15: 8 (8–9).
   TG Hardheartedness.
 c Titus 1: 14; D&C 3: 6
   (6–7); 46: 7; JS-H 1:
   19.
30a 2 Pet. 3: 12.
31a Isa. 28: 15; D&C 29:
   18 (14–21).
 c TG Sickness.
32a Ex. 3: 5; 2 Chr. 35: 5;
   Matt. 24: 15; D&C 87:
   8; 101: 22 (21–22, 64);
   115: 7.

holy places, and shall not be moved; but among the wicked, men shall lift up their voices and *b*curse God and die.

33 And there shall be *a*earthquakes also in divers places, and many desolations; yet men will harden their hearts against me, and they will take up the *b*sword, one against another, and they will kill one another.

34 And now, when I the Lord had spoken these words unto my disciples, they were troubled.

35 And I said unto them: Be not *a*troubled, for, when all these things shall come to pass, ye may know that the promises which have been made unto you shall be fulfilled.

36 And when the *a*light shall begin to break forth, it shall be with them like unto a parable which I will show you—

37 Ye look and behold the *a*fig-trees, and ye see them with your eyes, and ye say when they begin to shoot forth, and their leaves are yet tender, that summer is now nigh at hand;

38 Even so it shall be in that day when they shall see all these things, then shall they know that the hour is nigh.

39 And it shall come to pass that he that *a*feareth me shall be *b*looking forth for the great *c*day of the Lord to *d*come, even for the *e*signs of the coming of the *f*Son of Man.

40 And they shall see signs and *a*wonders, for they shall be shown forth in the heavens above, and in the earth beneath.

41 And they shall behold blood, and *a*fire, and vapors of *b*smoke.

42 And before the day of the Lord shall come, the *a*sun shall be darkened, and the moon shall be turned into blood, and the stars fall from heaven.

43 And the *a*remnant shall be gathered unto this place;

44 And then they shall look for me, and, behold, I will come; and they shall see me in the *a*clouds of heaven, clothed with power and great *b*glory; with all the holy angels; and he that *c*watches not for me shall be cut off.

45 But before the arm of the Lord shall fall, an angel shall sound his *a*trump, and the *b*saints that have slept shall *c*come forth to meet me in the *d*cloud.

46 Wherefore, if ye have slept in *a*peace blessed are you; for as you now behold me and know that I am, even so shall ye *b*come unto me and your souls shall *c*live, and your redemption shall be perfected; and the saints shall come forth from the *d*four quarters of the earth.

47 Then shall the *a*arm of the Lord fall upon the nations.

48 And then shall the Lord set his foot upon the *a*mount, and it shall cleave in twain, and the earth shall

32b Job 2:9; Rev. 16:11, 21.
33a D&C 43:18; 84:118; 88:87 (87, 90).
  b D&C 63:33.
35a Matt. 24:6.
36a Matt. 24:27; D&C 45:28.
37a Mark 13:28; Luke 21:29 (29–31); D&C 35:16.
39a Job 1:1; D&C 10:56 (55–56). TG Reverence.
  b 2 Pet. 3:12 (10–13); D&C 35:15 (15–16); 49:23; Moses 7:62.
  c TG Day of the Lord.
  d TG Jesus Christ, Second Coming.

  e D&C 68:11. TG Signs.
  f TG Jesus Christ, Son of Man.
40a Joel 2:30.
41a Joel 1:19 (19–20); D&C 29:21; 97:26 (25–26).
  b Gen. 19:28; 1 Ne. 19:11; 3 Ne. 10:13 (13–14); Morm. 8:29 (29–30).
42a Joel 2:10; Rev. 6:12; D&C 88:87; 133:49.
43a TG Israel, Gathering of; Israel, Remnant of.
44a Ex. 19:9 (9, 16).
  b TG Glory; Jesus Christ, Glory of; Jesus Christ,

    Second Coming.
  c Matt. 24:50 (43–51); Mark 13:33 (32–37); 1 Cor. 1:7 (7–8).
45a D&C 29:13; 43:18.
  b TG Resurrection; Saints.
  c D&C 88:97 (96–97); 133:56.
  d 1 Thes. 4:17.
46a Alma 40:12.
  b Isa. 55:3; Amos 5:6; D&C 88:63; 101:38.
  c Ps. 121:7.
  d TG Immortality.
  d D&C 33:6.
47a D&C 1:14 (13–14); 35:14.
48a Zech. 14:4 (4–7).

*b*tremble, and reel to and fro, and the *c*heavens also *d*shall shake.

49 And the Lord shall utter his voice, and all the ends of the earth shall hear it; and the nations of the earth shall *a*mourn, and they that have *b*laughed shall see their *c*folly.

50 And calamity shall cover the *a*mocker, and the scorner shall be consumed; and they that have watched for iniquity shall be hewn down and *b*cast into the *c*fire.

51 And then shall the *a*Jews *b*look upon me and say: What are these *c*wounds in thine hands and in thy feet?

52 Then shall they know that I am the Lord; for I will say unto them: These wounds are the wounds with which I was *a*wounded in the house of my friends. I am he who was lifted up. I am *b*Jesus that was *c*crucified. I am the *c*Son of God.

53 And then shall they *a*weep because of their iniquities; then shall they *b*lament because they *c*persecuted their *d*king.

54 And then shall the *a*heathen nations be *b*redeemed, and they that

*c*knew no *d*law shall have part in the *e*first *f*resurrection; and it shall be *g*tolerable for them.

55 And *a*Satan shall be *b*bound, that he shall have no place in the hearts of the children of men.

56 And at that day, when I shall come in my *a*glory, shall the parable be fulfilled which I spake concerning the ten *b*virgins.

57 For they that are wise and have received the *a*truth, and have taken the Holy Spirit for their *b*guide, and have not been deceived—verily I say unto you, they shall not be hewn down and cast into the *c*fire, but shall abide the day.

58 And the *a*earth shall be given unto them for an *b*inheritance; and they shall *c*multiply and wax strong, and their *d*children shall *e*grow up without *f*sin unto *g*salvation.

59 For the Lord shall be in their *a*midst, and his *b*glory shall be upon them, and he will be their *c*king and their *d*lawgiver.

60 And now, behold, I say unto you, it shall not be given unto you to know any further concerning this

---

48*b* D&C 43: 18; 84: 118;
      88: 87 (87, 90).
   c TG Last Days.
   d Joel 3: 16; D&C 21:
      6; 49: 23.
49*a* D&C 29: 15 (14–21);
      87: 6.
   b TG Laughter.
   c 2 Tim. 3: 9.
      TG Foolishness.
50*a* TG Mocking.
   b Isa. 29: 20.
   c TG Earth, Cleansing
      of.
51*a* TG Israel, Judah,
      People of.
   b Zech. 12: 10.
   c TG Jesus Christ,
      Second Coming.
52*a* Zech. 13: 6.
      TG Jesus Christ,
      Mission of.
   b TG Jesus Christ,
      Appearances,
      Postmortal.
   c Rom. 1: 4.
53*a* Rev. 1: 7 (7–8).
   b Ps. 4: 6; 119: 135;
      Zech. 12: 10.

   c TG Jesus Christ,
      Betrayal of.
   d Luke 23: 38; John 19:
      3 (3, 14–15).
54*a* Ezek. 36: 33 (23, 36);
      37: 28; 38: 16 (16, 23);
      39: 21 (7, 21, 23).
      TG Heathen.
   b TG Conversion.
   c TG Ignorance.
   d TG Accountability.
   e Rev. 20: 2; 1 Ne. 22:
      26; D&C 76: 71 (71–
      80).
   f TG Resurrection.
   g Matt. 11: 22; D&C 75:
      22.
55*a* TG Devil.
   b D&C 43: 31; 84: 100;
      88: 110; 101: 28.
56*a* TG Jesus Christ,
      Second Coming.
   b Matt. 25: 1 (1–13);
      D&C 63: 54.
57*a* TG Truth.
   b TG Guidance, Divine;
      Holy Ghost, Mission
      of; Motivations;

      Testimony.
   c D&C 29: 9 (9, 21, 23);
      63: 34 (34, 54); 64: 24;
      88: 94; 101: 24 (23–
      25).
58*a* TG Earth, Destiny of.
   b Isa. 29: 19; Matt. 5: 5;
      Col. 1: 12; 2 Ne. 9: 18;
      D&C 38: 20 (16–20);
      56: 20.
   c Gen. 1: 22 (20–25);
      Jer. 30: 19.
   d TG Children.
   e D&C 63: 51; 101: 30
      (29–31).
   f TG Sin.
   g TG Salvation; Salva-
      tion, of Little Children.
59*a* Matt. 18: 20; D&C 1:
      36 (35–36); 29: 11 (9–
      11); 84: 119 (118–119);
      104: 59.
   b TG Glory.
   c TG Kingdom of God,
      on Earth.
   d Gen. 49: 10; Zech.
      14: 9; D&C 38: 22;
      41: 4.

chapter, until the *a*New *b*Testament be translated, and in it all these things shall be made known;

61 Wherefore I give unto you that ye may now translate it, that ye may be prepared for the things to come.

62 For verily I say unto you, that great things await you;

63 Ye hear of *a*wars in foreign lands; but, behold, I say unto you, they are nigh, even at your *b*doors, and not many years hence ye shall hear of wars in your own lands.

64 Wherefore I, the Lord, have said, gather ye out from the *a*eastern lands, assemble ye yourselves together ye elders of my church; go forth into the western countries, call upon the inhabitants to repent, and inasmuch as they do repent, build up churches unto me.

65 And with one heart and with one mind, gather up your riches that ye may *a*purchase an inheritance which shall hereafter be appointed unto you.

66 And it shall be called the *a*New Jerusalem, a *b*land of *c*peace, a city of *d*refuge, a place of *e*safety for the saints of the Most High God;

67 And the *a*glory of the Lord shall be there, and the *b*terror of the Lord also shall be there, insomuch that the wicked will not come unto it, and it shall be called Zion.

68 And it shall come to pass among the wicked, that every man that will not take his sword against his *a*neighbor must needs flee unto *b*Zion for safety.

69 And there shall be *a*gathered unto it out of every *b*nation under heaven; and it shall be the only people that shall not be at *c*war one with another.

70 And it shall be said among the wicked: Let us not go up to battle against Zion, for the inhabitants of Zion are *a*terrible; wherefore we cannot stand.

71 And it shall come to pass that the righteous shall be gathered out from among all nations, and shall come to Zion, singing with *a*songs of everlasting *b*joy.

72 And now I say unto you, keep these things from going abroad unto the world until it is expedient in me, that ye may accomplish this work in the eyes of the people, and in the eyes of your enemies, that they may not know your works until ye have accomplished the thing which I have commanded you;

73 That when they shall know it, that they may consider these things.

74 For when the Lord shall appear he shall be *a*terrible unto them, that fear may seize upon them, and they shall stand afar off and tremble.

75 And all nations shall be afraid because of the terror of the Lord, and the power of his might. Even so. Amen.

60a D&C 42: 56; 73: 3 (3–4).
  b See an excerpt in the Pearl of Great Price, in Joseph Smith–Matthew. See also Bible, footnotes and Appendix, excerpts from the Joseph Smith Translation.
63a D&C 38: 29; 87: 2 (1–5); 130: 12.
  b Matt. 24: 33.
64a D&C 42: 64; 48: 2.
65a D&C 63: 27.
66a Isa. 35: 10; Ether 13:

6 (2–11); D&C 42: 9 (9, 35, 62); Moses 7: 62; A of F 10. TG Jerusalem, New; Zion.
  b D&C 29: 8 (7–8); 52: 2 (2, 42); 57: 1; 103: 24.
  c Ps. 72: 7; D&C 54: 10. TG Peace.
  d Isa. 4: 6; Joel 2: 32. TG Refuge.
  e TG Protection, Divine.
67a D&C 64: 41 (41–43); 84: 5 (4–5, 31); 97: 15

(15–20). TG Jesus Christ, Glory of.
  b D&C 64: 43.
68a Zech. 14: 13.
  TG Neighbor.
  b Isa. 31: 9. TG Zion.
69a Deut. 30: 3; Jer. 32: 37.
  b Zech. 2: 11 (10–12); D&C 49: 10; 97: 19 (18–21).
  c TG War.
70a Mal. 1: 14.
71a D&C 66: 11.
  b TG Joy.
74a Zeph. 2: 11.

SECTION 46

Revelation given through Joseph Smith the Prophet to the Church, at Kirtland, Ohio, March 8, 1831. HC 1: 163–165. In this early time of the Church, there had not yet developed a unified pattern for the conducting of Church services. However, a custom of admitting only members and earnest investigators to the sacrament meetings and other assemblies of the Church had become somewhat general. This revelation expresses the will of the Lord relative to governing and conducting meetings.

1–2, Elders are to conduct meetings as guided by the Holy Spirit; 3–6, Truth seekers should not be excluded from sacramental services; 7–12, Ask of God and seek the gifts of the Spirit; 13–26, An enumeration of some of these gifts; 27–33, Church leaders are given power to discern the gifts of the Spirit.

HEARKEN, O ye people of my church; for verily I say unto you that these things were spoken unto you for your *a*profit and learning.

2 But notwithstanding those things which are written, it always has been given to the *a*elders of my church from the beginning, and ever shall be, to *b*conduct all meetings as they are directed and guided by the Holy Spirit.

3 Nevertheless ye are commanded never to *a*cast any one out from your public *b*meetings, which are held before the world.

4 Ye are also commanded not to cast any one who belongeth to the church out of your sacrament meetings; nevertheless, if any have trespassed, let him *a*not *b*partake until he makes reconciliation.

5 And again I say unto you, ye shall not cast any out of your sacrament meetings who are earnestly *a*seeking the kingdom—I speak this concerning those who are not of the church.

6 And again I say unto you, concerning your *a*confirmation meetings, that if there be any that are not of the church, that are earnestly seeking after the kingdom, ye shall not cast them out.

7 But ye are commanded in all things to *a*ask of God, who giveth liberally; and that which the Spirit testifies unto you even so I would that ye should do in all *b*holiness of heart, walking uprightly before me, *c*considering the end of your salvation, doing all things with prayer and *d*thanksgiving, that ye may not be *e*seduced by evil *f*spirits, or doctrines of devils, or the *g*commandments of men; for some are of men, and others of devils.

8 Wherefore, beware lest ye not be deceived; and that ye may not be deceived *a*seek ye earnestly the best gifts, always remembering for what they are given;

9 For verily I say unto you, they

---

46 1a Deut. 10: 13 (12–13).
   2a Lev. 9: 1; Alma 6: 1.
      b Moro. 6: 9; D&C 20: 45.
   3a 3 Ne. 18: 22 (22–34).
      b TG Church; Fellowshipping; Meetings.
   4a 3 Ne. 12: 24 (23–26).
      b TG Reconciliation; Sacrament.
   5a TG Missionary Work.

6a IE for confirmation of those recently baptized, commonly done now in sacrament meeting.
7a James 1: 5 (5–6); D&C 6: 11; 88: 62 (62–65); 102: 23. TG Problem-Solving.
   b TG Holiness.
   c TG Meditation; Prayer.
   d Ps. 34: 1 (1–3); 69: 30

(30–31); Alma 34: 38. TG Thanksgiving.
   e 1 Tim. 4: 1 (1–4); D&C 28: 11; 43: 6 (5–7).
   f TG Spirits, Evil, Unclean.
   g Col. 2: 22 (18–22); Titus 1: 14; D&C 3: 6 (6–7); 45: 29; JS-H 1: 19.
8a 1 Cor. 12: 31; D&C 11: 10.

are given for the benefit of those who love me and keep all my commandments, and him that seeketh so to do; that all may be benefited that seek for that ask of me, that ask and not for a ^asign that they may ^bconsume it upon their lusts.

10 And again, verily I say unto you, I would that ye should always remember, and always retain in your ^aminds what those ^bgifts are, that are given unto the church.

11 For all have not every ^agift given unto them; for there are many gifts, and to every man is given a gift by the Spirit of God.

12 To some is given one, and to some is given another, that all may be profited thereby.

13 To some it is given by the ^aHoly Ghost to know that Jesus Christ is the Son of God, and that he was crucified for the sins of the world.

14 To others it is given to ^abelieve on their words, that they also might have eternal life if they continue faithful.

15 And again, to some it is given by the Holy Ghost to know the ^adifferences of administration, as it will be pleasing unto the same Lord, according as the Lord will, suiting his ^bmercies according to the conditions of the children of men.

16 And again, it is given by the Holy Ghost to some to know the diversities of operations, whether they be of God, that the manifestations of the ^aSpirit may be given to every man to profit withal.

17 And again, verily I say unto you, to some is given, by the Spirit of God, the word of ^awisdom.

18 To another is given the word of ^aknowledge, that all may be taught to be wise and to have knowledge.

19 And again, to some it is given to have ^afaith to be healed;

20 And to others it is given to have faith to ^aheal.

21 And again, to some is given the working of ^amiracles;

22 And to others it is given to ^aprophesy;

23 And to others the ^adiscerning of spirits.

24 And again, it is given to some to speak with ^atongues;

25 And to another is given the interpretation of tongues.

26 And all these ^agifts come from God, for the benefit of the ^bchildren of God.

27 And unto the ^abishop of the church, and unto such as God shall appoint and ordain to watch over the church and to be elders unto the church, are to have it given unto them to ^bdiscern all those gifts lest there shall be any among you professing and yet be not of God.

28 And it shall come to pass that he that asketh in ^aSpirit shall receive in Spirit;

29 That unto some it may be given to have all those gifts, that there may be a head, in order that every member may be profited thereby.

30 He that ^aasketh in the ^bSpirit asketh according to the ^cwill of God;

9a TG Sign Seekers.
  b James 4: 3.
10a TG Mind.
  b 1 Cor. 14: 12.
11a Rom. 1: 11.
      TG Holy Ghost, Gifts of.
13a TG Holy Ghost, Source of Testimony.
14a Rom. 10: 10 (4–11); Mosiah 26: 15 (15–16); Alma 19: 9; 56: 48 (47–48); 3 Ne. 12: 2.
15a Rom. 10: 5.
  b Gen. 32: 10; 1 Ne. 1: 20; Alma 34: 38.

16a 1 Cor. 12: 7 (3–8).
17a 1 Kgs. 5: 12; Moro. 10: 9 (9–10).
18a TG Education; Knowledge.
19a Mark 5: 34 (34–36); Hel. 15: 9 (9–10); D&C 42: 48 (48–52).
      TG Faith.
20a TG Healing.
21a TG Miracle.
22a TG Prophecy.
23a Acts 16: 18 (16–18); Moses 1: 15 (13–15).
24a TG Language.
26a TG God, Gifts of.

  b TG Man, a Spirit Child of Heavenly Father; Sons and Daughters of God.
27a TG Bishop.
  b TG Discernment, Spiritual.
28a Ezek. 36: 27; Rom. 8: 26 (26–27); D&C 88: 65 (64–65).
30a Hel. 10: 5; 3 Ne. 19: 24; D&C 50: 29.
      TG Holy Ghost, Mission of.
  b James 4: 3.
  c TG God, Will of.

wherefore it is done even as he asketh.

31 And again, I say unto you, all things must be done in the name of Christ, whatsoever you do in the Spirit;

32 And ye must give "thanks unto God in the Spirit for whatsoever blessing ye are blessed with.

33 And ye must practise "virtue and holiness before me continually. Even so. Amen.

SECTION 47

Revelation given through Joseph Smith the Prophet, at Kirtland, Ohio, March 8, 1831. HC 1: 166. Prior to this time Oliver Cowdery had acted as Church historian and recorder. John Whitmer had not sought an appointment as historian, but, being asked to serve in this capacity, he had said that he would obey the will of the Lord in the matter. He had already served as a secretary to the Prophet in recording many of the revelations received in the Fayette, New York, area.

1–4, John Whitmer is designated to keep the history of the Church and to write for the Prophet.

BEHOLD, it is expedient in me that my servant John should write and keep a regular "history, and assist you, my servant Joseph, in transcribing all things which shall be given you, until he is called to further duties.

2 Again, verily I say unto you that

he can also "lift up his voice in meetings, whenever it shall be expedient.

3 And again, I say unto you that it shall be appointed unto him to keep the church "record and history continually; for Oliver Cowdery I have appointed to another office.

4 Wherefore, it shall be given him, inasmuch as he is faithful, by the "Comforter, to write these things. Even so. Amen.

SECTION 48

Revelation given through Joseph Smith the Prophet, at Kirtland, Ohio, March 1831. HC 1: 166–167. The Prophet had inquired of the Lord as to the mode of procedure in procuring lands for the settlement of the saints. This was an important matter in view of the migration of members of the Church from the eastern United States, in obedience to the Lord's command that they should assemble in Ohio. See 37: 1–3; 45: 64.

1–3, The saints in Ohio are to share their lands with their brethren; 4–6, The saints are to purchase lands, build a city, and follow the counsel of their presiding officers.

IT is necessary that ye should remain for the present time in your places of abode, as it shall be suitable to your circumstances.

2 And inasmuch as ye have lands,

32a 1 Chr. 16: 8 (7–36);
 1 Thes. 1: 2; Alma 37:
 37; D&C 59: 7.
 TG Thanksgiving.

33a TG Holiness; Virtue.
47 1a D&C 21: 1; 69: 3
 (3–8); 85: 1.
2a TG Preaching.

3a TG Record Keeping.
4a TG Holy Ghost, Comforter.

ye shall ªimpart to the ᵇeastern brethren;

3 And inasmuch as ye have not lands, let them buy for the present time in those regions round about, as seemeth them good, for it must needs be necessary that they have places to live for the present time.

4 It must needs be necessary that ye ªsave all the money that ye can, and that ye obtain all that ye can in righteousness, that in time ye may be enabled to ᵇpurchase ᶜland for an ᵈinheritance, even the city.

5 It ªplace is not yet to be ᵇrevealed; but after your brethren come from the east there are to be

certain men appointed, and to them it shall be given to know the place, or to them it shall be revealed.

6 And they shall be appointed to ªpurchase the lands, and to make a commencement to lay the foundation of the city; and then shall ye begin to be gathered with your families, every man according to his ᵇfamily, according to his circumstances, and as is appointed to him by the presidency and the bishop of the church, according to the laws and commandments which ye have received, and which ye shall hereafter receive. Even so. Amen.

SECTION 49

Revelation given through Joseph Smith the Prophet to Sidney Rigdon, Parley P. Pratt, and Leman Copley, at Kirtland, Ohio, March 1831. HC 1: 167–169. (Some historical sources give the date of this revelation as May 1831.) Leman Copley had embraced the gospel, but still held to some of the teachings of the Shakers (United Society of Believers in Christ's Second Appearing) to which he had formerly belonged. Some of the beliefs of the Shakers were that Christ's second coming had already occurred and he had appeared in the form of a woman, Ann Lee; baptism by water was not considered essential; the eating of pork was specifically forbidden, and many did not eat any meat; and a celibate life was considered higher than marriage. In prefacing this revelation, the Prophet wrote, "In order to have a more perfect understanding on the subject, I inquired of the Lord, and received the following." The revelation refuted some of the basic concepts of the Shaker group. The aforementioned brethren took a copy of the revelation to the Shaker community (near Cleveland, Ohio) and read it to them in its entirety, but it was rejected.

1–7, Day and hour of Christ's coming shall remain unknown until he comes; 8–14, Men must repent, believe the gospel, and obey the ordinances to gain salvation; 15–16, Marriage is ordained of God; 17–21, Eating of meat

is approved; 22–28, Zion shall flourish and the Lamanites blossom as the rose before the Second Coming.

HEARKEN unto my word, my servants Sidney, and Parley, and

---

48 2a TG Welfare.
  b D&C 42: 64; 45: 64.
  4a TG Family, Managing Finances in.
  b D&C 57: 4.

  c D&C 57: 8.
  d D&C 42: 9 (9, 35, 62); 45: 66 (66–71); 64: 30.
  5a D&C 51: 16.
  b D&C 57: 2 (1–3).

  6a TG Jerusalem, New; Zion.
  b Num. 1: 2; Mosiah 6: 3; Ether 1: 41.

Leman; for behold, verily I say unto you, that I give unto you a commandment that you shall go and ᵃpreach my gospel which ye have received, even as ye have received it, unto the Shakers.

2 Behold, I say unto you, that they desire to know the truth in part, but not all, for they are not ᵃright before me and must needs repent.

3 Wherefore, I send you, my servants Sidney and Parley, to preach the gospel unto them.

4 And my servant Leman shall be ordained unto this work, that he may reason with them, not according to that which he has received of them, but according to that which shall be ᵃtaught him by my servants; and by so doing I will bless him, otherwise he shall not prosper.

5 Thus saith the Lord; for I am God, and have ᵃsent mine ᵇOnly Begotten Son into the world for the ᶜredemption of the world, and have decreed that he that receiveth him shall be saved, and he that receiveth him not shall be ᵈdamned—

6 And they have done unto the ᵃSon of Man even as they listed; and he has taken his power on the ᵇright hand of his ᶜglory, and now reigneth in the heavens, and will reign till he descends on the earth to put all enemies ᵈunder his feet, which time is nigh at hand—

7 I, the Lord God, have spoken it; but the hour and the ᵃday no man

knoweth, neither the angels in heaven, nor shall they know until he comes.

8 Wherefore, I will that all men shall repent, for all are under ᵃsin, except those which I have ᵇreserved unto myself, ᶜholy men that ye know not of.

9 Wherefore, I say unto you that I have sent unto you mine everlasting ᵃcovenant, even that which was from the beginning.

10 And that which I have promised I have so fulfilled, and the ᵃnations of the earth shall ᵇbow to it; and, if not of themselves, they shall come down, for that which is now exalted of itself shall be laid ᶜlow of power.

11 Wherefore, I give unto you a commandment that ye ᵃgo among this people, and say unto them, like unto mine apostle of old, whose name was ᵇPeter:

12 ᵃBelieve on the name of the Lord Jesus, who was on the earth, and is to come, the beginning and the end;

13 ᵃRepent and be baptized in the name of Jesus Christ, according to the holy commandment, for the remission of sins;

14 And whoso doeth this shall receive the ᵃgift of the Holy Ghost, by the laying on of the ᵇhands of the elders of the church.

15 And again, verily I say unto you, that whoso ᵃforbiddeth to marry is not ordained of God, for ᵇmarriage is ordained of God unto man.

49 1a TG Preaching.
2a Acts 8: 21.
4a TG Gospel; Truth.
5a John 3: 17 (16–17); D&C 132: 24 (24, 59). TG Jesus Christ, Authority of.
 b TG Jesus Christ, Divine Sonship.
 c TG Jesus Christ, Redeemer; Redemption.
 d TG Damnation.
6a TG Jesus Christ, Son of Man.
 b Acts 7: 56; D&C 76: 20 (20–23); 104: 7.
 c TG Jesus Christ, Glory of.

 d Ps. 66: 3; D&C 76: 61.
7a Matt. 24: 36; 25: 13; Mark 13: 32; Rev. 16: 15 (15–16); D&C 133: 11; JS-M 1: 40.
8a Gal. 3: 22; Mosiah 16: 3.
 b Rom. 11: 4.
 c Ex. 22: 31; Heb. 13: 2; W of M 1: 17; Alma 13: 26; D&C 107: 29.
9a Ps. 74: 20; Isa. 59: 21 (20–21); Rom. 11: 27; Heb. 10: 16 (16–17).
10a Zech. 2: 11 (10–12); D&C 45: 69 (66–69); 97: 19 (18–21).

 b Isa. 60: 14.
 c Matt. 23: 12.
11a TG Missionary Work.
 b Acts 2: 38 (37–38).
12a TG Baptism, Qualifications for.
13a TG Repentance.
14a TG Holy Ghost, Gift of.
 b TG Hands, Laying on of.
15a 1 Tim. 4: 3.
 b Gen. 2: 24 (23–24); D&C 42: 22; Moses 3: 24 (23–24); Abr. 5: 18 (17–18). TG Marriage; Marriage, Celestial.

16 Wherefore, it is lawful that he should have one ^awife, and they twain shall be ^bone flesh, and all this that the ^cearth might answer the end of its creation;

17 And that it might be filled with the measure of man, according to his ^acreation ^bbefore the world was made.

18 And whoso ^aforbiddeth to ^babstain from ^cmeats, that man should not eat the same, is not ordained of God;

19 For, behold, the ^abeasts of the field and the fowls of the air, and that which cometh of the earth, is ^bordained for the use of man for food and for ^craiment, and that he might have in abundance.

20 But it is not given that one man should ^apossess that which is above another, wherefore the ^bworld lieth in ^csin.

21 And wo be unto man that ^asheddeth blood or that ^bwasteth ^cflesh and hath no need.

22 And again, verily I say unto you, that the Son of Man ^acometh not in the form of a woman, neither of a man traveling on the earth.

23 Wherefore, be not ^adeceived, but continue in steadfastness, ^blooking forth for the heavens to be ^cshaken, and the earth to tremble and to reel to and fro as a drunken man, and for the ^dvalleys to be exalted, and for the ^emountains to be made low, and for the rough places to become smooth—and all this when the angel shall sound his ^ftrumpet.

24 But before the ^agreat day of the Lord shall come, ^aJacob shall flourish in the wilderness, and the Lamanites shall ^bblossom as the rose.

25 Zion shall ^aflourish upon the ^bhills, and rejoice upon the mountains, and shall be assembled together unto the place which I have appointed.

26 Behold, I say unto you, go forth as I have commanded you; repent of all your sins; ^aask and ye shall receive; knock and it shall be opened unto you.

27 Behold, I will go before you and be your ^arearward; and I will be in your ^bmidst, and you shall not be ^cconfounded.

28 Behold, I am Jesus Christ, and I come ^aquickly. Even so. Amen.

16a TG Marriage,
  Husbands; Marriage,
  Wives.
 b TG Family, Love
  within.
 c TG Earth, Purpose of.
17a TG Creation;
  Foreordination.
 b TG Man, Antemortal
  Existence of.
18a IE biddeth to abstain;
  see v. 19 and Gen. 9:
  3–4.
 b TG Abstinence.
 c TG Food; Meat; Word
  of Wisdom.
19a Gen. 1: 26; D&C 89:
  12.
 b 1 Tim. 4: 3. TG Food.
 c TG Clothing.
20a Acts 4: 32; D&C
  51: 3; 70: 14; 78: 5
  (5–6).

  TG Consecration;
  Covetousness.
 b TG World.
21a TG Life, Sanctity of.
  JST Gen. 9: 11 And
  surely, blood shall not
  be shed, only for meat,
  to save your lives;
  and the blood of every
  beast will I require at
  your hands.
 b TG Cruelty; Waste.
 c TG Food; Meat.
22a Matt. 24: 23 (23–27).
  TG Jesus Christ,
  Second Coming.
23a Matt. 24: 4 (4–5).
 b 2 Pet. 3: 12; D&C
  45: 39.
 c D&C 21: 6; 45: 48 (22,
  48).

 d Isa. 40: 4; D&C 109:
  74; 133: 22.
 e Micah 1: 4. TG Earth,
  Renewal of.
 f Isa. 27: 13;
  Matt. 24: 31.
24a 3 Ne. 5: 21 (21–26);
  D&C 52: 2 (1–3).
 b Isa. 35: 1 (1–2);
  2 Ne. 30: 6; 3 Ne.
  21: 25 (22–25);
  D&C 3: 20; 30: 6;
  109: 65.
25a D&C 35: 24; 39: 13;
  117: 7 (7–8).
 b Gen. 49: 26; 2 Ne. 12:
  2 (2–3).
26a D&C 88: 63 (62–64).
27a Isa. 52: 12.
 b Matt. 18: 20.
 c Ps. 22: 5; 1 Pet. 2: 6;
  D&C 84: 116.
28a D&C 1: 12.

SECTION 50

Revelation given through Joseph Smith the Prophet, at Kirtland, Ohio, May 1831. HC 1: 170–173. The Prophet states that some of the elders did not understand the manifestations of different spirits abroad in the earth, and that this revelation was given in response to his special inquiry on the matter. So-called spiritual phenomena were not uncommon among the members, some of whom claimed to be receiving visions and revelations.

1–5, Many false spirits are abroad in the earth; 6–9, Wo unto the hypocrites and those who are cut off from the Church; 10–14, Elders are to preach the gospel by the Spirit; 15–22, Both preachers and hearers need to be enlightened by the Spirit; 23–25, That which doth not edify is not of God; 26–28, The faithful are possessors of all things; 29–36, Prayers of the purified are answered; 37–46, Christ is the Good Shepherd and the Stone of Israel.

HEARKEN, O ye elders of my church, and give ear to the ªvoice of the living God; and attend to the words of wisdom which shall be given unto you, according as ye have asked and are agreed as touching the church, and the ᵇspirits which have gone abroad in the earth.

2 Behold, verily I say unto you, that there are many spirits which are false ªspirits, which have gone forth in the earth, deceiving the world.

3 And also ªSatan hath sought to deceive you, that he might overthrow you.

4 Behold, I, the Lord, have looked upon you, and have seen ªabominations in the church that ᵇprofess my name.

5 But blessed are they who are faithful and ªendure, whether in life or in death, for they shall inherit eternal life.

6 But wo unto them that are ªdeceivers and hypocrites, for, thus saith the Lord, I will bring them to judgment.

7 Behold, verily I say unto you, there are ªhypocrites among you, who have deceived some, which has given the ᵇadversary ᶜpower; but behold ᵈsuch shall be reclaimed;

8 But the ªhypocrites shall be detected and shall be ᵇcut off, either in life or in death, even as I will; and wo unto them who are cut off from my church, for the same are overcome of the world.

9 Wherefore, let every man beware lest he do that which is not in truth and righteousness before me.

10 And now come, saith the Lord, by the Spirit, unto the elders of his church, and let us ªreason together, that ye may understand;

11 Let us reason even as a man reasoneth one with another face to face.

12 Now, when a man reasoneth he is understood of man, because he reasoneth as a man; even so will I,

---

50 1a Josh. 3: 10; Jer. 23: 36.
　b Rev. 16: 14. TG Sorcery.
2a TG False Doctrine; Spirits, Evil, Unclean.
3a Luke 22: 31; 2 Ne. 2: 18 (17–18); 3 Ne. 18: 18; D&C 10: 22 (22–27). TG Devil.

4a D&C 1: 30; 20: 32 (32–34); 28: 11 (11–12).
　b D&C 41: 1; 56: 1; 112: 26. TG Jesus Christ, Taking the Name of.
5a TG Adversity; Steadfastness.
6a TG Deceit.
7a Prov. 11: 9 (5–11).
　b TG Devil.
　c Mosiah 27: 9 (8–9);

D&C 93: 39 (37, 39).
　d IE those who have been deceived.
8a TG Hypocrisy.
　b D&C 1: 14; 41: 1 (1, 5); 42: 37; 56: 3 (1, 3–4); 64: 35.
TG Excommunication.
10a Isa. 1: 18; 41: 1; D&C 45: 10.

the Lord, reason with you that you may ^aunderstand.

13 Wherefore, I the Lord ask you this question—unto what were ye ^aordained?

14 To preach my gospel by the ^aSpirit, even the ^bComforter which was sent forth to teach the truth.

15 And then received ye ^aspirits which ye could not understand, and received them to be of God; and in this are ye justified?

16 Behold ye shall answer this question yourselves; nevertheless, I will be ^amerciful unto you; he that is weak among you hereafter shall be made ^bstrong.

17 Verily I say unto you, he that is ordained of me and sent forth to ^apreach the word of truth by the Comforter, in the Spirit of truth, doth he ^bpreach it by the Spirit of truth or some other way?

18 And if it be by some other way it is not of God.

19 And again, he that receiveth the word of truth, doth he receive it by the Spirit of truth or some other way?

20 If it be some other way it is not of God.

21 Therefore, why is it that ye cannot understand and know, that he that receiveth the word by the ^aSpirit of truth receiveth it as it is preached by the Spirit of truth?

22 Wherefore, he that preacheth and he that receiveth, understand one another, and both are ^aedified and ^brejoice together.

23 And that which doth not ^aedify is not of God, and is ^bdarkness.

24 That which is of God is ^alight; and he that ^breceiveth ^clight, and ^ccontinueth in God, receiveth more ^elight; and that light groweth brighter and brighter until the perfect day.

25 And again, verily I say unto you, and I say it that you may know the ^atruth, that you may chase darkness from among you;

26 He that is ^aordained of God and sent forth, the same is appointed to be the ^bgreatest, notwithstanding he is the ^cleast and the ^dservant of all.

27 Wherefore, he is possessor of all things; for all things are ^asubject unto him, both in heaven and on the earth, the life and the light, the Spirit and the ^bpower, sent forth by the will of the Father through Jesus Christ, his Son.

28 But no man is possessor of all ^athings except he be ^bpurified and ^ccleansed from all sin.

29 And if ye are ^apurified and cleansed from all ^bsin, ye shall ^cask

12a Ps. 119: 27; D&C 1: 24.
13a TG Priesthood, Ordination.
14a D&C 43: 15.
  TG Teaching with the Spirit.
  b TG Holy Ghost, Comforter.
15a 1 Cor. 2: 12.
  TG Discernment, Spiritual.
16a Ps. 67: 1.
  b 2 Cor. 12: 10.
  TG Strength.
17a TG Missionary Work; Priesthood, Magnifying Callings within.
  b TG Holy Ghost, Mission of.
21a TG Truth.
22a TG Edification.
  b Neh. 8: 12; John 4:

36; D&C 18: 16 (13–16).
  TG Joy.
23a 1 Cor. 14: 26.
  b TG Darkness, Spiritual.
24a Eccl. 8: 1; 1 Jn. 2: 8; Moro. 7: 18 (14–19); D&C 67: 9; 84: 45 (45–47); 88: 49 (40–41, 49).
  TG Light of Christ.
  b TG Learning; Teachable.
  c Ps. 97: 11; Dan. 2: 21. TG Children of Light.
  d John 15: 4 (4–5, 10).
  e Isa. 28: 13 (9–13); 2 Ne. 28: 30. TG Light; Man, Potential to Become Like Heavenly Father; Perfection.
25a John 8: 32.
26a TG Leadership.

  b Luke 22: 24 (24–30).
  c Matt. 11: 11; Luke 7: 28.
  d Mark 10: 43 (43–44). TG Self-sacrifice; Servant; Service.
27a Dan. 7: 14 (13–14); Matt. 28: 18; John 3: 35; D&C 63: 59; 76: 55 (5–10, 50–60).
  b TG Priesthood, Power of.
28a D&C 76: 55 (55, 59).
  b TG Man, New, Spiritually Reborn; Purity.
  c 1 Jn. 1: 7.
29a Neh. 12: 30; 3 Ne. 8: 1; 19: 28 (28–29); D&C 29: 3; 88: 74 (74–75).
  b TG Sin.
  c Hel. 10: 5; D&C 46: 30.

whatsoever you will in the name of Jesus and it shall be done.

30 But know this, it shall be given you what you shall *a*ask; and as ye are appointed to the *b*head, the spirits shall be subject unto you.

31 Wherefore, it shall come to pass, that if you behold a *a*spirit manifested that you cannot understand, and you receive not that spirit, ye shall ask of the Father in the name of Jesus; and if he give not unto you that spirit, then you may know that it is not of God.

32 And it shall be given unto you, *a*power over that spirit; and you shall proclaim against that spirit with a loud voice that it is *b*not of God—

33 Not with *a*railing accusation, that ye be not overcome, neither with *b*boasting nor rejoicing, lest you be seized therewith.

34 He that receiveth of God, let him *a*account it of God; and let him rejoice that he is accounted of God worthy to receive.

35 And by giving heed and doing these things which ye have received, and which ye shall hereafter receive —and the *a*kingdom is given *b*you of the Father, and *c*power to *d*overcome all things which are not ordained of him—

36 And behold, verily I say unto you, blessed are you who are now hearing these words of mine from the mouth of my servant, for your sins are *a*forgiven you.

37 Let my servant Joseph Wakefield, in whom I am well pleased, and my servant *a*Parley P. Pratt go forth among the churches and strengthen them by the word of *b*exhortation;

38 And also my servant John Corrill, or as many of my servants as are ordained unto this office, and let them labor in the *a*vineyard; and let no man hinder them doing that which I have appointed unto them—

39 Wherefore, in this thing my servant *a*Edward Partridge is not justified; nevertheless let him repent and he shall be forgiven.

40 Behold, ye are little children and ye cannot *a*bear all things now; ye must *b*grow in *c*grace and in the knowledge of the truth.

41 *a*Fear not, little *b*children, for you are mine, and I have *c*overcome the world, and you are of them that my Father hath *d*given me;

42 And none of them that my Father hath given me shall be *a*lost.

43 And the Father and I are *a*one. I am *b*in the Father and the Father in me; and inasmuch as ye have received me, ye are in me and I in you.

44 Wherefore, I am in your midst, and I am the *a*good *b*shepherd, and the *c*stone of Israel. He that buildeth upon this *d*rock shall never *e*fall.

30a TG Prayer.
  b TG Authority.
31a Luke 11: 24 (24–26);
    1 Jn. 4: 1 (1–6).
  TG Spirits, Evil, Unclean.
32a Matt. 10: 1.
  b 1 Jn. 4: 3 (1–3).
33a Jude 1: 9.
  b Luke 10: 20 (17–20);
    D&C 84: 73; 105: 24.
  TG Boasting.
34a TG Ingratitude;
    Thanksgiving.
35a D&C 45: 1; 61: 37.
  TG Kingdom of God,
    on Earth.
  b D&C 6: 4; 35: 27.
  c TG Initiative.
  d 1 Jn. 4: 4.
36a TG Forgiveness.

37a D&C 32: 1; 52: 26;
    97: 3; 103: 30 (30–37).
  b TG Preaching.
38a TG Vineyard of the
    Lord.
39a D&C 42: 10; 51: 1
    (1–18).
40a John 16: 12; 3 Ne. 17:
    2 (2–4); D&C 78: 18
    (17–18).
  b 1 Cor. 3: 2 (2–3); Heb.
    5: 12 (11–14);
    D&C 19: 22.
  c TG Grace; Knowledge;
    Truth.
41a John 14: 1 (1–3); 1 Jn.
    2: 1–13; 4: 18 (7–21).
  b TG Sons and Daughters
    of God.
  c John 16: 33.
  d John 6: 37; 10: 29

(27–29); 17: 2 (2–12);
3 Ne. 15: 24; D&C
27: 14; 84: 63.
42a John 17: 12.
43a TG Jesus Christ,
    Relationships with the
    Father; Unity.
  b John 14: 11.
44a Ezra 3: 11; Alma 5:
    40.
  TG Jesus Christ, Good
    Shepherd; Shepherd.
  c Gen. 49: 24.
  TG Cornerstone; Jesus
    Christ, Prophecies
    about.
  d 1 Pet. 2: 4 (4–8).
  TG Rock.
  e 2 Pet. 1: 10; Hel. 5: 12.
  TG Apostasy of
    Individuals.

45 And the *day cometh that you shall hear my voice and *see me, and *know that I am.

46 *Watch, therefore, that ye may be *ready. Even so. Amen.

SECTION 51

Revelation given through Joseph Smith the Prophet, at Thompson, Ohio, May 1831. HC 1: 173–174. At this time the saints migrating from the eastern states began to arrive in Ohio, and it became necessary to make definite arrangements for their settlement. As this undertaking belonged particularly to the bishop's office, Bishop Edward Partridge sought instruction on the matter, and the Prophet inquired of the Lord.

1–8, Edward Partridge is appointed to regulate stewardships and properties; 9–12, The saints are to deal honestly and receive alike; 13–15, They are to have a bishop's storehouse and to organize properties according to the Lord's law; 16–20, Ohio is to be a temporary gathering place.

HEARKEN unto me, saith the Lord your God, and I will speak unto my servant *Edward Partridge, and give unto him directions; for it must needs be that he receive directions how to organize this people.

2 For it must needs be that they be *organized according to my *laws; if otherwise, they will be cut off.

3 Wherefore, let my servant Edward Partridge, and those whom he has chosen, in whom I am well pleased, appoint unto this people their *portions, every man *equal according to his family, according to his circumstances and his wants and *needs.

4 And let my servant Edward Partridge, when he shall appoint a man his *portion, give unto him a writing that shall secure unto him his portion, that he shall hold it, even this right and this inheritance in the church, until he transgresses and is not accounted worthy by the voice of the church, according to the *laws and *covenants of the church, to belong to the church.

5 And if he shall transgress and is not accounted worthy to belong to the church, he shall not have power to *claim that portion which he has consecrated unto the bishop for the poor and needy of my church; therefore, he shall not retain the gift, but shall only have *claim on that portion that is deeded unto him.

6 And thus all things shall be made sure, *according to the *laws of the land.

7 And let that which belongs to this people be appointed unto this people.

8 And the *money which is left unto this people—let there be an *agent appointed unto this people, to take the *money to provide food and raiment, according to the wants of this people.

9 And let every man deal *honestly,

45a TG Day of the Lord.
  b D&C 67: 10.
    TG God, Privilege of Seeing.
  c Acts 7: 56.
46a TG Watchfulness.
  b TG Procrastination.
51 1a D&C 50: 39; 52: 24.
2a TG Church Organization.
  b D&C 42: 30 (30–39);

51: 15; 105: 5.
3a TG Family, Managing Finances in.
  b D&C 49: 20.
  c Acts 2: 45.
4a D&C 83: 5.
  b D&C 42: 32 (30–39).
  c D&C 1: 6 (6, 37); 33: 14; 42: 13.
5a D&C 42: 37 (30–39).

See also Section 83.
  b D&C 56: 10.
6a 1 Pet. 2: 13 (13–14); D&C 44: 4; 98: 5 (5–7); 109: 54.
  b D&C 58: 21.
8a D&C 58: 51 (49–51); 60: 10; 84: 104.
  b D&C 84: 113.
  c D&C 63: 40 (40, 43, 46).
9a TG Honesty.

and be alike among this people, and receive alike, that ye may be *b*one, even as I have commanded you.

10 And let that which belongeth to this people not be taken and given unto that of *a*another church.

11 Wherefore, if another church would receive money of this church, let them *a*pay unto this church again according as they shall agree;

12 And this shall be done through the bishop or the agent, which shall be appointed by the *a*voice of the church.

13 And again, let the bishop appoint a *a*storehouse unto this church; and let all things both in money and in meat, which are more than is *b*needful for the wants of this people, be kept in the hands of the bishop.

14 And let him also reserve unto *a*himself for his own wants, and for the wants of his family, as he shall be employed in doing this business.

15 And thus I grant unto this people a privilege of organizing themselves according to my *a*laws.

16 And I consecrate unto them this land for a *a*little season, until I, the Lord, shall provide for them otherwise, and command them to go hence;

17 And the hour and the day is not given unto them, wherefore let them act upon this land as for years, and this shall turn unto them for their good.

18 Behold, this shall be *a*an example unto my servant Edward Partridge, in other places, in all churches.

19 And whoso is found a *a*faithful, a *b*just, and a wise *c*steward shall enter into the *d*joy of his Lord, and shall inherit eternal life.

20 Verily, I say unto you, I am Jesus Christ, who *a*cometh quickly, in an *b*hour you think not. Even so. Amen.

SECTION 52

Revelation given through Joseph Smith the Prophet, to the elders of the Church, at Kirtland, Ohio, June 7, 1831. HC 1: 175–179. A conference had been held at Kirtland, beginning on the 3rd, and closing on the 6th of June. At this conference the first distinctive ordinations to the office of high priest were made, and certain manifestations of false and deceiving spirits were discerned and rebuked.

1–2, The next conference is designated to be held in Missouri; 3–8, Appointments of certain elders to travel together are made; 9–11, The elders are to teach what the apostles and prophets have written; 12–21, Those enlightened by the Spirit bring forth fruits of praise and wisdom; 22–44, Various elders are appointed to go forth preaching the gospel, while traveling to Missouri for the conference.

BEHOLD, thus saith the Lord unto the elders whom he hath called and chosen in these last days, by the *a*voice of his Spirit—

2 Saying: I, the Lord, will make known unto you what I will that ye

---

9b TG Unity.
10a IE another branch of the Church; not another denomination. D&C 60: 9.
11a D&C 42: 54 (42, 53–54).
12a TG Common Consent.
13a D&C 42: 55; 58: 24 (24, 37). TG Welfare.

b D&C 42: 33 (33–34, 55); 82: 18 (17–19); 119: 1 (1–3).
14a D&C 31: 5.
15a D&C 42: 30 (30–39); 51: 2.
16a D&C 48: 5.
18a IE a pattern. D&C 72: 23 (19–26).

19a Matt. 24: 45; Luke 16: 10; D&C 6: 13; 138: 12.
   TG Trustworthiness.
b Prov. 11: 9 (9–11).
c TG Stewardship.
d TG Joy.
20a Rev. 22: 7 (6–16).
b Matt. 24: 44.
52 1a TG Called of God.

shall do from this time until the next conference, which shall be held in Missouri, upon the *a*land, which I will *b*consecrate unto my people, which are a *c*remnant of Jacob, and those who are heirs according to the *d*covenant.

3 Wherefore, verily I say unto you, let my servants Joseph Smith, Jun., and Sidney Rigdon take their journey as soon as preparations can be made to leave their homes, and journey to the land of *a*Missouri.

4 And inasmuch as they are faithful unto me, it shall be made known unto them what they shall do;

5 And it shall also, inasmuch as they are faithful, be made *a*known unto them the *b*land of your inheritance.

6 And inasmuch as they are not faithful, they shall be cut off, even as I will, as seemeth me good.

7 And again, verily I say unto you, let my servant Lyman Wight and my servant John Corrill take their journey speedily;

8 And also my servant John Murdock, and my servant Hyrum Smith, take their journey unto the same place by the way of Detroit.

9 And let them journey from thence preaching the word by the way, saying *a*none other things than that which the *b*prophets and apostles have written, and that which is taught them by the *c*Comforter through the prayer of faith.

10 Let them go *a*two by two, and thus let them preach by the way in every congregation, baptizing by *b*water, and the laying on of *c*hands by the water's side.

11 For thus saith the Lord, I will cut my work short in *a*righteousness, for the days come that I will send forth *b*judgment unto victory.

12 And let my servant Lyman Wight beware, for Satan desireth to *a*sift him as chaff.

13 And behold, he that is *a*faithful shall be made ruler over many things.

14 And again, I will give unto you a pattern in all things, that ye may not be deceived; for Satan is abroad in the land, and he goeth forth *a*deceiving the nations—

15 Wherefore he that prayeth, whose spirit is *a*contrite, the same is *b*accepted of me if he obey mine *c*ordinances.

16 He that *a*speaketh, whose spirit is contrite, whose language is meek and *b*edifieth, the same is of God if he obey mine ordinances.

17 And again, he that trembleth under my power shall be made *a*strong, and shall bring forth fruits of praise and *b*wisdom, according to the revelations and truths which I have given you.

18 And again, he that is overcome and *a*bringeth not forth fruits, even according to this pattern, is not of me.

19 Wherefore, by this pattern ye shall *a*know the spirits in all cases under the whole heavens.

20 And the days have come; according to men's faith it shall be *a*done unto them.

21 Behold, this commandment is

2*a* D&C 29: 8 (7–8); 45: 66 (64–66); 57: 1; 103: 24.
b D&C 58: 57; 84: 3 (3–4, 31); 103: 35; 105: 15.
c Ps. 135: 4; 3 Ne. 5: 21 (21–26); D&C 19: 27; 49: 24 (23–25); 109: 65.
d TG Abrahamic Covenant; Covenants.
3*a* D&C 54: 8 (7–8); 57: 1.
5*a* D&C 57: 2 (1–3).
b TG Lands of Inheritance.

9*a* Mosiah 18: 19 (19–20); D&C 42: 12; 52: 36.
b TG Prophets, Mission of; Scriptures, Value of.
c TG Holy Ghost, Comforter; Teaching with the Spirit.
10*a* Mark 6: 7; Luke 10: 1; D&C 61: 35; 62: 5.
b John 1: 26.
c TG Hands, Laying on of.
11*a* Rom. 9: 28.
b Matt. 12: 20.

12*a* Luke 22: 31.
13*a* Neh. 7: 2; Matt. 25: 23; D&C 132: 53.
14*a* Rev. 13: 14 (11–18).
15*a* TG Contrite Heart.
b Gen. 4: 7.
c TG Ordinance.
16*a* TG Communication.
b TG Edification.
17*a* D&C 66: 8; 133: 58.
b TG Wisdom.
18*a* Matt. 3: 10.
19*a* TG Discernment, Spiritual.
20*a* Matt. 8: 13.

given unto all the elders whom I have chosen.

22 And again, verily I say unto you, let my servant [a]Thomas B. Marsh and my servant [b]Ezra Thayre take their journey also, preaching the word by the way unto this same land.

23 And again, let my servant Isaac Morley and my servant Ezra Booth take their journey, also preaching the word by the way unto this same land.

24 And again, let my servants [a]Edward Partridge and Martin Harris take their journey with my servants Sidney Rigdon and Joseph Smith, Jun.

25 Let my servants David Whitmer and Harvey Whitlock also take their journey, and preach by the way unto this same land.

26 And let my servants [a]Parley P. Pratt and [b]Orson Pratt take their journey, and preach by the way, even unto this same land.

27 And let my servants Solomon Hancock and Simeon Carter also take their journey unto this same land, and preach by the way.

28 Let my servants Edson Fuller and Jacob Scott also take their journey.

29 Let my servants Levi W. Hancock and Zebedee Coltrin also take their journey.

30 Let my servants Reynolds Cahoon and Samuel H. Smith also take their journey.

31 Let my servants Wheeler Baldwin and William Carter also take their journey.

32 And let my servants [a]Newel Knight and [b]Selah J. Griffin both

be ordained, and also take their journey.

33 Yea, verily I say, let all these take their journey unto one place, in their several courses, and one man shall not build upon another's [a]foundation, neither journey in another's track.

34 He that is faithful, the same shall be kept and blessed with much [a]fruit.

35 And again, I say unto you, let my servants Joseph Wakefield and Solomon Humphrey take their journey into the eastern lands;

36 Let them labor with their families, [a]declaring none other things than the prophets and apostles, that which they have [b]seen and heard and most assuredly [c]believe, that the prophecies may be fulfilled.

37 In consequence of transgression, let that which be bestowed upon Heman Basset be [a]taken from him, and placed upon the head of Simonds Ryder.

38 And again, verily I say unto you, let Jared Carter be [a]ordained a priest, and also George James be ordained a [b]priest.

39 Let the residue of the elders [a]watch over the churches, and declare the word in the regions round about them; and let them[b]labor with their own hands that there be no [c]idolatry nor wickedness practised.

40 And remember in all things the [a]poor and the [b]needy, the [c]sick and the afflicted, for he that doeth not these things, the same is not my disciple.

41 And again, let my servants Joseph Smith, Jun., and Sidney

22a D&C 31: 1; 56: 5 (5-6); 75: 31.
  b D&C 33: 1.
24a D&C 51: 1 (1-18); 57: 7.
26a D&C 32: 1; 50: 37; 97: 3; 103: 30 (30-37).
  b D&C 34: 1; 103: 40; 124: 129; 136: 13.
32a D&C 54: 2.
  b D&C 56: 6.

33a Rom. 15: 20.
34a Col. 1: 6; Alma 32: 42 (28-42); 3 Ne. 14: 16.
36a Mosiah 18: 19 (18-20); D&C 5: 10; 31: 4; 42: 12; 52: 9.
  b John 3: 11 (11, 32).
  c TG Believe.
37a Matt. 13: 12 (10-13); 25: 29 (25-30).
38a D&C 79: 1.

  b TG Priest, Aaronic Priesthood.
39a Alma 6: 1.
  b Neh. 4: 6; 1 Cor. 4: 12; D&C 75: 3; 115: 10.
  c TG Idolatry.
40a Prov. 14: 21; Isa. 3: 15; D&C 104: 18.
  TG Generosity; Poor.
  b TG Compassion; Welfare.
  c TG Sickness.

Rigdon and Edward Partridge take with them a ᵐrecommend from the church. And let there be one obtained for my servant Oliver Cowdery also.

42 And thus, even as I have said, if ye are faithful ye shall assemble yourselves together to rejoice upon the land of ⁿMissouri, which is the land of your ᵇinheritance, which is now the land of your enemies.

43 But, behold, I, the Lord, will hasten the city in its time, and will crown the faithful with ᵒjoy and with rejoicing.

44 Behold, I am Jesus Christ, the Son of God, and I will ᵖlift them up at the last day. Even so. Amen.

SECTION 53

Revelation given through Joseph Smith the Prophet to Algernon Sidney Gilbert, at Kirtland, Ohio, June 1831. HC 1: 179–180. At Sidney Gilbert's request, the Prophet inquired of the Lord as to Brother Gilbert's work and appointment in the Church.

1–3, Sidney Gilbert's calling and election in the Church is to be ordained an elder; 4–7, He is also to serve as a bishop's agent.

BEHOLD, I say unto you, my servant Sidney Gilbert, that I have heard your prayers; and you have called upon me that it should be made known unto you, of the Lord your God, concerning your ᵃcalling and ᵇelection in the church, which I, the Lord, have raised up in these last days.

2 Behold, I, the Lord, who was ᵃcrucified for the sins of the world, give unto you a commandment that you shall ᵇforsake the world.

3 Take upon you mine ordination, even that of an elder, to preach faith and repentance and ᵈremission of sins, according to my word, and the reception of the Holy Spirit by the laying on of ᵇhands;

4 And also to be an ᵃagent unto this church in the place which shall be appointed by the bishop, according to commandments which shall be given hereafter.

5 And again, verily I say unto you, you shall take your journey with my servants Joseph Smith, Jun., and Sidney Rigdon.

6 Behold, these are the first ordinances which you shall receive; and the residue shall be made known in a time to come, according to your labor in my vineyard.

7 And again, I would that ye should learn that he only is saved who ᵃendureth unto the end. Even so. Amen.

SECTION 54

Revelation given through Joseph Smith the Prophet to Newel Knight, at Kirtland, Ohio, June 1831. HC 1: 180–181. Members of the Church in the branch at Thompson, Ohio, were divided on questions having to do with the consecration of properties. Selfishness and

41a Acts 14: 26; 15: 40;
    D&C 20: 64, 84; 72:
    17 (17, 19); 112: 21.
42a D&C 28: 9. TG Zion.
  b Num. 32: 18; D&C
    25: 2; 57: 2 (1–3);
    58: 51 (17, 28, 51).

43a TG Joy.
44a D&C 5: 35.
53 1a Compare with
    Sections 12, 14, 15, 16.
  b TG Election.
2a TG Jesus Christ,
    Crucifixion of.

  b 2 Cor. 6: 17.
  b TG World; Worldliness.
3a TG Remission of Sins.
  b TG Hands, Laying on of.
4a D&C 57: 6 (6–15); 83:
    113.
7a Matt. 10: 22.

greed were manifest, and Leman Copley had broken his covenant to consecrate his large farm as a place of inheritance for the saints arriving from Colesville, New York. Ezra Thayre was also involved in the controversy. As a consequence, Newel Knight (president of the branch at Thompson) and other elders had come to the Prophet asking how to proceed. The Prophet inquired of the Lord and received this revelation. See also Section 56, which is a continuation of the matter.

1–6, The saints must keep the gospel covenant to gain mercy; 7–10, They must be patient in tribulation.

BEHOLD, thus saith the Lord, even ^aAlpha and Omega, the beginning and the end, even he who was ^bcrucified for the sins of the world—

2 Behold, verily, verily, I say unto you, my servant Newel Knight, you shall stand fast in the office whereunto I have appointed you.

3 And if your brethren desire to escape their enemies, let them repent of all their sins, and become truly ^ahumble before me and contrite.

4 And as the covenant which they made unto me has been ^abroken, even so it has become ^bvoid and of none effect.

5 And wo to him by whom this ^aoffense cometh, for it had been better for him that he had been drowned in the depth of the sea.

6 But blessed are they who have kept the ^acovenant and observed the ^bcommandment, for they shall obtain ^cmercy.

7 Wherefore, go to now and flee the land, lest your enemies come upon you; and take your journey, and appoint whom you will to be your leader, and to pay moneys for you.

8 And thus you shall take your journey into the regions westward, unto the land of ^aMissouri, unto the borders of the Lamanites.

9 And after you have done journeying, behold, I say unto you, seek ye a ^aliving like unto men, until I prepare a place for you.

10 And again, be ^apatient in tribulation until I ^bcome; and, behold, I come quickly, and my ^creward is with me, and they who have ^dsought me early shall find ^erest to their souls. Even so. Amen.

SECTION 55

Revelation given through Joseph Smith the Prophet to William W. Phelps, at Kirtland, Ohio, June 1831. HC 1: 184–186. William W. Phelps, a printer, and his family had just arrived at Kirtland, and the Prophet sought the Lord for information concerning him.

54 1a Rev. 1:8; D&C 19:1; 75:1.
  b 1 Cor. 15:3.
    TG Jesus Christ, Crucifixion of.
3a Jer. 44:10.
4a Josh. 23:16 (15–16).
  b D&C 58:32 (32–33).
5a Matt. 18:6 (6–7);

Luke 17:2 (1–2).
  TG Offense.
6a 1 Kgs. 8:23.
  TG Covenants.
  b 1 Kgs. 3:14 (12–14).
  c TG Mercy.
8a D&C 52:3 (3, 42).
9a 1 Thes. 4:11.
10a TG Patience; Test,

Try; Prove; Tribulation.
  b Rev. 22:12. TG Jesus Christ, Second Coming.
  c TG Reward.
  d Prov. 8:17. TG Prayer.
  e Ps. 72:7; Matt. 11:29; D&C 45:66. TG Rest.

1–3, W. W. Phelps is called and chosen to be baptized, ordained an elder, and preach the gospel; 4, He is also to write books for children in church schools; 5–6, He is to travel to Missouri, which will be the area of his labors.

BEHOLD, thus saith the Lord unto you, my servant William, yea, even the Lord of the whole *a*earth, thou art called and chosen; and after thou hast been *b*baptized by water, which if you do with an eye single to my glory, you shall have a remission of your sins and a reception of the Holy Spirit by the laying on of *c*hands;

2 And then thou shalt be ordained by the hand of my servant Joseph Smith, Jun., to be an elder unto this church, to preach repentance and *a*remission of sins by way of baptism in the name of Jesus Christ, the Son of the living God.

3 And on whomsoever you shall *a*lay your hands, if they are contrite before me, you shall have power to give the Holy Spirit.

4 And again, you shall be ordained to assist my servant Oliver Cowdery to do the work of printing, and of selecting and writing *b*books for *b*schools in this church, that little *c*children also may receive *d*instruction before me as is pleasing unto me.

5 And again, verily I say unto you, for this cause you shall take your journey with my servants Joseph Smith, Jun., and Sidney Rigdon, that you may be *a*planted in the land of your inheritance to do this work.

6 And again, let my servant *a*Joseph Coe also take his journey with them. The residue shall be made known hereafter, even as I will. Amen.

SECTION 56

Revelation given through Joseph Smith the Prophet, at Kirtland, Ohio, June 1831. HC 1: 186–188. Ezra Thayre, who had been appointed to travel to Missouri with Thomas B. Marsh (52: 22), was unable to start on his mission when the latter was ready. Elder Thayre was not ready to depart on his journey because of his involvement in the problems at Thompson, Ohio. See heading to Section 54. The Lord answered the Prophet's inquiry on the matter by giving this revelation.

1–2, The saints must take up their cross and follow the Lord to gain salvation; 3–13, The Lord commands and revokes, and the disobedient are cast off; 14–17, Wo unto the rich who will not help the poor, and wo unto the poor whose hearts are not broken; 18–20, Blessed are the poor who are pure in heart, for they shall inherit the earth.

HEARKEN, O ye people who *a*profess my name, saith the Lord your God; for behold, mine anger is *b*kindled against the rebellious, and they shall know mine arm and mine indignation, in the day of *c*visitation and of wrath upon the nations.

2 And he that will not take up his *a*cross and *b*follow me, and keep my

---

55 1*a* Deut. 10: 14; 1 Ne. 11: 6; 2 Ne. 29: 7.
b TG Baptism, Essential.
c TG Hands, Laying on of.
2*a* TG Remission of Sins.
3*a* D&C 20: 41.
4*a* D&C 88: 118; 97: 3 (3–6); 109: 7 (7, 14).
b TG Education.

c TG Children.
d TG Family, Children, Responsibilities toward.
5*a* Amos 9: 15.
6*a* D&C 102: 3 (3, 34).
56 1*a* D&C 41: 1; 50: 4; 112: 26.
b TG Provoking.

c Jer. 10: 15; Hosea 9: 7; D&C 1: 14 (13–14).
2*a* Luke 14: 27.
b Matt. 8: 19; 2 Ne. 31: 10 (10–13); Moro. 7: 11. TG Jesus Christ, Exemplar.

commandments, the same shall not be saved.

3 Behold, I, the Lord, command; and he that will not ᵃobey shall be ᵇcut off in mine own due time, after I have commanded and the commandment is broken.

4 Wherefore I, the Lord, command and ᵃrevoke, as it seemeth me good; and all this to be answered upon the heads of the ᵇrebellious, saith the Lord.

5 Wherefore, I revoke the commandment which was given unto my servants ᵃThomas B. Marsh and Ezra Thayre, and give a new commandment unto my servant Thomas, that he shall take up his journey speedily to the land of Missouri, and my servant Selah J. Griffin shall also go with him.

6 For behold, the commandment which was given unto my servants ᵃSelah J. Griffin and Newel Knight, in consequence of the ᵇstiffneckedness of my people which are in Thompson, and their rebellions.

7 Wherefore, let my servant Newel Knight remain with them; and as many as will go may go, that are contrite before me, and be led by him to the land which I have appointed.

8 And again, verily I say unto you, that my servant Ezra Thayre must repent of his ᵃpride, and of his ᵇselfishness, and obey the former commandment which I have given him concerning the place upon which he lives.

9 And if he will do this, as there shall be no divisions made upon the land, he shall be appointed still to go to the land of Missouri;

10 Otherwise he shall receive the ᵃmoney which he has paid, and shall leave the place, and shall be ᵇcut off out of my church, saith the Lord God of hosts;

11 And though the heaven and the earth pass away, these words shall not ᵃpass away, but shall be fulfilled.

12 And if my servant Joseph Smith, Jun., must needs pay the money, behold, I, the Lord, will pay it unto him again in the land of Missouri, that those of whom he shall receive may be rewarded again according to that which they do;

13 For according to that which they do they shall receive, even in lands for their inheritance.

14 Behold, thus saith the Lord unto my people—you have many things to do and to repent of; for behold, your ᵃsins have come up unto me, and are not ᵇpardoned, because you seek to ᶜcounsel in your own ways.

15 And your hearts are not satisfied. And ye obey not the truth, but have ᵃpleasure in unrighteousness.

16 Wo unto you ᵃrich men, that will not ᵇgive your substance to the ᶜpoor, for your ᵈriches will canker your souls; and this shall be your lamentation in the day of visitation, and of judgment, and of indignation: The ᵉharvest is past, the summer is ended, and my soul is not saved!

17 Wo unto you ᵃpoor men, whose hearts are not broken, whose spirits are not contrite, and whose bellies are not satisfied, and whose hands are not stayed from laying hold upon

3a TG Disobedience; Obedience.
  b D&C 1: 14; 50: 8; 64: 35 (35–36).
4a Num. 14: 34; Jer. 18: 10 (6–10); D&C 19: 5; 58: 32 (31–33); 75: 6.
  b TG Rebellion.
5a D&C 31: 1; 52: 22; 75: 31.
6a D&C 52: 32.
  b TG Stiffneckedness.
8a TG Pride.

b TG Selfishness.
10a D&C 51: 5.
  b TG Apostasy of Individuals.
11a 2 Ne. 9: 16.
14a Mosiah 1: 2.
  TG Forgiveness.
  c Moses 6: 43.
15a Luke 21: 34.
16a Jer. 17: 11; Luke 21: 1 (1–4); 2 Ne. 9: 30; Mosiah 4: 23; D&C 84: 112. TG Treasure.

b TG Almsgiving; Generosity.
  c Prov. 14: 20 (20, 31); Alma 5: 55 (54–56); Hel. 6: 39 (39–40). TG Poor.
  d Ps. 62: 10; James 5: 3; Alma 5: 53 (53–56).
  e Jer. 8: 20; D&C 45: 2.
17a Ex. 23: 3 (1–3); Mosiah 4: 25 (24–27); D&C 42: 42; 68: 30 (30–32).

other men's goods, whose eyes are full of [b]greediness, and who will not [f]labor with your own hands!

18 But blessed are the [a]poor who are pure in heart, whose hearts are broken, and whose spirits are [b]contrite, for they shall see the [c]kingdom of God coming in power and great glory unto their deliverance; for the fatness of the [d]earth shall be theirs.

19 For behold, the Lord shall come, and his [a]recompense shall be with him, and he shall [b]reward every man, and the poor shall rejoice;

20 And their generations shall [a]inherit the earth from generation to generation, forever and ever. And now I make an end of speaking unto you. Even so. Amen.

SECTION 57

Revelation given through Joseph Smith the Prophet, in Zion, Jackson County, Missouri, July 20, 1831. HC 1: 189–190. In compliance with the Lord's command (Section 52), the elders had journeyed from Kirtland to Missouri with many varied experiences and some opposition. In contemplating the state of the Lamanites and the lack of civilization, refinement, and religion among the people generally, the Prophet exclaimed in yearning prayer: "When will the wilderness blossom as the rose? When will Zion be built up in her glory, and where will thy Temple stand, unto which all nations shall come in the last days?" Subsequently he received this revelation.

1–3, Independence, Missouri, is the place for the City of Zion and the temple; 4–7, The saints are to purchase lands and receive inheritances in that area; 8–16, Sidney Gilbert is to establish a store, W. W. Phelps is to be a printer, and Oliver Cowdery is to edit material for publication.

HEARKEN, O ye elders of my church, saith the Lord your God, who have assembled yourselves together, according to my commandments, in this land, which is the [a]land of [b]Missouri, which is the [b]land which

I have appointed and [c]consecrated for the [d]gathering of the saints.

2 Wherefore, this is the [a]land of promise, and the [b]place for the city of Zion.

3 And thus saith the Lord your God, if you will receive wisdom here is wisdom. Behold, the place which is now called Independence is the [a]center place; and a spot for the [b]temple is lying westward, upon a lot which is not far from the court-house.

4 Wherefore, it is wisdom that the land should be [a]purchased by the

---

17b TG Covetousness.
  c TG Labor; Laziness.
18a Ps. 35: 10; 86: 1; 109:
    31; Isa. 25: 4; Matt.
    5: 3 (3, 8); Luke 6: 20;
    3 Ne. 12: 3. TG Poor.
  b TG Contrite Heart;
    Humility; Meekness.
  c TG Kingdom of God,
    on Earth.
  d TG Earth, Destiny of.
19a Prov. 11: 31; Rev. 22:
    12; D&C 1: 10.

  b TG Reward.
20a Isa. 29: 19; Matt. 5: 5;
    D&C 45: 58; 57: 5.
57 1a D&C 52: 3 (3, 42).
  b D&C 29: 8 (7–8); 45:
    66 (64–66); 52: 2
    (2, 42); 58: 1; 103:
    24.
  c D&C 61: 17.
  d TG Mission of Latter-
    day Saints.
2a D&C 48: 5; 52: 5

    (5, 42).
  b D&C 28: 9; 42: 9 (9,
    62); 103: 24 (22–24).
  c D&C 62: 4; 78: 3.
    TG Zion.
3a D&C 69: 6.
  b D&C 58: 57; 84: 3
    (3–5, 31); 97: 10 (10–
    20); 124: 51 (49–51).
4a D&C 48: 4.
    TG Jerusalem, New;
    Zion.

saints, and also every tract lying westward, even unto the line running directly ᵇbetween Jew and Gentile;

5 And also every tract bordering by the prairies, inasmuch as my disciples are enabled to ᵃbuy lands. Behold, this is wisdom, that they may ᵇobtain it for an everlasting inheritance.

6 And let my servant Sidney Gilbert stand in the office to which I have appointed him, to receive moneys, to be an ᵃagent unto the church, to buy land in all the regions round about, inasmuch as can be done in righteousness, and as wisdom shall direct.

7 And let my servant ᵃEdward Partridge stand in the ᵇoffice to which I have appointed him, and ᶜdivide unto the saints their inheritance, even as I have commanded; and also those whom he has appointed to assist him.

8 And again, verily I say unto you, let my servant Sidney Gilbert plant himself in this place, and establish a ᵃstore, that he may sell goods ᵇwithout fraud, that he may obtain money to buy ᶜlands for the good of the saints, and that he may obtain whatsoever things the disciples may need to plant them in their inheritance.

9 And also let my servant Sidney Gilbert obtain a license—behold here is ᵃwisdom, and whoso readeth let him ᵇunderstand—that he may send goods also unto the people,

even by whom he will as clerks employed in his service;

10 And thus provide for my saints, that my gospel may be preached unto those who sit in ᵃdarkness and in the region and ᵇshadow of death.

11 And again, verily I say unto you, let my servant ᵃWilliam W. Phelps be planted in this place, and be established as a ᵇprinter unto the church.

12 And lo, if the world receive his writings—behold here is wisdom—let him obtain whatsoever he can obtain in righteousness, for the good of the saints.

13 And let my servant ᵃOliver Cowdery assist him, even as I have commanded, in whatsoever place I shall appoint unto him, to copy, and to correct, and select, that all things may be right before me, as it shall be proved by the Spirit through him.

14 And thus let those of whom I have spoken be planted in the land of Zion, as speedily as can be, with their ᵃfamilies, to do those things even as I have spoken.

15 And now concerning the gathering—Let the bishop and the agent make preparations for those families which have been commanded to come to this land, as soon as possible, and plant them in their inheritance.

16 And unto the residue of both elders and members further directions shall be given hereafter. Even so. Amen.

4b ıᴇ by metonymy
" Jew" here refers to the Lamanites, and "Gentile" to the white settlers.
5a D&C 42: 35; 58: 49 (49–51); 101: 70 (68–72); 103: 23 (22–24).
 b Matt. 5: 5; D&C 56: 20; 59: 2. ᴛɢ Lands of Inheritance.
6a D&C 53: 4; 64: 18;

70: 11.
7a D&C 52: 24; 58: 14 (14, 19, 24).
 b D&C 58: 40 (40–41); 61: 7 (7–12).
 c D&C 41: 9 (9–11); 51: 1 (1–20); 58: 17 (14–18).
8a D&C 63: 42; 64: 26.
 b ᴛɢ Honesty.
 c D&C 48: 4.
9a Rev. 13: 18.

 b Matt. 24: 15.
10a Matt. 4: 16.
 ᴛɢ Darkness, Spiritual.
 b Job 3: 5; Ps. 23: 4.
11a D&C 58: 40; 61: 7 (7–9); 70: 1.
 b D&C 58: 37 (37, 40–41).
13a See Index for many references to Oliver Cowdery.
14a ᴛɢ Family.

SECTION 58

Revelation given through Joseph Smith the Prophet, in Zion, Jackson County, Missouri, August 1, 1831. HC 1: 190–195. On the first Sabbath after the arrival of the Prophet and party in Jackson County, Missouri, a religious service was held and two members were received by baptism. During that week, members of the Colesville saints from the Thompson Branch and others arrived. Many were eager to learn the will of the Lord concerning them in the new place of gathering.

1–5, *Those who endure tribulation shall be crowned with glory; 6–12, The saints are to prepare for the marriage of the Lamb and the Supper of the Lord; 13–18, Bishops are judges in Israel; 19–23, The saints are to obey the laws of the land; 24–29, Men should use their agency to do good; 30–33, The Lord commands and revokes; 34–43, To repent, men must confess and forsake their sins; 44–58, The saints are to purchase their inheritance and gather in Missouri; 59–65, The gospel must be preached unto every creature.*

HEARKEN, O ye elders of my church, and give ^aear to my word, and learn of me what I will concerning you, and also concerning ^bthis land unto which I have sent you.

2 For verily I say unto you, blessed is he that ^akeepeth my commandments, whether in life or in ^bdeath; and he that is ^cfaithful in ^dtribulation, the ^ereward of the same is greater in the kingdom of heaven.

3 Ye cannot behold with your natural ^aeyes, for the present time, the design of your God concerning those things which shall come hereafter, and the ^bglory which shall follow after much tribulation.

4 For after much ^atribulation come the ^bblessings. Wherefore the day cometh that ye shall be ^ccrowned with much ^dglory; the hour is not yet, but is nigh at hand.

5 Remember this, which I tell you before, that you may ^alay it to heart, and receive that which is to follow.

6 Behold, verily I say unto you, for this cause I have sent you—that you might be obedient, and that your hearts might be ^aprepared to ^bbear ^ctestimony of the things which are to come;

7 And also that you might be honored in laying the foundation, and in bearing record of the land upon which the ^aZion of God shall stand;

8 And also that a feast of fat things might be prepared for the ^apoor; yea, a feast of fat things, of wine on the ^blees well refined, that the earth may know that the mouths of the prophets shall not fail;

9 Yea, a supper of the house of the Lord, well prepared, unto which all ^anations shall be invited.

10 First, the rich and the learned, the wise and the noble;

11 And after that cometh the day of my power; then shall the ^apoor,

---

58 1a Isa. 50: 5 (5–7).
  b D&C 57: 1 (1–8).
2a Ps. 19: 11 (9–11);
    Mosiah 2: 22.
  b 1 Pet. 4: 6.
  c 2 Thes. 1: 4.
    TG Steadfastness.
  d TG Adversity.
  e TG Reward.
3a TG God, Privilege of Seeing.

  b 1 Pet. 1: 11.
4a Ps. 30: 5; D&C 101: 2
    (2–7); 103: 12 (11–14);
    109: 76.
  b TG Blessings.
  c TG Exaltation.
  d Rom. 8: 18; D&C 63:
    66; 136: 31.
5a Deut. 11: 18.

6a 3 Ne. 17: 3; D&C 29:
    8; 132: 3.
  b Isa. 43: 10 (10–12);
    44: 8.
  c TG Testimony.
7a TG Zion.
8a Ps. 132: 15 (13–16).
    TG Poor.
  b Isa. 25: 6.
9a TG Nations.
11a TG Poor.

the lame, and the blind, and the deaf, come in unto the *b*marriage of the Lamb, and partake of the *c*supper of the Lord, prepared for the great day to come.

12 Behold, I, the Lord, have spoken it.

13 And that the *a*testimony might go forth from Zion, yea, from the mouth of the city of the heritage of God—

14 Yea, for this cause I have sent you hither, and have selected my servant *a*Edward Partridge, and have appointed unto him his mission in this land.

15 But if he repent not of his sins, which are *a*unbelief and blindness of *b*heart, let him take heed lest he *c*fall.

16 Behold his mission is given unto him, and it shall not be given again.

17 And whoso standeth in this mission is appointed to be a *a*judge in Israel, like as it was in ancient days, to *b*divide the lands of the heritage of God unto his *c*children;

18 And to judge his people by the testimony of the just, and by the assistance of his *a*counselors, according to the laws of the kingdom which are given by the *b*prophets of God.

19 For verily I say unto you, my law shall be kept on this land.

20 Let no man think he is *a*ruler; but let God rule him that judgeth, according to the counsel of his own *b*will, or, in other words, him that counseleth or sitteth upon the judgment seat.

21 Let no man break the *a*laws of the land, for he that keepeth the laws of God hath no need to break the laws of the land.

22 Wherefore, be *a*subject to the powers that be, *b*until he reigns whose right it is to reign, and subdues all enemies under his feet.

23 Behold, the *a*laws which ye have received from my hand are the laws of the church, and in this light ye shall hold them forth. Behold, here is wisdom.

24 And now, as I spake concerning my servant Edward Partridge, this land is the land of his *a*residence, and those whom he has appointed for his counselors; and also the land of the residence of him whom I have appointed to keep my *b*storehouse;

25 Wherefore, let them bring their families to this land, as they shall *a*counsel between themselves and me.

26 For behold, it is not meet that I should command in all things; for he that is *a*compelled in all things, the same is a *b*slothful and not a wise servant; wherefore he receiveth no reward.

27 Verily I say, men should be *a*anxiously engaged in a good cause, and do many things of their own free will, and bring to pass much righteousness;

28 For the power is in them, wherein they are *a*agents unto themselves. And inasmuch as men do good they shall in nowise lose their *b*reward.

11b Matt. 22: 2 (1–14); Rev. 19: 9; D&C 65: 3.
c Luke 14: 16 (16–24).
13a Micah 4: 2.
  TG Testimony.
14a D&C 57: 7; 60: 10.
15a TG Doubt.
  b TG Hardheartedness.
  c 1 Cor. 10: 12.
17a Deut. 16: 18; D&C 64: 40; 107: 72 (72–74). TG Bishop.
  b D&C 41: 9 (9–11); 51: 1 (1–21); 57: 7.
  c TG Sons and Daughters of God.
18a TG Counselors.

b TG Prophets, Mission of.
20a TG Unrighteous Dominion.
  b TG God, Will of.
21a Matt. 17: 24 (24–27); Luke 20: 22 (22–26); D&C 20: 1; 51: 6; 98: 9 (4–10); A of F 12. TG Citizenship; Governments.
22a Rom. 13: 1 (1–7). TG Governments; Submissiveness.
  b Gen. 49: 10; Ezek. 21: 27; Zech. 9: 10; D&C 76: 63. TG Jesus Christ, Messiah; Jesus

Christ, Millennial Reign.
23a D&C 42: 2 (2–8).
24a D&C 41: 9; 72: 6.
  b D&C 51: 13; 70: 7 (7–11).
25a TG Guidance, Divine.
26a TG Initiative.
  b Matt. 24: 45 (45–51); D&C 107: 100 (99–100). TG Apathy; Laziness.
27a TG Dedication; Diligence; Good Works; Industry; Zeal.
28a Amos 5: 14. TG Agency.
  b TG Reward.

29 But he that "doeth not anything until he is commanded, and receiveth a commandment with bdoubtful heart, and keepeth it with slothfulness, the same is cdamned.

30 Who am I that "made man, saith the Lord, that will hold him bguiltless that obeys not my commandments?

31 Who am I, saith the Lord, that have "promised and have not fulfilled?

32 I command and men aobey not; I brevoke and they receive not the blessing.

33 Then they "say in their hearts: This is not the work of the Lord, for his promises are not fulfilled. But wo unto such, for their breward lurketh cbeneath, and not from above.

34 And now I give unto you further directions concerning this land.

35 It is wisdom in me that my servant Martin Harris should be an example unto the church, in alaying his moneys before the bishop of the church.

36 And also, this is a law unto every man that cometh unto this land to receive an inheritance; and he shall do with his moneys according as the law directs.

37 And it is wisdom also that there should be lands purchased in Independence, for the place of the storehouse, and also for the house of the aprinting.

38 And other directions concerning my servant Martin Harris shall be given him of the Spirit, that he may receive his inheritance as seemeth him good;

39 And let him repent of his sins, for he seeketh the apraise of the world.

40 And also let my servant aWilliam W. Phelps stand in the office to which I have appointed him, and receive his inheritance in the land;

41 And also he hath need to repent, for I, the Lord, am not well pleased with him, for he seeketh to excel, and he is not sufficiently meek before me.

42 Behold, he who has arepented of his bsins, the same is cforgiven, and I, the Lord, remember them no more.

43 By this ye may know if a man repenteth of his sins—behold, he will aconfess them and bforsake them.

44 And now, verily, I say concerning the residue of the elders of my achurch, the time has not yet come, for many years, for them to receive their binheritance in this land, except they desire it through the prayer of faith, only as it shall be appointed unto them of the Lord.

45 For, behold, they shall apush the people together from the bends of the earth.

46 Wherefore, assemble yourselves together; and they who are not appointed to stay in this land, let them preach the gospel in the regions round about; and after that let them return to their homes.

47 Let them preach by the way, and abear testimony of the truth in all places, and call upon the rich, the high and the low, and the poor to repent.

48 And let them build up achurches, inasmuch as the inhabitants of the earth will repent.

49 And let there be an agent

29a Moro. 7: 6 (6-9).
  b TG Doubt.
  c TG Damnation.
30a Isa. 45: 9 (9-10);
  Hel. 12: 6 (6-22).
  b Ex. 20: 7; Mosiah 13: 15; Morm. 7: 7.
31a D&C 1: 37 (37-38); 82: 10.
32a 1 Sam. 28: 18.
  b Jer. 18: 10 (6-10); D&C 19: 5; 54: 4; 56: 4 (3-4).

33a 1 Ne. 15: 9 (7-11).
  b TG Reward.
  c D&C 29: 45.
35a D&C 42: 31 (30-32).
37a D&C 57: 11 (11-12).
39a 2 Ne. 26: 29; D&C 121: 35 (34-37).
40a D&C 57: 11; 61: 7 (7-9); 70: 1.
42a TG Repentance.
  b Ps. 25: 7.
  c Isa. 1: 18; Jer. 31: 34. TG Forgiveness.
43a Num. 5: 7 (6-10);

    D&C 19: 20; 64: 7.
    TG Confession.
  b D&C 82: 7.
44a TG Jesus Christ, Head of the Church.
  b TG Lands of Inheritance.
45a Deut. 33: 17.
  b Israel, Gathering of.
47a TG Jer. 19: 37; 63: 37; 68: 8; 71: 7.
48a IE branches of the Church.

appointed by the voice of the church, unto the church in Ohio, to receive moneys to ^apurchase lands in ^bZion.

50 And I give unto my servant Sidney Rigdon a commandment, that he shall ^awrite a description of the land of Zion, and a statement of the will of God, as it shall be made known by the Spirit unto him;

51 And an epistle and subscription, to be presented unto all the churches to obtain moneys, to be put into the hands of the bishop, of himself or the agent, as seemeth him good or as he shall direct, to ^apurchase lands for an ^binheritance for the children of God.

52 For, behold, verily I say unto you, the Lord willeth that the disciples and the children of men should open their hearts, even to purchase this whole region of country, as soon as time will permit.

53 Behold, here is wisdom. Let them do this lest they ^areceive none inheritance, save it be by the shedding of blood.

54 And again, inasmuch as there is land obtained, let there be workmen sent forth of all kinds unto this land, to labor for the saints of God.

55 Let all these things be done in ^aorder; and let the privileges of the lands be made known from time to time, by the bishop or the agent of the church.

56 And let the work of the ^agathering be not in ^bhaste, nor by flight; but let it be done as it shall be ^ccounseled by the elders of the church at the conferences, according to the knowledge which they receive from time to time.

57 And let my servant Sidney Rigdon ^aconsecrate and ^bdedicate this land, and the spot for the ^ctemple, unto the Lord.

58 And let a conference meeting be called; and after that let my servants Sidney Rigdon and Joseph Smith, Jun., return, and also Oliver Cowdery with them, to accomplish the residue of the work which I have appointed unto them in their own land, and the residue as shall be ^aruled by the conferences.

59 And let no man return from this land except he bear ^arecord by the way, of that which he knows and most assuredly believes.

60 Let that which has been bestowed upon ^aZiba Peterson be taken from him; and let him stand as a member in the church, and labor with his own hands, with the brethren, until he is sufficiently ^bchastened for all his sins; for he confesseth them not, and he thinketh to hide them.

61 Let the residue of the elders of this church, who are coming to this land, some of whom are exceedingly blessed even above measure, also hold a ^aconference upon this land.

62 And let my servant Edward Partridge direct the conference which shall be held by them.

63 And let them also return, preaching the gospel by the way, bearing record of the things which are revealed unto them.

64 For, verily, the sound must go forth from this place into all the world, and unto the uttermost parts of the earth—the gospel must be ^apreached unto every creature, with ^bsigns following them that believe.

65 And behold the Son of Man ^acometh. Amen.

49a D&C 42: 35; 57: 5
     (5–7); 101: 70 (68–
     74); 103: 23 (22–24).
  b TG Zion.
50a D&C 63: 56 (55–56);
     100: 9.
51a D&C 51: 8 (8–13); 84:
     104.
  b D&C 25: 12; 52: 42 (2,
     5, 42).
53a D&C 63: 29 (27–31);
     101: 70 (70–75).

55a D&C 101: 68.
  TG Order.
56a D&C 63: 24; 101: 68.
  b TG Haste; Rashness.
  c D&C 72: 24.
57a D&C 52: 2; 103: 35;
     105: 15.
  b TG Dedication.
  c D&C 57: 3; 84: 3 (3–5),
     31; 97: 10 (10–20);
     124: 51 (49–51).
58a TG Church Organiza-

tion; Common Consent.
59a TG Mission of Latter-
     day Saints; Testimony.
60a D&C 32: 3.
  b TG Chastening; For-
     giveness; Repentance.
61a TG Meetings.
64a TG Mission of Latter-
     day Saints.
  b TG Holy Ghost, Gifts
     of; Miracles; Signs.
65a D&C 1: 12.

SECTION 59

Revelation given through Joseph Smith the Prophet, in Zion, Jackson County, Missouri, August 7, 1831. HC 1: 196–201. Preceding his record of this revelation, the Prophet writes descriptively of the land of Zion wherein the people were then assembled. The land was consecrated, as the Lord had directed, and the site for the future temple was dedicated. The Lord makes these commandments especially applicable to the saints in Zion.

1–4, *The faithful saints in Zion shall be blessed;* 5–8, *They are to love and serve the Lord and keep his commandments;* 9–19, *By keeping the Lord's day holy, the saints are blessed temporally and spiritually;* 20–24, *The righteous are promised peace in this world and eternal life in the world to come.*

BEHOLD, blessed, saith the Lord, are they who have come up unto this land with an ᵃeye single to my glory, according to my commandments.

2 For those that live shall ᵃinherit the earth, and those that ᵇdie shall rest from all their labors, and their works shall follow them; and they shall receive a ᶜcrown in the ᵈmansions of my Father, which I have prepared for them.

3 Yea, blessed are they whose feet stand upon the land of Zion, who have obeyed my gospel; for they shall receive for their reward the good things of the earth, and it shall bring forth in its ᶜstrength.

4 And they shall also be crowned with blessings from above, yea, and with ᵃcommandments not a few, and with ᵇrevelations in their time—they that are ᶜfaithful and ᵈdiligent before me.

5 Wherefore, I give unto them a commandment, saying thus: Thou shalt ᵃlove the Lord thy God with all thy ᵇheart, with all thy might, mind, and strength; and in the name of Jesus Christ thou shalt ᶜserve him.

6 Thou shalt ᵃlove thy ᵇneighbor as thyself. Thou shalt not ᶜsteal; neither commit ᵈadultery, nor ᵉkill, nor do anything ᶠlike unto it.

7 Thou shalt ᵃthank the Lord thy God in all things.

8 Thou shalt offer a ᵃsacrifice unto the Lord thy God in ᵇrighteousness, even that of a broken heart and a ᶜcontrite spirit.

9 And that thou mayest more fully keep thyself ᵃunspotted from the

59 1a Matt. 6: 22 (22–24).
2a Matt. 5: 5; D&C 57: 5; 63: 20 (20, 48–49).
 b Isa. 57: 1 (1–2); Rev. 14: 13. TG Paradise.
 c TG Celestial Glory; Exaltation.
 d Ps. 65: 4; John 14: 2; D&C 72: 4; 76: 111; 81: 6; 98: 18; 106: 8.
3a Gen. 4: 12; Moses 4: 23 (23–24); 5: 37.
 TG Strength.
4a Alma 29: 9.
 b D&C 42: 61; 76: 7; 98: 12; 101: 32; 121: 28 (26–33).
 TG Revelation.

 c TG Steadfastness; Worthiness.
 d TG Diligence.
5a Deut. 11: 1; Matt. 22: 37; Mosiah 2: 4; Moro. 10: 32; D&C 20: 19. TG God, Love of; Love.
 b TG Heart.
 c TG Service; Worship.
6a TG Love.
 b Prov. 11: 12 (12–17). TG Fellowshipping; Neighbor.
 c TG Stealing.
 d TG Adultery; Chastity.
 e TG Murder.
 f Ex. 22: 19; Lev. 18:

22; 1 Cor. 6: 9; 1 Tim. 1: 10.
7a Ezra 3: 11; Ps. 34: 1 (1–3); 92: 1; Alma 37: 37; Ether 6: 9; D&C 46: 32.
 TG Communication; Thanksgiving.
8a TG Jesus Christ, Types of, in Memory; Self-sacrifice.
 b TG Righteousness.
 c TG Contrite Heart; Poor in Spirit.
9a James 1: 27.
 TG Abstinence; Self-mastery.

world, thou shalt go to the house of [b]prayer and offer up thy [c]sacraments upon thy [d]holy day;

10 For verily this is a [a]day appointed unto you to rest from your labors, and to pay thy devotions unto the Most High;

11 Nevertheless thy [a]vows shall be offered up in righteousness on all days and at all times;

12 But remember that on this, the [a]Lord's day, thou shalt offer thine [b]oblations and thy sacraments unto the Most High, [c]confessing thy sins unto thy brethren, and before the Lord.

13 And on this day thou shalt do none other thing, only let thy food be prepared with singleness of heart that thy [a]fasting may be perfect, or in other words, that thy [b]joy may be full.

14 Verily, this is fasting and prayer, or in other words, rejoicing and prayer.

15 And inasmuch as ye do these things with [a]thanksgiving, with [b]cheerful [c]hearts and countenances, not with [d]much [e]laughter, for this is sin, but with a glad heart and a cheerful countenance—

16 Verily I say, that inasmuch as ye do this, the [a]fulness of the earth is yours, the beasts of the field and the fowls of the air, and that which climbeth upon the trees and walketh upon the earth;

17 Yea, and the herb, and the [a]good things which come of the earth, whether for food or for [b]raiment, or for houses, or for barns, or for orchards, or for gardens, or for vineyards;

18 Yea, all things which come of the earth, in the season thereof, are made for the [a]benefit and the [b]use of man, both to please the eye and to [c]gladden the heart;

19 Yea, for [a]food and for raiment, for taste and for smell, to [b]strengthen the body and to enliven the soul.

20 And it pleaseth God that he hath given all these things unto man; for unto this end were they made to be used, with judgment, not to [a]excess, neither by extortion.

21 And in nothing doth man [a]offend God, or against none is his [b]wrath [c]kindled, save those who [d]confess not his hand in all things, and [e]obey not his commandments.

22 Behold, this is according to the law and the prophets; wherefore, trouble me no more concerning this matter.

23 But learn that he who doeth the works of [a]righteousness shall receive his [b]reward, even [c]peace in this world, and [d]eternal life in the world to come.

24 I, the Lord, have spoken it, and the Spirit beareth record. Amen.

9b TG Assembly for Worship; Prayer.
  c D&C 62:4.
    TG Sacrament.
  d Lev. 19:3; 23:3;
    Alma 1:26 (26–27);
    D&C 68:29.
    TG Sabbath.
10a Ex. 35:2; Lev. 23:25.
    TG Rest; Worship.
11a TG Commitment; Vows.
12a Neh. 8:10; Rev. 1:10.
  b IE offerings, whether of time, talents, or means, in service of God and fellowman.
    TG Sacrifice.
  c TG Confession.
13a IE hungering and thirsting after

righteousness; cf.
    Matt. 5:6; 3 Ne. 12:6.
    TG Fasting.
  b TG Joy.
15a TG Thanksgiving.
  b Ex. 25:2 (1–7); 35:5;
    D&C 64:22 (22, 34);
    97:8. TG Cheerfulness.
  c Prov. 17:22.
  d 1 Pet. 4:3; D&C 88:69.
  e TG Laughter.
16a TG Abundant Life.
17a Gen. 1:31; Moro. 7:
    12; Moses 2:31.
  b D&C 70:16 (15–16).
18a TG Earth, Purpose of;
    Meat.
  b Gen. 1:29; 9:3 (3–4).
  c TG Happiness.

19a TG Food.
  b TG Health.
20a TG Temperance.
21a TG Offenses.
  b TG God, Indignation of.
  c TG Provoking.
  d Neh. 12:24; Job 1:
    21; Ps. 97:12;
    Mosiah 2:20 (20–22);
    D&C 62:7.
  e TG Ingratitude.
  e TG Disobedience.
23a TG Righteousness.
  b TG Blessings; Reward.
  c Matt. 11:29 (28–30).
  d TG Happiness; Objectives; Peace; Peace of God.
  d D&C 14:7.

SECTION 60

Revelation given through Joseph Smith the Prophet, in Jackson County, Missouri, August 8, 1831. HC 1: 201-202. On this occasion the elders who had been appointed to return to the East desired to know how they should proceed, and by what route and manner they should travel.

1-9, *The elders are to preach the gospel in the congregations of the wicked;* 10-14, *They should not idle away their time, nor bury their talents;* 15-17, *They may wash their feet as a testimony against those who reject the gospel.*

BEHOLD, thus saith the Lord unto the elders of his church, who are to return speedily to the land from whence they came: Behold, it pleaseth me, that you have come up hither;

2 But with some I am not well pleased, for they will not open their ªmouths, but they hide the ᵇtalent which I have given unto them, because of the ᶜfear of man. Wo unto such, for mine ᵈanger is ᵉkindled against them.

3 And it shall come to pass, if they are not more faithful unto me, it shall be ªtaken away, even that which they have.

4 For I, the Lord, ªrule in the heavens above, and among the ᵇarmies of the earth; and in the day when I shall make up my ᶜjewels, all men shall know what it is that bespeaketh the power of God.

5 But, verily, I will speak unto you concerning your journey unto the land from whence you came. Let there be a craft made, or bought, as ªseemeth you good, it mattereth

not unto me, and take your journey speedily for the place which is called St. Louis.

6 And from thence let my servants, Sidney Rigdon, Joseph Smith, Jun., and Oliver Cowdery, take their journey for Cincinnati;

7 And in this place let them lift up their voice and declare my word with loud voices, without wrath or ªdoubting, lifting up holy hands upon them. For I am able to make you ᵇholy, and your sins are ᶜforgiven you.

8 And let the residue take their journey from St. Louis, ªtwo by two, and preach the word, not in haste, among the congregations of the wicked, until they return to the churches from whence they came.

9 And all this for the good of the ªchurches; for this intent have I sent them.

10 And let my servant ªEdward Partridge impart of the ᵇmoney which I have given him, a portion unto mine elders who are commanded to return;

11 And he that is able, let him return it by the way of the agent; and he that is not, of him it is not required.

12 And now I speak of the residue who are to come unto this land.

13 Behold, they have been sent to preach my gospel among the congre-

60 2a Ex. 4: 10 (10-12);
    Jer. 1: 6 (6-9);
    Luke 8: 16 (16-18);
    Eph. 6: 20 (19-20).
  b TG Talents.
  c Matt. 25: 25 (24-30).
    TG Fearfulness; Peer
    Influence.
  d TG Anger; God,
    Indignation of.

  e TG Provoking.
3a Matt. 25: 29 (29-30);
    Mark 4: 25; D&C 1: 33.
4a Judg. 8: 23 (22-23);
    Hel. 12: 6.
  b 2 Cor. 25: 8.
    TG War.
  c Isa. 62: 3; Zech. 9: 16;
    Mal. 3: 17; D&C
    101: 3.

5a TG Agency; Initiative.
7a TG Doubt.
  b TG Holiness.
  c TG Forgiveness.
8a Mark 6: 7.
9a D&C 51: 10.
10a D&C 58: 14 (14, 19,
    24); 64: 17.
  b D&C 51: 8 (8-13).

gations of the wicked; wherefore, I give unto them a commandment, thus: Thou shalt not *a*idle away thy time, neither shalt thou bury thy *b*talent that it may not be known.

14 And after thou hast come up unto the land of Zion, and hast proclaimed my word, thou shalt speedily return, proclaiming my word among the congregations of the wicked, not in *a*haste, neither in *b*wrath nor with *c*strife.

15 And shake off the *a*dust of thy feet against those who receive thee not, not in their presence, lest thou *b*provoke them, but in secret; and *c*wash thy feet, as a testimony against them in the day of judgment.

16 Behold, this is sufficient for you, and the will of him who hath sent you.

17 And by the mouth of my servant Joseph Smith, Jun., it shall be made known concerning Sidney Rigdon and Oliver Cowdery. The residue hereafter. Even so. Amen.

SECTION 61

Revelation given through Joseph Smith the Prophet, on the bank of the Missouri River, McIlwaine's Bend, August 12, 1831. HC 1: 202–205. On their return trip to Kirtland the Prophet and ten elders had traveled down the Missouri River in canoes. On the third day of the journey many dangers were experienced. Elder William W. Phelps, in daylight vision, saw the destroyer riding in power upon the face of the waters.

1–12, The Lord has decreed many destructions upon the waters; 13–22, The waters were cursed by John, and the destroyer rideth upon their face; 23–29, Some have power to command the waters; 30–35, Elders are to journey two by two and preach the gospel; 36–39, They are to prepare for the coming of the Son of Man.

BEHOLD, and hearken unto the voice of him who has all *a*power, who is from everlasting to everlasting, even *b*Alpha and Omega, the beginning and the end.

2 Behold, verily thus saith the Lord unto you, O ye elders of my church, who are assembled upon this spot, whose sins are now forgiven you, for I, the Lord, *a*forgive sins, and am *b*merciful unto those who *c*confess their sins with humble hearts;

3 But verily I say unto you, that it is not needful for this whole company of mine elders to be moving swiftly upon the waters, whilst the inhabitants on either side are perishing in unbelief.

4 Nevertheless, I suffered it that ye might bear record; behold, there are many dangers upon the waters, and more especially hereafter;

5 For I, the Lord, have decreed in mine anger many destructions upon the waters; yea, and especially upon these waters.

6 Nevertheless, all flesh is in mine hand, and he that is faithful among you shall not *a*perish by the waters.

7 Wherefore, it is expedient that

13*a* D&C 42: 42.
  TG Apathy;
  Idleness; Laziness;
  Priesthood, Magnifying Callings within;
  Procrastination;
  Waste; Zeal.
  b Matt. 25: 25 (14–30);
  D&C 82: 18.

14*a* TG Rashness.
  b Prov. 14: 29.
  c TG Strife.
15*a* Matt. 10: 14; Luke
  9: 5; Acts 13: 51; 18:
  6 (5–6); D&C 24: 15;
  75: 20; 84: 92 (92–95).

  b TG Provoking.
  c TG Washing.
61 1*a* TG God, Power of.
  b D&C 19: 1.
  2*a* Mosiah 4: 10 (10–11).
  TG Forgiveness.
  b TG God, Mercy of.
  c TG Confession.
  6*a* TG Protection, Divine.

my servant Sidney Gilbert and my servant ᵃWilliam W. Phelps be in haste upon their errand and mission.

8 Nevertheless, I would not suffer that ye should part until you were ᵃchastened for all your sins, that you might be one, that you might not perish in ᵇwickedness;

9 But now, verily I say, it behooveth me that ye should part. Wherefore let my servants Sidney Gilbert and William W. Phelps take their former company, and let them take their journey in haste that they may fill their mission, and through faith shall overcome;

10 And inasmuch as they are ᵃfaithful they shall be preserved, and I, the Lord, will be ᵇwith them.

11 And let the residue take that which is needful for clothing.

12 Let my servant Sidney Gilbert take that which is not needful with him, as you shall agree.

13 And now, behold, for your ᵃgood I gave unto you a ᵇcommandment concerning these things; and I, the Lord, will reason with you as with men in days of old.

14 Behold, I, the Lord, in the beginning blessed the ᵃwaters; but in the last days, by the mouth of my servant John, I ᵇcursed the waters.

15 Wherefore, the days will come that no flesh shall be safe upon the waters.

16 And it shall be said in days to come that none is able to go up to the land of Zion upon the waters, but he that is upright in heart.

17 And, as I, the Lord, in the beginning ᵃcursed the land, even so in the last days have I ᵇblessed it, in its time, for the use of my saints, that they may partake the fatness thereof.

18 And now I give unto you a commandment that what I say unto one

I say unto all, that you shall forewarn your brethren concerning these waters, that they come not in journeying upon them, lest their faith fail and they are caught in snares;

19 I, the Lord, have decreed, and the destroyer rideth upon the face thereof, and I revoke not the decree.

20 I, the Lord, was ᵃangry with you yesterday, but today mine anger is turned away.

21 Wherefore, let those concerning whom I have spoken, that should take their journey in haste—again I say unto you, let them take their journey in haste.

22 And it mattereth not unto me, after a little, if it so be that they fill their mission, whether they go by water or by land; let this be as it is made known unto them ᵃaccording to their judgments hereafter.

23 And now, concerning my servants, Sidney Rigdon, Joseph Smith, Jun., and Oliver Cowdery, let them come not again upon the waters, save it be upon the canal, while journeying unto their homes; or in other words they shall not come upon the waters to journey, save upon the canal.

24 Behold, I, the Lord, have appointed a way for the journeying of my saints; and behold, this is the way—that after they leave the canal they shall journey by land, inasmuch as they are commanded to journey and go up unto the land of Zion;

25 And they shall do ᵃlike unto the children of Israel, ᵇpitching their tents by the way.

26 And, behold, this commandment you shall give unto all your brethren.

27 Nevertheless, unto whom is given ᵃpower to command the

7a D&C 57: 11 (6–12);
  58: 40 (40–41); 70: 1.
8a TG Chastening.
  b TG Wickedness.
10a Ps. 31: 23.
  b Matt. 28: 20.
13a Deut. 10: 13; D&C
  21: 6.

b TG Commandments of
  God.
14a Gen. 1: 20.
  b Rev. 8: 10 (8–11).
  TG Curse; Last Days.
17a Moses 4: 23.
  b D&C 57: 1 (1–5).

20a TG God, Indignation
  of; God, Love of.
22a TG Agency; Initiative.
25a Num. 9: 18.
  b Num. 2: 34 (32–34).
27a TG Holy Ghost, Gifts
  of; Priesthood, Power
  of.

waters, unto him it is given by the Spirit to know all his ways;

28 Wherefore, let him do as the Spirit of the living God commandeth him, whether upon the land or upon the waters, as it remaineth with me to do hereafter.

29 And unto you is given the course for the saints, or the way for the saints of the camp of the Lord, to journey.

30 And again, verily I say unto you, my servants, Sidney Rigdon, Joseph Smith, Jun., and Oliver Cowdery, shall not open their mouths in the ᵃcongregations of the wicked until they arrive at Cincinnati;

31 And in that place they shall lift up their voices unto God against that people, yea, unto him whose anger is ᵃkindled against their wickedness, a people who are well-nigh ᵇripened for destruction.

32 And from thence let them journey for the congregations of their brethren, for their labors even now are wanted more abundantly among them than among the congregations of the wicked.

33 And now, concerning the residue, let them journey and ᵃdeclare the word among the congregations of the wicked, inasmuch as it is given;

34 And inasmuch as they do this they shall ᵃrid their garments, and they shall be spotless before me.

35 And let them journey together, or ᵃtwo by two, as seemeth them good, only let my servant Reynolds Cahoon, and my servant Samuel H. Smith, with whom I am well pleased, be not separated until they return to their homes, and this for a wise purpose in me.

36 And now, verily I say unto you, and what I say unto one I say unto all, be of good ᵃcheer, ᵇlittle children; for I am in your ᶜmidst, and I have not ᵈforsaken you;

37 And inasmuch as you have humbled yourselves before me, the blessings of the ᵃkingdom are yours.

38 Gird up your loins and be ᵃwatchful and be sober, looking forth for the coming of the Son of Man, for he cometh in an hour you think not.

39 Pray always that you enter not into ᵃtemptation, that you may abide the day of his coming, whether in life or in death. Even so. Amen.

SECTION 62

Revelation given through Joseph Smith the Prophet, on the bank of the Missouri River at Chariton, Missouri, August 13, 1831. HC 1 : 205–206. On this day the Prophet and his group, who were on their way from Independence to Kirtland, met several elders who were on their way to the land of Zion, and, after joyful salutations, received this revelation.

1–3, Testimonies are recorded in heaven; 4–9, The elders are to travel and preach according to judgment and as directed by the Spirit.

BEHOLD, and hearken, O ye elders of my church, saith the Lord your God, even Jesus Christ, your ᵃadvocate, who knoweth the weakness of

---

30a Micah 6 : 10 (10–15);
  D&C 62 : 5; 68 : 1.
31a TG Provoking.
  b Alma 37 : 31; Hel. 13 :
  14; D&C 101 : 11.
33a TG Preaching.
34a 2 Ne. 9 : 44; Jacob 2 :
  2 (2, 16); Mosiah 2 : 28.

35a Mark 6 : 7; Luke 10 : 1;
  D&C 52 : 10; 62 : 5.
  TG Missionary Work.
36a TG Cheerfulness.
  b John 13 : 33.
  c Matt. 18 : 20; 28 : 20
  (19–20).
  d Isa. 41 : 17 (15–17);
  1 Ne. 21 : 15 (14–15).

37a D&C 50 : 35; 62 : 9.
38a TG Watchfulness.
39a TG Temptation.
62 1a D&C 45 : 3.
  TG Jesus Christ,
  Advocate; Jesus
  Christ, Relationships
  with the Father.

man and how to ^{b}succor them who are ^{c}tempted.

2 And verily mine eyes are upon those who have not as yet gone up unto the land of Zion; wherefore your mission is not yet full.

3 Nevertheless, ye are ^{a}blessed, for the ^{b}testimony which ye have borne is ^{c}recorded in heaven for the angels to look upon; and they rejoice over you, and your ^{d}sins are forgiven you.

4 And now continue your journey. Assemble yourselves upon the land of ^{a}Zion; and hold a meeting and rejoice together, and offer a ^{b}sacrament unto the Most High.

5 And then you may return to bear record, yea, even altogether, or ^{a}two by two, as seemeth you good, it mattereth not unto me; only be faithful, and ^{b}declare glad tidings

unto the inhabitants of the earth, or among the ^{c}congregations of the wicked.

6 Behold, I, the Lord, have brought you together that the promise might be fulfilled, that the faithful among you should be preserved and rejoice together in the land of Missouri. I, the Lord, ^{a}promise the faithful and cannot ^{b}lie.

7 I, the Lord, am willing, if any among you ^{a}desire to ride upon horses, or upon mules, or in chariots, he shall receive this blessing, if he receive it from the hand of the Lord, with a ^{b}thankful heart in all things.

8 These things remain with you to do according to judgment and the directions of the Spirit.

9 Behold, the ^{a}kingdom is yours. And behold, and lo, I am ^{b}with the faithful always. Even so. Amen.

SECTION 63

Revelation given through Joseph Smith the Prophet, at Kirtland, Ohio, late in August 1831. HC 1: 206–211. The Prophet, Sidney Rigdon, and Oliver Cowdery had arrived in Kirtland on August 27, from their visit to Missouri. Prefacing his record of this revelation the Prophet wrote: "In these infant days of the Church, there was a great anxiety to obtain the word of the Lord upon every subject that in any way concerned our salvation; and as the land of Zion was now the most important temporal object in view, I inquired of the Lord for further information upon the gathering of the Saints, and the purchase of the land, and other matters."

1–6, A day of wrath shall come upon the wicked; 7–12, Signs come by faith; 13–19, The adulterous in heart shall deny the faith and be cast into the lake of fire; 20, The faithful shall receive an inheritance upon the transfigured earth; 21, Full account of the events on the Mount of Transfiguration has not yet been revealed; 22–23, The

obedient receive the mysteries of the kingdom; 24–31, Inheritances in Zion are to be purchased; 32–35, The Lord decrees wars, and the wicked slay the wicked; 36–48, The saints are to gather to Zion and provide moneys to build it up; 49–54, Blessings are assured the faithful at the Second Coming, in the resurrection, and dur-

1b Heb. 2: 18; Alma 7: 12.
  c Luke 4: 2.
3a TG Blessings.
  b Luke 12: 8 (8–9).
    TG Testimony.
  c TG Book of Life.
  d Matt. 9: 2; D&C 84: 61.
4a D&C 57: 2 (1–2).

  b TG Assembly for Worship; Sacrament.
5a Mark 6: 7; Luke 10: 1; D&C 52: 10; 61: 35.
  b TG Missionary Work.
  c D&C 61: 30.
6a Ezek. 36: 36.

  b TG God, Perfection of; Honesty.
7a TG Agency.
  b Job 1: 21; Mosiah 2: 20 (20–22); D&C 59: 21.
    TG Thanksgiving.
9a D&C 61: 37; 64: 4.
  b Matt. 28: 20.

ing the Millennium; 55–58, This is a day of warning; 59–66, The Lord's name is taken in vain by those who use it without authority.

HEARKEN, O ye people, and open your hearts and give ear from afar; and listen, you that call yourselves the *a*people of the Lord, and hear the word of the Lord and his will concerning you.

2 Yea, verily, I say, hear the word of him whose anger is *a*kindled against the wicked and *b*rebellious;

3 Who willeth to take even them whom he will *a*take, and *b*preserveth in life them whom he will preserve;

4 Who buildeth up at his own will and *a*pleasure; and destroyeth when he pleases, and is able to *b*cast the soul down to hell.

5 Behold, I, the Lord, utter my voice, and it shall be *a*obeyed.

6 Wherefore, verily I say, let the wicked take heed, and let the *a*rebellious *b*fear and tremble; and let the unbelieving hold their lips, for the *c*day of wrath shall come upon them as a *d*whirlwind, and all flesh shall *e*know that I am God.

7 And he that seeketh *a*signs shall see signs, but not unto salvation.

8 Verily, I say unto you, there are those among you who seek signs, and there have been such even from the beginning;

9 But, behold, faith cometh not by signs, but *a*signs follow those that believe.

10 Yea, *a*signs come by *b*faith, not by the will of men, nor as they please, but by the will of God.

11 Yea, signs come by faith, unto mighty works, for without *a*faith no man pleaseth God; and with whom God is *b*angry he is not well pleased; wherefore, unto such he showeth no signs, only in *c*wrath unto their *d*condemnation.

12 Wherefore, I, the Lord, am not pleased with those among you who have sought after signs and wonders for faith, and not for the good of men unto my glory.

13 Nevertheless, I give commandments, and many have turned away from my commandments and have *a*not kept them.

14 There were among you *a*adulterers and adulteresses, some of whom have turned away from you, and others remain with you that hereafter shall be revealed.

15 Let such beware and repent speedily, lest judgment shall come upon them as a *a*snare, and their *b*folly shall be made manifest, and their works shall follow them in the eyes of the people.

16 And verily I say unto you, as I have said before, he that *a*looketh on a *b*woman to *c*lust after her, or if any shall commit *c*adultery in their hearts, they shall not have the *d*Spirit, but shall deny the faith and shall fear.

17 Wherefore, I, the Lord, have said that the *a*fearful, and the *b*unbelieving, and all *c*liars, and whoso-

---

63 1a Lev. 26: 12;
   3 Ne. 20: 19.
 2a TG Provoking.
   b TG Rebellion.
 3a Job 1: 21; Isa. 57: 1.
   TG Death.
   b Mosiah 2: 20 (20–21).
 4a TG God, Justice of;
   Judgment.
   b Hel. 12: 21 (20–22).
 5a TG Obedience.
 6a TG Rebellion.
   b TG Day of the Lord.
   c D&C 1: 13 (13–14).
   d Jer. 30: 23; Dan. 11:
   40.
   e Isa. 49: 26.

 7a TG Sign Seekers.
   b Mark 8: 11 (11–21);
   D&C 46: 9.
 9a Mark 16: 17. TG Holy
   Ghost, Gifts of;
   Miracle; Signs.
 10a John 12: 18 (9, 17–18);
   Rom. 15: 19 (18–19);
   Morm. 9: 19 (19–21).
   b TG Faith.
 11a Heb. 11: 6.
   b TG God, Indignation
   of.
   c D&C 35: 11.
   d D&C 88: 65.
 13a TG Disobedience.
 14a D&C 42: 24 (24–25).

 15a Luke 21: 35.
   b 2 Tim. 3: 9.
   TG Foolishness.
 16a Matt. 5: 28 (27–28).
   b 2 Sam. 13: 4 (2–4).
   TG Lust; Sensuality;
   Sexual Immorality.
   c TG Adultery;
   Chastity.
   d TG Holy Ghost, Loss
   of.
 17a Rev. 21: 8.
   TG Fearfulness.
   b TG Unbelief,
   Unbelievers.
   c TG Honesty; Lying.

ever loveth and maketh a lie, and the*whoremonger, and the*sorcerer, shall have their part in that *lake which burneth with fire and brimstone, which is the *second death.

18 Verily I say, that they shall not have part in the *first resurrection.

19 And now behold, I, the Lord, say unto you that ye are not *justified, because these things are among you.

20 Nevertheless, he that *endureth in faith and doeth my *will, the same shall overcome, and shall receive an *inheritance upon the earth when the day of transfiguration shall come;

21 When the *earth shall be *transfigured, even according to the pattern which was shown unto mine apostles upon the *mount; of which account the fulness ye have not yet received.

22 And now, verily I say unto you, that as I said that I would make known my will unto you, behold I will make it known unto you, *not by the way of commandment, for there are many who observe not to keep my commandments.

23 But unto him that keepeth my commandments I will give the *mysteries of my kingdom, and the same shall be in him a well of living *water, *springing up unto everlasting life.

24 And now, behold, this is the will of the Lord your God concerning his saints, that they should *assemble themselves together unto the land of Zion, not in haste, lest there should be confusion, which bringeth pestilence.

25 Behold, the land of *Zion—I, the Lord, hold it in mine own hands;

26 Nevertheless, I, the Lord, render unto *Cæsar the things which are Cæsar's.

27 Wherefore, I the Lord will that you should *purchase the lands, that you may have advantage of the world, that you may have claim on the world, that they may not be *stirred up unto anger.

28 For *Satan *putteth it into their hearts to anger against you, and to the shedding of blood.

29 Wherefore, the land of Zion shall not be obtained but by *purchase or by blood, otherwise there is none inheritance for you.

30 And if by purchase, behold you are blessed;

31 And if by *blood, as you are forbidden to shed blood, lo, your enemies are upon you, and ye shall be scourged from city to city, and from synagogue to synagogue, and but *few shall stand to receive an inheritance.

32 I, the Lord, am *angry with the *wicked; I am holding my *Spirit from the inhabitants of the earth.

33 I have sworn in my wrath, and *decreed wars upon the face of the earth, and the wicked shall *slay the wicked, and fear shall come upon every man;

17d Rev. 22: 15 (14–15);
  D&C 76: 103.
e TG Sorcery.
f Rev. 19: 20; 2 Ne. 9:
  16 (8–19, 26); 28: 23;
  Jacob 6: 10; Alma 12:
  17 (16–18); D&C 76:
  36. TG Hell.
g TG Death, Spiritual,
  Second.
18a Rev. 20: 6.
19a TG Justification.
20a 2 Cor. 1: 6; D&C 101:
  35. TG Steadfastness.
b TG God, Will of.
c Isa. 29: 19; Matt. 5: 5;
  D&C 59: 2; 88: 26 (25–

26). TG Inheritance.
21a TG Earth, Destiny of.
b TG Transfiguration;
  World, End of.
22a 2 Cor. 8: 8; D&C 28: 5.
23a Alma 12: 9 (9–11);
  D&C 42: 61; 84: 19;
  107: 19 (18–19).
b TG Living Water.
c John 4: 14.
24a D&C 58: 56; 101: 68.
25a TG Zion.
26a Luke 20: 25; 23: 2;
  D&C 58: 22 (21–23).
  TG Governments.
27a D&C 45: 65.
b TG Provoking.

28a TG Devil.
b John 13: 2; 2 Ne. 28:
  20.
29a D&C 58: 53; 101: 70
  (70–75).
31a TG Blood, Shedding of.
b D&C 95: 5 (5–6);
  121: 34 (34–40).
32a Deut. 32: 21; 2 Ne.
  15: 25; Moses 6: 27.
  TG God, Indignation
  of.
b Isa. 57: 17.
c TG God, Spirit of.
33a D&C 45: 26 (26, 33);
  87: 2; 88: 91. TG War.
b Ps. 139: 19 (17–24);
  Isa. 11: 4 (3–4).

34 And the ªsaints also shall ᵇhardly ᶜescape; nevertheless, I, the Lord, am with them, and will ᵈcome down in heaven from the presence of my Father and ᵉconsume the wicked with unquenchable fire.

35 And behold, this is not yet, but ªby and by.

36 Wherefore, seeing that I, the Lord, have decreed all these things upon the face of the earth, I will that my saints should be assembled upon the land of Zion;

37 ªAnd that every man should take ᵇrighteousness in his hands and ᶜfaithfulness upon his loins, and lift a warning ᵈvoice unto the inhabitants of the earth; and declare both by word and by flight that ᵉdesolation shall come upon the wicked.

38 Wherefore, let my disciples in Kirtland arrange their temporal concerns, who dwell upon this farm.

39 Let my servant Titus Billings, who has the care thereof, dispose of the land, that he may be prepared in the coming spring to take his journey up unto the land of Zion, with those that dwell upon the face thereof, excepting those whom I shall reserve unto myself, that shall ªnot go until I shall command them.

40 And let all the moneys which can be spared, it mattereth not unto me whether it be little or much, be sent up unto the land of Zion, unto them whom I have appointed to ªreceive.

41 Behold, I, the Lord, will give unto my servant Joseph Smith, Jun., power that he shall be enabled to ªdiscern by the Spirit those who shall go up unto the land of Zion, and those of my disciples who shall tarry.

42 Let my servant ªNewel K. Whitney retain his ᵇstore, or in other words, the store, yet for a little season.

43 Nevertheless, let him impart all the money which he can impart, to be sent up unto the land of Zion.

44 Behold, these things are in his own hands, let him do ªaccording to wisdom.

45 Verily I say, let him be ordained as an agent unto the disciples that shall tarry, and let him be ªordained unto this power;

46 And now speedily visit the churches, expounding these things unto them, with my servant Oliver Cowdery. Behold, this is my will, obtaining moneys even as I have directed.

47 He that is ªfaithful and ᵇendureth shall overcome the world.

48 He that sendeth up treasures unto the land of Zion shall receive an ªinheritance in this world, and his works shall follow him, and also a ᵇreward in the world to come.

49 Yea, and blessed are the dead that ªdie in the Lord, from henceforth, when the Lord shall come, and old things shall ᵇpass away, and all things become new, they shall ᶜrise from the dead and shall not ᵈdie after, and shall receive an inheritance before the Lord, in the ᵉholy city.

50 And he that liveth when the Lord shall come, and hath kept the

---

34a TG Saints.
  b Matt. 24: 22; Luke 21: 36.
  c TG Protection, Divine.
  d TG Jesus Christ, Second Coming.
  e Jer. 8: 13; Matt. 3: 12; 2 Ne. 26: 6; D&C 29: 9 (9, 21, 23); 45: 57; 64: 24; 88: 94; 101: 24 (23–25, 66).
  TG Earth, Cleansing of.
35a JS-H 1: 41.
37a D&C 19: 37; 58: 47; 68: 8; 71: 7.
  b TG Righteousness.
  c Isa. 11: 5.

d D&C 1: 4.
e Isa. 47: 11.
  TG Judgment.
39a D&C 66: 6.
40a D&C 51: 8 (3–9).
41a TG Discernment, Spiritual.
42a D&C 64: 26.
  b D&C 57: 8.
44a TG Agency; Initiative.
45a TG Delegation of Responsibility; Stewardship.
47a Ps. 31: 23; Mosiah 2: 41; Ether 4: 19; D&C 6: 13.

b TG Perseverance.
48a D&C 25: 2; 64: 30; 85: 7 (1–3, 7, 9); 99: 7; 101: 18 (1, 6, 18); 103: 14 (11, 14).
  b TG Reward.
49a Rom. 14: 8 (5–9); Rev. 14: 13; D&C 42: 44 (44–47).
  b 2 Cor. 5: 17.
  c TG Resurrection.
  d John 5: 24; 8: 51; 11: 26; Rev. 21: 4; Alma 11: 45; 12: 18 (18, 20); D&C 88: 116.
  TG Immortality.
  e Jer. 31: 40 (38–40).

faith, ^ablessed is he; nevertheless, it is appointed to him to ^bdie at the age of man.

51 Wherefore, ^achildren shall ^bgrow up until they become old; old men shall die; but they shall not sleep in the dust, but they shall be ^cchanged in the twinkling of an eye.

52 Wherefore, for this cause preached the apostles unto the world the resurrection of the dead.

53 These things are the things that ye must look for; and, speaking after the manner of the Lord, they are now ^anigh at hand, and in a time to come, even in the day of the coming of the Son of Man.

54 And until that hour there will be foolish ^avirgins among the wise; and at that hour cometh an entire ^bseparation of the righteous and the wicked; and in that day will I send mine angels to ^cpluck out the wicked and cast them into unquenchable fire.

55 And now behold, verily I say unto you, I, the Lord, am not pleased with my servant ^aSidney Rigdon; he ^bexalted himself in his heart, and received not counsel, but ^cgrieved the Spirit;

56 Wherefore his ^awriting is not acceptable unto the Lord, and he shall make another; and if the Lord receive it not, behold he standeth no longer in the office to which I have appointed him.

57 And again, verily I say unto you, ^athose who desire in their hearts, in meekness, to ^bwarn sinners to repentance, let them be ordained unto this power.

58 For this is a day of ^awarning, and not a day of many words. For I, the Lord, am not to be ^bmocked in the last days.

59 Behold, I am from above, and my power lieth beneath. I am over all, and in all, and through all, and ^asearch all things, and the day cometh that all things shall be ^bsubject unto me.

60 Behold, I am ^aAlpha and Omega, even Jesus Christ.

61 Wherefore, let all men ^abeware how they take my ^bname in their lips—

62 For behold, verily I say, that many there be who are under this condemnation, who use the name of the Lord, and use it in vain, having not ^aauthority.

63 Wherefore, let the church repent of their sins, and I, the Lord, will ^aown them; otherwise they shall be cut off.

64 Remember that that which cometh from above is ^asacred, and must be ^bspoken with care, and by constraint of the Spirit; and in this there is no condemnation, and ye receive the Spirit ^cthrough prayer; wherefore, without this there remaineth condemnation.

65 Let my servants, Joseph Smith, Jun., and Sidney Rigdon, seek them a home, as they are ^ataught through prayer by the Spirit.

66 These things remain to overcome through patience, that such may receive a more exceeding and eternal ^aweight of ^bglory, otherwise, a greater condemnation. Amen.

50a TG Blessings.	c Ps. 52: 5; Matt. 13: 40	61a TG Self-mastery.
b TG Death.	(30, 39–41); Mosiah	b Ezek. 43: 8 (8–11).
51a TG Children; Mil-	16: 2.	TG Jesus Christ,
lennium.	55a Lev. 4: 22.	Taking the Name of;
b Isa. 65: 20 (20–22);	b TG Haughtiness; Pride.	Profanity.
D&C 45: 58; 101: 30	c TG Holy Ghost, Loss of.	62a TG Authority.
(29–31). TG Mortality;	56a D&C 58: 50 (50–51).	63a Rev. 3: 5.
Old Age.	57a D&C 4: 3 (3–6); 36: 5.	64a TG Sacred.
c 1 Cor. 15: 52 (51–52);	b D&C 18: 14.	b TG Reverence.
D&C 43: 32; 88: 28	TG Missionary Work.	c D&C 42: 14.
(20, 28).	58a TG Warnings.	65a TG God, Spirit of;
53a D&C 35: 15.	b TG Mocking.	Prayer; Teaching.
54a Matt. 25: 1; D&C 45:	59a 1 Cor. 2: 10.	66a 2 Cor. 4: 17.
56 (56–59).	b D&C 50: 27.	b Rom. 8: 18; D&C 58:
b TG Separation.	60a D&C 35: 1.	4; 136: 31.

SECTION 64

Revelation given through Joseph Smith the Prophet to the elders of the Church, at Kirtland, Ohio, September 11, 1831. HC 1 : 211-214. The Prophet was preparing to move to Hiram, Ohio, to renew his work on the translation of the Bible, which had been laid aside while he had been in Missouri. A company of brethren who had been commanded to journey to Zion (Missouri) was earnestly engaged in making preparations to leave in October. At this busy time, the revelation was received.

1–11, The saints are commanded to forgive one another, lest there remain in them the greater sin; 12–22, The unrepentant are to be tried in church courts; 23–25, He that is tithed shall not be burned at the Lord's coming; 26–32, The saints are warned against debt; 33–36, The rebellious shall be cut off out of Zion; 37–40, The Church shall judge the nations; 41–43, Zion shall flourish.

BEHOLD, thus saith the Lord your God unto you, O ye elders of my ^achurch, hearken ye and hear, and receive my will concerning you.

2 For verily I say unto you, I will that ye should ^aovercome the world; wherefore I will have ^bcompassion upon you.

3 There are those among you who have sinned; but verily I say, for this once, for mine own ^aglory, and for the salvation of souls, I have ^bforgiven you their sins.

4 I will be merciful unto you, for I have given unto you the ^akingdom.

5 And the ^akeys of the mysteries of the kingdom shall not be taken from

my servant Joseph Smith, Jun., through the means I have appointed, while he liveth, inasmuch as he obeyeth mine ^aordinances.

6 There are those who have sought occasion against him without cause;

7 Nevertheless, he has sinned; but verily I say unto you, I, the Lord, ^aforgive sins unto those who ^bconfess their sins before me and ask forgiveness, who have not ^csinned unto ^ddeath.

8 My disciples, in days of old, sought ^aoccasion against one another and forgave not one another in their hearts; and for this ^bevil they were ^cafflicted and sorely ^dchastened.

9 Wherefore, I say unto you, that ye ought to ^aforgive one another; for he that ^bforgiveth not his brother his trespasses standeth condemned before the Lord; for there remaineth in him the greater sin.

10 I, the Lord, will ^aforgive whom I will forgive, but of you it is required to ^bforgive all men.

11 And ye ought to say in your hearts—let God ^ajudge between me

---

64 1a TG Jesus Christ,
    Head of the Church.
2a 1 Jn. 5 : 4.
  b Micah 7 : 19.
    TG Compassion.
3a Moses 1 : 39.
  b Isa. 43 : 25; Luke 5 : 21.
4a D&C 62 : 9; 82 : 24.
5a D&C 28 : 7; 84 : 19.
    TG Priesthood, Keys of.
  b TG Ordinances.
7a Dan. 9 : 9.
    TG Remission of Sins.

  b Num. 5 : 7 (6–10);
    D&C 19 : 20; 58 : 43.
    TG Confession.
  c 1 Jn. 3 : 15; 5 : 17;
    Alma 5 : 42 (41–42).
  d D&C 76 : 33 (31–37).
8a Dan. 6 : 4.
    TG Contention;
    Disputations.
  b TG Evil.
  c TG Affliction.
  d TG Chastening.
9a Prov. 17 : 9;
    Mark 11 : 26 (25–26);

    D&C 82 : 1.
    TG Reconciliation.
  b Matt. 6 : 15 (14–15);
    Eph. 4 : 32.
10a Ex. 33 : 19; 34 : 7; Rom.
    9 : 18; Alma 39 : 6;
    D&C 56 : 14.
    TG Forgiveness.
  b Mosiah 26 : 31 (29–31).
    TG Benevolence;
    Forbearance.
11a 1 Sam. 24 : 12; Ps. 75 :
    7. TG Judgment.

and thee, and *b*reward thee according to thy *c*deeds.

12 And him that *a*repenteth not of his sins, and *b*confesseth them not, ye shall bring before the *c*church, and do with him as the *d*scripture saith unto you, either by commandment or by revelation.

13 And this ye shall do that God may be glorified—not because I forgive not, having not compassion, but that ye may be justified in the eyes of the law, that ye may not *a*offend him who is your lawgiver—

14 Verily I say, for this cause ye shall do these things.

15 Behold, I, the Lord, was angry with him who was my servant Ezra Booth, and also my servant Isaac Morley, for they *a*kept not the law, neither the commandment!

16 They sought *a*evil in their hearts, and I, the Lord, *b*withheld my Spirit. They *c*condemned for evil that thing in which there was no evil; nevertheless I have forgiven my servant Isaac Morley.

17 And also my servant *a*Edward Partridge, behold, he hath sinned, and *b*Satan seeketh to destroy his soul; but when these things are made known unto them, and they repent of the evil, they shall be forgiven.

18 And now, verily I say that it is expedient in me that my servant Sidney Gilbert, after a few weeks, shall return upon his business, and to his *a*agency in the land of Zion:

19 And that which he hath seen and heard may be made known unto my disciples, that they perish not. And for this cause have I spoken these things.

20 And again, I say unto you, that my servant Isaac Morley may not be *a*tempted above that which he is able to bear, and counsel wrongfully to your hurt, I gave commandment that his farm should be sold.

21 I will not that my servant Frederick G. Williams should sell his farm, for I, the Lord, will to retain a strong hold in the land of Kirtland, for the space of five years, in the which I will not overthrow the wicked, that thereby I may save some.

22 And after that day, I, the Lord, will not hold any *a*guilty that shall go with an open heart up to the land of Zion; for I, the Lord, require the *b*hearts of the children of men.

23 Behold, now it is called *a*today until the *b*coming of the Son of Man, and verily it is a day of *c*sacrifice, and a day for the tithing of my people; for he that is *d*tithed shall not be *e*burned at his coming.

24 For after today cometh the *a*burning—this is speaking after the manner of the Lord—for verily I say, tomorrow all the *b*proud and they that do wickedly shall be as *c*stubble; and I will burn them up, for I am the Lord of Hosts; and I will not *d*spare any that remain in *e*Babylon.

25 Wherefore, if ye believe me, ye will labor while it is called *a*today.

11b TG Reward.
  c 2 Tim. 4: 14.
12a TG Repentance.
  b TG Confession.
  c 1 Cor. 6: 1.
  d D&C 42: 81 (80–93).
13a TG Offenses.
15a D&C 42: 32 (32–35).
16a Prov. 1: 16; 2 Ne. 19: 17. TG Evil.
  b TG Holy Ghost, Loss of.
  c 2 Ne. 15: 20; D&C 121: 16.
17a D&C 60: 10; 115: 2 (2–6).
  b TG Devil.

18a D&C 57: 6.
20a TG Temptation.
22a TG Guilt.
  b Ex. 35: 5; D&C 59: 15; 64: 34.
23a John 9: 4; D&C 45: 6; 64: 25 (24–25).
  b TG Jesus Christ, Second Coming.
  c TG Sacrifice.
  d Mal. 3: 10 (10–11). See note on tithing in heading to Section 119.
24a Isa. 66: 15 (15–16);

Joel 2: 5; 2 Ne. 15: 24; 26: 6 (4, 6). TG Earth, Cleansing of; World, End of.
  b Job 40: 11; Prov. 15: 25; Mal. 3: 15; 2 Ne. 12: 12; 23: 11. TG Pride.
  c Mal. 4: 1; 3 Ne. 25: 1; JS-H 1: 37.
  d Gen. 18: 23; 1 Ne. 22: 15; Hel. 13: 13 (12–14).
  e D&C 1: 16. TG Babylon.
25a John 9: 4; D&C 45: 6; 64: 23. TG Procrastination.

26 And it is not meet that my servants, ^aNewel K. Whitney and Sidney Gilbert, should sell their ^bstore and their possessions here; for this is not wisdom until the residue of the church, which remaineth in this place, shall go up unto the land of Zion.

27 Behold, it is said in my laws, or forbidden, to get in ^adebt to thine enemies;

28 But behold, it is not said at any time that the Lord should not take when he please, and pay as seemeth him good.

29 Wherefore, as ye are agents, ye are on the Lord's errand; and whatever ye do according to the will of the Lord is the Lord's business.

30 And he hath set you to provide for his saints in these last days, that they may obtain an ^ainheritance in the land of Zion.

31 And behold, I, the Lord, declare unto you, and my ^awords are sure and shall not ^bfail, that they shall obtain it.

32 But all things must come to pass in their time.

33 Wherefore, be not ^aweary in ^bwell-doing, for ye are laying the foundation of a great work. And out of ^csmall things proceedeth that which is great.

34 Behold, the Lord ^arequireth the

^bheart and a ^cwilling mind; and the willing and ^dobedient shall ^eeat the good of the land of Zion in these last days.

35 And the ^arebellious shall be ^bcut off out of the land of Zion, and shall be sent away, and shall not inherit the land.

36 For, verily I say that the rebellious are not of the blood of ^aEphraim, wherefore they shall be plucked out.

37 Behold, I, the Lord, have made my church in these last days like unto a ^ajudge sitting on a hill, or in a high place, to ^bjudge the nations.

38 For it shall come to pass that the inhabitants of Zion shall ^ajudge all things pertaining to Zion.

39 And ^aliars and hypocrites shall be proved by them, and they who are ^bnot ^capostles and prophets shall be ^dknown.

40 And even the ^abishop, who is a ^bjudge, and his counselors, if they are not faithful in their ^cstewardships shall be condemned, and ^dothers shall be planted in their ^estead.

41 For, behold, I say unto you that ^aZion shall flourish, and the ^bglory of the Lord shall be upon her;

42 And she shall be an ^aensign unto the people, and there shall come

---

26a D&C 63:42.
  b D&C 57:8.
27a TG Debt.
30a D&C 63:48 (29, 31, 48); 85:7 (1–3, 7, 9).
31a Ps. 19:4; Mark 13:31; 2 Ne. 31:15.
  b 1 Ne. 20:14; D&C 76:3.
33a Gal. 6:9.
  TG Dedication; Laziness.
  b TG Benevolence; Good Works; Self-sacrifice.
  c D&C 123:16 (16–17).
34a Micah 6:8.
  b Deut. 32:46; Josh. 22:5; 1 Kgs. 2:4; Morm. 9:27; TG Heart.
  c Isa. 1:19; 2 Cor. 8:12; Moro. 7:8; D&C 64:22; 97:8.

d TG Loyalty; Obedience.
  e D&C 101:101.
  TG Abundant Life.
35a TG Rebellion.
36a Gen. 6:13; Obad. 1:9; D&C 41:5; 42:37; 50:8 (8–9); 56:3; Moses 8:30 (26, 30).
36a Gen. 48:16; 49:26 (22–26); Deut. 33:17 (16–17); Hosea 7:1 (1–16); Zech. 10:7 (7–12).
37a Obad. 1:21.
  b TG Judgment.
38a Isa. 2:3; Joel 3:16; D&C 133:21.
39a TG Honesty; Lying.

b TG False Prophets.
  c Rev. 2:2.
  TG Apostles.
  d Deut. 18:21 (21–22).
40a TG Bishop.
  b D&C 58:17; 107:72 (72–74).
  c TG Stewardship.
  d D&C 35:18 (17–18); 42:10; 104:77; 107:99 (99–100).
  e D&C 93:50 (47–50).
41a TG Zion.
  b D&C 45:67; 84:5 (4–5, 31); 97:15 (15–20); TG Glory.
42a TG Ensign; Mission of Latter-day Saints.

unto her out of every [b]nation under heaven.

43 And the day shall come when the nations of the earth shall [a]tremble because of her, and shall fear because of her terrible ones. The Lord hath spoken it. Amen.

SECTION 65

Revelation given through Joseph Smith the Prophet, at Hiram, Ohio, October 1831. HC 1: 218. The Prophet designates this revelation as a prayer.

1–2, Keys of the kingdom of God are committed to man on earth, and the gospel cause shall triumph; 3–6, The millennial kingdom of heaven shall come and join the kingdom of God on earth.

HEARKEN, and lo, a voice as of one sent down from on high, who is mighty and powerful, whose going forth is unto the ends of the earth, yea, whose voice is unto men— [a]Prepare ye the way of the Lord, make his paths straight.

2 The [a]keys of the [b]kingdom of God are committed unto man on the earth, and from thence shall the [c]gospel roll forth unto the ends of the earth, as the [d]stone which is cut out of the mountain without hands shall roll forth, until it has [e]filled the whole earth.

3 Yea, a voice crying— [a]Prepare ye the way of the Lord, prepare ye the [b]supper of the Lamb, make ready for the [c]Bridegroom.

4 Pray unto the Lord, [a]call upon his holy name, make known his wonderful [b]works among the people.

5 Call upon the Lord, that his kingdom may go forth upon the earth, that the inhabitants thereof may receive it, and be prepared for the days to come, in the which the Son of Man shall [a]come down in heaven, [b]clothed in the brightness of his [c]glory, to meet the [d]kingdom of God which is set up on the earth.

6 Wherefore, may the [a]kingdom of God go forth, that the [b]kingdom of heaven may come, that thou, O God, mayest be [c]glorified in heaven so on earth, that thine [d]enemies may be subdued; for [e]thine is the honor, power and glory, forever and ever. Amen.

SECTION 66

Revelation given through Joseph Smith the Prophet, at Orange, Ohio, October 25, 1831. HC 1: 219–221. This was the first day of an

---

42b 1 Kgs. 8: 41; Isa. 60: 9.
43a Isa. 40: 3; D&C 45: 67; 97: 19 (19–20).
65 1a Isa. 40: 3; Matt. 3: 3; John 1: 23.
  TG Millennium, Preparing a People for.
2a Matt. 16: 19; D&C 42: 69. TG Priesthood, Keys of; Priesthood, Melchizedek; Restoration of the Gospel.
  b Micah 4: 7; Luke 17: 21 (20–21); D&C 90: 3 (1–5).

  c TG Mission of Latter-day Saints.
  d Dan. 2: 45 (34–45); 8: 25.
  e Num. 14: 21; Ps. 72: 19. TG Last Days.
3a Matt. 3: 3; D&C 88: 66.
  b Matt. 22: 2 (1–14); Rev. 19: 9; D&C 58: 11.
  c Mark 2: 19 (19–20).
4a Gen. 4: 26; 1 Chr. 16: 8; Ps. 116: 17.
  b 1 Chr. 16: 24. TG God, Works of.

5a Matt. 16: 27; 24: 30.
  b Ps. 93: 1.
  c TG Glory.
  d Dan. 2: 44.
6a TG Kingdom of God, in Heaven; Kingdom of God, on Earth.
  b Rev. 11: 15.
  c John 17: 4.
  d 1 Chr. 17: 10; Ps. 89: 10; Micah 4: 10. TG Enemies.
  e 1 Chr. 29: 11; Matt. 6: 13; Rev. 11: 15.

important conference. In prefacing this revelation, the Prophet wrote: "At the request of William E. McLellin, I inquired of the Lord, and received the following."

1–4, The everlasting covenant is the fulness of the gospel; 5–8, Elders are to preach, testify, and reason with the people; 9–13, Faithful ministerial service assures an inheritance of eternal life.

BEHOLD, thus saith the Lord unto my servant *a*William E. McLellin— Blessed are you, inasmuch as you have *b*turned away from your iniquities, and have received my truths, saith the Lord your Redeemer, the *c*Savior of the world, even of as many as believe on my name.

2 Verily I say unto you, blessed are you for receiving mine *a*everlasting covenant, even the fulness of my gospel, sent forth unto the children of men, that they might have *b*life and be made *c*partakers of the *d*glories which are to be revealed in the last days, as it was written by the prophets and apostles in days of old.

3 Verily I say unto you, my servant William, that you are clean, but not *a*all; repent, therefore, of those things which are not pleasing in my sight, saith the Lord, for the Lord will *b*show them unto you.

4 And now, verily, I, the Lord, will show unto you what I *a*will concerning you, or what is my will concerning you.

5 Behold, verily I say unto you, that it is my will that you should *a*proclaim my gospel from land to land, and from *b*city to city, yea, in those regions round about where it has not been proclaimed.

6 Tarry not many days in this place; go *a*not up unto the land of Zion as yet; but inasmuch as you can *b*send, send; otherwise, think not of thy property.

7 *a*Go unto the eastern lands, bear *b*testimony in every place, unto every people and in their *c*synagogues, reasoning with the people.

8 Let my servant Samuel H. Smith go with you, and forsake him not, and give him thine instructions; and he that is *a*faithful shall be made *b*strong in every place; and I, the Lord, will go with you.

9 Lay your *a*hands upon the *b*sick, and they shall *c*recover. Return not till I, the Lord, shall send you. Be patient in affliction. *d*Ask, and ye shall receive; knock, and it shall be opened unto you.

10 Seek not to be *a*cumbered. Forsake all *b*unrighteousness. Commit not *c*adultery—a temptation with which thou hast been troubled.

11 *a*Keep these sayings, for they are true and *b*faithful; and thou shalt *c*magnify thine office, and push many people to *d*Zion with *e*songs of everlasting joy upon their heads.

12 *a*Continue in these things even unto the end, and you shall have a

66 1*a* D&C 68: 7; 75: 5; 90: 35.
b Mal. 2: 6.
c John 1: 12; 4: 42; 1 Jn. 4: 14.
2*a* TG New and Everlasting Covenant.
b John 5: 40; 10: 10.
c 1 Pet. 5: 1.
d 1 Pet. 4: 13. TG Glory.
3*a* John 13: 11 (10–11).
b Jacob 4: 7.
4*a* TG God, Will of; Guidance, Divine.
5*a* Mark 16: 15.

b Luke 8: 1; Alma 23: 4; D&C 75: 18.
6*a* D&C 63: 39 (24–39).
b D&C 63: 40 (40–46).
7*a* D&C 75: 6.
b John 1: 7.
c Acts 9: 20; 18: 4 (4–26); Alma 21: 4; D&C 68: 1.
8*a* Ps. 31: 23.
b D&C 52: 17; 133: 58.
9*a* TG Administrations to the Sick; Hands, Laying on of.

b TG Sickness.
c Matt. 9: 18.
d John 16: 24.
10*a* Luke 10: 40.
b Prov. 9: 6.
c Mark 10: 19.
TG Adultery.
11*a* D&C 35: 24; 103: 7.
b 2 Ne. 31: 15.
c Rom. 11: 13.
d D&C 45: 71. TG Singing.
e Isa. 35: 10; D&C 45: 71. TG Singing.
12*a* 2 Tim. 3: 14.

*b*crown of eternal life at the right hand of my Father, who is full of *c*grace and truth.

13 Verily, thus saith the Lord your *a*God, your Redeemer, even Jesus Christ. Amen.

SECTION 67

Revelation given through Joseph Smith the Prophet, at Hiram, Ohio, November 1831. HC 1: 224–225. The occasion was that of a special conference, and the publication of the revelations already received from the Lord through the Prophet was considered and acted upon. See heading to Section 1. It was decided that Oliver Cowdery and John Whitmer should take the manuscripts of the revelations to Independence, where W. W. Phelps would publish them as the "Book of Commandments." Many of the brethren bore solemn testimony that the revelations then compiled for publication were verily true, as was witnessed by the Holy Ghost shed forth upon them. The Prophet records that after the revelation known as Section 1 had been received, some negative conversation was had concerning the language used in the revelations. The present revelation followed.

1–3, The Lord hears the prayers and watches over his elders; 4–9, He challenges the wisest person to duplicate the least of his revelations; 10–14, Faithful elders shall be quickened by the Spirit and see the face of God.

BEHOLD and hearken, O ye *a*elders of my church, who have assembled yourselves together, whose *b*prayers I have heard, and whose *c*hearts I know, and whose desires have come up before me.

2 Behold and lo, mine *a*eyes are upon you, and the heavens and the earth are in mine *b*hands, and the riches of eternity are mine to give.

3 Ye endeavored to *a*believe that ye should receive the blessing which was offered unto you; but behold, verily I say unto you there were *b*fears in your hearts, and verily this is the reason that ye did not receive.

4 And now I, the Lord, give unto you a *a*testimony of the truth of these commandments which are lying before you.

5 Your eyes have been upon my servant Joseph Smith, Jun., and his *a*language you have known, and his imperfections you have known; and you have sought in your hearts knowledge that you might express beyond his language; this you also know.

6 Now, seek ye out of the Book of Commandments, even the least that is among them, and appoint him that is the most *a*wise among you;

7 Or, if there be any among you that shall make one *a*like unto it, then ye are justified in saying that ye do not know that they are true;

8 But if ye cannot make one like unto it, ye are under condemnation

---

12*b* Isa. 62: 3; Matt. 25: 21; 1 Pet. 5: 4; Rev. 2: 10.
  c John 1: 14.
13*a* Isa. 43: 12 (11–14); 44: 6.
67 1*a* TG Elders.

b 1 Kgs. 9: 3.
c Acts 1: 24.
  TG God, Omniscience of.
2*a* Ps. 34: 15; Amos 9: 8.
b Ps. 112: 8 (7–8);
Heb. 1: 10.
TG God, Works of.

3*a* TG Faith.
b TG Fearfulness.
4*a* TG Testimony; Truth.
5*a* D&C 1: 24 (18–24).
6*a* 2 Ne. 9: 29 (28–29, 42).
7*a* Prov. 30: 5 (5–6).

if ye do not *bear record that they are true.

9 For ye know that there is no unrighteousness in them, and that which is *righteousness cometh down from above, from the Father of *lights.

10 And again, verily I say unto you that it is your privilege, and a *promise I give unto you that have been ordained unto this ministry, that inasmuch as you *strip yourselves from *jealousies and *fears, and *humble yourselves before me, for ye are not sufficiently humble, the *veil shall be rent and you shall *see me and know that I am—not with the carnal neither natural mind, but with the spiritual.

11 For no *man has seen God at any time in the flesh, except quickened by the Spirit of God.

12 Neither can any *natural man abide the presence of God, neither after the carnal mind.

13 Ye are not able to abide the presence of God now, neither the ministering of angels; wherefore, *continue in patience until ye are *perfected.

14 Let not your minds *turn back; and when ye are *worthy, in mine own due time, ye shall see and know that which was conferred upon you by the hands of my servant Joseph Smith, Jun. Amen.

SECTION 68

Revelation given through Joseph Smith the Prophet, at Hiram, Ohio, November 1831, at the request of Orson Hyde, Luke S. Johnson, Lyman E. Johnson, and William E. McLellin. HC 1: 227–229. Although this revelation was given in response to supplication that the mind of the Lord be made known concerning the elders named, much of the content pertains to the whole Church.

1–5, Words of elders when moved upon by the Holy Ghost are scripture; 6–12, Elders are to preach and baptize, and signs follow true believers; 13–24, Firstborn among the sons of Aaron may serve as the Presiding Bishop (that is, hold the keys of presidency as a bishop) under the direction of the First Presidency; 25–28, Parents are commanded to teach the gospel to their children; 29–35, The saints are to

observe the Sabbath, labor diligently, and pray.

My servant, Orson Hyde, was called by his ordination to proclaim the *everlasting gospel, by the *Spirit of the living God, from people to people, and from land to land, in the *congregations of the wicked, in their *synagogues, reasoning with and *expounding all scriptures unto them.

8a TG Testimony;
  Witnesses.
9a Ps. 119:138; Isa. 45:
  19; James 1:17; Moro.
  7:16 (15–18).
  b D&C 50:24; 84:45;
  88:49.
10a TG Promises.
  b TG Humility; Purity.
  c TG Jealousy.
  d TG Fearfulness.
  e Prov. 6:3.
  TG Teachable.
  f TG Veil.

g Lev. 9:4; D&C 50:45;
  88:68; 93:1; 97:16;
  Moses 1:11.
11a Ex. 19:21; 33:20,
  esp. JST; John 1:18
  (JST 1 Jn. 4:12 No
  man hath seen God at
  any time, except them
  who believe); D&C 84:
  22; Moses 1:11(11,
  14). TG God, Privilege
  of Seeing.

12a JST Ex. 33:20; Mosiah
  3:19. TG Man, Natural,
  Not Spiritually
  Reborn.
13a Rom. 2:7.
  TG Patience.
  b Matt. 5:48.
14a D&C 133:15 (14–15).
  b TG Worthiness.
68 1a D&C 18:4.
  b TG God, Spirit of.
  c Ps. 26:5; D&C 61:30.
  d D&C 66:7.
  e Acts 28:23.

2 And, behold, and lo, this is an ensample unto all those who were ordained unto this priesthood, whose mission is appointed unto them to go forth—

3 And this is the [a]ensample unto them, that they shall [b]speak as they are moved upon by the Holy Ghost.

4 And whatsoever they shall speak when moved upon by the [a]Holy Ghost shall be scripture, shall be the will of the Lord, shall be the mind of the Lord, shall be the word of the Lord, shall be the voice of the Lord, and the [b]power of God unto salvation.

5 Behold, this is the promise of the Lord unto you, O ye my servants.

6 Wherefore, be of good [a]cheer, and do not [b]fear, for I the Lord am with you, and will stand by you; and ye shall bear record of me, even Jesus Christ, that I am the Son of the living God, that I [c]was, that I am, and that I am to come.

7 This is the word of the Lord unto you, my servant Orson Hyde, and also unto my servant Luke Johnson, and unto my servant Lyman Johnson, and unto my servant [a]William E. McLellin, and unto all the faithful elders of my church—

8 [a]Go ye into all the world, [b]preach the gospel to every [c]creature, acting in the [d]authority which I have given you, [e]baptizing in the name of the Father, and of the Son, and of the Holy Ghost.

9 And [a]he that believeth and is baptized shall be saved, and he that believeth not shall be [b]damned.

10 And he that believeth shall be blest with [a]signs following, even as it is written.

11 And unto you it shall be given to know the signs of the [a]times, and the [b]signs of the coming of the Son of Man;

12 And of as many as the Father shall bear record, to you shall be given power to [a]seal them up unto eternal life. Amen.

13 And now, concerning the items in addition to the [a]covenants and commandments, they are these—

14 There remain hereafter, in the due time of the Lord, other [a]bishops to be set apart unto the [b]church, to minister even according to the first;

15 Wherefore they shall be [a]high priests who are worthy, and they shall be appointed by the [b]First Presidency of the Melchizedek Priesthood, except they be literal descendants of [c]Aaron.

16 And if they be literal descendants of [a]Aaron they have a legal right to the bishopric, if they are the [b]firstborn among the sons of Aaron;

17 For the firstborn holds the right of the presidency over this priesthood, and the [a]keys or authority of the same.

18 No man has a legal right to this office, to hold the keys of this priesthood, except he be a [a]literal

---

3a TG Example.
 b Ex. 4: 12 (12–16);
   2 Pet. 1: 21; D&C 18:
   32; 34: 10; 42: 16;
   100: 5.
4a Acts 4: 31.
   TG Revelation.
 b Rom. 1: 16.
6a Matt. 9: 2.
 b Gen. 26: 24; Isa. 41:
   10; Dan. 10: 12;
   Philip. 1: 14 (12–17);
   D&C 98: 1; JS-H 1: 32.
 c Rev. 1: 4.
7a D&C 66: 1; 75: 6; 90:
   35.
8a D&C 1: 2; 19: 37; 58:
   47; 63: 37; 71: 7.
 b TG Preaching.

 c Mark 16: 15.
 d TG Authority;
   Priesthood, Authority.
 e TG Baptism.
9a Mark 16: 16; D&C
   20: 25.
 b TG Damnation.
10a TG Signs.
11a Acts 1: 7;
   D&C 121: 12 (12, 27,
   31).
 b D&C 1: 12.
12a D&C 1: 8; 132: 19, 49.
   TG Sealing.
13a D&C 1: 6. See also
   D&C "Explanatory
   Introduction."
14a D&C 41: 9.
   TG Bishop.

 b TG Church Organization.
15a D&C 72: 1.
 b D&C 81: 2; 107: 17
   (9, 17, 22).
 c Lev. 1: 7; D&C 84:
   30; 132: 59.
16a D&C 107: 16 (15–17,
   68–69).
   TG Priesthood,
   Aaronic.
 b TG Firstborn.
17a TG Priesthood, Keys
   of.
18a Ex. 40: 15 (12–15);
   D&C 84: 18 (18, 30);
   107: 16 (13–16,
   70–76).

descendant and the firstborn of Aaron.

19 But, as a [a]high priest of the Melchizedek Priesthood has authority to officiate in all the lesser offices he may officiate in the office of [b]bishop when no literal descendant of Aaron can be found, provided he is called and set apart and ordained unto this power, under the hands of the First Presidency of the Melchizedek Priesthood.

20 And a literal descendant of Aaron, also, must be designated by this Presidency, and found worthy, and [a]anointed, and ordained under the hands of this Presidency, otherwise they are not legally authorized to officiate in their priesthood.

21 But, by virtue of the decree concerning their right of the priesthood descending from father to son, they may claim their [a]anointing if at any time they can prove their lineage, or do ascertain it by revelation from the Lord under the [b]hands of the above named Presidency.

22 And again, no bishop or high priest who shall be set apart for this ministry shall be tried or [c]condemned for any crime, save it be before the [b]First Presidency of the church;

23 And inasmuch as he is found [a]guilty before this Presidency, by testimony that cannot be impeached, he shall be condemned;

24 And if he repent he shall be

[a]forgiven, according to the covenants and [b]commandments of the church.

25 And again, inasmuch as [a]parents have children in Zion, or in any of her [b]stakes which are organized, that [c]teach them not to understand the [d]doctrine of repentance, faith in Christ the Son of the living God, and of baptism and the gift of the Holy Ghost by the laying on of the hands, when [e]eight years old, the [f]sin be upon the heads of the parents.

26 For this shall be a law unto the [a]inhabitants of Zion, or in any of her stakes which are organized.

27 And their children shall be [a]baptized for the [b]remission of their sins when [c]eight years old, and receive the laying on of the hands.

28 And they shall also [a]teach their children to pray, and to walk uprightly before the Lord.

29 And the inhabitants of Zion shall also observe the [a]Sabbath day to keep it holy.

30 And the inhabitants of Zion also shall remember their [a]labors, inasmuch as they are appointed to labor, in all faithfulness; for the [b]idler shall be had in remembrance before the Lord.

31 Now, I, the Lord, am not well [a]pleased with the inhabitants of Zion, for there are [b]idlers among them; and their [c]children are also growing up in [d]wickedness; they also [e]seek not earnestly the riches of eternity, but their eyes are full of [f]greediness.

19a TG High Priest—
  Melchizedek Priesthood.
b TG Bishop.
20a D&C 109:35.
  TG Anointing; Priesthood, Ordination.
21a Num. 18:8.
b TG Hands, Laying on of.
22a TG Excommunication.
b D&C 107:78 (76–84).
23a TG Guilt.
24a TG Forgiveness.
b D&C 42:23 (13–29).
25a TG Family, Patriarchal; Marriage, Fatherhood; Marriage, Motherhood.

b TG Stakes.
c 1 Sam. 3:13; Ps. 78:4 (4–6). TG Family, Children, Responsibilities toward.
d Heb. 6:2.
e D&C 18:42; 20:71.
f Ezek. 33:4 (2–8); Jacob 1:18; D&C 29:48.
26a TG Zion.
27a TG Baptism, Essential; Salvation of Little Children.
b TG Remission of Sins.
c TG Baptism, Qualifications for.
28a Prov. 13:24.
  TG Learning; Prayer;

  Teaching.
29a Alma 1:26 (26–27);
  D&C 59:9.
  TG Sabbath.
30a TG Industry; Work, Value of.
b TG Laziness.
31a 1 Cor. 10:5.
b TG Idleness.
c Prov. 15:5.
  TG Children.
d TG Wickedness.
e Matt. 6:33 (25–34);
  Alma 39:14 (12–14);
  D&C 6:7 (6–7).
  TG Objectives; Treasure.
f TG Greed.

32 These things ought not to be, and must be done away from among them; wherefore, let my servant Oliver Cowdery ªcarry these sayings unto the land of Zion.

33 And a commandment I give unto them—that he that observeth not his ªprayers before the Lord in the season thereof, let him be had in ᵇremembrance before the judge of my people.

34 These sayings are ªtrue and faithful; wherefore, transgress them not, neither ᵇtake therefrom.

35 Behold, I am ªAlpha and Omega, and I ᵇcome quickly. Amen.

SECTION 69

Revelation given through Joseph Smith the Prophet, at Hiram, Ohio, November 1831. HC 1: 234–235. The compilation of revelations intended for early publication had been passed upon at the special conference of November 1. On November 3, the revelation herein appearing as Section 133 was added, and called the Appendix. By action of the conference, Oliver Cowdery was appointed to carry the manuscript of the compiled revelations and commandments to Independence, Missouri, for printing. He was also to take with him moneys that had been contributed for the building up of the Church in Missouri. As the course of travel would lead him through a sparsely settled country to the frontier, a traveling companion was desirable.

1–2, John Whitmer is to accompany Oliver Cowdery to Missouri; 3–8, He is also to preach and to collect, record, and write historical data.

HEARKEN unto me, saith the Lord your God, for my servant Oliver Cowdery's sake. It is not wisdom in me that he should be entrusted with the commandments and the moneys which he shall ªcarry unto the land of Zion, except one go with him who will be ᵇtrue and faithful.

2 Wherefore, I, the Lord, will that my servant, John Whitmer, should go with my servant Oliver Cowdery;

3 And also that he shall continue in ªwriting and making a ᵇhistory of all the important things which he shall observe and know concerning my church;

4 And also that he receive ªcounsel and assistance from my servant Oliver Cowdery and others.

5 And also, my servants who are abroad in the earth should send forth the accounts of their ªstewardships to the land of Zion;

6 For the land of Zion shall be a ªseat and a place to receive and do all these things.

7 Nevertheless, let my servant John Whitmer travel many times from place to place, and from church to church, that he may the more easily obtain knowledge—

8 Preaching and expounding, writing, copying, selecting, and obtaining all things which shall be for the good of the church, and for the rising generations that shall grow up on the land of Zion, to ªpossess it from generation to generation, forever and ever. Amen.

32a D&C 69:1.
33a TG Prayer.
  b TG Chastening;
    Reproof.
34a Rev. 22:6.
  b TG 20:35; 93:
    25 (24–25).

35a Rev. 1:8; D&C 19:1.
  b D&C 1:12.
69 1a D&C 68:32.
  b TG Dependability;
    Trustworthiness.
3a TG Record Keeping.

  b D&C 21:1; 47:1
    (1–3); 85:1.
4a Prov. 20:18.
  TG Counsel.
5a TG Stewardship.
6a D&C 57:3.
8a TG Zion.

SECTION 70

Revelation given through Joseph Smith the Prophet, at Kirtland, Ohio, November 12, 1831. HC 1: 235-237. The history written by the Prophet states that four special conferences were held from the 1st to the 12th of November, inclusive. In the last of these assemblies the great importance of the Book of Commandments, later called the Doctrine and Covenants, was considered; and the Prophet refers to it as being "the foundation of the Church in these last days, and a benefit to the world, showing that the keys of the mysteries of the kingdom of our Savior are again entrusted to man."

1-5, Stewards are appointed to publish the revelations; 6-13, Those who labor in spiritual things are worthy of their hire; 14-18, The saints should be equal in temporal things.

BEHOLD, and hearken, O ye inhabitants of Zion, and all ye people of my church who are afar off, and "hear the word of the Lord which I give unto my servant Joseph Smith, Jun., and also unto my servant Martin Harris, and also unto my servant Oliver Cowdery, and also unto my servant John Whitmer, and also unto my servant Sidney Rigdon, and also unto my servant *b*William W. Phelps, by the way of commandment unto them.

2 For I give unto them a commandment; wherefore hearken and hear, for thus saith the Lord unto them—

3 I, the Lord, have appointed them, and ordained them to be "stewards over the revelations and commandments which I have given unto them, and which I shall hereafter give unto them;

4 And an account of this "stewardship will I require of them in the day of judgment.

5 Wherefore, I have appointed unto them, and this is their business in the church of God, to "manage them and the concerns thereof, yea, the benefits thereof.

6 Wherefore, a commandment I give unto them, that they shall not give these things unto the church, neither unto the "world;

7 Nevertheless, inasmuch as they "receive more than is needful for their necessities and their wants, it shall be given into my *b*storehouse;

8 And the *a*benefits shall be consecrated unto the inhabitants of Zion, and unto their generations, inasmuch as they become *a*heirs according to the laws of the kingdom.

9 Behold, this is what the Lord requires of every man in his "stewardship, even as I, the Lord, have appointed or shall hereafter appoint unto any man.

10 And behold, none are exempt from this "law who belong to the church of the living God;

11 Yea, neither the bishop, neither the *a*agent who keepeth the Lord's storehouse, neither he who is appointed in a stewardship over *b*temporal things;

12 He who is appointed to administer spiritual things, the same is "worthy of his hire, even as those

---

70 1a Isa. 39:5.
    b D&C 57:11; 58:40;
       61:7 (7-9).
3a 1 Cor. 4:15; D&C 72:
    20.
4a TG Scriptures, Pres-
    ervation of;
    Stewardship.

5a TG Accountability;
   Delegation of
   Responsibility.
6a Moses 1:42; 4:32.
7a D&C 42:55.
   b D&C 58:24 (24, 37);
      72:10.

8a D&C 72:21.
   TG Wages.
   b D&C 38:20.
9a TG Stewardship.
10a D&C 85:3.
11a D&C 57:6.
    b D&C 107:68 (68-71).
12a Luke 10:7.

who are appointed to a stewardship to administer in temporal things;

13 Yea, even more abundantly, which abundance is multiplied unto them through the *manifestations of the Spirit.

14 Nevertheless, in your temporal things you shall be *equal, and this not grudgingly, otherwise the abundance of the manifestations of the Spirit shall be *withheld.

15 Now, this commandment I give unto my servants for their *benefit while they remain, for a manifestation of my blessings upon their

heads, and for a *reward of their *diligence and for their security;

16 For food and for *raiment; for an inheritance; for houses and for lands, in whatsoever circumstances I, the Lord, shall place them, and whithersoever I, the Lord, shall send them.

17 For they have been faithful over *many things, and have done well inasmuch as they have not sinned.

18 Behold, I, the Lord, am *merciful and will bless them, and they shall enter into the joy of these things. Even so. Amen.

SECTION 71

Revelation given to Joseph Smith the Prophet and Sidney Rigdon, at Hiram, Ohio, December 1, 1831. HC 1: 238–239. The Prophet had continued to translate the Bible with Sidney Rigdon as his scribe until this revelation was received, at which time it was temporarily laid aside so as to enable him to fulfill the instruction given herein. The brethren were to go forth to preach in order to allay the unfriendly feelings that had developed against the Church as a result of the publication of some newspaper articles by Ezra Booth, who had apostatized.

1–4, Joseph Smith and Sidney Rigdon are sent forth to proclaim the gospel; 5–11, Enemies of the saints shall be confounded.

BEHOLD, thus saith the Lord unto you my servants Joseph Smith, Jun., and Sidney Rigdon, that the time has verily come that it is necessary and expedient in me that you should open your mouths in *proclaiming my gospel, the things of the kingdom, expounding the *mysteries thereof out of the scriptures, according to that portion of Spirit and power which shall be given unto you, even as I will.

2 Verily I say unto you, proclaim unto the world in the regions round about, and in the church also, for the space of a season, even until it shall be *made known unto you.

3 Verily this is a mission for a season, which I give unto you.

4 Wherefore, *labor ye in my vineyard. Call upon the inhabitants of the earth, and bear record, and prepare the way for the commandments and revelations which are to come.

5 Now, behold this is wisdom; whoso readeth, let him *understand and *receive also;

6 For unto him that receiveth it

13*a* D&C 5: 16.
14*a* D&C 49: 20.
   TG Consecration; Selfishness.
  b TG Holy Ghost, Loss of.
15*a* Deut. 10: 13.

  b TG Reward.
  c TG Dependability; Diligence.
16*a* D&C 59: 17 (16–20).
17*a* Matt. 25: 21 (21–23).
18*a* Ps. 34: 8;
    Lam. 3: 25;
    Nahum 1: 7.

71 1*a* Matt. 4: 23.
   TG Missionary Work.
  b D&C 42: 61 (61–65).
2*a* D&C 73: 3.
4*a* D&C 24: 19.
5*a* TG Understanding.
  b Alma 12: 10 (9–11).

shall be given more *a*abundantly, even power.

7 Wherefore, *b*confound your *b*enemies; call upon them to *c*meet you both in public and in private; and inasmuch as ye are faithful their *d*shame shall be made manifest.

8 Wherefore, let them bring forth their *a*strong reasons against the Lord.

9 Verily, thus saith the Lord unto you—there is no *a*weapon that is formed against you shall prosper;

10 And if any man lift his voice against you he shall be *a*confounded in mine own due time.

11 Wherefore, *a*keep my commandments; they are true and faithful. Even so. Amen.

SECTION 72

Revelation given through Joseph Smith the Prophet, at Kirtland, Ohio, December 4, 1831. HC 1: 239–241. Several elders and members had assembled to learn their duty and to be further edified in the teachings of the Church. This section is a compilation of two revelations received on the same day. Verses 1–8 make known the calling of Newel K. Whitney as a bishop. He was then called and ordained, after which verses 9–26 were received giving additional information as to a bishop's duties.

1–8, Elders are to render an account of their stewardship unto the bishop; 9–15, The bishop keeps the storehouse and cares for the poor and needy; 16–26, Bishops are to certify worthiness of elders.

HEARKEN, and listen to the voice of the Lord, O ye who have assembled yourselves together, who are the *a*high priests of my church, to whom the *b*kingdom and power have been given.

2 For verily thus saith the Lord, it is expedient in me for a *a*bishop to be appointed unto you, or of you, unto the church in this part of the Lord's vineyard.

3 And verily in this thing ye have done wisely; for it is required of the Lord, at the hand of every *a*steward, to render an *b*account of his *c*stewardship, both in time and in eternity.

4 For he who is faithful and *a*wise in time is accounted worthy to inherit the *b*mansions prepared for him of my Father.

5 Verily I say unto you, the elders of the church in this part of my vineyard shall render an account of their stewardship unto the *a*bishop, who shall be appointed of me in this part of my vineyard.

6 These things shall be had on *a*record, to be handed over unto the *b*bishop in Zion.

7 And the duty of the *a*bishop shall be made known by the commandments which have been given, and tl e voice of the conference.

8 And now, verily I say unto you, my servant *a*Newel K. Whitney is

---

6*a* Matt. 13: 12.	**72** 1*a* D&C 68: 15 (15–19).	4*a* Matt. 24: 45.
7*a* Ps. 83: 17 (2–17);	*b* D&C 35: 27.	*b* D&C 59: 2.
2 Ne. 25: 14; Moses 7:	TG Kingdom of God,	5*a* TG Bishop.
15 (14–16).	on Earth.	6*a* TG Record Keeping.
b TG Enemies.	2*a* TG Bishop.	*b* D&C 41: 9; 58: 14
c D&C 19: 37; 58: 47;	3*a* Ezek. 34: 10; Matt.	(14–24).
63: 37; 68: 8.	25: 19; D&C 51: 19;	7*a* D&C 41: 9; 42: 31
8*a* Isa. 41: 21.	70: 9 (9–11); 104: 13	(30–31); 46: 27; 58:
9*a* Isa. 54: 17.	(11–13).	17 (17–18); 68: 16;
10*a* Jer. 17: 18 (15–18).	*b* D&C 42: 32 (30–42).	107: 88 (87–88).
11*a* Ex. 16: 28.	*c* Luke 19: 15 (11–27).	8*a* See Index.
	TG Stewardship.	

the man who shall be appointed and ordained unto this power. This is the will of the Lord your God, your Redeemer. Even so. Amen.

9 The word of the Lord, in addition to the "law which has been given, making known the *b*duty of the *c*bishop who has been ordained unto the church in this part of the vineyard, which is verily this—

10 To keep the Lord's *a*storehouse; to receive the funds of the church in this part of the vineyard;

11 To take an account of the elders as before has been commanded; and to *a*administer to their wants, who shall pay for that which they receive, inasmuch as they have wherewith to pay;

12 That this also may be consecrated to the good of the church, to the poor and needy.

13 And he who *a*hath not wherewith to pay, an account shall be taken and handed over to the bishop of Zion, who shall pay the debt out of that which the Lord shall put into his hands.

14 And the labors of the faithful who labor in spiritual things, in administering the gospel and the *a*things of the kingdom unto the church, and unto the world, shall answer the debt unto the bishop in Zion;

15 Thus it cometh out of the church, for according to the *a*law every man that cometh up to Zion must lay all things before the bishop in Zion.

16 And now, verily I say unto you, that as every elder in this part of the vineyard must give an account of his stewardship unto the bishop in this part of the vineyard—

17 A *a*certificate from the judge or bishop in this part of the vineyard, unto the bishop in Zion, rendereth every man acceptable, and answereth all things, for an inheritance, and to be received as a wise *a*steward and as a faithful *c*laborer;

18 Otherwise he shall not be *a*accepted of the bishop of Zion.

19 And now, verily I say unto you, let every elder who shall give an account unto the bishop of the church in this part of the vineyard be *a*recommended by the church or churches, in which he labors, that he may render himself and his accounts approved in all things.

20 And again, let my servants who are appointed as stewards over the *a*literary concerns of my church have claim for assistance upon the bishop or bishops in all things—

21 That the revelations may be *a*published, and go forth unto the ends of the earth; that they also may obtain *b*funds which shall benefit the church in all things;

22 That they also may render themselves approved in all things, and be accounted as *a*wise stewards.

23 And now, behold, this shall be an *a*ensample for all the extensive branches of my church, in whatsoever land they shall be established. And now I make an end of my sayings. Amen.

24 A few words in addition to the laws of the kingdom, respecting the members of the church—they that are *a*appointed by the Holy Spirit to go up unto Zion, and they who are *b*privileged to go up unto Zion—

25 Let them carry up unto the bishop a *a*certificate from three elders of the church, or a certificate from the bishop;

26 Otherwise he who shall go up unto the land of Zion shall not be accounted as a wise steward. This is also an ensample. Amen.

9a TG Bishop.
  b TG Duty.
  c D&C 58: 14–24.
10a D&C 70: 7 (7–11);
    78: 3. TG Welfare.
11a D&C 75: 24 (24–26).
13a D&C 58: 14. TG Poor.
14a TG Almsgiving;
    Generosity.

15a D&C 42: 30.
17a D&C 20: 64 (64, 84);
    52: 41; 72: 19 (18–26);
    112: 21.
  b D&C 42: 32.
  c TG Work, Value of.
18a D&C 72: 26.
19a D&C 20: 64.
20a D&C 70: 3 (3–5).

21a D&C 67: 6 (6–9).
  b D&C 70: 8 (5–8).
22a D&C 42: 32.
23a D&C 51: 18.
    TG Example.
24a TG Holy Ghost,
    Mission of.
  b D&C 58: 56.
25a D&C 72: 17 (17–18).

SECTION 73

Revelation given to Joseph Smith the Prophet and Sidney Rigdon, at Hiram, Ohio, January 10, 1832. HC 1: 241–242. Since the early part of the preceding December, the Prophet and Sidney had been engaged in preaching, and by this means much was accomplished in diminishing the unfavorable feelings that had arisen against the Church (see heading to Section 71).

1–2, Elders are to continue to preach; 3–6, Joseph Smith and Sidney Rigdon are to continue to translate the Bible until it is finished.

For verily, thus saith the Lord, it is expedient in me that ⁿthey should continue preaching the gospel, and in exhortation to the churches in the regions round about, until conference;

2 And then, behold, it shall be made known unto them, by the ⁿvoice of the conference, their several missions.

3 Now, verily I say unto you my servants, Joseph Smith, Jun., and Sidney Rigdon, saith the Lord, it is "expedient to ᵇtranslate again;

4 And, inasmuch as it is practicable, to preach in the regions round about until conference; and after that it is expedient to continue the work of ⁿtranslation until it is finished.

5 And let this be a pattern unto the elders until further knowledge, even as it is written.

6 Now I give no more unto you at this time. ⁿGird up your loins and be sober. Even so. Amen.

SECTION 74

Revelation given to Joseph Smith the Prophet, at Hiram, Ohio, January 1832. HC 1: 242. The Prophet writes, "Upon the reception of the foregoing word of the Lord [D&C 73], I recommended the translation of the Scriptures, and labored diligently until just before the conference, which was to convene on the 25th of January. During this period I also received the following, as an explanation of 1 Corinthians 7: 14."

1–5, Paul counsels the church of his day not to keep the law of Moses; 6–7, Little children are holy and are sanctified through the atonement.

For the ⁿunbelieving ᵇhusband is ᶜsanctified by the wife, and the unbelieving wife is sanctified by the husband; else were your children unclean, but now are they holy.

2 Now, in the days of the apostles the law of circumcision was had among all the Jews who believed not the gospel of Jesus Christ.

3 And it came to pass that there arose a great ⁿcontention among the

---

73 1a IE the others who were on missions; see Sections 57–68.
  2a D&C 20: 63.
  3a D&C 71: 2.
    b IE the translation of

the Bible. D&C 45: 60 (60–61); 76: 15.
  4a D&C 90: 13.
  6a 1 Pet. 1: 13.
74 1a 1 Cor. 7: 14 (14–19).
    b TG Marriage.

c TG Family, Love within; Sanctification.
3a Acts 15: 1 (1–35); Gal. 2: 3 (1–5); 5: 6 (1–14).

people concerning the law of [b]circumcision, for the unbelieving husband was desirous that his children should be circumcised and become subject to the [c]law of Moses, which law was fulfilled.

4 And it came to pass that the children, being brought up in subjection to the law of Moses, gave heed to the [a]traditions of their fathers and believed not the gospel of Christ, wherein they became unholy.

5 Wherefore, for this cause the apostle wrote unto the church, giving unto them a commandment, not of the Lord, but of himself, that a believer should not be [a]united to an [b]unbeliever; except the [c]law of Moses should be done away among them,

6 That their children might remain without circumcision; and that the [a]tradition might be done away, which saith that little children are unholy; for it was had among the Jews;

7 But little [a]children are [b]holy, being [c]sanctified through the [d]atonement of Jesus Christ; and this is what the scriptures mean.

SECTION 75

Revelation given through Joseph Smith the Prophet, at Amherst, Ohio, January 25, 1832. HC 1: 242–245. The occasion was that of a conference previously appointed. At this conference Joseph Smith was sustained and ordained President of the High Priesthood. Certain elders, who had encountered difficulty in bringing men to an understanding of their message, desired to learn more in detail as to their immediate duties. This revelation followed.

1–5, Faithful elders who preach the gospel will gain eternal life; 6–12, Pray to receive the Comforter, which teaches all things; 13–22, Elders shall sit in judgment on those who reject their message; 23–36, Families of missionaries are to receive help from the Church.

VERILY, verily, I say unto you, I who speak even by the [a]voice of my Spirit, even [b]Alpha and Omega, your Lord and your God—

2 Hearken, O ye who have [a]given your names to go forth to proclaim my gospel, and to [b]prune my vineyard.

3 Behold, I say unto you that it is my will that you should go forth and not tarry, neither be [a]idle but [b]labor with your might—

4 Lifting up your voices as with the sound of a trump, [a]proclaiming the [b]truth according to the revelations and commandments which I have given you.

5 And thus, if ye are faithful ye shall be laden with many [a]sheaves, and [b]crowned with honor, and glory, and immortality, and eternal life.

3b TG Circumcision.
  c TG Law of Moses.
4a TG Traditions of Men.
5a TG Marriage, Interfaith.
  b TG Unbelief, Unbelievers.
  c Rom. 7: 4 (4–6);
    2 Ne. 25: 25 (24–27).
6a TG Traditions of Men.
7a TG Children; Family.

  b Moro. 8: 8 (8–15);
    D&C 29: 46.
    TG Holiness.
  c TG Salvation of Little Children.
  d TG Jesus Christ, Atonement through.
75 1a TG Revelation.
  b Rev. 1: 8; D&C 68: 35.
2a D&C 75: 23.
    TG Initiative; Zeal.
  b Jacob 5: 62 (62–69).

3a TG Idleness.
  b Neh. 4: 6.
    TG Diligence; Industry.
4a TG Missionary Work.
  b 2 Cor. 4: 2; D&C 19: 37.
5a Ps. 126: 6; Alma 26: 5; D&C 4: 4; 33: 9.
    TG Eternal Life; Exaltation; Glory; Honor.

6 Therefore, verily I say unto my servant ^aWilliam E. McLellin, I ^brevoke the commission which I gave unto him to go unto the eastern countries;

7 And I give unto him a new commission and a new commandment, in the which I, the Lord, ^achasten him for the ^bmurmurings of his heart;

8 And he sinned; nevertheless, I forgive him and say unto him again, Go ye into the south countries.

9 And let my servant Luke Johnson go with him, and proclaim the things which I have commanded them—

10 Calling on the name of the Lord for the ^aComforter, which shall teach them all things that are expedient for them—

11 ^aPraying always that they ^bfaint not; and inasmuch as they do this, I will be with them even unto the end.

12 Behold, this is the will of the Lord your God concerning you. Even so. Amen.

13 And again, verily thus saith the Lord, let my servant Orson Hyde and my servant Samuel H. Smith take their journey into the eastern countries, and proclaim the things which I have commanded them; and inasmuch as they are faithful, lo, I will be ^awith them even unto the end.

14 And again, verily I say unto my servant Lyman Johnson, and unto my servant Orson Pratt, they shall also take their journey into the eastern countries; and behold, and lo, I am with them also, even unto the end.

15 And again, I say unto my servant Asa Dodds, and unto my servant Calves Wilson, that they also shall take their journey unto the western countries, and proclaim my gospel, even as I have commanded them.

16 And he who is faithful shall overcome all things, and shall be ^alifted up at the last day.

17 And again, I say unto my servant Major N. Ashley, and my servant Burr Riggs, let them take their journey also into the south country.

18 Yea, let all those take their journey, as I have commanded them, going from ^ahouse to house, and from village to village, and from city to city.

19 And in whatsoever house ye enter, and they receive you, leave your blessing upon that house.

20 And in whatsoever house ye enter, and they receive you not, ye shall depart speedily from that house, and ^ashake off the dust of your feet as a testimony against them.

21 And you shall be filled with ^ajoy and gladness; and know this, that in the day of judgment you shall be ^bjudges of that house, and condemn them;

22 And it shall be more ^atolerable for the ^bheathen in the day of judgment, than for that house; therefore, ^cgird up your loins and be faithful, and ye shall overcome all things, and be ^dlifted up at the last day. Even so. Amen.

23 And again, thus saith the Lord unto you, O ye elders of my church, who have ^agiven your names, that you might know his will concerning you—

24 Behold, I say unto you, that it is the ^aduty of the church to assist in ^bsupporting the families of

---

6a D&C 68: 7; 90: 35.
b D&C 66: 7 (1-13).
7a TG Chastening.
b Num. 11: 1 (1-2);
1 Ne. 17: 2.
10a TG Holy Ghost, Comforter.
11a 2 Ne. 32: 9.
b Luke 18: 1.

13a Matt. 28: 20.
16a D&C 5: 35.
18a Luke 8: 1; Alma 23: 4;
D&C 66: 5.
20a Matt. 10: 14 (12-14);
Luke 10: 11 (11-12);
D&C 24: 15; 60: 15;
99: 4 (4-5).
21a Matt. 5: 12 (11-12).
b TG Priesthood,

Authority.
22a Matt. 11: 22; D&C
45: 54.
b TG Heathen.
c D&C 27: 15 (15-18).
d D&C 5: 35.
23a D&C 75: 2.
24a D&C 72: 11 (11-12).
b D&C 31: 5.

those, and also to support the families of those who are called and must needs be sent unto the world to proclaim the gospel unto the world.

25 Wherefore, I, the Lord, give unto you this commandment, that ye obtain places for your "families, inasmuch as your brethren are willing to open their hearts.

26 And let all such as can obtain places for their families, and support of the church for them, not fail to go into the world, whether to the east or to the west, or to the north, or to the south.

27 Let them "ask and they shall receive, knock and it shall be opened unto them, and be made known from on high, even by the ᵇComforter, whither they shall go.

28 And again, verily I say unto you, that every "man who is obliged to ᵇprovide for his own ᶜfamily, let him provide, and he shall in nowise lose his crown; and let him labor in the church.

29 Let every man be "diligent in all things. And the ᵇidler shall not have place in the church, except he repent and mend his ways.

30 Wherefore, let my servant Simeon Carter and my servant Emer Harris be united in the ministry;

31 And also my servant Ezra Thayre and my servant "Thomas B. Marsh;

32 Also my servant Hyrum Smith and my servant Reynolds Cahoon;

33 And also my servant Daniel Stanton and my servant Seymour Brunson;

34 And also my servant Sylvester Smith and my servant Gideon Carter;

35 And also my servant Ruggles Eames and my servant "Stephen Burnett;

36 And also my servant Micah B. Welton and also my servant "Eden Smith. Even so. Amen.

SECTION 76

A vision given to Joseph Smith the Prophet and Sidney Rigdon, at Hiram, Ohio, February 16, 1832. HC 1: 245-252. Prefacing his record of this vision the Prophet wrote: "Upon my return from Amherst conference, I resumed the translation of the Scriptures. From sundry revelations which had been received, it was apparent that many important points touching the salvation of man had been taken from the Bible, or lost before it was compiled. It appeared self-evident from what truths were left, that if God rewarded every one according to the deeds done in the body, the term 'Heaven,' as intended for the Saints' eternal home, must include more kingdoms than one. Accordingly, while translating St. John's Gospel, myself and Elder Rigdon saw the following vision." It was after the Prophet had translated John 5: 29 that this vision was given.

1–4, *The Lord is God*; 5–10, *Mysteries of the kingdom will be revealed to all the faithful*; 11–17, *All shall come* forth in the resurrection of the just or the unjust; 18–24, *Inhabitants of many worlds are begotten sons and*

25a D&C 83: 2 (2–4).
27a D&C 4: 7.
   b TG Holy Ghost, Comforter.
28a TG Marriage, Husbands.

b 1 Tim. 5: 8.
   TG Family, Managing Finances in; Marriage, Fatherhood.
c TG Family; Family, Love within.

29a TG Diligence; Zeal.
   b TG Idleness; Laziness.
31a D&C 56: 5 (5–6).
35a D&C 80: 1.
36a D&C 80: 2.

daughters unto God through the atonement of Jesus Christ; 25–29, An angel of God fell and became the devil; 30–49, Sons of perdition suffer eternal damnation; all others gain some degree of salvation; 50–70, The glory and reward of exalted beings in the celestial kingdom; 71–80, Those who shall inherit the terrestrial kingdom; 81–113, Status of those in the telestial, terrestrial, and celestial glories; 114–119, All the faithful may see the vision of the degrees of glory.

^aHEAR, O ye heavens, and give ear, O earth, and rejoice ye inhabitants thereof, for the Lord is ^bGod, and beside him there is ^cno ^cSavior.

2 ^aGreat is his wisdom, ^bmarvelous are his ways, and the extent of his doings none can find out.

3 His ^apurposes fail not; neither are there any who can stay his hand.

4 From eternity to eternity he is the ^asame, and his years never ^bfail.

5 For thus saith the Lord—I, the Lord, am ^amerciful and gracious unto those who ^bfear me, and delight to honor those who ^cserve me in righteousness and in truth unto the end.

6 Great shall be their reward and eternal shall be their ^aglory.

7 And to them will I ^areveal all ^bmysteries, yea, all the hidden mysteries of my kingdom from days of old, and for ages to come, will

I make known unto them the good pleasure of my will concerning all things pertaining to my kingdom.

8 Yea, even the wonders of ^aeternity shall they know, and things to come will I show them, even the things of many generations.

9 And their ^awisdom shall be great, and their ^bunderstanding reach to heaven; and before them the wisdom of the wise shall ^cperish, and the understanding of the ^dprudent shall come to naught.

10 For by my ^aSpirit will I ^benlighten them, and by my ^cpower will I make known unto them the ^dsecrets of my ^ewill—yea, even those things which ^feye has not seen, nor ear heard, nor yet entered into the heart of man.

11 We, Joseph Smith, Jun., and Sidney Rigdon, being ^ain the Spirit on the sixteenth day of February, in the year of our Lord one thousand eight hundred and thirty-two—

12 By the power of the ^aSpirit our ^beyes were opened and our understandings were enlightened, so as to see and understand the things of God—

13 Even those things which were from the beginning before the world was, which were ordained of the Father, through his Only Begotten Son, who was in the bosom of the Father, even from the ^abeginning;

14 Of whom we bear record; and

76 1*a* Isa. 1: 2.
  b Josh. 22: 34; Jer. 10: 10.
  c Ex. 8: 10 (8–10); 1 Kgs. 8: 60; Isa. 43: 11; Hosea 13: 4.
  d TG Jesus Christ, Savior.
 2*a* Ex. 15: 11. TG God, Intelligence of; God, Wisdom of.
  b Ps. 25: 4 (1–5); 118: 23; Rev. 15: 3 (1–3).
 3*a* 1 Kgs. 8: 56; 1 Ne. 20: 14; D&C 64: 31.
 4*a* Mal. 3: 6; D&C 20: 12; 35: 1; 38: 1 (1–4); 39: 1 (1–3). TG God, Eternal Nature of; God, Perfection of.

  b Ps. 102: 27 (25–27); Heb. 1: 12.
 5*a* Ex. 34: 6; Ps. 103: 8; Prov. 8: 17. TG God, Mercy of.
  b Deut. 6: 13; Josh. 4: 24; 1 Kgs. 18: 3. TG Reverence.
  c 1 Sam. 7: 3; Ps. 34: 15; D&C 4: 2.
 6*a* Celestial Glory.
 7*a* D&C 42: 61; 59: 4; 98: 12; 101: 32; 121: 28 (26–33).
  b 2 Pet. 1: 2. TG Mysteries of Godliness.
 8*a* TG Eternity.
 9*a* TG Wisdom.
  b TG Understanding.

  c Isa. 29: 14; 2 Ne. 9: 28.
  d TG Prudence.
10*a* TG God, Spirit of.
  b TG Testimony.
  c TG Jesus Christ, Power of.
  d Dan. 2: 28.
  e TG God, Will of.
  f Isa. 64: 4; 1 Cor. 2: 9; 3 Ne. 17: 16 (15–25); D&C 76: 116 (114–119).
11*a* Rev. 1: 10; 4: 2.
12*a* TG Transfiguration.
  b Eph. 1: 18; D&C 11: 13; 110: 1; 137: 1; 138: 11 (11, 29). TG God, Privilege of Seeing.
13*a* TG Jesus Christ, Foreordained.

the record which we bear is the fulness of the gospel of Jesus Christ, who is the Son, whom we saw and with whom we ᵃconversed in the heavenly ᵇvision.

15 For while we were doing the work of ᵃtranslation, which the Lord had appointed unto us, we came to the twenty-ninth verse of the fifth chapter of John, which was given unto us as follows—

16 Speaking of the resurrection of the dead, concerning those who shall ᵃhear the voice of the ᵇSon of Man:

17 And shall come forth; ᵃthey who have done ᵇgood, in ᶜthe resurrection of the ᵈjust; and they who have done evil, in the resurrection of the unjust.

18 Now this caused us to marvel, for it was given unto us of the Spirit.

19 And while we ᵃmeditated upon these things, the Lord touched the eyes of our understandings and they were opened, and the ᵇglory of the Lord shone round about.

20 And we beheld the ᵃglory of the Son, on the ᵇright hand of the ᶜFather, and received of his fulness;

21 And saw the holy ᵃangels, and them who are ᵇsanctified before his throne, worshiping God, and the Lamb, who ᶜworship him forever and ever.

22 And now, after the many testimonies which have been given of him, this is the ᵃtestimony, last of all, which we give of him: That he ᵇlives!

23 For we ᵃsaw him, even on the ᵇright hand of ᶜGod; and we heard the voice bearing record that he is the Only ᵈBegotten of the Father—

24 That by ᵃhim, and through him, and of him, the ᵇworlds are and were created, and the ᶜinhabitants thereof are begotten ᵈsons and daughters unto God.

25 And this we saw also, and bear record, that an ᵃangel of God who was in authority in the presence of God, who ᵇrebelled against the Only Begotten ᶜSon whom the Father ᵈloved and who was in the bosom of the Father, was thrust down from the presence of God and the Son,

26 And was called ᵃPerdition, for the heavens ᵇwept over him—he was ᶜLucifer, a son of the morning.

27 And we beheld, and lo, he is ᵃfallen! is fallen, even a son of the morning!

14a D&C 109: 57.
  b TG Visions.
15a D&C 73: 3 (3–4); 93: 53.
16a John 5: 28.
  b TG Jesus Christ, Son of Man.
17a Joseph Smith Translation has the same wording as used here, which differs from the King James Version of John 5: 29.
  b TG Good Works.
  c TG Resurrection.
  d Dan. 12: 2 (1–3); Acts 24: 15; D&C 76: 65 (50, 64–65).
19a 1 Ne. 11: 1; D&C 138: 11 (1, 11); JS–H 1: 44. TG Meditation.
  b TG God, Glory of.
20a TG Jesus Christ, Glory of.
  b Acts 7: 56; D&C 49: 6; 104: 7.
  c TG God the Father—Elohim.

21a Matt. 25: 31; 2 Thes. 1: 7; Heb. 12: 22; D&C 130: 7; 136: 37.
  b TG Sanctification.
  c TG Worship.
22a TG Testimony; Witnesses.
  b Josh. 3: 10; 2 Sam. 22: 47; D&C 20: 17. TG Jesus Christ, Resurrection.
23a TG God, Privilege of Seeing; Jesus Christ, Appearances, Postmortal.
  b Heb. 1: 3.
  c TG Godhead.
  d John 1: 14.
24a Gen. 1: 1; John 1: 3 (1–3); Rom. 11: 36 (34–36); Heb. 1: 2 (1–3); Mosiah 4: 2; Morm. 9: 11; D&C 14: 9; 93: 10 (8–10).
  b Job. 9: 7 (7–9); Ps. 8: 3 (3–4); Moses 1: 33 (31–33); 7: 30 (29–31).

TG Astronomy; Creation; Jesus Christ, Creator; Jesus Christ, Power of.
  c D&C 88: 61.
  d Mal. 2: 10; 1 Cor. 15: 45 (45–48); 2 Ne. 2: 20 (19–20); D&C 27: 11; Moses 1: 34. TG Sons and Daughters of God.
25a D&C 29: 36 (36–39); Moses 4: 1 (1–3).
  b TG Council in Heaven; Rebellion.
  c TG Jesus Christ, Divine Sonship.
  d TG Jesus Christ, Relationships with the Father.
26a D&C 76: 32 (32–48); Moses 5: 24. TG Sons of Perdition.
  b Isa. 63: 9 (7–10); Moses 7: 29 (28–31).
  c Isa. 14: 12.
27a Luke 10: 18.

28 And while we were yet in the Spirit, the Lord commanded us that we should write the vision; for we beheld Satan, that old "serpent, even the ᵇdevil, who rebelled against God, and sought to take the kingdom of our ᶜGod and his Christ—

29 Wherefore, he maketh ᵃwar with the saints of God, and encompasseth them round about.

30 And we saw a vision of the ᵃsufferings of those with whom he made war and overcame, for thus came the voice of the Lord unto us:

31 Thus saith the Lord concerning all those who know my power, and have been made partakers thereof, and ᵃsuffered themselves through the power of the devil to be overcome, and to deny the truth and defy my power—

32 They are they who are the ᵃsons of ᵇperdition, of whom I say that it had been better for them never to have been born;

33 For they are ᵃvessels of wrath, doomed to suffer the wrath of God, with the devil and his angels in eternity;

34 Concerning whom I have said there is no ᵃforgiveness in this world nor in the world to come—

35 Having ᵃdenied the Holy Spirit after having received it, and having denied the Only Begotten Son of the Father, having ᵇcrucified him unto themselves and put him to an open ᶜshame.

36 These are they who shall go away into the ᵃlake of fire and brimstone, with the devil and his angels—

37 And the ᵃonly ones on whom the ᵇsecond ᶜdeath shall have any power;

38 Yea, verily, the only ones who shall ᵃnot be redeemed in the due time of the Lord, after the sufferings of his wrath.

39 For all the rest shall be ᵃbrought forth by the resurrection of the dead, through the ᵇtriumph and the glory of the Lamb, who was slain, who was in the bosom of the Father ᶜbefore the worlds were made.

40 And this is the ᵃgospel, the glad ᵇtidings, which the voice out of the heavens bore record unto us—

41 That he ᵃcame into the world, even Jesus, to be ᵇcrucified for the world, and to ᶜbear the sins of the ᵈworld, and to ᵉsanctify the world, and to ᶠcleanse it from all unrighteousness;

42 That through him all might be ᵃsaved whom the Father had put into his ᵇpower and made by him;

28a Rev. 12: 9.
   b TG Devil.
   c Isa. 14: 14; D&C 29: 36 (36–37); Moses 4: 1 (1–4).
29a Rev. 12: 9 (7–9); 13: 7; 2 Ne. 2: 18; 28: 20 (19–23); D&C 10: 27. TG War.
30a Jude 1: 6 (6–8); D&C 76: 44 (36, 44–49).
31a TG Apostasy of Individuals.
32a TG Sons of Perdition.
   b D&C 76: 26; Moses 5: 24.
33a Rom. 9: 22 (20–23); Rev. 2: 27 (26–27).
34a D&C 42: 18; 84: 41; 132: 27.
   b TG Forgiveness.
35a 2 Pet. 2: 20 (20–22); Alma 39: 6; D&C 76: 83. TG Holy Ghost,

Loss of; Holy Ghost, Unpardonable Sin against.
   b Heb. 6: 6 (4–6); 1 Ne. 19: 7; D&C 132: 27.
   c TG Shame.
36a Dan. 7: 11; Rev. 19: 20; 20: 10; 21: 8; 2 Ne. 9: 16 (8–19, 26); 28: 23; Jacob 6: 10; Mosiah 3: 27; Alma 12: 17 (16–18); D&C 63: 17.
37a D&C 76: 44 (44–49).
   b D&C 29: 28 (28, 41).
   c D&C 64: 7. TG Death, Spiritual, Second.
38a TG Sons of Perdition.
39a IE redeemed; see v. 38. All will be resurrected. See Alma 11: 41–45. D&C 88: 32.

   b TG Jesus Christ, Resurrection.
   c John 1: 1 (1–3, 10); Rev. 13: 8; D&C 93: 7.
40a 3 Ne. 27: 13 (13–22). TG Gospel; Salvation, Plan of.
   b Luke 8: 1.
41a TG Jesus Christ, Birth of; Jesus Christ, Mission of.
   b TG Jesus Christ, Crucifixion of.
   c Isa. 53: 12 (4–12); Heb. 9: 28.
   d 1 Jn. 2: 2 (1–2); Alma 11: 41 (40–41).
   e TG Salvation, Plan of; Sanctification.
   f TG Purification; Redemption.
42a TG Salvation.
   b TG Jesus Christ, Authority of.

43 Who ^aglorifies the Father, and saves all the works of his hands, except those sons of ^bperdition who deny the Son after the Father has revealed him.

44 Wherefore, he saves all ^aexcept them—they shall go away into ^beverlasting ^cpunishment, which is endless punishment, which is eternal punishment, to ^dreign with the ^edevil and his angels in eternity, where their ^fworm dieth not, and the fire is not quenched, which is their torment—

45 And the ^aend thereof, neither the place thereof, nor their torment, no man knows;

46 Neither was it revealed, neither is, neither will be revealed unto man, except to them who are made partakers thereof;

47 Nevertheless, I, the Lord, show it by ^avision unto many, but straightway shut it up again;

48 Wherefore, the end, the width, the height, and the ^adepth, and the misery thereof, they understand not, neither any man except those who are ^bordained unto this ^ccondemnation.

49 And we heard the voice, saying: ^aWrite the vision, for lo, this is the end of the vision of the sufferings of the ungodly.

50 And again we bear record—for we ^asaw and heard, and this is the ^btestimony of the ^cgospel of Christ concerning them who shall come forth in the resurrection of the ^djust—

51 They are they who received the ^atestimony of Jesus, and ^bbelieved on his name and were ^cbaptized after the ^dmanner of his burial, being ^eburied in the water in his name, and this according to the commandment which he has given;

52 That by ^akeeping the commandments they might be ^bwashed and ^ccleansed from all their sins, and receive the Holy Spirit by the laying on of the ^dhands of him who is ^eordained and sealed unto this power;

53 And who ^aovercome by faith, and are ^bsealed by the Holy Spirit of ^cpromise, which the Father ^dsheds forth upon all those who are just and true.

54 They are they who are the ^achurch of the ^bFirstborn.

55 They are they into whose hands the Father has given all things—

56 They are they who are ^apriests and ^bkings, who have received of his fulness, and of his glory;

57 And are ^apriests of the Most High, after the order of Melchizedek,

43a John 17: 4.
  TG Jesus Christ, Relationships with the Father.
  b TG Sons of Perdition.
44a D&C 76: 37.
  b TG D&C 19: 6.
  c D&C 76: 30. TG Damnation; Punishment.
  d D&C 88: 24.
  e TG Devil.
  f Isa. 66: 24; Mark 9: 48 (43–48).
45a D&C 29: 28 (28–29).
47a Moses 1: 20. TG Vision.
48a Rom. 2: 1.
  b IE sentenced, consigned.
  c Alma 42: 22.
49a TG Scriptures, Writing of.

50a TG Vision.
  b TG Testimony.
  c TG Gospel.
  d D&C 29: 13; 76: 17.
51a 1 Pet. 1: 9 (1–16). TG Baptism, Qualifications for.
  b D&C 20: 25.
  c TG Baptism, Essential.
  d D&C 124: 29; 128: 13.
  e Rom. 6: 4 (3–5). TG Baptism, Immersion.
52a TG D&C 138: 12.
  b 2 Ne. 9: 23; Moro. 8: 25.
  c TG Purification.
  d TG Hands, Laying on of; Holy Ghost, Gift of.
  e TG Authority.
53a TG Self-mastery.
  b TG Holy Ghost, Mission of; Sealing.

  c Eph. 1: 13; D&C 88: 3 (3–4); 124: 124; 132: 19 (18–26). TG Promise.
  d Acts 2: 33.
54a D&C 84: 34.
  b Heb. 12: 23; D&C 93: 22 (21–22). TG Jesus Christ, Firstborn.
55a Dan. 7: 14 (13–14); Matt. 28: 18; John 3: 35; 2 Pet. 1: 3; Rev. 2: 7; D&C 50: 28 (26–28); 84: 38.
56a Ex. 19: 6; Rev. 1: 6 (1–6); 5: 10; 20: 6; D&C 78: 15 (15, 18); 132: 19 (19–20).
  b D&C 104: 7.
57a TG High Priest—Melchizedek Priesthood; Priesthood, Melchizedek.

which was after the order of [b]Enoch, which was after the [c]order of the Only Begotten Son.

58 Wherefore, as it is written, they are [a]gods, even the [b]sons of [c]God—

59 Wherefore, [a]all things are theirs, whether life or death, or things present, or things to come, all are theirs and they are Christ's, and Christ is God's.

60 And they shall [a]overcome all things.

61 Wherefore, let no man [a]glory in man, but rather let him [b]glory in God, who shall [c]subdue all enemies under his feet.

62 These shall [a]dwell in the presence of God and his Christ forever and ever.

63 These are they whom he shall bring with him, when he shall [a]come in the [b]clouds of heaven to [c]reign on the earth over his people.

64 These are they who shall have part in the [a]first resurrection.

65 These are they who shall come forth in the resurrection of the [a]just.

66 These are they who are come unto [a]Mount [b]Zion, and unto the city of the living God, the heavenly place, the holiest of all.

67 These are they who have come to an innumerable company of [a]angels, to the general assembly and church of [b]Enoch, and of the [c]Firstborn.

68 These are they whose names are [a]written in heaven, where God and Christ are the [b]judge of all.

69 These are they who are [a]just men made [b]perfect through Jesus the mediator of the new [c]covenant, who wrought out this perfect [d]atonement through the shedding of his own [e]blood.

70 These are they whose bodies are [a]celestial, whose [b]glory is that of the [c]sun, even the glory of God, the [d]highest of all, whose glory the sun of the firmament is written of as being typical.

71 And again, we saw the [a]terrestrial world, and behold and lo, these are they who are of the terrestrial, whose glory differs from that of the church of the [b]Firstborn who have received the fulness of the Father, even as that of the [c]moon differs from the sun in the firmament.

57b Gen. 5: 23; Moses 6: 27 (27–68); 7: 1 (1–69).
  c D&C 107: 3 (2–4).
58a Ps. 82: 6 (1, 6); John 10:34 (34–36); 1 Cor. 8: 6 (5–6); D&C 121: 28. TG Exaltation; Man, Potential to Become Like Heavenly Father.
  b Luke 6: 35. TG Sons and Daughters of God.
  c Deut. 10: 17 (17–21); D&C 121: 32 (28–32).
59a Jer. 3: 1; Luke 12: 44; John 16: 15; 3 Ne. 28: 10; D&C 84: 38 (37–38).
60a Rev. 3: 5; 21: 7.
61a John 5: 44 (41–44); 1 Cor. 31 (21–23); 1 Thes. 2: 6.
  b Ps. 44: 8 (4–8); 2 Ne. 33: 6; Alma 26: 16 (11–16).
  c Ps. 66: 3; D&C 49: 6.
62a Ps. 15: 1 (1–5); 24: 3 (3–4); 27: 4; 1 Ne. 10:

21; 15: 33 (33–36); Mosiah 15: 23 (19–26); Morm. 7: 7; Moses 6: 57 (55–59).
  b D&C 76: 94 (94, 119); 130: 7. TG Eternal Life; God, Presence of.
63a TG Jesus Christ, Second Coming.
  b Matt. 24: 30.
  c Zech. 9: 10; D&C 58: 22. TG Jesus Christ, Millennial Reign.
64a Rev. 20: 6 (5–6).
65a D&C 76: 17.
66a Isa. 24: 23; Joel 2: 32; Obad. 1: 21; Heb. 11: 10; 12: 22 (22, 24); Rev. 14: 1; D&C 84: 2 (2, 18, 32); 133: 56 (18, 56).
  b TG Zion.
67a TG Angels.
  b D&C 38: 4; 45: 11 (11–12); Hel. 100 (99–100); 133: 54.
  c D&C 76: 54 (53–54).

68a TG Book of Life.
  b TG Jesus Christ, Judge; Judgment.
69a Ezek. 18: 9 (5–9); Heb. 12: 23; D&C 129: 3 (3–9); 138: 12.
  b TG Man, New, Spiritually Reborn; Perfection.
  c TG New and Everlasting Covenant.
  d TG Jesus Christ, Atonement through.
  e TG Blood, Symbolism of.
70a D&C 88: 29; 131: 1 (1–4); 137: 7. TG Celestial Glory.
  b Dan. 12: 3; D&C 137: 2 (2–4).
  c Matt. 13: 43; 1 Cor. 15: 41 (40–42).
  d TG God, Perfection of.
71a D&C 88: 30. TG Terrestrial Glory.
  b D&C 76: 54.
  c 1 Cor. 15: 41.

72 Behold, these are they who died *without *law;

73 And also who are the *spirits of men kept in *prison, whom the Son visited, and *preached the *gospel unto them, that they might be judged according to men in the flesh;

74 Who *received not the *testimony of Jesus in the flesh, but afterwards received it.

75 These are they who are *honorable men of the earth, who were *blinded by the craftiness of men.

76 These are they who receive of his glory, but not of his fulness.

77 These are they who receive of the *presence of the Son, but not of the fulness of the Father.

78 Wherefore, they are *bodies terrestrial, and not bodies celestial, and differ in glory as the moon differs from the sun.

79 These are they who are not *valiant in the *testimony of Jesus; wherefore, they obtain not the *crown over the kingdom of our God.

80 And now this is the end of the *vision which we saw of the terrestrial, that the Lord commanded us to *write while we were yet in the Spirit.

81 And again, we *saw the glory of the *telestial, which glory is that of the lesser, even as the *glory of the stars differs from that of the glory of the moon differs in the firmament.

82 These are they who received not the gospel of Christ, neither the *testimony of Jesus.

83 These are they who *deny not the Holy Spirit.

84 These are they who are thrust down to *hell.

85 These are they who shall not be redeemed from the *devil until the *last resurrection, until the Lord, even Christ the *Lamb, shall have finished his work.

86 These are they who receive not of his fulness in the eternal world, but of the Holy Spirit through the ministration of the terrestrial;

87 And the terrestrial through the *ministration of the celestial.

88 And also the telestial receive it of the administering of angels who are appointed to minister for them, or who are appointed to be *ministering spirits for them; for they shall be *heirs of salvation.

89 And thus we saw, in the heavenly vision, the glory of the *telestial, which surpasses all understanding;

90 And no man knows it except him to whom God has revealed it.

91 And thus we saw the glory of the *terrestrial which excels in all things the glory of the telestial, even in glory, and in power, and in might, and in dominion.

92 And thus we saw the *glory of the celestial, which *excels in all

72a Rom. 2:12; D&C 137:
  7 (7–10).
  b Acts 17:30.
    TG Accountability;
    Ignorance.
73a Job 14:10; Alma 11:
  45; 40:11 (11–14);
  Moses 7:57. TG Spirit
  Body; Spirits, Disembodied; Spirits in
  Prison.
  b D&C 88:99; 138:8.
    TG Genealogy and
    Temple Work; Salvation for the Dead.
  c 1 Pet. 3:19 (19–20);
    4:6; D&C 138:19.
  d TG Gospel.
74a D&C 138:32.
  b TG Salvation for the

Dead; Testimony.
75a TG Honorable.
  b TG Spiritual Blindness.
77a TG God, Presence of.
78a 1 Cor. 15:40 (40–42).
79a Jer. 8:20; D&C 45:2;
  56:16; 121:29.
    TG Apathy; Diligence;
    Trustworthiness.
  b TG Testimony.
80a TG Vision.
  b Moses 2:1. TG Record
    Keeping; Scriptures,
    Writing of.
81a TG Visions.
  b D&C 88:31.
    TG Telestial Glory.
  c TG Glory.
82a D&C 138:21.
    TG Testimony.

83a D&C 76:35.
84a Prov. 9:18; 2 Ne. 9:
  12 (11–12); Alma 12:
  11; D&C 29:38.
    TG Hell.
85a TG Devil.
  b Rev. 20:13 (12–13);
    Alma 11:41; D&C 43:
    18; 88:100 (100–101).
  c Gen. 22:8 (8–14);
    1 Ne. 13:35.
87a D&C 138:37.
88a TG Angels.
  b D&C 7:6.
89a TG Telestial Glory.
91a TG Terrestrial Glory.
92a TG Celestial Glory.
  b D&C 18:45; 84:38
    (35–38).

things—where God, even the Father, reigns upon his ^{c}throne forever and ever;

93 Before whose throne all things bow in humble ^{a}reverence, and give him glory forever and ever.

94 They who dwell in his ^{a}presence are the church of the ^{b}Firstborn; and they see as they are seen, and ^{c}know as they are known, having received of his fulness and of his ^{d}grace;

95 And he makes them ^{a}equal in power, and in might, and in dominion.

96 And the glory of the celestial is one, even as the glory of the ^{a}sun is one.

97 And the glory of the terrestrial is one, even as the glory of the moon is one.

98 And the glory of the telestial is one, even as the glory of the stars is one; for as one star differs from another star in glory, even so differs one from another in glory in the telestial world;

99 For these are they who are of ^{a}Paul, and of Apollos, and of Cephas.

100 These are they who say they are some of one and some of another —some of Christ and some of John, and some of Moses, and some of Elias, and some of ^{a}Esaias, and some of Isaiah, and some of Enoch;

101 But ^{a}received not the gospel, neither the testimony of Jesus, neither the prophets, neither the ^{b}everlasting covenant.

102 Last of all, these all are they who will not be ^{a}gathered with the saints, to be ^{b}caught up unto the ^{c}church of the Firstborn, and received into the cloud.

103 These are ^{a}they who are ^{b}liars, and ^{c}sorcerers, and ^{d}adulterers, and ^{e}whoremongers, and whosoever loves and makes a lie.

104 These are they who suffer the ^{a}wrath of God on earth.

105 These are they who suffer the ^{a}vengeance of eternal fire.

106 These are they who are cast down to ^{a}hell and ^{b}suffer the wrath of ^{c}Almighty God, until the ^{d}fulness of times, when Christ shall have ^{e}subdued all enemies under his ^{f}feet, and shall have ^{g}perfected his work;

107 When he shall ^{a}deliver up the ^{b}kingdom, and present it unto the Father, spotless, saying: I have ^{c}overcome and have ^{d}trodden the ^{e}wine-press ^{f}alone, even the wine-press of the fierceness of the wrath of Almighty God.

108 Then shall he be ^{a}crowned with the crown of his glory, to sit on the ^{b}throne of his power to reign forever and ever.

109 But behold, and lo, we saw the glory and the inhabitants of the telestial world, that they were as ^{a}innumerable as the stars in the

92c TG Kingdom of God, in Heaven.
93a TG Reverence.
94a D&C 76: 62; 130: 7. TG God, Presence of.
  b D&C 76: 54.
  c 1 Cor. 13: 12.
  d TG Grace.
95a D&C 29: 13 (12–13); 78: 5 (5–7); 84: 38 (35–39); 88: 107; 132: 20 (18–20).
96a 1 Cor. 15: 41 (40–41).
99a 1 Cor. 3: 22.
100a D&C 84: 13 (11–13).
101a TG Prophets, Rejection of.
  b TG New and Everlasting Covenant.
102a TG Separation.

b 1 Thes. 4: 16 (16–17); D&C 84: 100; 88: 96 (96–98); 101: 31.
  c D&C 78: 21.
103a Rev. 21: 8; 22: 15 (14–15); D&C 63: 17 (17–18).
  b TG Lying.
  c TG Sorcery.
  d TG Adultery; Sexual Immorality.
  e TG Whoredom.
104a TG Damnation.
105a Jude 1: 7.
106a TG Damnation; Hell.
  b D&C 19: 6.
  c D&C 87: 6.
  d Eph. 1: 10 (9–10).
  e 1 Cor. 15: 28; Philip. 3: 21.
  f Heb. 2: 8.

g Heb. 10: 14 (12–14).
107a 1 Cor. 15: 24 (24–28).
  b TG Jesus Christ, Relationships with the Father; Kingdom of God, on Earth.
  c John 16: 33.
  d Rev. 14: 20 (15–20); 19: 15; D&C 88: 106; 133: 50 (46–53).
  e Gen. 49: 11 (11–12); Isa. 63: 2 (1–3); Joel 3: 13; D&C 133: 48.
  f Mark 14: 37 (37, 40–41); D&C 122: 8 (7–8).
108a Rev. 19: 16.
  b D&C 137: 3.
109a Matt. 7: 13.

firmament of heaven, or as the sand upon the seashore;

110 And heard the voice of the Lord saying: These all shall bow the knee, and every tongue shall ^aconfess to him who sits upon the throne forever and ever;

111 For they shall be judged according to their ^aworks, and every man shall receive according to his own ^bworks, his own ^cdominion, in the ^dmansions which are prepared;

112 And they shall be ^aservants of the Most High; but ^bwhere God and Christ ^cdwell they ^dcannot come, ^eworlds without end.

113 This is the end of the vision which we saw, which we were commanded to write while we were yet in the Spirit.

114 But ^agreat and marvelous are the works of the Lord, and the ^bmysteries of his kingdom which he showed unto us, which surpass all understanding in glory, and in might, and in dominion;

115 Which he commanded us we should not write while we were yet in the Spirit, and are not ^alawful for man to utter;

116 Neither is man ^acapable to make them known, for they are only to be ^bseen and ^cunderstood by the power of the Holy Spirit, which God bestows on those who ^dlove him, and purify themselves before him;

117 To whom he grants this privilege of ^aseeing and knowing for themselves;

118 That through the power and manifestation of the Spirit, while in the flesh, they may be able to ^abear his ^bpresence in the world of glory.

119 And to God and the Lamb be ^aglory, and honor, and dominion forever and ever. Amen.

SECTION 77

Revelation given to Joseph Smith the Prophet, at Hiram, Ohio, March 1832. HC 1: 253–255. The Prophet wrote, "In connection with the translation of the Scriptures, I received the following explanation of the Revelation of St. John."

1–4, Beasts have spirits and shall dwell in eternal felicity on an immortal earth; 5–7, This earth has a temporal existence of 7,000 years; 8–10, Various angels restore the gospel and minister on earth; 11, The sealing of the 144,000; 12–13, Christ will come in the beginning of the seventh thousand years; 15, The two prophets who are to be slain in Jerusalem.

Q. What is the ^asea of glass spoken of by John, 4th chapter, and 6th verse of the Revelation?

A. It is the ^bearth, in its ^csanctified, ^dimmortal, and ^eeternal state.

2 Q. What are we to understand by the four beasts, spoken of in the same verse?

A. They are ^afigurative expressions, used by the Revelator, John,

110a Philip. 2: 10 (9–11).
111a TG Good Works.
  b Rev. 20: 12 (12–13).
  c Dan. 7: 27.
  d John 14: 2; D&C 59: 2; 81: 6.
112a TG Servants.
  b D&C 29: 29.
  c Rev. 21: 27 (9–27).
  d D&C 43: 33 (18, 33).
  e Eph. 3: 21.
114a 1 Chr. 16: 9; Ps. 9: 1; 26: 7; 40: 5; 92: 5; Rev. 15: 3; Morm. 9:

16 (16–20); D&C 88: 47; Moses 1: 4 (3–5).
  b Jacob 4: 8; D&C 19: 10.
115a 2 Cor. 12: 4; 3 Ne. 28: 14 (12–14).
116a 3 Ne. 5: 18; 17: 16 (15–25); 19: 32 (30–36); D&C 76: 10.
  b Ezek. 12: 2.
  c 1 Cor. 2: 11 (10–12). TG Holy Ghost, Mission of.
  d D&C 20: 31.

117a TG God, Privilege of Seeing.
118a D&C 88: 22.
  b TG God, Presence of.
119a Matt. 6: 13.
77 1a Ezek. 1: 22; Rev. 4: 6.
  b TG Earth, Destiny of.
  c D&C 130: 9. TG Sanctification.
  d TG Immortality.
  e TG Celestial Glory.
2a TG Symbolism.

in describing [b]heaven, the [c]paradise of God, the [d]happiness of man, and of beasts, and of creeping things, and of the fowls of the air; that which is spiritual being in the likeness of that which is temporal; and that which is temporal in the likeness of that which is spiritual; the [f]spirit of man in the likeness of his person, as also the spirit of the [f]beast, and every other creature which God has created.

3 Q. Are the four beasts limited to individual beasts, or do they represent classes or [a]orders?

A. They are limited to four individual beasts, which were shown to John, to represent the glory of the classes of beings in their destined [b]order or [c]sphere of creation, in the enjoyment of their [d]eternal [e]felicity.

4 Q. What are we to understand by the [a]eyes and [b]wings, which the beasts had?

A. Their eyes are a representation of light and knowledge, that is, they are full of [c]knowledge; and their wings are a [d]representation of [e]power, to move, to act, etc.

5 Q. What are we to understand by the four and twenty [a]elders, spoken of by John?

A. We are to understand that these elders whom John saw, were elders who had been [b]faithful in the work of the ministry and were dead; who belonged to the [c]seven churches, and were then in the paradise of God.

6 Q. What are we to understand by the book which John saw, which was [a]sealed on the back with seven seals?

A. We are to understand that it contains the revealed will, [b]mysteries, and the works of God; the hidden things of his economy concerning this [c]earth during the seven thousand years of its continuance, or its temporal existence.

7 Q. What are we to understand by the seven seals with which it was sealed?

A. We are to understand that the first seal contains the things of the [a]first thousand years, and the [b]second also of the second thousand years, and so on until the seventh.

8 Q. What are we to understand by the four [a]angels, spoken of in the 7th chapter and 1st verse of Revelation?

A. We are to understand that they are four angels sent forth from God, to whom is given power over the four parts of the earth, to save life and to destroy; these are they who have the [b]everlasting gospel to commit to every nation, kindred, tongue, and people; having power to [c]shut up the heavens, to seal up unto life, or to cast down to the [d]regions of darkness.

9 Q. What are we to understand by the angel [a]ascending from the east, Revelation 7th chapter and 2nd verse?

A. We are to understand that the angel ascending from the east is he to whom is given the seal of the living God over the twelve tribes of [b]Israel; wherefore, he crieth unto

2b TG Heaven.
  c TG Paradise.
  d TG Happiness.
  e D&C 93: 33; Abr. 5: 7 (7–8). TG Man, a Spirit Child of Heavenly Father; Spirit Body.
  f D&C 29: 24 (24–25); Moses 3: 19.
3a D&C 88: 42 (37–42); Abr. 3: 9.
  b TG Order.
  c D&C 93: 30; Moses 3: 9.
  d D&C 29: 24.

e TG Joy.
4a Zech. 3: 9; Rev. 5: 6.
  b 2 Chr. 5: 8; Isa. 6: 2 (2–7); Ezek. 1: 11.
  c TG God, Omniscience of.
  d TG Symbolism.
  e TG God, Power of.
5a Rev. 4: 4 (4, 10).
  b Rev. 14: 4 (2–5).
  c Rev. 1: 4.
6a Rev. 5: 1.
  b TG Mysteries of Godliness.
  c TG Earth, Destiny of.

7a TG Seal.
  b D&C 88: 108 (108–110).
  c Rev. 6: 3 (3–4); Moses 8: 28 (22, 28–29).
8a Rev. 7: 1 (1–8).
  b Rev. 14: 6.
  c 1 Kgs. 8: 35; Ether 4: 9.
  d Matt. 8: 12 (11–12); 22: 13 (1–14); D&C 133: 72 (71–73).
9a Rev. 7: 2.
  b Rev. 7: 4.

the four angels having the everlasting gospel, saying: Hurt not the earth, neither the sea, nor the trees, till we have sealed the servants of our God in their [f]foreheads. And, if you will receive it, this is [g]Elias which was to come to gather together the tribes of Israel, and [h]restore all things.

10 Q. What time are the things spoken of in this chapter to be accomplished?

A. They are to be accomplished in the [a]sixth thousand years, or the opening of the sixth seal.

11 Q. What are we to understand by sealing the one [a]hundred and forty-four thousand, out of all the tribes of Israel—twelve thousand out of every tribe?

A. We are to understand that those who are sealed are [b]high priests, ordained unto the holy order of God, to administer the everlasting gospel; for they are they who are ordained out of every nation, kindred, tongue, and people, by the angels to whom is given power over the nations of the earth, to bring as many as will come to the church of the [c]Firstborn.

12 Q. What are we to understand by the sounding of the [a]trumpets, mentioned in the 8th chapter of Revelation?

A. We are to understand that as God [b]made the world in six days, and on the seventh day he finished his work, and [c]sanctified it, and also formed man out of the [d]dust of the earth, even so, in the beginning of

the seventh thousand years will the Lord God [e]sanctify the earth, and complete the salvation of man, and [f]judge all things, and shall [g]redeem all things, except that which he hath not put into his power, when he shall have sealed all things, unto the end of all things; and the sounding of the trumpets of the seven angels are the preparing and finishing of his work, in the beginning of the seventh thousand years—the [h]preparing of the way before the time of his coming.

13 Q. When are the things to be accomplished, which are written in the 9th chapter of Revelation?

A. They are to be accomplished after the [a]opening of the seventh seal, [b]before the coming of Christ.

14 Q. What are we to understand by the little book which was [a]eaten by John, as mentioned in the 10th chapter of Revelation?

A. We are to understand that it was a mission, and an ordinance, for him to [b]gather the tribes of Israel; behold, this is Elias, who, as it is written, must come and [c]restore all things.

15 Q. What is to be understood by the two [a]witnesses, in the eleventh chapter of Revelation?

A. They are two prophets that are to be raised up to the [b]Jewish nation in the last days, at the time of the [c]restoration, and to prophesy to the Jews after they are gathered and have built the city of Jerusalem in the [d]land of their fathers.

9c Ezek. 9:4.
 d See "Elias" in BD.
    D&C 110:12.
 e TG Restoration of the
    Gospel.
10a Rev. 6:12 (12–17).
11a Rev. 7:4 (1–8); 14:3.
 b TG High Priest—
    Melchizedek Priest-
    hood.
 c D&C 76:54 (54, 67, 71,
    102). TG Jesus Christ,
    Firstborn.
12a Rev. 8:2.
 b TG Creation.

 c Gen. 2:3 (1–3);
    Ex. 20:11; Mosiah 13:
    19 (16–19); Moses 3:3
    (1–3); Abr. 5:3 (1–3).
 d Gen. 2:7; Morm. 9:17;
    D&C 93:35 (33–35).
 e TG Sanctification.
 f TG Jesus Christ, Judge;
    Judgment, The Last.
 g TG Jesus Christ,
    Redeemer.
 h TG Millennium, Pre-
    paring a People for.
13a Rev. 8:1.
 b Mal. 4:5.

14a Ezek. 2:9 (9–10); 3:2
    (1–3); Rev. 10:10.
 b TG Israel, Gathering of.
 c Matt. 17:11.
    TG Restoration of the
    Gospel.
15a Zech. 4:14 (12–14);
    Rev. 11:3 (1–14).
 b TG Israel, Judah,
    People of.
 c TG Last Days; Resto-
    ration of the Gospel.
 d Amos 9:15 (14–15).
    TG Israel, Land of.

SECTION 78

Revelation given through Joseph Smith the Prophet, at Hiram, Ohio, March 1832. The order given of the Lord to Joseph Smith for the purpose of establishing a storehouse for the poor. HC 1: 255-257. It was not always desirable that the identity of the individuals whom the Lord addressed in the revelations should be known by the world; hence, in the publication of this and some subsequent revelations the brethren were referred to by other than their own names. When the necessity had passed for keeping the names of the individuals unknown, their real names were thereafter given in brackets. Since there exists no vital need today to continue the code names, the real names only are now used herein, as given in the original manuscripts.

1-4, *The saints should organize and establish a storehouse;* 5 12, *Wise use of their properties will lead to salvation;* 13-14, *The Church should be independent of earthly powers;* 15-16, *Michael (Adam) serves under the direction of the Holy One (Christ);* 17-22, *Blessed are the faithful, for they shall inherit all things.*

THE Lord spake unto Joseph Smith, Jun., saying: Hearken unto me, saith the Lord your God, who are ordained unto the ᵃhigh priesthood of my church, who have assembled yourselves together;

2 And listen to the ᵃcounsel of him who has ᵇordained you from on high, who shall speak in your ears the words of ᶜwisdom, that salvation may be unto you in that thing which you have presented before me, saith the Lord God.

3 For verily I say unto you, the time has come, and is now at hand; and behold, and lo, it must needs be that there be an ᵃorganization of my people, in regulating and establishing the affairs of the ᵇstorehouse for the

ᶜpoor of my people, both in this place and in the land of ᵈZion—

4 For a permanent and everlasting establishment and order unto my church, to advance the cause, which ye have espoused, to the salvation of man, and to the glory of your Father who is in heaven;

5 That you may be ᵃequal in the bonds of heavenly things, yea, and earthly things also, for the obtaining of heavenly things.

6 For if ye are not equal in earthly things ye cannot be ᵃequal in obtaining heavenly things;

7 For if you will that I give you a place in the ᵃcelestial world, you must ᵇprepare yourselves by ᶜdoing the things which I have commanded you and required of you.

8 And now, verily thus saith the Lord, it is expedient that all things be done unto my ᵃglory, by you who are joined together in this ᵇorder;

9 Or, in other words, let my servant Newel K. Whitney and my servant Joseph Smith, Jun., and my

---

78 1a ᴛɢ Priesthood, Melchizedek.
  2a ᴛɢ Counsel.
    b ᴛɢ Priesthood, Authority; Priesthood, Ordination.
    c ᴛɢ God, Wisdom of; Wisdom.

3a D&C 51: 3; 82: 11 (11, 15-21).
    b D&C 72: 10; 83: 5.
    c D&C 42: 30 (30-42). ᴛɢ Poor; Welfare.
    d D&C 57: 2.
  5a ᴛɢ Consecration; Zion.
  6a D&C 49: 20.

7a ᴛɢ Celestial Glory; Objectives.
    b D&C 29: 8; 58: 6; 132: 3.
    c ᴛɢ Commitment.
  8a ᴛɢ Glory.
    b D&C 92: 1.

servant Sidney Rigdon sit in council with the saints which are in ^aZion;

10 Otherwise ^aSatan seeketh to turn their ^bhearts away from the truth, that they become ^cblinded and understand not the things which are prepared for them.

11 Wherefore, a commandment I give unto you, to prepare and organize yourselves by a ^abond or everlasting ^bcovenant that cannot be broken.

12 And he who breaketh it shall lose his office and standing in the church, and shall be ^adelivered over to the ^bbuffetings of Satan until the day of redemption.

13 Behold, this is the preparation wherewith I prepare you, and the foundation, and the ^aensample which I give unto you, whereby you may accomplish the commandments which are given you;

14 That through my providence, notwithstanding the ^atribulation which shall descend upon you, that the church may stand independent above all other creatures beneath the celestial world;

15 That you may come up unto the ^acrown prepared for you, and be made ^brulers over many kingdoms, saith the Lord God, the Holy One of Zion, who hath established the foundations of ^cAdam-ondi-Ahman;

16 Who hath appointed ^aMichael your prince, and established his feet, and set him upon high, and given unto him the keys of salvation under the counsel and direction of the ^bHoly One, who is without beginning of days or end of life.

17 Verily, verily, I say unto you, ye are ^alittle children, and ye have not as yet understood how great blessings the Father hath in his own hands and prepared for you;

18 And ye cannot ^abear all things now; nevertheless, be of good ^bcheer, for I will ^clead you along. The kingdom is yours and the blessings thereof are yours, and the ^driches of ^eeternity are yours.

19 And he who receiveth all things with ^athankfulness shall be made glorious; and the things of this earth shall be added unto him, even an ^bhundred fold, yea, more.

20 Wherefore, do the things which I have commanded you, saith your Redeemer, even the Son ^aAhman, who prepareth all things before he ^btaketh you;

21 For ye are the ^achurch of the ^bFirstborn, and he will take you up in a ^ccloud, and appoint every man his portion.

22 And he that is a faithful and ^awise ^bsteward shall inherit ^call things. Amen.

SECTION 79

Revelation given through Joseph Smith the Prophet, at Hiram, Ohio, March 1832. HC 1: 257.

9a D&C 72: 6 (1–26).	b Ex. 19: 6; Rev. 5: 10; 20: 6; D&C 76: 56; 132: 19 (19–20).	19a Ps. 34: 1 (1–3); Mosiah 2: 20 (20–21). TG Thanksgiving.
10a TG Devil.	c D&C 107: 53; 116: 1; 117: 8 (8, 11).	b Matt. 19: 29 (27–29).
b TG Hardheartedness.	16a D&C 27: 11. TG Adam.	20a D&C 95: 17; 107: 53; 116: 1.
c TG Spiritual Blindness.	b D&C 107: 54 (54–55).	b 1 Thes. 4: 17; Rev. 11: 12.
11a D&C 82: 11 (11, 15).	17a John 13: 33; 1 Cor. 2: 9; 1 Jn. 2: 1 (1, 12–13).	21a D&C 76: 102.
b TG Covenants.	18a John 16: 12; 3 Ne. 17: 2 (2–4); D&C 50: 40.	b D&C 76: 54 (53–54).
12a 1 Tim. 1: 20.	b TG Cheerfulness.	c D&C 88: 97.
b 1 Cor. 5: 5 (1–7); D&C 82: 21; 104: 10 (8–10).	c TG Guidance, Divine.	22a D&C 101: 61.
13a TG Millennium, Preparing a People for.	d TG Treasure.	b TG Stewardship.
14a D&C 58: 4 (3–4).	e TG Eternity.	c D&C 84: 38.
b TG Tribulation.		
15a TG Exaltation.		

1–4, *Jared Carter is called to preach the gospel by the Comforter.*

VERILY I say unto you, that it is my will that my servant Jared Carter should go again into the eastern countries, from place to place, and from city to city, in the power of the *a*ordination wherewith he has been ordained, proclaiming glad tidings of great joy, even the *b*everlasting gospel.

2 And I will send upon him the *a*Comforter, which shall teach him the truth and the *b*way whither he shall go;

3 And inasmuch as he is faithful, I will crown him again with *a*sheaves.

4 Wherefore, let your heart be glad, my servant Jared Carter, and *a*fear not, saith your Lord, even Jesus Christ. Amen.

SECTION 80

Revelation given through Joseph Smith the Prophet, at Hiram, Ohio, March 1832. HC 1: 257.

1–5, *Stephen Burnett and Eden Smith are called to preach in whatever place they choose.*

VERILY, thus saith the Lord unto you my servant *a*Stephen Burnett: Go ye, go ye into the world and preach the gospel to every *b*creature that cometh under the sound of your voice.

2 And inasmuch as you desire a companion, I will give unto you my servant *a*Eden Smith.

3 Wherefore, go ye and preach my gospel, whether to the north or to the south, to the east or to the west, it mattereth not, for ye cannot go amiss.

4 Therefore, declare the things which ye have heard, and verily believe, and *a*know to be true.

5 Behold, this is the will of him who hath *a*called you, your Redeemer, even Jesus Christ. Amen.

SECTION 81

Revelation given through Joseph Smith the Prophet, at Hiram, Ohio, March 1832. HC 1: 257–258. Frederick G. Williams is called to be a high priest and a counselor in the Presidency of the High Priesthood. The historical records show that when this revelation was received in March 1832, it called Jesse Gause to the office of counselor to Joseph Smith in the Presidency. However, when he failed to continue in a manner consistent with this appointment, the call was subsequently transferred to Frederick G. Williams. The revelation (dated March 1832) should be regarded as a step toward the formal organization of the First Presidency, specifically calling for the office of counselor in that body and explaining the dignity of the appointment. Brother Gause served for a time, but was excommunicated from the Church in December 1832. Brother Williams was ordained to the specified office on March 18, 1833.

---

79 1a D&C 52: 38 (38–39).
    b Rev. 14: 6.
   2a TG Holy Ghost,
      Comforter.

    b Ps. 25: 4 (1–5).
   3a D&C 31: 5.
   4a TG Fearfulness; Joy.
80 1a D&C 75: 35.
    b Mark 16: 15.

   2a D&C 75: 36.
   4a D&C 20: 17.
      TG Testimony.
   5a TG Called of God.

1–2, The keys of the kingdom are always held by the First Presidency; 3–7, If Frederick G. Williams is faithful in his ministry, he shall have eternal life.

VERILY, verily, I say unto you my servant Frederick G. Williams: Listen to the voice of him who speaketh, to the word of the Lord your God, and hearken to the calling wherewith you are called, even to be a [a]high priest in my church, and a [b]counselor unto my servant Joseph Smith, Jun.;

2 Unto whom I have given the [a]keys of the kingdom, which belong always unto the [b]Presidency of the High Priesthood:

3 Therefore, verily I acknowledge him and will bless him, and also thee, inasmuch as thou art faithful in counsel, in the office which I have ap-

pointed unto you, in prayer always, vocally and in thy heart, in public and in private, also in thy [a]ministry in proclaiming the gospel in the [b]land of the living, and among thy brethren.

4 And in doing these things thou wilt do the greatest [a]good unto thy fellow beings, and wilt promote the [g]glory of him who is your Lord.

5 Wherefore, be faithful; stand in the office which I have appointed unto you; [a]succor the [b]weak, lift up the hands which hang down, and [c]strengthen the [d]feeble knees.

6 And if thou art [a]faithful unto the end thou shalt have a [b]crown of [c]immortality, and eternal life in the [d]mansions which I have prepared in the house of my Father.

7 Behold, and lo, these are the words of Alpha and Omega, even Jesus Christ. Amen.

SECTION 82

Revelation given to Joseph Smith the Prophet, in Jackson County, Missouri, April 26, 1832. HC 1: 267–269. The occasion was a general council of the Church at which Joseph Smith the Prophet was sustained as the President of the High Priesthood, to which office he had previously been ordained at a conference of high priests, elders, and members, at Amherst, Ohio, January 25, 1832 (see heading to Section 75). Formerly unusual names were used in the publication of this revelation to conceal the identity of the persons named (see heading to Section 78). These unusual names have now been dropped, except in cases where the identification is not known (see verse 11).

1–4, Where much is given, much is required; 5–7, Darkness reigns in the world; 8–13, The Lord is bound when we do what he says; 14–18, Zion must increase in beauty and holiness; 19–24, Every man should seek the interest of his neighbor.

VERILY, verily, I say unto you, my servants, that inasmuch as you have [a]forgiven one another your trespasses, even so I, the Lord, forgive you.

2 Nevertheless, there are those among you who have sinned ex-

---

81 1a D&C 68: 15.
    TG High Priest—
    Melchizedek Priest-
    hood.
  b D&C 35: 22 (3–23);
    90: 6; 107: 24.
    TG Counselor.
  2a TG Priesthood, Keys
    of.
  b D&C 68: 15; 107:17

(9, 17, 22).
  3a TG Mission of Latter-
    day Saints.
  b Ps. 27: 13.
  4a TG Good Works.
  b D&C 124: 18;
    Moses 1: 39.
  5a TG Service.
  b Rom. 14: 1 (1–3).
  c D&C 23: 3; 31: 8;

108: 7.
  d Isa. 35: 3.
  6a TG Steadfastness.
  b TG Exaltation.
  c TG Immortality.
  d John 14: 2 (2–3);
    D&C 59: 2; 76: 111;
    98: 18; 106: 8.
82 1a Matt. 6: 14.
    TG Forgiveness.

ceedingly; yea, even *all of you have sinned; but verily I say unto you, beware from henceforth, and *refrain from sin, lest sore judgments fall upon your heads.

3 For of him unto whom *much is *given much is *required; and he who *sins against the greater *light shall *receive the greater *condemnation.

4 Ye call upon my name for *revelations, and I give them unto you; and inasmuch as ye keep not my sayings, which I give unto you, ye become transgressors; and *justice and judgment are the penalty which is affixed unto my law.

5 Therefore, what I say unto one I say unto all: *Watch, for the *adversary *spreadeth his dominions, and *darkness reigneth;

6 And the anger of God kindleth against the inhabitants of the earth; and *none doeth good, for all have gone out of the *way.

7 And now, verily I say unto you, I, the Lord, will not lay any *sin to your charge; go your ways and sin no more; but unto that soul who sinneth shall the *former sins return, saith the Lord your God.

8 And again, I say unto you, I give unto you a *new commandment, that you may understand my will concerning you;

9 Or, in other words, I give unto you directions how you may *act before me, that it may *turn to you for your salvation.

10 I, the Lord, am *bound when ye do what I say; but when ye do not what I say, ye have no *promise.

11 Therefore, verily I say unto you, that it is expedient for my servants Edward Partridge and Newel K. Whitney, A. Sidney Gilbert and Sidney Rigdon, and my servant Joseph Smith, and John Whitmer and Oliver Cowdery, and W. W. Phelps and Martin Harris to be bound *together by a bond and covenant that cannot be *broken by transgression, except judgment shall immediately follow, in your several *stewardships—

12 To manage the affairs of the poor, and all things pertaining to the bishopric *both in the land of Zion and in the land of Kirtland;

13 For I have consecrated the land of Kirtland in mine own due time for the benefit of the saints of the Most High, and for a *stake to Zion.

14 For *Zion must increase in *beauty, and in *holiness; her borders must be enlarged; her *stakes must be strengthened; yea, verily I say

2a Rom. 3: 23.
  b TG Abstinence.
3a Luke 12: 48; James 4: 17.
  TG Accountability; Talents.
  b Matt. 25: 29.
  TG Stewardship.
  c TG Mission of Latter-day Saints.
  d TG Apostasy of Individuals; Sin.
  e John 15: 22 (22–24); Rom. 7: 7 (7–8).
  TG Intelligence; Light.
  Luke 12: 47 (47–48); James 3: 1.
  f D&C 18: 46.
  TG Punishment.
4a TG Revelation.

  b TG God, Justice of; Justice.
5a TG Watchfulness.
  b TG Devil.
  c Isa. 60: 2; D&C 38: 11 (11–12).
  d TG Darkness, Spiritual.
6a Eccl. 7: 20; Matt. 19: 17.
  b Gen. 6: 12; Rom. 3: 12; D&C 1: 16; Moses 8: 29.
7a John 8: 11 (2–11).
  TG Sin.
  b Ps. 79: 8; Matt. 12: 45 (43–45); 18: 32–34; D&C 1: 33 (32–33); 58: 43.
8a John 13: 34.
9a D&C 43: 8; 103: 1.
  b Philip. 1: 19.

10a Josh. 23: 14; 1 Kgs. 8: 23; Ps. 97: 10; 145: 20 (1–21); Prov. 12: 2; 1 Ne. 15: 37 (37–38); 58: 31; 130: 20 (20–21).
  TG Blessing; Obedience.
  b TG Promise.
11a D&C 78: 3 (3–7, 11–15); 92: 1.
  b D&C 78: 11.
  c TG Stewardship.
12a D&C 104: 47.
13a Isa. 33: 20; 54: 2; D&C 68: 26; 94: 1.
14a TG Mission of Latter-day Saints.
  b TG Beauty.
  c Lev. 19: 2 (2–37).
  d TG Stake.

unto you, Zion must ᵉarise and put on her ᶠbeautiful garments.

15 Therefore, I give unto you this commandment, that ye bind yourselves by this covenant, and it shall be done according to the laws of the Lord.

16 Behold, here is ᵃwisdom also in me for your good.

17 And you are to be ᵃequal, or in other words, you are to have equal ᵇclaims on the ᶜproperties, for the benefit of ᵈmanaging the concerns of your stewardships, every man according to his wants and his needs, inasmuch as his wants are just—

18 And all this for the benefit of the church of the living God, that every man may ᵃimprove upon his ᵇtalent, that every man may ᶜgain other ᵈtalents, yea, even an hundred fold, to be cast into the Lord's ᶠstorehouse, to become the common ᵍproperty of the whole church—

19 ᵃEvery man seeking the interest of his ᵇneighbor, and doing all things with an ᶜeye single to the glory of God.

20 This order I have appointed to be an ᵃeverlasting ᵇorder unto you, and unto your successors, inasmuch as you sin not.

21 And the soul that sins against this covenant, and ᵃhardeneth his heart against it, shall be dealt with according to the laws of my church, and shall be delivered over to the ᵇbuffetings of Satan until the day of redemption.

22 And now, verily I say unto you, and this is wisdom, make unto yourselves friends with the ᵃmammon of unrighteousness, and they will not destroy you.

23 Leave judgment alone with me, for it is mine and I will ᵃrepay. Peace be with you; my blessings continue with you.

24 For even yet the ᵃkingdom is yours, and shall be forever, if you fall not from your ᵇsteadfastness. Even so. Amen.

SECTION 83

Revelation given through Joseph Smith the Prophet, at Independence, Missouri, April 30, 1832. HC 1: 269-270. This revelation was received as the Prophet sat in council with his brethren.

1-4, Women and children have claim upon their husbands and fathers for their support; 5-6, Widows and orphans have claim upon the Church for their support.

VERILY, thus saith the Lord, in addition to the ᵃlaws of the church concerning women and children, those who belong to the church, who have ᵇlost their husbands or fathers:

14e ᴛɢ Israel, Restoration of.
  f ᴛɢ Isa. 52: 1; D&C 113: 8 (7-8).
16a ᴛɢ God, Wisdom of.
17a ᴛɢ D&C 51: 3.
  b ᴛɢ Consecration.
  c ᴛɢ Wages.
  d ᴛɢ Family, Managing Finances in.
18a ᴛɢ Industry.
  b ᴛɢ Matt. 25: 25 (14-30); D&C 60: 13.
  c ᴛɢ Work, Value of.

d ᴛɢ Talents.
  e D&C 42: 33 (33-34, 55); 51: 13; 119: 1 (1-3).
  f D&C 42: 30.
19a 1 Cor. 10: 24.
  b ᴛɢ Neighbor.
  c Prov. 4: 21; D&C 88: 67. ᴛɢ Motivations.
20a D&C 104: 47.
  b D&C 78: 3 (3-6).
21a ᴛɢ Apostasy of Individuals; Hard-heartedness.
  b D&C 78: 12; 104: 9

(8-10); 132: 26.
22a Luke 16: 9.
23a Rom. 12: 19; Morm. 3: 15.
24a Luke 12: 32; D&C 64: 4.
  ᴛɢ Kingdom of God, on Earth.
  b ᴛɢ Dedication; Dependability.
83 1a D&C 51: 8 (7-14).
  b Deut. 10: 18; Isa. 1: 17 (16-17); James 1: 27.

2 "Women have *b*claim on their husbands for their maintenance, until their *c*husbands are taken; and if they are not found transgressors they shall have fellowship in the church.

3 And if they are not faithful they shall not have fellowship in the church; yet they may remain upon their inheritances according to the laws of the land.

4 All *a*children have claim upon their *b*parents for their *c*maintenance until they are of age.

5 And after that, they have *a*claim upon the church, or in other words upon the Lord's *b*storehouse, if their parents have not wherewith to give them inheritances.

6 And the storehouse shall be kept by the consecrations of the church; and *a*widows and orphans shall be provided for, as also the *b*poor. Amen.

SECTION 84

Revelation given through Joseph Smith the Prophet, at Kirtland, Ohio, September 22 and 23, 1832. HC 1: 286–295. During the month of September, elders had begun to return from their missions in the eastern states and to make reports of their labors. It was while they were together in this season of joy that the following communication was received. The Prophet designates it a revelation on priesthood.

1–5, The New Jerusalem and the temple shall be built in Missouri; 6–17, Line of priesthood is given from Moses to Adam; 18–25, The greater priesthood administers the gospel ordinances; 26–32, The lesser priesthood administers the preparatory law; 33–44, Men gain eternal life through the oath and covenant of the priesthood; 45–53, The Spirit of Christ enlightens men, and the world lies in sin; 54–61, The saints must testify of those things they have received; 62–76, They are to preach the gospel, and signs shall follow; 77–91, Elders are to go forth without purse or scrip, and the Lord will care for their needs; 92–97, Plagues and cursings await those who reject the gospel; 98–102, The new song

of the redemption of Zion; 103–110, Let every man stand in his own office and labor in his own calling; 111–120, The Lord's servants are to proclaim the abomination of desolation of the last days.

A *a*REVELATION of Jesus Christ unto his servant Joseph Smith, Jun., and six elders, as they *b*united their hearts and *c*lifted their voices on high.

2 Yea, the word of the Lord concerning his church, established in the last days for the *a*restoration of his people, as he has spoken by the mouth of his *b*prophets, and for the *c*gathering of his *d*saints to stand upon *e*Mount Zion, which shall be the city of *f*New Jerusalem.

2*a* D&C 75: 25.
  b 1 Tim. 5: 8 (8–16).
  c TG Family, Patriarchal; Marriage, Husbands.
4*a* Mosiah 4: 14 (14–15).
  TG Children.
  b TG Birth Control.
  c TG Family, Children, Responsibilities toward.
5*a* D&C 51: 4 (3–4).
  b D&C 78: 3. TG Welfare.

6*a* Deut. 14: 29; Mal. 3: 5; Acts 4: 35.
  TG Widows.
  b Zech. 7: 10; Mosiah 4: 26 (16–26); Hel. 4: 12; D&C 42: 30 (30–39, 71).
84 1*a* Gal. 1: 12.
  b 3 Ne. 27: 1 (1–2); D&C 29: 6.
  c TG Prayer.
2*a* TG Israel, Restoration of.

b Acts 3: 21.
c D&C 10: 65.
d TG Saints.
e Isa. 2: 3 (2–5); 18: 7; 24: 23; Heb. 12: 22 (22, 24); Rev. 14: 1; 3 Ne. 20: 33 (22–34); D&C 76: 66; 84: 32; 133: 56 (18, 56).
f Ether 13: 6 (2–11); D&C 42: 9; 45: 66 (66–67); A of F 10.
  TG Jerusalem, New.

3 Which city shall be ªbuilt, beginning at the ᵇtemple lot, which is appointed by the finger of the Lord, in the western boundaries of the State of Missouri, and ᶜdedicated by the hand of Joseph Smith, Jun., and others with whom the Lord was well pleased.

4 Verily this is the word of the Lord, that the city ªNew Jerusalem shall be built by the gathering of the saints, beginning at this place, even the place of the temple, which ᵇtemple shall be ᶜreared in this ᵈgeneration.

5 For verily this generation shall not all ªpass away until an ᵇhouse shall be built unto the Lord, and a ᶜcloud shall rest upon it, which cloud shall be even the ᵈglory of the Lord, which shall fill the house.

6 ªAnd the ᵇsons of Moses, according to the Holy Priesthood which he received under the ᶜhand of his father-in-law, ᵈJethro;

7 And Jethro received it under the hand of Caleb;

8 And Caleb received it under the hand of Elihu;

9 And Elihu under the hand of Jeremy;

10 And Jeremy under the hand of Gad;

11 And Gad under the hand of Esaias;

12 And Esaias received it under the hand of God.

13 ªEsaias also lived in the days of Abraham, and was blessed of him—

14 Which ªAbraham received the priesthood from ᵇMelchizedek, who received it through the lineage of his fathers, even till ᶜNoah;

15 And from Noah till ªEnoch, through the lineage of their fathers;

16 And from Enoch to ªAbel, who was slain by the ᵇconspiracy of his brother, who ᶜreceived the priesthood by the commandments of God, by the hand of his father ᵈAdam, who was the first man—

17 Which ªpriesthood ᵇcontinueth in the church of God in all generations, and is without ᶜbeginning of days or end of years.

18 And the Lord confirmed a ªpriesthood also upon ᵇAaron and his ᶜseed, throughout all their generations, which priesthood also continueth and ᵈabideth forever with the priesthood which is after the holiest order of God.

19 And this greater ªpriesthood administereth the gospel and holdeth the ᵇkey of the ᶜmysteries of

---

3a D&C 101: 18; 103: 11.
  b D&C 57: 3; 58: 57; 97: 10 (10–20); 124: 51 (49–51).
  c D&C 52: 2; HC 1: 199.
4a D&C 45: 66; Moses 7: 62. TG Mission of Latter-day Saints.
  b TG Temple.
  c D&C 124: 51 (49–54).
  d Matt. 23: 36; 24: 34; JS-M 1: 34.
5a D&C 45: 31.
  b D&C 124: 31 (25–55).
  c Ex. 33: 9; 40: 34; Num. 14: 14; 1 Kgs. 8: 10; 2 Chr. 5: 14 (11–14); 3 Ne. 18: 39. TG God, Presence of.
  d 2 Chr. 7: 2 (2–3); D&C 45: 67; 64: 41 (41–43); 97: 15 (15–20); 109: 12, 37. TG God, Manifestations of.
6a D&C 84: 31 (31–34).

b Lev. 8: 13; D&C 84: 34 (18–41).
  c TG Hands, Laying on of.
  d Ex. 2: 18 (16–18); 3: 1; 18: 1; Num. 10: 29.
   TG Priesthood, History of.
13a D&C 76: 100.
14a Abr. 1: 3 (1–4, 19, 31).
  b See "Melchizedek" in BD. Gen. 14: 18 (17–20); JST Gen. 14: 25–40; Alma 13: 14 (1–19); D&C 107: 2.
  c Gen. 5: 29.
15a Gen. 5: 21 (21–31); Moses 6: 21 (21–68); 7: 1 (1–69).
16a Gen. 4: 25 (2, 25).
  b Moses 5: 29 (29–32).
  c D&C 107: 42 (1, 40–57); Moses 6: 2.
  d 1 Cor. 15: 45. TG Adam.
17a Alma 13: 1 (1–19); Moses 6: 7; Abr. 2: 9

(9, 11). TG Priesthood, Melchizedek.
  b D&C 13: 1; 90: 3; 122: 9; 124: 130.
  d Heb. 7: 3.
18a TG Priesthood, History of.
  b Ex. 40: 15 (12–15); Num. 16: 40; 2 Chr. 26: 18; D&C 68: 18; 107: 13 (13–16, 70–76).
  c Lev. 8: 13; D&C 84: 6 (6–26, 33–41).
  d Num. 25: 13; D&C 13: 1.
19a TG Priesthood, Melchizedek.
  b D&C 28: 7; 35: 18; 64: 5. TG Priesthood, Keys of.
  c D&C 63: 23; 107: 19 (18–19). TG Mysteries of Godliness.

the kingdom, even the key of the [d]knowledge of God.

20 Therefore, in the [a]ordinances thereof, the power of [b]godliness is manifest.

21 And without the ordinances thereof, and the [a]authority of the priesthood, the power of godliness is [b]not manifest unto men in the flesh;

22 For without this [a]man can see the face of God, even the Father, and live.

23 Now this [a]Moses plainly taught to the children of Israel in the wilderness, and sought diligently to [b]sanctify his people that they might [c]behold the face of God;

24 But they [a]hardened their hearts and could not endure his [b]presence; therefore, the Lord in his [c]wrath, for his [d]anger was kindled against them, swore that they should not [e]enter into his rest while in the wilderness, which rest is the fulness of his glory.

25 Therefore, he took [a]Moses out of their midst, and the Holy [b]Priesthood also;

26 And the lesser [a]priesthood continued, which priesthood holdeth the [b]key of the [c]ministering of angels and the [d]preparatory gospel;

27 Which [a]gospel is the gospel of [b]repentance and of [c]baptism, and the [d]remission of sins, and the [e]law of [f]carnal commandments, which the Lord in his wrath caused to continue with the house of Aaron among the children of Israel until [g]John, whom God raised up, being [h]filled with the Holy Ghost from his mother's womb.

28 For he was baptized while he was yet in his childhood, and was [a]ordained by the angel of God at the time he was [b]eight days old unto this power, to overthrow the kingdom of the Jews, and to [c]make straight the way of the Lord before the face of his people, to prepare them for the [d]coming of the Lord, in whose hand is given [e]all power.

29 And [a]again, the [b]offices of elder and bishop are necessary [c]appendages belonging unto the high priesthood.

30 And again, the offices of [a]teacher and deacon are necessary appendages belonging to the lesser priesthood, which priesthood was confirmed upon [b]Aaron and his sons.

31 Therefore, as I said [a]concerning the sons of Moses—for the sons of Moses and also the sons of Aaron shall offer an acceptable [b]offering

19d Abr. 1: 2.
20a TG Ordinance.
 b TG Godliness.
21a TG Authority; Priesthood, Authority.
 b John 14: 21 (21–23).
22a John 1: 18; D&C 67: 11. TG God, Privilege of Seeing.
23a Ex. 19: 11 (5–11); 32: 19 (19–29); Deut. 4: 14; 30: 11 (11–14); 1 Ne. 20: 16; D&C 93: 31.
 b Lev. 8: 10. TG Sanctification.
 c TG God, Privilege of Seeing.
24a Ex. 20: 19 (18–21); 32: 8; Deut. 9: 23; 1 Ne. 17:30 (30–31,42). TG Hardheartedness.
 b Ex. 33: 3 (1–4); D&C 103: 19.

c Ex. 32: 10.
 d TG Anger; God, Indignation of.
 e JST Ex. 34: 1 (1–2); Num. 14: 23; Heb. 3: 11: 4:1 (1–11); Jacob 1: 7 (7–8).
25a Deut. 34: 5 (1–5).
 b TG Priesthood, History of; Priesthood, Melchizedek.
26a 2 Chr. 23: 6. TG Priesthood, Aaronic.
 b D&C 13: 1. TG Priesthood, Keys of.
 c D&C 107: 20.
 d Matt. 3: 3 (1–3); 1 Ne. 10: 8 (7–10).
27a D&C 107: 20.
 b TG Repentance.
 c TG Baptism.
 d TG Remission of Sins.
 e TG Law of Moses.

f Heb. 7: 16 (11–16).
 g John 5: 33; D&C 27: 7; 35: 4.
 h Luke 1: 15.
28a TG Priesthood, Ordination.
 b Gen. 17: 12.
 c Isa. 40: 3; Matt. 3: 3; Luke 3: 4; John 1: 23.
 d TG Jesus Christ, Prophecies about.
 e Matt. 28: 18; John 17: 2; 1 Cor. 15: 27; Heb. 1: 2; 1 Pet. 3: 22; D&C 93: 17.
29a TG Church Organization.
 b D&C 107: 5 (5, 7–88).
30a TG Deacon; Teacher.
 b Lev. 1: 7; D&C 132: 59.
31a D&C 13: 1; 84: 6; 124: 39.
 b D&C 128: 24.

and sacrifice in the house of the Lord, which house shall be built unto the Lord in this generation, upon the consecrated [c]spot as I have appointed—

32 And the sons of Moses and of Aaron shall be filled with the [a]glory of the Lord, upon [b]Mount Zion in the Lord's house, whose sons are ye; and also many whom I have called and sent forth to build up my [c]church.

33 For whoso is [a]faithful unto the obtaining these two [b]priesthoods of which I have spoken, and the [c]magnifying their calling, are [d]sanctified by the Spirit unto the [e]renewing of their bodies.

34 They become the [a]sons of Moses and of Aaron and the [b]seed of [c]Abraham, and the church and kingdom, and the [d]elect of God.

35 And also all they who receive this priesthood [a]receive me, saith the Lord;

36 For he that receiveth my servants [a]receiveth me;

37 And he that [a]receiveth me receiveth my Father;

38 And he that receiveth my Father receiveth my Father's [a]kingdom; therefore [b]all that my Father hath shall be given unto him.

39 And this is according to the [a]oath and covenant which belongeth to the priesthood.

40 Therefore, all those who receive the [a]priesthood, receive this [b]oath and covenant of my Father, which he cannot break, neither can it be moved.

41 But whoso breaketh this [a]covenant after he hath received it, and altogether turneth therefrom, shall [b]not have forgiveness of sins in this world nor in the world to come.

42 And wo unto all those who come not unto this priesthood which ye have received, which I now confirm upon you who are present this day, by mine own voice out of the heavens; and even I have given the heavenly hosts and mine angels [a]charge concerning you.

43 And I now give unto you a commandment to beware concerning yourselves, to give [a]diligent [b]heed to the words of eternal life.

44 For you shall [a]live by every word that proceedeth forth from the mouth of God.

45 For the [a]word of the Lord is truth, and whatsoever is truth is [b]light, and whatsoever is light is [c]Spirit, even the Spirit of Jesus Christ.

46 And the [a]Spirit giveth [b]light to

31c D&C 57:3.
32a TG Glory.
  b Isa. 24:23; Heb. 12:22 (22, 24); Rev. 14:1; D&C 76:66; 84:2 (2, 18); 133:56 (18, 56).
  c TG Jesus Christ, Head of the Church.
33a TG Loyalty; Worthiness.
  b TG Priesthood.
  c TG Israel, Mission of; Priesthood, Magnifying Callings within.
  d TG Sanctification.
  e Rom. 8:11.
34a D&C 84:6 (6–26).
  b Gal. 3:29; Abr. 2:10 (9–16). TG Seed of Abraham.
  c Lev. 26:42; D&C 132:30 (30–32). TG Abrahamic Covenant.

d Matt. 24:24; Mark 13:20; D&C 29:7. TG Election.
36a Matt. 10:40 (40–42); Luke 9:48; 10:16; 1 Jn. 4:6 (1–6).
37a John 13:20.
38a TG Exaltation; Kingdom of God, in Heaven.
  b Matt. 5:12 (3–12); Luke 12:44; 15:31 (31–32); John 16:15; Rom. 8:32 (22–34); Rev. 21:7; 3 Ne. 28:10; D&C 78:5 (5–7); 132:20 (18–20).
39a TG Covenant; Oath.
40a TG Priesthood, Melchizedek.
  b Ezek. 16:59 (44–63). TG Priesthood, Oath

and Covenant; Promise.
41a TG Apostasy of Individuals.
  b D&C 41:1; 42:18; 76:34; 132:27.
42a D&C 84:88.
43a TG Diligence.
  b 1 Kgs. 2:4; 1 Ne. 15:25 (23–25); D&C 1:14 (14, 37).
44a Deut. 8:3; Lev. 18:5; Matt. 4:4; D&C 98:11.
45a Ps. 33:4; 117:2. TG Truth.
  b D&C 67:9; 88:7 (6–13). TG Jesus Christ, Light of the World.
  c TG God, Spirit of.
46a Ezek. 36:27.
  b Rom. 2:15 (6–16). TG Conscience; Intelligence; Light of Christ.

'every man that cometh into the world; and the Spirit enlighteneth every man through the world, that hearkeneth to the voice of the Spirit.

47 And every one that hearkeneth to the voice of the Spirit ^acometh unto God, even the Father.

48 And the Father ^ateacheth him of the covenant which he has ^brenewed and confirmed upon you, which is confirmed upon you for your sakes, and not for your sakes only, but for the sake of the ^cwhole world.

49 And the whole ^aworld lieth in sin, and groaneth under ^bdarkness and under the ^cbondage of sin.

50 And by this you may know they are under the ^abondage of sin, because they come not unto me.

51 For whoso cometh not unto me is under the ^abondage of sin.

52 And whoso receiveth not my voice is not acquainted with ^amy voice, and is not of me.

53 And by this you may know the righteous from the wicked, and that the whole ^aworld ^bgroaneth under sin and darkness even now.

54 And your ^aminds in times past have been ^bdarkened because of ^cunbelief, and because you have treated ^dlightly the things you have received—

55 Which ^avanity and unbelief have brought the whole church under condemnation.

56 And this condemnation resteth upon the children of ^aZion, even all.

57 And they shall remain under this condemnation until they repent and remember the new ^acovenant, even the ^bBook of Mormon and the ^cformer commandments which I have given them, not only to say, but to ^ddo according to that which I have written—

58 That they may bring forth ^afruit meet for their Father's kingdom; otherwise there remaineth a ^bscourge and judgment to be poured out upon the children of Zion.

59 For shall the children of the kingdom ^apollute my holy land? Verily, I say unto you, Nay.

60 Verily, verily, I say unto you who now hear my ^awords, which are my voice, blessed are ye inasmuch as you receive these things;

61 For I will ^aforgive you of your sins with this commandment—that you remain ^bsteadfast in your minds in ^csolemnity and the spirit of prayer, in bearing ^dtestimony to all the world of those things which are communicated unto you.

62 Therefore, ^ago ye into all the world; and unto whatsoever place ye cannot go ye shall send, that the testimony may go from you into all the world unto every creature.

63 And as I said unto mine apostles, even so I say unto you, for you are mine ^aapostles, even God's high

---

46c John 1: 9; D&C 93: 2.
47a Moro. 7: 13 (12–13); D&C 35: 12.
  TG Guidance, Divine.
48a TG Inspiration; Teaching.
  b D&C 1: 22.
  TG Covenant.
  c Isa. 49: 6.
49a 1 Jn. 5: 19 (10–21).
  b TG Darkness, Spiritual.
  c TG Bondage, Spiritual.
50a Matt. 13: 19 (18–19); 2 Cor. 6: 17; D&C 93: 39 (38–39).
51a Gal. 4: 9. TG Sin.
52a John 10: 27 (7–27).
53a TG World.
  b Rom. 8: 22.

54a TG Mind.
  b TG Darkness, Spiritual; Light.
  c TG Apostasy of Individuals; Doubt; Unbelief, Unbelievers.
  d TG Levity.
55a Isa. 3: 16. TG Vanity.
56a Ps. 149: 2; Joel 2: 23; D&C 97: 21.
57a Jer. 31: 31 (31–34).
  b TG Book of Mormon.
  c Zech. 7: 7; Luke 16: 29 (29–31); 1 Ne. 13: 40.
  d James 1: 22 (22–25); D&C 42: 13 (13–29).
58a Luke 6: 44. TG Good Works; Mission of Latter-day Saints.

b D&C 90: 36.
  TG Punishment.
59a TG Pollution.
60a D&C 18: 34 (34–36).
61a Ex. 34: 7; Dan. 9: 9; D&C 62: 3.
  TG Forgiveness.
  b TG Dedication; Steadfastness.
  c D&C 43: 34; 88: 121; 100: 7.
  d TG Missionary Work.
62a Mark 16: 15; Acts 11: 18; D&C 1: 2.
  TG Israel, Mission of; Priesthood, Magnifying Callings within.
63a TG Apostles.

priests; ye are they whom my Father hath [b]given me; ye are my [c]friends;

64 Therefore, as I said unto mine apostles I say unto you again, that every [a]soul who [b]believeth on your words, and is baptized by water for the [c]remission of sins, shall [d]receive the Holy Ghost.

65 And these [a]signs shall follow them that believe:

66 In my name they shall do many wonderful [a]works;

67 In my [a]name they shall cast out devils;

68 In my name they shall [a]heal the sick;

69 In my name they shall [a]open the eyes of the blind, and unstop the ears of the deaf;

70 And the tongue of the dumb shall speak;

71 And if any man shall administer [a]poison unto them it shall not hurt them;

72 And the [a]poison of a serpent shall not have power to harm them.

73 But a commandment I give unto them, that they shall not [a]boast themselves of these things, neither speak them before the world; for these things are given unto you for your profit and for salvation.

74 Verily, verily, I say unto you, they who believe not on your words, and are not [a]baptized in water in

my name, for the [b]remission of their sins, that they may receive the Holy Ghost, shall be [c]damned, and shall not come into my Father's kingdom where my Father and I am.

75 And this revelation unto you, and commandment, is in force from this very hour upon all the [a]world, and the gospel is unto all who have not received it.

76 But, verily I say unto all those to whom the kingdom has been given—from you it [a]must be [b]preached unto them, that they shall repent of their former evil works; for they are to be upbraided for their evil [c]hearts of unbelief, and your brethren in Zion for their [d]rebellion against you at the time I sent you.

77 And again I say unto you, my friends, for from henceforth I shall call you [a]friends, it is expedient that I give unto you this commandment, that ye become even as my friends in days when I was with them, traveling to preach the gospel in my power;

78 For I suffered them not to have [a]purse or scrip, neither two coats.

79 Behold, I [a]send you out to [b]prove the world, and the laborer is worthy of his [c]hire.

80 And any man that shall go and preach this [a]gospel of the kingdom, and fail not to continue [b]faithful in all things, shall not be weary in

---

63b John 6: 37; 17: 9;
    3 Ne. 15: 24; D&C 27:
    14; 50: 41 (41–42).
  c Ex. 33: 11; John 15:
    14 (13–15); Ether 12:
    39; D&C 84: 77; 88:
    62; 93: 45.
64a TG Soul.
  b Mark 16: 16 (15–18).
    TG Believe.
  c TG Remission of Sins.
  d TG Holy Ghost, Gift of.
65a Mark 16: 17. TG Holy
    Ghost, Gifts of;
    Miracles; Signs.
66a TG God, Works of.
67a Matt. 7: 22; 10: 8;
    17: 21 (14–21).
68a Luke 4: 39.
    TG Healing.

69a Matt. 9: 28 (28–31);
    20: 30 (30–34);
    John 9: 1 (1–4);
    Mosiah 3: 5; 3 Ne. 17:
    9 (7–10). TG Sight.
71a Mark 16: 18.
72a Acts 28: 3 (3–9);
    D&C 24: 13; 124: 99
    (98–100).
73a Prov. 4: 24; Rom. 3:
    27; D&C 105: 24.
74a 2 Ne. 9: 23; D&C 76:
    52 (50–52); 137: 6.
    TG Baptism, Essential.
  b TG Remission of Sins.
  c John 3: 18; 12: 48.
75a TG Missionary Work;
    Revelation; World.

76a Isa. 49: 6 (5–7).
  b TG Priesthood,
    Magnifying Callings
    within.
  c TG Hardheartedness.
  d IE in April 1832
    according to HC 1:
    317–321.
77a D&C 84: 63.
    TG Friendship.
78a Matt. 10: 9 (9–10);
    Luke 10: 4; 22: 35
    (35–36); D&C 24: 18.
79a TG Delegation of
    Responsibility.
  b TG Test, Try, Prove.
  c D&C 31: 5.
80a Matt. 9: 35; JS-M 1:
    31.
  b TG Dependability.

mind, neither darkened, neither in body, limb, nor joint; and a ^a hair of his head shall not fall to the ground unnoticed. And they shall not go hungry, neither athirst.

81 Therefore, take ye no ^a thought for the morrow, for what ye shall eat, or what ye shall drink, or wherewithal ye shall be clothed.

82 For, ^a consider the ^b lilies of the field, how they grow, they toil not, neither do they spin; and the kingdoms of the world, in all their glory, are not arrayed like one of these.

83 For your ^a Father, who is in heaven, ^b knoweth that you have need of all these things.

84 Therefore, let the morrow take ^a thought for the things of itself.

85 Neither take ye thought beforehand ^a what ye shall say; but ^b treasure up in your minds continually the words of life, and it shall be ^c given you in the very hour that portion that shall be meted unto every man.

86 Therefore, let no man among you, for this commandment is unto all the ^a faithful who are called of God in the church unto the ministry, from this hour take purse or scrip, that goeth forth to proclaim this gospel of the kingdom.

87 Behold, I send you out to ^a reprove the world of all their unrighteous deeds, and to teach them of a judgment which is to come.

88 And whoso ^a receiveth you, there I will be also, for I will go ^b before your face. I will be on your right hand and on your left, and my ^c Spirit shall be in your hearts, and mine ^d angels round about you, to bear you up.

89 Whoso receiveth you receiveth me; and the same will feed you, and clothe you, and give you money.

90 And he who feeds you, or clothes you, or gives you money, shall in nowise ^a lose his reward.

91 And he that doeth not these things is not my disciple; by this you may know ^a my disciples.

92 He that receiveth you not, go away from him alone by yourselves, and ^a cleanse your feet even with water, pure water, whether in heat or in cold, and bear testimony of it unto your Father which is in heaven, and return not again unto that man.

93 And in whatsoever village or city ye enter, do likewise.

94 Nevertheless, search diligently and spare not; and wo unto that house, or that village or city that rejecteth you, or your words, or your testimony concerning me.

95 Wo, I say again, unto that house, or that village or city that rejecteth you, or your words, or your testimony of me;

96 For I, the ^a Almighty, have laid my hands upon the nations, to ^b scourge them for their ^c wickedness.

97 And ^a plagues shall go forth, and they shall not be taken from the earth until I have completed my work, which shall be cut ^b short in righteousness—

98 Until all shall ^a know me, who remain, even from the least unto the greatest, and shall be filled with

80c Luke 21:18.
81a Matt. 6:25;
     Luke 12:22.
82a Matt. 6:28.
  b TG Nature.
83a TG Man, a Spirit Child
     of Heavenly Father.
  b Matt. 6:8, 32.
84a Matt. 6:34.
85a Matt. 10:19 (19–20);
     Luke 12:11 (11–12);
     21:14; D&C 100:6.
  b Alma 17:2 (2–3);
     Hel. 5:18 (18–19);
     D&C 6:20; 11:26 (21–
     26); 24:6; 100:5 (5–8).

     TG Meditation; Mind;
       Motivations; Study.
  c TG Teaching with the
       Spirit.
86a Matt. 24:45; D&C 58:
     26 (26–29); 107:100
     (99–100).
87a TG Missionary Work.
88a Matt. 10:40 (40–42);
     John 13:20; 3 Jn. 1:5
     (1–14).
  b Ex. 23:23; Lev. 26:
     12 (13–13); Judg. 4:
     14; Ether 1:42 (42–43).
  c TG God, Spirit of.

  d D&C 84:42.
     TG Angels.
90a Matt. 10:42; Mark 9:
     41.
91a John 13:35.
92a Matt. 10:14; Luke 9:
     5; D&C 60:15.
     TG Washing.
96a TG God, Power of.
  b D&C 1:14 (13–14).
  c TG Wickedness.
97a TG Plague.
  b Matt. 24:22.
98a TG God, Knowledge
     about.

the knowledge of the Lord, and shall *b*see eye to eye, and shall lift up their voice, and with the voice together *c*sing this new song, saying:

99 The Lord hath brought again Zion;

The Lord hath *a*redeemed his people, *b*Israel,

According to the *c*election of *d*grace,

Which was brought to pass by the faith

And *e*covenant of their fathers.

100 The Lord hath redeemed his people;

And Satan is *a*bound and *b*time is no longer.

The Lord hath gathered all things in *c*one.

The Lord hath brought down *d*Zion from above.

The Lord hath *e*brought up Zion from beneath.

101 The *a*earth hath travailed and *b*brought forth her strength;

And truth is established in her bowels;

And the heavens have smiled upon her;

And she is clothed with the *c*glory of her God;

For he *d*stands in the midst of his *e*people.

102 Glory, and honor, and power, and might,

Be ascribed to our God; for he is full of *a*mercy,

Justice, grace and truth, and *b*peace, Forever and ever, Amen.

103 And again, verily, verily, I say unto you, it is expedient that every man who goes forth to proclaim mine everlasting gospel, that inasmuch as they have *a*families, and receive *b*money by gift, that they should send it unto them or make use of it for their benefit, as the Lord shall direct them, for thus it seemeth me good.

104 And let all those who have not families, who receive *a*money, send it up unto the bishop in Zion, or unto the bishop in Ohio, that it may be consecrated for the bringing forth of the revelations and the printing thereof, and for establishing Zion.

105 And if any man shall give unto any of you a coat, or a suit, take the old and cast it unto the *a*poor, and go on your way rejoicing.

106 And if any man among you be *a*strong in the Spirit, let him take with him that is *b*weak, that he may be *c*edified in all *d*meekness, that he may become strong also.

107 Therefore, take with you those who are ordained unto the *a*lesser priesthood, and send them *b*before you to make appointments, and to prepare the way, and to fill appointments that you yourselves are not able to fill.

108 Behold, this is the way that mine apostles, in ancient days, built up my church unto me.

109 Therefore, let every man stand in his own *a*office, and *b*labor in his own calling; and let not the *c*head say unto the feet it hath no need of the feet; for without the feet how shall the body be able to stand?

98b Isa. 52: 8.
   c Ps. 96: 1; Rev. 15: 3; D&C 25: 12; 133: 56. TG Singing.
99a Deut. 21: 8; Ps. 25: 22; Rom. 11: 26 (25–28); D&C 43: 29; 100: 13; 136: 18.
   b TG Israel, Restoration of.
   c TG Election.
   d TG Grace.
   e TG Abrahamic Covenant.
100a Num. 20: 2 (2–3); D&C 43: 31; 45: 55; 88: 110; 101: 28.

   b Alma 40: 8. TG Time.
   c Eph. 1: 10; D&C 27: 13.
   d D&C 45: 12 (11–14); Moses 7: 63 (62–64). TG Zion.
   e D&C 76: 102; 88: 96.
101a TG Earth, Destiny of.
   b Moses 7: 64 (54–67).
   c TG Glory.
   d TG God, Presence of.
   e Jer. 30: 22.
102a TG God, Mercy of.
   b TG Peace of God.
103a TG Family.
   b TG Family, Managing Finances in.

104a D&C 51: 8 (8–13); 58: 51 (49–51).
105a TG Poor.
106a TG Fellowshipping.
   b Rom. 14: 1 (1–4, 10, 13).
   c TG Edification.
   d TG Meekness.
107a TG Priesthood, Aaronic.
   b Luke 10: 1 (1–12).
109a TG Church Organization.
   b TG Priesthood, Magnifying Callings within.
   c 1 Cor. 12: 21.

110 Also the body hath need of every "member, that all may be "edified together, that the system may be kept perfect.

111 And behold, the "high priests should travel, and also the elders, and also the lesser "priests; but the "deacons and "teachers should be appointed to "watch over the church, to be standing ministers unto the church.

112 And the bishop, Newel K. Whitney, also should travel round about and among all the churches, searching after the poor to "administer to their wants by "humbling the rich and the proud.

113 He should also employ an "agent to take charge and to do his secular business as he shall direct.

114 Nevertheless, let the bishop go unto the city of New York, also to the city of Albany, and also to the city of Boston, and warn the people of those "cities with the sound of the gospel, with a loud voice, of the "desolation and utter abolishment which await them if they do reject these things.

115 For if they do reject these

things the hour of their judgment is nigh, and their "house shall be left unto them "desolate.

116 Let him "trust in me and he shall not be "confounded; and a "hair of his head shall not fall to the ground unnoticed.

117 And verily I say unto you, the rest of my servants, go ye forth as your circumstances shall permit, in your several callings, unto the great and notable cities and villages, "reproving the world in righteousness of all their unrighteous and ungodly deeds, setting forth clearly and understandingly the desolation of "abomination in the last days.

118 For, with you saith the Lord "Almighty, I will "rend their "kingdoms; I will not only "shake the earth, but the "starry heavens shall tremble.

119 For I, the Lord, have put forth my hand to exert the "powers of heaven; ye cannot see it now, yet a "little while and ye shall see it, and know that I am, and that "I will "come and reign with my people.

120 I am "Alpha and Omega, the beginning and the end. Amen.

SECTION 85

Revelation given through Joseph Smith the Prophet, at Kirtland, Ohio, November 27, 1832. HC 1: 298-299. This section is an extract from a letter of the Prophet to W. W. Phelps, who was living in Independence, Missouri. It was given to answer questions about those saints who had moved to Zion, but who had not received their inheritances according to the established order in the Church.

110a TG Church.
  b TG Edification.
111a TG High Priest—Melchizedek Priesthood.
  b TG Priest, Aaronic Priesthood.
  c TG Deacon.
  d TG Teacher.
  e TG Watchfulness.
112a TG Poor; Welfare.
  b D&C 56:16.
113a D&C 51:8 (8-12); 53:4; 90:22.
114a Matt. 11:20; Alma 34:31 (31-36);

3 Ne. 9:3.
  b D&C 1:13 (13-14).
115a Luke 13:35.
116a Prov. 28:25 (25-26); Isa. 50:10; D&C 11:12. TG Trust in God.
  b Ps. 22:5; 1 Pet. 2:6; D&C 49:27.
  c Matt. 10:30; Luke 21:18.
117a Titus 1:13.
  b TG Abomination of Desolation; Warnings.
118a TG God, Power of.
  b Dan. 2:44 (34-35,

44-45).
  c TG Kings, Earthly.
  d Joel 2:10; D&C 43:18; 45:33 (33, 48); 88:87 (87,90). TG Last Days.
  e D&C 21:6.
119a Matt. 24:29.
  b Heb. 10:37.
  c Ex. 15:18.
  d D&C 1:36 (12, 35-36); 29:11 (9-11); 45:59; 104:59. TG Jesus Christ, Millennial Reign; Jesus Christ, Second Coming.
120a D&C 35:1.

1–5, Inheritances in Zion are to be received through consecration; 6–12, One mighty and strong shall give the saints their inheritance in Zion.

It is the duty of the Lord's clerk, whom he has appointed, to keep a [a]history, and a general church [b]record of all things that transpire in Zion, and of all those who [c]consecrate properties, and receive [d]inheritances legally from the bishop;

2 And also their manner of life, their faith, and works; and also of the [a]apostates who apostatize after receiving their inheritances.

3 It is contrary to the will and commandment of God that those who receive not their [a]inheritance by [b]consecration, agreeable to his [c]law, which he has given, that he may [d]tithe his people, to prepare them against the day of [e]vengeance and burning, should have their [f]names enrolled with the people of God.

4 Neither is their [a]genealogy to be kept, or to be had where it may be found on any of the records or history of the church.

5 Their names shall not be found, neither the names of the fathers, nor the names of the children written in the [a]book of the law of God, saith the Lord of Hosts.

6 Yea, thus saith the [a]still small voice, which whispereth through and [b]pierceth all things, and often times it maketh my bones to quake while it maketh manifest, saying:

7 And it shall come to pass that I, the Lord God, will send one mighty and strong, holding the scepter of power in his hand, clothed with light for a covering, whose mouth shall utter words, eternal words; while his bowels shall be a fountain of truth, to set in [a]order the house of God, and to arrange by [b]lot the inheritances of the saints whose names are found, and the names of their fathers, and of their children, enrolled in the book of the law of God;

8 While that man, who was called and appointed, that putteth forth his hand to [a]steady the [b]ark of God, shall fall by the shaft of death, like as a tree that is smitten by the vivid shaft of lightning.

9 And all they who are not found written in the [a]book of remembrance shall find none inheritance in that day; but they shall be cut asunder, and their portion shall be appointed them among [b]unbelievers, where are [c]wailing and gnashing of teeth.

10 These things I say not of [a]myself; therefore, as the Lord speaketh, he will also fulfil.

11 And they who are of the High Priesthood, whose names are not found written in the [a]book of the law, or that are found to have [b]apostatized, or to have been [c]cut off from the church, as well as the lesser priesthood, or the members, in that day shall [d]not find an inheritance among the saints of the Most High;

85 1a D&C 21: 1; 47: 1;
69: 3 (3–8).
  b TG Record Keeping.
  c D&C 42: 30 (30–35).
  d D&C 51: 3 (1–3); 90:
30 (30–31).
2a TG Apostasy of
Individuals.
3a Num. 34: 13.
  b D&C 42: 30.
  TG Consecration.
  c D&C 70: 10.
  d TG Tithing.
  e Mal. 3: 11 (11, 17);
D&C 1: 13 (13–14);
97: 26.

  f Mal. 3: 16; D&C 20:
82.
4a Ezra 2: 62 (62–63).
5a TG Book of Life;
Record Keeping.
6a 1 Kgs. 19: 12 (11–13);
Job 4: 16 (12–21);
Hel. 5: 30 (30–31);
3 Ne. 11: 3 (3–6).
  b Heb. 4: 12.
7a TG Order.
  b Num. 33: 54.
  c D&C 64: 30; 99: 7.
8a Num. 1: 51; D&C 64:
17.
  b 2 Sam. 6: 6 (6–7);
1 Chr. 13: 10 (9–12).

  TG Ark of the
Covenant.
9a 3 Ne. 24: 16;
Moses 6: 5.
  TG Book of
Remembrance.
  b TG Unbelief,
Unbelievers.
  c D&C 19: 5.
10a D&C 1: 38.
11a TG Book of Life.
  b TG Apostasy of
Individuals.
  c TG Excommunication;
Worthiness.
  d D&C 51: 5 (4–5).

12 Therefore, it shall be done unto them as unto the *children of the *priest, as will be found recorded in the second chapter and sixty-first and second verses of Ezra.

SECTION 86

Revelation given through Joseph Smith the Prophet, at Kirtland, Ohio, December 6, 1832. HC 1: 300. This revelation was received while the Prophet was reviewing and editing the manuscript of the translation of the Bible.

1–7, The Lord gives the meaning of the parable of the wheat and tares ; 8–11, Priesthood blessings to those who are lawful heirs according to the flesh.

VERILY, thus saith the Lord unto you my servants, concerning the *parable of the *wheat and of the tares:

2 Behold, verily I say, the field was the world, and the apostles were the *sowers of the seed;

3 And after they have fallen asleep the great persecutor of the church, the apostate, the *whore, even *Babylon, that maketh all nations to drink of her cup, in whose hearts the enemy, even Satan, sitteth to reign—behold he soweth the *tares; wherefore, the tares choke the wheat and drive the *church into the wilderness.

4 But behold, in the *last days, even now while the Lord is beginning to bring forth the word, and the blade is springing up and is yet tender—

5 Behold, verily I say unto you, the *angels are crying unto the Lord day and night, who are ready and waiting to be sent forth to *reap down the fields;

6 But the Lord saith unto them, pluck not up the tares while the blade is yet tender (for verily your faith is weak), lest you destroy the wheat also.

7 Therefore, let the wheat and the *tares grow together until the harvest is fully ripe; then ye shall first gather out the wheat from among the tares, and after the gathering of the wheat, behold and lo, the tares are bound in bundles, and the field remaineth to be *burned.

8 Therefore, thus saith the Lord unto you, with whom the *priesthood hath continued through the lineage of your fathers—

9 For ye are lawful *heirs, according to the flesh, and have been *hid from the world with Christ in God—

10 Therefore your life and the *priesthood have remained, and must needs remain through you and your lineage until the *restoration of all things spoken by the mouths of all the holy prophets since the world began.

12a Ezra 2: 61 (61–62); Neh. 7: 63 (63–64).
  b TG Priesthood, Qualifying for.
86 1a D&C 101: 65 (64–75).
  b Matt. 13: 36 (6–43).
2a Matt. 13: 39; Mark 4: 3.
  TG Mission of Early Saints.
3a TG Whoredom.
  b Rev. 17: 5 (1–9).

  TG Babylon.
  c TG Apostasy of the Early Christian Church.
  d Rev. 12: 6 (6, 14).
4a TG Last Days.
5a D&C 38: 12.
  b TG Harvest.
7a D&C 101: 66.
  b Matt. 13: 40; Rev. 18: 8 (6–8).
8a D&C 113: 8.
  TG Priesthood,

History of.
9a Abr. 2: 9 (9–11).
  TG Abrahamic Covenant; Birthright; Seed of Abraham.
  b Col. 3: 3 (3–4).
10a TG Priesthood, Melchizedek.
  b Acts 3: 21; D&C 132: 45.
  TG Restoration of the Gospel.

11 Therefore, blessed are ye if ye continue in my ᵃgoodness, a ᵇlight unto the Gentiles, and through this priesthood, a ᶜsavior unto my people ᵈIsrael. The Lord hath said it. Amen.

SECTION 87

Revelation and prophecy on war, given through Joseph Smith the Prophet, December 25, 1832. HC 1: 301–302. This section was received at a time when the brethren were reflecting and reasoning upon African slavery on the American continent and the slavery of the children of men throughout the world.

1–4, War foretold between the Northern States and the Southern States; 5–8, Great calamities shall fall upon all the inhabitants of the earth.

VERILY, thus saith the Lord concerning the ᵃwars that will ᵇshortly come to pass, beginning at the rebellion of ᶜSouth Carolina, which will eventually terminate in the death and misery of many souls;

2 And the ᵃtime will come that ᵇwar will be poured out upon all nations, beginning at this place.

3 For behold, the Southern States shall be divided against the Northern States, and the Southern States will call on other nations, even the nation of Great Britain, as it is called, and they shall also call upon other nations, in order to defend themselves against other nations; and then ᵃwar shall be poured out upon all nations.

4 And it shall come to pass, after many days, ᵃslaves shall rise up against their masters, who shall be marshaled and disciplined for war.

5 And it shall come to pass also that the ᵃremnants who are left of the land will marshal themselves, and shall become exceedingly angry, and shall vex the Gentiles with a sore vexation.

6 And thus, with the ᵃsword and by bloodshed the inhabitants of the earth shall ᵇmourn; and with ᶜfamine, and plague, and earthquake, and the thunder of heaven, and the fierce and vivid lightning also, shall the inhabitants of the earth be made to feel the wrath, and indignation, and ᵈchastening ᵉhand of an Almighty God, until the consumption decreed hath made a full ᶠend of all ᵍnations;

7 That the cry of the saints, and of the ᵃblood of the saints, shall cease to come up into the ears of the Lord of ᵇSabaoth, from the earth, to be avenged of their enemies.

8 Wherefore, ᵃstand ye in holy places, and be not moved, until the day of the Lord come; for behold, it cometh ᵇquickly, saith the Lord. Amen.

11a Ex. 34: 6 (5–7);
2 Ne. 4: 17; 9: 10.
b Isa. 49: 6. TG Mission
of Latter-day Saints;
Peculiar People.
c Obad. 1: 21.
d Neh. 1: 10;
D&C 109: 59 (59–67).

87 1a D&C 45: 26.
b JS-H 1: 41 (40–41).
c D&C 130: 12 (12–13).
2a TG Last Days.
b Joel 3: 9 (9–16);
Matt. 24: 6 (6–7);
D&C 38: 29; 45: 63 (26,

63); 63: 33; 130: 12.
3a D&C 45: 69.
4a D&C 134: 12.
5a Micah 5: 8 (8–15); 3 Ne.
16: 15 (7–15); 20: 16
(15–21); 21: 12 (12–21);
D&C 109: 65 (65–67).
TG Israel, Remnant of.
6a Deut. 32: 41; 2 Ne. 1:
12.
b D&C 29: 15 (14–21);
45: 49. TG Mourning.
c Joel 1: 10; D&C 43: 25
(24–25); JS-M 1: 29.
TG Drought; Famine;

Plague.
d TG Chastening.
e Ether 1: 1.
f TG World, End of.
g Mark 13: 8; 1 Ne. 14:
15.
7a Rev. 6: 10 (1, 10); 19:
2; 2 Ne. 28: 10;
Morm. 8: 27 (27, 40–41);
Ether 8: 22 (22–24).
b James 5: 4; D&C 88:
2; 95: 7.
8a Matt. 24: 15; D&C 45:
32; 101: 22 (21–22, 64).
b Rev. 3: 11; D&C 1: 12.

SECTION 88

Revelation given through Joseph Smith the Prophet at Kirtland, Ohio, December 27, 1832. HC 1: 302–312. It was designated by the Prophet as the "olive leaf... plucked from the Tree of Paradise, the Lord's message of peace to us." It appears from the historical records that portions of this revelation were received on December 27 and 28, 1832, and January 3, 1833.

1–5, Faithful saints receive that Comforter which is the promise of eternal life; 6–13, All things are controlled and governed by the light of Christ; 14–16, The resurrection comes through the redemption; 17–31, Obedience to celestial, terrestrial, or telestial law prepares men for those respective kingdoms and glories; 32–35, Those who will to abide in sin remain filthy still; 36–41, All kingdoms are governed by law; 42–45, God hath given a law unto all things; 46–50, Man shall comprehend even God; 51–61, The parable of the man sending his servants into the field and visiting them in turn; 62–73, Draw near unto the Lord, and ye shall see his face; 74–80, Sanctify yourselves and teach one another the doctrines of the kingdom; 81–85, Every man who hath been warned should warn his neighbor; 86–94, Signs, upheavals of the elements, and angels prepare the way for the coming of the Lord; 95–102, Angelic trumps call forth the dead in their order; 103–116, Angelic trumps proclaim the restoration of the gospel, the fall of Babylon, and the battle of the great God; 117–126, Seek learning, establish a house of God [a temple], and clothe yourselves with the bond of charity; 127–141, Order of the school of the prophets set forth, including the ordinance of washing of feet.

VERILY, thus saith the Lord unto you who have assembled yourselves together to receive his will concerning you:

2 Behold, this is pleasing unto your Lord, and the angels ^arejoice over you; the ^balms of your prayers have come up into the ears of the Lord of ^cSabaoth, and are recorded in the ^dbook of the names of the sanctified, even them of the celestial world.

3 Wherefore, I now send upon you another ^aComforter, even upon you my friends, that it may abide in your hearts, even the Holy Spirit of ^bpromise; which other Comforter is the same that I promised unto my disciples, as is recorded in the testimony of John.

4 This Comforter is the ^apromise which I give unto you of ^beternal life, even the ^cglory of the celestial kingdom;

5 Which glory is that of the church of the ^aFirstborn, even of God, the holiest of all, through Jesus Christ his Son—

6 He that ^aascended up on high, as also he ^bdescended below all things, that he might be in and through all things, the ^dlight of truth;

7 Which truth shineth. This is the ^alight of Christ. As also he is in the

---

88 2a Luke 15: 7 (7–10).
   b Acts 10: 2 (1–4);
       D&C 112: 1.
       TG Almsgiving;
       Prayer.
       James 5: 4; D&C 87: 7; 95: 7.
   d TG Book of Life.
 3a John 14: 16.

   b 2 Pet. 1: 19; D&C 76: 53; 132: 19 (19, 26, 49).
 4a 1 Jn. 2: 25.
   b D&C 14: 7; 131: 5.
   c TG Celestial Glory.
 5a D&C 77: 11.
 6a Ps. 68: 18; Eph. 4: 8.
   b D&C 122: 8.
       TG Jesus Christ,

       Condescension of.
   c TG God, Omniscience of.
   d D&C 93: 2 (2, 8–39).
       TG Light; Truth.
 7a Moro. 7: 19 (15–19); D&C 84: 45; 93: 36.
       TG God, Spirit of; Light of Christ.

sun, and the light of the sun, and the power thereof by which it was [b]made.

8 As also he is in the moon, and is the light of the moon, and the power thereof by which it was made;

9 As also the light of the stars, and the power thereof by which they were made;

10 And the earth also, and the power thereof, even the earth upon which you [a]stand.

11 And the light which shineth, which giveth you light, is through him who enlighteneth your eyes, which is the same light that quickeneth your [a]understandings;

12 Which [a]light proceedeth forth from the presence of God to [b]fill the immensity of space—

13 The [a]light which is in all things, which giveth [b]life to all things, which is the [c]law by which all things are governed, even the [d]power of God who [e]sitteth upon his throne, who is in the bosom of eternity, who is in the midst of all things.

14 Now, verily I say unto you, that through the [a]redemption which is made for you is brought to pass the resurrection from the dead.

15 And the [a]spirit and the [b]body are the [c]soul of man.

16 And the [a]resurrection from the dead is the redemption of the soul.

17 And the redemption of the soul is through him that [a]quickeneth all things, in whose bosom it is decreed that the [b]poor and the [c]meek of the [d]earth shall inherit it.

18 Therefore, it must needs be [a]sanctified from all [b]unrighteousness, that it may be prepared for the celestial [c]glory;

19 For after it hath filled the measure of its creation, it shall be crowned with [a]glory, even with the presence of God the Father;

20 That bodies who are of the [a]celestial kingdom may [b]possess it forever and ever; for, for this [c]intent was it made and created, and for this intent are they [d]sanctified.

21 And they who are not [a]sanctified through the [b]law which I have given unto you, even the law of Christ, must inherit [c]another kingdom, even that of a terrestrial kingdom, or that of a telestial kingdom.

22 For he who is not able to abide the [a]law of a celestial kingdom cannot [b]abide a [c]celestial glory.

23 And he who cannot abide the law of a [a]terrestrial kingdom cannot abide a terrestrial glory.

24 And he who cannot abide the law of a [a]telestial [b]kingdom cannot abide a telestial [c]glory; therefore he is not meet for a kingdom of glory. Therefore he must abide a kingdom which is not a kingdom of glory.

25 And again, verily I say unto

7b Gen. 1:16. TG Creation; Jesus Christ, Creator; Jesus Christ, Power of; Moses 2:1.
10a Moses 2:1.
11a TG Understanding.
12a 1 Tim. 6:16. TG Light of Christ.
　b Ps. 139:7 (7–12); Jer. 23:24.
13a Col. 1:17 (16–17).
　b Deut. 30:20; D&C 10:70. TG Jesus Christ, Creator.
　c Job 38:33 (1–41); D&C 88:38 (36–38). TG God, Law of.
　d 2 Cor. 4:7. TG Jesus Christ, Power of.
　e Ps. 47:8; Rev. 7:15.
14a TG Jesus Christ, Atonement through;

Redemption; Resurrection.
15a TG Man, a Spirit Child of Heavenly Father; Spirit Body; Spirit Creation.
　b TG Body, Sanctity of.
　c Gen. 2:7; Ezek. 37:14 (6–14); Alma 40:23 (16–24). TG Soul.
16a Alma 11:45 (40–45).
17a 1 Tim. 6:13.
　b Luke 6:20; D&C 104:16. TG Poor.
　c Zeph. 2:3 (1–3); Matt. 5:5; D&C 38:20. TG Meekness.
　d TG Earth, Destiny of.
18a Gen. 6:11; Moses 8:28 (28–30).

　c TG Celestial Glory.
19a D&C 130:7 (7–9). TG Earth, Destiny of.
20a TG Earth, Purpose of.
　b D&C 38:20.
　c Moses 1:39. TG Man, Potential to Become Like Heavenly Father.
　d TG Man, New, Spiritually Reborn.
21a TG Sanctification.
　b TG God, Law of.
　c D&C 43:33 (18, 33); 76:112 (102, 112).
22a D&C 105:5.
　b D&C 76:118.
　c TG Celestial Glory.
23a TG Terrestrial Glory.
24a TG Telestial Glory.
　b D&C 76:44 (44–48).
　c Moses 1:13.

you, the ^aearth abideth the law of a celestial kingdom, for it filleth the ^bmeasure of its creation, and transgresseth not the law—

26 Wherefore, it shall be ^asanctified; yea, notwithstanding it shall ^bdie, it shall be ^cquickened again, and shall abide the power by which it is quickened, and the ^drighteous shall ^einherit it.

27 For notwithstanding they die, they also shall ^arise again, a ^bspiritual body.

28 They who are of a celestial ^aspirit shall receive the same ^bbody which was a natural body; even ye shall receive your bodies, and your ^cglory shall be that glory by which your bodies are ^dquickened.

29 Ye who are ^aquickened by a portion of the celestial ^bglory shall then receive of the same, even a fulness.

30 And they who are quickened by a portion of the ^aterrestrial glory shall then receive of the same, even a fulness.

31 And also they who are quickened by a portion of the ^atelestial glory shall then receive of the same, even a fulness.

32 And they who remain shall also be ^aquickened; nevertheless, they shall return again to their own place, to enjoy that which they are ^bwilling to receive, because they were not willing to enjoy that which they might have received.

33 For what doth it profit a man if a gift is bestowed upon him, and he receive not the gift? Behold, he rejoices not in that which is given unto him, neither rejoices in him who is the giver of the gift.

34 And again, verily I say unto you, that which is ^agoverned by law is also preserved by law and perfected and ^bsanctified by the same.

35 That which ^abreaketh a law, and ^babideth not by ^claw, but seeketh to become a law unto itself, and willeth to abide in sin, and altogether abideth in sin, cannot be sanctified by law, neither by ^dmercy, ^ejustice, nor ^fjudgment. Therefore, they must remain ^gfilthy still.

36 All kingdoms have a law given;

37 And there are many ^akingdoms; for there is no ^bspace in the which there is no ^ckingdom; and there is no kingdom in which there is no space, either a greater or a lesser kingdom.

38 And unto every kingdom is given a ^alaw; and unto every law there are certain bounds also and conditions.

39 All beings who abide not in those ^aconditions are not ^bjustified.

40 For ^aintelligence cleaveth unto intelligence; ^bwisdom receiveth wisdom; ^ctruth embraceth truth; ^dvirtue loveth virtue; ^elight cleaveth unto light; ^fmercy hath ^gcompassion on mercy and claimeth her own; ^hjustice continueth its course and

25a TG Earth, Destiny of.
  b 2 Ne. 2: 12.
26a TG Sanctification.
  b TG World, End of.
  c TG Earth, Renewal of.
  d 2 Pet. 3: 13 (11–13).
  e Matt. 5: 5; D&C 38: 20;
    45: 58; 56: 20; 57: 5; 59:
    2; 63: 20 (20, 48–49).
27a TG Resurrection.
  b 1 Cor. 15: 44.
28a TG Spirit Body.
  b TG Body, Sanctity of.
  c TG Judgment, The
    Last.
  d 1 Cor. 15: 35; D&C 43:
    32; 63: 51; 101: 31.
29a D&C 76: 70 (50–70).
    TG Celestial Glory.

  b TG Man, Potential to
    Become Like Heavenly
    Father.
30a D&C 76: 71 (71–80).
    TG Terrestrial Glory.
31a D&C 76: 81 (81–90, 98).
    TG Telestial Glory.
32a Alma 11: 41 (41–45);
    D&C 76: 39.
  b TG Agency.
34a TG Governments;
    Order.
  b TG Sanctification.
35a TG Disobedience.
  b TG Rebellion.
  c Prov. 28: 9.
  d TG God, Justice of.
  e TG Judgment.
  f Rev. 22: 11; 1 Ne. 15:
    33 (33–35); 2 Ne. 9: 16;

    Alma 7: 21; Morm. 9:
    14. TG Filthiness.
37a D&C 76: 24; Moses 1:
    33.
  b TG Astronomy.
  c TG Order.
38a Job 38: 33 (1–41);
    D&C 88: 13. TG God,
    Law of.
39a D&C 130: 21 (20–21).
  b TG Justification.
40a TG Intelligence.
  b TG Wisdom.
  c TG Truth.
  d TG Chastity; Virtue.
  e TG Light.
  f TG Mercy.
  g TG Compassion.
  h TG God, Justice of;
    Justice.

claimeth its own; judgment goeth before the face of him who sitteth upon the throne and governeth and executeth all things.

41 He *a*comprehendeth all things, and all things are before him, and all things are round about him; and he is above all things, and in all things, and is through all things, and is round about all things; and all things are by him, and of him, even God, forever and ever.

42 And again, verily I say unto you, he hath given a *a*law unto all things, by which they move in their *b*times and their seasons;

43 And their courses are fixed, even the courses of the heavens and the earth, which comprehend the earth and all the planets.

44 And they give *a*light to each other in their times and in their seasons, in their minutes, in their hours, in their days, in their weeks, in their months, in their years—all these are *b*one year with God, but not with man.

45 The earth *a*rolls upon her wings, and the *b*sun giveth his light by day, and the moon giveth her light by night, and the stars also give their light, as they roll upon their wings in their glory, in the midst of the *c*power of God.

46 Unto what shall I liken these kingdoms, that ye may understand?

47 Behold, all these are *a*kingdoms, and any man who hath *b*seen any or the least of these hath *c*seen God *d*moving in his majesty and power.

48 I say unto you, he hath seen him; nevertheless, he who came unto his *a*own was not comprehended.

49 The *a*light shineth in darkness, and the darkness comprehendeth it

not; nevertheless, the day shall come when you shall *b*comprehend even God, being quickened in him and by him.

50 Then shall ye know that ye have *a*seen me, that I am, and that I am the true *b*light that is in you, and that you are in me; otherwise ye could not abound.

51 Behold, I will liken these kingdoms unto a man having a field, and he sent forth his servants into the field to dig in the field.

52 And he said unto the first: Go ye and labor in the field, and in the first hour I will come unto you, and ye shall behold the joy of my countenance.

53 And he said unto the second: Go ye also into the field, and in the second hour I will visit you with the joy of my countenance.

54 And also unto the third, saying: I will visit you;

55 And unto the fourth, and so on unto the twelfth.

56 And the lord of the field went unto the first in the first hour, and tarried with him all that hour, and he was made glad with the light of the countenance of his lord.

57 And then he withdrew from the first that he might visit the second also, and the third, and the fourth, and so on unto the twelfth.

58 And thus they all received the light of the countenance of their lord, every man in his hour, and in his time, and in his season—

59 Beginning at the first, and so on unto the *a*last, and from the last unto the first, and from the first unto the last;

60 Every man in his own *a*order,

41a Job 22: 13 (13–14); Ps. 94: 9 (7–10); D&C 38: 2; Moses 1: 35 (35–37); 7: 36; Abr. 3: 2 (1–16).
42a Dan. 2: 21 (19–22, 28); Abr. 3: 9. TG God, Law of; Order.
  b Abr. 3: 4 (4–19). TG Nature; Time.
44a TG Light.
45a Hel. 12: 15 (8–15).
  b Gen. 1: 16; D&C 76: 71 (70–71); Abr. 4: 16.
  c D&C 88: 13 (7–13).
47a D&C 88: 61.
  b Moses 1: 27 (27–28); 7: 23; Abr. 3: 21 (21–23).
  c Alma 30: 44; Moses 6: 63.
  d D&C 76: 114.
48a John 1: 11.
49a D&C 6: 21; 50: 24 (23–24); 67: 9; 84: 45 (45–47).
  b John 17: 3; D&C 93: 28; 101: 32 (32–34). TG Revelation.
50a John 14: 7.
  b Dan. 2: 22. TG Light of Christ.
59a Matt. 20: 8 (1–16).
60a TG Order.

until his hour was finished, even according as his lord had commanded him, that his lord might be glorified in him, and he in his lord, that they all might be glorified.

61 Therefore, unto this parable I will liken all these *a*kingdoms, and the *b*inhabitants thereof—every kingdom in its hour, and in its time, and in its season, even according to the decree which God hath made.

62 And again, verily I say unto you, my *a*friends, I leave these *b*sayings with you to *c*ponder in your hearts, with this commandment which I give unto you, that ye shall *d*call upon me while I am near—

63 *a*Draw *b*near unto me and I will draw near unto you; *c*seek me diligently and ye shall *d*find me; ask, and ye shall receive; knock, and it shall be opened unto you.

64 Whatsoever ye *a*ask the Father in my name it shall be given unto you, that is *b*expedient for you;

65 And if ye ask anything that is not *a*expedient for you, it shall turn unto your *b*condemnation.

66 Behold, that which you hear is as the *a*voice of one crying in the wilderness—in the wilderness, because you cannot see him—my voice, because my voice is *b*Spirit; *c*truth abideth

and hath no end; and if it be in you it shall abound.

67 And if your eye be *a*single to my *b*glory, your whole bodies shall be filled with light, and there shall be no darkness in you; and that body which is filled with light *c*comprehendeth all things.

68 Therefore, *a*sanctify yourselves that your *b*minds become *c*single to God, and the days will come that you shall *d*see him; for he will unveil his face unto you, and it shall be in his own time, and in his own way, and according to his own will.

69 Remember the great and last promise which I have made unto you; cast away your *a*idle thoughts and your *b*excess of *c*laughter far from you.

70 Tarry ye, tarry ye in this place, and call a *a*solemn assembly, even of those who are the first *b*laborers in this last kingdom.

71 And let those whom they have warned in their traveling call on the Lord, and *a*ponder the *b*warning in their hearts which they have received, for a little season.

72 Behold, and lo, I will take care of your *a*flocks, and will raise up elders and send unto them.

73 Behold, I will *a*hasten my work in its time.

61*a* D&C 88: 47.
  b D&C 76: 24.
62*a* Ex. 33: 11; Ether 12: 39; D&C 84: 63; 93: 45.
  b Deut. 6: 6.
  c TG Meditation.
  d Isa. 55: 6; James 1: 5 (5–6); D&C 46: 7.
63*a* Ps. 69: 18; Zech. 1: 3 (3–4); James 4: 8; Rev. 3: 20 (20–21).
  TG God, Access to; God, Presence of.
  b Deut. 4: 7; Lam. 3: 57; Ezek. 36: 9 (8–15).
  c 1 Chr. 28: 9; Ezra 8: 22 (22–23); Ether 12: 41; D&C 101: 38; Abr. 2: 12.
  d 2 Chr. 15: 15; D&C 4: 7; 49: 26.
64*a* TG Communication; Prayer.

  b D&C 18: 18.
65*a* Rom. 8: 26 (26–27); James 4: 3; D&C 46: 28 (28–30).
  b D&C 63: 11 (7–12).
66*a* Ps. 95: 7; Isa. 40: 3; 1 Ne. 17: 13; Alma 5: 37 (37–38); D&C 65: 3; 97: 1; 128: 20.
  b TG God, Spirit of.
  c TG Truth.
67*a* Matt. 6: 22; D&C 82: 19. TG Dedication; Motivations; Priesthood, Magnifying Callings within.
  b John 7: 18.
  c Prov. 28: 5; D&C 93: 28. TG Discernment, Spiritual.
68*a* TG Man, New, Spiritually Reborn; Sanctification.
  b TG Mind.

  c Luke 11: 34 (34–36). TG Commitment.
  d Lev. 9: 4; D&C 67: 10 (10–12); 93: 1; 97: 16. TG God, Privilege of Seeing.
69*a* Matt. 12: 36; Alma 12: 14.
  b TG Rioting and Reveling; Temperance.
  c 1 Pet. 4: 3; D&C 59: 15; 88: 121.
  TG Laughter; Levity.
70*a* D&C 88: 117 (117–119); 124: 39. TG Solemn Assembly.
  b TG Missionary Work.
71*a* D&C 101: 78. TG Agency.
  b TG Warnings.
72*a* TG Church; Sheep; Shepherd.
73*a* Isa. 60: 22 (1–22).

74 And I give unto you, who are the first *a*laborers in this last kingdom, a commandment that you assemble yourselves together, and organize yourselves, and prepare yourselves, and *b*sanctify yourselves; yea, purify your hearts, and *c*cleanse your hands and your feet before me, that I may make you *d*clean;

75 That I may testify unto you *a*Father, and your God, and my *b*God, that you are clean from the *c*blood of this wicked generation; that I may fulfil this promise, this great and last *d*promise, which I have made unto you, when I will.

76 Also, I give unto you a commandment that ye shall continue in *a*prayer and fasting from this time forth.

77 And I give unto you a commandment that you shall *a*teach one another the *b*doctrine of the kingdom.

78 Teach ye diligently and my *a*grace shall attend you, that you may be *b*instructed more perfectly in theory, in principle, in doctrine, in the law of the gospel, in all things that pertain unto the kingdom of God, that are expedient for you to understand;

79 Of things both in *a*heaven and in the earth, and under the earth; things which have been, things which are, things which must

*b*shortly come to pass; things which are at home, things which are abroad; the wars and the perplexities of the *c*nations, and the judgments which are on the land; and a *d*knowledge also of countries and of kingdoms—

80 That ye may be prepared in all things where I shall send you again to *a*magnify the calling whereunto I have called you, and the *b*mission with which I have commissioned you.

81 Behold, I sent you out to *a*testify and warn the people, and it becometh every man who hath been warned to *b*warn his neighbor.

82 Therefore, they are left *a*without excuse, and their sins are upon their *b*own heads.

83 He that *a*seeketh me *b*early shall find me, and shall not be forsaken.

84 Therefore, tarry ye, and labor diligently, that you may be perfected in your ministry to go forth among the *a*Gentiles for the last time, as many as the mouth of the Lord shall name; to *b*bind up the law and *c*seal up the testimony, and to prepare the saints for the hour of judgment which is to come;

85 That their souls may escape the wrath of God, the *a*desolation of abomination which awaits the wicked, both in this world and in the world to come. Verily, I say unto you, let those who are not the *b*first

74*a* Matt. 9: 37; 20: 1.
　b Lev. 20: 7 (7–8); 2 Chr. 35: 6; Neh. 12: 30; 3 Ne. 19: 28 (28–29); D&C 50: 29 (28–29); 133: 62.
　c D&C 88: 139; 124: 37. TG Cleanliness; Washing.
　d Ether 12: 37; D&C 135: 5 (4–5).
75*a* TG Man, a Spirit Child of Heavenly Father.
　b TG Jesus Christ, Relationships with the Father.
　c Acts 2: 40; D&C 88: 138.
　d TG Promise.
76*a* 4 Ne. 1: 12; Moro. 6: 5. TG Fasting; Prayer.
77*a* Ex. 35: 34; Moro. 10: 9 (9–10); D&C 38: 23; 43: 8; 107: 85 (85–89). TG Teaching.
　b Titus 2: 1.
78*a* TG Grace.
　b D&C 88: 118; 90: 15; 93: 53. TG Education.
79*a* TG Heaven.
　b Rev. 1: 1; 22: 6.
　c TG Nations; War.
　d TG Knowledge.
80*a* TG Priesthood, Magnifying Callings within.
　b TG Mission of Latter-day Saints.
81*a* TG Testimony.
　b Ex. 18: 20; Ezra 7:

25; Ezek. 33: 6 (6–9); D&C 63: 58. TG Warnings; Watchman.
82*a* Rom. 1: 20 (17–21).
　b Acts 18: 6.
83*a* Deut. 4: 29 (29–31); Isa. 26: 9; Jer. 29: 13 (10–14); D&C 54: 10.
　b TG Procrastination.
84*a* Isa. 42: 6; D&C 133: 37 (37–60); JS–H 1: 41.
　b Isa. 8: 16 (16–17).
　c TG Seal.
85*a* Dan. 9: 27; Matt. 24: 15. TG Abomination of Desolation.
　b D&C 20: 2 (2, 5); 105: 7 (7, 33).

elders continue in the vineyard until the mouth of the Lord shall ^ccall them, for their time is not yet come; their garments are not ^dclean from the blood of this generation.

86 Abide ye in the ^aliberty wherewith ye are made ^bfree; ^centangle not yourselves in ^dsin, but let your hands be ^eclean, until the Lord comes.

87 For not many days hence and the ^aearth shall ^btremble and reel to and fro as a drunken man; and the ^csun shall ^dhide his face, and shall refuse to give light; and the moon shall be bathed in ^eblood; and the stars shall become exceedingly angry, and shall ^fcast themselves down as a fig that falleth from off a fig-tree.

88 And after your ^atestimony cometh wrath and indignation upon the people.

89 For after your testimony cometh the testimony of ^aearthquakes, that shall cause groanings in the midst of her, and men shall fall upon the ground and shall not be able to stand.

90 And also cometh the testimony of the ^avoice of thunderings, and the voice of lightnings, and the voice of tempests, and the voice of the waves of the sea heaving themselves beyond their bounds.

91 And all things shall be in ^acommotion; and surely, men's ^bhearts shall fail them; for fear shall come upon all people.

92 And ^aangels shall fly through the midst of heaven, crying with a loud voice, sounding the trump of God, saying: Prepare ye, prepare ye, O inhabitants of the earth; for the ^bjudgment of our God is come. Behold, and lo, the ^cBridegroom cometh; go ye out to meet him.

93 And immediately there shall appear a ^agreat sign in heaven, and all people shall see it together.

94 And another angel shall sound his trump, saying: That ^agreat ^bchurch, the ^cmother of abominations, that made all nations drink of the wine of the wrath of her ^dfornication, that ^epersecuteth the saints of God, that shed their blood—she who sitteth upon many waters, and upon the islands of the sea—behold, she is the ^ftares of the earth; she is bound in bundles; her bands are made strong, no man can loose them; therefore, she is ready to be burned. And he shall sound his trump both long and loud, and all nations shall hear it.

95 And there shall be ^asilence in ^bheaven for the space of half an hour; and immediately after shall the curtain of heaven be unfolded, as a ^cscroll is unfolded after it is rolled up, and the ^dface of the Lord shall be unveiled;

96 And the saints that are upon

85c　D&C 11:15.
　d　Lev. 6:11 (10–11);
　　1 Ne. 12:10 (10–11);
　　Jacob 1:19; 2:2;
　　D&C 4:2; 112:33.
　　TG Purification.
86a　1 Cor. 7:22; Mosiah 5:
　　8. TG Liberty.
　b　John 8:36; Alma 61:
　　9 (9, 21). TG Agency.
　c　Gal. 5:1.
　d　TG Bondage, Spiritual;
　　Sin.
　e　Job 17:9; 2 Ne. 25:
　　16. TG Chastity;
　　Cleanliness; Purification;
　　Worthiness.
87a　Isa. 13:13 (4–13); 14:
　　26 (22–26).

　h　D&C 43:18; 45:33;
　　84:118; 133:22.
　c　Joel 2:10; D&C 45:
　　42; 133:49.
　d　D&C 29:14.
　e　Rev. 6:12.
88a　TG Testimony.
89a　Rev. 11:13 (13–14);
　　D&C 45:33.
90a　Joel 2:11; Rev. 8:5;
　　D&C 35:21; 43:18
　　(17–25); 133:50 (50–
　　52).
91a　D&C 45:26; 63:33.
　b　Luke 21:26.
　　TG Fearfulness; Last
　　Days.
92a　Rev. 8:13; D&C 43:
　　18 (18, 25); 133:17.

　b　TG Jesus Christ, Judge.
　　Matt. 25:6; D&C 33:
　　17; 133:19 (10, 19).
93a　Matt. 24:30; Luke 21:
　　25 (25–27). TG Signs.
94a　1 Ne. 13:6 (4–9).
　b　TG Devil, Church of.
　c　Rev. 17:5 (5–15).
　d　Rev. 14:8.
　e　TG Hate; Persecution.
　f　Matt. 13:38; D&C 64:
　　24 (23–24); 101:24
　　(23–25). TG Earth,
　　Cleansing of.
95a　D&C 38:12.
　b　D&C 133:40 (40–46).
　c　Rev. 6:14.
　d　TG Jesus Christ,
　　Second Coming.

the earth, who are alive, shall be quickened and be [a]caught up to meet him.

97 And they who have slept in their graves shall [a]come forth, for their graves shall be opened; and they also shall be caught up to meet him in the midst of the [b]pillar of heaven—

98 They are Christ's, the [a]first fruits, they who shall descend with him first, and they who are on the earth and in their graves, who are first caught up to meet him; and all this by the voice of the sounding of the trump of the angel of God.

99 And after this another angel shall sound, which is the second trump; and then cometh the redemption of those who are Christ's at his [a]coming; who have received their part in that [b]prison which is prepared for them, that they might receive the gospel, and be [c]judged according to men in the flesh.

100 And again, another trump shall sound, which is the third trump; and then come [a]the spirits of men who are to be judged, and are found under [b]condemnation;

101 And these are the rest of the [a]dead; and they live not again until the [b]thousand years are ended, neither again, until the end of the earth.

102 And another trump shall sound, which is the fourth trump, saying: There are found among those who are to remain until that great and last day, even the end, who shall [a]remain [b]filthy still.

103 And another trump shall sound, which is the fifth trump, which is the fifth angel who committeth the [a]everlasting gospel—flying through the midst of heaven, unto all nations, kindreds, tongues, and people;

104 And this shall be the sound of his trump, saying to all people, both in heaven and in earth, and that are under the earth—for [a]every ear shall hear it, and every knee shall [b]bow, and every tongue shall confess, while they hear the sound of the trump, saying: [c]Fear God, and give glory to him who sitteth upon the throne, [d]forever and ever; for the hour of his judgment is come.

105 And again, another angel shall sound his trump, which is the sixth angel, saying: She is [a]fallen who made all nations drink of the wine of the wrath of her fornication; she is fallen, is fallen!

106 And again, another angel shall sound his trump, which is the seventh angel, saying: It is finished; it is finished! The [a]Lamb of God hath [b]overcome and [c]trodden the wine-press alone, even the winepress of the fierceness of the wrath of Almighty God.

107 And then shall the angels be crowned with the glory of his might, and the [a]saints shall be filled with his [b]glory, and receive their [c]inheritance and be made [d]equal with him.

108 And then shall the first angel

96a 1 Thes. 4: 16 (16–17);
    D&C 76: 102; 84: 100;
    101: 31.
97a 1 Thes. 2: 19;
    D&C 29: 13; 45: 45
    (45–46); 133: 56.
    TG Resurrection.
  b D&C 78: 21.
98a 1 Cor. 15: 23 (1–58).
99a TG Jesus Christ,
    Second Coming.
  b D&C 76: 73 (71–74);
    138: 8; Moses 7: 57.
    TG Salvation for the
    Dead; Spirits in
    Prison.

c 1 Pet. 4: 6.
100a Rev. 20: 13 (12–13);
    Alma 11:41; D&C 43:
    18; 76: 85.
  b Damnation.
101a Rev. 20: 5.
  b Millennium.
102a D&C 43: 18.
  b TG Filthiness.
103a Rev. 14: 6 (6–7).
    TG Restoration of the
    Gospel.
104a Ps. 86: 9; Rev. 5: 13.
  b Rom. 66: 4; 72: 9 (9–10);
    Mal. 1: 11; Philip. 2:
    10 (9–11).

c Rev. 14: 7.
    TG Reverence.
  d Heb. 1: 8.
105a Rev. 14: 8; D&C 1:
    16.
106a TG Jesus Christ, Lamb
    of God.
  b 1 Cor. 15: 25.
  c Isa. 63: 3 (3–4);
    Rev. 14: 20 (15–20);
    19: 15; D&C 76: 107;
    133: 50 (46–53).
107a TG Angels; Saints.
  b TG Celestial Glory.
  c TG Exaltation.
  d John 5: 18;
    D&C 76: 95.

again sound his trump in the ears of all living, and ᵃreveal the secret acts of men, and the mighty works of God in the ᵇfirst thousand years.

109 And then shall the second angel sound his trump, and reveal the secret acts of men, and the thoughts and intents of their hearts, and the mighty ᵃworks of God in the second thousand years—

110 And so on, until the seventh angel shall sound his trump; and he shall ᵃstand forth upon the land and upon the sea, and ᵇswear in the name of him who sitteth upon the throne, that there shall be ᶜtime no longer; and ᵈSatan shall be bound, that old serpent, who is called the devil, and shall not be loosed for the space of a ᵉthousand years.

111 And then he shall be ᵃloosed for a little season, that he may gather together his armies.

112 And ᵃMichael, the seventh angel, even the archangel, shall gather together his armies, even the hosts of heaven.

113 And the devil shall gather together his ᵃarmies; even the hosts of hell, and shall come up to battle against Michael and his armies.

114 And then cometh the ᵃbattle of the great God; and the devil and his armies shall be ᵇcast away into their own place, that they shall not have power over the saints any more at all.

115 For Michael shall fight their battles, and shall overcome him who ᵃseeketh the throne of him who sitteth upon the throne, even the Lamb.

116 This is the glory of God, and the ᵃsanctified; and they shall not any more see ᵇdeath.

117 Therefore, verily I say unto you, my ᵃfriends, call your solemn assembly, as I have ᵇcommanded you.

118 And as all have not ᵃfaith, seek ye diligently and ᵇteach one another words of ᶜwisdom; yea, seek ye out of the best ᵈbooks words of wisdom; seek learning, even by study and also by faith.

119 ᵃOrganize yourselves; prepare every needful thing; and establish a ᵇhouse, even a house of prayer, a house of fasting, a house of faith, a house of learning, a house of glory, a house of order, a house of God;

120 That your ᵃincomings may be in the name of the Lord; that your outgoings may be in the name of the Lord; that all your salutations may be in the name of the Lord, with ᵇuplifted hands unto the Most High.

121 Therefore, ᵃcease from all your light speeches, from all ᵇlaughter, from all your ᶜlustful desires, from all your ᵈpride and light-mindedness, and from all your wicked doings.

122 Appoint among yourselves a teacher, and let ᵃnot all be spokesmen at once; but let one speak at a

---

108a Ps. 64: 5 (4–6);
   Alma 37: 25;
   D&C 1: 3.
   b D&C 77: 6 (6–7, 12).
109a TG God, Works of.
110a Rev. 10: 5.
   b Dan. 12: 7.
   c D&C 84: 100.
   d Rev. 20: 2 (1–10);
   1 Ne. 22: 26;
   D&C 101: 28.
   e TG Millennium.
111a Rev. 20: 3 (3–10);
   Jacob 5: 77 (76–77);
   D&C 29: 22; 43: 31
   (30–31).
112a TG Adam.
113a Rev. 20: 8.
114a Rev. 16: 14.

b Rom. 16: 20; 1 Jn. 3:
   8; Rev. 20: 10 (9–10);
   D&C 19: 3; 29: 28
   (27–30, 44).
115a Isa. 14: 14 (12–15);
   Moses 4: 1 (1–4).
116a TG Saints; Sanctification.
   b Rev. 21: 4; Alma 11:
   45; 12: 18 (18, 20);
   D&C 63: 49.
   TG Immortality.
117a D&C 109: 6.
   b D&C 88: 70 (70–75).
118a TG Faith.
   b Prov. 9: 9; 23: 12;
   D&C 88: 78 (76–80);
   90: 15; 93: 53.
   TG Education; Learn-
   ing; Study; Teaching.

c TG Wisdom.
   d D&C 55: 4; 97: 3 (3–
   6); 109: 7 (7, 14).
119a TG Family, Managing
   Finances in; Priest-
   hood, Magnifying
   Callings within.
   b Hag. 1: 8; D&C 95: 3;
   97: 12 (10–17); 109: 8
   (2–9); 115: 8.
   TG Temple.
120a Ezek. 43: 11 (11–12).
   b Ps. 63: 4; 134: 2 (1–3).
121a Rom. 1: 30; D&C 59: 15;
   100: 7.
   b D&C 59: 15; 88: 69.
   c TG Carnal Mind; Lust;
   Sensuality.
   d TG Levity; Pride.
122a TG Order.

time and let all listen unto his sayings, that when all have spoken that all may be *b*edified of all, and that every man may have an equal privilege.

123 See that ye *a*love one another; cease to be *b*covetous; learn to impart one to another as the gospel requires.

124 Cease to be *a*idle; cease to be *b*unclean; cease to *c*find fault one with another; cease to *d*sleep longer than is needful; retire to thy bed early, that ye may not be weary; arise early, that your bodies and your minds may be *e*invigorated.

125 And above all things, clothe yourselves with the bond of *a*charity, as with a mantle, which is the bond of perfectness and *b*peace.

126 *a*Pray always, that ye may not faint, until I *b*come. Behold, and lo, I will come quickly, and receive you unto myself. Amen.

127 And again, the order of the house prepared for the *a*presidency of the *b*school of the *c*prophets, established for their instruction in all things that are expedient for them, even for all the *d*officers of the church, or in other words, those who are called to the ministry in the church, beginning at the high priests, even down to the deacons—

128 And this shall be the order of the house of the presidency of the school: He that is appointed to be president, or teacher, shall be found standing in his place, in the house which shall be prepared for him.

129 Therefore, he shall be first in the house of God, in a place that the congregation in the house may hear

his words carefully and distinctly, not with loud speech.

130 And when he cometh into the house of God, for he should be first in the house—behold, this is *a*beautiful, that he may be an *b*example—

131 Let him offer himself in prayer upon his knees before God, in *a*token or remembrance of the everlasting covenant.

132 And when any shall come in after him, let the teacher arise, and, with *a*uplifted hands to heaven, yea, even directly, salute his brother or brethren with these words:

133 Art thou a brother or brethren? I salute you in the name of the Lord Jesus Christ, in token or remembrance of the everlasting covenant, in which covenant I receive you to *a*fellowship, in a determination that is fixed, immovable, and unchangeable, to be your *b*friend and *c*brother through the grace of God in the bonds of love, to walk in all the commandments of God blameless, in thanksgiving, forever and ever. Amen.

134 And he that is found *a*unworthy of this salutation shall not have place among you; for ye shall not suffer that mine house shall be *b*polluted by him.

135 And he that cometh in and is faithful before me, and is a brother, or if they be brethren, they shall salute the president or teacher with uplifted hands to heaven, with this same prayer and covenant, or by saying Amen, in token of the same.

136 Behold, verily, I say unto you, this is an ensample unto you for a salutation to one another in the

---

122*b* TG Edification.
123*a* TG Love.
　b TG Covetousness.
124*a* TG Idleness;
　　Laziness.
　b TG Uncleanness.
　c Isa. 29:21;
　　D&C 64:8 (7–10).
　　TG Backbiting;
　　Gossip.
　d TG Sleep.
　e TG Health.
125*a* TG Charity.

　b TG Peace; Peacemakers.
126*a* TG Prayer.
　b Rev. 22:7 (7, 20);
　　D&C 1:12.
127*a* D&C 90:13.
　b D&C 90:7; 95:10
　　(10, 17); 97:5 (5–6).
　　TG Education.
　c 2 Kgs. 2:3 (3–15).
　d Num. 11:16;
　　D&C 107:21.
130*a* Isa. 52:7.

　b TG Example.
131*a* TG Everlasting
　　Covenant; Prayer;
　　Worship.
132*a* Lev. 9:22.
133*a* TG Fellowshipping.
　b TG Friendship.
　c TG Brotherhood and
　　Sisterhood.
134*a* Jer. 7:10 (9–10).
　b D&C 97:15 (15–17);
　　110:8 (7–8).

house of God, in the school of the prophets.

137 And ye are called to do this by prayer and thanksgiving, as the Spirit shall give utterance in all your doings in the house of the Lord, in the school of the prophets, that it may become a sanctuary, a tabernacle of the Holy Spirit to your *edification.

138 And ye shall not receive any among you into this school save he is clean from the *blood of this generation;

139 And he shall be received by

the ordinance of the *washing of feet, for unto this end was the ordinance of the washing of feet instituted.

140 And again, the ordinance of washing feet is to be administered by the president, or presiding elder of the church.

141 It is to be commenced with prayer; and after partaking of *bread and wine, he is to gird himself according to the *pattern given in the thirteenth chapter of John's testimony concerning me. Amen.

SECTION 89

Revelation given through Joseph Smith the Prophet, at Kirtland, Ohio, February 27, 1833. HC 1: 327–329. As a consequence of the early brethren using tobacco in their meetings, the Prophet was led to ponder upon the matter; consequently he inquired of the Lord concerning it. This revelation, known as the Word of Wisdom, was the result. The first three verses were originally written as an inspired introduction and description by the Prophet.

1–9, Use of wine, strong drinks, tobacco, and hot drinks proscribed; 10–17, Herbs, fruits, flesh, and grain are ordained for the use of man and of animals; 18–21, Obedience to gospel law, including the Word of Wisdom, brings temporal and spiritual blessings.

A *WORD OF WISDOM, for the benefit of the council of high priests, assembled in Kirtland, and the church, and also the saints in Zion—

2 To be sent greeting; not by commandment or constraint, but by revelation and the *word of wisdom, showing forth the order and *will of

God in the temporal salvation of all saints in the last days—

3 Given for a principle with *promise, adapted to the capacity of the *weak and the weakest of all *saints, who are or can be called saints.

4 Behold, verily, thus saith the Lord unto you: In consequence of *evils and designs which do and will exist in the hearts of *conspiring men in the last days, I have *warned you, and forewarn you, by giving unto you this word of wisdom by revelation—

5 That inasmuch as any man *drinketh *wine or strong drink

137a TG Edification; Worship.
138a D&C 88: 75 (75, 85).
139a D&C 88: 74.
    TG Washing.
141a TG Sacrament.
    b John 13: 5 (4–17).
89 1a TG Word of Wisdom.
2a 1 Cor. 12: 8; D&C 84: 44.

b D&C 29: 34.
    TG Commandments of God; God, Will of.
3a Eph. 2: 12; 6: 2;
    D&C 89: 18 (18–21).
    b 2 Cor. 12: 10; D&C 1: 19. TG Humility.
    c TG Saints.
4a TG Deceit; Evil.
    b TG Conspiracy;

Wickedness.
    c TG Warnings.
5a TG Abstinence.
    b Lev. 10: 9 (9–11);
    Isa. 5: 22 (11, 22);
    Rom. 14: 21 (20–23);
    D&C 27: 3.
    TG Drunkenness;
    Temperance; Word of
    Wisdom.

among you, behold it is not good, neither meet in the sight of your Father, only in assembling yourselves together to offer up your sacraments before him.

6 And, behold, this should be wine, yea, ^apure wine of the grape of the vine, of your own make.

7 And, again, ^astrong drinks are not for the belly, but for the washing of your bodies.

8 And again, tobacco is not for the ^abody, neither for the belly, and is not good for man, but is an herb for bruises and all sick cattle, to be used with judgment and skill.

9 And again, hot drinks are not for the body or belly.

10 And again, verily I say unto you, all wholesome ^aherbs God hath ordained for the constitution, nature, and use of man—

11 Every herb in the season thereof, and every fruit in the season thereof; all these to be used with ^aprudence and ^bthanksgiving.

12 Yea, ^aflesh also of ^bbeasts and of the fowls of the air, I, the Lord, have ordained for the use of man with thanksgiving; nevertheless they are to be used ^csparingly;

13 And it is pleasing unto me that they should not be ^aused, only in times of winter, or of cold, or ^bfamine.

14 All ^agrain is ordained for the use of man and of beasts, to be the staff of life, not only for man but for the beasts of the field, and the fowls of heaven, and all wild animals that run or creep on the earth;

15 And ^athese hath God made for the use of man only in times of famine and excess of hunger.

16 All grain is good for the ^afood of man; as also the ^bfruit of the vine; that which yieldeth fruit, whether in the ground or above the ground—

17 Nevertheless, wheat for man, and corn for the ox, and oats for the horse, and rye for the fowls and for swine, and for all beasts of the field, and barley for all useful animals, and for mild drinks, as also other grain.

18 And all saints who remember to keep and do these sayings, walking in obedience to the commandments, ^ashall receive ^bhealth in their navel and marrow to their bones;

19 And shall ^afind ^bwisdom and great ^ctreasures of ^dknowledge, even hidden treasures;

20 And shall ^arun and not be ^bweary, and shall walk and not faint.

21 And I, the Lord, give unto them a promise, that the ^adestroying angel shall ^bpass by them, as the children of Israel, and not slay them. Amen.

SECTION 90

Revelation to Joseph Smith the Prophet, given at Kirtland, Ohio, March 8, 1833. HC 1: 329–331. This revelation is a continuing step in the establishment of the First Presidency (see heading to Section 81), and as a consequence thereof the counselors mentioned were ordained on March 18, 1833.

6a D&C 27: 3 (1–14).
7a Prov. 20: 1; 23: 30 (29–35); Luke 1: 15.
8a TG Body, Sanctity of; Health.
10a IE plants. Gen. 1: 29; D&C 59: 17 (17–20).
11a TG Prudence; Temperance.
  b 1 Tim. 4: 3 (3–4). TG Thanksgiving.
12a Gen. 9: 3; Lev. 11: 2 (1–8). TG Meat.

  b D&C 49: 19.
  c TG Temperance.
13a D&C 59: 20 (16–20).
  b TG Famine.
14a See "Corn" in BD.
15a D&C 49: 18; 89: 13.
16a TG Food.
  b Gen. 1: 29.
18a D&C 89: 3.
  b Prov. 3: 8; Dan. 1: 13 (6–20). TG Health.

19a D&C 84: 80.
  b TG Wisdom.
  c TG Treasure.
  d Dan. 1: 17 (6–20). TG Knowledge; Testimony.
20a Prov. 4: 12; Isa. 40: 31. TG Strength.
  b Prov. 24: 10 (10–12); D&C 84: 80.
21a TG Protection, Divine.
  b Ex. 12: 23 (23, 29).

1–5, Keys of the kingdom are committed to Joseph Smith and through him to the Church; 6–7, Sidney Rigdon and Frederick G. Williams are to serve in the First Presidency; 8–11, The gospel is to be preached to the nations of Israel, to the Gentiles, and to the Jews, every man hearing in his own tongue; 12–18, Joseph Smith and his counselors are to set in order the Church; 19–37, Various individuals are counseled by the Lord to walk uprightly and serve in his kingdom.

THUS saith the Lord, verily, verily I say unto you my son, thy sins are ^aforgiven thee, according to thy petition, for thy prayers and the prayers of thy brethren have come up into my ears.

2 Therefore, thou art blessed from henceforth that bear the ^akeys of the kingdom given unto you; which ^bkingdom is coming forth for the last time.

3 Verily I say unto you, the keys of this ^akingdom shall ^bnever be taken from you, while thou art in the world, neither in the world to come;

4 Nevertheless, through you shall the ^aoracles be given to another, yea, even unto the church.

5 And all they who receive the ^aoracles of God, let them beware how they hold them lest they are accounted as a light thing, and are brought under condemnation thereby, and stumble and fall when the storms descend, and the winds blow, and the ^brains descend, and beat upon their house.

6 And again, verily I say unto thy brethren, Sidney Rigdon and ^aFrederick G. Williams, their sins are forgiven them also, and they are accounted as ^bequal with thee in holding the keys of this last kingdom;

7 As also through your administration the keys of the ^aschool of the prophets, which I have commanded to be organized;

8 That thereby they may be ^aperfected in their ministry for the salvation of Zion, and of the nations of Israel, and of the Gentiles, as many as will believe;

9 That through your administration they may receive the word, and through their administration the word may go forth unto the ends of the earth, unto the ^aGentiles ^bfirst, and then, behold, and lo, they shall turn unto the Jews.

10 And then cometh the day when the arm of the Lord shall be ^arevealed in power in convincing the nations, the ^bheathen nations, the house of ^cJoseph, of the gospel of their salvation.

11 For it shall come to pass in that day, that every man shall ^ahear the fulness of the gospel in his own tongue, and in his own ^blanguage, through those who are ^cordained unto this ^dpower, by the administration of the ^eComforter, shed forth upon them for the ^frevelation of Jesus Christ.

12 And now, verily I say unto you, I give unto you a commandment that you continue in the ^aministry and presidency.

90 1a TG Forgiveness.
2a TG Priesthood, Keys of.
  b TG Jesus Christ, Prophecies about.
3a Matt. 21:43; D&C 65:2.
  b D&C 43:3 (3–4); 84:17; 122:9; 124:130.
4a IE revelations from the Lord. Heb. 5:12; D&C 124:91 (91–96). TG Prophets, Mission of.
5a Acts 13:8. TG Prophets, Rejection of.
  b Matt. 7:25.
6a D&C 92:1.

  b D&C 35:22 (3–23); 81:1 (1–7); 107:24 (22–24).
7a D&C 88:127.
8a Eph. 4:12 (11–13).
9a 1 Ne. 13:42; D&C 18:6 (6, 26–27); 19:27; 21:12; 107:33; 112:4; 133:8.
  b Matt. 19:30; Acts 13:46 (46–51); Ether 13:12 (10–12).
10a D&C 42:58 (58–60); 43:25 (23–27); 58:64 (63–64); 88:84 (84, 87–92); 133:37 (37–60).

  b Ps. 98:2; 1 Ne. 15:13. TG Heathen.
  c Gen. 49:22 (22–26); Deut. 33:17 (13–17); Hosea 14:8 (4–9); D&C 133:26 (26–30).
11a TG Missionary Work.
  b TG Language.
  c TG Called of God.
  d TG Priesthood, Power of.
  e TG Holy Ghost, Comforter.
  f TG Testimony.
12a TG Leadership; Service.

13 And when you have finished the ^atranslation of the prophets, you shall from thenceforth ^bpreside over the affairs of the church and the school;

14 And from time to time, as shall be manifested by the Comforter, receive ^arevelations to unfold the ^bmysteries of the kingdom;

15 And set in order the churches, and ^astudy and ^blearn, and become acquainted with all good books, and with ^clanguages, tongues, and people.

16 And this shall be your business and mission in all your lives, to preside in council, and set in ^aorder all the affairs of this church and kingdom.

17 Be not ^aashamed, neither confounded; but be admonished in all your high-mindedness and ^bpride, for it bringeth a snare upon your souls.

18 Set in ^aorder your houses; keep ^bslothfulness and ^cuncleanness far from you.

19 Now, verily I say unto you, let there be a ^aplace provided, as soon as it is possible, for the family of thy counselor and scribe, even Frederick G. Williams.

20 And let mine ^aaged servant, Joseph Smith, Sen., continue with his family upon the place where he now lives; and let it not be sold until the mouth of the Lord shall name.

21 And let my counselor, even Sidney ^aRigdon, remain where he now resides until the mouth of the Lord shall name.

22 And let the bishop search diligently to obtain an ^aagent, and

let him be a man who has got ^briches in store—a man of God, and of strong faith;

23 That thereby he may be enabled to discharge every debt; that the storehouse of the Lord may not be brought into disrepute before the eyes of the people.

24 Search ^adiligently, ^bpray always, and be believing, and ^call things shall work together for your good, if ye walk uprightly and remember the ^dcovenant wherewith ye have covenanted one with another.

25 Let your families be ^asmall, especially mine aged servant Joseph Smith's, Sen., as pertaining to those who do not belong to your families;

26 That those things that are provided for you, to bring to pass my work, be not taken from you and given to those that are not worthy—

27 And thereby you be hindered in accomplishing those things which I have commanded you.

28 And again, verily I say unto you, it is my will that my hand-maid Vienna Jaques should receive ^amoney to bear her expenses, and go up unto the land of Zion;

29 And the residue of the money may be consecrated unto me, and she be rewarded in mine own due time.

30 Verily I say unto you, that it is meet in mine eyes that she should go up unto the land of Zion, and receive an ^ainheritance from the hand of the bishop;

31 That she may settle down in peace inasmuch as she is faithful,

---

13a D&C 73:4 (3–4).
  b D&C 88:127 (127–138); 90:32 (32–33); 107:91.
14a TG Revelation.
  b TG Mysteries of Godliness.
15a D&C 88:78 (76–80), 118; 93:53.
  TG Education; Scriptures, Study of; Study.
  b Mal. 2:7 (7–9); D&C 107:99 (99–100); 131:6. TG Learning.
  c D&C 90:11.

16a TG Language.
  b Titus 1:5. TG Order.
17a Micah 3:7 (6–7); 2 Ne. 6:13 (7, 13).
  b D&C 88:121.
  TG Shame.
18a TG Order.
  b TG Apathy; Idleness; Laziness; Procrastination.
  c D&C 94:9; 97:15.
  TG Uncleanness.
19a D&C 41:7 (7–8).
20a D&C 124:19.
21a D&C 93:51.

22a D&C 84:113.
  b Jacob 2:19 (17–19).
24a TG Dedication; Diligence.
  b TG Prayer.
  c Deut. 23:5; Ezra 8:22; Rom. 8:28; D&C 97:18 (18–20); 100:15.
  d Ps. 132:12.
  TG Commitment; Covenants.
25a Mosiah 4:27 (26–27).
28a D&C 60:10 (10–11).
30a D&C 51:3 (1–3); 85:1 (1–3).

and not be idle in her days from thenceforth.

32 And behold, verily I say unto you, that ye shall ^awrite this commandment, and say unto your brethren in Zion, in love greeting, that I have called you also to ^bpreside over Zion in mine own due time.

33 Therefore, let them cease wearying me concerning this matter.

34 Behold, I say unto you that your brethren in Zion begin to repent, and the angels rejoice over them.

35 Nevertheless, I am not well pleased with many things; and I am not well pleased with my servant ^aWilliam E. McLellin, neither with my servant Sidney Gilbert; and the bishop also, and others have many things to repent of.

36 But verily I say unto you, that I, the Lord, will contend with ^aZion, and plead with her strong ones, and ^bchasten her until she overcomes and is ^cclean before me.

37 For she shall not be removed out of her place. I, the Lord, have spoken it. Amen.

SECTION 91

Revelation given through Joseph Smith the Prophet, at Kirtland, Ohio, March 9, 1833. HC 1 : 331–332. The Prophet was at this time engaged in the translation of the Old Testament. Having come to that portion of the ancient writings called the Apocrypha, he inquired of the Lord and received this instruction.

1–3, The Apocrypha is mostly translated correctly but contains many interpolations by the hands of men that are not true; 4–6, It benefits those enlightened by the Spirit.

VERILY, thus saith the Lord unto you concerning the ^aApocrypha— There are many things contained therein that are true, and it is mostly translated correctly;

2 There are many things contained therein that are not true, which are ^ainterpolations by the hands of men.

3 Verily, I say unto you, that it is not needful that the Apocrypha should be ^atranslated.

4 Therefore, whoso readeth it, let him ^aunderstand, for the Spirit manifesteth truth;

5 And whoso is enlightened by the ^aSpirit shall obtain benefit therefrom;

6 And whoso receiveth not by the Spirit, cannot be benefited. Therefore it is not needful that it should be translated. Amen.

SECTION 92

Revelation given to Joseph Smith the Prophet, at Kirtland, Ohio, March 15, 1833. HC 1 : 333. The revelation is directed to Frederick G. Williams, who had recently been appointed a counselor in the First Presidency.

32a TG Record Keeping;
     Scriptures, Writing
     of.
  b D&C 90: 13; 107: 91.
35a D&C 66: 1; 68: 7;
     75: 6.
36a TG Zion.

  b D&C 84: 58.
     TG Chastening.
  c TG Cleanliness;
     Purification.
91 1a See "Apocrypha"
     in BD.
  2a TG Record Keeping;

Scriptures, Preservation of.
3a D&C 45: 60 (60–61);
     93: 53.
4a TG Understanding.
5a TG Holy Ghost,
     Mission of; Inspiration.

1–2, A commandment relative to admission to the United Order.

VERILY, thus saith the Lord, I give unto the *a*united order, organized agreeable to the commandment previously given, a revelation and commandment concerning my servant *b*Frederick G. Williams, that

ye shall receive him into the order. What I say unto one I say unto all.

2 And again, I say unto you my servant Frederick G. Williams, you shall be a lively member in this order; and inasmuch as you are faithful in keeping all former commandments you shall be blessed forever. Amen.

SECTION 93

Revelation given through Joseph Smith the Prophet, at Kirtland, Ohio, May 6, 1833. HC 1: 343–346.

1–5, All who are faithful shall see the Lord; 6–18, John bore record that the Son of God went from grace to grace until he received a fulness of the glory of the Father; 19–20, Faithful men, going from grace to grace, shall also receive of his fulness; 21–22, Those who are begotten through Christ are the Church of the Firstborn; 23–28, Christ received a fulness of all truth, and man by obedience may do likewise; 29–32, Man was in the beginning with God; 33–35, The elements are eternal, and man may receive a fulness of joy in the resurrection; 36–37, The glory of God is intelligence; 38–40, Children are innocent before God because of the redemption of Christ; 41–53, The leading brethren are commanded to set their families in order.

VERILY, thus saith the Lord: It shall come to pass that every soul who *a*forsaketh his *b*sins and cometh unto

me, and *c*calleth on my name, and *d*obeyeth my voice, and keepeth my commandments, shall *e*see my *f*face and *g*know that I am;

2 And that I am the true *a*light that lighteth every man that cometh into the world;

3 And that I am *a*in the Father, and the Father in me, and the Father and I are one—

4 The Father *a*because he *b*gave me of his fulness, and the Son because I was in the world and made *c*flesh my *d*tabernacle, and dwelt among the sons of men.

5 I was in the world and received of my Father, and the *a*works of him were plainly manifest.

6 And *a*John saw and bore record of the fulness of my *b*glory, and the fulness of *c*John's record is hereafter to be revealed.

7 And he bore record, saying: I saw his glory, that he was in the *a*beginning, before the world was;

---

92 1a D&C 82: 11 (11, 15–21); 96: 8 (6–9).
  b D&C 90: 6.
93 1a Rom. 12: 1 (1–3).
  b TG Worthiness.
  c Joel 2: 32.
  d TG Obedience.
  e Lev. 9: 4; John 14: 23 (18, 21–23); D&C 38: 8; 67: 10 (10–12); 88: 68; 101: 23; 130: 3. TG God, Presence of; Jesus Christ, Appearances, Postmortal.
  f 1 Jn. 4: 12 (7–21) (esp.

JST). TG God, Privilege of Seeing.
  g TG God, Access to; God, Knowledge about.
2a John 1: 4 (7–9); D&C 14: 9; 84: 46 (45–47); 88: 6. TG Light of Christ.
3a John 10: 30 (28–31); 14: 10; 17: 22; D&C 50: 43.
  b TG Jesus Christ, Authority of; Jesus

Christ, Relationships with the Father.
  c TG Flesh and Blood; Jesus Christ, Birth of; Jesus Christ, Condescension of.
  d 2 Pet. 1: 13.
5a John 5: 36; 10: 25; 14: 10 (10–12).
6a John 1: 34.
  b TG Jesus Christ, Glory of.
  c John 20: 30 (30–31).
7a John 1: 1 (1–3, 14); D&C 76: 39.

8 Therefore, in the beginning the "Word was, for he was the Word, even the messenger of salvation—

9 The "light and the Redeemer of the world; the Spirit of truth, who came into the world, because the world was made by him, and in him was the life of men and the light of men.

10 The worlds were "made by him; men were made by him; all things were made by him, and through him, and of him.

11 And I, John, "bear record that I beheld his "glory, as the glory of the Only Begotten of the Father, full of grace and truth, even the Spirit of truth, which came and dwelt in the flesh, and dwelt among us.

12 And I, John, saw that he received not of the "fulness at the first, but received "grace for grace;

13 And he received not of the fulness at first, but continued from "grace to grace, until he received a fulness;

14 And thus he was called the "Son of God, because he received not of the fulness at the first.

15 And I, "John, bear record, and lo, the heavens were opened, and the Holy Ghost descended upon him in the form of a dove, and sat upon him, and there came a voice out of

heaven saying: This is my "beloved Son.

16 And I, John, bear record that he received a fulness of the glory of the Father;

17 And he received "all "power, both in heaven and on earth, and the glory of the Father was with him, for he dwelt in him.

18 And it shall come to pass, that if you are faithful you shall receive the "fulness of the record of John.

19 I give unto you these sayings that you may understand and know how to worship, and "know what you worship, that you may come unto the Father in my name, and in due time receive of his fulness.

20 For if you keep my "commandments you shall receive of his "fulness, and be "glorified in me as I am in the Father; therefore, I say unto you, you shall receive "grace for grace.

21 And now, verily I say unto you, I was in the "beginning with the Father, and am the "Firstborn;

22 And all those who are begotten through me are "partakers of the "glory of the same, and are the "church of the Firstborn.

23 Ye were also in the beginning with the Father; that which is "Spirit, even the Spirit of truth;

8a TG Jesus Christ, Jehovah; Jesus Christ, Messenger of the Covenant; Salvation.
9a TG Jesus Christ, Creator; Jesus Christ, Light of the World; Jesus Christ, Mission of.
10a John 1: 3 (1-3); Rom. 11: 36; Heb. 1: 2 (1-3); D&C 76: 24.
11a John 1: 14 (14, 32).
 b TG Jesus Christ, Glory of.
12a Philip. 2: 8 (6-9); Heb. 5: 8 (8-9).
 b John 1: 16.
13a Luke 2: 52. TG Grace.
14a Matt. 1: 16 (1-16); Luke 20: 41. TG Jesus Christ, Divine Sonship.
15a John 1: 32 (15-32).

TG Holy Ghost, Dove, Sign of.
 b TG Witness of the Father.
17a Matt. 28: 18; John 17: 2; 1 Cor. 15: 27; Heb. 1: 2; 1 Pet. 3: 22; D&C 84: 28.
 b TG God, Power of; God the Father—Elohim, Jesus Christ, Authority of; Jesus Christ, Power of.
18a TG Scriptures to Come Forth.
19a Luke 4: 8; John 4: 22 (5-26);
 Acts 17: 22 (22-25);
 Alma 21: 22 (21-22);
 D&C 43: 8 (8-9); 134: 4 (1-4); A of F 11.
 TG Discernment, Spiritual; Worship.

20a Deut. 8: 1 (1-2).
 b John 1: 16.
 c John 17: 22 (5, 22).
 TG Man, Potential to Become Like Heavenly Father.
 d Isa. 28: 13 (9-13).
 TG Grace.
21a TG Jesus Christ, Foreordained; Jesus Christ, Relationships with the Father.
 b TG Jesus Christ, Divine Sonship; Jesus Christ, Firstborn.
22a 1 Pet. 5: 1; D&C 133: 57.
 b TG Celestial Glory.
 c D&C 76: 54 (53-54).
23a TG Man, a Spirit Child of Heavenly Father; Spirit Creation.

24 And ^atruth is ^bknowledge of things as they are, and as they were, and as they are to come;

25 And whatsoever is ^amore or less than this is the spirit of that wicked one who was a ^bliar from the beginning.

26 The Spirit of ^atruth is of God. I am the Spirit of truth, and John bore record of me, saying: He ^breceived a fulness of truth, yea, even of all truth;

27 And no man receiveth a ^afulness unless he keepeth his commandments.

28 He that ^akeepeth his commandments receiveth ^btruth and ^clight, until he is glorified in truth and ^dknoweth all things.

29 Man was also in the ^abeginning with God. ^bIntelligence, or the ^clight of ^dtruth, was not ^ecreated or made, neither indeed can be.

30 All truth is independent in that ^asphere in which God has placed it, to ^bact for itself, as all intelligence also; otherwise there is no existence.

31 Behold, here is the ^aagency of man, and here is the condemnation of man; because that which was from the beginning is ^bplainly manifest unto them, and they receive not the light.

32 And every man whose spirit receiveth not the ^alight is under condemnation.

33 For man is ^aspirit. The elements are ^beternal, and ^cspirit and element, inseparably connected, receive a fulness of joy;

34 And when ^aseparated, man cannot receive a fulness of joy.

35 The ^aelements are the ^btabernacle of God; yea, man is the tabernacle of God, even ^ctemples; and whatsoever temple is ^ddefiled, God shall destroy that temple.

36 The ^aglory of God is ^bintelligence, or, in other words, ^clight and truth.

37 Light and truth forsake that ^aevil one.

38 Every ^aspirit of man was ^binnocent in the beginning; and God having ^credeemed man from the ^dfall, men became again, in their infant state, ^einnocent before God.

39 And that ^awicked one cometh and ^btaketh away light and truth,

24a Ps. 117:2. TG Truth.
  b TG Knowledge.
25a D&C 20:35; 68:34.
  b John 8:44; Moses 4:4 (1-4).
26a John 14:6. TG God, Intelligence of.
  b John 1:16 (16-17).
27a TG Abundant Life; Perfection.
28a TG Obedience.
  b TG Truth.
  c Matt. 6:22 (22-23); D&C 50:24.
  d John 17:3; 2 Pet. 1:4; D&C 88:67 (49, 67); 101:32 (32-34). TG Mysteries of Godliness.
29a Prov. 8:23; Abr. 3:18. TG Man, Antemortal Existence of; Man, Potential to Become Like Heavenly Father.
  b TG God, Intelligence of; Intelligence.
  c TG Light.
  d TG Truth.
  e TG Creation.

30a D&C 77:3.
  b 2 Ne. 2:14 (13-26).
31a TG Agency.
  b Deut. 30:11 (11-14); 1 Ne. 20:16; D&C 84:23.
32a TG Conscience; Ignorance.
33a John 4:24; D&C 77:2; Abr. 5:7 (7-8). TG Man, a Spirit Child of Heavenly Father; Spirit Body; Spirit Creation.
  b TG Eternity.
  c D&C 138:17. TG Eternal Life; Joy; Resurrection.
34a 2 Ne. 9:8 (8-10). TG Spirits, Disembodied.
35a Gen. 2:7; Morm. 9:17; D&C 77:12.
  b 2 Pet. 1:13; D&C 88:41 (12, 41, 45).
  c TG Body, Sanctity of.
  d Mark 7:15; 1 Cor. 3:17 (16-17); Titus 1:15; 2 Ne. 19:17.

36a TG God, Glory of; Jesus Christ, Glory of.
  b D&C 130:18; Abr. 3:19. TG God, Intelligence of; Intelligence.
  c D&C 88:7 (6-13).
37a 2 Ne. 30:18; Moses 1:15 (12-16). TG Devil.
38a TG Spirit Body.
  b TG Conceived in Sin; Purity.
  c Ps. 49:15; Mosiah 27:24 (24-26); Moses 5:9; A of F 3.
  d TG Redemption.
  e TG Fall of Man.
  e Moro. 8:12 (8, 12, 22); D&C 29:46. TG Justification; Salvation of Little Children; Sanctification.
39a TG Devil.
  b Matt. 13:19 (18-19); 2 Cor. 4:4 (3-4); Mosiah 27:9 (8-9); Alma 12:10 (9-11); D&C 50:7; 84:50 (49-53).

through ᶜdisobedience, from the children of men, and because of the ᵈtradition of their fathers.

40 But I have commanded you to bring up your ᵃchildren in ᵇlight and truth.

41 But verily I say unto you, my servant Frederick G. Williams, you have continued under this condemnation;

42 You have not ᵃtaught your children light and truth, according to the commandments; and that wicked one hath power, as yet, over you, and this is the cause of your ᵇaffliction.

43 And now a commandment I give unto you— if you will be delivered you shall set in ᵃorder your own house, for there are many things that are not right in your house.

44 Verily, I say unto my servant Sidney Rigdon, that in some things he hath not kept the commandments concerning his children; therefore, first set in order thy house.

45 Verily, I say unto my servant Joseph Smith, Jun., or in other words, I will call you ᵃfriends, for you are my friends, and ye shall have an inheritance with me—

46 I called you ᵃservants for the world's sake, and ye are their servants for my sake—

47 And now, verily I say unto Joseph Smith, Jun.—You have not kept the commandments, and must needs stand ᵃrebuked before the Lord;

48 Your ᵃfamily must needs repent and forsake some things, and give more earnest heed unto your sayings, or be removed out of their place.

49 What I say unto one I say unto all; ᵃpray always lest that wicked one have power in you, and remove you out of your place.

50 My servant Newel K. Whitney also, a bishop of my church, hath need to be ᵃchastened, and set in ᵇorder his family, and see that they are more ᶜdiligent and concerned at home, and pray always, or they shall be removed out of their ᵈplace.

51 Now, I say unto you, my friends, let my servant Sidney Rigdon go on his journey, and make haste, and also proclaim the ᵃacceptable year of the Lord, and the ᵇgospel of salvation, as I shall give him utterance; and by your prayer of faith with one consent I will uphold him.

52 And let my servants Joseph Smith, Jun., and Frederick G. Williams make haste also, and it shall be given them even according to the prayer of faith; and inasmuch as you keep my sayings you shall not be confounded in this world, nor in the world to come.

53 And, verily I say unto you, that it is my will that you should ᵃhasten to ᵇtranslate my scriptures, and to ᶜobtain a ᵈknowledge of history, and of countries, and of kingdoms, of ᵉlaws of God and man, and all this for the salvation of Zion. Amen.

39c ᴛɢ Disobedience.
  d Jer. 16: 19; Ezek. 20: 18; Alma 3: 8.
    ᴛɢ Traditions of Men.
40a ᴛɢ Family, Children, Responsibilities toward; Marriage, Fatherhood; Marriage, Motherhood.
  b ᴛɢ Children of Light.
42a ᴛɢ Ex. 10: 2 (1–2); 1 Sam. 3: 13 (11–13); D&C 68: 25 (25–31); Moses 6: 58.

  b ᴛɢ Accountability.
43a Esth. 1: 22; 1 Tim. 3: 5 (4–5). ᴛɢ Order.
45a Ex. 33: 11; D&C 84: 63; 88: 62; 94: 1.
    ᴛɢ Friendship.
46a Lev. 25: 55; 1 Ne. 21: 3 (3–6). ᴛɢ Servant.
47a D&C 95: 1 (1–2).
    ᴛɢ Chastening.
48a ᴛɢ Family, Children, Duties of.
49a 3 Ne. 18: 15 (15–21).
50a ᴛɢ Reproof; Warning.
  b ᴛɢ Order.

  c ᴛɢ Diligence.
  d D&C 64: 40.
51a Luke 4: 19; 2 Cor. 6: 2.
  b Eph. 1: 13.
53a D&C 45: 60 (60–61); 73: 3; 76: 15; 91: 3; 94: 10.
  b ɪᴇ the translation of the Bible.
  c D&C 88: 78 (76–80), 118; 90: 15.
  d ᴛɢ Education; Knowledge; Learning.
  e ᴛɢ God, Law of.

SECTION 94

Revelation given through Joseph Smith the Prophet, at Kirtland, Ohio, May 6, 1833. HC 1: 346-347. Hyrum Smith, Reynolds Cahoon, and Jared Carter are appointed as a Church building committee.

1–9, A commandment relative to the erection of a house for the work of the Presidency; 10–12, A printing house is to be built; 13–17, Certain inheritances are assigned.

AND again, verily I say unto you, my *a*friends, a commandment I give unto you, that ye shall commence a work of laying out and preparing a beginning and foundation of the city of the *b*stake of Zion, here in the land of Kirtland, beginning at my house.

2 And behold, it must be done according to the *a*pattern which I have given unto you.

3 And let the first lot on the south be consecrated unto me for the building of a house for the presidency, for the work of the presidency, in obtaining revelations; and for the work of the ministry of the *a*presidency, in all things pertaining to the church and kingdom.

4 Verily I say unto you, that it shall be built fifty-five by sixty-five feet in the width thereof and in the length thereof, in the inner court.

5 And there shall be a lower court and a higher court, according to the pattern which shall be given unto you hereafter.

6 And it shall be *a*dedicated unto the Lord from the foundation thereof, according to the *b*order of the priesthood, according to the pattern

which shall be given unto you hereafter.

7 And it shall be wholly dedicated unto the Lord for the work of the "presidency."

8 And ye shall not suffer any *a*unclean thing to come in unto it; and my *b*glory shall be there, and my *c*presence shall be there.

9 But if there shall come into it any *a*unclean thing, my glory shall not be there; and my presence shall not come into it.

10 And again, verily I say unto you, the second lot on the south shall be dedicated unto me for the building of a house unto me, for the work of the *a*printing of the *b*translation of my scriptures, and all things whatsoever I shall command you.

11 And it shall be fifty-five feet in the width thereof and the length thereof, in the inner court; and there shall be a lower and a higher court.

12 And this house shall be wholly dedicated unto the Lord from the foundation thereof, for the work of the printing, in all things whatsoever I shall command you, to be holy, undefiled, according to the pattern in all things as it shall be given unto you.

13 And on the third lot shall my servant Hyrum Smith receive his *a*inheritance.

14 And on the first and second lots

---

94 1a D&C 93: 45.
  b D&C 68: 26; 82: 13;
    96: 1; 104: 48; 109: 59.
  2a Heb. 8: 5; D&C 52: 14;
    95: 14; 97: 10; 115: 14
    (14–16).
  3a D&C 107: 9 (8–78).
  6a TG Dedication; Sacred.
  b 1 Chr. 6: 32.

7a D&C 107: 9 (8–78).
8a Luke 19: 46 (46–48);
    D&C 109: 20 (19–20).
    TG Uncleanness.
  b 1 Kgs. 8: 11 (10–11);
    Ezek. 43: 2; D&C 101:
    25. TG Glory.
  c TG God, Presence of.
9a Lev. 15: 31; D&C 90:
    18; 97: 15.

10a D&C 104: 58.
  TG Scriptures, Writing
    of.
  b IE the translation of
    the Bible. D&C 93: 53;
    124: 89.
13a TG Inheritance. See
    also "Inheritance" in
    Index.

on the north shall my servants Reynolds Cahoon and Jared Carter receive their inheritances—

15 That they may do the work which I have appointed them, to be a committee to build mine houses, according to the commandment, which I, the Lord God, have given unto you.

16 These two houses are not to be built until I give unto you a commandment concerning them.

17 And now I give unto you no more at this time. Amen.

SECTION 95

Revelation given through Joseph Smith the Prophet, at Kirtland, Ohio, June 1, 1833. HC 1: 350–352. This revelation is a continuation of divine directions to build houses for worship and instruction, especially the House of the Lord. See Section 88: 119–136 and Section 94.

1–6, The saints are chastened for their failure to build the House of the Lord; 7–10, The Lord desires to use his house to endow his people with power from on high; 11–17, The house is to be dedicated as a place of worship and for the school of the apostles.

VERILY, thus saith the Lord unto you whom I love, and whom I ᵃlove I also chasten that their sins may be ᵇforgiven, for with the ᶜchastisement I prepare a way for their ᵈdeliverance in all things out of ᵉtemptation, and I have loved you—

2 Wherefore, ye must needs be chastened and stand rebuked before my face;

3 For ye have sinned against me a very grievous sin, in that ye have not considered the great commandment in all things, that I have given unto you concerning the building of mine ᵃhouse;

4 For the preparation wherewith I design to prepare mine apostles to ᵃprune my vineyard for the last time, that I may bring to pass my ᵇstrange act, that I may ᶜpour out my Spirit upon all flesh—

5 But behold, verily I say unto you, that there are many who have been ordained among you, whom I have called but few of them are ᵃchosen.

6 They who are not chosen have sinned a very grievous sin, in that they are ᵃwalking in ᵇdarkness at noon-day.

7 And for this cause I gave unto you a commandment that you should call your ᵃsolemn assembly, that your ᵇfastings and your ᶜmourning might come up into the ears of the Lord of ᵈSabaoth, which is by interpretation, the ᵉcreator of the first day, the beginning and the end.

8 Yea, verily I say unto you, I gave

---

95 1a 2 Sam. 7: 14;
Prov. 13: 18; Heb. 12:
6 (5–12); Hel. 15: 3;
D&C 101: 4 (4–5); 103:
4. TG Chastening; God,
Love of.
  b TG Forgiveness.
  c Deut. 11: 2 (1–8);
D&C 105: 6.
  d 2 Sam. 14: 14;
1 Cor. 10: 13.
TG Deliverance;
Forgiveness.
  e TG Temptation.

3a Hag. 1: 8; D&C 88:
119.
4a Jacob 5: 61 (61–75);
D&C 24: 19; 33: 3
(3–4); 39: 17.
  b Isa. 28: 21; D&C 101:
95.
  c Prov. 1: 23; Ezek. 36:
27; Joel 2: 28; Acts 2:
17; D&C 19: 38.
TG Holy Ghost,
Gifts of.
5a Matt. 20: 16; D&C 63:
31; 105: 36 (35–36);
121: 34 (34–40).

TG Called of God;
Election; Worthiness.
6a TG Walking in
Darkness.
  b Deut. 28: 29 (15–45).
TG Darkness, Spiritual.
7a D&C 88: 117 (70–119).
TG Solemn Assembly.
  b TG Fasting.
  c TG Mourning;
Repentance.
  d James 5: 4; D&C 87:
7; 88: 2.
  e TG Jesus Christ,
Creator.

unto you a commandment that you should ^abuild a house, in the which house I design to ^bendow those whom I have ^cchosen with power from on high;

9 For this is the ^apromise of the Father unto you; therefore I command you to tarry, even as mine apostles at Jerusalem.

10 Nevertheless, my servants sinned a very grievous sin; and ^acontentions arose in the ^bschool of the prophets; which was very grievous unto me, saith your Lord; therefore I sent them forth to be chastened.

11 Verily I say unto you, it is my will that you should build a house. ^aIf you keep my commandments you shall have power to build it.

12 If you ^akeep not my commandments, the ^blove of the Father shall not continue with you, therefore you shall ^cwalk in darkness.

13 Now here is wisdom, and the ^amind of the Lord—let the house be built, not after the manner of the world, for I give not unto you that ye shall live after the manner of the world;

14 Therefore, let it be built after the ^amanner which I shall show unto three of you, whom ye shall appoint and ordain unto this power.

15 And the size thereof shall be fifty and five feet in width, and let it be sixty-five feet in length, in the inner court thereof.

16 And let the lower part of the inner court be dedicated unto me for your sacrament offering, and for your preaching, and your fasting, and your praying, and the ^aoffering up of your most holy desires unto me, saith your Lord.

17 And let the higher part of the inner court be dedicated unto me for the ^aschool of mine apostles, saith Son ^bAhman; or, in other words, Alphus; or, in other words, Omegus; even Jesus Christ your ^cLord. Amen.

SECTION 96

Revelation given to Joseph Smith the Prophet, showing the order of the City or Stake of Zion at Kirtland, Ohio, June 4, 1833. Given as an example to the saints in Kirtland. HC 1: 352–353. The occasion was a conference of high priests, and the chief subject of consideration was the disposal of certain lands, known as the French farm, possessed by the Church near Kirtland. Since the conference could not agree who should take charge of the farm, all agreed to inquire of the Lord concerning the matter.

1, The Kirtland Stake of Zion is to be made strong; 2–5, The bishop is to divide the inheritances for the saints; 6–9, John Johnson is to be a member of the United Order.

BEHOLD, I say unto you, here is wisdom, whereby ye may know how to act concerning this matter, for it is expedient in me that this ^astake that I have set for the strength of Zion should be made strong.

8a D&C 88: 119; 104: 43; 115: 8.
 b D&C 38: 32; 39: 15; 43: 16; 110: 9 (9–10). TG Genealogy and Temple Work.
 c TG Election.
9a Luke 24: 49; Acts 1: 4.
10a D&C 88: 134 (133–134). TG Contention;

Disputations.
 b D&C 88: 127; 97: 5 (5–6).
12a John 15: 10; Mosiah 2: 4.
 b 1 Jn. 2: 10 (10, 15).
 c 2 Pet. 2: 17. TG Walking in Darkness.

13a D&C 68: 4.
14a D&C 92: 2; 124: 42.
16a D&C 59: 9 (9–14).
17a D&C 88: 127 (127–141).
 b D&C 78: 20.
 c TG Jesus Christ, Lord.
96 1a Isa. 33: 20; 54: 2; D&C 94: 1; 104: 48.

2 Therefore, let my servant Newel K. ^aWhitney take charge of the place which is named among you, upon which I design to build mine ^bholy house.

3 And again, let it be divided into lots, according to wisdom, for the benefit of those who seek ^ainheritances, as it shall be determined in council among you.

4 Therefore, take heed that ye see to this matter, and that portion that is necessary to benefit mine ^aorder, for the purpose of bringing forth my word to the children of men.

5 For behold, verily I say unto you, this is the most expedient in me, that my word should go forth unto the children of men, for the purpose of subduing the hearts of the children of men for your good. Even so. Amen.

6 And again, verily I say unto you, it is wisdom and expedient in me, that my servant ^aJohn Johnson whose offering I have accepted, and whose prayers I have heard, unto whom I give a promise of eternal life inasmuch as he keepeth my commandments from henceforth—

7 For he is a descendant of ^aJoseph and a partaker of the blessings of the promise made unto his fathers—

8 Verily I say unto you, it is expedient in me that he should become a member of the ^aorder, that he may assist in bringing forth my word unto the children of men.

9 Therefore ye shall ordain him unto this blessing, and he shall seek diligently to take away ^aincumbrances that are upon the house named among you, that he may dwell therein. Even so. Amen.

SECTION 97

Revelation given through Joseph Smith the Prophet, at Kirtland, Ohio, August 2, 1833. HC 1: 400–402. This revelation deals particularly with the affairs of the saints in Zion, Jackson County, Missouri, in response to the Prophet's inquiry of the Lord for information. Members of the Church in Missouri were at this time subjected to severe persecution, and on July 23, 1833, had been forced to sign an agreement to leave Jackson County.

1–2, Many of the saints in Zion (Jackson County, Missouri) are blessed for their faithfulness; 3–5, Parley P. Pratt is commended for his labors in the school in Zion; 6–9, Those who observe their covenants are accepted by the Lord; 10–17, A house is to be built in Zion in which the pure in heart shall see God; 18–21, Zion is the pure in heart; 22–28, Zion shall escape the Lord's scourge if she is faithful.

VERILY I say unto you my friends, I speak unto you with my ^avoice,

even the voice of my Spirit, that I may show unto you my will concerning your brethren in the land of ^bZion, many of whom are truly humble and are seeking diligently to learn wisdom and to find truth.

2 Verily, verily I say unto you, blessed are such, for they shall obtain; for I, the Lord, show mercy unto all the ^ameek, and upon all whomsoever I will, that I may be ^bjustified when I shall bring them unto judgment.

3 Behold, I say unto you, con-

2a D&C 72: 8 (7–8).
  b 2 Chr. 3: 8.
3a D&C 38: 20.
4a D&C 78: 3.
6a D&C 102: 3 (3, 34).
7a Gen. 49: 26 (22–26);

Rev. 7: 8; 1 Ne. 5: 14 (14–16); D&C 133: 32.
8a D&C 92: 1; 104: 1 (1, 47–53).
9a D&C 90: 23 (22–23).

97 1a TG Revelation; Wisdom.
  b D&C 64: 26 (18–41); 66: 6.
2a Matt. 5: 5.
  b Ps. 51: 4.

cerning the school in Zion, I, the Lord, am well pleased that there should be a *a*school in Zion, and also with my servant *b*Parley P. Pratt, for he abideth in me.

4 And inasmuch as he continueth to abide in me he shall continue to preside over the school in the land of Zion until I shall give unto him other commandments.

5 And I will bless him with a multiplicity of blessings, in expounding all scriptures and mysteries to the edification of the *a*school, and of the church in Zion.

6 And to the residue of the school, I, the Lord, am willing to show mercy; nevertheless, there are those that must needs be *a*chastened, and their works shall be made known.

7 The *a*ax is laid at the root of the trees; and every tree that bringeth not forth good fruit shall be hewn down and cast into the fire. I, the Lord, have spoken it.

8 Verily I say unto you, all among them who know their hearts are *a*honest, and are broken, and their spirits contrite, and are *b*willing to observe their covenants by *c*sacrifice—yea, every sacrifice which I, the Lord, shall command—they are *d*accepted of me.

9 For I, the Lord, will cause them to bring forth as a very fruitful *a*tree which is planted in a goodly land, by a pure stream, that yieldeth much precious fruit.

10 Verily I say unto you, that it is my will that a *a*house should be built unto me in the land of Zion, like unto the *b*pattern which I have given you.

11 Yea, let it be built speedily, by the tithing of my people.

12 Behold, this is the *a*tithing and the *b*sacrifice which I, the Lord, require at their hands, that there may be a *c*house built unto me for the salvation of Zion—

13 For a place of *a*thanksgiving for all saints, and for a place of instruction for all those who are called to the work of the ministry in all their several callings and offices;

14 That they may be perfected in the *a*understanding of their ministry, in theory, in principle, and in doctrine, in all things pertaining to the *b*kingdom of God on the earth, the *c*keys of which kingdom have been *d*conferred upon you.

15 And inasmuch as my people *a*build a *b*house unto me in the *c*name of the Lord, and do not suffer any *d*unclean thing to come into it, that it be not defiled, my *e*glory shall rest upon it;

16 Yea, and my *a*presence shall be there, for I will come into it, and all the *b*pure in heart that shall come into it shall see God.

17 But if it be defiled I will not come into it, and my glory shall not be there; for I will not come into *a*unholy temples.

3a D&C 55: 4; 88: 118; 109: 7 (7, 14).
  b D&C 32: 1; 50: 37; 52: 26; 103: 30 (30–37).
5a D&C 88: 127.
6a TG Chastening.
7a Matt. 3: 10; 7: 19; Luke 3: 9; 6: 44; Alma 5: 52 (36–52); 3 Ne. 14: 19.
8a TG Contrite Heart; Honesty.
  b Ex. 5: 2 (1–7); D&C 64: 34.
  c TG Commitment; Sacrifice.
  d Gen. 4: 7; D&C 52: 15; 132: 50; Moses 5: 23.

9a Ps. 1: 3 (1–3); Jer. 17: 8.
10a D&C 57: 3; 58: 57; 84: 3 (3–5, 31); 88: 119; 124: 31 (25–51).
  b Num. 8: 4; D&C 52: 14; 94: 2; 115: 14 (14–16).
12a TG Tithing.
  b TG Sacrifice.
  c 1 Kgs. 5: 5.
13a 2 Chr. 5: 13.
  TG Thanksgiving.
14a TG Understanding.
  b TG Kingdom of God, on Earth.
  c TG Priesthood, Keys of.
  d TG Delegation of

Responsibility.
15a 2 Chr. 2: 4.
  b TG Temple.
  c 1 Kgs. 8: 29.
  d D&C 94: 9; 109: 20; 110: 8 (7–8).
  e 2 Chr. 5: 14 (13–14); Hag. 2: 7; D&C 84: 5 (4–5, 31). TG Glory.
16a Lev. 16: 2; D&C 124: 27. TG God, Presence of.
  b Matt. 5: 8; D&C 67: 10; 88: 68. TG God, Knowledge about; God, Privilege of Seeing; Purity.
17a 1 Cor. 3: 16 (16–17); Eph. 5: 5.

18 And, now, behold, if Zion do these things she shall ªprosper, and spread herself and become very glorious, very great, and very terrible.

19 And the ªnations of the earth shall honor her, and shall say: Surely ᵇZion is the city of our God, and surely Zion cannot fall, neither be moved out of her place, for God is there, and the hand of the Lord is there;

20 And he hath sworn by the power of his might to be her salvation and her high ªtower.

21 Therefore, verily, thus saith the Lord, let Zion rejoice, for this is ªZion—THE PURE IN HEART; therefore, let Zion rejoice, while all the wicked shall mourn.

22 For behold, and lo, ªvengeance cometh speedily upon the ungodly as the whirlwind; and who shall escape it?

23 The Lord's ªscourge shall pass over by night and by day, and the report thereof shall vex all people;

yea, it shall not be stayed until the Lord come;

24 For the ªindignation of the Lord is kindled against their abominations and all their wicked works.

25 Nevertheless, Zion shall ªescape if she observe to do all things whatsoever I have commanded her.

26 But if she ªobserve not to do whatsoever I have commanded her, I will ᵇvisit her ªaccording to all her works, with sore affliction, with ᵈpestilence, with ᵉplague, with sword, with ᶠvengeance, with ᵍdevouring fire.

27 Nevertheless, let it be read this once to her ears, that I, the Lord, have accepted of her offering; and if she sin no more ªnone of these things shall come upon her;

28 And I will bless her with ªblessings, and multiply a multiplicity of blessings upon her, and upon her generations forever and ever, saith the Lord your God. Amen.

SECTION 98

Revelation given through Joseph Smith the Prophet, at Kirtland, Ohio, August 6, 1833. HC 1: 403–406. This revelation came in consequence of the persecution upon the saints in Missouri. It is natural that the saints in Missouri, having suffered physically and also having lost property, should feel an inclination toward retaliation and revenge. Therefore the Lord gave this revelation. Although some news of the problems in Missouri had no doubt reached the Prophet in Kirtland (nine hundred miles away), the seriousness of the situation could have been known to him at this date only by revelation.

18a Josh. 1: 7; D&C 90: 24; 100: 15.
19a Isa. 60: 14; Zech. 2: 11 (10–12); D&C 45: 69 (66–69); 49: 10.
  b TG Jerusalem, New.
20a 2 Sam. 22: 3.
21a Moses 7: 18 (18–19).
  b TG Purity; Zion.
22a Prov. 10: 25; Isa. 66: 15; Jer. 23: 19.

23a Isa. 28: 15; D&C 45: 31. TG World, End of.
24a TG God, Indignation of; Wickedness.
25a D&C 63: 34; JS-M 1: 20.
  b TG Protection, Divine.
26a Deut. 28: 15.
  b TG Punishment; Reproof.
  c D&C 84: 58.
  d Luke 21: 11 (10–13);

2 Ne. 6: 15;
Mosiah 12: 4.
  e TG Plague.
  f Isa. 34: 8; 61: 2;
Mal. 4: 1 (1, 3);
3 Ne. 21: 21 (20–21).
  g Isa. 29: 6; Joel 1: 19 (19–20); Mal. 3: 11;
D&C 85: 3.
27a Jer. 18: 8; Jonah 3: 10 (9–10).
28a TG Blessing.

1–3, Afflictions of the saints shall be for their good; 4–8, The saints are to befriend the constitutional law of the land; 9–10, Honest, wise, and good men should be supported for secular offices; 11–15, Those who lay down their lives in the Lord's cause shall have eternal life; 16–18, Renounce war and proclaim peace; 19–22, The saints in Kirtland are reproved and commanded to repent; 23–32, The Lord reveals his laws governing the persecutions and afflictions imposed on his people; 33–38, War is justified only when the Lord commands it; 39–48, The saints are to forgive their enemies, who, if they repent, shall also escape the Lord's vengeance.

VERILY I say unto you my friends, ᵃfear not, let your hearts be comforted; yea, rejoice evermore, and in everything give ᵇthanks;

2 ᵃWaiting patiently on the Lord, for your prayers have entered into the ears of the Lord of Sabaoth, and are recorded with this seal and testament—the Lord hath sworn and decreed that they shall be granted.

3 Therefore, he giveth this promise unto you, with an immutable covenant that they shall be fulfilled; and all things wherewith you have been ᵃafflicted shall work together for your ᵇgood, and to my name's glory, saith the Lord.

4 And now, verily I say unto you concerning the ᵃlaws of the land, it is my will that my people should observe to do all things whatsoever I command them.

5 And that ᵃlaw of the land which is ᵇconstitutional, supporting that principle of freedom in maintaining rights and privileges, belongs to all mankind, and is justifiable before me.

6 Therefore, I, the Lord, justify you, and your brethren of my church, in befriending that law which is the ᵃconstitutional law of the land;

7 And as pertaining to law of man, whatsoever is more or less than this, cometh of evil.

8 I, the Lord God, make you ᵃfree, therefore ye are free indeed; and the law also maketh you free.

9 Nevertheless, when the ᵃwicked ᵇrule the people mourn.

10 Wherefore, ᵃhonest men and wise men should be sought for diligently, and good men and wise men ye should observe to uphold; otherwise whatsoever is less than these cometh of evil.

11 And I give unto you a commandment, that ye shall forsake all evil and cleave unto all ᵃgood, that ye shall live by every ᵇword which proceedeth forth out of the mouth of God.

12 For he will ᵃgive unto the faithful line upon line, precept upon precept; and I will ᵇtry you and prove you herewith.

13 And whoso ᵃlayeth down his life in my cause, for my name's sake, shall find it again, even life eternal.

14 Therefore, be not ᵃafraid of your enemies, for I have decreed in my heart, saith the Lord, that I will ᵇprove you in all things, whether you will abide in my covenant, ᶜeven

98 1a D&C 68: 6.
  b TG Thanksgiving.
2a Gen. 49: 18; Ps. 27: 14; 37: 34; 40: 1; Prov. 20: 22; Isa. 30: 18 (18–19); 1 Ne. 21: 23; 2 Ne. 6: 13; D&C 133: 45.
3a TG Affliction.
  b D&C 122: 7.
4a TG Citizenship.
5a 1 Pet. 2: 13 (13–14); D&C 44: 4; 51: 6; 58:

21; 109: 54; 134: 5.
  b TG Governments; Liberty.
6a D&C 44: 4; 101: 80.
8a John 8: 32; 2 Cor. 3: 17.
  b TG Agency; Liberty.
9a Prov. 28: 28; 29: 2.
  b TG Tyranny.
10a TG Citizenship; Honesty.
11a TG Good Works.
  b Deut. 8: 3; Matt. 4: 4; D&C 84: 44 (43–44).
12a Isa. 28: 10; D&C 42:

61; 59: 4; 76: 7; 101: 32; 121: 28 (26–33).
  b Judg. 7: 4; Alma 27: 15; Abr. 3: 25.
13a Luke 9: 24; 21: 17 (15–19); Philip. 2: 17; D&C 101: 35; 103: 27 (27–28).
  TG Martyrdom.
14a Neh. 4: 14; D&C 122: 9.
  b D&C 124: 55; 132: 51.
  TG Test, Try, Prove.
  c Rev. 2: 10; D&C 136: 39 (31, 39).

unto death, that you may be found worthy.

15 For if ye will not abide in my covenant ye are not worthy of me.

16 Therefore, ^arenounce war and proclaim peace, and seek diligently to ^bturn the hearts of the children to their fathers, and the hearts of the fathers to the children;

17 And again, the hearts of the ^aJews unto the prophets, and the prophets unto the Jews; lest I come and smite the whole earth with a curse, and all flesh be consumed before me.

18 Let not your hearts be troubled; for in my Father's house are ^amany mansions, and I have prepared a place for you; and where my Father and I am, there ye shall be also.

19 Behold, I, the Lord, am not well ^apleased with many who are in the church at Kirtland;

20 For they do not ^aforsake their sins, and their wicked ways, the pride of their hearts, and their covetousness, and all their detestable things, and observe the words of wisdom and eternal life which I have given unto them.

21 Verily I say unto you, that I, the Lord, will ^achasten them and will do whatsoever I list, if they do not repent and observe all things whatsoever I have said unto them.

22 And again I say unto you, if ye observe to ^ado whatsoever I command you, I, the Lord, will turn away all ^bwrath and indignation from you, and the ^cgates of hell shall not prevail against you.

23 Now, I speak unto you concerning your families—if men will ^asmite you, or your families, once,

and ye ^bbear it patiently and ^crevile not against them, neither seek ^drevenge, ye shall be ^crewarded;

24 But if ye bear it not patiently, it shall be accounted unto you as being ^ameted out as a just measure unto you.

25 And again, if your enemy shall smite you the second time, and you revile not against your enemy, and bear it patiently, your reward shall be an ^ahundredfold.

26 And again, if he shall smite you the third time, and ye bear it ^apatiently, your reward shall be doubled unto you four-fold;

27 And these three ^atestimonies shall stand against your enemy if he repent not, and shall not be blotted out.

28 And now, verily I say unto you, if that enemy shall escape my vengeance, that he be not brought into judgment before me, then ye shall see to it that ye ^awarn him in my name, that he come no more upon you, neither upon your family, even your children's children unto the third and fourth generation.

29 And then, if he shall come upon you or your children, or your children's children unto the third and fourth generation, I have delivered thine ^aenemy into thine hands;

30 And then if thou wilt spare him, thou shalt be rewarded for thy ^arighteousness; and also thy children and thy children's children unto the third and fourth generation.

31 Nevertheless, thine enemy is in thine hands; and if thou rewardest him according to his works thou art justified; if he has sought thy life, and thy life is endangered by him,

16a Alma 48: 14. TG Peace; Peacemakers; War.
  b Mal. 4: 6 (5–6); D&C 2: 2.
17a TG Israel, Judah, People of; Israel, Restoration of.
18a John 14: 2; D&C 59: 2; 76: 111; 81: 6; 106: 8.
19a Rom. 8: 8 (5–9); 1 Cor. 10: 5 (1–6).
20a TG Repentance.

21a Deut. 11: 2 (1–8); Mosiah 23: 21; Hel. 12: 3.
22a TG Obedience.
  b Isa. 60: 10; D&C 101: 9.
  c Matt. 16: 18; D&C 33: 13; 109: 26.
23a Luke 6: 29; Alma 43: 46 (46–47).
  TG Persecution.
  b TG Forbearance.
  c TG Reviling.

d Deut. 19: 6.
  TG Retribution.
  e 2 Sam. 16: 12.
  TG Reward.
24a Matt. 7: 2 (1–2).
25a Gen. 26: 12.
26a TG Patience.
27a TG Judgment.
28a TG Warnings.
29a Deut. 7: 23 (16–23).
30a TG Reward; Righteousness.

thine enemy is in thine hands and thou art justified.

32 Behold, this is the law I gave unto my servant Nephi, and thy *fathers, Joseph, and Jacob, and Isaac, and Abraham, and all mine ancient prophets and apostles.

33 And again, this is the *law that I gave unto mine ancients, that they should not go out unto battle against any nation, kindred, tongue, or people, save I, the Lord, commanded them.

34 And if any nation, tongue, or people should proclaim war against them, they should first lift a standard of *peace unto that people, nation, or tongue;

35 And if that people did not accept the offering of peace, neither the second nor the third time, they should bring these testimonies before the Lord;

36 Then I, the Lord, would give unto them a commandment, and justify them in going out to battle against that nation, tongue, or people.

37 And I, the Lord, would *fight their battles, and their children's battles, and their children's children's, until they had avenged themselves on all their enemies, to the third and fourth generation.

38 Behold, this is an *ensample unto all people, saith the Lord your God, for justification before me.

39 And again, verily I say unto you, if after thine *enemy has come upon thee the first time, he repent and come unto thee praying their forgiveness, thou shalt forgive him, and shalt hold it no more as a testimony against thine enemy—

40 And so on unto the second and third time; and as oft as thine

enemy repenteth of the trespass wherewith he has trespassed against thee, thou shalt *forgive him, until seventy times seven.

41 And if he trespass against thee and repent not the first time, nevertheless thou shalt forgive him.

42 And if he trespass against thee the second time, and repent not, nevertheless thou shalt forgive him.

43 And if he trespass against thee the third time, and repent not, thou shalt also forgive him.

44 But if he trespass against thee the fourth time thou shalt not forgive him, but shalt bring these testimonies before the Lord; and they shall not be blotted out until he repent and *reward thee four-fold in all things wherewith he has trespassed against thee.

45 And if he do this, thou shalt forgive him with all thine heart; and if he do not this, I, the Lord, will *avenge thee of thine enemy an hundred-fold;

46 And upon his children, and upon his children's *children of all them that *hate me, unto the *third and fourth generation.

47 But if the *children shall repent, or the children's children, and *turn to the Lord their God, with all their hearts and with all their might, mind, and strength, and *restore four-fold for all their trespasses wherewith they have trespassed, or wherewith their fathers have trespassed, or their fathers' fathers, then thine indignation shall be turned away;

48 And vengeance shall *no more come upon them, saith the Lord thy God, and their trespasses shall never be brought any more as a testimony before the Lord against them. Amen.

32a D&C 27:10.
33a Deut. 20:10 (10–12);
   Josh. 8:2 (1–29);
   1 Kgs. 8:44; Alma 48:
   16 (10–25).
34a TG Peace; Peace-
   makers.
37a Josh. 23:5 (5–11);
   Ps. 35:1; Isa. 49:25;

D&C 105:14.
   TG Protection, Divine.
38a TG Example.
39a TG Enemies.
40a Matt. 18:22 (21–22).
   TG Forgiveness.
44a TG Recompense.
45a Deut. 32:35.
46a TG Accountability.

b TG Hate.
c Deut. 5:9.
47a Ex. 20:5 (5–6);
   Ezek. 18:20 (19–23).
b Lam. 5:21; Mosiah 7:
   33; Morm. 9:6.
c Lev. 5:16; 6:4; 24:
   21 (18–21).
48a TG Forgiveness.

SECTION 99

Revelation given through Joseph Smith the Prophet to John Murdock, August 1832, at Hiram, Ohio. Although editions of the Doctrine and Covenants beginning with 1876 have listed this revelation as Kirtland, August 1833, earlier editions and other historical records certify to the proper information.

1–8, John Murdock is called to proclaim the gospel, and those who receive him receive the Lord and shall obtain mercy.

BEHOLD, thus saith the Lord unto my servant John Murdock—thou art "called to go into the eastern countries from house to house, from village to village, and from city to city, to proclaim mine everlasting gospel unto the inhabitants thereof, in the midst of *b*persecution and wickedness.

2 And who *a*receiveth you receiveth me; and you shall have power to declare my word in the *b*demonstration of my Holy Spirit.

3 And who receiveth you *a*as a little child, receiveth my *b*kingdom; and blessed are they, for they shall obtain *c*mercy.

4 And whoso rejecteth you shall be *a*rejected of my Father and his house; and you shall cleanse your *b*feet in the secret places by the way for a testimony against them.

5 And behold, and lo, I *a*come quickly to *b*judgment, to convince all of their ungodly deeds which they have committed against me, as it is written of me in the volume of the book.

6 And now, verily I say unto you, that it is not expedient that you should go until your children are *a*provided for, and set up kindly unto the bishop of Zion.

7 And after a few years, if thou desirest of me, thou mayest go up also unto the goodly land, to possess thine *a*inheritance;

8 Otherwise thou shalt continue proclaiming my gospel *a*until thou be taken. Amen.

SECTION 100

Revelation given to Joseph Smith the Prophet and Sidney Rigdon, at Perrysburg, New York, October 12, 1833. HC 1: 416, 419–421. The two brethren, having been absent from their families for several days, felt some concern about them.

1–4, Joseph and Sidney to preach the gospel for the salvation of souls; 5–8, It shall be given them in the very hour what they shall say; 9–12, Sidney is to be a spokesman and Joseph is to be a revelator and mighty in testimony;

13–17, The Lord will raise up a pure people, and the obedient shall be saved.

VERILY, thus saith the Lord unto you, my friends Sidney and Joseph, your families are well; they are in

---

99 1a Luke 10: 1 (1–20).
   b TG Persecution.
  2a Matt. 10: 40 (40–42).
   b 1 Cor. 2: 4.
  3a Matt. 18: 4 (1–14).
   b Kingdom of God,

in Heaven; Kingdom
of God, on Earth.
  c TG Mercy.
  4a John 12: 49 (44–49).
   b D&C 75: 20 (19–22).
  5a D&C 1: 12.
   b Jude 1: 15 (14–15).

TG Jesus Christ, Judge.
6a D&C 75: 24 (24–26).
7a D&C 85: 7 (1–3, 7, 9);
   101: 18 (1, 6, 18).
8a Matt. 19: 29.
  TG Self-sacrifice.

"mine hands, and I will do with them as seemeth me good; for in me there is all power.

2 Therefore, follow me, and listen to the counsel which I shall give unto you.

3 Behold, and lo, I have much people in this place, in the regions round about; and an effectual door shall be opened in the regions round about in this eastern land.

4 Therefore, I, the Lord, have suffered you to come unto this place; for thus it was expedient in me for the "salvation of souls.

5 Therefore, verily I say unto you, lift up your voices unto this people; "speak the thoughts that I shall put into your hearts, and you shall not be "confounded before men;

6 For it shall be "given you in the very hour, yea, in the very moment, what ye shall say.

7 But a commandment I give unto you, that ye shall declare whatsoever thing ye "declare in my name, in solemnity of heart, in the spirit of meekness, in all things.

8 And I give unto you this promise, that inasmuch as ye do this the "Holy Ghost shall be shed forth in bearing record unto all things whatsoever ye shall say.

9 And it is expedient in me that you, my servant Sidney, should be a "spokesman unto this people; yea, verily, I will ordain you unto this calling, even to be a spokesman unto my servant Joseph.

10 And I will give unto him power to be mighty in "testimony.

11 And I will give unto thee power to be "mighty in expounding all scriptures, that thou mayest be a spokesman unto him, and he shall be a "revelator unto thee, that thou mayest know the certainty of all things "pertaining to the things of my kingdom on the earth.

12 Therefore, continue your journey and let your hearts rejoice; for behold, and lo, I am with you even unto the end.

13 And now I give unto you a word concerning Zion. "Zion shall be "redeemed, although she is chastened for a little season.

14 Thy brethren, my servants Orson Hyde and John Gould, are in my hands; and inasmuch as they keep my commandments they shall be saved.

15 Therefore, let your hearts be comforted; for "all things shall work together for good to them that walk uprightly, and to the sanctification of the church.

16 For I will raise up unto myself a "pure people, that will serve me in righteousness;

17 And all that "call upon the name of the Lord, and keep his commandments, shall be saved. Even so. Amen.

SECTION 101

Revelation given to Joseph Smith the Prophet, at Kirtland, Ohio, December 16, 1833. HC 1: 458-464. At this time the saints who had gathered in Missouri were suffering great persecution. Mobs had

100 1a TG Protection, Divine.
4a TG Mission of Latter-day Saints.
5a Ex. 4: 12 (12–16); Prov. 16: 1; Hel. 5: 18 (18–19); 13: 3; D&C 68: 3 (3–4).
b Acts 6: 10.
6a Matt. 10: 19 (19–20); D&C 84: 85.

7a D&C 18: 21; 43: 34; 84: 61; 88: 121.
TG Meekness; Sincerity.
8a Rom. 10: 17 (13–17); 2 Ne. 33: 1 (1–4).
9a Ex. 4: 16 (14–16); 2 Ne. 3: 17 (17–18); D&C 124: 104.
10a TG Testimony.
11a Acts 18: 24; Alma 17: 3 (2–3).

b TG Revelation.
c Acts 1: 3.
13a TG Zion.
b D&C 84: 99; 103: 15 (15, 20, 29).
15a Rom. 8: 28; D&C 90: 24; 105: 40.
16a TG Peculiar People; Purity.
17a Ps. 50: 15; Joel 2: 32; Alma 38: 5 (4–5).

driven them from their homes in Jackson County, and some of them had tried to establish themselves in Van Buren County, but persecution followed them. The main body of the saints was at that time in Clay County, Missouri. Threats of death against individuals of the Church were many. The people had lost household furniture, clothing, livestock, and other personal property, and many of their crops had been destroyed.

1–8, The saints are chastened and afflicted because of their transgressions; 9–15, The Lord's indignation shall fall upon the nations, but his people will be gathered and comforted; 16–21, Zion and her stakes shall be established; 22–31, The nature of life during the Millennium is set forth; 32–42, The saints shall be blessed and rewarded then; 43–62, Parable of the nobleman and the olive trees signifying the troubles and eventual redemption of Zion; 63–75, The saints are to continue their gathering together; 76–80, The Lord established the Constitution of the United States; 81–101, The saints are to importune for the redress of grievances, according to the parable of the woman and the unjust judge.

VERILY I say unto you, concerning your brethren who have been afflicted, and *a*persecuted, and *b*cast out from the land of their inheritance—

2 I, the Lord, have suffered the *a*affliction to come upon them, wherewith they have been afflicted, in consequence of their *b*transgressions;

3 Yet I will own them, and they shall be *a*mine in that day when I shall come to make up my jewels.

4 Therefore, they must needs be *a*chastened and tried, even as *b*Abraham, who was commanded to offer up his only son.

5 For all those who will not *a*endure chastening, but *b*deny me, cannot be sanctified.

6 Behold, I say unto you, there were jarrings, and *a*contentions, and *b*envyings, and *c*strifes, and *d*lustful and covetous desires among them; therefore by these things they polluted their inheritances.

7 They were slow to *a*hearken unto the voice of the Lord their God; therefore, the Lord their God is slow to hearken unto their prayers, to answer them in the day of their trouble.

8 In the day of their peace they esteemed lightly my counsel; but, in the day of their *a*trouble, of necessity they *b*feel after me.

9 Verily I say unto you, notwithstanding their sins, my bowels are filled with *a*compassion towards them. I will not utterly *b*cast them off; and in the day of *c*wrath I will remember mercy.

10 I have sworn, and the decree hath gone forth by a former commandment which I have given unto

---

101 1a TG Persecution.
  b D&C 103:2 (2, 11);
    104:51; 109:47; 121:
    23.
2a Ps. 119:67; D&C 58:
    4. TG Affliction.
  b Jer. 30:15; 40:3;
    Lam. 1:5; Mosiah 7:
    29; D&C 103:4; 105:9
    (2–10).
3a Isa. 62:3; Mal. 3:17;
    D&C 60:4.
4a 2 Sam. 7:14; D&C 95:
    1 (1–2); 136:31.
  b Gen. 22:2 (1–14);

Jacob 4:5; D&C 132:
    51.
5a Prov. 5:12; Alma 61:9.
  b Prov. 30:9; Matt. 10:
    33 (32–33); Rom. 1:16
    (15–18); 2 Tim. 2:12
    (10–15); 2 Ne. 31:14
    (12–21).
6a TG Contention;
    Disputations.
  b TG Envy.
  c TG Strife.
  d TG Carnal Mind; Lust;
    Sensuality.
7a Lev. 26:14 (14–20);

1 Sam. 8:18; Isa. 1:
    15; 59:2; Jer. 2:27;
    11:11; Ezek. 20:3;
    Mosiah 11:24 (22–25);
    21:15; Alma 5:38 (38–
    42).
8a Neh. 9:33; Mosiah 13:
    29; Alma 46:8;
    Hel. 12:3.
  b Hosea 5:15; Acts 17:
    27; Alma 32:6.
9a TG Compassion; Mercy.
  b Jer. 30:11.
  c Isa. 60:10; D&C 98:
    22 (21–22).

you, that I would let fall the "sword of mine indignation in behalf of my people; and even as I have said, it shall come to pass.

11 Mine indignation is soon to be poured out without measure upon all nations; and this will I do when the cup of their iniquity is "full.

12 And in that day all who are found upon the "watch-tower, or in other words, all mine Israel, shall be saved.

13 And they that have been scattered shall be "gathered.

14 And all they who have "mourned shall be comforted.

15 And all they who have given their "lives for my name shall be crowned.

16 Therefore, let your hearts be comforted concerning Zion; for all flesh is in mine "hands; be still and "know that I am God.

17 "Zion shall not be moved out of her place, notwithstanding her children are scattered.

18 They that remain, and are pure in heart, shall return, and come to their "inheritances, they and their children, with "songs of everlasting joy, to 'build up the waste places of Zion—

19 And all these things that the prophets might be fulfilled.

20 And, behold, there is none other "place appointed than that which I have appointed; neither shall there

be any other place appointed than that which I have appointed, for the work of the gathering of my saints—

21 Until the day cometh when there is found no more room for them; and then I have other places which I will appoint unto them, and they shall be called "stakes, for the curtains or the strength of Zion.

22 Behold, it is my will, that all they who call on my name, and worship me according to mine everlasting gospel, should "gather together, and "stand in holy places;

23 And "prepare for the revelation which is to come, when the "veil of the covering of my temple, in my tabernacle, which hideth the earth, shall be taken off, and all flesh shall 'see me together.

24 And every "corruptible thing, both of man, or of the beasts of the field, or of the fowls of the heavens, or of the fish of the sea, that dwells upon all the face of the earth, shall be "consumed;

25 And also that of element shall "melt with fervent heat; and all things shall become "new, that my knowledge and 'glory may dwell upon all the "earth.

26 And in that day the enmity of man, and the "enmity of beasts, yea, the "enmity of all flesh, shall cease from before my face.

27 And in that day "whatsoever any

10a D&C 1: 13 (13–14).
11a Gen. 15: 16; Alma 37:
     31; Hel. 13: 14;
     D&C 61: 31.
12a Ezek. 3: 17; 33: 9
     (6–10).
13a Deut. 30: 3; Ps. 60: 1
     (1–3); Micah 7: 12 (11–
     12); 1 Ne. 10: 14.
14a Matt. 5: 4.
     TG Comfort; Israel,
     Restoration of;
     Mourning.
15a Matt. 5: 10 (10–11);
     10: 39. TG Martyrdom.
16a Moses 6: 32.
   b Ex. 14: 13; Ps. 46: 10;
     Jer. 5: 3.
17a D&C 101: 20 (20–22).
     TG Zion.

18a D&C 99: 7; 103: 14
     (11, 14).
   b Isa. 35: 10; D&C 45:
     71. TG Singing.
   c Amos 9: 14; D&C 84:
     3 (2–5); 103: 11.
20a D&C 57: 2 (1–4).
21a D&C 82: 13; 115: 18
     (6, 17–18). TG Stakes.
22a D&C 10: 65.
     TG Israel, Gathering of;
     Mission of Latter-day
     Saints.
   b 2 Chr. 35: 5; Matt. 24:
     15; D&C 45: 32; 87:
     8; JS-M 1: 12.
23a TG Millennium,
     Preparing a People for.
   b TG Veil.

c Isa. 40: 5; D&C 38: 8;
     93: 1.
24a Ps. 72: 4; D&C 29: 24.
   b Zeph. 1: 2 (2–3);
     Mal. 4: 1; D&C 88: 94;
     JS-H 1: 37.
25a Amos 9: 5; 2 Pet. 3: 10
     (10–12). TG Earth,
     Cleansing of; World,
     End of.
   b Rev. 21: 5. TG Earth,
     Renewal of.
   c Isa. 6: 3; Ezek. 43: 2;
     Rev. 18: 1; D&C 94: 8.
     TG Glory.
   d TG Earth, Destiny of.
26a Isa. 11: 9 (6–9).
   b TG Peace.
27a Isa. 65: 24; D&C 4: 7.

man shall ask, it shall be given unto him.

28 And in that day ^aSatan shall not have power to tempt any man.

29 And there shall be no ^asorrow because there is no death.

30 In that day an ^ainfant shall not die until he is old; and his life shall be as the age of a tree;

31 And when he dies he shall not sleep, that is to say in the earth, but shall be ^achanged in the twinkling of an eye, and shall be ^bcaught up, and his rest shall be glorious.

32 Yea, verily I say unto you, in that ^aday when the Lord shall come, he shall ^breveal all things—

33 Things which have passed, and ^ahidden things which no man knew, things of the ^bearth, by which it was made, and the purpose and the end thereof—

34 Things most precious, things that are above, and things that are beneath, things that are in the earth, and upon the earth, and in heaven.

35 And all they who suffer ^apersecution for my name, and endure in faith, though they are called to lay down their lives for my ^bsake yet shall they partake of all this glory.

36 Wherefore, ^afear not even unto death; for in this world your joy is not full, but in me your ^bjoy is full.

37 Therefore, care not for the body, neither the life of the body; but care for the ^asoul, and for the life of the soul.

38 And ^aseek the face of the Lord always, that in ^bpatience ye may possess your souls, and ye shall have eternal life.

39 When men are called unto mine ^aeverlasting gospel, and covenant with an everlasting covenant, they are accounted as the ^bsalt of the earth and the savor of men;

40 They are called to be the savor of men; therefore, if that ^asalt of the earth lose its savor, behold, it is thenceforth good for nothing only to be cast out and trodden under the feet of men.

41 Behold, here is wisdom concerning the children of Zion, even many, but not all; they were found transgressors, therefore they must needs be ^achastened—

42 He that ^aexalteth himself shall be abased, and he that ^babaseth himself shall be exalted.

43 And now, I will show unto you a parable, that you may know my will concerning the ^aredemption of Zion.

44 A certain ^anobleman had a spot of land, very choice; and he said unto his servants: Go ye unto my ^bvineyard, even upon this very choice piece of land, and plant twelve olive-trees;

45 And set ^awatchmen round about

28a Rev. 20: 2 (2–3);
1 Ne. 22: 26; D&C 88:
110.
29a TG Immortality;
Sorrow.
30a Isa. 65: 20 (20–22);
D&C 45: 58; 63: 50
(49–50).
31a 1 Cor. 15: 52; D&C 43:
32; 88: 28 (20, 28).
  TG Resurrection.
  b 1 Thes. 4: 16 (16–17);
D&C 76: 102; 88: 96
(96–98).
32a D&C 29: 11; 43: 30.
  TG Jesus Christ, Second
Coming; Millennium.
  b D&C 98: 12; 121: 28
(26–33).
33a TG Mysteries of Godliness.

b TG Earth, Destiny of;
Earth, Purpose of.
35a 2 Cor. 1: 6; 4: 9;
D&C 63: 20. TG Malice;
Persecution; Perseverance.
  b Luke 21: 17 (15–19);
D&C 98: 13.
36a D&C 98: 13.
  TG Comfort; Death,
Power over.
  b 2 Ne. 27: 30. TG Joy.
37a TG Soul; Worth of
Souls.
38a 2 Chr. 7: 14; Ps. 27: 8;
69: 32; Amos 5: 6;
D&C 45: 46.
  b TG Patience.
39a TG New and Everlasting Covenant.
  b Matt. 5: 13; 1 Tim. 4:

16; D&C 103: 10.
  TG Mission of Latter-day Saints; Peculiar
People; Salt.
40a D&C 103: 10.
41a TG Chastening;
Reproof.
42a Obad. 1: 3 (3–4);
Luke 14: 11; 2 Ne. 20:
33; Hel. 4: 12 (12–13).
  TG Leadership.
  b Luke 18: 14; D&C 101:
10; 104: 82; 124: 114.
43a D&C 103: 1.
44a D&C 101: 21 (21–22).
  b Isa. 5: 1 (1–7);
Matt. 2: 31 (33–41);
Jacob 5: 3 (3–77).
45a D&C 52: 2 (2, 7); 3 Ne.
16: 18. TG Watchmen.

them, and build a tower, that one may overlook the land round about, to be a watchman upon the tower, that mine olive-trees may not be broken down when the enemy shall come to spoil and take upon themselves the fruit of my vineyard.

46 Now, the servants of the nobleman went and did as their lord commanded them, and planted the olive-trees, and built a hedge round about, and set watchmen, and began to build a tower.

47 And while they were yet laying the foundation thereof, they began to say among themselves: And what need hath my lord of this tower?

48 And consulted for a long time, saying among themselves: What need hath my lord of this tower, seeing this is a time of peace?

49 Might not this money be given to the exchangers? For there is no need of these things.

50 And while they were at variance one with another they became very *slothful, and they hearkened not unto the commandments of their lord.

51 And the enemy came by night, and broke down the *hedge; and the servants of the nobleman arose and were affrighted, and fled; and the enemy destroyed their works, and broke down the olive-trees.

52 Now, behold, the nobleman, the lord of the *vineyard, called upon his servants, and said unto them, Why! what is the cause of this great evil?

53 Ought ye not to have done even as I commanded you, and—after ye had planted the vineyard, and built the hedge round about, and set watchmen upon the walls thereof—built the tower also, and set a *watchman upon the tower, and watched for my vineyard, and not

have fallen asleep, lest the enemy should come upon you?

54 And behold, the watchman upon the tower would have seen the enemy while he was yet afar off; and then ye could have made ready and kept the enemy from breaking down the hedge thereof, and saved my vineyard from the hands of the destroyer.

55 And the lord of the vineyard said unto one of his *servants: Go and gather together the residue of my servants, and take *all the strength of mine house, which are my warriors, my young men, and they that are of middle age also among all my servants, who are the strength of mine house, save those only whom I have appointed to tarry;

56 And go ye straightway unto the land of my vineyard, and redeem my vineyard; for it is mine; I have bought it with money.

57 Therefore, get ye straightway unto my land; break down the *walls of mine enemies; throw down their tower, and scatter their watchmen.

58 And inasmuch as they gather together against you, *avenge me of mine enemies, that by and by I may come with the residue of mine house and possess the land.

59 And the servant said unto his lord: When shall these things be?

60 And he said unto his servant: When I will; go ye straightway, and do all things whatsoever I have commanded you;

61 And this shall be my seal and *blessing upon you—a faithful and *wise steward in the midst of mine house, a *ruler in my kingdom.

62 And his servant went straightway, and did all things whatsoever his lord commanded him; and *after many days all things were fulfilled.

63 Again, verily I say unto you, I will show unto you wisdom in me concerning all the churches, inas-

50a TG Dependability; Laziness.
51a Isa. 5: 5 (1–7).
52a TG Vineyard of the Lord.
53a Ezek. 33: 2 (2–7).

55a D&C 103: 21. TG Stewardship.
  b D&C 103: 22 (22, 29–30); 105: 30 (16, 29–30).
57a Josh. 6: 20.
58a Num. 31: 2; Isa. 1: 24;

  D&C 97: 22; 103: 26; 105: 30 (15, 30).
61a TG Blessing; Reward.
  b D&C 78: 22.
  c Matt. 25: 21 (20–23).
62a D&C 105: 37 (15, 37).

much as they are [a]willing to be guided in a right and proper way for their salvation—

64 That the work of the [a]gathering together of my saints may continue, that I may build them up unto my name upon [b]holy places; for the time of [c]harvest is come, and my word must needs be [d]fulfilled.

65 Therefore, I must gather together my people, according to the parable of the wheat and the [a]tares, that the wheat may be secured in the garners to possess eternal life, and be crowned with celestial [b]glory, when I shall come in the kingdom of my Father to reward every man according as his work shall be;

66 While the [a]tares shall be bound in bundles, and their bands made strong, that they may be [b]burned with unquenchable fire;

67 Therefore, a commandment I give unto all the churches, that they shall continue to gather together unto the places which I have appointed.

68 Nevertheless, as I have said unto you in a former commandment, let not your [a]gathering be in haste, nor by flight; but let all things be prepared before you.

69 And in order that all things be prepared before you, observe the commandment which I have given concerning these things—

70 Which saith, or teacheth, to [a]purchase all the lands with money, which can be purchased for money, in the region round about the land which I have appointed to be the land of Zion, for the beginning of the gathering of my saints;

71 All the land which can be purchased in Jackson county, and the counties round about, and leave the residue in mine hand.

72 Now, verily I say unto you, let all the churches gather together all their moneys; let these things be done in their time, but not in [a]haste; and observe to have all things prepared before you.

73 And let honorable men be appointed, even [a]wise men, and send them to purchase these lands.

74 And the churches in the [a]eastern countries, when they are built up, if they will hearken unto this counsel they may buy lands and gather together upon them; and in this way they may establish Zion.

75 There is even now already in store sufficient, yea, even an abundance, to redeem Zion, and establish her waste places, no more to be thrown down, were the churches, who call themselves after my name, [a]willing to hearken to my voice.

76 And again I say unto you, those who have been scattered by their enemies, it is my will that they should continue to importune for redress, and redemption, by the hands of those who are placed as rulers and are in authority over you—

77 According to the laws and [a]constitution of the people, which I have suffered to be established, and should be maintained for the [b]rights and protection of all flesh, according to just and holy principles;

78 That every man may act in doctrine and principle pertaining to futurity, according to the moral [a]agency which I have given unto him, that every man may be [b]accountable for his own sins in the day of [c]judgment.

79 Therefore, it is not right that

63a TG Teachable.
64a D&C 10:65.
  b D&C 87:8.
  c Joel 3:13; D&C 33:3 (3, 7). TG Harvest.
    D&C 1:38.
65a Matt. 13:36 (6–43); D&C 86:1 (1–7).
  b Celestial Glory; Glory; Reward.
66a D&C 38:12.

b Nahum 1:5; Matt. 3:12; D&C 63:34 (33–34).
68a D&C 58:56; 63:24.
70a D&C 42:35; 57:5 (5–7); 58:49 (49–53); 63:27 (27–29); 103:23 (22–24).
72a Isa. 52:12 (10–12); D&C 58:56. TG Haste; Rashness.
73a D&C 105:28 (28–30).

74a D&C 100:3.
75a Alma 5:37 (37–39); D&C 105:2.
77a TG Citizenship; Governments.
  b TG Liberty.
78a TG Agency.
  b TG Accountability; Punishment.
  c TG Judgment, The Last.

any man should be in "bondage one to another.

80 And for this purpose have I established the "Constitution of this land, by the hands of wise men whom I raised up unto this very purpose, and redeemed the land by the ^{b}shedding of blood.

81 Now, unto what shall I liken the children of Zion? I will liken them unto the "parable of the woman and the unjust judge, for men ought always to ^{b}pray and not to faint, which saith—

82 There was in a city a judge which feared not God, neither regarded man.

83 And there was a widow in that city, and she came unto him, saying: Avenge me of mine adversary.

84 And he would not for a while, but afterward he said within himself: Though I fear not God, nor regard man, yet because this widow troubleth me I will avenge her, lest by her continual coming she weary me.

85 Thus will I liken the children of Zion.

86 Let them importune at the "feet of the judge;

87 And if he heed them not, let them importune at the feet of the governor;

88 And if the governor heed them not, let them importune at the feet of the president;

89 And if the president heed them not, then will the Lord arise and come forth out of his "hiding place, and in his fury vex the nation;

90 And in his hot displeasure, and in his fierce anger, in his time, will cut off those wicked, unfaithful, and

"unjust ^{b}stewards, and appoint them their portion among ^{c}hypocrites, and ^{d}unbelievers;

91 Even in outer darkness, where there is "weeping, and wailing, and gnashing of teeth.

92 Pray ye, therefore, that their ears may be opened unto your cries, that I may be "merciful unto them, that these things may not come upon them.

93 What I have said unto you must needs be, that all men may be left without "excuse;

94 That wise men and rulers may hear and know that which they have never "considered;

95 That I may proceed to bring to pass my act, my "strange act, and perform my work, my strange work, that men may ^{b}discern between the righteous and the wicked, saith your God.

96 And again, I say unto you, it is contrary to my commandment and my will that my servant Sidney Gilbert should sell my "storehouse, which I have appointed unto my people, into the hands of mine enemies.

97 Let not that which I have appointed be polluted by mine enemies, by the consent of those who "call themselves after my name;

98 For this is a very sore and grievous sin against me, and against my people, in consequence of those things which I have decreed and which are soon to befall the nations.

99 Therefore, it is my will that my people should claim, and hold claim upon that which I have appointed unto them, though they should not be permitted to dwell thereon.

79a 2 Chr. 28: 11; 1 Ne. 17: 25; Mosiah 11: 21.
  TG Bondage, Physical; Slavery.
80a 2 Ne. 1: 7 (7–9); D&C 98: 5 (5–6).
  b 1 Ne. 13: 18 (13–19).
81a Luke 18: 1 (1–8).
  b TG Prayer.
86a TG Humility.
89a Isa. 45: 15 (15–17);

Zech. 2: 13; D&C 121: 1 (1, 4); 123: 6.
90a TG Injustice.
  b TG Stewardship.
  c TG Hypocrisy.
  d Rev. 21: 8.
  TG Unbelief, Unbelievers.
91a Matt. 25: 30; D&C 19: 5; 29: 15 (15–20); 124: 8.
92a TG God, Mercy of.

93a Rom. 1: 20 (18–21).
94a Isa. 52: 15 (13–15); 3 Ne. 20: 45; 21: 8.
95a Isa. 28: 21; D&C 95: 4.
  b Mal. 3: 18.
  TG Discernment, Spiritual.
96a D&C 58: 37; 72: 10 (8–10); 90: 35 (35–37).
97a D&C 103: 4; 112: 26; 125: 2.

100 Nevertheless, I do not say they shall not dwell thereon; for inasmuch as they bring forth fruit and works meet for my kingdom they *a*shall dwell thereon.

101 They shall build, and another shall not *a*inherit it; they shall plant vineyards, and they shall eat the fruit thereof. Even so. Amen.

SECTION 102

Minutes of the organization of the first high council of the Church, at Kirtland, Ohio, February 17, 1834. HC 2: 28–31. The original minutes were recorded by Elders Oliver Cowdery and Orson Hyde. Two days later, the minutes were corrected by the Prophet, read to the high council, and accepted by the council. Verses 30–32, having to do with the Council of the Twelve Apostles, were added by the Prophet Joseph Smith in 1835 when he prepared this section for publication in the Doctrine and Covenants.

1–8, A high council is appointed to settle important difficulties that arise in the Church; 9–18, Procedures are given for hearing cases; 19–23, The president of the council renders the decision; 24–34, Appellate procedure is set forth.

THIS day a general council of twenty-four high priests assembled at the house of Joseph Smith, Jun., by revelation, and proceeded to organize the *a*high council of the church of Christ, which was to consist of twelve high priests, and one or three presidents as the case might require.

2 The *a*high council was appointed by revelation for the purpose of *b*settling important difficulties which might arise in the church, which could not be settled by the church or the *c*bishop's council to the satisfaction of the parties.

3 Joseph Smith, Jun., Sidney Rigdon and Frederick G. Williams were acknowledged presidents by the voice of the council; and Joseph Smith, Sen., John Smith, Joseph Coe, John Johnson, Martin Harris, John S. Carter, Jared Carter, Oliver Cowdery, Samuel H. Smith, Orson Hyde, Sylvester Smith, and Luke Johnson, high priests, were chosen

to be a standing council for the church, by the unanimous voice of the council.

4 The above-named councilors were then asked whether they accepted their appointments, and whether they would act in that office according to the *a*law of heaven, to which they all answered that they accepted their appointments, and would fill their offices according to the grace of God bestowed upon them.

5 The number composing the council, who voted in the name and for the church in appointing the above-named councilors were forty-three, as follows: nine high priests, seventeen elders, four priests, and thirteen members.

6 Voted: that the high council cannot have power to act without seven of the above-named councilors, or their regularly appointed successors are present.

7 These seven shall have power to appoint other high priests, whom they may consider worthy and capable to act in the place of absent councilors.

8 Voted: that whenever any vacancy shall occur by the death, removal from office for transgression,

---

100a D&C 103: 15 (15–28).
101a Isa. 65: 21; D&C 64:
   34. TG Millennium.

102 1a D&C 42: 34.
  2a D&C 20: 67.
   b TG Judgment.

  c D&C 107: 73 (72–75).
  4a TG God, Law of.

or removal from the bounds of this church government, of any one of the above-named councilors, it shall be filled by the nomination of the ᵃpresident or presidents, and sanctioned by the voice of a general council of high priests, convened for that purpose, to act in the name of the church.

9 The president of the church, who is also the president of the council, is appointed by ᵃrevelation, and ᵇacknowledged in his administration by the voice of the church.

10 And it is according to the dignity of his office that he should preside over the council of the church; and it is his privilege to be assisted by two other presidents, appointed after the same manner that he himself was appointed.

11 And in case of the absence of one or both of those who are appointed to assist him, he has power to preside over the council without an assistant; and in case he himself is absent, the other presidents have power to preside in his stead, both or either of them.

12 Whenever a high council of the church of Christ is regularly organized, according to the foregoing pattern, it shall be the duty of the twelve councilors to cast lots by numbers, and thereby ascertain who of the twelve shall speak first, commencing with number one and so in succession to number twelve.

13 Whenever this council convenes to act upon any case, the twelve councilors shall consider whether it is a difficult one or not; if it is not, two only of the councilors shall speak upon it, according to the form above written.

14 But if it is thought to be difficult, four shall be appointed; and if more difficult, six; but in no case shall more than six be appointed to speak.

15 The accused, in all cases, has a right to one-half of the council, to prevent insult or ᵃinjustice.

16 And the councilors appointed to speak before the council are to present the case, after the evidence is examined, in its true light before the council; and every man is to speak according to equity and ᵃjustice.

17 Those councilors who ᵃdraw even numbers, that is, 2, 4, 6, 8, 10, and 12, are the individuals who are to stand up in behalf of the accused, and prevent insult and ᵇinjustice.

18 In all cases the accuser and the accused shall have a privilege of speaking for themselves before the council, after the evidences are ᵃheard and the councilors who are appointed to speak on the case have finished their remarks.

19 After the evidences are heard, the councilors, accuser and accused have spoken, the president shall give a decision according to the understanding which he shall have of the case, and call upon the twelve councilors to ᵃsanction the same by their vote.

20 But should the remaining councilors, who have not spoken, or any one of them, after hearing the evidences and pleadings impartially, discover an ᵃerror in the decision of the president, they can manifest it, and the case shall have a rehearing.

21 And if, after a careful re-hearing, any additional light is shown upon the case, the decision shall be altered accordingly.

22 But in case no additional light is given, the first decision shall stand, the majority of the council having power to determine the same.

23 In case of difficulty respecting ᵃdoctrine or principle, if there is not a sufficiency written to make the

8a D&C 68: 15 (15, 19, 22).
9a TG Called of God. See also the headings to Sections 81 and 90.
b   TG Sustaining Church Leaders.
15a TG Injustice.
16a TG Justice.
17a See BD Lots, Casting of.
b   TG Injustice.
18a John 7: 51; Acts 25: 16.
19a TG Common Consent.
20a Isa. 56: 1.
23a Num. 9: 8.

case clear to the minds of the council, the president may inquire and obtain the *b*mind of the Lord by revelation.

24 The high priests, when abroad, have power to call and organize a council after the manner of the foregoing, to settle difficulties, when the parties or either of them shall request it.

25 And the said council of high priests shall have power to appoint one of their own number to preside over such council for the time being.

26 It shall be the duty of said council to *a*transmit, immediately, a copy of their proceedings, with a full statement of the testimony accompanying their decision, to the high council of the seat of the First Presidency of the Church.

27 Should the parties or either of them be dissatisfied with the decision of said council, they may appeal to the high council of the seat of the First Presidency of the Church, and have a re-hearing, which case shall there be conducted, according to the former pattern written, as though no such decision had been made.

28 This council of high priests abroad is only to be called on the most *d*difficult cases of church matters; and no common or ordinary case is to be sufficient to call such council.

29 The traveling or located high priests abroad have power to say whether it is necessary to call such a council or not.

30 There is a distinction between the *a*high council or traveling high priests abroad, and the traveling high council composed of the twelve *b*apostles, in their decisions.

31 From the decision of the former there can be an appeal; but from the decision of the latter there cannot.

32 The latter can only be called in question by the general authorities of the church in case of transgression.

33 Resolved: that the president or presidents of the seat of the First Presidency of the Church shall have power to determine whether any such case, as may be appealed, is justly entitled to a re-hearing, after examining the appeal and the evidences and statements accompanying it.

34 The twelve councilors then proceeded to cast lots or ballot, to ascertain who should speak first, and the following was the result, namely: 1, Oliver Cowdery; 2, Joseph Coe; 3, Samuel H. Smith; 4, Luke Johnson; 5, John S. Carter; 6, Sylvester Smith; 7, John Johnson; 8, Orson Hyde; 9, Jared Carter; 10, Joseph Smith, Sen.; 11, John Smith; 12, Martin Harris.

After prayer the conference adjourned.

OLIVER COWDERY,
ORSON HYDE,
Clerks

SECTION 103

Revelation given through Joseph Smith the Prophet, at Kirtland, Ohio, February 24, 1834. HC 2: 36–39. This revelation was received after the arrival in Kirtland, Ohio, of Parley P. Pratt and Lyman Wight, who had come from Missouri to counsel with the Prophet as to the relief and restoration of the saints to their lands in Jackson County.

23b Lev. 24: 12; D&C 68: 4. TG Revelation.
26a TG Church Organization; Order.
28a D&C 107: 78.
30a D&C 107: 23–24, 31, 35–38.
  b TG Apostles.

1–4, Why the Lord permitted the saints in Jackson County to be persecuted; 5–10, The saints shall prevail if they keep the commandments; 11–20, The redemption of Zion shall come by power, and the Lord will go before his people; 21–28, The saints are to gather in Zion, and those who lay down their lives shall find them again; 29–40, Various brethren are called to organize Zion's Camp and go to Zion; they are promised victory if they are faithful.

VERILY I say unto you, my friends, behold, I will give unto you a revelation and commandment, that you may know how to ᵃact in the discharge of your duties concerning the salvation and ᵇredemption of your brethren, who have been scattered on the land of Zion;

2 Being ᵃdriven and smitten by the hands of mine enemies, on whom I will pour out my ᵇwrath without measure in mine own time.

3 For I have suffered them thus far, that they might ᵃfill up the measure of their iniquities, that their cup might be full;

4 And that those who call themselves after my name might be ᵃchastened for a little season with a sore and grievous chastisement, because they did not ᵇhearken altogether unto the precepts and commandments which I gave unto them.

5 But verily I say unto you, that I have decreed a decree which my people shall ᵃrealize, inasmuch as they hearken from this very hour

unto the ᵇcounsel which I, the Lord their God, shall give unto them.

6 Behold they shall, for I have decreed it, begin to ᵃprevail against mine ᵇenemies from this very hour.

7 And by ᵃhearkening to observe all the words which I, the Lord their God, shall speak unto them, they shall never cease to prevail until the ᵇkingdoms of the world are subdued under my feet, and the earth is ᶜgiven unto the saints, to ᵈpossess it forever and ever.

8 But inasmuch as they ᵃkeep not my commandments, and hearken not to observe all my words, the kingdoms of the world shall prevail against them.

9 For they were set to be a ᵃlight unto the world, and to be the ᵇsaviors of men;

10 And inasmuch as they are not the saviors of men, they are as ᵃsalt that has lost its savor, and is thenceforth good for nothing but to be cast out and trodden under foot of men.

11 But verily I say unto you, I have decreed that your brethren which have been scattered shall return to the ᵃlands of their inheritances, and shall ᵇbuild up the waste places of Zion.

12 For after ᵃmuch tribulation, as I have said unto you in a former commandment, cometh the blessing.

13 Behold, this is the blessing which I have promised after your tribulations, and the tribulations of your brethren—your redemption, and the redemption of your

---

103 1a D&C 43: 8; 82: 9.
  b D&C 101: 43 (43–62).
2a D&C 101: 1; 104: 51;
    109: 47.
  b Rom. 12: 19 (17–20);
    Morm. 3: 15 (9–15).
    TG Protection, Divine.
3a Gen. 15: 16; Matt. 23:
    32 (30–36); Alma 14:
    11 (10–11); 60: 13.
4a D&C 95: 1.
    TG Chastening.
  b Lam. 1: 5; D&C 101:
    2; 105: 9 (2–10).
    TG Disobedience.

5a D&C 130: 20.
  b TG Counsel.
6a Hosea 6: 1.
  b Deut. 33: 27.
7a D&C 35: 24.
    TG Obedience.
  b Dan. 2: 44 (34–45).
    TG Earth, Destiny of;
    Kings, Earthly.
  c Dan. 7: 27. TG Saints.
  d D&C 38: 20.
8a Lev. 26: 17 (16–17);
    1 Kgs. 8: 33;
    Mosiah 11: 13 (13–14);
    D&C 82: 10.
9a Ezek. 5: 5; 1 Ne. 21:

6; Alma 4: 11; 39: 11.
    TG Children of Light;
    Example; Light.
  b Obad. 1: 21.
10a Matt. 5: 13; D&C 101:
    39 (39–41).
    TG Salt.
11a D&C 101: 18; 109: 47.
  b Amos 9: 14; D&C 84:
    3 (2–5).
12a John 16: 33; Rev. 7:
    14 (13–14); D&C 58:
    4; 109: 76; 112: 13.
    TG Probation; Test,
    Try, Prove.

brethren, even their restoration to the land of Zion, to be established, no more to be thrown down.

14 Nevertheless, if they pollute their inheritances they shall be thrown down; for I will not spare them if they pollute their inheritances.

15 Behold, I say unto you, the *a*redemption of Zion must needs come by power;

16 Therefore, I will raise up unto my people a man, who shall *a*lead them like as Moses led the children of Israel.

17 For ye are the children of Israel, and of the *a*seed of Abraham, and ye must needs be *b*led out of *c*bondage by power, and with a stretched-out arm.

18 And as your fathers were *a*led at the first, even so shall the redemption of Zion be.

19 Therefore, let not your hearts faint, for I say not unto you as I said unto your fathers: Mine *a*angel shall go up before you, but not my *b*presence.

20 But I say unto you: Mine *a*angels shall go up before you, and also my *b*presence, and in time ye shall *c*possess the goodly land.

21 Verily, verily I say unto you, that my servant Joseph Smith, Jun., is the *a*man to whom I likened the servant *b*of whom the Lord of the *b*vineyard spake in the parable which I have given unto you.

22 Therefore let my servant Joseph Smith, Jun., say unto the *a*strength of my house, my young men and the middle aged—Gather yourselves together unto the land of Zion, upon the land which I have bought with money that has been consecrated unto me.

23 And let all the churches send up wise men with their moneys, and *a*purchase lands even as I have commanded them.

24 And inasmuch as mine enemies come against you to drive you from my goodly *a*land, which I have consecrated to the land of Zion, even from your own lands after these testimonies, which ye have brought before me against them, ye shall curse them;

25 And whomsoever ye *a*curse, I will curse, and ye shall avenge me of mine enemies.

26 And my presence shall be with you even in *a*avenging me of mine enemies, unto the third and fourth generation of them that hate me.

27 Let no man be afraid to lay down his *a*life for my sake; for whoso *b*layeth down his life for my sake shall find it again.

28 And whoso is not willing to lay down his life for my sake is not my disciple.

29 It is my will that my servant *a*Sidney Rigdon shall lift up his voice in the congregations in the eastern countries, in preparing the churches to keep the commandments which I have given unto them concerning the restoration and redemption of Zion.

30 It is my will that my servant Parley P. Pratt and my servant Lyman Wight should not return to the land of their brethren, until they

15a D&C 100: 13; 105: 1 (1–16, 34).
16a D&C 3: 10 (2–10); Mosiah 7: 19; Alma 36: 28; D&C 107: 91 (91–92).
17a TG Abrahamic Covenant; Seed of Abraham.
    b Ex. 13: 21 (21–22).
    c TG Bondage, Physical.
18a D&C 136: 22 (18, 22).
19a TG Angels.
    b Ex. 33: 3 (1–4);

D&C 84: 24 (23–28).
20a Ex. 14: 19 (19–20).
    b 1 Cor. 10: 1.
    c D&C 100: 13.
21a D&C 101: 44 (44, 55).
    b TG Vineyard of the Lord.
22a D&C 35: 13 (13–14); 101: 55; 105: 16 (16, 29–30).
23a D&C 42: 35; 57: 5 (5–7); 58: 49 (49–51); 101: 70 (68–74).
24a D&C 28: 9; 29: 8 (7–8);

45: 66 (64–66); 52: 2 (2, 42); 57: 1 (1–2).
25a Deut. 30: 7; D&C 124: 93.
26a D&C 97: 22; 101: 58; 105: 30 (15, 30).
27a Luke 14: 33.
    b Matt. 10: 39; Luke 9: 24; D&C 98: 13 (13–15); 124: 54.
29a See Index for references to the names in this verse and succeeding verses.

have obtained companies to go up unto the land of Zion, by tens, or by twenties, or by fifties, or by an hundred, until they have obtained to the number of five hundred of the *strength of my house.

31 Behold this is my will; ask and ye shall receive; but men do *not always do my will.

32 Therefore, if you cannot obtain five hundred, seek diligently that peradventure you may obtain three hundred.

33 And if ye cannot obtain three hundred, seek diligently that peradventure ye may obtain one hundred.

34 But verily I say unto you, a commandment I give unto you, that ye shall not go up unto the land of Zion until you have obtained a hundred of the strength of my house, to go up with you unto the land of Zion.

35 Therefore, as I said unto you, ask and ye shall receive; pray earnestly that peradventure my servant Joseph Smith, Jun., may go with you, and preside in the midst of my people, and organize my kingdom upon the *consecrated land, and establish the children of Zion upon the laws and commandments which have been and which shall be given unto you.

36 All victory and glory is brought to pass unto you through your *diligence, faithfulness, and *prayers of faith.

37 Let my servant Parley P. Pratt journey with my servant Joseph Smith, Jun.

38 Let my servant Lyman Wight journey with my servant Sidney Rigdon.

39 Let my servant Hyrum Smith journey with my servant Frederick G. Williams.

40 Let my servant Orson Hyde journey with my servant Orson Pratt, whithersoever my servant Joseph Smith, Jun., shall counsel them, in obtaining the fulfilment of these commandments which I have given unto you, and leave the residue in my hands. Even so. Amen.

SECTION 104

Revelation given to Joseph Smith the Prophet, April 23, 1834, concerning the United Order, or the order of the Church for the benefit of the poor. HC 2: 54-60. The occasion was that of a council meeting of the First Presidency and other high priests, in which the pressing temporal needs of the people had been given consideration. The United Order at Kirtland was to be temporarily dissolved and reorganized, and the properties as stewardships were to be divided among members of the order.

1-10, Saints who transgress against the United Order shall be cursed; 11-16, The Lord provides for his saints in his own way; 17-18, Gospel law governs the care of the poor; 19-46, Stewardships and blessings of various brethren are designated; 47-53, The United Order in Kirtland and the order in Zion are to operate separately;

54-66, The sacred treasury of the Lord is set up for the printing of the scriptures; 67-77, The general treasury of the United Order is to operate on the basis of common consent; 78-86, Those in the United Order are to pay all their debts, and the Lord will deliver them from financial bondage.

30a D&C 101: 55.
31a D&C 82: 10.
35a D&C 84: 3 (3-4, 31);

105: 15.
36a TG Dedication;
    Diligence;

    Steadfastness;
    Trustworthiness.
  b D&C 104: 82 (79-82).

VERILY I say unto you, my friends, I give unto you counsel, and a commandment, concerning all the ^aproperties which belong to the order which I commanded to be organized and established, to be a ^bunited order, and an everlasting order for the benefit of my ^cchurch, and for the salvation of men until I come—

2 With promise immutable and unchangeable, that inasmuch as those whom I commanded were faithful they should be blessed with a ^amultiplicity of blessings;

3 But inasmuch as they were not faithful they were nigh unto ^acursing.

4 Therefore, inasmuch as some of my servants have not kept the commandment, but have broken the covenant through ^acovetousness, and with feigned words, I have ^bcursed them with a very sore and grievous curse.

5 For I, the Lord, have decreed in my heart, that inasmuch as any man belonging to the order shall be found a transgressor, or, in other words, shall break the ^acovenant with which ye are bound, he shall be cursed in his life, and shall be trodden down by whom I will;

6 For I, the Lord, am not to be ^amocked in these things—

7 And all this that the innocent among you may not be condemned with the ^aunjust; and that the guilty among you may not escape; because I, the Lord, have promised unto you a ^bcrown of glory at my ^cright hand.

8 Therefore, inasmuch as you are found transgressors, you cannot escape my wrath in your lives.

9 Inasmuch as ye are ^acut off for transgression, ye cannot escape the ^bbuffetings of ^cSatan until the day of redemption.

10 And I now give unto you power from this very hour, that if any man among you, of the order, is found a transgressor and repenteth not of the evil, that ye shall ^adeliver him over unto the buffetings of Satan; and he shall not have power to ^bbring evil upon you.

11 It is wisdom in me; therefore, a commandment I give unto you, that ye shall organize yourselves and appoint every man his ^astewardship;

12 That every man may give an account unto me of the stewardship which is appointed unto him.

13 For it is expedient that I, the Lord, should make every man ^aaccountable, as a ^bsteward over earthly blessings, which I have made and prepared for my creatures.

14 I, the Lord, stretched out the heavens, and ^abuilt the earth, my very ^bhandiwork; and all things therein are mine.

15 And it is my purpose to provide for my saints, for all things are mine.

16 But it must needs be done in mine own ^away; and behold this is the way that I, the Lord, have decreed to provide for my saints, that the ^bpoor shall be exalted, in that the rich are made low.

17 For the ^aearth is full, and there is enough and to spare; yea, I have prepared all things, and have given unto the children of men to be ^bagents unto themselves.

18 Therefore, if any man shall take

---

104 1a D&C 104: 19 (19–46).
  b D&C 78: 3 (3–15); 96: 8 (6–9); 105: 4 (4–5).
  c TG Jesus Christ, Second Coming.
2a Luke 18: 30.
3a Heb. 6: 8.
4a TG Covetousness.
  b D&C 82: 21. TG Curse.
5a Hosea 10: 4; 3 Ne. 24: 5.
6a Gal. 6: 7 (7–9).
7a TG Mocking.
  b TG Injustice; Justice.
  b Isa. 62: 3; D&C 76: 56 (50–70). TG Glory.
  c D&C 76: 20 (20–23).
9a TG Excommunication.
10a 1 Tim. 1: 20.
  b D&C 109: 26 (25–27).
11a D&C 42: 32.
  TG Stewardship.
13a TG Accountability.
  b D&C 72: 3 (3–5, 16–22).
  TG Creation.
14a Isa. 42: 5; 45: 12.
  b Ps. 19: 1; 24: 1.
16a D&C 105: 5. TG Welfare.
  b 1 Sam. 2: 8 (7–8); Luke 1: 52 (51–53).
  c D&C 88: 17.
17a Ps. 136: 25; D&C 59: 16 (16–20). TG Earth, Purpose of; Nature.
  b TG Agency.

of the ᵃabundance which I have made, and impart not his portion, according to the ᵇgospel, unto the ᶜpoor and the needy, he shall, with the wicked, lift up his eyes in ᵈhell, being in torment.

19 And now, verily I say unto you, concerning the ᵃproperties of the ᵇorder—

20 Let my servant Sidney Rigdon have appointed unto him the place where he now resides, and the lot of the tannery for his stewardship, for his support while he is laboring in my vineyard, even as I will, when I shall command him.

21 And let all things be done according to the counsel of the order, and united consent or voice of the order, which dwell in the land of Kirtland.

22 And this stewardship and blessing, I, the Lord, confer upon my servant Sidney Rigdon for a blessing upon him, and his seed after him;

23 And I will multiply blessings upon him, inasmuch as he will be humble before me.

24 And again, let my servant Martin Harris have appointed unto him, for his stewardship, the lot of land which my servant John Johnson obtained in exchange for his former inheritance, for him and his seed after him;

25 And inasmuch as he is faithful, I will multiply blessings upon him and his seed after him.

26 And let my servant Martin Harris devote his moneys for the proclaiming of my words, according as my servant Joseph Smith, Jun., shall direct.

27 And again, let my servant Frederick G. Williams have the place upon which he now dwells.

28 And let my servant Oliver Cowdery have the lot which is set off joining the house, which is to be for the printing office, which is lot

number one, and also the lot upon which his father resides.

29 And let my servants Frederick G. Williams and Oliver Cowdery have the printing office and all things that pertain unto it.

30 And this shall be their stewardship which shall be appointed unto them.

31 And inasmuch as they are faithful, behold I will bless, and multiply blessings upon them.

32 And this is the beginning of the stewardship which I have appointed them, for them and their seed after them.

33 And, inasmuch as they are faithful, I will multiply blessings upon them and their ᵃseed after them, even a multiplicity of blessings.

34 And again, let my servant John Johnson have the house in which he lives, and the inheritance, all save the ground which has been reserved for the ᵃbuilding of my houses, which pertains to that inheritance, and those lots which have been named for my servant Oliver Cowdery.

35 And inasmuch as he is faithful, I will multiply blessings upon him.

36 And it is my will that he should sell the lots that are laid off for the building up of the ᵃcity of my saints, inasmuch as it shall be made known to him by the ᵇvoice of the Spirit, and according to the counsel of the order, and by the voice of the order.

37 And this is the beginning of the stewardship which I have appointed unto him, for a blessing unto him and his seed after him.

38 And inasmuch as he is faithful, I will multiply a multiplicity of blessings upon him.

39 And again, let my servant Newel K. Whitney have appointed unto him the houses and lot where he now resides, and the lot and building on which the mercantile establishment stands, and also the lot which

18a Luke 3: 11; James 2:
  16. TG Selfishness.
  b D&C 42: 30.
  c Job 29: 12; Prov. 14:

21; Mosiah 4: 26;
  D&C 52: 40.
  d Luke 16: 23 (20-31).
19a D&C 104: 1.
  b D&C 92: 1.

33a Ps. 112: 2.
34a D&C 94: 3 (3, 10, 16).
36a D&C 48: 4; 51: 16.
  b TG Revelation.

is on the the corner south of the mercantile establishment, and also the lot on which the ashery is situated.

40 And all this I have appointed unto my servant Newel K. Whitney for his stewardship, for a blessing upon him and his seed after him, for the benefit of the mercantile establishment of my order which I have established for my stake in the land of Kirtland.

41 Yea, verily, this is the stewardship which I have appointed unto my servant N. K. Whitney, even this whole mercantile establishment, him and his ^aagent, and his seed after him.

42 And inasmuch as he is faithful in keeping my commandments, which I have given unto him, I will multiply blessings upon him and his seed after him, even a multiplicity of blessings.

43 And again, let my servant Joseph Smith, Jun., have appointed unto him the lot which is laid off for the ^abuilding of my house, which is forty rods long and twelve wide, and also the inheritance upon which his father now resides;

44 And this is the beginning of the stewardship which I have appointed unto him, for a blessing upon him, and upon his father.

45 For behold, I have reserved an inheritance for his ^afather, for his support; therefore he shall be reckoned in the house of my servant Joseph Smith, Jun.

46 And I will multiply blessings upon the house of my servant Joseph Smith, Jun., inasmuch as he is faithful, even a multiplicity of blessings.

47 And now, a commandment I give unto you concerning Zion, that you shall no longer be bound as a ^aunited order to your brethren of Zion, only on this wise—

48 After you are organized, you shall be called the United Order of the ^aStake of Zion, the City of Kirtland. And your brethren, after they are organized, shall be called the United Order of the City of Zion.

49 And they shall be organized in their own names, and in their own name; and they shall do their business in their own name, and in their own names;

50 And you shall do your business in your own name, and in your own names.

51 And this I have commanded to be done for your salvation, and also for their salvation, in consequence of their being ^adriven out and that which is to come.

52 The ^acovenants being broken through transgression, by ^bcovetousness and feigned words—

53 Therefore, you are dissolved as a united order with your brethren, that you are not bound only up to this hour unto them, only on this wise, as I said, by ^aloan as shall be agreed by this order in council, as your circumstances will admit and the voice of the council direct.

54 And again, a commandment I give unto you concerning your stewardship which I have appointed unto you.

55 Behold, all these properties are mine, or else your faith is vain, and ye are found hypocrites, and the ^acovenants which ye have made unto me are broken;

56 And if the properties are mine, then ye are ^astewards; otherwise ye are no stewards.

57 But, verily I say unto you, I have appointed unto you to be stewards over mine house, even stewards indeed.

58 And for this purpose I have commanded you to organize yourselves,

---

41a D&C 84: 113.
43a D&C 95: 8.
45a D&C 90: 20; 124: 19.
47a D&C 82: 12 (11-12, 20).
48a D&C 68: 26; 82: 13; 94: 1; 96: 1; 109: 59.
51a D&C 101: 1; 103: 2 (2, 11); 109: 47.
52a TG Covenants.
  b TG Covetousness.
53a TG Loan.
55a TG Consecration.
56a TG Stewardship.

even to print "my words, the fulness of my scriptures, the revelations which I have given unto you, and which I shall, hereafter, from time to time give unto you—

59 For the purpose of building up my church and kingdom on the earth, and to "prepare my people for the time when I shall "dwell with them, which is nigh at hand.

60 And ye shall prepare for yourselves a place for a "treasury, and consecrate it unto my name.

61 And ye shall appoint one among you to keep the treasury, and he shall be ordained unto this blessing.

62 And there shall be a seal upon the treasury, and all the sacred things shall be delivered into the treasury; and no man among you shall call it his own, or any part of it, for it shall belong to you all with one accord.

63 And I give it unto you from this very hour; and now see to it, that ye go to and make use of the stewardship which I have appointed unto you, exclusive of the sacred things, for the purpose of printing these sacred things as I have said.

64 And the "avails of the sacred things shall be had in the treasury, and a seal shall be upon it; and it shall not be used or taken out of the treasury by any one, neither shall the seal be loosed which shall be placed upon it, only by the voice of the order, or by commandment.

65 And thus shall ye preserve the avails of the sacred things in the treasury, for sacred and holy purposes.

66 And this shall be called the "sacred treasury of the Lord; and a seal shall be kept upon it that it may be holy and consecrated unto the Lord.

67 And again, there shall be another treasury prepared, and a treasurer

appointed to keep the treasury, and a seal shall be placed upon it;

68 And all moneys that you receive in your stewardships, by improving upon the properties which I have appointed unto you, in houses, or in lands, or in cattle, or in all things save it be the holy and sacred writings, which I have reserved unto myself for holy and sacred purposes, shall be cast into the treasury as fast as you receive moneys, by hundreds, or by fifties, or by twenties, or by tens, or by fives.

69 Or in other words, if any man among you obtain five dollars let him cast them into the treasury; or if he obtain ten, or twenty, or fifty, or a hundred, let him do likewise;

70 And let not any among you say that it is his own; for it shall not be called his, nor any part of it.

71 And there shall not any part of it be used, or taken out of the treasury, only by the voice and common consent of the order.

72 And this shall be the voice and common consent of the order—that any man among you say to the treasurer: I have need of this to help me in my stewardship—

73 If it be five dollars, or if it be ten dollars, or twenty, or fifty, or a hundred, the treasurer shall give unto him the sum which he requires to help him in his stewardship—

74 Until he be found a transgressor, and it is manifest before the council of the order plainly that he is an unfaithful and an "unwise steward.

75 But so long as he is in full fellowship, and is faithful and wise in his stewardship, this shall be his token unto the treasurer that the treasurer shall not withhold.

76 But in case of transgression, the

58a IE the Bible translation. D&C 94: 10; 124: 89; 133: 60.
  TG Scriptures, Preservation of; Scriptures to Come Forth.

59a TG Millennium, Preparing a People for.
  b D&C 1: 36 (35–36); 29: 11 (9–11); 45: 59; 84: 119 (118–119).
  TG Jesus Christ, Second Coming.

60a 2 Kgs. 22: 4 (4–7); 2 Chr. 34: 9 (8–14).
64a IE profits, or proceeds.
66a TG Sacred.
74a Luke 16: 1 (1–12).

treasurer shall be subject unto the council and voice of the order.

77 And in case the treasurer is found an unfaithful and an unwise steward, he shall be subject to the council and voice of the order, and shall be removed out of his place, and ª another shall be appointed in his stead.

78 And again, verily I say unto you, concerning your debts—behold it is my will that you shall ª pay all your ᵇ debts.

79 And it is my will that you shall ª humble yourselves before me, and obtain this blessing by your ᵇ diligence and humility and the prayer of faith.

80 And inasmuch as you are diligent and humble, and exercise the ª prayer of faith, behold, I will soften the hearts of those to whom you are in debt, until I shall send means unto you for your ᵇ deliverance.

81 Therefore write speedily to New York and write according to that which shall be dictated by my ª Spirit; and I will soften the hearts of those to whom you are in debt, that it shall be taken away out of their minds to bring affliction upon you.

82 And inasmuch as ye are ª humble and faithful and ᵇ call upon my name, behold, I will give you the ᶜ victory.

83 I give unto you a promise, that you shall be delivered this once out of your ª bondage.

84 Inasmuch as you obtain a chance to loan money by hundreds, or thousands, even until you shall loan enough to deliver yourself from bondage, it is your privilege.

85 And pledge the properties which I have put into your hands, this once, by giving your names by common consent or otherwise, as it shall seem good unto you.

86 I give unto you this privilege, this once; and behold, if you proceed to do the things which I have laid before you, according to my commandments, all these things are mine, and ye are my stewards, and the master will not suffer his house to be ª broken up. Even so. Amen.

SECTION 105

Revelation given through Joseph Smith the Prophet, on Fishing River, Missouri, June 22, 1834. HC 2: 108–111. Mob violence against the saints in Missouri had increased, and organized bodies from several counties had declared their intent to destroy the people. The Prophet had come from Kirtland at the head of a party known as Zion's Camp, bringing clothing and provisions. While this party was encamped on Fishing River, the Prophet received the revelation.

1–5, Zion shall be built up by conformity to celestial law; 6–13, Redemption of Zion deferred for a little season; 14–19, The Lord will fight the battles of Zion; 20–26, The saints are to be wise and not boast of mighty works as they gather; 27–30, Lands in Jackson and adjoining counties should be purchased; 31–34, The elders are to *receive an endowment in the House of the Lord in Kirtland; 35–37, Saints who are both called and chosen shall be sanctified; 38–41, Saints are to lift an ensign of peace to the world.*

VERILY I say unto you who have assembled yourselves together that you may learn my will concerning

---

77a D&C 64: 40; 107: 99
        (99–100).
78a D&C 42: 54.
   b TG Debt.
79a TG Humility.

   b TG Diligence.
80a James 5: 15.
   b TG Deliverance.
81a TG God, Spirit of.
82a Luke 14: 11; D&C 67:

10; 101: 42.
   b D&C 103: 36.
   c TG Objectives.
83a TG Bondage, Physical.
86a Matt. 24: 43.

the "redemption of mine afflicted people—

2 Behold, I say unto you, were it not for the "transgressions of my people, speaking concerning the church and not individuals, they might have been redeemed even now.

3 But behold, they have not learned to be obedient to the things which I required at their hands, but are full of all manner of evil, and do not "impart of their substance, as becometh saints, to the poor and afflicted among them;

4 And are not "united according to the union required by the law of the celestial kingdom;

5 And "Zion cannot be built up "unless it is by the "principles of the "law of the celestial kingdom; otherwise I cannot receive her unto myself.

6 And my people must needs be "chastened until they learn "obedience, if it must needs be, by the things which they "suffer.

7 I speak not concerning those who are appointed to lead my people, who are the "first elders of my church, for they are not all under this condemnation;

8 But I speak concerning my churches abroad—there are many who will say: Where is their God? Behold, he will "deliver them in time of trouble, otherwise we will not go up unto Zion, and will keep our moneys.

9 Therefore, in consequence of the "transgressions of my people, it is

expedient in me that mine elders should wait for a little season for the "redemption of Zion—

10 That they themselves may be prepared, and that my people may be "taught more perfectly, and have experience, and know more perfectly concerning their "duty, and the things which I require at their hands.

11 And this cannot be brought to pass until mine "elders are "endowed with power from on high.

12 For behold, I have prepared a great endowment and blessing to be "poured out upon them, inasmuch as they are faithful and continue in humility before me.

13 Therefore it is expedient in me that mine elders should wait for a little season, for the redemption of Zion.

14 For behold, I do not require at their hands to fight the battles of Zion; for, as I said in a former commandment, even so will I fulfil—I will "fight your battles.

15 Behold, the "destroyer I have sent forth to destroy and lay waste mine "enemies; and not many years hence they shall not be left to pollute mine heritage, and to "blaspheme my name upon the lands which I have "consecrated for the gathering together of my saints.

16 Behold, I have commanded my servant Joseph Smith, Jun., to say unto them the "strength of my house, even my warriors, my young men, and middle-aged, to gather together for the redemption of my

105 1a D&C 100: 13; 103: 15.
  2a D&C 104: 52 (1–18, 52).
   TG Transgression.
  3a Acts 5: 2 (1–11);
    D&C 42: 30.
   TG Consecration;
    Welfare.
  4a D&C 78: 3 (3–7), (11–15); 104: 1 (1, 47–53).
  5a TG Zion.
   b D&C 104: 16 (15–16).
   c D&C 11: 9.
   d D&C 51: 2; 88: 22.
  6a Deut. 11: 2 (1–8);
    D&C 95: 1.

TG Chastening;
    Suffering.
   b TG Obedience.
   c Heb. 5: 8.
  7a D&C 20: 2 (2, 5); 88:
    85. TG Leadership.
  8a 2 Kgs. 17: 39; 2 Ne.
    6: 17; D&C 108: 8.
   TG Deliverance.
  9a Lam. 1: 5; D&C 101:
    2; 103: 4.
   b D&C 105: 31.
 10a TG Teachable.
   b TG Duty.
 11a TG Elders.
   b D&C 38: 32; 95: 8.

12a Zech. 12: 10; D&C 110:
    10.
 14a Josh. 10: 14 (12–14);
    2 Chr. 20: 15; Ps. 35:
    1; Isa. 49: 25; D&C 98:
    37. TG Protection,
    Divine.
 15a D&C 1: 13 (13–14).
   b Ex. 23: 22 (20–23);
    D&C 8: 4; 136: 40.
   c Ps. 74: 10; D&C 112:
    26 (24–26).
   d D&C 52: 2; 58: 57;
    84: 3 (3–4, 31); 103: 35.
 16a D&C 101: 55; 103: 22
    (22, 30). TG Strength.

people, and throw down the towers of mine enemies, and scatter their [b]watchmen;

17 But the strength of mine house have not hearkened unto my words.

18 But inasmuch as there are those who have hearkened unto my words, I have prepared a blessing and an [a]endowment for them, if they continue faithful.

19 I have heard their prayers, and will accept their offering; and it is expedient in me that they should be brought thus far for a [a]trial of their [b]faith.

20 And now, verily I say unto you, a commandment I give unto you, that as many as have come up hither, that can stay in the region round about, let them stay;

21 And those that cannot stay, who have families in the east, let them tarry for a little season, inasmuch as my servant Joseph shall appoint unto them;

22 For I will counsel him concerning this matter, and all things whatsoever he shall appoint unto them shall be fulfilled.

23 And let all my people who dwell in the regions round about be very faithful, and prayerful, and humble before me, and reveal not the things which I have revealed unto them, until it is wisdom in me that they should be revealed.

24 Talk not of judgments, neither [a]boast of faith nor of mighty [b]works, but carefully gather together, as much in one region as can be, consistently with the feelings of the people;

25 And behold, I will give unto you favor and grace in their eyes, that you may rest in [a]peace and safety, while you are saying unto the people: Execute judgment and justice for us

according to law, and redress us of our [b]wrongs.

26 Now, behold, I say unto you, my friends, in this way you may find favor in the eyes of the people, until the [a]army of Israel becomes very great.

27 And I will soften the hearts of the people, as I did the heart of [a]Pharaoh, from time to time, until my servant Joseph Smith, Jun., and mine elders, whom I have appointed, shall have time to gather up the strength of my house,

28 And to have sent [a]wise men, to fulfil that which I have commanded concerning the [b]purchasing of all the lands in Jackson county that can be purchased, and in the adjoining counties round about.

29 For it is my will that these lands should be purchased; and after they are purchased that my saints should possess them according to the laws of [a]consecration which I have given.

30 And after these lands are purchased, I will hold the [a]armies of Israel guiltless in taking possession of their own lands, which they have previously purchased with their moneys, and of throwing down the towers of mine enemies that may be upon them, and scattering their watchmen, and [b]avenging me of mine enemies unto the third and fourth generation of them that hate me.

31 But first let my army become very great, and let it be [a]sanctified before me, that it may become fair as the sun, and clear as the [b]moon, and that her banners may be terrible unto all nations;

32 That the kingdoms of this world may be constrained to acknowledge that the kingdom of Zion is in very deed the [a]kingdom of our God and

16b TG Watchmen.
18a D&C 110:9 (8–10).
19a TG Probation; Test,
      Try, Prove.
  b TG Faith.
24a D&C 50:33 (32–33);
      84:73. TG Boasting.
  b TG Good Works.
25a TG Grace; Protection,

Divine.
  b TG Injustice; Justice.
26a Joel 2:11 (11, 25).
27a Gen. 47:6 (1–12).
28a D&C 101:73.
  b D&C 42:35.
29a D&C 42:30.
30a D&C 35:13 (13–14);
      101:55 (55, 58); 103:

22 (22, 26, 29).
  b D&C 97:22.
31a D&C 105:9.
      TG Sanctification.
  b Song. 6:10; D&C 5:
      14; 109:73.
32a Rev. 11:15.
      TG Kingdom of God,
      on Earth.

his Christ; therefore, let us become [b]subject unto her laws.

33 Verily I say unto you, it is expedient in me that the first elders of my church should receive their [a]endowment from on high in my house, which I have commanded to be built unto my name in the land of Kirtland.

34 And let those commandments which I have given concerning Zion and her [a]law be executed and fulfilled, after her redemption.

35 There has been a day of [a]calling, but the time has come for a day of choosing; and let those be chosen that are [b]worthy.

36 And it shall be [a]manifest unto my servant, by the voice of the Spirit, those that are [b]chosen; and they shall be [c]sanctified.

37 And inasmuch as they follow the [a]counsel which they receive, they shall have power [b]after many days to accomplish all things pertaining to Zion.

38 And again I say unto you, sue for [a]peace, not only to the people that have smitten you, but also to all people;

39 And lift up an [a]ensign of [b]peace, and make a proclamation of peace unto the ends of the earth;

40 And make proposals for peace unto those who have smitten you, according to the voice of the Spirit which is in you, and [a]all things shall work together for your good.

41 Therefore, be faithful; and behold, and lo, I am [a]with you even unto the end. Even so. Amen.

SECTION 106

Revelation given through Joseph Smith the Prophet, at Kirtland, Ohio, November 25, 1834. HC 2: 170–171. This revelation is directed to Warren A. Cowdery, an older brother of Oliver Cowdery.

1–3, Warren A. Cowdery is called as a local presiding officer; 4–5, The Second Coming shall not overtake the children of light as a thief; 6–8, Great blessings follow faithful service in the Church.

IT is my will that my servant Warren A. Cowdery should be appointed and ordained a presiding high priest over my church, in the land of [a]Freedom and the regions round about;

2 And should preach my [a]everlasting gospel, and lift up his voice and

warn the people, not only in his own place, but in the adjoining counties;

3 And devote his whole time to this high and holy calling, which I now give unto him, [a]seeking diligently the kingdom of heaven and its righteousness, and all things necessary shall be added thereunto; for the [b]laborer is worthy of his hire.

4 And again, verily I say unto you, the [a]coming of the Lord draweth nigh, and it overtaketh the world as a [b]thief in the night—

5 Therefore, gird up your loins, that

32b TG Governments; Submissiveness.
33a D&C 95: 8 (8–9).
34a D&C 42: 2 (2, 18–69); 78: 3 (1–22).
35a TG Called of God.
 b TG Worthiness.
36a TG Guidance, Divine.
 b D&C 95: 5 (5–6).
 c TG Man, New, Spiritually Reborn; Sanctification.

37a Prov. 15: 22. TG Counsel.
 b D&C 101: 62.
38a Deut. 20: 10.
39a TG Ensign.
 b TG Peace; Peacemakers.
40a Rom. 8: 28; D&C 90: 24; 100: 15.
41a Matt. 28: 20 (19–20).
106 1a IE the city of Freedom, N.Y., and

environs.
2a D&C 18: 4.
3a Matt. 6: 33. TG Kingdom of God, in Heaven.
 b Matt. 10: 10; D&C 31: 5. TG Reward; Wages.
4a James 5: 8. TG Jesus Christ, Second Coming; Last Days.
 b 1 Thes. 5: 2.

you may be the *a*children of light, and that day shall not *b*overtake you as a thief.

6 And again, verily I say unto you, there was joy in heaven when my servant Warren bowed to my scepter, and separated himself from the crafts of men;

7 Therefore, blessed is my servant Warren, for I will have mercy on him; and, notwithstanding the *a*vanity of his heart, I will lift him up inasmuch as he will humble himself before me.

8 And I will give him *a*grace and assurance wherewith he may stand; and if he continue to be a faithful witness and a *b*light unto the church I have prepared a crown for him in the *c*mansions of my Father. Even so. Amen.

SECTION 107

Revelation on priesthood, given through Joseph Smith the Prophet, at Kirtland, Ohio, dated March 28, 1835. HC 2: 209–217. On the date named the Twelve met in council, confessing their individual weaknesses and shortcomings, expressing repentance, and seeking the further guidance of the Lord. They were about to separate on missions to districts assigned. Although portions of this section were received on the date named, the historical records affirm that various parts were received at sundry times, some as early as November 1831.

1–6, There are two priesthoods: the Melchizedek and the Aaronic; 7–12, Those who hold the Melchizedek Priesthood have power to officiate in all offices in the Church; 13–17, The bishopric presides over the Aaronic Priesthood, which administers in outward ordinances; 18–20, The Melchizedek Priesthood holds the keys of all spiritual blessings; the Aaronic Priesthood holds the keys of the ministering of angels; 21–38, The First Presidency, the Twelve, and the Seventy constitute the presiding quorums, whose decisions are to be made in unity and righteousness; 39–52, Patriarchal order established from Adam to Noah; 53–57, Ancient saints assembled at Adam-ondi-Ahman, and the Lord appeared to them; 58–67, The Twelve are to set the officers of the Church in order; 68–76, Bishops serve as common judges in Israel; 77–84, The First Presidency and the Twelve constitute the highest court in the Church; 85–100, Priesthood presidents govern their respective quorums.

THERE are, in the church, two *a*priesthoods, namely, the Melchizedek and *b*Aaronic, including the Levitical Priesthood.

2 Why the first is called the *a*Melchizedek Priesthood is because *b*Melchizedek was such a great high priest.

3 Before his day it was called the Holy *a*Priesthood, after the *b*Order of the Son of God.

4 But out of *a*respect or *b*reverence to the name of the Supreme Being, to avoid the too frequent repetition

---

5*a* TG Children of Light.
  b Rev. 16: 15 (15–16).
7*a* TG Vanity.
8*a* TG Grace.
  b TG Example; Light.
  c John 14: 2; Ether 12: 32 (32–37); D&C 59: 2; 76: 111; 81: 6; 98: 18.

107 1*a* TG Priesthood.
  b TG Priesthood, Aaronic.
2*a* See BD Melchizedek.
  TG Priesthood, Melchizedek.
  b JST Gen. 14: 25–40;

Alma 13: 14 (3–19);
D&C 84: 14.
3*a* TG Jesus Christ, Authority of.
  b D&C 76: 57.
4*a* TG Respect.
  b TG Reverence.

of his name, they, the church, in ancient days, called that priesthood after Melchizedek, or the Melchizedek Priesthood.

5 All other authorities or offices in the church are *appendages to this priesthood.

6 But there are two divisions or grand heads—one is the Melchizedek Priesthood, and the other is the Aaronic or *Levitical Priesthood.

7 The office of an *elder comes under the priesthood of Melchizedek.

8 The *Melchizedek Priesthood holds the right of presidency, and has power and *authority over all the offices in the church in all ages of the world, to administer in spiritual things.

9 The *Presidency of the High Priesthood, after the order of Melchizedek, have a right to officiate in all the offices in the church.

10 *High priests after the order of the Melchizedek Priesthood have a *right to officiate in their own *standing, under the direction of the presidency, in administering spiritual things, and also in the office of an elder, *priest (of the Levitical order), teacher, deacon, and member.

11 An elder has a right to officiate in his stead when the high priest is not present.

12 The high priest and *elder are to administer in spiritual things, agreeable to the covenants and commandments of the church; and they have a right to officiate in all these offices of the church when there are no higher authorities present.

13 The second priesthood is called the Priesthood of *Aaron, because it was conferred upon Aaron and his seed, throughout all their generations.

14 Why it is called the lesser priesthood is because it is an *appendage to the greater, or the Melchizedek Priesthood, and has power in administering outward ordinances.

15 The *bishopric is the presidency of this priesthood, and holds the *keys or authority of the same.

16 No man has a legal right to this office, to hold the keys of this priesthood, except he be a *literal descendant of *Aaron.

17 But as a high priest of the *Melchizedek Priesthood has authority to officiate in all the lesser offices, he may officiate in the office of *bishop when no literal descendant of Aaron can be found, provided he is called and *set apart and ordained unto this power by the hands of the *Presidency of the Melchizedek Priesthood.

18 The power and authority of the higher, or Melchizedek Priesthood, is to hold the *keys of all the spiritual blessings of the church—

19 To have the privilege of receiving the *mysteries of the kingdom of heaven, to have the *heavens opened unto them, to commune with the *general assembly and church of the *Firstborn, and to enjoy the communion and *presence of God the

---

5a D&C 84: 29; 107: 14.
6a Deut. 10: 8 (8–9); 18: 5.
7a TG Elders.
8a Acts 6: 4.
 b TG Authority; Priesthood, Authority.
9a D&C 81: 2; 107: 22 (22, 65–67, 91–92).
10a TG High Priest—Melchizedek Priesthood.
 b D&C 20: 38 (38–67); 121: 36 (35–46).
 c D&C 124: 133 (133–136).
 d TG Priest, Aaronic Priesthood.

12a D&C 124: 137.
13a Ex. 27: 21; 2 Chr. 26: 18; D&C 27: 8; 84: 18 (18–27). TG Priesthood, Aaronic.
14a D&C 20: 52; 107: 5.
15a D&C 124: 141. TG Bishop.
 b TG Priesthood, Keys of.
16a Ex. 40: 15 (12–15); D&C 68: 16 (14–24); 84: 18 (18, 30); 107: 69 (68–78).
 b Neh. 11: 22.
17a TG Priesthood, Melchizedek.

 b TG Bishop.
 c TG Setting Apart.
 d D&C 68: 15; 81: 2.
18a TG Priesthood, Keys of.
19a Eph. 1: 9; Alma 12: 9 (9–11); D&C 63: 23; 84: 19 (19–22). TG Mysteries of Godliness.
 b Ezek. 1: 1; Acts 7: 56; 10: 11.
 c Heb. 12: 23 (22–24).
 d TG Jesus Christ, Firstborn.
 e TG God, Presence of; God, Privilege of Seeing.

Father, and Jesus the *mediator of the new covenant.

20 And the *power and authority of the lesser, or *Aaronic Priesthood, is to hold the *keys of the ministering of angels, and to *administer in outward *ordinances, the letter of the gospel, the baptism of repentance for the *remission of sins, agreeable to the covenants and commandments.

21 Of necessity there are presidents, or presiding *officers growing out of, or appointed of or from among those who are ordained to the several offices in these two priesthoods.

22 Of the *Melchizedek Priesthood, three *Presiding High Priests, chosen by the body, appointed and ordained to that office, and *upheld by the confidence, faith, and prayer of the church, form a quorum of the Presidency of the Church.

23 The *twelve traveling councilors are called to be the Twelve *Apostles, or special *witnesses of the name of Christ in all the world—thus differing from other officers in the church in the duties of their calling.

24 And they form a quorum, *equal in authority and power to the three presidents previously mentioned.

25 The *Seventy are also called to *preach the gospel, and to be especial witnesses unto the Gentiles and in all the world—thus differing from other officers in the church in the duties of their calling.

26 And they form a quorum, equal in *authority to that of the Twelve

special witnesses or Apostles just named.

27 And every decision made by either of these quorums must be by the *unanimous voice of the same; that is, every member in each quorum must be agreed to its decisions, in order to make their decisions of the same power or validity one with the other—

28 A majority may form a quorum when circumstances render it impossible to be otherwise—

29 Unless this is the case, their decisions are not entitled to the same blessings which the decisions of a quorum of three presidents were anciently, who were ordained after the order of Melchizedek, and were *righteous and holy men.

30 The decisions of these quorums, or either of them, are to be made in all *righteousness, in holiness, and lowliness of heart, meekness and *long suffering, and in *faith, and *virtue, and knowledge, temperance, patience, godliness, brotherly kindness and charity;

31 Because the promise is, if these things abound in them they shall not be *unfruitful in the knowledge of the Lord.

32 And in case that any decision of these quorums is made in unrighteousness, it may be brought before a general assembly of the several quorums, which constitute the spiritual authorities of the church; otherwise there can be no *appeal from their decision.

19f TG Jesus Christ, Messenger of the Covenant.
20a Lev. 7: 35.
  b TG Priesthood, Aaronic.
  c D&C 13: 1; 84: 27 (26–27).
  d Num. 18: 5 (1–6).
  e TG Ordinance.
  f TG Baptism; Remission of Sins; Repentance.
21a Num. 11: 16; D&C 88: 127; 124: 123.
22a TG Priesthood, Melchizedek.

  b D&C 68: 15; 90: 6; 107: 9 (9, 65–67, 78–84, 91–92).
  c TG Sustaining Church Leaders.
23a D&C 18: 31 (31–37); 107: 33 (33–35).
  b 2 Pet. 1: 1. TG Apostles.
  c TG Witnesses.
24a D&C 90: 6.
25a D&C 107: 34. TG Seventy.
  b TG Missionary Work; Preaching.
26a Luke 10: 1 (1–12,

17–20).
27a TG Unity.
29a Ex. 22: 31; Alma 13: 26; D&C 49: 8.
30a D&C 121: 36. TG Priesthood, Magnifying Callings within; Righteousness.
  b TG Forbearance.
  c 2 Pet. 1: 5 (5–7).
  d D&C 121: 41 (41–46). TG Benevolence; Godliness; Kindness; Temperance; Virtue.
31a 2 Pet. 1: 8 (5–8).
32a D&C 102: 20 (12–34).

33 The ^aTwelve are a ^bTraveling Presiding High Council, to officiate in the name of the Lord, under the direction of the Presidency of the Church, agreeable to the institution of heaven; to build up the church, and regulate all the affairs of the same in all nations, first unto the ^cGentiles and secondly unto the Jews.

34 The ^aSeventy are to act in the name of the Lord, under the direction of the ^bTwelve or the traveling high council, in building up the church and regulating all the affairs of the same in all nations, first unto the Gentiles and then to the Jews;

35 The Twelve being ^asent out, holding the keys, to open the door by the proclamation of the gospel of Jesus Christ, and first unto the Gentiles and then unto the Jews.

36 The standing ^ahigh councils, at the stakes of Zion, form a quorum equal in authority in the affairs of the church, in all their decisions, to the quorum of the presidency, or to the traveling high council.

37 The ^ahigh council in Zion form a quorum equal in authority in the affairs of the church, in all their decisions, to the councils of the Twelve at the stakes of Zion.

38 It is the duty of the traveling high council to call upon the ^aSeventy, when they need assistance, to fill the several calls for preaching and administering the gospel, instead of any others.

39 It is the duty of the ^aTwelve, in all large branches of the church, to ordain ^bevangelical ministers, as they shall be designated unto them by revelation—

40 The order of this priesthood was

confirmed to be handed down from father to son, and rightly belongs to the literal descendants of the chosen seed, to whom the promises were made.

41 This ^aorder was instituted in the days of ^bAdam, and came down by ^clineage in the following manner:

42 From Adam to ^aSeth, who was ^bordained by Adam at the age of sixty-nine years, and was blessed by him three years previous to his (Adam's) death, and received the promise of God by his father, that his posterity should be the chosen of the Lord, and that they should be ^cpreserved unto the end of the earth;

43 Because he (Seth) was a ^aperfect man, and his ^blikeness was the express likeness of his father, insomuch that he seemed to be like unto his father in all things, and could be distinguished from him only by his age.

44 Enos was ordained at the age of one hundred and thirty-four years and four months, by the hand of Adam.

45 God called upon Cainan in the wilderness in the fortieth year of his age; and he met Adam in journeying to the place Shedolamak. He was eighty-seven years old when he received his ordination.

46 Mahalaleel was four hundred and ninety-six years and seven days old when he was ordained by the hand of Adam, who also blessed him.

47 Jared was two hundred years old when he was ordained under the hand of Adam, who also blessed him.

48 ^aEnoch was twenty-five years old when he was ordained under the hand of Adam; and he was sixty-five and Adam blessed him.

33a D&C 107: 23 (23–24, 38–39). TG Apostles.
  b D&C 124: 139.
  c 1 Ne. 13: 42; 3 Ne. 16: 7 (4–13); D&C 18: 6 (6, 26); 19: 27; 21: 12; 90: 9 (8–9); 112: 4.
34a D&C 107: 25 (25, 38). TG Seventy.
  b D&C 112: 21.

35a Matt. 10: 5 (5–42).
36a D&C 102: 30 (27–32).
37a D&C 124: 131.
38a D&C 107: 34 (34, 90–98).
39a D&C 107: 33 (33–35, 58).
  b D&C 124: 91 (91–92).
41a D&C 84: 16.
  TG Patriarch; Priesthood, History of.

  b Gen. 5: 4 (1–32).
  c Moses 6: 22 (10–25).
42a Gen. 4: 25.
  b D&C 84: 16;
    Moses 6: 2.
  c Gen. 45: 7 (1–8);
    2 Ne. 3: 16.
43a TG Perfection.
  b Gen. 5: 3.
48a Moses 6: 25 (21–68;
    Moses 7).

49 And he ^asaw the Lord, and he walked with him, and was before his face continually; and he ^bwalked with God three hundred and sixty-five years, making him four hundred and thirty years old when he was translated.

50 Methuselah was one hundred years old when he was ordained under the hand of Adam.

51 Lamech was thirty-two years old when he was ordained under the hand of Seth.

52 Noah was ten years old when he was ^aordained under the hand of Methuselah.

53 Three years previous to the death of Adam, he called Seth, Enos, Cainan, Mahalaleel, Jared, Enoch, and Methuselah, who were all ^ahigh priests, with the residue of his posterity who were righteous, into the valley of ^bAdam-ondi-Ahman, and there bestowed upon them his last blessing.

54 And the Lord appeared unto them, and they rose up and blessed ^aAdam, and called him Michael, the prince, the archangel.

55 And the Lord administered comfort unto Adam, and said unto him: I have set thee to be at the head; a multitude of nations shall come of thee, and thou art a ^aprince over them forever.

56 And Adam stood up in the midst of the congregation; and, notwithstanding he was bowed down with age, being full of the Holy Ghost, ^apredicted whatsoever should befall his posterity unto the latest generation.

57 These things were all written in the book of ^aEnoch, and are to be testified of in due time.

58 It is the duty of the ^aTwelve, also, to ^bordain and set in order all the other officers of the church, agreeable to the revelation which says:

59 To the church of Christ in the land of Zion, in addition to the church ^alaws respecting church business—

60 Verily, I say unto you, saith the Lord of Hosts, there must needs be ^apresiding elders to preside over those who are of the office of an elder;

61 And also ^apriests to preside over those who are of the office of a priest;

62 And also teachers to preside over those who are of the office of a teacher, in like manner, and also the ^adeacons—

63 Wherefore, from deacon to teacher, and from teacher to priest, and from priest to elder, severally as they are appointed, according to the covenants and commandments of the church.

64 Then comes the High Priesthood, which is the greatest of all.

65 Wherefore, it must needs be that one be appointed of the High ^aPriesthood to preside over the priesthood, and he shall be called President of the High Priesthood of the Church;

66 Or, in other words, the ^aPresiding High Priest over the High Priesthood of the Church.

67 From the same comes the administering of ordinances and blessings upon the church, by the ^alaying on of the hands.

68 Wherefore, the office of a bishop

49a TG Jesus Christ, Appearances, Antemortal.
 b Gen. 5: 22; Heb. 11: 5; Moses 7: 69.
  TG Translated Beings; Walking with God.
52a Moses 8: 19.
53a TG High Priest— Melchizedek Priesthood.
 b Dan. 7: 13 (13–14);

D&C 78: 15 (15–20); 116: 1.
54a 2 Ne. 9: 21; D&C 128: 21; TG Adam.
55a D&C 78: 16.
56a Moses 5: 10.
57a Moses 6: 46 (5, 46). TG Scriptures, Lost.
58a D&C 107: 39 (38–39). TG Apostles.
 b TG Priesthood, Ordination.

59a D&C 42: 59; 43: 2–9; 72: 9; 83: 1; 103: 35.
60a D&C 107: 89 (89–90).
61a D&C 20: 46; 84: 111; 107: 87.
62a D&C 107: 85 (85–86).
65a TG Priesthood, Melchizedek.
66a D&C 107: 91 (9, 22, 91–92).
67a TG Blessing; Hands, Laying on of; Ordinance.

is not equal unto it; for the office of a °bishop is in administering all °temporal things;

69 Nevertheless a °bishop must be chosen from the High °Priesthood, unless he is a °literal descendant of Aaron;

70 For unless he is a °literal descendant of Aaron he cannot hold the keys of that priesthood.

71 Nevertheless, a high priest, that is, after the order of Melchizedek, may be set apart unto the ministering of temporal things, having a °knowledge of them by the Spirit of truth;

72 And also to be a °judge in Israel, to do the business of the church, to sit in °judgment upon transgressors upon testimony as it shall be laid before him according to the laws, by the assistance of his °counselors, whom he has chosen or will choose among the elders of the church.

73 This is the duty of a bishop who is not a literal descendant of Aaron, but has been ordained to the High Priesthood after the order of Melchizedek.

74 Thus shall he be a °judge, even a common judge among the inhabitants of Zion, or in a stake of Zion, or in any branch of the church where he shall be °set apart unto this ministry, until the borders of Zion are enlarged and it becomes necessary to have other bishops or judges in Zion or elsewhere.

75 And inasmuch as there are other bishops appointed they shall act in the same office.

76 But a literal descendant of Aaron has a legal right to the presidency of this priesthood, to the °keys of this ministry, to act in the office of bishop independently, without

counselors, except in a case where a President of the High Priesthood, after the order of Melchizedek, is tried, to sit as a judge in Israel.

77 And the decision of either of these councils, agreeable to the commandment which says:

78 Again, verily, I say unto you, the most important business of the church, and the most °difficult cases of the church, inasmuch as there is not satisfaction upon the decision of the bishop or judges, it shall be handed over and carried up unto the council of the church, before the °Presidency of the High Priesthood.

79 And the Presidency of the council of the High Priesthood shall have power to call other high priests, even twelve, to assist as counselors; and thus the Presidency of the High Priesthood and its counselors shall have power to decide upon testimony according to the laws of the church.

80 And after this decision it shall be had in remembrance no more before the Lord; for this is the highest council of the church of God, and a final decision upon controversies in spiritual matters.

81 There is not any person belonging to the church who is exempt from this council of the church.

82 And inasmuch as a President of the High Priesthood shall transgress, he shall be had in remembrance before the °common council of the church, who shall be assisted by twelve counselors of the High Priesthood;

83 And their decision upon his head shall be an end of controversy concerning him.

84 Thus, none shall be exempted from the °justice and the °laws of God, that all things may be done in

68a TG Bishop.
  b Acts 6: 3; D&C 70: 11 (11–12).
69a Ex. 40: 15 (12–15);

D&C 84: 18 (18, 30).
71a TG Holy Ghost, Mission of; Knowledge.
72a D&C 58: 17 (17–18); 64: 40.
  b TG Judgment.
  c TG Counselor.
74a Ex. 18: 13; Mosiah 29: 11 (11–44); Alma 46: 4.

  b TG Setting Apart.
76a TG Priesthood, Keys of (28).
78a D&C 102: 28 (13–14, 28).
  b D&C 88: 22.
82a D&C 107: 74 (74–76).
84a TG God, Justice of; Justice.
  b TG God, Law of.

ᶜorder and in solemnity before him, according to truth and righteousness.

85 And again, verily I say unto you, the duty of a president over the office of a ᵃdeacon is to preside over twelve deacons, to sit in council with them, and to ᵇteach them their duty, ᶜedifying one another, as it is given according to the covenants.

86 And also the duty of the president over the office of the ᵃteachers is to preside over twenty-four of the teachers, and to sit in council with them, teaching them the duties of their office, as given in the covenants.

87 Also the duty of the president over the Priesthood of Aaron is to preside over forty-eight ᵃpriests, and sit in council with them, to teach them the duties of their office, as is given in the covenants.

88 This president is to be a ᵃbishop; for this is one of the duties of this priesthood.

89 Again, the duty of the president over the office of ᵃelders is to preside over ninety-six elders, and to sit in council with them, and to teach them according to the covenants.

90 This presidency is a distinct one from that of the seventy, and is designed for those who do not ᵃtravel into all the world.

91 And again, the duty of the President of the office of the High Priesthood is to ᵃpreside over the whole church, and to be like unto ᵇMoses—

92 Behold, here is wisdom; yea, to be a ᵃseer, a ᵇrevelator, a translator, and a ᶜprophet, having all the ᵈgifts of God which he bestows upon the head of the church.

93 And it is according to the vision showing the order of the ᵃSeventy, that they should have seven presidents to preside over them, chosen out of the number of the seventy;

94 And the seventh president of these presidents is to preside over the six;

95 And these seven presidents are to choose other seventy besides the first seventy to whom they belong, and are to preside over them;

96 And also other seventy, until seven times seventy, if the labor in the vineyard of necessity requires it.

97 And these ᵃseventy are to be ᵇtraveling ministers, unto the Gentiles first and also unto the Jews.

98 Whereas other officers of the church, who belong not unto the Twelve, neither to the Seventy, are not under the responsibility to travel among all nations, but are to travel as their circumstances shall allow, notwithstanding they may hold as high and responsible offices in the church.

99 Wherefore, now let every man learn his ᵃduty, and to act in the office in which he is appointed, in all ᵇdiligence.

100 He that is ᵃslothful shall not be counted ᵇworthy to stand, and he that learns not his duty and shows himself not approved shall not be counted worthy to stand. Even so. Amen.

84c ᴛɢ Order.
85a ᴛɢ Deacons.
  b Ex. 35: 34; Moro. 10: 9 (9–10); D&C 38: 23; 88: 77 (77–79, 118).
  c ᴛɢ Edification.
86a D&C 20: 53 (53–60).
  ᴛɢ Teachers.
87a ᴛɢ Priest, Aaronic Priesthood.
88a ᴛɢ Bishop.
89a ᴛɢ Elders.
90a D&C 124: 37.
91a D&C 90: 13 (13, 32–33); 107: 66 (9, 22, 65–67).

  b D&C 28: 2; 103: 16 (16–21).
92a Mosiah 8: 16 (13–18).
  ᴛɢ Seer.
  b ᴛɢ Revelation.
  c D&C 21: 1.
    ᴛɢ Prophets, Mission of.
  d ᴛɢ God, Gifts of; Holy Ghost, Gifts of.
93a D&C 107: 38.
97a ᴛɢ Seventy.
  b D&C 124: 138 (138–139).
99a Deut. 4: 5 (5–8); Mal. 2: 7 (7–9).

  ᴛɢ Duty; Leadership; Priesthood, Magnifying Callings within; Priesthood, Oath and Covenant.
  b ᴛɢ Dedication; Diligence; Steadfastness; Zeal.
100a Matt. 24: 45; D&C 58: 26 (26–29); 84: 85 (85–86).
  ᴛɢ Apathy; Idleness; Laziness.
  b ᴛɢ Priesthood, Oath and Covenant; Worthiness.

SECTION 108

Revelation given through Joseph Smith the Prophet, at Kirtland, Ohio, December 26, 1835. HC 2: 345. This section was received at the request of Lyman Sherman, who had previously been ordained a high priest and a seventy, and who had come to the Prophet with a request for a revelation to make known his duty.

1–3, Lyman Sherman forgiven of his sins; 4–5, He is to be numbered with the leading elders of the Church; 6–8, He is called to preach the gospel and strengthen his brethren.

VERILY thus saith the Lord unto you, my servant Lyman: Your sins are forgiven you, because you have obeyed my *"voice* in coming up hither this morning to receive counsel of him whom I have appointed.

2 Therefore, let your soul be at *"rest* concerning your spiritual standing, and resist no more my voice.

3 And arise up and be more careful henceforth in observing your *"vows,* which you have made and do make, and you shall be blessed with exceeding great blessings.

4 Wait patiently until the *"solemn assembly* shall be called of my servants, then you shall be remembered with the *"first* of mine elders, and receive right by ordination with the rest of mine elders whom I have chosen.

5 Behold, this is the *"promise* of the Father unto you if you continue faithful.

6 And it shall be fulfilled upon you in that day that you shall have right to *"preach* my gospel wheresoever I shall send you, from henceforth from that time.

7 Therefore, *"strengthen* your brethren in all your conversation, in all your prayers, in all your exhortations, and in all your doings.

8 And behold, and lo, I am with you to bless you, and *"deliver* you forever. Amen.

SECTION 109

Prayer offered at the dedication of the temple at Kirtland, Ohio, March 27, 1836. HC 2: 420–426. According to the Prophet's written statement, this prayer was given to him by revelation.

1–5, Kirtland Temple built as a place for the Son of Man to visit; 6–21, It is to be a house of prayer, fasting, faith, learning, glory, and order, and a house of God; 22–33, May the unrepentant who oppose the Lord's people be confounded; 34–42, May the saints go forth in power to gather the righteous to Zion; 43–53, May the saints be delivered from the terrible things to be poured out upon the wicked in the last days; 54–58, May nations and peoples and churches be prepared for the gospel; 59–67, May the Jews, the Lamanites, and all Israel be redeemed; 68–80, May the saints be crowned with glory and honor and gain eternal salvation.

---

108 1a TG Counsel;
     Guidance, Divine;
     Inspiration.
  2a TG Peace of God.
  3a TG Integrity; Vows.

4a D&C 88: 70; 95: 7;
     109: 6 (6–10).
  b D&C 88: 85; 105: 7
     (7, 33).
  5a D&C 82: 10.

6a TG Missionary Work.
  7a Luke 22: 32.
  8a Dan. 6: 27; 2 Ne. 9: 19
     (18–19); D&C 105: 8.
     TG Deliverance.

^aTHANKS be to thy name, O Lord God of Israel, who keepest ^bcovenant and showest mercy unto thy servants who walk uprightly before thee, with all their hearts—

2 Thou who hast commanded thy servants to ^abuild a house to thy name in this place [Kirtland].

3 And now thou beholdest, O Lord, that thy servants have done according to thy commandment.

4 And now we ask thee, Holy Father, in the name of Jesus Christ, the Son of thy bosom, in whose name alone salvation can be administered to the children of men, we ask thee, O Lord, to accept of this ^ahouse, the ^bworkmanship of the hands of us, thy servants, which thou didst command us to build.

5 For thou knowest that we have done this work through great tribulation; and out of our poverty we have ^agiven of our substance to build a ^bhouse to thy name, that the Son of Man might have a place to ^cmanifest himself to his people.

6 And as thou hast said in a ^arevelation, given to us, calling us thy friends, saying—Call your solemn assembly, as I have commanded you;

7 And as all have not faith, seek ye diligently and teach one another words of wisdom; yea, seek ye out of the best ^abooks words of wisdom, seek learning even by study and also by faith;

8 Organize yourselves; ^aprepare every needful thing, and establish a house, even a ^bhouse of prayer, a house of fasting, a house of faith, a house of learning, a house of glory, a house of ^corder, a ^dhouse of God;

9 That your ^aincomings may be in the name of the Lord, that your outgoings may be in the name of the Lord, that all your salutations may be in the name of the Lord, with uplifted hands unto the Most High—

10 And now, Holy Father, we ask thee to assist us, thy people, with thy grace, in calling our ^asolemn assembly, that it may be done to thine honor and to thy divine acceptance;

11 And in a manner that we may be found worthy, in thy sight, to secure a fulfilment of the ^apromises which thou hast made unto us, thy people, in the revelations given unto us;

12 That thy ^aglory may rest down upon thy people, and upon this thy house, which we now dedicate to thee, that it may be ^bsanctified and consecrated to be holy, and that thy holy presence may be continually in this house;

13 And that all people who shall enter upon the threshold of the Lord's house may feel thy power, and feel constrained to acknowledge that thou hast sanctified it, and that it is thy house, a ^aplace of thy holiness.

14 And do thou grant, Holy Father, that all those who shall worship in this house may be taught words of wisdom out of the best ^abooks, and that they may seek learning even by study, and also by faith, as thou hast said;

15 And that they may grow up in thee, and receive a fulness of the Holy Ghost, and be organized according to thy laws, and be prepared to obtain every needful thing;

16 And that this house may be a house of prayer, a house of fasting, a house of faith, a house of glory and of God, even thy house;

---

109 1a 1 Chr. 16:8 (7–36);
    Alma 37:37; D&C 46:
    32.
  b 1 Kgs. 8:23 (22–61);
    Dan. 9:4 (4, 9).
  2a D&C 88:119.
  4a 1 Kgs. 9:1.
  b 2 Ne. 5:16.
  5a Mark 12:44 (41–44).
  b D&C 124:27 (27–28).

  c Lev. 16:2.
  6a D&C 88:117 (117–120).
  7a D&C 88:118.
  8a TG Skills.
  b TG Temple.
  c TG Order.
  d 1 Kgs. 8:17.
  9a D&C 88:120.

  10a TG Solemn Assembly.
  11a D&C 38:32; 105:33
    (11–12, 18, 33); 110:9.
  12a Ex. 40:34; 1 Kgs. 8:11
    (10–13); 2 Chr. 7:2
    (2–3); D&C 84:5; 109:
    37.
  13a Lev. 16:23.
  14a D&C 88:118 (118–119).

17 That all the incomings of thy people, into this house, may be in the name of the Lord;

18 That all their outgoings from this house may be in the name of the Lord;

19 And that all their salutations may be in the name of the Lord, with holy hands, uplifted to the Most High;

20 And that no *a*unclean thing shall be permitted to come into thy house to *b*pollute it;

21 And when thy people *a*transgress, any of them, they may speedily repent and return unto thee, and find favor in thy sight, and be restored to the blessings which thou hast ordained to be poured out upon those who shall *b*reverence thee in thy house.

22 And we ask thee, Holy Father, that thy servants may go forth from this house armed with thy power, and that thy *a*name may be upon them, and thy glory be round about them, and thine *b*angels have charge over them;

23 And from this place they may bear exceedingly great and glorious tidings, in truth, unto the *a*ends of the earth, that they may know that this is thy work, and that thou hast put forth thy hand, to fulfil that which thou hast spoken by the mouths of the prophets, concerning the last days.

24 We ask thee, Holy Father, to establish the people that shall worship, and honorably hold a name and standing in this thy house, to all generations and for eternity;

25 That no weapon *a*formed against them shall prosper; that he who

diggeth a *b*pit for them shall fall into the same himself;

26 That no combination of wickedness shall have power to rise up and *a*prevail over thy people upon whom thy *b*name shall be put in this house;

27 And if any people shall rise against this people, that thine anger be kindled against them;

28 And if they shall smite this people thou wilt smite them; thou wilt *a*fight for thy people as thou didst in the day of battle, that they may be delivered from the hands of all their enemies.

29 We ask thee, Holy Father, to confound, and astonish, and to bring to *a*shame and confusion, all those who have spread *b*lying reports abroad, over the world, against thy servant or servants, if they will not repent, when the everlasting gospel shall be proclaimed in their ears;

30 And that all their works may be brought to naught, and be swept away by the *a*hail, and by the judgments which thou wilt send upon them in thine anger, that there may be an end to *b*lyings and slanders against thy people.

31 For thou knowest, O Lord, that thy servants have been innocent before thee in *a*bearing record of thy name, for which they have suffered these things.

32 Therefore we plead before thee for a full and complete *a*deliverance from under this *b*yoke;

33 Break it off, O Lord; break it off from the necks of thy servants, by thy power, that we may rise up in the midst of this generation and do thy work.

34 O Jehovah, have mercy upon

20a Luke 19: 46 (46–48); D&C 94: 8 (8–9); 97: 15 (15–17).
 b TG Pollution.
21a 1 Kgs. 8: 31 (31–34).
 b TG Reverence.
22a TG Jesus Christ, Power of; Jesus Christ, Taking the Name of.
 b TG Angels; Protection, Divine.

23a D&C 1: 2.
25a Isa. 54: 17.
 b Prov. 26: 27; 1 Ne. 14: 3; 22: 14.
26a Matt. 16: 18; D&C 98: 22.
 b 1 Kgs. 8: 29; D&C 112: 12 (11–12).
28a TG Protection, Divine.
29a TG Shame.

 b TG Lying.
30a Ex. 9: 18 (13–35); Isa. 28: 17 (15–19); Mosiah 12: 6; D&C 29: 16 (16–21).
 b TG Lying.
31a TG Deliverance.
32a TG Deliverance.
 b TG Bondage, Spiritual.

this people, and as all men *a*sin forgive the transgressions of thy people, and let them be blotted out forever.

35 Let the *a*anointing of thy ministers be sealed upon them with power from on high.

36 Let it be fulfilled upon them, as upon those on the day of Pentecost; let the gift of *a*tongues be poured out upon thy people, even *b*cloven tongues as of fire, and the interpretation thereof.

37 And let thy house be filled, as with a rushing mighty *a*wind, with thy *b*glory.

38 Put upon thy servants the *a*testimony of the covenant, that when they go out and proclaim thy word they may *b*seal up the law, and prepare the hearts of thy saints for all those judgments thou art about to send, in thy wrath, upon the inhabitants of the *c*earth, because of their transgressions, that thy people may not faint in the day of trouble.

39 And whatsoever city thy servants shall enter, and the people of that city *a*receive their testimony, let thy peace and thy salvation be upon that city; that they may gather out of that city the righteous, that they may come forth to *b*Zion, or to her stakes, the places of thine appointment, with songs of everlasting joy;

40 And until this be accomplished, let not thy judgments fall upon that city.

41 And whatsoever city thy servants shall enter, and the people of that city receive not the testimony of thy servants, and thy servants

warn them to save themselves from this untoward generation, let it be upon that city according to that which thou hast spoken by the mouths of thy prophets.

42 But deliver thou, O Jehovah, we beseech thee, thy servants from their hands, and *a*cleanse them from their blood.

43 O Lord, we delight not in the destruction of our fellow men; their *a*souls are precious before thee;

44 But thy word must be fulfilled. Help thy servants to say, with thy *a*grace assisting them: Thy will be done, O Lord, and not ours.

45 We know that thou hast spoken by the mouth of thy prophets terrible things concerning the *a*wicked, in the last days—that thou wilt pour out thy judgments, without measure;

46 Therefore, O Lord, deliver thy people from the calamity of the wicked; enable thy servants to seal up the law, and *a*bind up the testimony, that they may be prepared against the day of burning.

47 We ask thee, Holy Father, to remember those who have been *a*driven by the inhabitants of Jackson county, Missouri, from the lands of their inheritance, and break off, O Lord, this *b*yoke of affliction that has been put upon them.

48 Thou knowest, O Lord, that they have been greatly *a*oppressed and afflicted by wicked men; and our *b*hearts flow out with sorrow because of their grievous *c*burdens.

49 O Lord, *a*how long wilt thou suffer this people to bear this affliction, and the *b*cries of their innocent ones to ascend up in thine ears, and

---

34a Rom. 3: 23; 5: 1-12:
  21. TG Sin.
35a Ex. 25: 6; Lev. 8: 12
  (12-13); D&C 68: 20.
  TG Anointing.
36a TG Holy Ghost, Gifts
  of.
  b Acts 2: 3.
37a Acts 2: 2.
  b 2 Chr. 7: 2 (2-3);
  D&C 84: 5; 109: 12.
  TG God, Manifestations of.

38a TG Testimony.
  b Isa. 8: 16; D&C 1: 8.
  c TG Earth, Cleansing of.
39a Matt. 10: 13 (11-15).
  b Isa. 35: 10.
42a Purification.
43a TG Life, Sanctity of;
  Worth of Souls.
44a TG God, Will of; Grace.
45a TG Last Days; Wickedness.

46a Isa. 8: 16. TG Seal;
  Sealing; Testimony.
47a D&C 101: 1; 103: 2
  (2, 11); 104: 51.
  b TG Bondage, Physical.
48a TG Oppression.
  b TG Compassion.
  c Ps. 81: 6 (5-6).
49a Ps. 13: 2 (1-6); 74: 10
  (10-23).
  b Ex. 3: 9 (7, 9); 2 Ne. 26:
  15; Mosiah 21: 15.

their ᵇblood come up in testimony before thee, and not make a display of thy testimony in their behalf?

50 Have ᵃmercy, O Lord, upon the wicked mob, who have driven thy people, that they may cease to spoil, that they may repent of their sins if repentance is to be found;

51 But if they will not, make bare thine arm, O Lord, and ᵃredeem that which thou didst appoint a Zion unto thy people.

52 And if it cannot be otherwise, that the cause of thy people may not fail before thee may thine anger be kindled, and thine ᵃindignation fall upon them, that they may be wasted away, both root and branch, from under heaven;

53 But inasmuch as they will repent, thou art ᵃgracious and merciful, and wilt turn away thy wrath when thou lookest upon the face of thine Anointed.

54 Have mercy, O Lord, upon all the ᵃnations of the earth; have mercy upon the rulers of our land; may those principles, which were so honorably and nobly defended, namely, the ᵇConstitution of our land, by our fathers, be established forever.

55 ᵃRemember the kings, the princes, the nobles, and the great ones of the earth, and all people, and the churches, all the poor, the needy, and afflicted ones of the earth;

56 That their hearts may be softened when thy servants shall go out from thy house, O Jehovah, to bear testimony of thy name; that

their prejudices may give way before the ᵃtruth, and thy people may obtain favor in the sight of all;

57 That all the ends of the earth may know that we, thy servants, have ᵃheard thy voice, and that thou hast sent us:

58 That from among all these, thy servants, the sons of Jacob, may gather out the righteous to build a holy ᵃcity to thy name, as thou hast commanded them.

59 We ask thee to appoint unto Zion other ᵃstakes besides this one which thou hast appointed, that the gathering of thy ᵇpeople may roll on in great power and majesty, that thy work may be cut ᶜshort in righteousness.

60 Now these words, O Lord, we have spoken before thee, concerning the revelations and commandments which thou hast given unto us, who are identified with the ᵃGentiles.

61 But thou knowest that thou hast a great love for the children of Jacob, who have been ᵃscattered upon the ᵇmountains for a long time, in a ᶜcloudy and dark day.

62 We therefore ask thee to have mercy upon the children of Jacob, that ᵃJerusalem, from this hour, may begin to be redeemed;

63 And the yoke of bondage may begin to be broken off from the house of ᵃDavid;

64 And the children of ᵃJudah may begin to return to the ᵇlands which thou didst give to Abraham, their father.

65 And cause that the ᵃremnants

49c ᴛɢ Martyrdom.
50a ᴛɢ Mercy; Repentance.
51a D&C 100: 13; 105: 2.
52a ᴛɢ God, Indignation of; Punishment.
53a ᴛɢ Forgiveness; Grace.
54a ᴛɢ Governments; Nations.
  b 1 Pet. 2: 13 (13–14); D&C 44: 4; 51: 6; 98: 5 (5–7); 101: 77 (77, 80).
55a ᴛɢ Compassion.
56a ᴛɢ Hardheartedness; Teachable; Truth.
57a D&C 20: 16; 76: 14

58a D&C 28: 9.
59a Isa. 54: 2; D&C 104: 48.
  b D&C 86: 11. ᴛɢ Israel, Gathering of.
  c Matt. 24: 22.
60a 1 Ne. 13: 4 (1–32); 15: 13 (13–18).
61a Hosea 1: 6; 13: 9 (9–14).
  b Gen. 49: 26.
  c Ezek. 30: 3.
62a 3 Ne. 20: 29.
  ᴛɢ Jerusalem.

63a 1 Kgs. 11: 39. ᴛɢ Israel, Restoration of.
64a Hosea 1: 7; Zech. 12: 6 (6–9); Mal. 3: 4; D&C 133: 35 (13, 35).
  ᴛɢ Israel, Judah, People of.
  b Gen. 17: 8 (1–8).
  ᴛɢ Promised Land.
65a 2 Ne. 30: 3; Alma 46: 23 (23–24); 3 Ne. 20: 16 (15–21); D&C 3: 18; 10: 48 (46–52); 19: 27; 52: 7; 87: 5 (4–5).
  ᴛɢ Israel, Remnant of.

of Jacob, who have been cursed and smitten because of their transgression, be [b]converted from their wild and savage condition to the fulness of the everlasting gospel;

66 That they may lay down their weapons of bloodshed, and cease their rebellions.

67 And may all the scattered remnants of [a]Israel, who have been driven to the ends of the earth, come to a knowledge of the truth, believe in the Messiah, and be redeemed from [b]oppression, and rejoice before thee.

68 O Lord, remember thy servant, Joseph Smith, Jun., and all his afflictions and persecutions—how he has [a]covenanted with [b]Jehovah, and vowed to thee, O Mighty God of Jacob—and the commandments which thou hast given unto him, and that he hath sincerely striven to do thy will.

69 Have mercy, O Lord, upon his [a]wife and children, that they may be exalted in thy presence, and preserved by thy fostering hand.

70 Have mercy upon all their [a]immediate connections, that their prejudices may be broken up and swept away as with a flood; that they may be [b]converted and redeemed with Israel, and know that thou art God.

71 Remember, O Lord, the presidents, even all the presidents of thy church, that thy right hand may exalt them, with all their families, and their immediate connections, that their names may be perpetuated and had in everlasting remembrance from generation to generation.

72 Remember all thy church, O Lord, with all their families, and all their immediate connections, with all their sick and afflicted ones, with all the poor and meek of the earth; that the [a]kingdom, which thou hast set up without hands, may become a great mountain and fill the whole earth;

73 That thy [a]church may come forth out of the wilderness of darkness, and shine forth fair as the [b]moon, clear as the sun, and terrible as an army with banners;

74 And be adorned as a bride for that day when thou shalt unveil the heavens, and cause the mountains to [a]flow down at thy presence, and the [b]valleys to be exalted, the rough places made smooth; that thy glory may fill the earth;

75 That when the trump shall sound for the dead, we shall be [a]caught up in the cloud to meet thee, that we may ever be with the Lord;

76 That our garments may be pure, that we may be clothed upon with [a]robes of [b]righteousness, with palms in our hands, and [c]crowns of glory upon our heads, and reap eternal [d]joy for all our [e]sufferings.

77 O Lord God Almighty, hear us in these our petitions, and answer us from heaven, thy holy habitation, where thou sittest enthroned, with [a]glory, honor, power, majesty, might, dominion, truth, justice, judgment, mercy, and an infinity of fulness, from everlasting to everlasting.

78 O hear, O hear, O hear us, O Lord! And answer these petitions, and accept the [a]dedication of this

---

65b 2 Ne. 30: 6; 3 Ne. 21: 25 (22–25); D&C 49: 24. TG Conversion.

67a TG Israel, Restoration of; Israel, Scattering of.
  b TG Bondage, Spiritual; Oppression.

68a TG Covenants.
  b TG Jesus Christ, Jehovah.

69a TG Family; Family, Eternal.

70a TG close relatives.
  b TG Conversion.

72a Dan. 2: 44 (44–45); D&C 35: 27; 65: 2.

73a TG Mission of Latter-day Saints.
  b Song. 6: 10; D&C 5: 14; 105: 31.

74a Judg. 5: 5; D&C 133: 22 (21–22, 40); Moses 6: 34.
  b Isa. 40: 4; Luke 3: 5; Hel. 14: 23; D&C

49: 23.

75a 1 Thes. 4: 17.

76a Lev. 8: 7; 2 Ne. 9: 14.
  b TG Righteousness.
  c TG Exaltation.
  d Heb. 12: 2 (1–11); D&C 58: 4; 103: 12 (11–14).
  e Heb. 11: 40, esp. in JST. TG Suffering.

77a TG God, Glory of.

78a TG Dedication.

house unto thee, the *b*work of our hands, which we have built unto thy name;

79 And also this church, to put upon it thy *a*name. And help us by the power of thy Spirit, that we may *b*mingle our voices with those bright,

shining *c*seraphs around thy throne, with acclamations of *d*praise, singing Hosanna to God and the *e*Lamb!

80 And let these, thine *a*anointed ones, be clothed with salvation, and thy saints *b*shout aloud for joy. Amen, and Amen.

SECTION 110

Visions manifested to Joseph Smith the Prophet and Oliver Cowdery in the temple at Kirtland, Ohio, April 3, 1836. HC 2: 435-436. The occasion was that of a Sabbath day meeting. The Prophet prefaces his record of the manifestations with these words: "In the afternoon, I assisted the other Presidents in distributing the Lord's Supper to the Church, receiving it from the Twelve, whose privilege it was to officiate at the sacred desk this day. After having performed this service to my brethren, I retired to the pulpit, the veils being dropped, and bowed myself, with Oliver Cowdery, in solemn and silent prayer. After rising from prayer, the following vision was opened to both of us."

1-10, The Lord Jehovah appears in glory and accepts the Kirtland Temple as his house; 11-12, Moses and Elias each appear and commit their keys and dispensations; 13-16, Elijah returns and commits the keys of his dispensation as promised by Malachi.

THE *a*veil was taken from our minds, and the *b*eyes of our *c*understanding were opened.

2 We *a*saw the Lord *b*standing on the breastwork of the pulpit, before us; and under his feet was a paved

work of pure *c*gold, in color like amber.

3 His *a*eyes were as a flame of fire; the hair of his head was white like the pure snow; his *b*countenance shone above the brightness of the sun; and his *c*voice was as the sound of the rushing of great waters, even the voice of *d*Jehovah, saying:

4 I am the *a*first and the last; I am he who *b*liveth, I am he who was slain; I am your *c*advocate with the Father.

5 Behold, your sins are *a*forgiven

78b TG Industry.
79a TG Jesus Christ, Taking the Name of.
  b D&C 20: 16, 36 (35-36).
  c Isa. 6: 2 (1-6).
  d Ezra 3: 11 (11-13);
    D&C 136: 28.
  e TG Jesus Christ, Lamb of God.
80a Ps. 18: 50; 20: 6.
    TG Anointing;
    Salvation.
  b Ps. 132: 16.
110 1a TG Veil.
  b D&C 76: 12 (10, 12, 19); 136: 32; 138: 11.

  c TG Understanding.
2a TG God, Privilege of Seeing; Jesus Christ, Appearances, Postmortal.
  b 1 Sam. 3: 10; 1 Ne. 1: 11 (8-15); JS-H 1: 17.
  c Ezek. 1: 27 (26-28);
    Rev. 21: 21;
    D&C 137: 4.
3a Rev. 1: 14; 2: 18.
    TG God, Body of (Corporeal Nature).
  b Ex. 34: 29 (29-35);
    Rev. 1: 16; Hel. 5: 36;
    JS-H 1: 32.

  c Ezek. 1: 24; 43: 2;
    Rev. 1: 15; D&C 133: 22.
  d TG Jesus Christ, Jehovah.
4a TG Jesus Christ, First-born.
  b Deut. 5: 24 (22-24);
    Zech. 13: 6; D&C 45: 52 (51-52).
  c TG God, Access to;
    Jesus Christ, Authority of;
    Jesus Christ, Relationships with the Father.
5a Luke 5: 21.
    TG Forgiveness.

you; you are clean before me; therefore, lift up your heads and *b*rejoice.

6 Let the hearts of your brethren rejoice, and let the hearts of all my people rejoice, who have, with their might, *a*built this house to my name.

7 For behold, I have *a*accepted this *b*house, and my name shall be here; and I will *c*manifest myself to my people in mercy in this house.

8 Yea, I will *a*appear unto my servants, and speak unto them with mine own voice, if my people will keep my commandments, and do not *b*pollute this *c*holy house.

9 Yea the hearts of thousands and tens of thousands shall greatly rejoice in consequence of the *a*blessings which shall be poured out, and the *b*endowment with which my servants have been endowed in this house.

10 And the fame of this house shall spread to foreign lands; and this is the beginning of the blessing which shall be *a*poured out upon the heads of my people. Even so. Amen.

11 After this *a*vision closed, the heavens were again *b*opened unto us; and *c*Moses appeared before us, and committed unto us the *d*keys of the *e*gathering of Israel from the four parts of the earth, and the leading of the ten tribes from the land of *f*north.

12 After this, *a*Elias appeared, and committed the *b*dispensation of the *c*gospel of Abraham, saying that in us and our seed all *d*generations after us should be *e*blessed.

13 After this vision had closed, another great and glorious *a*vision burst upon us; for *b*Elijah the prophet, who was taken to heaven without tasting death, stood before us, and said:

14 Behold, the time has fully come, which was spoken of by the mouth of Malachi—testifying that he [Elijah] should be sent, before the great and dreadful day of the Lord come—

15 To *a*turn the *b*hearts of the fathers to the children, and the children to the fathers, lest the whole earth be smitten with a curse—

16 Therefore, the *a*keys of this *b*dispensation are committed into your hands; and by this ye may know that the great and dreadful *c*day of the Lord is near, even at the doors.

5*b* TG Joy.
6*a* D&C 109: 4 (4–5).
7*a* 2 Chr. 7: 16.
  TG Dedication.
  b TG Temple.
  c TG God, Manifestations of.
8*a* Ex. 19: 11 (10–11); D&C 50: 45.
  b D&C 88: 134; 97: 15 (15–17). TG Pollution.
  c TG Holiness.
9*a* Gen. 12: 3 (1–3); D&C 39: 15; Abr. 2: 11 (8–11).
  b D&C 95: 8 (8–9).
10*a* Zech. 12: 10; D&C 105: 12.
11*a* TG Vision.
  b Ezek. 1: 1.
  c Matt. 17: 3; D&C 133: 55.

d D&C 113: 6.
  TG Priesthood, Keys of.
  e 1 Ne. 22: 12 (10–12); Jacob 6: 2; D&C 29: 7; 45: 43; 127: 6.
  TG Israel, Gathering of.
  f D&C 133: 26.
  TG Israel, Tribes of, Ten Lost.
12*a* D&C 77: 9 (9, 14).
  b TG Dispensations.
  c Gal. 3: 8 (6–29); D&C 124: 58.
  TG Abrahamic Covenant.
  d Gen. 18: 18 (17–19).
  e TG Mission of Latter-day Saints.
13*a* TG Vision.

b 1 Kgs. 17: 1; Mal. 4: 5 (5–6); Matt. 17: 3 (1–4); Luke 4: 25; 3 Ne. 25: 5 (5–6); D&C 2: 1; 35: 4; 128: 17; 138: 46.
  TG Translated Beings.
15*a* JS-H 1: 39 (38–39).
  b TG Family, Love within; Genealogy and Temple Work; Salvation for the Dead.
16*a* TG Authority; Priesthood, Keys of; Sealing.
  b TG Dispensations; Restoration of the Gospel.
  c Zeph. 1: 14.
  TG Jesus Christ, Second Coming; Last Days.

SECTION 111

Revelation given through Joseph Smith the Prophet, at Salem, Massachusetts, August 6, 1836. HC 2: 465-466. At this time the leaders of the Church were heavily in debt due to their labors in the ministry. Hearing that a large amount of money would be available to them in Salem, the Prophet, Sidney Rigdon, Hyrum Smith, and Oliver Cowdery traveled there from Kirtland, Ohio, to investigate this claim, along with preaching the gospel. The brethren transacted several items of church business and did some preaching. When it became apparent that no money was to be forthcoming, they returned to Kirtland. Several of the factors prominent in the background are reflected in the wording of this revelation.

1-5, The Lord looks to the temporal needs of his servants; 6-11, He will deal mercifully with Zion and arrange all things for the good of his servants.

I, THE Lord your God, am ᵃnot displeased with your coming this journey, notwithstanding your follies.

2 I have much ᵃtreasure in this city for you, for the benefit of Zion, and many people in this city, whom I will gather out in due time for the benefit of Zion, through your instrumentality.

3 Therefore, it is expedient that you should form ᵃacquaintance with men in this city, as you shall be led, and as it shall be given you.

4 And it shall come to pass in due time that I will ᵃgive this city into your hands, that you shall have power over it, insomuch that they shall not ᵇdiscover your secret parts; and its wealth pertaining to gold and silver shall be yours.

5 Concern not yourselves about your ᵃdebts, for I will give you power to pay them.

6 Concern not yourselves about Zion, for I will deal mercifully with her.

7 Tarry in this place, and in the regions round about;

8 And the place where it is my will that you should tarry, for the main, shall be signalized unto you by the ᵃpeace and power of my ᵇSpirit, that shall flow unto you.

9 This place you may obtain by hire. And inquire diligently concerning the more ancient inhabitants and founders of this city;

10 For there are more treasures than one for you in this city.

11 Therefore, be ye as ᵃwise as serpents and yet without ᵇsin; and I will order all things for your ᶜgood, as fast as ye are able to receive them. Amen.

SECTION 112

Revelation given through Joseph Smith the Prophet to Thomas B. Marsh, at Kirtland, Ohio, July 23, 1837. HC 2: 499-501. The word of the Lord unto Thomas B. Marsh, concerning the Twelve Apostles

111 1a TG God, Mercy of.
2a TG Acts 18: 10 (9-11);
Rom. 1: 13.
TG Treasure.
3a TG Fellowshipping;
Missionary Work.

4a TG Conversion.
b TG Shame.
5a D&C 64: 27 (27-29).
8a Micah 5: 5; D&C 27:
16. TG Peace of God.

b TG God, Spirit of.
11a TG Matt. 10: 16.
b Heb. 4: 15.
c Rom. 8: 28; D&C 100:
15.

of the Lamb. The Prophet records that this revelation was received on the day on which the gospel was first preached in England. Thomas B. Marsh was at this time president of the Quorum of the Twelve Apostles.

1–10, The Twelve are to send the gospel and raise the warning voice to all nations and people; 11–15, They are to take up their cross, follow Jesus, and feed his sheep; 16–20, Those who receive the First Presidency receive the Lord; 21–29, Darkness covers the earth, and only those who believe and are baptized shall be saved; 30–34, The First Presidency and the Twelve hold the keys of the dispensation of the fulness of times.

VERILY thus saith the Lord unto you my servant Thomas: I have heard thy prayers; and thine ᵃalms have come up as a ᵇmemorial before me, in behalf of those, thy brethren, who were chosen to bear testimony of my name and to ᶜsend it abroad among all nations, kindreds, tongues, and people, and ordained through the instrumentality of my servants,

2 Verily I say unto you, there have been some few things in thine heart and with thee with which I, the Lord, was not well pleased.

3 Nevertheless, inasmuch as thou hast ᵃabased thyself thou shalt be exalted; therefore, all thy sins are forgiven thee.

4 Let thy heart be of good ᵃcheer before my face; and thou shalt bear record of my name, not only unto the ᵇGentiles, but also unto the Jews; and thou shalt send forth my word unto the ends of the earth.

5 ᵃContend thou, therefore, morning by morning; and day after day let thy ᵇwarning voice go forth; and when the night cometh let not the inhabitants of the earth slumber, because of thy ᶜspeech.

6 Let thy habitation be known in Zion, and ᵃremove not thy house; for I, the Lord, have a great work for thee to do, in publishing my name among the children of men.

7 Therefore, ᵃgird up thy loins for the work. Let thy feet be shod also, for thou art chosen, and thy path lieth among the mountains, and among many nations.

8 And by thy word many high ones shall be brought low, and by thy word many low ones shall be ᵃexalted.

9 Thy voice shall be a rebuke unto the transgressor; and at thy ᵃrebuke let the tongue of the slanderer cease its perverseness.

10 Be thou ᵃhumble; and the Lord thy God shall ᵇlead thee by the hand, and give thee answer to thy prayers.

11 I know thy heart, and have heard thy prayers concerning thy brethren. Be not partial towards them in love above many others, but let thy ᵃlove be for them as for thyself; and let thy love abound unto all men, and unto all who love my name.

12 And pray for thy brethren of the Twelve. ᵃAdmonish them sharply for my name's sake, and let them be admonished for all their sins, and be ye faithful before me unto my ᵇname.

13 And after their ᵃtemptations,

---

112 1a TG Almsgiving.
   b Acts 10:4.
   c D&C 18:28.
  3a Matt. 23:12; Luke 14:11.
  4a Matt. 9:2; John 16:33.
   b 1 Ne. 13:42; D&C 18:6 (6–26); 19:27; 21:12; 90:9 (8–9); 107:33.
  5a Jude 1:3.

   b Ether 12:3 (2–3).
   c TG Zeal.
  6a Ps. 125:1; Micah 4:2.
  7a Eph. 6:15 (14–17).
  8a Ezek. 17:24; Matt. 23:12; 2 Ne. 20:33.
  9a Luke 17:2; 2 Tim. 4:2.
  10a Prov. 18:12.
   TG Humility; Meekness.

   b Isa. 57:18 (16–18).
   TG Guidance, Divine.
  11a Matt. 5:43 (43–48).
   TG Charity; Love.
  12a Rom. 15:14; 2 Thes. 3:15 (14–15).
   b TG Jesus Christ, Taking the Name of.
  13a TG Temptation; Test, Try, Prove.

and much ^btribulation, behold, I, the Lord, will feel after them, and if they harden not their hearts, and ^cstiffen not their necks against me, they shall be ^dconverted, and I will heal them.

14 Now, I say unto you, and what I say unto you, I say unto all the Twelve: Arise and gird up your loins, take up your ^across, follow me, and ^bfeed my sheep.

15 Exalt not yourselves; ^arebel not against my servant Joseph; for verily I say unto you, I am with him, and my hand shall be over him; and the ^bkeys which I have given unto him, and also to youward, shall not be taken from him till I come.

16 Verily I say unto you, my servant Thomas, thou art the man whom I have chosen to hold the ^akeys of my kingdom, as pertaining to the Twelve, abroad among all nations—

17 That thou mayest be my servant to unlock the door of the kingdom in all places where my servant Joseph, and my servant Sidney, and my servant Hyrum, ^acannot come:

18 For on them have I laid the burden of all the churches for a little season.

19 Wherefore, whithersoever they shall send you, go ye, and I will be with you; and in whatsoever place ye shall proclaim my name an ^aeffectual door shall be opened unto you, that they may receive my word.

20 Whosoever ^areceiveth my word receiveth me, and whosoever receiveth me, receiveth those, the First Presidency, whom I have sent, whom I have made counselors for my name's sake unto you.

21 And again, I say unto you, that whosoever ye shall send in my name, by the voice of your brethren, the ^aTwelve, duly recommended and ^bauthorized by you, shall have power to open the door of my kingdom unto any nation whithersoever ye shall send them—

22 Inasmuch as they shall humble themselves before me, and abide in my word, and ^ahearken to the voice of my Spirit.

23 Verily, verily, I say unto you, ^adarkness covereth the earth, and gross darkness the minds of the people, and all flesh has become ^bcorrupt before my face.

24 Behold, ^avengeance cometh speedily upon the inhabitants of the earth, a day of wrath, a day of burning, a day of ^bdesolation, of ^cweeping, of mourning, and of lamentation; and as a whirlwind it shall come upon all the face of the earth, saith the Lord;

25 And upon my ^ahouse shall it ^bbegin, and from my house shall it go forth, saith the Lord;

26 First among those among you, saith the Lord, who have ^aprofessed to know my ^bname and have not ^cknown me, and have ^dblasphemed

13b John 16: 33;
   Rev. 7: 14 (13–14);
   D&C 103: 12.
   TG Tribulation.
c TG Stiffneckedness.
d John 12: 40; 2 Ne. 26:
   9; 3 Ne. 9: 13 (13–14);
   18: 32. TG Conversion;
   Man, New, Spiritually
   Reborn.
14a Matt. 16: 24; Luke 9:
   23.
b John 21: 16 (15–17).
15a TG Rebellion.
b D&C 28: 7.
16a TG Priesthood, Keys
   of.
17a Luke 10: 1.
19a 1 Cor. 16: 9.

20a D&C 84: 35.
   TG Teachable.
21a D&C 107: 34 (34–35).
b TG Authority; Delega-
   tion of Responsibility.
22a TG God, Spirit of;
   Obedience.
23a Isa. 60: 2; Micah 3: 6;
   D&C 38: 11 (11–12);
   Moses 7: 61 (61–62).
   TG Apostasy of the
   Early Christian
   Church; Darkness,
   Spiritual.
b Gen. 6: 11 (5–6, 11–13);
   Ps. 14: 1; D&C 10: 21
   (20–23).
24a TG Day of the Lord;
   Retribution;

   Vengeance.
b Mal. 4: 5.
c Matt. 8: 12; D&C 101:
   91; 124: 8.
   TG Mourning.
25a TG Chastening.
b 1 Pet. 4: 17 (17–18).
26a D&C 41: 1; 50: 4; 56:
   1. TG Hypocrisy.
b TG Jesus Christ,
   Taking the Name of.
c Hosea 8: 2 (1–4);
   Luke 6: 46; Mosiah 26:
   25 (24–27); 3 Ne. 14:
   23 (21–23).
d D&C 105: 15.
   TG Apostasy of
   Individuals;
   Blasphemy.

against me in the midst of my house, saith the Lord.

27 Therefore, see to it that ye trouble not yourselves concerning the affairs of my church *a*in this place, saith the Lord.

28 But *a*purify your hearts before me; and then *b*go ye into all the world, and preach my gospel unto every creature who has not received it;

29 And he that *a*believeth and is *b*baptized shall be saved, and he that believeth not, and is not baptized, shall be *c*damned.

30 For unto you, the *a*Twelve, and those, the First Presidency, who are appointed with you to be your *b*counselors and your leaders, is the *c*power of this priesthood given, for the last days and for the last time,

in the which is the dispensation of the *d*fulness of times.

31 Which power you hold, in connection with all those who have received a *a*dispensation at any time from the beginning of the creation;

32 For verily I say unto you, the *a*keys of the dispensation, which ye have received, have *b*come down from the fathers, and last of all, being sent down from heaven unto you.

33 Verily I say unto you, behold how great is your calling. *a*Cleanse your hearts and your garments, lest the blood of this generation be *b*required at your hands.

34 Be faithful until I come, for I *a*come quickly; and my reward is with me to recompense every man according as his *b*work shall be. I am Alpha and Omega. Amen.

SECTION 113

Answers to certain questions on the writings of Isaiah, given by Joseph Smith the Prophet, March 1838. HC 3: 9–10.

1–6, The Stem of Jesse, the rod coming therefrom, and the root of Jesse are identified; 7–10, The scattered remnants of Zion have a right to the priesthood and are called to return to the Lord.

Who is the *a*Stem of Jesse spoken of in the 1st, 2d, 3d, 4th, and 5th verses of the 11th chapter of Isaiah?

2 Verily thus saith the Lord: It is Christ.

3 What is the *a*rod spoken of in the

first verse of the 11th chapter of Isaiah, that should come of the Stem of Jesse?

4 Behold, thus saith the Lord: It is a servant in the hands of Christ, who is partly a descendant of Jesse as well as of *a*Ephraim, or of the house of Joseph, on whom there is laid much *b*power.

5 What is the *a*root of Jesse spoken of in the 10th verse of the 11th chapter?

6 Behold, thus saith the Lord, it is a *a*descendant of Jesse, as well as of

---

27a D&C 107: 33 (33–39).
28a TG Purification;
   Purity.
   b Mark 16: 15 (15–16);
   D&C 18: 28.
29a Morm. 9: 23 (22–24);
   D&C 20: 25.
   b TG Baptism, Essential.
   c TG Damnation.
30a TG Apostles; Church
   Organization.
   b TG Counselor;
   Leadership.
   c TG Priesthood, Power
   of.

d Eph. 1: 10 (9–10);
   D&C 27: 13; 76: 106;
   124: 41.
   TG Restoration of the
   Gospel.
31a TG Dispensations.
32a TG Priesthood, Keys
   of.
   a Abr. 1: 3.
   TG Priesthood, History
   of.
33a Jacob 1: 19; 2: 2;
   D&C 88: 85.
   b Ezek. 34: 10; D&C
   72: 3.

34a Rev. 3: 11; 22: 7 (7,
   12); D&C 1: 12.
   b TG Good Works;
   Reward.
113 1a Isa. 11: 1 (1–5).
   TG Jesus Christ,
   Davidic Descent of.
3a Ps. 110: 2 (1–4).
4a Gen. 41: 52 (50–52);
   D&C 133: 34 (30–34).
   TG Israel, Joseph,
   People of.
5a 2 Ne. 21: 10 (10–12).
6a Isa. 11: 10.

Joseph, unto whom rightly belongs the [b]priesthood, and the [c]keys of the kingdom, for an [d]ensign, and for the gathering of my people in the [e]last days.

7 Questions by Elias Higbee: What is meant by the command in Isaiah, 52d chapter, 1st verse, which saith: Put on thy strength, O Zion—and what people had Isaiah reference to?

8 He had reference to those whom God should call in the last days, who should hold the [a]power of [b]priesthood to bring again [c]Zion, and the redemption of Israel; and to put on her [d]strength is to put on the [e]authority of the [f]priesthood, which

she, Zion, has a [g]right to by lineage; also to return to that power which she had lost.

9 What are we to understand by Zion loosing herself from the bands of her neck; 2d verse?

10 We are to understand that the [a]scattered [b]remnants are exhorted to [c]return to the Lord from whence they have fallen; which if they do, the promise of the Lord is that he will speak to them, or give them revelation. See the 6th, 7th, and 8th verses. The [d]bands of her neck are the curses of God upon her, or the remnants of Israel in their scattered condition among the Gentiles.

SECTION 114

Revelation given through Joseph Smith the Prophet, at Far West, Missouri, April 17, 1838. HC 3: 23.

1–2, Church positions held by those who are not faithful shall be given to others.

VERILY thus saith the Lord: It is wisdom in my servant David W. Patten, that he settle up all his business as soon as he possibly can, and make a disposition of his merchandise, that he may [a]perform a mission unto me next spring, in

company with others, even twelve including himself, to testify of my name and bear glad tidings unto all the world.

2 For verily thus saith the Lord, that inasmuch as there are those among you who [a]deny my name, others shall be [b]planted in their [c]stead and receive their [d]bishopric. Amen.

SECTION 115

Revelation given through Joseph Smith the Prophet, at Far West, Missouri, April 26, 1838, making known the will of God concerning the building up of that place and of the Lord's House. HC 3: 23–25. This revelation is addressed to the presiding officers of the Church.

6b TG Priesthood, Melchizedek.
  c D&C 110: 11.
    TG Priesthood, Keys of.
  d Isa. 30: 17; D&C 45: 9. TG Ensign.
  e TG Israel, Gathering of; Last Days.
8a TG Priesthood, Power of.
  b D&C 86: 8.
    TG Priesthood, Keys of.
  c TG Zion.

  d Isa. 45: 24; 52: 1;
    1 Ne. 17: 3; D&C 82: 14. TG Israel, Restoration of; Strength.
  e TG Authority; Mission of Latter-day Saints; Priesthood, Authority.
  f TG Priesthood, History of.
  g TG Birthright.
10a TG Israel, Scattering of.
  b Micah 5: 3. TG Israel,

Remnant of.
  c Hosea 3: 5; 2 Ne. 6: 11.
  d Isa. 52: 2 (2, 6–8).
    TG Bondage, Spiritual.
114 1a D&C 118: 5.
2a TG Apostasy of Individuals.
  b 1 Sam. 2: 35; D&C 118: 1 (1, 6).
  c D&C 35: 18; 42: 10; 64: 40.
  d Acts 1: 20 (20–26).

1–4, The Lord names his church, The Church of Jesus Christ of Latter-day Saints; 5–6, Zion and her stakes are places of defense and refuge for the saints; 7–16, The saints are commanded to build a House of the Lord at Far West; 17–19, Joseph Smith holds the keys of the kingdom of God on earth.

VERILY thus saith the Lord unto you, my servant Joseph Smith, Jun., and also my servant Sidney Rigdon, and also my servant Hyrum Smith, and your *^acounselors who are and shall be appointed hereafter;

2 And also unto you, my servant *^aEdward Partridge, and his counselors;

3 And also unto my faithful servants who are of the high council of my *^achurch in Zion, for thus it shall be called, and unto all the elders and people of my Church of Jesus Christ of Latter-day Saints, scattered abroad in all the world;

4 For thus shall *^amy *^bchurch be called in the last days, even The Church of Jesus Christ of Latter-day *^cSaints.

5 Verily I say unto you all: *^aArise and shine forth, that thy *^blight may be a *^cstandard for the *^dnations;

6 And that the *^agathering together upon the land of *^bZion, and upon her *^cstakes, may be for a defense, and for a *^drefuge from the storm, and from wrath when it shall be *^epoured out without mixture upon the whole earth.

7 Let the city, Far West, be a holy and consecrated land unto me; and

it shall be called most holy, for the ground upon which thou standest is *^aholy.

8 Therefore, I command you to *^abuild a house unto me, for the gathering together of my saints, that they may *^bworship me.

9 And let there be a beginning of this work, and a foundation, and a preparatory work, this following summer;

10 And let the beginning be made on the fourth day of July next; and from that time forth let my people *^alabor diligently to build a house unto my name;

11 And in *^aone year from this day let them re-commence laying the foundation of my *^bhouse.

12 Thus let them from that time forth labor diligently until it shall be finished, from the corner stone thereof unto the top thereof, until there shall not anything remain that is not finished.

13 Verily I say unto you, let not my servant Joseph, neither my servant Sidney, neither my servant Hyrum, get in *^adebt any more for the building of a house unto my name;

14 But let a house be built unto my name according to the *^apattern which I will show unto them.

15 And if my people build it not according to the pattern which I shall show unto their presidency, I will not accept it at their hands.

16 But if my people do build it according to the pattern which I shall show unto their presidency, even my servant Joseph and his

---

115 1a D&C 81: 1; 112: 20; 124: 91.
2a D&C 64: 17; 124: 19.
3a Jesus Christ, Head of the Church.
4a 3 Ne. 27: 8.
  b 1 Cor. 1: 10 (10–13); D&C 20: 1 (1–4); 136: 2 (2–8). TG Kingdom of God, on Earth.
  c TG Saints.
5a Isa. 60: 1 (1–3). TG Mission of Latter-day Saints.

  b TG Light; Peculiar People.
  c Gen. 18: 18 (17–19); Isa. 11: 12. TG Ensign; Example.
  d TG Nations.
6a TG Last Days.
  b TG Zion.
  c D&C 101: 21; 115: 18 (17–18). TG Stake.
  d Isa. 25: 4 (3–5); D&C 45: 66 (62–71). TG Refuge.

  e Rev. 14: 10; D&C 1: 13 (13–14).
7a Ex. 3: 5; Josh. 5: 15; D&C 101: 64.
8a D&C 88: 119; 95: 8.
  b TG Worship.
10a Neh. 4: 6; D&C 52: 39; 75: 3. TG Industry.
11a D&C 118: 5.
  b D&C 124: 45 (45–54).
13a D&C 64: 86 (78–86).
14a Num. 8: 4; Heb. 8: 5; D&C 97: 10.

counselors, then I will accept it at the hands of my people.

17 And again, verily I say unto you, it is my will that the city of Far West should be built up speedily by the gathering of my saints;

18 And also that other places should be appointed for [a]stakes in the regions round about, as they shall be manifested unto my servant Joseph, from time to time.

19 For behold, I will be with him, and I will sanctify him before the people; for unto him have I given the [a]keys of this kingdom and ministry. Even so. Amen.

SECTION 116

Revelation given to Joseph Smith the Prophet, near Wight's Ferry, at a place called Spring Hill, Daviess County, Missouri, May 19, 1838. HC 3: 35.

SPRING Hill is named by the Lord [a]Adam-ondi-Ahman, because, said he, it is the place where [b]Adam shall come to visit his people, or the Ancient of Days shall sit, as spoken of by Daniel the prophet.

SECTION 117

Revelation given through Joseph Smith the Prophet, at Far West, Missouri, July 8, 1838, concerning the immediate duties of William Marks, Newel K. Whitney, and Oliver Granger. HC 3: 45–46.

1–9, The Lord's servants should not covet temporal things, for "what is property unto the Lord?"; 10–16, They are to forsake littleness of soul, and their sacrifices shall be sacred unto the Lord.

VERILY thus saith the Lord unto my servant [a]William Marks, and also unto my servant Newel K. Whitney, let them settle up their business speedily and journey from the land of Kirtland, before I, the Lord, [b]send again the snows upon the earth.

2 Let them awake, and arise, and [a]come forth, and not tarry, for I, the Lord, command it.

3 Therefore, if they [a]tarry it shall not be well with them.

4 Let them repent of all their sins, and of all their covetous desires, before me, saith the Lord; for what is [a]property unto me? saith the Lord.

5 Let the properties of Kirtland be turned out for [a]debts, saith the Lord. Let them go, saith the Lord, and whatsoever remaineth, let it remain in your hands, saith the Lord.

6 For have I not the fowls of heaven, and also the fish of the sea, and the beasts of the mountains? Have I not [a]made the earth? Do I not hold the [b]destinies of all the armies of the nations of the earth?

18a D&C 101: 21; 115: 6.
  TG Stake.
19a TG Priesthood, Keys of.
116 1a Dan. 7: 13 (13–14, 22); D&C 78: 15 (15, 20); 95: 17; 107: 53; 117: 8 (8, 11). Note that a song titled "Adam-ondi-Ahman," written by W. W.

Phelps, was sung at the Kirtland Temple dedication (HC 2: 417).
  b TG Adam.
117 1a D&C 124: 79 (79–80).
  b Job 37: 6 (5–6); Ps. 148: 8; Hel. 11: 17 (13–17); Ether 2: 24.
2a IE from Kirtland.

3a TG Disobedience; Procrastination.
4a Mark 14: 4 (3–4); D&C 104: 14.
5a D&C 90: 23 (22–23).
6a TG Creation; God, Works of; Jesus Christ, Creator.
  b Isa. 45: 1 (1–3); 1 Ne. 17: 37.

7 Therefore, will I not make [a]solitary places to bud and to [b]blossom, and to bring forth in abundance? saith the Lord.

8 Is there not room enough on the mountains of [a]Adam-ondi-Ahman, and on the plains of Olaha [b]Shinehah, or the land where [c]Adam dwelt, that you should covet that which is but the drop, and neglect the more weighty matters?

9 Therefore, come up hither unto the land of my people, even Zion.

10 Let my servant William Marks be [a]faithful over a few things, and he shall be a ruler over many. Let him preside in the midst of my people in the city of Far West, and let him be blessed with the blessings of my people.

11 Let my servant Newel K. Whitney be ashamed of the [a]Nicolaitane band and of all their [b]secret abominations, and of all his littleness of soul before me, saith the Lord, and come up to the land of Adam-ondi-Ahman, and be a [c]bishop unto my people, saith the Lord, not in name but in deed, saith the Lord.

12 And again, I say unto you,

I remember my servant [a]Oliver Granger; behold, verily I say unto him that his name shall be had in sacred remembrance from generation to generation, forever and ever, saith the Lord.

13 Therefore, let him contend earnestly for the redemption of the First Presidency of my Church, saith the Lord; and when he falls he shall rise again, for his [a]sacrifice shall be more sacred unto me than his increase, saith the Lord.

14 Therefore, let him come up hither speedily, unto the land of Zion; and in the due time he shall be made a merchant unto my name, saith the Lord, for the benefit of my people.

15 Therefore let no man despise my servant Oliver Granger, but let the blessings of my people be on him forever and ever.

16 And again, verily I say unto you, let all my servants in the land of Kirtland remember the Lord their God, and mine house also, to keep and preserve it holy, and to overthrow the moneychangers in mine own due time, saith the Lord. Even so. Amen.

SECTION 118

Revelation given through Joseph Smith the Prophet, at Far West, Missouri, July 8, 1838, in response to the supplication: "Show us thy will, O Lord, concerning the Twelve." HC 3: 46–47.

1–3, *The Lord will provide for the families of the Twelve; 4–6, Vacancies in the Twelve are filled.*

VERILY, thus saith the Lord: Let a conference be held immediately; let the Twelve be organized; and let men be appointed to [a]supply the place of those who are fallen.

2 Let my servant [a]Thomas remain for a season in the land of Zion, to publish my word.

3 Let the residue continue to preach from that hour, and if they will do this in all [a]lowliness of heart, in meekness and humility, and [b]long-suffering, I, the Lord, give unto them a [c]promise that I will

7a Isa. 35: 1 (1–2).
  b D&C 35: 24; 39: 13;
    49: 25. TG Earth,
    Renewal of.
8a D&C 116: 1.
  b Abr. 3: 13.
  c TG Adam; Eden.
10a Matt. 25: 23.

11a Rev. 2: 6 (6, 15).
  b TG Secret Combinations.
  c D&C 72: 8 (6–8).
12a IE the agent left by the
    prophet to settle his
    affairs in Kirtland
    (HC 3: 164–165, 345).

13a TG Self-sacrifice.
118 1a Acts 1: 25 (23–26);
    D&C 114: 2.
2a IE Thomas B. Marsh.
3a Eph. 4: 2.
  b TG Perseverance.
  c TG Promises.

provide for their families; and an effectual door shall be opened for them, from henceforth.

4 And next spring let them depart to go over the great waters, and there promulgate my gospel, the fulness thereof, and bear record of my name.

5 Let them *take leave of my saints in the city of Far West, on the *b*twenty-sixth day of April next, on the building-spot of my house, saith the Lord.

6 Let my servant John Taylor, and also my servant John E. Page, and also my servant Wilford Woodruff, and also my servant Willard Richards, be appointed to fill the places of those who have *a*fallen, and be officially notified of their appointment.

SECTION 119

Revelation given through Joseph Smith the Prophet, at Far West, Missouri, July 8, 1838, in answer to his supplication: "O Lord, show unto thy servants how much thou requirest of the properties of thy people for a tithing." HC 3: 44. The law of tithing, as understood today, had not been given to the Church previous to this revelation. The term "tithing" in the prayer just quoted and in previous revelations (64: 23; 85: 3; 97:11) had meant not just one-tenth, but all free-will offerings, or contributions, to the Church funds. The Lord had previously given to the Church the law of consecration and stewardship of property, which members (chiefly the leading elders) entered into by a covenant that was to be ever-lasting. Because of failure on the part of many to abide by this covenant, the Lord withdrew it for a time, and gave instead the law of tithing to the whole Church. The Prophet asked the Lord how much of their property he required for sacred purposes. The answer was this revelation.

1–5, The saints are to pay their surplus property and then give, as tithing, one-tenth of their interest annually; 6–7, Such a course will sanctify the land of Zion.

VERILY, thus saith the Lord, I require all their *a*surplus property to be put into the hands of the bishop of my church in Zion,

2 For the building of mine *a*house, and for the laying of the foundation of Zion and for the priesthood, and for the debts of the Presidency of my Church.

3 And this shall be the beginning of the *a*tithing of my people.

4 And after that, those who have thus been *a*tithed shall pay one-tenth of all their interest annually; and this shall be a standing law unto them forever, for my holy priesthood, saith the Lord.

5 Verily I say unto you, it shall come to pass that all those who gather unto the land of *a*Zion shall be tithed of their surplus properties, and shall observe this law, or they shall not be found worthy to abide among you.

5a D&C 114: 1.
  b D&C 115: 11.
6a D&C 114: 2.
119 1a D&C 42: 33 (33–

34), 55; 51: 13; 82: 18
  (17–19).
2a 2 Chr. 3: 3 (3–4);
  D&C 115: 8 (8–13).

3a D&C 42: 30; 64: 23;
  120: 1.
4a TG Tithing.
5a D&C 52: 42 (42–43).

6 And I say unto you, if my people observe not this law, to keep it holy, and by this law sanctify the land of Zion unto me, that my statutes and my judgments may be kept therein, that it may be most holy, behold,

verily I say unto you, it shall not be a land of *a*Zion unto you.

7 And this shall be an ensample unto all the *a*stakes of Zion. Even so. Amen.

SECTION 120

Revelation given through Joseph Smith the Prophet, at Far West, Missouri, July 8, 1838, making known the disposition of the properties tithed as named in the preceding revelation, Section 119. HC 3: 44.

VERILY, thus saith the Lord, the time is now come, that *a*it shall be *b*disposed of by a council, composed of the First Presidency of my

Church, and of the bishop and his council, and by my high council; and by mine own voice unto them, saith the Lord. Even so. Amen.

SECTION 121

Prayer and prophecies written by Joseph Smith the Prophet, while he was a prisoner in the jail at Liberty, Missouri, dated March 20, 1839. HC 3: 289–300. The Prophet with several companions had been months in prison. Their petitions and appeals directed to the executive officers and the judiciary had failed to bring them relief.

1–6, The Prophet pleads with the Lord for the suffering saints; 7–10, The Lord speaks peace to him; 11–17, Cursed are all those who raise false cries of transgression against the Lord's people; 18–25, They shall not have right to the priesthood and shall be damned; 26–32, Glorious revelations promised those who endure valiantly; 33–40, Many are called and few chosen; 41–46, The priesthood should be used only in righteousness.

O GOD, *a*where art thou? And where is the pavilion that covereth thy *b*hiding place?

2 *a*How long shall thy hand be stayed, and thine eye, yea thy pure

eye, behold from the eternal heavens the wrongs of thy people and of thy servants, and thine ear be penetrated with their cries?

3 Yea, O Lord, *a*how long shall they suffer these wrongs and unlawful *b*oppressions, before thine heart shall be softened toward them, and thy bowels be moved with *c*compassion toward them?

4 O Lord God *a*Almighty, maker of *b*heaven, earth, and seas, and of all things that in them are, and who controllest and subjectest the devil, and the dark and benighted dominion of Sheol— stretch forth thy hand; let thine eye pierce; let thy *c*pavilion be taken up; let thy *d*hiding place no longer be covered; let thine ear be

6a TG Zion.
7a D&C 82: 13.
120 1a D&C 119: 1 (1–4).
   b TG Accountability;
    Church Organization.
121 1a Matt. 27: 46.
   b Ps. 13: 1 (1–2); 18: 11;

102: 1; Isa. 45: 15.
2a Ex. 5: 22; Ps. 35: 17
  (17–28); 89: 46;
  Hab. 1: 2 (2–4).
3a Ps. 69: 14 (1–2, 14);
  Alma 14: 26 (26–29).

b TG Cruelty; Oppression; Persecution.
c TG Compassion.
4a TG God, Power of.
  b Gen. 1: 1.
  c 2 Sam. 22: 7.
  d D&C 101: 89; 123: 6.

inclined; let thine ^{e}heart be softened, and thy bowels moved with compassion toward us.

5 Let thine ^{a}anger be kindled against our enemies; and, in the fury of thine heart, with thy ^{b}sword ^{c}avenge us of our wrongs.

6 Remember thy ^{a}suffering saints, O our God; and thy servants will rejoice in thy name forever.

7 My son, ^{a}peace be unto thy soul; thine ^{b}adversity and thine afflictions shall be but a ^{c}small moment;

8 And then, if thou ^{a}endure it well, God shall exalt thee on high; thou shalt triumph over all thy ^{b}foes.

9 Thy ^{a}friends do stand by thee, and they shall hail thee again with warm hearts and friendly hands.

10 Thou art not yet as Job; thy ^{a}friends do not contend against thee, neither charge thee with transgression, as they did Job.

11 And they who do charge thee with transgression, their hope shall be blasted, and their prospects shall ^{a}melt away as the hoar frost melteth before the burning rays of the rising sun;

12 And also that God hath set his hand and seal to change the ^{a}times and seasons, and to blind their ^{b}minds, that they may not understand his ^{c}marvelous workings; that he may ^{d}prove them also and take them in their own craftiness;

13 Also because their hearts are

corrupted, and the things which they are willing to bring upon others, and love to have others suffer, may come upon ^{a}themselves to the very uttermost;

14 That they may be ^{a}disappointed also, and their hopes may be cut off;

15 And not many years hence, that they and their ^{a}posterity shall be ^{b}swept from under heaven, saith God, that not one of them is left to stand by the wall.

16 ^{a}Cursed are all those that shall lift up the ^{b}heel against mine ^{c}anointed, saith the Lord, and cry they have ^{d}sinned when they have not sinned before me, saith the Lord, but have done that which was meet in mine eyes, and which I commanded them.

17 But ^{a}those who cry transgression do it because they are the servants of sin, and are the ^{b}children of disobedience themselves.

18 And those who ^{a}swear ^{b}falsely against my servants, that they might bring them into bondage and death—

19 Wo unto them; because they have ^{a}offended my little ones they shall be severed from the ^{b}ordinances of mine house.

20 Their ^{a}basket shall not be full, their houses and their barns shall perish, and they themselves shall be ^{b}despised by those that flattered them.

4e	TG Compassion; God, Mercy of.	10a	Job 4:1 (1–8); 13:4; 16:2.
5a	Ps. 119:84.	11a	Ps. 58:7 (3–11);
b	D&C 1:13 (13–14).		Jer. 1:19 (7–19).
c	Ps. 35:1 (1–10);	12a	Dan. 2:21 (19–22, 28); Acts 1:7;
	Luke 18:7.		D&C 68:11 (7–12).
6a	D&C 122:5 (5–7).		TG Time.
	TG Suffering.	b	2 Kgs. 6:18 (18–23).
7a	Acts 23:11 (11–14).		TG Mind.
	TG Comfort.	c	Ex. 8:19; 1 Ne. 19: 22; Alma 23:6;
b	TG Adversity; Affliction.		D&C 84:3.
c	Isa. 54:7.	d	TG Test, Try, Prove.
8a	1 Pet. 2:20 (19–23).	13a	Prov. 28:10; 1 Ne. 14: 3.
	TG Perseverance; Probation.	14a	3 Ne. 4:10.
b	TG Enemies.	15a	Ps. 37:28; 109:13.
9a	D&C 122:3.	b	D&C 124:52.
	TG Friendship.	16a	TG Curse.

b	Ps. 41:9; John 13:18. TG Prophets, Rejection of; Reviling.
c	1 Sam. 26:9; Ps. 2:2 (2–4); 105:15.
d	2 Ne. 15:20; Moro. 7: 14 (14, 18); D&C 64: 16.
17a	Rev. 12:10; Alma 15: 15.
b	Eph. 5:6 (2–6).
18a	TG Swearing.
b	Mal. 3:5. TG Lying; Slander.
19a	Matt. 18:6. TG Offenses.
b	TG Ordinance; Salvation.
20a	Deut. 28:17 (15–26).
b	Prov. 24:24 (23–26).

21 They shall not have right to the "priesthood, nor their posterity after them from generation to generation.

22 It had been "better for them that a millstone had been hanged about their necks, and they drowned in the depth of the sea.

23 Wo unto all those that "discomfort my people, and drive, and "murder, and testify against them, saith the Lord of Hosts; a "generation of vipers shall not escape the damnation of hell.

24 Behold, mine eyes "see and know all their works, and I have in reserve a swift "judgment in the season thereof, for them all;

25 For there is a "time "appointed for every man, according to his "works shall he.

26 God shall give unto you "knowledge by his Holy "Spirit, yea, by the unspeakable "gift of the Holy Ghost, that has not been revealed since the world was until now;

27 Which our forefathers have awaited with "anxious expectation to be revealed in the last times, which their minds were pointed to by the angels, as held in reserve for the fulness of their glory;

28 A time to come in the which "nothing shall be withheld, whether there be "one God or many "gods, they shall be manifest.

29 All thrones and dominions, principalities and powers, shall be "revealed and set forth upon all who have endured "valiantly for the gospel of Jesus Christ.

30 And also, if there be "bounds set to the heavens or to the seas, or to the dry land, or to the sun, moon, or stars—

31 All the times of their revolutions, all the appointed days, months, and years, and all the days of their days, months, and years, and all their "glories, laws, and set times, shall be revealed in the days of the "dispensation of the fulness of times—

32 According to that which was "ordained in the midst of the "Council of the Eternal "God of all other gods before this "world was, that should be reserved unto the finishing and the end thereof, when every man shall enter into his eternal "presence and into his immortal "rest.

33 How long can rolling waters remain impure? What "power shall stay the heavens? As well might man stretch forth his puny arm to stop the Missouri river in its decreed course, or to turn it up stream, as to "hinder the "Almighty from pouring down "knowledge from heaven

---

21a Alma 13: 4 (3–5).
 TG Priesthood,
 Qualifying for.
22a Matt. 18: 6; D&C 54:
 5.
 b Esth. 3: 13.
 c Matt. 12: 34; 23: 33.
24a Job 10: 4; Ps. 139: 1;
 Jonah 3: 10. TG God,
 Omniscience of.
 b Ps. 109: 7 (3–7);
 Hel. 8: 25; D&C 10:
 23 (20–23).
25a D&C 122: 9.
 b Job 7: 1;
 Alma 12: 27 (26–28);
 D&C 42: 48.
 c TG Good Works.
26a Dan. 2: 28 (22–29, 49);
 Amos 3: 7; A of F 9.
 TG Mysteries of Godliness; Revelation.

 b TG God, Spirit of.
 c TG Holy Ghost, Gift
 of.
 d Alma 12: 10 (9–11);
 40: 3. TG Scriptures to
 Come Forth.
27a Rom. 16: 25; D&C 6: 7
 (7–11); 42: 65 (61–65).
28a D&C 42: 61; 59: 4; 76:
 7; 98: 12; 101: 32.
 b Rom. 3: 30 (28–31);
 1 Tim. 2: 5.
 c Ps. 82: 6; John 10: 34;
 1 Cor. 8: 6 (5–6);
 D&C 76: 58; Abr. 4: 1
 (1–31); 5: 1 (1–21).
29a D&C 101: 32.
 b D&C 76: 79.
 TG Diligence; Trustworthiness.
30a Job 26: 10 (7–14); 38:
 33 (1–41); Ps. 104: 9

 (1–35); Acts 17: 26
 (24–28).
31a Abr. 3: 4 (2–10).
 TG Glory; God, Law of.
 b TG Dispensations.
32a TG Earth, Purpose of.
 b TG Council in Heaven.
 c Deut. 10: 17 (17–21);
 Dan. 11: 36.
 d TG Earth, Destiny of;
 World.
 e TG Man, Potential to
 Become Like Heavenly
 Father.
 f Ps. 95: 11; Heb. 3: 11;
 4: 1; Alma 12: 34;
 3 Ne. 27: 19;
 D&C 84: 24.
33a Rom. 8: 39 (35–39).
 b Dan. 4: 35.
 c TG God, Power of.
 d Dan. 12: 4.
 TG Knowledge.

upon the heads of the Latter-day Saints.

34 Behold, there are many [a]called, but few are chosen. And why are they not chosen?

35 Because their [a]hearts are set so much upon the things of this [b]world, and [c]aspire to the [d]honors of men, that they do not learn this one lesson—

36 That the [a]rights of the priesthood are inseparably connected with the powers of heaven, and that the powers of heaven cannot be [b]controlled nor handled only upon the [c]principles of righteousness.

37 That they may be conferred upon us, it is true; but when we undertake to [a]cover our [b]sins, or to gratify our [c]pride, our vain ambition, or to exercise control or [d]dominion or compulsion upon the souls of the children of men, in any degree of unrighteousness, behold, the heavens [e]withdraw themselves; the Spirit of the Lord is grieved; and when it is withdrawn, Amen to the priesthood or the authority of that man.

38 Behold, ere he is aware, he is left unto himself, to [a]kick against the pricks, to [b]persecute the saints, and to [c]fight against God.

39 We have learned by sad experience that it is the [a]nature and disposition of almost all men, as soon as they get a little [b]authority, as they suppose, that they will immediately begin to exercise [c]unrighteous dominion.

40 Hence many are called, but [a]few are chosen.

41 No [a]power or influence can or ought to be maintained by virtue of the [b]priesthood, only by [c]persuasion, by [d]long-suffering, by gentleness and meekness, and by love unfeigned;

42 By [a]kindness, and pure [b]knowledge, which shall greatly enlarge the [c]soul without [d]hypocrisy, and without [e]guile—

43 [a]Reproving betimes with [b]sharpness, when [c]moved upon by the Holy Ghost; and then showing forth afterwards an increase of [d]love toward him whom thou hast reproved, lest he esteem thee to be his enemy;

44 That he may know that thy faithfulness is stronger than the cords of [a]death.

45 Let thy [b]bowels also be full of charity towards all men, and to the

---

34a Matt. 20: 16; 22: 14 (1–14); Luke 13: 23; D&C 63: 31; 95: 5 (5–6). TG Called of God.
35a Luke 14: 18 (18–20).
  b TG Selfishness; Worldliness.
  c TG Motivations.
  d Matt. 6: 2; 2 Ne. 26: 29; D&C 58: 39. TG Honor.
36a D&C 107: 10. TG Priesthood, Authority; Priesthood, Keys of; Priesthood, Oath and Covenant; Priesthood, Power of.
  b TG Priesthood, Magnifying Callings within.
  c D&C 107: 30. TG Righteousness.
37a Prov. 28: 13. TG Apostasy of Individuals; Honesty; Hypocrisy.
  b TG Sin.

c TG Haughtiness; Pride.
  d Gen. 1: 26 (26–28); D&C 76: 111 (110–112).
  e 1 Sam. 18: 12; D&C 1: 33; 3: 11; JS–H 1: 46.
  f TG Holy Ghost, Loss of.
38a Acts 9: 5; 26: 14.
  b TG Persecution.
  c Micah 3: 5; 1 Ne. 11: 35 (34–36).
39a TG Man, Natural, Not Spiritually Reborn.
  b TG Authority.
  c 1 Kgs. 16: 2. TG Leadership; Unrighteous Dominion.
40a Matt. 20: 16; D&C 95: 5.
41a TG Priesthood, Power of.
  b 1 Pet. 5: 3 (1–3). TG Priesthood; Priesthood, Magnifying Callings within.

c Prov. 25: 15. TG Communication; Marriage, Husbands.
  d 2 Cor. 6: 6. TG Forbearance; Love; Meekness; Patience.
42a TG Courtesy; Kindness.
  b 1 Pet. 3: 7. TG Knowledge.
  c TG Understanding.
  d James 3: 17.
  e TG Guile; Sincerity.
43a TG Chastening; Reproof.
  b D&C 15: 2.
  c TG Holy Ghost, Mission of.
  d TG Charity.
44a TG Dependability.
45a 1 Thes. 3: 12; 1 Jn. 3: 17 (16–17). TG Benevolence; Charity; Priesthood, Magnifying Callings within.

household of faith, and let *b*virtue garnish thy thoughts unceasingly; then shall thy *c*confidence wax strong in the *d*presence of God; and the doctrine of the priesthood shall distil upon thy soul as the *e*dews from heaven.

46 The Holy Ghost shall be thy constant *a*companion, and thy scepter an unchanging scepter of *b*righteousness and truth; and thy *c*dominion shall be an everlasting dominion, and without compulsory means it shall flow unto thee forever and ever.

SECTION 122

The word of the Lord to Joseph Smith the Prophet, while he was a prisoner in the jail at Liberty, Missouri, March 1839. HC 3: 300–301.

1–4, The ends of the earth shall inquire after the name of Joseph Smith; 5–7, All his perils and travails shall give him experience and be for his good; 8–9, The Son of Man hath descended below them all.

THE ends of the earth shall inquire after thy *a*name, and fools shall have thee in *b*derision, and hell shall rage against thee;

2 While the pure in heart, and the wise, and the noble, and the virtuous, shall seek *a*counsel, and authority, and blessings constantly from under thy hand.

3 And thy *a*people shall never be turned against thee by the testimony of traitors.

4 And although their influence shall cast thee into trouble, and into bars and walls, thou shalt be had in *a*honor; and but for a small *b*moment and thy voice shall be more terrible in the midst of thine enemies than the fierce *c*lion, because of thy righteousness; and thy God shall stand by thee forever and ever.

5 If thou art called to pass through *a*tribulation; if thou art in perils among false brethren; if thou art in *b*perils among robbers; if thou art in perils by land or by sea;

6 If thou art *a*accused with all manner of false accusations; if thine enemies fall upon thee; if they tear thee from the society of thy father and mother and brethren and sisters; and if with a drawn sword thine enemies tear thee from the bosom of thy wife, and of thine offspring, and thine elder son, although but six years of age, shall cling to thy garments, and shall say, My father, my father, why can't you stay with us? O, my father, what are the men going to do with you? and if then he shall be thrust from thee by the sword, and thou be dragged to *b*prison, and thine enemies prowl around thee like *c*wolves for the blood of the lamb;

7 And if thou shouldst be cast into the *a*pit, or into the hands of murderers, and the sentence of death passed upon thee; if thou be cast

45*b* TG Chastity; Modesty; Virtue.
  c TG Trust in God.
  d TG God, Presence of; God, Privilege of Seeing.
  e Deut. 32: 2; D&C 128: 19.
46*a* TG Holy Ghost, Mission of; Spirituality.
  b TG Righteousness.
  c Dan. 7: 14.

122 1*a* JS–H 1: 33.
  b Job 30: 1; Ps. 119: 51 (49–52); Jer. 20: 7 (7–9).
2*a* TG Counsel.
3*a* D&C 121: 9.
  TG Friendship.
4*a* TG Respect.
  b D&C 121: 7 (7–8).
  c 3 Ne. 20: 16 (16–21).
  TG Protection, Divine.

5*a* D&C 121: 6.
  TG Tribulation.
  b 2 Cor. 11: 26 (23–28).
6*a* Job 8: 6 (1–22).
  b Jer. 36: 5; Acts 5: 18 (15, 18); 12: 5; 16: 23 (19–40); Alma 14: 22 (22–28).
  c Luke 10: 3.
7*a* Gen. 37: 24; Jer. 38: 6 (6–13).

into the [b]deep; if the billowing surge conspire against thee; if fierce winds become thine enemy; if the heavens gather blackness, and all the elements combine to [c]hedge up the way; and above all, if the very jaws of [d]hell shall gape open the mouth wide after thee, know thou, my son, that all these things shall give thee [e]experience, and shall be for thy good.

8 The [a]Son of Man hath [b]descended below them all. Art thou greater than he?

9 Therefore, [a]hold on thy way, and the priesthood shall [b]remain with thee; for their [c]bounds are set, they cannot pass. Thy [d]days are known, and thy years shall not be numbered less; therefore, [e]fear not what man can do, for God shall be with you forever and ever.

SECTION 123

Duty of the saints in relation to their persecutors, as set forth by Joseph Smith the Prophet, while a prisoner in the jail at Liberty, Missouri, March 1839. HC 3: 302–303.

1–6, The saints should collect and publish an account of their sufferings and persecutions; 7–10, The same spirit that established the false creeds also leads to persecution of the saints; 11–17, Many among all sects will yet receive the truth.

AND again, we would suggest for your consideration the propriety of all the saints [a]gathering up a knowledge of all the facts, and [b]sufferings and abuses put upon them by the people of this State;

2 And also of all the property and amount of damages which they have sustained, both of character and personal [a]injuries, as well as real property;

3 And also the names of all persons that have had a hand in their [a]oppressions, as far as they can get hold of them and find them out.

4 And perhaps a committee can be appointed to find out these things, and to take [a]statements and affidavits; and also to gather up the libelous publications that are afloat;

5 And all that are in the magazines, and in the encyclopedias, and all the libelous histories that are published, and are writing, and by whom, and present the whole concatenation of diabolical rascality and nefarious and murderous impositions that have been practised upon this people—

6 That we may not only publish to all the world, but present them to the [a]heads of government in all their dark and hellish hue, as the last effort which is enjoined on us by our Heavenly Father, before we can fully and completely claim that promise which shall call him forth from his [b]hiding place; and also that the whole nation may be left without excuse before he can

---

7b Ps. 69: 2 (1–2, 14);
    Jonah 2: 3 (3–9);
    2 Cor. 11: 25.
c Lam. 3: 7 (7–8).
    TG Despair.
d 2 Sam. 22: 6 (5–7);
    JS-H 1: 16 (15–16).
e Job 2: 10 (10–13); 3:
    20 (20–30); 5: 27;
    Eccl. 3: 10 (9–10);
    Jer. 24: 5; 2 Cor. 4: 17;
    Heb. 12: 10 (10–11);
    1 Pet. 2: 20 (20–21);

    2 Ne. 2: 11.
8a TG Jesus Christ, Son of
    Man.
b Matt. 14: 37 (37, 40–
    41); Heb. 2: 17 (9–18);
    D&C 76: 107; 88: 6.
9a TG Steadfastness.
b D&C 13: 1; 84: 17; 90:
    3; 124: 130.
c Deut. 32: 8; Job 11: 20
    (19–20).
d D&C 121: 25.
e Neh. 4: 14; Ps. 56: 4

    (4, 11); 118: 6; Jer. 1:
    17 (17–19); Luke 12: 5
    (4–5); 2 Ne. 8: 7
    (7–12); D&C 3: 7; 98:
    14.
123 1a D&C 69: 8.
    b Ezra 4: 1 (1–24).
2a TG Injustice.
3a TG Oppression.
4a TG Record Keeping.
6a Ezra 5: 8 (8–17).
    b D&C 101: 89; 121: 4
    (1, 4).

send forth the power of his mighty arm.

7 It is an imperative duty that we owe to God, to angels, with whom we shall be brought to stand, and also to ourselves, to our wives and [a]children, who have been made to bow down with grief, sorrow, and care, under the most damning hand of murder, tyranny, and [b]oppression, supported and urged on and upheld by the influence of that spirit which hath so strongly riveted the [c]creeds of the fathers, who have inherited lies, upon the hearts of the children, and filled the world with confusion, and has been growing stronger and stronger, and is now the very mainspring of all corruption, and the whole [d]earth groans under the weight of its iniquity.

8 It is an iron [a]yoke, it is a strong band; they are the very handcuffs, and chains, and shackles, and fetters of [b]hell.

9 Therefore it is an imperative duty that we owe, not only to our own wives and children, but to the [a]widows and fatherless, whose husbands and fathers have been [b]murdered under its iron hand;

10 Which dark and blackening deeds are enough to make hell itself [a]shudder, and to stand aghast and pale, and the hands of the very devil to tremble and palsy.

11 And also it is an imperative duty that we owe to all the rising generation, and to all the pure in heart—

12 For there are many yet on the earth among all sects, parties, and denominations, who are [a]blinded by the subtle [b]craftiness of men, whereby they lie in wait to [c]deceive, and who are only kept from the truth because they [d]know not where to find it—

13 Therefore, that we should waste and [a]wear out our lives in bringing to light all the [b]hidden things of darkness, wherein we know them; and they are truly manifest from heaven—

14 These should then be attended to with great [a]earnestness.

15 Let no man count them as small things; for there is much which lieth in futurity, pertaining to the saints, which depends upon these things.

16 You know, brethren, that a very large ship is [a]benefited very much by a very small helm in the time of a storm, by being kept workways with the wind and the waves.

17 Therefore, dearly beloved brethren, let us [a]cheerfully [b]do all things that lie in our power; and then may we stand still, with the utmost assurance, to see the [c]salvation of God, and for his arm to be revealed.

SECTION 124

Revelation given to Joseph Smith the Prophet, at Nauvoo, Illinois, January 19, 1841. HC 4: 274–286. Because of increasing persecutions and illegal procedures against them by public officers, the saints had been compelled to leave Missouri. The exterminating order issued by Lilburn W. Boggs, Governor of Missouri, dated

7a TG Family, Children, Responsibilities toward.
  b TG Cruelty.
  c Alma 24: 7; JS-H 1: 19. TG Traditions of Men.
  d Isa. 33: 9; Moses 7: 49.
8a TG Bondage, Physical; Bondage, Spiritual.
  b TG Hell.

9a TG Children; Widows.
  b D&C 98: 13; 103: 27 (27–28); 124: 54.
10a Isa. 14: 9 (4–11).
12a Col. 2: 8; D&C 76: 75. TG Spiritual Blindness.
  b TG False Doctrine; False Prophets.
  c Col. 2: 18 (16–23).
  d 1 Ne. 8: 21 (19–24). TG Mission of Latter-

day Saints.
13a TG Dedication.
  b 1 Cor. 4: 5. TG Secret Combinations.
14a TG Zeal.
16a James 3: 4; 1 Ne. 16: 29; Alma 37: 6 (6–8); D&C 64: 33.
17a TG Cheerfulness.
  b TG Initiative.
  c Ex. 14: 13; Isa. 30: 15,

October 27, 1838, had left them no alternative. See HC 3: 175. In 1841, when this revelation was given, the city of Nauvoo, occupying the site of the former village of Commerce, Illinois, had been built up by the saints, and here the headquarters of the Church had been established.

1–14, *Joseph Smith is commanded to make a solemn proclamation of the gospel to the president of the United States, the governors, and the rulers of all nations;* 15–21, *Hyrum Smith, David W. Patten, Joseph Smith, Sen., and others among the living and the dead are blessed for their integrity and virtues;* 22–28, *The saints are commanded to build both a house for the entertainment of strangers and a temple in Nauvoo;* 29–36, *Baptisms for the dead are to be performed in temples;* 37–44, *The Lord's people always build temples for the performance of holy ordinances;* 45–55, *The saints are excused from building the temple in Jackson County because of the oppression of their enemies;* 56–83, *Directions are given for the building of the Nauvoo House;* 84–96, *Hyrum Smith is called to be a patriarch and to receive the keys and stand in the place of Oliver Cowdery;* 97–122, *William Law and others are counseled in their labors;* 123–145, *General and local officers are named, along with their duties and quorum affiliations.*

VERILY, thus saith the Lord unto you, my servant Joseph Smith, I am well pleased with your *a*offering and acknowledgments, which you have made; for unto this end have I raised you up, that I might show forth my *b*wisdom through the *c*weak things of the earth.

2 Your prayers are acceptable before me; and in answer to them I say unto you, that you are now called immediately to make a solemn *a*proclamation of my gospel, and of this *b*stake which I have planted to be a *c*cornerstone of Zion, which shall be polished with the refinement which is after the similitude of a palace.

3 This proclamation shall be made to all the *a*kings of the world, to the four corners thereof, to the honorable president-elect, and the high-minded governors of the nation in which you live, and to all the nations of the earth scattered abroad.

4 Let it be *a*written in the spirit of meekness and by the power of the Holy Ghost, which shall be in you at the time of the writing of the same;

5 For it shall be *a*given you by the Holy Ghost to know my *b*will concerning those *c*kings and authorities, even what shall befall them in a time to come.

6 For, behold, I am about to call upon them to give heed to the light and glory of Zion, for the time has come to favor her.

7 Call ye, therefore, upon them with loud proclamation, and with your testimony, fearing them not, for they are as *a*grass, and all their glory as the flower thereof which soon falleth, that they may be left also without excuse—

8 And that I may *a*visit them in the day of visitation, when I shall *b*unveil the face of my covering, to

124 1a Rom. 12: 1; 1 Tim.
  2: 3 (1–4); 1 Pet. 2: 5.
  b TG God, Wisdom of.
  c 1 Cor. 1: 27 (26–29);
    D&C 1: 19; 35: 13.
 2a TG Mission of Latter-
    day Saints.
  b TG Stake.
  c TG Cornerstone.

3a Ps. 119: 46; 138: 4
  (1–5); Matt. 10: 18;
  Acts 9: 15; D&C 1: 23.
4a TG Holy Ghost, Gifts
  of; Meekness.
5a Dan. 2: 22 (19–22,
  28).
  b TG God, Will of.

c Gen. 41: 25; Dan. 2:
  21 (20–22).
  TG Kings, Earthly.
7a Ps. 90: 5; 103: 15 (15–
  16); Isa. 40: 6 (6–8);
  1 Pet. 1: 24.
8a Isa. 10: 3 (1–4);
  1 Pet. 2: 12.
  b D&C 1: 12. TG Veil.

appoint the portion of the [c]oppressor among hypocrites, where there is [d]gnashing of teeth, if they reject my servants and my testimony which I have revealed unto them.

9 And again, I will visit and soften their hearts, many of them for your good, that ye may find grace in their eyes, that they may come to the [d]light of truth, and the Gentiles to the exaltation or lifting up of Zion.

10 For the day of my visitation cometh speedily, in an [a]hour when ye think not of; and where shall be the safety of my people, and refuge for those who shall be left of them?

11 Awake, O kings of the earth! Come ye, O, come ye, with your [a]gold and your silver, to the help of my people, to the house of the daughters of Zion.

12 And again, verily I say unto you, let my servant Robert B. Thompson help you to write this proclamation, for I am well pleased with him, and that he should be with you;

13 Let him, therefore, hearken to your counsel, and I will bless him with a multiplicity of blessings; let him be faithful and true in all things from henceforth, and he shall be great in mine eyes;

14 But let him remember that his [a]stewardship will I require at his hands.

15 And again, verily I say unto you, blessed is my servant Hyrum Smith; for I, the Lord, love him because of the [a]integrity of his heart, and because he loveth that which is right before me, saith the Lord.

16 Again, let my servant John C. Bennett help you in your labor in sending my word to the kings and people of the earth, and stand by you, even you my servant Joseph Smith, in the hour of affliction; and

his reward shall not fail if he receive [a]counsel.

17 And for his love he shall be great, for he shall be mine if he do this, saith the Lord. I have seen the work which he hath done, which I accept if he continue, and will crown him with blessings and great glory.

18 And again, I say unto you that it is my will that my servant Lyman Wight should continue in preaching for Zion, in the spirit of meekness, confessing me before the world; and I will bear him up as on [a]eagles' wings; and he shall beget glory and honor to himself and unto my name.

19 That when he shall finish his work that I may [a]receive him unto myself, even as I did my servant David Patten, who is with me at this time, and also my servant [b]Edward Partridge, and also my aged servant Joseph Smith, Sen., who sitteth [c]with Abraham at his right hand, and blessed and holy is he, for he is mine.

20 And again, verily I say unto you, my servant George Miller is without [a]guile; he may be trusted because of the [b]integrity of his heart; and for the love which he has to my testimony I, the Lord, love him.

21 I therefore say unto you, I seal upon his head the office of a bishopric, like unto my [a]servant Edward Partridge, that he may receive the consecrations of mine house, that he may administer blessings upon the heads of the poor of my people, saith the Lord. Let no man despise my servant George, for he shall honor me.

22 Let my servant George, and my servant Lyman, and my servant John Snider, and others, build a [a]house unto my name, such a one as my servant Joseph shall show unto

---

8c TG Cruelty;
    Oppression.
  d D&C 29: 15 (15–20);
    101: 91; 112: 24.
9a Isa. 60: 3 (1–12).
    TG Light.
10a Matt. 24: 44.

11a Isa. 60: 6 (6, 11–17);
    61: 6 (4–6).
14a TG Stewardship.
15a TG Integrity; Sincerity.
16a TG Counsel.
18a Ex. 19: 4; Isa. 40: 31.
19a D&C 124: 130.
   b D&C 115: 2 (2–6).

c Luke 16: 22;
  D&C 137: 5.
20a TG Guile; Sincerity.
  b Prov. 19: 1.
    TG Integrity.
21a D&C 41: 9. TG Bishop.
22a D&C 124: 56 (56–82,
    111–122).

them, upon the place which he shall show unto them also.

23 And it shall be for a house for boarding, a house that strangers may come from afar to lodge therein; therefore let it be a good house, worthy of all acceptation, that the weary [a]traveler may find health and safety while he shall contemplate the word of the Lord; and the [b]corner-stone I have appointed for Zion.

24 This house shall be a healthful habitation if it be built unto my name, and if the governor which shall be appointed unto it shall not suffer any pollution to come upon it. It shall be holy, or the Lord your God will not [a]dwell therein.

25 And again, verily I say unto you, let all my saints [a]come from afar.

26 And send ye [a]swift messengers, yea, chosen messengers, and say unto them: Come ye, with all your [b]gold, and your silver, and your precious stones, and with all your antiquities; and with all who have [c]knowledge of antiquities, that will come, may come, and bring the [d]box-tree, and the fir-tree, and the pine-tree, together with all the precious trees of the earth;

27 And with iron, with copper, and with brass, and with zinc, and with all your precious things of the earth; and build a [a]house to my name, for the Most High to [b]dwell therein.

28 For there is not a place found on earth that he may come to and [a]restore again that which was lost unto you, or which he hath taken away, even the fulness of the priesthood.

29 For a [a]baptismal font there is not upon the earth, that they, my saints, may be [b]baptized for those who are dead—

30 For this ordinance belongeth to my house, and cannot be acceptable to me, only in the days of your poverty, wherein ye are not able to build a house unto me.

31 But I command you, all ye my saints, to [a]build a house unto me; and I grant unto you a sufficient time to build a house unto me; and during this time your baptisms shall be acceptable unto me.

32 But behold, at the end of this appointment your baptisms for your dead shall not be acceptable unto me; and if you do not these things at the end of the appointment ye shall be rejected as a church, with your dead, saith the Lord your God.

33 For verily I say unto you, that [a]after you have had sufficient time to build a house to me, wherein the ordinance of baptizing for the dead belongeth, and for which the same was instituted from before the foundation of the world, your baptisms for your dead cannot be acceptable unto me;

34 For therein are the [a]keys of the holy priesthood ordained, that you may receive honor and glory.

35 And after this time, your baptisms for the dead, by those who are scattered abroad, are not acceptable unto me, saith the Lord.

36 For it is ordained that in Zion, and in her stakes, and in Jerusalem, those places which I have appointed for [a]refuge, shall be the places for your baptisms for your dead.

37 And again, verily I say unto

23a Lev. 25: 35 (35–38);
    Deut. 31: 12 (12–13);
    Matt. 25: 35 (35, 38,
    43–44).
  b D&C 124: 2.
24a D&C 97: 16 (15–17).
25a D&C 10: 65.
26a Isa. 18: 2 (1–7).
  b 1 Kgs. 6: 21 (21–22);
    2 Ne. 5: 15.
  c D&C 93: 53.
  d Ex. 26: 15; Isa. 41:

19; 60: 13.
27a D&C 109: 5.
    TG Temple.
  b Ex. 25: 8; 1 Kgs. 6:
    13; D&C 97: 16 (15–
    17); 104: 59.
28a TG Priesthood,
    Melchizedek; Restora-
    tion of the Gospel.
29a D&C 76: 51; 128: 13.
  b 1 Cor. 15: 29;
    D&C 127: 6; 138: 33.

TG Baptism for the
    Dead; Salvation for the
    Dead.
31a 2 Chr. 3: 1 (1–17);
    2 Ne. 5: 16 (15–17);
    D&C 84: 5 (5, 31); 97:
    10.
33a IE Oct. 3, 1841; see
    HC 4: 426, 446–447.
34a D&C 110: 16 (14–16).
36a Isa. 4: 6 (4–6);
    D&C 133: 13 (4–14).

you, how shall your *washings be acceptable unto me, except ye perform them in a house which you have built to my name?

38 For, this cause I commanded Moses that he should build a *tabernacle, that they should bear it with them in the wilderness, and to build a house in the land of promise, that those ordinances might be revealed which had been hid from before the world was.

39 Therefore, verily I say unto you, that your *anointings, and your washings, and your *baptisms for the dead, and your *solemn assemblies, and your *memorials for your *sacrifices by the sons of Levi, and for your *oracles in your most *holy places wherein you receive conversations, and your statutes and judgments, for the beginning of the revelations and foundation of Zion, and for the glory, honor, and endowment of all her municipals, are ordained by the ordinance of my holy house, which my people are always commanded to build unto my holy name.

40 And verily I say unto you, let this *house be built unto my name, that I may reveal mine ordinances therein unto my people;

41 For I deign to *reveal unto my church things which have been kept *hid from before the foundation of the world, things that pertain to the dispensation of the *fulness of times.

42 And *I will show unto my servant Joseph all things pertaining to this house, and the priesthood there-

of, and the place whereon it shall be built.

43 And ye shall build it on the place where you have contemplated building it, for that is the spot which I have chosen for you to build it.

44 If ye labor with all your might, I will consecrate that spot that it shall be made *holy.

45 And if my people will hearken unto my voice, and unto the voice of my *servants whom I have appointed to lead my people, behold, verily I say unto you, they shall not be moved out of their place.

46 But if they will not *hearken to my voice, nor unto the voice of these men whom I have appointed, they shall not be blest, because they *pollute mine holy grounds, and mine holy ordinances, and charters, and my holy words which I give unto them.

47 And it shall come to pass that if you build a house unto my name, and do not do the things that I say, I will not perform the *oath which I make unto you, neither fulfil the promises which ye expect at my hands, saith the Lord.

48 For *instead of blessings, ye, by your own works, bring cursings, wrath, indignation, and judgments upon your own heads, by your follies, and by all your abominations, which you practise before me, saith the Lord.

49 Verily, verily, I say unto you, that when I give a commandment to any of the sons of men to do a work unto my name, and those sons of men go with all their might and with

37a Lev. 8: 6; D&C 88: 74.
  TG Washing.
38a Ex. 25: 9 (1–9); 29: 4;
  33: 7; 35: 11;
  Ezek. 37: 27.
  TG Temple.
39a Ex. 25: 6; 29: 7;
  Lev. 10: 7; 14: 28;
  Num. 18: 8; D&C 68:
  21. TG Anointing.
  b TG Baptism for the
  Dead; Genealogy and
  Temple Work.

c D&C 88: 70 (70, 117).
  TG Solemn Assembly.
d Ex. 12: 14 (14–17);
  Lev. 2: 2 (2, 9, 16).
e Deut. 10: 8; D&C 13:
  1; 84: 31; 128: 24;
  JS–H 1: 69.
f D&C 90: 4.
g Ex. 26: 33; 1 Kgs. 6:
  16; Ezek. 41: 4.
40a TG Ordinances;
  Temple.
41a A of F 9.

b TG Alma 40: 3; D&C 121:
  26 (26–31).
c Eph. 1: 10 (9–10);
  D&C 27: 13; 76: 106;
  112: 30.
42a D&C 95: 14 (14–17).
44a TG Holiness.
45a TG Leadership;
  Prophets, Mission of.
46a TG Prophets, Rejection
  of.
  b TG Pollution.
47a TG Oath; Promise.
48a Deut. 28: 15 (1–47).

all they have to perform that work, and cease not their ᵃdiligence, and their enemies come upon them and ᵇhinder them from performing that work, behold, it behooveth me to ᶜrequire that work no more at the hands of those sons of men, but to accept of their offerings.

50 And the iniquity and transgression of my holy laws and commandments I will ᵃvisit upon the heads of those who hindered my work, unto the third and fourth ᵇgeneration, so long as they repent not, and hate me, saith the Lord God.

51 Therefore, for this cause have I accepted the offerings of those whom I commanded to build up a city and a ᵃhouse unto my name, in Jackson county, Missouri, and were hindered by their enemies, saith the Lord your God.

52 And I will answer ᵃjudgment, wrath, and indignation, wailing, and anguish, and gnashing of teeth upon their heads, unto the third and fourth generation, so long as they repent not, and hate me, saith the Lord your God.

53 And this I make an ᵃexample unto you, for your consolation concerning all those who have been commanded to do a work and have been hindered by the hands of their enemies, and by ᵇoppression, saith the Lord your God.

54 For I am the Lord your God, and will save all those of your brethren who have been ᵃpure in heart, and have been ᵇslain in the land of Missouri, saith the Lord.

55 And again, verily I say unto you, I command you again to build a

ᵃhouse to my name, even in this place, that you may ᵇprove yourselves unto me that ye are ᶜfaithful in all things whatsoever I command you, that I may bless you, and crown you with honor, immortality, and eternal life.

56 And now I say unto you, as pertaining to my boarding ᵃhouse which I have commanded you to build for the boarding of strangers, let it be built unto my name, and let my name be named upon it, and let my servant Joseph and his house have place therein, from generation to generation.

57 For this ᵃanointing have I put upon his head, that his blessing shall also be put upon the head of his posterity after him.

58 And as I said unto ᵃAbraham concerning the kindreds of the earth, even so I say unto my servant Joseph: In thee and in thy ᵇseed shall the kindred of the earth be blessed.

59 Therefore, let my servant Joseph and his seed after him have place in that house, from generation to generation, forever and ever, saith the Lord.

60 And let the name of that house be called ᵃNauvoo House; and let it be a delightful habitation for man, and a resting-place for the weary traveler, that he may contemplate the glory of Zion, and the glory of this, the corner-stone thereof;

61 That he may receive also the counsel from those whom I have set to be as ᵃplants of renown, and as ᵇwatchmen upon her walls.

62 Behold, verily I say unto you, let my servant George Miller, and

49a TG Diligence.
  b Ezra 4: 21.
  c D&C 56: 4.
50a Jer. 9: 9; Mosiah 12: 1.
  TG Accountability.
  b Deut. 5: 9.
  TG Procrastination; Repentance.
51a D&C 115: 11.
52a D&C 121: 15 (11–23).
  TG Punishment; Sorrow.

53a Num. 26: 10.
  b TG Oppression.
54a TG Purity.
  b Matt. 10: 39; D&C 98: 13; 103: 27 (27–28); 123: 9 (7, 9).
55a D&C 127: 4.
  b Ex. 15: 25 (23–26); D&C 98: 14 (12–14); Abr. 3: 25. TG Test, Try, Prove.
  c 1 Kgs. 6: 12 (11–13).
56a D&C 124: 22 (22–24).

57a TG Anointing.
58a Gen. 12: 3; 22: 18; Abr. 2: 11.
  TG Abrahamic Covenant.
  b D&C 110: 12.
60a IE beautiful, delightful, as used in Isa. 52: 7 in Hebrew.
61a Isa. 60: 21; Ezek. 37: 29.
  b TG Watchmen.

my servant Lyman Wight, and my servant John Snider, and my servant Peter Haws, organize themselves, and appoint one of them to be a president over their quorum for the purpose of building that house.

63 And they shall form a constitution, whereby they may receive stock for the building of that house.

64 And they shall not receive less than fifty dollars for a share of stock in that house, and they shall be permitted to receive fifteen thousand dollars from any one man for stock in that house.

65 But they shall not be permitted to receive over fifteen thousand dollars stock from any one man.

66 And they shall not be permitted to receive under fifty dollars for a share of stock from any one man in that house.

67 And they shall not be permitted to receive any man, as a stockholder in this house, except the same shall pay his stock into their hands at the time he receives stock;

68 And in proportion to the amount of stock he pays into their hands he shall receive stock in that house; but if he pays nothing into their hands he shall not receive any stock in that house.

69 And if any pay stock into their hands it shall be for stock in that house, for himself, and for his generation after him, from generation to generation, so long as he and his heirs shall hold that stock, and do not sell or convey the stock away out of their hands by their own free will and act, if you will do my will, saith the Lord your God.

70 And again, verily I say unto you, if my servant George Miller, and my servant Lyman Wight, and my servant John Snider, and my servant Peter Haws, receive any stock into their hands, in moneys, or in properties wherein they receive the real value of moneys, they shall not appropriate any portion of that stock to any other purpose, only in that house.

71 And if they do appropriate any portion of that stock anywhere else, only in that house, without the consent of the stockholder, and do not repay fourfold for the stock which they appropriate anywhere else, only in that house, they shall be accursed, and shall be moved out of their place, saith the Lord God; for I, the Lord, am God, and cannot be *mocked in any of these things.

72 Verily I say unto you, let my servant Joseph pay stock into their hands for the building of that house, as seemeth him good; but my servant Joseph cannot pay over fifteen thousand dollars stock in that house, nor under fifty dollars; neither can any other man, saith the Lord.

73 And there are others also who wish to know my will concerning them, for they have asked it at my hands.

74 Therefore, I say unto you concerning my servant Vinson Knight, if he will do my will let him put stock into that house for himself, and for his generation after him, from generation to generation.

75 And let him lift up his voice long and loud, in the midst of the people, to *plead the cause of the poor and the needy; and let him not fail, neither let his heart faint; and I will *accept of his offerings, for they shall not be unto me as the offerings of Cain, for he shall be mine, saith the Lord.

76 Let his family rejoice and turn away their hearts from affliction; for I have chosen him and anointed him, and he shall be honored in the midst of his house, for I will forgive all his sins, saith the Lord. Amen.

77 Verily I say unto you, let my servant Hyrum put stock into that house as seemeth him good, for himself and his generation after him, from generation to generation.

78 Let my servant Isaac Galland put stock into that house; for I, the Lord, love him for the work he hath done, and will forgive all his sins; therefore, let him be remembered for

---

71a Gal. 6: 7.   75a Prov. 22: 23; 31: 9.   b Gen. 4: 4–5.

an interest in that house from generation to generation.

79 Let my servant Isaac Galland be appointed among you, and be ordained by my servant William Marks, and be blessed of him, to go with my servant Hyrum to accomplish the work that my servant Joseph shall point out to them, and they shall be greatly blessed.

80 Let my servant William Marks pay stock into that house, as seemeth him good, for himself and his generation, from generation to generation.

81 Let my servant Henry G. Sherwood pay stock into that house, as seemeth him good, for himself and his seed after him, from generation to generation.

82 Let my servant William Law pay stock into that house, for himself and his seed after him, from generation to generation.

83 If he will do my will let him not take his family unto the eastern lands, even unto Kirtland; nevertheless, I, the Lord, will build up ªKirtland, but I, the Lord, have a scourge prepared for the inhabitants thereof.

84 And with my servant Almon Babbitt, there are many things with which I am not pleased; behold, he aspireth to establish his counsel instead of the counsel which I have ordained, even that of the Presidency of my Church; and he setteth up a ªgolden calf for the worship of my people.

85 Let no man ªgo from this place who has come here essaying to keep my commandments;

86 If they live here let them live unto me; and if they die let them die unto me; for they shall ªrest from all their labors here, and shall continue their works.

87 Therefore, let my servant William put his trust in me, and cease to fear concerning his family, because of the sickness of the land. If ye ªlove me, keep my commandments; and the sickness of the land shall ªredound to your glory.

88 Let my servant William go and proclaim my everlasting gospel with a loud voice, and with great joy, as he shall be moved upon by my ªSpirit, unto the inhabitants of Warsaw, and also unto the inhabitants of Carthage, and also unto the inhabitants of Burlington, and also unto the inhabitants of Madison, and await patiently and diligently for further instructions at my general conference, saith the Lord.

89 If he will do my ªwill let him from henceforth hearken to the counsel of my servant Joseph, and with his interest support the ªcause of the poor, and publish ªthe new translation of my holy word unto the inhabitants of the earth.

90 And if he will do this I will ªbless him with a multiplicity of blessings, that he shall not be forsaken, nor his seed be found ªbegging bread.

91 And again, verily I say unto you, let my servant William be appointed, ordained, and anointed, as counselor unto my servant Joseph, in the room of my servant Hyrum, that my servant Hyrum may take the office of Priesthood and ªPatriarch, which was appointed unto him by his father, by blessing and also by right;

92 That from henceforth he shall hold the keys of the ªpatriarchal blessings upon the heads of all my people,

93 That whoever he blesses shall be blessed, and whoever he ªcurses shall be cursed; that whatsoever he

---

83a D&C 117: 16.
84a Ex. 32: 4.
85a Luke 9: 62; D&C 124:
    108 (87, 108–110).
86a Rev. 14: 13.
    TG Paradise.
87a John 14: 15.

b D&C 121: 8; 122: 7.
88a TG God, Spirit of.
89a TG God, Will of.
  b D&C 78: 3.
  c IE the Joseph Smith
     Translation of the
     Bible. D&C 94: 10.
90a TG Blessing.

b Ps. 37: 25.
91a D&C 107: 40 (39–40).
    See also HC 4: 227.
92a TG Patriarch;
    Patriarchal Blessings.
93a D&C 103: 25; 132: 47
    (45–48). TG Curse.

shall *b*bind on earth shall be bound in heaven; and whatsoever he shall loose on earth shall be loosed in heaven.

94 And from this time forth I appoint unto him that he may be a prophet, and a *a*seer, and a revelator unto my church, as well as my servant Joseph;

95 That he may act in concert also with my *a*servant Joseph; and that he shall receive counsel from my servant Joseph, who shall show unto him the *b*keys whereby he may ask and receive, and be crowned with the same blessing, and glory, and honor, and priesthood, and gifts of the priesthood, that once were put upon him that was my servant *c*Oliver Cowdery;

96 That my servant Hyrum may bear record of the things which I shall show unto him, that his name may be had in honorable remembrance from generation to generation, forever and ever.

97 Let my servant William Law also receive the keys by which he may ask and receive blessings; let him be *a*humble before me, and be without *b*guile, and he shall receive of my Spirit, even the *c*Comforter, which shall manifest unto him the truth of all things, and shall give him, in the very hour, what he shall say.

98 And these *a*signs shall follow him—he shall heal the *b*sick, he shall cast out devils, and shall be delivered from those who would administer unto him deadly poison;

99 And he shall be led in paths where the poisonous serpent *a*cannot lay hold upon his heel, and he shall mount up in the *b*imagination of his thoughts as upon eagles' wings.

100 And what if I will that he

should *a*raise the dead, let him not withhold his voice.

101 Therefore, let my servant William cry aloud and spare not, with joy and rejoicing, and with hosannas to him that sitteth upon the throne forever and ever, saith the Lord your God.

102 Behold, I say unto you, I have a mission in store for my servant William, and my servant Hyrum, and for them alone; and let my servant Joseph tarry at home, for he is needed. The remainder I will show unto you hereafter. Even so. Amen.

103 And again, verily I say unto you, if my servant Sidney will serve me and be *a*counselor unto my servant Joseph, let him arise and come up and stand in the office of his calling, and humble himself before me.

104 And if he will offer unto me an acceptable offering, and acknowledgments, and remain with my people, behold, I, the Lord your God, will heal him that he shall be healed; and he shall lift up his voice again on the mountains, and be a *a*spokesman before my face.

105 Let him come and locate his family in the neighborhood in which my servant Joseph resides.

106 And in all his journeyings let him lift up his voice as with the sound of a trump, and warn the inhabitants of the earth to flee the wrath to come.

107 Let him assist my servant Joseph, and also let my servant William Law assist my servant Joseph, in making a solemn *a*proclamation unto the kings of the earth, even as I have before said unto you.

108 If my servant Sidney will do my will, let him not remove his family unto the *a*eastern lands, but

93b Matt. 16: 19; 18: 18.
  TG Priesthood, Keys of; Sealing.
94a D&C 107: 92. TG Seer.
95a D&C 6: 18 (18–19).
  b D&C 6: 28.
  c See his name in the Index for references to his callings.

97a TG Teachable.
  b TG Guile; Sincerity.
  c TG Holy Ghost, Comforter.
98a Mark 16: 17 (17–18).
  TG Holy Ghost, Gifts of.
  b TG Heal; Sickness.
99a Acts 28: 3 (3–9);
  D&C 24: 13; 84: 72

  (71–72).
  b Isa. 40: 31.
100a TG Death, Power over.
103a D&C 90: 21.
104a Ex. 4: 16 (14–16);
  2 Ne. 3: 17 (17–18);
  D&C 100: 9 (9–11).
107a D&C 124: 2.
108a D&C 124: 83.

let him change their habitation, even as I have said.

109 Behold, it is not my will that he shall seek to find safety and refuge out of the city which I have appointed unto you, even the city of Nauvoo.

110 Verily I say unto you, even now, if he will hearken unto my voice, it shall be well with him. Even so. Amen.

111 And again, verily I say unto you, let my servant Amos Davies pay stock into the hands of those whom I have appointed to build a house for boarding, even the Nauvoo House.

112 This let him do if he will have an interest; and let him hearken unto the counsel of my servant Joseph, and labor with his own hands that he may obtain the confidence of men.

113 And when he shall *prove himself faithful in all things that shall be *bentrusted unto his care, yea, even a few things, he shall be made ruler over many;

114 Let him therefore *abase himself that he may be exalted. Even so. Amen.

115 And again, verily I say unto you, if my servant Robert D. Foster will obey my voice, let him build a house for my servant Joseph, according to the contract which he has made with him, as the door shall be open to him from time to time.

116 And let him repent of all his *folly, and clothe himself with *bcharity; and *ccease to do evil, and lay aside all his hard *dspeeches;

117 And pay stock also into the hands of the quorum of the Nauvoo House, for himself and for his generation after him, from generation to generation;

118 And hearken unto the counsel of my servants Joseph, and Hyrum, and William Law, and unto the authorities which I have called to lay the foundation of Zion; and it shall be well with him forever and ever. Even so. Amen.

119 And again, verily I say unto you, let no man pay stock to the quorum of the Nauvoo House unless he shall be a believer in the Book of Mormon, and the revelations I have given unto you, saith the Lord your God;

120 For that which is *amore or less than this cometh of evil, and shall be attended with cursings and not blessings, saith the Lord your God. Even so. Amen.

121 And again, verily I say unto you, let the quorum of the Nauvoo House have a just recompense of wages for all their labors which they do in building the Nauvoo House; and let their wages be as shall be agreed among themselves, as pertaining to the price thereof.

122 And let every man who pays stock bear his proportion of their wages, if it must needs be, for their support, saith the Lord; otherwise, their labors shall be accounted unto them for stock in that house. Even so. Amen.

123 Verily I say unto you, I now give unto you the *aofficers belonging to my Priesthood, that ye may hold the *bkeys thereof, even the Priesthood which is after the order of Melchizedek, which is after the order of mine *cOnly Begotten Son.

124 First, I give unto you Hyrum Smith to be a *apatriarch unto you, to hold the *bsealing blessings of my church, even the Holy Spirit of *cpromise, whereby ye are *dsealed up

113a TG Test, Try, Prove.
  b 1 Thes. 2 : 4.
114a Matt. 23 : 12;
  D&C 101 : 42.
116a TG Foolishness.
  b Col. 3 : 14.
  c TG Self-mastery.
  d TG Slander.

120a Deut. 28 : 14;
  Matt. 5 : 37.
123a D&C 107 : 21; 124 :
  143. TG Church
  Organization:
  Delegation of
  Responsibility.
  b TG Priesthood, Keys
  of.

  c TG Jesus Christ,
  Authority of.
124a D&C 124 : 91.
  TG Patriarch.
  b TG Sealing.
  c D&C 76 : 53; 88 : 3
  (3–4); 132 : 19 (18–
  26).
  d Eph. 4 : 30.

unto the day of redemption, that ye may not fall notwithstanding the [c]hour of temptation that may come upon you.

125 I give unto you my servant Joseph to be a presiding elder over all my church, to be a translator, a revelator, a [a]seer, and prophet.

126 I give unto him for [a]counselors my servant Sidney Rigdon and my servant William Law, that these may constitute a quorum and First Presidency, to receive the [b]oracles for the whole church.

127 I give unto you my servant [a]Brigham Young to be a president over the Twelve traveling council;

128 Which [a]Twelve hold the keys to open up the authority of my kingdom upon the four corners of the earth, and after that to send my word to every [b]creature.

129 [a]They are Heber C. Kimball, Parley P. Pratt, Orson Pratt, Orson Hyde, William Smith, John Taylor, John E. Page, Wilford Woodruff, Willard Richards, George A. Smith;

130 David Patten I have [a]taken unto myself; behold, his [b]priesthood no man [c]taketh from him; but, verily I say unto you, another may be appointed unto the same calling.

131 And again, I say unto you, I give unto you a [a]high council, for the corner-stone of Zion—

132 Namely, Samuel Bent, Henry G. Sherwood, George W. Harris, Charles C. Rich, Thomas Grover, Newel Knight, David Dort, Dunbar Wilson—Seymour Brunson I have taken unto myself; no man taketh his priesthood, but another may be appointed unto the same priesthood in his stead; and verily I say unto you, let my servant Aaron Johnson

be ordained unto this calling in his stead—David Fullmer, Alpheus Cutler, William Huntington.

133 And again, I give unto you Don C. Smith to be a president over a quorum of high priests;

134 Which ordinance is instituted for the purpose of qualifying those who shall be appointed standing presidents or servants over different [a]stakes scattered abroad;

135 And they may travel also if they choose, but rather be ordained for standing presidents; this is the office of their calling, saith the Lord your God.

136 I give unto him Amasa Lyman and Noah Packard for counselors, that they may preside over the quorum of high priests of my church, saith the Lord.

137 And again, I say unto you, I give unto you John A. Hicks, Samuel Williams, and Jesse Baker, which priesthood is to preside over the quorum of [a]elders, which quorum is instituted for standing ministers; nevertheless they may travel, yet they are ordained to be standing ministers to my church, saith the Lord.

138 And again, I give unto you Joseph Young, Josiah Butterfield, Daniel Miles, Henry Herriman, Zera Pulsipher, Levi Hancock, James Foster, to preside over the quorum of [a]seventies;

139 Which quorum is instituted for [a]traveling elders to bear record of my name in all the world, wherever the traveling high council, mine apostles, shall send them to prepare a way before my face.

140 The difference between this quorum and the quorum of elders is that one is to travel continually, and the other is to preside over the

124e Rev. 3: 10.
125a D&C 20: 2; 21: 1.
    TG Seer.
126a D&C 68: 15; 90: 21;
    124: 91. TG Counselor.
  b D&C 90: 4 (4–5).
    TG Revelation.
127a D&C 18: 27; 107: 23;
    126: 1.

128a TG Apostles.
  b Mark 16: 15.
129a See Index for
    reference to each
    name.
130a D&C 124: 19.
  b Heb. 5: 6.
  c D&C 90: 3.
    TG Priesthood.

131a D&C 102: 30 (27–32);
    107: 36 (36–37).
134a TG Stakes.
137a D&C 20: 38; 107: 12
    (11–12, 89–90).
    TG Elders.
138a TG Seventy.
139a D&C 107: 33 (33, 93–
    98).

churches from time to time; the one has the responsibility of presiding from time to time, and the other has no responsibility of presiding, saith the Lord your God.

141 And again, I say unto you, I give unto you Vinson Knight, Samuel H. Smith, and Shadrach Roundy, if he will receive it, to preside over the [a]bishopric; a knowledge of said bisnophic is given unto you in the book of Doctrine and Covenants.

142 And again, I say unto you, Samuel Rolfe and his counselors for [a]priests, and the president of the teachers and his counselors, and also the president of the deacons and his counselors, and also the president of the stake and his counselors.

143 The above [a]offices I have given unto you, and the keys thereof, for helps and for governments, for the work of the ministry and the [b]perfecting of my saints.

144 And a commandment I give unto you, that you should fill all these offices and [a]approve of those names which I have mentioned, or else disapprove of them at my general conference;

145 And that ye should prepare rooms for all these offices in my [a]house when you build it unto my name, saith the Lord your God. Even so. Amen.

SECTION 125

Revelation given through Joseph Smith the Prophet, at Nauvoo, Illinois, March 1841, concerning the saints in the Territory of Iowa. HC 4: 311–312.

1–4, The saints are to build cities and to gather to the stakes of Zion.

WHAT is the will of the Lord concerning the saints in the Territory of Iowa?

2 Verily, thus saith the Lord, I say unto you, if those who [a]call themselves by my name and are essaying to be my saints, if they will do my will and keep my commandments concerning them, let them gather themselves together unto the places which I shall appoint unto them by my servant Joseph, and build up cities unto my name, that they may be prepared for that which is in store for a time to come.

3 Let them build up a city unto my name upon the land opposite the city of Nauvoo, and let the name of [a]Zarahemla be named upon it.

4 And let all those who come from the east, and the west, and the north, and the south, that have desires to dwell therein, take up their inheritance in the same, as well as in the city of [a]Nashville, or in the city of Nauvoo, and in all the [b]stakes which I have appointed, saith the Lord.

SECTION 126

Revelation given through Joseph Smith the Prophet, in the house of Brigham Young, at Nauvoo, Illinois, July 9, 1841. HC 4: 382. At this time Brigham Young was president of the Quorum of the Twelve Apostles.

141a D&C 68: 14 (14–24);
   107: 15 (15–17), 68
   (68–76).
142a TG Deacon; Priest,
   Aaronic Priesthood;
   Teachers.
143a D&C 107: 21; 124: 23.

b 1 Cor. 12: 28; Eph. 4:
   11 (11–16).
144a D&C 26: 2.
   TG Common Consent;
   Sustaining Church
   Leaders.
145a D&C 27: 1 (27–28).

125 2a TG Jesus Christ,
   Taking the Name of.
3a Omni 1: 14 (14, 18);
   Alma 2: 26.
4a IE Nashville in Lee
   County, Iowa.
   b TG Stake.

1–3, Brigham Young is commended for his labors and is relieved of future travel abroad.

DEAR and well-beloved brother, [a]Brigham Young, verily thus saith the Lord unto you: My servant Brigham, it is [b]no more required at your hand to leave your family as in times past, for your offering is acceptable to me.

2 I have seen your [a]labor and toil in journeyings for my name.

3 I therefore command you to [a]send my word abroad, and take especial [b]care of your family at this time, henceforth and forever. Amen.

SECTION 127

An epistle from Joseph Smith the Prophet to the Latter-day Saints at Nauvoo, Illinois, containing directions on baptism for the dead; dated at Nauvoo, September 1, 1842. HC 5: 142–144.

1–4, Joseph Smith glories in persecution and tribulation; 5–12, Records must be kept relative to baptisms for the dead.

FORASMUCH as the Lord has revealed unto me that my enemies, both in Missouri and this State, were again in the pursuit of me; and inasmuch as they pursue me without a [a]cause, and have not the least shadow or coloring of justice or right on their side in the getting up of their prosecutions against me; and inasmuch as their pretensions are all founded in falsehood of the blackest dye, I have thought it expedient and wisdom in me to leave the place for a short season, for my own safety and the safety of this people. I would say to all those with whom I have business, that I have left my [b]affairs with agents and clerks who will transact all business in a prompt and proper manner, and will see that all my debts are canceled in due time, by turning out property, or otherwise, as the case may require, or as the circumstances may admit of. When I learn that the storm is fully blown over, then I will return to you again.

2 And as for the [a]perils which I am called to pass through, they seem but a small thing to me, as the [b]envy and wrath of man have been my common lot all the days of my life; and for what cause it seems mysterious, unless I was [c]ordained from before the foundation of the world for some good end, or bad, as you may choose to call it. Judge ye for yourselves. God [d]knoweth all these things, whether it be good or bad. But nevertheless, deep water is what I am wont to swim in. It all has become a second nature to me; and I feel, like Paul, to glory in [e]tribulation; for to this day has the God of my fathers delivered me out of them all, and will deliver me from henceforth; for behold, and lo, I shall triumph over all my enemies, for the Lord God hath spoken it.

3 Let all the saints rejoice, therefore, and be exceedingly glad; for Israel's [a]God is their God, and he will mete out a just recompense of [b]reward upon the heads of all their [c]oppressors.

---

126 1a See D&C 136,
          heading. D&C 124:127.
     b D&C 18: 28 (27–28).
2a TG Good Works.
3a D&C 107: 38; 124: 39.
     b TG Family, Children,
          Responsibilities
          toward; Family, Love
          within.

127 1a Job 2: 3; Matt. 5:
          10 (10–12); 10: 22
          (22–23).
     b TG Accountability.
2a Ps. 23: 4 (1–6); 138: 7.
     TG Persecution.
     b TG Envy.
     c Alma 13: 3.

     d TG God, Omniscience
          of; God, Perfection of.
     e 2 Cor. 6: 4 (4–5).
     TG Test, Try, Prove.
3a Isa. 29: 23 (22–24);
          45: 3; 3 Ne. 11: 14;
          D&C 36: 1.
     b TG Reward.
     c TG Oppression.

4 And again, verily thus saith the Lord: Let the work of my *temple, and all the works which I have appointed unto you, be continued on and not cease; and let your *diligence, and your perseverance, and patience, and your works be redoubled, and you shall in nowise lose your reward, saith the Lord of Hosts. And if they *persecute you, so persecuted they the prophets and righteous men that were before you. For all this there is a reward in heaven.

5 And again, I give unto you a word in relation to the *baptism for your dead.

6 Verily, thus saith the Lord unto you concerning your dead: When any of you are *baptized for your dead, let there be a *recorder, and let him be eye-witness of your baptisms; let him hear with his ears, that he may testify of a truth, saith the Lord;

7 That in all your recordings it may be *recorded in heaven; whatsoever you *bind on earth, may be bound in heaven; whatsoever you loose on earth, may be loosed in heaven;

8 For I am about to *restore many things to the earth, pertaining to the *priesthood, saith the Lord of Hosts.

9 And again, let all the *records be had in order, that they may be put in the archives of my holy temple, to be held in remembrance from generation to generation, saith the Lord of Hosts.

10 I will say to all the saints, that I desired, with exceedingly great desire, to have addressed them from the stand on the subject of baptism for the dead, on the following Sabbath. But inasmuch as it is out of my power to do so, I will write the word of the Lord from time to time, on that subject, and send it to you by mail, as well as many other things.

11 I now close my letter for the present, for the want of more time; for the enemy is on the alert, and as the Savior said, the *prince of this world cometh, but he hath nothing in me.

12 Behold, my prayer to God is that you all may be saved. And I subscribe myself your servant in the Lord, prophet and *seer of the Church of Jesus Christ of Latter-day Saints.

JOSEPH SMITH.

SECTION 128

An epistle from Joseph Smith the Prophet to The Church of Jesus Christ of Latter-day Saints, containing further directions on baptism for the dead; dated at Nauvoo, Illinois, September 6, 1842. HC 5: 148–153.

1–5, Local and general recorders must certify to the fact of baptisms for the dead; 6–9, Their records are binding and recorded on earth and in heaven; 10–14, The baptismal font is a similitude of the grave; 15–17, Elijah restored power relative to baptism for the dead; 18–21, All of the keys, powers, and authorities of past dispensations have been restored; 22–25, Glad and glorious tidings acclaimed for the living and the dead.

4a TG D&C 124: 55 (25–48, 55).
 b TG Dedication; Diligence; Patience.
 c TG Hate; Malice; Reward.
5a TG Baptism for the Dead; Genealogy and Temple Work; Salva-

tion for the Dead.
6a 1 Cor. 15: 29;
   D&C 124: 29; 128: 18 (13, 18).
 b D&C 128: 2 (2–4, 7).
7a TG Book of Life.
 b TG Priesthood, Keys of.
8a TG Restoration of

the Gospel.
 b TG Priesthood, Melchizedek.
9a D&C 128: 24.
   TG Record Keeping.
11a John 14: 30.
   TG Satan.
12a D&C 124: 125.
   TG Seer.

As I stated to you in my letter before I left my place, that I would write to you from time to time and give you information in relation to many subjects, I now resume the subject of the ªbaptism for the dead, as that subject seems to occupy my mind, and press itself upon my feelings the strongest, since I have been pursued by my enemies.

2 I wrote a few words of revelation to you concerning a recorder. I have had a few additional views in relation to this matter, which I now certify. That is, it was declared in my former letter that there should be a ªrecorder, who should be eye-witness, and also to hear with his ears, that he might make a record of a truth before the Lord.

3 Now, in relation to this matter, it would be very difficult for one recorder to be present at all times, and to do all the business. To obviate this difficulty, there can be a recorder appointed in each ward of the city, who is well qualified for taking accurate minutes; and let him be very particular and precise in taking the whole proceedings, certifying in his record that he saw with his eyes, and heard with his ears, giving the date, and names, and so forth, and the history of the whole transaction; naming also some three individuals that are present, if there be any present, who can at any time when called upon certify to the same, that in the mouth of two or three ªwitnesses every word may be established.

4 Then, let there be a general ªrecorder, to whom these other records can be handed, being attended with certificates over their own signatures, certifying that the record they have made is true. Then the general church recorder can enter the record on the general church book, with the certificates and all the attending witnesses, with his own statement that he verily believes the above statement and records to be true, from his knowledge of the general character and appointment of those men by the church. And when this is done on the general church book, the record shall be just as holy, and shall answer the ordinance just the same as if he had seen with his eyes and heard with his ears, and made a record of the same on the general church book.

5 You may think this order of things to be very particular; but let me tell you that it is only to answer the will of God, by conforming to the ordinance and preparation that the Lord ordained and prepared before the foundation of the world, for the ªsalvation of the dead who should die without a ᵇknowledge of the gospel.

6 And further, I want you to remember that John the Revelator was contemplating this very subject in relation to the dead, when he declared, as you will find recorded in Revelation 20:12— *And I saw the dead, small and great, stand before God; and the books were opened; and another book was opened, which is the book of life; and the dead were judged out of those things which were ᵃwritten in the books, according to their works.*

7 You will discover in this quotation that the books were opened; and another book was opened, which was the book of life; but the dead were judged out of those things which were written in the books, according to their works; consequently, the books spoken of must be the books which contained the record of their works, and refer to the ªrecords which are kept on the earth. And the book which was the ᵇbook of life is the record which is

128 1a TG Baptism for the   3a D&C 6: 28.   6a Heb. 12: 23.
        Dead; Genealogy and   TG Witnesses.   7a D&C 21: 1.
        Temple Work.   4a D&C 47: 1 (1–4).   b Rev. 20: 12; D&C 127:
     2a 1 Kgs. 4: 3;   5a TG Salvation for the   6 (6–7). TG Book of
        D&C 127: 6.   Dead.   Life.
                             b 1 Pet. 4: 6; D&C 138: 2.

kept in heaven; the principle agreeing precisely with the doctrine which is commanded you in the revelation contained in the letter which I wrote to you previous to my leaving my place—that in all your recordings it may be recorded in heaven.

8 Now, the nature of this ordinance consists in the "power of the priesthood, by the revelation of Jesus Christ, wherein it is granted that whatsoever you *bind on earth shall be bound in heaven, and whatsoever you loose on earth shall be loosed in heaven. Or, in other words, taking a different view of the translation, whatsoever you record on earth shall be recorded in heaven, and whatsoever you do not record on earth shall not be recorded in heaven; for out of the books shall your dead be judged, according to their own works, whether they themselves have attended to the *ordinances in their own *propria persona*, or by the means of their own agents, according to the ordinance which God has prepared for their salvation from before the foundation of the world, according to the records which they have kept concerning their dead.

9 It may seem to some to be a very bold doctrine that we talk of—a power which records or binds on earth and binds in heaven. Nevertheless, in all ages of the world, whenever the Lord has given a *dispensation of the priesthood to any man by actual revelation, or any set of men, this power has always been given. Hence, whatsoever those men did in *authority, in the name of the Lord, and did it truly and faithfully, and kept a proper and faithful record of the same, it became a law on earth and in heaven, and could not be annulled, according to the decrees

of the great "Jehovah. This is a faithful saying. Who can hear it?

10 And again, for the precedent, Matthew 16:18, 19: *And I say also unto thee, That thou art Peter, and upon this "rock I will build my church; and the gates of hell shall not prevail against it. And I will give unto thee the keys of the kingdom of heaven: and whatsoever thou shalt bind on earth shall be bound in heaven; and whatsoever thou shalt loose on earth shall be loosed in heaven.*

11 Now the great and grand secret of the whole matter, and the *summum bonum* of the whole subject that is lying before us, consists in obtaining the "powers of the Holy Priesthood. For him to whom these keys are given there is no difficulty in obtaining a *knowledge of facts in relation to the *salvation of the children of men, both as well for the dead as for the living.

12 Herein is "glory and honor, and immortality and eternal life—The ordinance of baptism by water, to be *immersed therein in order to answer to the likeness of the dead, that one principle might accord with the other; to be immersed in the water and come forth out of the water is in the likeness of the resurrection of the dead in coming forth out of their graves; hence, this ordinance was instituted to form a relationship with the ordinance of baptism for the dead, being in likeness of the dead.

13 Consequently, the "baptismal font was instituted as a similitude of the grave, and was commanded to be in a place underneath where the living are wont to assemble, to show forth the living and the dead, and that all things may have their likeness, and that they may accord one with another—that which is earthly

8a TG Priesthood, Power of.
b TG Priesthood, Keys of; Sealing.
c TG Ordinance.
9a TG Dispensations.
b TG Authority; Priesthood, Authority.
c TG Jesus Christ, Jehovah.
10a Matt. 16: 18 (18–19).
11a TG Priesthood, Power of.
b TG Learning.
c TG Salvation.
12a TG Glory; Honor; Immortality.
b TG Baptism, Immersion.
13a Rom. 6: 4 (3–5); D&C 76: 51; 124: 29.

conforming to that which is *bheavenly, as Paul hath declared, 1 Corinthians 15:46, 47, and 48:

14 *Howbeit that was not first which is spiritual, but that which is natural; and afterward that which is spiritual. The first man is of the earth, earthy; the second man is the Lord from heaven. As is the earthy, such are they also that are earthy; and as is the heavenly, such are they also that are heavenly.* And as are the records on the earth in relation to your dead, which are truly made out, so also are the records in heaven. This, therefore, is the *asealing and binding power, and, in one sense of the word, the *bkeys of the kingdom, which consist in the key of *cknowledge.

15 And now, my dearly beloved brethren and sisters, let me assure you that these are principles in relation to the dead and the living that cannot be lightly passed over, as pertaining to our salvation. For their *asalvation is necessary and essential to our salvation, as Paul says concerning the fathers—that they without us cannot be made perfect—neither can we without our dead be made *bperfect.

16 And now, in relation to the baptism for the dead, I will give you another quotation of Paul, 1 Corinthians 15:29: *Else what shall they do which are baptized for the dead, if the dead rise not at all? Why are they then baptized for the dead?*

17 And again, in connection with this quotation I will give you a quotation from one of the prophets, who had his eye fixed on the *arestoration of the priesthood, the glories to be revealed in the last days, and in an especial manner this most glorious of all subjects belonging to the ever-

lasting gospel, namely, the baptism for the dead; for Malachi says, last chapter, verses 5th and 6th: *Behold, I will send you *bElijah the prophet before the coming of the great and dreadful day of the Lord: And he shall turn the heart of the fathers to the children, and the heart of the children to their fathers, lest I come and smite the earth with a curse.*

18 I might have rendered a *aplainer translation to this, but it is sufficiently plain to suit my purpose as it stands. It is sufficient to know, in this case, that the earth will be smitten with a *bcurse unless there is a welding *clink of some kind or other between the fathers and the *dchildren, upon some subject or other—and behold what is that subject? It is the *ebaptism for the dead. For we without them cannot be made perfect; neither can they without us be made perfect. Neither can they nor we be made perfect without those who have died in the gospel also; for it is necessary in the ushering in of the dispensation of the *ffulness of times, which dispensation is now beginning to usher in, that a whole and complete and perfect union, and welding together of dispensations, and keys, and powers, and glories should take place, and be revealed from the days of Adam even to the present time. And not only this, but those things which never have been revealed from the *gfoundation of the world, but have been kept hid from the wise and prudent, shall be revealed unto *hbabes and sucklings in this, the dispensation of the fulness of times.

19 Now, what do we hear in the gospel which we have received? A voice of *agladness! A voice of

13b TG Symbolism.
14a TG Sealing.
  b TG Priesthood, Keys of.
  c Luke 11: 52.
    TG Knowledge.
15a TG Mission of Latter-day Saints; Salvation, Plan of.
  b Heb. 11: 40.
    TG Perfection.

17a TG Restoration of the Gospel.
  b 3 Ne. 25: 5 (5–6);
    D&C 2: 1; 35: 4; 110: 14 (13–16).
18a D&C 2: 2 (1–3);
    JS-H 1: 39 (36–39).
  b TG Curse.
  c TG Genealogy and Temple Work.

d TG Family, Children, Duties of.
e 1 Cor. 15: 29;
  D&C 124: 29 (28–29); 127: 6.
f D&C 138: 53.
g D&C 35: 18.
h Matt. 11: 25; Luke 10: 21; Alma 32: 23.
19a TG Happiness; Joy.

mercy from heaven; and a voice of *b*truth out of the earth; glad tidings for the dead; a voice of gladness for the living and the dead; glad tidings of great *c*joy. How beautiful upon the mountains are the *d*feet of those that bring glad tidings of good things, and that say unto Zion: Behold, thy God reigneth! As the *e*dews of Carmel, so shall the knowledge of God descend upon them!

20 And again, what do we hear? Glad tidings from *a*Cumorah! *b*Moroni, an angel from heaven, declaring the fulfilment of the prophets— the *c*book to be revealed. A voice of the Lord in the wilderness of Fayette, Seneca county, declaring the three witnesses to *d*bear record of the book! The voice of *e*Michael on the banks of the Susquehanna, detecting the *f*devil when he appeared as an angel of *g*light! The voice of *h*Peter, James, and John in the wilderness near Harmony, Susquehanna county, and Colesville, Broome county, on the Susquehanna river, declaring themselves as possessing the *i*keys of the kingdom, and of the dispensation of the fulness of times!

21 And again, the voice of God in the chamber of old *a*Father Whitmer, in Fayette, Seneca county, and at sundry times, and in divers places through all the travels and tribulations of this Church of Jesus Christ of Latter-day Saints! And the voice of Michael, the archangel; the voice of *b*Gabriel, and of Raphael, and of divers *c*angels, from Michael or

*d*Adam down to the present time, all declaring their *e*dispensation, their rights, their *f*keys, their honors, their majesty and glory, and the power of their priesthood; giving line upon line, *g*precept upon precept; here a little, and there a little; giving us consolation by holding forth that which is to come, confirming our *h*hope!

22 Brethren, shall we not go on in so great a cause? Go forward and not backward. *a*Courage, brethren; and on, on to the victory! Let your hearts rejoice, and be exceedingly glad. Let the earth break forth into *b*singing. Let the *c*dead speak forth anthems of eternal praise to the *d*King Immanuel, who hath ordained, before the world was, that which would enable us to *e*redeem them out of their *f*prison; for the prisoners shall go free.

23 Let the *a*mountains shout for joy, and all ye valleys cry aloud; and all ye seas and dry lands tell the wonders of your Eternal King! And ye rivers, and brooks, and rills, flow down with gladness. Let the woods and all the trees of the field praise the Lord; and ye solid *b*rocks weep for joy! And let the sun, moon, and the *c*morning stars sing together, and let all the sons of God shout for joy! And let the eternal creations declare his name forever and ever! And again I say, how glorious is the voice we hear from heaven, proclaiming in our ears, glory, and salvation, and honor, and *d*immortality,

---

19b Ps. 85: 11 (9-11).
c Luke 2: 10.
d Nahum 1: 15; Isa. 52: 7 (7-10); Mosiah 15: 18 (13-18); 3 Ne. 20: 40.
e Deut. 32: 2; Isa. 26: 19; Hosea 14: 5; D&C 121: 45.
20a JS-H 1: 51 (51-52).
b D&C 27: 5 (5-16).
c Isa. 29: 11 (4, 11-14); 2 Ne. 27: 6 (6-29).
d D&C 17: 3 (1-9).
e D&C 27: 11. TG Adam.
f TG Devil.
g 2 Cor. 11: 14 (13-15).

h Matt. 17: 1; D&C 27: 12.
i TG Priesthood, History of; Priesthood, Keys of; Priesthood, Melchizedek.
21a D&C 30: 4. See also HC 1: 60-61.
b Dan. 8: 16; Luke 1: 19 (19, 26).
c TG Angels.
d 2 Ne. 9: 21; D&C 107: 54 (53-56).
e TG Dispensations.
f TG Priesthood, Keys of.
g Isa. 28: 10.
h 1 Cor. 15: 19. TG Hope.

22a TG Courage; Zeal.
b Isa. 49: 13.
c Isa. 25: 8; 26: 19.
d Isa. 7: 14; Matt. 2: 2; 2 Ne. 10: 14; Alma 5: 50; Moses 7: 53; Abr. 3: 27.
e TG Redemption; Salvation, Plan of.
f Isa. 24: 22; 49: 9; D&C 76: 73 (72-74).
23a Isa. 42: 11 (10-14); 44: 23; 55: 1.
b Luke 19: 40.
c Job 38: 7.
d TG Eternal Life; Immortality.

and eternal life; kingdoms, principalities, and powers!

24 Behold, the great *"day of the Lord is at hand; and who can *abide the day of his coming, and who can stand when he appeareth? For he is like a *refiner's *fire, and like fuller's soap; and he shall sit as a *refiner and purifier of silver, and he shall purify the sons of *Levi, and purge them as gold and silver, that they may offer unto the Lord an *offering in righteousness. Let us, therefore, as a church and a people, and as Latter-

day Saints, offer unto the Lord an offering in righteousness; and let us present in his holy temple, when it is finished, a book containing the *records of our dead, which shall be worthy of all acceptation.

25 Brethren, I have many things to say to you on the subject; but shall now close for the present, and continue the subject another time. I am, as ever, your humble servant and never deviating friend,

JOSEPH SMITH.

SECTION 129

Instructions given by Joseph Smith the Prophet, at Nauvoo, Illinois, February 9, 1843, making known three grand keys by which the correct nature of ministering angels and spirits may be distinguished. HC 5: 267.

1–3, There are both resurrected and spirit bodies in heaven; 4–9, Keys are given whereby messengers from beyond the veil may be identified.

THERE are two kinds of beings in *heaven, namely: *Angels, who are *resurrected personages, having *bodies of flesh and bones—

2 For instance, Jesus said: *Handle me and see, for a spirit hath not *flesh and bones, as ye see me have.*

3 Secondly: the *"spirits of *just men made *perfect, they who are not resurrected, but inherit the same glory.

4 When a messenger comes saying he has a message from God, offer him your hand and request him to shake hands with you.

5 If he be an angel he will do so, and you will feel his hand.

6 If he be the spirit of a just man made perfect he will come in his glory; for that is the only way he can appear—

7 Ask him to shake hands with you, but he will not move, because it is contrary to the *order of heaven for a just man to *deceive; but he will still deliver his message.

8 If it be the *devil as an angel of light, when you ask him to shake hands with you he will offer you his hand, and you will not *feel anything; you may therefore detect him.

9 These are three grand *keys whereby you may know whether any administration is from God.

24a TG Day of the Lord.
  b Mal. 3: 2 (1–3).
  c TG Earth, Cleansing of; Jesus Christ, Second Coming.
  d Num. 11: 1 (1, 10); D&C 35: 14; Moses 7: 34.
  e Prov. 17: 3; Zech. 13: 9; 3 Ne. 24: 2 (2–3).
  f Deut. 10: 8; 3 Ne. 24: 3; D&C 13: 1; 124: 39.
  g D&C 84: 31.
     TG Sacrifice.

  h Num. 1: 18; D&C 127: 9 (5–10). TG Genealogy and Temple Work; Mission of Latter-day Saints; Salvation for the Dead.
129 1a TG Heaven.
   b TG Angels.
   c TG Resurrection.
   d Matt. 27: 52 (52–53).
  2a Luke 24: 39.
  3a TG Spirit Body; Spirits, Disembodied.

   b Gen. 6: 9; Heb. 12: 23; D&C 76: 69.
   c TG Man, Potential to Become Like Heavenly Father.
  7a TG Order.
   b TG Deceit; Lying.
  8a 2 Cor. 11: 14; 2 Ne. 9: 9.
     TG Spirits, Evil, Unclean.
   b D&C 131: 8 (7–8).
  9a 1 Jn. 4: 1 (1–6).
     TG Discernment, Spiritual.

SECTION 130

Items of instruction given by Joseph Smith the Prophet, at Ramus, Illinois, April 2, 1843. HC 5: 323–325.

1–3, The Father and the Son may appear personally to men; 4–7, Angels reside in a celestial sphere; 8–9, The celestial earth will be a great Urim and Thummim; 10–11, A white stone is given to all who enter the celestial world; 12–17, The time of the Second Coming is withheld from the Prophet; 18–19, Intelligence gained in this life rises with us in the resurrection; 20–21, All blessings come by obedience to law; 22–23, The Father and the Son have bodies of flesh and bones.

WHEN the Savior shall *a*appear we shall see him as he is. We shall see that he is a *b*man like ourselves.

2 And that same *a*sociality which exists among us here will exist among us there, only it will be coupled with *b*eternal glory, which glory we do not now enjoy.

3 John 14:23—The *a*appearing of the Father and the Son, in that verse, is a personal *a*appearance; and the idea that the Father and the Son *c*dwell in a man's heart is an old sectarian notion, and is false.

4 In answer to the question—Is not the reckoning of God's *a*time, angel's time, prophet's time, and man's time, according to the planet on which they reside?

5 I answer, Yes. But there are no *a*angels who *b*minister to this earth but those who do belong or have belonged to it.

6 The angels do not reside on a planet like this earth;

7 But *a*they reside in the *b*presence of God, on a globe *c*like a *d*sea of glass and *e*fire, where all things for their glory are manifest, past, present, and future, and are continually before the Lord.

8 The place where God resides is a great *a*Urim and Thummim.

9 This *a*earth, in its *b*sanctified and *c*immortal state, will be made like unto *d*crystal and will be a Urim and Thummim to the inhabitants who dwell thereon, whereby all things pertaining to an inferior kingdom, or all kingdoms of a lower order, will be manifest to those who dwell on it; and this earth will be *e*Christ's.

10 Then the white *a*stone mentioned in Revelation 2:17, will become a Urim and Thummim to each individual who receives one, whereby things pertaining to a *b*higher order of kingdoms will be made known;

11 And a *a*white stone is given to each of those who come into the celestial kingdom, whereon is a new *b*name written, which no man

---

130 1a 1 Jn. 3: 2.
    TG Jesus Christ,
    Second Coming.
  b TG God, Body of
    (Corporeal Nature);
    Man, Potential to
    Become Like Heavenly
    Father.
2a TG Family, Eternal;
    Family, Love within;
    Marriage, Continuing
    Courtship in.
  b TG Celestial Glory;
    Eternal Life.
3a TG God, Privilege of
    Seeing.
  b John 14: 23 (21–23);

D&C 93: 1.
    TG Revelation.
  c Alma 34: 36;
    D&C 130: 22.
4a Abr. 3: 9 (4–10); 4: 13
    (13–14); 5: 13.
    TG Time.
5a TG Angels.
  b D&C 7: 6; 43: 25; 129:
    3 (3, 6–7).
7a Matt. 18: 10; 25: 31;
    2 Thes. 1: 7; D&C 76:
    21; 136: 37.
  b 1 Tim. 6: 16; D&C 76:
    62, 94 (94, 119); 88:
    19. TG God, Presence of.
  c Ezek. 1: 4 (4, 26–28);

Hel. 5: 23; D&C 133:
    41; 137: 2.
  d Rev. 4: 6; 15: 2 (1–4).
  e Isa. 33: 14.
8a TG Urim and
    Thummim.
9a TG Earth, Destiny of.
  b D&C 77: 1.
  c TG Immortality.
  d Ezek. 1: 22.
  e TG Jesus Christ, King.
10a TG Urim and
    Thummim.
  b Abr. 3: 3 (3–17).
11a Rev. 2: 17.
  b Isa. 54: 2; 65: 15;
    Mosiah 5: 12 (9–14).

knoweth save he that receiveth it. The new name is the key word.

12 I prophesy, in the name of the Lord God, that the commencement of the *a*difficulties which will cause much bloodshed previous to the coming of the Son of Man will be in South Carolina.

13 It may probably arise through the slave question. This *a*voice declared to me, while I was praying earnestly on the subject, December 25th, 1832.

14 I was once praying very earnestly to know the time of the *a*coming of the Son of Man, when I heard a voice repeat the following:

15 Joseph, my son, if thou livest until thou art eighty-five years old, thou shalt see the face of the Son of Man; therefore *a*let this suffice, and trouble me no more on this matter.

16 I was left thus, without being able to decide whether this coming referred to the beginning of the millennium or to some previous appearing, or whether I should die and thus see his face.

17 I believe the coming of the Son of Man will not be any sooner than that time.

18 Whatever principle of *a*intelligence we attain unto in this life, it will rise with us in the *b*resurrection.

19 And if a person gains more *a*knowledge and intelligence in this life through his *b*diligence and obedience than another, he will have so much the *c*advantage in the world to come.

20 There is a *a*law, irrevocably decreed in *b*heaven before the foundations of this world, upon which all *c*blessings are predicated—

21 And when we obtain any *a*blessing from God, it is by *b*obedience to that law upon which it is predicated.

22 The *a*Father has a *b*body of flesh and bones as tangible as man's; the Son also; but the Holy Ghost has not a body of flesh and bones, but is a personage of *c*Spirit. Were it not so, the Holy Ghost could not *d*dwell in us.

23 A man may receive the *a*Holy Ghost, and it may descend upon him and not *b*tarry with him.

SECTION 131

Instructions by Joseph Smith the Prophet, given at Ramus, Illinois, May 16 and 17, 1843. HC 5: 392–393.

1 4, Celestial marriage is essential to exaltation in the highest heaven; 5–6,	How men are sealed up unto eternal life; 7–8, All spirit is matter.

12a D&C 38: 29; 45: 63 (26, 63); 87: 2 (1–5).
   TG War.
13a TG Revelation.
14a TG Jesus Christ, Prophecies about; Jesus Christ, Second Coming.
15a Matt. 24: 36 (36–42); D&C 49: 7.
18a 2 Ne. 9: 13 (13–14); D&C 93: 36.
   TG Intelligence; Learning.
   b TG Resurrection.
19a TG Education; Knowledge; Objectives.

   b TG Diligence.
   c Matt. 25: 21 (14–29); Alma 12: 10 (9–11).
20a Jer. 26: 4; D&C 82: 10.
   b TG Council in Heaven; God, Law of.
   c Ex. 32: 29; Deut. 11: 27 (26–28); D&C 132: 5.
21a Deut. 6: 24; Alma 45: 16 (15–17).
   TG Blessing.
   b TG Obedience.
22a TG God the Father—Elohim; Godhead; Man, Potential to

Become Like Heavenly Father.
   b John 4: 24 (23–24); 14: 9; Acts 17: 28 (25–29); Heb. 1: 3. TG God, Body of (Corporeal Nature); God, Knowledge about; God, Manifestations of.
   c TG Spirit Body.
   d 2 Tim. 1: 14. TG Holy Ghost, Mission of.
23a TG Holy Ghost, Gift of.
   b TG Holy Ghost, Loss of.

IN the ^acelestial glory there are three ^bheavens or degrees;

2 And in order to obtain the ^ahighest, a man must enter into this ^border of the ^cpriesthood [meaning the new and ^deverlasting covenant of ^emarriage];

3 And if he does not, he cannot obtain it.

4 He may enter into the other, but that is the end of his kingdom; he cannot have an ^dincrease.

5 (May 17th, 1843.) The more sure word of ^aprophecy means a man's

knowing that he is ^bsealed up unto ^ceternal life, by revelation and the spirit of prophecy, through the power of the Holy Priesthood.

6 It is impossible for a man to be ^asaved in ^bignorance.

7 There is no such thing as immaterial matter. All ^aspirit is matter, but it is more fine or pure, and can only be discerned by ^bpurer eyes;

8 We cannot ^asee it; but when our bodies are purified we shall see that it is all ^bmatter.

SECTION 132

Revelation given through Joseph Smith the Prophet, at Nauvoo, Illinois, recorded July 12, 1843, relating to the new and everlasting covenant, including the eternity of the marriage covenant, as also plurality of wives. HC 5: 501–507. Although the revelation was recorded in 1843, it is evident from the historical records that the doctrines and principles involved in this revelation had been known by the Prophet since 1831.

1–6, Exaltation is gained through the new and everlasting covenant; 7–14, The terms and conditions of that covenant are set forth; 15–20, Celestial marriage and a continuation of the family unit enable men to become gods; 21–25, The strait and narrow way that leads to eternal lives; 26–27, Law given relative to blasphemy against the Holy Ghost; 28–39, Promises of eternal increase and exaltation made to prophets and saints in all ages; 40–47, Joseph Smith is given the power to bind and seal on earth and in heaven; 48–50, The Lord seals upon him his exaltation; 51–57, Emma Smith is counseled to be faithful and true; 58–66, Laws governing the plurality of wives are set forth.

VERILY, thus saith the Lord unto you my servant Joseph, that inasmuch as you have inquired of my hand to know and understand wherein I, the Lord, justified my servants Abraham, Isaac, and Jacob, as also Moses, David and Solomon, my servants, as touching the principle

131 1*a* D&C 76: 70.
    TG Celestial Glory.
  b TG Heaven. See also "Heaven" in BD.
  2*a* D&C 132: 21 (5–21).
    TG Family, Eternal; Man, Potential to Become Like Heavenly Father.
  b TG Genealogy and Temple Work.
  c TG Priesthood, Melchizedek.

  d TG New and Everlasting Covenant.
  4*a* Matt. 22: 30 (23–33); D&C 132: 16–17.
    TG Marriage, Fatherhood; Marriage, Motherhood.
  5*a* 2 Pet. 1: 19 (3–21).
    TG Prophecy.
  b TG Election; Eternal Life; Sealing.
  c D&C 68: 12; 88: 4.
  6*a* TG Salvation.

  b Mal. 2: 7 (7–9); D&C 90: 15 (14–15); 107: 99 (99–100).
    TG Apathy; Education; Ignorance; Knowledge; Learning.
  7*a* TG Spirit Body; Spirit Creation.
  b D&C 76: 12; 97: 16; Moses 1: 11.
  8*a* D&C 129: 8.
  b D&C 77: 2; Moses 3: 5 (5–9).

and doctrine of their having many ^awives and ^bconcubines—

2 Behold, and lo, I am the Lord thy God, and will answer thee as touching this matter.

3 Therefore, ^aprepare thy heart to receive and ^bobey the instructions which I am about to give unto you; for all those who have this law revealed unto them must obey the same.

4 For behold, I reveal unto you a new and an everlasting ^acovenant; and if ye abide not that covenant, then are ye ^bdamned; for no one can ^creject this covenant and be permitted to enter into my glory.

5 For all who will have a ^ablessing at my hands shall abide the ^blaw which was appointed for that blessing, and the conditions thereof, as were instituted from before the foundation of the world.

6 And as pertaining to the new and ^aeverlasting covenant, it was instituted for the fulness of my ^bglory; and he that receiveth a fulness thereof must and shall abide the law, or he shall be damned, saith the Lord God.

7 And verily I say unto you, that the ^aconditions of this law are these: All covenants, contracts, bonds, obligations, ^boaths, ^cvows, performances, connections, associations, or expectations, that are not made and entered into and ^dsealed by the Holy Spirit of ^epromise, of him who is ^fanointed, both as well for time and for all eternity, and

that too most holy, by ^frevelation and commandment through the medium of mine anointed, whom I have appointed on the earth to hold this ^gpower (and I have appointed unto my servant Joseph to hold this ^hpower in the last days, and there is never but one on the earth at a time on whom this power and the ⁱkeys of this priesthood are conferred), are of no efficacy, virtue, or force in or after the resurrection from the dead; for all contracts that are not made unto this end have an end when men are dead.

8 Behold, mine house is a house of ^aorder, saith the Lord God, and not a house of confusion.

9 Will I ^aaccept of an offering, saith the Lord, that is not made in my name?

10 Or will I receive at your hands that which I have not ^aappointed?

11 And will I appoint unto you, saith the Lord, except it be by law, even as I and my Father ^aordained unto you, before the world was?

12 I am the Lord thy God; and I give unto you this commandment—that no man shall ^acome unto the Father but by me or by my word, which is my law, saith the Lord.

13 And everything that is in the world, whether it be ordained of men, by ^athrones, or principalities, or powers, or things of name, whatsoever they may be, that are not by me or by my word, saith the Lord, shall be thrown down, and shall ^bnot remain after men are dead, neither

---

132 1a Ex. 21: 10 (1, 7–11); Jacob 2: 24 (23–30); D&C 132: 38 (34, 37–39). TG Marriage, Plural.
  b Gen. 25: 6.
    TG Concubine.
3a Ezra 7: 10; D&C 29: 8; 58: 6; 78: 7.
  b TG Obedience.
4a TG Covenants.
  b D&C 84: 24.
  c D&C 131: 2 (1–4).
5a Ex. 32: 29; D&C 130: 20; 132: 11 (11, 28, 32).
  b TG God, Law of.

6a D&C 66: 2. TG New and Everlasting Covenant.
  b D&C 76: 70 (50–70, 92–96). TG Celestial Glory.
7a D&C 88: 39 (38–39).
  b TG Oath.
  c TG Vow.
  d TG Holy Ghost, Mission of; Holy Spirit; Sealing.
  e TG Priesthood, Authority.
  f Prophets, Mission of; Revelation.
  g TG Priesthood,

Power of.
  h TG Priesthood, Authority.
  i TG Priesthood, Keys of.
8a TG Order.
9a Lev. 7: 18 (16–18); 17: 8 (8–9); Moro. 7: 6 (5–6). TG Sacrifice.
10a Lev. 22: 20 (20–25); Moses 5: 21.
11a D&C 49: 15; 132: 5 (5, 63).
12a Isa. 55: 3; John 14: 6. TG God, Access to.
13a TG Governments; Kings, Earthly.
  b 3 Ne. 27: 11 (10–11).

in nor after the resurrection, saith the Lord your God.

14 For whatsoever things remain are by me; and whatsoever things are not by me shall be shaken and destroyed.

15 Therefore, if a "man marry him a wife in the world, and he marry her not by me nor by my word, and he covenant with her so long as he is in the world and she with him, their covenant and marriage are not of force when they are dead, and when they are out of the world; therefore, they are not bound by any law when they are out of the world.

16 Therefore, when they are out of the world they neither marry nor are given in "marriage; but are appointed angels in "heaven, which angels are ministering "servants, to minister for those who are worthy of a far more, and an exceeding, and an eternal weight of glory.

17 For these angels did not abide my law; therefore, they cannot be enlarged, but remain separately and singly, without exaltation, in their saved condition, to all eternity; and from henceforth are not gods, but are "angels of God forever and ever.

18 And again, verily I say unto you, if a man marry a wife, and make a covenant with her for time and for all eternity, if that "covenant is not by me or by my word, which is my law, and is not sealed by the Holy Spirit of promise, through him whom I have anointed and appointed unto this power, then it is not valid neither of force when they are out of the world, because they are not joined by me, saith the Lord, neither by

my word; when they are out of the world it cannot be received there, because the angels and the gods are appointed there, by whom they cannot pass; they cannot, therefore, inherit my glory; for my house is a house of order, saith the Lord.

19 And again, verily I say unto you, if a man "marry a wife by my word, which is my law, and by the new and "everlasting covenant, and it is "sealed unto them by the Holy Spirit of "promise, by him who is anointed, unto whom I have appointed this power and the "keys of this priesthood; and it shall be said unto them—Ye shall come forth in the first resurrection; and if it be after the first resurrection, in the next resurrection; and shall inherit "thrones, kingdoms, principalities, and powers, dominions, all heights and depths—then shall it be written in the Lamb's "Book of Life, that he shall commit no "murder whereby to shed innocent "blood, and if ye abide in my covenant, and commit no murder whereby to shed innocent blood, it shall be done unto them in all things whatsoever my servant hath put upon them, in time, and through all eternity; and shall be of full force when they are out of the world; and they shall pass by the angels, and the gods, which are set there, to their "exaltation and glory in all things, as hath been sealed upon their heads, which glory shall be a fulness and a continuation of the "seeds forever and ever.

20 Then shall they be gods, because they have no end; therefore shall they be from "everlasting to ever-

---

15a TG Marriage, Husbands; Marriage, Interfaith; Marriage, Temporal; Marriage, Wives.
16a Matt. 22: 30 (23–33); Mark 12: 25; Luke 20: 35 (27–36).
  TG Marriage.
  b D&C 131: 4 (1–4).
  TG Heaven.
  c TG Servant.
17a Luke 20: 36.

18a D&C 132: 7 (7, 46–47).
19a TG Marriage, Celestial; Marriage, Wives.
  b TG New and Everlasting Covenant.
  c TG Sealing.
  d 2 Pet. 1: 19; D&C 68: 12; 76: 53; 88: 3 (3–4); 124: 124; 132: 49.
  e TG Priesthood, Keys of.
  f Ex. 19: 6; Rev. 5: 10;

   20: 6; D&C 76: 56; 78: 15 (15, 18).
  g TG Book of Life.
  h TG Murder.
  i Jer. 22: 3. TG Blood, Shedding of; Life, Sanctity of.
  j TG Celestial Glory; Election; Exaltation; Glory.
  k TG Family, Eternal; Family, Patriarchal.
20a Rev. 22: 5 (1–5).

lasting, because they continue; then shall they be above all, because all things are subject unto them. Then shall they be [b]gods, because they have [c]all power, and the angels are subject unto them.

21 Verily, verily, I say unto you, except ye abide my [a]law ye cannot attain to this glory.

22 For [a]strait is the gate, and narrow the [b]way that leadeth unto the exaltation and continuation of the [c]lives, and few there be that find it, because ye receive me not in the world neither do ye know me.

23 But if ye receive me in the world, then shall ye know me, and shall receive your exaltation; that [a]where I am ye shall be also.

24 This is [a]eternal lives—to [b]know the only wise and true God, and Jesus Christ, whom he hath [c]sent. I am he. Receive ye, therefore, my law.

25 [a]Broad is the gate, and wide the way that leadeth to the [b]deaths; and many there are that go in thereat, because they [c]receive me not, neither do they abide in my law.

26 Verily, verily, I say unto you, if a man marry a wife according to my word, and they are sealed by the [a]Holy Spirit of promise, according to mine appointment, and he or she shall commit any sin or transgres-

sion of the new and everlasting covenant whatever, and all manner of blasphemies, and if they [b]commit no murder wherein they shed innocent blood, yet they shall come forth in the first resurrection, and enter into their exaltation; but they shall be destroyed in the flesh, and shall be [c]delivered unto the buffetings of [d]Satan unto the day of [e]redemption, saith the Lord God.

27 The [a]blasphemy against the Holy Ghost, which shall [b]not be [c]forgiven in the world nor out of the world, is in that ye commit [d]murder wherein ye shed innocent blood, and assent unto my death, after ye have received my new and everlasting covenant, saith the Lord God; and he that abideth not this law can in nowise enter into my glory, but shall be [e]damned, saith the Lord.

28 I am the Lord thy God, and will give unto thee the [a]law of my Holy Priesthood, as was ordained by me and my Father before the world was.

29 [a]Abraham received all things, whatsoever he received, by revelation and commandment, by my word, saith the Lord, and hath entered into his exaltation and sitteth upon his throne.

30 [a]Abraham received promises concerning his seed, and of the fruit of his loins—from whose [b]loins ye

20b Matt. 25: 21; D&C 132: 37.
  TG Exaltation; Man, Potential to Become Like Heavenly Father.
  c D&C 29: 13 (12–13); 50: 27 (26–28); 76: 95; 78: 5 (5–7); 84: 38 (35–39).
21a TG God, Law of.
22a Luke 13: 24 (22–30); 2 Ne. 33: 9; Hel. 3: 29 (29–30).
  b Matt. 7: 23 (esp. JST); 2 Ne. 9: 41; 31: 21 (17–21).
  c D&C 132: 30 (30–31).
23a John 14: 3 (2–3).
24a John 17: 3. TG Eternal Life.
  b TG God, Knowledge about.

c John 3: 17 (16–17); D&C 49: 5.
25a Gen. 6: 12; 2 Ne. 28: 11; Hel. 6: 31; 3 Ne. 14: 13 (13–15).
  b Matt. 7: 13 (13–14).
  TG Death, Spiritual, First; Death, Spiritual, Second.
  c John 5: 43.
26a D&C 88: 3 (3–4); 132: 19 (7, 19–20).
  b Alma 39: 5 (5–6).
  TG Blood, Shedding of.
  c 1 Tim. 1: 20; D&C 82: 21; 104: 9 (9–10).
  d TG Devil.
  e TG Redemption.
27a Blasphemy; Holy Ghost, Unpardonable Sin against; Sin.
  b Matt. 12: 32 (31–32);

Heb. 6: 4 (4–6); 10: 29 (26–29); D&C 42: 18; 76: 34 (31, 34–35); 84: 41.
  c TG Death, Spiritual, Second; Forgiveness; Sons of Perdition.
  d TG Murder.
28a Acts 17: 26; D&C 132: 5.
  TG Damnation.
29a D&C 132: 5; D&C 132: 37; 133: 55; 137: 5; Abr. 2: 11 (9–11).
30a Gen. 12: 3 (1–3); 13: 16; 2 Ne. 26: 42; Gal. 3: 14 (7–14, 26–29); 2 Ne. 29: 14; D&C 84: 34.
  TG Abrahamic Covenant; Seed of Abraham.
  b 2 Ne. 3: 6 (6–16).

are, namely, my servant Joseph—which were to continue so long as they were in the world; and as touching Abraham and his seed, out of the world they should continue; both in the world and out of the world should they continue as innumerable as the [f]stars; or, if ye were to count the sand upon the seashore ye could not number them.

31 This promise is yours also, because ye are of [a]Abraham, and the promise was made unto Abraham; and by this law is the continuation of the works of my Father, wherein he glorifieth himself.

32 Go ye, therefore, and do the [a]works of Abraham; enter ye into my law and ye shall be saved.

33 But if ye enter not into my law ye cannot receive the promise of my Father, which I made unto Abraham.

34 God [a]commanded Abraham, and Sarah gave [b]Hagar to Abraham to wife. And why did she do it? Because this was the law; and from Hagar sprang many people. This, therefore, was fulfilling, among other things, the promises.

35 Was Abraham, therefore, under condemnation? Verily I say unto you, Nay; for I, the Lord, [a]commanded it.

36 Abraham was [a]commanded to offer his son Isaac; nevertheless, it was written: Thou shalt not [b]kill. Abraham, however, did not refuse, and it was accounted unto him for [c]righteousness.

37 Abraham received [a]concubines,

and they bore him children; and it was accounted unto them for righteousness, because they were given unto him, and he abode in my law; as Isaac also and [b]Jacob did none other things than that which they were commanded; and because they did none other things than that which they have commanded, they have entered into their [c]exaltation, according to the promises, and sit upon thrones, and are not angels but are gods.

38 David also received [a]many wives and concubines, and also Solomon and Moses my servants, as also many others of my servants, from the beginning of creation until this time; and in nothing did they sin save in those things which they received not of me.

39 [a]David's wives and concubines were [b]given unto him of me, by the hand of Nathan, my servant, and others of the prophets who had the [c]keys of this power; and in none of these things did he [d]sin against me save in the case of [e]Uriah and his wife; and, therefore he hath [f]fallen from his exaltation, and received his portion; and he shall not inherit them out of the world, for I [g]gave them unto another, saith the Lord.

40 I am the Lord thy God, and I gave unto thee, my servant Joseph, an [a]appointment, and restore all things. Ask what ye will, and it shall be given unto you according to my word.

41 And as ye have asked concerning adultery, verily, verily, I

30c Gen. 15: 5; 22: 17;
Deut. 1: 10; 1 Chr. 27:
23; Neh. 9: 23;
Hosea 1: 10.
31a D&C 86: 9 (8–11);
110: 12.
32a John 8: 39; Alma 5: 24
(22–24).
34a Gen. 16: 2 (1–3);
Gal. 4: 22 (21–31);
D&C 132: 65.
b Gen. 25: 12 (12–18).
35a Jacob 2: 30 (24–30).
36a Gen. 22: 2 (2–12).
b Ex. 20: 13.

c Gen. 15: 6; Jacob 4: 5.
TG Righteousness.
37a Gen. 25: 6.
b Gen. 30: 4 (3–4);
D&C 133: 55.
c TG Exaltation; Man,
Potential to Become
Like Heavenly Father.
38a Ex. 21: 10 (1, 7–11);
1 Sam. 25: 43 (42–43);
2 Sam. 5: 13; 1 Kgs.
11: 3 (1–3); Jacob 1:
15; D&C 132: 1.
39a 1 Sam. 27: 3; 2 Sam. 2:
2; 1 Chr. 14: 3;

Jacob 2: 24 (23–24).
b 2 Sam. 12: 8.
c TG Priesthood, Keys
of.
d 2 Sam. 11: 27.
TG Adultery; Sin.
e 2 Sam. 11: 4; 12: 9
(1–15); 1 Kgs. 15: 5;
1 Chr. 11: 41.
f Ps. 89: 39.
TG Punishment.
g Jer. 8: 10.
40a JS-H 1: 33 (18–20, 26,
33). TG Prophets,
Mission of; Restoration of the Gospel.

say unto you, if a man [a]receiveth a wife in the new and everlasting covenant, and if she be with another man, and I have not appointed unto her by the holy [b]anointing, she hath committed [c]adultery and shall be destroyed.

42 If she be not in the new and everlasting covenant, and she be with another man, she has [a]committed adultery.

43 And if her husband be with another woman, and he was under a [a]vow, he hath broken his vow and hath committed adultery.

44 And if she hath not committed adultery, but is innocent and hath not broken her vow, and she knoweth it, and I reveal it unto you, my servant Joseph, then shall you have power, by the power of my Holy Priesthood, to take her and [a]give her unto him that hath not committed [b]adultery but hath been [c]faithful; for he shall be made ruler over many.

45 For I have conferred upon you the [a]keys and power of the priesthood, wherein I [b]restore all things, and make known unto you all things in due time.

46 And verily, verily, I say unto you, that whatsoever you [a]seal on earth shall be sealed in heaven; and whatsoever you [b]bind on earth, in my name and by my word, saith the Lord, it shall be eternally bound in the heavens; and whosoever sins you [c]remit on earth shall be remitted eternally in the heavens; and whosoever sins you retain on earth shall be retained in heaven.

47 And again, verily I say, whomsoever you bless I will bless, and whomsoever you curse I will [a]curse, saith the Lord; for I, the Lord, am thy God.

48 And again, verily I say unto you, my servant Joseph, that whatsoever you give on earth, and to whomsoever you [a]give any one on earth, by my word and according to my law, it shall be visited with blessings and not cursings, and with my power, saith the Lord, and shall be without condemnation on earth and in heaven.

49 For I am the Lord thy God, and will be [a]with thee even unto the [b]end of the world, and through all eternity; for verily I [c]seal upon you your [d]exaltation, and prepare a throne for you in the kingdom of my Father, with Abraham your [e]father.

50 Behold, I have seen your [a]sacrifices, and will forgive all your sins; I have seen your [b]sacrifices in obedience to that which I have told you. Go, therefore, and I make a way for your escape, and I [c]accepted the offering of Abraham of his son Isaac.

51 Verily, I say unto you: A commandment I give unto mine handmaid, Emma Smith, your wife, whom I have given unto you, that she stay herself and partake not of that which I commanded you to offer unto her; for I did it, saith the Lord, to [a]prove you all, as I did Abraham, and that I might require an offering at your hand, by covenant and sacrifice.

52 And let mine handmaid, Emma Smith, [a]receive all those that have

---

41a TG D&C 132: 19 (4–7, 19).
 b TG Anointing.
 c TG Adultery.
42a TG D&C 42: 24 (22–26).
43a TG Covenants; Marriage; Vows.
44a TG Divorce.
 b TG Chastity.
 c Luke 16: 10 (10–12); 19: 26 (12–26).
45a TG Priesthood, Keys of.
 b Acts 3: 21; D&C 86: 10. TG Restoration of the Gospel.

46a TG Marriage, Celestial; Sealing.
 b TG Priesthood, Authority.
 c TG Remission of Sins.
47a D&C 3: 1 (1–3); D&C 103: 25; 124: 93.
48a TG D&C 132: 39.
49a TG God, Presence of; Walking with God.
 b Matt. 28: 20.
 c 2 Pet. 1: 19; D&C 68: 12; 132: 19.
 d D&C 5: 22. TG Election.

e Gen. 17: 4 (1–8); 2 Ne. 8: 2; D&C 109: 64.
50a Luke 14: 33 (28–33).
 b TG Sacrifice.
 c Gen. 22: 12 (1–18); Gal. 3: 6; D&C 52: 15; 97: 8; Moses 5: 23.
51a Gen. 22: 1; Ex. 15: 25 (23–26); D&C 98: 14 (12–14); 101: 4; 124: 55; Abr. 3: 25. TG Test, Try, Prove.
52a D&C 132: 65.

been given unto my servant Joseph, and who are virtuous and pure before me; and those who are not pure, and have said they were pure, shall be destroyed, saith the Lord God.

53 For I am the Lord thy God, and ye shall obey my voice; and I give unto my servant Joseph that he shall be made ruler over many things; for he hath been *a*faithful over a few things, and from henceforth I will strengthen him.

54 And I command mine handmaid, Emma Smith, to abide and *a*cleave unto my servant Joseph, and to none else. But if she will not abide this commandment she shall be *b*destroyed, saith the Lord; for I am the Lord thy God, and will destroy her if she abide not in my law.

55 But if she will not abide this commandment, then shall my servant Joseph do all things for her, even as he hath said; and I will bless him and multiply him and give unto him an *a*hundredfold in this world, of fathers and mothers, brothers and sisters, houses and lands, wives and children, and crowns of *b*eternal lives in the eternal worlds.

56 And again, verily I say, let mine handmaid *a*forgive my servant Joseph his trespasses; and then shall she be forgiven her trespasses, wherein she hath trespassed against me; and I, the Lord thy God, will bless her, and multiply her, and make her heart to *b*rejoice.

57 And again, I say, let not my servant Joseph put his property out of his hands, lest an enemy come and destroy him; for *a*Satan *b*seeketh to destroy; for I am the Lord thy God, and he is my servant; and

behold, and lo, I am with him, as I was with Abraham, thy father, even unto his *c*exaltation and glory.

58 Now, as touching the law of the *a*priesthood, there are many things pertaining thereunto.

59 Verily, if a man be called of my Father, as was *a*Aaron, by mine own voice, and by the voice of him that *b*sent me, and I have endowed him with the *c*keys of the power of this priesthood, if he do anything in my name, and according to my law and by my word, he will not commit *d*sin, and I will justify him.

60 Let no one, therefore, set on my servant Joseph; for I will justify him; for he shall do the sacrifice which I require at his hands for his transgressions, saith the Lord your God.

61 And again, as pertaining to the law of the priesthood—if any man espouse a virgin, and desire to espouse *a*another, and if the first give her consent, and if he espouse the second, and they are virgins, and have vowed to no other man, then is he justified; he cannot commit adultery for they are given unto him; for he cannot commit adultery with that that belongeth unto him and to no one else.

62 And if he have *a*ten virgins given unto him by this law, he cannot commit adultery, for they belong to him, and they are given unto him; therefore is he justified.

63 But if one or either of the ten virgins, after she is espoused, shall be with another man, she has committed adultery, and shall be destroyed; for they are given unto him to *a*multiply and replenish the earth, according to my commandment, and

53a Matt. 25: 21 (14–28);
  D&C 52: 13.
54a D&C 42: 22.
  TG Marriage, Husbands.
  b Acts 3: 23; D&C 25: 15.
55a D&C 132: 22 (22–24).
  b D&C 132: 22 (22–24).
  TG Family, Eternal.
56a Matt. 6: 15 (12–15).

TG Family, Love within; Forgiveness.
57a TG Devil; Enemies.
  b Matt. 10: 28; Rev. 12: 12 (12–17).
  c D&C 132: 37.
58a D&C 84: 19 (19–26).
59a Heb. 5: 4 (1–6).
  TG Priesthood, Qualifying for.

b TG Jesus Christ, Authority of.
c TG Priesthood, Keys of.
d 1 Jn. 5: 18.
61a TG Marriage, Plural.
62a D&C 132: 48. See also D&C, Official Declaration 1.
63a Gen. 1: 22 (20–25); Jacob 2: 30.

to fulfil the promise which was given by my Father before the foundation of the world, and for their exaltation in the eternal worlds, that they may bear the souls of men; for herein is the work of my Father continued, that he may be [b]glorified.

64 And again, verily, verily, I say unto you, if any man have a wife, who holds the keys of this power, and he teaches unto her the law of my priesthood, as pertaining to these things, then shall she believe and administer unto him, or she shall be destroyed, saith the Lord your God; for I will destroy her; for I will magnify my name upon all those who receive and abide in my law.

65 Therefore, it shall be lawful in me, if she receive not this law, for him to receive all things whatsoever I, the Lord his God, will give unto him, because she did not believe and administer unto him according to my word; and she then becomes the transgressor; and he is exempt from the law of Sarah, who administered unto Abraham according to the law when I commanded Abraham to take [a]Hagar to wife.

66 And now, as pertaining to this law, verily, verily, I say unto you, I will reveal more unto you, hereafter; therefore, let this suffice for the present. Behold, I am Alpha and Omega. Amen.

SECTION 133

Revelation given through Joseph Smith the Prophet, at Hiram, Ohio, November 3, 1831. HC 1: 229–234. Prefacing this revelation the Prophet wrote: "At this time there were many things which the Elders desired to know relative to preaching the Gospel to the inhabitants of the earth, and concerning the gathering; and in order to walk by the true light, and be instructed from on high, on the 3rd of November, 1831, I inquired of the Lord and received the following important revelation." This section was first added to the book of Doctrine and Covenants as an appendix, and was subsequently assigned a section number.

1–6, The saints are commanded to prepare for the Second Coming; 7–16, All men are commanded to flee from Babylon, come to Zion, and prepare for the great day of the Lord; 17–35, He shall stand on Mount Zion, the continents shall become one land, and the lost tribes of Israel shall return; 36–40, The gospel was restored through Joseph Smith to be preached in all the world; 41–51, The Lord shall come down in vengeance upon the wicked; 52–56, It shall be the year of his redeemed; 57–74, The gospel is to be sent forth to save the saints and for the destruction of the wicked.

HEARKEN, O ye people of my church, saith the Lord your God, and hear the word of the Lord concerning you—

2 The Lord who shall suddenly [a]come to his temple; the Lord who shall come down upon the world with a curse to [b]judgment; yea, upon all nations that [c]forget God, and upon all the ungodly among you.

3 For he shall make [a]bare his holy arm in the eyes of all the nations,

---

63b Moses 1: 39.
65a Gen. 16: 2 (1–3); 25:
12; Gal. 4: 22;
D&C 132: 34 (34, 61).
133 2a Mal. 3: 1; D&C

36: 8. TG Jesus Christ,
Second Coming.
b D&C 1: 36. TG Jesus
Christ, Judge; Judgment, The Last.

c 2 Kgs. 17: 38;
Alma 46: 8.
3a Isa. 52: 10. TG God,
Power of.

and all the ends of the earth shall see the ^{b}salvation of their God.

4 Wherefore, prepare ye, prepare ye, O my people; sanctify yourselves; gather ye together, O ye people of my church, upon the land of Zion, all you that have not been commanded to ^{a}tarry.

5 Go ye out from ^{a}Babylon. Be ye ^{b}clean that bear the vessels of the Lord.

6 Call your ^{a}solemn assemblies, and ^{b}speak often one to another. And let every man call upon the name of the Lord.

7 Yea, verily I say unto you again, the time has come when the voice of the Lord is unto you: Go ye out of Babylon; ^{a}gather ye out from among the nations, from the ^{b}four winds, from one end of heaven to the other.

8 Send forth the elders of my church unto the ^{a}nations which are afar off; unto the ^{b}islands of the sea; send forth unto foreign lands; call upon all nations, first upon the ^{c}Gentiles, and then upon the Jews.

9 And behold, and lo, this shall be their cry, and the voice of the Lord unto all people: Go ye forth unto the land of Zion, that the borders of my people may be enlarged, and that her ^{a}stakes may be strengthened, and that ^{b}Zion may go forth unto the regions round about.

10 Yea, let the cry go forth among all people: Awake and arise and go forth to meet the ^{a}Bridegroom; behold and lo, the Bridegroom cometh; go ye out to meet him. Prepare yourselves for the ^{b}great day of the Lord.

11 ^{a}Watch, therefore, for ye ^{b}know neither the day nor the hour.

12 Let them, therefore, who are ^{a}among the Gentiles flee unto ^{b}Zion.

13 And let them who be of ^{a}Judah flee unto ^{b}Jerusalem, unto the ^{c}mountains of the Lord's ^{d}house.

14 Go ye ^{a}out from among the nations, even from ^{b}Babylon, from the midst of ^{c}wickedness, which is spiritual Babylon.

15 But verily, thus saith the Lord, let not your flight be in ^{a}haste, but let all things be prepared before you; and he that goeth, let him ^{b}not look back lest sudden destruction shall come upon him.

16 Hearken and hear, O ye inhabitants of the earth. ^{a}Listen, ye elders of my church together, and hear the voice of the Lord; for he calleth upon all men, and he commandeth all men everywhere to ^{b}repent.

17 For behold, the Lord God hath ^{a}sent forth the angel crying through the midst of heaven, saying: Prepare ye the way of the Lord, and make his

3b Isa. 12:2; 52:10.
  TG Salvation.
4a D&C 62:4; 63:41 (24, 39–41).
5a Alma 5:57; D&C 1:16. TG Worldliness.
  b Isa. 52:11; 2 Tim. 2:21; 3 Ne. 20:41; D&C 38:42. TG Body, Sanctity of; Cleanliness.
6a TG Solemn Assembly.
  b Mal. 3:16 (16–18).
7a D&C 29:8. TG Israel, Gathering of; Mission of Latter-day Saints.
  b Zech. 2:6 (6–7).
8a TG Missionary Work; Nations.
  b Isa. 11:11; 51:5;

1 Ne. 22:4; 2 Ne. 10:8 (8, 20); 29:7.
  c Matt. 19:30; Acts 13:46; D&C 18:26 (26–27); 90:9 (8–9).
9a Isa. 54:2. TG Stakes.
  b D&C 58:25 (25, 56); 63:24; 101:68 (68–71). TG Zion.
10a Matt. 25:6; D&C 33:17 (17–18); 45:56 (54–59).
  b D&C 1:12. TG Day of the Lord.
11a Prov. 27:18; Mark 13:35 (24–37); 1 Ne. 21:23; 2 Ne. 6:13.
  b D&C 49:7.
12a Isa. 4:2; D&C 38:31 (31, 42).
  b TG Jerusalem.

New; Zion.
13a D&C 45:25 (24–25). TG Israel, Judah, People of.
  b TG Jerusalem.
  c Ezek. 38:8; Dan. 11:45; JS-M 1:13.
  d Ps. 122:1 (1–9).
14a TG Israel, Gathering of; Separation.
  b D&C 1:16.
  c TG Wickedness.
15a Isa. 52:12 (10–12); D&C 58:56. TG Haste.
  b Gen. 19:17; Luke 9:62; D&C 67:14.
16a D&C 1:1 (1–6).
  b TG Repentance.
17a D&C 1:1; 27:5 (5–10); 88:92.

paths straight, for the hour of his ᵇcoming is nigh—

18 When the ᵃLamb shall stand upon ᵇMount Zion, and with him a ᶜhundred and forty-four thousand, having his Father's name written on their foreheads.

19 Wherefore, prepare ye for the ᵃcoming of the Bridegroom; go ye, go ye out to meet him.

20 For behold, he shall ᵃstand upon the mount of Olivet, and upon the mighty ocean, even the great deep, and upon the islands of the sea, and upon the land of Zion.

21 And he shall ᵃutter his voice out of ᵇZion, and he shall speak from Jerusalem, and his ᶜvoice shall be heard among all people;

22 And it shall be a voice as the ᵃvoice of many waters, and as the voice of a great ᵇthunder, which shall ᶜbreak down the mountains, and the valleys shall not be found.

23 He shall command the great deep, and it shall be driven back into the north countries, and the ᵃislands shall become one land;

24 And the ᵃland of Jerusalem and the land of ᵇZion shall be turned back into their own place, and the ᶜearth shall be like as it was in the days before it was ᵈdivided.

25 And the Lord, even the Savior, shall ᵃstand in the midst of his people, and shall ᵇreign over all flesh.

26 And they who are in the ᵃnorth countries shall come in remembrance before the Lord; and their prophets shall hear his voice, and shall no longer stay themselves; and they shall ᵇsmite the rocks, and the ice shall flow down at their presence.

27 And an ᵃhighway shall be cast up in the midst of the great deep.

28 Their enemies shall become a prey unto them,

29 And in the ᵃbarren deserts there shall come forth pools of ᵇliving water; and the parched ground shall no longer be a thirsty land.

30 And they shall bring forth their rich ᵃtreasures unto the children of Ephraim, my servants.

31 And the boundaries of the everlasting ᵃhills shall tremble at their presence.

32 And there shall they fall down and be ᵃcrowned with glory, even in Zion, by the hands of the servants of the Lord, even the children of ᵇEphraim.

33 And they shall be filled with ᵃsongs of everlasting joy.

34 Behold, this is the ᵃblessing of the ᵇeverlasting God upon the ᵈtribes

17b Isa. 40: 3 (3–5);
     Mal. 3: 1; Rev. 14: 6
     (6–8). TG Jesus Christ,
     Prophecies about.
18a Rev. 14: 1.
   b D&C 84: 2.
   c Rev. 7: 4 (1–4).
19a Matt. 25: 6 (1–13);
     D&C 33: 17 (17–18);
     88: 92.
20a Isa. 51: 5 (3–6);
     Zech. 14: 4 (4–9);
     3 Ne. 20: 22; 21: 25
     (23–25); D&C 45: 48
     (48–53). TG Jesus
     Christ, Second
     Coming.
21a Joel 3: 16; Amos 1: 2.
   b Isa. 2: 3 (2–4).
   c D&C 45: 49 (48–49).
22a Ezek. 43: 2; Rev. 1:
     15; 19: 6; D&C 110: 3.
   b Ps. 77: 18; Rev. 14: 2.
   c Judg. 5: 5; Isa. 40: 4;

     64: 1; Rev. 16: 20
     (17–21); D&C 49: 23;
     88: 87; 109: 74;
     Moses 6: 34.
23a Rev. 6: 14 (13–17).
24a TG Israel, Land of.
   b TG Zion.
   c TG Earth, Destiny of.
   d Gen. 10: 25. TG Earth,
     Dividing of; Earth,
     Renewal of.
25a Isa. 12: 6.
   b TG Jesus Christ, King;
     Jesus Christ, Second
     Coming; Millennium.
26a Jer. 16: 15 (14–15);
     D&C 110: 11.
     TG Israel, Bondage of,
     in Other Lands; Israel,
     Tribes of, Ten Lost.
   b Ex. 17: 6 (6–7).
27a Num. 14: 29; Isa. 11: 16
     (15–16); 35: 8 (8–10);
     51: 11 (9–11); 62: 10
     (10–12); 2 Ne. 21: 16.

     TG Israel, Gathering
     of.
29a Isa. 35: 7 (6–7).
   b TG Living Water.
30a Isa. 60: 9 (8–12).
     TG Treasure.
31a Gen. 49: 26; 1 Ne. 3: 6;
     D&C 49: 25.
32a Deut. 33: 16 (13–17).
     TG Exaltation.
   b Gen. 48: 20 (16–20);
     49: 26 (22–26);
     Zech. 10: 7 (7–12).
     TG Israel, Joseph,
     People of; Mission of
     Latter-day Saints.
33a Isa. 35: 10 (8–10);
     51: 11; Jer. 31: 12
     (10–14); D&C 66: 11.
     TG Singing.
34a TG Israel, Blessings of.
   b Gen. 21: 33.
   c TG Israel, Tribes of,
     Twelve.

of [a]Israel, and the richer blessing upon the head of [c]Ephraim and his fellows.

35 And they also of the tribe of [a]Judah, after their pain, shall be [b]sanctified in [c]holiness before the Lord, to dwell in his [d]presence day and night, forever and ever.

36 And now, verily saith the Lord, that these things might be known among you, O inhabitants of the earth, I have sent forth mine [a]angel flying through the midst of heaven, having the everlasting [b]gospel, who hath appeared unto some and hath committed it unto man, who shall appear unto [c]many that dwell on the earth.

37 And this [a]gospel shall be [b]preached unto [c]every nation, and kindred, and tongue, and people.

38 And the [a]servants of God shall go forth, saying with a loud voice: Fear God and give glory to him, for the hour of his judgment is come;

39 And [a]worship him that made heaven, and earth, and the sea, and the [b]fountains of waters—

40 Calling upon the name of the Lord day and night, saying: O that thou wouldst [a]rend the heavens, that thou wouldst come down, that the mountains might flow down at thy presence.

41 And it shall be answered upon their heads; for the presence of the Lord shall be [a]as the melting fire that burneth, and as the fire which causeth the waters to boil.

42 O Lord, thou shalt come down to make thy name known to thine adversaries, and all nations shall tremble at thy presence—

43 When thou doest [a]terrible things, things they look not for;

44 Yea, when thou comest down, and the mountains flow down at thy presence, thou shalt [a]meet him who rejoiceth and worketh righteousness, who remembereth thee in thy ways.

45 For since the beginning of the world have not men heard nor perceived by the ear, neither hath any eye seen, O God, besides thee, how great things thou hast [a]prepared for him that [b]waiteth for thee.

46 And it shall be said: [a]Who is this that cometh down from God in heaven with dyed [b]garments; yea, from the regions which are not known, clothed in his glorious apparel, traveling in the greatness of his strength?

47 And he shall say: [a]I am he who spake in [b]righteousness, mighty to save.

48 And the Lord shall be [a]red in his apparel, and his garments like him that treadeth in the wine-vat.

49 And so great shall be the glory of his presence that the [a]sun shall hide his face in shame, and the moon

---

34d TG Israel, Mission of.
  e Gen. 41: 52 (50–52);
    48: 14 (14–20); 1 Chr. 5:
    1 (1–2); Jer. 31: 9
    (6–9); Ether 13: 7
    (7–10); D&C 113: 4.
35a Hosea 1: 7; D&C 109:
    64. TG Israel, Judah,
    People of.
  b Gen. 49: 11.
  c TG Holiness.
  d TG God, Presence of.
36a Rev. 14: 6 (6–7);
    D&C 20: 6 (6–12);
    133: 17.
  b TG Restoration of the
    Gospel.
  c D&C 77: 8; 88: 103
    (103–104).
37a Ps. 67: 2 (1–2).

TG Last Days.
  b TG Mission of Latter-
    day Saints; Preaching.
  c Gen. 12: 3; D&C 42:
    58 (58–60); 43: 25 (23–
    27); 58: 64 (63–64);
    88: 84 (84, 87–92);
    90: 10; Abr. 2: 11
    (9–11).
38a Rev. 14: 7.
  TG Missionary Work.
39a Zech. 14: 16.
  b TG Worship.
40a Isa. 64: 1 (1–8);
    D&C 88: 95.
41a Ex. 24: 17; Job 41: 31;
    Jer. 9: 7; Hel. 5: 23;
    D&C 130: 7; 137: 2.
  TG Earth, Cleansing
    of.

43a Deut. 10: 21.
44a 1 Thes. 4: 17 (15–18).
45a Isa. 64: 4; 1 Cor. 2: 9.
  b Lam. 3: 25 (25–26);
    1 Ne. 21: 23; 2 Ne. 6:
    7, 13; D&C 98: 2.
46a Isa. 63: 1 (1–2).
  b Luke 22: 44;
    Mosiah 3: 7; D&C 19:
    18. TG Jesus Christ,
    Second Coming.
47a 2 Ne. 8: 12; D&C 136:
    22.
  b Dan. 9: 16.
48a Gen. 49: 11; D&C 19:
    23; Joel 2: 10;
    Amos 5: 18; D&C 45:
    42; 88: 87.
49a Isa. 13: 10 (9–13); 24:
    23; Joel 2: 10;
    Amos 5: 18; D&C 45:
    42; 88: 87.

shall withhold its light, and the stars shall be hurled from their places.

50 And his *voice shall be: I have *trodden the wine-press alone, and have brought judgment upon all people; and none were with me;

51 And I have *trampled them in my fury, and I did tread upon them in mine anger, and their blood have I *sprinkled upon my garments, and stained all my raiment; for this was the *day of vengeance which was in my heart.

52 And now the year of my *redeemed is come; and they shall mention the loving kindness of their Lord, and all that he has bestowed upon them according to his *goodness, and according to his loving kindness, forever and ever.

53 In all their *afflictions he was afflicted. And the angel of his presence saved them; and in his *love, and in his pity, he *redeemed them, and bore them, and carried them all the days of old;

54 Yea, and *Enoch also, and they who were with him; the prophets who were before him; and *Noah also, and they who were before him; and *Moses also, and they who were before him;

55 And from *Moses to Elijah, and from Elijah to John, who were with

Christ in his *resurrection, and the holy apostles, with Abraham, Isaac, and Jacob, shall be in the presence of the Lamb.

56 And the *graves of the *saints shall be *opened; and they shall come forth and stand on the *right hand of the Lamb, when he shall stand upon *Mount Zion, and upon the holy city, the New Jerusalem; and they shall *sing the *song of the *Lamb, day and night forever and ever.

57 And for this cause, that men might be made *partakers of the *glories which were to be revealed, the Lord sent forth the fulness of his *gospel, his everlasting covenant, reasoning in plainness and simplicity—

58 To *prepare the *weak for those things which are coming on the earth, and for the Lord's errand in the day when the weak shall *confound the *wise, and the little one become a *strong *nation, and two shall put their tens of thousands to *flight.

59 And by the weak things of the earth the Lord shall *thrash the nations by the power of his Spirit.

60 And for this cause these commandments were given; they were commanded to be kept from the world in the day that they were

50a Joel 2: 11; D&C 35: 21; 43: 18 (17–25).
 b Isa. 63: 3 (3–9); Rev. 19: 15 (11–15); D&C 76: 107; 88: 106.
51a Ps. 110: 6 (1–7); 1 Cor. 15: 27 (24–28); Heb. 10: 13 (12–14).
 b Lev. 8: 30; Num. 18: 17; Isa. 63: 3 (2–4).
 c TG Day of the Lord; Vengeance.
52a Isa. 63: 4.
53a Isa. 63: 9; Lam. 3: 33 (1–39).
 b TG Charity; Compassion; God, Love of.
 c TG Jesus Christ, Redeemer.
54a Gen. 5: 23; D&C 38: 4; 45: 11 (11–12).
 b Gen. 7: 23 (1–24); 8:1 (1–22).

c Ex. 3: 8 (1–22).
55a TG Dispensation.
 b Alma 40: 20 (18–21).
 TG Jesus Christ, Resurrection.
56a D&C 29: 13.
 b TG Saints.
 c D&C 45: 45 (45–46); 88: 97 (96–97).
 TG Resurrection.
 d Matt. 25: 34 (31–46).
 TG Exaltation.
 e Isa. 24: 23; Heb. 12: 22 (22, 24); Rev. 14: 1; D&C 76: 66; 84: 2 (2, 18, 32).
 f Isa. 12: 5 (1–6).
 g Rev. 15: 3 (3–4); D&C 84: 98 (98–102).
 h TG Jesus Christ, Lamb of God.
57a D&C 93: 22.

TG Man, Potential to Become Like Heavenly Father.
 b TG Celestial Glory; Glory; Telestial Glory; Terrestrial Glory.
 c TG Gospel; New and Everlasting Covenant; Restoration of the Gospel.
58a TG Mission of Latter-day Saints.
 b D&C 35: 13; 124: 1.
 c Matt. 11: 25; 1 Cor. 1: 27; Alma 32: 23; 37: 7 (6–7).
 d Isa. 44: 25; 1 Cor. 1: 20.
 e Josh. 1: 6 (6–9); Isa. 60: 22; D&C 52: 17; 66: 8.
 f TG Kingdom of God, on Earth.
 g Deut. 32: 30 (29–30).
59a Micah 4: 13 (11–13).

given, but now are to "go forth unto ᵇall flesh—

61 And this according to the mind and will of the Lord, who ruleth over all flesh.

62 And unto him that repenteth and "sanctifieth himself before the Lord shall be given eternal life.

63 And upon them that "hearken not to the voice of the Lord shall be fulfilled that which was written by the prophet Moses, that they should be ᵇcut off from among the people.

64 And also that which was written by the prophet "Malachi: For, behold, the ᵇday cometh that shall ʳburn as an oven, and all the proud, yea, and all that do ᵈwickedly, shall be stubble; and the day that cometh shall burn them up, saith the Lord of hosts, that it shall leave them neither root nor branch.

65 Wherefore, this shall be the answer of the Lord unto them:

66 In that day when I came unto mine own, no man among you "received me, and you were driven out.

67 When I called again there was none of you to answer; yet my "arm was not shortened at all that I could not redeem, neither my ᵇpower to deliver.

68 Behold, at my rebuke I "dry up the sea. I make the rivers a wilderness; their fish stink, and die for thirst.

69 I clothe the heavens with blackness, and make sackcloth their covering.

70 And "this shall ye have of my hand—ye shall lie down in sorrow.

71 Behold, and lo, there are none to deliver you; for ye "obeyed not my voice when I called to you out of the heavens; ye ᵇbelieved not my servants, and when they were ᶜsent unto you ye received them not.

72 Wherefore, they sealed up the testimony and bound up the law, and ye were delivered over unto "darkness.

73 These shall go away into outer darkness, where there is "weeping, and wailing, and gnashing of teeth.

74 Behold the Lord your God hath spoken it. Amen.

SECTION 134

A declaration of belief regarding governments and laws in general, adopted by unanimous vote at a general assembly of the Church held at Kirtland, Ohio, August 17, 1835. HC 2: 247–249. The occasion was a meeting of Church leaders, brought together to consider the proposed contents of the first edition of the Doctrine and Covenants. At that time this declaration was given the following preamble: "That our belief with regard to earthly governments and

60a D&C 104: 58.
  b D&C 1: 2.
62a 2 Chr. 35: 6; D&C 88: 74. TG Sanctification.
63a Deut. 28: 15.
  TG Disobedience.
  b Acts 3: 23; 1 Ne. 22: 20 (20–21); 3 Ne. 20: 23; 21: 11; D&C 1: 14; JS-H 1: 40.
64a Mal. 4: 1.
  b D&C 5: 19; JS-H 1: 37. TG Last Days.
  c Isa. 24: 6; 66: 15 (15–

16); Joel 2: 5; 1 Ne. 22: 15; 3 Ne. 25: 1; D&C 29: 9; 64: 24.
  TG Earth, Cleansing of.
  d JS-M 1: 4.
66a Matt. 23: 38 (37–39); John 1: 11.
67a 2 Ne. 28: 32.
  b Isa. 50: 2; Ezek. 37: 12 (11–14); Hosea 13: 14.
68a Ex. 14: 21 (1–31); Josh. 3: 17 (14–17); 2 Ne. 7: 2.

TG Drought.
70a Isa. 50: 11.
71a TG Apostasy of Israel.
  b Luke 16: 31.
  TG Prophets, Rejection of.
  c 2 Chr. 36: 15; Jer. 44: 4 (4–5).
72a Isa. 8: 15 (16–15); Matt. 8: 12 (11–12); D&C 77: 8.
  TG Darkness, Spiritual.
73a Luke 13: 28; D&C 19: 5; 101: 91 (90–91).

laws in general may not be misinterpreted nor misunderstood, we have thought proper to present at the close of this volume our opinion concerning the same."

1–4, Governments should preserve freedom of conscience and worship; 5–8, All men should uphold their governments, and owe respect and deference to the law; 9–10, Religious societies should not exercise civil powers; 11–12, Men are justified in defending themselves and their property.

WE believe that ᵃgovernments were instituted of God for the benefit of man; and that he holds men ᵇaccountable for their acts in relation to them, both in making laws and administering them, for the good and safety of society.

2 We believe that no government can exist in ᵃpeace, except such laws are framed and held inviolate as will secure to each individual the ᵇfree exercise of ᶜconscience, the right and control of property, and the ᵈprotection of life.

3 We believe that all governments necessarily require ᵃcivil ᵇofficers and magistrates to enforce the laws of the same; and that such as will administer the law in equity and justice should be sought for and upheld by the voice of the people if a republic, or the will of the sovereign.

4 We believe that religion is instituted of God; and that men are amenable to him, and to him only, for the exercise of it, unless their religious opinions prompt them to infringe upon the rights and liberties of others; but we do not believe that human law has a right to interfere in prescribing rules of ᵃworship to bind the consciences of men, nor dictate forms for public or private devotion; that the civil magistrate should restrain crime, but never control conscience; should punish ᵇguilt, but never suppress the freedom of the soul.

5 We believe that all men are bound to ᵃsustain and uphold the respective ᵇgovernments in which they reside, while protected in their inherent and inalienable rights by the laws of such governments; and that sedition and ᶜrebellion are unbecoming every citizen thus protected, and should be punished accordingly; and that all governments have a right to enact such laws as in their own judgments are best calculated to secure the public interest; at the same time, however, holding sacred the freedom of conscience.

6 We believe that every man should be ᵃhonored in his station, rulers and magistrates as such, being placed for the protection of the innocent and the punishment of the guilty; and that to the ᵇlaws all men show ᶜrespect and deference, as without them peace and harmony would be supplanted by anarchy and terror; human laws being instituted for the express purpose of regulating our interests as individuals and nations, between man and man; and divine laws given of heaven, prescribing rules on spiritual concerns, for faith and worship, both to be answered by man to his Maker.

---

134 1a Jer. 27:6 (4–11);
  John 19:11; Rom. 13:
  1 (1–4); D&C 98:5
  (4–7); 101:77; A of F
  12. TG Citizenship;
  Governments.
 b TG Accountability;
  Judgment.
2a TG Peace.
 b TG Agency; Liberty.

 c TG Conscience.
 d Josh. 20:3; D&C 42:
  18 (18–19).
3a Ezra 7:25; 2 Pet. 2:
  13 (13–17).
 b D&C 98:10 (8–10).
  TG Delegation of
  Responsibility.
4a Matt. 22:21; Alma 21:
  22 (21–22); D&C 63:
  26; A of F 11.

  TG Worship.
 b TG Guilt; Punishment.
5a TG Loyalty;
  Obedience; Order.
 b TG Citizenship;
  Governments.
 c TG Rebellion.
6a Rom. 13:7.
 b D&C 58:21; 88:34.
 c TG Respect.

7 We believe that rulers, states, and governments have a right, and are bound to enact laws for the protection of all *a*citizens in the free exercise of their religious *b*belief; but we do not believe that they have a right in justice to deprive citizens of this privilege, or proscribe them in their opinions, so long as a regard and reverence are shown to the laws and such religious opinions do not justify sedition nor conspiracy.

8 We believe that the commission of crime should be *a*punished according to the nature of the offense; that murder, treason, robbery, theft, and the breach of the general peace, in all respects, should be punished according to their criminality and their tendency to evil among men, by the laws of that government in which the offense is committed; and for the public *b*peace and tranquility all men should step forward and use their ability in bringing *c*offenders against good laws to punishment.

9 We do not believe it just to *a*mingle religious influence with civil government, whereby one religious society is fostered and another proscribed in its spiritual privileges, and the individual rights of its members, as citizens, denied.

10 We believe that all religious societies have a right to deal with their members for disorderly conduct, *a*according to the rules and regulations of such societies; provided that such dealings be for fellowship and good standing; but we do not believe that any religious society has *b*authority to try men on

the right of property or life, to take from them this world's goods, or to put them in jeopardy of either life or limb, or to inflict any physical punishment upon them. They can only excommunicate them from their society, and withdraw from them their fellowship.

11 We believe that men should appeal to the civil law for redress of all *a*wrongs and grievances, where personal abuse is inflicted or the right of property or character infringed, where such laws exist as will protect the same; but we believe that all men are justified in *b*defending themselves, their friends, and property, and the government, from the unlawful assaults and encroachments of all persons in times of exigency, where immediate appeal cannot be made to the laws, and relief afforded.

12 We believe it just to *a*preach the gospel to the nations of the earth, and warn the righteous to save themselves from the corruption of the world; but we do not believe it right to interfere with *b*bondservants, neither preach the gospel to, nor baptize them contrary to the will and wish of their masters, nor to meddle with or influence them in the least to cause them to be dissatisfied with their situations in this life, thereby jeopardizing the lives of men; such interference we believe to be unlawful and unjust, and dangerous to the peace of every government allowing human beings to be held in *c*servitude.

SECTION 135

Martyrdom of Joseph Smith the Prophet and his brother, Hyrum Smith the Patriarch, at Carthage, Illinois, June 27, 1844. HC 6: 629–

7a TG Citizenship.
  b Micah 4: 5; A of F 11.
8a Alma 1: 14 (11–18);
   D&C 42: 84 (84–87).
  b TG Peace.
  c Ex. 18: 22 (17–26).
   TG Offenses.

9a Alma 30: 7 (7–11).
   TG Governments.
10a D&C 42: 81.
  b TG Authority;
   Excommunication.
11a TG Injustice; Malice;
   Oppression;

   Persecution.
  b TG Deliverance.
12a TG Mission of Latter-
   day Saints; Warnings.
  b Philem. 1: 10 (10–19).
   TG Bondage, Physical.
  c TG Slavery.

631. *This document was written by Elder John Taylor of the Council of the Twelve, who was a witness to the events.*

1–2, Joseph and Hyrum martyred in Carthage Jail; 3, Preeminent position of the Prophet acclaimed; 4–7, Their innocent blood testifies of the truth and divinity of the work.

To seal the testimony of this book and the Book of Mormon, we announce the [a]martyrdom of Joseph Smith the Prophet, and Hyrum Smith the Patriarch. They were shot in Carthage jail, on the 27th of June, 1844, about five o'clock p.m., by an armed mob—painted black—of from 150 to 200 persons. [b]Hyrum was shot first and fell calmly, exclaiming: *I am a [c]dead man!* Joseph leaped from the window, and was shot dead in the attempt, exclaiming: *[d]O Lord my God!* They were both shot after they were dead, in a brutal manner, and both received four balls.

2 John Taylor and Willard Richards, two of the Twelve, were the only persons in the room at the time; the former was wounded in a savage manner with four balls, but has since recovered; the latter, through the providence of God, escaped, without even a hole in his robe.

3 Joseph Smith, the [a]Prophet and [b]Seer of the Lord, has done more, [c]save Jesus only, for the salvation of men in this world, than any other man that ever lived in it. In the short space of twenty years, he has brought forth the Book of Mormon, which he translated by the gift and power of God, and has been the means of publishing it on two continents; has sent the [d]fulness of the everlasting gospel, which it con-

tained, to the four quarters of the earth; has brought forth the revelations and commandments which compose this book of Doctrine and Covenants, and many other wise documents and instructions for the benefit of the children of men; gathered many thousands of the Latter-day Saints, founded a great city, and left a fame and name that cannot be slain. He lived great, and he died great in the eyes of God and his people; and like most of the Lord's anointed in ancient times, has sealed his mission and his works with his own [b]blood; and so has his brother Hyrum. In life they were not divided, and in death they were not [f]separated!

4 When Joseph went to Carthage to deliver himself up to the pretended requirements of the law, two or three days previous to his assassination, he said: "I am going like a [a]lamb to the slaughter; but I am calm as a summer's morning; I have a [b]conscience [c]void of offense towards God, and towards all men. I SHALL DIE INNOCENT, AND IT SHALL YET BE SAID OF ME—HE WAS MURDERED IN COLD BLOOD."—The same morning, after Hyrum had made ready to go—shall it be said to the slaughter? yes, for so it was—he read the following paragraph, near the close of the twelfth chapter of Ether, in the Book of Mormon, and turned down the leaf upon it:

5 *And it came to pass that I prayed unto the Lord that he would give unto the Gentiles grace, that they might have charity. And it came to pass that the Lord said unto me: If they have not charity it mattereth not unto thee,*

---

135 1a D&C 5: 22; 6: 30.
   TG Martyrdom.
   b JS-H 1: 4.
   c TG Death; Murder.
   d Ps. 38: 21 (21–22);
     71: 12.
   3a Prophets, Mission
     of.

   b TG Seer.
   c TG Jesus Christ,
     Savior; Salvation.
   d D&C 35: 17; 42: 12.
     TG Restoration of the
     Gospel.
   e Mosiah 17: 20; D&C

   136: 39. TG Blood,
     Symbolism of.
   f 2 Sam. 1: 23.
   4a Isa. 53: 7; Jer. 11: 19;
     Mosiah 14: 7.
   b TG Conscience.
   c TG Purity.

thou hast been *a*faithful; wherefore thy garments shall be made *b*clean. And because thou hast seen thy weakness, thou shalt be made strong, even unto the sitting down in the place which I have prepared in the mansions of my Father. And now I ... bid farewell unto the Gentiles; yea, and also unto my brethren whom I love, until we shall meet before the *c*judgment-seat of Christ, where all men shall know that my garments are not spotted with your blood. The *d*testators are now dead, and their *e*testament is in force.

6 Hyrum Smith was forty-four years old in February, 1844, and Joseph Smith was thirty-eight in December, 1843; and henceforward their names will be classed among the *a*martyrs of religion; and the reader in every nation will be reminded that the Book of Mormon, and this book of Doctrine and Covenants of the church, cost the best blood of the nineteenth century to bring them forth for the salvation of a ruined world; and that if the fire can scathe a *b*green tree for the glory of God, how easy it will burn up the dry trees to purify the vineyard of corruption. They lived for glory;

they died for glory; and glory is their eternal *c*reward. From age to age shall their names go down to posterity as gems for the sanctified.

7 They were innocent of any crime, as they had often been proved before, and were only confined in jail by the conspiracy of traitors and wicked men; and their *innocent blood* on the floor of Carthage jail is a broad seal affixed to "Mormonism" that cannot be rejected by any court on earth, and their *innocent blood* on the escutcheon of the State of Illinois, with the broken faith of the State as pledged by the governor, is a witness to the truth of the everlasting gospel that all the world cannot impeach; and their *innocent blood* on the banner of liberty, and on the *magna charta* of the United States, is an ambassador for the religion of Jesus Christ, that will touch the hearts of honest men among all nations; and their *innocent blood*, with the innocent blood of all the martyrs under the *a*altar that John saw, will cry unto the Lord of Hosts till he avenges that blood on the earth. Amen.

SECTION 136

The word and will of the Lord, given through President Brigham Young at the Winter Quarters of the Camp of Israel, Omaha Nation, West Bank of the Missouri River, near Council Bluffs, Iowa. Journal History of the Church, January 14, 1847.

1–16, How the Camp of Israel is to be organized for the westward journey; 17–27, The saints are commanded to live by numerous gospel standards; 28–33, The saints should sing, dance, pray, and learn wisdom; 34–42, Prophets are slain that they might be honored and the wicked condemned.

THE Word and *a*Will of the Lord concerning the Camp of *b*Israel in their journeyings to the West:

2 Let all the people of the *c*Church of Jesus Christ of Latter-day Saints, and those who journey with them, be organized into companies, with a covenant and promise to *b*keep all

5a TG Loyalty; Steadfastness.
  b D&C 88: 74 (74–75).
  c Ether 12: 36–38.
  d 1 Tim. 2: 6; Heb. 9: 16 (16–17).

e Heb. 9: 17.
  TG Testimony.
6a TG Martyrdom.
  b Luke 23: 31.
  c TG Reward.
7a Rev. 6: 9.

136 1a TG God, Will of.
  b D&C 133: 32 (32–35); A of F 1.
2a D&C 20: 1 (1–4); 115: 4.
  b D&C 41: 5 (5–6); 56: 2 (2–3).

the commandments and statutes of the Lord our God.

3 Let the companies be organized with captains of [a]hundreds, captains of fifties, and captains of tens, with a president and his two counselors at their head, under the direction of the Twelve [b]Apostles.

4 And this shall be our [c]covenant—that we will [d]walk in all the [e]ordinances of the Lord.

5 Let each company provide themselves with all the teams, wagons, provisions, clothing, and other necessaries for the journey, that they can.

6 When the companies are organized let them go to with their [a]might, to prepare for those who are to tarry.

7 Let each company, with their captains and presidents, decide how many can go next spring; then choose out a sufficient number of able-bodied and expert men, to take teams, seeds, and farming utensils, to go as pioneers to prepare for putting in spring crops.

8 Let each company [a]bear an equal proportion, according to the dividend of their property, in taking the poor, the [b]widows, the [c]fatherless, and the families of those who have gone into the army, that the cries of the widow and the [d]fatherless come not up into the ears of the Lord against this people.

9 Let each company prepare houses, and fields for raising [a]grain, for those who are to remain behind this season; and this is the will of the Lord concerning his people.

10 Let every man use all his influence and property to remove this people to the place where the Lord shall locate a [a]stake of Zion.

11 And if ye do this with a pure heart, in all faithfulness, ye shall be [a]blessed; you shall be [b]blessed in your flocks, and in your herds, and in your fields, and in your houses, and in your families.

12 Let my servants Ezra T. Benson and Erastus Snow organize a company.

13 And let my servants Orson Pratt and Wilford Woodruff organize a company.

14 Also, let my servants Amasa Lyman and George A. Smith organize a company.

15 And appoint presidents, and [a]captains of hundreds, and of fifties, and of tens.

16 And let my servants that have been appointed go and [a]teach this, my will, to the saints, that they may be ready to go to a land of peace.

17 Go thy way and do as I have told you, and [a]fear not thine enemies; for they shall not have power to stop my work.

18 Zion shall be [a]redeemed in mine own due time.

19 And if any man shall seek to build up himself, and seeketh not my [a]counsel, he shall have no power, and his [b]folly shall be made manifest.

20 [a]Seek ye; and keep all your [b]pledges one with another; and [c]covet not that which is thy brother's.

21 [a]Keep yourselves from evil to take the name of the Lord in vain, for I am the Lord your God, even the [b]God of your fathers, the God of Abraham and of Isaac and of Jacob.

3a TG Apostles.
 b TG Apostles.
4a TG Covenants.
 b TG Walking with God.
 c TG Ordinances.
6a Judg. 6: 14.
8a D&C 38: 24 (24-27).
 b TG Poor; Widows.
 c Ps. 68: 5; 146: 9 (1-10); James 1: 27 (25-27).

d 3 Ne. 24: 5.
9a TG Bread; Self-sacrifice.
10a TG Stake; Zion.
11a Gen. 26: 12; Deut. 28: 4 (1-14); Alma 34: 20 (17-27).
 TG Blessing.
15a Deut. 1: 15.
16a TG Teaching.
17a TG Courage; Enemies; Fearfulness.
18a D&C 100: 13.

19a TG Counsel; Problem-Solving.
 b TG Foolishness.
20a IE Seek the Lord's counsel; see v. 19.
 b TG Honesty; Promise; Vow.
 c TG Covetousness.
21a TG Profanity; Self-mastery.
 b Ex. 3: 6; Matt. 22: 32; 1 Ne. 19: 10.

22 I am he who ^aled the children of Israel out of the land of Egypt; and my arm is stretched out in the last days, to ^bsave my people Israel.

23 Cease to ^acontend one with another; cease to speak ^bevil one of another.

24 Cease ^adrunkenness; and let your words tend to ^bedifying one another.

25 If thou ^aborrowest of thy ^bneighbor, thou shalt ^crestore that which thou hast borrowed; and if thou canst not repay then go straightway and tell thy neighbor, lest he condemn thee.

26 If thou shalt find that which thy neighbor has ^alost, thou shalt make diligent search till thou shalt ^bdeliver it to him again.

27 Thou shalt be ^adiligent in ^bpreserving what thou hast, that thou mayest be a wise ^csteward; for it is the free gift of the Lord thy God, and thou art his steward.

28 If thou art ^amerry, ^bpraise the Lord with singing, with music, with ^cdancing, and with a ^dprayer of praise and ^ethanksgiving.

29 If thou art ^asorrowful, call on the Lord thy God with supplication, that your souls may be ^bjoyful.

30 Fear not thine ^aenemies, for they are in mine hands and I will do my pleasure with them.

31 My people must be ^atried in all things, that they may be prepared to receive the ^bglory that I have for them, even the glory of Zion; and he that will not ^cbear chastisement is not worthy of my kingdom.

32 Let him that is ^aignorant ^blearn ^cwisdom by ^dhumbling himself and calling upon the Lord his God, that his ^eeyes may be opened that he may see, and his ears opened that he may hear;

33 For my ^aSpirit is sent forth into the world to enlighten the ^bhumble and contrite, and to the ^ccondemnation of the ungodly.

34 Thy brethren have rejected you and your testimony, even the nation that has ^adriven you out;

35 And now cometh the day of their calamity, even the days of sorrow, like a woman that is taken in travail; and their ^asorrow shall be great unless they speedily repent, yea, very speedily.

36 For they ^akilled the prophets,

22a Gen. 15: 14 (13–14);
  Ex. 13: 18 (18, 20);
  Amos 3: 1 (1–2);
  1 Ne. 5: 15; D&C 103:
  18.
23a Isa. 9: 12; Jer. 30: 10;
  32: 17; Ezek. 20: 34
  (33–34); Hosea 13: 9;
  D&C 38: 33.
23a Prov. 17: 14; 2 Tim.
  2: 24; 3 Ne. 11: 29
  (29–30). TG Contention;
  Disputations;
  Strife.
 b D&C 20: 54.
  TG Backbiting.
24a TG Drunkenness;
  Word of Wisdom.
 b 1 Pet. 1: 15.
  TG Edification.
25a TG Borrowing; Debt;
  Honesty.
 b TG Neighbor.
 c Ps. 27: 21; Mosiah 4:
  28.
26a Lev. 6: 4; Deut. 22: 3.

 b TG Honesty.
27a TG Diligence.
 b Prov. 21: 20.
 c TG Stewardship.
28a TG Happiness.
 b Ps. 33: 1; 147: 7; Isa.
  12: 4; Eph. 5: 19 (19–
  20); 1 Ne. 18: 16;
  Mosiah 2: 20 (20–21);
  Alma 26: 8; D&C 25:
  11 (11–12); 109: 79.
  TG Communication;
  Singing.
 c 2 Sam. 6: 14.
 d TG Prayer.
 e 2 Chr. 5: 13; D&C 97:
  13. TG Thanksgiving.
29a 2 Sam. 22: 7.
  TG Sorrow.
 b TG Joy.
30a Deut. 30: 7.
  TG Enemies.
31a Gen. 22: 1 (1–19).
  TG Adversity;
  Millennium, Preparing
  a People for;

  Test, Try, Prove.
 b Rom. 8: 18; D&C 58:
  4; 63: 66. TG Celestial
  Glory.
 c Lam. 3: 27 (24–27).
  TG Chastening.
32a TG Education;
  Learning.
 b TG Ignorance.
 c TG Wisdom.
 d TG Humility;
  Teachable.
 e Gen. 3: 5 (3–6);
  Mosiah 27: 22;
  D&C 88: 11 (11–13);
  110: 1.
33a TG God, Spirit of.
 b TG Contrite Heart;
  Meekness.
 c TG Chastening.
34a TG Persecution.
35a TG Punishment;
  Sorrow.
36a Zech. 1: 4 (2–5).
  TG Prophets, Rejection
  of.

and them that were sent unto them; and they have [b]shed innocent blood, which crieth from the ground against them.

37 Therefore, marvel not at these things, for ye are not yet [a]pure; ye can not yet bear my glory; but ye shall behold it if ye are faithful in keeping all my words that I have [b]given you, from the days of Adam to Abraham, from Abraham to Moses, from Moses to Jesus and his apostles, and from Jesus and his apostles to Joseph Smith, whom I did call upon by mine [c]angels, my ministering servants, and by mine own voice out of the heavens, to bring forth my work;

38 Which [a]foundation he did lay, and was faithful; and I took him to myself.

39 Many have marveled because of his death; but it was needful that he should [a]seal his [b]testimony with his [c]blood, that he might be [d]honored and the wicked might be condemned.

40 Have I not delivered you from your [a]enemies, only in that I have left a witness of my name?

41 Now, therefore, hearken, O ye people of my [a]church; and ye elders listen together; you have received my [b]kingdom.

42 Be [a]diligent in keeping all my commandments, lest judgments come upon you, and your faith fail you, and your enemies triumph over you. So no more at present. Amen and Amen.

SECTION 137

A vision given to Joseph Smith the Prophet, in the temple at Kirtland, Ohio, January 21, 1836. HC 2: 380—381. The occasion was the administration of the ordinances of the endowment as far as they had then been revealed.

1—6, *The Prophet sees his brother Alvin in the celestial kingdom;* 7—9, *The doctrine of salvation for the dead is revealed;* 10, *All children are saved in the celestial kingdom.*

THE [a]heavens were [b]opened upon us, and I beheld the [c]celestial kingdom of God, and the glory thereof, whether in the [d]body or out I cannot tell.

2 I saw the transcendent [a]beauty of the [b]gate through which the heirs of that kingdom will enter, which was [c]like unto [d]circling flames of fire;

3 Also the [a]blazing [b]throne of God, whereon was seated the [c]Father and the [d]Son.

4 I saw the beautiful streets of that kingdom, which had the appearance of being paved with [a]gold.

5 I saw Father [a]Adam and [b]Abra-

36b Rev. 19: 2; Morm. 8: 41 (40—41).	of the Church.	c Ex. 24: 17; Isa. 33: 14 (14—15); Hel. 5: 23; D&C 130: 7; 133: 41.
37a TG Purity.	b Dan. 7: 27.	
b Hel. 8: 18 (16—19).	42a TG Steadfastness.	d Ezek. 1: 4 (4—25).
c Rev. 14: 6; D&C 27: 16; 111—16; 128: 20 (19—21); 133: 36; JS-H 1: 30—47.	**137** 1a Acts 7: 56 (55—56); 1 Ne. 1: 8; Hel. 5: 48 (45—49). TG Heaven.	3a Ezek. 1: 27 (26—27); Dan. 7: 9.
		b Isa. 6: 1; Ezek. 1: 26 (26—28); D&C 76: 108 (106—108).
	b JS-H 1: 43.	
38a D&C 135: 3.	c TG Celestial Glory; Kingdom of God, in Heaven.	c TG God the Father— Elohim; Godhead.
39a Rev. 2: 10; Mosiah 17: 20; D&C 98: 14; 135: 3.		d Acts 7: 55 (55—56).
b TG Testimony.	d 2 Cor. 12: 2 (2—4); Rev. 21: 10; 1 Ne. 11: 1; Moses 1: 11.	4a Rev. 21: 21 (10—27); D&C 110: 2.
c TG Martyrdom.		5a TG Adam.
d TG Honor; Justice.	2a Rev. 21: 19 (10—27); D&C 76: 70.	b D&C 132: 29; Abr. 2: 11 (9—11).
40a Ex. 23: 22 (20—23); D&C 8: 4; 105: 15.	b TG Beauty.	
41a TG Jesus Christ, Head	b 2 Ne. 9: 41.	

ham; and my *father and my mother; my brother *Alvin, that has long since *slept;

6 And *marveled how it was that he had obtained an *inheritance in that kingdom, seeing that he had departed this life before the Lord had set his hand to *gather Israel the second time, and had not been *baptized for the remission of sins.

7 Thus came the *voice of the Lord unto me, saying: All who have died *without a knowledge of this gospel, who would have received it if they had been permitted to tarry, shall be *heirs of the celestial kingdom of God;

8 Also all that shall die henceforth without a knowledge of it, who *would have received it with all their hearts, shall be heirs of that kingdom;

9 For I, the Lord, will *judge all men according to their *works, according to the *desire of their hearts.

10 And I also beheld that all *children who die before they arrive at the *years of accountability are *saved in the celestial kingdom of heaven.

SECTION 138

A vision, given to President Joseph F. Smith in Salt Lake City, Utah, on October 3, 1918. In his opening address at the eighty-ninth Semi-annual General Conference of the Church, on October 4, 1918, President Smith declared that he had received several divine communications during the previous months. One of these, concerning the Savior's visit to the spirits of the dead while his body was in the tomb, he had received the previous day. It was written immediately following the close of the conference; on October 31, 1918, it was submitted to the counselors in the First Presidency, the Council of the Twelve, and the Patriarch, and it was unanimously accepted by them.

1–10, President Joseph F. Smith ponders upon the writings of Peter and our Lord's visit to the spirit world; 11–24, He sees the righteous dead assembled in paradise and Christ's ministry among them; 25–37, How the preaching of the gospel was organized among the spirits; 38–52, President Smith sees Adam, Eve, and many of the holy prophets in the spirit world who considered their spirit state before their resurrection as a bondage; 53–60, The righteous dead of this day continue their labors in the world of spirits.

ON the third of October, in the year nineteen hundred and eighteen, I

5c D&C 124: 19.
  TG Family, Eternal.
 d JS-H 1: 4.
 e 1 Cor. 15: 20.
6a D&C 138: 25.
 b TG Salvation for the Dead.
 c Isa. 11: 11;
   1 Ne. 22: 12 (10–12);
   Jacob 6: 2. TG Israel,
   Gathering of; Israel,
   Restoration of.
 d Luke 24: 47; John
   3: 5 (3–5); 2 Ne. 9: 23;

Ether 4: 18 (18–19);
   D&C 76: 52 (50–52);
   84: 74. TG Baptism,
   Essential.
7a Hel. 5: 30.
   TG Revelation.
 b 1 Pet. 4: 6; 2 Ne. 9: 26
   (25–26); Mosiah 15:
   24; D&C 29: 50.
 c Heb. 9: 15 (14–15);
   D&C 76: 70 (50–70).
   TG Exaltation; Salva-
   tion for the Dead.

8a Alma 18: 32; D&C 6:
   16.
9a Rev. 20: 12 (12–14).
   TG God, Justice of;
   Judgment, The Last.
 b TG Good Works;
   Justice.
 c D&C 64: 22 (22, 34).
   TG Agency; Motiva-
   tions.
10a TG Children.
 b D&C 68: 27 (25–27).
 c TG Salvation of Little
   Children.

sat in my room ªpondering over the scriptures;

2 And ªreflecting upon the great ᵇatoning ᶜsacrifice that was made by the Son of God, for the ᵈredemption of the world;

3 And the great and wonderful ªlove made manifest by the Father and the Son in the coming of the ᵇRedeemer into the world;

4 That through his ªatonement, and by ᵇobedience to the principles of the gospel, mankind might be saved.

5 While I was thus engaged, my mind reverted to the writings of the apostle Peter, to the ªprimitive saints scattered abroad throughout ᵇPontus, Galatia, Cappadocia, and other parts of Asia, where the gospel had been ᶜpreached after the crucifixion of the Lord.

6 I opened the Bible and read the third and fourth chapters of the first epistle of ªPeter, and as I read I was greatly ᵇimpressed, more than I had ever been before, with the following passages:

7 "For Christ also hath once suffered for sins, the just for the unjust, that he might bring us to God, being put to death in the flesh, but quickened by the Spirit;

8 "By which also he went and preached unto the spirits in ªprison;

9 "Which sometime were disobedient, when once the long-suffering of God waited in the days of Noah, while the ark was a preparing, wherein few, that is, eight souls were saved by water." (1 Peter 3:18–20.)

10 "For for this cause was the gospel preached also to them that are dead, that they might be judged according to men in the flesh, but live according to God in the spirit." (1 Peter 4:6.)

11 As I ªpondered over these things which are ᵇwritten, the ᶜeyes of my ᵈunderstanding were opened, and the Spirit of the Lord ᵉrested upon me, and I saw the hosts of the ᶠdead, both small and great.

12 And there were gathered together in one place an innumerable company of the spirits of the ªjust, who had been ᵇfaithful in the ᶜtestimony of Jesus while they lived in mortality;

13 And who had offered ªsacrifice in the ᵇsimilitude of the great sacrifice of the Son of God, and had suffered ᶜtribulation in their Redeemer's ᵈname.

14 All these had departed the mortal life, firm in the ªhope of a glorious ᵇresurrection, through the ᶜgrace of God the ᵈFather and his ᵉOnly Begotten Son, Jesus Christ.

15 I beheld that they were filled with ªjoy and gladness, and were rejoicing together because the day of their ᵇdeliverance was at hand.

---

138 1a TG Meditation; Scriptures, Study of.
2a JS-H 1:12.
  b Matt. 20:28. TG Jesus Christ, Atonement through.
  c TG Sacrifice.
  d TG Redemption.
3a John 3:16 (14–17). TG God, Love of.
  b Isa. 63:9 (1–9). TG Jesus Christ, Redeemer.
4a 2 Ne. 25:23; A of F 3.
  b Matt. 7:21 (21–27). TG Obedience.
5a IE former-day saints.
  b 1 Pet. 1:1.
  c Acts 16:6 (6–9); 19:26 (10–26).
6a See 1 Pet. 3:18–20 and 4:6 in the New Testament for additional notes and cross references.
  b JS-H 1:12 (11–13).
8a Isa. 61:1 (1–2); Luke 4:18 (18–21); D&C 76:73 (73–74); 88:99.
11a D&C 76:19.
  b TG Scriptures, Value of.
  c Luke 24:31; Eph. 1:18; D&C 76:12 (10, 12, 19); 110:1.
  d TG Understanding.
  e Num. 11:25; Isa. 11:2.
  f TG Spirits, Disembodied.
12a Ezek. 18:5 (5–9); D&C 76:69 (69–70).
  b D&C 6:13; 51:19; 76:52 (51–53).
  c TG Testimony.
13a TG Sacrifice.
  b TG Jesus Christ, Types, in Anticipation; Jesus Christ, Types, in Memory.
  c TG Persecution; Tribulation.
  d Matt. 5:11 (10–12).
14a 1 Cor. 15:19 (18–21); Ether 12:4; Moro. 7:41 (3, 40–48).
  b TG Resurrection.
  c TG Grace.
  d TG God the Father—Elohim.
  e TG Jesus Christ, Mission of.
15a Isa. 51:11; Alma 40:12 (11–13).
  b TG Salvation.

16 They were assembled awaiting the advent of the Son of God into the *spirit world, to declare their *redemption from the *bands of death.

17 Their sleeping *dust was to be *restored unto its *perfect frame, *bone to his bone, and the sinews and the flesh upon them, the *spirit and the body to be united never again to be divided, that they might receive a fulness of *joy.

18 While this vast multitude waited and conversed, rejoicing in the hour of their *deliverance from the chains of death, the Son of God appeared, declaring *liberty to the *captives who had been faithful;

19 And there he *preached to them the everlasting *gospel, the doctrine of the *resurrection and the redemption of mankind from the *fall, and from individual sins on conditions of *repentance.

20 But unto the *wicked he did not go, and among the ungodly and the unrepentant who had *defiled themselves while in the flesh, his voice was not raised;

21 Neither did the *rebellious who rejected the *testimonies and the warnings of the ancient *prophets behold his *presence, nor look upon his face.

22 Where there were, *darkness reigned, but among the righteous there was *peace;

23 And the saints rejoiced in their *redemption, and bowed the *knee and acknowledged the Son of God as their Redeemer and Deliverer from death and the *chains of *hell.

24 Their countenances *shone, and the *radiance from the presence of the Lord rested upon them, and they *sang praises unto his holy name.

25 I marveled, for I understood that the Savior spent about three years in his *ministry among the Jews and those of the house of Israel, endeavoring to *teach them the everlasting gospel and call them unto repentance;

26 And yet, notwithstanding his mighty works, and miracles, and proclamation of the truth, in great *power and authority, there were but *few who hearkened to his voice, and rejoiced in his presence, and received salvation at his hands.

27 But his ministry among those who were dead was limited to the *brief time intervening between the crucifixion and his resurrection;

28 And I wondered at the words of Peter—wherein he said that the Son of God preached unto the *spirits in prison, who sometime were disobedient, when once the long-suffering of God waited in the days of Noah—and how it was possible for him to preach to those spirits and perform the necessary labor among them in so short a time.

16a Luke 23: 43; Alma 40:
20 (20–21).
TG Paradise.
b TG Redemption.
c Alma 36: 18; Morm.
9: 13.
17a Job 34: 15.
b 2 Ne. 9: 13 (10–13);
Alma 41: 4 (3–5).
c TG Perfection.
d Ezek. 37: 7 (1–14).
e D&C 93: 33 (33–34).
f TG Joy.
18a 2 Ne. 9: 12.
b TG Jesus Christ,
Redeemer; Salvation
for the Dead.
c Isa. 61: 1.
19a D&C 76: 73 (72–74).
TG Preaching.

b TG Gospel.
c 2 Ne. 9: 13 (4–22).
d TG Fall of Man.
e TG Repentance.
20a Alma 40: 14 (13–14).
TG Spirits in Prison;
Wickedness.
b 1 Ne. 10: 21; D&C 138:
37; Moses 6: 57.
21a Matt. 23: 37.
TG Rebellion.
b D&C 76: 82.
c TG Prophets, Re-
jection of.
d Moses 6: 57.
22a TG Darkness, Spiritual.
b TG Peace of God.
23a Heb. 9: 12 (11–15).
TG Joy; Redemption.
b Rom. 14: 11; Mosiah

27: 31.
c Alma 5: 7.
d TG Hell.
24a Ex. 34: 30 (29–30, 35);
Hel. 5: 36 (23–48);
JS-H 1: 32 (31–32).
TG Light.
b Ps. 104: 2; Isa. 60: 19;
Rev. 22: 5; JS-H 1: 17.
c 2 Chr. 29: 30.
TG Singing; Worship.
25a TG Jesus Christ,
Mission of.
b TG Teaching.
26a 1 Ne. 11: 28 (28, 31).
b Matt. 7: 14 (13–14);
1 Ne. 11: 31 (28–32),
14: 12.
27a Mark 8: 31.
28a TG Spirits in Prison.

29 And as I wondered, my eyes were opened, and my understanding [a]quickened, and I perceived that the Lord went not in person among the [b]wicked and the disobedient who had rejected the truth, to teach them;

30 But behold, from among the righteous, he [a]organized his forces and appointed [b]messengers, [c]clothed with power and authority, and [d]commissioned them to go forth and carry the light of the gospel to them that were in [e]darkness, even to [f]all the spirits of men; and thus was the gospel preached to the dead.

31 And the chosen messengers went forth to declare the [a]acceptable day of the Lord and proclaim [b]liberty to the captives who were bound, even unto all who would [c]repent of their sins and receive the gospel.

32 Thus was the gospel preached to those who had [a]died in their sins, without a [b]knowledge of the truth, or in [c]transgression, having [d]rejected the prophets.

33 These were taught [a]faith in God, repentance from sin, [b]vicarious baptism for the [c]remission of sins, the [d]gift of the Holy Ghost by the laying on of hands,

34 And all other principles of the gospel that were necessary for them to know in order to qualify them-selves that they might be [a]judged according to men in the flesh, but live according to God in the spirit.

35 And so it was made known among the dead, both small and great, the unrighteous as well as the faithful, that redemption had been wrought through the [a]sacrifice of the Son of God upon the [b]cross.

36 Thus was it made known that our Redeemer spent his time during his sojourn in the world of [a]spirits, instructing and preparing the faithful spirits of the [b]prophets who had testified of him in the flesh;

37 That they might carry the message of redemption unto all the dead, unto whom he could not go personally, because of their [a]rebellion and transgression, that they through the ministration of his servants might also hear his words.

38 Among the great and [a]mighty ones who were assembled in this vast congregation of the righteous were Father [b]Adam, the [c]Ancient of Days and father of all,

39 And our glorious [a]Mother [b]Eve, with many of her faithful [c]daughters who had lived through the ages and worshiped the true and living God.

40 [a]Abel, the first [b]martyr, was there, and his brother [c]Seth, one of the mighty ones, who was in the express [d]image of his father, Adam.

41 [a]Noah, who gave warning of the

29a D&C 76: 12.
  b D&C 138: 20.
30a TG Kingdom of God, in Heaven.
  b TG Missionary Work.
  c Luke 24: 49.
    TG Delegation of Responsibility; Priesthood, Authority; Priesthood, Power of.
  d D&C 20: 73.
  e TG Darkness, Spiritual.
  f D&C 1: 2 (2, 11).
31a Isa. 61: 2; Luke 4: 19.
  b TG Liberty.
  c TG Repentance; Teachable.
32a John 8: 24 (21–24).
  b D&C 128: 5. TG Knowledge.
  c TG Transgression.

d D&C 76: 74 (73–74).
33a A of F 4. TG Faith.
  b D&C 124: 33 (28–39). TG Baptism, Essential; Baptism for the Dead.
  c TG Remission of Sins.
  d TG Holy Ghost, Gift of.
34a 1 Pet. 4: 6. TG Judgment, The Last; Justice.
35a Alma 34: 14 (9–16). TG Jesus Christ, Atonement through; Sacrifice.
36a TG Jesus Christ, Crucifixion of.
  b TG Paradise.
  b TG Prophets, Mission of.

37a 1 Ne. 10: 21; D&C 138: 20; Moses 6. 57.
38a Abr. 3: 22 (22–26).
  b Moses 1: 34. TG Adam.
  c Dan. 7: 9 (9–14); 2 Ne. 2: 20; D&C 27: 11.
39a Moses 4: 26.
  b Gen. 3: 20; Moses 5: 12 (4, 11–12).
  c Moses 5: 2 (2–3). TG Sons and Daughters of God; Woman.
40a Gen. 4: 2 (1–8); Moses 5: 17 (17–32).
  b TG Martyrdom.
  c Gen. 4: 25 (25–26); Moses 6: 3 (2–13).
  d Gen. 5: 3; Moses 6: 10.
41a Gen. 6: 8 (1–22); Moses 8: 13 (8–30).

flood; [b]Shem, the great [c]high priest; [d]Abraham, the father of the faithful; [e]Isaac, [f]Jacob, and Moses, the great [g]law-giver of Israel;

42 And [a]Isaiah, who declared by prophecy that the Redeemer was anointed to bind up the broken-hearted, to proclaim liberty to the [b]captives, and the opening of the [c]prison to them that were bound, were also there.

43 Moreover, Ezekiel, who was shown in vision the great valley of [a]dry bones, which were to be [b]clothed upon with flesh, to come forth again in the resurrection of the dead, living souls;

44 Daniel, who foresaw and foretold the establishment of the [a]kingdom of God in the latter days, never again to be destroyed nor given to other people;

45 [a]Elias, who was with Moses on the Mount of Transfiguration;

46 And [a]Malachi, the prophet who testified of the coming of [b]Elijah— of whom also Moroni spake to the Prophet Joseph Smith, declaring that he should come before the ushering in of the great and dreadful [c]day of the Lord—were also there.

47 The Prophet Elijah was to plant in the [a]hearts of the children the promises made to their fathers,

48 Foreshadowing the great work to be done in the [a]temples of the Lord in the [b]dispensation of the fulness of times, for the redemption of the dead, and the [c]sealing of the children to their parents, lest the whole earth be smitten with a curse and utterly wasted at his coming.

49 All these and many more, even the [a]prophets who dwelt among the Nephites and [b]testified of the coming of the Son of God, mingled in the vast assembly and waited for their deliverance,

50 For the [a]dead had looked upon the long absence of their [b]spirits from their bodies as a [c]bondage.

51 These the Lord taught, and gave them [a]power to come forth, after his resurrection from the dead, to enter into his Father's kingdom, there to be crowned with [b]immortality and eternal life,

52 And continue thenceforth their labor as had been promised by the Lord, and be partakers of all [a]blessings which were held in reserve for them that love him.

53 The Prophet Joseph Smith, and my father, Hyrum Smith, Brigham Young, John Taylor, Wilford Woodruff, and other choice [a]spirits who were [b]reserved to come forth in the fulness of times to take part in laying the [c]foundations of the great latter-day work,

54 Including the building of the [a]temples and the performance of ordinances therein for the redemption of the [b]dead, were also in the spirit world.

55 I observed that they were also

41b Gen. 5: 32.
  c TG High Priest— Melchizedek Priesthood; Priesthood, Melchizedek.
  d Gen. 17: 5 (1–27).
  e Gen. 21: 3 (1–8).
  f Gen. 35: 10 (1–29).
  g TG Law of Moses.
42a Isa. 1: 1.
  b Isa. 61: 1 (1–2).
  c TG Spirits in Prison.
43a Ezek. 1: 3; 37: 1 (1–14).
  b TG Resurrection.
44a Dan. 2: 44 (44–45).
  TG Kingdom of God, on Earth.
45a See "Elias" in BD.

46a Mal. 4: 5 (5–6); JS—H 1: 38 (36–39).
  b 1 Kgs. 17: 1 (1–24); D&C 110: 13 (13–15).
  c TG Day of the Lord.
47a Mal. 4: 6 (5–6); D&C 128: 17; JS—H 1: 39 (36–39).
48a TG Genealogy and Temple Work; Salvation for the Dead.
  b TG Dispensations.
  c TG Family, Eternal; Sealing.
49a TG Jesus Christ, Prophecies about.
  b Hel. 8: 22 (19–22).
50a Luke 1: 79.

  b TG Spirits, Disembodied.
  c D&C 45: 17.
51a Rom. 8: 11; 1 Cor. 6: 14; Alma 40: 20 (19–21).
  b D&C 29: 43.
  TG Eternal Life.
52a Deut. 7: 13 (6–14); Isa. 64: 4; 1 Cor. 2: 9.
  TG Blessing.
53a TG Man, Antemortal Existence of.
  b TG Foreordination.
  c D&C 128: 18.
  d D&C 64: 33.
54a TG Temple.
  b TG Salvation for the Dead.

among the ᵃnoble and great ones who were ᵇchosen in the beginning to be rulers in the Church of God.

56 Even before they were born, they, with many others, received their first ᵃlessons in the world of spirits and were ᵇprepared to come forth in the due ᶜtime of the Lord to labor in his ᵈvineyard for the salvation of the souls of men.

57 I beheld that the faithful ᵃelders of this dispensation, when they depart from mortal life, continue their labors in the ᵇpreaching of the ᶜgospel of repentance and redemption, through the sacrifice of the Only Begotten Son of God, among those who are in darkness and under the bondage of sin in the great world of the ᵈspirits of the dead.

58 The dead who ᵃrepent will be redeemed, through obedience to the ᵇordinances of the house of God,

59 And after they have paid the ᵃpenalty of their transgressions, and are ᵇwashed clean, shall receive a ᶜreward according to their ᵈworks, for they are heirs of salvation.

60 Thus was the ᵃvision of the redemption of the dead revealed to me, and I bear record, and I know that this ᵇrecord is ᶜtrue, through the blessing of our Lord and Savior, Jesus Christ, even so. Amen.

55a Abr. 3: 22 (22-24).
  b TG Foreordination.
56a TG Earth, Purpose of;
      Learning.
  b Job 38: 7 (1-7);
      Alma 13: 3 (3-7).
  c Acts 17: 26.
  d Jacob 6: 2 (2-3).
57a TG Elders; Missionary
      Work.

  b TG Mission of Latter-
      day Saints.
  c TG Gospel.
  d TG Spirits in Prison.
58a TG Redemption;
      Repentance.
  b Matt. 16: 19.
      TG Covenants;
      Ordinance.

59a TG Punishment.
  b Alma 5: 21 (17-22).
      TG Forgiveness.
  c TG Justice; Reward.
  d TG Good Works.
60a Rev. 20: 12.
  b TG Testimony.
  c John 21: 24.
      TG True.

OFFICIAL DECLARATION—1

To Whom It May Concern:

Press dispatches having been sent for political purposes, from Salt Lake City, which have been widely published, to the effect that the Utah Commission, in their recent report to the Secretary of the Interior, allege that plural marriages are still being solemnized and that forty or more such marriages have been contracted in Utah since last June or during the past year, also that in public discourses the leaders of the Church have taught, encouraged and urged the continuance of the practice of polygamy—

I, therefore, as President of the Church of Jesus Christ of Latter-day Saints, do hereby, in the most solemn manner, declare that these charges are false. We are not teaching polygamy or plural marriage, nor permitting any person to enter into its practice, and I deny that either forty or any other number of plural marriages have during that period been solemnized in our Temples or in any other place in the Territory.

One case has been reported, in which the parties allege that the marriage was performed in the Endowment House, in Salt Lake City, in the Spring of 1889, but I have not been able to learn who performed the ceremony; whatever was done in this matter was without my knowledge. In consequence of this alleged occurrence the Endowment House was, by my instructions, taken down without delay.

Inasmuch as laws have been enacted by Congress forbidding plural marriages, which laws have been pronounced constitutional by the court of last resort, I hereby declare my intention to submit to those laws, and to use my influence with the members of the Church over which I preside to have them do likewise.

There is nothing in my teachings to the Church or in those of my associates, during the time specified, which can be reasonably construed to inculcate or encourage polygamy; and when any Elder of the Church has used language which appeared to convey any such teaching, he has been promptly reproved. And I now publicly declare that my advice to the Latter-day Saints is to refrain from contracting any marriage forbidden by the law of the land.

WILFORD WOODRUFF
President of the Church of Jesus Christ
of Latter-day Saints.

President Lorenzo Snow offered the following:

"I move that, recognizing Wilford Woodruff as the President of the Church of Jesus Christ of Latter-day Saints, and the only man on the earth at the present time who holds the keys of the sealing ordinances, we consider him fully authorized by virtue of his position to issue the Manifesto which has been read in our hearing, and which is dated September 24th, 1890, and that as a Church in General Conference assembled, we accept his declaration concerning plural marriages as authoritative and binding."

The vote to sustain the foregoing motion was unanimous.

Salt Lake City, Utah, October 6, 1890.

EXCERPTS FROM THREE ADDRESSES BY PRESIDENT WILFORD WOODRUFF REGARDING THE MANIFESTO

The Lord will never permit me or any other man who stands as President of this Church to lead you astray. It is not in the programme. It is not in the mind of God. If I were to attempt that, the Lord would remove me out of my place, and so He will any other man who attempts to lead the children of men astray from the oracles of God and from their duty. (Sixty-first Semiannual General Conference of the Church, Monday, October 6, 1890, Salt Lake City, Utah. Reported in *Deseret Evening News*, October 11, 1890, p. 2.)

It matters not who lives or who dies, or who is called to lead this Church, they have got to lead it by the inspiration of Almighty God. If they do not do it that way, they cannot do it at all. . . .

I have had some revelations of late, and very important ones to me, and I will tell you what the Lord has said to me. Let me bring your minds to what is termed the manifesto. . . .

The Lord has told me to ask the Latter-day Saints a question, and He also told me that if they would listen to what I said to them and answer the question put to them, by the Spirit and power of God, they would all answer alike, and they would all believe alike with regard to this matter.

The question is this: Which is the wisest course for the Latter-day Saints to pursue—to continue to attempt to practice plural marriage, with the laws of the nation against it and the opposition of sixty millions of people, and at the cost of the confiscation and loss of all the Temples, and the stopping of all the ordinances therein, both for the living and the dead, and the imprisonment of the First Presidency and Twelve and the heads of families in the Church, and the confiscation of personal property of the people (all of which of themselves would stop the practice); or, after doing and suffering what we have through our adherence to this principle to cease the practice and submit to the law, and through doing so leave the Prophets, Apostles and fathers at home, so that they can instruct the people and attend to the duties of the Church, and also leave the Temples in the hands of the Saints, so that they can attend to the ordinances of the Gospel, both for the living and the dead?

The Lord showed me by vision and revelation exactly what would take place if we did not stop this practice. If we had not stopped it, you would have had no use for . . . any of the men in this temple at Logan; for all ordinances would be stopped throughout the land of Zion. Confusion would reign throughout Israel, and many men would be made prisoners. This trouble would have come upon the whole Church, and we should have been compelled to stop the practice. Now, the question is, whether it should be stopped in this manner, or in the way the Lord has manifested to us, and leave our Prophets and Apostles and fathers free men, and the temples in the hands of the people, so that the dead may be redeemed. A large number have already been delivered from the prison house in the spirit world by this people, and shall the work go on or stop? This is the question I lay before the Latter-day Saints. You have to judge for yourselves. I want you to answer it for yourselves. I shall not answer it; but I say to you that that is exactly the condition we as a people would have been in had we not taken the course we have.

. . . I saw exactly what would come to pass if there was not something done. I have had this spirit upon me for a long time. But I want to say this: I should have let all the temples go out of our hands; I should have gone to prison myself, and let every other man go there, had not the God of heaven commanded me to do what I did do; and when the hour came that I was commanded to do that, it was all clear to me. I went before the Lord, and I wrote what the Lord told me to write. . . .

I leave this with you, for you to contemplate and consider. The Lord is at work with us. (Cache Stake Conference, Logan, Utah, Sunday, November 1, 1891. Reported in *Deseret Weekly*, November 14, 1891.)

Now I will tell you what was manifested to me and what the Son of God performed in this thing. . . . All these things would have come to pass, as God Almighty lives, had not that Manifesto been given. Therefore, the Son of God felt disposed to have that thing presented to the Church and to the world for purposes in his own mind. The Lord had decreed the establishment of Zion. He had decreed the finishing of this temple. He had decreed that the salvation of the living and the dead should be given in these valleys of the mountains. And Almighty God decreed that the Devil should not thwart it. If you can understand that, that is a key to it. (From a discourse at the sixth session of the dedication of the Salt Lake Temple, April 1893, Typescript of Dedicatory Services, Archives, Church Historical Department, Salt Lake City, Utah.)

OFFICIAL DECLARATION—2

To Whom It May Concern:

On September 30, 1978, at the 148th Semiannual General Conference of The Church of Jesus Christ of Latter-day Saints, the following was presented by President N. Eldon Tanner, First Counselor in the First Presidency of the Church:

In early June of this year, the First Presidency announced that a revelation had been received by President Spencer W. Kimball extending priesthood and temple blessings to all worthy male members of the Church. President Kimball has asked that I advise the conference that after he had received this revelation, which came to him after extended meditation and prayer in the sacred rooms of the holy temple, he presented it to his counselors, who accepted it and approved it. It was then presented to the Quorum of the Twelve Apostles, who unanimously approved it, and was subsequently presented to all other General Authorities, who likewise approved it unanimously.

President Kimball has asked that I now read this letter:

June 8, 1978
To all general and local priesthood officers of The Church of Jesus Christ of Latter-day Saints throughout the world:

Dear Brethren:

As we have witnessed the expansion of the work of the Lord over the earth, we have been grateful that people of many nations have responded to the message of the restored gospel, and have joined the Church in ever-increasing numbers. This, in turn, has inspired us with a desire to extend to every worthy member of the Church all of the privileges and blessings which the gospel affords.

Aware of the promises made by the prophets and presidents of the Church who have preceded us that at some time, in God's eternal plan, all of our brethren who are worthy may receive the priesthood, and witnessing the faithfulness of those from whom the priesthood has been withheld, we have pleaded long and earnestly in behalf of these, our faithful brethren, spending many hours in the Upper Room of the Temple supplicating the Lord for divine guidance.

He has heard our prayers, and by revelation has confirmed that the long-promised day has come when every faithful, worthy man in the Church may receive the holy priesthood, with power to exercise its divine authority, and enjoy with his loved ones every blessing that flows therefrom, including the blessings of the temple. Accordingly, all worthy male members of the Church may be ordained to the priesthood without regard for race or color. Priesthood leaders are instructed to follow the policy of carefully interviewing all candidates for ordination to either the Aaronic or the Melchizedek Priesthood to insure that they meet the established standards for worthiness.

We declare with soberness that the Lord has now made known his will for the blessing of all his children throughout the earth who will hearken to the voice of his authorized servants, and prepare themselves to receive every blessing of the gospel.

Sincerely yours,

SPENCER W. KIMBALL
N. ELDON TANNER
MARION G. ROMNEY

The First Presidency

Recognizing Spencer W. Kimball as the prophet, seer, and revelator, and president of The Church of Jesus Christ of Latter-day Saints, it is proposed that we as a constituent assembly accept this revelation as the word and will of the Lord. All in favor please signify by raising your right hand. Any opposed by the same sign.

The vote to sustain the foregoing motion was unanimous in the affirmative.

Salt Lake City, Utah, September 30, 1978.

Canada

Vermont

Maine

Sharon•
Norwich• •Lebanon

New York

New
Hampshire

Atlantic

Albany•

•Topsfield

Massachusetts

Salem•
Boston•

Ocean

Connecticut

R.I.

•New York City

The New England Area

N.J.

| 0 | 10 | 50 | 100 | Miles |
| 0 | 16 | 80 | 160 | Km |

BYU Geography Dept.

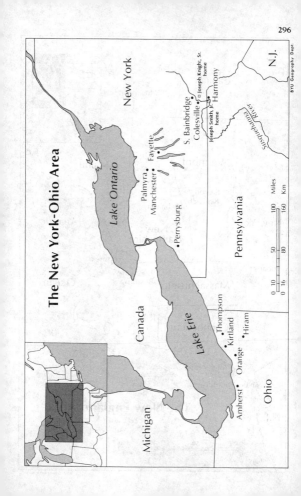

The New York-Ohio Area

New York

Lake Ontario

Canada

Lake Erie

Michigan

Ohio

Pennsylvania

N.J.

Susquehanna River

Palmyra
Manchester
Fayette
S. Bainbridge
Colesville
Joseph Knight, Sr.
Harmony
Joseph Smith Jr.
home

Perrysburg

Thompson
Kirtland
Orange
Hiram
Amherst

BYU Geography Dept.

0   10   50   100   Miles
0 16   80   160   Km

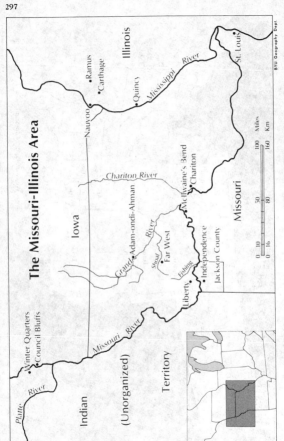

The Missouri-Illinois Area

297

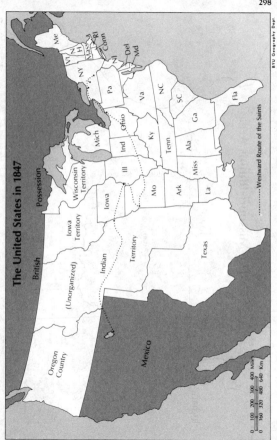

The United States in 1847

British Possession

Oregon Country

Iowa Territory

Indian Territory (Unorganized)

Texas

Mexico

Wisconsin Territory

Mich

Ill

Iowa

Mo

Ark

La

Miss

Ala

Tenn

Ky

Ohio

Ind

Ga

SC

NC

Va

Pa

Fla

Me

Vt

N.H.

Mass

R.I.

Conn

NY

NJ

Del

Md

.... Westward Route of the Saints

BYU Geography Dept.

0 100 200 300 400 Miles
0 160 320 480 640 Km

THE
PEARL OF GREAT PRICE

A SELECTION FROM THE REVELATIONS,
TRANSLATIONS, AND NARRATIONS OF
JOSEPH SMITH

FIRST PROPHET, SEER, AND REVELATOR TO
THE CHURCH OF JESUS CHRIST OF
LATTER-DAY SAINTS

PUBLISHED BY
THE CHURCH OF JESUS CHRIST
OF LATTER-DAY SAINTS
SALT LAKE CITY, UTAH, U.S.A.

INTRODUCTORY NOTE

The Pearl of Great Price is a selection of choice materials touching many significant aspects of the faith and doctrine of The Church of Jesus Christ of Latter-day Saints. These items were produced by the Prophet Joseph Smith and were published in the Church periodicals of his day.

The first collection of materials carrying the title Pearl of Great Price was made in 1851 by Elder Franklin D. Richards, then a member of the Council of the Twelve and president of the British Mission. Its purpose was to make more readily accessible some important articles that had had limited circulation in the time of Joseph Smith. As Church membership increased throughout Europe and America there was a need to make these items available. The Pearl of Great Price received wide use and subsequently became a standard work of the Church by action of the First Presidency and the general conference in Salt Lake City on October 10, 1880.

Several revisions have been made in the contents as the needs of the Church have required. In 1878 portions of the Book of Moses not contained in the first edition were added. In 1902 certain parts of the Pearl of Great Price that duplicated material also published in the Doctrine and Covenants were omitted. Arrangement into chapters and verses, with footnotes, was done in 1902. The first publication in double-column pages, with index, was in 1921. No other changes were made until April 1976, when two items of revelation were added. In 1979 these two items were removed from the Pearl of Great Price and placed in the Doctrine and Covenants, where they now appear as sections 137 and 138. In the present edition some changes have been made to bring the text into conformity with earlier documents.

Following is a brief introduction to the present contents:

Selections from the Book of Moses. An extract from the book of Genesis of Joseph Smith's Translation of the Bible, which he began in June 1830. See *History of the Church,* vol. 1, pp. 98–101, 131–139.

The Book of Abraham. A translation from some Egyptian papyri that came into the hands of Joseph Smith in 1835, containing writings of the patriarch Abraham. The translation was published serially in the *Times and Seasons* beginning March 1, 1842, at Nauvoo, Illinois. See *History of the Church,* vol. 4, pp. 519–534.

Joseph Smith—Matthew. An extract from the testimony of Matthew in Joseph Smith's Translation of the Bible. See Doctrine and Covenants 45: 60–61 for the divine injunction to begin the translation of the New Testament.

Joseph Smith—History. Excerpts from Joseph Smith's official testimony and history, which he prepared in 1838, and which was published serially in the *Times and Seasons* in Nauvoo, Illinois, beginning on March 15, 1842. See *History of the Church,* vol. 1, pp. 1–44, for the complete account.

The Articles of Faith of The Church of Jesus Christ of Latter-day Saints. A statement by Joseph Smith published in the *Times and Seasons* March 1, 1842, in company with a short history of the Church that was popularly known as the Wentworth Letter. See *History of the Church,* vol. 4, pp. 535–541.

CONTENTS

	Page
Selections from the Book of Moses . . .	1
The Book of Abraham	29
Facsimile No. 1	28
Facsimile No. 2	36
Facsimile No. 3	41
Joseph Smith—Matthew	43
Joseph Smith—History	47
The Articles of Faith	60

CONTENTS

THE
PEARL OF GREAT PRICE

SELECTIONS FROM THE
BOOK OF MOSES

*An extract from the translation of the Bible as revealed to
Joseph Smith the Prophet, June 1830—February 1831*

CHAPTER 1
(June 1830)

God reveals himself to Moses—Moses transfigured—Confrontation with Satan—Many inhabited worlds seen—Worlds without number created by the Son—God's work and glory to bring to pass the immortality and eternal life of man.

THE words of God, which he ^aspake unto Moses at a time when Moses was caught up into an exceedingly high ^bmountain,

2 And he ^asaw God ^bface to face, and he ^ctalked with him, and the ^dglory of God was upon Moses; therefore Moses could endure his presence.

3 And God spake unto Moses, saying: Behold, I am the Lord God ^aAlmighty, and ^bEndless is my ^cname; for I am without beginning of days or end of years; and is not this endless?

4 And, behold, thou art my son; wherefore ^alook, and I will show thee the ^bworkmanship of mine ^chands; but not all, for my ^dworks are without ^eend, and also my ^fwords, for they never cease.

5 Wherefore, no man can behold all my ^aworks, except he behold all my ^bglory; and no man can ^cbehold all my ^dglory, and afterwards remain in the flesh on the earth.

6 And I have a work for thee, Moses, my son; and thou art in the ^asimilitude of mine ^bOnly ^cBegotten; and mine Only Begotten is and shall be the ^dSavior, for he is full of ^egrace

---

1 1a Alma 12: 30; Moses 1: 42.
b Isa. 19: 3; Ezek. 40: 2; Rev. 21: 10; Moses 1: 42.
2a Ex. 3: 6; 33: 20 (11–23); John 1: 18; Ether 3: 15; Moses 1: 11. TG God, Privilege of Seeing; Jesus Christ, Appearances, Antemortal; Vision.
b Num. 12: 8; Deut. 34: 10; D&C 17: 1. TG God, Manifestations of.
c Ex. 25: 1. TG Communication.
d Deut. 5: 24; Moses 1: 14 (13–14, 25).

3a Rev. 19: 6. TG Jesus Christ, Power of.
b Isa. 63: 16; D&C 19: 10 (9–12); Moses 7: 35. TG God, Eternal Nature of.
c Ex. 3: 15.
4a Moses 7: 4.
b Job 9: 12.
c Moses 7: 32 (32–37).
d Ps. 40: 5; 92: 5; Morm. 9: 16 (16–20); D&C 76: 114. TG God, Works of.
e Ps. 111: 8 (7–8); 1 Ne. 14: 7; D&C 29: 33; Moses 1: 38.

f Ps. 33: 11; 2 Ne. 9: 16; D&C 1: 38 (37–39).
5a TG God, Works of.
b TG Glory; Jesus Christ, Glory of.
c TG God, Privilege of Seeing.
d Ex. 24: 17; John 12: 41. TG Celestial Glory.
6a Gen. 1: 26; Deut. 18: 15; Acts 3: 22; 1 Ne. 22: 21; Moses 1: 16 (13–16).
b Moses 1: 33.
c Moses 6: 57.
d 1 Ne. 13: 40. TG Jesus Christ, Savior.
e John 1: 17 (17, 17); 2 Ne. 2: 6; Alma 13: 9. TG Grace.

and ^f truth; but there is ^g no God beside me, and all things are present with me, for I ^h know them all.

7 And now, behold, this one thing I show unto thee, Moses, my son, for thou art in the world, and now I show it unto thee.

8 And it came to pass that Moses looked, and beheld the ^a world upon which he was created; and Moses ^b beheld the world and the ends thereof, and all the children of men which are, and which were created; of the same he greatly ^c marveled and wondered.

9 And the ^a presence of God withdrew from Moses, that his ^b glory was not upon Moses; and Moses was left unto himself. And as he was left unto himself, he ^c fell unto the earth.

10 And it came to pass that it was for the space of many hours before Moses did again receive his natural ^a strength like unto man; and he said unto himself: Now, for this cause I know that ^b man is ^c nothing, which thing I never had supposed.

11 But now mine own eyes have ^a beheld God; but not my ^b natural, but my ^c spiritual eyes, for my ^d natural eyes could not have ^e beheld; for I should have ^f withered and ^g died in his presence; but his ^h glory was upon me; and I beheld his ^i face, for I was ^j transfigured before him.

12 And it came to pass that when Moses had said these words, behold, ^a Satan came ^b tempting him, saying: Moses, son of man, worship me.

13 And it came to pass that Moses looked upon Satan and said: Who art thou? For behold, I am a ^a son of God, in the similitude of his Only Begotten; and where is thy ^b glory, that I should worship thee?

14 For behold, I could not look upon God, except his ^a glory should come upon me, and I were transfigured before him. But I ^b can look upon thee in the natural man. Is it not so, surely?

15 And blessed be the name of my God, for his ^a Spirit hath not altogether withdrawn from me, or else where is thy glory, for it is darkness unto me? And I can judge between thee and God; for God said unto me: ^b Worship God, for him only shalt thou ^c serve.

16 Get thee hence, Satan; deceive me not; for God said unto me: Thou art after the ^a similitude of mine Only Begotten.

17 And he also gave me commandments when he ^a called unto me out of the burning ^b bush, saying: ^c Call upon God in the name of mine Only Begotten, and worship me.

18 And again Moses said: I will not cease to call upon God, I have other

---

6f Moses 5:7.
g Deut. 32:17; 1 Kgs. 8: 60; Isa. 44:8; 45:5 (5–22); 46:9.
h Isa. 48:3 (3–7); 1 Ne. 9:6; Moses 1:35. TG God, Foreknowledge of; God, Omniscience of.
8a Moses 2:1.
b Moses 1:27.
c Ps. 8:3 (3–4).
9a Job 10:12.
b TG Glory.
c Isa. 6:5; Acts 9:4; JS-H 1:20.
10a Num. 10:8 (8, 17); 1 Ne. 17:47; 19:20; Alma 27:17.
b TG Mortality.
c Job 42:6 (1–6).

Dan. 4:35; Hel. 12:7; Ether 3:2.
TG Humility.
11a Moses 1:2. TG God, Privilege of Seeing.
b Moses 6:36.
c Moses 1:31.
d Ex. 33:20.
e D&C 67:10 (10–13).
f Ex. 19:21; D&C 67:11 (11–13).
g Ex. 20:19.
h TG Glory.
i Gen. 32:30; Moses 7: 4.
j Matt. 17:2 (1–8); D&C 110:3.
TG Transfiguration.
12a Moses 4:4 (1, 4).
TG Devil.
b Luke 4:2 (1–13);

2 Cor. 11:14 (13–15);
Rev. 12:9 (7–9);
2 Ne. 1:18 (17–18);
Moses 1:21; 6:49.
13a Job 1:6; Isa. 14:12 (12–15).
b D&C 88:24.
14a Moses 1:2 (2, 25).
TG Glory.
b Rev. 1:17.
15a TG God, Spirit of.
b Matt. 4:10.
TG Worship.
c 1 Sam. 7:3; 3 Ne. 13: 24.
16a Moses 1:6. TG God, Body of (Corporeal Nature).
17a Ex. 19:3.
b Ex. 3:2 (2–15).
c Moses 5:8.

things to inquire of him: for his [a]glory has been upon me, wherefore I can judge between him and thee. [b]Depart hence, Satan.

19 And now, when Moses had said these words, [a]Satan cried with a loud voice, and ranted upon the earth, and commanded, saying: I am the [b]Only Begotten, worship me.

20 And it came to pass that Moses began to [a]fear exceedingly; and as he began to fear, he saw the bitterness of [b]hell. Nevertheless, [c]calling upon God, he received [d]strength, and he commanded, saying: Depart from me, Satan, for this one God only will I worship, which is the God of [e]glory.

21 And now Satan began to tremble, and the earth [a]shook; and Moses received strength, and called upon God, saying: In the name of the Only Begotten, [b]depart hence, [c]Satan.

22 And it came to pass that Satan cried with a loud voice, with weeping, and wailing, and [a]gnashing of teeth; and he departed hence, even from the presence of Moses, that he beheld him not.

23 And now of this thing Moses bore record; but because of [a]wickedness it is [b]not had among the children of men.

24 And it came to pass that when Satan had departed from the presence of Moses, that Moses lifted up his eyes unto heaven, being filled with the [a]Holy Ghost, which bear-

eth record of the Father and the Son;

25 And calling upon the name of God, he beheld his [a]glory again, for it was upon him; and he heard a [b]voice, saying: Blessed art thou, Moses, for I, the Almighty, have [c]chosen thee, and thou shalt be made stronger than many [d]waters; for they shall obey thy [e]command as if thou wert [f]God.

26 And lo, I am [a]with thee, even unto the end of thy days; for thou shalt [b]deliver my people from [c]bondage, even [d]Israel my [e]chosen.

27 And it came to pass, as the voice was still speaking, Moses cast his eyes and [a]beheld the earth, yea, even all of it; and there was not a particle of it which he did not behold, [b]discerning it by the [c]spirit of God.

28 And he beheld also the inhabitants thereof, and there was not a [a]soul which he beheld not; and he discerned them by the Spirit of God; and their numbers were great, even numberless as the sand upon the sea shore.

29 And he beheld many lands; and each land was called [a]earth, and there were [b]inhabitants on the face thereof.

30 And it came to pass that Moses called upon God, saying: [a]Tell me, I pray thee, why these things are so, and by what thou madest them?

31 And behold, the glory of the Lord was upon Moses, so that Moses stood in the presence of God, and

18a TG Glory; Jesus Christ, Glory of.
  b Matt. 4:10.
19a TG False Christs.
  b JS-M 1:6 (5-9).
20a TG Fearfulness.
  b D&C 76:47 (44-47). TG Hell.
  c JS-H 1:16 (15-16). TG Prayer.
  d TG God, Power of; Strength.
  e TG Glory.
21a Moses 1:12.
  b Matt. 10:1. TG Spirits, Evil, Unclean.
22a Matt. 13:42 (41-42); Mosiah 16:2 (1-3).

23a Luke 11:52. TG Record Keeping.
  b Moses 1:41.
24a 3 Ne. 11:32 (32, 36); Moses 8:24.
25a TG Glory.
  b Hel. 5:30; 3 Ne. 11:3.
  c Abr. 3:23.
  d Ex. 14:21.
  e TG Priesthood, Authority.
  f Ex. 4:16.
26a TG Walking with God.
  b Ex. 3:10 (7-12). TG Israel, Deliverance of.
  c Ex. 20:2; Ps. 80:8; 1 Ne. 17:23 (23-25). TG Israel, Bondage

of, in Egypt.
  d 1 Kgs. 8:53 (51, 53). TG Israel, Twelve Tribes of.
  e Ps. 33:12.
27a D&C 88:47 (45-47); Moses 1:8; 7:23; Abr. 3:21 (21-23). TG Vision.
  b TG Discernment, Spiritual; Holy Ghost, Mission of.
  c TG God, Spirit of.
28a Moses 7:23.
29a Gen. 1:10. TG Earth, Dividing of.
  b 1 Ne. 17:36.
30a Moses 2:1.

talked with him ^aface to face. And the Lord God said unto Moses: For mine own ^bpurpose have I made these things. Here is ^cwisdom and it remaineth in me.

32 And by the ^aword of my power, have I created them, which is mine Only Begotten Son, who is full of ^bgrace and truth.

33 And ^aworlds without number have I ^bcreated; and I also created them for mine own purpose; and by the ^cSon I ^dcreated them, which is mine ^eOnly Begotten.

34 And the ^afirst man of all men have I called ^bAdam, which is ^cmany.

35 But only an account of this earth, and the inhabitants thereof, give I unto you. For behold, there are many worlds that have passed away by the word of my power. And there are many that now stand, and innumerable are they unto man; but all things are numbered unto me, for they are mine and I ^aknow them.

36 And it came to pass that Moses spake unto the Lord, saying: Be merciful unto thy servant, O God, and ^atell me concerning this earth, and the inhabitants thereof, and also the heavens, and then thy servant will be content.

37 And the Lord God spake unto Moses, saying: The ^aheavens, they are many, and they cannot be numbered unto man; but they are numbered unto me, for they are mine.

38 And as one earth shall pass away, and the heavens thereof even so shall another come; and there is no ^aend to my works, neither to my words.

39 For behold, this is my ^awork and my ^bglory—to bring to pass the ^cimmortality and ^deternal ^elife of man.

40 And now, Moses, my son, I will speak unto thee concerning this earth upon which thou standest; and thou shalt ^awrite the things which I shall speak.

41 And in a day when the children of men shall esteem my words as ^anaught and ^btake many of them from the ^cbook which thou shalt write, behold, I will raise up another ^dlike unto thee; and they shall be ^ehad again among the children of men—among as many as shall believe.

42 (These words were ^aspoken unto Moses in the mount, the name of which shall not be known among the children of men. And now they are spoken unto you. Show them not unto any except them that believe. Even so. Amen.)

31a Deut. 5:4; Moses 1:11.
  b Isa. 45:18 (17–18);
    Eph. 3:11 (7–12);
    2 Ne. 2:15 (14–30).
    TG Earth, Purpose of.
  c TG God, Intelligence of.
32a John 1:3 (1–4); Heb. 1:
    2 (1–3); Rev. 19:13
    (13–15); Jacob 4:9;
    Moses 2:1 (1, 5).
    TG Jesus Christ,
    Authority of.
  b Moses 5:7 (7–8).
    TG Grace.
33a Job 9:9 (7–9); Ps. 8:3
    (3–4); Amos 9:6; D&C
    76:24; Moses 7:30
    (29–31). TG Astronomy;
    Creation; God, Works
    of.; World.
  b TG God, Creator.
  c TG Jesus Christ,
    Divine Sonship; Jesus
    Christ, Jehovah.

  d TG Jesus Christ,
    Creator.
  e Moses 1:6.
34a Moses 3:7.
  b Abr. 1:3. TG Adam.
  c 1 Cor. 15:45 (45–48);
    2 Ne. 2:20 (19–20);
    D&C 27:11; 76:24;
    138:38; Moses 4:26;
    6:9.
35a 1 Ne. 9:6; D&C 38:2;
    88:41; Moses 1:6; 7:
    36; Abr. 3:2 (1–16).
    TG God, Omniscience
    of.
36a Moses 2:1.
37a Gen. 1:1; Moses 2:1;
    Abr. 4:1. TG Heaven.
38a Moses 1:4.
39a Ps. 90:16; Matt. 5:48;
    Rom. 8:17 (14–21);
    2 Ne. 2:15 (14–30);
    Alma 42:26; D&C 29:
    43 (42–44). TG God,

    Works of.
  b Micah 2:9; Mosiah 4:
    12; D&C 81:4 (3–4).
    TG Glory; Jesus Christ,
    Glory of.
  c Moses 6:59.
    TG Immortality;
    Jesus Christ, Mission
    of.; Resurrection.
  d TG Eternal Life; Man,
    Potential to Become
    Like Heavenly Father.
  e TG Earth, Purpose of.
40a Neh. 13:1 (1–3);
    2 Tim. 3:16; 2 Ne. 29:
    11 (11–12).
41a Moses 1:23.
  b 1 Ne. 13:26 (23–32).
  c Ex. 17:14; 1 Ne. 5:11;
    19:23.
  d 2 Ne. 3:9 (7–19).
  e 1 Ne. 13:32, 39–40;
    D&C 9:2.
42a Moses 1:6.

CHAPTER 2
(June–October 1830)

God creates the heavens and the earth—All forms of life created—God makes man and gives him dominion over all else.

AND it came to pass that the Lord spake unto Moses, saying: Behold, I *a*reveal unto you concerning this *b*heaven, and this *c*earth; *d*write the words which I speak. I am the Beginning and the End, the *e*Almighty God; by mine *f*Only Begotten I *g*created these things; yea, in the beginning I *h*created the *i*heaven, and the earth upon which thou standest.

2 And the earth was without *a*form, and void; and I caused *b*darkness to come up upon the face of the deep; and my *c*Spirit *d*moved upon the face of the water; for I am God.

3 And I, God, said: Let there be *a*light; and there was light.

4 And I, God, saw the light; and that light was *a*good. And I, God, divided the *b*light from the darkness.

5 And I, God, called the light Day; and the darkness, I called Night; and this I did by the *a*word of my power, and it was done as I *b*spake; and the evening and the morning were the first *c*day.

6 And again, I, God, said: Let there be a *a*firmament in the midst of the water, and it was so, even as I spake; and I said: Let it divide the waters from the waters; and it was done;

7 And I, God, made the firmament and divided the *a*waters, yea, the great waters under the firmament from the waters which were above the firmament, and it was so even as I spake.

8 And I, God, called the firmament *a*Heaven; and the evening and the morning were the second day.

9 And I, God, said: Let the *a*waters under the heaven be gathered together unto *b*one place, and it was so; and I, God, said: Let there be dry land; and it was so.

10 And I, God, called the dry land *a*Earth; and the gathering together of the waters, called I the Sea; and I, God, saw that all things which I had made were good.

11 And I, God, said: Let the earth bring forth *a*grass, the herb yielding seed, the fruit tree yielding fruit, after his kind, and the tree yielding fruit, whose seed should be in itself upon the earth, and it was so even as I spake.

12 And the earth brought forth grass, every herb yielding seed after his kind, and the tree yielding fruit, whose seed should be in itself, after his *a*kind; and I, God, saw that all things which I had made were good;

13 And the evening and the morning were the third day.

14 And I, God, said: Let there be *a*lights in the firmament of the heaven, to divide the day from the night, and let them be for signs, and

2 1*a* Moses 1: 30 (30, 36).
  b TG Heaven.
  c Moses 1 : 8.
  d D&C 76: 80. TG Record Keeping; Scribe; Scriptures, Writing of.
  e 1 Ne. 1: 14.
  f Moses 1: 32; Abr. 4: 1.
  g TG Creation; Jesus Christ, Creator.
  h TG God, Creator; God, Works of.
  i Gen. 1: 1.
 2*a* Jer. 4: 23 (23–25).
  b TG Darkness, Physical.
  c TG God, Spirit of.
  d Gen. 1: 2; Abr. 4: 2.

 3*a* D&C 88: 7 (6–13).
  TG Light.
 4*a* Gen. 1: 4; Abr. 4: 4.
  b TG Light.
 5*a* Moses 1: 32.
  b Ps. 33: 9; 2 Cor. 4: 6.
  c Gen. 1: 5.
 6*a* See Abr., Fac. 2, fig. 4 concerning the firmament or expanse. See also Gen. 1: 6 (6–8); Moses 2: 14–18.
 7*a* Amos 9: 6; Abr. 4: 9 (9–10).
 8*a* IE The whole expanse around about the earth, its atmosphere, and beyond are

generically here called "Heaven." The same word is also used sometimes to refer to paradise, to the dwelling place of God, and to the kingdoms of glory.
 9*a* TG Earth, Dividing of.
  b Gen. 1: 9; Abr. 4: 9.
 10*a* IE The whole sphere or any of its parts above the seas is called "Earth."
 11*a* Gen. 1: 11 (11–12); Abr. 4: 11 (11–12).
 12*a* Gen. 1: 12.
 14*a* Ps. 104: 19.

for seasons, and for days, and for years;

15 And let them be for lights in the firmament of the heaven to give light upon the earth; and it was so.

16 And I, God, made two great lights; the greater *a*light to rule the day, and the lesser light to rule the night, and the *b*greater light was the sun, and the lesser light was the moon; and the stars also were made even according to my word.

17 And I, God, set them in the firmament of the heaven to give light upon the earth,

18 And the *a*sun to rule over the day, and the moon to rule over the night, and to divide the light from the *b*darkness; and I, God, saw that all things which I had made were good;

19 And the evening and the morning were the fourth day.

20 And I, God, said: Let the waters bring forth abundantly the moving creature that hath life, and fowl which may fly above the earth in the open firmament of heaven.

21 And I, God, created great *a*whales, and every living creature that moveth, which the waters brought forth abundantly, after their kind, and every winged fowl after his kind; and I, God, saw that all things which I had created were good.

22 And I, God, blessed them, saying: Be fruitful, and *a*multiply, and fill the waters in the sea; and let fowl multiply in the earth;

23 And the evening and the morning were the fifth day.

24 And I, God, said: Let the earth bring forth the living creature after

his kind, cattle, and creeping things, and beasts of the earth after their kind, and it was so;

25 And I, God, made the beasts of the earth after their kind, and cattle after their kind, and everything which creepeth upon the earth after his kind; and I, God, saw that all these things were good.

26 And I, God, said unto mine *a*Only Begotten, which was with me from the *b*beginning: Let *c*us *d*make man in our *e*image, after our likeness; and it was so. And I, God, said: Let them have *f*dominion over the fishes of the sea, and over the fowl of the air, and over the cattle, and over all the earth, and over every creeping thing that creepeth upon the earth.

27 And I, God, created man in mine own *a*image, in the image of mine Only Begotten created I him; male and female created I them.

28 And I, God, blessed them, and said unto them: Be *a*fruitful, and *b*multiply, and replenish the earth, and subdue it, and have dominion over the fish of the sea, and over the fowl of the air, and over every living thing that moveth upon the earth.

29 And I, God, said unto man: Behold, I have given you every herb bearing seed, which is upon the face of all the earth, and every tree in the which shall be the fruit of a tree yielding seed; to you it shall be for *d*meat.

30 And to every beast of the earth, and to every fowl of the air, and to everything that creepeth upon the earth, wherein I grant life, there shall be given every clean herb for meat; and it was so, even as I spake.

16a TG Light.
  b Gen. 1: 16.
18a TG Astronomy.
  b TG Darkness, Physical.
21a Gen. 1: 21; Abr. 4: 21.
22a Gen. 1: 22 (20–25);
    D&C 45: 58; 132: 63
    (55–56, 63); Abr. 4:
    22.
26a TG Jesus Christ, Divine
    Sonship.

b TG Jesus Christ,
  Firstborn.
c TG Jesus Christ,
  Creator.
d TG Man, Physical
  Creation of.
e Gen. 1: 26 (26–28);
  Moses 6: 9 (8–10);
  Abr. 4: 26 (26–31).
f Gen. 1: 26 (26–28);
  D&C 76: 111 (110–
  112); 121: 37 (34–46);

Moses 5: 1; Abr. 4: 26
  (26–28).
27a TG God, Body of
  (Corporeal Nature).
28a TG Birth Control.
  b Moses 5: 2.
  TG Marriage, Father-
  hood.
29a Gen. 1: 29 (29–30);
  Ps. 136: 25; D&C 104:
  17 (15–18); Abr. 4: 29
  (29–30).

31 And I, God, saw everything that I had made, and, behold, all things which I had made were very *a*good; and the evening and the morning were the *b*sixth day.

CHAPTER 3
(June–October 1830)

God created all things spiritually before they were naturally upon the earth—First man and first flesh created—Woman a help meet for man.

THUS the *a*heaven and the earth were finished, and all the *b*host of them.

2 And on the seventh day I, God, ended my work, and all things which I had made; and I *a*rested on the *b*seventh day from all my work, and all things which I had made were finished, and I, God, saw that they were good;

3 And I, God, *a*blessed the seventh day, and *b*sanctified it; because that in it I had rested from all my *c*work which I, God, had created and made.

4 And now, behold, I say unto you, that these are the generations of the heaven and of the earth, when they were *a*created, in the day that I, the Lord God, made the *b*heaven and the earth,

5 And every plant of the field before it was in the earth, and every herb of the field before it grew. For I, the Lord God, *a*created all things, of which I have spoken, *b*spiritually, before they were *c*naturally upon the face of the earth. For I, the Lord God, had not caused it to rain upon the face of the earth. And I, the Lord God, had *d*created all the children of men; and not yet a man to till the *e*ground; for in *f*heaven *g*created I them; and there was not yet flesh upon the earth, neither in the water, neither in the air;

6 But I, the Lord God, spake, and there went up a *a*mist from the earth, and watered the whole face of the ground.

7 And I, the Lord God, formed man from the *a*dust of the ground, and breathed into his nostrils the *b*breath of life; and *c*man became a living *d*soul, the *e*first flesh upon the earth, the first man also; nevertheless, all things were before created; but spiritually were they created and made according to my word.

8 And I, the Lord God, planted a garden eastward in *a*Eden, and there I put the man whom I had formed.

9 And out of the ground made I, the Lord God, to grow every tree, *a*naturally, that is pleasant to the sight of man; and man could behold it. And it became also a *b*living soul. For it was spiritual in the day that I created it; for it remaineth in the sphere in which I, God, created it, yea, even all things which I prepared for the use of man; and man saw that it was good for food. And I, the Lord God, planted the *c*tree of life also in the midst of the garden,

31a Gen. 1:31; Moro. 7: 12; D&C 59:17 (16–20).
  b Ex. 20:11 (8–11); 31:17; Mosiah 13:19; Abr. 4:31.
3 1a TG Creation.
  b Gen. 2:1; D&C 29: 36; 38:1; 45:1; Abr. 5:1.
2a Gen. 2:2 (1–3); Abr. 5:2 (1–3). TG Rest.
  b TG Sabbath.
3a Ex. 20:11; Mosiah 13: 19; D&C 77:12.
  b Abr. 5:3 (1–3).
  c Ex. 31:15 (14–15); Mosiah 13:18 (16–19).

4a Gen. 2:4 (4–5); Abr. 5: 4 (4–5).
  b Neh. 9:6.
5a Moses 6:51. TG Creation; God, Creator.
  b Abr. 3:23; D&C 29: 31–34. TG Life, Sanctity of; Spirit Creation.
  c Moses 3:9. TG Man, Physical Creation of.
  d TG Man, a Spirit Child of Heavenly Father.
  e Gen. 2:5.
  f TG Heaven.

g TG Man, Antemortal Existence of.
6a Gen. 2:6.
7a Gen. 2:7; Moses 4:25 (25–29); 6:59; Abr. 5: 7.
  b TG Breath of Life.
  c TG Adam.
  d Isa. 57:16. TG Soul.
  e Moses 1:34.
8a Isa. 51:3. TG Eden.
9a Moses 3:5.
  b TG Life, Sanctity of.
  c Gen. 2:9; 1 Ne. 11:25; 15:22 (22, 28, 36); Alma 42:5 (2–6); Moses 4:28 (28, 31); Abr. 5:9.

and also the tree of knowledge of good and evil.

10 And I, the Lord God, caused a river to go out of ᵃEden to water the garden; and from thence it was parted, and became into four ᵇheads.

11 And I, the Lord God, called the name of the first Pison, and it compasseth the whole land of ᵃHavilah, where I, the Lord God, created much gold;

12 And the gold of that land was good, and there was bdellium and the ᵃonyx stone.

13 And the name of the second river was called Gihon; the same that compasseth the whole land of ᵃEthiopia.

14 And the name of the third river was Hiddekel; that which goeth toward the east of Assyria. And the fourth river was the Euphrates.

15 And I, the Lord God, took the man, and put him into the Garden of ᵃEden, to dress it, and to keep it.

16 And I, the Lord God, commanded the man, saying: Of every tree of the garden thou mayest freely eat,

17 But of the tree of the ᵃknowledge of good and evil, thou shalt not eat of it, nevertheless, thou mayest ᵇchoose for thyself, for it is given unto thee; but, remember that I ᶜforbid it, for in the ᵈday thou eatest thereof thou shalt surely ᵉdie.

18 And I, the Lord God, said unto mine ᵃOnly Begotten, that it was not good that the man should be ᵇalone; wherefore, I will make an ᶜhelp meet for him.

19 And out of the ground I, the

Lord God, formed every ᵃbeast of the field, and every fowl of the air; and commanded that they should come unto Adam, to see what he would call them; and they were also living souls; for I, God, breathed into them the ᵇbreath of life, and commanded that whatsoever Adam called every living creature, that should be the name thereof.

20 And Adam gave ᵃnames to all cattle, and to the fowl of the air, and to every beast of the field; but as for Adam, there was not found an help meet for him.

21 And I, the Lord God, caused a deep sleep to fall upon Adam; and he slept, and I took one of his ribs and closed up the flesh in the stead thereof;

22 And the rib which I, the Lord God, had taken from man, made I a ᵃwoman, and brought her unto the man.

23 And ᵃAdam said: This I know now is bone of my bones, and ᵇflesh of my flesh; she shall be called Woman, because she was taken out of man.

24 Therefore shall a man leave his father and his mother, and shall ᵃcleave unto his ᵇwife; and ᶜthey shall be ᵈone flesh.

25 And they were both naked, the man and his wife, and were not ashamed.

CHAPTER 4
(June–October 1830)

How Satan became the devil—He tempts Eve—Adam and Eve fall and death enters the world.

10a TG Eden.
  b Gen. 2: 10.
11a Gen. 2: 11.
12a Ex. 25: 7.
13a TG In the area of Eden and Adam-ondi-Ahman there were rivers and lands that received names that were later attached to other lands and rivers. As to the location of Eden and its environs, see D&C 117: 8–9. Gen. 2: 13.

15a TG Eden.
17a TG Knowledge.
  b Moses 7: 32.
     TG Agency.
  c 2 Ne. 2: 15.
  d Abr. 5: 13.
  e Gen. 2: 17; Moses 4: 17 (17–19). TG Mortality.
18a TG Jesus Christ, Divine Sonship.
  b TG Family, Eternal.
  c Gen. 2: 18; Abr. 5: 14.
19a Prov. 12: 10; D&C 29: 24 (24–25); 49: 19 (18–21); 77: 2. TG Creation.

  b TG Breath of Life.
20a TG Language.
22a TG Creation.
23a TG Adam.

  b Gen. 2: 23; Jacob 2: 21; Abr. 5: 17.
24a Gen. 2: 24 (23–24); D&C 42: 22; 49: 15 (15–16); Abr. 5: 18 (17–18).
  b TG Family, Love within.
  c Eccl. 4: 9 (9–12).
  d TG Divorce; Marriage, Celestial.

AND I, the ^aLord God, spake unto Moses, saying: That ^bSatan, whom thou hast commanded in the name of mine Only Begotten, is the same which was from the ^cbeginning, and he came before me, saying—Behold, here am I, send me, I will be thy son, and I will ^dredeem all mankind, that one soul shall not be lost, and surely ^eI will do it; wherefore ^fgive me thine honor.

2 But, behold, my Beloved ^aSon, which was my Beloved and ^bChosen from the beginning, said unto me—^cFather, thy ^dwill be done, and the ^eglory be thine forever.

3 Wherefore, because that ^aSatan ^brebelled against me, and sought to destroy the ^cagency of man, which I, the Lord God, had given him, and also, that I should give unto him mine own power; by the power of mine Only Begotten, I caused that he should be ^dcast down;

4 And he became ^aSatan, yea, even the ^bdevil, the father of all ^clies, to ^ddeceive and to blind men, and to lead them ^ecaptive at his will, even as many as would not ^fhearken unto my voice.

5 And now the serpent was more ^asubtle than any beast of the field which I, the Lord God, had made.

6 And ^aSatan put it into the heart of the serpent, (for he had drawn away ^bmany after him,) and he sought also to ^cbeguile Eve, for he ^dknew not the ^emind of God, wherefore he sought to destroy the world.

7 And he said unto the woman: Yea, hath God said—Ye shall not eat of every tree of the garden? (And he spake by the mouth of the serpent.)

8 And the woman said unto the serpent: We may eat of the fruit of the trees of the garden;

9 But of the fruit of the tree which thou beholdest in the midst of the garden, God hath said—Ye shall not eat of it, neither shall ye touch it, lest ye die.

10 And the serpent said unto the ^awoman: Ye shall not surely die;

11 For God doth know that in the day ye eat thereof, then your ^aeyes shall be opened, and ye shall be as gods, ^bknowing good and evil.

12 And when the woman saw that the tree was good for food, and that it became pleasant to the eyes, and a tree to be ^adesired to make her wise, she took of the ^bfruit thereof, and did ^ceat, and also gave unto her husband with her, and he did eat.

13 And the eyes of them both were opened, and they knew that they had been ^anaked. And they sewed fig-leaves together and made themselves ^baprons.

14 And they heard the voice of the Lord God, as they were ^awalking in

4 1a Moses 5: 58.
  b D&C 29: 36 (36–39);
    76: 25 (25–26); Abr. 3:
    27.
  c Moses 5: 24.
  d TG Redemption.
  e Isa. 14: 13 (12–15).
  f TG Selfishness.
 2a TG Jesus Christ, Divine
    Sonship; Witness of
    the Father.
  b Moses 7: 39; Abr. 3:
    27. TG Foreordination;
    Jesus Christ, Authority
    of; Jesus Christ, Fore-
    ordained; Jesus Christ,
    Messenger of the Cove-
    nant; Jesus Christ,
    Messiah.
  c TG God the Father—
    Elohim.

  d Luke 22: 42. TG God,
    the Standard of Right-
    eousness.
  e Ps. 96: 8; John 7: 18.
    TG Glory.
 3a TG Sons of Perdition.
  b Abr. 3: 28. TG Council
    in Heaven; Rebellion.
  c TG Agency.
  d D&C 76: 25 (25–27).
 4a Moses 1: 12.
  b TG Devil.
  c 2 Ne. 2: 18; D&C 10:
    25. TG Honesty; Lying.
  d 1 Thes. 3: 5; D&C 29:
    39 (39–40, 47).
    TG Deceit.
  e TG Bondage, Spiritual.
  f TG Disobedience.
 5a Gen. 3: 1; Mosiah 16:

    3; Alma 12: 4;
    D&C 123: 12.
 6a TG Devil.
  b D&C 29: 36.
  c TG Honesty.
  d John 16: 3 (1–3).
  e 1 Cor. 2: 16. TG Mind.
10a 1 Tim. 2: 14.
11a Gen. 3: 5 (3–6);
    D&C 76: 12 (12, 19);
    Moses 5: 10.
  b Alma 12: 31.
    TG Knowledge.
12a Gen. 3: 6; 1 Ne. 8: 12
    (10–15); 15: 36.
  b D&C 29: 40.
  c TG Fall of Man.
13a Gen. 2: 25; 2 Ne. 9: 14.
  b TG Apparel.
14a Gen. 3: 8.

the garden, in the cool of the day; and Adam and his wife went to hide themselves from the ᵇpresence of the Lord God amongst the trees of the garden.

15 And I, the Lord God, called unto Adam, and said unto him: Where ᵃgoest thou?

16 And he said: I heard thy voice in the garden, and I was afraid, because I beheld that I was naked, and I hid myself.

17 And I, the Lord God, said unto Adam: Who told thee thou wast naked? Hast thou eaten of the tree whereof I commanded thee that thou shouldst not eat, if so thou shouldst surely ᵃdie?

18 And the man said: The woman thou gavest me, and commanded that she should remain with me, she gave me of the fruit of the tree and I did eat.

19 And I, the Lord God, said unto the woman: What is this thing which thou hast done? And the woman said: The serpent ᵃbeguiled me, and I did eat.

20 And I, the Lord God, said unto the serpent: Because thou hast done this thou shalt be ᵃcursed above all cattle, and above every beast of the field; upon thy belly shalt thou go, and dust shalt thou eat all the days of thy life;

21 And I will put ᵃenmity between thee and the woman, between thy seed and her seed; and he shall ᵇbruise thy head, and thou shalt bruise his heel.

22 Unto the woman, I, the Lord God, said: I will greatly multiply thy sorrow and thy conception. In

ᵃsorrow thou shalt bring forth children, and thy desire shall be to thy ᵇhusband, and he shall rule over thee.

23 And unto Adam,ᵃ I, the Lord God, said: Because thou hast hearkened unto the voice of thy wife, and hast eaten of the fruit of the tree of which I commanded thee, saying—Thou shalt not eat of it, ᵃcursed shall be the ground for thy sake; in ᵇsorrow shalt thou eat of it all the days of thy life.

24 Thorns also, and thistles shall it bring forth to thee, and thou shalt eat the herb of the field.

25 By the ᵃsweat of thy ᵇface shalt thou eat bread, until thou shalt return unto the ground—for thou shalt surely die—for out of it wast thou taken: for ᵈdust thou wast, and unto dust shalt thou return.

26 And Adam called his wife's name Eve, because she was the mother of all living; for thus have I, the Lord God, called the first of all women, which are ᵃmany.

27 Unto Adam, and also unto his wife, did I, the Lord God, make coats of ᵃskins, and ᵇclothed them.

28 And I, the Lord God, ᵃsaid unto mine Only Begotten: Behold, the ᵇman is become as one of us to ᶜknow good and evil; and now lest he put forth his hand and ᵈpartake also of the ᵉtree of life, and eat and live forever,

29 Therefore I, the Lord God, will send him forth from the Garden of ᵃEden, to till the ground from whence he was taken;

30 For as I, the Lord God, liveth, even so my ᵃwords cannot return

14b Jonah 1: 3.
15a Gen. 3: 9.
17a Moses 3: 17.
19a Gen. 3: 13 (1–13);
　2 Ne. 9: 9; Mosiah 16: 3;
　Ether 8: 25.
20a Gen. 3: 14 (13–16).
21a Gen. 3: 15.
　b Ps. 68: 21; Rom. 16:
　20; Heb. 2: 14.
22a Gen. 3: 16. TG Pain.
　b TG Marriage, Husbands;
　Marriage, Wives.

23a Job 14: 1; Moses 8: 9.
　TG Earth, Curse of.
　b TG Suffering.
25a Gen. 3: 19 (17–19).
　TG Mortality.
　b Moses 5: 1.
　c Gen. 2: 7; Job 10: 9;
　Ps. 104: 29; Alma 42:
　30; Moses 3: 7; 6: 59;
　Abr. 5: 7.
26a Moses 1: 34; 6: 9.
27a Gen. 27: 16; Alma 49:
　6.

　b TG Apparel; Clothing;
　Modesty.
28a Gen. 3: 22.
　b TG Man, Potential to
　Become Like Heavenly
　Father.
　c TG Knowledge; Proba-
　tion.
　d Alma 42: 5 (4–5).
　e Gen. 2: 9; 1 Ne. 11: 25;
　Moses 3: 9; Abr. 5: 9.
29a TG Eden.
30a 1 Kgs. 8: 56; Jer. 44: 28.

void, for as they go forth out of my mouth they must be fulfilled.

31 So I drove out the man, and I placed at the east of the Garden of [a]Eden, [b]cherubim and a flaming sword, which turned every way to keep the way of the tree of life.

32 (And these are the words which I spake unto my servant Moses, and they are true even as I will; and I have spoken them unto you. See thou show them unto no man, until I command you, except to them that believe. Amen.)

CHAPTER 5
(June–October 1830)

Adam and Eve bring forth children— Adam offers sacrifice, serves God— Cain and Abel born—Cain rebels, loves Satan more than God, and becomes Perdition—Murder and wickedness spread—The gospel preached from the beginning.

AND it came to pass that after I, the Lord God, had driven them out, that Adam began to till the earth, and to have [a]dominion over all the beasts of the field, and to eat his bread by the sweat of his [b]brow, as I the Lord had commanded him. And Eve, also, his wife, did [c]labor with him.

2 And [a]Adam knew his wife, and she bare unto him [b]sons and [c]daughters, and they began to [d]multiply and to replenish the earth.

3 And from that time forth, the sons and [a]daughters of Adam began to divide two and two in the land, and to till the land, and to tend flocks, and they also begat sons and daughters.

4 And Adam and Eve, his wife, [a]called upon the name of the Lord, and they heard the voice of the Lord from the way toward the Garden of [b]Eden, speaking unto them, and they saw him not; for they were shut out from his [c]presence.

5 And he gave unto them commandments, that they should [a]worship the Lord their God, and should offer the [b]firstlings of their [c]flocks, for an offering unto the Lord. And Adam was [d]obedient unto the commandments of the Lord.

6 And after many days an [a]angel of the Lord appeared unto Adam, saying: Why dost thou offer [b]sacrifices unto the Lord? And Adam said unto him: I know not, save the Lord commanded me.

7 And then the angel spake, saying: This thing is a [a]similitude of the [b]sacrifice of the Only Begotten of the Father, which is full of [c]grace and [d]truth.

8 Wherefore, thou shalt do all that thou doest in the [a]name of the Son, and thou shalt [b]repent and [c]call upon God in the name of the Son forevermore.

9 And in that day the [a]Holy Ghost fell upon Adam, which beareth record of the Father and the Son, saying: I am the [b]Only Begotten of the Father from the beginning, henceforth and forever, that as thou hast [c]fallen thou mayest be [d]re-

---

31a TG Eden.
 b Alma 42: 3.
 TG Cherubim.
5 1a Moses 2: 26.
 b Moses 4: 25.
 c TG Labor.
2a Gen. 5: 4 (3–32).
 b Gen. 4: 1 (1–2);
    Moses 5: 16 (16–17).
 c D&C 138: 39.
 d Gen. 9: 1; Moses 2: 28.
3a Gen. 4: 17; Moses 5: 28.
4a Gen. 4: 26; Moses 6: 4.
 b TG Eden.
 c Alma 42: 9.
5a TG Worship.

b Ex. 13: 12 (12–13);
   Num. 18: 17; Mosiah 2: 3. TG Firstborn.
 c Moses 5: 19 (19–20).
 d TG Obedience.
6a TG Angels.
 b TG Ordinance; Sacrifice.
7a TG Jesus Christ, Types, in Anticipation.
 b Gen. 4: 5 (3–7); 1 Chr. 6: 49; Alma 34: 10 (10–15); Moses 5: 21 (20–26). TG Blood, Symbolism of; Jesus Christ, Atonement through.

c Moses 1: 32. TG Grace.
 d Moses 1: 6.
8a Moses 1: 17.
 b Moses 6: 57; 7: 10.
   TG Repentance.
 c TG Prayer.
9a TG Holy Ghost, Baptism of.
 b Jesus Christ, Divine Sonship.
 c TG Death, Spiritual, First; Fall of Man.
 d Ps. 49: 15; Mosiah 27: 24 (24–26); D&C 93: 38; A of F 3.
   TG Redemption; Salvation, Plan of.

deemed, and all mankind, even as many as will.

10 And in that day Adam blessed God and was [a]filled, and began to [b]prophesy concerning all the families of the earth, saying: Blessed be the name of God, for because of my [c]transgression my [d]eyes are opened, and in this life I shall have [e]joy, and again in the [f]flesh I shall see God.

11 And Eve, his wife, heard all these things and was glad, saying: Were it not for our transgression we never should have [a]seed, and never should have [b]known good and evil, and the joy of our redemption, and the eternal life which God giveth unto all the obedient.

12 And Adam and [a]Eve blessed the name of God, and they made all things [b]known unto their sons and their daughters.

13 And [a]Satan came among them, saying: I am also a son of God; and he commanded them, saying: [b]Believe it not; and they believed it not, and they [c]loved Satan more than God. And men began from that time forth to be [d]carnal, sensual, and devilish.

14 And the Lord God called upon men by the [a]Holy Ghost everywhere and commanded them that they should repent;

15 And as many as [a]believed in the Son, and repented of their sins, should be [b]saved; and as many as believed not and repented not, should be [c]damned; and the words went forth out of the mouth of God

in a firm decree; wherefore they must be fulfilled.

16 And Adam and Eve, his wife, ceased not to call upon God. And Adam knew Eve his wife, and she conceived and bare [a]Cain, and said: I have gotten a man from the Lord; wherefore he may not reject his words. But behold, Cain [b]hearkened not, saying: Who is the Lord that I should [c]know him?

17 And she again conceived and bare his brother Abel. And Abel [a]hearkened unto the voice of the Lord. And [b]Abel was a keeper of sheep, but Cain was a tiller of the ground.

18 And Cain [a]loved Satan more than God. And Satan commanded him, saying: [b]Make an offering unto the Lord.

19 And in process of time it came to pass that Cain brought of the [a]fruit of the ground an offering unto the Lord.

20 And Abel, he also brought of the [a]firstlings of his flock, and of the fat thereof. And the Lord had [b]respect unto Abel, and to his [c]offering;

21 But unto Cain, and to his [a]offering, he had not respect. Now Satan knew this, and it [b]pleased him. And Cain was very wroth, and his countenance fell.

22 And the Lord said unto Cain: Why art thou wroth? Why is thy countenance fallen?

23 If thou doest well, thou shalt be [a]accepted. And if thou doest not well, sin lieth at the door, and Satan [b]desireth to have thee; and except

10a TG Man, New, Spiritually Reborn.
  b D&C 107: 56 (41–56).
  c TG Transgression.
  d Gen. 3: 5 (3–6);
    D&C 76: 12 (12, 19);
    Moses 4: 11 (10–13).
  e TG Joy.
  f Job 19: 26; 2 Ne. 9: 4.
11a 2 Ne. 2: 23 (22–25).
    TG Birth Control;
    Family; Marriage,
    Motherhood.
  b Gen. 3: 22.
12a Gen. 3: 20; D&C 138: 39.

b Deut. 4: 9 (9–10).
13a TG Devil.
  b TG Spiritual Blindness;
    Unbelief, Unbelievers.
  c Moses 5: 28; 6: 15.
  d TG Carnal Mind; Man,
    Natural, Not Spiritually Reborn.
14a John 14: 26 (16–26).
15a TG Faith.
  b TG Jesus Christ,
    Savior.
  c D&C 42: 60.
16a Gen. 4: 1 (1–2).
  b 1 Sam. 3: 13; 1 Ne. 2:
    12 (12–13); Mosiah 27:

8 (7–37).
  c Ex. 5: 2; Alma 9: 6.
17a Heb. 11: 4.
  b D&C 138: 40.
18a D&C 10: 21 (20–21).
  b D&C 132: 9 (8–11).
19a Moses 5: 5.
20a Mosiah 2: 3.
  b TG Respect.
  c TG Sacrifice.
21a Gen. 4: 5 (3–7);
    Moses 5: 7 (4–8).
  b Moses 7: 26.
23a Gen. 4: 7; D&C 52: 15;
    97: 8; 132: 50.
  b Gen. 4: 7.

thou shalt hearken unto my commandments, I will ᶜdeliver thee up, and it shall be unto thee according to his desire. And thou shalt ᵈrule over him;

24 For from this time forth thou shalt be the father of his ᵃlies; thou shalt be called ᵇPerdition; for thou wast also ᶜbefore the world.

25 And it shall be said in time to come—That these abominations were had from ᵃCain; for he rejected the greater counsel which was had from God; and this is a ᵇcursing which I will put upon thee, except thou repent.

26 And Cain was wroth, and listened not any more to the voice of the Lord, neither to Abel, his brother, who walked in holiness before the Lord.

27 And Adam and his wife ᵃmourned before the Lord, because of Cain and his brethren.

28 And it came to pass that Cain took one of his brothers' daughters to ᵃwife, and they ᵇloved Satan more than God.

29 And Satan said unto Cain: ᵃSwear unto me by thy throat, and if thou tell it thou shalt die; and swear thy brethren by their heads, and by the living God, that they tell it not; for if they tell it, they shall surely die; and this that thy father may not know it; and this day I will deliver thy brother Abel into thine hands.

30 And Satan sware unto Cain that he would do according to his ᵃcommands. And all these things were done in secret.

31 And Cain said: Truly I am Mahan, the master of this great ᵈsecret, that I may ᵇmurder and get

ᶜgain. Wherefore Cain was called Master ᵈMahan, and he gloried in his wickedness.

32 And Cain went into the field, and Cain talked with Abel, his brother. And it came to pass that while they were in the field, Cain rose up against Abel, his brother, and slew him.

33 And Cain ᵃgloried in that which he had done, saying: I am free; surely the ᵇflocks of my brother falleth into my hands.

34 And the Lord said unto Cain: Where is Abel, thy brother? And he said: I know not. Am I my brother's ᵃkeeper?

35 And the Lord said: What hast thou done? The voice of thy brother's ᵃblood cries unto me from the ground.

36 And now thou shalt be ᵃcursed from the earth which hath opened her mouth to receive thy brother's blood from thy hand.

37 When thou tillest the ground it shall not henceforth yield unto thee her ᵃstrength. A ᵇfugitive and a vagabond shalt thou be in the earth.

38 And Cain said unto the Lord: Satan ᵃtempted me because of my brother's flocks. And I was wroth also; for his offering thou didst accept and not mine; my ᵇpunishment is greater than I can bear.

39 Behold thou hast driven me out this day from the face of the Lord, and from thy face shall I be hid; and I shall be a fugitive and a vagabond in the earth; and it shall come to pass, that he that findeth me will slay me, because of mine iniquities, for these things are not hid from the Lord.

40 And I the Lord said unto him:

23c ᴛɢ Bondage, Spiritual.
  d Moses 5:30.
24a ᴛɢ Honesty.
  b D&C 76: 26, 32 (32–48).
    ᴛɢ Sons of Perdition.
  c Moses 4: 1.
25a Hel. 6: 27 (26–28).
  b Moses 5: 36. ᴛɢ Curse.
27a ᴛɢ Mourning.
28a Moses 5: 3 (2–3).

b Moses 5: 13.
29a Matt. 5: 36.
30a Moses 5: 23.
31a Deut. 27: 24.
  b ᴛɢ Murder.
  c Deut. 27: 25.
  d ɪᴇ "Mind," "destroyer," and "great one" are possible meanings of the roots evident in "Mahan."

33a ᴛɢ Boasting.
  b ᴛɢ Covetousness.
34a Gen. 4: 9 (8–15).
35a ᴛɢ Life, Sanctity of.
36a D&C 29: 41. ᴛɢ Curse.
37a ᴛɢ Strength.
  b Gen. 4: 12 (11–12).
38a ᴛɢ Covetousness; Temptation.
  b ᴛɢ Punishment.

Whosoever slayeth thee, vengeance shall be taken on him sevenfold. And I the Lord set a ^{a}mark upon Cain, lest any finding him should kill him.

41 And Cain was ^{a}shut out from the ^{b}presence of the Lord, and with his wife and many of his brethren dwelt in the land of Nod, on the east of Eden.

42 And Cain knew his wife, and she conceived and bare Enoch, and he also begat many sons and daughters. And he builded a city, and he called the name of the ^{a}city after the name of his son, Enoch.

43 And unto Enoch was born Irad, and other sons and daughters. And Irad begat Mahujael, and other sons and daughters. And Mahujael begat Methusael, and other sons and daughters. And Methusael begat Lamech.

44 And Lamech took unto himself two wives; the name of one being Adah, and the name of the other, Zillah.

45 And Adah bare Jabal; he was the father of such as dwell in ^{a}tents, and they were keepers of cattle; and his brother's name was Jubal, who was the father of all such as handle the harp and organ.

46 And Zillah, she also bare Tubal Cain, an instructor of every artificer in brass and iron. And the sister of Tubal Cain was called Naamah.

47 And Lamech said unto his wives, Adah and Zillah: Hear my voice, ye wives of Lamech, hearken unto my speech; for I have slain a man to my wounding, and a young man to my hurt.

48 If Cain shall be avenged sevenfold, truly Lamech shall be ^{a}seventy and seven fold;

49 For ^{a}Lamech having entered into a covenant with Satan, after the manner of Cain, wherein he became Master Mahan, master of that great secret which was administered unto Cain by Satan; and Irad, the son of Enoch, having known their secret, began to reveal it unto the sons of Adam;

50 Wherefore Lamech, being angry, slew him, not like unto Cain, his brother Abel, for the sake of getting gain, but he slew him for the ^{a}oath's sake.

51 For, from the days of Cain, there was a secret ^{a}combination, and their works were in the dark, and they knew every man his brother.

52 Wherefore the Lord ^{a}cursed Lamech, and his house, and all them that had covenanted with Satan; for they kept not the commandments of God, and it displeased God, and he ministered not unto them, and their works were abominations, and began to spread among all the ^{b}sons of men. And it was among the sons of men.

53 And among the daughters of men these things were not spoken, because that Lamech had spoken the secret unto his wives, and they rebelled against him, and declared these things abroad, and had not compassion;

54 Wherefore Lamech was despised, and cast out, and came not among the sons of men, lest he should die.

55 And thus the works of ^{a}darkness began to prevail among all the sons of men.

56 And God ^{a}cursed the earth with a sore curse, and was angry with the wicked, with all the sons of men whom he had made;

40a Gen. 4: 15; Alma 3: 7 (7–16).
41a TG Bondage, Spiritual.
  b Moses 6: 49.
42a IE There was a man named Enoch in Cain's lineage, and a city by that name among his people. Do not confuse these with the Enoch

of the righteous line of Seth and with his city, Zion, also called "City of Enoch."
45a Moses 6: 38; 7: 5 (5–6).
48a IE Lamech presumptively boasted that far more would be done for him than for Cain. The reasons for his assump-

tion are given in verses 49 and 50.
49a Gen. 4: 24.
50a TG Oath.
51a TG Secret Combinations.
52a TG Curse.
  b Moses 8: 14 (14–15, 19).
55a TG Darkness, Spiritual.
56a TG Earth, Curse of.

57 For they would not ᵃhearken unto his voice, nor believe on his Only Begotten Son, even him whom he declared should ᵇcome in the meridian of time, who was ᶜprepared from before the foundation of the world.

58 And thus the ᵃGospel began to be ᵇpreached, from the beginning, being declared by ᶜholy ᵈangels sent forth from the presence of God, and by his own voice, and by the gift of the Holy Ghost.

59 And thus all things were confirmed unto ᵃAdam, by an holy ordinance, and the Gospel preached, and a decree sent forth, that it should be in the world, until the end thereof; and thus it was. Amen.

CHAPTER 6
(November–December 1830)

Adam's seed keep a book of remembrance—His righteous posterity preach repentance—God reveals himself to Enoch—Enoch preaches the gospel—The plan of salvation was revealed to Adam—He received baptism and the priesthood.

AND Adam hearkened unto the voice of God, and called upon his sons to repent.

2 And Adam knew his wife again, and she bare a son, and he called his name ᵃSeth. And Adam glorified the name of God; for he said: God hath appointed me another seed, instead of Abel, whom Cain slew.

3 And God revealed himself unto ᵃSeth, and he rebelled not, but offered an acceptable ᵇsacrifice, like unto his brother Abel. And to him also was born a son, and he called his name Enos.

4 And then began these men to ᵃcall upon the name of the Lord, and the Lord blessed them;

5 And a ᵃbook of ᵇremembrance was kept, in the which was recorded, in the ᶜlanguage of Adam, for it was given unto as many as called upon God to write by the spirit of ᵈinspiration;

6 And by them their ᵃchildren were taught to read and write, having a ᵇlanguage which was ᶜpure and undefiled.

7 Now this same ᵃPriesthood, which was in the beginning, shall be in the end of the world also.

8 Now this prophecy Adam spake, as he was moved upon by the ᵃHoly Ghost, and a ᵇgenealogy was kept of the ᶜchildren of God. And this was the ᵈbook of the generations of Adam, saying: In the day that God created man, in the likeness of God made he him;

9 In the ᵃimage of his own ᵇbody, male and female, ᶜcreated he them, and blessed them, and called their ᵈname Adam, in the day when they were created and became living ᵉsouls in the land upon the ᶠfootstool of God.

10 And ᵃAdam lived one hundred and thirty years, and begat a son

---

57a Disobedience; Unbelief, Unbelievers.
b TG Jesus Christ, Birth of.
c Jesus Christ, Authority of.
58a TG Gospel.
b TG Preaching.
c Alma 12: 29 (28–30); Moro. 7: 25 (25, 31).
d Acts 7: 53.
59a TG Adam.
6 2a Gen. 4: 25.
3a D&C 138: 40.
b TG Sacrifice.
4a Gen. 4: 26; Moses 5: 4.
TG Prayer.
5a Abr. 1: 28 (28, 31).

TG Scriptures, Lost; Scriptures, Writing of.
b TG Book of Remembrance.
c Moses 6: 46.
d TG Guidance, Divine; Inspiration.
6a TG Education; Family, Children, Responsibilities toward.
b TG Language.
c Zeph. 3: 9.
7a TG Priesthood; Priesthood, History of; Priesthood, Melchizedek.
8a Ex. 4: 12 (12–16); 2 Pet. 1: 21; D&C 24: 6

(5–6); 28: 1 4; Moses 6: 32.
b TG Genealogy and Temple Work.
c TG Sons and Daughters of God.
d Gen. 5: 1.
9a Gen. 1: 26 (26–28); Moses 2: 26 (26–29); Abr. 4: 26 (26–31).
b TG God, Body of (Corporeal Nature).
c TG Man, Physical Creation of.
d Moses 1: 34; 4: 26.
e TG Soul.
f Moses 6: 44; Abr. 2: 7.
10a D&C 107: 41 (41–56).

in his own likeness, after his own *b*image, and called his name Seth.

11 And the days of Adam, after he had begotten Seth, were eight hundred years, and he begat many sons and daughters;

12 And all the days that Adam lived were nine hundred and thirty years, and he died.

13 Seth lived one hundred and five years, and begat Enos, and *a*prophesied in all his days, and taught his son Enos in the ways of God; wherefore Enos prophesied also.

14 And Seth lived, after he begat Enos, eight hundred and seven years, and begat many sons and daughters.

15 And the children of *a*men were numerous upon all the face of the land. And in those days *b*Satan had great *c*dominion among men, and raged in their hearts; and from thenceforth came *d*wars and bloodshed; and a man's hand was against his own brother, in administering death, because of *e*secret *f*works, seeking for *g*power.

16 All the days of Seth were nine hundred and twelve years, and he died.

17 And Enos lived ninety years, and begat *a*Cainan. And Enos and the residue of the people of God came out from the land, which was called Shulon, and dwelt in a land of promise, which he called after his own son, whom he had named *b*Cainan.

18 And Enos lived, after he begat Cainan, eight hundred and fifteen years, and begat many sons and daughters. And all the days of Enos were nine hundred and five years, and he died.

19 And Cainan lived seventy years, and begat Mahalaleel; and Cainan lived after he begat Mahalaleel eight hundred and forty years, and begat sons and daughters. And all the days of *a*Cainan were nine hundred and ten years, and he died.

20 And Mahalaleel lived sixty-five years, and begat Jared; and Mahalaleel lived, after he begat Jared, eight hundred and thirty years, and begat sons and daughters. And all the days of Mahalaleel were eight hundred and ninety-five years, and he died.

21 And Jared lived one hundred and sixty-two years, and begat *a*Enoch; and Jared lived, after he begat Enoch, eight hundred years, and begat sons and daughters. And Jared *b*taught Enoch in all the ways of God.

22 And this is the genealogy of the sons of Adam, with whom God, himself, conversed.

23 And they were *a*preachers of *b*righteousness, and spake and *c*prophesied, and called upon all men, everywhere, to repent; and *d*faith was *e*taught unto the children of men.

24 And it came to pass that all the days of Jared were nine hundred and sixty-two years, and he died.

25 And Enoch lived sixty-five years, and begat Methuselah.

26 And it came to pass that Enoch journeyed in the land, among the people; and as he journeyed, the *a*Spirit of God descended out of heaven, and abode upon him.

27 And he heard a *a*voice from heaven, saying: *b*Enoch, my son,

---

10*b* IE Seth was in the likeness and image of Adam, as Adam was in the image of God. Gen. 5: 3; D&C 107: 42–43; 138: 40.
13*a* Moses 5: 23.
15*a* Moses 8: 14 (13–15).
  b 3 Ne. 6: 15.
  c Moses 5: 13.
  d TG War.

e TG Conspiracy.
f TG Secret Combinations.
g TG Selfishness.
17*a* D&C 107: 45, 53.
  b Moses 6: 41.
19*a* Gen. 5: 14 (4–24);
  D&C 107: 45 (45, 53).
21*a* Gen. 5: 22 (5–24);
  Moses 7: 69; 8: 1 (1–2).
  b Moses 6: 41.

22*a* Luke 3: 38.
23*a* Moses 6: 13.
  TG Preaching.
  b TG Righteousness.
  c Moses 8: 3, 16.
  TG Prophets, Mission of.
  d TG Faith.
  e TG Education.
26*a* TG God, Spirit of.
27*a* TG Guidance, Divine.
  b Jude 1: 14 (14–16).

*prophesy unto this people, and say unto them—Repent, for thus saith the Lord: I am *d*angry with this people, and my fierce anger is kindled against them; for their hearts have waxed *e*hard, and their *f*ears are dull of hearing, and their eyes *g*cannot see afar off;

28 And for these many generations, ever since the day that I created them, have they gone astray, and have *a*denied me, and have sought their own counsels in the dark; and in their own abominations have they devised murder, and have not kept the commandments, which I gave unto their father, Adam.

29 Wherefore, they have foresworn themselves, and, by their oaths, they have brought upon themselves death; and a *a*hell I have prepared for them, if they repent not;

30 And this is a decree, which I have sent forth in the beginning of the world, from my own mouth, from the foundation thereof, and by the mouths of my servants, thy fathers, have I decreed it, even as it shall be sent forth in the world, unto the ends thereof.

31 And when Enoch had heard these words, he *a*bowed himself to the earth, before the Lord, and spake before the Lord, saying: *b*Why is it that I have found favor in thy sight, and am but a lad, and all the people *c*hate me; for I am *d*slow of speech; wherefore am I thy servant?

32 And the Lord said unto Enoch: Go forth and do as I have com-manded thee, and no man shall pierce thee. Open thy *d*mouth, and it shall be filled, and I will give thee utterance, for all flesh is in my hands, and I will do as seemeth me good.

33 Say unto this people: *a*Choose ye *b*this day, to serve the Lord God who made you.

34 Behold my *a*Spirit is upon you, wherefore all thy words will I justify; and the *b*mountains shall flee before you, and the *c*rivers shall turn from their course; and thou shalt abide in me, and I in you; therefore *d*walk with me.

35 And the Lord spake unto Enoch, and said unto him: Anoint thine eyes with *a*clay, and wash them, and thou shalt see. And he did so.

36 And he beheld the *a*spirits that God had created; and he beheld also things which were not visible to the *b*natural eye; and from thenceforth came the saying abroad in the land: A *c*seer hath the Lord raised up unto his people.

37 And it came to pass that Enoch went forth in the land, among the people, standing upon the hills and the high places, and cried with a loud voice, testifying against their works; and all men were *a*offended because of him.

38 And they came forth to hear him, upon the high places, saying unto the *a*tent-keepers: Tarry ye here and keep the tents, while we go yonder to behold the seer, for he prophesieth, and there is a strange thing in the land; a *b*wild man hath come among us.

27c Moses 8: 19.
    d Deut. 32: 21; 2 Ne. 15:
      25; D&C 63: 32.
    e TG Hardheartedness.
    f Ps. 78: 1; 2 Ne. 9: 31;
      Mosiah 26: 28; D&C 1:
      14 (2, 11, 14).
    g Prov. 7: 9; Alma 10:
      25; 14: 6; Moses 7: 26.
28a TG Rebellion.
29a Moses 7: 37. TG Hell.
31a Ex. 34: 8.
    b Ex. 3: 11 (10–21).
    c Jer. 11: 19; Matt. 10:

      22; JS–H 1: 20.
    TG Hate.
    d Ex. 4: 10; Jer. 1: 6 (6–
      9).
32a Ex. 4: 12 (12–16);
      D&C 24: 6 (5–6); 28: 4;
      Moses 6: 8; 7: 13.
    TG Prophets, Mission of.
33a TG Agency.
    b TG Procrastination.
34a TG Teaching with the
      Spirit.
    b Judg. 5: 5; Matt. 17:
      20; D&C 109: 74; 133:
      22 (21–22, 40).

    c Moses 7: 13.
    d Gen. 5: 24; Moses 7:
      69. TG Walking with
      God.
35a John 9: 6 (6, 15).
36a TG Man, Antemortal
      Existence of; Spirit
      Body; Spirit Creation.
    b Moses 1: 11.
    c TG Seer.
37a Matt. 11: 6; 1 Ne. 16: 2
      (1–3); Mosiah 13: 7.
38a Moses 5: 45; 7: 5 (5–6).
    b Gen. 6: 12; Matt. 3: 4
      (1–12).

39 And it came to pass when they heard him, no man laid hands on him; for *a*fear came on all them that heard him; for he *b*walked with God.

40 And there came a man unto him, whose name was Mahijah, and said unto him: Tell us plainly who thou art, and from whence thou comest?

41 And he said unto them: I came out from the land of *a*Cainan, the land of my fathers, a land of *b*righteousness unto this day. And my father *c*taught me in all the ways of God.

42 And it came to pass, as I journeyed from the land of Cainan, by the sea east, I beheld a vision; and lo, the heavens I saw, and the Lord spake with me, and gave me commandment; wherefore, for this cause, to keep the commandment, I speak forth these words.

43 And Enoch continued his speech, saying: The Lord which spake with me, the same is the God of heaven, and he is my God, and your God, and ye are my brethren, and why *a*counsel ye yourselves, and deny the God of heaven?

44 The heavens he made; the *a*earth is his *b*footstool; and the foundation thereof is his. Behold, he laid it, an host of men hath he brought in upon the face thereof.

45 And death hath come upon our fathers; nevertheless we know them, and cannot deny, and even the first of all we know, even *a*Adam.

46 For a book of *a*remembrance we have *b*written among us, according to the pattern given by the finger of God; and it is given in our own *c*language.

47 And as Enoch spake forth the words of God, the people trembled, and could not *a*stand in his presence.

48 And he said unto them: Because that Adam *a*fell, we are; and by his fall came *b*death; and we are made partakers of misery and woe.

49 Behold Satan hath come among the children of men, and *a*tempteth them to *b*worship him; and men have become *c*carnal, *d*sensual, and devilish, and are shut out from the *e*presence of God.

50 But God hath made known unto our fathers that all men must repent.

51 And he called upon our father Adam by his own voice, saying: I am God; I *a*made the world, and *b*men *c*before they were in the flesh.

52 And he also said unto him: If thou wilt turn unto me, and hearken unto my voice, and believe, and repent of all thy transgressions, and be *a*baptized, even in water, in the name of mine Only Begotten Son, who is full of *b*grace and truth, which is Jesus *c*Christ, the only *d*name which shall be given under heaven, whereby *e*salvation shall come unto the children of men, ye shall receive the gift of the Holy Ghost, asking all things in his name, and whatsoever ye shall ask, it shall be given you.

53 And our father Adam spake un-

39a Luke 7: 16; Alma 19: 25 (24–27).
  b TG God, Privilege of Seeing; Walking with God.
41a Moses 6: 17.
  b TG Righteousness.
  c Moses 6: 21.
43a Prov. 1: 25 (24–33); D&C 56: 14 (14–15).
44a Deut. 10: 14; 1 Ne. 11: 6; 2 Ne. 29: 7; D&C 55: 1.
  b Moses 6: 9; Abr. 2: 7.
45a TG Adam.
46a TG Book of Remembrance; Genealogy and

Temple Work.
  b TG Scriptures, Writing of.
47a 1 Ne. 17: 48 (48–55).
48a 2 Ne. 2: 25.
  TG Fall of Man.
  b TG Death; Mortality.
49a Moses 1: 12.
  TG Temptation.
  b TG Worship.
  c Mosiah 16: 3 (3–4); Moses 5: 13.
  TG Carnal Mind; Man, Natural, Not Spiritually Reborn.

d TG Sensuality.
  e Gen. 4: 16; Moses 5: 41.
51a Moses 3: 5.
  b TG Man, a Spirit Child of Heavenly Father.
  c TG Spirit Creation.
52a 3 Ne. 11: 26 (23–26).
  TG Baptism, Essential.
  b TG Grace.
  c TG Jesus Christ, Messiah.
  d Acts 4: 12. TG Jesus Christ, Authority of; Name.
  e TG Jesus Christ, Savior; Salvation.

to the Lord, and said: Why is it that men must repent and be baptized in water? And the Lord said unto Adam: Behold I have *ᵉforgiven thee thy transgression in the Garden of Eden.

54 Hence came the saying abroad among the people, that the *ᵃSon of God hath *ᵇatoned for original guilt, wherein the sins of the parents cannot be answered upon the heads of the *ᶜchildren, for they are *ᵈwhole from the foundation of the world.

55 And the Lord spake unto Adam, saying: Inasmuch as thy children are *ᵃconceived in sin, even so when they begin to grow up, *ᵇsin conceiveth in their hearts, and they taste the *ᶜbitter, that they may know to prize the good.

56 And it is given unto them to know good from evil; wherefore they are *ᵃagents unto themselves, and I have given unto you another law and commandment.

57 Wherefore teach it unto your children, that all men, everywhere, must *ᵃrepent, or they can in nowise inherit the kingdom of God, for no *ᵇunclean thing can dwell there, or *ᶜdwell in his *ᵈpresence; for, in the language of Adam, *ᵉMan of Holiness is his name, and the name of his Only Begotten is the *ᶠSon of Man,

even *ᵍJesus Christ, a righteous *ʰJudge, who shall come in the meridian of time.

58 Therefore I give unto you a *ᵃcommandment, to *ᵇteach these things freely unto your *ᶜchildren, saying:

59 That by reason of transgression cometh the fall, which fall bringeth death, and inasmuch as ye were born into the world by water, and blood, and the *ᵃspirit, which I·have made, and so became of *ᵇdust a living soul, even so ye must be *ᶜborn again into the kingdom of heaven, of *ᵈwater, and of the Spirit, and be cleansed by blood, even the blood of mine Only Begotten; that ye might be sanctified from all sin, and *ᵉenjoy the *ᶠwords of *ᵍeternal life in this world, and eternal life in the world to come, even immortal *ʰglory;

60 For by the *ᵃwater ye keep the commandment; by the Spirit ye are *ᵇjustified, and by the *ᶜblood ye are *ᵈsanctified;

61 Therefore it is given to abide in you; the *ᵃrecord of heaven; the *ᵇComforter; the *ᶜpeaceable things of immortal glory; the truth of all things; that which quickeneth all things, which maketh alive all things; that which knoweth all things, and hath all *ᵈpower accord-

---

53a ᴛɢ Forgiveness.
54a ᴛɢ Jesus Christ, Divine Sonship.
  b Mosiah 3: 16. ᴛɢ Jesus Christ, Atonement through.
  d ᴛɢ Children.
  d ᴛɢ Salvation of Little Children.
55a ᴛɢ Conceived in Sin.
  b ᴛɢ Death, Spiritual, First; Man, Natural, Not Spiritually Reborn.
  c D&C 29: 39. ᴛɢ Opposition.
56a Gal. 5: 1; 2 Ne. 2: 27 (26–27); Hel. 14: 30 (29–30). ᴛɢ Agency.
57a 1 Cor. 6: 9 (9–10); Moses 5: 8; 7: 10. ᴛɢ Baptism, Qualifications for; Repentance.
  b Lev. 15: 31.

ᴛɢ Chastity; Cleanliness; God, Perfection of; Modesty; Uncleanness.
  c Ps. 15: 1 (1–5); 24: 3 (3–4); 27: 4; 1 Ne. 10: 21; 15: 33 (33–36); Mosiah 15: 23 (19–26); Morm. 7: 7; D&C 76: 62 (50–62).
  d ᴛɢ God, Presence of.
  e Moses 7: 35.
  f Matt. 20: 28; John 3: 13 (13–14).
  g ᴛɢ Jesus Christ, Prophecies about.
  h ᴛɢ God, Justice of; Jesus Christ, Judge.
58a ᴛɢ Authority.
  b ᴛɢ Education.
  c ᴛɢ Family, Children, Responsibilities toward.
59a 1 Jn. 5: 8.

  b Gen. 2: 7; Moses 3: 7; 4: 25 (25–29); Abr. 5: 7.
  c ᴛɢ Holy Ghost, Baptism of; Man, New, Spiritually Reborn.
  d ᴛɢ Baptism; Baptism Essential.
  e 2 Ne. 4: 15 (15–16).
  f John 6: 68.
  g Abr. 2: 11.
  h ᴛɢ Celestial Glory; Glory.
60a Moro. 8: 25.
  b ᴛɢ Justification.
  c ᴛɢ Blood, Shedding of; Blood, Symbolism of.
  d ᴛɢ Sanctification.
61a ᴛɢ Holy Ghost, Source of Testimony.
  b ᴛɢ Holy Ghost, Comforter.
  c ᴛɢ Peace of God.
  d ᴛɢ Jesus Christ, Power of.

ing to wisdom, mercy, truth, justice, and judgment.

62 And now, behold, I say unto you: This is the *a*plan of salvation unto all men, through the *b*blood of mine *c*Only Begotten, who shall come in the meridian of time.

63 And behold, all things have their *a*likeness, and all things are created and made to bear record of me, both things which are temporal, and things which are spiritual; things which are in the heavens above, and things which are on the earth, and things which are in the earth, and things which are under the earth, both above and beneath: all things bear record of me.

64 And it came to pass, when the Lord had spoken with Adam, our father, that Adam cried unto the Lord, and he was *a*caught away by the Spirit of the Lord, and was carried down into the water, and was laid under the *b*water, and was brought forth out of the water.

65 And thus he was baptized, and the Spirit of God descended upon him, and thus he was *a*born of the Spirit, and became quickened in the *b*inner man.

66 And he heard a voice out of heaven, saying: Thou art baptized with *a*fire, and with the Holy Ghost. This is the *b*record of the Father, and the Son, from henceforth and forever;

67 And thou art after the *a*order of him who was without beginning of days or end of years, from all eternity to all eternity.

68 Behold, thou art *a*one in me, a son of God; and thus may all become my *b*sons. Amen.

CHAPTER 7
(December 1830)

Enoch teaches, leads the people, moves mountains—The City of Zion is established—Enoch foresees the coming of the Son of Man, his atoning sacrifice, and the resurrection of the saints—He foresees the restoration, the gathering, the Second Coming, and the return of Zion.

AND it came to pass that Enoch continued his speech, saying: Behold, our father Adam taught these things, and many have believed and become the *a*sons of God, and many have believed not, and have perished in their sins, and are looking forth with *b*fear, in torment, for the fiery indignation of the wrath of God to be poured out upon them.

2 And from that time forth Enoch began to prophesy, saying unto the people, that: As I was journeying, and stood upon the place Mahujah, and cried unto the Lord, there came a voice out of heaven, saying—Turn ye, and get ye upon the mount *a*Simeon.

3 And it came to pass that I turned and went up on the mount; and as I stood upon the mount, I beheld the heavens open, and I was clothed upon with *a*glory;

4 And I *a*saw the Lord; and he stood before my face, and he talked with me, even as a man talketh one with another, *b*face to face; and he

---

62*a* TG Gospel; Salvation, Plan of.
   b TG Blood, Symbolism of.
   c TG Jesus Christ, Birth of.
63*a* Heb. 8: 5; D&C 77: 2.
   b Alma 30: 44; D&C 88: 47 (45–47).
64*a* 1 Kgs. 18: 12; 2 Kgs. 2: 16. TG Holy Ghost, Mission of.
   b TG Baptism, Immersion.

65*a* TG Man, New, Spiritually Reborn.
   b Mosiah 27: 25; Alma 5: 14 (12–15).
66*a* D&C 19: 31.
   b 2 Ne. 31: 18 (17–21); 3 Ne. 28: 11.
67*a* TG Priesthood, Melchizedek.
68*a* John 17: 21; 1 Jn. 1: 3; D&C 35: 2.
   b John 1: 12 (9–13); Mosiah 27: 25 (24–26); D&C 34: 3. TG Sons and Daughters of God.

7 1*a* TG Sons and Daughters of God.
   b Alma 40: 14 (11–14).
2*a* The Hebrew equivalent of Simeon is *Shim'on*, which means "hearing."
3*a* TG Transfiguration.
4*a* TG God, Privilege of Seeing; Jesus Christ, Appearances, Antemortal.
   b Gen. 32: 30; Deut. 5: 4; Moses 1: 11 (2, 11, 31).

said unto me: [c]Look, and I will [d]show unto thee the world for the space of many generations.

5 And it came to pass that I beheld in the valley of Shum, and lo, a great people which dwelt in [a]tents, which were the people of Shum.

6 And again the Lord said unto me: Look; and I looked towards the north, and I beheld the people of [a]Canaan, which dwelt in tents.

7 And the Lord said unto me: Prophesy; and I prophesied, saying: Behold the people of Canaan, which are numerous, shall go forth in battle array against the people of Shum, and shall slay them that they shall utterly be destroyed; and the people of Canaan shall divide themselves in the land, and the land shall be barren and unfruitful, and none other people shall dwell there but the people of Canaan;

8 For behold, the Lord shall [a]curse the land with much heat, and the [b]barrenness thereof shall go forth forever; and there was a blackness came upon all the children of Canaan, that they were despised among all people.

9 And it came to pass that the Lord said unto me: Look; and I looked, and I beheld the land of Sharon, and the land of Enoch, and the land of Omner, and the land of Heni, and the land of Shem, and the land of Haner, and the land of Hanannihah, and all the inhabitants thereof;

10 And the Lord said unto me: Go to this people, and say unto them— [a]Repent, lest I come out and smite them with a curse, and they die.

11 And he gave unto me a commandment that I should [a]baptize in the name of the Father, and of the

Son, which is full of [b]grace and truth, and of the Holy Ghost, which beareth record of the Father and the Son.

12 And it came to pass that Enoch continued to call upon all the people, save it were the people of Canaan, to repent;

13 And so great was the [a]faith of Enoch that he led the people of God, and their enemies came to battle against them; and he [b]spake the word of the Lord, and the earth trembled, and the [c]mountains fled, even according to his command; and the [d]rivers of water were turned out of their course; and the roar of the lions was heard out of the wilderness; and all nations feared greatly, so [e]powerful was the word of Enoch, and so great was the power of the language which God had given him.

14 There also came [a]up a land out of the depth of the sea, and so great was the fear of the enemies of the people of God, that they fled and stood afar off and went upon the land which came up out of the depth of the sea.

15 And the [a]giants of the land, also, stood afar off; and there went forth a [b]curse upon all people that fought against God;

16 And from that time forth there were wars and bloodshed among them; but the Lord came and [d]dwelt with his people, and they dwelt in righteousness.

17 The [a]fear of the Lord was upon all nations, so great was the [b]glory of the Lord, which was upon his people. And the Lord blessed the [c]land, and they were blessed upon the mountains, and upon the high places, and did flourish.

4c Moses 1: 4.
  d TG God, Omniscience of; Revelation.
5a Moses 5: 45; 6: 38.
6a Abr. 1: 21.
8a TG Earth, Curse of.
  b TG Barrenness.
10a Moses 5: 8; 6: 57.
11a TG Baptism, Essential.

b TG Grace.
13a TG Faith.
  b Moses 6: 32.
  c Matt. 17: 20; Luke 17: 6 (5–6).
  d Moses 6: 34.
  e TG Priesthood, Power of.
14a TG Ne. 9: 8.
15a Num. 13: 33; Moses 8: 18.

b Ps. 83: 17 (2–17);
  2 Ne. 25: 14;
  D&C 71: 7.
16a TG God, Presence of.
17a Ex. 33: 27 (27–28);
  Alma 14: 26; D&C 64: 43.
  b TG Glory.
  c 1 Chr. 28: 8 (7–8);
  1 Ne. 2: 20.

18 And the Lord called his people ^aZion, because they were of ^bone heart and one mind, and dwelt in righteousness; and there was no poor among them.

19 And Enoch continued his preaching in righteousness unto the people of God. And it came to pass in his days, that he built a city that was called the City of Holiness, even Zion.

20 And it came to pass that Enoch talked with the Lord; and he said unto the Lord: Surely ^aZion shall dwell in safety forever. But the Lord said unto Enoch: Zion have I blessed, but the ^bresidue of the people have I cursed.

21 And it came to pass that the Lord showed unto Enoch all the inhabitants of the earth; and he beheld, and lo, ^aZion, in process of time, was ^btaken up into heaven. And the Lord said unto Enoch: Behold mine abode forever.

22 And Enoch also beheld the residue of the people which were the sons of Adam; and they were a mixture of all the seed of Adam save it was the seed of Cain, for the seed of Cain were black, and had not place among them.

23 And after that Zion was taken up into ^aheaven, Enoch ^bbeheld, and lo, ^call the nations of the earth were before him;

24 And there came generation upon generation; and Enoch was high and ^alifted up, even in the bosom of the Father, and of the Son of Man; and behold, the power of Satan was upon all the face of the earth.

25 And he saw angels descending

out of heaven; and he heard a loud voice saying: Wo, wo be unto the inhabitants of the earth.

26 And he beheld Satan; and he had a great ^achain in his hand, and it veiled the whole face of the earth with ^bdarkness; and he looked up and ^claughed, and his ^dangels rejoiced.

27 And Enoch beheld ^aangels descending out of heaven, bearing ^btestimony of the Father and Son; and the Holy Ghost fell on many, and they were caught up by the powers of heaven into Zion.

28 And it came to pass that the God of heaven looked upon the ^aresidue of the people, and he wept; and Enoch bore record of it, saying: How is it that the heavens weep, and shed forth their tears as the rain upon the mountains?

29 And Enoch said unto the Lord: How is it that thou canst ^aweep, seeing thou art holy, and from all eternity to all eternity?

30 And were it possible that man could number the particles of the earth, yea, millions of ^aearths like this, it would not be a beginning to the number of thy ^bcreations; and thy curtains are stretched out still; and yet thou art there, and thy bosom is there; and also thou art just; thou art merciful and kind forever;

31 And thou hast taken ^aZion to thine own bosom, from all thy creations, from all eternity to all eternity; and naught but peace, ^bjustice, and truth is the habitation of thy throne; and mercy shall go before thy face and have no end; how is it thou canst ^cweep?

18a D&C 38: 4. TG Zion.
  b 2 Chr. 30: 12; Acts 4:
    32 (31-32); Philip. 2:
    1-4. TG Unity.
20a Moses 7: 63 (62-63).
  TG Jerusalem, New.
  b Moses 7: 28.
21a Moses 7: 31.
  b Moses 7: 47, 69.
23a TG Heaven.
  b TG Visions.
  c D&C 88: 47 (45-47);

Moses 1: 28 (27-29);
  Abr. 3: 21 (21-23).
24a 2 Cor. 12: 2 (1-4).
26a Prov. 5: 22; 2 Tim. 2:
    26 (24-26); Alma 12:
    11 (10-11).
  b Isa. 60: 2 (1-3);
    Alma 10: 25; 14: 6;
    Moses 6: 27.
  c Moses 5: 21.
  d 2 Pet. 2: 4; Jude 1: 6;
    D&C 29: 37 (36-45).
27a TG Angels.

b TG Testimony.
28a Moro. 7: 32; Moses 7:
    20.
29a Isa. 63: 9 (7-10).
30a Job 9: 9 (7-9); Ps. 8: 3
    (3-4); D&C 76: 24;
    Moses 1: 33.
  TG Astronomy.
  b TG Creation.
31a Moses 7: 21.
  b TG God, Justice of.
  c Moses 7: 37 (37, 40).

32 The Lord said unto Enoch: Behold these thy brethren; they are the workmanship of mine own ^ahands, and I gave unto them their ^bknowledge, in the day I created them; and in the Garden of Eden, gave I unto man his ^cagency;

33 And unto thy brethren have I said, and also given commandment, that they should ^alove one another, and that they should choose me, their Father; but behold, they are without affection, and they ^bhate their own blood;

34 And the ^afire of mine ^bindignation is kindled against them; and in my hot displeasure will I send in the ^cfloods upon them, for my fierce anger is kindled against them.

35 Behold, I am God; ^aMan of Holiness is my name; Man of Counsel is my name; and Endless and Eternal is my ^bname, also.

36 Wherefore, I can stretch forth mine hands and hold all the ^acreations which I have made; and mine eye can pierce them also, and among all the workmanship of mine hands there has not been so great ^bwickedness as among thy brethren.

37 But behold, their sins shall be upon the heads of their fathers; Satan shall be their father, and misery shall be their doom; and the whole heavens shall weep over them, even all the workmanship of mine hands; wherefore should not the heavens weep, seeing these shall suffer?

38 But behold, these which thine eyes are upon shall perish in the floods; and behold, I will shut them up; a ^aprison have I prepared for them.

39 And That which I have chosen hath pled before my face. Wherefore, he ^asuffereth for their sins; inasmuch as they will repent in the day that my ^bChosen shall return unto me, and until that day shall be in ^ctorment;

40 Wherefore, for this shall the heavens weep, yea, and all the workmanship of mine hands.

41 And it came to pass that the Lord spake unto Enoch, and ^atold Enoch all the doings of the children of men; wherefore Enoch knew, and looked upon their wickedness, and their misery, and wept and stretched forth his arms, and his ^bheart swelled wide as eternity; and his bowels yearned; and all eternity shook.

42 And Enoch also saw Noah, and his ^afamily; that the posterity of all the sons of Noah should be saved with a temporal salvation;

43 Wherefore Enoch saw that Noah built an ^aark; and that the Lord smiled upon it, and held it in his own hand; but upon the residue of the wicked the ^bfloods came and swallowed them up.

44 And as Enoch saw this, he had ^abitterness of soul, and wept over his brethren, and said unto the heavens: I will refuse to be ^bcomforted; but the Lord said unto Enoch: Lift up your heart, and be glad; and look.

45 And it came to pass that Enoch looked; and from Noah, he beheld all the families of the earth; and he cried unto the Lord, saying: When shall the day of the Lord come? When shall the blood of the Right-

---

32a Moses 1:4.
  b TG God, Intelligence
    of; Knowledge.
  c TG Agency.
33a TG Love.
  b Gen. 6:11. TG Hate.
34a Num. 11:1 (1, 10);
    D&C 35:14.
  b Ps. 106:40.
  c Gen. 7:10 (4, 10);
    Moses 8:17 (17, 24).
    TG Flood.
35a Moses 6:57.

b Ex. 3:15; Moses 1:3.
36a D&C 38:2; 88:41;
    Moses 1:35 (35–37).
    TG God, Omniscience of.
  b Gen. 6:5 (5–6);
    3 Ne. 9:9; Morm. 4:12
    (10–12); D&C 112:23;
    Moses 8:22 (22, 28–
    30).
38a 1 Pet. 3:20 (18–21).
    TG Spirits in Prison.
39a Ezek. 33:11.
  b Moses 4:2; Abr. 3:27.

c TG Damnation.
41a TG God, Omniscience of.
  b Mosiah 28:3.
    TG Compassion.
42a Gen. 8:16; Moses 8:12.
43a Gen. 6:14–22; Ether 6:7 (6–8).
  b TG Flood; Punishment.
44a Job 10:1; Isa. 38:15.
  b Ps. 77:2; Ether 15:3.

eous be shed, that all they that mourn may be ^asanctified and have eternal life?

46 And the Lord said: It shall be in the ^ameridian of time, in the days of wickedness and vengeance.

47 And behold, Enoch ^asaw the day of the coming of the Son of Man, even in the flesh; and his soul rejoiced, saying: The Righteous is lifted up, and the ^bLamb is slain from the foundation of the world; and through ^cfaith I am in the bosom of the Father, and behold, ^dZion is with me.

48 And it came to pass that Enoch looked upon the ^aearth; and he heard a voice from the bowels thereof, saying: Wo, wo is me, the mother of men; I am ^bpained, I am weary, because of the wickedness of my children. When shall I ^crest, and be ^dcleansed from the ^efilthiness which is gone forth out of me? When will my Creator sanctify me, that I may rest, and righteousness for a season abide upon my face?

49 And when Enoch heard the earth mourn, he wept, and cried unto the Lord, saying: O Lord, wilt thou not have compassion on the earth? Wilt thou not bless the children of Noah?

50 And it came to pass that Enoch continued his cry unto the Lord, saying: I ask thee, O Lord, in the name of thine Only Begotten, even Jesus Christ, that thou wilt have mercy upon Noah and his seed, that the earth might never more be covered by the ^afloods.

51 And the Lord could not withhold; and he ^acovenanted with Enoch, and sware unto him with an oath, that he would stay the ^bfloods; that he would call upon the children of Noah;

52 And he sent forth an unalterable decree, that a ^aremnant of his seed should always be found among all nations, while the earth should stand;

53 And the Lord said: Blessed is he through whose seed Messiah shall come; for he saith—I am ^aMessiah, the ^bKing of Zion, the ^cRock of Heaven, which is broad as ^deternity; whoso cometh in at the gate and ^eclimbeth up by me shall never fall; wherefore, blessed are they of whom I have spoken, for they shall come forth in ^fsongs of everlasting ^gjoy.

54 And it came to pass that Enoch cried unto the Lord, saying: When the Son of Man cometh in the flesh, shall the earth rest? I pray thee, show me these things.

55 And the Lord said unto Enoch: Look, and he looked and beheld the ^aSon of Man lifted up on the ^bcross, after the manner of men;

56 And he heard a loud voice; and the heavens were ^aveiled; and all the creations of God mourned; and the earth ^bgroaned; and the rocks were rent; and the ^csaints arose, and were ^dcrowned at the ^eright hand of the Son of Man, with crowns of glory;

57 And as many of the ^aspirits as were in ^bprison came forth, and stood on the right hand of God; and

---

45a TG Sanctification.
46a Moses 5: 57.
47a TG Jesus Christ,
    Appearances,
    Antemortal.
  b TG Jesus Christ, Lamb
    of God; Passover.
  c TG Faith.
  d Moses 7: 21.
48a TG Earth, Purpose of.
  b TG Pain.
  c Moses 7: 64 (54, 58,
    64).
  d TG Earth, Cleansing of.
  e TG Filthiness.
50a TG Flood.

51a Moses 7: 60.
  b Ps. 104: 9.
52a Moses 8: 2.
53a TG Jesus Christ,
    Messiah.
  b Matt. 2: 2; 2 Ne. 10:
    14; Alma 5: 50;
    D&C 128: 22 (22–23).
  c Ps. 71: 3; 78: 35;
    Hel. 5: 12.
    TG Corner-stone; Rock.
  d TG Eternity.
  e 2 Ne. 31: 19 (19–20).
  f TG Singing.
  g TG Joy.

55a TG Jesus Christ,
    Prophecies about.
  b 3 Ne. 27: 14. TG Jesus
    Christ, Crucifixion of.
56a TG Veil.
  b Matt. 27: 51 (45, 50–
    51).
  c TG Saints.
  d TG Exaltation.
  e Matt. 25: 34.
57a TG Spirits, Disem-
    bodied.
  b D&C 76: 73 (71–74);
    88: 99. TG Salvation,
    for the Dead; Spirits in
    Prison.

the remainder were reserved in chains of darkness until the judgment of the great day.

58 And again Enoch wept and cried unto the Lord, saying: When shall the earth *a*rest?

59 And Enoch beheld the Son of Man ascend up unto the Father; and he called unto the Lord, saying: Wilt thou not come again upon the earth? Forasmuch as thou art God, and I know thee, and thou hast sworn unto me, and commanded me that I should ask in the name of thine Only Begotten; thou hast made me, and given unto me a right to thy throne, and not of myself, but through thine own grace; wherefore, I ask thee if thou wilt not come again on the earth.

60 And the Lord said unto Enoch: As I live, even so will I come in the *a*last days, in the days of wickedness and vengeance, to fulfil the *b*oath which I have made unto you concerning the children of Noah;

61 And the day shall come that the earth shall *a*rest, but before that day the heavens shall be *b*darkened, and a *c*veil of darkness shall cover the earth; and the heavens shall shake, and also the earth; and great tribulations shall be among the children of men, but my people will I *d*preserve;

62 And *a*righteousness will I send down out of heaven; and truth will I send forth out of the earth, to bear *b*testimony of mine Only Begotten; his *c*resurrection from the dead; yea, and also the resurrection of all men; and righteousness and truth will I cause to sweep the earth as with a flood, to *d*gather out mine elect from

the four quarters of the earth, unto a place which I shall prepare, an Holy City, that my people may gird up their loins, and be looking forth for the time of my coming; for there shall be my tabernacle, and it shall be called *e*Zion, a New *f*Jerusalem.

63 And the Lord said unto Enoch: Then shalt thou and all thy *a*city meet them there, and we will *b*receive them into our bosom, and they shall see us; and we will fall upon our necks, and they shall fall upon our necks, and we will kiss each other;

64 And there shall be mine abode, and it shall be Zion, which shall come forth out of all the creations which I have made; and for the space of a *a*thousand years the *b*earth shall *c*rest.

65 And it came to pass that Enoch saw the *a*day of the *b*coming of the Son of Man, in the last days, to dwell on the earth in righteousness for the space of a thousand years;

66 But before that day he saw great tribulations among the wicked; and he also saw the sea, that it was troubled, and men's hearts *a*failing them, looking forth with fear for the *b*judgments of the Almighty God, which should come upon the wicked.

67 And the Lord showed Enoch all things, even unto the end of the world; and he saw the day of the righteous, the hour of their redemption, and received a fulness of *a*joy;

68 And all the days of *a*Zion, in the days of Enoch, were three hundred and sixty-five years.

69 And Enoch and all his people *a*walked with God, and he dwelt in the midst of Zion; and it came to

58a Dan. 12: 8 (8–13).
60a TG Last Days.
  b Moses 7: 51.
61a TG Rest.
  b Micah 3: 6; D&C 38:
    11 (11–12); 112: 23.
  c TG Veil.
  d 1 Ne. 22: 17 (15–22);
    2 Ne. 30: 10.
    TG Protection, Divine.
62a TG Righteousness.
  b TG Testimony.

c TG Jesus Christ,
    Resurrection.
d TG Israel, Gathering of.
e TG Zion.
f TG Jerusalem, New.
63a Rev. 21: 10 (9–11);
    D&C 45: 12 (11–12);
    Moses 7: 20 (20–21).
  b Rev. 14: 13 (12–13).
64a TG Millennium.
  b TG Earth, Destiny of.

c Moses 7: 48.
    TG Earth, Purpose of.
65a 1 Cor. 5: 5.
  b Jude 1: 14.
66a Isa. 13: 7.
  b TG Judgment, The
    Last.
67a TG Joy.
68a Gen. 5: 23; Moses 8: 1.
69a Gen. 5: 24; Moses 6:
    34. TG Walking with
    God.

pass that Zion was not, for God received it up into his own bosom; and from thence went forth the saying, ZION IS FLED.

CHAPTER 8
(February 1831)

Methuselah prophesies—Noah and his sons preach the gospel—Great wickedness prevails—The call to repentance unheeded—God decrees destruction of all flesh by the flood.

AND all the days of [a]Enoch were four hundred and thirty years.

2 And it came to pass that Methuselah, the son of Enoch, was [a]not taken, that the covenants of the Lord might be fulfilled, which he made to Enoch; for he truly covenanted with Enoch that Noah should be of the fruit of his loins.

3 And it came to pass that Methuselah [a]prophesied that from his loins should spring all the kingdoms of the earth (through Noah), and he took glory unto himself.

4 And there came forth a great [a]famine into the land, and the Lord [b]cursed the earth with a sore curse, and many of the inhabitants thereof died.

5 And it came to pass that Methuselah lived one hundred and eighty-seven years, and begat Lamech;

6 And Methuselah lived, after he begat Lamech, seven hundred and eighty-two years, and begat sons and daughters;

7 And all the days of Methuselah were nine hundred and sixty-nine years, and he died.

8 And Lamech lived one hundred and eighty-two years, and begat a son,

9 And he called his name Noah,

saying: This son shall comfort us concerning our work and toil of our hands, because of the ground which the Lord hath [a]cursed.

10 And Lamech lived, after he begat Noah, five hundred and ninety-five years, and begat sons and daughters;

11 And all the days of Lamech were seven hundred and seventy-seven years, and he died.

12 And Noah was four hundred and fifty years old, and [a]begat Japheth; and forty-two years afterward he begat [b]Shem of her who was the mother of Japheth, and when he was five hundred years old he begat [c]Ham.

13 And [a]Noah and his sons hearkened unto the Lord, and gave heed, and they were called the [b]sons of God.

14 And when these men began to multiply on the face of the earth, and daughters were born unto them, the [a]sons of men saw that those daughters were fair, and they took them [b]wives, even as they chose.

15 And the Lord said unto Noah: The daughters of thy sons have sold themselves; for behold mine anger is kindled against the sons of men, for they will not [a]hearken to my voice.

16 And it came to pass that Noah [a]prophesied, and taught the things of God, even as it was in the beginning.

17 And the Lord said unto Noah: My Spirit shall not always [a]strive with man, for he shall know that all [b]flesh shall die; yet his days shall be an [c]hundred and twenty years; and if men do not repent, I will send in the [d]floods upon them.

18 And in those days there were

8 1a Moses 7: 68–69.
   2a Moses 7: 52 (51–52).
   3a Moses 6: 23.
   4a TG Famine.
    b TG Curse.
   9a Moses 4: 23. TG Curse.
  12a Gen. 5: 32; 9: 18 (18–27).
    b 1 Chr. 1: 4.

    c Abr. 1: 11 (11–27).
  13a Gen. 6: 8; 7: 5;
     D&C 138:41.
     TG Obedience.
    b TG Sons and Daughters of God.
  14a Moses 5: 52; 6: 15.
    b TG Marriage; Marriage, Interfaith.
  15a TG Disobedience.

  16a Moses 6: 23.
  17a 2 Ne. 26: 11; Ether 2: 15. TG God, Access to.
    b Gen. 6: 3; 2 Ne. 9: 4 (4–8). TG Flesh and Blood.
    c Gen. 6: 3.
    d Gen. 7: 10 (4, 10); Moses 7: 34.

^agiants on the earth, and they sought Noah to take away his ^blife; but the Lord was with Noah, and the ^cpower of the Lord was upon him.

19 And the Lord ^aordained ^bNoah after his own ^corder, and commanded him that he should go forth and ^ddeclare his Gospel unto the children of men, even as it was given unto Enoch.

20 And it came to pass that Noah called upon the children of men that they should ^arepent; but they hearkened not unto his words;

21 And also, after that they had heard him, they came up before him, saying: Behold, we are the sons of God; have we not taken unto ourselves the ^adaughters of men? And are we not ^beating and drinking, and marrying and giving in marriage? And our wives bear unto us children, and the same are mighty men, which are like unto men of old, men of great renown. And they hearkened not unto the words of Noah.

22 And God saw that the ^awickedness of men had become great in the earth; and every man was lifted up in the ^bimagination of the thoughts of his heart, being only evil continually.

23 And it came to pass that Noah continued his ^apreaching unto the people, saying: Hearken, and give heed unto my words;

24 ^aBelieve and repent of your sins and be ^bbaptized in the name of

Jesus Christ, the Son of God, even as our fathers, and ye shall receive the Holy Ghost, that ye may have all things made ^cmanifest; and if ye do not this, the floods will come in upon you; nevertheless they hearkened not.

25 And it ^arepented Noah, and his heart was pained that the Lord had made man on the earth, and it grieved him at the heart.

26 And the Lord said: I will ^adestroy man whom I have created, from the face of the earth, both man and beast, and the creeping things, and the fowls of the air; for it repenteth Noah that I have created them, and that I have made them; and he hath called upon me; for they have sought his ^blife.

27 And thus Noah found ^agrace in the eyes of the Lord; for Noah was a just man, and ^bperfect in his generation; and he ^cwalked with God, as did also his three sons, Shem, Ham, and Japheth.

28 The ^aearth was ^bcorrupt before God, and it was filled with violence.

29 And God looked upon the earth, and, behold, it was corrupt, for all flesh had corrupted its ^away upon the earth.

30 And God said unto Noah: The end of all flesh is come before me, for the earth is filled with violence, and behold I will ^adestroy all flesh from off the earth.

18a Gen. 6: 4; Num. 13:
   33; Deut. 2: 20;
   Josh. 17: 15; Moses 7:
   15 (14–15).
  b Moses 8: 26.
  c TG Priesthood, Power
   of.
19a D&C 107: 52.
   TG Priesthood, Ordina-
   tion.
  b Abr. 1: 19.
  c TG Priesthood, Melchizedek.
  d TG Missionary Work.

20a Gen. 5: 29.
   TG Repentance.
21a Matt. 24: 38.
   TG Disobedience.
22a Gen. 6: 5 (5–6);
   3 Ne. 9: 9; Morm. 4: 1
   (10–12); D&C 112: 23;
   Moses 7: 36 (36–37).
  b Alma 12: 14 (3, 7, 14);
   D&C 124: 99.
23a TG Preaching.
24a TG Baptism, Qualifications for.
  b TG Baptism, Essential.
  c 2 Ne. 31: 5 (2–5);

   Moses 1: 24.
25a Gen. 6: 6; Ps. 106: 45.
26a TG Earth, Cleansing of.
  b Moses 8: 18.
27a TG Grace.
  b Gen. 6: 9; D&C 129: 3
   (3, 6).
  c TG Walking with God.
28a Rev. 6: 3 (3–4);
   D&C 77: 7.
  b Gen. 6: 11 (11–13);
   D&C 10: 21; 112: 23.
29a Gen. 6: 12; D&C 82: 6.
30a Gen. 6: 13; 7: 23;
   D&C 56: 3; 64: 35.

A FACSIMILE FROM THE BOOK OF ABRAHAM

No. 1

EXPLANATION

Fig. 1. The Angel of the Lord.

Fig. 2. Abraham fastened upon an altar.

Fig. 3. The idolatrous priest of Elkenah attempting to offer up Abraham as a sacrifice.

Fig. 4. The altar for sacrifice by the idolatrous priests, standing before the gods of Elkenah, Libnah, Mahmackrah, Korash, and Pharaoh.

Fig. 5. The idolatrous god of Elkenah.

Fig. 6. The idolatrous god of Libnah.

Fig. 7. The idolatrous god of Mahmackrah.

Fig. 8. The idolatrous god of Korash.

Fig. 9. The idolatrous god of Pharaoh.

Fig. 10. Abraham in Egypt.

Fig. 11. Designed to represent the pillars of heaven, as understood by the Egyptians.

Fig. 12. Raukeeyang, signifying expanse, or the firmament over our heads; but in this case, in relation to this subject, the Egyptians meant it to signify Shaumau, to be high, or the heavens, answering to the Hebrew word, Shaumahyeem.

THE BOOK OF ABRAHAM

TRANSLATED FROM THE PAPYRUS, BY JOSEPH SMITH

A Translation of some ancient Records, that have fallen into our hands from the catacombs of Egypt.—The writings of Abraham while he was in Egypt, called the Book of Abraham, written by his own hand, upon papyrus. See History of the Church, vol. 2, pp. 235, 236, 348–351.

CHAPTER 1

Abraham seeks the blessings of the patriarchal order—He is persecuted by false priests in Chaldea—Jehovah saves him—Origins and government of Egypt reviewed.

IN the land of the ªChaldeans, at the residence of my fathers, I, ᵇAbraham, saw that it was needful for me to obtain another place of ᶜresidence;

2 And, finding there was greater ªhappiness and peace and rest for me, I sought for the blessings of the fathers, and the right whereunto I should be ordained to administer the same; having been myself a follower of ᵇrighteousness, desiring also to be one who possessed great ᶜknowledge, and to be a greater follower of righteousness, and to possess a greater knowledge, and to be a father of many ªnations, a prince of peace, and ªdesiring to receive instructions, and to keep the commandments of God, I became a rightful heir, a ᶠHigh Priest, holding the right belonging to the fathers.

3 It was ªconferred upon me from the fathers; it came down from the fathers, from the beginning of time, yea, even from the beginning, or before the foundation of the earth, down to the present time, even the right of the ᵇfirstborn, or the first man, who is ᶜAdam, or first father, through the fathers unto me.

4 I sought for mine ªappointment unto the Priesthood according to the appointment of God unto the ᵇfathers concerning the seed.

5 My ªfathers, having turned from their righteousness, and from the holy commandments which the Lord their God had given unto them, unto the worshiping of the ᵇgods of the ᶜheathen, utterly refused to hearken to my voice;

6 For their ªhearts were set to do ᵇevil, and were wholly turned to the god of ᶜElkenah, and the god of Libnah, and the god of Mahmackrah, and the god of Korash, and the god of Pharaoh, king of Egypt;

7 Therefore they turned their hearts to the sacrifice of the ªheathen in offering up their children unto these dumb idols, and hearkened not unto my voice, but endeavored to

1 1a Abr. 1: 20 (20–30); 2: 4 (1, 4).
  b Gen. 11: 26 (10–26); Hel. 8: 18 (16–19).
  c Acts 7: 3 (2–4).
2a TG Happiness; Priesthood, Qualifying for; Rest; Righteousness.
  b TG God, the Standard of Righteousness.
  c Prov. 19: 2; D&C 42: 61.

d Gen. 12: 2; 17: 6; 18: 18.
e Gen. 13: 4.
f TG High Priest; Priesthood, History of; Priesthood, Melchizedek.
3a D&C 84: 14 (6–17). TG Authority; Patriarch.
  b D&C 68: 17. TG Firstborn.
  c Moses 1: 34. TG Adam.

4a TG Birthright.
  b D&C 84: 14 (6–17).
5a Gen. 12: 1.
  b Josh. 24: 14.
  c TG Heathen.
6a TG Hardheartedness.
  b Alma 40: 13.
  c IE "gods," as illustrated in Facsimile No. 1 of the Book of Abraham.
7a TG Heathen.

take away my [b]life by the hand of the priest of Elkenah. The priest of Elkenah was also the priest of Pharaoh.

8 Now, at this time it was the custom of the priest of Pharaoh, the king of Egypt, to offer up upon the altar which was built in the land of Chaldea, for the offering unto these strange gods, men, women, and children.

9 And it came to pass that the priest made an offering unto the god of Pharaoh, and also unto the god of Shagreel, even after the manner of the Egyptians. Now the god of Shagreel was the sun.

10 Even the thank-offering of a child did the [a]priest of Pharaoh offer upon the altar which stood by the hill called Potiphar's Hill, at the head of the plain of Olishem.

11 Now, this priest had offered upon this altar three virgins at one time, who were the daughters of Onitah, one of the royal descent directly from the loins of [a]Ham. These virgins were offered up because of their virtue; they would not [b]bow down to worship gods of wood or of stone, therefore they were killed upon this altar, and it was done after the manner of the Egyptians.

12 And it came to pass that the priests laid violence upon me, that they might slay me also, as they did those virgins upon this altar; and that you may have a knowledge of this altar, I will refer you to the representation at the commencement of this record.

13 It was made after the form of a bedstead, such as was had among the Chaldeans, and it stood before the gods of Elkenah, Libnah, Mahmackrah, Korash, and also a god

like unto that of Pharaoh, king of Egypt.

14 That you may have an understanding of these gods, I have given you the fashion of them in the figures at the beginning, which manner of figures is called by the Chaldeans Rahleenos, which signifies hieroglyphics.

15 And as they lifted up their hands upon me, that they might offer me up and take away my life, behold, I lifted up my voice unto the Lord my God, and the Lord [a]hearkened and heard, and he filled me with the vision of the Almighty, and the angel of his presence stood by me, and immediately [b]unloosed my bands;

16 And his voice was unto me: [a]Abraham, Abraham, behold, my [b]name is Jehovah, and I have heard thee, and have come down to deliver thee, and to take thee away from thy [c]father's house, and from all thy kinsfolk, into a strange [d]land which thou knowest not of;

17 And this because they have turned their [a]hearts away from me, to worship the god of Elkenah, and the god of Libnah, and the god of Mahmackrah, and the god of Korash, and the god of Pharaoh, king of Egypt; therefore I have come down to [b]visit them, and to destroy him who hath lifted up his hand against them, Abraham, my son, to take away thy life.

18 Behold, I will lead thee by my hand, and I will take thee, to put upon thee my name, even the Priesthood of thy father, and my power shall be over thee.

19 As it was with [a]Noah so shall it be with thee; but through thy ministry my [b]name shall be known in the earth [c]forever, for I am thy God.

7b Abr. 1: 15, 17, 30.
10a TG False Priesthoods.
11a Moses 8: 12.
  b Dan. 3: 18 (1–23).
15a Mosiah 9: 18 (17–18);
    D&C 35: 3.
  b Abr. 2: 13; 3: 20.
16a "Abram" in 1: 16, 17;
    2: 3, 6, 14, 17, in *Times*

and Seasons, March 1,
1842, but "Abraham"
in all publications
since *Millennial Star*,
July 1842.
  b Jer. 16: 21. TG Jesus
    Christ, Jehovah.
  c Gen. 12: 1.
  d TG Promised Lands.

17a TG Worship.
  b 1 Ne. 13: 34; D&C 124:
    8.
19a Moses 8: 19.
  b Gen. 12: 3 (1–3);
    Abr. 2: 6 (6–11).
  c Ps. 48: 14; D&C 20:
    12.

20 Behold, Potiphar's Hill was in the land of ªUr, of Chaldea. And the Lord broke down the altar of Elkenah, and of the gods of the land, and utterly destroyed them, and smote the priest that he died; and there was great mourning in Chaldea, and also in the court of Pharaoh; which Pharaoh signifies king by royal blood.

21 Now this king of Egypt was a descendant from the ªloins of ᵇHam, and was a partaker of the blood of the ᶜCanaanites by birth.

22 From this descent sprang all the Egyptians, and thus the blood of the ªCanaanites was preserved in the land.

23 The land of ªEgypt being first discovered by a woman, who was the daughter of Ham, and the daughter of Egyptus, which in the Chaldean signifies Egypt, which signifies that which is forbidden;

24 When this woman discovered the land it was under water, who afterward settled her sons in it; and thus, from Ham, sprang that race which preserved the curse in the land.

25 Now the first ªgovernment of Egypt was established by Pharaoh, the eldest son of Egyptus, the daughter of Ham, and it was after the manner of the government of Ham, which was patriarchal.

26 Pharaoh, being a righteous man, established his kingdom and judged his people wisely and justly all his days, seeking earnestly to imitate that ªorder established by the fathers in the first generations, in the days of the first patriarchal reign, even in the reign of Adam, and also

of Noah, his father, who blessed him with the ᵇblessings of the earth, and with the blessings of wisdom, but cursed him as pertaining to the Priesthood.

27 Now, Pharaoh being of that lineage by which he could not have the right of ªPriesthood, notwithstanding the Pharaohs would fain ᵇclaim it from Noah, through Ham, therefore my father was led away by their idolatry;

28 But I shall endeavor, hereafter, to delineate the chronology running back from myself to the beginning of the creation, for the ªrecords have come into my hands, which I hold unto this present time.

29 Now, after the priest of Elkenah was smitten that he died, there came a fulfilment of those things which were said unto me concerning the land of Chaldea, that there should be a ªfamine in the land.

30 Accordingly a famine prevailed throughout all the land of Chaldea, and my father was sorely tormented because of the famine, and he repented of the evil which he had determined against me, to take away my ªlife.

31 But the ªrecords of the fathers, even the patriarchs, concerning the right of Priesthood, the Lord my God preserved in mine own hands; therefore a knowledge of the beginning of the creation, and also of the ᵇplanets, and of the stars, as they were made known unto the fathers, have I kept even unto this day, and I shall endeavor to write some of these things upon this ᶜrecord, for the benefit of my posterity that shall come after me.

20a Gen. 11: 28; Abr. 1: 1; 2: 4 (1–4).
21a Gen. 10: 6 (6–8); Abr. 1: 25 (20–25).
  b Ps. 78: 51; Moses 8: 12.
  c Ps. 105: 23;
    Moses 7: 6 (6–8).
22a Gen. 10: 15 (6–20); Moses 7: 7 (6–8).
23a Ps. 105: 23; Gen. 10: 6.

25a TG Governments.
26a TG Order.
  b TG Blessing.
27a TG Priesthood, Qualifying for.
  b TG Unrighteous Dominion.
28a Moses 6: 5.
  TG Scriptures, Writing of.

29a Abr. 2: 1, 17.
  TG Famine.
30a Abr. 1: 7 (7, 12).
31a TG Record Keeping; Scriptures, Preservation of.
  b Abr. 3: 2 (1–21).
  TG Astronomy.
  c TG Book of Remembrance.

CHAPTER 2

Abraham leaves Ur to go to Canaan—Jehovah appears to him at Haran—All gospel blessings are promised to his seed, and through his seed to all—He goes to Canaan, and on to Egypt.

Now the Lord God caused the *a*famine to wax sore in the land of Ur, insomuch that *b*Haran, my brother, died; but *c*Terah, my father, yet lived in the land of Ur, of the Chaldees.

2 And it came to pass that I, Abraham, took *a*Sarai to wife, and *b*Nahor, my brother, took Milcah to wife, who was the *c*daughter of Haran.

3 Now the Lord had *a*said unto me: Abraham, get thee out of thy country, and from thy kindred, and from thy father's house, unto a land that I will show thee.

4 I left the land of *a*Ur, of the Chaldees, to go into the land of Canaan; and I took Lot, my brother's son, and his wife, and Sarai my wife; and also my *b*father followed after me, unto the land which we denominated Haran.

5 And the famine abated; and my father tarried in Haran and dwelt there, as there were many flocks in Haran; and my father turned again unto his *a*idolatry, therefore he continued in Haran.

6 But I, Abraham, and Lot, my brother's son, prayed unto the Lord, and the Lord *a*appeared unto me, and said unto me: Arise, and take Lot with thee; for I have purposed to take thee away out of Haran, and to make of thee a *b*minister to bear my *c*name in a strange *d*land which I will give unto thy seed after thee for an everlasting possession, when they hearken to my voice.

7 For I am the Lord thy God; I dwell in *a*heaven; the earth is my *b*footstool; I stretch my hand over the sea, and it obeys my voice; I cause the wind and the fire to be my *c*chariot; I say to the mountains—Depart hence—and behold, they are taken away by a whirlwind, in an instant, suddenly.

8 My *a*name is Jehovah, and I *b*know the end from the beginning; therefore my hand shall be over thee.

9 And I will make of thee a great *a*nation, and I will *b*bless thee above measure, and make thy name great among all nations, and thou shalt be a blessing unto thy seed after thee, that in their hands they shall bear this ministry and *c*Priesthood unto all nations;

10 And I will *a*bless them through thy name; for as many as receive this *b*Gospel shall be called after thy *c*name, and shall be accounted thy *d*seed, and shall rise up and bless thee, as their *e*father;

2 1*a* Abr. 1: 29.
  b Gen. 11: 28.
  c Gen. 11: 24 (24–26);
     1 Chr. 1: 26.
2*a* Gen. 11: 29; 12: 5.
  b Gen. 11: 27; 22: 23
     (20–24).
  c Gen. 20: 12 (12, 16).
3*a* Gen. 12: 1; 20: 13;
     Acts 7: 2 (1–8, 16).
4*a* Neh. 9: 7; Abr. 1: 1,
     20, 29–30.
  b Gen. 11: 31 (31–32).
5*a* Josh. 24: 2 (2–3).
6*a* Gen. 17: 1; 48: 3;
     Ex. 6: 2–3; D&C 107:
     54; Abr. 3: 11. TG God,
     Manifestations of;
     Jesus Christ, Appearances,
     Antemortal.

  b TG Delegation of
     Responsibility.
  c Gen. 12: 3; Abr. 1: 19.
  d Gen. 13: 15; 17: 8; 48:
     4; Ex. 33: 1; 1 Ne. 10:
     3; Abr. 2: 19.
     TG Israel, Land of.
7*a* Moses 6: 42.
  b Lam. 2: 1; Is. 1* Ne. 17:
     39; D&C 38: 17;
     Moses 6: 9, 44.
  c 2 Kgs. 2: 11; Isa. 66:
     15 (15–16).
8*a* Jer. 16: 21.
  b TG God, Foreknowledge
     of; God, Omniscience of.
9*a* 2 Sam. 7: 23; Neh. 9:
     23; Isa. 9: 3; 26: 15;

     Acts 13: 26; Abr. 3:
     14.
  b Gen. 12: 2 (1–3); 49:
     26; Ps. 105: 10 (8–10);
     1 Ne. 17: 40; 2 Ne. 29:
     14; 3 Ne. 20: 27;
     Morm. 5: 20.
     TG Seed of Abraham.
  c D&C 84: 17 (17–19);
     Moses 6: 7.
10*a* TG Israel, Blessings of.
   b Acts 15: 14; Gal. 3: 8
     (7–9).
   c Gen. 12: 2 (2–3);
     Isa. 44: 5.
   d Gen. 13: 16 (14–16);
     Rom. 4: 11; Gal. 3: 29
     (26–29); 2 Ne. 30: 2.
   e TG Patriarch.

11 And I will ᵃbless them that bless thee, and ᵇcurse them that curse thee; and in thee (that is, in thy Priesthood) and in thy ᶜseed (that is, thy Priesthood), for I give unto thee a promise that this ᵈright shall continue in thee, and in thy seed after thee (that is to say, the literal seed, or the seed of the body) shall all the families of the earth be blessed, even with the blessings of the Gospel, which are the blessings of salvation, even of life eternal.

12 Now, after the Lord had withdrawn from speaking to me, and withdrawn his face from me, I said in my heart: Thy servant has ᵃsought thee earnestly; now I have found thee;

13 Thou didst send thine angel to ᵃdeliver me from the gods of Elkenah, and I will do well to hearken unto thy voice, therefore let thy servant rise up and depart in peace.

14 So I, Abraham, departed as the Lord had said unto me, and Lot with me; and I, Abraham, was ᵃsixty and two years old when I departed out of Haran.

15 And I took Sarai, whom I took to wife when I was in Ur, in Chaldea, and Lot, my brother's son, and all our substance that we had gathered, and the souls that we had ᵃwon in Haran, and came forth in the way to the land of Canaan, and dwelt in tents as we came on our way;

16 Therefore, ᵃeternity was our covering and our ᵇrock and our salvation, as we journeyed from Haran by the way of ᶜJershon, to come to the land of Canaan.

17 Now I, Abraham, built an ᵃaltar in the land of Jershon, and made an offering unto the Lord, and prayed that the ᵇfamine might be turned away from my father's house, that they might not perish.

18 And then we passed from Jershon through the land unto the place of Sechem; it was situated in the plains of Moreh, and we had already come into the borders of the land of the ᵃCanaanites, and I offered ᵇsacrifice there in the plains of Moreh, and called on the Lord devoutly, because we had already come into the land of this idolatrous nation.

19 And the Lord ᵃappeared unto me in answer to my prayers, and said unto me: Unto thy seed will I give this ᵇland.

20 And I, Abraham, arose from the place of the altar which I had built unto the Lord, and removed from thence unto a mountain on the east of ᵃBethel, and pitched my tent there, Bethel on the west, and ᵇHai on the east; and there I built another ᶜaltar unto the Lord, and ᵈcalled again upon the name of the Lord.

21 And I, Abraham, journeyed, going on still towards the south; and there was a continuation of a famine in the land; and I, Abraham, concluded to go down into Egypt, to sojourn there, for the famine became very grievous.

22 And it came to pass when I was come near to enter into Egypt, the Lord ᵃsaid unto me: Behold, Sarai, thy wife, is a very fair woman to look upon;

11a TG Israel, Blessings of.
  b TG Curse.
  c Isa. 49: 3; 61: 9.
  d TG Birthright; Israel,
    Mission of; Priesthood, Melchizedek.
12a Jer. 29: 13; D&C 88: 63.
13a Abr. 1: 15 (15–17).
14a Gen. 12: 4.
15a Gen. 12: 5.
    TG Conversion.
16a TG Eternity.
  b TG Rock.
  c IE There is a possi-

bility that Abram
traveled southward on
the ancient route by
way of Damascus to the
site of ancient Jerash
(Jershon), thence
down the Jabbok,
across the Jordan, and
up the Wadi Farah to
Sechem (also spelled
Shechem, Sichem, and
Sychem).
17a Gen. 12: 7 (7–8);
  1 Ne. 2: 7.

  b Abr. 1: 29; 2: 1.
18a Gen. 12: 6.
  b TG Sacrifice.
19a D&C 107: 54 (53–54).
  b Gen. 11: 31 (27–31);
    13: 15; 17: 8 (1–27);
    Ex. 3: 8 (1–10);
    Num. 34: 2 (1–29).
    TG Promised Lands.
20a Gen. 28: 19.
  b Gen. 13: 3.
  c Gen. 13: 4.
  d Gen. 12: 8.
22a Gen. 12: 11.

23 Therefore it shall come to pass, when the Egyptians shall see her, they will say—She is his wife; and they will kill you, but they will save her alive; therefore see that ye do on this wise:

24 Let her say unto the Egyptians, she is thy sister, and thy soul shall live.

25 And it came to pass that I, Abraham, told Sarai, my wife, all that the Lord had said unto me—Therefore say unto them, I pray thee, thou art my *a*sister, that it may be well with me for thy sake, and my soul shall live because of thee.

CHAPTER 3

Abraham learns about the sun, moon, and stars by means of the Urim and Thummim—The Lord reveals to him the eternal nature of spirits—He learns of pre-earth life, foreordination, the creation, the choosing of a Redeemer, and the second estate of man.

AND I, Abraham, had the *a*Urim and Thummim, which the Lord my God had given unto me, in Ur of the Chaldees;

2 And I saw the *a*stars, that they were very great, and that one of them was nearest unto the throne of God; and there were many great ones which were near unto it;

3 And the Lord said unto me: These are the governing ones; and the name of the great one is *a*Kolob, because it is near unto me, for I am the Lord thy God: I have set this one to govern all those which belong to the same order as that upon which thou standest.

4 And the Lord said unto me, by the Urim and Thummim, that Kolob was after the manner of the Lord, according to its *a*times and

seasons in the revolutions thereof; that one revolution was a *b*day unto the Lord, after his manner of reckoning, it being one thousand *c*years according to the time appointed unto that whereon thou standest. This is the reckoning of the Lord's *d*time, according to the reckoning of Kolob.

5 And the Lord said unto me: The planet which is the lesser light, lesser than that which is to rule the day, even the night, is above or *a*greater than that upon which thou standest in point of reckoning, for it moveth in order more slow; this is in order because it standeth above the earth upon which thou standest, therefore the reckoning of its time is not so many as to its number of days, and of months, and of years.

6 And the Lord said unto me: Now, Abraham, these *a*two facts exist, behold thine eyes see it; it is given unto thee to know the times of reckoning, and the set time, yea, the set time of the earth upon which thou standest, and the set time of the greater light which is set to rule the day, and the set time of the lesser light which is set to rule the night.

7 Now the set time of the lesser light is a longer time as to its reckoning than the reckoning of the time of the earth upon which thou standest.

8 And where these two facts exist, there shall be another fact above them, that is, there shall be another planet whose reckoning of time shall be longer still;

9 And thus there shall be the reckoning of the time of one *a*planet above another, until thou come nigh unto Kolob, which Kolob is after the reckoning of the Lord's time; which Kolob is set nigh unto the throne of God, to govern all those planets which belong to the same *b*order as that upon which thou standest.

25a Gen. 12: 10 (9–20); 20: 12.

3 1a Ex. 28: 30; Mosiah 8: 13 (13–19); 28: 13 (13–16); JS-H 1: 35.
 TG Urim and Thummim.

2a Moses 1: 35 (35–37); 7: 36; Abr. 1: 31.
3a See also Facsimile No. 2, figs. 1–5. Abr. 3: 16; 5: 13. TG Astronomy.
4a Dan. 2: 21.
 b Abr. 5: 13.
 c Ps. 90: 4; 2 Pet. 3: 8.

d TG Time.
5a IE It rotates on its axis more slowly. See also v. 7.
6a Abr. 3: 16 (16–19).
9a TG Astronomy.
 b D&C 77: 3; 88: 42 (37–42). TG Order.

10 And it is given unto thee to know the set time of all the stars that are set to give light, until thou come near unto the throne of God.

11 Thus I, Abraham, *talked with the Lord, face to face, as one man talketh with another; and he told me of the works which his hands had made;

12 And he said unto me: My son, my son (and his hand was stretched out), behold I will show you all these. And he put his hand upon mine eyes, and I saw those things which his hands had made, which were many; and they multiplied before mine eyes, and I could not see the end thereof.

13 And he said unto me: This is Shinehah, which is the sun. And he said unto me: Kokob, which is star. And he said unto me: Olea, which is the moon. And he said unto me: Kokaubeam, which signifies stars, or all the great lights, which were in the firmament of heaven.

14 And it was in the night time when the Lord spake these words unto me: I will *multiply thee, and thy *seed after thee, like unto these; and if thou canst count the *number of sands, so shall be the number of thy seeds.

15 And the Lord said unto me: Abraham, I *show these things unto thee before ye go into Egypt, that ye may declare all these words.

16 If *two things exist, and there be one above the other, there shall be greater things above them; therefore *Kolob is the greatest of all the Kokaubeam that thou hast seen, because it is nearest unto me.

17 Now, if there be two things, one above the other, and the moon be above the earth, then it may be that a planet or a star may exist above it; and there is nothing that the Lord thy God shall take in his heart to do but what he will *do it.

18 Howbeit that he made the greater star; as, also, if there be two *spirits, and one shall be more intelligent than the other, yet these two spirits, notwithstanding one is more intelligent than the other, have no beginning; they existed before, they shall have no end, they shall exist after, for they are *gnolaum, or eternal.

19 And the Lord said unto me: These two facts do exist, that there are two spirits, one being more intelligent than the other; there shall be another more intelligent than they; I am the Lord thy God, I am *more intelligent than they all.

20 The Lord thy God sent his angel to *deliver thee from the hands of the priest of Elkenah.

21 I dwell in the midst of them all; I now, therefore, have come down unto thee to declare unto thee the *works which my hands have made, wherein my *wisdom excelleth them all, for I *rule in the heavens above, and in the earth beneath, in all wisdom and prudence, over all the intelligences thine eyes have seen from the beginning; I came down in the beginning in the midst of all the intelligences thou hast seen.

22 Now the Lord had shown unto me, Abraham, the *intelligences that were organized before the world was; and among all these

11a Gen. 17: 1; Abr. 2: 6 (6, 8, 19). TG God, Access to; God, Manifestations of; God, Privilege of Seeing.
14a Abr. 2: 9.
  b Gen. 13: 16; D&C 132: 30.
  c 1 Kgs. 9: 8; Hosea 1: 10.
15a TG Guidance, Divine.
16a Abr. 3: 6 (6, 8).
  b Abr. 3: 3.

17a Job 9: 4 (4–12).
18a TG Spirit Body; Spirit Creation.
  b Gnolaum is a transliteration of a Hebrew word meaning eternal.
19a Isa. 55: 9 (8–9). TG God, Intelligence of; God, Omniscience of; Intelligence.
20a Abr. 1: 15.
21a D&C 88: 47 (45–47); Moses 1: 27 (27–28);

7: 23.
  b Job 12: 13 (7–25); 2 Ne. 9: 8.
  c TG God, Perfection of; Kingdom of God, in Heaven.
22a TG Council in Heaven; Intelligence; Man, a Spirit Child of Heavenly Father; Man, Antemortal Existence of; Spirit Creation.

EXPLANATION

Fig. 1. Kolob, signifying the first creation, nearest to the celestial, or the residence of God. First in government, the last pertaining to the measurement of time. The measurement according to celestial time, which celestial time signifies one day to a cubit. One day in Kolob is equal to a thousand years according to the measurement of this earth, which is called by the Egyptians Jah-oh-eh.

Fig. 2. Stands next to Kolob, called by the Egyptians Oliblish, which is the next grand governing creation near to the celestial or the place where God resides; holding the key of power also, pertaining to other planets; as revealed from God to Abraham, as he offered sacrifice upon an altar, which he had built unto the Lord.

Fig. 3. Is made to represent God, sitting upon his throne, clothed with power and authority; with a crown of eternal light upon his head; representing also the grand Key-words of the Holy Priesthood, as revealed to Adam in the Garden of Eden, as also to Seth, Noah, Melchizedek, Abraham, and all to whom the Priesthood was revealed.

Fig. 4. Answers to the Hebrew word Raukeeyang, signifying expanse, or the firmament of the heavens; also a numerical figure, in Egyptian signifying one thousand; answering to the measuring of the time of Oliblish, which is equal with Kolob in its revolution and in its measuring of time.

Fig. 5. Is called in Egyptian Enish-go-on-dosh; this is one of the governing planets also, and is said by the Egyptians to be the Sun, and to borrow its light from Kolob through the medium of Kae-e-vanrash, which is the grand Key, or, in other words, the governing power, which governs fifteen other fixed planets or stars, as also Floeese or the Moon, the Earth and the Sun in their annual revolutions. This planet receives its power through the medium of Kli-flos-is-es, or Hah-ko-kau-beam, the stars represented by numbers 22 and 23, receiving light from the revolutions of Kolob.

Fig. 6. Represents this earth in its four quarters.

Fig. 7. Represents God sitting upon his throne, revealing through the heavens the grand Key-words of the Priesthood; as, also, the sign of the Holy Ghost unto Abraham, in the form of a dove.

Fig. 8. Contains writings that cannot be revealed unto the world; but is to be had in the Holy Temple of God.

Fig. 9. Ought not to be revealed at the present time.

Fig. 10. Also.

Fig. 11. Also. If the world can find out these numbers, so let it be. Amen.

Figures 12, 13, 14, 15, 16, 17, 18, 19, 20, and 21 will be given in the own due time of the Lord.

The above translation is given as far as we have any right to give at the present time.

there were many of the [b]noble and great ones;

23 And God saw these souls that they were good, and he stood in the midst of them, and he said: These I will make my rulers; for he stood among those that were spirits, and he saw that they were good; and he said unto me: Abraham, thou art one of them; thou wast [a]chosen before thou wast born.

24 And there stood [a]one among them that was like unto God, and he said unto those who were with him: We will go down, for there is space there, and we will take of these materials, and [b]we will make an earth whereon these may [c]dwell;

25 And we will [a]prove them herewith, to see if they will [b]do all things whatsoever the Lord their God shall command them;

26 And they who [a]keep their first [b]estate shall be added upon; and they who keep not their first estate shall not have glory in the same kingdom with those who keep their first estate; and they who keep their second [c]estate shall have [d]glory added upon their heads for ever and ever.

27 And the [a]Lord said: Whom shall I [b]send? And one answered like unto the Son of Man: Here am I, send me. And [c]another answered and said: Here am I, send me. And the Lord said: I will [d]send the first.

28 And the [a]second was angry, and kept not his first [b]estate; and, at that day, many followed after him.

CHAPTER 4

The Gods plan the creation of the earth and all life thereon—Their plans for the six days of creation are set forth.

AND then the Lord said: Let us go down. And they went down at the beginning, and they, that is the [a]Gods, [b]organized and formed the [c]heavens and the earth.

2 And the earth, after it was formed, was empty and desolate, because they had not formed anything but the earth; and [a]darkness reigned upon the face of the deep, and the Spirit of the Gods [b]was brooding upon the face of the waters.

3 And they (the Gods) said: Let there be light; and there was light.

4 And they (the Gods) comprehended the light, for it was [a]bright; and they divided the light, or caused it to be divided, from the darkness.

5 And the Gods called the light Day, and the darkness they called Night. And it came to pass that from the evening until morning they called [a]night; and from the morning until the evening they called day; and this was the first, or the beginning, of that which they called day and night.

6 And the Gods also said: Let there be an [a]expanse in the midst of the waters, and it shall divide the waters from the waters.

7 And the Gods ordered the expanse, so that they divided the waters which were under the expanse from

---

23a Isa. 49: 1 (1–5); Jer. 1: 5; Moses 1: 25; 3: 5. TG Election; Foreordination.
24a TG Jesus Christ, Firstborn.
 b TG Jesus Christ, Creator.
 c TG Earth, Purpose of.
25a D&C 98: 14 (12–14); 124: 55. TG Agency; Salvation, Plan of; Test, Try, Prove.

 b TG Obedience.
26a TG Dependability.
 b Jude 1: 6.
 c TG Mortality.
 d Titus 1: 2. TG Glory; Reward.
27a TG God the Father—Elohim.
 b Moses 7: 39.
 c Moses 4: 1 (1–2).
 d TG Jesus Christ, Authority of; Jesus Christ, Foreordained; Jesus Christ, Messenger of the Covenant; Jesus

Christ, Messiah; Jesus Christ, Mission of.
28a TG Devil.
 b TG Sons of Perdition.
4 1a Gen. 1: 1; Moses 2: 1. TG Jesus Christ, Creator.
 b Prov. 3: 19 (19–20).
 c Moses 1: 37 (36–38).
2a TG Darkness, Physical.
 b Gen. 1: 2; Moses 2: 2.
4a Gen. 1: 4; Moses 2: 4.
5a Gen. 1: 5.
6a Gen. 1: 6.

the waters which were above the expanse; and it was so, even as they ordered.

8 And the Gods called the expanse, Heaven. And it came to pass that it was from evening until morning that they called night; and it came to pass that it was from morning until evening that they called day; and this was the second ^atime that they called night and day.

9 And the Gods ordered, saying: Let the ^awaters under the heaven be gathered together unto ^bone place, and let the earth come up dry; and it was so as they ordered.

10 And the Gods pronounced the dry land, Earth; and the gathering together of the waters, pronounced they, ^aGreat Waters; and the Gods saw that they were obeyed.

11 And the Gods said: Let us prepare the earth to bring forth ^agrass; the herb yielding seed; the fruit tree yielding fruit, after his kind, whose seed in itself yieldeth its own likeness upon the earth; and it was so, even as they ordered.

12 And the Gods organized the ^aearth to bring forth grass from its own seed, and the herb to bring forth herb from its own seed, yielding seed after his kind; and the earth to bring forth the tree from its own seed, yielding fruit, whose seed could only bring forth the same in itself, after his kind; and the Gods saw that they were obeyed.

13 And it came to pass that they numbered the days; from the evening until the morning they called night; and it came to pass, from the morning until the evening they called day; and it was the third time.

14 And the Gods organized the ^alights in the expanse of the heaven, and caused them to divide the day from the night; and organized them to be for signs and for seasons, and for days and for years;

15 And organized them to be for lights in the expanse of the heaven to give light upon the earth; and it was so.

16 And the Gods organized the two great lights, the ^agreater light to rule the day, and the lesser light to rule the night; with the lesser light they set the stars also;

17 And the Gods set them in the expanse of the heavens, to give light upon the earth, and to rule over the day and over the night, and to cause to divide the light from the ^adarkness.

18 And the Gods watched those things which they had ^aordered until they obeyed.

19 And it came to pass that it was from evening until morning that it was night; and it came to pass that it was from morning until evening that it was day; and it was the fourth time.

20 And the Gods said: Let us prepare the waters to bring forth abundantly the moving creatures that have life; and the fowl, that they may fly above the earth in the open expanse of heaven.

21 And the Gods prepared the waters that they might bring forth great ^awhales, and every living creature that moveth, which the waters were to bring forth abundantly after their kind; and every winged fowl after their kind. And the Gods saw that they would be obeyed, and that their plan was good.

22 And the Gods said: We will bless them, and cause them to be fruitful and multiply, and fill the waters in the seas or ^agreat waters; and cause the fowl to multiply in the earth.

23 And it came to pass that it was from evening until morning that they called night; and it came to

---

8a Gen. 1:8.
9a Amos 9:6; Moses 2:7 (6–9).
  b Gen. 1:9.
10a Gen. 1:10; Abr. 4:22.
11a Gen. 1:11 (11–12);

Moses 2:11 (11–12).
12a Ex. 9:29; D&C 14:9;
  15:2.
14a D&C 88:7 (7–11).
16a Gen. 1:16; D&C 76:
  71 (70–71); 88:45.

17a TG Darkness, Physical.
18a TG Order.
21a Gen. 1:21; Moses 2:
  21.
22a Abr. 4:10.

pass that it was from morning until evening that they called day; and it was the fifth time.

24 And the Gods prepared the earth to bring forth the living creature after his kind, cattle and creeping things, and beasts of the earth after their kind; and it was so, as they had said.

25 And the Gods organized the earth to bring forth the beasts after their kind, and cattle after their kind, and every thing that creepeth upon the earth after its kind; and the Gods saw they would obey.

26 And the Gods took [a]counsel among themselves and said: Let us go down and [b]form man in our [c]image, after our likeness; and we will give them dominion over the fish of the sea, and over the fowl of the air, and over the cattle, and over all the earth, and over every creeping thing that creepeth upon the earth.

27 So the [a]Gods went down to organize man in their own [b]image, in the image of the Gods to form him, male and female to form they them.

28 And the Gods said: We will bless them. And the Gods said: We will cause them to be fruitful and multiply, and replenish the earth, and subdue it, and to have dominion over the fish of the sea, and over the fowl of the air, and over every living thing that moveth upon the earth.

29 And the Gods said: Behold, we will give them every herb bearing seed that shall come upon the face of all the earth, and every tree which shall have fruit upon it; yea, the fruit of the tree yielding seed to them we will give it; it shall be for their [a]meat.

30 And to every beast of the earth, and to every fowl of the air, and to

every thing that creepeth upon the earth, behold, we will give them life, and also we will give to them every green herb for meat, and all these things shall be thus organized.

31 And the Gods said: We will do everything that we have said, and organize them; and behold, they shall be very obedient. And it came to pass that it was from evening until morning they called night; and it came to pass that it was from morning until evening that they called day; and they numbered the [a]sixth time.

CHAPTER 5

The Gods finish their planning of the creation of all things—They bring to pass the creation according to their plans—Adam names every living creature.

AND thus we will finish the heavens and the earth, and all the [a]hosts of them.

2 And the Gods said among themselves: On the seventh time we will end our work, which we have counseled; and we will [a]rest on the [b]seventh time from all our work which we have counseled.

3 And the Gods concluded upon the seventh time, because that on the seventh time they would [a]rest from all their [b]works which they (the Gods) counseled among themselves to form; and [c]sanctified it. And thus were their decisions at the time that they counseled among themselves to form the heavens and the earth.

4 And the Gods came down and formed these the generations of the heavens and of the earth, when they were formed in the day that the [a]Gods formed the earth and the heavens,

5 According to all that which they had said concerning every plant of

26a TG Counsel.
  b TG Man, Physical
    Creation of.
  c Moses 6: 9 (8–10).
27a Gen. 1: 26; Abr. 5: 7.
  b TG God, Body of
    (Corporeal Nature).

29a Gen. 1: 29 (29–30).
31a Ex. 31: 17; Mosiah 13:
    19.
5 1a D&C 38: 1; 45: 1.
2a TG Rest.
  b TG Sabbath.

3a Ex. 20: 8 (8–11).
  b Ex. 31: 15 (15–16);
    Mosiah 13: 18 (16–19).
  c Mosiah 13: 19 (16–19);
    D&C 77: 12.
4a Neh. 9: 6.

A FACSIMILE FROM THE BOOK OF ABRAHAM

No. 3

ENG BY R. HEDLOCK

EXPLANATION

Fig. 1. Abraham sitting upon Pharaoh's throne, by the politeness of the king, with a crown upon his head, representing the Priesthood, as emblematical of the grand Presidency in Heaven; with the scepter of justice and judgment in his hand.

Fig. 2. King Pharaoh, whose name is given in the characters above his head.

Fig. 3. Signifies Abraham in Egypt as given also in Figure 10 of Facsimile No. 1.

Fig. 4. Prince of Pharaoh, King of Egypt, as written above the hand.

Fig. 5. Shulem, one of the king's principal waiters, as represented by the characters above his hand.

Fig. 6. Olimlah, a slave belonging to the prince.

Abraham is reasoning upon the principles of Astronomy, in the king's court.

the field before it was in the *a*earth, and every herb of the field before it grew; for the Gods had not caused it to rain upon the earth when they counseled to do them, and had not formed a man to till the ground.

6 But there went up a mist from the earth, and watered the whole face of the ground.

7 And the *a*Gods formed man from the *b*dust of the ground, and took his *c*spirit (that is, the man's spirit), and put it into him; and breathed into his nostrils the breath of life, and man became a living *d*soul.

8 And the Gods planted a garden, eastward in *a*Eden, and there they put the man, whose spirit they had put into the body which they had formed.

9 And out of the ground made the Gods to grow every tree that is pleasant to the sight and good for food; the *a*tree of life, also, in the midst of the garden, and the tree of knowledge of good and evil.

10 There was a river running out of Eden, to water the garden, and from thence it was parted and became into four heads.

11 And the Gods took the man and put him in the Garden of Eden, to dress it and to keep it.

12 And the Gods commanded the man, saying: Of every tree of the garden thou mayest freely eat,

13 But of the tree of knowledge of good and evil, thou shalt not eat of it; for in the time that thou eatest thereof, thou shalt surely die. Now I, Abraham, saw that it was after

the Lord's *a*time, which was after the time of *b*Kolob; for as yet the Gods had not appointed unto Adam his reckoning.

14 And the Gods said: Let us make an help meet for the man, for it is not good that the man should be alone, therefore we will form an help meet for him.

15 And the Gods caused a deep sleep to fall upon Adam; and he slept, and they took one of his ribs, and closed up the flesh in the stead thereof;

16 And of the rib which the Gods had taken from man, formed they a *a*woman, and brought her unto the man.

17 And Adam said: This was bone of my bones, and *a*flesh of my flesh; now she shall be called Woman, because she was taken out of man;

18 Therefore shall a man leave his father and his mother, and shall *a*cleave unto his wife, and they shall be *b*one flesh.

19 And they were both naked, the man and his wife, and were not *a*ashamed.

20 And out of the ground the Gods formed every beast of the field, and every fowl of the air, and brought them unto Adam to see what he would call them; and whatsoever *a*Adam called every living creature, that should be the name thereof.

21 And Adam gave *a*names to all *b*cattle, to the fowl of the air, to every beast of the field; and for Adam, there was found an *c*help meet for him.

5a TG Spirit Creation.
7a Abr. 4: 27 (26–31).
  b Moses 4: 25 (25–29); 6: 59.
  c Gen. 2: 7; 2 Ne. 9: 26; D&C 77: 2; 93: 33.
    TG Man, Antemortal Existence of; Spirit Body.
d TG Soul.
8a TG Eden.
9a 1 Ne. 11: 25; Moses 4: 28, 31.
13a Abr. 3: 4, 10. TG Time.
  b Abr. 3: 3 (2–4).
16a TG Woman.
17a Jacob 2: 21.
18a D&C 42: 22; 49: 15

(15–16).
  b TG Divorce; Marriage, Celestial.
19a TG Shame.
20a TG Adam.
21a TG Language.
  b Enos 1: 21; Ether 9: 18.
  c Abr. 5: 14.

JOSEPH SMITH—MATTHEW

An extract from the translation of the Bible as revealed to Joseph Smith the Prophet in 1831: Matthew 23: 39 and chapter 24.

Jesus foretells the impending destruction of Jerusalem—He also discourses on the second coming of the Son of Man, and the destruction of the wicked.

[a]FOR I say unto you, that ye shall not see me henceforth and know that I am he of whom it is written by the prophets, until ye shall say: Blessed is he who [b]cometh in the name of the Lord, in the clouds of heaven, and all the holy angels with him. Then understood his disciples that he should come again on the earth, after that he was glorified and [c]crowned on the right hand of God.

2 And Jesus went out, and departed from the temple; and his disciples came to him, for to [d]hear him, saying: Master, show us concerning the buildings of the temple, as thou hast said—They shall be thrown down, and left unto you desolate.

3 And Jesus said unto them: See ye not all these things, and do ye not understand them? Verily I say unto you, there shall not be left here, upon this temple, one [a]stone upon another that shall not be thrown down.

4 And Jesus left them, and went upon the Mount of Olives. And as he sat upon the Mount of Olives, the disciples came unto him privately, saying: Tell us when shall these things be which thou hast said concerning the destruction of the temple, and the Jews; and what is the [a]sign of thy [b]coming, and of the [c]end of the world, or the destruction of the [d]wicked, which is the end of the world?

5 And Jesus answered, and said unto them: Take heed that no man deceive you;

6 For many shall come in my name, saying—I am [a]Christ—and shall deceive many;

7 Then shall they deliver you up to be [a]afflicted, and shall kill you, and ye shall be [b]hated of all nations, for my name's sake;

8 And then shall many be [a]offended, and shall betray one another, and shall hate one another;

9 And many [a]false prophets shall arise, and shall deceive many;

10 And because iniquity shall abound, the [a]love of many shall wax cold;

11 But he that remaineth [a]steadfast and is not overcome, the same shall be saved.

12 When you, therefore, shall see the [a]abomination of [b]desolation, spoken of by Daniel the prophet, concerning the destruction of [c]Jerusalem, then you shall stand in the

1 1a Matt. 23: 39.
 b Ps. 118: 26 (24–26);
  Matt. 26: 64; Acts 1:
  11.
 c TG Jesus Christ, Relationships with the
  Father.
2a Matt. 24: 1–51.
3a Luke 19: 44 (41–44).
4a Luke 21: 7 (7–36);

D&C 45: 16 (16–75).
  TG Last Days.
 b TG Jesus Christ,
  Second Coming.
 c TG World, End of.
 d Mal. 4: 1; D&C 133: 64
  (64–74).
6a Moses 1: 19. TG False
  Christs.
7a 1 Pet. 4: 13 (12–16).

 b TG Hate; Malice.
8a Ezek. 32: 9 (7–9).
  TG Offenses.
9a TG False Prophets.
10a D&C 45: 27.
11a 2 Pet. 3: 17.
12a JS-M 1: 32.
 b TG Abomination of
  Desolation.
 c TG Jerusalem.

*d*holy place; whoso readeth let him understand.

13 Then let them who are in Judea flee into the *a*mountains;

14 Let him who is on the housetop flee, and not return to take anything out of his house;

15 Neither let him who is in the field return back to take his clothes;

16 And wo unto them that are with *a*child, and unto them that give suck in those days;

17 Therefore, pray ye the Lord that your flight be not in the winter, neither on the Sabbath day;

18 For then, in those days, shall be great *a*tribulation on the *b*Jews, and upon the inhabitants of *c*Jerusalem, such as was not before sent upon Israel, of God, since the beginning of their kingdom until this time; no, nor ever shall be sent again upon Israel.

19 All things which have befallen them are only the beginning of the sorrows which shall come upon them.

20 And except those days should be shortened, there should none of their flesh be *a*saved; but for the elect's sake, according to the *b*covenant, those days shall be shortened.

21 Behold, these things I have spoken unto you concerning the Jews; and again, after the tribulation of those days which shall come upon Jerusalem, if any man shall say unto you, Lo, here is Christ, or there, believe him not;

22 For in those days there shall also arise false *a*Christs, and false prophets, and shall show great signs and wonders, insomuch, that, if possible, they shall deceive the very elect, who are the elect according to the covenant.

23 Behold, I speak these things unto you for the *a*elect's sake; and you also shall hear of *b*wars, and rumors of wars; see that ye be not troubled, for all I have told you must come to pass; but the end is not yet.

24 Behold, I have told you before;

25 Wherefore, if they shall say unto you: Behold, he is in the desert; go not forth: Behold, he is in the secret chambers; believe it not;

26 For as the light of the morning cometh out of the *a*east, and shineth even unto the west, and covereth the whole earth, so shall also the coming of the Son of Man be.

27 And now I show unto you a parable. Behold, wheresoever the *a*carcass is, there will the eagles be *b*gathered together; so likewise shall mine elect be gathered from the four quarters of the earth.

28 And they shall hear of wars, and rumors of wars.

29 Behold I speak for mine elect's sake; for nation shall rise against nation, and kingdom against kingdom; there shall be *a*famines, and pestilences, and earthquakes, in divers places.

30 And again, because iniquity shall abound, the love of men shall wax *a*cold; but he that shall not be overcome, the same shall be saved.

31 And again, this *a*Gospel of the Kingdom shall be preached in all the world, for a witness unto all *b*nations, and then shall the end come, or the destruction of the wicked.

32 And again shall the *a*abomination of desolation, spoken of by Daniel the prophet, be fulfilled.

33 And immediately after the tribulation of those days, the *a*sun shall be *b*darkened, and the moon shall not give her light, and the

---

12d D&C 101: 22 (22–25).
13a D&C 133: 13 (9–13).
16a Luke 23: 29 (29–31).
18a *TG* Dan. 12: 1; JS-M 1: 36.
  b TG Israel, Judah, People of.
  c Zech. 12: 3 (1–14); 14: 2 (1–5).
20a D&C 97: 25 (21–28).

  b 2 Ne. 30: 2; 3 Ne. 21: 22–24.
22a *TG* False Christs.
23a D&C 29: 7 (7–23).
  b D&C 45: 26 (18–59).
26a Eccl. 43: 2 (1–9).
27a *b* Deut. 28: 26.
  b Ps. 74: 1 (1–2); Matt. 24: 28; 1 Ne. 19: 16 (15–16); D&C 35: 25.

29a Joel 1: 10; D&C 43: 25 (24–25); 87: 6 (1–8).
30a Isa. 9: 19; Mosiah 9: 2.
31a Matt. 9: 35; D&C 84: 80 (79–80).
  b TG Nations.
32a JS-M 1: 12.
33a Joel 2: 10; D&C 29: 14.
  b Amos 5: 18.

*stars shall fall from heaven, and the powers of heaven shall be shaken.

34 Verily, I say unto you, this *generation, in which these things shall be shown forth, shall not pass away until all I have told you shall be fulfilled.

35 Although, the days will come, that heaven and earth shall pass away; yet my *words shall not pass away, but all shall be fulfilled.

36 And, as I said before, after the *tribulation of those days, and the powers of the heavens shall be shaken, then shall appear the sign of the Son of Man in heaven, and then shall all the tribes of the earth *mourn; and they shall see the *Son of Man *coming in the clouds of heaven, with power and great glory;

37 And whoso *treasureth up my word, shall not be deceived, for the Son of Man shall *come, and he shall send his *angels before him with the great sound of a trumpet, and they shall gather together the *remainder of his elect from the four winds, from one end of heaven to the other.

38 Now learn a parable of the *fig-tree—When its branches are yet tender, and it begins to put forth leaves, you know that summer is nigh at hand;

39 So likewise, mine elect, when they shall see all these things, they shall know that he is near, even at the doors;

40 But of that day, and hour, no one *knoweth; no, not the angels of God in heaven, but my Father only.

41 But as it was in the days of *Noah, so it shall be also at the coming of the Son of Man;

42 For it shall be with them, as it was in the days which were before

the *flood; for until the day that Noah entered into the ark they were eating and drinking, marrying and giving in marriage;

43 And *knew not until the flood came, and took them all away; so shall also the coming of the Son of Man be.

44 Then shall be fulfilled that which is written, that in the *last days, two shall be in the field, the one shall be taken, and the other *left;

45 Two shall be grinding at the mill, the one shall be taken, and the other left;

46 And what I say unto one, I say unto all men; *watch, therefore, for you know not at what hour your Lord doth come.

47 But know this, if the good man of the house had known in what watch the thief would come, he would have watched, and would not have suffered his house to have been broken up, but would have been ready.

48 Therefore be ye also *ready, for in such an hour as ye think not, the Son of Man cometh.

49 Who, then, is a *faithful and wise servant, whom his lord hath made ruler over his household, to give them meat in due season?

50 Blessed is that *servant whom his lord, when he cometh, shall find so doing; and verily I say unto you, he shall make him ruler over all his goods.

51 But if that evil servant shall say in his heart: My lord *delayeth his coming,

52 And shall begin to smite his fellow-servants, and to eat and drink with the drunken,

53 The lord of that servant shall come in a day when he looketh not

33c Ezek. 32: 7 (7–9).
34a Matt. 24: 34; D&C 45: 31.
35a D&C 1: 38; 29: 33.
36a JS–M 1: 18.
  TG Tribulation.
  b TG Millennium.
  d Matt. 25: 31.
37a TG Scriptures, Study of;

Study; Treasure.
  b TG Jesus Christ, Second Coming.
  c D&C 29: 11 (11–15);
  Moses 7: 25 (25–26).
  d TG Israel, Remnant of.
38a D&C 35: 16.
40a D&C 39: 21 (20–22);
  49: 7.
41a Gen. 6: 5.

42a TG Flood.
43a TG Apathy.
44a TG Earth, Cleansing of.
  b Zech. 13: 8.
46a TG Watchfulness.
48a TG Procrastination.
49a TG Trustworthiness.
50a TG Millennium,
  Preparing a People for.
51a D&C 45: 26.

for him, and in an hour that he is not aware of,

54 And shall cut him asunder, and shall appoint him his portion with the hypocrites; there shall be weeping and *a*gnashing of teeth.

55 And thus cometh the *a*end of the wicked, according to the prophecy of Moses, saying: They shall be cut off from among the people; but the end of the earth is not yet, but by and by.

54a Matt. 8: 12.

55a Ps. 36: 11–12; 73: 17 (3–17); 2 Ne. 30: 10;

D&C 1: 9 (9–10); 29: 17. TG World, End of.

JOSEPH SMITH—HISTORY

EXTRACTS FROM THE HISTORY OF JOSEPH SMITH, THE PROPHET

History of the Church, Vol. 1, Chapters 1–5

Joseph Smith tells of his ancestry, family members, and their early abodes—An unusual excitement about religion prevails in western New York—He determines to seek wisdom as directed by James —The Father and the Son appear and Joseph is called to his prophetic ministry. (Verses 1–20.)

OWING to the many reports which have been put in circulation by evil-disposed and designing persons, in relation to the rise and progress of the Church of Jesus Christ of *a*Latter-day Saints, all of which have been designed by the authors thereof to militate against its character as a Church and its progress in the world—I have been induced to write this history, to disabuse the public mind, and put all inquirers after truth in possession of the *b*facts, as they have transpired, in relation both to myself and the Church, so far as I have such facts in my possession.

2 In this history I shall present the various events in relation to this Church, in truth and righteousness, as they have transpired, or as they at present exist, being now [1838] the *a*eighth *b*year since the organization of the said Church.

3 *a*I was born in the year of our Lord one thousand eight hundred and five, on the twenty-third day of December, in the town of Sharon, Windsor county, State of Vermont

... My father, *b*Joseph Smith, Sen., left the State of Vermont, and moved to Palmyra, Ontario (now Wayne) county, in the State of New York, when I was in my tenth year, or thereabouts. In about four years after my father's arrival in Palmyra, he moved with his family into Manchester in the same county of Ontario—

4 His family consisting of eleven souls, namely, my father, Joseph Smith; my *a*mother, Lucy Smith (whose name, previous to her marriage, was Mack, daughter of Solomon Mack); my brothers, *b*Alvin (who died November 19th, 1823, in the 26th year of his age), *c*Hyrum, myself, *d*Samuel Harrison, William, Don Carlos; and my sisters, Sophronia, Catherine, and Lucy.

5 Some time in the second year after our removal to Manchester, there was in the place where we lived an unusual excitement on the subject of religion. It commenced with the Methodists, but soon became general among all the sects in that region of country. Indeed, the whole district of country seemed affected by it, and great multitudes united themselves to the different religious parties, which created no small stir and division amongst the people, some crying, *a*"Lo, here!" and others, "Lo, there!" Some were contending for the Methodist faith, some for the Presbyterian, and some for the Baptist.

---

1 1*a* TG Restoration of the Gospel.
  b Luke 1: 4 (1–4).
2*a* JS-H 1: 60.
  b D&C 20: 1.

3*a* TG Joseph Smith.
  b 2 Ne. 3: 15.
4*a* JS-H 1: 20 (7, 20).
  b D&C 137: 5 (5–6);
    JS-H 1: 56.

  c D&C 11: 23 (1–30);
    135: 1 (1–4).
  d D&C 23: 4 (3–5).
5*a* Matt. 24: 23.

6 For, notwithstanding the great ᵃlove which the converts to these different faiths expressed at the time of their conversion, and the great zeal manifested by the respective clergy, who were active in getting up and promoting this extraordinary scene of religious feeling, in order to have everybody converted, as they were pleased to call it, let them join what sect they pleased; yet when the converts began to file off, some to one party and some to another, it was seen that the seemingly good feelings of both the priests and the converts were more ᵇpretended than real; for a scene of great confusion and bad feeling ensued—priest contending against priest, and convert against convert; so that all their good feelings one for another, if they ever had any, were entirely lost in a strife of words and a contest about opinions.

7 I was at this time in my fifteenth year. My father's family was proselyted to the Presbyterian faith, and four of them joined that church, namely, my mother, Lucy; my brothers Hyrum and Samuel Harrison; and my sister Sophronia.

8 During this time of great excitement my mind was called up to serious reflection and great uneasiness; but though my feelings were deep and often poignant, still I kept myself aloof from all these parties, though I attended their several meetings as often as occasion would permit. In process of time my mind became somewhat partial to the Methodist sect, and I felt some desire to be united with them; but so great were the confusion and ᵃstrife among the different denominations, that it was impossible for a person young as I was, and so unacquainted with men and things, to come to any certain conclusion who was ᵇright and who was wrong.

9 My mind at times was greatly excited, the cry and tumult were so great and incessant. The Presbyterians were most decided against the Baptists and Methodists, and used all the powers of both reason and sophistry to prove their errors, or, at least, to make the people think they were in error. On the other hand, the Baptists and Methodists in their turn were equally zealous in endeavoring to establish their own tenets and disprove all others.

10 In the midst of this war of words and tumult of opinions, I often said to myself: What is to be done? Who of all these parties are right; or, are they all wrong together? If any one of them be ᵃright, which is it, and how shall I know it?

11 While I was laboring under the extreme difficulties caused by the contests of these parties of religionists, I was one day reading the Epistle of ᵃJames, first chapter and fifth verse, which reads: *If any of you lack ᵇwisdom, let him ask of God, that giveth to all men liberally, and upbraideth not; and it shall be given him.*

12 Never did any passage of ᵃscripture come with more power to the heart of man than this did at this time to mine. It seemed to enter with great force into every feeling of my heart. I reflected on it again and again, knowing that if any person needed ᵇwisdom from God, I did; for how to act I did not know, and unless I could get more wisdom than I then had, I would never know; for the teachers of religion of the different sects ᶜunderstood the same passages of scripture so differently as to destroy all confidence in settling the question by an appeal to the Bible.

13 At length I came to the conclusion that I must either remain in ᵃdarkness and confusion, or else I must do as James directs, that is, ask of God. I at length came to the determination to "ask of God," concluding that if he gave wisdom to

---

6a 1 Pet. 1: 22.
  b TG Guile; Hypocrisy.
8a TG Strife.
  b D&C 101: 95 (93–95).

10a TG Truth.
11a James 1: 5 (1–7).
  b 1 Kgs. 3: 12; 2 Ne. 28: 15; Jacob 6: 12.

12a D&C 138: 6.
  b TG Guidance, Divine.
  c 1 Cor. 2: 11 (10–16).
13a Micah 7: 8.

them that lacked wisdom, and would [b]give liberally, and not upbraid, I might venture.

14 So, in accordance with this, my determination to ask of God, I retired to the [a]woods to make the attempt. It was on the morning of a [b]beautiful, clear day, early in the spring of eighteen hundred and twenty. It was the first time in my life that I had made such an attempt, for amidst all my anxieties I had never as yet made the attempt to [c]pray [d]vocally.

15 After I had retired to the place where I had previously designed to go, having looked around me, and finding myself alone, I kneeled down and began to offer up the desires of my heart to God. I had scarcely done so, when immediately I was [a]seized upon by some power which entirely overcame me, and had such an astonishing influence over me as to bind my tongue so that I could not speak. Thick [b]darkness gathered around me, and it seemed to me for a time as if I were doomed to sudden destruction.

16 But, exerting all my powers to [a]call upon God to deliver me out of the power of this enemy which had seized upon me, and at the very moment when I was ready to sink into [b]despair and abandon myself to destruction—not to an imaginary ruin, but to the power of some actual being from the unseen world, who had such marvelous power as I had never before felt in any being—just

at this moment of great alarm, I saw a pillar of [c]light exactly over my head, above the brightness of the [d]sun, which descended gradually until it fell upon me.

17 It no sooner appeared than I found myself [a]delivered from the enemy which held me bound. When the light rested upon me I [b]saw two [c]Personages, whose brightness and [d]glory defy all description, [e]standing above me in the air. One of them spake unto me, calling me by name and said, pointing to the other— *This is My [f]Beloved [g]Son. Hear Him!*

18 My object in going to [a]inquire of the Lord was to know which of all the sects was right, that I might know which to join. No sooner, therefore, did I get possession of myself, so as to be able to speak, than I asked the Personages who stood above me in the light, which of all the sects was right (for at this time it had never entered into my heart that all were wrong)—and which I should join.

19 I was answered that I must join none of them, for they were all [a]wrong; and the Personage who addressed me said that all their creeds were an abomination in his sight; that those [b]professors were all [c]corrupt; that: "they [d]draw near to me with their lips, but their [e]hearts are far from me, they teach for doctrines the [f]commandments of men, having a form of godliness, but they deny the [g]power thereof."

13b TG Communication.
14a Matt. 14: 23.
  b TG Beauty.
  c TG Prayer.
  d Ps. 77: 1.
15a Eph. 6: 12 (11–18).
  b Gen. 15: 12 (1–21).
    TG Darkness, Physical.
16a Moses 1: 20.
  b Isa. 6: 5 (1–7).
    TG Despair.
  c Acts 26: 13.
  d Rev. 1: 16.
17a TG Deliverance.
  b TG God, Privilege of Seeing; Vision.
  c Jer. 10: 10; 1 Jn. 4: 12

(7–21); JS-H 1: 25.
  TG God, Father; God, Manifestations of; Godhead; Jesus Christ, Appearances, Postmortal; Restoration of the Gospel; Revelation.
  d TG Jesus Christ, Glory of.
  e 1 Sam. 3: 10.
  f Matt. 3: 17; 17: 5;
3 Ne. 11: 7. TG Witness of the Father.
  g TG Jesus Christ, Divine Sonship.
18a Ex. 18: 15; 1 Sam. 9: 9; Alma 27: 10 (7, 10);

D&C 6: 11; 46: 7.
19a TG Apostasy of the Early Christian Church.
  b Jude 1: 4. TG False Prophets.
  c TG False Doctrine.
  d Isa. 29: 13; Ezek. 33: 31 (30–33); Luke 6: 46.
  e Jer. 3: 10. TG Apostasy of Individuals; Hardheartedness; Hypocrisy.
  f Col. 2: 22 (18–22); Titus 1: 14; D&C 3: 6 (6–7); 45: 29; 46: 7.
  g 2 Tim. 3: 5.

20 He again forbade me to join with any of them; and many other things did he say unto me, which I cannot write at this time. When I came to myself again, I found myself [a]lying on my back, looking up into heaven. When the light had departed, I had no strength; but soon recovering in some degree, I went home. And as I leaned up to the fireplace, [b]mother inquired what the matter was. I replied, "Never mind, all is well—I am well enough off." I then said to my mother, "I have learned for myself that Presbyterianism is not true." It seems as though the [c]adversary was aware, at a very early period of my life, that I was destined to prove a disturber and an annoyer of his kingdom; else why should the powers of darkness combine against me? Why the [d]opposition and persecution that arose against me, almost in my infancy?

Some preachers and other professors of religion reject account of First Vision—Persecution heaped upon Joseph Smith—He testifies of the reality of the vision. (Verses 21–26.)

21 Some few days after I had this vision, I happened to be in company with one of the Methodist preachers, who was very active in the before mentioned religious excitement; and, conversing with him on the subject of religion, I took occasion to give him an account of the vision which I had had. I was greatly surprised at his behavior; he treated my communication not only lightly, but with great contempt, saying it was all of the devil, that there were no such things as [a]visions or [b]revelations in these days; that all such things had ceased with the apostles, and that there would never be any more of them.

22 I soon found, however, that my telling the story had excited a great deal of prejudice against me among professors of religion, and was the cause of great [a]persecution, which continued to increase; and though I was an [b]obscure boy, only between fourteen and fifteen years of age, and my circumstances in life such as to make a boy of no consequence in the world, yet men of high standing would take notice sufficient to excite the public mind against me, and create a bitter persecution; and this was common among all the sects—all united to persecute me.

23 It caused me serious reflection then, and often has since, how very strange it was that an obscure [a]boy, of a little over fourteen years of age, and one, too, who was doomed to the necessity of obtaining a scanty maintenance by his daily [b]labor, should be thought a character of sufficient importance to attract the attention of the great ones of the most popular sects of the day, and in a manner to create in them a spirit of the most bitter [c]persecution and [d]reviling. But strange or not, so it was, and it was often the cause of great sorrow to myself.

24 However, it was nevertheless a fact that I had beheld a [a]vision. I have thought since, that I felt much like Paul, when he made his defense before King Agrippa, and related the account of the vision he had when he saw a light, and heard a voice; but still there were but few who believed him; some said he was dishonest, others said he was [b]mad; and he was ridiculed and reviled. But all this did not destroy the reality of his vision. He had seen a

20a Dan. 10: 9; 1 Ne. 1: 7; Moses 1: 9.
    b JS-H 1: 4. TG Family, Love within.
    c TG Devil.
    d Jer. 11: 19; Matt. 10: 22; Moses 6: 31 (31–37).

21a 1 Sam. 3: 1.
    b TG Revelation.
22a James 5: 10 (10–11); Mosiah 17: 13 (10–20); Alma 14: 26 (20–27).
    b 1 Sam. 17: 33 (32–51); 1 Chr. 29: 1.
23a Amos 7: 14 (14–15); Acts 5: 38 (38–39).

    b TG Industry.
    c Jer. 1: 19 (6–19).
    TG Malice; Persecution.
    d TG Reviling.
24a Ezek. 1: 1; 1 Ne. 1: 16. TG Vision.
    b Acts 26: 24 (1–32).

vision, he knew he had, and all the *persecution under heaven could not make it otherwise; and though they should persecute him unto death, yet he knew, and would know to his latest breath, that he had both seen a light and heard a voice speaking unto him, and all the world could not make him think or believe otherwise.

25 So it was with me. I had actually seen a light, and in the midst of that light I saw two *d*Personages, and they did in reality speak to me; and though I was *b*hated and *c*persecuted for saying that I had seen a vision, yet it was true; and while they were persecuting me, reviling me, and speaking all manner of evil against me *d*falsely for so saying, I was led to say in my heart: Why persecute me for telling the truth? I have actually seen a vision; and who am I that I can withstand God, or why does the world think to make me deny what I have actually seen? For I had seen a vision; I knew it, and I knew that God knew it, and I could not *d*deny it, neither dared I do it; at least I knew that by so doing I would offend God, and come under condemnation.

26 I had now got my mind satisfied so far as the sectarian world was concerned—that it was not my duty to join with any of them, but to continue as I was until further *d*directed. I had found the testimony of James to be true—that a man who lacked wisdom might ask of God, and obtain, and not be *b*upbraided.

Moroni appears to Joseph Smith—Joseph's name is to be known for good and evil among all nations—Moroni tells him of the Book of Mormon and of the coming judgments of the Lord, and quotes many scriptures—The hiding place of the gold plates is re-

vealed—Moroni continues to instruct the Prophet. (Verses 27–54.)

27 I continued to pursue my common vocations in life until the twenty-first of September, one thousand eight hundred and twenty-three, all the time suffering severe persecution at the hands of all classes of men, both religious and irreligious, because I continued to *a*affirm that I had seen a vision.

28 During the space of time which intervened between the time I had the vision and the year eighteen hundred and twenty-three—having been forbidden to join any of the religious sects of the day, and being of very tender years, and persecuted by those who ought to have been my *a*friends and to have treated me kindly, and if they supposed me to be deluded to have endeavored in a proper and affectionate manner to have reclaimed me—I was left to all kinds of *b*temptations; and, mingling with all kinds of society, I frequently fell into many foolish *c*errors, and displayed the weakness of youth, and the foibles of human nature; which, I am sorry to say, led me into divers temptations, offensive in the sight of God. In making this confession, no one need suppose me guilty of any great or malignant sins. A disposition to commit such was never in my nature. But I was guilty of *d*levity, and sometimes associated with jovial company, etc., not consistent with that character which ought to be maintained by one who was *e*called of God as I had been. But this will not seem very strange to any one who recollects my youth, and is acquainted with my native *f*cheery temperament.

29 In consequence of these things, I often felt condemned for my weak-

24c 1 Thes. 3: 3.
25a JS-H 1: 17.
  b TG Hate.
  c TG Adversity.
  d TG Injustice.

e TG Courage; Honesty; Integrity.
26a JS-H 1: 33 (33–50).
  b Ps. 20: 6; James 1: 5.
27a 2 Cor. 1: 12.
28a TG Friendship.

b TG Temptation.
c Ps. 25: 7; D&C 20: 5.
d TG Levity.
e TG Called of God.
f TG Cheerfulness.

ness and imperfections; when, on the evening of the above-mentioned twenty-first of September, after I had retired to my bed for the night, I betook myself to ^aprayer and supplication to Almighty God for forgiveness of all my sins and follies, and also for a manifestation to me, that I might know of my state and standing before him; for I had full ^bconfidence in obtaining a divine manifestation, as I previously had one.

30 While I was thus in the act of calling upon God, I discovered a ^alight appearing in my room, which continued to increase until the room was lighter than at noonday, when immediately a ^bpersonage appeared at my bedside, standing in the air, for his feet did not touch the floor.

31 He had on a loose robe of most exquisite ^awhiteness. It was a whiteness beyond anything earthly I had ever seen; nor do I believe that any earthly thing could be made to appear so exceedingly white and brilliant. His hands were naked, and his arms also, a little above the wrist; so, also, were his feet naked, as were his legs, a little above the ankles. His head and neck were also bare. I could discover that he had no other clothing on but this robe, as it was open, so that I could see into his bosom.

32 Not only was his robe exceedingly white, but his whole person was ^aglorious beyond description, and his countenance truly like ^blightning. The room was exceedingly light, but not so very bright as immediately around his person.

When I first looked upon him, I was ^cafraid; but the ^dfear soon left me.

33 He called me by ^aname, and said unto me that he was a ^bmessenger sent from the presence of God to me, and that his name was Moroni; that God had a work for me to do; and that my name should be had for ^cgood and evil among all nations, kindreds, and tongues, or that it should be both good and evil spoken of among all people.

34 He said there was a ^abook deposited, written upon gold plates, giving an account of the former inhabitants of this continent, and the source from whence they sprang. He also said that the ^bfulness of the everlasting Gospel was contained in it, as delivered by the Savior to the ancient inhabitants;

35 Also, that there were two stones in silver bows—and these stones, fastened to a ^abreastplate, constituted what is called the ^bUrim and Thummim—deposited with the plates; and the possession and use of these stones were what constituted ^c"seers" in ancient or former times; and that God had prepared them for the purpose of translating the book.

36 After telling me these things, he commenced quoting the prophecies of the Old Testament. He first quoted part of the third chapter of ^aMalachi; and he quoted also the fourth or last chapter of the same prophecy, though with a little variation from the way it reads in our Bibles. Instead of quoting the first verse as it reads in our books, he quoted it thus:

37 For behold, the ^aday cometh that shall ^bburn as an oven, and all the

29a TG Prayer.
  b James 1: 6 (5–7).
30a 1 Ne. 1: 6.
  b TG Angels.
31a Acts 10: 30 (30–33);
    1 Ne. 8: 5; 3 Ne. 11: 8.
32a TG Glory.
  b Ex. 34: 29 (29–35);
    Hel. 5: 36; D&C 110: 3.
  c Ex. 3: 6; Ether 3: 6 (6–8, 19).

d Dan. 10: 12; Hel. 5: 26; D&C 68: 6; 98: 1.
33a Ex. 33: 12 (12, 17); Isa. 45: 3 (3–4).
  b JS-H 1: 26.
  c Isa. 5: 20.
34a TG Book of Mormon; Scriptures, Preservation of.
  b Rom. 15: 29. TG Restoration of the Gospel.

35a Ex. 25: 7; Lev. 8: 8 (7–9).
  b Ex. 28: 30. TG Urim and Thummim.
  c 1 Sam. 9: 9.
36a Mal. chs. 3; 4.
37a TG Day of the Lord.
  b Mal. 9: 5 (5, 18–19); 3 Ne. 25: 1–6; D&C 64: 23 (23–24). TG Earth, Cleansing of; World, End of.

proud, yea, and all that do wickedly shall burn as ᶜ*stubble; for they that come shall burn them, saith the Lord of Hosts, that it shall leave them neither root nor branch.*

38 And again, he quoted the fifth verse thus: *Behold, I will reveal unto you the* ᵃ*Priesthood, by the hand of* ᵇ*Elijah the prophet, before the coming of the great and dreadful day of* ᶜ*Lord.*

39 He also quoted the next verse differently: *And he shall plant in the hearts of the* ᵃ*children the* ᵇ*promises made to the fathers, and the hearts of the children shall turn to their fathers. If it were not so, the whole earth would be utterly wasted at his coming.*

40 In addition to these, he quoted the eleventh chapter of ᵃIsaiah, saying that it was about to be fulfilled. He quoted also the third chapter of Acts, twenty-second and twenty-third verses, precisely as they stand in our New Testament. He said that that ᵇprophet was Christ; but the day had not yet come when "they who would not hear his voice should be ᶜcut off from among the people," but soon would come.

41 He also quoted the second chapter of ᵃJoel, from the twenty-eighth verse to the last. He also said that this was not yet fulfilled, but was soon to be. And he further stated that the fulness of the ᵇGentiles was soon to come in. He quoted many other passages of scripture, and offered many explanations which ᶜcannot be mentioned here.

42 Again, he told me, that when I got those plates of which he had spoken—for the time that they should be obtained was not yet ful-

filled—I should not show them to any person; neither the breastplate with the Urim and Thummim; only to those to whom I should be commanded to show them; if I did I should be ᵃdestroyed. While I was conversing with me about the plates, the vision was opened to my ᵇmind that I could see the place where the plates were deposited, and that so clearly and distinctly that I knew the place again when I visited it.

43 After this communication, I saw the light in the room begin to gather immediately around the person of him who had been speaking to me, and it continued to do so until the room was again left dark, except just around him; when, instantly I saw, as it were, a conduit open right up into heaven, and he ᵃascended till he entirely disappeared, and the room was left as it had been before this heavenly light had made its appearance.

44 I lay musing on the singularity of the scene, and marveling greatly at what had been told to me by this extraordinary messenger; when, in the midst of my ᵃmeditation, I suddenly discovered that my room was again beginning to get lighted, and in an instant, as it were, the same heavenly messenger was again by my bedside.

45 He commenced, and ᵃagain related the very same things which he had done at his first visit, without the least variation; which having done, he informed me of great ᵇjudgments which were coming upon the earth, with great desolations by ᶜfamine, ᵈsword, and pestilence; and

---

37c Ex. 15: 7 (7–8);
  Nahum 1: 10; 1 Ne. 22:
  23 (15, 23); 2 Ne. 26: 6
  (4–6); D&C 29: 9.
38a TG Priesthood; Priesthood, Keys of.
 b Mal. 4: 5 (5–6);
  D&C 27: 9; 110: 13–16;
  138: 46.
 c TG Millennium.
39a TG Genealogy and
  Temple Work;

Salvation for the Dead.
 b Gal. 3: 5, 8, 18, 29.
40a Isa. 11: 10 (1–16).
 b Deut. 18: 15 (15–19);
  Acts 3: 22 (22–23); 7:
  37.
 c 3 Ne. 20: 23; 21: 10.
41a Joel 2: 28 (28–32);
  Acts 2: 16 (16–21).
 b Isa. 42: 6; Rom. 11: 25
  (11–27); D&C 88: 84
  (84–85). TG Gentiles.

 c 2 Cor. 12: 4.
42a JS–H 1: 59.
 b TG Mind.
43a Acts 1: 9.
44a D&C 76: 19.
 a TG Meditation.
45a Ezek. 2: 3 (1–10); 3: 4
  (1–27).
 b TG Judgment.
 c TG Famine.
 d Deut. 32: 25; 1 Ne. 1:
  13; Alma 10: 22.

that these grievous judgments would come on the earth in this generation. Having related these things, he again ascended as he had done before.

46 By this time, so deep were the impressions made on my mind, that sleep had fled from my eyes, and I lay overwhelmed in *astonishment* at what I had both seen and heard. But what was my surprise when again I beheld the same messenger at my bedside, and heard him rehearse or repeat over again to me the same things as before; and added a caution to me, telling me that Satan would try to *tempt me (in consequence of the indigent circumstances of my father's family), to get the plates for the purpose of getting *rich. This he forbade me, saying that I must have no other object in view in getting the plates but to glorify God, and must not be influenced by any other *motive than that of building his kingdom; otherwise I could not get them.

47 After this third visit, he again ascended into heaven as before, and I was again left to *ponder on the strangeness of what I had just experienced; when almost immediately after the heavenly messenger had ascended from me for the third time, the cock crowed, and I found that day was approaching, so that our interviews must have occupied the whole of that night.

48 I shortly after arose from my bed, and, as usual, went to the necessary labors of the day; but, in attempting to work as at other times, I found my *strength so exhausted as to render me entirely unable. My father, who was laboring along with me, discovered something to be wrong with me, and told me to go home. I started with the intention of going to the house; but, in attempting to cross the fence out of the field where we were, my strength entirely failed me, and I *fell helpless on the ground, and for a time was quite unconscious of anything.

49 The first thing that I can recollect was a voice speaking unto me, calling me by name. I looked up, and beheld the same messenger standing over my head, surrounded by light as before. He then again related unto me all that he had related to me the previous night, and commanded me to go to my *father and tell him of the vision and commandments which I had received.

50 I obeyed; I returned to my *father in the field, and rehearsed the whole matter to him. He *replied to me that it was of God, and told me to go and do as commanded by the messenger. I left the field, and went to the place where the messenger had told me the plates were deposited; and owing to the distinctness of the vision which I had had concerning it, I knew the place the instant that I arrived there.

51 Convenient to the village of Manchester, Ontario county, New York, stands a *hill of considerable size, and the most elevated of any in the neighborhood. On the west side of this hill, not far from the top, under a stone of considerable size, lay the plates, deposited in a stone box. This stone was thick and rounding in the middle on the upper side, and thinner towards the edges, so that the middle part of it was visible above the ground, but the edge all around was covered with earth.

52 Having removed the earth, I obtained a lever, which I got fixed under the edge of the stone, and with a little exertion raised it up. I looked in, and there indeed did I behold the *plates, the *Urim and Thummim, and the breastplate, as

46a Dan. 8: 27.
  b TG Temptation.
  c TG Sacrilege.
  d Luke 11: 34 (34–36);
    D&C 121: 37.
47a TG Meditation.

48a TG Strength.
  b Acts 9: 4 (4–8).
49a TG Family, Love within.
50a TG Honoring Father
    and Mother.

  b TG Counsel.
51a D&C 128: 20.
52a Morm. 6: 6; Ether 4: 5
    (4–7); D&C 17: 1.
  b TG Urim and
    Thummim.

stated by the messenger. The box in which they lay was formed by laying stones together in some kind of cement. In the bottom of the box were laid two stones crossways of the box, and on these stones lay the plates and the other things with them.

53 I made an attempt to take them out, but was forbidden by the messenger, and was again informed that the time for bringing them forth had not yet arrived, neither would it, until four years from that time; but he told me that I should come to that place precisely in one year from that time, and that he would there meet with me, and that I should continue to do so until the time should come for obtaining the plates.

54 Accordingly, as I had been commanded, I went at the end of each year, and at each time I found the same messenger there, and received instruction and intelligence from him at each of our interviews, respecting what the Lord was going to do, and how and in what manner his *a*kingdom was to be conducted in the last days.

Joseph Smith marries Emma Hale— He receives the gold plates from Moroni and translates some of the characters—Martin Harris shows characters and translation to Professor Anthon, who says: "I cannot read a sealed book." (Verses 55–65.)

55 As my father's worldly circumstances were very limited, we were under the necessity of *a*laboring with our hands, hiring out by day's work and otherwise, as we could get opportunity. Sometimes we were at home, and sometimes abroad, and by continuous *b*labor were enabled to get a comfortable maintenance.

56 In the year 1823 my father's family met with a great *a*affliction by the death of my eldest brother, *b*Alvin. In the month of October,

1825, I hired with an old gentleman by the name of Josiah Stoal, who lived in Chenango county, State of New York. He had heard something of a silver mine having been opened by the Spaniards in Harmony, Susquehanna county, State of Pennsylvania; and had, previous to my hiring to him, been digging, in order, if possible, to discover the mine. After I went to live with him, he took me, with the rest of his hands, to dig for the silver mine, at which I continued to work for nearly a month, without success in our undertaking, and finally I prevailed with the old gentleman to cease digging after it. Hence arose the very prevalent story of my having been a money-digger.

57 During the time that I was thus employed, I was put to board with a Mr. Isaac Hale, of that place; it was there I first saw my wife (his daughter), Emma Hale. On the 18th of January, 1827, we were married, while I was yet employed in the service of Mr. Stoal.

58 Owing to my continuing to assert that I had seen a vision, *a*persecution still followed me, and my wife's father's family were very much opposed to our being married. I was, therefore, under the necessity of taking her elsewhere; so we went and were married at the house of Squire Tarbill, in South Bainbridge, Chenango county, New York. Immediately after my marriage, I left Mr. Stoal's, and went to my father's, and *b*farmed with him that season.

59 At length the time arrived for obtaining the plates, the Urim and Thummim, and the breastplate. On the twenty-second day of September, one thousand eight hundred and twenty-seven, having gone as usual at the end of another year to the place where they were deposited, the same heavenly messenger delivered them up to *a*me with this

---

54*a* TG Kingdom of God, on Earth.
55*a* TG Industry.

b TG Work, Value of.
56*a* TG Affliction.
b JS-H 1: 4.

58*a* TG Hate; Persecution.
b TG Industry.
59*a* Isa. 29: 12.

charge: that I should be [b]responsible for them; that if I should let them go carelessly, or through any [c]neglect of mine, I should be cut off; but that if I would use all my endeavors to [d]preserve them, until he, the messenger, should call for them, they should be protected.

60 I soon found out the reason why I had received such strict charges to keep them safe, and why it was that the messenger had said that when I had done what was required at my hand, he would call for them. For no sooner was it known that I had them, than the most strenuous exertions were used to [e]get them from me. Every stratagem that could be invented was resorted to for that purpose. The persecution became more bitter and severe than before, and multitudes were on the alert continually to get them from me if possible. But by the wisdom of God, they remained safe in my hands, until I had accomplished by them what was required at my hand. When, according to arrangements, the messenger called for them, I delivered them up to him; and he has them in his charge until this [b]day, being the second day of May, one thousand eight hundred and thirty-eight.

61 The excitement, however, still continued, and rumor with her thousand tongues was all the time employed in circulating [e]falsehoods about my father's family, and about myself. If I were to relate a thousandth part of them, it would fill up volumes. The persecution, however, became so intolerable that I was under the necessity of leaving Manchester, and going with my wife to Susquehanna county, in the State of Pennsylvania. While preparing to start—being very poor, and the persecution so heavy upon us that there was no probability that we would ever be otherwise—in the midst of

our afflictions we found a friend in a gentleman by the name of [b]Martin Harris, who came to us and gave me fifty dollars to assist us on our journey. Mr. Harris was a resident of Palmyra township, Wayne county, in the State of New York, and a farmer of respectability.

62 By this timely aid was I enabled to reach the place of my destination in Pennsylvania; and immediately after my arrival there I commenced copying the characters off the plates. I copied a considerable number of them, and by means of the [a]Urim and Thummim I translated some of them, which I did between the time I arrived at the house of my wife's father, in the month of December, and the February following.

63 Sometime in this month of February, the aforementioned Mr. Martin Harris came to our place, got the characters which I had drawn off the plates, and started with them to the city of New York. For what took place relative to him and the characters, I refer to his own account of the circumstances, as he related them to me after his return, which was as follows:

64 "I went to the city of New York, and presented the characters which had been translated, with the translation thereof, to Professor Charles Anthon, a gentleman celebrated for his literary attainments. Professor Anthon stated that the translation was correct, more so than any he had before seen translated from the Egyptian. I then showed him those which were not yet translated, and he said that they were Egyptian, Chaldaic, Assyriac, and Arabic; and he said they were true characters. He gave me a certificate, certifying to the people of Palmyra that they were true characters, and that the translation of such of them as had been translated

---

59b TG Dependability; Trustworthiness.
c JS-H 1:42.

d TG Scriptures, Preservation of.
60a TG Stealing.
b JS-H 1:2.

61a TG Injustice.
b D&C 5:1 (1–32).
62a TG Urim and Thummim.

was also correct. I took the certificate and put it into my pocket, and was just leaving the house, when Mr. Anthon called me back, and asked me how the young man found out that there were gold plates in the place where he found them. I answered that an angel of God had revealed it unto him.

65 "He then said to me, 'Let me see that certificate.' I accordingly took it out of my pocket and gave it to him, when he took it and tore it to pieces, saying that there was no such thing now as ministering of *angels, and that if I would bring the plates to him he would translate them. I informed him that part of the plates were *sealed, and that I was forbidden to bring them. He replied, 'I cannot read a sealed book.' I left him and went to Dr. Mitchell, who sanctioned what Professor Anthon had said respecting both the characters and the translation."

. . . .

Oliver Cowdery serves as scribe in translating the Book of Mormon— Joseph and Oliver receive the Aaronic Priesthood from John the Baptist— They are baptized, ordained, and receive the spirit of prophecy. (Verses 66–75.)

66 On the 5th day of April, 1829, *Oliver Cowdery came to my house, until which time I had never seen him. He stated to me that having been teaching school in the neighborhood where my father resided, and my father being one of those who sent to the school, he went to board for a season at his house, and while there the family related to

him the circumstances of my having received the plates, and accordingly he had come to make inquiries of me.

67 Two days after the arrival of Mr. Cowdery (being the 7th of April) I commenced to translate the Book of Mormon, and he began to *write for me.

. . . .

68 We still continued the work of translation, when, in the ensuing month (May, 1829), we on a certain day went into the woods to pray and inquire of the Lord respecting *baptism for the *remission of sins, that we found mentioned in the translation of the plates. While we were thus employed, praying and calling upon the Lord, a messenger from heaven descended in a *cloud of light, and having laid his *hands upon us, he *ordained us, saying:

69 *Upon you my fellow servants, in the name of Messiah, I confer the *Priesthood of *Aaron, which holds the keys of the ministering of angels, and of the gospel of repentance, and of *baptism by immersion for the remission of sins; and this shall never be taken again from the earth until the sons of *Levi do offer again an offering unto the Lord in *righteousness.*

70 He said this Aaronic Priesthood had not the power of laying on hands for the gift of the Holy Ghost, but that this should be conferred on us hereafter; and he commanded us to go and be baptized, and gave us directions that I should baptize Oliver Cowdery, and that afterwards he should baptize me.

71 Accordingly we went and were baptized. I *baptized him first, and afterwards he baptized me—after

65a TG Angels, Ministering.
  b Isa. 29:11 (11–12);
    Dan. 12:9; 1 Ne. 14:
    26; 2 Ne. 27:10;
    Ether 4:5 (4–7);
    D&C 35:18.
66a D&C 8:1 (1–12).
67a D&C 9:1.
  TG Scriptures, Writing
  of.

68a TG Baptism; Baptism,
    Essential; Baptism,
    Immersion.
  b TG Remission of Sins.
  c Num. 11:25; Ether 2:
    4 (4–5, 14); D&C 34:7
    (7–9).
  d A of F 5. TG Hands,
    Laying on of.
  e TG Priesthood, Authority; Priesthood,

    History of.
69a TG Restoration of the
    Gospel.
  b TG Priesthood, Aaronic.
  c TG Baptism.
  d Deut. 10:8; D&C 13:
    1; 124:39.
  e TG Righteousness.
71a Mosiah 18:13–15;
    3 Ne. 19:10–13.

which I laid my hands upon his head and ordained him to the Aaronic Priesthood, and afterwards he laid his hands on me and ordained me to the same Priesthood—for so we were commanded.*

72 The [a]messenger who visited us on this occasion and conferred this Priesthood upon us, said that his name was John, the same that is called [b]John the Baptist in the New Testament, and that he acted under the direction of [c]Peter, James and John, who held the keys of the Priesthood of Melchizedek, which Priesthood, he said, would in due time be conferred on us, and that I should be called the first [d]Elder of the Church, and he (Oliver Cowdery) the second. It was on the fifteenth day of May, 1829, that we were ordained under the hand of this messenger, and baptized.

73 Immediately on our coming up out of the water after we had been baptized, we experienced great and glorious blessings from our Heavenly Father. No sooner had I baptized Oliver Cowdery, than the Holy Ghost fell upon him, and he stood up and [a]prophesied many things which should shortly come to pass. And again, so soon as I had been baptized by him, I also had the spirit of prophecy, when, standing up, I prophesied concerning the rise of

this Church, and many other things connected with the Church, and this generation of the children of men. We were filled with the Holy Ghost, and rejoiced in the God of our salvation.

74 Our minds being now enlightened, we began to have the [a]scriptures laid open to our understandings, and the [b]true meaning and intention of their more [c]mysterious passages revealed unto us in a manner which we never could attain to previously, nor ever before had thought of. In the meantime we were forced to keep secret the circumstances of having received the Priesthood and our having been baptized, owing to a spirit of persecution which had already manifested itself in the neighborhood.

75 We had been threatened with being mobbed, from time to time, and this, too, by professors of religion. And their intentions of mobbing us were only counteracted by the influence of my wife's father's family (under Divine providence), who had become very [a]friendly to me, and who were opposed to mobs, and were willing that I should be allowed to continue the work of translation without interruption; and therefore offered and promised us protection from all unlawful proceedings, as far as in them lay.

---

* Oliver Cowdery describes these events thus: "These were days never to be forgotten—to sit under the sound of a voice dictated by the inspiration of heaven, awakened the utmost gratitude of this bosom! Day after day I continued, uninterrupted, to write from his mouth, as he translated with the Urim and Thummim, or, as the Nephites would have said, 'Interpreters,' the history or record called 'The Book of Mormon.'

"To notice, in even few words, the interesting account given by Mormon and his faithful son, Moroni, of a people once beloved and favored of heaven, would supersede my present design; I shall therefore defer this to a future period, and, as I said in the introduction, pass more directly to some few incidents immediately connected with the rise of this Church, which may be entertaining to some thousands who have stepped forward, amid the frowns of bigots and the calumny of hypocrites, and embraced the Gospel of Christ.

"No men, in their sober senses, could translate and write the directions given to the Nephites from the mouth of the Savior, of the precise manner in which men should

---

72a Luke 3:4.
  b Matt. 3:1 (1–12).
  c D&C 7:7 (5–7); 27:12.
    TG Priesthood, Keys of; Priesthood,

Melchizedek.
  d TG Elder.
73a TG Holy Ghost, Gifts of; Holy Ghost, Mission of.

74a D&C 32:4.
  b John 16:13.
  c TG Mysteries of Godliness.
75a TG Friendship.

build up His Church, and especially when corruption had spread an uncertainty over all forms and systems practiced among men, without desiring a privilege of showing the willingness of the heart by being buried in the liquid grave, to answer a 'good conscience by the resurrection of Jesus Christ.'

"After writing the account given of the Savior's ministry to the remnant of the seed of Jacob, upon this continent, it was easy to be seen, as the prophet said it would be, that darkness covered the earth and gross darkness the minds of the people. On reflecting further it was so easy to be seen that amid the great strife and noise concerning religion, none had authority from God to administer the ordinances of the Gospel. For the question might be asked, have men authority to administer in the name of Christ, who deny revelations, when His testimony is no less than the spirit of prophecy, and His religion based, built, and sustained by immediate revelations, in all ages of the world when He has had a people on earth? If these facts were buried, and carefully concealed by men whose craft would have been in danger if once permitted to shine in the faces of men, they were no longer to us; and we only waited for the commandment to be given 'Arise and be baptized.'

"This was not long desired before it was realized. The Lord, who is rich in mercy, and ever willing to answer the consistent prayer of the humble, after we had called upon Him in a fervent manner, aside from the abodes of men, condescended to manifest to us His will. On a sudden, as from the midst of eternity, the voice of the Redeemer spake peace to us, while the veil was parted and the angel of God came down clothed with glory, and delivered the anxiously looked for message, and the keys of the Gospel of repentance. What joy! what wonder! what amazement! While the world was racked and distracted—while millions were groping as the blind for the wall, and while all men were resting upon uncertainty, as a general mass, our eyes beheld, our ears heard, as in the 'blaze of day'; yes, more—above the glitter of the May sunbeam, which then shed its brilliancy over the face of nature! Then his voice, though mild, pierced to the center, and his words, 'I am thy fellow-servant,' dispelled every fear. We listened, we gazed, we admired! 'Twas the voice of an angel from glory, 'twas a message from the Most High! And as we heard we rejoiced, while His love enkindled upon our souls, and we were wrapped in the vision of the Almighty! Where was room for doubt? Nowhere; uncertainty had fled, doubt had sunk no more to rise, while fiction and deception had fled forever!

"But, dear brother, think, further think for a moment, what joy filled our hearts, and with what surprise we must have bowed, (for who would not have bowed the knee for such a blessing?) when we received under his hand the Holy Priesthood as he said, 'Upon you my fellow-servants, in the name of Messiah, I confer this Priesthood and this authority, which shall remain upon earth, that the Sons of Levi may yet offer an offering unto the Lord in righteousness!'

"I shall not attempt to paint to you the feelings of this heart, nor the majestic beauty and glory which surrounded us on this occasion; but you will believe me when I say, that earth, nor men, with the eloquence of time, cannot begin to clothe language in as interesting and sublime a manner as this holy personage. No; nor has this earth power to give the joy, to bestow the peace, or comprehend the wisdom which was contained in each sentence as they were delivered by the power of the Holy Spirit! Man may deceive his fellow-men, deception may follow deception, and the children of the wicked one may have power to seduce the foolish and untaught, till naught but fiction feeds the many, and the fruit of falsehood carries in its current the giddy to the grave; but one touch with the finger of his love, yes, one ray of glory from the upper world, or one word from the mouth of the Savior, from the bosom of eternity, strikes it all into insignificance, and blots it forever from the mind. The assurance that we were in the presence of an angel, the certainty that we heard the voice of Jesus, and the truth unsullied as it flowed from a pure personage, dictated by the will of God, is to me past description, and I shall ever look upon this expression of the Savior's goodness with wonder and thanksgiving while I am permitted to tarry; and in those mansions where perfection dwells and sin never comes, I hope to adore in that day which shall never cease."—*Messenger and Advocate*, vol. 1 (October 1834), pp. 14–16.

THE ARTICLES OF FAITH

OF THE CHURCH OF JESUS CHRIST OF LATTER-DAY SAINTS

History of the Church, Vol. 4, pp. 535–541

WE [a]believe in [b]God, the Eternal Father, and in His [c]Son, Jesus Christ, and in the [d]Holy Ghost.

2 We believe that men will be [a]punished for their [b]own sins, and not for Adam's [c]transgression.

3 We believe that through the [a]Atonement of Christ, all [b]mankind may be [c]saved, by obedience to the laws and ordinances of the Gospel.

4 We believe that the first principles and [a]ordinances of the Gospel are: first, [b]Faith in the Lord Jesus Christ; second, [c]Repentance; third, [d]Baptism by [e]immersion for the [f]remission of sins; fourth, Laying on of [g]hands for the [h]gift of the Holy Ghost.

5 We believe that a man must be [a]called of God, by [b]prophecy, and by the laying on of [c]hands by those who are in [d]authority, to [e]preach the Gospel and administer the [f]ordinances thereof.

6 We believe in the same [a]organization that existed in the Primitive Church, namely, apostles, [b]prophets, [c]pastors, [d]teachers, [e]evangelists, and so forth.

7 We believe in the [a]gift of [b]tongues, [c]prophecy, [d]revelation, [e]visions, [f]healing, [g]interpretation of tongues, and so forth.

8 We believe the [a]Bible to be the [b]word of God as far as it is translated [c]correctly; we also believe the [d]Book of Mormon to be the word of God.

9 We believe all that God has [a]revealed, all that He does now reveal, and we believe that He will yet [b]reveal many great and important things pertaining to the Kingdom of God.

1a TG Believe.
b TG God the Father—Elohim; Godhead.
c TG Jesus Christ, Divine Sonship.
d TG Holy Ghost.
2a TG Punishment.
b Ex. 32: 33; Deut. 24: 16; Ezek. 18: 20 (1–20). TG Accountability; Agency.
c TG Fall of Man.
3a TG Jesus Christ, Atonement through.
b Jude 1: 3.
c Ps. 49: 15; Mosiah 27: 24 (24–26); D&C 93: 38; Moses 5: 9. TG Salvation.
4a TG Ordinances.
b D&C 138: 33. TG Baptism, Qualifications for; Faith.
c TG Repentance.
d TG Baptism.

e TG Baptism, Immersion.
f TG Remission of Sins.
g TG Hands, Laying on of.
h TG Holy Ghost, Gift of.
5a Num. 27: 16 (15–20). TG Called of God; Priesthood, Qualifying for.
b TG Prophecy.
c TG Hands, Laying on of.
d D&C 11: 15 (15–21). TG Authority; Priesthood, Authority.
e D&C 11: 15 (15–21). TG Preaching.
f Alma 13: 16 (8–16).
6a TG Church Organization.
b TG Prophets, Mission of.
c TG Bishop.
d TG Teachers.

e TG Patriarchs.
7a TG Holy Ghost, Gifts of.
b TG Language.
c TG Prophecy.
d TG Revelation.
e TG Visions.
f TG Healing.
g 1 Cor. 12: 10; Morm. 9: 7.
8a TG Bible; Revelation; Scriptures, Preservation of; Scriptures, Value of; Scriptures, Writing of.
b Isa. 8: 20 (16–22).
c 1 Ne. 13: 26 (20–40); 14: 21 (20–26).
d TG Book of Mormon.
9a TG Revelation.
b Dan. 2: 28 (22–29, 49); Amos 3: 7; D&C 121: 26 (25–33). TG Scriptures to Come Forth.

10 We believe in the literal ^agathering of Israel and in the restoration of the ^bTen Tribes; that ^cZion (the New Jerusalem) will be built upon the American continent; that Christ will ^dreign personally upon the earth; and, that the earth will be ^erenewed and receive its ^fparadisiacal ^gglory.

11 We claim the ^aprivilege of worshiping Almighty God according to the ^bdictates of our own ^cconscience, and allow all men the same privilege, let them ^dworship how, where, or what they may.

12 We believe in being ^asubject to ^bkings, presidents, rulers, and magistrates, in ^cobeying, honoring, and sustaining the ^dlaw.

13 ^aWe believe in being ^bhonest, true, ^cchaste, ^dbenevolent, virtuous, and in doing ^egood to all men; indeed, we may say that we follow the admonition of Paul—We believe all things, we ^fhope all things, we have endured many things, and hope to be able to ^gendure all things. If there is anything ^hvirtuous, ⁱlovely, or of good report or praiseworthy, we seek after these things.

JOSEPH SMITH.

10a Isa. 49: 22 (20–22); 60: 4; 1 Ne. 19: 16 (16–17).
TG Israel, Gathering of.
 b TG Israel, Tribes of, Ten Lost.
 c Ether 13: 6 (2–11); D&C 42: 9; 45: 66 (66–67); 84: 2 (2–5); Moses 7: 62.
TG Jerusalem, New; Zion.
 d Micah 4: 7. TG Jesus Christ, Millennial Reign.
 e TG Earth, Cleansing of; Earth, Renewal of;

Eden.
 f IE a condition like the Garden of Eden; see Isa. 11: 1–9; 35: 1–10; 51: 1–3; 65: 17–25; Ezek. 36: 35 (1–38); 2 Ne. 8: 1–3.
TG Paradise.
 g TG Glory.
11a Alma 21: 22 (21–22); D&C 93: 19; 134: 4 (1–4).
 b TG Agency.
 c TG Conscience.
 d Micah 4: 5; D&C 134: 7 (4, 7). TG Worship.

12a D&C 134: 1 (1–11).
TG Citizenship; Governments.
 b TG Kings, Earthly.
 c TG Obedience.
 d D&C 58: 21 (21–23).
13a Philip. 4: 8.
 b TG Honesty; Integrity.
 c TG Chastity.
 d TG Benevolence.
 e TG Good Works.
 f TG Hope.
 g TG Perseverance; Steadfastness.
 h TG Modesty; Virtue.
 i TG Beauty.

INDEX

INDEX

AARON—brother of Moses (see also Bishop; Priesthood; Aaronic; BD Aaron)

D&C 8: 6–9 gift of A.; 84: 18 the Lord confirmed priesthood on A. and his seed; 84: 27 law of carnal commandments continues with house of A.; 84: 31 sons of Moses and A. to offer sacrifice in house of the Lord; 84: 33–34 those who magnify callings in priesthood become sons of Moses and A.; 132: 59 the Lord will justify actions of those called of the Father as was A.

AARON, DESCENDANTS OF (see Bishop; Priesthood, Aaronic)

ABASE (see also Humble)

D&C 101: 42 he who exalts himself shall be a.; 112: 3 he who has a. himself shall be exalted.

ABEL—son of Adam (see also BD Abel)

D&C 84: 16 priesthood from A. to Enoch; 84: 16 A. is slain by Cain; 84: 16 A. receives priesthood from Adam; 138: 40 A. is first martyr, slain in spirit world.

Moses 5: 17 birth of A.; 5: 17 A. is keeper of sheep; 5: 20 A. offers firstlings of flock; 5: 32 A. is slain by Cain; 5: 35 blood of A. cries from ground; 6: 2–3 Seth[1] is born to take place of A.

ABIDE (see also Dwell; Obedience; Remain)

D&C 1: 39 truth a. forever; 35: 18 Joseph Smith to hold keys if he a. in the Lord; 35: 21 elect shall a. day of the Lord's coming; 38: 8 he who is not purified shall not a. the Lord's coming; 84: 18 Aaronic Priesthood to a. forever with priesthood after holiest order of God; 88: 22–24 he who cannot a. law of a kingdom cannot a. glory of that kingdom; 88: 25 earth a. law of celestial kingdom; 88: 26 earth shall a. power by which it is quickened; 88: 35 that which a. not by law remains filthy; 88: 35 that which a. in sin cannot be sanctified by law; 128: 24 who can a. the Lord's coming; 132: 4 if ye a. not the new and everlasting covenant, ye are damned; 132: 5 all who will have blessing shall a. law appointed for that blessing; 132: 5 he who receives fulness of the Lord's glory must a. the law.

ABOMINATION, ABOMINABLE (see also Abomination of Desolation; Church, Great and Abominable; Church of the Devil; Evil; Sin; TG Abomination)

D&C 3: 18 Nephites destroyed because of a.; 10: 21 hearts of those who obtained manuscript are full of a.; 29: 21 great and a. church to be cast down; 29: 21 a. shall not reign; 50: 4 the Lord has seen a. in church; 88: 94 mother of a. ready to be burned; 97: 24 indignation of the Lord kindled against a.

ABOMINATION OF DESOLATION (see also Abomination; Desolation; TG Abomination of Desolation; BD Abomination of Desolation)

D&C 84: 117 desolation of a. in last days; 88: 85 desolation of a. awaits the wicked.

JS-M 1: 12, 32 (Dan. 11: 31; 12: 11; Matt. 24: 15) a. of desolation concerning destruction of Jerusalem.

ABRAHAM—father of faithful (see also Abrahamic Covenant; BD Abraham)

D&C 27: 5, 10 the Lord will drink of fruit of vine with A.; 84: 13 A. blessed Esaias; 84: 14 A. receives priesthood from Melchizedek; 84: 33–34, 103–117 (138: 41) faithful become the seed of A.; 98: 32 law of forbearance given to A.; 101: 4 (132: 36) commanded to sacrifice his only son; 101: 4 saints to be tried as A.; 110: 12 dispensation of gospel of A. committed by Elias; 124: 58 (132: 31) promise to A. repeated to Joseph Smith; 132: 1, 37 the Lord gave wives and concubines to A.; 132: 29 received all things by revelation; 132: 29 (137: 5) has received his exaltation; 132: 34 God commanded and Sarah gave Hagar to A.; 132: 65 Sarah administered to A. according to the law; 138: 41 Joseph F. Smith sees A. in spirit world.

Abr. 1: 2 high priest; 1: 2 desires more knowledge and righteousness; 1: 2 desires to be father of many nations; 1: 2 seeks blessings of fathers; 1: 4 seeks appointment to priesthood; 1: 7, 12 in hands of idolatrous priests; 1: 16 is delivered from priests by Jehovah; 1: 16 Jehovah speaks to A.; 1: 18 Jehovah to give his name and priesthood to A.; 2: 3 is commanded to leave Chaldea; 2: 4 goes to Haran; 2: 6 is commanded to leave Haran; 2: 6, 19 Jehovah appears to A.; 2: 24 is told to say Sarai his sister; 2: 15 takes family and followers to land of Canaan; 2: 17 builds altar, makes an offering; 2: 21 decides to go to Egypt; 3: 11 talks with the Lord face to face; 3: 14 seed of A. to be multiplied as number of sands; 3: 23 was chosen before he was born.

ABRAHAMIC COVENANT (see also Covenant; Israel; TG Abrahamic Covenant; BD Abraham, Covenant of)

D&C 52: 2 (86: 9) the Lord's people are heirs according to the covenant; 84: 34 they who magnify callings become seed of A.; 84: 99 election brought to pass by faith and covenant of Israel's fathers; 110: 12 Elias commits dispensation of gospel of A.; 124: 58 through A. and his seed shall kindreds of earth be blessed; 132: 32 do the works of A.

Abr. 2: 9–11 promises given to A.

ABRIDGMENT (see also Plates; Record)

D&C 10: 44 lost manuscript contained only an a. of account of Nephi¹.

ABSENCE (see also Separation)

D&C 45: 17 (138: 50) a. of spirits from bodies viewed as bondage.

ABSTINENCE (see also Temperance; Word of Wisdom)

D&C 49: 18 a. from meats is not ordained of God; 59: 9 keep thyself unspotted from the world; 82: 2 refrain from sin; 88: 124 cease to be idle, unclean; 89: 5 not good to drink wine or strong drink; 136: 21 keep yourselves from evil.

ABUNDANCE (see also Fulness; TG Abundant Life)

D&C 59: 16 fulness of the earth is yours; 64: 34 obedient shall eat the good of the land; 70: 13 a. is multiplied through manifestations of Spirit; 101: 75 an a. is in store to redeem Zion; 104: 18 take of a. which the Lord made; 104: 18 greed with a. shall be punished; 117: 7 solitary places to bring forth in a.

ACCEPT (see also Acceptable; Approve; Embrace; Receive)

D&C 132: 9 will the Lord a. offering not made in his name.

ACCEPTABLE (see also Accept; Approve)

D&C 84: 31 sons of Aaron¹ shall offer an a. offering; 93: 51 (138: 31) proclaim the a. year of the Lord; 124: 2 your prayers are a. before me; 124: 30, 33–37

baptism for dead cannot be a. to the Lord outside his house; 124: 31 baptisms are a. while saints build temple; 124: 104 if Sidney Rigdon offers an a. offering, the Lord will heal him.

ACCOUNTABILITY, AGE OF (see also Accountable)

D&C 18: 42 all who have arrived at years of a. should repent and be baptized; 20: 71 none to be received into church unless they have reached years of a.; 29: 47 Satan cannot tempt little children until they become a.; 68: 25, 27 children to be baptized when eight years old; 137: 10 children who die before a. are saved in celestial kingdom.

ACCOUNTABLE (see also Accountability, Age of; Count; Responsibility; TG Accountability)

D&C 42: 32 every man shall be made a.; 69: 5 servants shall send accounts of stewardships to Zion; 72: 3 (104: 12) each steward to render an account to the Lord; 72: 5, 16 elders to render an account of stewardship to bishop; 101: 78 every man is a. for his own sins; 104: 13 the Lord to make every man a. as steward; 134: 1 men are a. for their acts in relation to governments.

ACCUSER

D&C 102: 15–19 a. and accused in church courts.

ACKNOWLEDGE (see also Confess)

D&C 102: 3 First Presidency is a. by voice of the Twelve; 102: 9 president of church is a. in his administration by voice of church; 138: 23 saints a. the Son as their Redeemer.

ACQUAINT, ACQUAINTANCE (see also Knowledge)

D&C 84: 52 whoso receives not the Lord's voice is not a. with it; 90: 15 become a. with all good books; 111: 3 expedient to form a. with men.

ACT (see also Agency; Deed; Walk; Work [noun])

D&C 1: 3 (88: 108–110) secret a. shall be revealed; 43: 8 saints to instruct each other how to a.; 43: 9 bind yourselves to a. in holiness before the Lord; 101: 78 every man to a. in doctrine and principle; 107: 34 the Seventy are to a. in name of the Lord; 107: 99 every man to learn his duty and a. in his office; 134: 1 God holds men accountable for their a. in relation to government.

ADAM—*first man created on earth* (*see also* Adam-ondi-Ahman; Eden; Garden of; Eve; Fall of Man; Man; Michael; TG Adam; BD Adam)

D&C 27: 11 the father of all; 27: 11 (107: 54; 116: 1; 128: 21; 138: 38) is Michael, the ancient of days; 29: 35 was made an agent unto himself; 29: 36, 40 was tempted by devil; 29: 40 partook of forbidden fruit; 29: 40 became subject to will of devil; 29: 41 spiritual death of A.; 29: 42 angels declared repentance and redemption to A.; 84: 16 Abel received priesthood from A.; 107: 42–53 ordained Seth[1], Cainan, Mahalaleel, Jared[1], Enoch[1], Methuselah; 107: 53–57 called posterity together at Adam-ondi-Ahman; 107: 54 the Lord blessed A. and called him Michael; 116: 1 will visit his people at Adam-ondi-Ahman; 117: 8 dwelled in Olaha Shinehah; 128: 20–21 voice of Michael, or A., came to Joseph Smith.

Moses 1: 34 was first man of all men; 3: 20 (Abr. 5: 21) gives names to beasts and fowls; 3: 22 (Abr. 5: 15) rib of A. taken to make woman; 4: 12 partakes of fruit of tree; 4: 13 recognizes his nakedness; 4: 14 hides from God; 4: 25 to partake of death; 4: 27 coat of skins made for A.; 4: 29, 31 is sent forth from Garden of Eden; 5: 1 begins to till the earth; 5: 1 to have dominion over beasts of field; 5: 1 to eat bread by sweat of brow; 5: 2 (6: 11) begets sons and daughters; 5: 3 children of A. beget sons and daughters; 5: 4 shut out from presence of the Lord; 5: 5 commanded to worship the Lord and offer firstlings; 5: 6 is asked by angel why he offers sacrifice; 5: 8 is commanded to repent and to call upon God in name of the Son; 5: 9 Holy Ghost falls upon A.; 5: 10 begins to prophesy; 5: 10 eyes of A. opened because of transgression; 5: 12 blesses name of God; 5: 12 makes all things known to sons and daughters; 5: 27 mourns because of Cain; 6: 1 hearkens to voice of God; 6: 1 calls upon sons to repent; 6: 2 glorifies name of God; 6: 6 language of A. is pure and undefiled; 6: 12 lives 930 years; 6: 22 A., son of God, conversed with God; 6: 23 posterity of A. are preachers of righteousness; 6: 48 death comes through fall of A.; 6: 53 is forgiven transgression in Garden of Eden; 6: 64–65 is caught away by Spirit and baptized; 6: 55 children of A. are conceived in sin; 6: 65 is born of Spirit; 6: 65 becomes quickened in the inner man; 6: 66 is baptized with fire and Holy Ghost; 6: 67 is after the order of God; **Abr.** 1: 3 priesthood comes down to Abraham from A.; 5: 7 is formed from dust of the ground; 5: 11 is placed in Garden of Eden; **A of F**

2 men will be punished for own sins, not for transgression of A.

ADAM-ONDI-AHMAN (*see also* Adam; Eden, Garden of; D&C map, p. 297)

D&C 78: 15 the Lord established foundations of A.; 107: 53–57 Adam called posterity together at A.; 116: 1 Adam shall visit his people at A.

ADD (*see also* Increase)

D&C 11: 22–23 (106: 3) study the Lord's word, and all things shall be *a.* thereto; 20: 35 neither *a.* to nor diminish from revelation of John; 78: 19 things of this earth to be *a.* to the faithful.

Abr. 3: 26 they who keep first estate shall be *a.* upon; 3: 26 they who keep second estate shall have glory *a.* upon heads forever.

ADMINISTRATION, ADMINISTER (*see also* Administration to the Sick; Impart; Minister [verb])

D&C 20: 40, 46, 58 duty of priesthood bearers to *a.* sacrament; 20: 75–79 manner of *a.* sacrament; 46: 15 spiritual gift of knowing differences of *a.*; 76: 88 the telestial receive of Christ's fulness through *a.* of angels; 84: 19 Melchizedek Priesthood *a.* gospel; 107: 8, 12 Melchizedek Priesthood has authority to *a.* spiritual things; 107: 20 Aaronic Priesthood *a.* outward ordinances.

ADMINISTRATION TO THE SICK (*see also* Blessing; Hands, Laying on of; Heal; Ordinance; Sick, Sickness; TG Administrations to the Sick)

D&C 24: 14 elders not to heal the sick unless they request it; 42: 44, 48 (66: 9) two or more elders to lay hands upon the sick.

ADULTERY, ADULTERER (*see also* Fornication; Lust; Pure; Whore; TG Adulterer, Adultery; Sexual Abuse; BD Adultery)

D&C 42: 22 cleave unto thy wife and none else; 42: 23 (63: 16) he who lusts after woman denies the faith, shall not have Spirit; 42: 24 (59: 6; 66: 10) thou shalt not commit *a.*; 42: 24 (59: 6) those who commit *a.* and repent not shall be cast out; 42: 25–26 repentant *a.* to be forgiven; 42: 74–75 those who leave companions for sake of *a.* shall be cast out; 42: 80 those who commit *a.* are to be tried by elders; 42: 80–83 deal with *a.* according to law of God; 63: 14 some *a.* among members; 63: 15 works of *a.* to follow them in eyes of people; 76: 103 *a.* to inherit telestial glory; 132: 41–45 instructions concerning those who have entered covenant of eternal marriage.

ADVANTAGE (see also Blessings; Gain)

D&C 130: 19 a. in hereafter gained through diligence here.

ADVERSARY (see also Devil)

D&C 3: 8 the Lord supports against fiery darts of a.; 50: 7 hypocrites have given the a. power; 82: 5 a. spreads his dominions.

ADVERSITY (see also Affliction; Experience; Infirmity; Oppression; Patience; Persecution; Suffering; Tear [verb]; Tempt; Trial, Try; Tribulation; Wind)

D&C 121: 7 a. shall be but a small moment; 122: 7 a. gives experience.

ADVOCATE (see also Jesus Christ—Advocate)

AFFIXED (see Punishment)

AFFLICTION (see also Chasten; Needy; Oppression; Pain; Persecution; Suffering; Trial, Try; Tribulation)

D&C 24: 1 the Lord lifts men out of a.; 24: 8 (31: 9; 66: 9) be patient in a.; 93: 42 a. is caused by failure to teach children; 97: 26 the Lord will visit Zion with sore a.; 98: 3 (122: 7) a. to work for your good; 101: 2 a consequence of transgression; 109: 47 break off, O Lord, this yoke of a.; 121: 7 a. to be but a small moment; 122: 7 a. give experience; 133: 53 the Lord was afflicted in all a. of the redeemed.

AFRAID (see also Fear; Fear of God)

D&C 45: 75 all nations to be a. because of terror of the Lord; 98: 14 be not a. of enemies.

Moses 4: 16 Adam hears God's voice and is a.; JS-H 1: 32 Joseph Smith is a. when he first sees angel.

AGE (see also Accountability, Age of; Old)

D&C 63: 50 the faithful who live when the Lord comes shall die at a. of man; 83: 4 children have claim upon parents for maintenance until they are of a.; 101: 30 infant's life shall be as a. of tree.

AGENCY, AGENT (see also Accountability, Age of; Accountable; Act; Agent, Financial; Choose; Control; Evil; Fall of Man; Freedom; Fruit, Forbidden; Knowledge; Law; Liberty; Obedience; Tempt; Transgression; Will; TG Agency)

D&C 29: 35 the Lord gives unto man to be a. unto himself; 29: 36 third part of hosts of heaven were lost because of their

a.; 29: 39 devil must tempt men or they could not be a.; 37: 4 let every man choose for himself; 58: 27 men should do many things of free will; 58: 28 men have power to be a. unto themselves; 64: 29 as ye are a., ye are on the Lord's errand; 88: 86 abide in liberty wherewith ye are made free; 93: 31 here is the a. of man; 98: 8 the Lord makes men free; 101: 78 men to act according to moral a. given by the Lord; 134: 2 governments to secure free exercise of conscience.

Moses 4: 3 Satan sought to destroy a. of man; 6: 56 because men know good from evil, they are a. unto themselves; 7: 32 a. given in Garden of Eden.

AGENT, FINANCIAL (see also Treasury)

D&C 51: 8 (57: 6; 58: 49) financial a. to be appointed for church; 51: 12 bishop or a. to pay money; 84: 113 (90: 22–23) bishop to search for a. for secular business, storehouse.

AGREE (see also Common Consent; Unite)

D&C 27: 18 be a. as to what ye ask; 29: 33 knowledge was given because it was asked by those who were a.; 41: 2 assemble yourselves to a. upon my word; 107: 27 each member of quorum must be a. to its decision.

AGRIPPA (see also BD Agrippa)

JS-H 1: 24 Joseph Smith feels like Paul before A.

AHMAN

D&C 78: 20 (95: 17) Christ, the Son A.

ALBANY, NEW YORK (see also D&C map, p. 295)

D&C 84: 114 people of A. to be warned.

ALCOHOL (see Word of Wisdom)

ALIVE (see also Living; Quicken)

D&C 88: 96 saints who are a. shall be quickened, caught up to meet Christ.

Moses 6: 61 that which makes a. all things is given to abide in you.

ALLOWANCE (see also God, Goodness of)

D&C 1: 31 the Lord cannot look upon sin with least degree of a.

ALMIGHTY (see God, Power of)

ALMS (see also Charity; Impart; Needy; Poor; Relief; TG Almsgiving; BD Almsgiving)

D&C 88: 2 a. of prayers have come

up to the Lord; 112 : 1 *a.* have come up as memorial before the Lord.

ALPHA, ALPHUS (*see also* TG Omega; BD Alpha; Omega)

D&C 19 : 1 (35 : 1; 38 : 1; 45 : 7; 54 : 1; 61 : 1; 63 : 60; 68 : 35; 75 : 1; 81 : 7; 84 : 120; 112 : 34; 132 : 66) Christ is A. and Omega; 95 : 17 Christ, the Son Ahman, or in other words, A., or Omegus.

ALTAR (*see also* Idolatry; Offering; Sacrifice; BD Altar)

D&C 135 : 7 (Rev. 6 : 9) John the Revelator saw innocent blood of martyrs under *a.*

Abr. 1 : 13 description of *a.* of idolatrous priests; 2 : 17, 20 *a.* built by Abraham.

ALTER (*see also* Change)

D&C 10 : 10–11, 29 lost manuscript to be *a.* by wicked men.

AMBITION (*see also* Aspire)

D&C 121 : 37 vain *a.* grieves the Spirit.

AMEN (*see also* BD Amen)

D&C 88 : 135 say A. in token of prayer of salutation in house of God; 121 : 37 *a.* to priesthood of man who exercises compulsion.

AMERICA, AMERICAN

D&C 10 : 49–50 prophets blessed land in prayers; 10 : 51 A. to be free.

A of F 10 Zion to be built upon A. continent.

AMHERST, OHIO (*see also* D&C map, p. 296)

D&C 75 revelation received at A.

ANCIENT (*see also* Old; Primitive)

D&C 8 : 1 Oliver Cowdery to receive knowledge of *a.* records; 98 : 32 the Lord gave law to all *a.* prophets; 107 : 4 church in *a.* days called priesthood after Melchizedek.

ANCIENT OF DAYS (*see* Adam)

ANGEL (*see also* Angels, Ministering of; Angels of the Devil; Archangel; Messenger; Moroni²; Servant; TG Angels; BD Angels)

D&C 20 : 6 description of *a.*; 29 : 42 *a.* sent to declare repentance and redemption to Adam; 38 : 12 (86 : 5) *a.* wait to reap the earth; 42 : 6 ye shall declare the word like unto *a.* of God; 45 : 45 (49 : 23; 77 : 12; 88 : 92–112) *a.* to sound trumps;

49 : 7 *a.* know not the time of the Lord's coming; 62 : 3 (88 : 2; 90 : 34) *a.* rejoice over elders' testimonies; 63 : 54 *a.* shall cast wicked unto unquenchable fire; 76 : 21 *a.* worship God at his throne; 77 : 9 (Rev. 7 : 2) explanation of *a.* ascending from the east; 84 : 28 John the Baptist ordained by *a.*; 84 : 42 (109 : 22) *a.* are given charge concerning elders; 88 : 92 (133 : 17) *a.* shall fly through the midst of heaven; 88 : 107 *a.* to be crowned with glory; 89 : 21 destroying *a.* shall pass by those who obey Word of Wisdom; 103 : 19–20 *a.* shall go before the Lord's servants; 123 : 7 duty owed to *a.*; 128 : 21 voices of diverse *a.* heard; 129 : 1 *a.* are resurrected personages, having bodies of flesh; 129 : 4–8 test for recognizing *a.*; 130 : 4 reckoning of *a's* time; 130 : 5 only *a.* who belong to this earth minister to it; 130 : 6–7 *a.* reside in presence of God; 132 : 18–19 those who enter covenant of eternal marriage shall pass by appointed gods and *a.*; 132 : 20 *a.* are subject to the gods; 132 : 37 Abraham, Isaac, and Jacob are gods, not *a.*; 133 : 53 *a.* of the Lord's presence saved the redeemed.

Moses 5 : 6 *a.* of the Lord asks Adam why he offers sacrifice; 5 : 58 *a.* begin to declare gospel; 7 : 25, 27 *a.* seen by Enoch²; Abr. 1 : 15 (2 : 13; 3 : 20) *a.* of God's presence delivers Abraham; JS-H 1 : 64 *a.* reveals plates.

ANGELS, MINISTERING OF (*see also* Angel; Minister [verb] TG Angels, Ministering)

D&C 7 : 6 Peter the apostle was to be made ministering *a.*; 10 : 14 to another is given gift of beholding *a.* and ministering spirits; 13 : 1 (84 : 26; 107 : 20) the Aaronic Priesthood holds keys of ministering of *a.*; 20 : 6 *a.* ministers to Joseph Smith; 20 : 10 (27 : 16) gospel confirmed to others by ministering of *a.*; 20 : 35 scriptures and revelations come through ministering of *a.*; 43 : 25 the Lord calls upon nations by ministering of *a.*; 67 : 13 natural man cannot abide ministering of *a.*; 76 : 88 the telestial receive Christ's fulness through administering of *a.*; 130 : 5 only *a.* who belong to this earth minister to it; 132 : 16–17 celestial heirs not married in covenant are appointed ministering *a.*; 136 : 7 Joseph Smith called upon by *a.* and ministering spirits.

ANGELS OF THE DEVIL (*see also* Devil; Spirit; Evil)

D&C 29 : 28 (76 : 33) the wicked will suffer with devil and his *a.*; 29 : 36–37 third part of hosts of heaven become devil's *a.*; 76 : 25 *a.* who was in authority rebelled against Only Begotten; 128: 20 devil appeared as *a.* of light.

ANGER, ANGRY (*see also* Fury; Indignation; Offend; Rage; Wrath)

D&C 1: 13 (5: 8; 56: 1; 60: 2; 61: 31; 2, 32; 82: 6; 84: 24; 97: 24; 101: 90; 133: 51) the Lord's *a.* is kindled; 10: 24, 32 (63: 27–28) Satan stirs men's *a.* against this now; 19: 15 repent, lest I smite you by my *a.*; 63: 11 with whom the Lord is *a.* he is not well pleased; 88: 87 stars shall become *a.*; 121: 5 may the Lord's *a.* be kindled against saints' enemies.

Moses 6: 27 (7: 34; 8: 15) the Lord's *a.* is kindled; **Abr.** 3: 28 the second was *a.* and kept not his first estate.

ANGUISH (*see also* Misery; Pain; Punishment; Suffering; Torment)

D&C 124: 52 the Lord to answer *a.* on those who hate him.

ANIMAL (*see also* Beast; Calf; Cattle; Chickens; Creep; Creature; Dove; Eagle; Firstling; Flock; Food; Fowl; Hen; Horse; Lamb; Meat; Ox; Serpent; Sheep; Swine; Viper; BD Animals)

D&C 89: 14 *a.* are for use of man; 89: 17 barley for all useful *a.*

Moses 2: 24–25 (3: 19; **Abr.** 4: 24–25) creation of *a.*

ANOINTED, THE (*see also* Anointing; BD Anointed One)

D&C 109: 80 let the Lord's *a.* be clothed with salvation; 121: 16 cursed are those who lift up heel against the Lord's *a.*; 132: 7 covenants and performances must be sealed through medium of the Lord's *a.*

ANOINTING, ANOINT (*see also* Anointed, the; Consecrate; Ordinance; TG Anointing; BD Anoint)

D&C 68: 20–21 descendant of Aaron[1] must be designated and *a.* by Presidency to serve as bishop; 109: 35 *a.* of ministers to be sealed from on high; 124: 39 your *a.* are ordained by ordinance of the Lord's holy house; 124: 57 *a.* put upon Joseph Smith's head; 138: 42 the Redeemer was *a.* to bind up the brokenhearted.

Moses 6: 35 the Lord tells Enoch[2] to *a.* eyes with clay.

ANSWER (*see also* Prayer; Receive)

D&C 101: 7 the Lord is slow to *a.* prayers of those slow to hearken; 112: 10 be humble, and the Lord will give *a.* to prayers.

Abr. 3: 27 one *a.* like unto Son of Man.

ANTHON, CHARLES

JS-H 1: 63–65 (2 Ne. 27: 15–18) certifies characters and translation from plates.

ANXIETY, ANXIOUS, ANXIOUSLY (*see also* Fear; Trouble; Worry)

D&C 58: 27 men should be *a.* engaged in good cause.

APOCRYPHA (*see also* BD Apocrypha)

D&C 91: 1–2 many things both true and untrue in A.; 91: 3 need not be translated; 91: 4–6 whoso is enlightened by the Spirit can obtain benefit from A.

APOSTASY (*see also* Apostate; Church, Great and Abominable; Church of the Devil; Darkness; Spiritual; Priestcraft; Prophets, False; Sin; Transgression; Unbelief; TG Apostasy of Individuals)

D&C 1: 15 those who reject prophets have strayed from ordinances, broken everlasting covenant; 3: 4 those who have received revelation may fall if they follow own will; 3: 9–11 because of transgression, if thou art not aware thou wilt fall; 5: 32 if Martin Harris does not humble himself and receive witness, he will fall into transgression; 10: 26 Satan causes men to catch themselves in own snare; 11: 25 wo unto him who denies revelation; 20: 9 Book of Mormon contains record of fallen people; 20: 32 possibility that many may fall from grace; 40: 2 fear of persecution and cares of world cause James Covill to reject word; 50: 44 he who builds upon this rock shall never fall; 58: 15 if he repent not of his sins, let him take heed lest he fall; 82: 3 he who sins against greater light receives greater condemnation; 82: 21 those who sin against covenant are delivered to buffetings of Satan; 84: 41 whoso breaks covenant shall not have forgiveness; 84: 54 minds darkened because of unbelief; 85: 11 those who have apostatized shall have no inheritance among saints; 86: 3 Satan sows tares; 112: 26 some have blasphemed against the Lord in midst of his house; 114: 2 some among saints deny the Lord's name; 118: 1 let men be appointed to supply place of those who are fallen; 121: 37 amen to priesthood of those who cover their sins.

JS-H 1: 19 (Isa. 29: 13) churches are wrong, draw near the Lord with lips, but hearts are far from him.

APOSTATE

D&C 86: 3 Babylon, the *a.*

APOSTLE (*see also* Council; Disciple; James; John; Paul; Peter; Priesthood, Melchizedek; TG Apostles; BD Apostle)

D&C 1: 14 those who heed not words of prophets and *a.* shall be cut off; 18: 9 Oliver Cowdery and David Whitmer called with same calling as Paul the *a.*; 18: 26–28 (107: 35) the Twelve called to declare gospel to both Gentile and Jew; 18: 27 the Twelve to be the Lord's disciples; 18: 29 *a.* ordained to baptize; 18: 32 (20: 39; 107: 39, 58) *a.* ordained to ordain other priesthood officers; 18: 37 the Twelve searched out by Oliver Cowdery and David Whitmer; 20: 2 (21: 1) Joseph Smith ordained an *a.*; 20: 38 *a.* is an elder; 20: 40 *a.* to administer sacrament; 20: 41, 43 *a.* confirm baptized members; 20: 42 *a.* teach and watch over the church; 20: 44 *a.* take lead in meetings; 27: 12 (107: 23) *a.* are special witnesses of Christ's name; 27: 12 Joseph Smith and Oliver Cowdery ordained by Peter, James, and John; 29: 12 the Twelve from Jerusalem shall judge the righteous of house of Israel; 35: 6 *a.* of old bestowed Holy Ghost by laying on of hands; 52: 9, 36 elders to preach that which prophets and *a.* have written; 63: 52 *a.* preached resurrection; 84: 39 false *a.* and prophets to be known; 84: 63 you are mine *a.*, even God's high priests; 84: 108 *a.* built up ancient church; 95: 4 *a.* are to prune vineyard; 102: 30 traveling high council composed of twelve *a.*; 107: 23, 33 twelve traveling councilors are called to twelve *a.*; 107: 24 quorum of *a.* equal in authority to First Presidency; 107: 34 (124: 139) direct work of the Seventy; 107: 35 (124: 128) the Twelve sent out, holding keys to proclaim gospel; 112: 14–32 power of priesthood given to the Twelve; 112: 21 the Twelve to send out ministers; sec. 118 revelation of God's will concerning the Twelve; 136: 3 Camp of Israel under direction of Twelve.

A of F 6 *a.* part of Church organization.

APPAREL (see also Clothing; Garment; Raiment; TG Apparel)

D&C 42: 40 let all thy garments be plain; 133: 46, 48 the Lord will come clothed in glorious red *a.*

APPEAL (see also Plead; Trial; Judicial)

D&C 11: 18 *a.* to the Spirit; 102: 33 *a.* to First Presidency in judicial proceedings; 107: 32 conditions of no *a.* from decisions; 134: 11 men should *a.* to civil law for redress of wrongs.

APPEAR (see also Jesus Christ, Appearances of; Show)

D&C 128: 20 devil *a.* as angel of light; 129: 6 spirit of just man can only *a.*

in glory; 133: 36 angel has *a.* to some and committed gospel to man.

JS–H 1: 30 light and personage *a.* in Joseph Smith's room.

APPENDAGE

D&C 84: 29 offices of elder and bishop are *a.* to high priesthood; 84: 30 offices of teacher and deacon are *a.* to lesser priesthood; 107: 5 other authorities or offices are *a.* to Melchizedek Priesthood; 107: 14 Aaronic Priesthood is *a.* to the Melchizedek.

APPENDIX

D&C sec. 133 revelation designated as the A.

APPOINT (see also Appointment; Ordain)

D&C 28: 12 nothing shall be *a.* unto church covenants to church covenants; 42: 48 those not *a.* unto death shall be healed; 43: 3 no one to receive revelations and commandments except he be *a.*; 84: 31 house of the Lord to be built upon consecrated spot as he has *a.*; 101: 20 none other place *a.* for Zion than that *a.* by the Lord; 104: 11 *a.* every man his stewardship; 121: 25 a time *a.* for every man, according to his works; 132: 10 the Lord will not receive that which he has not *a.*; 132: 11 the Lord will not *a.* except by law.

APPOINTMENT (see also Appoint)

D&C 107: those of lesser priesthood to make and fill *a.*

Abr. 1: 4 Abraham sought for *a.* unto priesthood.

APPROVE (see also Accept; Acceptable)

D&C 107: 100 he who shows himself not *a.* will not be counted worthy to stand; 124: 144 names to be *a.* at conference.

ARABIC (see also Language)

JS–H 1: 64 characters on plates resemble A.

ARCHANGEL (see also Angel)

D&C 29: 26 (88: 112; 107: 54; 128: 21) Michael, the *a.*

ARCHIVES

D&C 127: 9 records to be put in *a.* of temple.

ARISE (see also Rise)

D&C 82: 14 Zion must *a.*; 88: 124 *a.* early; 115: 5 *a.* and shine forth.

ARK (see also BD Ark; Ark of the Covenant)

D&C 85: 8 man who puts forth hand to steady the *a.* will die.

Moses 7: 43 Enoch² sees Noah¹ build *a.*; **JS-M** 1: 42 until day Noah¹ entered *a.*, people were eating and drinking.

ARM (see also Might; Strength; TG Trust Not in the Arm of Flesh)

D&C 1: 14 (90: 10; 133: 3) *a.* of the Lord shall be revealed; 1: 19 trust not in *a.* of flesh; 3: 8 the Lord would have extended his *a.* and supported you; 6: 20 the faithful are encircled in *a.* of the Lord's love; 15: 2 (16: 2) the Lord's *a.* is over all the earth; 29: 1 *a.* of mercy hath atoned for sins; 35: 8 (133: 67) the Lord's *a.* is not shortened; 45: 45, 47 the Lord's *a.* to fall upon nations; 56: 1 the rebellious to know the Lord's *a.*; 121: 33 as well might man stretch forth his puny *a.* to stop the Missouri; 133: 3 the Lord shall make bare his *a.* in eyes of all nations.

ARMOR (see also Shield)

D&C 27: 15 take upon you the Lord's whole *a.*

ARMY, ARMIES (see also Battle; War)

D&C 5: 14 (109: 73) church to come forth terrible as *a.* with banners; 60: 4 God rules among *a.*; 88: 111–113 battle between *a.* of devil and Michael; 105: 26 *a.* of Israel to become very great; 105: 31 let the Lord's *a.* be sanctified.

ASHAMED (see also Shame)

D&C 42: 91 those who offend openly should be rebuked openly, that they may be *a.*; 90: 17 be not *a.*

Moses 3: 25 (Abr. 5: 19) Adam and Eve were naked and were not *a.*

ASHLEY, MAJOR N.

D&C 75: 17 called to journey into South.

ASK (see also Inquire; Knock; Prayer; Question; Seek; TG Prayer)

D&C 4: 7 (6: 5; 8: 1; 11: 5; 12: 5; 14: 5; 29: 6; 42: 3, 61; 49: 26; 66: 9; 75: 27; 88: 63; 101: 27; 103: 35) *a.* and ye shall receive; 8: 9 *a.* and receive knowledge; 8: 10 (18: 18) *a.* in faith; 8: 10 do not *a.* for that which you ought not; 8: 11 *a.* that you may know mysteries of God; 9: 7 you took no thought save to *a.* the Lord; 9: 8 study, then *a.*; 10: 21 because of corrupt hearts men do not *a.* the Lord; 14: 8 (18: 18) *a.* the Father in Christ's name; 18: 18 *a.* and you shall have Holy Ghost; 42: 56 *a.* and scriptures will be given; 42: 61–62 if thou shalt *a.*, thou

shalt receive revelation; 42: 68 (46: 7; James 1: 5) he who lacks wisdom should *a.* the Lord, who gives liberally; 46: 7 ye are commanded in all things to *a.* of God; 46: 28 he who *a.* in Spirit will receive in Spirit; 46: 30 he who *a.* in Spirit *a.* according to will of God; 50: 29 if purified, whatever ye *a.* in the Lord's name will be done; 50: 30 it will be given what to *a.*; 88: 65 do not *a.* for things not expedient; 132: 45 *a.* what ye will, and it shall be given.

Moses 6: 52 (7: 59) *a.* all things in name of the Son; 7: 50 Enoch² *a.* the Lord to have mercy on Noah¹ and his seed; **JS-H** 1: 11, 26 (James 1: 5) if any of you lack wisdom, let him *a.* of God.

ASLEEP (see also Sleep; Watch)

D&C 35: 21 the elect to hear the Lord's voice and not be *a.*; 86: 3 after apostles sleep *a.*, Satan sows tares; 101: 53 ye should not fall *a.*, lest enemy come upon you.

ASPIRE (see also Ambition)

D&C 121: 35 few are chosen, because they *a.* to honors of men; 124: 84 Almon Babbitt *a.* to establish his counsel instead of Presidency's.

ASSEMBLE (see also Church of God; Conference; Congregation; Meet; Meeting; Solemn Assembly; Worship)

D&C 37: 3 (39: 15) church commanded to *a.* at the Ohio; 41: 2 elders commanded to *a.* to agree on word; 43: 8 when *a.* together, church to instruct one another; 49: 25 Zion to *a.* before the Lord's coming; 52: 42 faithful to *a.* in Missouri; 59: 9–13 go to house of prayer on the Lord's holy day; 62: 4 (63: 24, 36) elders to *a.* in land of Zion; 138: 16, 38, 49 the dead *a.* awaiting the Son's advent.

ASTRAY (see also Apostasy; Err; Lose)

Moses 6: 28 since creation, men have gone *a.*

ASTRONOMY (see also Moon; Star; Sun; World)

D&C 88: 37 no space in which there is no kingdom; 130: 7 angels reside in presence of God, on globe like sea of glass and fire.

Moses 1: 33 the Lord has created worlds without number; 7: 30 the Lord's creations cannot be numbered; **Abr.** 1: 31 records of the fathers contain knowledge of creation, planets, stars; 3: 3, 9 Kolob, nearest to God, governs all planets in order of earth; 3: 4 one revolution of Kolob is day unto the Lord, thousand years.

ATE (see Eat)

ATHIRST (see also Thirst, Thirsty)

D&C 84: 80 those who preach gospel faithfully shall not go *a*.

ATONE, ATONEMENT (see Jesus Christ, Atonement through)

ATTAIN (see also Obtain)

D&C 130: 18 whatever principle of intelligence we *a*. unto in this life will rise with us; 132: 21 except ye abide the Lord's law ye cannot *a*. celestial glory.

AUTHORITIES (see also Authority; Officer)

D&C 102: 32 decisions of the Twelve can be questioned only by general *a*.; 107: 5 all *a*. in church other than Melchizedek Priesthood are appendages to it; 107: 32 appeal may be brought to quorums which constitute spiritual *a*. of church; 124: 5 kings and *a*. to be appealed to; 124: 118 hearken unto *a*. called to lay foundation of Zion.

AUTHORITY (see also Calling; Dominion; Office; Ordain; Ordinance; Power; Priesthood; Reign; Rule; Scepter; tg Authority)

D&C 1: 6 this is mine *a*. and *a*. of my servants; 20: 2 Joseph Smith called of God; 20: 63–64 license permitting elder to perform duty; 25: 3 Emma Smith called by the Lord; 27: 8 Joseph Smith and Oliver Cowdery called and ordained, even as Aaron; 28: 2 (43: 2–7) no one to receive commandments and revelation for church except one appointed; 28: 3 declare the commandments with *a*.; 28: 5 Oliver Cowdery to write by way of wisdom, not commandment; 42: 11 no one to preach gospel unless ordained by someone who has *a*.; 63: 62 many use name of the Lord in vain, having not *a*.; 68: 8 elders to preach gospel, acting in *a*.; 68: 20 descendant of Aaron[1] not authorized unless designated and ordained by Presidency; 76: 25 angel who was in *a*. rebelled; 84: 21 power of godliness not manifest without *a*.; 107: 8, 18–19 Melchizedek Priesthood has *a*. to administer in spiritual things; 107: 20 *a*. of Aaronic Priesthood is to administer in outward ordinances; 112: 21 the Twelve are duly recommended and authorized; 113: 8 put on *a*. of priesthood; 121: 39 unrighteous dominion practiced by those who get a little *a*.; 124: 128 pure in heart shall seek *a*.; 124: 128 the Twelve hold keys to open up *a*. of kingdom; 128: 9 what is done by divine *a*. becomes law; 134: 10 religious society has *a*. to deal

with men for fellowship; 138: 26 truth proclaimed in great power and *a*.; 138: 30 Lord appointed messengers clothed with power and *a*.

A of F 5 man must be called of God by those in *a*.

AVENGE (see also Revenge; Vengeance)

D&C 87: 7 blood of saints to be *a*.; 98: 45 the Lord will *a*. thee of thine enemy an hundredfold; 101: 58 (103: 25) *a*. me of mine enemies; 121: 5 with thy sword, *a*. us of our wrongs.

Moses 5: 48 Cain shall be *a*. seven-fold.

AVOID

D&C 107: 4 *a*. too frequent repetition of the Lord's name.

AWAKE (see also Quicken)

D&C 29: 26 all the dead shall *a*.; 124: 11 *a*., O kings of earth.

BABBITT, ALMON

D&C 124: 84 seeks to establish his counsel over that of Presidency.

BABE (see also Child; Infant)

D&C 128: 18 that which has never been revealed will be revealed to *b*. and sucklings.

BABYLON—capital of Babylonia, in southwest Asia (see also Church of the Devil; tg Babylon; bd Babylon)

D&C 1: 16 B. the great shall fall; 35: 11 desolations upon B.; 64: 24 the Lord will not spare any that remain in B.; 86: 3 B., the great persecutor of church, the apostate; 133: 5, 7, 14 go out from B.; 133: 14 wickedness is spiritual B.

BACKBITING (see also Gossip; Revile; Slander)

D&C 20: 54 teachers to see there is no *b*. in church; 42: 27 thou shalt not speak evil of thy neighbor; 88: 124 cease to find fault one with another; 136: 23 cease to speak evil one of another.

BACKWARD (see Forward)

BAKER, JESSE

D&C 124: 137 member of elders quorum presidency.

BALDWIN, WHEELER

D&C 52: 31 to journey to Missouri.

BAND (see also Bind; Chain; Cord; Robber)

D&C 113: 10 (Isa. 52: 2) *b*. of Zion's

neck in Isaiah are God's curses; 138: 16 the Son declares redemption from b. of death.

BANNER

D&C 5: 14 (109: 73) church to rise terrible as army with b.; 105: 31 b. of the Lord's army to be terrible unto all nations; 135: 7 innocent blood of martyrs on b. of liberty is ambassador of religion of Christ.

BAPTISM, BAPTIZE (see also Accountability, Age of; Baptism for the Dead; Born of God; Church of God; Convert; Faith; Fire; Font; Forgive; Grave; Holy Ghost; Immersion; Name; Ordinance; Rebaptism; Remission; Repentance; Sacrament; Salvation; Wash; Water; Witness; TG Baptism; Baptism, Essential; Baptism, Immersion; Baptism, Qualifications for; BD Baptism)

D&C 13: 1 (84: 26–27) Aaronic Priesthood holds keys of b.; 13: 1 (19: 31; 33: 11; 55: 1–2; 68: 27; 76: 52; 84: 27, 74; 107: 20) b. for remission of sins; 18: 22 (20: 25; 68: 9; 112: 29) those who are b. shall be saved; 18: 29 (20: 38, 42) the Twelve are ordained to b.; 18: 41–42 (33: 11; 49: 13; 84: 27) repent and be b.; 18: 42 (20: 71; 68: 25, 27) all who come to years of accountability must be b.; 19: 31 (20: 41; 33: 11; 39: 6) b. of fire and Holy Ghost; 20: 37 requirements for b. explained; 20: 46 duty of priests to b.; 20: 68 duty of members after b.; 20: 73 (68: 8) b. in name of Father, Son, Holy Ghost; 20: 73–74 manner of performing b.; 20: 74 (76: 51; 128: 12) b. by immersion; 33: 11–12 (39: 6) one of first principles of gospel; 35: 5 Sidney Rigdon b. without giving Holy Ghost; 39: 20 (42: 7; 52: 10; 68: 8) elders to go forth b. with water; 39: 23 (55: 1; 84: 64) those who are b. shall receive gift of Holy Ghost; 55: 1 after b. comes remission of sins; 68: 25 parents must teach children doctrine of b.; 76: 51 (128: 12) b. after manner of Christ's burial; 76: 51 those b. in the Lord's name shall inherit celestial glory; 84: 27 preparatory gospel of repentance and b.; 84: 28 John the Baptist was b. in his childhood; 84: 74 those who are not b. shall be damned; 137: 5–7 Alvin Smith inherited celestial kingdom without being b. in this life; 138: 33 the dead are taught vicarious b. for remission of sins.

Moses 6: 52 (8: 24) those b. in name of the Son will receive Holy Ghost; 6: 52 Adam is commanded to be b. in water in name of the Son; 6: 59 ye must be born into kingdom of heaven, of water and of Spirit; 6: 60 by the water ye keep the

commandment; 6: 64–66 Adam is b. in water and with fire; 7: 11 the Lord commands Enoch² to b. in name of Father, Son, Holy Ghost; **JS-H** 1: 69 Aaronic Priesthood holds keys of gospel of b. by immersion for remission of sins; 1: 70–71 Joseph Smith and Oliver Cowdery b. each other; **A of F** 4 b. by immersion for remission of sins.

BAPTISM FOR THE DEAD (see also Baptism; Temple; TG Baptism for the Dead)

D&C 124: 29 no place yet on earth where saints can be b. for dead; 124: 33 b. for dead to be performed in the Lord's house; 127: 5–10 the Lord's instructions on b. for dead; sec. 128 Joseph Smith's teachings on b. for dead; 138: 33 spirits of the dead are taught vicarious b. for remission of sins.

BAPTIST (see John the Baptist)

BARE (see also Naked)

D&C 133: 3 the Lord shall make b. his arm in eyes of all nations.

BARLEY (see also Grain)

D&C 89: 17 b. for all useful animals.

BASSET, HEMAN

D&C 52: 37 because of transgression, loses what had been given to him.

BATHE (see Tears)

BATTLE (see also Army; Fight; Slaughter; War; TG God to Fight Our Battles)

D&C 45: 70 the wicked to say, Let us not go to b. against Zion; 88: 112–115 devil and his armies shall b. against Michael and his army; 98: 33 saints should not go to b. with any nation unless the Lord commands it; 98: 37 the Lord to fight b. of those who bring complaints before him; 105: 14 the Lord to fight Zion's b.

BEAR, BORE, BORNE (see also Born; Burden; Endure; Record; Tolerable)

D&C 38: 42 (133: 5) those that b. vessels of Lord to be clean; 42: 52 infirmities b. by those who believe; 50: 40 (78: 18) elders cannot b. all things yet; 76: 41 Jesus to b. sins of world; 76: 118 men can b. God's presence only through manifestation of spirit; 98: 23 those who b. persecution patiently will be rewarded; 124: 18 the Lord will b. servant up on eagles' wings; 136: 31 he who will not b. chastisement is not worthy.

Abr. 2: 9 Abraham's seed to b. ministry and priesthood.

BEAST (see also Animal)

D&C 49: 19 (89: 12) b. given for use of man; 77: 2–3 (Rev. 4: 6) four b. used by John in describing heaven represent glory of classes of beings; 77: 4 represent light and knowledge; 77: 4 wings of b. represent power; 89: 14, 17 grains ordained for use of man and b.; 101: 26 enmity of b. to cease at the Lord's coming.

Moses 2: 24 (3: 19; Abr. 4: 24–25) creation of b.

BEAUTY, BEAUTIFUL (see also Fair)

D&C 42: 40 let b. of garments be work of own hands; 82: 14 Zion must increase in b.; 128: 19 how b. upon mountains are feet of those that bring glad tidings; 137: 2 transcendent b. of gates of celestial kingdom.

BEDSTEAD

Abr. 1: 13 idolatrous altar is made after form of b.

BEGIN (see Beginning)

BEGINNING (see also Creation; End)

D&C 8: 12 the Lord spoke from b.; 19: 1 (35: 1; 38: 1; 45: 7; 49: 12; 54: 1; 61: 1; 84: 120; 95: 7) Christ is the b. and the end; 22: 1 covenant was from b.; 29: 32 all things created first spiritual, second temporal, which is b. of the Lord's work; 29: 33 the Lord's works have no end, neither b.; 29: 38 hell prepared from b.; 76: 13 Son was with Father from b.; 78: 16 Holy One without b. of days or end of life; 84: 17 priesthood without b. of days or end of years; 87: 1–2 b. of wars at rebellion of South Carolina; 93: 7, 21 Christ was in the b.; 93: 8 (John 1: 1) in b. was the Word; 93: 23, 29 man was in b. with God; 93: 38 spirit of man was innocent in b.; 112: 31 Twelve hold power in connection with all who have received a dispensation since b.; 119: 3 b. of tithing of the Lord's people; 132: 38 the Lord's servants from b. received many wives and concubines; 138: 55 noble and great spirits chosen in b. to be rulers.

Moses 1: 3 (6: 67) the Lord is without b. of days or end of years; 2: 1 the Lord is the B. and the End; 2: 1 (Abr. 4: 1) in b. the Lord created heaven and earth; 2: 26 Only Begotten was with God from b.; 4: 1 Satan was from b.; 5: 58 gospel was preached from b.; 6: 7 priesthood was in b.; 8: 16 Noah[1] taught things of God, as it was in b.; **Abr.** 1: 3 priesthood came down from fathers from b. of time; 1: 31 Abraham keeps knowledge of b. of creation; 2: 8 Jehovah knows end from b.; 3: 18 spirits have no b.; 3: 21 the

Lord came down in b. in midst of all intelligences; 4: 5 b. of day and night.

BEGOTTEN (see also Born of God; Children of God; Jesus Christ—Only Begotten Son; Son)

D&C 76: 24 inhabitants of the world are b. sons and daughters of God; 93: 22 those who are b. through the Lord are of church of the Firstborn.

BEGUILE (see also Deceit; Lying)

Moses 4: 6 Satan sought to b. Eve.

BEHOLD, BEHELD (see also Look; See; Sin)

D&C 5: 13 witnesses to be given power to b. plates; 6: 37 b. wounds which pierced the Lord's side; 45: 4 Father b. death of him who did no sin; 76: 20 Joseph Smith and Sidney Rigdon b. glory of the Son; 76: 28 we b. Satan; 84: 23 those who are sanctified might b. face of God; 88: 52 those who labor in the field will b. joy of the Lord's countenance; 93: 11 John b. glory of the Lord; 121: 2 how long shall the Lord b. from heaven the wrongs of his people; 136: 37 the faithful will b. the Lord's glory.

Moses 1: 5 no man can b. the Lord's glory and remain in flesh; 1: 11 Moses' spiritual eyes b. God; 7: 59 Enoch[2] b. the Son ascend to the Father.

BELIEF, BELIEVE, BELIEVING (see also Believer; Doubt; Faith; Opinion; Religion; Unbelief; TG Belief)

D&C 3: 20 plates were preserved that Lamanites may b.; 5: 7 if men will not b. the Lord's words, they will not b. Joseph Smith; 5: 16 whosoever b. on the Lord's words will be given manifestation of Spirit; 8: 1 (11: 10, 14; 14: 8) ask in faith, b. that you will receive; 10: 50 whosoever b. in gospel in this life will have eternal life; 11: 30 (34: 3; 35: 2; 45: 5; 49: 12) those who b. on the Lord's name become sons of God; 14: 8 those who ask in faith, b., shall receive Holy Ghost; 20: 25–26 (68: 9) b. leads to salvation; 20: 29 all men must repent and b. on name of Jesus Christ; 29: 43 those who b. are raised in immortality unto eternal life; 29: 44 those who do not b. are raised to eternal damnation; 35: 8 the Lord will show wonders to those who b.; 38: 4 the Lord pleads before the Father for those who b.; 42: 52 those without faith to heal, but who b. in the Lord, will become sons; 45: 8 (76: 52) to them that b., the Lord gave power to obtain eternal life; 46: 14 spiritual gift of b. in others' words; 49: 12 b. on name of Jesus; 58: 64 (68: 10;

84: 65) signs follow those who b.; 67: 3 elders endeavor to b. that they should receive blessing; 68: 9 (84: 74; 112: 29) he who b. and is baptized shall be saved; 90: 24 pray always and be b.; 109: 67 scattered remnants of Israel to b. in Messiah; 133: 71 men b. not the Lord's servants; 134: 7 governments are bound to protect free exercise of religious b.

Moses 1: 42 (4: 32) words spoken to Moses on mount should be shown only to those who b.; 5: 13 Satan commands men to b. not; 6: 52 those who b., repent, and are baptized shall receive Holy Ghost; 7: 1 many have believed things taught by Adam.

BELIEVER (*see also* Saint)

D&C 74: 5 b. should not be united to unbeliever.

BELLY

D&C 89: 7–9 strong drinks not for the b.

BELOVED (*see* Jesus Christ—Son of God; John the Beloved)

BENEFIT (*see also* Blessing; Gain; Profit)

D&C 46: 9 best gifts are given for b. of those who love and obey the Lord; 59: 18 all things that come from earth are made for b. of man; 70: 8 b. from revelations and commandments to be consecrated unto inhabitants of Zion; 91: 5 whoso is enlightened by Spirit shall obtain b.; 134: 1 governments instituted of God for b. of man.

BENNETT, JOHN C.

D&C 124: 16–17 to help in sending out the Lord's word.

BENSON, EZRA T.

D&C 136: 12 to organize company for journey west.

BENT, SAMUEL

D&C 124: 132 a member of high council.

BETHEL (*see also* BD Bethel)

Abr. 2: 20 Abraham goes east of B.

BETTER (*see also* Good)

D&C 54: 5 b. for him that he had been drowned; 76: 32 b. for sons of perdition never to have been born; 121: 22 b. that millstone had been hanged about neck.

BEWARE

D&C 23: 1 (25: 14; 38: 39) b. of pride;

46: 8 b. lest ye be deceived; 63: 61 let all men b. how they take the Lord's name.

BIBLE (*see also* New Testament; Old Testament; Scriptures; BD Bible)

D&C 42: 12 elders to teach principles of gospel in B. and Book of Mormon.

A of F 8 we believe B. to be word of God.

BILLINGS, TITUS

D&C 63: 39 to dispose of land.

BIND, BOUND (*see also* Band; Bondage; Priesthood; Seal)

D&C 35: 24 (104: 5) keep all commandments by which ye are b.; 43: 9 b. yourselves to act in all holiness; 43: 31 (45: 55; 84: 100; 88: 110) Satan to be b. during Millennium; 82: 10 I, the Lord, am b. when ye do what I say; 82: 11, 15 the Lord's servants are b. together by covenant; 86: 7 (88: 94) after gathering of wheat, tares to be b. in bundles; 88: 84 (133: 72) elders to b. up law; 109: 46 enable thy servants to b. up testimony; 124: 93 (127: 7; 128: 8; 132: 46) what the Lord's servants b. on earth shall be b. in heaven; 128: 14 binding power explained; 134: 4 human law has no right to b. men's consciences; 134: 5 men are b. to sustain their governments; 134: 7 rulers are b. to enact laws to protect citizens' exercise of beliefs; 138: 31, 42 Redeemer and chosen messengers proclaim liberty to captive spirits who were b.; 138: 42 Redeemer anointed to b. up the broken-hearted.

BIRTH (*see* Bear, Bore, Borne; Born)

BIRTHRIGHT (*see* Heir; Inherit, Inheritance; Lineage; BD Birthright)

BISHOP (*see also* Bishopric; Judge [noun]; Judge [verb]; Pastor; Priesthood, Aaronic; BD Bishop)

D&C 20: 66 traveling b. have privilege of ordaining where there is no branch; 20: 67 b. to be ordained by direction of high council or general conference; 41: 9 Edward Partridge to be ordained a b.; 42: 31 (51: 5) properties consecrated for support of poor are given to b.; 42: 34 (51: 13) to administer storehouse; 42: 73 (51: 14) b. to receive support or just remuneration for service; 42: 82 b. to be present at church courts; 46: 27, 29 b. is responsible for discerning spiritual gifts; 48: 6 families to be gathered to new city as appointed by presidency and b.; 58: 17 b. is responsible for dividing lands among saints; 58: 17 (64: 40) b. to be judge in Israel; 64: 40 (68: 23) if unfaithful in stewardship, b. will be condemned;

68: 14 (72: 2; 107: 75) other *b.* to be set apart; 68: 15, 19 (107: 17, 69–76) worthy high priests may be appointed *b.*; 68: 15–21 (107: 16, 69, 76) literal descendants of Aaron[1] have legal right to office of *b.*; 68: 20 descendants of Aaron[1] must be ordained to office of *b.*; 68: 22–24 *b.* to be tried only before Presidency; 70: 11 *b.* not exempt from law of stewardship; 72: 5 (72: 16) elders to render account of their stewardship unto *b.*; 72: 7 duty of *b.* to be made known by commandments; 72: 8 Newel K. Whitney called to be a *b.*; 72: 10–16 (107: 73–76) duties of *b.*; 84: 29 office of *b.* a necessary appendage to High Priesthood; 84: 112 *b.* to care for the poor; 107: 17 *b.* must be ordained by Presidency; 107: 68 *b.* administers all temporal things; 107: 76 descendant of Aaron[1] may act in office of *b.* without counselors; 107: 87–88 (68: 16–17) president of Aaronic Priesthood is to be *b.*; 120: 1 *b.* is to aid in disposition of tithing.

BISHOPRIC (*see also* Bishop; Counselor)

D&C 42: 31, 71 two elders or high priests to be appointed counselors; 42: 71–72 counselors to be supported out of storehouse or remuneration; 58: 18 (107: 72) counselors to assist bishop according to laws of kingdom; 64: 40 if unfaithful in stewardship, *b.* will be condemned; 68: 15–21 (107: 16) literal descendants of Aaron[1] have legal right to *b.*; 107: 15 *b.* is presidency of Aaronic Priesthood; 124: 141 knowledge of *b.* given in Doctrine and Covenants.

BITTER, BITTERNESS (*see also* Experience)

D&C 19: 18 Christ would that he might not drink *b.* cup; 29: 39 if men never had *b.*, they could not know the sweet; 42: 47 *b.* death of those who die not in the Lord.

Moses 1: 20 Moses saw *b.* of hell; 6: 55 men taste *b.* that they may know to prize the good; 7: 44 Enoch[2] has *b.* of soul because of destruction of the wicked.

BLACK, BLACKNESS (*see also* Darkness, Physical)

D&C 122: 7 if the heavens gather *b.*, these things shall give experience; 133: 69 the Lord to clothe heavens with *b.*

Moses 7: 8 *b.* came upon children of Canaan; 7: 22 seed of Cain were *b.*

BLAMELESS (*see also* Guiltless; Innocent; Spotless)

D&C 4: 2 those who serve God with all mind and strength stand *b.*; 38: 31 the

Lord's revelation to help people gather without spot and *b.*

BLASPHEMY, BLASPHEME (*see also* TG Blaspheme; BD Blasphemy)

D&C 105: 15 the Lord's enemies not to be left to *b.* his name; 112: 25–26 desolation upon those who *b.* against the Lord in midst of his house; 132: 26 if those sealed by Holy Spirit of promise commit *b.*; 132: 27 *b.* against Holy Ghost.

BLEED (*see also* Blood)

D&C 19: 18 suffering caused Savior to *b.* at every pore.

BLESSED [adj.] (*see also* Blessing; Happiness; BD Beatitudes)

D&C 6: 31 (84: 60) *b.* are they who reject not the Lord's words; 15: 5 (16: 5) *b.* are you for speaking the Lord's words; 34: 4 *b.* are you because you have believed; 34: 5 more *b.* are you because you are called to preach gospel; 50: 5 *b.* are they who are faithful and endure; 50: 36 *b.* are you, for your sins are forgiven; 56: 18 *b.* are the poor who are pure in heart; 59: 1 *b.* are they who come unto land with eye single to the Lord's glory; 63: 49 *b.* are the dead that die in the Lord; 63: 50 *b.* is he who has kept the faith when the Lord comes; 66: 2 (84: 60) *b.* are you for receiving everlasting covenant of gospel; 97: 1–2 *b.* are they who seek wisdom and truth, for they shall obtain.

Moses 1: 15 (5: 10) *b.* be the name of my God; 7: 53 *b.* is he through whose seed Messiah shall come; JS-M 1: 1 *b.* is he who comes in the name of the Lord.

BLESSING, BLESS (*see also* Administration to the Sick; Benefit; Blessed [adj.]; Obedience; Ordinance; Patriarch; Privilege; Reward)

D&C 1: 28 the humble shall be *b.* from on high; 6: 9 (11: 9; 14: 11) assist to bring forth the Lord's work and you shall be *b.*; 6: 10 art thou *b.* because of thy gift; 10: 50 Nephite prophets left *b.* upon land; 18: 8 the diligent to be *b.* unto eternal life; 18: 45 *b.* of the Lord are above all things; 19: 38 pray always, and great shall be your *b.*; 20: 70 elders to *b.* children; 20: 76–79 *b.* of sacrament; 21: 9 the Lord will *b.* all who labor in vineyard; 24: 4, 6, 15 (41: 1) the Lord will send curses instead of *b.* upon those who reject his servants; 38: 14 saints are not *b.* because of iniquity or unbelief; 41: 1 the Lord gives greatest *b.* to those who hear him; 58: 4 (103: 12) after much tribulation come *b.*; 58: 32 *b.* revoked for disobedience; 59: 3 those in Zion who obey gospel will be crowned with *b.* from above; 61:

14 in beginning, the Lord *b.* the waters;
61: 37 those who humble themselves
receive *b.* of kingdom; 62: 3 men are *b.*
for testimony they have borne; 67: 3 *b.*
withheld because of fears; 75: 19 elders to
leave *b.* on whatever house receives them;
78: 17 saints understand not how great *b.*
the Father has prepared; 104: 2, 46 (124:
90) the faithful to be *b.* with multiplicity
of *b.*; 104: 13 the Lord makes men
stewards over earthly *b.*; 105: 12 the Lord
has prepared a great endowment, and *b.*
will be poured out; 110: 10 beginning
of *b.* to be poured out upon the Lord's
people; 110: 12 in saints their seed
all generations will be *b.*; 124: 124
patriarch holds the sealing *b.*; 130: 20,
21 all *b.* are predicated upon obedience to
laws; 132: 47 the Lord will *b.* those whom
elders *b.*; 133: 34 richer *b.* upon Ephraim;
138: 52 prophets to be partakers of all *b.*
held in reserve for them who love the Lord.

Moses 3: 3 God *b.* the seventh day;
5: 10–12 Adam and Eve *b.* God; 6: 4 men
began to call upon the Lord, and he *b.*
them; 6: 9 (Abr. 4: 22, 28) God created
male and female and *b.* them; 7: 17 the
Lord *b.* the land; **Abr.** 1: 2 Abraham
seeks for *b.* of fathers; 1: 26 Noah [1] *b.* man
with *b.* of earth and of wisdom; 2: 9 the
Lord will *b.* Abraham above measure;
2: 9–10 Abraham's seed to be *b.* through
him; 2: 10 those who receive gospel will
b. Abraham as their father; 2: 11 I will *b.*
them that *b.* thee; 2: 11 in Abraham's
seed shall all families of earth be *b.* with
b. of gospel.

BLINDNESS, BLIND (see also Darkness, Spiritual; Ignorance; BD Blindness)

D&C 35: 9 (84: 69) they who ask in
faith shall cause the *b.* to receive sight;
58: 15 sins of unbelief and *b.* of heart;
76: 75 (123: 12) terrestrial glory includes
honorable men *b.* by craftiness of men;
78: 10 Satan seeks to turn hearts from
truth, that men become *b.*; 84: 69 in Lord's
name believers to open eyes of *b.*

Moses 4: 4 Satan deceives and *b.*
men.

BLOOD (see also Blood, Shedding of; Jesus Christ, Atonement through; Sacrament; Sacrifice; TG Blood; Blood, Eating of; Blood, Shedding of; Blood, Symbolism of; BD Blood)

D&C 20: 40, 79 (27: 2) sacrament
wine is emblem of Christ's *b.*; 27: 2 the
Lord's *b.* shed for remission of sins; 29: 14
(34: 9; 45: 42; 88: 87) moon to turn to *b.*;
29: 17 the Lord's *b.* shall not cleanse
wicked who hear not; 38: 4 by virtue of
spilt *b.*, the Lord pleads before the Father

for believers; 45: 41 *b.* and fire at the
Lord's coming; 76: 69 Jesus wrought
perfect atonement through shedding *b.*;
87: 7 (109: 9; 136: 36) *b.* of saints cries to
the Lord to be avenged; 88: 75, 85, 138
clean from *b.* of this wicked generation;
109: 49 how long will the Lord suffer
saints' *b.* to come up in testimony before
him; 133: 51 the Lord has sprinkled the
people's *b.* upon his garments; 135: 3
(136: 39) Joseph Smith sealed mission
with own *b.*

Moses 5: 35 voice of Abel's *b.* cries
to the Lord; 6: 59 men born into world
by water, *b.*, spirit; 6: 59 men must be
cleansed by *b.* of Only Begotten; 6: 60 by
b. ye are sanctified; 6: 62 plan of salvation
unto all men through *b.* of Only Begotten;
7: 33 men hate their own *b.*; 7: 45 when
shall *b.* of the Righteous be shed; **Abr.** 1:
20 Pharaoh signifies king by royal *b.*; 1:
21 king of Egypt was partaker of *b.* of
Canaanites by birth.

BLOOD, SHEDDING OF (see also Blood; Kill; Martyrdom; Murder; Sacrifice; War; TG Blood, Shedding of)

D&C 20: 79 wine in remembrance of
b. which Christ shed for men; 27: 2 the
Lord's *b.* was shed for remission of sin;
49: 21 wo to man who sheds *b.* or wastes
flesh without need; 58: 52–53 (63: 30–31)
inheritances to be obtained by purchase
and not by shedding of *b.*; 63: 28 shedding
of *b.* prompted by Satan; 76: 69 Jesus
wrought perfect atonement through shedding of *b.*; 87: 6 by bloodshed, inhabitants
of earth shall mourn; 88: 94 church that
sheds *b.* of saints is cause of earth; 101: 80
land redeemed by shedding of *b.*; 130: 12
bloodshed to begin in South Carolina;
132: 19 those who enter covenant and
do not shed innocent *b.* will be exalted;
132: 27 blasphemy against Holy Ghost is
shedding of innocent *b.* and assenting to
Christ's death.

Moses 6: 15 (7: 16) Satan rages in
men's hearts and bloodshed comes; 7: 45
when shall *b.* of the Righteous be shed.

BLOSSOM (see also Flourish)

D&C 49: 24 Lamanites to *b.* as rose;
117: 7 solitary places to bud and to *b.*

BLOT (see also Cast; Cut; Excommunication)

D&C 20: 83 names of excommunicated to be *b.* out of record.

BOAST (see also TG Boast, Boasting)

D&C 3: 4, 13 men who *b.* in own
strength must fall; 50: 33 *b.* not in proclaiming evil spirit lest you be seized;

84: 73 believers not to *b.* themselves; 105: 24 *b.* not of faith nor of mighty works.

BODY, BODIES (*see also* Death, Physical; Flesh; Resurrection; Soul; Tabernacle; TG Body; Body, Sanctity of; Spirit Body)

D&C 19: 18 Christ suffered both *b.* and spirit; 20: 40, 77 (27: 2) sacrament bread to be eaten in remembrance of Savior's *b.*; 45: 17 (138: 50) absence of spirits from *b.* viewed as bondage; 59: 19 things of earth given to strengthen *b.*; 76: 70 celestial *b.* have glory of sun; 76: 78 glory of terrestrial *b.* compared to moon; 84: 33 those who magnify callings are sanctified unto renewing of *b.*; 84: 109 *b.* has need of every member; 88: 15 spirit and *b.* are soul of man; 88: 27 the righteous shall rise again a spiritual *b.*; 88: 28 celestial spirit shall receive natural *b.*; 88: 67 if eye single to God's glory, *b.* shall be filled with light; 89: 7 strong drinks for washing of *b.*; 89: 8 tobacco not for *b.*; 89: 9 hot drinks not for *b.*; 101: 37 care not for the *b.*, neither the life of the *b.*; 129: 1 angels are resurrected beings with *b.* of flesh and bones; 130: 22 Father and Son have *b.* of flesh and bones; 130: 22 Holy Ghost has not a *b.* of flesh, but of Spirit; 131: 8 when our *b.* are purified, we shall see that spirit is matter; 137: 1 Joseph Smith knew not whether he saw vision in *b.*; 138: 17 spirit and *b.* to be reunited, never again to be divided.

Moses 6: 9 God created male and female in image of his own *b.*; **Abr.** 2: 11 right of priesthood to continue in seed of Abraham's *b.*

BOGGS, LILBURN B.—*Governor of Missouri*

D&C 124: Intro. had issued exterminating order.

BOND (*see also* Bondage)

D&C 24: 11 in the Lord, man to have glory, whether in *b.* or free; 43: 20 call upon nations to repent, both *b.* and free; 78: 5 saints to be equal in *b.* of heavenly things and earthly things; 78: 11 (82: 11) organize yourselves by a *b.* of everlasting covenant; 88: 125 clothe yourselves with the *b.* of charity; 88: 133 be friend and brother in *b.* of love; 132: 7 all *b.* entered into without being sealed by Holy Spirit of promise are of no force after resurrection.

BONDAGE (*see also* Blindness; Bond; Liberty; Slavery; Yoke; TG Bondage, Physical; Bondage, Spiritual)

D&C 19: 35 pay the debt, release

thyself from *b.*; 45: 17 (138: 50) men look upon absence of spirits from bodies as *b.*; 84: 49 whole world lies under *b.* of sin; 101: 79 not right that any man should be in *b.*; 103: 17 Israel to be led out of *b.*; 104: 83–84 church to be delivered from *b.*; 123: 8 they are the chains, shackles, and fetters of hell; 138: 57 elders preach among spirits under *b.* of sin.

BONE (*see also* Body)

D&C 29: 19 flesh of wicked shall fall from *b.*; 85: 6 still small voice makes *b.* quake; 89: 18 saints who keep Word of Wisdom shall receive marrow to their *b.*; 129: 1 angels are resurrected personages, having bodies of flesh and *b.*; 130: 22 Father and Son have bodies of flesh and *b.*; 138: 17 sleeping dust of dead to be restored to perfect frame, *b.* to *b.*; 138: 43 (Ezek. 37: 1–14) Ezekiel shown valley of dry *b.*

Moses 3: 23 (Abr. 5: 17) this is *b.* of my *b.*

BOOK (*see also* Bible; Book of Commandments; Book of Lehi; Book of Mormon; Plates; Record; Scriptures; Write; TG Book; Book of Life; Book of Remembrance; BD Book of Life)

D&C 20: 82 names of whole church to be kept in *b.*; 77: 6 (Rev. 5: 1) explanation of *b.* sealed with seven seals; 77: 14 (Rev. 10: 2, 8–10) explanation of little *b.* eaten by John; 85: 5, 11 names of those who apostatize shall not be found in *b.* of law of God; 85: 7 saints whose names are found in *b.* of law shall receive inheritance; 85: 9 they who are not written in *b.* of remembrance shall find no inheritance; 88: 2 alms of your prayers are recorded in *b.* of the names of the sanctified; 88: 118 (90: 15; 109: 7–14) seek ye out of the best *b.*; 107: 57 *b.* of Enoch²; 128: 7 *b.* of life is the record kept in heaven; 128: 8 dead to be judged out of *b.*; 128: 24 saints to present in temple a *b.* containing records of their dead; 132: 19 Lamb's *B.* of Life; 135: 3 Joseph Smith brought forth revelations composing this *b.* of Doctrine and Covenants.

Moses 6: 5 *b.* of remembrance kept in language of Adam; 6: 8 Adam keeps *b.* of generations; 6: 46 *b.* of remembrance written according to pattern given.

BOOK OF COMMANDMENTS (*see also* Book; Doctrine and Covenants)

D&C 1: 6 Lord's preface to *b.* of his commandments; 67: Intro. W. W. Phelps to publish *B.* of *C.*; 67: 4 the Lord testifies to truth of *B.* of *C.*; 67: 7 the Lord counsels to study *B.* of *C.*; 69: Intro.

Oliver Cowdery to take manuscript of *B. of C.* to Missouri; sec. 70 importance of *B. of C.*

BOOK OF LEHI (*see also* Book; Book of Mormon; Manuscript, Lost)

    D&C 3: Intro. comprised lost 116 pages of Book of Mormon manuscript; 10: Intro., 10–12 alterations made in translation of *B. of L.*

BOOK OF MORMON (*see also* Book; Book of Lehi; Manuscript, Lost; Plates; Scriptures; Smith, Joseph, Jr.; Translation; Urim and Thummim; Witnesses, Three; TG Book of Mormon; BD Ephraim, Stick of)

    D&C 1: 29 (17: 6; 20: 8; 135: 3) Joseph Smith to translate *B. of M.* by power of God; **3:** Intro. (10: 1) Martin Harris loses 116 pages of translation; **5:** 19–20 plates preserved that Lamanites might be brought to knowledge of fathers; **5:** 3 Joseph Smith not to show plates unless commanded; **5:** 4 (20: 8) Joseph Smith given gift to translate plates; **6:** Intro. Oliver Cowdery has testimony of *B. of M.;* **8:** Intro. Oliver Cowdery desires gift of translating *B. of M.;* sec. 10 revelation regarding loss of manuscript; **10:** 1 *B. of M.* translated by means of Urim and Thummim; **10:** 38–40 account of lost translation is engraven on plates of Nephi; **10:** 41–42 translation of plates of Nephi to be substituted for lost pages; **10:** 45–46 many things on plates of Nephi and remainder of plates throw greater views upon gospel; sec. 17 revelation to Three Witnesses regarding *B. of M.;* **17:** 6 the Lord testifies that *B. of M.* is true; **19:** 26 impart freely of property to printing of *B. of M.;* **19:** 26–27 contains truth and word of God; **20:** 8–12 (27: 5; 42: 12) contains fulness of gospel; **20:** 9 is record of fallen people; **20:** 10 is given by inspiration and confirmed to others by ministering of angels; **20:** 14 those who accept *B. of M.* receive crown of eternal life; **20:** 15 those who reject *B. of M.* will be condemned; **24:** 1 Joseph Smith called and chosen to write *B. of M.;* **27:** 5 Moroni² sent to reveal *B. of M.;* **33:** 16 given for instruction; **42:** 12 elders to teach from *B. of M.;* **84:** 57 Zion condemned until they remember new covenant, even *B. of M.;* **128:** 20 Moroni² declares the *B. of M.*

    Moses 7: 62 God will send righteousness out of earth to bear testimony of Only Begotten; **JS-H:** 1: 29–54, 59–60 Joseph Smith obtains plates; 1: 67 Joseph Smith begins to translate *B. of M.;* **A of F** 8 we believe *B. of M.* to be word of God.

BOOTH, EZRA

    D&C 52: 23 to take journey, preaching all the way; **64:** 15–16 the Lord's anger toward *E.B.;* **71:** Intro. apostates published anti-Church newspaper articles.

BORDERS (*see also* Boundaries)

    D&C 82: 14 (107: 74; 133: 9) Zion's *b.* must be enlarged.

BORN (*see also* Bear, Bore, Borne; Born of God; Firstborn; Jesus Christ, First Coming of)

    D&C 76: 32 better for sons of perdition never to have been *b.;* **138:** 56 noble spirits received first lessons before they were *b.*

BORN OF GOD (*see also* Baptism; Convert; Fire; Holy Ghost; Spirit, Holy/Spirit of the Lord; TG Man, New, Spiritually Reborn)

    D&C 5: 16 those who believe will be *b.* of water and Spirit.

    Moses 6: 59 man must be *b.* again; **6:** 65 Adam is *b.* of Spirit.

BORNE (*see* Bear, Bore, Borne)

BORROW

    D&C 136: 25 return that which thou hast *b.*

BOSOM

    D&C 9: 8 if it is right, the Lord will cause *b.* to burn; **38:** 4 the Lord took Zion of Enoch² into his *b.;* **88:** 13 God is in the *b.* of eternity; **109:** 4 (76: 13, 25, 39) Jesus Christ, Son of the Father's *b.*

    Moses 7: 24, 47, 69 Enoch² is in *b.* of the Father; **7:** 63 city of Enoch² to be received into the Lord's *b.*

BOSTON (*see also* D&C map, p. 295)

    D&C 84: 114 people of *B.* to be warned.

BOUGHT (*see* Buy, Bought)

BOUND (*see* Bind, Bound; Bounds)

BOUNDARIES (*see also* Borders)

    D&C 133: 31 *b.* of everlasting hills to tremble.

BOUNDS

    D&C 88: 38 unto every law there are certain *b.;* **122:** 9 *b.* of enemies set.

BOW [noun] (*see also* Urim and Thummim)

    JS-H 1: 35 two stones in silver *b.* are called Urim and Thummim.

BOW [verb]

D&C 5: 24 if Martin Harris *b.* before the Lord, he will see plates; 49: 10 nations of earth to *b.*; 76: 93 all things in humble reverence before God's throne; 76: 110 (88: 104) every knee to *b.*; 123: 7 wives and children *b.* down with grief; 138: 23 saints *b.* knee and acknowledge the Son.

BOWELS (see also Mercy)

D&C 84: 101 truth established in earth's *b.*; 101: 9 (121: 3) the Lord's *b.* are filled with compassion; 121: 45 let thy *b.* be full of charity.

BRANCH (see also Israel; TG Branch; Jesus Christ, Davidic Descent of; Vineyard of the Lord)

D&C 10: 60 (John 10: 16) other sheep were *b.* of house of Jacob; 20: 65 where there is *b.* of church, no person to be ordained without voice of church; 107: 74 bishop is common judge in any *b.* of church where he is set apart; 109: 52 many saints' enemies be wasted, both root and *b.*; 133: 64 day of the Lord will burn the wicked, leaving neither root nor *b.*

BRASS

D&C 124: 27 come with all your *b.* and precious things to build a house to my name.

Moses 5: 46 Tubal Cain an instructor of every artificer in *b.*

BREAD (see also Sacrament; TG Bread; Bread of Life)

D&C 20: 40, 46, 77 *b.* is emblem of Christ's flesh; 20: 75 church should meet often to partake of *b.* and wine; 20: 76–77 manner of administering sacrament *b.*; 42: 42 the idle not to eat *b.* of laborer; 88: 140–41 washing of feet includes partaking of *b.* and wine.

Moses 4: 25 (5: 1) Adam to eat *b.* by sweat of face.

BREAK, BROKEN (see also Broken Heart and Contrite Spirit)

D&C 1: 15 (3: 13; 40: 3; 54: 4; 104: 4, 52, 55) they have *b.* the everlasting covenant; 1: 19 the weak to be *b.* down; 42: 30 property to be consecrated with covenant and deed that cannot be *b.*; 58: 21 let no man *b.* laws of land; 78: 11 (82: 11) organize yourselves with covenant that cannot be *b.*; 84: 40 Father cannot *b.* oath and covenant of priesthood; 88: 35 *b.* law cannot be sanctified; 101: 57 *b.* down walls of the Lord's enemies; 104: 5 those who *b.* covenant will be cursed; 104: 86 master will not suffer house to be *b.* up; 109: 33, 47 *b.* yoke off neck of the Lord's servants; 109:

63 yoke of bondage to be *b.* off house of David; 109: 70 prejudices to be *b.* up; 132: 43–44 vow is *b.* through adultery; 133: 22 the Lord's voice to *b.* down mountains.

BREASTPLATE (see also Urim and Thummim; BD Breastplate)

D&C 17: 1 view of *b.* promised to Three Witnesses; 27: 16 have on the *b.* of righteousness.

JS-H 1: 35 two stones fastened to *b.* constitute Urim and Thummim; 1: 35 *b.* is deposited with ancient records; 1: 52 Joseph Smith's first view of *b.*

BREATH (see also TG Breath of Life)

Moses 3: 7, 19 (Abr. 5: 7) the Lord breathes *b.* of life into Adam, beasts.

BRETHREN (see Brother)

BRIDE (see also Bridegroom; TG Bride; BD Bride, Bridegroom)

D&C 109: 74 church to be adorned as *b.* for the Lord's coming.

BRIDEGROOM (see also Bride; TG Bridegroom; BD Bride, Bridegroom)

D&C 33: 17 (65: 3; 133: 19) ready at coming of the *B.*; 65: 3 make ready for the *B.*; 88: 92 (133: 10) the *B.* comes.

BRIGHTNESS, BRIGHTER (see also Light)

D&C 5: 19 inhabitants of earth destroyed by *b.* of the Lord's coming; 50: 24 light groweth *b.* and *b.* until perfect day; 65: 5 the Son to come clothed in *b.* of his glory; 110: 3 the Lord's countenance shines above *b.* of sun.

JS-H 1: 16–17 *b.* of Father and Son is above that of sun.

BRIMSTONE (see Lake; BD Brimstone)

BRING

D&C 6: 6 seek to *b.* forth the cause of Zion; 18: 12 Christ has risen, that he might *b.* all men unto him; 58: 27 men should *b.* to pass much righteousness.

BROAD (see also Wide)

D&C 132: 25 *b.* is gate that leads to death.

Moses 7: 53 I am Messiah, the Rock of Heaven, which is *b.* as eternity.

BROKEN HEART AND CONTRITE SPIRIT (see also Humble; Sacrifice; TG Contrite Heart)

D&C 20: 37 (59: 8) those who come with *b.h.* and contrite spirit should be baptized; 56: 17 wo unto the poor whose hearts are not *b.* and spirits are not contrite; 56: 18 blessed are the poor whose hearts are b. and spirits are contrite; 59: 8 offer sacrifice of b.h. and contrite spirit; 97: 8 all whose hearts are b. and whose spirits are contrite are accepted of the Lord; 138: 42 (Isa. 61: 1) the Redeemer anointed to bind up the b-hearted.

BROTHER, BRETHREN (see also Jared[2], Brother of; TG Brethren; Brother; Brotherhood and Sisterhood)

D&C 4: 6 remember brotherly kindness; 38: 24–25 let every man esteem his b. as himself; 42: 88 if a b. offends, take him alone; 45: 5 Father, spare my b. who believe on my name; 88: 133 art thou a b. or brethren; 108: 7 strengthen your b.; 128: 22 b., shall we not go on in so great a cause; 136: 20 covet not that which is thy b's.

Moses 5: 34 am I my b's keeper.

BRUISE (see also Hurt; Wound)

D&C 89: 8 tobacco an herb for b. and all sick cattle.

BRUNSON, SEYMOUR

D&C 75: 33 to preach with Daniel Stanton; 124: 132 member of high council, has been taken by the Lord to himself.

BUCKLER

D&C 35: 14 the Lord to be shield and b. of the weak.

BUFFETING

D&C 78: 12 (82: 21; 104: 9–10; 132: 26) he who breaks covenant is delivered to b. of Satan.

BUILD, BUILT (see also Foundation; House; Rock; Synagogue)

D&C 10: 52, 54 gospel given to b., not to destroy; 63: 4 the Lord, at his pleasure, b. up; 101: 18 they that remain shall b. up waste places of Zion; 101: 101 they shall b. and another shall not inherit; 104: 14 the Lord b. the earth; 138: 53–54 choice spirits reserved for latter-day work, including b. temples.

BUILDING COMMITTEE

D&C 94: Intro. appointment of b.c.

BURDEN (see also Affliction; Oppression; Suffering)

D&C 109: 48 saints sorrow because of grievous b.; 112: 18 the Lord has laid b. of all the churches upon Presidency.

BURLINGTON, ILLINOIS

D&C 124: 88 gospel to be proclaimed to inhabitants of B.

BURN, BURNING (see also Destruction; Fire; Hell; Oven, Stubble; BD Burnt Offering)

D&C 9: 8 if it is right, bosom shall b.; 29: 9 (64: 24; 133: 64) the Lord will b. the proud; 31: 4 field is white already to be b.; 33: 17 have lamps trimmed and b. ready for Bridegroom; 38: 12 (86: 7; 101: 66) tares to be gathered that they may be b.; 64: 23 he who is tithed shall not be b.; 64: 24 after today comes the b.; 88: 94 great church is ready to be b.; 112: 24 day of b. to come speedily; 133: 41 presence of the Lord to be as melting fire that b.

BURNETT, STEPHEN

D&C 75: 35 to preach with Ruggles Eames; 80: 1 directed to preach gospel; 80: 2 given Eden Smith as companion.

BURROUGHS, PHILIP

D&C 30: 10 John Whitmer to proclaim gospel to P.B.

BURY (see also Grave; BD Burial)

D&C 60: 13 do not b. talent; 76: 51 baptize by being b. in water.

BUSH (see also BD Burning Bush)

Moses 1: 17 the Lord gave Moses commandments out of burning b.

BUSINESS (see also Gain)

D&C 20: 62 conferences to do necessary church b.; 107: 59 church laws respecting church b.; 107: 72 bishop to do b. of church.

BUTTERFIELD, JOSIAH

D&C 124: 138 one of seven presidents of seventies.

BUY, BOUGHT

D&C 48: 3 (57: 6; 101: 74) saints to b. land; 101: 55 redeem my vineyard, for I have b. it with money; 103: 22 Lord has b. Zion with money consecrated unto him.

CAESAR (see also BD Caesar)

D&C 63: 26 the Lord renders unto C. things that are C's.

CAHOON, REYNOLDS

D&C 52: 30 to journey to Missouri; 61: 35 to travel with Samuel Smith; 75: 32 to preach with Hyrum Smith; 94: 14 assigned a lot in Kirtland as inheritance.

CAIN—son of Adam (see also BD Cain)

D&C 124: 75 offerings of Vinson Knight shall not be as those of C.

Moses 5: 16 birth of C.; 5: 17 was tiller of ground; 5: 18 was commanded by Satan to make offering unto the Lord; 5: 18, 28 loves Satan more than God; 5: 19 makes offering unto the Lord; 5: 23 Satan desires to have C.; 5: 23 to rule over Satan; 5: 24 was before the world; 5: 24 to be called Perdition; 5: 24 to be father of lies; 5: 25 to receive great cursing unless he repents; 5: 28 takes one of his brothers' daughters to wife; 5: 29 is sworn to secrecy by Satan; 5: 31 is called Master Mahan; 5: 32 slays Abel; 5: 36 to be cursed from the earth; 5: 37, 39 to be fugitive and vagabond; 5: 39 is driven from face of the Lord; 5: 40 marked by the Lord; 5: 41 is shut out from presence of the Lord; 5: 42 begets many sons and daughters; 5: 42 builds a city, named after son, Enoch[1]; 5: 43 genealogy of descendants of C. to Lamech[1]; 7: 22 seed of C. have no place among sons of Adam.

CAINAN—*son of Enos*

D&C 107: 45 called upon by God, ordained by Adam; 107: 53 called to gathering of Adam's posterity at Adam-ondi-Ahman.

Moses 6: 17 Enos[1] calls promised land after his son C.

CALAMITY (*see also* Destruction)

D&C 1: 17 c. to come upon inhabitants; 45: 50 c. to cover the mocker.

CALEB

D&C 84: 7 gave priesthood to Jethro; 84: 8 received priesthood from Elihu.

CALF (*see also* BD Calves)

D&C 124: 84 Almon Babbitt sets up golden c. for worship.

CALL (*see also* Calling; Name; Ordain; Prayer, TG Called of God)

D&C 4: 3 if ye have desires to serve God, ye are c.; 6: 4 (11: 4; 12: 4; 14: 4) whosoever will thrust in his sickle is c.; 9: 14 stand fast in the work wherewith I have c. you; 11: 15 not suppose that you are c. to preach until you are c.; 18: 14 Oliver Cowdery and David Whitmer are c. with same calling as Paul, to c. repentance; 18: 24 all men to be c. by name of Jesus Christ at last day; 18: 26 Twelve are c. to declare gospel to Gentile and Jew; 29: 7 elders are c. to bring to pass gathering of elect; 43: 25 how oft have I c. you by mouth of my servants; 52: 1 elders are c. and chosen by voice of Spirit; 64: 25 labor while it is c. today; 65: 4 c. upon the Lord's holy name; 84: 77 (93: 45) the Lord c. elders his friends; 87: 3 southern states will c. on other nations;

88: 62 c. upon the Lord while he is near; 93: 1 those who repent and c. on the Lord's name will see his face; 95: 5 (105: 35; 121: 34, 40) many are c., but few are chosen; 136: 29 if sorrowful, c. on the Lord; 138: 25 the Savior spent three years c. Israel to repentance.

Moses 1: 17–18 Moses is commanded to c. upon God in name of Only Begotten; **Abr.** 2: 10 those who receive gospel shall be c. after Abraham's name; **A of F** 5 man must be c. of God by prophecy and laying on of hands by those in authority.

CALLING (*see also* Authority; Call; Office; TG Called of God; Calling)

D&C 18: 9 Oliver Cowdery and David Whitmer are called with same c. as Paul; 18: 32 declare gospel according to c.; 20: 27 those who believe in gifts and c. of God should be saved; 60: 60 every priesthood bearer ordained according to c. of God; 84: 33 those who magnify c. will be sanctified by Spirit; 84: 109 let every man labor in his own c.; 105: 35 day of c. to be followed by day of choosing; 112: 33 how great is your c.

CALM

D&C 135: 4 Joseph Smith is c. as summer's morning.

CAMP

D&C 61: 21 way given for saints of c. of the Lord to journey; sec. 136 revelation concerning c. of Israel.

CANAAN, CANAANITES (*see also* BD Canaan)

Moses 7: 7 prophecy of Enoch[2] concerning children of C.; 7: 8 children of C. become black; **Abr.** 1: 22 blood of C. perpetuated by Egyptians; 2: 15 Abraham takes family and followers to land of C.; 2: 19 land of C. promised to seed of Abraham.

CANKER

D&C 56: 16 riches c. souls.

CAPITAL PUNISHMENT (*see also* Blood, Shedding of; Murder; Punishment; TG Capital Punishment)

D&C 42: 19 he who kills shall die; 42: 79 those who kill will be delivered to law of land.

CAPTAIN (*see also* Officer)

D&C 136: 3, 7, 15 companies to be organized with c. of hundreds, fifties, and tens.

CARCASS

JS-M 1: 27 (Matt. 24: 28) where c. is, there will eagles be gathered.

CARE

D&C 39: 9 James Covill has rejected God because of c. of world; 63: 64 speak of sacred things with c.; 101: 37 c. not for the body, but c. for the soul.

CARMEL (see also BD Carmel)

D&C 128: 19 knowledge to descend as dews of C.

CARNAL (see also Devilish; Fall of Man; Lust; Sensual; TG Carnal Mind)

D&C 3: 4 c. desires lead to fall; 29: 35 commandments are spiritual, not c.; 67: 10 man cannot see God but with c. mind; 67: 12 c. mind cannot abide God's vengeance; 84: 27 preparatory gospel is law of c. commandments.

Moses 5: 13 (6: 49) men began to be c., sensual, devilish.

CARTER, GIDEON

D&C 75: 34 to preach with Sylvester Smith.

CARTER, JARED

D&C 52: 38 to be ordained a priest; 79: 1 to go to eastern countries; 94: Intro. appointed to building committee; 94: 1 assigned lot in Kirtland as inheritance; 102: 3 member of high council.

CARTER, JOHN S.

D&C 102: 3 member of high council.

CARTER, SIMEON

D&C 52: 27 to journey to Missouri preaching gospel; 75: 30 to preach with Emer Harris.

CARTER, WILLIAM

D&C 52: 31 to journey to Missouri.

CARTHAGE, ILLINOIS (see also D&C map, p. 297)

D&C 124: 88 gospel proclaimed in C.; 135: 1 Joseph and Hyrum Smith martyred at C.

CAST (see also Blot; Cut; Devils; Fire)

D&C 29: 41 Adam c. out of garden from the Lord's presence; 41: 5 members who do not keep law will be c. out; 20, 24, 28, 75 those who will not repent shall be c. out; 46: 3 none to be c. out of public meetings; 101: 9 the Lord will not utterly c. weak saints off.

Moses 4: 3 because Satan rebelled, God c. him down.

CATCH, CAUGHT

D&C 10: 13, 25-26 evil men try to c. Joseph Smith in discrepancies of trans-

lation; 88: 96 (101: 31; 109: 75) saints alive at the Lord's coming shall be quickened and c. up.

Moses 1: 1 Moses is c. up into mountain; 6: 64 Adam is c. up by Spirit; 7: 27 many c. up into Zion.

CATTLE (see also Animal, Beast)

D&C 89: 8 tobacco for sick c.

Moses 2: 24 (Abr. 4: 24) let earth bring forth c.; 3: 20 (Abr. 5: 21) Adam gives names to all c.; 5: 45 Jabal is father of keepers of c.

CAUSE (see also Reason)

D&C 6 (11: 6; 12: 6; 21: 7) seek to bring forth and establish c. of Zion; 45: 3 Christ pleads men's c. before the Father; 58: 27 men should be anxiously engaged in good c.; 124: 75, 89 plead the c. of poor and needy.

CEASE (see also Miracle; Stop; Strive)

D&C 88: 121 c. from all light speeches; 88: 124 c. to be idle, to be unclean, to find fault; 124: 116 c. to do evil.

Moses 1: 4 the Lord's works and words never c.

CELESTIAL GLORY (see also Telestial Glory; Terrestrial Glory)

D&C 76: 50–70 (137: 1) Joseph Smith sees vision of c. glory; 76: 51–53 c. heirs fulfilled first principles of gospel; 76: 53, 60 c. heirs overcome all things by faith; 76: 54, 67, 94 (88: 5) c. heirs are church of Firstborn; 76: 55, 59 c. heirs receive all things; 76: 56–57 c. heirs are priests after order of Melchizedek; 76: 58 c. heirs are gods and sons of God; 76: 62 c. heirs dwell in presence of God and Christ; 76: 64–65 c. heirs have part in first resurrection, resurrection of the just; 76: 69 c. heirs are just men made perfect through Christ's atonement; 76: 70 c. heirs have c. bodies; 76: 70, 96 c. glory compared with glory of sun; 76: 87 the terrestrial receive of Christ's fulness through ministration of c.; 76: 92 glory of c. excels all things; 78: 7 if saints desire place in c. world, they must prepare; 88: 2 the sanctified inherit c. world; 88: 3 c. world is c. kingdom; 88: 18 soul must be sanctified to be prepared for c. glory; 88: 20 c. bodies to possess the earth; 88: 22 those not able to abide law of c. kingdom cannot abide c. glory; 88: 25 earth abides c. law; 88: 28 c. spirits receive natural bodies; 101: 65 those given eternal life will be crowned with c. glory; 105: 4 c. union required by law; 105: 5 Zion built by law of c. kingdom; 130: 11 those who enter c. kingdom are given white stone with new name; 131: 1 in c. glory there are three heavens; 131: 2 conditions for attaining highest degree in c. kingdom; 132: 19 c. glory to be a fulness and continuation of seeds forever; 137: 6–8 those who would have accepted gospel shall inherit c. kingdom; 137: 10 children who die before age of accountability inherit c. kingdom.

CENTER
D&C 10: 56 the Lord will cause the wicked to shake to c.; 57: 3 Independence is the c. place.

CERTIFICATE
D&C 20: 64 priesthood bearer to take c. of ordination authorizing him to perform duties; 20: 84 c. to be furnished to removing members; 72: 17–18 c. from bishop renders man acceptable; 72: 25 members must bring c.; 128: 4 recorder to sign c. that record is true.

CHAFF
D&C 52: 12 Satan desires to sift him as c.

CHAIN (see also Band; Hell; TG Bondage, Spiritual)
D&C 38: 5 wicked kept in c. of darkness until judgment; 123: 8 they are c. of hell; 138: 18 dead spirits rejoice in deliverance from c.; 138: 23 saints acknowledge the Son as their Deliverer from c. of hell.
Moses 7: 26 Enoch² sees Satan with great c.; 7: 57 remainder of spirits are reserved in c. of darkness until judgment.

CHALDEA, CHALDEAN, CHALDAIC (see also BD Chaldea)
Abr. 1: 1 Abraham resides in land of C.; 1: 8, 13, 20 Pharaoh offers human sacrifices on altar in C.; 1: 23 Egyptus in the C. signifies Egypt, which signifies that which is forbidden; 1: 29–30 famine in C.; 2: 4 Abraham leaves land of C.; JS-H 1: 64 characters on plates resemble C.

CHANGE (see also Alter; Born of God; Convert; Repentance)
D&C 43: 32 (63: 51; 101: 31) the righteous to be c. in twinkling of eye; 121: 12 God to c. the times and seasons.

CHARACTERS (see also Language; Writing)
JS-H 1: 63–65 Martin Harris takes c. drawn from plates.

CHARGE
D&C 84: 42 (109: 22) the Lord gives angels c. concerning elders.

CHARIOT (see also BD Chariot)
Abr. 2: 7 wind and fire are c. of the Lord.

CHARITY (see also Alms; Compassion; Impart; Love; TG Charity; BD Charity)
D&C 4: 5 (12: 8) c. qualifies men for the Lord's work; 18: 19 you can do nothing without faith, hope, c.; 88: 125 (124: 116) clothe yourselves with bond of c.; 121: 45 let bowels be full of c. toward all men.

CHASTEN, CHASTISEMENT (see also Affliction; Prove; Punishment; Reprove; Tribulation; Trial, Try; TG Chastening)
D&C 1: 27 sinners are c. that they might repent; 42: 88–92 offenders to be c. publicly or privately according to offense; 58: 60 that bestowed upon Ziba Peterson to be taken until he is sufficiently c. for sins; 61: 8 c. saints for sins, that they might be one; 64: 8 disciples were c. because they forgave not; 75: 7 William McLellin is c. for murmurings of heart; 87: 6 nations to feel c. hand of God; 90: 36 Zion to be c. until she overcomes and is clean; 95: 1 whom the Lord loves he c.; 95: 1 with c. the Lord prepares way for saints' deliverance out of temptation; 97: 6 school in Zion must be c.; 98: 21 the Lord to c. church in Kirtland if they do not repent; 100: 13 Zion shall be redeemed, although she is c.; 101: 5 those who will not endure c. cannot be sanctified; 101: 41 transgressors must be c.; 103: 4 those who call themselves after the Lord's name will be c.; 105: 6 people must be c. until they learn; 136: 31 he that will not bear c. is not worthy of God's kingdom.

CHASTITY, CHASTE (see also Adultery; Clean; Fornication; Lust; Pure; Virtue; TG Chastity, Chaste)
D&C 61: 36 be of good c., little children; 68: 6 be of good c. and do not fear; 78: 18 be of good c., for the Lord will lead you; 112: 4 let your heart be of good c. before the Lord's face.

CHEER (see also Cheerful; Happiness; Joy; TG Cheer)
D&C 59: 15 feast with c. hearts and countenances; 123: 17 c. do all things.

CHEERFUL, CHEERFULLY (see also Cheer; TG Cheerful, Cheerfulness)
D&C 59: 15 feast with c. hearts and countenances; 123: 17 c. do all things.

CHERUBIM (see also TG Cherubim; BD Cherubim)
Moses 4: 31 c. and flaming sword keep way of tree of life.

CHICKENS (*see also* Animal)

D&C 10: 65 (29: 2; 43: 24) the Lord gathers people as hen gathers her c.

CHILD, CHILDREN (*see also* Babe; Children of God; Daughter; Son; TG Child; Children; Family, Children, Duties of; Family, Children, Responsibilities toward; Honoring Father and Mother; Salvation of Little Children)

D&C 2: 2 (27: 9; 98: 16; 110: 15; 128: 17–18; 138: 47; Mal. 4: 6) promises made to fathers will be planted in hearts of c.; 18: 42 c. who have arrived at years of accountability must repent; 20: 70 c. to be blessed by elders before the church; 29: 46 (74: 7) c. redeemed from foundation of world through Savior; 29: 47 c. cannot sin because they cannot be tempted; 45: 54–58 c. of those who abide the Lord's coming will grow up without sin unto salvation; 50: 40 (78: 17) elders are still little c., cannot bear all things yet; 55: 4 establish school, that c. may receive instruction; 63: 51 during Millennium, c. to grow up until they become old; 68: 25–28 (93: 40) c. to be taught principles of gospel by parents; 68: 31 c. in Zion are growing up in wickedness; 74: 7 c. are holy through atonement of Christ; 83: 4 c. have claim upon parents for maintenance; 83: 5 c. have claim on church if parents cannot provide inheritance; 93: 40 parents commanded to bring up c. in light and truth; 93: 42 neglect of c. is causing affliction; 98: 16 saints to seek diligently to turn hearts of c. to their fathers; 98: 44–47 the Lord takes vengeance upon c. of those who repent not; 99: 3 he who receives you as a little c. receives my kingdom; 99: 6 elders should not take until c. are provided for; 121: 17 those who cry transgression are c. of disobedience; 128: 18 earth to be smitten unless there is welding link between fathers and c.; 137: 10 c. who die before accountability are saved in celestial kingdom; 138: 48 c. to be sealed to parents in dispensation of fulness of times.

Moses 6: 6 c. are taught to read and write in undefiled language; 6: 54 c. are whole from foundation of world; 6: 55 c. are conceived in sin; **Abr.** 1: 7, 10 c. are sacrificed to idols; **JS-M** 1: 16 wo unto them who are with c. in those days; **JS-H** 1: 39 (Mal. 4: 6) the Lord will plant in hearts of c. the promises made to the fathers.

CHILDREN OF GOD (*see also* Born of God; Heir; Son; TG Children of Light)

D&C 41: 6 things belonging to c. of kingdom should not be given to the un-

worthy; 50: 41 fear not, little c., for you are mine; 106: 5 gird up your loins that you may be the c. of light.

CHOOSE, CHOSEN (*see also* Agency; Chosen [adj.]; Elect)

D&C 1: 4 (29: 4) the Lord has c. disciples to warn all people; 3: 9 thou wast c. to do work of the Lord; 37: 4 let every man c. for himself; 55: 1 thou art called and c.; 95: 5 (121: 34, 40) many called, but few c.; 95: 8 the Lord will endow with power those whom he has c.; 105: 35–36 difference between calling and c.; 138: 55 noble and great spirits who were c. in beginning to be rulers in church of God.

Moses 3: 17 Adam may c. for himself; 6: 33 c. ye this day to serve the Lord; 7: 33 men are commanded to c. Father; 7: 39 That which God has c. has pled before him; **Abr.** 3: 23 Abraham was c. before he was born.

CHOSEN [adj.]

D&C 107: 40 order of priesthood belongs to descendants of c. seed.

Moses 1: 26 the Lord to deliver Israel his c.; 4: 2 Son was God's C. from beginning; 7: 39 God's C. will suffer for men's sins, return to God.

CHRIST (*see* Jesus Christ)

CHURCH (*see* Church, Great and Abominable; Church of Enoch²; Church of God; Church of the Devil; Church of the Firstborn; Churches, False; TG Church)

CHURCH, GREAT AND ABOMINABLE (*see also* Church of the Devil; Churches, False; Whore)

D&C 29: 21 great and abominable c. to be cast down by devouring fire; 88: 94 great and abominable c. persecutes saints, is tares of earth.

CHURCH OF CHRIST (*see* Church of God)

CHURCH OF ENOCH²

D&C 76: 67 celestial heirs come to general assembly and c. of Enoch² and the Firstborn.

CHURCH OF GOD (*see also* Church of Enoch²; Church of the Firstborn; Priesthood, Aaronic; Priesthood, Melchizedek; TG Church; Church, Name of; Church before Christ; Church Organization; BD Church)

D&C 1: 30 this c. is only true and living c.; 1: 30 (5: 14; 33: 5; 109: 73) c. to be brought out of obscurity; 1: 30 the Lord gave men power to lay foundation of c.; 1: 30 the Lord is pleased with c. collectively; 10: 53 the Lord will establish c. if generation harden not hearts; 10: 55 those who belong to c. inherit kingdom of heaven; 10: 67 whosoever repents and comes to the Lord is his c.; 10: 69 whosoever is of my c. will I establish upon my rock; 11: 16 wait until you have my word, my rock, my c.; 18: 4 in scriptures are written all things concerning foundation of c.; 18: 5 if you build up my c., gates of hell shall not prevail; sec. 20 revelation on c. organization and government; 20: 1 (21: 3) c. organized April 6, 1830; 20: 37 the repentant to be received by baptism into c.; 20: 53–55 teacher's duty to watch over c.; 20: 55 c. to meet often; 20: 83 names of those expelled from c. shall be blotted out; 21: 2 Joseph Smith inspired by Holy Ghost to lay foundation of c.; 26: 2 (28: 13; 102: 9) all things to be done by common consent in c.; 28: 2 one appointed to receive revelation in c.; 30: 6 c. to be built up among Lamanites; 33: 13 (128: 10) upon this rock I will build my c.; 37: 2 c. to assemble at the Ohio; 38: 36 (51: 5–15) instructions concerning c. property; 39: 13 (42: 8) calls to build up c.; 41: 3 (58: 23) the Lord's law teaches how to govern c.; 42: 13 observe the covenants and c. articles; 42: 59 commandments in scriptures to be law governing c.; 42: 67 c. covenants promised; 43: 2 commandment given for law unto c.; 43: 8–9 when assembled together, c. to instruct each other how to act; 43: 11 purge out iniquity in c.; 45: 64 (58: 48) if inhabitants repent, build c.; 50: 4 the Lord has seen abominations in c.; 50: 37 strengthen c.; 58: 23 laws given are laws of c.; 59: 9 go to house of prayer to offer sacraments on Sabbath; 60: 8 preach word among congregations of wicked until they return to c. whence they came; 63: 63 let c. repent of sins; 64: 12 he who repents not should be brought before c.; 64: 37 the Lord made c. like judge to judge nations; 68: 14 (72: 2) bishops to be set apart unto c.; 69: 3, 7 history of c. to be kept; 70: 1–5 stewards to manage business in c.; 75: 24 duty of c. to support families of those called to preach; 78: 14 c. to stand independent; 82: 17 saints to be equal for benefit of c.; 82: 18 talents to be cast into storehouse, become common property of c.; 82: 21 sinners to be dealt with according to laws of c.; 83: 4 laws of c. concerning women and children; 84: 2 c. established for gathering of saints; 84: 17 priesthood continues in c.; 84: 34 those who magnify callings become

c. and kingdom of God; 84: 55 c. under condemnation because of vanity and unbelief; 84: 108 apostles built c. in ancient days; 84: 110 (1 Cor. 12: 12–27) body hath need of every member; 85: 11 apostates to have no inheritance in c.; 86: 3 Babylon, great persecutor of c.; 90: 4 oracles to be given to c. through Joseph Smith; 90: 13 Joseph Smith to preside over c.; 98: 19 God not pleased with some in c.; 101: 64–65, 72 the Lord commands c. to gather to appointed places; 103: 29 prepare c. for redemption of Zion; 104: 58–59 scriptures established to build up c.; 105: 2 but for transgression of c., they might have been redeemed; 107: 22 Presidency upheld by confidence, faith, and prayer of c.; 107: 33 the Twelve build up and regulate c. in all nations; 107: 34 the Seventy act under direction of Twelve to build and regulate c.; 107: 59 revelation to c. of Christ in addition to c. laws respecting c. business; 107: 72 high priest can serve as bishop to do business of c.; 107: 78 most important business of c. to be carried to council of c. before Presidency; 107: 80 the Presidency, highest council in c.; 107: 91 duty of President of High Priesthood to preside over whole c.; 115: 3–4 (127: 12; 128: 21; 136: 2; OD–1; OD–2) C. of Jesus Christ of Latter-day Saints; 124: 41 the Lord to reveal unto c. things which have been kept hid; 124: 94 Hyrum Smith appointed prophet, seer, revelator unto c.; 138: 55 noble spirits chosen in beginning to be rulers in c.

JS-H: 1: 1 Joseph Smith to write history of c.; 1: 73 Joseph Smith prophesies concerning rise of c.; **A of F** 6 we believe in same organization that existed in Primitive C.

CHURCH OF THE DEVIL (see also Church, Great and Abominable; Churches, False; Devil; TG Devil, Church of)

D&C 10: 56 the Lord will cause those who build up kingdom of devil to tremble and shake; 18: 20 contend against no c., save c. of devil.

CHURCH OF THE FIRSTBORN (see also Celestial Glory)

D&C 76: 54, 67, 71, 94 celestial heirs are c. of F.; 76: 102 telestial heirs will not be caught up to c. of F.; 77: 11 as many as come will be brought to c. of F.; 78: 21 ye are c. of F.; 88: 5 celestial glory is glory of c. of F.; 93: 22 those who are begotten through Christ are c. of F.; 107: 19 priesthood to commune with c. of F.

CHURCH OF THE LAMB (see Church of God)

CHURCHES, FALSE (see also Church, Great and Abominable; Church of the Devil; Doctrine, False; Priestcraft; Prophets, False; Tradition)

D&C 10: 56 the Lord will cause those who build c. to get gain to shake and tremble.

CINCINNATI, OHIO

D&C 60: 6 (61: 30) elders sent to C.

CIRCUMCISION (see also TG Circumcision; BD Circumcision)

D&C sec. 74 contention in days of apostles concerning law of c.

CITIZENSHIP (see also Government, Civil)

D&C 42: 27 do not speak evil of neighbor, nor do him any harm; 58: 21 (98: 4) let no man break laws of land; 98: 10 uphold good men and wise men; 134: 1 governments are instituted of God for benefit of man; 134: 5 all men are bound to uphold their governments; 134: 6 all men owe respect and deference to laws; 134: 7 governments establish laws for protection of all citizens.

A of F 12 we believe in being subject to rulers and in obeying the law.

CITY (see also Enoch[2]; Jerusalem; Jerusalem, New; Zion)

D&C 63: 31 if saints obtain land by blood, they will be scourged from c. to c.; 63: 49 those who die in the Lord will receive inheritance in holy c.; 66: 5 proclaim gospel from c. to c.; 84: 93 (109: 41) wo to c. that rejects elders; 109: 39-40 peace and salvation to come to c. that accept elders; 125: 2 saints to gather and build up c.; 128: 3 recorder to be appointed in each ward of c.

CITY OF HOLINESS (see also Enoch[2]; Zion)

CLAIM (see also Justice; Mercy)

D&C 51: 5 transgressor shall not have power to c. what he has consecrated to bishop; 63: 27 saints to purchase lands, that they might have c. on world; 68: 21 descendant of Aaron[1] may c. anointing if he can prove lineage; 72: 20 stewards over literary concerns have c. for assistance upon bishop; 82: 17 saints to have equal c. on properties; 83: 2 women have c. upon husbands for maintenance; 83: 4-5 children have c. upon parents, then church, for maintenance.

Abr. 1: 27 Pharaoh c. right of priesthood from Noah[1].

CLAY (see also Tabernacle)

Moses 6: 35 Enoch[2] is told to anoint eyes with c.

CLEAN, CLEANLINESS (see also Cleanse; Holy; Pure; Purify; TG Cleanliness; BD Clean and Unclean)

D&C 38: 10 (66: 3) you are c., but not all; 38: 42 (133: 5) be ye c. that bear vessels of the Lord; 42: 41 all things to be done in c. before the Lord; 88: 74 purify your hearts that I may make you c.; 88: 75 Christ to testify to the Father that saints are c. from blood of generation; 88: 85 garments of laborers in vineyard not c. from blood of generation; 88: 86 let your hands be c.; 88: 138 those who enter school must be c. from blood of generation; 90: 36 the Lord will chasten Zion until she is c.; 138: 59 dead who repent are washed c.

CLEANSE (see also Baptism; Clean; Purify; Sanctification; Wash)

D&C 29: 17 Christ's blood shall not c. the wicked if they do not hear him; 50: 28 no man is possessor of all things except he be c. from all sin; 76: 41 Jesus came into world to c. it; 76: 52 those who keep commandments are c. from sins; 84: 92 (99: 4) elders to c. feet as testimony against those who reject them; 88: 74 laborers in kingdom to c. hands and feet before the Lord; 109: 42 c. thy servants from blood of generation; 112: 33 c. your hearts and your garments.

Moses 6: 59 men must be c. by blood of Only Begotten; 7: 48 when shall earth be c. from filthiness.

CLEAR

D&C 5: 14 (105: 31) church to come out of wilderness, c. as moon; 109: 73 church to come out of wilderness, c. as sun.

CLEAVE, CLAVE [join] (see also Mount, Mountain; Rock)

D&C 11: 19 c. unto the Lord with all thy heart; 25: 13 c. unto covenants thou hast made; 42: 22 husbands to c. unto wives and none else; 88: 40 intelligence c. unto intelligence; 98: 11 c. unto all good.

Moses 3: 24 (Abr. 5: 18) man shall c. unto his wife.

CLERK (see also Recorder)

D&C 85: 1 duty of the Lord's c.

CLOTHE

D&C 29: 12 Twelve to stand with Christ, c. in robes of righteousness; 38: 26 what father c. one son in robes, other in rags; 45: 44 the Lord will come c. with power and great glory; 65: 5 the Lord will come c. in brightness of his glory; 84: 81 take no thought wherewith you shall be c.; 84: 89 whoso receives the Lord will c. elders; 84: 101 earth c. with God's glory; 85: 7 the Lord will send forth mighty one, c. with light; 88: 125 c. yourselves with bond of charity; 133: 69 heavens c. in blackness; 138: 30 the Lord c. his messengers with power and authority; 138: 43 dry bones to be c. upon with flesh.

Moses 4: 27 the Lord c. Adam and Eve in coats of skins; 7: 3 Enoch² is c. upon with glory.

CLOTHING

D&C 61: 11 elders to take what is needful for c.; 136: 5 each company to provide themselves with c.

CLOUD (see also Smoke; Vapor)

D&C 34: 7 (45: 44; 76: 63) the Lord to come in c.; 45: 45 (78: 21; 109: 75) saints to meet Christ in c.; 76: 102 telestial heirs not to be received into c.; 84: 5 c. shall be glory of the Lord.

JS-M 1: 36 (Matt. 24: 30) Son of Man coming in c. of heaven; **JS-H** 1: 68 John the Baptist descends in c. of light.

COAT (see also Clothing)

D&C 24: 18 (84: 78) commandment not to take two c.; 84: 105 if any man give you c. give old to the poor.

Moses 4: 27 c. of skins given to Adam and Eve.

CODE NAMES

D&C 78: Intro. explanation concerning c. names.

COE, JOSEPH

D&C 55: 6 to journey to Missouri; 102: 3 member of high council.

COLD

D&C 45: 27 love of men shall wax c.; 89: 13 flesh not to be used, only in times of c. or famine.

JS-M 1: 10 love of many shall wax c.; 1: 30 love of men shall wax c.

COLESVILLE, NEW YORK (see also D&C map, p. 296)

D&C 24: 3 Joseph Smith to go to C.; 26: 1 Joseph Smith to confirm church in C.; 37: 2 saints in C. pray with much faith; 54: Intro. saints arriving in Ohio from C.; sec. 58 revelation given in behalf of saints from C.; 128: 20 voice of Peter, James, and John heard near C.

COLTRIN, ZEBEDEE

D&C 52: 29 to journey to Missouri.

COMBINATION (see Secret Combination)

COME, CAME (see also Enter; Jesus Christ, First Coming of; Jesus Christ, Second Coming of)

D&C 10: 67 those who c. unto the Lord are his church; 18: 11 the Lord suffered that all might repent and c. unto him; 29: 26 dead to awake and c. forth; 45: 46 c. unto the Lord and live; 67: 9 that which is righteous c. down from the Father; 98: 10 (124: 120) whatsoever is less c. of evil.

COMFORT (see also Consolation; Holy Ghost—Comforter; Mourn, Rest)

D&C 25: 5 Emma Smith's calling to be c. unto Joseph; 101: 14 blessed are they that mourn, for they shall be c.; 107: 55 the Lord administered c. unto Adam.

COMFORTER (see Holy Ghost—Comforter)

COMING (see Jesus Christ, Appearances of; Jesus Christ, First Coming of; Jesus Christ, Second Coming of)

COMMAND (see also Commandments of God)

D&C 46: 7 be not seduced by c. of men.

Moses 1: 18 (4: 1) Moses c. Satan to depart; 5: 18 Satan c. Cain to make offering unto the Lord; **JS-H** 1; 19 false churches teach for doctrines the c. of men.

COMMANDMENTS OF GOD (see also Obedience; Statute; TG Commandments of God)

D&C 1: 17 the Lord called upon Joseph Smith and gave him c.; 1: 18 the Lord gave c. to proclaim gospel; 1: 24 c. are given to servants in their weakness; 1: 24-30 (133: 57-60) why c. are given; 1: 37 search these c.; 3: 10 repent of what is contrary to c.; 5: 22 (6: 6, 9, 37; 8: 5; 11: 6, 9, 18, 20; 12: 6; 14: 6-7; 18: 43; 19: 13; 25: 15; 30: 8; 35: 24; 43: 35; 71: 11; 136: 42) keep my c.; 5: 33 c. are given that thy days may be prolonged; 5: 35 if thou art faithful in keeping c., thou shalt be lifted up; 10: 56 (18: 46; 56: 2; 58: 30; 95: 12; 103: 8) violators of c. to suffer; 11: 20 (14: 7; 15: 5; 17: 8; 58: 2; 59: 1, 4; 63: 23; 76: 52; 89: 18; 93: 20, 28; 95: 11; 124: 87) keepers of c. to be blessed; 18: 9 (133: 16) the Lord c. all men to repent; 18: 46 (25: 15; 56: 2) they who keep not c. cannot be saved; 19: 32 great and last c.; 20: 19 God gave c. to love and serve him; 25: 15 if men keep not the c., they cannot come where the Lord is; 28: 2

Commission *(cont.)*

(43: 2–3, 5) only one to receive c. for church; 28: 5, 8 Oliver Cowdery to write by way of wisdom, not c.; 28: 6 thou shalt not c. him who is at thy head; 29: 35 the Lord's c. are spiritual, not natural or temporal; 29: 40 Adam transgressed the c. by partaking of fruit; 38: 16 for your salvation the Lord gave a c.; 42: 4 first c., to go forth in the Lord's name; 42: 15 do as the Lord has c. concerning teaching; 42:29 (124: 87) if thou lovest God, keep c.; 42: 58 c. will be taught to all nations; 42: 59 c. are given in scriptures to be law governing church; 43: 2 Joseph Smith appointed to receive c.; 43: 8–9 church to assemble, instruct each other how to act upon points of c.; 46: 7 ye are c. in all things to ask of God; 56: 4 (58: 32) the Lord c. and revokes; 58: 2 those who keep c. will receive greater reward in kingdom of heaven; 58: 26 not meet that the Lord should c. in all things; 58: 29 he who does nothing until c. is damned; 58: 29 he who receives c. with doubtful heart is damned; 59: 4 the diligent will be blessed with c. and revelations; 59: 21 wrath of God kindled against those who do not obey c.; 63: 13 the Lord gives c. for men's good; 63: 13 many have turned from the Lord's c.; 63: 23 he who keeps c. is given mysteries of kingdom; 67: 4 the Lord gives testimony of c. in Book of C.; 70: 3 stewards over revelations and c. appointed; 71: 4 elders to prepare way for c. which are to come; 75: 3 proclaim truth according to the c.; 76: 52 those who keep c. are washed and cleansed from sins; 78: 13 the Lord prepares saints to accomplish his c.; 82: 8 c. are given that saints may understand the Lord's will; 82: 9 c. are directions; 84: 27 preparatory gospel is law of carnal c.; 89: 2 Word of Wisdom given not by c. or constraint, but by revelation; 89: 18 those who walk in obedience to c. receive health; 93: 1 those who keep c. shall see the Lord's face; 93: 20 those who keep c. receive of the Lord's fulness; 98: 33 go not out to battle, save the Lord c.; 101: 60 do whatsoever the Lord has c.; 124: 49 when saints are prevented from fulfilling c., the Lord requires work no more; 132: 29 Abraham received all things by c.; 132: 36 Abraham was c. to offer his son; 133: 23 the Lord to c. the deep to be driven back into north countries; 136: 2 saints under covenant to keep all the c.

Moses 3: 16–17 (4: 23; Abr. 5: 13) the Lord c. Adam not to partake of tree of knowledge of good and evil; 5: 5 Adam received c. from the Lord; 5: 6 I know not, save the Lord c. me; 5: 14 the Lord c. men to repent; 6: 60 by the water ye keep the c.; **Abr.** 3: 25 the Lord will prove men to see if they will do all that he c. them.

COMMISSION

D&C 20: 73 having been c. of Jesus Christ, I baptize you; 88: 80 saints to be prepared to magnify mission with which the Lord has c. them; 138: 30 the Lord c. messengers to carry gospel to spirits in darkness.

COMMIT (see Adultery; Murder; Sin)

COMMITTEE

D&C 94: 15 c. appointed to build the Lord's houses; 123: 4–6 c. to gather libelous publications.

COMMON (see also Common Consent)

D&C 82: 18 c. property put in storehouse; 102: 28 no c. case is sufficient to call council of high priests; 107: 74 bishop to be c. judge in Israel; 107: 82 if President transgress, he is to be tried before c. council of church.

COMMON CONSENT (see also TG Sustaining Church Leaders)

D&C 20: 63 elders to receive license by vote of church; 20: 65–66 vote required for ordination in church; 26: 2 (28: 13) all things to be done by c. c.; 38: 34 men to be appointed by voice of church; 41: 9 Edward Partridge to be appointed bishop by voice of church; 51: 4 transgressors to be accounted unworthy by voice of church; 104: 21 let all things be done by united c.; 104: 64, 71–72 nothing to be taken from treasury except by voice or c. c. of order; 124: 144 fill all these offices and approve of those names.

COMMOTION

D&C 45: 26 whole earth shall be in c.; 88: 91 all things shall be in c.

COMMUNICATION (see Hear; Hearken; Speak; Think; Understand; TG Communication)

COMMUNION, COMMUNE (see also TG Sacrament; BD Communion)

D&C 107: 19 Melchizedek Priesthood holds keys to c. with church of Firstborn, to enjoy c. and presence of God.

COMPANION (see also Holy Ghost, Gift of; Husband; Wife)

D&C 42: 74 those who put away c. because of fornication shall not be cast out; 42: 75 those who leave c. to commit adultery shall be cast out; 121: 46 Holy Ghost shall be thy constant c.

COMPANY, COMPANIES

D&C 76: 67 celestial inhabitants come to innumerable c. of angels; 103: 30 c. to go to land of Zion; 136: 2–3 c. to cross plains.

COMPASS (see Liahona)

COMPASSION (see also Charity; Love; Mercy; Pity; TG Compassion)

D&C 64: 2 the Lord to have c. upon elders; 88: 40 mercy hath c. on mercy; 109: 9 (121: 3) the Lord's bowels to be moved with c. toward saints.

COMPEL, COMPULSION, COMPULSORY (see also Agency; Constraint; Dominion; Liberty)

D&C 58: 26 he who is c. in all things is slothful servant; 121: 37 when men exercise c. upon souls of men, heavens withdraw themselves; 121: 46 without c. means thy dominion shall flow unto thee forever.

COMPREHEND (see also God, Omniscience of; Know; Understand)

D&C 6: 21 (10: 58; 34: 2; 39: 2; 45: 7; 88: 49) darkness c. not the light; 88: 6, 41 the Lord c. all things; 88: 49 he who is quickened by God will c. God; 88: 67 body filled with light c. all things.

Abr. 4: 4 the Gods c. the light.

COMPULSION, COMPULSORY (see Compel)

CONCEIVE (see also Bear; TG Conceived in Sin)

Moses 6: 55 children are c. in sin; 6: 55 when children begin to grow up, sin c. in their hearts.

CONCUBINE (see also Adultery; Wife; TG Concubine)

D&C 132: 1, 37–39 ancient prophets were given many wives and c.

CONDEMN, CONDEMNATION (see also Judge [verb])

D&C 5: 27 covenant breakers are c.; 6: 35 I do not c. thee, sin no more; 10: 23 cunning plan shall turn to c.; 20: 15 unbelief of hardhearted shall turn to their own c.; 42: 81 adulterer to be c. by two witnesses; 61: 11 unto those without faith, God shows signs to their c.; 63: 62 c. for using name of the Lord in vain; 64: 9 he who forgives not, stands c.; 68: 22 no bishop to be c. except before First Presidency; 75: 21 elders to judge and c. houses that reject them; 76: 48 c. of sons of perdition incomprehensible; 82: 3 he who sins against greater light shall

receive greater c.; 84: 55–57 church under c. because of vanity and unbelief; 88: 65 asking for things not expedient brings c.; 88: 100 spirits under c. to be judged; 93: 31–32 those who receive not the light are under c.; 136: 25 those who cannot repay borrowing should tell neighbor lest he c. them; 136: 33 Spirit sent forth to c. of the ungodly.

CONDITION

D&C 46: 15 mercies suited according to c. of men; 88: 38–39 every law has certain c.; 130: 20 (132: 5) c. for obtaining blessings; 138: 19 men redeemed from individual sins of c.

CONFER (see also Confirm; Ordain; Priesthood)

D&C 13: 1 John the Baptist c. Aaronic Priesthood; 67: 14 elders to know that which Joseph Smith c. upon them; 97: 14 keys of kingdom have been c. upon you; 107: 13 second priesthood called Aaronic Priesthood because it was c. upon Aaron¹ and seed; 121: 37 that rights of priesthood may be c. upon us is true; 132: 7 never but one on earth at time upon whom keys of priesthood are c.; 132: 45 the Lord has c. upon you keys of priesthood wherein he restores all things.

Abr. 1: 3 priesthood is c. upon Abraham from fathers; JS-H 1: 68–69, 72 John the Baptist c. Aaronic Priesthood upon Joseph Smith and Oliver Cowdery; 1: 70 Melchizedek Priesthood to be c. hereafter.

CONFERENCE (see also Assemble; Meet; Meetings)

D&C 20: 61 c. to be held every three months; 20: 67 (124: 144) officers to be ordained by direction of general c.; 44: 1 (58: 56, 61) elders to gather for c.; 58: 62 Edward Partridge to direct c.; 73: 2 elders sent on missions by voice of c.; 124: 88 missionary to await further instructions at general c.

CONFESS (see also Acknowledge; Confession of Sins; TG Confess)

D&C 59: 12 those offend God who c. not his hand; 76: 110 (88: 104) every knee shall bow and every tongue c.; 124: 18 the Lord's servant to c. him before the world.

CONFESSION OF SINS (see also Confess; Forgive; Humble; Repentance; TG Confession; BD Confession)

D&C 19: 20 c. your sins, lest you suffer punishments; 42: 88 if offender c., thou shalt be reconciled; 42: 91 offenders who c. not will be delivered to law of God; 42: 92 those who offend in secret will be given opportunity to c. in secret; 58: 43 if man repents of sins, he will c. them; 61: 2 (64: 7) the Lord forgives those who c. sins with humble hearts; 64: 12 he who does not repent and c. will be brought before church.

CONFIDENCE

D&C 107: 22 First Presidency upheld by c. of church; 121: 45 then shall thy c. wax strong in presence of God.

JS-H 1: 29 Joseph Smith prays with full c. he will obtain divine manifestation.

CONFIRM (see also Confer; Hands, Laying on of; Holy Ghost, Gift of; Ordinance; BD Confirmation)

D&C 20: 10 Book of Mormon is c. to others by ministering of angels; 20: 41, 43, 68 those baptized to be c. by laying on of hands for baptism of fire; 20: 43 (33: 15) those baptized to be c. by laying on of hands for gift of Holy Ghost; 20: 68 church members to be instructed before being c.; 24: 9 continue in laying on of hands and c. churches; 27: 12 Joseph Smith and Oliver Cowdery are c. apostles by Peter, James, and John; 84: 18, 30 the Lord c. priesthood upon Aaron'; 84: 42 the Lord c. upon elders priesthood which they have received; 84: 48 the Father c. covenant upon priesthood for sake of world; 107: 40 order of priesthood c. to be handed down from father to son; 128: 21 angels from Michael to the present c. our hope.

Moses 5: 59 all things are c. unto Adam by holy ordinance.

CONFOUND (see also Confusion)

D&C 10:42 the Lord to c. those who altered his words; 49: 27 elders shall not be c.; 71: 7 c. your enemies; 71: 10 any man who lifts voice against elders will be c.; 84: 116 let him trust in me and he shall not be c.; 93: 52 if you keep my sayings, you shall not be c.; 100: 5 the Lord's servants shall not be c. before men; 133: 58 the weak shall c. the wise.

CONFUSION (see also Order)

D&C 63: 24 assemble not in haste lest there be c.; 123: 7 Satan has filled world with c.; 132: 8 God's house not one of c.

CONGREGATION (see also Assemble; Meet, Meeting)

D&C 52: 10 elders to preach by the way in every c.; 60: 8, 13–14 (61: 33; 62: 5; 68: 1) preach gospel among c. of wicked; 61: 30, 32 restrict teaching among c. of wicked; 61: 32 elders to

journey for c. of their brethren; 107: 56 Adam stood up in c. of his posterity; 138: 38 great spirits gathered in c. of righteous.

CONQUER (see also Overcome; Subdue)

D&C 10: 5 pray always that you may c. Satan.

CONSCIENCE (see also Light; TG Conscience; BD Conscience)

D&C 84: 46 (93: 2) the Spirit gives light to every man; 88: 11 light which quickens understandings is through him who enlightens your eyes; 134: 2 government to secure free exercise of c.; 135: 4 Joseph Smith has c. void of offense towards God.

A of F 11 we claim privilege of worshipping God according to dictates of c.

CONSECRATE (see also Anointing; Consecration, Law of; Dedicate; Ordain; Sanctification)

D&C 52: 2 conference to be held upon land the Lord has c. to his people; 58: 57 (84: 31) spot for temple to be c. and dedicated; 133: 35 kingdom to be organized on c. land; 105: 15 enemies not to pollute land c. for gathering of saints; 109: 12 temple to be sanctified and c. to be holy.

CONSECRATION, LAW OF (see also Order; Zion)

D&C 42: 30–39 (51: 2–19; 58: 35–37) principles of c. explained; 42: 30, 39 c. of thy properties for support of the poor; 42: 32 c. properties not to be taken from church; 49: 20 one man should not possess above another; 51: 3 every man equal according to his family; 51: 5 transgressor not to have claim upon portion c. to bishop; 58: 36 (85: 3) a law for inheritance in Zion; 78: 5 order established that saints may be equal in bonds of heavenly and earthly things; 83: 6 storehouse kept by c.; 105: 5 Zion can only be built up by principles of celestial law; 105: 29 lands to be purchased according to laws of c.; 105: 34 let commandments concerning Zion's law be executed and fulfilled; 124: 21 bishop to receive c. of the Lord's house.

CONSENT (see also Common Consent; Unite, Unity)

D&C 93: 51 by saints' prayer of faith with one c. the Lord will uphold servant.

CONSIDER

D&C 95: 3 ye have not c. the great commandment.

CONSOLATION (see also Comfort)

D&C 124: 53 the Lord makes an example for saints' c.; 128: 21 angels give c. by holding forth that which is to come.

CONSPIRACY, CONSPIRING (see also Fraud; Secret; Secret Combination; TG Conspiracy)

D&C 84: 16 Abel slain by c. of brother; 89: 4 evils and designs in hearts of c. men in last days; 134: 7 religious opinions not to justify sedition nor c.; 135: 7 Joseph and Hyrum Smith confined in jail by c. of wicked men.

CONSTITUTION (see also Government, Civil)

D&C 98: 5–6 c. law should be befriended; 101: 77, 80 the Lord caused c. to be established; 109: 54 prayer that c. be maintained.

CONSTRAINT (see also Compel)

D&C 63: 64 that which comes from above must be spoken by c. of Spirit; 89: 2 Word of Wisdom given not by commandment or c., but by revelation.

CONSUME, CONSUMPTION (see also Devour)

D&C 5: 19 inhabitants of earth to be c. by brightness of the Lord's coming; 29: 23 heaven and earth to be c. after Millennium; 45: 50 scorner shall be c.; 46: 9 men should not ask for sign to c. it upon their lusts; 63: 34 wicked to be c. with unquenchable fire; 87: 6 c. decreed shall make full end of all nations; 98: 17 hearts to be turned lest all flesh be c.; 101: 24 every corruptible thing to be c.

CONTENTION, CONTEND (see also Hardheartedness; Prophets, False; Strife; TG Contention)

D&C 10: 63 establish gospel that there not be so much c.; 10: 63 Satan stirs hearts to c.; 18: 20 c. against no church, except church of devil; 74: 3 c. among people concerning law of circumcision during days of apostles; 95: 10 c. arose in school of prophets; 101: 6 c. in Zion pollute saints' inheritances; 112: 5 c. thou, and let thy warning voice go forth; 121: 10 thy friends do not c. against thee; 136: 23 cease to c. one with another.

CONTINUE, CONTINUATION

D&C 33: 13 if ye c., gates of hell shall not prevail; 50: 24 he who receives light and c. in God receives more light; 66: 12 c. in these things even unto end; 67: 13 c. in patience until ye are perfected;

132: 19 c. of seeds forever; 132: 22 narrow is the way to exaltation and c. of the lives; 138: 52, 57 prophets, faithful elders c. labors after this life.

Abr. 2: 11 right of priesthood to c. in Abraham's seed.

CONTRITE (see also Broken Heart and Contrite Spirit; Humble; TG Contrite Heart)

D&C 21: 9 Jesus crucified for remission of sins unto c. heart; 52: 15 he whose spirit is c. is accepted; 54: 3 those who are c. will escape enemies; 55: 3 Holy Spirit promised to those who are c.; 136: 33 Spirit is sent to enlighten the c.

CONTROL (see also Agency; Compel)

D&C 121: 36 powers of heaven can be c. only upon principles of righteousness; 121: 37 when men exercise c. over souls of men, the heavens withdraw; 134: 2 governments must frame laws that secure right and c. of property; 134: 4 magistrate should never c. conscience.

CONTROVERSY (see Contention)

CONVERSATION, CONVERSE (see also BD Conversation)

D&C 20: 69 members manifest by godly walk and c. that they are worthy of sacrament; 108: 7 strengthen brethren in all your c.

Moses 6: 22 God c. with Adam.

CONVERT (see also Baptism; Born of God; Change; Fire; Holy Ghost; Repentance; TG Conversion; Convert; BD Conversion)

D&C 44: 4 many to be c. by elders; 109: 65 remnants of Jacob to be c. from savage condition; 109: 70 scattered remnants to be c. and redeemed with Israel; 112: 13 the Twelve shall be c.

CONVINCE, CONVINCING (see also Conversion; Persuade; Witness; BD Convince)

D&C 6: 11 find out mysteries to c. others of error of their ways; 11: 21 you shall have power of God unto the c. of men; 18: 44 the Lord to work marvelous work c. many of their sins; 90: 10 arm of the Lord to be revealed in c. nations of gospel.

COPLEY, LEMAN

D&C sec. 49 revelation to; 49: 1 called to preach gospel to Shakers; 54: Intro. broke covenant of consecration.

CORD (see also Band)

D&C 121: 44 that he may know thy faithfulness is stronger than c. of death.

CORINTHIANS, FIRST (see also Paul; BD Corinthians, Epistles to)

D&C sec. 74 revelation regarding 1 Cor. 7: 14; 128: 13 the earthly conforms to the heavenly, as Paul declared in 1 Cor. 15: 46–48; 128: 16 Paul mentions baptism for dead in 1 Cor. 15: 29.

CORN (see also Grain; BD Corn)

D&C 89: 17 c. for the ox.

CORNERSTONE (see also Rock; Stone; TG Cornerstone)

D&C 50: 44 Christ is the stone of Israel; 124: 2, 60 stake planted to be a c.; 124: 131 high council given for c. of Zion.

CORRILL, JOHN

D&C 50: 38 called to labor in vineyard; 52: 7 to journey to Missouri.

CORRUPT, CORRUPTION (see also Corruptible; Defile; Filthiness; Pervert; Wicked)

D&C 10: 21 hearts are c.; 38: 11 (112: 23) flesh is c. before the Lord; 123: 7 evil spirit is mainspring of all c.; 134: 12 preach gospel to warn the righteous to save themselves from c.; 135: 6 easy to burn dry trees to purify vineyard of c.

CORRUPTIBLE (see also Corrupt)

D&C 101: 24 every c. thing shall be consumed.

COUNCIL (see also Apostle; High Council; Quorum; TG Council in Heaven)

D&C 78: 9 the Lord's servants to sit in c. with saints; 90: 16 First Presidency presides in c.; 96: 3 division of land to be determined in c. among saints; 102: 2 high c. settles important difficulties not settled by bishop's c.; 102: 8 replacements in standing c. to be sanctioned by general c. of high priests; 102: 9 president of church is president of c. of church; 102 30 (107: 33–34, 36, 38; 124: 127, 139) traveling high c. of apostles; 107: 78–81 cases to be appealed to c. of church; 107: 79 presidency of c. of High Priesthood; 107: 80 First Presidency is highest c. of church; 107: 82 if president transgress, to be tried before common c. of church; 107: 85–89 quorum presidents sit in c. with members; 120: 1 tithed property to be disposed of by c.; 121: 32 ordained in C. of Eternal God before world was.

COUNCIL BLUFFS, NEBRASKA (see D&C map, p. 297)

COUNSEL (see also God, Wisdom of)

D&C 1: 19 man should not c. fellow man; 3: 4 those who set at naught c. of God will incur his vengeance; 3: 15 thou hast suffered c. of thy director to be trampled; 19: 33 receive misery if thou slight these c.; 22: 4 seek not to c. your God; 56: 14 you are not pardoned, because you seek to c. in your own ways; 78: 2 (103: 5) listen to c. of him who hath ordained you; 101: 8 saints who were cast out of inheritance esteemed lightly the Lord's c.; 103: 5 people should hearken to the Lord's c.; 105: 37 if the chosen follow c., they shall receive power; 108: 1 (124: 89) receive c. of him whom I have appointed; 122: 2 the virtuous shall seek c.; 124: 16 his reward shall not fail if he receive c.; 136: 19 those who seek not the Lord's c. shall have no power.

Moses 5: 25 Cain rejects greater c. from God; 6: 28 men have sought their own c. in dark; 6: 43 why c. ye yourselves and deny God; 7: 35 Man of C. is God's name; Abr. 4: 26 (5: 2–3, 5) the Gods took c. among themselves.

COUNSELOR (see also Bishopric)

D&C 42: 31, 71 two elders or high priests to be appointed bishop's c.; 42: 71–72 bishop's c. to be supported out of storehouse or remuneration; 58: 18 (107: 72) bishop to judge by assistance of c.; 81: 1 Frederick G. Williams called as c. to Joseph Smith; 107: 78 descendant of Aaron can act as bishop without c.; 107: 79 twelve are called to assist Presidency as c.; 112: 20, 30 the Lord has made First Presidency c. and leaders of the Twelve; 124: 126 Sidney Rigdon is called as c. to Joseph Smith; 124: 142 c. given for presidents of priests, teachers, deacons, stake.

COUNT (see also Account; Sand)

D&C 107: 100 slothful shall not be c. worthy to stand; 123: 15 let no man c. them as small things.

COUNTENANCE (see also Face)

D&C 20: 6 c. of angel is like lightning; 59: 15 do these things with cheerful c.; 88: 52 labor in field, and ye shall behold joy of my c.; 110: 3 the Lord's c. shines above brightness of sun; 138: 24 c. of dead saints shines.

Moses 5: 21–22 Cain's c. falls; JS–H 1: 32 c. of Moroni[2] is like lightning.

COUNTRY, COUNTRIES (see also Government, Civil; Nation; North)

D&C 38: 29 ye hear of wars in far c.;

88: 79 (93: 53) acquire knowledge of c.

Abr. 2: 3 Abraham, get thee out of c.

COURAGE (see also Faith; Fear)

D&C 128: 22 c., brethren, and on to victory.

COURSE (see also Path)

D&C 3: 2 (35: 1) the Lord's c. is one eternal round; 88: 40 justice continues its c.; 88: 43 c. of heavens and earth are fixed.

COURT (see also Excommunication)

D&C 42: 80 adulterers to be tried before two or more elders; 42: 82 bishop to be present at c.; 42: 89 unreconciled disputes among members to be dealt with by church, not before world; 42: 91 offenders who confess not are to be delivered to law of God; 64: 12 those who do not repent and confess are to be brought before church; 64: 13 hold c. to be justified in eyes of law; 68: 22–24 c. for bishop or high priest; 102: 12–33 procedures for high council c.; 107: 77–84 c. involving presidency of high priesthood; 135: 7 martyrs' blood cannot be rejected by any c. on earth.

COVENANT (see also Abraham; Abrahamic Covenant; Baptism; Chosen; Gospel; Israel; Oath; Priesthood; Promise; Promised Land; Sacrament; TG Covenants; Priesthood, Oath and Covenant; Seed of Abraham; BD Abrahamic Covenant; Covenant)

D&C 1: 15 (54: 4; 104: 4, 52) men have broken the Lord's everlasting c.; 1: 22 (45: 9; 49: 9) the Lord will establish everlasting c.; 22: 1 (sec. 132) old c. done away, the Lord gives new and everlasting c.; 25: 13 cleave unto c.; 38: 20 c. regarding land of inheritance; 42: 13 observe the c. and church articles; 42: 30 consecrate of properties for support of the poor with c.; 42: 67 saints hereafter to receive church c.; 42: 78 members to keep all c. of church; 49: 9 c. was from beginning; 52: 2 the Lord's people are heirs according to c.; 54: 4 saints' c. with the Lord has been broken; 54: 6 they who keep c. will obtain mercy; 66: 2 everlasting c., fulness of gospel; 76: 69 (107: 19) Jesus, mediator of the new c.; 76: 101 celestial heirs received new everlasting c.; 78: 11 (82: 11, 15) saints to organize themselves by bond or covenant c.; 78: 12 he who breaks c. will lose standing in church; 82: 21 he who sins against c. to be dealt with according to laws of church; 84: 33–41 oath and c. of priesthood; 84: 57 children of Zion to remain condemned until they remember new c., even Book of Mormon

and former commandments; 88: 131 prayer enjoined in token of everlasting c.; 88: 133 I salute you in token or remembrance of everlasting c.; 90: 24 remember the c. wherewith ye have c. one with another; 97: 8 those willing to observe c. by sacrifice are accepted by the Lord; 98: 3 the Lord promises with immutable c. to grant saints' prayers; 98: 14 the Lord to prove saints, whether they will abide in c.; 101: 39 when men are called unto everlasting gospel and c., an everlasting c., they are salt of earth; 104: 4–5 the Lord curses those who break c. of united order; 104: 52 c. broken through transgression; sec. 132 (131: 2–4) revelation of new and everlasting c. of marriage; 136: 4 saints c. to walk in all ordinances of the Lord.

Abr. 2: 9–11 the Lord's c. with Abraham.

COVER, COVERING (see also Hide)

D&C 112: 23 darkness c. earth; 121: 37 when man c. sins, amen to his priesthood.

Abr. 2: 16 eternity was our c.

COVET, COVETOUSNESS (see also Desire; Envy; Greediness; Jealousy; Lust; TG Covet, Covetousness)

D&C 19: 25 (Ex. 20: 17) thou shalt not c. thy neighbor's wife; 19: 26 thou shalt not c. thine own property; 88: 123 cease to be covetous; 104: 4, 52 some of the Lord's servants have broken covenant through c.; 136: 20 c. not that which is thy brother's.

COVILL, JAMES

D&C sec. 39 revelation to; 39: 8 heart of, is right before the Lord; 39: 9 sorrows from rejecting the Lord because of pride and worldly cares; 39: 10 is promised a blessing; 39: 11 to preach fulness of gospel; 40: 2 rejects call because of fear of persecution; 40: 3 breaks covenant.

COWDERY, OLIVER

D&C secs. 6–9, 17–18, 23–24, 26, 28 revelations to; 6: 10–11 (8: 4) possesses gift of revelation; 6: 17, 22–24 receives witness of translation; 6: 18 is admonished to stand by Joseph Smith; 6: 25–28 is given gift to translate; 8: 1 to receive knowledge of records; 8: 6 has gift of Aaron; 9: 1 does not translate; 9: 1, 4 continues as scribe; 9: 2 to be given other records to translate; 9: 3, 5, 10–11 loses privilege of translating; sec. 13 (27: 8) is ordained by John the Baptist; 17: 3, 5 to testify that he has seen sacred plates; 17: 7 receives same gift of faith and power as Joseph Smith; 18: 2 receives testimony of

Spirit that writings are true; 18: 7 is baptized by Joseph Smith; 18: 9 is called with same calling as Paul; 18: 37 called to search out the Twelve; 20: 3 is called an apostle; 20: 3 is ordained by Joseph Smith; 21: Intro. sustained as presiding officer of church; 21: 10 to ordain Joseph Smith; 21: 12 first preacher unto church; 23: 1 counseled to beware of pride; 24: 10–12 (28: 16) to continue bearing the Lord's name before world; 24: 11 to glory in the Lord, not self; 28: 3 to declare Joseph Smith's revelations as Aaron[1]; 28: 4 to speak whenever led by Comforter; 28: 5 to write by way of wisdom, not commandment; 28: 8 (30: 6) called to preach to Lamanites; 28: 8 is promised revelations; 28: 11 to warn Hiram Page; 30: 5 to be accompanied by Peter Whitmer, Jun.; 32: 2 Parley P. Pratt to go with; 55: 4 to be assisted by William W. Phelps in providing books for schools; 57: 13 to assist William W. Phelps in printing; 58: 58 (60: 6; 68: 32; 69: 1) journeys of; 61: 23 not to travel on waters; 61: 32 is needed more among brethren than among congregations of the wicked; 63: Intro. arrives in Kirtland from Missouri; 63: 46 and Newell K. Whitney to visit the churches; 67: Intro. (69: Intro.) to take manuscript of revelations to Independence; 68: 32 to carry the Lord's warning to Zion; 70: 3 is appointed and ordained over stewards over revelations and commandments; 82: 11 to be bound by bond and covenant to brethren; 102: Intro. records minutes of first high council; 102: 3, 34 member of first high council; 104: 28–29 to have printing house; 104: 34 lots assigned to; sec. 110 visions manifested to Joseph Smith and; 111: Intro. goes to Salem, Mass., with Joseph Smith; 124: 94–95 place of, given to Hyrum Smith.

JS-H 1: 66 boards at home of Joseph Smith, Sen.; 1: 67 scribe in translating Book of Mormon; 1: 68–73 receives Aaronic Priesthood, is baptized; 1: 73 prophesies following baptism.

COWDERY, WARREN

D&C sec. 106 revelation to; 106: 1 to be ordained presiding high priest in land of Freedom.

CRAFTINESS (see also Cunning; Deceit; Guile; Skill; Subtlety)

D&C 76: 75 (123: 12) honorable men blinded by c. of men; 121: 12 the Lord to take men in their own c.

CREATION, CREATE (see also Adam; Beginning; Creature; Earth; God—Creator;

Jesus Christ—Creator; TG Creation, Create; Earth, Purpose of; Man, Physical Creation of; Spirit Creation)

D&C 14: 9 (45: 1; 76: 24; 93: 10; 104: 14; 117: 6) heavens and earth c. by Jesus Christ; 20: 18 God c. male and female after his image; 29: 30–31 (45: 1) the Lord c. all things by power of his Spirit; 29: 31–33 relationships of temporal and spiritual c.; 38: 3 the Lord spoke and world was made; 45: 1 all things that live were made by the Lord; 49: 16 earth to answer end of its c.; 49: 17 man c. before world was made; 77: 12 God made world in six days; 88: 7 Christ is power by which sun was made; 88: 19, 25 earth to fill the measure of its c.; 88: 20 earth c. for celestial beings; 93: 29 intelligence, or the light of truth, was not c.; 104: 12 the Lord makes every man steward over earthly blessings he has made for his creatures; 128: 23 let eternal c. declare the Lord's name.

Moses 1: 30–31 Moses asks God about his c.; ch. 2–3 c. of heaven and earth revealed to Moses; 2: 27 (6: 9) God c. man in his own image; 3: 5, 7 the Lord c. all things spiritually before naturally; 6: 36 Enoch[2] beholds spirits that God c.; 7: 30 impossible to number God's c.; 7: 31 the Lord has taken Zion from all his c.; 7: 36 the Lord can stretch forth his hands and hold all his c.; 7: 64 Zion shall come forth out of all the Lord's c.

CREATOR (see God—Creator; Jesus Christ—Creator)

CREATURE

D&C 18: 28 (58: 64; 68: 8; 80: 1; 84: 62; 112: 28; 124: 128) gospel to be preached to every c.; 77: 2 spirit of every c. in likeness of its body; 78: 14 church to stand independent of all other c.

Moses 2: 20–25 (3: 19; Abr. 4: 24–25; 5: 20) creation of living c.

CREEP, CREEPING (see also Animal)

D&C 77: 2 (Rev. 4: 6) four beasts represent happiness of man, beast, c. things; 89: 14 grain is ordained for use of wild animals that run on c.

Moses 2: 25 (Abr. 4: 25) creation of everything that c. upon earth.

CRIME (see also Law; Law, Civil; Offense; Sin; Transgression)

D&C 68: 22 bishop or high priest to be tried for c. only before First Presidency; 134: 8 commission of c. should be punished according to nature of offense.

CROOKED (see also Straight)

D&C 3: 2 God does not walk in c.

paths; 33: 2 (34: 6) gospel to be declared unto a c. generation.

CROP (see also Food)

D&C 29: 16 great hailstorm to destroy c.

CROSS (see also Jesus Christ, Death of)

D&C 23: 6 (112: 14) take up your c.; 56: 2 he who will not take up his c. shall not be saved.

CROWN (see also Exaltation; Glory; Reward)

D&C 20: 14 (66: 12; 75: 5; 81: 6; 138: 51) those who accept gospel will receive c. of eternal life, immortality; 25: 15 thou shalt receive c. of righteousness; 29: 13 dead who die in the Lord will receive c. of righteousness; 52: 43 faithful to be c. with joy; 58: 4 after tribulation, saints to be c. with glory; 59: 2 those who die in Zion will receive c. in mansions of the Father; 76: 79 those not valiant obtain not the c.; 76: 108 Christ to be c. with c. of glory; 78: 15 the Lord prepares saints to come up unto c. prepared for them; 81: 6 Frederick G. Williams to have c. of immortality; 88: 19 earth to be c. with glory; 88: 107 angels to be c. with glory; 101: 15 martyrs to be c. with glory; 101: 65 (109: 76) saints to be c. with celestial glory; 104: 7 the Lord has promised saints a c. of glory at his right hand; 124: 95 Hyrum Smith to be c. with same blessings as Joseph Smith; 132: 55 the Lord to give Joseph Smith c. of eternal lives; 133: 32 those from north countries to be c. with glory.

Moses 7: 56 saints c. with glory at right hand of Son; JS-M 1: 1 Christ to come again after he is c. on God's right hand.

CRUCIFIXION (see Jesus Christ, Death of)

CRY (see also Mourn; Plead; Prayer; Wailing; Weep)

D&C 6: 22 cast your mind upon night you c. unto me to know truth; 18: 14–15 (34: 6; 36: 6) c. repentance; 19: 37 (39: 19; 128: 23) declare truth, c. with joy and hosannas; 65: 3 (88: 92; 133: 17) a voice c., Prepare way of the Lord; 86: 5 angels are c. to be sent forth; 87: 7 (109: 49) c. of saints ascend to heaven; 88: 66 voice of one c. in wilderness; 101: 92 pray that ears of government leaders will be open to your c.; 136: 36 innocent blood c. from ground against murderers.

CRYSTAL (see also Glass)

D&C 130: 9 earth to become like c.

CUMORAH, HILL

D&C 128: 20 glad tidings from C. JS-H 1: 42, 50–54, 59 Joseph Smith takes plates from Hill C.

CUNNING (see also Craftiness; Deceit; Subtlety)

D&C 10: 12, 23 c. plan laid by Satan; 10: 43 God's wisdom greater than c.

CUP (see also Drink)

D&C 19: 18 suffering caused Christ to shrink from bitter c.; 29: 17 (43: 26) c. of the Lord's indignation is full, 86: 3 Babylon makes all nations drink her c.; 101: 11 when c. of iniquity is full, the Lord will pour out indignation; 103: 3 the Lord has suffered saints' enemies that their c. might be full.

CURSE, CURSING (see also Cursed [adj.]; Mark; Punishment; TG Curse)

D&C 24: 4, 6, 15 those who reject elders will receive c. instead of blessing; 24: 15 elders to c. those who reject them by casting dust from feet; 24: 17 those who go to law against Joseph Smith will be c. by law; 27: 9 (98: 16–17; 110: 15; 128: 17–18; 138: 48) Elijah to turn hearts of children and fathers to each other, lest earth be smitten with c.; 38: 18 the Lord gives saints a land on which there shall be no c.; 41: 1 the Lord c. those who profess his name but hear not; 61: 14 the Lord c. waters in last days; 61: 17 in beginning, the Lord c. the land; 98: 17 turn hearts of Jews to prophets lest the Lord smite whole earth with c.; 103: 24 saints to c. enemies of God; 103: 25 (124: 93; 132: 47–48) whomsoever ye c., I will c.; 124: 48 ye bring c. by your own works; 128: 18 earth to be smitten with c. unless there is welding link; 133: 2 the Lord to come down upon world with c. to judgment.

Moses 5: 25 God puts c. upon Cain, except he repents; 5: 56 (8: 4) God c. earth with sore c.; 7: 8 the Lord shall c. land with heat and barrenness; Abr. 1: 24 from Ham sprang race that preserved c.; 1: 26 Noah[1] c. Ham as pertaining to priesthood; 2: 11 the Lord will c. those who c. Abraham.

CURSED [adj.] (see also Curse)

D&C 121: 16 c. are they who lift heel against the Lord's anointed.

Moses 4: 23 c. shall be ground for thy sake.

CURTAIN (see also Veil)

D&C 88: 95 c. of heaven to be unfolded; 101: 21 stakes appointed for c. or strength of Zion.

Moses 7: 30 thy c. are stretched out still.

CUSTOM (see also Tradition)

Abr. 1: 8 c. of priest of Pharaoh to offer human sacrifice.

CUT (see also Blot; Cast; Excommunication; Hew; Prune)

D&C 1: 14 those who do not hear voice of the Lord will be c. off; 45: 44 he who watches not for the Lord will be c. off; 50: 8 hypocrites will be c. off; 52: 6 those who are not faithful will be c. off; 52: 11 (84: 97; 109: 59) the Lord will c. his work short; 56: 3 those who do not obey will be c. off; 64: 35 the rebellious will be c. off; 65: 2 (Dan. 2: 34) gospel to roll forth as stone c. out without hands; 85: 11 those c. off from church will not find inheritance; 104: 9 those c. off for transgression cannot escape Satan's buffetings.

CUTLER, ALPHEUS

D&C 124: 132 member of high council.

DAMNATION, DAMNED (see also Condemn; Death, Spiritual; Hell; Punishment; BD Damnation)

D&C 29: 44 (68: 9) those who believe not will receive eternal d.; 42: 60 (68: 9; 84: 74; 112: 29) the disobedient shall be d.; 49: 5 he that receives not the Son shall be d.; 58: 29 he that does not anything until he is commanded is d.; 112: 29 he that is not baptized shall be d.; 121: 23 those who discomfort the Lord's people shall not escape d.; 132: 4 he that does not abide covenant will be d.; 132: 27 those who commit blasphemy against Holy Ghost shall be d.

Moses 5: 15 disbelievers in Son will be d.

DANCE, DANCING (see also BD Dancing)

D&C 136: 28 praise the Lord with d.

DANGER (see also Peril)

D&C 61: 4 many d. upon the waters.

DANIEL (see also Stone; BD Daniel)

D&C 116: 1 (Dan. 7: 9–14) spoke of Adam's visit to Adam-ondi-Ahman; 138: 44 (Dan. 2: 34–35, 44–45) foresaw establishing of God's kingdom.

DARK, DARKEN (see Darkness, Physical; Darkness, Spiritual; Light)

DARKNESS, PHYSICAL (see also Black; Blackness; Darkness, Spiritual; Light; Night)

D&C 29: 14 (34: 9; 45: 42) sun shall be d.

Moses 2: 4, 18 (Abr. 4: 4) light is divided from d.; 7: 61 heavens to be darkened, veil of d. to cover earth; JS-M 1: 33 (Matt. 24: 29) sun shall be darkened as sign of Christ's coming; JS-H 1: 15 d. gathers around Joseph Smith.

DARKNESS, SPIRITUAL (see also Apostasy; Ignorance; Light; Obscurity; Wicked; TG Darkness, Spiritual; Walking in Darkness; BD Darkness)

D&C 1: 30 church to be brought forth out of d.; 6: 21 (10: 58; 34: 2; 39: 2; 45: 7) d. does not comprehend light; 10: 2 because of loss of translation, Joseph Smith's mind is darkened; 10: 21 (29: 45) men love d. rather than light; 11: 11 Christ is light which shines in d.; 14: 9 Jesus Christ, a light which cannot be hid in d.; 21: 6 the Lord to disperse powers of d.; 24: 1 Joseph Smith delivered from powers of Satan and d.; 38: 5 the wicked kept in chains of d. until judgment; 38: 8 veil of d. soon to be rent; 38: 11 powers of d. prevail among men; 38: 12 powers of d. cause silence to reign; 45: 28 (57: 10) those in d. to hear gospel; 50: 23 that which does not edify is d.; 50: 25 know truth to chase d. away; 82: 5 adversary spreads dominions, and d. reigns; 84: 49 world groans under d.; 84: 54 minds are darkened because of unbelief; 84: 80 those who preach gospel shall not be d.; 88: 67 if eye single to the Lord's glory, no d. in you; 95: 6 (95: 12) sin of walking in d. at noonday; 91: 10 (133: 72–73) wicked to have portion in outer d.; 112: 23 d. covers earth, and gross d. minds of people; 138: 22 where rebellious spirits are, d. reigns; 138: 30, 57 righteous spirits carry gospel to those in d.

Moses 5: 51 from days of Cain, men's works were in the d.; 5: 55 works of d. prevail; 6: 28 men have sought own counsels with d.; JS-H 1: 15 d. gathers around Joseph Smith.

DART

D&C 3: 8 faithful to be supported against fiery d. of adversary; 27: 1 shield of faith quenches fiery d. of the wicked.

DAUGHTER (see also Child)

D&C 25: 1 all who receive gospel are sons and d. in kingdom; 76: 24 inhabitants of worlds are begotten sons and d. unto God; 138: 39 Eve and many other

d. seen among the righteous in spirit world.

Abr. 1: 23, 25 Egypt discovered by d. of Ham.

DAVID—*King of Israel (see also* BD *David)*

D&C 109: 63 bondage may be taken from house of D.; 132: 1, 38 D. was given many wives; 132: 39 D. has fallen from exaltation.

DAVIES, AMOS

D&C 124: 111–114 to pay stock in Nauvoo House.

DAY *(see* Day of the Lord; Judgment; Light; Sabbath; Time; BD Day of Atonement)

DAY OF THE LORD *(see also* Day; Jesus Christ, Second Coming of; TG Day of the Lord)

D&C 1: 9 the unbelieving and rebellious to be sealed unto d. of wrath; 1: 10 d. when the Lord comes to recompense men according to works; 1: 14 d. when the wicked shall be cut off; 1: 35 d. of the Lord speedily cometh; 2: 1 (110: 14; 128: 17) Elijah to be sent before great and dreadful d. of the Lord; 29: 9 (43: 17; 110: 16; 128: 24) d. of the Lord is near at hand; 29: 12 the Twelve to stand at Christ's right hand at d. of his coming; 29: 14 (45: 16–33; 49: 24) signs before great d. shall come; 34: 8 all nations to tremble at d. of the Lord's coming; 35: 21 (61: 39) abide d. of the Lord's coming; 39: 10 d. of deliverance are come; 39: 21 (49: 7; 51: 17; 133: 11) no man knows d. or hour of the Lord's coming; 42: 36 covenant people to be gathered in d. when the Lord comes to temple; 43. 21 (58: 11; 133: 10) prepare for great d. of the Lord; 45: 39 he who fears the Lord will look for signs of d. of the Lord's coming; 45: 56 parable of ten virgins to be fulfilled in d. when the Lord comes in glory; 50: 45 d. to come when saints will see the Lord; 56: 1 the rebellious to know the Lord's indignation in d. of visitation; 56: 16 lamentation of the rich in d. of visitation; 58: 11 d. of the Lord's power comes; 63: 6 d. of wrath to come upon the rebellious and unbelieving as whirlwind; 63: 20 he who endures will receive inheritance when d. of transfiguration comes; 85: 3 tithing to prepare saints against d. of vengeance and burning; 87: 8 stand in holy places until d. of the Lord comes; 88: 102 some who remain until great and last d. will be filthy still; 101: 9 in d. of wrath the Lord will remember mercy; 106: 5 gird up loins, that d. of

the Lord may not overtake you; 109: 46 seal up law to prepare against d. of burning; 112: 24 d. of wrath, of burning, of desolation, of weeping, of mourning, of lamentation; 124: 10 d. of visitation comes speedily; 133: 51 the Lord treads upon the wicked in d. of vengeance; 133: 64 d. cometh that shall burn as oven.

Moses 7: 45 when shall d. of the Lord come; 7: 65 Enoch² saw d. of coming of Son; JS-M 1: 40 (Matt. 24: 36) no one knows d. or hour of the Lord's coming.

DEACON *(see also* Priesthood, Aaronic; BD Deacon)

D&C 20: 38, 57–59 (84: 30, 111) office and duty of d.; 20: 57 to assist teachers; 20: 58 has no authority to baptize, administer sacrament, or lay on hands; 20: 60, 64 ordination of d.; 84: 111 d. and teachers appointed to watch over church; 107: 62 need for one to preside over d.; 107: 85 duty of president over d.; 124: 142–143 keys given president of d. and his counselors.

DEAD *(see also* Baptism for the Dead; Death, Physical; Death, Spiritual; Jesus Christ, Resurrection of; Raise; Resurrection)

D&C 22: 2 futility of d. works; 29: 13 the d. which die in the Lord will receive crown of righteousness; 42: 45 weep for the d.; 63: 49 blessed are the d. who die in the Lord; 110: 14–16 Elijah commits keys for work for the d.; 128: 6, 8 the d. are judged out of books; 128: 11 he who has keys can obtain knowledge pertaining to salvation for the d.; 128: 14 records of the d. kept in heaven; 128: 15, 18 without our d. we cannot be made perfect; 128: 19 in gospel we hear voice of gladness for the living and the d.; 128: 24 book containing records of the d. to be presented in temple; 138: 10, 30, 35, 37, 57 gospel preached to spirits of the d.; 138: 48, 54 great work for redemption of the d. to be done in temples; 138: 58 the d. who repent will be redeemed through obedience.

DEAF, DEAFNESS *(see also* Heal; Hear)

D&C 35: 9 the Lord's servants to cause the d. to hear; 58: 11 the d. come to marriage of the Lamb; 84: 69 ears of the d. shall be unstopped.

DEARTH *(see* Famine)

DEATH, PHYSICAL *(see also* Body; Capital Punishment; Dead; Death, Spiritual;

Die; Jesus Christ, Death of; Jesus Christ, Resurrection of; Martyrdom; Raise; Resurrection; Sleep; TG Death; Death, Power over; BD Death)

D&C 7: 2 John the apostle asks for power over d.; 29: 42 Adam was not to die temporal d. until the Lord sent angels to teach him; 29: 43 by natural d. men are raised in immortality unto eternal life; 42: 46 those who die in the Lord shall not taste d.; 42: 47 bitter d. of those who die not in the Lord; 42: 48 those not appointed unto d. shall be healed; 45: 2 hearken unto the Lord's voice lest d. overtake you and soul not saved; 50: 5 they who are faithful in life or d. shall inherit eternal life; 50: 8 hypocrites shall be cut off, in life of d.; 58: 2 he who keeps commandments, whether in life or d., receives greater reward; 63: 50–51 during Millennium, the old will be changed in twinkling of eye; 88: 116 the sanctified shall not any more see d.; 98: 14 the Lord will test you unto d.; 101: 29 there shall be no sorrow because there is no d.; 101: 36 fear not even unto d.; 110: 13 Elijah did not taste d.; 121: 44 show love, that thy faithfulness may be seen as stronger than cords of d.; 124: 130 man's priesthood remains after d.; 132: 13 whatever is not of the Lord ceases at d.; 138: 16 the Son declares redemption from bands of d.; 138: 18 spirits rejoice in deliverance from chains of d.; 138: 23 saints acknowledge Christ as Deliverer from d.

Moses 4: 25 d. came through disobedience; 6: 48, 59 d. came by fall of Adam.

DEATH, SPIRITUAL (see also Damnation; Dead; Death, Physical; Die; Fall of Man; God, Presence of; Hell; Redemption; Repentance; Sin; TG Death, Spiritual, First; Death, Spiritual, Second)

D&C 29: 41 Adam suffered first spiritual d. when cast out of garden; 29: 41 to be cast from God's presence is first d., same as last d., which is spiritual; 29: 44 those who believe not cannot be redeemed from spiritual (old); 63: 17–18 lake which burns with fire and brimstone is second d.; 64: 7 forgiveness for those who have not sinned unto d.; 67: 12 natural man cannot abide presence of God; 76: 37 sons of perdition are only ones on whom second d. shall have power; 132: 25 wide is way that leads to d.; 132: 27 those who commit blasphemy against Holy Ghost will not be forgiven.

Moses 6: 48, 59 d. came by fall of Adam.

DEBT (see also Borrow; TG Debt)

D&C 19: 35 pay d., release thyself from bondage; 64: 27 forbidden to get in d. to enemies; 72: 13 d. of those unable to pay should be paid by bishop; 104: 78 pay all your d.; 111: 5 concern not yourselves about your d.; 115: 13 d. not to be incurred for building house of the Lord; 119: 1–2 surplus property in hands of bishop for payment of d.

DECEIT, DECEIVE, DECEIVING (see also Beguile; Craftiness; Cunning; False, Falsehood; Hypocrisy; Lying)

D&C 10: 25 Satan tells men to d.; 10: 28 wo unto him who lies to d.; 43: 6 saints should not receive those who come with revelations, so that they may not be d.; 45: 57 they who take Holy Spirit for guide and have not been d. shall abide the Lord's coming; 46: 8 that ye may not be d., seek best gifts; 50: 3 Satan seeks to d.; 50: 6 wo unto them that are deceivers and hypocrites; 52: 14 the Lord gives pattern that saints may not be d.; 123: 12 many are blinded by those who lie in wait to d.; 129: 7 contrary to order of heaven for just man to d.

Moses 1: 16 Satan, d. me not; 4: 4 Satan d. and blinds men; JS-M 1: 5 take heed that no man d. you; 1: 6, 22 (Matt. 24: 5, 23–24) false Christs will d. many.

DECISION

D&C 102: 19–22 after hearing evidence in church court, president gives d.; 102: 31 d. of high council may be appealed, but not d. of the Twelve; 107: 27–28 d. of quorums must be unanimous; 107: 30 d. of quorums are to be made in righteousness; 107: 32 unrighteous d. may be appealed to general assembly of quorums; 107: 78 d. of bishop or judges may be appealed to council of church.

DECLARE (see also Preach; Proclamation; Prophecy; Tell)

D&C 10: 68 whoso d. more or less is not of the Lord; 11: 21 obtain word before you d. it; 19: 29 (62: 5) d. glad tidings; 28: 3 d. faithfully the commandments; 29: 4 elders chosen out of world to d. gospel; 60: 7 elders to d. the Lord's word; 128: 21 all angels d. their dispensation; 138: 16, 18 the Son d. redemption from bands of death.

Moses 5: 58 gospel d. by angels from beginning.

DECREE (see also Command; Commandments of God; Consume; Law; Ordain; Statute)

D&C 1: 7 what the Lord d. shall be

fulfilled; **98**: 14 the Lord has d. he will prove saints.

Moses 5: 59 (6: 30) d. sent forth that gospel should be in world until end.

DEDICATE, DEDICATION (see also Consecrate; Devote)

D&C 58: 57 Sidney Rigdon to d. spot for temple; **94**: 6–7, 10, 12 houses to be d. unto the Lord for work of presidency, translation, printing; **95**: 16–17 house to be d. to sacrament offerings and school of apostles; sec. 109 prayer of d. for Kirtland Temple; **109**: 78 (110: 7) accept the d. of this house.

DEED (see also Act; Do; Work [noun])

D&C 10: 21 because d. of the wicked are evil, they do not ask the Lord, **29**: 45 those whose d. are evil will receive their wages; **42**: 30 consecrate properties with a d. which cannot be broken; **64**: 11 let God reward according to d.; **84**: 117 elders to reprove world because of ungodly d.; **99**: 5 the Lord will come quickly to convince all of their ungodly d.; **117**: 11 Newel K. Whitney to be bishop, not in name but in d.

DEEP (see also Depth, Sea)

D&C 122: 7 if thou be cast into the d., it shall be for thy good; **133**: 20 the Lord to stand upon mighty ocean, even great d.; **133**: 23 the Lord to command great d., to be driven back into north countries; **133**: 27 highway to be cast up in midst of d.

Moses 2: 2 (Abr. 4: 2) darkness comes upon face of d.

DEFENCE, DEFENSE, DEFEND (see also Fight; Preserve)

D&C 87: 3 southern states to call upon other nations to d. themselves; **115**: 6 gathering in Zion to be for a d.; **134**: 11 all men are justified in d. themselves.

DEFILE (see also Corrupt; Filthiness; Unclean)

D&C 93: 35 God to destroy whatsoever temple is d.; **138**: 20 the Lord's voice not raised among those who d. themselves while in flesh.

DEGREE (see also Celestial Glory; BD Degrees of Glory)

DELAY

D&C 45: 26 men shall say Christ d. his coming.

DELICATE (see Tender)

DELIGHT (see also Joy; Pleased; Pleasure)

D&C 25: 12 the Lord d. in song of heart; **25**: 14 wife's soul to d. in husband; **41**: 1 the Lord d. to bless his people with greatest of all blessings; **76**: 5 the Lord d. to honor those who serve him in righteousness.

DELIVER, DELIVERANCE (see also Escape; Give; Redemption; Salvation; Save)

D&C 8: 4 gift of revelation shall d. Oliver Cowdery out of hands of enemies; **24**: 1 Joseph Smith is d. from powers of Satan; **30**: 6 ever pray for d.; **39**: 10 days of d. are come; **56**: 18 kingdom of God to come in power and glory unto d. of the poor; **78**: 12 (82: 21; 104: 10; 132: 26) transgressors to be d. over to buffetings of Satan; **95**: 1 the Lord prepares way for those he loves to be d. from temptation; **104**: 80 the Lord to send means for d.; **105**: 8 the Lord to d. churches in time of trouble; **108**: 8 the Lord to bless and d. saints forever; **109**: 32 saints plead for full and complete d.; **109**: 46 d. thy people from calamity; **133**: 67 the Lord's power to d. was not shortened; **133**: 71 none to d. the disobedient; **136**: 26 find that which neighbor has lost and d. it to him; **138**: 15, 18, 49 spirits of dead rejoice because d. was at hand; **138**: 23 saints acknowledge Son as their deliverer from death.

DENOMINATIONS (see also Churches, False; Sect)

D&C 123: 12 many pure in heart among d.

DENY (see also Reject; Renounce)

D&C 11: 25 d. not spirit of revelation; **39**: 16 the Lord cannot d. his word; **42**: 23 (63: 16) he who lusts after woman shall d. the faith; **76**: 35, 43 sons of perdition d. Holy Ghost and Son; **101**: 5 those who will not endure chastening, but d. the Lord, cannot be sanctified; **114**: 2 some among saints d. the Lord's name.

Moses 6: 28 men have d. God.

DEPART (see also Die; Flight; Go; Journey; Leave)

D&C 137: 6 those who d. mortality before restoration may inherit celestial kingdom; **138**: 57 faithful elders who d. this life continue labors in spirit world.

Moses 1: 18, 21 d. hence, Satan.

DEPRIVE (see also Take)

D&C 134: 7 governments have no right to d. people of free exercise of religious belief.

DEPTH (see also Deep)

D&C 54: 5 (121: 22) better if sinner had been drowned in d. of sea; 76: 48 d. of torment no man knows except those ordained to it; 132: 19 he whose marriage is sealed by Holy Spirit of promise shall inherit all heights and d.

DESCEND (see also Descendant; Fall; Jesus Christ, Condescension of; Jesus Christ, Second Coming of)

D&C 6 Christ to reign in heavens till he d. on earth; 88: 6 (122: 8) Savior d. below all things; 93: 15 Holy Ghost d. upon Christ; 128: 19 knowledge of God to d. upon saints; 130: 23 Holy Ghost may d. upon man and not tarry.

Moses 6: 26 Spirit d. upon Enoch²; 6: 65 Spirit d. upon Adam after baptism; 7: 25 Enoch² sees angels d. out of heaven; **JS-H** 1: 16 pillar of light d. upon Joseph Smith; 1: 68 John the Baptist d. in cloud of light.

DESCENDANT (see also Genealogy; Lineage)

D&C 68: 18–20 (107: 16–17, 69–70, 76) no man has legal right to bishopric except d. of Aaron¹; 107: 40 order of priesthood belongs rightly to d. of chosen seed; 107: 69 bishop must be chosen from High Priesthood unless he is d. of Aaron¹; 107: 72–73 bishop who is not d. of Aaron¹ should call counselors; 113: 4, 6 rod from stem of Jesse and root of Jesse are d. of both Jesse and Joseph¹.

DESIGN (see also Plan)

D&C 3: 1 d. of God cannot be frustrated; 10: 31 those who have stolen translation must not accomplish evil d.; 89:4 conspiring men in latter days to have d.

DESIRE (see also Covet; Lust)

D&C 3: 4 man who follows dictates of carnal d. must fall; 4: 3 if ye have d. to serve God, ye are called; 6: 3 (11: 3; 12: 3; 14: 3) who d. to reap, let him reap; 6: 8 (7: 8; 11: 8, 17) as you d. of me, so shall it be done; 6: 20 the Lord speaks to Oliver Cowdery because of his d.; 6: 27 d. to lay up treasures in heaven; 7: 8 Joseph Smith and Oliver Cowdery to have their d., for they joy in that which they d.; 11: 1 Hyrum Smith to have gift if he d. it of the Lord in faith; 11: 21 if you d., you shall have my Spirit; 18: 38 by their d. you shall know the Twelve; 20: 37 all who d. to be baptized shall be received by baptism into church; 42: 12–13 if ye d. glories and mysteries, uphold the prophet; 52: 12 Satan d. to sift you as chaff; 67: 1

d. of elders came up before the Lord; 88: 121 cease from all lustful d.; 95: 16 part of the Lord's house dedicated to offering of most holy d.; 101: 6 because of covetous d., saints polluted inheritances; 137: 9 the Lord judges according to works and d. of men's hearts.

Moses 4: 12 tree to be d. to make wise; 4: 22 thy d. shall be to thy husband; 5: 23 Satan d. to have thee; **JS-H** 1: 15 Joseph offers up d. of heart unto God.

DESOLATION, DESOLATE (see also Abomination of Desolation; Destruction; Empty; Waste)

D&C 5: 19 d. scourge to go forth; 29: 8 saints are gathered to prepare against day when d. is sent forth; 35: 11 nothing to be shown forth except d. upon Babylon; 45: 17 d. to come upon this generation; 45: 31 d. sickness to cover the land; 63: 37 d. to come upon the wicked; 84: 115 house of those who reject gospel shall be left d.; 112: 24 d. to come speedily.

Abr. 4: 2 earth was empty and d.

DESPISE (see also Hate; Reject)

D&C 3: 7 men d. the Lord's words; 35: 13 the Lord calls those who are unlearned and d. to thrash nations; 121: 20 those who persecute saints will be d. by those who flattered them.

DESTROY (see Destruction)

DESTROYER

D&C 61: 19 d. rides upon the waters; 101: 54 watchman could have saved vineyard from d.; 105: 15 d. sent forth to destroy the Lord's enemies.

DESTROYING ANGEL

D&C 89: 21 to pass by those who obey Word of Wisdom.

DESTRUCTION, DESTROY (see also Burn; Calamity; Desolation; Destroyer; Destroying Angel; Earthquake; Famine; Fire; Flood; Iniquity; Scatter; Slaughter; Slay; Waste)

D&C 3: 18 the Lord allowed Lamanites to d. Nephites because of iniquities; 5: 20 the Lord told people of d. of Jerusalem; 5: 33 many lie in wait to d.; 10: 6 servants of Satan have sought to d. Joseph Smith; 10: 22 Satan leads souls to d.; 10: 23 Satan lays cunning plan to d. work of God; 10: 27 (64: 10) Satan seeks to d. souls; 10: 43 the Lord will not suffer those who alter translation to d. his work; 10: 52, 54 the Lord does not bring gospel to d., but to build up; 19: 3 Christ to d. Satan at end of world; 19: 33 d. of self and property if Martin Harris slights the Lord's counsel; 29: 16 great hailstorm to be sent to d. crops; 34: 9 d. await the wicked at the Lord's coming; 61: 31 people ripe for d.; 63: 4 the Lord d. when he pleases; 93: 35 whatsoever temple is defiled, God shall d.; 105: 15 the Lord has sent forth destroyer to d. enemies; 109: 43 delight not in d. of fellow men; 132: 26 those who break new and everlasting covenant shall be d.; 133: 15 he who goes should not look back, lest d. come upon him.

Moses 4: 3 Satan sought to d. man's agency; 4: 6 Satan sought to d. the world.

DETECT (*see also* Revelation; Reveal)

D&C 50: 8 hypocrites shall be d.; 128: 20 voice of Michael d. when he appeared as angel of light; 129: 8 if devil appears as angel of light, shake hands to d. him.

DETERMINE, DETERMINATION

D&C 20: 37 d. to serve the Lord to the end; 88: 133 I receive you to fellowship with unchangeable d.

DETROIT, MICHIGAN (*see also* D&C map, p. 296)

D&C 52: 8 elders to go by way of D.

DEVIL (*see also* Adversary; Angels of the Devil; Church of the Devil; Contention; Devilish; Devils; Evil; Hell; Lucifer; Lying; Perdition; Rebel, Rebellion; Satan; Serpent; Tempt; Wicked; TG Devil; BD Devil)

D&C 1: 35 d. to have power over own dominion; 10: 12 d. seeks to lay cunning plan to destroy the Lord's work; 10: 27 d. goes to and fro in earth to destroy; 10: 43 the Lord's wisdom is greater than cunning of d.; 29: 28 d. and his angels to be cast into everlasting fire; 29: 29 d. and his angels cannot dwell with God; 29: 36 d. tempted Adam; 29: 36 d. rebelled against God; 29: 37 d. and angels thrust down; 29: 39 d. must tempt so that men can be agents unto themselves; 29: 40 Adam became subject to will of d. because of transgression; 76: 28 Satan, that old serpent, the d.; 76: 33, 44 sons of perdition to reign with d. and his angels; 76: 36, 44 d. and his angels go away into lake of fire and brimstone; 76: 85 they who are not to be redeemed from d. until last resurrection are telestial heirs; 88: 110 d. to be bound for thousand years; 88: 113-115 d. shall gather armies to battle against Michael; 121: 4 God controls and subjects the d.; 123: 10 murder of husbands and fathers is enough to make hands of d.

tremble; 128: 20 (129: 8) voice of Michael detected d. when he appeared as angel of light.

Moses 4: 4 Satan became d.

DEVILISH (*see also* Carnal; Devil)

D&C 20: 20 by transgression of laws man became sensual and d.

DEVILS (*see also* Angels of the Devil; Devil; Spirit, Evil)

D&C 24: 13 (35: 9; 84: 67; 124: 98) cast out d. in the Lord's name; 46: 7 do all things in prayer that ye be not seduced by doctrines of d.

DEVOTE, DEVOTION (*see also* Consecrate; Consecration, Law of; Worship)

D&C 59: 10 pay d. to Most High on Sabbath; 104: 26 Martin Harris to d. moneys for proclaiming the Lord's word; 106: 3 Warren Cowdery to d. time to preaching gospel; 134: 4 human law has no right to dictate forms of public or private d.

DEVOUR (*see also* Burn; Consume; Eat; Fire)

D&C 29: 20 beasts shall d. the wicked; 29: 21 great and abominable church to be cast down by d. fire; 97: 26 if Zion disobeys, the Lord will visit her with d. fire.

DEW

D&C 121: 45 doctrine of priesthood to distil upon soul as d. from heaven; 128: 19 knowledge of God to descend as d. of Carmel.

DIE (*see also* Death, Physical; Death, Spiritual; Jesus Christ, Death of; Depart; Perish)

D&C 29: 42 Adam should not d. temporal death until angels sent to teach him; 42: 44 (124: 86) if those blessed by elders d., they shall d. unto the Lord; 42: 45 weep for those who d.; 42: 46 those who d. in the Lord shall not taste death, for it is sweet; 42: 47 bitter death of those who d. not in the Lord; 59: 2 those who d. in Zion shall receive crown in mansions of Father; 63: 49 those who d. in the Lord rise from dead and do not d. after; 63: 50 the faithful who live when the Lord comes will d. at age of man; 76: 72 terrestrial glory includes those who d. without law; 88: 26 although earth shall d., it shall be quickened; 88: 27 although the righteous d., they shall rise again; 101: 30 in day of the Lord, infant shall not d. until old; 101: 35 faithful who d. shall partake of glory; 137: 7-8 those who d. without gospel but would have received it may inherit celestial kingdom; 137: 10 children who d. before age of accountability are saved.

Moses 3: 17 (4: 9–10; Abr. 5: 13) in day thou eatest thereof thou shalt surely d.; 5: 29 if thou tell it, thou shalt d.

DIG (see also Pit)

D&C 88: 51 kingdom likened to man who sent servants to d. in field.

DILIGENCE, DILIGENT, DILIGENTLY (see also Earnest; Endure; Faithful; Obedience)

D&C 4: 6 d. a requirement for serving God; 6: 20 (136: 42) be d. in keeping commandments; 10: 4 be d. unto the end; 18: 8 he who is d. in keeping commandments will be blessed unto eternal life; 21: 7 the Lord knows Joseph Smith's d.; 59: 4 those who are d. to be blessed with commandments and revelations; 90: 15 commandment given for reward of d.; 75: 29 let every man be d. in all things; 84: 43 give d. heed to words of eternal life; 88: 78 teach ye d.; 88: 118 seek d. and teach one another words of wisdom; 90: 24 search d., pray always; 93: 50 see that children are more d. and concerned at home; 98: 10 honest and wise men should be sought for d.; 103: 36 victory and glory brought through d.; 104: 79 blessing obtained by d.; 107: 99 each man to learn his duty and to act d. in office; 124: 49 promise given those who cease not their d.; 127: 4 let your d. be redoubled; 130: 19 person who gains more knowledge and intelligence through d. has advantage in world to come; 136: 27 be d. in preserving what thou hast.

DIRECTION, DIRECT (see also Course; Director; Guide; Inspire; Lead)

D&C 20: 67 priesthood officers to be ordained by d. of high council or general conference; 20: 80 transgressors to be dealt with as scriptures d.; 42: 13 elders to teach church covenants, d. by Spirit; 46: 2 elders to conduct meetings as d. by Spirit; 82: 9 commandments given as d.; 107: 10 high priests officiate under d. of presidency; 107: 33 the Twelve officiate under d. of the Presidency; 107: 34 the Seventy act under d. of the Twelve.

DIRECTOR (see also Liahona)

D&C 3: 15 you suffered counsel of your d. to be trampled upon.

DISCERN (see also Discerner; Enlighten; Light; Perceive; TG Discernment, Spiritual)

D&C 46: 8 seek best gifts to avoid being deceived; 46: 23 (50: 31–33) spiritual gift to d. spirits; 46: 27 bishop and elders to d. whether gifts are of God; 52: 19 pattern for knowing spirits; 63: 41 Joseph Smith given power to d. who should go to Zion; 101: 95 men may d. between the righteous and the wicked; sec. 129 d. of angels and spirits; 131: 7 spirit can only be d. by purer eyes.

Moses 1: 27–28 Moses d. whole earth by Spirit.

DISCERNER

D&C 33: 1 the Lord a d. of thoughts and intents.

DISCIPLE (see also Apostle; Follow, Follower; Servant; TG Disciple; BD Disciple)

D&C 1: 4 voice of warning to all people by voice of the Lord's d.; 1: 5 none shall stay the Lord's d.; 18: 27 Twelve shall be the Lord's d.; 41: 5 he who does the law is the Lord's d.; 45: 32 the Lord's d. shall stand in holy places; 52: 40 he who does not remember poor and needy is not the Lord's d.; 64: 8 d. of old were chastened; 84: 91 d. to be known by their works; 103: 27–28 he who is not willing to lay down life for the Lord's sake is not the Lord's d.

DISOBEDIENCE, DISOBEDIENT (see also Obedience; Rebel; Sin; Transgression; TG Disobedience; Disobey)

D&C 56: 3 (1: 14) he who will not obey shall be cut off; 58: 32 the Lord commands and men obey not; 59: 21 those who obey not his commandments offend God; 88: 35 that which breaks law cannot be sanctified by law; 93: 39 wicked one takes away light and truth through d.; 97: 26 results of d.; 103: 8 world shall prevail if saints are d.; 121: 17 some cry transgression because of d.; 133: 63 punishment of the d.; 133: 71 none to deliver you, for you obeyed not my voice; 138: 8–9 Savior preached to spirits who were d.; 138: 29 the Lord went not in person among the d.

DISPENSATION (see also BD Dispensation)

D&C 27: 13 (112: 30; 121: 31; 128: 18) the Lord commits d. of gospel for last times, for fulness of times; 110: 12 Elias committed d. of gospel of Abraham; 110: 16 keys of this d. are committed; 112: 31 power of priesthood held in connection with that of earlier d.; 112: 32 keys of this d. come down from the fathers; 121: 31 all knowledge revealed in this d.; 128: 9 whenever the Lord has given d. of priesthood, power which binds in heaven also given; 128: 18 welding together of d.; 128: 20 Peter, James, and John possess keys of d.; 128: 21 voices of angels all declaring their d.; 138: 48 great work to be done in temples in d. of fulness of times; 138: 57 faithful elders of this d. continue labors among the dead.

DISPERSE (see also Scatter; TG Israel, Scattering of; BD Dispersions)

D&C 21: 6 the Lord will d. powers of darkness.

DISPLEASURE, DISPLEASE (see also Anger; Wrath)

D&C 58: 41 (60: 2; 68: 31; 90: 35; 98: 19) the Lord is not well pleased with some saints; 63: 11 with whom the Lord is angry he is not well pleased.

Moses 5: 52 Lamech¹ and his house d. God because of disobedience; 7: 34 in his hot d. God will send floods.

DISPOSITION

D&C 121: 39 it is d. of almost all men to exercise unrighteous dominion.

DISSENSION (see also Contention)

D&C 10: 48 some Nephites became Lamanites because of d.

DIVERSITY

D&C 46: 16 given by Holy Ghost to know d. of operations.

DIVIDE, DIVISION (see also Separation)

D&C 6: 2 (11: 2; 12: 2; 14: 2; 33: 1) the Lord's word sharper than sword to d. asunder joints and marrow; 133: 24 earth to be as it was before it was d.; 138: 17 reunited body and spirit shall never be d. again.

DIVORCE (see also Marriage; BD Divorce)

D&C 42: 22 thou shalt love thy wife and cleave unto her; 42: 74–76 manner of dealing with persons who have left their companions.

DO, DID, DONE (see also Deed; Labor; Obedience; Perform; Walk; Wrought)

D&C 1: 32 he who d. commandments shall be forgiven; 41: 5 he who d. law is disciple; 42: 38 as ye d. it to the least, ye d. it to the Lord; 82: 10 I, the Lord, am bound when ye d. what I say; 98: 22 if ye observe to d. whatsoever I command, I will turn away wrath.

Moses 4: 19 what is this thing thou hast d.; 5: 23 if thou d. well, thou shalt be accepted.

DOCTRINE (see also Gospel; Law; Precept; Principle)

D&C 10: 62 other sheep shall bring to light true points of the Lord's d.; 10: 63 Satan stirs up hearts to contention concerning d.; 10: 67 this is my d.; 11: 16 wait, that you may know of a surety the Lord's d.; 68: 25 teach children d. of repentance, faith, baptism; 88: 77 teach one another d. of kingdom; 97: 14 saints to be perfected in d.; 102: 23 presidency to obtain revelation to resolve difficulties respecting d.; 121: 45 d. of priesthood shall distil upon soul.

DOCTRINE, FALSE (see also Apostasy; Churches, False; Contention; Err; Precept; Prophets, False)

D&C 43: 5 receive not the teachings of any who come before you as revelations or commandments; 46: 7 be not seduced by d. of devils; 50: 23 that which does not edify is not of God; 123:12 many are blinded by subtle craftiness of men.

JS-H 1: 19 professors of religion teach for d. the commandments of men.

DOCTRINE AND COVENANTS (see also Book of Commandments)

D&C 70: Intro. importance of D. and C.; 124: 141 knowledge of bishopric given in D. and C.; 135: 3 Joseph Smith brought forth revelations of D. and C.; 135: 6 D. and C. cost best blood of century; 138: Intro. meeting to consider contents of first edition of D. and C.

DODDS, ASA

D&C 75: 15 called to proclaim gospel in west.

DOG (see also Animal; BD Dog)

D&C 41: 6 things of kingdom not to be given to unworthy, or to d.

DOMINION (see also Authority; Kingdom; Power; Reign; Rule)

D&C 1: 35 devil shall have power over his own d.; 76: 95 celestial heirs to be equal in power, might, and d.; 76: 111 each man to receive d. according to works; 76: 114 works of the Lord surpass understanding in d.; 82: 5 adversary spreads his d.; 121: 29 d. to be revealed to the valiant; 121: 37 when men exercise unrighteous d., Spirit withdraws; 121: 39 nature of almost all men to exercise unrighteous d.; 121: 46 everlasting d. promised.

Moses 2: 26 (Abr. 4: 26) man to have d.; 6: 15 Satan has great d. among men.

DOOR (see also Gate)

D&C 45: 63 wars are nigh, even at d.; 100: 3 (112: 19; 118: 3) effectual d. shall be opened; 107: 35 the Twelve hold keys to open d. by proclamation of gospel; 110: 16 day of the Lord is at the d.

Moses 5: 23 if thou doest not well, sin lieth at the d.; **JS-M** 1: 39 (Matt. 24: 33) by signs the elect shall know Son's coming is at the d.

DORT, DAVID

D&C 124: 132 member of high council.

DOUBT, DOUBTINGS (see also Belief; Faith; Unbelief; TG Doubt, Doubtful)

D&C 6: 36 d. not, fear not; 8: 8 d. not, for gift of Aaron[1] is of God; 58: 29 he who receives commandment with d. heart is damned; 60: 7 declare the Lord's word without wrath or d.

DOVE (see also Holy Ghost; TG Holy Ghost, Sign of; BD Dove; Dove, Sign of)

D&C 93: 15 Holy Ghost descends upon Savior in form of d.

DRAW

D&C 88: 63 d. nigh to the Lord, and he will d. nigh to you.

JS-H 1: 19 they d. near me with lips, but hearts are far from me.

DREADFUL (see Day of the Lord)

DRINK, DRUNK (see also Cup; Drunken; Eat; Sacrament; Wine)

D&C 27: 5 I will d. of fruit of vine with you; 89: 5, 7 strong d. is not good; 89: 9 hot d. not for body or belly; 89: 17 barley and other grain for mild d.

DROUGHT (see Famine)

DRUNKEN, DRUNKENNESS (see also Wine; TG Drunkenness)

D&C 49: 23 (88: 87) earth to reel as d. man; 89: 5 wine or strong drink is not good; 136: 24 cease d.

DRY (see also Ground)

D&C 133: 68 at his rebuke the Lord d. up the sea.

Moses 2: 9–10 (Abr. 4: 9–10) creation of d. land.

DUMB (see also Heal)

D&C 35: 9 (84: 70) the Lord's servants to cause d. to speak.

Abr. 1: 7 fathers offered up children to d. idols.

DUST (see also Earth; Ground)

D&C 24: 15 (60: 15; 75: 20) elders to curse those who reject them by casting d. off feet; 63: 51 old men shall die, but not sleep in d.; 75: 21 elders to be judges over house where they shake off d. of feet; 77: 12 God formed man out of d.; 138: 17 sleeping d. of dead shall be restored to perfect frame.

Moses 3: 7 (Abr. 5: 7) man formed from d.; 4: 20 d. shalt thou eat; 4: 25 d. thou wast, unto d. shalt thou return.

DUTY (see also Perform; Responsibility)

D&C 20: 38–67 d. of elders, priests, teachers, deacons; 20: 47, 51 members to attend to all family d.; 20: 68–69 d. of the members after baptism; 72: 9 d. of bishop; 105: 10 elders to know more perfectly their d.; 107: 38 d. of Twelve to call upon seventy; 107: 39 d. of Twelve to ordain evangelical ministers; 107: 85–91 d. of presidents; 107: 99 let every man learn his d.; 123: 7 imperative d. that saints owe to God.

DWELL, DWELLING (see also Abide; God, Presence of)

D&C 6: 30 those persecuted will d. with the Lord in glory; 8: 2 Holy Ghost shall d. in heart; 76: 62 those in celestial glory d. in presence of God and Christ; 76: 112 telestial inhabitants cannot d. where God and Christ are; 93: 4, 11 Son d. in flesh among men; 104: 59 the Lord to d. with his people; 124: 27 build house for the Most High to d. in; 130: 22 if Holy Ghost were not a spirit, he could not d. in men; 133: 35 Judah to d. in the Lord's presence.

DWINDLE, DWINDLING (see Unbelief)

EAGLE (see also Animal)

D&C 124: 18 the Lord will bear his servant up as on e's wings; 124: 19 he shall mount up in imagination as upon e's wings.

EAMES, RUGGLES

D&C 75: 35 to preach with Stephen Burnett.

EAR (see also Hear)

D&C 1: 2 no e. that shall not hear; 43: 1 (45: 1; 50: 1; 58: 1; 63: 1; 76: 1) give e. to the Lord's word; 76: 10 the Lord will make known things that no e. has heard; 78: 2 the Lord will speak in your e. words of wisdom; 84: 69 elders shall unstop e. of the deaf; 88: 104 every e. shall hear; 101: 92 pray that the e. of unfaithful stewards may be opened;

121: 2 how long shall the Lord's *e.* be penetrated with saints' cries; 121: 4 let the Lord's *e.* be inclined; 133: 45 men have not perceived by *e.* how great things God has prepared.

Moses 6: 27 *e.* are dull of hearing.

EARLY

D&C 54: 10 (88: 83) those that seek the Lord *e.* shall find him; 88: 124 retire to thy bed *e.*, arise *e.*

EARNEST, EARNESTLY (see also Diligence)

D&C 46: 5–6 *e.* seek the kingdom; 46: 8 seek ye *e.* the best gifts; 68: 31 saints' children seek not *e.* the riches of eternity; 93: 48 Joseph Smith's family must give more *e.* heed to his sayings; 103: 35 (130: 14) pray *e.*; 117: 13 contend *e.* for redemption; 130: 13–14 Joseph Smith receives revelations while praying *e.*

EARTH (see also Creation; Dust; Earthly; Earthquake; Ground; Land; World; TG Earth, Cleansing of; Earth, Curse of; Earth, Destiny of; Earth, Dividing of; Earth, Purpose of; Earth, Renewal of)

D&C 1: 35 peace shall be taken from *e.*; 1: 38 (29: 23; 43: 31–32; 56: 11) *e.* shall pass away; 2: 3 (27: 9; 128: 18; 138: 48; Mal. 3: 5–6) hearts of children to be turned to fathers lest *e.* be smitten with curse; 10: 27 Satan goes up and down in *e.*; 14: 9 Christ created heavens and *e.*; 15: 2 the Lord's arm is over all the *e.*; 20: 17 God is framer of *e.*; 29: 9 hour is nigh when *e.* is ripe; 29: 23 there shall be new heaven and new *e.*; 29: 26 the dead to awake before *e.* passes away; 38: 17 the Lord made *e.* rich; 43: 31 after Satan is loosed comes end of *e.*; 45: 48 (88: 87) *e.* shall tremble; 45: 58 (56: 20; 63: 20; 103: 7) *e.* shall be given to saints for inheritance; 49: 19 (59: 17–19) products of *e.* are ordained for use of man; 55: 1 the Lord of whole *e.*; 56: 18 (88: 17) the poor and meek shall inherit *e.*; 59: 3 those who obey gospel shall receive good things of *e.*; 59: 3 *e.* shall bring forth in its strength; 59: 15–16 fulness of *e.* belongs to those who remember Sabbath and fast with thanksgiving; 59: 20 things of *e.* to be used in judgment, not to excess; 63: 21 *e.* to be transfigured; 67: 2 heavens and *e.* are in the Lord's hands; 76: 63 the Lord to come in glory to reign on *e.*; 77: 1 (130: 7) *e.* in its sanctified, immortal, and eternal state; 77: 6 seven thousand years of *e.*'s continuance; 78: 19 things of *e.* shall be added to him who receives with thankfulness; 84: 101 *e.* clothed with glory of her God; 84: 118 the Lord will shake *e.*; 88: 10

Christ the light of the *e.*; 88: 18 *e.* to be sanctified in preparation for celestial glory; 88: 19 (130: 7) *e.* to be crowned with glory, with presence of God; 88: 20 celestial inhabitants shall possess *e.*; 88: 25 *e.* abides law of celestial kingdom; 88: 26 *e.* shall die, be quickened again, and shall abide; 88: 43 course of *e.* is fixed; 101: 25 all things shall become new upon *e.*; 104: 14 *e.* is the Lord's handiwork; 104: 17 *e.* is full; 123: 7 *e.* groans under iniquity; 130: 5 angels who minister to this *e.*; 130: 9 *e.* sanctified, to be made like crystal, will be a Urim and Thummim; 133: 24 *e.* to be like it was before it was divided.

Moses 1: 27 Moses beholds whole *e.*; 1: 29 each land was called *e.*; 1: 38 as one *e.* passes away, another shall come; 1: 40 the Lord speaks to Moses concerning *e.* upon which he stands; 2: 10 (Abr. 4: 9–10) creation of *e.*; 5: 56 *e.* cursed with sore curse; 6: 44 (Abr. 2: 7) *e.* is God's footstool; 7: 30 God has created millions of earths like this *e.*; 7: 48 *e.*, mother of men, yearns for rest; 7: 49 *e.* mourns; 7: 61 *e.* to rest after tribulation; 7: 64 *e.* to rest a thousand years; 8: 28–30 *e.* corrupt before God, filled with violence; **Abr.** 3: 6–7 Abraham knows set time of *e.*; **JS—M** 1: 1 Christ to come again upon *e.*

EARTHLY (see also Earth; Temporal; World)

D&C 78: 5 saints to be equal in *e.* things; 104: 13 every man is accountable as steward over *e.* things.

EARTHQUAKE (see also Earth; Shake; Tremble; TG Earthquake)

D&C 29: 13 (43: 18; 45: 33, 48; 49: 23; 84: 118; 88: 87) *e.* at the Lord's coming; 43: 25 the Lord calls by voice of *e.*; 87: 6 with *e.* shall inhabitants of earth feel wrath of God; 88: 89 after elders' testimony comes testimony of *e.*

JS—M 1: 29 (Matt. 24: 7) there shall be *e.* in divers places.

EAT, EATEN (see also Consume; Devour; Drink; Food; Partake; Taste)

D&C 20: 77 *e.* bread in remembrance of the Son's body; 27: 2 it matters not what saints *e.* to partake of sacrament; 29: 18 flies to *e.* flesh of the wicked; 42: 42 the idle shall not *e.* bread of laborer; 64: 34 the willing and obedient shall *e.* the good of land; 77: 14 book which was *e.* by John; 84: 81 take no thought what ye shall *e.*; 101: 101 saints to plant vineyards and *e.* fruit.

Moses 4: 12 Eve and Adam *e.* forbidden fruit.

EDEN, GARDEN OF—*home of Adam and Eve (see also* Adam; Creation; Fall of Man; Fruit, Forbidden; Tree of Life; BD Eden, Garden of)

D&C 29: 41 Adam was cast out of E. because of transgression.

Moses 3: 8, 15 (Abr. 5: 8, 11) man put into garden in E.; 3: 9 tree of life planted in E.; 3: 9 (Abr. 5: 13) tree of knowledge of good and evil in E.; 3: 10 the Lord causes river to go out of E. to water garden; 4: 29 the Lord sends man forth from E.; 4: 31 cherubim and flaming sword to guard E.; 5: 4 Adam and Eve hear voice from way toward E.; 6: 53 Adam's transgression in E. forgiven; 7: 32 the Lord gave man his agency in E.

EDGE (*see* Sharp)

EDIFICATION, EDIFY (*see also* Enlighten; Instruction)

D&C 43: 8 (88: 122; 107: 85) instruct and e. each other; 50: 22 he that preaches and he that receives understand each other and are e.; 50: 23 that which does not e. is not of God; 52: 16 he whose language is meek and e. is of God; 84: 106 the strong in spirit should e. the weak in meekness; 84: 110 body needs every member, that all may be e. together; 88: 137 house of the Lord a tabernacle of Holy Spirit to saints' e.; 136: 24 let words e. one another.

EDUCATION (*see* TG Education)

EFFECT

D&C 54: 4 broken covenant becomes void and of none e.

EGYPT—*land of Israel's captivity (see also* Egyptian; Egyptus; BD Egypt)

D&C 136: 22 the Lord led children of Israel out of E.

Abr. 1: 8, 21, 26 Pharaoh, king of E.; 1: 23 E. was discovered by daughter of Ham; 1: 23 E. signifies that which is forbidden; 1: 25 first government of E. established after manner of patriarchal government of Ham; 2: 21 (3: 15) Abraham journeys toward E.

EGYPTIAN (*see also* Egypt; Language)

Abr. 1: 11 virgins killed upon altar after manner of E.; 1: 21–22 E. are descendants of Ham; JS-H 1: 64 characters on plates resemble E.

EGYPTUS (*see also* Egypt)

Abr. 1: 23 Egypt discovered by daughter of E.; 1: 23 E. signifies Egypt, that which is forbidden.

EIGHT (*see also* Accountability, Age of)

D&C 138: 9 in days of Noah[1], e. souls were saved.

ELDER (*see also* Priesthood, Melchizedek; TG Elder; Elder—Melchizedek Priesthood; BD Elders)

D&C 20: 2 Joseph Smith, first e. of church; 20: 3 Oliver Cowdery, second e. of church; 20: 16 e. to bear witness of God's words; 20: 38 apostle is an e.; 20: 45 (46: 2) duty of e. to conduct meetings as led by Spirit; 20: 60 every e. to be ordained according to gifts and callings of God unto him; 20: 70 e. to bless children; 21: 1 Joseph Smith to be called an e.; 42: 12 e. to teach gospel from scriptures; 42: 31, 71 two e. or high priests to be appointed bishop's counselors; 42: 44 e. to lay hands on sick; 43: 15 e. sent forth to teach, not to be taught; 43: 16 e. to be taught from on high; 53: 3 ordination of e. to teach first principles; 68: 8–12 (133: 8) e. called to missionary work; 72: 5, 16, 19, 25 e. to render account of stewardship; 84: 29 (107: 7) office of e. a necessary appendage to high priesthood; 84: 111 (124: 137) e. called to travel; 105: 11 e. to be endowed with power; 105: 33 first e. should receive their endowment; 107: 10 high priests may officiate in office of e.; 107: 12 high priest and e. are to administer in spiritual things; 107: 60 presiding e. needed to preside over e.; 107: 89 duty of president over office of e.; 124: 125 Joseph Smith, presiding e. over church; 124: 139 seventies to be traveling e.; 133: 8 send forth e. unto nations; 138: 57 faithful e. continue labors in spirit world.

ELECTION, ELECT (*see also* Choose; Chosen; Exaltation; Heir; Premortal Existence; Seal; TG Election; Elect; BD Election)

D&C 25: 3 Emma Smith, an e. lady; 29: 7 (33: 6) elders called to bring to pass gathering of the e.; 29: 7 (33: 6; 35: 21) the e. hear the Lord's voice and harden not hearts; 35: 20 scriptures given for salvation of the e.; 35: 21 the e. to abide the Lord's coming because they will be purified; 84: 34 those who magnify callings in priesthood become the e. of God; 84: 99 the Lord has redeemed Israel according to e. of grace.

Moses 7: 62 (JS-M 1: 27) the Lord to gather his e. unto Zion; JS-M 1: 20 (Matt. 24: 22) for the e's sake, days of tribulation shall be shortened; 1: 22 (Matt. 24: 24) false Christs shall deceive the e., if possible.

ELEMENT (see also Materials; Matter)

D&C 93: 33 e. are eternal; 93: 33 spirit and e. inseparably connected receive fulness of joy; 93: 35 e. are tabernacle of God; 101: 25 e. shall melt with fervent heat.

ELIAS (see also Elijah; BD Elias)

D&C 27: 6 E. given keys to bring to pass restoration of all things; 27: 7 E. visited Zacharias; 27: 7 John the Baptist was filled with spirit of E.; 77: 9, 14 E. to come to gather tithes of Israel and restore all things; 110: 12 E. commits dispensation of gospel of Abraham; 138: 45 Joseph F. Smith saw E., who was with Moses on Mount of Transfiguration.

ELIHU (see also BD Elihu)

D&C 84: 8 gave priesthood to Caleb; 84: 9 received priesthood from Jeremy.

ELIJAH—prophet of Israel [ca. 900 B.C.] (see also Elias; BD Elijah)

D&C 2: 1 the Lord to reveal priesthood by hand of E.; 27: 9 (110: 15; 128: 17; 138: 47) E. was given keys of turning hearts of children and fathers to each other; 35: 4 Sidney Rigdon is called to prepare way before E.; 110: 13–16 E. appears at dedication of Kirtland Temple; 138: 46 Malachi prophesied of coming of E.

ELKENAH (see also Gods; Idolatry)

Abr. 1: 6 people's hearts turned to god of E.; 1: 7 priest of E. tries to take Abraham's life; 1: 13 altar stands before god of E.; 1: 20 the Lord breaks down altar of E.; (3: 20) the Lord sent angels to deliver Abraham from gods of E.

EMBLEM (see also Remember, Remembrance; Representation; Sacrament; Token; Type)

D&C 20: 40, 75–79 bread and wine e. of Christ's flesh and blood.

EMBRACE (see also Accept; Receive)

D&C 36: 7 every man who e. church with singleness of heart should be ordained and sent out; 42: 39 the Lord to consecrate unto the poor of Israel the riches of Gentiles who e. gospel; 88: 40 truth e. truth.

EMPTY (see also Desolation, Desolate; Void; Waste)

D&C 5: 19 scourge to be poured out until earth is e.

END, ENDS (see also Beginning; Endless; Endure; Finish; Last; Last Days; Pass; TG World, End of)

D&C 6: 13 (18: 22; 20: 25, 29; 31: 13; 53: 7; 81: 1) be faithful to e.; 10: 4 be diligent unto e.; 19: 3 Satan to be destroyed at e. of world; 20: 28 Father, Son, and Holy Ghost are one God without e.; 20: 37 (76: 5) serve the Lord to the e.; 24: 8, 10 (75: 11, 13–14; 100: 12; 105: 41; 132: 49) I am with thee to the e.; 29: 23 (43: 31; 45: 22) e. shall come; 29: 33 the Lord's work to have no e.; 38: 5 judgment at e. of earth; 43: 31 Satan reigns previous to the e.; 43: 33 (76: 45, 48) no man knows e. of the wicked; 45: 26 men shall say Christ delays coming until e. of earth; 46: 7 consider e. of your salvation; 49: 16 earth to answer e. of its creation; 59: 20 unto this e. were things of earth made; 76: 112 worlds without e.; 87: 6 consumption to make e. of all nations; 88: 66 truth has no e.; 88: 101 final resurrection at the e.; 88: 102 some who remain until e. shall remain filthy; 88: 138–139 unto this e. was washing of feet instituted; 101: 32–33 the Lord to reveal purpose and e. of earth; 107: 42 posterity of Seth[1] to be preserved to e. of earth; 122: 1 e. of earth shall inquire; 124: 1 unto this e. have I raised you up; 131: 4 those who enter not the covenant of marriage have e. of kingdom; 132: 7 all contracts not made to this e. have e. when men are dead; 132: 20 they shall be gods because they have no e.

Abr. 3: 18 spirits shall have no e.; JS-M 1: 4 what is sign of e. of world.

ENDLESS (see also End; Eternal; Everlasting; God, Eternal Nature of; Infinite; Misery; Torment)

D&C 19: 12 E. is God's name; 19: 12 (76: 44) e. punishment is God's punishment.

Moses 1: 3 (7: 35) name of God is E.

ENDOW, ENDOWMENT (see also Endowment House; Ordinance; Temple)

D&C 38: 32, 38 (43: 16; Luke 24: 49) saints to be e. with power; 95: 8 the Lord to e. with power those whom he has chosen; 105: 11–12 the Lord has prepared great e. for elders; 110: 9 rejoicing because of e. with which the Lord's servants have been e.; 124: 39 e. ordained by ordinance of the Lord's holy house; 132: 59 those called by the Father, as Aaron, are e. with keys of priesthood; 137: Intro. administration of ordinances of e.

ENDOWMENT HOUSE

D&C OD-1 taken down because of unauthorized marriage.

ENDURE, ENDURANCE (see also Bear; Continue; Diligence; Faint; Faithful; Firmness; Obedience; Perseverance; Probation; Steadfast)

D&C 10: 69 those who e. to end will be established upon the Lord's rock; 14: 7 (50: 5; 66: 12) those who e. to end shall inherit eternal life; 18: 22 (20: 25, 29; 53: 7) those who e. to end shall be saved; 24: 8 e. afflictions, for the Lord is with you; 63: 20, 47 he who e. in faith shall overcome; 84: 24 those who harden hearts could not e. the Lord's presence; 101: 5 those who will not e. chastening cannot be sanctified; 101: 35 those who e. in faith shall partake of glory; 121: 8 e. adversity well, and God shall exalt thee; 121: 29 those who e. valiantly will receive thrones and dominions.

Moses 1: 2 Moses could e. God's presence; A of F 13 we have e. many things and hope to be able to e. all things.

ENEMY (see also Adversary; Foe; Oppressor)

D&C 8: 4 spirit of revelation to deliver Joseph Smith out of hands of e.; 24: 1 Joseph Smith delivered from e.; 27: 3 saints not to purchase wine of e.; 35: 14 e. of the Lord's servants shall be under their feet; 37: 1 translation is stopped because of e.; 38: 9 e. shall not overcome; 38: 28 e. seeks lives of saints; 38: 31 the Lord commands saints to go to the Ohio to escape e.; 42: 43 sick not to be nourished by e.; 44: 5 church to organize so that e. do not have power to destroy; 49: 6 Christ will descend to put all e. under his feet; 54: 3 to escape e. repent and be humble; 58: 22 (76: 61, 106) the Lord will subdue all e.; 63: 31 if land of Zion is obtained by blood, e. will scourge saints; 64: 27 forbidden to get in debt to e.; 65: 5 kingdom to go forth that the Lord's e. may be subdued; 71: 7 confound your e.; 87: 7 blood of saints to be avenged of e.; 98: 14 (136: 17, 30) be not afraid of e.; 98: 23–31 reward for long-suffering toward e.; 98: 39–40 if e. repent, forgive him seventy times seven; 101: 51 e. came by night and broke down hedge; 103: 2 conditions upon which saints should prevail against e.; 103: 24–25 e. to be cursed; 105: 15 destroyer to lay waste e.; 121: 5 prayer that the Lord's anger be kindled against e.; 121: 43 show increase of love, lest he esteem thee to be e.; 133: 28 e. shall become a prey; 136: 40 the Lord has delivered saints from e.

ENGAGED (see also Idleness)

D&C 58: 27 men should be anxiously e. in good cause.

ENGRAVINGS (see also Plates; Record; Writing)

D&C 8: 1 Oliver Cowdery to receive knowledge concerning e. of ancient records.

ENLARGE (see also Grow; Increase)

D&C 82: 14 (107: 74; 133: 9) Zion's borders must be e.; 121: 42 kindness and pure knowledge shall greatly e. the soul; 132: 17 angels did not abide law, so could not be e.

ENLIGHTEN (see also Discern; Edification; Illuminate; Inspire; Light; Quicken; Shine)

D&C 6: 15 thou hast inquired and I did e. thy mind; 76: 12 eyes were opened and understanding e.; 84: 46 Spirit e. every man; 88: 11 light is through him who e. your eyes; 91: 5 whoso is e. by Spirit shall benefit from Apocrypha.

ENMITY

D&C 101: 26 e. of men, of beasts, of all flesh to cease.

Moses 4: 21 I will put e. between thee and the woman.

ENOCH¹—son of Cain (see also BD Enoch)

Moses 5: 42 Cain names city after his son, E.

ENOCH²—great prophet, leader of city of Zion (see also Translated Beings; Zion)

D&C 38: 4 the Lord took Zion of E. to his bosom; 45: 12–14 (107: 49) E. and his city were separated from earth; 76: 57 priesthood after order of Melchizedek is after order of E.; 76: 67 those who inherit celestial glory come to church of E.; 84: 15–16 priesthood was passed through lineage of fathers from E. to Noah¹ to Abel; 107: 49 E. saw the Lord and walked with him continually; 107: 53 E. was called to gathering of Zion at Adam-ondi-Ahman; 107: 57 gathering of Adam's posterity recorded in book of E.

Moses 6: 21 son of Jared¹; 6: 21, 41 is taught in ways of God; 6: 26, 34 Spirit of God descends upon E.; 6: 21 is commanded to prophesy; 6: 31 bows before the Lord; 6: 32–33 receives instructions from the Lord; 6: 34 is given power and blessing; 6: 34, 39 (7: 69) walks with God; 6: 36 beholds spirits that God has created; 6: 36 is called a seer; 6: 37 goes forth in the land, testifying; 6: 41 comes out from land of Cainan; 6: 42 sees a vision and receives commandments; 6: 47 people tremble in presence of E.; 7: 2 begins to prophesy; 7: 4 talks with God; 7: 9

beholds land of E.; 7: 10 is commanded to cry repentance; 7: 11 is commanded to baptize; 7: 13 faith of E.; 7: 13 leads people in battle; 7: 19 builds city, called City of Holiness; 7: 21 is lifted up in bosom of the Father; 7: 32 sees Garden of Eden in vision; 7: 41, 44 weeps for wickedness of children of men; 7: 45 beholds all families of earth; 7: 47 sees day of coming of the Son; 7: 49 cries for compassion upon the earth; 7: 49–50 pleads for Noah[1] and his seed; 7: 63 E. and his city to meet the elect in New Jerusalem; 7: 67 is shown all things even to end of world; 8: 1 lives 430 years; 8: 2–12 genealogy of E. to sons of Noah.[1]

ENOS—*grandson of Adam (see also* BD *Enos)*

D&C 107: 44 ordained by Adam; 107: 53 is called to gathering of Adam's posterity at Adam-ondi-Ahman.

Moses 6:3, 13 son of Seth[1]; 6: 13 prophesies; 6: 17 dwells in a land of promise; 6: 17 father of Cainan.

ENOUGH (*see also* Sufficient)

D&C 104: 17 earth is full, there is e. and to spare.

ENSAMPLE (*see* Example)

ENSIGN (*see also* Standard)

D&C 64: 42 Zion to be e. unto people; 105: 39 lift an e. of peace; 113: 6 root of Jesse belong keys of kingdom, for an e.

ENTANGLE

D&C 20: 5 Joseph Smith e. again in vanities of world; 88: 86 e. not yourselves in sin.

ENTER (*see also* Come, Gate; Rest)

D&C 132: 4 no one can reject covenant and e. into the Lord's glory; 138: 51 righteous spirits given power to e. the Father's kingdom.

ENTRUSTED (*see also* Give)

D&C 3: 5 Joseph Smith has been e. with records; 12: 8 he who assists in work must be temperate in all things e. his care.

ENVY, ENVYING (*see also* Covet; Jealousy; Pride; TG Envy)

D&C 101: 6 e. among saints polluted their inheritances; 127: 2 e. and wrath of man have been Joseph Smith's common lot.

EPHRAIM—*kingdom of Israel (see also* Israel; Joseph[1], Seed of; BD Ephraim; Israel; Israel, Kingdom of; Joseph, People of)

D&C 27: 5 the Lord has committed keys of record of stick of E. to Moroni[2]; 64: 36 the rebellious are not of blood of E.; 113: 4 rod that should come from Stem of Jesse is descendant of Jesse and of E.; 133: 30 lost tribes to bring treasures to children of E.; 133: 32 lost tribes to be crowned with glory by children of E.; 133: 34 blessing of God upon E.

EPISTLE (*see also* Letter)

D&C 58: 51 Sidney Rigdon to write e. to be presented to all churches to obtain moneys; 127: Intro. e. from Joseph Smith to saints at Nauvoo.

EQUAL (*see also* Consecration, Law of; Judgment; Respect; Same)

D&C 51: 3, 9 every man e. according to his family; 70: 14 be e. in temporal things; 76: 95 church of Christ e. in power, might, dominion; 78: 5 saints to be e. in both heavenly and earthly things; 78: 6 if not e. in earthly things, cannot be e. in obtaining heavenly things; 82: 17 saints to have e. claims on property to manage stewardships; 88: 107 saints to be made e. with the Lamb; 88: 122 every man to have e. privilege; 90: 6 counselor accounted e. with prophet in holding keys of kingdom; 102: 16 every man to speak according to e. and justice before court; 107: 24 Quorum of Twelve e. in authority to that of Presidency; 107: 36–37 standing high councils form quorum e. in authority to quorum of presidency or traveling high council; 107: 68 office of bishop not e. to Presiding High Priest over High Priesthood; 134: 3 magistrates required to administer law in e. and justice.

ERR (*see also* Astray; Sin; Stumble; Transgression)

D&C 1: 24–25 commandments given so that if people e., it might be made known; 6: 11 exercise gift to convince many of e. of their ways; 10: 63 men e. for they wrest scriptures; 33: 4 people e. because of priestcrafts.

ERRAND (*see also* Calling; Commission; Mission)

D&C 64: 29(133:58) as ye are agents, ye are on the Lord's e.

ESAIAS (*see also* BD Esaias)

D&C 84: 11 gave priesthood to Gad; 84: 12 received priesthood under hand of God; 84: 13 was blessed by Abraham.

ESCAPE (*see also* Deliver; Flight; Refuge; Release; Salvation)

D&C 1: 2 none to *e*. voice of the Lord; 10: 5 pray to *e*. servants of Satan; 38: 31 saints to go to the Ohio to *e*. power of enemy; 63: 34 saints shall hardly *e*. wars; 97: 25 Zion to *e*. if she obeys; 104: 7 guilty not to *e*.; 104: 8–9 those who transgress cannot *e*. the Lord's wrath, buffetings of Satan; 121: 23 generations of vipers shall not *e*. damnation of hell; 132: 50 the Lord will make way for saints' *e*.

ESTABLISH, ESTABLISHMENT (see also Confirm; Organize; Prepare)

D&C 33: 5 the Lord has *e*. this church; 138: 44 Daniel foresaw *e*. of kingdom of God.

ESTATE (see also Premortal Existence)

Abr. 3: 26 those who keep first and second *e*. shall be added upon; 3: 28 the second kept not his first *e*.

ESTEEM (see also Love; Regard; Respect; Worth)

D&C 38: 24–25 let every man *e*. his brother; 101: 8 in day of peace, saints *e*. lightly the Lord's counsel.

ETERNAL, ETERNALLY (see also Endless; Eternal Life; Eternity; Everlasting; God, Eternal Nature of; Infinite)

D&C 3: 2 (35: 1) God's course one *e*. round; 19: 7 *e*. damnation; 19: 11 *e*. punishment is God's punishment; 20: 17 God is infinite and *e*.; 20: 28 Godhead is *e*.; 29: 44 those who believe not are raised unto *e*. damnation; 77: 1 earth *e*. in its sanctified, *e*. state; 93: 33 elements are *e*.; 109: 76 reap *e*. joy for sufferings; 121: 32 council of the E. God of all other gods; 130: 2 coupled with *e*. glory; 132: 46 that which elders bind on earth shall be *e*. bound in heavens.

Abr. Fac. 2, fig. 3 God clothed with crown of *e*. light.

ETERNAL FATHER, GOD THE (see God, Eternal Nature of; God the Father)

ETERNAL LIFE (see also Celestial Glory; Continue; Continuation; Exaltation; Immortality; Live; Redemption; Resurrection; Salvation; TG Eternal Life)

D&C 5: 22 Joseph Smith granted *e*. life if obedient; 6: 7 (11: 7) he who has *e*. life is rich; 10: 50 those in this land who believe in gospel shall have *e*. life; 14: 7 (50: 5; 66: 12) those who endure to end will have *e*. life; 14: 7 *e*. life is greatest of all gifts of God; 18: 8 the diligent are blessed unto *e*. life; 20: 14 those who accept Book of Mormon receive crown of *e*. life; 20: 26 those who believe words of

prophets have *e*. life; 29: 27 the righteous will be gathered on the Lord's right hand unto *e*. life; 29: 43 by natural death men are raised in immortality unto *e*. life; 42: 61 if thou shalt ask, thou shalt receive that which brings *e*. life; 45: 5 come unto God and have everlasting life; 45: 8 those who believe on the Lord's name are given power to obtain *e*. life; 51: 19 faithful steward to inherit *e*. life; 59: 23 he who does work of righteousness shall receive peace and *e*. life; 68: 12 power given to seal up unto *e*. life those of whom the Father bears record; 75: 5 (138: 51) he who is faithful to be crowned with immortality and *e*. life; 88: 4 Comforter is promise of *e*. life; 98: 13 he who lays down life for the Lord's sake shall find *e*. life; 130: 2 same sociality existing here will exist there, coupled with *e*. glory; 132: 24 this is *e*. lives—to know the only wise and true God; 132: 55 Joseph Smith to be given crowns of *e*. lives in *e*. worlds; 133: 62 the Lord will give *e*. life to him who repents and sanctifies himself.

Moses 1: 39 work and glory of God is to bring to pass immortality and *e*. life; 5: 11 *e*. life given to the obedient.

ETERNITY (see also Eternal; God, Eternal Nature of; Time)

D&C 38: 1 the Lord looked upon wide expanse of *e*.; 38: 12 all *e*. is pained because of powers of darkness; 38: 20 saints shall possess land as inheritance in *e*.; 38: 39 those who seek riches which Father gives shall have riches of *e*.; 39: 22 those who receive gospel shall be gathered in time and *e*.; 43: 34 let the solemnities of *e*. rest upon your minds; 67: 2 riches of *e*. are the Lord's to give; 68: 31 saints do not seek earnestly riches of *e*.; 72: 3 accounts to be rendered in time and *e*.; 76: 4 from *e*. to *e*. the Lord is the same; 76: 5–8 the Lord reveals wonders of *e*. to those who serve him; 78: 18 riches of *e*. are yours; 88: 13 God is in bosom of *e*.; 132: 7, 18–19 anointed both for time and for all *e*.

Moses 7: 41 *e*. shook when the Lord spoke to Enoch².

ETHER, BOOK OF

D&C 135: 4–5 (Ether 12: 36–38) quotation from.

EUPHRATES (see River)

EVANGELICAL (see Minister [noun])

EVE—*mother of all living* (see also Adam; Eden, Garden of; Parent; Woman; BD Eve)

D&C 138: 39 Joseph F. Smith saw E. among noble spirits.

Moses 4: 6 Satan seeks to beguile E.; 4: 12 partakes of forbidden fruit; 4: 13 recognizes nakedness; 4: 14 hides from the Lord; 4: 22 to bring forth children in sorrow; 4: 26 mother of all living; 5: 27 God makes coat of skins for E.; 5: 2, 16–17 bears sons and daughters; 5: 4 shut out from God's presence; 5: 11 recognizes effects of transgression; 5: 12 blesses name of God; 5: 12 makes all things known to sons and daughters; 5: 16 bears Cain; 5: 17 bears Abel.

EVERLASTING (see also Endless; Eternal; Eternal Life; God, Eternal Nature of)

D&C 1: 15 (45: 9; 49: 9; 66: 2; 76: 101) e. covenant; 6: 3 (11: 3; 12: 3; 14: 3; 43: 25) e. salvation; 22: 1 a new and an e. covenant; 27: 5 (79: 1; 101: 39; 138: 19, 25) e. gospel; 121: 46 e. dominion; 131: 2 (132: 6, 19) new and e. covenant of marriage; 132: 20 they shall be gods from e. to e.; 133: 31 e. hills.

EVIL (see also Abomination; Agency; Carnal; Devil; Filthiness; Iniquity; Sin; Spirit, Evil; Transgression; Unclean; Wicked; Wrong)

D&C 10: 21 wicked men love darkness because deeds are e.; 20: 54 teachers to see that there is no e. speaking in church; 27: 15 take up God's armor to withstand the e. day; 29: 45 men's deeds are e.; 42: 27 not speak e. of neighbor; 64: 8 for e. of not forgiving, ancient disciples were sorely chastened; 64: 16 they sought e., and the Spirit was withheld; 64: 16 they condemned for e. that in which there was no e.; 76: 17 resurrection of those who have done e.; 89: 4 e. in hearts of conspiring men; 93: 37 light and truth forsake e. one; 98: 7, 10 (124: 120) whatever is more or less than this cometh of e.; 98: 11 forsake all e. and cleave unto all good; 136: 21 keep yourselves from e.; 136: 23 cease to speak e.

Moses 4: 11 ye shall be as gods, knowing good and e.; 8: 22 every man was lifted up in imagination, being only e. continually; **JS-H 1**: 33 Joseph Smith's name to be both good and e. spoken of.

EXALT, EXALTED (see also Exaltation; Life; Raise; TG Exalt)

D&C 49: 23 valleys to be e.; 101: 42 (112: 3; 124: 114) he who abases himself shall be e.; 104: 16 the poor shall be e.; 112: 8 many low ones shall be e.; 112: 15 e. not yourselves; 121: 8 endure it well, God shall e. thee.

EXALTATION (see also Celestial Glory; Continue; Continuation; Crown; Dominion; Elect; Eternal Life; Glory [noun]; Gods; Inherit; Marriage; Throne; TG Exaltation; Jesus Christ, Misson of; Man, Potential to Become Like Heavenly Father)

D&C 124: 9 Gentiles to come to e. or lifting up of Zion; 132: 17 ministering angels remain without e.; 132: 29, 37 Abraham, Isaac, and Jacob have entered into their e.; 132: 49 the Lord seals upon Joseph Smith his e.

EXAMPLE (see also Ensign; Light; Standard; TG Example)

D&C 58: 35 Martin Harris to be e. to church in laying moneys before bishop; 68: 1–3 calling for Orson Hyde to preach by the Spirit is e. to all ordained to priesthood; 72: 23 e. of stewards for all branches of church; 78: 13 the Lord gives e. whereby saints accomplish commandments; 98: 38 e. unto all people for justification before the Lord.

EXCESS

D&C 59: 20 things of earth to be used with judgment, not to e.; 88: 69 cast away your e. of laughter; 89: 15 flesh made for use only in times of famine and e. of hunger.

EXCOMMUNICATION (see also Blot; Cast; Court; Cut)

D&C 20: 80 any member transgressing shall be dealt with as scriptures direct; 134: 10 religious societies have right to e. members from their society.

EXCUSE (see also Exempt; Forgive; Pardon)

D&C 88: 82 those who have been warned are without e.; 101: 93 what the Lord has said must be, that all men may be left without e.; 123: 6 abuses against saints should be published, that nation be left without e.

EXEMPT (see also Excuse)

D&C 10: 28 those who lie because others lie are not e. from God's justice; 70: 10 none are e. from law of consecration; 107: 81 no member of church is e. from council of church.

EXERCISE (see Conscience; Dominion; Faith)

EXHORT, EXHORTATION (see also Persuasion; Preach; Warn)

D&C 19: 37 preach, e., declare; 20: 42, 46–47, 50, 59 priesthood bearers' duty to e.; 20: 51 teachers are to visit members, e. them to pray; 23: 3 Hyrum Smith's calling is to e.; 25: 7 Emma Smith ordained to e. the church as led by Spirit; 50: 37 elders called to strengthen churches by e.; 108: 7 strengthen your brethren in all your e.; 113: 10 scattered remnants are e. to return to the Lord.

EXPANSE

D&C 38: 1 the Lord looked upon wide e. of eternity.

Abr. 4: 6–7 an e. formed in midst of waters.

EXPEDIENT (see also Meet [adj.])

D&C 18: 18 Holy Ghost manifests all things that are e.; 88: 65 if ye ask anything that is not e. for you, it shall turn to condemnation; 78 saints to be instructed in all things e. for them to understand; 96: 5 e. that the Lord's word should go forth; 105: 13 e. to wait for the redemption of Zion.

EXPERIENCE (see also Affliction; Suffering)

D&C 105: 10 elders to wait, that the Lord's people may have e.; 121: 39 we have learned by sad e.; 122: 7 afflictions shall give thee e.

EXPOUND (see also Preach; Teach)

D&C 20: 42, 46, 52 duty of priesthood bearers to e.; 24: 5 continue e. all scripture to church; 68: 1 elders to reason and e. all scriptures; 97: 5 the Lord to bless Parley P. Pratt in e. all scriptures and mysteries; 100: 11 the Lord to give Sidney Rigdon power to be mighty in e. scriptures.

EXQUISITE

D&C 19: 15 repent, lest sufferings be so e. that you know not.

EYE (see also See; Sight)

D&C 1: 1 (38: 8; 67: 2) the Lord's e. are upon all men; 1: 2 no e. that shall not see: 4: 5 (27: 2; 55: 1; 59: 1; 82: 19; 88:67) e. single to glory of God; 29: 19 e. of the wicked shall fall from sockets; 38: 2 all things present before the Lord's e.; 43: 32 (63: 51; 101: 31) the righteous shall be changed in twinkling of e.; 58: 3 man cannot behold design of God with natural e.; 59: 17–19 good things of earth made to please e.; 76: 10 the Lord to reveal secrets which e. hath not seen; 76: 12 (110: 1) our e. were opened and understandings enlightened; 76: 19 (110: 1) the Lord touched e. of understanding, and they were opened; 77: 4 e. of beasts explained; 84: 69 elders

shall open e. of the blind; 84: 98 all shall see e. to e.; 88: 11 light is through him who enlightens your e.; 110: 3 the Lord's e. were as flame; 121: 2 how long shall the Lord's pure e. behold wrongs of his people; 121: 24 the Lord's e. see all; 131: 7 spirit matter can only be discerned by pure e.

Moses 1: 11 Moses beholds God with spiritual e.; 5: 10 because of transgression, Adam's e. are opened; 6: 35 anoint thine e. with clay; 6: 36 Enoch² beholds things not visible to natural e.

FACE (see also Countenance; God, Presence of)

D&C 17: 1 (50: 11) brother of Jared² talked with the Lord f. to f.; 84: 22 without priesthood no man can see f. of the Father and live; 84: 23 Moses sought to sanctify his people, that they might behold f. of God; 88: 68, 95 (124: 8) f. of the Lord shall be unveiled; 93: 1 the obedient shall see the Lord's f.; 101: 38 seek f. of the Lord always; 107: 49 Enoch² was before the Lord's f. continually; 124: 8 in day of visitation the Lord will unveil f. of his covering; 130: 15–16 Joseph Smith to see the Lord's f.; 133: 49 sun shall hide f. in shame; 138: 21 spirits of the rebellious did not look on the Savior's f.

Moses 1: 2, 31 God speaks to Moses f. to f.; 7: 4 Enoch² talks with God f. to f.; **Abr.** 3: 11 Abraham talks with the Lord f. to f.

FAIL

D&C 45: 26 (88: 91) men's hearts f. them for fear; 64: 31 the Lord's words shall not f.; 76: 3 the Lord's purposes f. not.

FAINT (see also Continue; Endure; Perseverance)

D&C 75: 11 (88: 126) missionaries to pray always that they f. not; 89: 20 saints who keep Word of Wisdom shall walk and not f.; 101: 81 men ought always to pray and f. not.

FAIR (see also Beauty)

D&C 5: 14 (105: 31) church to come forth f. as sun; 109: 73 church to come forth f. as moon.

Abr. 2: 22 Sarai is f. to look upon.

FAITH (see also Baptism; Belief; Born of God; Confidence; Doubt; Faithful; Forgive; Gospel; Hope; Knowledge; Miracle; Obedience; Prayer; Religion; Repentance; Salvation; Sanctification; Sign; Testimony; Trial; Trust; TG Faith; BD Faith)

D&C 1: 21 commandments given that *f.* might increase; 3: 20 glorified through *f.* in the Lord's name; 4: 5–6 *f.* is qualification for the work; 5: 24, 28 blessings promised on condition of *f.*; 6: 19 have *f.*; 8: 1 knowledge granted by *f.*; 8: 10 (18: 19) without *f.* you can do nothing; 8: 11 (11: 10, 14, 17; 52: 20) according to *f.* shall it be done; 10: 47, 49, 52 desires are granted according to *f.* in prayers; 12: 8 *f.* required for establishment of God's work; 14: 8 ask in *f.*; 17: 2–3, 5, 7 sacred things to be shown by *f.*; 17: 3 Three Witnesses see plates by *f.*; 18: 31 in *f.* and you shall have Holy Ghost; 19: 31 declare repentance and *f.* on Savior; 20: 25, 29 endure in *f.* to end; 21: 5 receive word in patience and *f.*; 26: 2 all things you shall receive by *f.*; 27: 17 shield of *f.* quenches adversary's darts; 29: 6 whatsoever ye ask in *f.*, ye shall receive; 29: 42 angels declare to Adam redemption through *f.* on Son; 33: 12 men must have *f.* or they cannot be saved; 33: 15 whoso has *f.* should be confirmed; 35: 9 whoso asks in *f.* shall cast out devils; 35: 11 without *f.* nothing will be shown; 41: 3 by prayer of *f.* ye shall receive my law; 42: 14 Spirit given by prayer of *f.*; 42: 23 (63: 16) he who looks upon a woman to lust shall deny the *f.*; 42: 48–52 he who has *f.* in the Lord to be healed shall be healed; 44: 2 if they exercise *f.*, the Lord will pour out Spirit; 46: 19–20 spiritual gift of *f.* to be healed or to heal; 53: 3 elders to preach *f.*; 61: 9 (63: 20; 76: 53) overcome through *f.*; 61: 18 warning against failing in *f.*; 63: 9–11 signs come by *f.*, not by will of men; 63: 11 without *f.* no man pleases God; 63: 16 adulterers deny the *f.*; 68: 25 parents to teach children *f.* in Christ; 88: 118 (109: 7) as all have not *f.*, teach one another words of wisdom; 88: 118 (109: 14) seek learning by study and by *f.*; 88: 119 (109: 8, 16) temple to be a house of *f.*; 93: 51 by saints' prayer of *f.* with one consent, the Lord to uphold missionary; 105: 19 saints brought thus far for trial of *f.*; 105: 24 boast not of *f.*; 107: 22 Presidency upheld by *f.* of church; 107: 30 decisions of quorums to be made in *f.*; 136: 42 keep my commandments lest your *f.* fail; 138: 32–33 those who die without knowledge of God will be taught *f.* in God.

Moses 6: 23 *f.* was taught to children of men; 7: 13 great *f.* of Enoch²; 7: 47 through *f.* Enoch² is in bosom of the Father; **A of F** 4 *f.* one of first principles of gospel.

D&C 1: 37 (71: 11) search commandments, for they are true and *f.*; 3: 8 Joseph Smith should have been *f.*; 5: 35 if thou art *f.*, thou shalt be lifted up; 6: 13 (31: 13) hold out *f.* to end; 6: 37 be *f.*, and ye shall inherit kingdom of heaven; 9: 13 be *f.* and yield to no temptation; 27: 18 if *f.* till the Lord comes, ye shall be caught up; 42: 66 observe laws and be *f.*; 46: 14 men to have eternal life if they continue *f.*; 51: 19 whoso is found a *f.* steward shall enter joy of the Lord; 52: 4 if missionaries are *f.*, they shall know what to do; 52: 5 if people are *f.*, land of inheritance to be made known; 52: 13 (101: 61; 117: 10; 124: 113; 132: 53) he who is *f.* in least is also *f.* in much; 52: 34 the *f.* to be blessed with much fruit; 52: 42 the *f.* to assemble themselves; 52: 43 the Lord to crown the *f.* with joy; 58: 2 he who is *f.* in tribulation will receive greater reward; 59: 4 (75: 5; 79: 3; 81: 6) the *f.* and diligent before the Lord shall be crowned with blessings; 60: 3 if not *f.*, that which they have shall be taken away; 62: 5 (81: 5) be *f.*; 62: 6 the *f.* shall be preserved; 62: 9 (75: 13) the Lord is with the *f.* always; 63: 47 every man should take *f.* upon his loins; 63: 47 (75: 16, 22) the *f.* to overcome world; 66: 8 he who is *f.* shall be made strong; 70: 17 the Lord's servants have been *f.* over many things; 72: 4 he who is *f.* and wise in time will inherit the Father's mansions; 78: 22 (81: 6; 106: 8) *f.* steward shall inherit all things; 83: 3 those not *f.* shall be denied fellowship in church; 84: 33 whoso is *f.* in obtaining two priesthoods shall be sanctified; 84: 80 those who preach gospel and continue *f.* shall not be weary in mind; 98: 12 the Lord gives unto the *f.* line upon line; 103: 36 all victory and glory brought to pass through elders' *f.*; 104: 82 victory promised to the *f.*; 105: 12 a great endowment for the *f.*; 121: 44 show increased love that he may know thy *f.* is stronger than cords of death; 124: 55 saints to build house unto the Lord to prove that they are *f.*; 132: 44 wife of adulterer to be given unto him who has been *f.*; 138: 12 spirits of those *f.* in mortality are gathered in one place; 138: 18 the Son declares liberty to captives who have been *f.*; 138: 36 the Redeemer prepares *f.* spirits of prophets to teach all the dead; 138: 41 Abraham, father of the *f.*; 138: 57 *f.* elders of this dispensation to teach the dead.

FAITHFUL, FAITHFULNESS (see also Diligence; Faith; Obedience; Righteousness; Steadfast; Work [noun]; Worthy)

FALL, FALLEN (see also Apostasy; Descend; Fall of Man)

D&C 1: 16 Babylon shall *f.*; 29: 14 (45: 42; 88: 87) stars to *f.* from heaven;

29: 19 flesh of wicked shall *f.* from bones; 76: 27 son of morning is *f.*; 84: 80 hair of missionary's head shall not *f.* unnoticed; 85: 8 he who steadies ark shall *f.* by shaft of death; 88: 87 stars to *f.* as figs that *f.* from tree; 88: 105 she is *f.* who made all nations drink wine of wrath; 101: 53 watchman not to *f.* asleep lest enemy come.

FALL OF MAN (see also Adam; Carnal; Death, Physical; Death, Spiritual; Fruit, Forbidden; Jesus Christ, Atonement through; Nature, Natural; Resurrection; Sin; Transgression; TG Fall of Man; BD Fall of Adam)

D&C 20: 20 by transgression of holy laws man became fallen man; 29: 40–41 man was cast out of Eden because of transgression; 93: 38 God redeemed man from the *f.*; 138: 19 the Son preached to spirits doctrine of redemption from the *f.*

Moses 5: 9 as Adam has fallen, he may be redeemed; 6: 48 because Adam fell, we are; 6: 59 by reason of transgression cometh the *f.*, which *f.* bringeth death; **A of F** 2 men will be punished for own sins, not for Adam's transgression.

FALLEN (see Fall, Fallen; Fall of Man)

FALSE, FALSEHOOD (see also Churches, False; Deceit; Lying; Prophets, False; Wrong)

D&C 45: Intro. *f.* reports led to receiving of revelation; 50: 2 many *f.* spirits have gone forth in earth; 121: 18 those who swear *f.* against the Lord's servants will be severed from ordinance; 122: 5–7 if thou art in peril because of *f.* brethren, *f.* accusations, these things will give thee experience; 127: 1 pretensions of Joseph Smith's enemies founded in *f.*; 130: 3 idea that Father and Son dwell in man's heart is *f.*

FALSE PROPHETS (see Prophets, False)

FAMILY (see also Brother; Child; Daughter; Father; Husband; Mother; Patriarch; Sister; Son; Wife; TG Family, Children, Duties of; Family, Children, Responsibilities toward; Family, Eternal; Family, Love within; Family, Patriarchal; BD Family)

D&C 19: 34 impart all property, save for support of *f.*; 20: 47, 51 priests to exhort members to attend to all *f.* duties; 23: 3 Hyrum Smith's duty is to church because of *f.*; 51: 3 portions appointed to every man equal according to *f.*; 52: 36 elders to labor with their *f.*; 57: 14 the

Lord's servants to be planted in land of Zion with *f.*; 75: 24 duty of church to support *f.* of those called to preach; 75: 28 every man obliged to provide for own *f.*; 83: 2 women have claim on husbands for maintenance of *f.*; 84: 103 those who preach gospel and are given money should send it to *f.*; 90: 25 let *f.* be small as pertaining to those who do not belong to *f.*; 93: 48 Joseph Smith's *f.* must repent; 93: 50 Newel K. Whitney needs to set *f.* in order; 107: 41 patriarchal order of priesthood instituted in days of Adam; 118: 3 I will provide for their *f.*; 136: 11 you shall be blessed in your *f.*

Moses 5: 10 Adam prophesies concerning all *f.* of earth; 7: 45 Enoch² beholds all *f.* of earth; **Abr.** 2: 11 in Abraham's seed shall all *f.* of earth be blessed.

FAMINE (see also Chasten; Destruction; Hunger; Punishment)

D&C 29: 16 hailstorm to destroy crops of earth; 43: 25 how oft has the Lord called upon nations by voice of *f.*; 87: 6 with *f.* shall inhabitants of earth feel wrath of God; 89: 13, 15 flesh should not be used, only in times of winter or *f.*

Moses 8: 4 *f.* in Methuselah's day; **Abr.** 1: 29 (2: 1) *f.* in Chaldea; **JS-M** 1: 29 *f.* in last days; **JS-H** 1: 45 judgments to come with great desolations by *f.*

FAR WEST, MISSOURI (see also D&C map, p. 297)

D&C secs. 113–115, 117–120 revelations received at F.W.; 115: 7 city of F.W. to be holy and consecrated; 115: 8 commandment to build house of God at F.W.; 115: 17 city of F.W. to be built quickly for gathering of saints; 117: 10 William Marks to preside in F.W.; 118: 5 the Twelve to take leave of saints in city of F.W.

FAST (see also Faster; Fasting; Firmness; Steadfast)

D&C 9: 14 (54: 2) stand *f.* in calling.

FASTER (see also Run)

D&C 10: 4 do not run *f.* than you have strength.

FASTING (see also Humble; Prayer; TG Fasting; BD Fasts)

D&C 59: 13 on Sabbath prepare food with singleness of heart that *f.* be perfect; 59: 13–14 *f.* is joy; 88: 76 commandment to continue in prayer and *f.*; 88: 119 (109: 8, 16) establish house of *f.*; 95: 7 call solemn assembly that *f.* come up into the ears of the Lord.

FATHER (see also Abraham; Family; God the Father; Husband; Mother; Parent; Patriarch; Son; TG Honoring Father and Mother; Marriage, Fatherhood)

D&C 2: 2 (27: 9; 98: 16); 110: 15; 128: 17; 138: 47) promises made to f. to be planted in hearts of children; 27: 10 Joseph, Jacob, Isaac, and Abraham, your f. by whom promises remain; 27: 11 (29: 34; 138: 38) Adam, f. of all; 29: 48 great things required of children's f.; 75: 28 every man obliged to provide for his family; sec. 83 law of church concerning those who have lost husband or f.; 84: 14–16 priesthood received through lineage of f.; 85: 7 names of saints' f. to be found in book of law of God; 86: 8 priesthood continues through lineage of f.; 107: 40 patriarchal order from f. to son; 112: 32 keys have come down from the f.; 128: 18 welding link necessary between f. and children; 136: 21 I am the God of your f.; 137: 5 Joseph Smith saw his f. in celestial kingdom; 138: 41 f. of the faithful, Abraham; 138: 53 Joseph F. Smith saw f. in spirit world.

Moses 3: 24 man shall leave f. and mother and cleave to wife; 4: 4 Satan the f. of all lies; Abr. 1: 2 Abraham has high priest, holding right belonging to f.; 2: 10 Abraham to be blessed by his seed as their f.; JS-H 1: 49 Joseph Smith commanded to tell f. of vision.

FATHERLESS (see Orphan)

FAULT (see also Transgression; Weak, Weakness)

D&C 6: 19 Oliver Cowdery to admonish Joseph Smith in his f.; 20: 80 member overtaken in f. to be dealt with as scriptures direct; 88: 124 cease to find f. one with another.

FAYETTE, NEW YORK (see also D&C map, p. 296)

D&C secs. 14–18, 20–21, 28–40 revelations given at F.; 24: 3 Joseph Smith sent to F.; 128: 20 voice of the Lord in wilderness of F.

FEAR, FEARFUL (see also Afraid; Anxiety; Courage; Fear of God; Quake; Shake; Terror; Tremble)

D&C 1: 7 f. and tremble, for the Lord's decrees will be fulfilled; 3: 7 (30: 1, 11; 122: 9) you should not f. man more than God; 6: 33 f. not to do good; 6: 34 (35: 27) f. not, little flock; 6: 36 doubt not, f. not; 9: 11 Oliver Cowdery to translate, then time was past; 10: 55 those who belong to the Lord's church need not f.; 30: 11 (122: 9) do not f. what

man can do; 38: 15 f. not, for kingdom is yours; 38: 30 if ye are prepared, ye shall not f.; 50: 41 f. not, little children, for you are mine; 60: 2 elders do not open mouths because of f. of man; 63: 6 let the rebellious f. and tremble; 63: 16 those who commit adultery in hearts shall deny the faith and shall f.; 63: 17 the f. will have part in lake of fire and brimstone; 63: 33 (88: 91) f. to come upon every man; 67: 3 saints did not receive blessings because of f.; 67: 10 if elders strip themselves from f., they shall see God; 68: 6 be of good cheer, and do not f.; 98: 1 f. not, let your hearts be comforted; 101: 36 f. not even unto death; 136: 17 f. not thine enemies.

Moses 1: 20 Moses begins to f. and sees bitterness of hell; 6: 39 no man touches Enoch² because of f.; JS-H 1: 32 Joseph Smith's f. soon leaves him.

FEAR OF GOD (see also Fear; Obedience; Reverence; Worship; TG Fear of God)

D&C 10: 56 those who do not f. the Lord will tremble; 45: 39 he who f. the Lord will look for the Lord's coming; 52: 17 he who trembles under the Lord's power will be made strong; 76: 5 the Lord is merciful to those who f. him; 88: 104 (133: 38) f. God and give glory to him.

Moses 6: 39 f. comes on all who hear Enoch²; 7: 17 f. of the Lord is upon all nations.

FEAST (see also Food)

D&C 58: 8 f. of fat things to be prepared for the poor.

FEEBLE (see also Weak)

D&C 81: 5 strengthen the f. knees.

FEED (see also Eat; Food; Impart; Nourish)

D&C 84: 89–90 they who receive the Lord's servants f. them and shall not lose reward; 112: 14 f. my sheep.

FEEL (see also Handle; Touch)

D&C 9: 8 by burning in bosom you shall f. it is right; 101: 8 in day of saints' trouble, they f. after the Lord; 109: 13 all who enter the Lord's house may f. his power; 112: 13 after their temptations, the Lord will f. after the Twelve; 129: 5–8 man can f. angel's hand, but not spirit's.

FEET (see Foot, Feet)

FELLOWSHIP (see also TG Brotherhood and Sisterhood; Fellowship; Fellowshipping)

D&C 83: 2 women are to have f. in church; 83: 3 those not faithful are denied *f.* in church; 88: 133 saints to receive each other to *f.* in covenant; 134: 10 religious societies have right to deal with members regarding *f.*

FEMALE (*see also* Woman)

D&C 20: 18 God created male and *f.* **Moses** 2: 27 (6: 9; Abr. 4: 27) male and *f.* created in image of Son.

FEW

D&C 3: 4 none good save a *f.*; 59: 4 Zion to be blessed with commandments not a *f.*; 117: 10 (124: 113; 132: 53) those who are faithful over a *f.* things will be made rulers over many; 121: 34, 40 many called, but *f.* chosen; 132: 22 *f.* find the way that leads to exaltation; 138: 26 *f.* hearkened to Savior during ministry among Jews.

FIELD

D&C 4: 4 (6: 3; 11: 3; 12: 3; 14: 3; 31: 4; 33: 3, 7) *f.* is white already to harvest; 86: 2 in parable of wheat and tares, *f.* is the world; 88: 51 kingdom likened to maid who sends servants to dig in *f.*; 136: 11 he who helps saints move to Zion will be blessed in his *f.*

FIERY (*see* Dart; Fire)

FIG (*see also* Tree; BD Fig Tree)

D&C 35: 16 poor and meek will learn parable of *f.*-tree; 45: 37 when *f.*-trees shoot forth leaves, summer is nigh; 88: 87 stars to cast themselves down as *f.* that falls from *f.*-tree.

Moses 4: 13 aprons of *f.* leaves; JS-M 1: 38 (Matt. 24: 32) when *f.*-tree puts forth leaves, summer is nigh.

FIGHT, FOUGHT (*see also* Battle; Persecution; War)

D&C 88: 115 Michael shall *f.* saints' battles; 98: 37 (105: 14; 109: 28) the Lord will *f.* his people's battles; 121: 38 he who exercises dominion will be left unto himself to *f.* against God.

FILL (*see also* Full)

D&C 11: 13 Spirit shall *f.* your soul with joy; 27: 7 John the Baptist was *f.* with spirit of Elias; 33: 8, 10 open your mouths and they shall be *f.*; 49: 17 earth to be *f.* with measure of man; 65: 2 (109: 72; Dan. 2: 34–38, 44–45) stone cut out without hands shall *f.* earth; 75: 21 elders shall be *f.* with joy; 84: 27 John the Baptist was *f.* with Holy Ghost from mother's womb; 84: 32 sons of Moses and Aaron[1] shall be *f.* with glory of the Lord; 84: 98 all shall be *f.* with knowledge of the Lord; 88: 12 light proceeds from

God's presence to *f.* immensity of space; 88: 19 earth to *f.* measure of its creation; 88: 67 if eye single to God's glory, body shall be *f.* with light; 88: 67 body *f.* with light comprehends all things; 88: 107 saints shall be *f.* with God's glory; 109: 74 glory of the Lord to *f.* earth.

Moses 1: 24 Moses is *f.* with Holy Ghost; 5: 10 Adam blesses God and is *f.*; 6: 32 open thy mouth and it shall be *f.*; 8: 28, 30 earth is *f.* with violence; **Abr.** 1: 15 Abraham is *f.* with vision of the Almighty; JS-H 1: 73 Joseph Smith and Oliver Cowdery are *f.* with Holy Ghost.

FILTHINESS, FILTHY (*see also* Corrupt; Defile; Evil; Pollute; Spot; Stain; Unclean; Wicked)

D&C 88: 35 those who will to abide in sin must remain *f.*

Moses 7: 48 when earth shall be cleansed from *f.*

FIND

D&C 76: 2 none can *f.* out extent of the Lord's doings; 88: 63 those who seek the Lord diligently shall *f.* him; 132: 22 *f.* narrow way to exaltation.

FINISH (*see also* End)

D&C 19: 2 Christ *f.* will of the Father; 76: 85 resurrection of telestial beings must wait until Christ *f.* his work; 77: 12 on seventh day God *f.* his work; 88: 106 seventh angel to say, It is *f.*

FIRE (*see also* Born of God; Burn; Cleanse; Destruction; Hell; Holy Ghost, Baptism of; Purify; Remission; TG Earth, Cleansing of; Fire, Baptism of; Holy Ghost, Baptism of; BD Fire)

D&C 7: 6 the Lord will make John the Apostle as a flaming *f.*; 19: 31 remission of sins by baptism and by *f.*; 29: 12 the Lord to come in pillar of *f.*; 29: 21 abominable church cast down by devouring *f.*; 29: 28 devil and his angels cast into everlasting *f.*; 33: 11 after baptism by water comes baptism of *f.* and Holy Ghost; 35: 14 the Lord to preserve the weak by *f.* in his indignation; 43: 32 earth shall pass away so as by *f.*; 43: 33 (63: 34, 54; 101: 66) wicked to suffer unquenchable *f.*; 45: 41 *f.* to be seen as sign of the Lord's coming; 45: 50 they who have watched for iniquity shall be cast into *f.*; 63: 17 (76: 36–37) lake of *f.* and brimstone; 76: 44 where devil reigns, *f.* is not quenched; 76: 105 those in telestial glory suffer vengeance of eternal *f.*; 97: 7 tree not bearing good fruit shall be cast into *f.*; 97: 26 the Lord will visit Zion according to her works, with devouring *f.*; 110: 3 the Lord's eyes as flame of *f.*; 128: 24 he is like refiner's *f.*; 130: 7 angels reside in presence of God on globe like sea of glass and *f.*; 133: 41 presence of the Lord shall be as melting *f.*; 137: 2 gates of celestial kingdom appear as circling flames of *f.*

Moses 6: 66 Adam is baptized with *f.* and Holy Ghost; 7: 34 *f.* of the Lord's indignation is kindled; **Abr.** 2: 7 the Lord causes wind and *f.* to be his chariot.

FIRMAMENT (*see also* Heaven; Star; Sun)

Moses 2: 26 (Abr. 4: 6) creation of *f.*

FIRMNESS, FIRM, FIRMER (*see also* Endure; Fast; Fixed; Immovable; Steadfast)

D&C 5: 22 be *f.* in keeping commandments; 138: 14 spirits of faithful were *f.* in hope of resurrection.

FIRST (*see also* Death, Spiritual; Estate; First Presidency; Firstborn; Firstling; Resurrection)

D&C 11: 21 *f.* seek to obtain the Lord's word; 20: 2, 5 (21: 11) Joseph Smith, *f.* elder of church; 29: 30 *f.* shall be last and last shall be *f.*; 29: 32 the Lord created all things *f.* spiritual, secondly temporal; 84: 16 Adam was the *f.* man; 88: 59 all servants receive their lord's countenance beginning at *f.* and unto last, and from last to *f.*, and *f.* to last; 88: 70, 74 *f.* laborers in this last kingdom; 90: 9 (107: 33–35, 97; 133: 8) gospel to be preached *f.* to Gentiles; 93: 12–14 Christ received not of fulness at *f.*; 95: 7 the Lord of Sabaoth is creator of *f.* day; 110: 4 Jehovah says, I am the *f.* and the last; 128: 14 *f.* man is of the earth.

Moses 1: 34 (3: 7) Adam was *f.* of all men; **JS-H** 1: 72 Joseph Smith to be *f.* elder of church.

FIRST PRESIDENCY (*see also* Presidency; Priesthood, Melchizedek)

D&C 48: 6 saints to be gathered as appointed by presidency; 68: 15, 19 (107: 17) high priests may be appointed bishops by F.P.; 68: 19–20 literal descendant of Aaron must be designated and ordained by F.P.; 68: 22 bishops to be tried before F.P.; 81: Intro. (90: Intro) calling of F.P.; 81: 2 keys of kingdom belong to Presidency of High Priesthood; 90: 12–16, 32 duties of presidency; 94: 3 house to be built for work of presidency; 102: 26–27, 33 (107: 78–80) role of F.P. in appeals from church tribunals; 107: 9 Presidency of High Priesthood to have right to officiate in all offices; 107: 22 three Presiding High Priests form quorum of Presidency; 107:

33 the Twelve officiate under direction of Presidency; 112: 20, 30 the Lord has made F.P. counselors unto the Twelve; 112: 30 power of priesthood given to the Twelve and the F.P.; 117: 13 Oliver Granger to contend for redemption of F.P.; 119: 2 tithing required for debts of presidency; 120: 1 tithing to be disposed of by council including F.P.; 124: 126 Sidney Rigdon and William Law given as counselors to constitute quorum of F.P.; 124: 126 F.P. to receive oracles for whole church.

FIRSTBORN (*see also* Church of Firstborn; Firstling; BD Firstborn)

D&C 68: 16–17 *f.* among sons of Aaron[1] holds right of presidency over Aaronic Priesthood.

Abr. 1: 3 priesthood, right of *f.*, came down from fathers.

FIRSTLING

Moses 5: 5 Adam and Eve commanded to offer *f.* of flock; 5: 20 *f.* of flock offered by Abel.

FISHING RIVER, MISSOURI (*see also* D&C map, p. 297)

D&C sec. 105 revelation received at.

FIXED (*see also* Firmness)

D&C 88: 43 courses of heaven and earth are *f.*; 88: 133 I receive you to fellowship in determination that is *f.* to be your friend; 128: 17 Malachi had eye *f.* on restoration of priesthood.

FLATTER (*see also* Deceit; Hypocrisy; Lying)

D&C 10: 25–26, 29 Satan *f.* men.

FLEE (*see* Flight)

FLESH (*see also* Body; Carnal; Man; Mankind; Nature; Natural; Sacrament; Sensual; Temporal; TG Flesh; Flesh and Blood; Trust Not in the Arm of Flesh; BD Flesh)

D&C 1: 19 not trust in arm of *f.*; 18: 11 (138: 17) the Lord suffered death in *f.*; 20: 26 Son came in meridian of time in the *f.*; 20: 40 sacrament bread is emblem of Christ's *f.*; 29: 18 God will send flies to eat men's *f.*; 36: 6 hate garments spotted with *f.*; 38: 11 (112: 23) all *f.* is corrupted before the Lord; 38: 16 (61: 6; 101: 16) all *f.* is the Lord's; 49: 16 man and wife shall be one *f.*; 49: 21 wo unto man who wastes *f.*; 61: 5 no *f.* will be safe upon waters; 63: 6 all *f.* to know the Lord is God; 67: 11 no man has seen God in *f.* except quickened by Spirit; 76: 73

(88: 99; 138: 10, 34; 1 Pet. 4: 6) spirits of dead to be judged according to men in the *f.*; 76: 74 telestial glory includes those who accepted not gospel in *f.*; 84: 21 power of godliness not manifest unto men in *f.* without priesthood; 86: 9 ye are lawful heirs according to *f.*; 89: 12-13 *f.* of beasts and fowls ordained for use of man; 93: 4 the Lord made *f.* his tabernacle; 93: 11 the Lord dwelt in *f.* among us; 95: 4 Spirit to be poured out upon all *f.*; 101: 16 all *f.* is in the Lord's hands; 101: 26 enmity of all *f.* shall cease; 129: 2 a spirit has not *f.* and bones; 130: 22 Father and Son have bodies of *f.* and bones; 138: 17, 43 bones to be clothed with *f.* in resurrection; 138: 20 Christ went not among spirits who had defiled themselves while in *f.*

Moses 3: 5 (6: 51) not yet *f.* upon earth when the Lord created man; 3: 7 man became first *f.* upon earth; 3: 23 (Abr. 5: 17) this is *f.* of my *f.*; 7: 47, 54 Enoch¹ saw coming of Son in *f.*; 8: 17 all *f.* shall die.

FLIES (see also Plague)

D&C 29: 18 God will send *f.* to eat the wicked.

FLIGHT, FLEE (see also Depart; Escape; Journey; Leave)

D&C 45: 68 those who will not fight neighbors must *f.* unto Zion; 54: 7 *f.* the land to escape enemies; 58: 56 (101: 68) gathering not to be by *f.*; 124: 106 inhabitants of earth to *f.* wrath; 133: 12 let those among Gentiles *f.* unto Zion; 133: 13 Judah *f.* unto Jerusalem; 133: 15 let not your *f.* be in haste; 133: 58 two shall put tens of thousands to *f.*

Moses 6: 34 mountains shall *f.* before Enoch²; 7: 69 Zion is *f.*; **JS-M** 1: 17 (Matt. 24: 20) pray that your *f.* be not in winter.

FLOCK (see also Church of God; Congregation; Fold; Sheep)

D&C 6: 34 (35: 27) fear not, little *f.*; 88: 72 the Lord will care for elders' *f.*; 136: 11 saints to be blessed in their *f.*

Moses 5: 33, 38 Satan tempts Cain because of Abel's *f.*; **Abr.** 2: 15 many *f.* in Haran.

FLOOD (see also Destruction; Noah; Sea; Water; **TG** Flood, Noah's)

Moses 7: 34 (8: 17) *f.* predicted because of sin; 7: 38 wicked shall perish in *f.*; 7: 51 the Lord to stay *f.*; 8: 24 Noah¹ is warned of *f.*

FLOURISH (see also Blossom; Enlarge; Grow; Increase)

D&C 35: 24 (39: 13; 49: 25; 64: 41) Zion shall *f.*

FLOW

D&C 109: 74 (133: 40, 44) mountains to *f.* down at the Lord's presence; 133: 26 ice shall *f.* down at presence of lost tribes.

FLY (see also Flies)

D&C 88: 92, 103 (133: 36) angels *f.* through heaven.

FOE (see also Adversary; Enemy)

D&C 121: 8 Joseph Smith to triumph over all *f.*

FOLD (see also Flock; Sheep)

D&C 10: 59 other sheep have I not of this *f.*

FOLLOW, FOLLOWER (see also Disciple; Obedience)

D&C 38: 22 hear my voice and *f.* me; 56: 2 (112: 14) he who will not take up cross and *f.* the Lord will not be saved; 59: 2 (63: 15) works of those who die will *f.* them; 63: 9 (84: 65) signs *f.* those who believe.

FOLLY (see also Foolish)

D&C 35: 7 (63: 15) *f.* of Gentiles shall be made manifest; 45: 49 they who have laughed shall see their *f.*; 63: 15 *f.* of adulterous members shall be made manifest; 124: 48 saints bring judgments upon own heads by *f.*; 124: 116 Robert D. Foster called to repent of *f.*; 136: 19 *f.* of those who seek not the Lord's counsel shall be made manifest.

FONT (see also Baptism)

D&C 124: 29 no baptismal *f.* upon earth for baptism for dead; 128: 13 *f.* is similitude of grave.

FOOD (see also Eat; Feast; Feed; Fruit; Grain; Herb; Meat; Nourish; Partake; Word of Wisdom)

D&C 42: 43 the sick should be nourished with herbs and mild *f.*; 49: 19 (59: 16-19; 89: 12) beasts ordained for use of man for *f.*; 51: 8 agent to purchase *f.*; 59: 13 on Sabbath prepare *f.* with singleness of heart; 59: 17, 19 good things of earth provided for *f.*; 89: 16 all grain is good for *f.* of man.

Moses 3: 9 (Abr. 5: 9) tree good for *f.*

FOOLISH (see also False; Folly)

D&C 63: 54 *f.* virgins among the wise

FOOT, FEET (see also Footstool; Tread)

D&C 6: 37 behold prints in the Lord's *f.*; 24: 15 (60: 15; 75: 20; 99: 4) elders to shake dust off *f.* as testimony against those who reject them; 27: 16 (112: 7) *f.* shod with gospel of peace; 45: 48 the Lord shall set his *f.* upon this mount; 45: 51 Jews to ask Christ, What are these wounds in thy *f.*; 49: 6 (58: 22; 76: 61) the Lord to put all enemies under his *f.*; 84: 92 (99: 4) elders to wash *f.* as testimony against those who reject them; 84: 109 head shall not say it needs not the *f.*; 88: 139–140 ordinance of washing of *f.*; 110: 2 paved work of pure gold under the Lord's *f.*; 128: 19 how beautiful upon the mountains are *f.* of those who bring glad tidings.

FOOTSTOOL

> D&C 38: 17 earth is God's *f.*
> Moses 6: 9, 44 (Abr. 2: 7) earth is God's *f.*

FORBID, FORBIDDEN (*see also* Commandments of God; Fruit, Forbidden; Hinder)

> D&C 49: 15 whoso *f.* to marry is not ordained of God; 49: 18 whoso *f.* to abstain from meats is not ordained of God; 63: 31 you are *f.* to shed blood; 64: 27 *f.* to get in debt to enemies.
> Abr. 1: 23 Egypt signifies that which is *f.*

FOREHEAD (*see also* Countenance)

> D&C 77: 9 servants of God to be sealed in their *f.*; 133: 18 hundred and forty-four thousand to have Father's name written in their *f.*

FOREKNOWLEDGE (*see* God, Foreknowledge of)

FORORDINATION (*see* Calling; Elect; God, Foreknowledge of; Premortal Existence; TG Foreordination; Jesus Christ, Foreordained; Man, Antemortal Existence of)

FORESHADOW (*see also* Shadow)

> D&C 138: 48 Elijah's mission *f.* great work to be done in temples.

FOREWARN (*see also* Warn)

> D&C 61: 18 *f.* your brethren concerning these waters; 89: 4 the Lord *f.* men by giving Word of Wisdom by revelation.

FORGET, FORGOT, FORGOTTEN (*see also* Forgive; Remember)

> D&C 9: 9 stupor of thought shall cause you to *f.* thing which is wrong; 133: 2 the Lord to curse all nations that *f.* God.

FORGIVE, FORGIVEN, FORGIVENESS (*see also* Baptism; Confession of Sins; Forget; Forsake; Jesus Christ, Atonement through; Pardon; Reconcile; Remission; Repentance; TG Forgive, Forgiven)

> D&C 1: 32 (42: 25; 58: 42; 64: 17; 68: 24; 98: 39) he who repents shall be *f.*; 29: 3 (36: 1; 50: 36; 60: 7; 62: 3; 64: 3; 84: 61) your sins are *f.* you; 31: 5 thrust in your sickle and your sins are *f.*; 42: 18, 79 he who kills shall not be *f.*; 42: 25 he who forsakes adultery and does it no more shall be *f.*; 61: 2 (64: 7) the Lord *f.* sins of those who confess; 64: 8 disciples did not *f.* each other; 64: 10 the Lord will *f.* whom he will *f.*, but men must *f.* all; 76: 34, 38 no *f.* for sons of perdition; 82: 1 inasmuch as men *f.* one another, the Lord will *f.* them; 84: 41 no *f.* for those who break covenants; 95: 1 the Lord chastens those he loves that their sins may be *f.*; 98: 40 *f.* enemy until seventy times seven; 98: 44 when not to *f.*; 132: 27 blasphemy against Holy Ghost shall not be *f.*
> Moses 6: 53 the Lord *f.* Adam his transgression in garden; JS-H 1: 29 Joseph Smith prays for *f.* of sins.

FORM [noun] (*see also* Frame [noun]; Image; TG Holy Ghost, Dove, Sign of)

> D&C 49: 22 Son comes not in *f.* of woman; 93: 15 Holy Ghost descended upon Savior in *f.* of dove.

FORMED [verb] (*see also* Creation; Organize)

> D&C 77: 12 God *f.* man from dust.

FORNICATION, FORNICATOR (*see also* Adultery; Lust; Whore; TG Fornication; Sexual Immorality)

> D&C 35: 11 (88: 94, 105) Babylon made nations drink of wine of wrath of her *f.*; 42: 74–75 those who put away spouse for *f.* should not be cast out; 42: 76 receive no *f.* if they are married; 42: 77 *f.* must repent to enter church.

FORSAKE, FORSAKEN (*see also* Forgive, Forgiveness; Leave; Repentance)

> D&C 42: 25 adulterers who repent and *f.* sin shall be forgiven; 53: 2 the world; 58: 43 he who repents will confess sins and *f.* them; 61: 36 (124: 90) the Lord has not *f.* his children; 66: 10 (93: 48; 98: 11) *f.* all unrighteousness; 88: 83 he who seeks the Lord shall not be *f.*; 93: 1 every soul who *f.* his sins shall see my face; 93: 37 light and truth *f.* evil one.

FORWARD

D&C 128: 22 go *f.*, not backward.

FOSTER, JAMES

D&C 124: 138 one of seven presidents of seventies quorum.

FOSTER, ROBERT D.

D&C 124: 115 to build house for Joseph Smith; 124: 116 warned to repent and clothe himself in charity; 124: 117 to pay stock in Nauvoo House.

FOUGHT (see Fight)

FOUND (see Find)

FOUNDATION (see also Cornerstone; Formation; Founded; Founder; Premortal Existence; Preparator; Rock)

D&C 1: 30 elders given power to lay *f.* of church; 18: 4–5 build church upon *f.* of gospel; 21: 2 (136: 38) Joseph Smith inspired to lay *f.* of church; 45: 1 the Lord laid *f.* of earth; 52: 33 one man shall not build upon another's *f.*; 58: 7 saints sent to Missouri to lay *f.* of Zion; 64: 33 ye are laying *f.* of great work; 124: 33, 41 (128: 5) ordinances prepared before *f.* of world; 132: 20 (132: 5) law decreed in heaven before *f.* of world; 138: 53 choice spirits reserved to lay *f.* of great latter-day work.

Moses 5: 57 Son prepared from *f.* of world; 6: 44 *f.* of earth is the Lord's; 6: 54 children are whole from *f.* of world; 7: 47 Lamb is slain from *f.* of world; Abr. 1: 3 priesthood came down from before *f.* of earth to present.

FOUNTAIN (see also River; Water; Well)

D&C 85: 7 the Lord to send one whose bowels shall be *f.* of truth; 133: 39 worship him who made *f.* of waters.

FOWL (see also Animal)

D&C 29: 20 *f.* shall devour the wicked; 49: 19 (89: 12) *f.* ordained for use of man; 89: 14, 17 grain ordained for use of beasts and *f.*

Moses 2: 21 (3: 19) creation of *f.*; 8: 26 the Lord to destroy *f.*

FRAME [noun] (see also Body)

D&C 138: 17 sleeping dust of the dead will be restored to perfect *f.*

FRAUD (see also Conspiracy; Deceit; Lying)

D&C 57: 8 sell goods without *f.*

FREEDOM, FREE (see also Agency; Bondage; Deliver; Freely; Government, Civil; Liberty; Redemption; Salvation)

D&C 10: 51 land to be *f.*; 38: 22 follow the Lord and be *f.* people; 58: 27 men should do many things of own *f.* will; 88: 86 abide in the liberty wherewith ye are made *f.*; 98: 5 constitution supports principle of *f.*; 98: 8 law makes you *f.*; 134: 2, 5, 7 governments to protect right of *f.* exercise of religious belief.

Moses 5: 33 Cain says, I am *f.*

FREEDOM, LAND OF

D&C 106: 1 Warren A. Cowdery appointed high priest over church in F.

FREELY

D&C 10: 66 partake *f.* of waters of life.

Moses 6: 58 teach these things *f.* to your children.

FRENCH FARM

D&C 96: Intro. disposal of.

FRIEND (see also TG Brotherhood and Sisterhood; Fellowshipping)

D&C 45: 52 the Lord was wounded in house of *f.*; 82: 22 wisdom to make *f.* with mammon of unrighteousness; 84: 77 (93: 45; 94: 1; 98: 1; 100: 1; 104: 1) the Lord calls his servants *f.*; 88: 133 greeting with determination to be *f.* and brother through grace of God; 121: 9 stand by Joseph Smith; 134: 11 all men are justified in defending their *f.*

JS-H 1: 28 Joseph Smith is persecuted by those who should be his *f.*

FRUIT, FRUITFUL (see also Food; Fruit, Forbidden; Tree; Tree of Life; Work [noun])

D&C 27: 5 the Lord will drink of *f.* of vine; 52: 17 he who trembles under the Lord's power will bring forth *f.* of praise and wisdom; 52: 18 he who brings no *f.* forth is not of God; 52: 34 the faithful will be blessed with much *f.*; 84: 58 bring forth *f.* meet for Father's kingdom; 89: 11, 16 *f.* in their seasons ordained for man's use; 97: 7 every tree that does not produce good *f.* will be hewn down; 97: 9 the Lord will cause saints to bring forth as *f.* tree; 101: 100 if saints bring forth *f.*, they will dwell in the Lord's kingdom; 101: 101 saints shall plant and eat the *f.*; 132: 30 Abraham received promises concerning *f.* of his loins.

Moses 3: 11 (Abr. 4: 11) let the *f.* tree yield *f.* after his kind; 2: 28 (Abr. 4: 22) God commands Adam and Eve to be *f.*

FRUIT, FORBIDDEN (see also Agency; Eden, Garden of; Fall of Man; Tree)

D&C 29: 40 Adam partook of *f.f.* and transgressed commandment.

Moses 4: 6–11 serpent tempts Eve to eat *f.*; 4: 12, 18, 23 Adam and Eve eat *f.*

FRUSTRATED (*see also* Hinder)

D&C 3: 1 purposes of God cannot be *f.*; 3: 3 it is not the work of God that is *f.*

FULFIL (*see also* Perform)

D&C 1: 7 what the Lord has decreed shall be *f.*; 1: 18 (42: 39) that which was written by prophets will be *f.*; 1: 38 (101: 64) the Lord's word shall not pass away, but shall all be *f.*; 3: 19 plates preserved that God's promises might be *f.*; 24: 14 scriptures to be *f.*; 29: 10 that spoken by apostles must be *f.*; 45: 23 things I have told you shall all be *f.*; 45: 25, 30 times of Gentiles to be *f.*; 56: 11 these words shall be *f.*; 58: 31 have I promised and have not *f.*; 58: 33 some say the Lord's promises are not *f.*; 74: 3 law of Moses was *f.*; 85: 10 as the Lord speaks, he will also *f.*; 105: 34 commandments concerning Zion and her law to be *f.*

FULL (*see also* Fill; Fulness)

D&C 29: 17 (43: 26) cup of the Lord's indignation is *f.*; 87: 6 consumption decreed will make *f.* end of all nations; 93: 11 Only Begotten, *f.* of grace and truth; 101: 11 the Lord's indignation to be poured out when cup of iniquity is *f.*; 104: 17 earth is *f.* and there is enough and to spare; 107: 56 Adam is *f.* of Holy Ghost; 121: 45 let bowels be *f.* of charity toward all men.

FULLER [noun]

D&C 128: 24 the Lord is like refiner's fire and *f*'s soap.

FULLER, EDSON

D&C 52: 28 to journey to Missouri.

FULLMER, DAVID

D&C 124: 132 member of high council.

FULNESS (*see also* Abundance; Full; Gospel)

D&C 27: 13 (76: 106; 112: 30; 121: 31; 124: 41; 128: 18–20; 138: 48, 53) dispensation of *f.* of times; 42: 15 observe commandment concerning teaching until *f.* of scriptures is given; 59: 16 *f.* of earth is yours; 76: 20, 56, 94 (88: 29) those in celestial glory receive *f.* and glory of Father; 76: 76–77, 86 those in terrestrial and telestial glories receive the Lord's glory but not

f.; 84: 24 Lord's rest is *f.* of his glory; 93: 4, 12, 16, 19, 27 Father gave of his *f.* to Son; 93: 12–13 Son received not *f.* at first; 93: 13 Son continued from grace to grace until he received *f.*; 93: 18 if faithful, saints to receive *f.* of John's record; 93: 27 no man receives *f.* unless he keeps commandments; 93: 33 (138: 17) spirit and element, inseparably connected, receive *f.* of joy; 104: 58 *f.* of scriptures to be printed; 109: 15 receive *f.* of Holy Ghost; 124: 28 *f.* of priesthood revealed; 132: 6 everlasting covenant instituted for *f.* of the Lord's glory.

Moses 7: 67 the righteous to receive *f.* of joy; **JS-H 1**: 41 *f.* of Gentiles soon to come.

FURY (*see also* Anger; Wrath)

D&C 101: 89 the Lord to vex the nation in his *f.*; 121: 5 Joseph Smith asks the Lord to avenge his people in *f.* of his heart; 133: 51 the Lord trampled people in his *f.*

GABRIEL (*see also* BD Gabriel)

D&C 128: 21 voice of G.

GAD

D&C 84: 10 gave priesthood to Jeremy; 84: 11 received priesthood from Esaias.

GAIN (*see also* Advantage; Benefit; Business; Profit; Riches; Wealth)

D&C 10: 56 those who build up churches to get *g.* will tremble; 82: 18 every man to *g.* other talents; 130: 19 if person *g.* more knowledge in this life, he will have advantage in world to come.

Moses 5: 31 Cain is master of great secret to murder and get *g.*; 5: 50 Cain slew Abel for *g.*

GALL (*see also* Bitter; BD Gall)

GALLAND, ISAAC

D&C 124: 78–79 to put stock in Nauvoo House.

GARDEN (*see also* Eden, Garden of)

D&C 59: 17 good things of earth for *g.* made for benefit of man.

GARMENT (*see also* Apparel; Clothing; Raiment; Robe)

D&C 20: 6 *g.* of angel, pure and white; 36: 6 hate *g.* spotted with flesh; 42: 40 let beauty of *g.* be work of own hands; 42: 42 the idle shall not wear *g.* of laborer; 42: 54 thou shalt not take thy brother's *g.*; 61: 34 those who declare word shall rid *g.*; 82: 14

Zion must arise and put on beautiful g.; 88: 85 saints' g. are not clean from blood of this generation; 109: 76 saints' g. to be pure; 112: 33 cleanse your hearts and your g.; 133: 46, 48 the Lord to come down from God with dyed g.; 133: 51 their blood have I sprinkled upon my g.; 135: 5 g. of Moroni² are clean; 135: 5 all men shall know my g. are not spotted with your blood.

GARNISH

D&C 121: 45 let virtue g. thy thoughts unceasingly.

GATE (see also Door; Path; Way)

D&C 10: 69 (17: 8; 18: 5; 21: 6; 33: 13; 98: 22; 128: 10) g. of hell shall not prevail; 22: 2 you cannot enter at strait g. by law of Moses; 22: 4 enter in at g.; 43: 7 he who is ordained of the Lord shall come in at g.; 132: 22 strait is g. to exaltation; 132: 25 broad is g. to the deaths; 137: 2 transcendent beauty of g. to celestial kingdom.

GATHER (see also Assemble; Israel; Recover; Remnant; Restoration; Return; Scatter; Zion)

D&C 6: 32 where two or three are g., there is the Lord; 10: 65 (29: 2; 43: 24) the Lord will g. them as a hen g. her chickens; 27: 13 the Lord to g. all things in one; 29: 7 elders called to bring to pass g. of elect; 29: 8 g. of elect to prepare for tribulation; 29: 27 righteous to be g. on the Lord's right hand; 33: 6 (45: 46) the Lord will g. the elect from four quarters of earth; 38: 12 angels to g. tares; 38: 31 saints to be g. unto the Lord a righteous people without spot and blameless; 39: 22 those who receive gospel will be g. in time and eternity; 42: 9, 36 (45: 66-71) saints to be g. in New Jerusalem; 42: 36 covenant people to be g. in one; 45: 25 Christ prophesies to disciples that Jews will be g.; 45: 43 remnant will be g. at the Lord's coming; 45: 69 people to be g. unto Zion out of every nation; 45: 71 righteous to be g. from among nations; 48: 6 families to be g. to new city; 57: 1, 15 saints to be g. in Missouri; 58: 56 (101: 68) let work of g. be done in haste; 76: 102 celestial heirs will not be g. with saints; 77: 15 two prophets will testify to Jews after they are g.; 84: 2 church established for g. of saints; 84: 4 New Jerusalem built by g.; 86: 7 wheat to be g. from among tares; 101: 13 the scattered shall be g.; 101: 22 those who worship the Lord should be g. together; 101: 64 work of g. of saints may continue; 101: 65 g. the Lord's people, according to parable of wheat and tares; 101: 74 g. together and

establish Zion; 105: 15 lands consecrated for g.; 110: 11 Moses commits keys of g. of Israel; 133: 4 those not commanded to tarry should g. upon land of Zion; 133: 7, 14 g. ye out from the nations; 138: 12 spirits of the just are g. in one place.

Moses 7: 62 Enoch² foretells g. of God's elect; **JS-M** 1: 27 g. of elect compared to g. of eagles to carcass; 1: 37 angels to g. elect from four winds; **A of F** 10 we believe in literal g. of Israel.

GAUSE, JESSE

D&C 81: Intro. called as counselor in First Presidency.

GENEALOGY (see also Descendant; Father; Lineage; TG Genealogy and Temple Work; BD Genealogy)

D&C 85: 4 g. not kept for those who receive inheritance by g.

Moses 6: 8 g. kept of children of God; 6: 10–22 g. from Adam to Enoch²; 8: 2–12 g. from Enoch² to sons of Noah¹.

GENERAL AUTHORITY (see also Apostle; Authorities; First Presidency; Seventy)

D&C 102: 32 decision of twelve apostles can be questioned only by g.a.

GENERATION

D&C 5: 8 unbelieving and stiffnecked g.; 5: 10 this g. shall have the Lord's word; 5: 18 elders' testimony will condemn this g.; 6: 9 (11: 9) say nothing but repentance to this g.; 10: 33 Satan thinks to overpower testimony in this g.; 10: 53 if this g. harden not hearts, the Lord will establish church; 20: 11 God inspires men in this g.; 33: 2 (34: 6) elders called to declare gospel unto crooked and perverse g.; 35: 12 fulness of gospel sent forth unto this g.; 36: 6 save yourselves from this untoward g.; 45: 21 this g. of Jews shall not pass away until desolations come; 45: 31 men standing in that g. shall see scourge; 84: 4–5, 31 temple in New Jerusalem to be built in this g.; 88: 75, 85, 138 ye are clean from blood of this wicked g.; 98: 28–30, 37, 46 (103: 26; 105: 30; 124: 50) the Lord to avenge saints on enemies unto third and fourth g.; 110: 12 in us and our seed all g. after us should be blessed; 112: 33 cleanse your garments lest blood of this g. be required at your hands; 124: 50 the Lord visits iniquities of fathers upon children unto third and fourth g.

Moses 3: 4 (Abr. 5: 4) g. of heaven and earth; 6: 8 book of g. of Adam is kept; 8: 27 Noah¹ is perfect in his g.

GENTILE (see also Heathen; Nation; BD Gentile)

D&C 14: 10 (19: 27; 90: 9; 107: 33, 97) the Lord to bring forth fulness of gospel from G. unto Israel; 18: 6 G. to be stirred up unto repentance; 18: 26–27 the Twelve called to declare gospel, both to G. and Jew; 19: 27 Book of Mormon is the Lord's word to G.; 35: 7 there shall be great work among G.; 35: 7 abominations of G. to be manifest; 42: 39 the Lord to consecrate riches of G. unto poor of Israel; 45: 9 G. to seek everlasting covenant; 45: 25, 28, 30 times of the G.; 57: 4 saints to buy land unto line running directly between Jew and G.; 86: 11 elders to be light unto G.; 87: 5 remnants of slaves left in land shall vex the G.; 88: 84 go forth among G. for last time; 90: 9 (107: 33–35, 97; 133: 8) word to go forth unto the G. first; 107: 25 the Seventy are especial witnesses unto G.; 109: 60 saints identified with G.; 124: 9 G. come to exaltation of Zion; 133: 12 those among G. should flee to Zion.

JS-H 1: 41 fulness of G. soon to come.

GENTLE, GENTLENESS (see also Kindness; Meek; Tender)

D&C 121: 41 power or influence to be maintained only by g.

GIANT (see also BD Giants)

Moses 7: 15 g. in days of Enoch[2]; 8: 18 g. in days of Noah[1].

GIFT (see also Give; Holy Ghost, Gift of; Spirit, Gifts of; TG God, Gifts of)

D&C 3: 11 except Joseph Smith repent, he will have no more g.; 5: 4 Joseph Smith given g. to translate; 6: 10 blessed art thou because of thy g.; 6: 10 g. is sacred and comes from above; 6: 11 thou shalt exercise thy g.; 6: 12 make not thy g. known; 6: 13 (14: 7) salvation in kingdom of God is greatest of all g.; 8: 4 thy g. shall deliver thee; 8: 6 g. of Aaron; 10: 3 g. to translate is restored; 11: 10 Hyrum Smith to receive a g.; 14: 7 eternal life is greatest g. of all g. of God; 17: 5 Three Witnesses receive same g. as Joseph Smith; 18: 32 declare gospel according to g. of God; 20: 60 priesthood bearers ordained according to g. of God; 46: 8 seek earnestly the best g.; 46: 9 g. given for benefit of those who love the Lord and keep commandments; 46: 10–26 there are many g. of Spirit; 46: 11 every man is given g. by Spirit; 46: 26 (84: 73) all spiritual g. come from God; 46: 27, 29 bishop responsible for discerning spiritual g.; 88: 33 no profit if g. is bestowed and not received; 107: 92 President of High Priesthood is prophet, having

all g. of God; 109: 36 g. of tongues to be poured out; 124: 95 Hyrum Smith to be given g. once put upon Oliver Cowdery.

GIHON (see River)

GILBERT, SIDNEY

D&C sec. 53 revelation to; 53: 2 commanded to forsake world; 53: 5 to journey to Missouri; 57: 6 to be agent in buying land for saints; 57: 8–9 to establish store; 64: 18–19 to return to business.

GIRD, GIRT

D&C 27: 15 (35: 14, 36: 8; 38: 9; 43: 19; 61: 38; 73: 6; 75: 22; 106: 5; 112: 7, 14) g. your loins.

GIVE, GIVEN (see also Confer; Deliver; Entrusted; Gift; Grant; Impart; Mete; Provide; Render)

D&C 34: 3 Christ so loved the world that he g. his own life; 42: 68 (46: 7) ask the Lord for wisdom and he will g. liberally; 56: 16 wo unto rich men who will not g. of their substance; 82: 3 of him unto whom much is g. much is required; 84: 85 in the very hour the portion for each is g.; 100: 6 it shall be g. you what ye shall say.

JS-H 1: 11, 13 (James 1: 5) if any lack wisdom, let him ask God, who g. liberally.

GLAD, GLADDEN, GLADNESS (see also Delight; Happiness; Joy; Pleased; Pleasure)

D&C 19: 29 (31: 3; 62: 5; 76: 40; 114: 1) declare g. tidings; 19: 39 canst thou read this without lifting up heart for g.; 29: 5 be g. for the Lord is in your midst; 59: 17–19 good things of earth made to g. the heart; 128: 19 we hear in gospel a voice of g., of g. tidings; 138: 15 spirits of just are filled with g.

GLASS (see also Crystal; BD Glass)

D&C 77: 1 (Rev. 4: 6) sea of g. is sanctified earth; 130: 7 angels dwell in presence of God on globe like sea of g. and fire.

GLORIFY (see also Exaltation; Glorious; Glory [noun]; Honor; Praise; Sanctification)

D&C 3: 20 Lamanites to be g. through faith in the Lord's name; 45: 4 Father gave Son that he might be g.; 64: 13 deal with transgressor as scripture says, that God may be g.; 65: 6 kingdom of God to go forth that God may be g.; 76: 43 Jesus the Father; 88: 60 lord to visit laborers in order, that they might be g. in each other; 93: 20 those who keep commandments will receive of Father's fulness and be g.; 93: 28 he who keeps commandments receives truth and light until he is g.; 132: 63 work of Father continues that he may be g.

Moses 6: 2 Adam g. name of God; **JS-H** 1: 46 have no other object in getting plates but to g. God.

GLORIOUS (see also Glorify; Glory [noun])

D&C 42: 45 weep for those who have not hope of g. resurrection; 78: 19 he who is thankful shall be made g.; 97: 18 Zion shall become g.; 101: 31 rest of those who die in Millennium shall be g.; 110: 13 another great and g. vision burst upon us; 133: 46 the Lord to come clothed in his g. apparel.

JS-H 1: 32 whole person of Moroni² was g. beyond description.

GLORY [noun] (see also Celestial Glory; Eternal Life; Exaltation; Glorify; Glory [verb]; Glory of the World; Light; Majesty; Power; Reward; Telestial Glory; Terrestrial Glory; Transfiguration; TG Glory; God, Glory of)

D&C 5: 27 (2; 55: 1; 59: 1; 82: 19; 88: 67) keep eye single to g. of God; 6: 30 those who are rejected, as was the Lord, shall dwell with him in g.; 7: 3 (45: 16, 44; 65: 5–6) Christ to come in g.; 19: 7 scripture to work upon men's hearts for g. of the Lord's name; 19: 19 g. be to the Father; 21: 6 heavens to shake for g. of the Lord's name; 24: 1 in the Lord shall Oliver Cowdery have g.; 25: 15 Emma Smith to delight in g. that shall come to husband; 29: 12 apostles shall stand in g.; 43: 9–10 g. added to those who bind themselves to act in the Lord; 43: 12 if g. of kingdom is desired, uphold Joseph Smith by prayer of faith; 45: 16 signs of Christ's coming in g.; 45: 59 g. of the Lord to be upon those who abide his coming; 45: 67 (64: 41; 84: 101) g. of the Lord to be in New Jerusalem; 49: 6 Son has taken his power on right hand of his g.; 56: 18 kingdom of God to come in great g.; 58: 3–4 g. shall follow after much tribulation; 63: 66 those who overcome through patience receive more exceeding and eternal weight of g.; 65: 5 Son to come clothed in brightness of g.; 66: 2 (133: 57) gospel sent that men might be partakers of g.; 75: 5 faithful shall be crowned with honor and g.; 76: 6 eternal shall be g. of those who serve the Lord; 76: 19 g. of the Lord shone round about; 76: 20 Joseph Smith and Sidney Rigdon behold g. of the Son; 76: 56 celestial in-

habitants receive of Father's fulness and g.; 76: 70, 92 g. of celestial is that of sun, even g. of God; 76: 76 those in terrestrial g. receive the Lord's g. but not fulness; 76: 81–119 degrees of g. compared; 78: 8 all things be done to the Lord's g.; 81: 4 promote g. of your Lord; 84: 5 (97: 15; 109: 37) g. of the Lord to fill his house; 84: 24 the Lord's rest is fulness of his g.; 84: 32 sons of Moses and Aaron¹ shall be filled with g. of the Lord; 88: 4 Comforter is promise of g. of celestial kingdom; 88: 22–31 who cannot abide law cannot abide g.; 88: 28–31 your g. shall be that g. by which your bodies are quickened; 88: 107 saints shall be filled with God's g.; 88: 116 this is the g. of God and the sanctified; 88: 119 (109: 8, 16) establish a house of g.; 93: 6 John saw and bore record of the Lord's g.; 93: 11 I beheld his g., as the g. of the Only Begotten; 93: 16 Christ received fulness of Father's g.; 93: 36 g. of God is intelligence; 97: 17 the Lord's g. shall not be in defiled temple; 98: 3 afflictions to work for your good and to my name's g.; 101: 25 all things to become new, that the Lord's knowledge and g. may dwell upon earth; 101: 35 whoso lays down his life shall receive g.; 101: 65 the Lord's people to be crowned with celestial g.; 103: 36 victory and g. brought to pass through diligence; 104: 7 the Lord promises the innocent a crown of g.; 121: 31 g., laws, and set times of heavenly bodies; 124: 17 (132: 57) the Lord to crown Joseph Smith with blessings and great g.; 124: 87 sickness of land shall redound to your g.; 128: 12 in sealing keys of priesthood is g.; 128: 21 angels declaring their majesty and g.; 130: 2 earthly sociality will be coupled with eternal g.; 132: 6, 19, 21 new and everlasting covenant instituted for fulness of g.; 132: 19 g. is fulness and continuation of seeds forever; 133: 32 they who are in north countries shall be crowned with g.; 133: 38 fear God and give g. to him; 133: 49 great shall be g. of the Lord's presence; 135: 6 Joseph and Hyrum Smith lived for g., died for g., and g. is their reward; 136: 31 the Lord will try his people to prepare them to receive g.

Moses 1: 2 g. of God is upon Moses; 1: 5 no man can behold God's g. and remain in flesh; 1: 20 Moses will worship only the one God of g.; 1: 39 this is my work and my g.; 4: 2 the g. be thine forever; 6: 59 the sanctified to enjoy immortal g.; 6: 61 peaceable things of immortal g. to abide in the sanctified; 7: 3 Enoch² is clothed upon with g.; 7: 17 fear of the Lord is upon all nations because of his great g.; 7: 56 saints to be crowned with crowns of g.; 8: 3 Methuselah takes g. unto himself; **Abr.** 3: 26 they who keep not first estate shall not have g. in same kingdom; JS-H 1: 17 g. of Father and Son defies description; **A of F** 10 earth to receive its paradisiacal g.

GLORY [verb] (see also Boast; Glory [noun]; Glory of the World; Praise)

D&C 76: 61 let no man g. in man, but let him g. in God.

GLORY OF THE WORLD (see also Boast; Pride; Vanity)

D&C 10: 19 evil men desire to destroy the work to get g. of world.

GNASHING (see also Hell; Torment)

D&C 19: 5 (85: 9; 101: 91; 124: 8; 133: 73) wailing and g. of teeth among the wicked.

GO

D&C 1: 5 disciples shall g. forth, and none shall stay them; 49: 11 the Lord commands elders to g. among people; 49: 27 the Lord will g. before saints; 133: 5 g. ye out from Babylon.

GOD (see also Born of God; Children of God; Church of God; Commandments of God; Faith; Fear of God; Gift; Glory [noun]; God, Body of; God—Creator; God, Eternal Nature of; God, Foreknowledge of; God, Goodness of; God, Love of; God, Manifestations of; God, Omniscience of; God, Power of; God, Presence of; God, Wisdom of; God the Father; Godhead; Godliness; Gods; Grace; Holy Ghost; Indignation; Kingdom of God; Jesus Christ; Jesus Christ—Creator; Jesus Christ—Holy One of Israel; Jesus Christ—Jehovah; Jesus Christ—Lord; Judgment; Justice; Knowledge; Law; Mercy; Mystery; Name of the Lord; Praise; Prayer; Redemption; Spirit, Holy/Spirit of the Lord; Trust; Will; Word of God/Word of the Lord; Work [noun]; Worship; Wrath; TG God; BD God)

D&C 3: 1, 3 works of G. cannot be frustrated; 3: 2 G. does not walk in crooked paths; 3: 2 G's course is one eternal round; 6: 2 (11: 2; 12: 2; 14: 2) I am G.; 6: 16 only G. knows thoughts and intents of heart; 8: 1 the Lord is your G. and Redeemer; 14: 9 (20: 19, 32; 42: 1; 50: 1; 55: 2; 61: 28; 68: 1, 6, 25; 70: 10; 76: 66; 77: 9; 82: 18) the living G.; 18: 10 worth of souls great in sight of G.; 18: 33 (27: 1) Jesus Christ your Lord and G.; 19: 10 Endless is G's name; 20: 1 G. inspires and calls men in this generation;

21: 5 word of Joseph Smith should be received as from mouth of G.; 45: 15 (50: 12) G. will reason with men; 49: 5 G. sent Only Begotten Son for redemption of world; 50: 17 G. speaks only by spirit of truth; 56: 4 G. commands and revokes as seems to him good; 76: 1 the Lord is G., and beside him there is no Savior; 76: 22 Joseph Smith's testimony that G. lives; 88: 41 G. comprehends all things; 88: 41 all things are before and round about G.; 88: 75 I may testify unto your Father, your G., my G., that you are clean; 93: 35 man is tabernacle of G.; 93: 36 glory of G. is intelligence; 112: 10 G. leads men and answers their prayers; 136: 21 G. of Abraham, Isaac, Jacob.

Moses 1: 1 words of G. to Moses; 1: 2, 11, 31 Moses talks with G. face to face; 1: 3 (7: 35) Endless is G's name; 1: 3 G. is without beginning or end; 1: 4, 38 works of G. are without end; 1: 6 no G. beside me; 1: 6 all things are present with G.; 1: 15 worship G., for him only shalt thou serve; 1: 21 Moses called upon G. to repel Satan; 1: 35 all things are numbered unto G.; 1: 39 glory of G. is to bring to pass immortality and eternal life; 4: 11 ye shall be as G., knowing good and evil; 5: 13, 18 men love Satan more than G.; 5: 29 the living G.; 6: 22, 51–52 G. conversed with Adam; 6: 43 the Lord who spoke with Enoch² is G. of heaven; 6: 57 (7: 35) Man of Holiness is G's name; 7: 24 Enoch² is lifted up in bosom of G.; 7: 28 G. of heaven wept; 7: 35 Man of Counsel is G's name; 7: 35 Endless and Eternal is G's name; 7: 69 G. walked with Enoch²; **Abr.** 3: 19 G. is more intelligent than all.

GOD, BODY OF (see also TG God, Body of—Corporeal Nature)

D&C 20: 18 G. created man after his own image; 110: 3 appearance of the Lord is described; 130: 1 when Savior appears, we shall see that he is a man like ourselves; 130: 22 Father and Son have bodies of flesh and bones.

Moses 1: 2, 11, 31 Moses sees G. face to face; 1: 16 Moses is after similitude of Only Begotten; 6: 9 in image of his own body, G. created man; **Abr.** 3: 11 Abraham talks with the Lord face to face; 4: 27 the G. organized man in their own image.

GOD—CREATOR (see also Creation; Jesus Christ—Creator; TG God, Creator)

D&C 20: 18 G. created male and female after his image; 45: 1 I give ear to him who laid foundations of earth, made heavens and all the hosts thereof; 77: 12

G. made the world in six days; 95: 7 Lord of Sabaoth, by interpretation, is creator of the first day; 121: 4 the Lord G. Almighty, maker of heaven, earth, and seas; 134: 6 human and divine laws are to be answered by man unto his Maker.

Moses 1: 33 worlds without number has G. created; 2: 1 by his Only Begotten, G. created heaven and earth; 2: 2–19 (Abr. 4: 1–19) G. created the heavens and earth; 2: 20–26 (Abr. 4: 20–25) G. created every living creature; 2: 27 (6: 8–9; Abr. 4: 26–27) G. created man in his own image; 3: 5, 7 G. created all things spiritually before naturally; 6: 36 Enoch² beholds spirits that G. created; 7: 30 impossible to number G's creations; 7: 48 when will my G. sanctify me.

GOD, ETERNAL NATURE OF (see also God the Father; TG God, Eternal Nature of)

D&C 3: 2 (35: 1) G's course is one eternal round; 19: 4, 10 G. is endless; 19: 10 name of G. is Endless; 19: 11–12 eternal or endless punishment is G's punishment; 20: 12 G. is the same yesterday, today, forever; 20: 17 G. is infinite, eternal, unchangeable, from everlasting to everlasting; 20: 28 Father, Son, and Holy Ghost are one G., infinite, eternal, without end; 29: 33 works of G. have no end, nor beginning; 35: 1 (38: 1; 45: 7; 54: 1; 61: 1) the Lord is Alpha and Omega, the beginning and the end; 76: 4 from eternity to eternity, the Lord is the same; 78: 16 Holy One is without beginning of days or end of life; 121: 32 council of the Eternal G. of all other gods.

Moses 1: 3 Endless is G's name; 1: 3 (6: 67) G. is without beginning of days or end of years; 7: 35 Endless and Eternal is G's name.

GOD, FOREKNOWLEDGE OF (see also Elect; God, Omniscience of; TG God, Foreknowledge of)

D&C 1: 17 the Lord knows calamities to come; 5: 32 the Lord foresees Martin Harris will fall if not humble; 130: 7 past, present, and future are continually before the Lord.

Moses 1: 6 all things are present with G.; 7: 67 the Lord showed Enoch² all things unto end of world; **Abr.** 2: 8 Jehovah knows the end from the beginning.

GOD, GOODNESS OF (see also God, Love of)

D&C 86: 11 blessed are ye if ye continue in my goodness; 133: 52 the redeemed shall mention all that the Lord has bestowed upon them in his goodness.

GOD, LOVE OF (see also Charity; Compassion; Love; Mercy; TG God, Love of)

D&C 6: 20 be diligent and I will encircle thee in arms of my love; 18: 10 worth of souls is great in sight of G.; 20: 19 G. commanded men to love and serve him; 34: 3 Christ so loved world that he gave life; 41: 1 G. delights to bless his people; 76: 25 Father loves Only Begotten Son; 76: 116 G. bestows Holy Spirit on those who love him; 95: 1 whom the Lord loves he chastens; 133: 53 in his love the Lord redeemed men; 138: 3 love made manifest by Father and Son in coming of Redeemer.

GOD, MANIFESTATIONS OF (see also God, Presence of; Jesus Christ, Appearances of; Jesus Christ, Second Coming of; Revelation; Vision; Voice; TG God, Manifestations of; God, Privilege of Seeing)

D&C 29: 11 the Lord to reveal himself from heaven; 35: 21 (50: 45) the elect will hear the Lord's voice and see him; 58: 3 ye cannot behold with natural eyes, for present time, the design of G.; 67: 12 natural man cannot abide G's presence; 76: 23 Joseph Smith and Sidney Rigdon see the Lord on right hand of G.; 76: 117 G. grants privilege of seeing him to those who purify themselves; 84: 5 cloud resting upon house of the Lord shall be his glory; 84: 22 without ordinances of priesthood, no man can see face of G. and live; 84: 23 Moses seeks to sanctify his people that they might behold face of G.; 88: 68 sanctify yourselves that mind is single to G., and he will unveil his face; 93: 1 those who forsake sins and obey commandments shall see the Lord's face; 93: 15 voice out of heaven says, This is my beloved Son; 97: 16 pure in heart shall come to house of the Lord and see G.; 109: 5 Son to have place to manifest himself; 110: 2–10 Joseph Smith and Oliver Cowdery see the Lord at dedication of Kirtland Temple; 110: 7 the Lord will manifest himself to his people; 130: 3 appearing of Father and Son in John 14: 23 is personal appearance; 133: 20 Christ shall stand upon mount of Olivet; 133: 25 the Lord shall stand in midst of his people.

Moses 1: 2 Moses talks with G. face to face; 1: 5 no man can behold all G's glory and remain in flesh; 1: 11 Moses' spiritual eyes have beheld G.; 6: 39 Enoch² walks with God; 7: 4 the Lord stands before Enoch² and talks with him face to face; **Abr.** 3: 11 Abraham talks with the Lord face to face; **JS-H** 1: 17–20 Father and Son appear to Joseph Smith.

GOD, OMNISCIENCE OF (see also God, Foreknowledge of; God, Wisdom of; Knowledge; TG God, Omniscience of)

D&C 1: 1 the Lord's eyes are on all men; 6: 16 (33: 1) G. alone knows men's thoughts; 6: 24 (15: 3) the Lord tells things no man knows; 38: 2 (130: 7) the Lord knows all things; 67: 1 the Lord knows men's hearts; 88: 6, 41 the Lord comprehends all things; 121: 24 the Lord's eyes see and know all men's secret; 130: 7 past, present, and future are continually before the Lord.

Moses 1: 6 all things are present with G.; 1: 35 the Lord knows all worlds that stand or have passed away; 7: 41 the Lord tells Enoch[2] all the doings of men; 7: 67 the Lord showed Enoch[2] all things, unto end of world; **Abr.** 2: 8 Jehovah knows the end from the beginning; 3: 19 G. is more intelligent than all.

GOD, POWER OF

D&C 1: 36 the Lord shall have power over his saints; 3: 1 purposes of G. cannot be frustrated; 10: 14 the Lord will not suffer Satan to accomplish evil design; 10: 43 the Lord will not suffer men to destroy his work; 11: 11 (18: 47) by my power I give these words unto thee; 11: 21 if you desire, you shall have power of G. unto convincing of men; 15: 2 (16: 2) I speak unto you with sharpness and power; 18: 35 by my power you can read these words to one another; 19: 3 the Lord retains all power; 19: 14 commandments received by the Lord's almighty power; 19: 20 the Lord humbles men with his almighty power; 20: 21 (76: 106–7; 87: 6; 88: 106; 109: 77; 121: 4, 33) Almighty G.; 20: 24 Son to reign with almighty power; 34: 7 the Lord to come in power and glory; 45: 75 all nations shall be afraid because of power of the Lord's might; 49: 6 Son has taken his power on right hand of his glory; 58: 11 after that cometh the day of my power; 61: 1 hearken to voice of him who has all power; 63: 59 I am from above, and my power lieth beneath; 65: 6 thine is the honor, power, and glory; 68: 4 whatsoever they speak when moved by Holy Ghost shall be power of G. unto salvation; 76: 10 by my power will I make known the secrets of my will; 76: 31–33 fate of those who defy the Lord's power; 76: 108 Christ to sit on throne of his power to reign forever; 84: 96, 118 (109: 77; 121: 4) the Lord Almighty; 88: 7 Christ is power of sun by which it was made; 88: 13 light which is in all things is power of G.; 93: 17 the Son received all power from Father;

100: 1 in the Lord there is all power; 133: 47 the Lord is mighty to save.

Moses 1: 3, 25 (2: 1; **Abr.** 1: 15; JS-H 1: 29) the Lord Almighty.

GOD, PRESENCE OF (see also Death, Spiritual; Redemption; Resurrection)

D&C 29: 41 Adam cast out from Eden, from G's presence; 67: 12 no natural man can abide presence of G.; 76: 62 celestial inhabitants shall dwell in presence of G. and Christ; 76: 77 terrestrial inhabitants receive of presence of the Son; 76: 94 those who dwell in Father's presence are church of Firstborn; 76: 118 only through power of Spirit can men bear G's presence in world of glory; 84: 5 glory of G. to fill his house; 84: 24 those who harden hearts cannot endure the Lord's presence; 84: 88 the Lord will be with those who receive his servants; 84: 119 the Lord will come and reign with his people; 88: 63 the Lord will draw near to those who draw near unto him; 93: 1 those who keep commandments shall see the Lord's face; 94: 8–9 (97: 16) no unclean thing can come into the Lord's presence; 97: 16 the Lord's presence to be in his house; 101: 38 seek the face of the Lord always; 103: 19–20, 26 the Lord's presence will go up with saints to possess Zion; 107: 19 Melchizedek Priesthood holds keys to enjoy communion and presence of G.; 110: 8 the Lord will appear unto his servants; 121: 32 every man shall enter into G's eternal presence; 121: 45 thy confidence shall wax strong in presence of G.; 130: 7 angels reside in presence of G.; 133: 35 tribe of Judah to be sanctified to dwell in the Lord's presence; 133: 41 presence of the Lord shall be as melting fire; 133: 42 nations shall tremble at the Lord's presence; 133: 44 mountains shall flow down at the Lord's presence; 138: 21 spirits of the rebellious do not behold Christ's presence; 138: 24 radiance from presence of the Lord rests upon saints in spirit world; 138: 26 few rejoiced in Christ's presence during ministry among Jews.

Moses 1: 2, 31 glory of G. is upon Moses, so that he can endure G's presence; 1: 9 presence of G. withdraws from Moses; 5: 4 Adam and Eve are shut out from G's presence; 5: 41 Cain is shut out from presence of the Lord; 6: 49 men have become carnal, and are shut out from presence of G.; 6: 57 no unclean thing can dwell in G's presence; 7: 16, 69 the Lord dwells with his people, Zion; **Abr.** 1: 15 angel of G's presence unlooses Abraham; JS-H 1: 33 messenger sent from presence of G. to Joseph Smith.

GOD, WISDOM OF (see also God, Omniscience of; TG God, Wisdom of)

D&C 9: 3 men should be patient because of the Lord's wisdom; 9: 6 do not murmur, for it is wisdom in me that I have dealt with you after this manner; 10: 35 the Lord reveals wisdom to preserve saints; 10: 43 the Lord's wisdom is greater than cunning of devil; 42: 68 he who lacks wisdom should ask the Lord; 76: 2 great is the Lord's wisdom; 78: 2 the Lord will speak words of wisdom in saints' ears; 105: 13 saints not to reveal what the Lord has revealed to them until it is wisdom in the Lord; 124: 1 the Lord to show forth his wisdom through the weak.

Abr. 3: 21 G's wisdom excelleth them all.

GOD THE FATHER (see also Children of God; Jesus Christ—Creator; Jesus Christ—Jehovah; TG God the Father—Elohim/Eloheim; God the Father—Jehovah; Man, a Spirit Child of Heavenly Father)

D&C 18: 18, 40 ask Father in Christ's name; 19: 2 Christ accomplished will of Father; 19: 24 Christ came by will of Father; 20: 24 Son ascended to sit on right hand of God; 20: 28 (50: 43; 93: 3) Father, Son, and Holy Ghost are one God; 20: 29 worship Father in Christ's name; 20: 77, 79 O God the Eternal Father; 27: 14 (84: 63) those whom Father has given to Son; 29: 5 (110: 4) Christ is man's advocate with Father; 35: 2 (93: 3) Christ is one in Father and Father is one in Christ; 63: 34 the Lord will come down from presence of Father; 66: 12 those who continue to end will have eternal life at right hand of Father; 68: 8 baptize in name of Father, Son, and Holy Ghost; 76: 20, 23 glory of Son seen on right hand of Father; 76: 43 Christ glorifies Father; 76: 77 they who receive not of fulness of Father; 76: 107 Christ shall deliver up kingdom to Father; 81: 6 (98: 18) faithful shall have eternal life in mansions in house of Father; 84: 37, 40 he who receives the Lord receives Father; 84: 83 Father knows men's needs; 88: 19 earth to be crowned with presence of God the Father; 88: 75 the Lord to testify unto Father whether saints are clean; 93: 3 Christ and Father are one; 93: 17 glory of Father was with Christ; 93: 19 come unto Father in Christ's name; 93: 20 Christ is glorified in Father; 93: 21 Christ was in beginning with Father; 93: 23 men were in beginning with Father; 99: 4 Father shall reject those who reject elders; 123: 6 last effort enjoined by Heavenly Father; 130: 22 Father has body of flesh and bones; 132: 12 no man shall come to Father but by Christ; 137: 3 Joseph Smith saw Father and Son on throne; 138: 3 love of Father and Son manifest in coming of Redeemer; 138: 14 resurrection through grace of Father and Son.

Moses 1: 24 (5: 9; 7: 11) Holy Ghost bears record of Father and Son; 4: 2 Father, thy will be done; 6: 66 this is record of Father and Son; 7: 11 baptize in name of Father, Son, Holy Ghost; 7: 33 the Lord gives commandment that men should choose him, their Father; 7: 47 through faith Enoch² is in bosom of Father; JS-H 1: 17 Eternal Father bears witness of Son to Joseph Smith; 1: 73 at baptism, Joseph Smith and Oliver Cowdery experience glorious blessings from Heavenly Father; AofF 1 we believe in God the Eternal Father.

GODHEAD (see also God; God the Father; Holy Ghost; Jesus Christ; TG Godhead)

D&C 20: 28 Father, Son, and Holy Ghost are one God; 20: 73 I baptize you in name of Father, Son, Holy Ghost; 35: 2 (50: 43; 93: 3) Son is one in Father, as Father is one in Son; 130: 22 Father and Son have bodies of flesh and bone, Holy Ghost is personage of spirit.

JS-H 1: 17 Joseph Smith sees two Personages; A of F 1 we believe in God, the Eternal Father, and in His son, Jesus Christ, and in the Holy Ghost.

GODLINESS, GODLY (see also Mystery; TG Godliness; Mysteries of Godliness)

D&C 4: 6 remember g.; 19: 10 mystery of g., how great it is; 20: 69 members shall manifest by g. walk and conversation that they are worthy of sacrament; 84: 20 in ordinances of Melchizedek Priesthood the power of g. is manifest; 84: 21 without the fulness of the power of g. is not manifest in the flesh; 84: 22 without power of g. no man can see God; 107: 30 decisions of quorums are to be made in all g.

GODS (see also Elkenah; Exaltation; Idolatry; Korash; Libnah; Mahmackrah)

D&C 76: 58 inhabitants of celestial glory become g.; 121: 28 whether there be one God or many g. shall be manifest; 121: 32 council of Eternal God of all other g.; 132: 17 angels who do not abide law become not g., but angels of God; 132: 18–19 if marriage sealed by Holy Spirit of promise, they can pass the g. appointed; 132: 20, 37 those who receive exaltation are g. and have no end; 132: 37 Abraham, Isaac, and Jacob are g., not angels.

Moses 4: 11 ye shall be as g., knowing good and evil; **Abr.** 1: 5–6 Abraham's fathers have turned to worshipping g. of heathens.

GOLD, GOLDEN

D&C 110: 2 under the Lord's feet was paved work of pure g.; 124: 11 kings to bring g. and silver to help people of Zion; 124: 84 Almon Babbitt sets up g. calf; 128: 24 the Lord will purge sons of Levi¹ as g. and silver; 137: 4 streets of celestial kingdom had appearance of g.

GOOD (see also Better; God, Goodness of; Goods, Praiseworthy; Tidings; Work [noun])

D&C 6: 13 those who do g. will be saved; 6: 33 fear not to do g.; 11: 12 trust in that Spirit which leads to do g.; 21: 6 (35: 24) the Lord will cause heavens to shake for saints' g.; 33: 4 (35: 12) none do g. except a few; 58: 28 if men do g., they shall not lose their reward; 59: 17–18 g. things of earth given for use and benefit of men; 64: 34 the obedient shall eat the g. of the land; 76: 17 they who have done g. will come forth in resurrection of just; 81: 4 doing g. to fellow men promotes glory of the Lord; 90: 24 (100: 15; 105: 40; 122: 7) all things shall work together for your g.; 97: 7 every tree that brings not forth g. fruit will be hewn down; 98: 10 uphold wise and g. men; 98: 11 cleave unto g.; 122: 7 afflictions shall be for thy g.

Moses 2: 31 (3: 2) all things which God had made were g.; 3: 18 (Abr. 5: 14) not g. that man should be alone; 5: 11 without transgression we never should have known g. and evil; **Abr.** 3: 23 God saw premortal intelligences that they were g.; 4: 21 the Gods saw that their plan was g.; **JS–H** 1: 33 Joseph Smith's name to be had for g. and evil among nations; **A of F** 13 we believe in doing g. to all men.

GOODS

D&C 56: 17 wo unto poor who lay hands on other men's g.; 57: 8–9 sell g. without fraud; 134: 10 religious societies have no right to take world's g. from members.

GOSPEL (see also Baptism; Covenant; Faith; Holy Ghost, Gift of; Jesus Christ; Message; Obedience; Plan; Religion; Repentance; Salvation; Tidings; Truth; Word of God/Word of the Lord)

D&C 1: 23 fulness of g. to be proclaimed; 6: 26 records kept back contain much of g.; 10: 48 g. to be preached to Lamanites; 10: 49 g. made known to other nations; 10: 50 those who believe in

g. will have eternal life; 10: 52 the Lord to bring g. to build up, not to destroy; 11: 16 wait to preach until you shall have my g.; 11: 24 (18: 17) build upon the Lord's rock, which is his g.; 14: 10 the Lord to bring g. from Gentiles to Israel; 18: 4 foundation of g. in scriptures; 18: 26 the Twelve called to declare g. to Gentile and Jew; 18: 28 (58: 64) g. to be preached to every creature; 18: 32 declare g. according to Holy Ghost; 20: 9 (27: 5; 42: 12) Book of Mormon contains fulness of g.; 24: 12 declare g. at all times in all places; 25: 1 those who receive g. are sons and daughters in the Lord's kingdom; 27: 13 keys of dispensation of g. for last times committed to Peter, James, and John; 27: 16 g. of peace; 28: 16 (29: 4) g. to be declared with sound of rejoicing; 29: 42 g. promised to Adam and his seed; 33: 11–12 (39: 6; 49: 12–14; 53: 3; 68: 25) first principles of g.; 35: 12 fulness of g. sent forth to this generation; 35: 15 g. to be preached to the poor and meek; 35: 17 (135: 3) fulness of g. sent forth by Joseph Smith; 36: 5 those who embrace calling should be ordained and sent forth to preach everlasting g.; 36: 7 those who embrace g. with singleness of heart to be ordained and sent forth; 38: 33 (42: 63) g. to be preached among all nations; 39: 5 he who receives g. receives the Lord; 39: 6 this is my g.; 39: 11 fulness of g. sent to recover Israel; 39: 18 if people receive fulness of g., the Lord will stay his hand; 39: 22 those who receive g. will be gathered; 42: 6 go forth in power of Spirit, preaching g.; 42: 6 g. to be preached two by two; 42: 12 fulness of g. contained in Bible and Book of Mormon; 45: 28 fulness of g. to come to those in darkness; 60: 14 manner of preaching g.; 65: 2 g. to roll forth from church; 66: 2 everlasting covenant, fulness of g.; 68: 1, 8 (99: 1) elders called to proclaim everlasting g.; 76: 1 record we hear is g. of Christ; 76: 40–43 g. is atonement of Christ; 76: 73 Son visited and preached g. to spirits in prison; 76: 82 fate of those who refuse g.; 76: 101 telestial glory includes those who receive not g.; 79: 1 (128: 19) everlasting g. is glad tidings of great joy; 84: 19 Melchizedek Priesthood administers g.; 84: 26 lesser priesthood holds keys of preparatory g.; 88: 78 saints to be instructed more perfectly in law of g.; 90: 11 every man shall have fulness of g.; 93: 51 proclaim g. of salvation as the Lord gives utterance; 110: 12 Elias has committed dispensation of g. of Abraham; 128: 5 (137: 7; 138: 10, 19, 30–34, 57) the Lord prepared for salvation of those who die without knowledge of g.; 133: 36

everlasting g. committed by angel; 133:
57 that men might be partakers of glories,
the Lord sent forth fulness of g.; 137: 7
those who die without knowledge of g.
but would have accepted it will inherit
celestial glory; 138: 4 through atonement
and obedience to g., mankind may be
saved; 138: 18–21, 28–37 g. preached to
spirits of dead; 138: 25 Savior taught g.
to Jews during mortal ministry.

Moses 5: 58 g. was preached from
beginning; 5: 58 g. declared by holy
angels; 5: 59 g. to remain until end
of world; 8: 19 Noah' commanded to
declare g.; **Abr.** 2: 10 those who receive g.
will be called after Abraham's name; 2:
11 blessings of g. are blessings of salvation; **JS-H** 1: 34 fulness of g. contained in
gold plates; **A of F** 3 all mankind may be
saved by obedience to laws and ordinances
of g.; 4 first principles and ordinances of g.;
5 man must be called of God to preach g.

GOSSIP (see also Lying; Slander)
   D&C 42: 27 (136: 23) thou shalt not
speak evil of thy neighbor; 88: 124 cease
to find fault one with another; 136: 24 let
your words tend to edifying one another.

GOULD, JOHN
   D&C 100: 14 to be saved if obedient.

GOVERN, GOVERNMENT (see also Government, Civil; Order; Regulate; Rule)
   D&C 31: 9 g. your house in meekness; 38: 36 officers to g. affairs of church
property; 41: 3 (42: 59) scriptures given
for law to g. church; 88: 34 that which
is g. by law is preserved by law; 88: 40
the Lord g. and executes all things; 124:
143 priesthood offices given for helps
and g.
   Abr. 3: 3, 9 the Lord sets Kolob to
g. the planets.

GOVERNMENT, CIVIL (see also Constitution; Country; Freedom; Govern; Governor; Law, Civil; Liberty; Nation;
President; Right [noun]; TG Governments)
   D&C 42: 79, 84–86 members who
kill, steal, lie are to be delivered to law of
land; 42: 89 unreconciled disputes among
members resolved by church, not before
world; 58: 21 let no man break law of
land; 58: 21 he who keeps law of God
has no need to break law of land; 58: 22
saints should be subject to powers that be
until the Lord reigns; 63: 26 the Lord
renders unto Caesar that which is Caesar's;
98: 4–7 saints to befriend law of land; 98: 5
(101: 77) constitutional law is justifiable
before the Lord; 98: 9 when the wicked

rule, the people mourn; 101: 76–80 g. to
protect rights; 105: 32 kingdoms of world
to acknowledge kingdom of Zion; 109:
54–55 prayer for nation; 123: 6 abuses
against saints to be presented to heads of
g.; 134: 1 g. are instituted of God for
benefit of man; 134: 2, 4–5, 7 g. must
protect freedom of religion; 134: 3, 5–6
people should seek and uphold just g.;
134: 3, 5–7 human law instituted to
protect individual rights, justice; 134: 8
g. should punish commission of crime;
134: 9 religious influence and civil g.
should not be mingled; 134: 11 men
should appeal to civil law for redress of
wrongs.
   Abr. 1: 25 first g. of Egypt
established by Pharaoh.

GOVERNOR (see also Government, Civil)
   D&C 124: 3 proclamation of gospel
to g.

GRACE (see also Gracious; Jesus Christ,
Atonement through; Mercy; Redemption; Salvation; Work [noun]; BD Grace)
   D&C 17: 8 (18: 31) the Lord's g. is
sufficient for you; 20: 30 justification
through g. of the Lord; 20: 31 sanctification through g. of the Lord; 20: 32
possibility that man may fall from g.;
50: 40 elders must grow in g. and knowledge; 66: 12 Father full of g. and truth;
76: 94 church of Firstborn receives of
God's fulness and g.; 84: 99 the Lord has
redeemed Israel according to election of
g.; 88: 78 teach ye diligently and my g.
shall attend you; 93: 11 Son full of g. and
truth; 93: 12–13 Son received g. for g.
until he received fulness; 93: 20 those
who keep commandments shall receive
g.; 93: 20 ye shall receive g. for g.; 106: 8
the Lord gives g. and assurance; 124: 1
the Lord to soften hearts of wicked, that
saints may find g. in their eyes; 138: 14
resurrection comes through g. of Father
and Son.
   Moses 7: 59 thou hast given me
right to throne through g.

GRACIOUS (see also Grace)
   D&C 76: 5 the Lord is g. to those
who fear him; 109: 53 the Lord is g. and
merciful to those who repent.

GRAIN (see also Barley; Corn; Crop; Food;
Oats; Rye; Wheat)
   D&C 89: 14 (89: 16–17) all g. is
ordained for use of man; 136: 9 each
company to prepare fields for raising g.

GRANGER, OLIVER
   D&C 117: Intro. revelation concern-

ing duties of; 117: 12–13 to contend for redemption of First Presidency.

GRAPE (see also Vineyard; Wine)

D&C 89: 6 pure wine of the g. to be used in sacrament.

GRASS (see also Herb; Plant)

D&C 124: 7 do not fear kings and authorities, for they are as g.

GRAVE (see also Baptism; Bury; Death, Physical; Resurrection)

D&C 29: 26 (88: 97; 133: 56) g. shall be opened; 88: 97 they who have slept in g. shall come forth; 88: 98 they who are in g. shall be caught up to meet the Lord; 128: 12–13 baptismal font a similitude of g.

GREAT, GREATER, GREATEST (see also Day of the Lord; Mighty)

D&C 29: 1 (38: 1; 39: 1) Christ, the G. I AM; 50: 26 he who is ordained of God is appointed to be g., notwithstanding he is least; 64: 33 out of small things proceed the g.; 82: 3 he who sins against g. light receives g. condemnation; 107: 64 High Priesthood is g. of all; 109: 56 hearts of g. ones of earth to be softened; 122: 8 Son hath descended below all, art thou g. than he; 128: 6 (138: 11) gospel made known to the dead, both g. and small; 138: 38 Joseph F. Smith saw g. and mighty ones among righteous spirits; 138: 55 noble and g. spirits chosen to be rulers in church.

Abr. 3: 22 among premortal intelligences were many noble and g. ones.

GREAT BRITAIN

D&C 87: 3 southern states to call upon G.B. for aid.

GREEDINESS (see also Covet; Riches; Selfishness)

D&C 56: 17 wo unto poor who are full of g.; 68: 31 inhabitants of Zion filled with g.

GRIEVE (see also Grievous; Lament; Mourn)

D&C 63: 55 Sidney Rigdon exalted himself and g. the Spirit; 121: 37 Spirit of the Lord is g. by those who exercise compulsion upon men.

Moses 8: 25 Noah[1] g. that the Lord made man.

GRIEVOUS (see also Gross)

D&C 95: 3, 6, 10 (101: 98) saints have sinned with g. sins; 103: 4 saints to be chastened with g. chastisement; 104: 4 those who break covenant shall be cursed

with g. curse; 109: 48 burdens of saints are g.

Abr. 2: 21 famine becomes g.

GRIFFIN, SELAH J.

D&C 52: 32 to be ordained and to journey to Missouri; 56: 5–6 to accompany Thomas B. Marsh to Missouri.

GROAN, GROANING (see also Cry; Mourn)

D&C 84: 49 (84: 53) whole world lies in sin and g.; 88: 89 earthquakes to cause g.; 123: 7 whole earth g. under its iniquity.

Moses 7: 56 earth g.

GROSS, GROSSER, GROSSEST (see also Grievous)

D&C 112: 23 g. darkness covers minds of people.

GROUND (see also Dust; Earth)

D&C 88: 89 earthquakes to cause men to fall to g.; 89: 16 that which yields fruit, whether in g. or above g., is for man's use; 104: 34 g. reserved for building of the Lord's houses; 115: 7 g. upon which Far West stands is holy; 133: 29 parched g. shall no longer be thirsty land; 136: 36 blood of prophets cries from g.

Moses 3: 5 (Abr. 5: 5) the Lord had not yet created man to till g.; 4: 23 g. cursed through fall of Adam.

GROVER, THOMAS

D&C 124: 132 member of high council.

GROW (see also Enlarge; Flourish; Increase; Multiply; Spread; Swell; Wax)

D&C 45: 58 (63: 51) in Millennium children shall g. up without sin; 50: 24 light to g. brighter and brighter; 50: 40 elders must g. in grace and knowledge; 68: 31 children in Zion are g. up in wickedness; 84: 82 consider how lilies of field g.; 86: 7 wheat and tares g. together; 109: 15 saints to g. up in the Lord; 123: 7 wicked spirit g. stronger and stronger.

GRUDGINGLY

D&C 70: 14 be equal, and this not g.

GUIDE (see also Counsel; Direction; Enlighten; God, Wisdom of; Holy Ghost; Inspire; Revelation; TG Guidance, Divine)

D&C 19: 40 canst thou run about as blind g.; 45: 57 the wise take Holy Ghost as g.; 46: 2 meetings to be conducted as g. by Spirit; 101: 63 the Lord to show wisdom if churches will be g. in right way.

GUILE (see also Deceit; Hypocrisy)

D&C 41: 11 Edward Partridge is without g.; 121: 42 pure knowledge shall greatly enlarge soul without g.; 124: 97 William Law admonished to be humble and without g.

GUILT, GUILTY (see also Bondage; Repentance; Shame; Sin; Spot; Stain; Torment; Transgression)

D&C 38: 14 some saints are g. before the Lord; 64: 22 the Lord will not hold any g. who go with open heart to Zion; 68: 1 bishops found g. before First Presidency should be condemned; 104: 7 the g. shall not escape; 134: 4 civil authorities should punish g., but never suppress freedom of soul.

Moses 6: 54 Son atones for original g.

GUILTLESS (see also Blameless; Spotless)

D&C 58: 30 The Lord will not hold him g. who obeys not his commandments.

HAGAR (see also BD Hagar)

D&C 132: 34, 65 given to Abraham.

HAIL (see also Destruction; Storm)

D&C 29: 16 great h. sent to destroy crops; 43: 25 the Lord calls nations by voice of great h.; 109: 30 works of those who lie against the Lord's servants to be swept away by h.

HAIR (see also Head)

D&C 9: 14 (29: 25) stand fast in the work, and h. of head shall not be lost; 84: 80, 116 h. of missionary's head shall not fall to ground unnoticed; 110: 3 h. of the Lord's head was white.

HALE, EMMA (see Smith, Emma Hale)

HALE, ISAAC

JS-H 1: 57 Joseph Smith lives at home of.

HAM (see also BD Ham)

Moses 8: 12, 27 son of Noah[1]; Abr. 1: 11 virgins offered as sacrifice were descended from H.; 1: 21, 23–24 progenitor of the Egyptians; 1: 23 father of discoverer of Egypt; 1: 25 government of H. was patriarchal; 1: 26 blessed as to things of earth and wisdom, but not as to priesthood.

HANANNIAH

Moses 7: 9 Enoch[2] beholds land of H.

HANCOCK, LEVI W.

D&C 52: 29 to journey to Missouri;

124: 138 one of seven presidents of seventies quorum.

HANCOCK, SOLOMON

D&C 52: 27 to journey to Missouri, preaching along the way.

HAND (see also Hand of the Lord; Handiwork; Hands, Laying on of; Labor; Right Hand)

D&C 2: 1 priesthood to be revealed by h. of Elijah; 5: 37 behold prints of nails in the Lord's h. and feet; 39: 19 (42: 7) kingdom of heaven is at h.; 45: 51 Jews to ask about wounds in the Lord's h. and feet; 60: 7 elders to lift up holy h.; 63: 37 every man should take righteousness in his h.; 65: 2 (Dan. 2: 34–35, 44–45) gospel to roll forth as stone cut out without h.; 81: 5 (Heb. 12: 12) lift up h. that hang down; 85: 8 man who puts forth h. to steady ark will fall by death; 88: 74, 86 the Lord's laborers commanded to cleanse h. and feet before him; 88: 120, 132 salutations may be with uplifted h. unto the Most High; 105: 3, 10 saints have not been obedient to what the Lord requires at their h.; 107: 44 Enos[1] ordained by h. of Adam; 129: 4, 7–8 ask messenger from the Lord to shake h.; 132: 10 will I receive at your h. that which I have not appointed.

HAND OF THE LORD (see also God, Power of)

D&C 59: 21 God is displeased with those who confess not his h. in all things; 61: 6 (101: 16) all flesh is in the Lord's h.; 67: 2 heavens and earth are in the Lord's h.; 76: 3 none can stay the Lord's h.; 84: 119 the Lord has put forth h. to exert powers of heaven; 87: 6 inhabitants of earth to feel chastening h. of Almighty God; 97: 19 h. of the Lord is in Zion; 112: 10 be humble, and the Lord shall lead thee by h.; 121: 4 Lord, stretch forth thy h.; 136: 30 saints' enemies are in the Lord's h.

Moses 1: 4 a Lord to show Moses workmanship of his h.; 6: 32 all flesh is in God's h.; 7: 32 men are workmanship of God's h.; Abr. 1: 18 I will lead thee by my h.

HANDIWORK (see also Creation; Workmanship)

D&C 104: 14 heavens and earth are the Lord's h.

HANDLE (see also Control; Feel)

D&C 121: 36 powers of heaven can be h. only upon principles of righteousness; 129: 2 (Luke 24: 39) h. me and see, for spirit has not flesh and bones.

HANDMAID

D&C 90: 28 Vienna Jaques is addressed as h.; 132: 51 Emma Smith is addressed as h.

HANDS, LAYING ON OF (see also Administration to the Sick; Anointing; Confer; Confirm; Holy Ghost, Gift of; Ordain; Ordinance; Priesthood; Melchizedek; TG Hands, Laying on of; BD Laying on of Hands)

D&C 20: 41, 43, 68 laying on of h. for baptism of fire; 20: 58 teachers and deacons do not have authority to lay on h.; 20: 68 (33: 15) confirmed by laying on of h.; 20: 68 instruction to precede the laying on of h.; 20; 70 elders to lay h. upon children for blessing; 24: 9 continue in laying on of h.; 25: 8 (33: 15; 35: 6; 39: 23; 49: 14; 53: 3; 55: 3; 68: 25; 76: 52; 138: 33) receive Holy Ghost by laying on of h.; 36: 2 the Lord will lay h. upon Edward Partridge by h of his servant; 42: 44 (66: 9) elders shall lay h. upon sick; 52: 10 elder is to baptize and lay on h. by water's side; 68: 21 lineage to be ascertained by revelation from the Lord under h. of Presidency; 68: 27 children to receive laying on of h. after baptism; 84: 6–16 (107: 44) priesthood received by laying on of h.; 107: 67 from President of High Priesthood comes administering of ordinances and blessings upon church, by laying on of h.

JS-H 1: 68 John the Baptist ordains Joseph Smith and Oliver Cowdery by laying on of h.; 1: 70 Aaronic Priesthood has not power of laying on of h. for gift of Holy Ghost; **A of F** 4 laying on of h. for gift of Holy Ghost; 5 man must be called of God by prophecy and laying on of h.

HANG (see also Capital Punishment; Sword)

D&C 81: 5 (Heb. 12: 12) lift up hands that h. down.

HAPPINESS, HAPPY, HAPPIER (see also Blessed [adj.]; Cheer; Delight; Glad; Joy; Merry; Pleased; Pleasure)

D&C 77: 2 four beasts in Rev. 4: 6 represent h. of man and beasts.

Abr. 1: 2 no greater h. for Abraham than blessing of fathers.

HARAN (see also BD Haran)

Abr. 2: 1 brother of Abraham.

HARAN, LAND OF (see also BD Haran)

Abr. 2: 4 temporary abode of Abraham; 2: 6 Abraham and Lot to leave H.; 2: 14 Abraham departs out of H.

HARD (see also Hardheartedness)

D&C 19: 15 men know not how h. their suffering will be to bear; 20: 54 teachers to see that there is no h. with each other among members.

HARDHEARTEDNESS (see also Contention; Doubt; Hate; Pride; Rebel; Resist; Soften; Stiffnecked; Unbelief; Wicked; TG Hardheartedness)

D&C 5: 18 testimony of Three Witnesses to condemn this generation if they harden hearts; 10: 32 (10: 63) Satan hardens hearts of people; 10: 53 the Lord will establish church if this generation hardens not hearts; 10: 65 the Lord will gather them if they will not harden hearts; 29: 7 the elect hear the Lord's voice and harden not hearts; 38: 6 the wicked who do not hear the Lord's voice but harden hearts will be kept in chains; 45: 6 members warned not to harden hearts; 45: 29 those in darkness turn hearts from the Lord because of precepts of men; 45: 33 in last days men will harden hearts against the Lord; 58: 15 blindness of heart may cause a man to fall; 78: 10 Satan turns men's hearts away from truth; 82: 21 soul that hardens heart against covenant will be delivered to Satan's buffetings; 84: 24 children of Israel hardened hearts and could not endure the Lord's presence; 84: 76 men to be upbraided for evil hearts of unbelief; 112: 13 the Lord will feel after the Twelve if they harden not their hearts.

Moses 6: 27 hearts have waxed hard; **Abr.** 1: 6 hearts of Abraham's fathers were set to do evil.

HARM (see also Hurt)

D&C 10: 25 Satan teaches there is no h. in deceiving and lying; 42: 27 thou shalt not do any h. to neighbor; 84: 72 poison of serpent shall not have power to h. apostles.

HARMONY, PENNSYLVANIA (see also D&C map, p. 296)

D&C sec. 3–13, 24–27 revelations received at H.

HARRIS, EMER

D&C 75: 30 to preach with Simeon Carter.

HARRIS, GEORGE W.

D&C 124: 132 member of high council.

HARRIS, MARTIN

D&C 3: Intro. is given 116 pages of

Book of Mormon manuscript; 3: 12–13 has broken most sacred promises; 5: Intro. revelation given at request of; 5: 1 desires witness of plates; 5: 24 does not humble himself sufficiently; 5: 25 to serve as witness if humble; 5: 28 must confess transgressions; 10: 6–7 has sought to destroy Joseph Smith; 17: Intro. revelation to, prior to viewing plates; 19: Intro. revelation to, as commandment of God; 19: 26–27, 35 to impart of property to printing of Book of Mormon; 52: 24 to journey to Missouri; 58: 35 to lay money before bishop; 58: 38–39 warned to repent, for he seeks praise of world; 70: 1–3 one of stewards over revelations and commandments; 82: 11 to be bound to other elders by covenant that cannot be broken by transgression; 102: 3, 34 member of high council; 104: 24 appointed lot of land for stewardship; 104: 26 to devote moneys to proclaiming the Lord's words.

JS-H 1: 61 gives money to Joseph Smith; 1: 63 takes translation to New York City.

HARVEST (see also Reap; Thrash)

D&C 4: 4 (6: 3; 11: 3; 12: 3; 14: 3; 33: 3, 7) field is white already to h.; 45: 2 (56: 16) h. shall be ended and your souls not saved; 86: 7 wheat and tares to grow together until h. is ripe; 101: 64 gathering of saints for time of h. is come.

HASTE, HASTEN

D&C 58: 56 (101: 58, 72) work of gathering should not be in h.; 60: 8, 14 preach the word, not in h.; 63: 24 saints to assemble in Zion, not in h. lest there be confusion; 88: 73 the Lord will h. his work in its time; 101: 72 all things to be done in their time, not in h.; 133: 15 flight should not be in h.

HATE, HATRED (see also Despise; Malice; Persecution; Prejudice; Revile)

D&C 43: 21 if the Lord calls upon men to repent and they h. him, what will they say when thunder speaks; 98: 46 (103: 26; 105: 30; 124: 50, 52) the Lord takes vengeance on children's children of them that h. him.

HAWS, PETER

D&C 124: 62, 70 to help in building Nauvoo House.

HEAD (see also Hair; Order)

D&C 28: 6 thou shalt not command him who is at thy h. and at h. of church; 16: 29 some are given all spiritual gifts that there may be a h.; 50: 30 spirits

subject to him who is appointed to h.; 68: 25 sin to be upon h. of parents who do not teach children; 107: 55 Adam set to be at the h.; 107: 92 gifts of God bestowed upon h. of church; 121: 33 the Lord pours down knowledge upon h. of saints; 123: 6 libelous publication to be presented to h. of government; 124: 50 iniquity to be visited upon h. of those who hinder the Lord's work; 132: 19 exaltation sealed upon h. of those whose marriage is sealed by Holy Spirit of promise; 133: 34 richer blessing upon h. of Ephraim.

Moses 4: 21 seed of woman shall bruise serpent's h.; **JS-H** 1: 16 Joseph Smith sees pillar of light over his h.; 1: 31 h. and neck of Moroni² are bare.

HEAL, HEALING (see also Administration to the Sick; Deaf; Dumb; Hands, Laying on of; Jesus Christ, Atonement through; Miracle; Ordinance; Raise; Recover; Save; Sick; TG Heal, Healing)

D&C 24: 13 require not miracles, except casting out devils, h. the sick; 35: 9 (84: 68) whoso asks in the Lord's name in faith shall h. the sick; 42: 43 he who has not faith to be h. should be nourished; 42: 48–51 he who has faith in the Lord to be h. shall be; 46: 19 spiritual gift of faith to be h.; 46: 20 spiritual gift of faith to h.; 112: 13 if the Twelve harden not their hearts, the Lord will h. them; 124: 98 signs that will follow the Lord's servants include h. the sick.

A of F 7 we believe in gift of h.

HEALTH (see also Body; Heal; Sick; Strength; Word of Wisdom; TG Health)

D&C 89: 18 saints who obey Word of Wisdom receive in navels; 124: 23 boarding house to be established that weary traveler may find h. and safety.

HEAR, HEARD (see also Deaf; Ear; Hearken; Heed; Listen)

D&C 1: 2 no ear that shall not h. the Lord's voice; 1: 14 they who will not h. voice of the Lord or his servants will be cut off; 18: 36 testify that you have h. my voice; 29: 7 the elect h. the Lord's voice; 38: 29 (45: 26, 63) ye h. of wars; 70: 1 inhabitants of the Lord admonished to h. the Lord's word to his servants; 76: 16 dead shall h. Son's voice and come forth; 90: 11 every man shall h. gospel in his own tongue; 138: 37 spirits of rebellious h. gospel through ministration of the Lord's servants.

Moses 4: 14 Adam and Eve h. voice of God while walking in garden; 5: 4 Adam and Eve h. the Lord's voice from way toward Eden; 6: 27 Enoch² h. voice

from heaven; 7: 49 Enoch[2] h. earth
mourn; **JS-H** 1: 24 Joseph Smith felt like
Paul, who saw vision, h. voice.

HEARKEN (see also Hear; Heed; Listen;
Obedience)

D&C 29: 2 the Lord will gather
those who h. to his voice; 84: 46–47 those
who h. to voice of Spirit are enlightened
and come to Father; 101: 7 God is slow
to h. unto prayers of those slow to h.
his voice; 103: 4 members chastened
because they did not h. to commandments; 138: 26 few h. to Savior during
mortal ministry.

Moses 4: 4 Satan leads captive those
who h. not to God's voice; 5: 16 Cain h.
not; 6: 1 Adam h. unto voice of God.

HEART (see also Bosom; Broken Heart and
Contrite Spirit; Change; Convert; Hard-
heartedness; Humble; Intent; Lowliness;
Pride; Purpose)

D&C 1: 2 no h. that shall not be
penetrated; 2: 1–2 (27: 9; 110: 15; 128:
17; 138: 47) Elijah to turn h. of children
and fathers to each other; 4: 2 serve
the Lord with all thy h.; 6: 20 (11:
26; 43: 34) treasure up these words in
thy h.; 8: 2 the Lord speaks in mind and
h.; 10: 15 Satan puts it into men's h. to
tempt the Lord; 10: 20 Satan has great
hold upon men's h.; 10: 21 h. are corrupt;
10: 63 Satan stirs h. to contention; 11: 19
cleave unto the Lord with all your h.; 19:
7 words "eternal damnation" to work on
men's h.; 19: 28 thou shalt pray in thy h.;
19: 39 lift up thy h. for gladness; 21: 9
Christ crucified for remission of sin unto
contrite h.; 25: 12 the Lord delights in
song of h.; 38: 19 the Lord will give land
for inheritance if saints seek it with all
their h.; 38: 29 ye know not the h. of men
in your own land regarding war; 42: 22
love thy wife with all thy h.; 42: 25
adulterer who repents with all his h. shall
be forgiven; 42: 69 lift up your h. and
rejoice; 45: 26 (88: 91) men's h. will fail
them in last days; 45: 29 those in darkness
turn h. from the Lord because of precepts
of men; 45: 55 Satan to have no place in
men's h. during Millennium; 45: 65 with
one h. and mind, gather riches to purchase
land; 59: 5 love the Lord thy God with
all thy h.; 59: 17–19 good things of earth
made to gladden h.; 64: 22 (64: 34) the
Lord requires men's h.; 78: 10 Satan seeks
to turn men's h. from truth; 81: 3 pray
always, vocally and in h.; 84: 88 Spirit
shall be in your h.; 88: 3 Comforter to
abide in your h.; 88: 62 ponder these sayings in your h.; 89: 4 evils and designs to
exist in h. of conspiring men in last days;

98: 17 seek to turn h. of Jews unto
prophets; 121: 4 Lord, let thine h. be
softened; 121: 35 men's h. are set upon
things of world; 124: 9 the Lord will
soften h. of saints' enemies for their good;
137: 9 the Lord judges men according to
works and desires of h.

Moses 4: 6 Satan influences h. of
serpent; 6: 27 men's h. have waxed hard;
6: 55 when children begin to grow up,
sin conceives in their h.; 7: 18 people of
Zion are of one h.; **Abr.** 1: 6 father's h.
were set to do evil; 3: 17 nothing that the
Lord takes in his h. to do but he does it;
JS-H 1: 19 men's h. are far from God;
1: 39 (Mal. 4: 6) Elijah shall plant in h.
of children the promises made to the
fathers.

HEAT (see also Hot)

D&C 101: 25 elements to melt with
fervent h.

Moses 7: 8 the Lord shall curse land
with much h.

HEATHEN (see also Gentile)

D&C 45: 54 h. nations shall be
redeemed after Jews; 75: 22 more tolerable for h. in day of judgment than for
house that rejects elders; 90: 10 arm of
the Lord to be revealed in power in convincing h. nations of gospel.

Abr. 1: 5 fathers turned to worshipping h. gods.

HEAVEN (see also Astronomy; Celestial
Glory; Creation; God—Creator; Heavenly; Host; Jesus Christ—Creator; Kingdom of God; Paradise; **BD** Heaven)

D&C 1: 8 (128: 8, 10; 132: 46)
power given to seal on earth and in h.;
1: 17 the Lord spoke to Joseph Smith
from h.; 21: 6 (35: 24; 43: 18; 45: 48;
49: 23; 84: 118) God will cause the h. to
shake; 29: 14 (45: 42) stars shall fall from
h.; 29: 23 (45: 22; 56: 11) h. and earth to
pass away; 29: 23 new h. and new earth;
45: 16 the Lord will come in clouds of h.;
49: 6 Son reigns in h.; 63: 34 the Lord
will come down in h. from Father's
presence; 67: 2 h. and earth are in the
Lord's hands; 76: 26 h. wept over Lucifer;
77: 2 beasts used by John in describing h.;
84: 42 priesthood confirmed by voice from
h.; 84: 101 h. have smiled on earth; 88: 43
courses of the h. are fixed; 88: 79 saints
to be instructed of things in both h. and
earth; 88: 92–93, 103 angels shall fly
through midst of h.; 88: 95 silence in h.;
88: 97 the quickened will meet the Lord
in pillar of h.; 93: 17 Son received all
power, both in h. and on earth; 107: 19
Melchizedek Priesthood holds keys to

have *h.* opened; 112: 32 keys of this dispensation sent from *h.;* 121: 33 what power shall stay the *h.;* 121: 36 rights of priesthood are inseparably connected with powers of *h.;* 121: 45 doctrine of priesthood shall distill upon soul as dews from *h.;* 124: 93 (127: 7; 128: 8, 10; 132: 46) what you bind on earth shall be bound in *h.;* 128: 14 as are records on earth, so those in *h.;* 128: 19, 23 voice of mercy from *h.;* 129: 1 two kinds of beings in *h.;* 131: 1 in celestial glory there are three *h.,* or degrees; 133: 17, 36 angel crying through midst of *h.;* 133: 69 the Lord clothes *h.* with blackness.

Moses 1: 37 *h.* cannot be numbered to man, but are numbered to God; 1: 38 heavens and earth pass away, another shall come; ch. 2–3 creation of *h.* and earth revealed to Moses; 2: 8 firmament called *h.;* 7: 56 the *h.* were veiled; 7: 61 (JS-M 1: 36) the *h.* shall be darkened; **Abr.** 2: 7 God dwells in *h.;* 4: 8 the Gods called the expanse, *H.;* 5: 1–4 the Gods finished the *h.* and the earth; **JS-M** 1: 33 (Matt. 24: 29) stars shall fall from *h.;* 1: 33, 36 (Matt. 24: 29) powers of the *h.* shall be shaken; 1: 36 (Matt. 24: 30) signs of Son appear in *h.;* 1: 36 (Matt. 24: 30) Son will come in clouds of *h.*

HEAVENLY (see also Heaven)

D&C 76: 14, 89 Joseph Smith and Sidney Rigdon see *h.* vision; 76: 66 city of the living God, *h.* place; 78: 5 saints to be equal in bonds of *h.* things; 78: 5–6 if saints are not equal in earthly things, they cannot be equal in *h.* things; 84: 42 *h.* hosts given charge concerning saints; 128: 13–14 the earthly conforms to the *h.*

HEAVENLY FATHER (see God the Father)

HEED (see also Hear; Hearken; Listen; Obedience; Regard)

D&C 1: 14 they who will not give *h.* to voice of the Lord and his servants will be cut off; 20: 33 let church take *h.* and pray always; 20: 34 let those who are sanctified take *h.;* 21: 4 church should *h.* words and commandment Joseph Smith receives; 63: 6 let the wicked take *h.;* 84: 43 give diligent *h.* to words of eternal life; 93: 48 Joseph Smith's family must give more earnest *h.* to your words.

Moses 8: 13 Noah[1] and sons give *h.* to the Lord; 8: 23 Noah[1] preaches, Give *h.* to my words.

HEEL (see also Foot)

D&C 121: 16 cursed are those who lift up *h.* against the Lord's anointed.

Moses 4: 21 serpent shall bruise *h.* of seed of woman.

HEIGHT (see Depth)

HEIR (see also Children of God; Elect; Exaltation; Inherit; Seed)

D&C 7: 6 (76: 88) John to minister to *h.* of salvation who dwell on earth; 52: 2 the Lord's people a remnant of Jacob, *h.* according to covenant; 70: 8 inhabitants of Zion to become *h.* according to laws of kingdom; 86: 9 those who hold priesthood by lineage are lawful *h.* according to flesh; 137: 7–8 those who would have accepted gospel are *h.* of celestial kingdom; 138: 59 repentant sinners who pay penalty are *h.* of salvation.

Abr. 1: 2 Abraham became rightful *h.,* a high priest.

HELL (see also Bondage; Damnation; Darkness, Spiritual; Death, Spiritual; Devil; Jesus Christ, Atonement through; Lake; Redemption; Resurrection; Torment; Wicked; TG Hell; BD Hell)

D&C 6: 34 earth and *h.* cannot prevail; 10: 26 Satan drags souls down to *h.;* 10: 69 (17: 8; 18: 5; 21: 6; 33: 13; 98: 22; 128: 10) gates of *h.* shall not prevail; 29: 38 place prepared from beginning for devil and his angels; 63: 4 the Lord able to cast soul down to *h.;* 76: 84, 106 heirs of telestial glory are thrust down to *h.;* 88: 113 devil to gather together his armies, hosts of *h.;* 104: 18 those who impart not portion will be with wicked in *h.;* 121: 23 generation of vipers shall not escape damnation of *h.;* 122: 1 *h.* shall rage against thee; 122: 7 very jaws of *h.* shall gape open; 123: 8 handcuffs, chains, shackles, and fetters of *h.;* 123: 10 black deeds are enough to make *h.* shudder; 138: 23 saints acknowledge Son as Deliverer from chains of *h.*

Moses 1: 20 Moses sees bitterness of *h.;* 6: 29 *h.* prepared for the wicked.

HELM

D&C 123: 16 large ship is benefited by small *h.*

HELMET (see also Armor)

D&C 27: 18 take *h.* of salvation.

HELP (see also Deliver; Relief; Serve; Succor; Support; BD Help)

D&C 124: 143 the Lord gives priesthood offices for *h.* and governments.

Moses 3: 18 (Abr. 5: 14, 21) the Lord makes an *h.* meet for Adam.

HEN (see also Animal)

D&C 10: 65 (29: 2; 43: 24) the Lord would gather his people as h. gathers her chickens.

HENI, LAND OF

Moses 7: 9 Enoch² beholds land of H.

HERB (see also Food; Grass)

D&C 42: 43 those without faith to be healed shall be nourished with h.; 59: 17–18 (89: 10–11) h. made for benefit and use of man.

HERD (see also Animal; Cattle; Flock; Fold)

D&C 136: 11 if Saints remove to Zion, they will be blessed in h.

HERITAGE (see also Inherit, Inheritance)

D&C 58: 13 (58: 17) Zion, city of h. of God; 105: 15 the Lord's enemies shall not be left to pollute his h.

HERRIMAN, HENRY

D&C 124: 138 one of seven presidents of seventies.

HEW, HEWN (see also Cut; Prune)

D&C 45: 50 they who have watched for iniquity shall be h. down; 45: 57 those who take Holy Ghost for guide shall not be h. down; 97: 7 trees that bring not forth good fruit shall be h. down.

HICKS, JOHN A.

D&C 124: 137 member of elders quorum presidency.

HIDDEKEL (see River)

HIDE, HID, HIDDEN (see also Cover)

D&C 6: 27 scriptures are h. because of iniquity; 14: 9 Christ a light which cannot be h. in darkness; 60: 2 the Lord not pleased with those who h. talent; 77: 6 sealed book contains h. things of God's economy; 86: 9 saints have been h. from world; 88: 87 (133: 49) sun shall h. his face; 89: 19 those who obey Word of Wisdom shall find h. treasures; 101: 23 veil of covering of temple, which h. earth, shall be taken off; 101: 32–33 the Lord shall reveal things no man knew; 101: 89 (123: 6) the Lord to arise and come forth out of h. place; 121: 1 where is pavilion that covers thy h. place; 123: 13 saints to bring to light h. things of darkness; 124: 38, 41 ordinances h. from before world was.

Moses 4: 16 Adam h. himself because he was naked; 5: 39 from the Lord's face shall Cain be h.

HIEROGLYPHICS (see also Characters; Language; Writing)

Abr. 1: 14 Rahleenos signifies h.

HIGBEE, ELIAS

D&C 113: 7–10 answers to questions asked by.

HIGH, HIGHER, HIGHEST (see also High Council; High Priest; Highway; Pride, Proud)

D&C 19: 29 (64: 37) publish glad tidings upon every h. place; 20: 8 (38: 32, 38; 78: 2; 95: 8; 105: 11, 33; 109: 35) receive power from on h.; 39: 19 (45: 66; 59: 10; 62: 4; 76: 57, 112; 82: 13; 85: 11) the Most H.; 42: 9 building of New Jerusalem to be revealed from on h.; 43: 16 ye are to be taught from on h.; 58: 47 call upon the h. to repent; 64: 37 the Lord has made church like judge sitting in h. place; 76: 27 ask and it shall be made known from on h.; 76: 70 of God, the h. of all; 78: 16 Michael set upon h.; 90: 17 h-mindedness brings snare; 112: 8 h. ones shall be brought low; 130: 10 things pertaining to h. order of kingdoms made known through Urim and Thummim; 131: 2 those who will obtain h. degree of celestial glory must enter new and everlasting covenant of marriage.

Moses 6: 37–38 Enoch² preaches from h. places; 7: 17 people are blessed upon the h. places and flourish; JS-H 1: 22 men of h. standing excite public against Joseph Smith.

HIGH COUNCIL, HIGH COUNCILOR (see also Council)

D&C 20: 66 h.c. have privilege of ordaining where there is no branch; 20: 67 every h.c. to be ordained by direction of h.c. or general conference; 20: 67 those to be ordained by direction of h.c.; 42: 34 h.c. to administer storehouse; 102: Intro. minutes of h.c.; 102: 1–2 h.c. of church organized; 102: 2 h.c. settles differences not settled by bishop's council; 102: 6 h.c. cannot act without at least seven members present; 102: 12–26 h.c. courts; 102: 27, 30–33 appeals of decisions of h.c. court; 102: 30 distinction between the h.c. and the traveling h.c. of apostles; 107: 33–34 (124: 139) the Twelve are a Traveling Presiding H.c.; 107: 36–37 standing h.c. in stakes are equal in authority to presidency and traveling h.c.; 120: 1 tithes to be disposed of by council including h.c.; 124: 131 h.c. given for cornerstone of Zion.

HIGH PRIEST (see also Bishop; Priesthood, Melchizedek; TG High Priest—Melchizedek Priesthood; BD High Priest)

D&C 20: 66 h.p. may have privilege of ordaining where there is no branch; 20: 67 h.p. to be ordained by direction of high council or general conference; 42: 31, 71 two elders or h.p. to be appointed bishop's counselors; 52: Intro. first ordinations to office of h.p.; 68: 15, 19, 22 h.p. may be appointed to office of bishop; 68: 19 (107: 17) h.p. have authority to officiate in all lesser offices; 72: 1 revelation to h.p.; 76: 57 (107: 10) priests of Most High, after the order of Melchizedek; 77: 11 those who are sealed are h.p.; 84: 63 apostles are God's h.p.; 84: 111 h.p. should travel; 102: 1 high council to consist of twelve h.p.; 107: 2 Melchizedek, a great h.p.; 107: 10, 12 h.p. administer in spiritual things; 107: 22 three presiding h.p. form Presidency of Church; 107: 53 descendants of Adam who were h.p. were called together; 107: 66 President of Church is Presiding H.P. over High Priesthood; 107: 71 h.p. may administer in temporal things; 124: 134 ordinance instituted to qualify standing presidents over stakes; 138: 41 Shem, the great h.p.

Abr. 1: 2 Abraham is h.p.

HIGH PRIESTHOOD (see also Priesthood, Melchizedek)

HIGHWAY (see also Path; Street; Way)

D&C 133: 27 h. to be cast up in great deep.

HILL (see also Cumorah, Hill; Mount, Mountain)

D&C 35: 24 (39: 13) Zion to rejoice upon h.; 49: 25 Zion shall flourish upon h.; 64: 37 church compared to judge sitting on h.; 133: 31 everlasting h. shall tremble at presence of lost tribes.

Abr. 1: 10, 20 priest offers sacrifices upon Potiphar's H.

HINDER (see also Forbid; Frustrated; Stay; Stop; Withhold)

D&C 50: 38 let no man h. elders in labors appointed by the Lord; 121: 33 man cannot h. the Almighty from pouring down knowledge; 124: 49 when enemies h. saints from performing work, the Lord requires it no more.

HIRAM, OHIO (see also D&C map, p. 296)

D&C secs. 1, 65, 67–70, 73–74, 76–81, 99, 133 revelations received at H.; 64: Intro. Joseph Smith prepares to move to H.

HIRE (see also Wages)

D&C 31: 5 (84: 79; 106: 3) laborer is worthy of his h.; 70: 12 he who is appointed to administer spiritual things is worthy of his h.

HISTORY (see also Record)

D&C 47: 1, 3 (69: 2–3) John Whitmer to keep regular church h.; 85: 1 clerk to keep h. and general church record; 93: 53 elders to obtain knowledge of h.; 123: 5–6 saints to present libelous h. to heads of government; 128: 3 recorders to be appointed in each ward to record h. of transactions.

JS-H 1: 1 Joseph Smith writes h. to disabuse public mind.

HOLD (see also Keep; Power; Retain; Withhold)

D&C 10: 20 Satan has great h. upon hearts.

HOLINESS (see also Godliness; Holy; Purity; Righteous; Sacred; Sanctification)

D&C 20: 69 (21: 4) walk in h. before the Lord; 38: 24 (46: 33) practice virtue and h. before the Lord; 46: 7 do that which Spirit testifies should be done in all h.; 109: 13 the Lord's house, a place of h.; 133: 35 after their pain, Judah shall be sanctified in h.

Moses 5: 26 Abel walked in h. before the Lord; 6: 57 (7: 35) Man of H. is God's name; 7: 19 city of Enoch[2] called City of H.

HOLY (see also Holiness; Holy Ghost; Jesus Christ—Holy One of Israel; Order; Spirit, Holy/Spirit of the Lord)

D&C 20: 11 God calls men to his h. work in this age; 45: 12 h. men sought day of righteousness; 45: 32 (87: 8; 101: 22, 64) disciples shall stand in h. places; 49: 8 all men are under sin except h. men whom the Lord has reserved unto himself; 59: 9 saints to offer sacraments upon the Lord's h. day; 60: 7 the Lord is able to make men h.; 63: 49 the faithful shall receive an inheritance in h. city; 74: 7 little children are h.; 84: 59 h. land must not be polluted; 101: 64 the Lord to build saints up unto his name upon h. places; 115: 7 Far West, a h. city; 119: 6 if saints do not keep law of tithing, h. land will not be Zion to them; 124: 44 the Lord will consecrate spot for temple and it shall be made h.

Moses 7: 62 the Lord's elect will be gathered to H. City.

HOLY GHOST (see also Born of God; Fire; Holy Ghost, Baptism of; Holy Ghost—Comforter; Holy Ghost, Gift of; Holy Spirit of Promise; Spirit, Gifts of; Spirit, Holy/Spirit of the Lord; TG God, Spirit of; Holy Ghost; Holy Ghost, Dove, Sign of; Holy Ghost, Gifts of; Holy Ghost, Loss of; Holy Ghost, Mission of; Holy Ghost, Source of Testimony; Holy Ghost, Unpardonable Sin against; Holy Spirit; Lord, Spirit of; Spirit; BD Holy Ghost)

D&C 8: 2 the Lord speaks in mind and heart by H.G.; 8: 2 H.G. shall dwell in your heart; 8: 3 H.G. is spirit of revelation; 14: 8 H.G. gives utterance; 18: 18 H.G. manifests all things that are expedient; 18: 32 the Twelve should declare the gospel according to power of H.G.; 20: 26 prophets spake as inspired by gift of H.G.; 20: 26–27 H.G. bears record of Father and Son; 20: 28 Father, Son, and H.G. are one; 20: 35 scripture and revelations given through gift and power of H.G.; 20: 45 (46: 2) elders to conduct meetings as led by H.G.; 20: 60 priesthood bearers ordained by power of H.G. in the one who ordains them; 35: 19 H.G. knows all things; 35: 19 (121: 26) knowledge given by H.G.; 39: 6 H.G. teaches peaceable things of kingdom; 68: 2–4 priesthood bearers should preach as directed by H.G.; 68: 4 H.G. gives scriptures; 68: 8 baptism in name of Father, Son, and H.G.; 84: 27 John filled with H.G.; 93: 15 H.G. descended upon Christ in form of dove; 100: 8 H.G. to be shed forth in bearing record to all things elders say; 121: 26 God gives knowledge by unspeakable gift of H.G.; 121: 43 reprove with sharpness when moved by H.G.; 121: 46 H.G. shall be thy constant companion; 130: 22 H.G. has not a body of flesh and bones, but is personage of spirit; 130: 23 man may receive H.G. without its tarrying with him; 132: 27 blasphemy against H.G.

Moses 1: 24 Moses filled with H.G.; 1: 24 (5: 9; 7: 11) H.G. bears record of Father and Son; 5: 9 H.G. fell upon Adam; 5: 14 the Lord called upon men by H.G.; 5: 58 gospel declared by gift of H.G.; 6: 8 Adam moved upon by H.G.; 7: 27 H.G. fell upon many in time of Enoch[2]; **A of F** 1 we believe in the H.G.

HOLY GHOST, BAPTISM OF (see also Born of God; Convert; Fire; Holy Ghost, Gift of; Remission; Sanctification; TG Holy Ghost, Baptism of)

D&C 5: 16 those who believe shall be born of fire, and of water and of Spirit; 19: 31 (20: 41, 43; 33: 11; 39: 6) remission of sins by baptism and by fire; 84: 64 every soul baptized by water for remission of sins shall receive H.G.

Moses 6: 59 ye must be born again of water and of Spirit; 6: 65–66 Adam is baptized with fire and H.G.; **JS-H** 1: 73 after baptism, Joseph Smith and Oliver Cowdery are filled with H.G.

HOLY GHOST—COMFORTER (see also Holy Ghost; TG Holy Ghost, Comforter; BD Comforter)

D&C 21: 9 (24: 5; 31: 11; 75: 27; 90: 14) revelation given through the Comforter; 28: 1, 4 (50: 14; 52: 9) elders teach by Comforter; 31: 11 (75: 27; 79: 2) Comforter will guide missionaries in travels; 35: 19 (42: 17) Comforter knows all things; 36: 2 (39: 6) H.G. is the Comforter; 36: 2 (39: 6) Comforter teaches peaceable things of kingdom; 42: 16 (52: 9; 90: 14) elders to speak and prophesy by Comforter; 42: 17 Comforter bears record of Father and Son; 47: 4 given by Comforter to write things of God; 50: 14 (52: 9; 75: 10; 79: 2; 124: 97) Comforter teaches the truth; 88: 3–4 the Lord sends another Comforter, Holy Spirit of promise; 90: 11 every man to hear gospel in own tongue by administration of Comforter.

Moses 6: 61 Comforter to abide in righteousness.

HOLY GHOST, GIFT OF (see also Confirm; Gift; Gospel; Hands, Laying on of; Holy Ghost; Holy Ghost, Baptism of; Ordinance; Spirit, Gifts of; TG Holy Ghost, Gift of)

D&C 20: 43 (33: 15; 35: 6; 39: 23; 49: 14; 55: 1; 68: 25) the Lord bestows gift of H.G. on those who are confirmed in church; 35: 5 Sidney Rigdon baptized by water, but they did not receive H.G.; 35: 6 (55: 1) after baptism, receive H.G. by laying on of hands; 53: 3 elders ordained to preach reception of H.G. by laying on of hands; 68: 25 parents must teach children doctrine of gift of H.G.; 76: 52 those in celestial glory have received Holy Spirit by laying on of hands; 84: 64 every soul who is baptized shall receive H.G.; 121: 46 H.G. shall be thy constant companion; 138: 33 spirits of dead are taught gift of H.G. by laying on of hands.

Moses 6: 52 he who is baptized shall receive gift of H.G.; **JS-H** 1: 70 Aaronic Priesthood has not power of laying on hands for gift of H.G.; **A of F** 4 laying on of hands for gift of H.G., one of first ordinances of gospel.

HOLY ONE (see Jesus Christ—Holy One of Israel)

HOLY SPIRIT OF PROMISE (see also Holy Ghost; Seal; Spirit; Spirit, Gifts of; Spirit, Holy/Spirit of the Lord)

D&C 76: 53 (132: 26) those who come forth in resurrection of the just are sealed by H.S. of promise; 88: 3 the Lord sends another Comforter, the H.S. of promise; 124: 124 Hyrum Smith, as patriarch, holds sealing blessings, the H.S. of promise by which men are sealed up until day of redemption; 132: 7, 18–19, 26 all covenants and performances must be sealed by H.S. of promise to have force after this life.

HOME (see also Dwell, Dwelling)

D&C 88: 79 saints to receive knowledge of things at h. and abroad; 93: 50 Newel K. Whitney to be more diligent and concerned at h.

HONEST, HONESTLY (see also Integrity; Uprightness; TG Honesty)

D&C 8: 1 (11: 10) ask in faith, with h. heart; 51: 9 let every man deal h.; 97: 8 sacrifices of those who know their hearts are h.; 98: 10 seek h. and wise men; 135: 7 innocent blood of martyrs will touch hearts of h. men among all nations.

A of F 13 we believe in being h.

HONEY

D&C 38: 18 the Lord to give saints land flowing with milk and h.

HONOR (see also Esteem; Glorify; Glory; Honorable; Integrity; Praise; Respect; Reverence)

D&C 20: 36 (65: 6; 84: 102) h., power, and glory be rendered to the Lord; 29: 36 devil sought God's h.; 58: 7 the Lord sends Joseph Smith that he might be h. in laying foundation; 75: 5 (124: 55) faithful to be crowned with h.; 76: 5 the Lord h. those who serve him in righteousness; 97: 19 nations of earth shall h. Zion; 121: 35 few are chosen because they aspire to h. of men; 124: 34 keys of priesthood ordained, that elders may receive h.; 128: 21 voice of angels declaring their h.; 134: 6 every man should be h. in his station; 136: 39 Joseph Smith died that he might be h. and the wicked might be condemned.

Moses 4: 1 Satan asks Father to give him the h.; A of F 12 we believe in h. the law.

HONORABLE (see also Noble; Worthy)

D&C 76: 75 h. men of earth blinded by craftiness of men; 101: 73 h. men to be appointed to purchase lands.

HOPE (see also Faith; Trust)

D&C 4: 5 (6: 19; 12: 8) h. a qualification for the ministry; 18: 19 he who has not faith, h., and charity can do nothing; 42: 45 weep for death of those that have not h. of glorious resurrection; 128: 21 voices of messengers confirm our h.; 138: 14 the just have firm h. of resurrection.

A of F 13 we h. all things.

HORSE (see also Animal)

D&C 89: 17 oats for h.

HOSANNA (see also BD Hosanna)

D&C 19: 37 (36: 3; 39: 19; 124: 101) elders to preach gospel by crying h.; 109: 79 saints to mingle voices with seraphs singing h. to God and the Lamb.

HOST (see also Jesus Christ—Lord of Hosts)

D&C 29: 11 (29: 36; 38: 1, 11; 45: 1; 84: 42; 88: 112) h. of heaven; 29: 15 weeping and wailing among h. of men; 88: 113 devil shall gather h. of hell; 138: 11 Joseph F. Smith saw h. of dead.

HOT (see also Heat; Word of Wisdom)

D&C 89: 9 h. drinks are not for the body.

HOUR (see also Time; BD Hour)

D&C 1: 35 (29: 9–10; 45: 38; 58: 4; 133: 17) h. is nigh; 33: 3 it is eleventh h.; 39: 21 (49: 7; 133: 11, 17) no man knows h. of the Lord's coming; 45: 2 (51: 20; 61: 38; 124: 10) the Lord comes in h. you think not; 84: 85 (100: 6) it shall be given you in the very h. what to say; 88: 58 each received light of the Lord's countenance in his h.; 88: 84, 104 (133: 38) h. of judgment to come; 88: 95 silence in heaven for half an h.

Moses 7: 67 Enoch² sees h. of redemption of the righteous; JS-M 1: 40 that day and h. no one knoweth; 1: 48 in such an h. when ye think not, the Son cometh.

HOUSE (see also Housetop; Israel; Temple; BD House)

D&C 19: 36 Martin Harris is commanded to leave his h.; 20: 47, 51 the duty of priests and teachers to visit h. of each member; 31: 9 govern my h. in meekness; 41: 7 Joseph Smith to have h. built; 42: 35 residue in storehouse used to build h. of worship; 45: 52 Christ wounded in h. of friends; 58: 9 supper of h. of the

Lord; 59: 9 go to *h.* of prayer on the Lord's holy day; 75: 18–20 elders to go from *h.* to *h.*; 81: 6 the Lord has prepared mansions in *h.* of Father; 84: 5 *h.* shall be built unto the Lord; 84: 31 *h.* of the Lord to be built in this generation; 84: 32 sons of Moses and Aaron to be filled with glory upon Mount Zion in the Lord's *h.*; 84: 94 wo unto *h.* that rejects elders; 85: 7 one mighty and strong to set in order the *h.* of God; 88: 119 (109: 8–16) establish a *h.* of prayer; 88: 127 order of *h.* prepared for presidency of school of prophets; 88: 137 salutation by prayer in *h.* of the Lord; 93: 43 set in order your own *h.*; 95: 3 neglect of commandment to build the Lord's *h.*; 95: 8, 11 (97: 15; 105: 33; 115: 8; 124: 31) commandment to build the Lord's *h.* for endowments; 97: 12 tithing and sacrifice required to build *h.* unto the Lord for salvation of Zion; 110: 7 the Lord will manifest himself in his *h.*; 112: 25 desolation to go forth from the Lord's *h.*; 117: 16 keep the Lord's *h.* holy; 119: 2 surplus property for building of the Lord's *h.*; 121: 19 those who persecute saints to be severed from ordinances of the Lord's *h.*; 124: 22, 24 commandment to build boarding *h.*; 124: 25–27 saints to gather to build *h.* for the Most High; 124: 28 the Lord to restore fulness of priesthood in his *h.*; 124: 29–30 baptisms for dead must be performed in the Lord's *h.*; 124: 39 ordained by ordinance of the Lord's holy *h.*; 124: 55 commandment to build *h.* in Nauvoo; 132: 8, 18 *h.* of the Lord is *h.* of order; 133: 13 those who are of Judah will flee unto Jerusalem, unto the mountains of the Lord's *h.*; 138: 58 repentant dead will be redeemed through ordinances of the Lord's *h.*

HOUSETOP

D&C 1: 3 iniquities shall be spoken upon the *h.*

JS-M 1: 14 (Matt. 24: 17) let him on *h.* flee.

HUMAN (see also Man; Mankind)

D&C 134: 4 *h.* law has no right to prescribe rules of worship; **JS-H** 1: 28 Joseph Smith displays foibles of *h.* nature.

HUMBLE, HUMILITY (see also Abase; Boast; Broken Heart and Contrite Spirit; Fasting; Low; Lowliness; Meek; Poor; Weak; TG Humility, Humble)

D&C 1: 28 the Lord's servants are *h.* that they might be made strong and receive knowledge; 11: 12 trust in Spirit which leads men to walk *h.*; 12: 8 no one can assist except he be *h.*; 19: 20 repent lest I *h.* you; 19: 30 preach with *h.*; 19: 41

canst thou be *h.* and meek; 20: 37 *h.* required for baptism; 29: 2 the Lord will gather those who *h.* themselves; 54: 3 those who desire to escape their enemies must repent and become truly *h.*; 61: 2 the Lord forgives those who confess sins with *h.* hearts; 61: 37 as saints *h.* themselves before the Lord, blessings of kingdom are theirs; 67: 10 if elders *h.* themselves, they will see God; 84: 112 wants of the poor to be met by *h.*; the rich and the proud; 104: 79 saints to obtain blessings by diligence and *h.*; 105: 12 endowment and blessing to be poured out on those who continue in *h.*; 112: 10 be thou *h.*, and the Lord shall lead thee by hand; 136: 32 the ignorant will learn wisdom by *h.* himself.

HUMPHREY, SOLOMON

D&C 52: 35 to journey to eastern lands.

HUNGER, HUNGRY (see also Charity; Famine; Food)

D&C 84: 80 those who preach gospel shall not go *h.*; 89: 15 these to be used only in times of excess *h.*

HUNTINGTON, WILLIAM

D&C 124: 132 member of high council.

HURT (see also Harm; Wound)

D&C 77: 9 *h.* not the earth; 84: 71 poison shall not *h.* apostles.

HUSBAND (see also Companion; Family; Marriage; Wife; TG Husband; Marriage, Husband)

D&C 25: 9 *h.* shall support thee in church; 25: 14 let thy soul delight in thy *h.*; 74: 1 unbelieving *h.* is sanctified by wife; 74: 1 unbelieving wife is sanctified by *h.*; 83: 2 women have claim on *h.* for maintenance.

Moses 4: 12 woman gave fruit to her *h.*; 4: 22 thy desire shall be to thy *h.*

HYDE, ORSON

D&C 68: Intro. revelation given at request of; 68: 1–3 example of preaching gospel by Spirit; 75: 13 sent on mission; 100: 14 to be saved if obedient; 102: Intro. recorded minutes of first high council; 102: 3 member of high council; 103: 40 to accompany Orson Pratt; 124: 129 member of the Twelve.

HYMN (see also Music; Song)

D&C 25: 11 Emma Smith to make selection of sacred *h.*

HYPOCRISY, HYPOCRITE (see also Deceit; Guile; Lying; Sincerity; Wicked; BD Hypocrite)

D&C 41: 5 he who says he receives law but does it not is not the Lord's disciple; 50: 6–8 h. among saints shall be detected and cut off; 64: 39 h. to be proved by inhabitants of Zion; 101: 90 unjust stewards to be appointed portion among h.; 104: 55 all consecrated properties are the Lord's or else saints are h.; 112: 26 desolation to begin among those who profess to know the Lord's name but have not known him; 121: 37 when men undertake to cover their sins, Spirit withdraws; 121: 42 pure knowledge shall greatly enlarge soul without h.; 124: 8 oppressor to be appointed portion among h.

I AM (see also Jesus Christ—Jehovah; BD Jehovah)

D&C 29: 1 (38: 1; 39: 1) Jesus Christ, the Great I Am; 67: 10 you shall see me and know that I Am.

ICE

D&C 133: 26 i. shall flow down at presence of lost tribes.

IDLENESS, IDLE, IDLER (see also Engaged; Labor; Sleep; Slothful)

D&C 42: 42 thou shalt not be i.; 60: 13 thou shalt not i. away thy time; 68: 30–31 the Lord is not well pleased with i. among inhabitants of Zion; 75: 3 men should not be i., but should labor with might; 75: 29 the i. shall not have place in church; 88: 69 cast away i. thoughts; 88: 124 cease to be i.

IDOLATRY, IDOLATROUS, IDOL (see also Altar; Gods; Image; Priests, False; Sacrifice; BD Idol)

D&C 1: 16 every man walks after image of his own God, whose substance is that of an i.; 52: 39 elders to labor that no i. be practised.

Abr. 1: 7 fathers offered children to dumb i.; 1: 27 Abraham's father led away by Egyptians' i.; 2: 5 Abraham's father turns again to his i.

IDUMEA

D&C 1: 36 I. is the world.

IGNORANCE, IGNORANT (see also Accountable; Blindness; Darkness, Spiritual; Knowledge; Unlearned)

D&C 131: 6 impossible for man to be saved in i.; 136: 32 let him who is i. learn wisdom.

ILLINOIS (see D&C maps, pp. 297, 298)

IMAGE (see also Creation; Form [noun]; Idolatry; Similarity)

D&C 1: 16 every man walks after i. of his own God; 20: 18 man created after i. of God; 138: 40 Seth was express i. of Adam.

Moses 2: 26–27 (6: 9–10; Abr. 4: 26–27) man created in i. of God.

IMAGINATION (see also Think)

D&C 124: 99 he shall mount up in i. of thoughts.

Moses 8: 22 every man lifted up in i. of thoughts of heart.

IMITATE

Abr. 1: 26 Pharaoh i. order established by fathers.

IMMANUEL (see Jesus Christ—Immanuel)

IMMATERIAL (see Matter)

IMMENSITY

D&C 88: 12 light from God fills i. of space.

IMMERSION (see also Baptism; Water; TG Baptism, Immersion)

D&C 13: 1 (20: 74) baptism by i.; 76: 51 celestial heirs were baptized, being buried in water after manner of Christ's burial; 128: 12 baptism by i. to answer likeness of dead.

Moses 6: 64 Adam is laid under the water; A of F 4 baptism by i. for remission of sins, one of first ordinances of gospel.

IMMORTALITY, IMMORTAL (see also Body; Death, Physical; Eternal Life; Jesus Christ, Resurrection of; Life; Live; Redemption; Resurrection; TG Immortality)

D&C 29: 43 by natural death man may be raised in i. unto eternal life; 45: 46 souls of those who come unto the Lord shall live; 63: 49 those who rise from dead shall not die after; 75: 5 (81: 6; 124: 55; 138: 51) the faithful to be crowned with i.; 77: 1 (130: 9) earth in its sanctified, i. state; 88: 116 the sanctified will not any more see death; 121: 32 every man shall enter God's i. rest; 128: 23 glorious voice from heaven proclaiming i. and eternal life.

Moses 1: 39 God's work and glory, to bring to pass i. and eternal life of man.

IMMOVABLE (see also Firmness; Immutable; Steadfast)

D&C 88: 133 I receive you to fellowship in i. determination to be friend.

IMMUTABLE (see also Change; Immovable; Unalterable; Unchangeable)

D&C 98: 3 (104: 2) the Lord gives promise with i. covenant.

IMPART (see also Alms; Charity; Give; Poor)

D&C 11: 13 the Lord will i. his Spirit; 19: 26 Martin Harris is to i. freely to printing of Book of Mormon; 19: 34 i. all save that needed to support family; 42: 31 i. of substance unto the poor; 88: 123 learn to i. one to another as gospel requires; 104: 18 he who takes of abundance but i. not his portion to the poor will lift up eyes in hell; 105: 3 saints do not i. of substance to poor as becometh saints.

IMPOSSIBLE

D&C 131: 6 i. for a man to be saved in ignorance.

IMPROVE (see also Increase)

D&C 82: 18 man may i. upon his talent; 104: 68 cast into treasury moneys received in stewardship by i. properties.

IMPURE (see Roll, Rolling)

INCOMING

D&C 88: 120 (109: 9, 17–18) i. and outgoing should be in the Lord's name.

INCREASE (see also Add; Continue; Continuation; Enlarge; Flourish; Grow; Improve; Multiply; Prolong; Reward; Seed; Spread; Swell; Wax)

D&C 1: 21 faith to i. in earth; 82: 14 Zion must i. in beauty; 121: 43 after reproving, show i. of love; 131: 4 those who do not enter new and everlasting covenant of marriage cannot have i.

INDEPENDENCE, MISSOURI (see also D&C map, p. 297)

D&C 57: 3 center place of Zion; 58: 37 land to be purchased in I.; sec. 83 revelation received at I.

INDEPENDENT, INDEPENDENTLY

D&C 78: 14 church to stand i. above all other creatures; 93: 30 all truth is i. in sphere in which God has placed it; 107: 76 descendant of Aaron may act in office of bishop i., without counselors.

INDIAN TRIBES (see also Lamanites)

D&C 32: Intro. revelation concerning missionary work to I.

INDIGNATION (see also Anger; Displeasure; Judgment; Punishment; Wrath)

D&C 29: 17 (35: 14; 43: 26) cup of the Lord's i. is full; 56: 1 the rebellious shall know the Lord's i.; 87: 6 inhabitants of earth will feel i. of Almighty God; 97: 24 the Lord's i. is kindled against abominations of the wicked; 98: 47 the Lord's i. shall be turned away from those who repent; 101: 10 the Lord will let fall the sword of his i. on behalf of his people; 109: 52 the Lord's i. to fall upon the wicked mob.

Moses 7: 1 unbelievers look forth for God's i. to be poured upon them.

INDIVIDUAL, INDIVIDUALLY

D&C 1: 30 the Lord is pleased with church collectively, not i.; 105: 2 transgressions of the Lord's people, speaking of church, not i., have prevented redemption; 130: 10 each i. to receive white stone; 134: 2 laws must secure to each i. the free exercise of conscience.

INFANT (see also Accountability, Age of; Babe; Child)

D&C 93: 38 men became again innocent in their i. state; 101: 30 in that day i. will not die until old.

INFINITE (see also Endless; Eternal; God, Eternal Nature of; Innumerable)

D&C 20: 17, 28 God is i. and eternal.

INFIRMITY (see also Affliction; Suffering; Weak)

D&C 42: 52 saints to bear i. of those who have not faith to do great things.

INFLICT

D&C 134: 10–11 religious societies do not have right to i. physical punishment or personal abuse.

INFLUENCE (see also Power)

D&C 121: 41 no power or i. can be maintained by virtue of priesthood; 122: 4 i. of traitors causes trouble; 123: 7 wives and children upheld by i. of spirit; 134: 9 not just to mingle religious i. with civil government; 136: 10 let every man use all his i. to remove saints to Zion.

JS-H 1: 15 Joseph Smith seized by power with astonishing i. in bind tongue; 1: 75 intentions of mob counteracted by i. of Hales family.

INHERIT, INHERITANCE (see also Celestial Glory; Children of God; Consecration, Law of; Covenant; Heir; Heritage; Possess; Promised Land; BD Inheritance)

D&C 6: 37 those who keep commandments will i. kingdom of heaven; 10: 55 those who belong to church will i. kingdom of heaven; 38: 19–20 the Lord to give saints land of *i.*; 38: 20 saints and children to possess land of *i.* in eternity; 45: 58 (56: 20) those who abide the Lord's coming will be given earth for *i.*; 45: 65 (48: 4; 57: 5) saints to gather riches to purchase *i.*; 50: 5 those who endure to end will *i.* eternal life; 51: 4 saints to hold portions as *i.* until they transgress; 51: 19 (78: 22) faithful steward to *i.* eternal life; 52: 5 land of *i.* to be made known; 52: 42 Missouri is land of *i.*; 58: 36 the law to those who came to receive *i.*; 59: 1–2 those who survive in Zion will *i.* earth; 63: 20 he who endures shall receive *i.* on earth in day of transfiguration; 63: 49 resurrected saints to receive *i.* in holy city; 72: 4 those who are faithful in time will *i.* mansions of Father; 72: 17 certificate from bishop answers for *i.*; 85: 3 those who receive not their *i.* by consecration should not be numbered among saints; 85: 7 one mighty and strong to arrange *i.* by lot; 85: 9, 11 those whose names are not written in book of remembrance shall find no *i.*; 88: 17 the poor and meek of earth will *i.* it; 88: 26 the righteous will *i.* earth; 88: 107 saints shall receive *i.* and be made equal with God; 101: 6 *i.* polluted by strife; 101: 101 what saints build, another shall not *i.*; 103: 14 saints will be thrown down if they pollute *i.*; 123: 7 fathers have *i.* lies; 132: 19 those who marry in new and everlasting covenant will *i.* thrones, kingdoms; 132: 39 David will not *i.* his wives and concubines; 137: 6 those who died before restoration of gospel may obtain *i.* in celestial kingdom.

Moses 6: 57 men must repent or they cannot *i.* kingdom of God.

INIQUITY (*see also* Destruction; Evil; Judgment; Rebel; Sin; Transgression; Trespass; Ungodliness; Unrighteous; Wicked; TG Iniquity)

D&C 1: 3 *i.* of rebellious to be spoken from housetops; 3: 18 Lamanites dwindled in unbelief because of *i.* of fathers; 3: 18 Nephites destroyed because of *i.*; 6: 27 scriptures hidden because of *i.*; 10: 20 Satan stirs men up to *i.*; 10: 29 Satan flatters men to do *i.*; 18: 6 world ripe in *i.*; 20: 54 teachers to see there is no *i.* in church; 38: 14 saints are blessed, but not because of *i.*; 42: 87 members who do *i.* to be delivered to law of God; 43: 11 purge out *i.* among saints; 45: 27 because *i.* will abound, love of men shall wax cold; 45: 50 they who have watched for *i.* shall be hewn down; 45: 53 Jews to weep because of *i.*; 101: 11 God's indignation to be poured out when cup of *i.* is full; 103: 3 the Lord suffers enemies to fill up measure

of their *i.*; 123: 7 earth groans under weight of *i.*

Moses 5: 39 he that findeth me shall slay me because of mine *i.*; JS-M 1: 10 because *i.* shall abound, love of many shall wax cold; 1: 30 because *i.* shall abound, love of men shall wax cold.

INJUSTICE (*see also* Justice; Persecution; Unjust; Unlawful)

D&C 102: 15 half of high council appointed to prevent insult or *i.* in court.

INNOCENT (*see also* Blameless; Blood, Shedding of; Guiltless; Pure; Righteousness; Spotless)

D&C 93: 38 man was *i.* in the beginning; 93: 38 through redemption men become again *i.* before God in infant state; 104: 7 is *i.* are not to be condemned with the unjust; 134: 6 rulers and magistrates placed for protection of the *i.*; 135: 7 Joseph and Hyrum Smith were *i.* of any crime; 136: 36 *i.* blood cries from ground.

INNUMERABLE (*see also* Count; Infinite; Number; Sand)

D&C 76: 109 inhabitants of telestial world were *i.* as stars; 132: 30 Abraham's seed to continue *i.* as stars.

INQUIRE (*see also* Ask; Prayer; Question; Seek)

D&C 6: 11 he who *i.* shall know mysteries; 6: 14 as often as thou hast *i.*, thou hast received instructions of the Spirit; 30: 3 you are left to *i.*; 102: 23 in case of difficulty regarding doctrine, the president may *i.* for revelation; 122: 1 ends of earth shall *i.* after Joseph Smith's name.

Moses 1: 18 Moses has other things to *i.* of God; JS-H 1: 18 Joseph Smith *i.* of the Lord to know which sect is right.

INSEPARABLY

D&C 93: 33 spirit and element *i.* connected receive fulness of joy; 121: 36 rights of priesthood are *i.* connected with powers of heaven.

INSPIRE, INSPIRATION (*see also* Calling; Enlighten; Holy Ghost; Revelation; Spirit, Holy/Spirit of the Lord; TG Inspiration)

D&C 8: 2 the Lord will tell you in your mind and in your heart, by Holy Ghost; 9: 8 if it is right, the Lord will cause bosom to burn; 20: 7 God gave Joseph Smith commandments which *i.* him; 20: 10 Book of Mormon given by *i.*;

20: 11 God *i.* men and calls them to his holy work; 20: 26 prophets spoke as *i.* by Holy Ghost; 21: 2, 7 Joseph Smith *i.* to lay foundation of church; 21: 9 Joseph Smith's words given by Comforter; 24: 6 it is given in the very moment what to speak or write; 28: 4 speak or teach whenever led by Comforter; 33: 8 open your mouths and they shall be filled; 34: 10 prophesy, and it shall be given by power of Holy Ghost; 43: 16 elders to be taught from on high; 85: 6 still small voice whispers through and pierces all things.

Moses 6: 5 those called of God write by spirit of *i.*

INSTRUCTION, INSTRUCT (*see also* Charge; Command; Commandments of God; Counsel; Edification; Revelation; Teach)

D&C 1: 26 commandments *i.* those who seek wisdom; 6: 14 those who inquire receive *i.* of Spirit; 33: 16 Book of Mormon scriptures given for *i.*; 43: 8 saints should assemble to *i.* and edify each other; 55: 4 schools to be established so that children may receive *i.*; 88: 78 those who teach diligently will be *i.* more perfectly in doctrine; 88: 127 school of prophets established for *i.* in all things; 97: 13 the Lord's house a place of *i.* for those called to ministry; 124: 88 await *i.* at general conference; 132: 3 obey *i.* given by the Lord; 138: 36 the Redeemer *i.* faithful spirits to teach gospel.

JS-H 1: 54 Joseph Smith receives *i.* from Moroni² each year.

INSTRUMENTALITY

D&C 112: 1 missionaries are ordained through *i.* of the Lord's servants.

INTEGRITY (*see also* Honest; Righteousness; Sincerity; Uprightness)

D&C 124: 15 the Lord loves Hyrum Smith because of *i.*; 124: 20 George Miller may be trusted because of *i.*

INTELLIGENCE, INTELLIGENT (*see also* Knowledge; Learning; Light; Mind; Premortal Existence; Truth)

D&C 88: 40 *i.* cleaveth unto *i.*; 93: 29 *i.* was not created or made; 93: 30 all *i.* is independent in sphere in which God has placed it; 93: 36 glory of God is *i.*; 130: 18–19 whatever principle of *i.* man attains in this life will rise with him in resurrection.

Abr. 3: 19 one spirit more *i.* than another, the Lord more *i.* than they all; 3: 21–22 the Lord rules over all *i.*; 3: 22 Abraham beholds premortal *i.*

INTENT (*see also* Desire; Purpose; Sincerity; Thoughts; Will)

D&C 6: 16 (33: 1) only God knows *i.* of heart; 88: 20 for this *i.* was earth made and created; 88: 109 *i.* of hearts to be made known.

INTERCESSION (*see* Jesus Christ—Mediator)

INTEREST (*see also* Tithing)

D&C 82: 19 every man to seek *i.* of neighbor; 119: 4 saints to pay one-tenth of *i.* annually as tithing; 134: 6 human laws to regulate our *i.* as individuals and nations.

INTERPRETATION OF TONGUES (*see also* Language; Spirit, Gifts of; Tongue; Translation)

D&C 46: 25 to another is given the *i.* of tongues; 109: 36 *i.* of tongues to be poured out.

A of F 7 we believe in gift of *i.* of tongues.

INVITE (*see also* Lead)

D&C 20: 59 deacons and teachers to *i.* all to come unto Christ; 58: 9 all nations shall be *i.* to supper of house of the Lord.

IOWA (*see also* D&C maps, pp. 297, 298)

D&C sec. 125 will of the Lord concerning saints in *I.*

IRAD—*grandson of Cain*

Moses 5: 43 son of Enoch¹, father of Mahujael; 5: 45 reveals Cain's secret to sons of Adam; 5: 50 slain by Lamech¹.

IRON (*see also* Rod; Yoke)

Moses 5: 46 Tubal Cain an instructor of every artificer in *i.*

ISAAC—*son of Abraham* (*see also* BD Isaac)

D&C 98: 32 law given to *I.*; 132: 36 Abraham commanded to offer *I.*; 132: 37 *I.* abode in God's law; 133: 55 shall be in presence of Lamb; 138: 41 seen by Joseph F. Smith among noble spirits.

ISAIAH—*Hebrew prophet* [c. eighth century B.C.] (*see also* BD Isaiah)

D&C sec. 113 answers questions on writings of *I.*; 138: 42 seen by Joseph F. Smith among noble spirits.

JS-H 1: 40 quoted by angel to Joseph Smith.

ISLAND

D&C 1: 1 (88: 94; 133: 20) ye who are upon *i.* of sea, listen together; 88: 94

abominable church sits upon *i.* of sea; 133: 8 send elders unto *i.* of sea; 133: 20 Bridegroom shall stand upon *i.* of sea; 133: 23 *i.* shall become one land.

ISRAEL—*name of Jacob and, by extension, of all his descendants* (see also Abrahamic Covenant; Branch; Covenant; Ephraim; Israel, Gathering of; Israel, Scattering of; Israel, Ten Lost Tribes of; Jacob; Jacob, House of; Jew; Joseph; Joseph, Seed of; Judah; Remnant; TG Israel; Israel, Blessings of; Israel, Bondage of, in Other Lands; Israel, Deliverance of; Israel, Joseph, People of; Israel, Judah, People of; Israel, Land of; Israel, Mission of; Israel, Origins of; Israel, Remnant of; Israel, Twelve Tribes of; BD Israel; Israel, Kingdom of)

D&C 18: 6 house of *I.* must be stirred up to repent; 42: 39 the Lord to consecrate riches of Gentiles to the poor of house of *I.*; 77: 11 144,000 to be sealed out of all tribes of *I.*; 84: 23 Moses taught *I.* in wilderness; 103: 17 saints are children of *I.*; 113: 10 bands on Zion's neck are God's curses on *I.* in scattered condition; 133: 34 blessings of God upon tribes of *I.*; 136: 22 I am he who led children of *I.*; 138: 25 Savior spent three years in ministry to those of house of *I.*

Moses 1: 26 God calls *I.* his chosen; 1: 26 *I.* to be delivered by Moses.

ISRAEL, GATHERING OF (see also Israel, Scattering of; TG Israel, Gathering of; Israel, Restoration of)

D&C 10: 65 (29: 2) the Lord will gather his people as hen gathers chickens; 14: 10 Christ to bring fulness of gospel from Gentiles to house of *I.*; 29: 7 ye are called to bring to pass gathering of the Lord's elect; 35: 25 (38: 33) *I.* shall be saved in the Lord's due time; 39: 11 fulness of gospel to be preached, the covenant sent forth to recover *I.*; 42: 9 New Jerusalem to be prepared that the Lord's people may be gathered in one; 45: 17, 25 Christ teaches disciples about restoration of *I.*; 77: 14 (Rev. 10: 2, 9–11) little book mentioned in Rev. 10 is mission and ordinance to gather house of *I.*; 84: 2 church established for restoration of the Lord's people and gathering of saints; 84: 99 the Lord to redeem his people; 86: 11 (113: 8) priesthood bearers to be saviors unto *I.*; 101: 12 *I.* shall be saved; 101: 13 they who have been scattered shall be gathered; 109: 64 prayer that children of Judah may begin to return to lands given to Abraham; 110: 11 Moses commits keys of gathering of *I.*; 113: 10 scattered remnants are exhorted to return

to the Lord; 133: 12–14 those who are among Gentiles should go out from the nations and flee unto Zion; 137: 6 the Lord set his hand to gather *I.* the second time.

A of F 10 we believe in the literal gathering of *I.* and in the restoration of the Ten Tribes.

ISRAEL, SCATTERING OF (see also Destruction; Israel, Gathering of; Israel, Ten Lost Tribes of; Remnant; TG Israel, Scattering of)

D&C 45: 19 Christ prophesied that Jews would be destroyed and scattered among all nations; 113: 10 scattered remnants are exhorted to return to the Lord.

ISRAEL, TEN LOST TRIBES OF (see also Israel, Gathering of; Israel, Scattering of; TG Israel, Ten Lost Tribes of)

D&C 110: 11 Moses commits keys of leading of ten tribes from north; 133: 26–34 those in north countries shall come.

A of F 10 we believe in the restoration of the Ten Tribes.

JABAL—*Son of Lamech*

Moses 5: 45 father of those who dwell in tents.

JACKSON COUNTY, MISSOURI (see also Jerusalem, New; Zion)

D&C secs. 57–60, 82 revelations received at; 101: 71 (105: 28) saints to purchase land in; 124: 5 God accepts offerings of those commanded to build city in.

JACOB—*father of twelve tribes, name changed to Israel [c. 1800 B.C.]* (see also Israel; Jacob, House of; BD Israel; Jacob)

D&C 27: 10 Joseph[1], J., Isaac, Abraham, by whom promises remain; 98: 32 law given unto J.; 132: 1, 37 the Lord justified J. in having many wives and concubines; 133: 55 J. shall be in presence of the Lamb; 136: 21 God of Abraham, Isaac, J.; 138: 41 Joseph F. Smith saw J. among noble spirits.

JACOB, HOUSE OF (see also Israel; Jacob; Remnant)

D&C 10: 60 the Lord's other sheep are branch of house of J.; 49: 24 J. to flourish in wilderness before the Lord's coming; 52: 2 the Lord's people are remnant of J.; 109: 58, 61 prayer for children of J.; 109: 62 have mercy upon children of J.; 109: 65 remnant of J. smitten because of transgression will be converted.

JACQUES, VIENNA

D&C 90: 28–31 to go up to land of Zion.

JAMES (see also Apostle; Priesthood, Melchizedek; BD James)

D&C 27: 12 Joseph Smith and Oliver Cowdery ordained and confirmed apostles by Peter, J., and John; 128: 20 voice of Peter, J., and John declaring themselves as possessing keys of kingdom.

JS-H 1: 11, 13, 21 Joseph Smith read in epistle of J.; 1: 72 Peter, J., and John hold keys of Melchizedek Priesthood.

JAMES, GEORGE

D&C 52: 38 to be ordained a priest.

JAPHETH (see also BD Japheth)

Moses 8: 12, 27 son of Noah¹.

JARED¹—father of Enoch²

D&C 107: 47 ordained and blessed by Adam¹; 107: 53 called to gathering of Adam's posterity at Adam-ondi-Ahman.

Moses 6: 20 son of Mahalaleel; 6: 21 teaches Enoch² in all the ways of God.

JARED²—founder of Jaredites

There are no references to Jared² in the Doctrine and Covenants and Pearl of Great Price.

JARED², BROTHER OF—first Jaredite prophet

D&C 17: 1 received Urim and Thummim and spoke with the Lord face to face.

JEALOUSY (see also Covet; Envy)

D&C 67: 10 elders to strip themselves from j.

JEHOVAH (see Jesus Christ—Jehovah)

JEREMY

D&C 84: 9 gave priesthood to Elihu; 84: 10 received priesthood from God.

JERSHON, LAND OF

Abr. 2: 16 Abraham travels by way of J.; 2: 17 Abraham builds altar in J.

JERUSALEM—chief city of Jews and surrounding area (see also Jerusalem, New; Jew; BD Jerusalem; Judea)

D&C 5: 20 the Lord told people of destruction of J.; 45: 18–25 Christ's prediction concerning J.; 77: 15 Jews to gather and build city of J.; 109: 62 J. to be redeemed; 124: 36 baptisms for the dead in J.; 133: 13 let Judah flee to J.; 133: 21 the Lord shall speak from J.; 133: 24 land of J. to be turned back into its own place.

JS-M 1: 12, 18, 21 tribulation and destruction to come upon J. in latter days.

JERUSALEM, NEW (see also Jackson County; Zion; TG Jerusalem, New)

D&C 28: 9 (42: 9, 35, 62; 48: 5) time and place for building N.J. shall be revealed; 42: 35 consecration of properties for building N.J.; 42: 36 N.J. built for gathering of covenant people; 42: 67 covenants promised to saints in N.J.; 45: 66 69 N.J. a place of peace, refuge, safety; 45: 67 glory of the Lord shall be in N.J., and it shall be called Zion; 45: 68, 70 wicked to fear Zion; 52: 43 the Lord to hasten the city of N.J.; 84: 2, 4 saints to be gathered to Mount Zion, city of N.J.; 84: 3–4 N.J. to be built beginning at temple lot; 124: 51 reason why N.J. was not built; 133: 56 resurrected saints to stand with Lamb upon holy city.

Moses 7: 62 the Lord to gather his elect to Holy City called Zion, a N.J.; A of F 10 Zion (the N.J.) will be built upon American continent.

JESSE—father of David [c. 1100 B.C.] (see also BD Jesse)

D&C 113: 1–6 Stem of J.

JESUS CHRIST (see also Baptism; Belief; Blood; Charity; Church of God; Church of the Firstborn; Cornerstone; Day of the Lord; Faith; Fall of Man; Firstborn; Glory [noun]; God; God, Body of; God—Creator; God, Eternal Nature of; God, Foreknowledge of; God, Goodness of; God, Love of; God, Manifestations of; God, Omniscience of; God, Power of; God, Presence of; God, Wisdom of; God the Father; Gospel; Grace; Hand of the Lord; Jesus Christ—Advocate; Jesus Christ, Appearances of; Jesus Christ, Atonement through; Jesus Christ, Condescension of; Jesus Christ—Creator; Jesus Christ, Death of; Jesus Christ, First Coming of; Jesus Christ—Good Shepherd; Jesus Christ—Holy One of Israel; Jesus Christ—Immanuel; Jesus Christ—Jehovah; Jesus Christ—Lamb of God; Jesus Christ—Lord; Jesus Christ—Lord of Hosts; Jesus Christ—Mediator; Jesus Christ—Messiah; Jesus Christ—Only Begotten Son; Jesus Christ—Redeemer; Jesus Christ, Resurrection of; Jesus Christ—Savior; Jesus Christ, Second Coming of; Jesus Christ—Son of God; Jesus Christ—Son of Man; Jesus Christ,

Types of; Judgment; Justice; King; Light; Love; Mercy; Name of the Lord; Rest; Rock; Spirit, Holy/Spirit of the Lord; Word of God/Word of the Lord; TG Jesus Christ; Jesus Christ, Antemortal Existence of; Jesus Christ, Ascension of; Jesus Christ, Authority of; Jesus Christ, Baptism of; Jesus Christ, Betrayal of; Jesus Christ, Davidic Descent of; Jesus Christ, Exemplar; Jesus Christ, Family of; Jesus Christ, Firstborn; Jesus Christ, Foreordained; Jesus Christ, Glory of; Jesus Christ, Head of the Church; Jesus Christ, Judge; Jesus Christ, King; Jesus Christ, Light of the World; Jesus Christ, Messenger of the Covenant; Jesus Christ, Millennial Reign of; Jesus Christ, Mission of; Jesus Christ, Power of; Jesus Christ, Prophecies about; Jesus Christ, Relationship with the Father; Jesus Christ, Rock; Jesus Christ, Second Comforter; Jesus Christ, Spirit of; Jesus Christ, Taking the Name of; Jesus Christ, Teaching Mode of; Jesus Christ, Temptation of; Jesus Christ, Trials of; BD Jesus)

D&C 1: 36 (29: 11; 43: 29; 58: 22; 76: 63, 108) millennial reign of Jesus Christ; 5: 14 (10: 67; 11: 16; 18: 5; 30: 6; 33: 5; 39: 13; 41: 3; 42: 59; 43: 15; 45: 1; 69: 3; 84: 32; 104: 1; 115: 3; 119: 3; 124: 41, 94; 133: 4, 16; 136: 41) head of church; 6: 21 (10: 57; 11: 28; 14: 9; 17: 9; 18: 33, 47; 19: 24; 35: 2; 36: 8; 38: 1; 43: 34; 45: 52; 49: 28; 51: 20; 52: 44) I am Christ; 6: 21 (10: 58; 11: 11; 34: 2; 39: 2; 45: 7) the light which shines in darkness; 10: 70 (11: 28; 34: 2; 39: 2; 45: 7; 84: 45; 93: 9) light and life of world; 19: 1 (35: 1; 38: 1; 45: 7; 54: 1; 61: 1; 84: 120) Alpha and Omega, the beginning and the end; 19: 2 Christ accomplished will of Father; 19: 3 (50: 27; 76: 10, 24; 88: 7, 13; 93: 17) power of Jesus Christ; 19: 3 Christ will destroy Satan; 19: 3 (39: 18; 43: 33; 76: 68; 77: 12; 99: 5; 133: 2) Christ will judge every man; 19: 18 suffering caused Christ to tremble and bleed; 19: 24 Jesus Christ came by will of Father and does his will; 19: 24 (20: 24; 93: 4, 17; 107: 3; 124: 123) authority of Jesus Christ; 20: 22 Son suffered temptation, but gave no heed; 20: 24 Christ ascended to reign with Father; 20: 30–31 justification through grace of Jesus Christ; 34: 3 Christ so loved the world that he gave his life; 35: 2 (50: 43) Christ is one with Father; 45: 11 the God of Enoch²; 45: 52 Jesus will proclaim himself to Jews; 45: 53, 59 (128: 22–23) the King; 50: 41 Christ has overcome the world; 59: 5 serve God in the name of Jesus Christ; 60: 4 Christ

rules in heavens above; 62: 1 Jesus Christ knows men's weaknesses and how to succor them; 62: 6 he cannot lie; 68: 6 elders to bear record of Jesus Christ; 76: 13 (93: 21) premortal existence of Jesus Christ; 76: 43 Jesus glorifies Father; 76: 107 Jesus to deliver kingdom to Father; 76: 108 Jesus to be crowned with glory and reign forever; 84: 45 whatsoever is light is Spirit of Christ; 93: 8 the messenger of salvation; 110: 4 the first and the last; 113: 1–2 (Isa. 11: 1–5) the Stem of Jesse; 132: 24 to have eternal lives is to know God and Jesus Christ.

Moses 6: 52, 57 (7: 50) name of Only Begotten is Son of Man, even Jesus Christ; **JS-H** 1: 40 prophet mentioned in Acts 3: 22–23 is Christ; **A of F** 1 we believe in God, the Eternal Father, and in His son, Jesus Christ; 10 we believe that Christ will reign personally upon earth.

JESUS CHRIST—ADVOCATE (see also Jesus Christ, Atonement through; Jesus Christ—Mediator)

D&C 29: 5 (32: 3; 45: 3; 62: 1; 110: 4) I am your advocate with the Father; 38: 4 Christ pleads before the Father for those who believe in him.

JESUS CHRIST, APPEARANCES OF (see also Day of the Lord; God, Manifestations of; Vision; Visitation; TG God, Manifestations of; God, Privilege of Seeing; Jesus Christ, Appearances, Antemortal; Jesus Christ, Appearances, Postmortal)

D&C 6: 37 behold the wounds which pierced my side; 45: 74 when the Lord appears, he shall be terrible unto saints' enemies; 67: 10 if you strip yourselves of fears and humble yourselves, veil shall be rent and you shall see me; 76: 23 Joseph Smith and Sidney Rigdon see glory of Son on right hand of Father; 93: 1 those who come unto the Lord and obey will see his face; 107: 49 Enoch³ saw the Lord; 107: 54 the Lord appeared to Adam's family at Adam-ondi-Ahman; 110: 1–10 the Lord appears at dedication of Kirtland Temple; 110: 8 the Lord will appear to his servants; 130: 1 when Savior appears, saints will see him; 130: 3 personal appearing of Father and Son in John 14: 23 is personal appearance; 138: 8 (1 Pet. 3: 18–19) Son appears to spirits in spirit world.

Moses 1: 2 Moses sees God face to face; 7: 4 Enoch³ saw the Lord; **Abr.** 2: 6–11 the Lord appears to Abraham; **JS-H** 1: 17 20 Father and Son appear to Joseph Smith.

JESUS CHRIST, ATONEMENT THROUGH (see also Fall of Man; Forgive; Grace; Jesus Christ—Advocate; Jesus Christ, Death of; Jesus Christ, First Coming of; Jesus Christ—Lamb of God; Jesus Christ—Mediator; Jesus Christ—Messiah; Jesus Christ—Only Begotten Son; Jesus Christ—Redeemer; Jesus Christ, Resurrection of; Jesus Christ—Savior; Jesus Christ, Types of; Mercy; Merit; Offering; Plan; Reconcile; Remission; Sacrifice; Salvation; Sanctification; TG Jesus Christ, Atonement through; BD Atonement)

D&C 18: 11 Redeemer suffered pain of all men; 19: 16, 18 God suffered that men might not; 29: 1 the LORD's arm of mercy atones for sins; 29: 46 (74: 7) children are redeemed from foundation of world through atonement of Savior; 38: 4 by virtue of his spilt blood Christ pleads before Father for men; 45: 4 Father, behold sufferings and death of him who did no sin; 76: 69 Jesus wrought out perfect atonement through shedding of blood; 138: 2 great atoning sacrifice made by Son for redemption of world; 138: 4 mankind to be saved through atonement of Son.

Moses 5: 7 sacrifice of firstling of flock is similitude of sacrifice of Only Begotten; 6: 54 Son has atoned for original guilt; **A of F** 3 through Atonement of Christ all mankind may be saved.

JESUS CHRIST, CONDESCENSION OF (see also TG Jesus Christ, Condescension of)

D&C 88: 6 (122: 8) Son has descended below all things.

JESUS CHRIST—CREATOR (see also Creation; God—Creator; God the Father; Jesus Christ—Jehovah)

D&C 29: 30–31 by power of his spirit Christ created all things, spiritual and temporal; 38: 1–3 Christ spake and the world was made; 45: 1 hearken to him who laid foundations of earth and made heavens; 76: 24 by Only Begotten the worlds are and were created; 88: 7 Christ is light of sun and power by which it was made; 93: 9 world was made by Redeemer.

Moses 1: 33 (2: 1) worlds without number have I created by Son; **Abr.** 3: 24 spirit like unto God says, We will go down and make a world; 4: 1 the Gods organized and formed heavens and earth.

JESUS CHRIST, DEATH OF (see also Death, Physical; Jesus Christ, Resurrection of; TG Jesus Christ, Crucifixion of; Jesus Christ, Death of)

D&C 18: 11 Redeemer suffered death, pain of all men that all might repent; 20: 23 (45: 52) Son was crucified, died; 21: 9 (35: 2; 46: 13; 53: 2) Christ was crucified for sins of world; 45: 4 Father, behold sufferings and death of him who did no sin; 45: 52 I am Jesus who was crucified; 76: 39 resurrection through glory of Lamb who was slain; 76: 41 Jesus was crucified to bear sins of world, sanctify world, cleanse it from all unrighteousness; 110: 4 I am he who was slain; 138: 27 Christ's ministry among dead during time between crucifixion and resurrection; 138: 35 redemption wrought through sacrifice of Son upon cross.

Moses 7: 47 Righteous is lifted up; 7: 55 Enoch[2] beholds Son lifted up on cross.

JESUS CHRIST, FIRST COMING OF (see also Jesus Christ, Second Coming of; TG Jesus Christ, Birth of)

D&C 19: 24 Christ came by will of Father; 20: 1 rise of Church 1830 years after coming of Christ in flesh; 76: 41 Jesus came into world to be crucified; 93: 4 Christ called Son because he made flesh his tabernacle and dwelt among men.

Moses 5: 57 (6: 57, 62) Only Begotten Son to come in meridian of time; 7: 53 blessed is he through whose seed Messiah shall come; 7: 54 when Son comes, earth shall rest.

JESUS CHRIST—HOLY ONE OF ISRAEL (see also BD Holy One of Israel)

D&C 78: 16 Michael under direction of Holy One.

JESUS CHRIST—IMMANUEL (see also BD Immanuel)

D&C 128: 22 let the dead praise Immanuel.

JESUS CHRIST—JEHOVAH (see also I Am; Jesus Christ—Creator; BD Jehovah)

D&C 109: 34 O Jehovah, have mercy; 109: 42 deliver, O Jehovah, thy servants from hands of those who reject them; 109: 56 servants to bear testimony to Jehovah's name; 109: 68 Joseph Smith covenanted with Jehovah; 110: 1–3 appearance and voice of Jehovah; 128: 9 decrees of Jehovah concerning records.

Abr. 1: 16 (2: 8) Jehovah declares his name to Abraham.

JESUS CHRIST—LAMB OF GOD (see also TG Jesus Christ, Lamb of God)

D&C 58: 11 the poor, lame, and deaf to come into marriage of Lamb; 65: 3 prepare supper of Lamb; 76: 39 resur-

rection through triumph of Lamb; 76: 39
Lamb was in bosom of Father before
worlds were made; 76: 85 Christ the
Lamb; 76: 119 glory, honor, and dominion
to God and Lamb; 88: 106 Lamb has
overcome and trodden the wine-press;
109: 79 sing Hosanna to God and Lamb;
133: 18 Lamb shall stand upon Mount
Zion; 133: 55 prophets shall be in
presence of Lamb; 133: 56 saints shall
sing song of Lamb.

Moses 7: 47 Son is the Lamb slain
from foundation of world.

JESUS CHRIST—LORD (see also Day of
the Lord; God; Jesus Christ—Lord of
Hosts; Name of the Lord; Spirit,
Holy/Spirit of the Lord; Word of
God/Word of the Lord; TG Jesus Christ,
Lord; Lord; BD Lord)

D&C 1: 17 the Lord called upon
Joseph Smith; 1: 39 (5: 2) the Lord is
God; 10: 70 (18: 33; 34: 12) Jesus Christ,
your Redeemer, your Lord and your
God; 15: 1 (17: 9; 19: 1; 95: 17) listen to
words of Jesus Christ, your Lord; 17: 1
brother of Jared² talked with the Lord;
19: 1 (35: 1; 38: 1; 54: 1; 75: 1) the Lord
is Alpha and Omega; 21: 1 an apostle by
grace of your Lord, Jesus Christ; 21: 6
the Lord God will disperse powers of
darkness from before you; 33: 10 (34: 6;
65: 1, 3; 133: 17) prepare way of the
Lord; 53: 2 the Lord was crucified for
sins of world; 55: 1 the Lord of the whole
earth; 59: 5 (Matt. 22: 37) thou shalt love
the Lord thy God with all thy heart; 61: 2
the Lord forgives sins; 63: 34 the Lord
is with the saints; 64: 10 the Lord will
forgive whom he will; 64: 34 the Lord
requires the heart; 68: 4 that which is
spoken under influence of Holy Ghost is
will, mind, word, voice of the Lord; 70:
18 the Lord is merciful; 77: 12 the Lord
will sanctify the earth; 82: 1 the Lord
forgives those who forgive; 82: 10 I, the
Lord, am bound when ye do what I say;
84: 35 all who receive priesthood receive
the Lord; 84: 98 all shall know the Lord
and be filled with knowledge of the Lord;
85: 10 as the Lord speaketh, he will also
fulfil; 87: 7 (88: 2; 95: 7; 98: 2) the Lord
of Sabaoth; 112: 10 be humble, and the
Lord thy God will lead thee; 124: 24
house shall be holy, or the Lord thy God
will not dwell therein; 133: 25 the Lord
shall stand in midst of his people; 133:
48 the Lord shall be red in his apparel;
137: 9 the Lord will judge all men; 138:
29–37 the Lord went not personally
among spirits of wicked; 138: 60 our Lord
and Savior, Jesus Christ.

Moses 1: 3 I am the Lord God

Almighty; 5: 14 the Lord God called upon
men by Holy Ghost to repent; 7: 16 the
Lord dwells with his people in days of
Enoch²; 7: 30 the Lord is just, merciful,
kind; 8: 19 the Lord ordains Noah¹ after
his own order; **Abr.** 3: 21 the Lord dwells
in midst of all intelligences; **A of F** 4 faith
in the Lord Jesus Christ, one of first
principles of gospel.

JESUS CHRIST—LORD OF HOSTS (see
also Jesus Christ—Lord; TG Lord of
Hosts; BD Lord of Hosts)

D&C 1: 33 Spirit shall not always
strive with man, saith the Lord of Hosts;
29: 9 (64: 24; 133: 64; Mal. 4: 1) I will
burn the wicked up, saith the Lord of
Hosts; 85: 5 names of the unfaithful will
not be written in book of law of God,
saith the Lord of Hosts; 127: 4 you shall
in nowise lose reward, saith the Lord of
Hosts.

JS-H 1: 37 the wicked shall be
burned, saith the Lord of Hosts.

JESUS CHRIST—MEDIATOR (see also
Jesus Christ, Atonement through; Jesus
Christ—Advocate; TG Jesus Christ,
Mediator)

D&C 76: 69 (107: 19) Jesus the
mediator of new covenant.

JESUS CHRIST—MESSIAH (see also TG
Jesus Christ—Messiah; BD Messiah)

D&C 13: 1 priesthood conferred in
name of Messiah; 19: 27 Jews to stop
looking for Messiah to come who has
come; 109: 67 scattered remnants of
Israel to believe in Messiah.

Moses 7: 53 blessed is he through
whose seed Messiah shall come; 7: 53 the
Lord saith, I am Messiah, King of Zion;
JS-H 1: 69 priesthood conferred in name
of Messiah.

**JESUS CHRIST—ONLY BEGOTTEN
SON** (see also Jesus Christ—Son of God;
TG Jesus Christ, Only Begotten Son)

D&C 20: 21 (49: 5) Almighty God
gave his Only Begotten Son; 29: 42
redemption through faith on Only
Begotten Son; 29: 46 little children are
redeemed through Only Begotten; 49: 5
redemption only to those who receive
Only Begotten Son; 76: 13 things ordained
of Father through Only Begotten Son;
76: 23 voice bears record of Only Begotten; 76: 25–26 Lucifer rebelled against
Only Begotten Son; 76: 35 sons of
perdition deny Only Begotten Son; 76:
57 (124: 123) priests after order of
Melchizedek, which is order of Only Begotten Son; 93: 11 Christ's glory is glory

of Only Begotten; 138: 14 resurrection through grace of Father and Only Begotten Son, Jesus Christ; 138: 57 redemption through sacrifice of Only Begotten Son.

Moses 1: 6 Only Begotten is and shall be Savior; 1: 17 call upon God in name of Only Begotten; 1: 21 (4: 1) Moses commands Satan to depart in name of Only Begotten; 1: 32-33 (2: 1) by word of power, which is Only Begotten Son, God created worlds; 2: 27 God created man in image of Only Begotten; 4: 3 by power of Only Begotten, God cast Satan down; 5: 7 sacrifice of firstlings is similitude of sacrifice of Only Begotten; 5: 9 I am the Only Begotten of the Father from the beginning; 5: 57 (6: 62) Only Begotten Son to come in meridian of time; 6: 52 be baptized in name of Only Begotten is Son of Man, even Jesus Christ; 6: 59 be cleansed by blood of Only Begotten; 6: 62 plan of salvation unto all men through blood of Only Begotten; 7: 59 ask in name of Only Begotten; 7: 62 God will send truth out of earth to testify of Only Begotten.

JESUS CHRIST—REDEEMER (see also Jesus Christ, Atonement through; Jesus Christ—Savior; Redemption; TG Jesus Christ, Redeemer)

D&C 10: 70 remember words of him who is your Redeemer; 18: 11–12 Redeemer has suffered that all men might repent; 18: 47 Jesus Christ, your Redeemer; 19: 1 (93: 9) I am the Redeemer of the world; 19: 16 God has suffered these things that they might not suffer; 29: 46 little children are redeemed through Only Begotten; 49: 5 God sent Only Begotten into world for redemption of world; 77: 12 in beginning of seventh thousand years God will redeem all things; 138: 3 love of Father and Son manifest in coming of Redeemer; 138: 18 Son declares liberty to captive spirits; 138: 23 saints acknowledge Son as Redeemer; 138: 42 Redeemer anointed to bind up brokenhearted.

JESUS CHRIST, RESURRECTION OF (see also Death, Physical; Immortality; Jesus Christ, Atonement through; Jesus Christ, Death of; Jesus Christ—Redeemer; Resurrection; TG Jesus Christ, Resurrection of)

D&C 18: 12 the Lord is risen from dead to bring men unto him; 20: 23 resurrection of Christ on third day; 76: 39 resurrection through triumph and glory of Lamb; 133: 55 those who were with Christ in his resurrection.

Moses 7: 62 God will send truth out of earth to testify of resurrection of Christ and all men.

JESUS CHRIST—SAVIOR (see also Jesus Christ, Atonement through; Jesus Christ—Redeemer; Salvation; Save; TG Jesus Christ—Savior)

D&C 1: 20 every man to speak in name of Savior; 3: 16 knowledge of Savior comes through Jews; 43: 34 I am Jesus Christ, Savior of world; 76: 1 beside the Lord there is no Savior; 130: 1 we shall see Savior is a man like ourselves.

Moses 1: 6 Only Begotten is and shall be Savior.

JESUS CHRIST, SECOND COMING OF (see also Day of the Lord; Last Days; Millennium; TG Jesus Christ, Second Coming of)

D&C 1: 12 (34: 7; 35: 15; 43: 17; 49: 6; 104: 59; 106: 4; 110: 16; 133: 17) time of coming is nigh at hand; 2: 1 (138: 47–48) Elijah to come before coming of day of the Lord; 5: 19 (93: 34 133: 64) unrepentant to be destroyed by brightness of the Lord's coming; 29: 11 (34: 7; 45: 16; 65: 5) the Lord to reveal himself from heaven with power and glory; 29: 13–16 (34: 9; 43: 18; 45: 16–33, 39; 49: 23–25; 63: 53; 68: 11; 77: 12; 88: 93; 133: 41–52) signs of the Lord's coming; 33: 17 have lamps and oil ready for coming of Bridegroom; 33: 18 (34: 12, 35: 27; 39: 24; 41: 4; 49: 28; 51: 20; 54: 10; 68: 35) the Lord to come quickly; 34: 6 (39: 20; 77: 12; 84: 28) cry repentance, preparing way of the Lord for second coming; 34: 7 (45: 16, 44–50; 76: 63) the Lord to come in clouds; 34: 8 all nations to tremble at the Lord's coming; 35: 21 the elect to abide day of the Lord's coming; 35: 27 kingdom is yours until 1 come; 36: 8 (133: 2) the Lord to come suddenly to temple; 38: 8 day soon cometh that ye shall see me; 38: 21 (41: 4) the Lord to be ruler when he comes; 38: 22 no laws but the Lord's at his coming; 39: 21 (49: 7; 61: 38; Matt. 24: 36) no man knows hour and day of the Lord's coming; 39: 23 (61: 38) look for signs of the Lord's coming; 43: 29 the Lord to come in judgment in own due time; 45: 39 he who fears the Lord will look for signs of coming; 49: 22 Son not to come in form of woman; 56: 18 the poor who are pure in heart to see the Lord's coming; 61: 38 Son comes in hour you think not; 61: 39 pray to abide day of the Lord's coming; 63: 34 the wicked to be consumed in fire at the Lord's coming; 63: 49 (133: 56) the dead to rise when the Lord comes; 63: 50 blessed is he who lives at the Lord's coming; 64: 23 it is called today until coming of Son; 64: 23 he who is tithed shall not be burned at the Lord's coming; 64: 24 after today comes the burning; 65: 5 Son to come down to meet kingdom of God on earth; 76: 63 those in resurrection of the just to come with the Lord to reign; 88: 86 let hands be clean until the Lord comes; 88: 92 (133: 19) Bridegroom cometh, go out to meet him; 88: 95 after space of silence in heaven, the Lord's face will be unveiled; 88: 96 saints to be caught up to meet the Lord; 88: 99 redemption of those who are Christ's at his coming; 97: 23 the Lord's scourge not to be stayed until he comes; 101: 23 all flesh shall see the Lord; 101: 24 corruptible things to be consumed at the Lord's coming; 101: 32 all things to be revealed at the Lord's coming; 101: 65 saints to be crowned at the Lord's coming; 104: 58–59 scriptures to be published to prepare people for time when the Lord will dwell with them; 106: 4 the Lord to come as thief in night; 128: 24 who can abide day of the Lord's coming; 130: 1 when Savior appears, we shall see he is man like ourselves; 130: 12 bloodshed before the Lord's coming; 130: 14–17 Joseph Smith's prayer concerning time of the Lord's coming; 133: 2 the Lord shall come down upon world with curse to judgment; 133: 25 Savior shall stand in midst of his people and reign over all flesh; 133: 46 it shall be said, Who is this that comes down from God in heaven with dyed garments; 133: 64 (Mal. 4: 1) day cometh that shall burn as oven.

Moses 7: 47, 65 Enoch² saw day of coming of Son; JS-M 1: 26 (Matt. 24: 27) coming of Son shall be as light of morning which comes out of east and shines unto west; 1: 33, 36 (Matt. 24: 29–30) signs of the Lord's coming to appear in heaven; 1: 36 (Matt. 24: 30) all shall see Son coming with power and glory; 1: 40 (Matt. 24: 36) of day and hour of the Lord's coming no man knoweth, only Father.

JESUS CHRIST—SON OF GOD (see also God the Father; Jesus Christ—Creator; Jesus Christ—Immanuel; Jesus Christ—Jehovah; Jesus Christ—Lamb of God; Jesus Christ—Messiah; Jesus Christ—Only Begotten Son; Jesus Christ—Son of Man; TG Jesus Christ, Divine Sonship; BD Son of God)

D&C 6: 21 (10: 57; 11: 28; 14: 9; 20: 77, 79; 35: 2; 36: 8; 42: 1; 45: 52; 46: 13; 50: 27; 52: 44; 55: 2; 68: 6, 25; 76: 14; 88: 5; 109: 4) Jesus Christ, the Son of God; 20: 21 (49: 5) God gave his Son; 20: 27 (42: 17) Holy Ghost bears record of Father and Son; 20: 28 Father, Son, and Holy Ghost are one God; 20: 73 (68: 8) baptize in name of Son; 20: 77, 79 sacrament is in remembrance of body and blood of Son; 20: 77 saints take upon them the name of Son; 29: 42 redemption through faith in Son; 45: 4 blood of Son was shed; 45: 39 (61: 38; 63: 53; 68: 11) look forward to signs of coming of Son; 46: 13 spiritual gift of knowing that Christ is Son of God; 49: 5 Son was sent for redemption of world; 49: 6 (137: 3) Son has taken power on right hand of glory; 49: 6 Son to reign till he descends to earth; 49: 22 Son comes not in form of woman; 58: 65 (65: 5) Son shall come; 76: 13 things ordained of Father through Son from beginning; 76: 14 in resurrection, the dead will hear voice of Son and come forth; 76: 20 glory of Son seen; 76: 25 Lucifer rebelled against Son; 76: 25 Lucifer thrust down from presence of God and Son; 76: 35, 43 sons of perdition denied the Son; 76: 57 (107: 3; 124: 123) Melchizedek Priesthood is after the order of the Son; 76: 73 (138: 18–21, 29–30; 1 Pet. 3: 18–20) Son visits spirits in prison; 76: 77 terrestrial inhabitants receive presence of Son; 78: 20 (95: 17) your Redeemer, Son Ahman; 93: 4 Christ called Son because he made flesh his tabernacle; 93: 13–17 Christ called Son because he received not of fulness at first; 93: 15 this is my beloved Son; 109: 5 saints build house where Son might manifest himself; 122: 8 Son has descended below them all; 130: 12 much bloodshed before coming of Son; 130: 22 Son has body of flesh and bones; 138: 2, 13, 35, 57 great atoning sacrifice of the Son; 138: 14 resurrection through grace of Father and Son.

Moses 1: 24 Holy Ghost bears record of Father and Son; 1: 32–33 (2: 1) God created worlds by his Son; 2: 1 Son says, Father, thy will be done; 5: 8 do all in name of Son; 5: 8 call upon Son in name of Son; 5: 9 Holy Ghost bears record of Father and Son; 6: 54 Son of God has atoned for original guilt; 7: 11 baptize in name of Father, Son, Holy Ghost; 7: 27 Enoch² beholds angels descending from heaven, bearing testimony of Father and Son; 8: 24 be baptized in name of Jesus Christ, the Son of God; JS-H 1: 17 this is my beloved Son, hear him; **A of F** 1 We believe in God, the Eternal Father, and in his Son, Jesus Christ.

JESUS CHRIST—SON OF MAN (see also Jesus Christ—Only Begotten Son; Jesus Christ—Son of God; TG Jesus Christ, Son of Man; BD Son of Man)

D&C 45: 39 (61: 38; 63: 53; 68: 11) look for signs of coming of Son of Man; 49: 6 world has done unto Son of Man as they listed; 49: 22 Son of Man comes not in form of woman; 58: 65 Son of Man cometh; 64: 23 called today until coming of Son of Man; 65: 5 prepare for days to come in which Son of Man shall come down in heaven; 76: 16 those who shall hear voice of Son of Man and come forth in resurrection; 109: 5 saints build house, that Son of Man might have place to manifest himself; 122: 8 Son of Man has descended below them all; 130: 14–15, 17 Joseph Smith prays to know time of coming of Son of Man.

Moses 6: 57 name of Only Begotten is Son of Man; 7: 24 Enoch² is lifted up in bosom of Father and Son of Man; 7: 47, 65 Enoch² sees day of coming of Son of Man; 7: 54 when Son of Man comes in flesh, shall earth rest; 7: 55 Enoch² sees Son of Man lifted up on cross; 7: 56 Enoch² sees saints crowned at right hand of Son of Man; 7: 59 Enoch² beholds Son of Man ascend to Father; 7: 65 Son of Man to dwell on earth in righteousness a thousand years; **Abr.** 3: 27 one like unto Son of Man say, Here am I, send me; **JS-M** 1: 26 (Matt. 24: 27) coming of Son of Man to be as light from east that covers earth; 1: 36 (Matt. 24: 30) all tribes of earth shall see Son of Man coming in clouds of heaven; 1: 37 (Matt. 24: 31) Son of Man to send angels before him; 1: 41–43 (Matt. 24: 37–39) coming of Son of Man to be like coming of flood in days of Noah¹; 1: 48 (Matt. 24: 44) Son of Man comes in hour when men think not.

JESUS CHRIST, TYPES OF (see also Type; TG Jesus Christ, Types of, in Anticipation; Jesus Christ, Types of, in Memory)

D&C 20: 40 (27: 2) bread and wine are emblems of Christ's flesh and blood; 76: 70 glory of sun is typical of glory of God; 128: 13 baptismal font instituted as similitude of grave; 138: 13 offering of sacrifice is in similitude of great sacrifice of Son.

Moses 5: 5–7 sacrifice of firstlings of flock is similitude of sacrifice of Only Begotten; 6: 63 all things have their likeness, are made to bear record of God.

JEW, JEWISH—descendant of Judah, or inhabitant of kingdom of Judah (see also Israel; Israel, Gathering of; Israel, Scattering of; Jacob, House of; Jerusalem; Judah; TG Israel, Judah, People of; Jew, Jewish; BD Jew)

D&C 3: 16 knowledge of Savior came through testimony of J.; 18: 26–27 (107: 33) Twelve called to declare gospel to Gentile and J.; 14: 10 (19: 27) J. receive gospel from Gentiles; 19: 27 Lamanites a remnant of J.; 20: 9 Book of Mormon for the J.; 45: 51–52 J. to see Christ's wounds; 45: 53 J. to weep because of iniquities, because they persecuted their king; 77: 15 two prophets to be raised up to J. nation; 84: 28 John the Baptist ordained to power to overthrow kingdom of J.; 90: 9 (107: 33–34; 133: 8) gospel to go to Gentiles first, then to J.; 98: 17 hearts of J. to be turned to prophets; 138: 25 Savior spent three years in ministry among J.

JS-M 1: 4 disciples ask Christ about destruction of J.; 1: 18, 21 great tribulation to come upon J.

JEWEL

D&C 60: 4 (101: 3) day when the Lord will come to make up his j.

JOHN THE BAPTIST (see also Zacharias; BD John the Baptist)

D&C 13: 1 (27: 8) ordains Joseph Smith and Oliver Cowdery to Aaronic Priesthood; 27: 7 birth of J. the Baptist foretold by Elias; 27: 7 filled with spirit of Elias; 27: 8 sent to restore Aaronic Priesthood; 35: 4 Sidney Rigdon sent forth even as J.; 84: 27 law of carnal commandments continued until J.; 84: 28 baptized in childhood and ordained when eight days old; 93: 6, 18 J's record to be revealed; 93: 6–17 J. saw and bore record of fulness of Christ's glory.

JS-H 1: 68–72 confers Aaronic Priesthood on Joseph Smith and Oliver Cowdery.

JOHN THE BELOVED—also known as the Revelator [c. first century A.D.] (see also BD John)

D&C sec. 7 translation from parchment written by J.; 7: 1 J., my beloved; 7: 1–3 given power over death; 7: 4 desired to bring souls to the Lord; 7: 7 a ministering angel; 7: 7 Peter, James, and J. receive keys of ministry; 20: 35 we know these things are true and according to revelations of J.; 27: 12 Joseph Smith and Oliver Cowdery ordained apostles by Peter, James, and J.; 61: 14 the Lord cursed waters by mouth of J.; 76: 15–17 (John 5: 29) Joseph Smith reads J's words about resurrection; sec. 77 explanation of Revelation of J.; 88: 3 (John 14: 16–17, 26) recorded promise of another Comforter; 88: 141 ordinance of washing of feet, according to pattern in John 13;

93: 6, 18 fulness of J's record to be revealed; 93: 6–17 saw and bore record of Christ's glory; 128: 6 (Rev. 20: 12) J. declares the dead will be judged from books; 128: 20 we hear voice of Peter, James, and J.; 130: 3 explanation of John 14: 23.

JOHNSON, AARON

D&C 124: 132 ordained to calling on high council.

JOHNSON, JOHN

D&C 102: 3 member of high council; 104: 24, 34 exchange of land of.

JOHNSON, LUKE

D&C sec. 68 revelation given at request of; 68: 7–8 commanded to go into world preaching; 75: 9 to accompany William McLellin to south; 102: 3 member of high council.

JOHNSON, LYMAN

D&C sec. 68 revelation given at request of; 68: 7–8 commanded to go into world preaching; 75: 14 to travel with Orson Pratt.

JOIN (see also Cleave; Unite)

JS-H 1: 18–20 Joseph Smith is told not to j. any church.

JOINT

D&C 6: 2 (11: 2; 12: 2; 14: 2; 33: 1) the Lord's word is sharper than sword, to dividing of j. and marrow; 84: 80 those who preach shall not be darkened in body, limb, or j.

JOSEPH—son of Jacob [c. 1700 B.C.] (see also Ephraim; Israel; Joseph, Seed of; Smith, Joseph, Jr.; BD Joseph; Joseph, Stick of)

D&C 27: 10 Christ will drink fruit of vine with J. and other prophets; 98: 32 law of forgiveness given to J.

JOSEPH, SEED OF—descendants of Joseph (see also Israel; Joseph)

D&C 90: 10 house of J. to be convinced of gospel; 113: 6 root of Jesse to be descendant of J.

JOURNEY (see also Depart; Flight; Sojourn; Travel)

D&C 33: 8 Nephi[1] of old j. from Jerusalem in wilderness; 52: 3 Joseph Smith and Sidney Rigdon j. to Missouri; 136: 1 word of the Lord concerning camp of Israel in j. in West.

Moses 6: 26 (7: 2) Enoch[2] j. among people; Abr. 2: 16 Abraham j. from Haran to Canaan; 2: 21 Abraham j. toward Egypt.

JOY, JOYOUS (see also Cheer; Delight; Glad; Happiness; Pleasure; Rejoice)

D&C 6: 31 have j. in fruit of labors; 11: 13 Spirit shall fill soul with j.; 18: 13 the Lord's great j. in soul that repents; 18: 15 great j. of those who bring one soul to God; 18: 16 great j. of those who bring many souls; 25: 13 (27: 15) lift up thy heart and rejoice; 42: 61 knowing peaceable things of kingdom brings j.; 45: 71 (66: 11; 101: 18; 133: 33) come to Zion, singing with songs of everlasting j.; 51: 19 wise steward will enter into j. of his Lord; 52: 43 the Lord to crown the faithful with j.; 59: 13 perfect fasting means full j.; 88: 52 laborer to be visited by lord, behold j. of his countenance; 93: 33 (138: 17) spirit and element inseparably connected receive fulness of j.; 101: 36 in this world j. is not full, but in the Lord j. is full; 136: 29 call on the Lord that souls may be joyful; 138: 15 spirits of the just filled with j.

Moses 5: 10–11 in this life I shall have j.; 7: 67 Enoch[2] receives fulness of j.

JUBAL—son of Lamech

Moses 5: 45 the father of all who handle harp and organ.

JUDAH—southern kingdom of Israelites (see also Israel; Jacob; Jacob, House of; Jerusalem; Jew; TG Israel, Judah, People of; BD Judah, Kingdom of)

D&C 109: 64 children of J. to return to lands; 133: 13 J. to flee to Jerusalem; 133: 35 tribe of J. to be sanctified after pain.

JUDGE [noun] (see also Bishop; Judge; [verb]; Judgment)

D&C 58: 17–18 (64: 40; 107: 72, 74) bishop appointed to be j. in Israel; 64: 37 the Lord made church like j. to judge the nations; 68: 33 he who observes not his prayers should be had in remembrance before j.; 72: 17 certificate from j. or bishop renders every man acceptable; 75: 21 elders to be j. of houses where they shake off dust; 76: 68 God and Christ the j. of all; 101: 81–89 parable of woman and unjust j. likened to children of Zion; 107: 76 descendant of Aaron[1] has right to sit as j. in Israel.

Moses 6: 57 Jesus Christ is righteous J.

JUDGE [verb] (see also Condemn; Judge [noun]; Judgment; Justice)

D&C 10: 37 men cannot always j. the righteous; 11: 12 Spirit leads to j. righteously; 19: 3 (76: 111; 137: 9) Christ to j. all men according to works; 20: 13

world to be j. by witnesses; 29: 12 Twelve from Jerusalem to j. whole house of Israel; 58: 20 let God rule him who j.; 64: 11 let God j. between me and thee; 64: 37 the Lord made church like unto a judge to j. the nations; 64: 38 inhabitants of Zion to j. all things pertaining to Zion; 76: 73 (88: 99; 138: 34; 1 Pet. 4: 6) Son preached gospel to those in prison, to be j. according to men in flesh; 128: 6-8 (Rev. 20: 12) the dead to be j. out of books.

Moses 1: 15, 18 Moses can j. between Satan and God; Abr. 1: 26 Pharaoh j. his people wisely.

JUDGMENT (see also Anger; Condemn; Day of the Lord; Destruction; Equal; Iniquity; Jesus Christ; Judge [verb]; Judgment-seat; Just; Justice; Last Days; Reward; Scourge; Thrash; Transgression; Visitation; Wicked; Wrath; TG God, Justice of; Judgment, Judgment, the Last)

D&C 1: 36 (43: 29; 133: 2) the Lord to come down in j.; 19: 3 works of Satan to be destroyed in day of j.; 19: 5 the Lord revokes not his j.; 29: 30 not all God's j. to be given to men; 38: 5 the wicked kept in chains of darkness until j.; 39: 16 prayers that the Lord will stay his hand in j.; 39: 18 j. to be stayed on condition of repentance; 41: 12 the Lord's words to be answered unless elders' souls in day of j.; 43: 25 nations to be called upon by voice of j.; 52: 11 the Lord to send forth j. unto victory; 59: 20 things of earth to be used in j., not to excess; 75: 21 in day of j. elders will be judges of those who reject them; 75: 22 more tolerable for heathen in day of j. than for those who reject elders; 82: 4 justice and j. are penalty against law; 82: 23 leave j. to the Lord; 84: 87 elders to teach the world of j.; 88: 35 that which seeks to become a law unto itself cannot be sanctified by law, mercy, justice, or j.; 88: 40 j. goes before face of the Lord; 88: 84 prepare saints for hour of j.; 88: 92 angels to proclaim j.; 88: 104 (133: 38) hour of God's j. is come; 89: 8 tobacco to be used with j.; 99: 5 the Lord comes quickly to j.; 107: 72-74, 78 bishops to sit in j. upon transgressers; 121: 24 the Lord has reserved swift j. for persecutors of saints; 136: 42 be diligent lest j. come upon you.

Moses 7: 66 j. to come upon the wicked; JS-H 1: 45 great j. to come upon earth.

JUDGMENT-SEAT (see also Bar; Judge; Chief; Judgment; Throne; Tribunal)

D&C 135: 5 (Ether 12: 38) all must stand before j-s. of Christ.

JUST (see also Justice; Perfect; Righteousness; Uprightness)

D&C 3: 4 those who follow own will instead of God's incur displeasure of j. God; 51: 19 j. and wise steward shall enter joy of the Lord; 58: 18 bishop to judge by testimony of j.; 76: 17, 50-70 those who will come forward in resurrection of the j.; 76: 69 (129: 3, 6) those in celestial glory are j. men made perfect; 82: 17 every man to have according to his j. wants and needs; 138: 7 (1 Pet. 3: 18) Christ suffered, the j. for the unjust; 138: 12 spirits of the j. gather in one place in spirit world.

Moses 7: 30 Lord is j.; 8: 27 Noah¹ a j. man.

JUSTICE (see also Injustice; Judge [verb]; Judgment; Just; Mercy; Punishment; Sacrifice; Vengeance; TG God, Justice of)

D&C 10: 28 he who lies to deceive is not exempt from j. of God; 82: 4 j. and judgment are penalty against law; 84: 102 God is full of j.; 88: 35 that which breaks law cannot be sanctified by j.; 88: 40 j. claims its own; 107: 84 none shall be exempted from j. and laws; 109: 77 the Lord enthroned with j.; 134: 3 seek for those who will administer law with j.; 134: 7 governments have no right in j. to deprive citizens of free exercise of conscience.

JUSTIFICATION, JUSTIFY (see also Jesus Christ, Atonement through; Sanctification; TG Justification)

D&C 20: 30 j. through grace of the Lord and Savior; 64: 12-13 bring unrepentant sinner before church, that ye may be j. in eyes of law; 88: 39 those who abide not in conditions of law are not j.; 98: 34-38 j. in going to battle if peace is offered three times.

Moses 6: 60 by the Spirit men are j.

KEEP, KEPT (see also Keeper; Maintain; Obedience; Observe; Preserve; Reserve; Retain; Withhold)

D&C 5: 28 (6: 9, 37; 8: 5; 10: 56; 11: 6, 9, 18, 20; 12: 6; 14: 6-7; 18: 43, 46; 19: 13; 20: 77; 25: 15; 29: 12; 35: 24; 42: 1, 29, 78; 43: 35; 46: 9; 56: 2; 63: 22; 71: 11; 93: 20, 44, 47; 95: 11-12; 100: 14, 17; 103: 8, 29; 104: 4; 110: 8; 124: 85, 87; 125: 2; 136: 2) k. the commandments; 21: 1 (47: 1, 3; 85: 1; 128: 7-9) k. church history; 33: 14 k. church articles and covenants; 41: 4 (44: 5; 58: 19; 64: 15;

119: 6) k. the Lord's laws; 42: 34 (58: 24; 72: 10) k. the Lord's storehouse; 59: 9 k. thyself unspotted; 66: 11 (82: 4; 89: 18; 93: 52) k. the Lord's sayings; 68: 29 k. the Sabbath day holy; 90: 18 k. slothfulness and uncleanness far from you; 104: 61, 67 (105: 8) k. the treasury; 117: 16 k. temple holy; 136: 20 k. pledges with each other; 136: 21 k. yourselves from evil.

Moses 3: 15 (Abr. 5: 11) the Lord puts man in garden to dress and k. it; 4: 31 the Lord places cherubim and flaming sword to k. way of tree of life; **Abr.** 3: 26 they who k. their first estate shall be added upon; 3: 28 the second k. not his first estate.

KEEPER

Moses 5: 17 Abel a k. of sheep; 5: 34 am I my brother's k.

KEY (see also Priesthood, Melchizedek; TG Priesthood, Keys of)

D&C 6: 28 k. of gift to translate given; 7: 7 (27: 12–13; 128: 20) k. of ministry committed to Peter, James, and John; 13: 1 (84: 26) Aaronic Priesthood holds k. of ministering of angels and gospel of baptism; 27: 5 k. of record of stick of Ephraim committed to Moroni[1]; 27: 6 k. of restoration committed to Elias; 27: 9 k. of turning hearts of fathers and children committed to Elijah; 27: 12–13 (97: 14) Joseph Smith and Oliver Cowdery ordained to bear k. of ministry; 28: 7 (35: 18; 64: 5; 115: 19) Joseph Smith given k. of mysteries of sealed revelations; 35: 25 Israel to be led by k.; 42: 69 (65: 2) k. of church given; 64: 5 (90: 3; 112: 15) k. not to be taken from Joseph Smith; 65: 2 k. committed to man on earth; 68: 17 firstborn holds right to k. of Aaronic Priesthood; 78: 16 the Lord gave Michael k. of salvation; 81: 2 Joseph Smith holds k. of Presidency; 81: 2 k. belong always to Presidency; 84: 19 (107: 18–19; 128: 14) Melchizedek Priesthood holds k. of mysteries of knowledge of God; 90: 2 you are blessed who bear k. of kingdom; 107: 15–17 bishopric holds k. of Aaronic Priesthood; 107: 16, 70, 76 descendant of Aaron[1] has legal right to k. of Aaronic Priesthood; 107: 18–19 authority of Melchizedek Priesthood is to hold k. of spiritual blessings of church; 107: 20 authority of Aaronic Priesthood is to hold k. of ministering of angels; 110: 11 k. of gathering of Israel committed by Moses; 110: 16 k. of this dispensation committed to Joseph Smith and Oliver Cowdery; 112: 16 (124: 128) k. held by the Twelve; 112:

32 k. sent down from heaven; 113: 6 priesthood and k. of kingdom belong rightly to root of Jesse; 124: 34 k. of holy Priesthood ordained in temple for honor and glory; 124: 91–92 k. of patriarchal blessings given to Hyrum Smith; 124: 97 k. by which to receive blessings; 124: 143 offices and k. for perfecting of saints; 128: 11 he who has k. obtains knowledge; 128: 14 k. of kingdom consist in k. of knowledge; 128: 21 angels declare their k.; 129: 9 three grand k. whereby you may know whether any administration is of God; 132: 7 only one holds k. at a time; 132: 64 man holding k. of power should teach wife law of priesthood.

JS-H 1: 69 Aaronic Priesthood holds k. of ministering of angels and gospel of repentance and baptism; 1: 72 Peter, James, and John hold k. of Melchizedek Priesthood.

KILL (see also Blood, Shedding of; Capital Punishment; Death, Physical; Martyrdom; Murder; Slaughter; Slay; Smite)

D&C 19: 25 commandment not to seek one's neighbor's life; 42: 18, 79 he who k. shall not have forgiveness; 42: 18 (59: 6; 132: 36) thou shalt not k.; 42: 19 he who k. shall die; 42: 79 members who k. shall be dealt with according to laws of land; 45: 33 in last days men will k. one another; 136: 36 brethren of nation k. the prophets.

Moses 5: 40 the Lord sets mark on Cain lest any k. him; **Abr.** 1: 11 virgins are k. upon altar; 2: 23 Egyptians will k. Abraham because of his wife.

KIMBALL, HEBER C.

D&C 124: 129 member of the Twelve.

KIMBALL, SPENCER W.

D&C OD–2 receives revelation extending priesthood to all worthy male members; OD–2 recognized as prophet, seer, and revelator.

KINDLE (see Anger)

KINDNESS (see also Charity; Compassion; Gentle; Love)

D&C 4: 6 remember brotherly k.; 107: 30 decisions to be made in brotherly k.; 121: 41–42 influence to be maintained by k.; 133: 52 the redeemed shall mention loving k. of their Lord.

KINDRED (see also Nation)

D&C Abr. 1: 58 the Lord spoke unto Abraham concerning k. of earth.

KING (see also Jesus Christ; Kingdom; Prince; Reign; Rule; TG Jesus Christ, King; Kings, Earthly)

D&C 1: 23 gospel proclaimed before k. and rulers; 38: 21 no k. in land, for the Lord will be k.; 45: 53 Jews lament because they persecuted their k.; 45: 59 the Lord will be k. and lawgiver of righteous; 76: 56 those in celestial glory are priests and k.; 109: 55 remember the k. and great ones of earth; 124: 3, 16 proclamation to be made to k. of world; 124: 5 church to know the Lord's will concerning k. and authorities; 124: 11 Awake, O k. of earth.

Moses 7: 53 the Lord is K. of Zion;
Abr. 1: 21 k. of Egypt a descendant of Ham; **A of F** 12 we believe in being subject to k.

KINGDOM (see also Celestial Glory; Church of the Devil; Dominion; Government, Civil; King; Kingdom of God; Nation; Telestial Glory; Terrestrial Glory)

D&C 10: 56 the Lord will disturb those who build up k. of devil; 84: 82 k. of world are not arrayed like lilies of field; 84: 118 the Lord will rend k. of the wicked; 88: 22–24 laws and glories of three k.; 88: 34–38 all k. have a law given; 88: 37 no space in which there is no k.; 88: 42–45 sun and planets are k.; 88: 51–61 k. are likened to man having a field; 88: 79 (93: 53) obtain knowledge of countries and k.; 103: 7 k. of world to be subdued; 105: 32 k. of world to acknowledge k. of Zion is k. of God; 130: 10 things pertaining to higher order of k. made known by Urim and Thummim; 132: 19 those married by new and everlasting covenant inherit k., principalities.

Moses 8: 3 Methuselah prophesies that through his loins will spring all k. of earth; **Abr.** 1: 26 Pharaoh established his k.; 3: 26 those who do not keep first estate will not have glory in same k. as those who do; **JS-M** 1: 29 k. shall rise up against k.

KINGDOM OF GOD (see also Celestial Glory; Church of God; Heaven; Millennium; TG Kingdom of God, in Heaven; Kingdom of God, on Earth; BD Kingdom of Heaven, or Kingdom of God)

D&C 6: 3 (11: 3; 12: 3; 14: 3) he who thrusts in sickle will treasure up salvation in k. of God; 6: 13 he who is faithful to end will be saved in k. of God; 6: 37 saints shall inherit k. of heaven; 7: 4 Peter desired to come speedily unto the Lord in his k.; 10: 55 those who belong to church shall inherit k. of heaven; 11: 23

(106: 3) seek diligently the k. and all things shall be added; 15: 6 (18: 16) those who bring souls to the Lord shall rest with them in Father's k.; 18: 25 those who know not the name by which they are called cannot have place in Father's k.; 25: 1 those who receive gospel are sons and daughters in the Lord's k.; 29: 5 (50: 35) Father's good will to give saints the k.; 33: 10 (42: 7) k. of heaven is at hand; 35: 27 (38: 9, 15; 62: 9; 78: 18; 82: 24) k. is yours; 36: 2 Holy Ghost teaches peaceable things of k.; 41: 6 things belonging to children of k. should not be given to the unworthy; 42: 69 (64: 4–5) unto elders the k., or keys of church, have been given; 45: 1 k. has been given to people of church; 46: 5–6 those earnestly seeking k. should not be cast out of meetings; 56: 18 poor who are pure in heart shall see k. of God coming in power; 58: 2 he who is faithful receives greater reward in k. of heaven; 65: 2 keys of k. of God are committed unto man; 65: 5–6 pray that the Lord's k. may go forth; 65: 6 k. of God to go forth that k. of heaven may come; 72: 1 k. and power have been given to high priests; 76: 107 Christ shall deliver up k. to Father; 76: 114 marvelous are mysteries of k.; 84: 33–38 those who magnify callings receive Father's k.; 84: 74 unbelievers shall not enter Father's k.; 88: 70, 74 first laborers in this last k.; 90: 3 keys of this k. shall never be taken; 97: 14 saints to be perfected in all things pertaining to k. of God; 99: 3 he who receives elders as little child receives the Lord's k.; 105: 32 k. of world shall acknowledge that k. of Zion is k. of God; 136: 31 he who will not bear chastisement is not worthy of the Lord's k.; 138: 44 (Dan. 2: 31–45) Daniel foretold establishment of k. of God in latter days; 138: 51 the Lord gives the just power to enter Father's k.

Moses 6: 57 no unclean thing can enter k. of God; **A of F** 9 we believe all that God has revealed pertaining to k. of God.

KIRTLAND, OHIO (see also Kirtland Temple; D&C map, p. 296)

D&C secs. 41–50, 52–56, 63–64, 70, 72, 84–98, 101–104, 106–110, 112, 134, 137 revelations received at; 82: 13 (94: 1) consecrated for a stake; sec. 96 revelation concerning stake at; 98: 19 offenders in the church at; 104: 40 mercantile establishment in; 104: 48 United Order at; 117: 5 properties of K. to be turned out for debt; 117: 16 servants in K. admonished; 124: 83 the Lord will build up K.

KIRTLAND TEMPLE

D&C 105: 33 endowment in; sec. 109 prayer at dedication of; sec. 110 visions received in; sec. 137 vision of celestial kingdom given to Joseph Smith in.

KNEE (see also Kneel)

D&C 76: 110 in telestial kingdom all shall bow the k.; 81: 5 (Heb. 12: 12) strengthen the feeble k.; 88: 104 every k. shall bow to the Lord; 88: 131 offer prayer upon k.; 138: 23 saints' spirits bow k. and acknowledge Son.

KNEEL (see also Knee)

D&C 20: 76 elder or priest shall k. to offer sacrament prayer.

KNIGHT, JOSEPH, SR.

D&C secs. 12, 23 revelations to; 23: 6–7 is told to pray.

KNIGHT, NEWEL

D&C 52: 32 to be ordained and to journey to Missouri; sec. 54 revelation to; 56: 6–7 original commandment to, revoked because of people's stiffneckedness; sec. 72 revelation making known the calling of; 124: 32 member of high council.

KNIGHT, VINSON

D&C 124: 74 to put stock in Nauvoo House; 124: 141 to preside over a bishopric.

KNOCK (see also Ask)

D&C 4: 7 (6: 5; 11: 5; 12: 5; 14: 5; 49: 26; 66: 9; 75: 27; 88: 63) k. and it shall be opened.

KNOW, KNEW (see also Comprehend; God, Omniscience of; Knowledge; Learn; Perceive; Revelation; Testimony; Understand)

D&C 1: 17 the Lord k. calamity to come; 5: 25 witness shall say, I k. of a surety these things are true; 6: 11 if thou wilt inquire, thou shalt k. great and marvelous things; 6: 16 only God k. thoughts; 6: 24 (15: 3) the Lord will tell what no man k.; 11: 14 by faith ye shall k.; 11: 16 Hyrum Smith to wait until he k. doctrine of surety; 18: 25 men who k. not name by which they are called will have no place in kingdom of Father; 19: 8 Martin Harris to k. even as apostles; 19: 22 world must not k. these things, lest they perish; 20: 17 we k. there is a God in heaven; 38: 2 the Lord k. all things, for all things are present before his eyes; 38: 8 (67: 10) day comes that ye shall see me and k. that I am; 39: 21 (49. 7) no man k.

day or hour of the Lord's coming; 42: 61 he who asks will receive revelation to k. mysteries of kingdom; 45: 22 ye k. heavens and earth shall pass away; 45: 54 they who k. no law shall have part in first resurrection; 46: 13 spiritual gift to k. that Jesus Christ is Son of God; 46: 15–16 Holy Ghost gives some to k. differences of administration, diversities of operations; 50: 31 (52: 19) way to k. whether spirit is of God; 50: 45 (93: 1) saints shall hear my voice and k. that I am; 63: 6 all flesh shall k. that I am God; 67: 1 the Lord k. elders' hearts; 76: 116–117 God grants privilege of seeing and k. for themselves to those who love him; 84: 50–53 way to k. the righteous from the wicked; 84: 83 Father k. that elders have need of all these things; 84: 98 after destruction, all who remain shall k. the Lord; 93: 28 he who keeps commandments receives truth and light until he k. all; 101: 16 be still and k. that I am God; 101: 32–33 the Lord to reveal hidden things which no man k.; 112: 26 vengeance to come upon those who have professed to k. the Lord's name and have not k. him; 121: 24 mine eyes see and k. all men's works; 127: 2 God k. all things; 131: 5 more sure word of prophecy means a man k. he is sealed unto eternal life; 132: 22 few find way to exaltation because they do not k. the Lord; 132: 24 eternal lives is to k. the only wise and true God.

Moses 1: 10 Moses k. that man is nothing; 4: 11, 28 man becomes as gods to k. good and evil; 6: 56 given unto men to k. good from evil; JS-M 1: 47 (Matt. 24: 34) no man k. hour or day of the Lord's coming; 1: 47 (Matt. 24: 43) if man of house had k. in what watch thief would come, he would have watched.

KNOWLEDGE (see also Agency; Faith; God, Omniscience of; Holy Ghost; Ignorance; Intelligence; Know; Learn; Mystery; Scriptures; Study; Testimony; Truth; Understand; Wisdom; TG Knowledge; BD Knowledge)

D&C 1: 28 the humble to receive k.; 3: 16 k. of Savior has come through testimony of Jews; 3: 19–20 plates preserved that Lamanites might come to k. of fathers and the Lord's promises; 4: 6 remember faith, virtue, k.; 8: 1 Oliver Cowdery to receive k. of whatever he asks in faith; 8: 9, 11 ask and receive k. through gift of Aaron[1]; 20: 13 those who have k. will be judged; 29: 49 whoso has k. is commanded to repent; 42: 61 if thou ask, thou shalt receive k. upon k., to know mysteries and peaceable things; 46: 18 spiritual gift of word of k.; 50: 40

elders must grow in grace and k. of truth;
67: 5 elders have sought k. that they
might express beyond this language; 84:
19 Melchizedek Priesthood holds key of
k. of God; 84: 98 all who remain will be
filled with k. of the Lord; 88: 79 (93: 53)
obtain k. of countries and kingdoms; 89:
19 those who obey Word of Wisdom shall
find great treasures of k.; 93: 24 truth is
k. of things as they are, were, and are to
come; 93: 53 elders should obtain k. of
history, laws of God and men; 101: 25 the
Lord's k. and glory will dwell upon all the
earth; 107: 31 if these qualities abound,
quorums will not be unfruitful in k. of
the Lord; 107: 71 high priest has k. of
temporal things; 109: 67 Israel to come
to k. of truth; 121: 26 hitherto un-
revealed k. to be given to saints; 121: 33
Almighty pours down k. from heaven
upon saints; 121: 42 pure k. shall greatly
enlarge soul; 128: 14 keys of kingdom
consist in key of k.; 128: 19 k. of God
shall descend as dews of Carmel; 130: 19
if person gains more k. in this life, he will
have advantage in world to come.

Moses 3: 9, 17 (4: 9, 28; Abr. 5: 13)
tree of k. of good and evil; Abr. 1: 2
Abraham to possess great k.

KOKAUBEAM (see Star)

KOKOB (see Star)

KOLOB

Abr. 3: 2–18 Abraham's revelation
concerning K. and the stars; 3: 4, 9 (5:
13) the Lord's reckoning according to time of K.; 3: 9 K. is set nigh unto
God's throne, to govern other planets.

KORASH (see Gods; Idolatry)

Abr. 1: 13, 17 heathen god of K.

LABOR (see also Do; Idleness; Laborer;
Travail; Wages; Work [verb])

D&C 6: 31 have joy in fruit of l.;
10: 4 do not l. more than you have
strength; 38: 40 (52: 39) every man
should go to with l. of hands to prepare
and accomplish commandments; 39: 13
(43: 28; 50: 38; 71: 4) called to l. in the
Lord's vineyard; 52: 39 elders to l. with
own hands; 56: 17 wo unto poor who will
not l. with own hands; 59: 2 (124: 86)
those who die shall rest from l.; 64:
23 l. while it is called today; 68: 30 inhabitants of Zion appointed to l. in faithfulness; 75: 3 be not idle, but l. with your
might; 75: 28 let every man l. in church;
84: 109 let every man l. in own calling;

88: 51–52 the Lord sends servants into
field to l.; 115: 10 the Lord's people to
l. diligently to build his house; 124:
121 quorum of Nauvoo House to have
just recompense for l.; 126: 2 the Lord
has seen Brigham Young's l. in his
name; 138: 51–52, 56–57 faithful elders
continue l. in Father's kingdom in spirit
world.

Moses 5: 1 Eve l. with Adam.

LABORER (see also Labor)

D&C 23: 7 give language to exhortation, that you may receive reward
of l.; 31: 5 (84: 79; 106: 3) l. is worthy of
his hire; 33: 3 last time the Lord shall
call l. into vineyard; 39: 17 call faithful l.
into vineyard; 42: 42 idle shall not eat
bread of l.; 88: 70 call solemn assembly
of first l. in last kingdom.

LADEN (see also Burden)

D&C 31: 5 (33: 9; 75: 5) the faithful
will be l. with sheaves.

LAKE (see also Hell; Torment)

D&C 63: 17 (76: 36–37) l. of fire and
brimstone is second death; 76: 36 sons of
perdition cast into l. of fire and brimstone.

LAMANITE—descendant of Laman, later any
person who rejects the gospel

D&C 3: 18, 20 L. come to knowledge
of fathers through Book of Mormon; 10:
48 gospel to be preached to L. and those
who became L. because of dissensions;
19. 27 L. are remnant of Jews; 28: 8 (30:
6) Oliver Cowdery called to preach to L.;
32: 2 first missionaries to L.; 49: 24 L. to
blossom as rose before the Lord's coming;
54: 8 saints commanded to flee to borders
of L.; sec. 57 revelation concerning L.

LAMB (see also Animal; Jesus Christ—
Lamb of God; Sheep)

D&C 122: 6 enemies prowl like
wolves for blood of l.; 135: 4 Joseph
Smith going like l. to slaughter.

LAME (see also Heal)

D&C 35: 9 they who ask in the
Lord's name in faith shall cause the l. to
walk; 42: 51 the l. who hath faith to leap
shall leap; 58: 11 the l. to come unto
marriage of Lamb.

LAMECH[1]—descendant of Cain

Moses 5: 42–43 son of Methusael;
5: 44, 47 takes two wives; 5: 45–46 father
of Jabal, Jubal, and Tubal Cain; 5: 47–51
slays Irad; 5: 49 enters covenant with
Satan, becomes Master Mahan; 5: 52 the

Lord curses *L.* and his house; 5: 54 is despised and cast out.

LAMECH²—*father of Noah¹*

Moses 8: 5–6 son of Methuselah; 8: 8–10 father of Noah¹; 8: 11 lives seven hundred and seventy-seven years and dies.

LAMENT, LAMENTATION (*see also* Cry; Grieve; Mourn; Wailing; Weep)

D&C 45: 53 Jews shall *l.* because they persecuted their king; 56: 16 riches that canker soul are *l.* of rich men; 112: 24 day of *l.* comes speedily upon inhabitants of earth.

LAMP (*see also* Light; BD Lamp)

D&C 33: 17 have *l.* trimmed and burning, ready for Bridegroom.

LAND (*see also* Country; Earth; Ground; Inherit; Law, Civil; Nation; Promised Land)

D&C 10: 49–51 Nephite prophets left blessing upon *l.* regarding gospel and freedom; 19: 34 Martin Harris commanded to impart part of his *l.*; 42: 34–35 residue in storehouse used to purchase *l.*; 42: 79, 84–86 (51: 6; 58: 21; 98: 4–6) laws of *l.*; 45: 63 ye shall hear of wars in your own *l.*; 45: 66 New Jerusalem to be *l.* of peace; 48: 2–3 *l.* to be shared with new members migrating from east; 48: 4 (57: 5; 58: 51–52) save money to purchase *l.* for inheritance; 48: 5–6 men to be appointed to purchase *l.* for city; 52: 14 Satan is abroad in *l.*; 58: 19 God's law to be kept on this *l.*; 63: 27 saints to purchase *l.*, to have advantage of world; 77: 15 Jews to build city of Jerusalem in *l.* of their fathers; 81: 3 gospel to be proclaimed in *l.* of the living; 101: 43–62 parable of nobleman who had choice spot of *l.*; 101: 70–71, 74 *l.* round about *l.* of Zion to be purchased for gathering of saints; 101: 80 God has redeemed the *l.* by shedding of blood; 105: 30 after *l.* are purchased, armies of Israel to possess them; 109: 64 Judah to begin to return to *l.* given to Abraham; 110: 11 Moses commits keys of leading ten tribes from *l.* of north; 115: 7 city of Far West to be holy and consecrated *l.* unto the Lord; 133: 23 islands to become one *l.*; 133: 24 *l.* of Jerusalem and of Zion to be turned back.

Moses 1: 29 Moses beholds many *l.*, each called earth; 2: 10 (Abr. 4: 10) God calls dry *l.* Earth; 6: 41 Enoch² came from *l.* of Cainan; 7: 13 of fathers, *l.* of righteousness; 7: 14 *l.* comes up from depth of sea.

LANGUAGE (*see also* Arabic; Chaldea; Chaldaic; Characters; Egyptian; Interpretation; Speak; Speech; Tongue; Translation; Word; Write; Writing; TG Language)

D&C 1: 24 commandments given to servants after manner of their *l.*; 29: 33 the Lord speaks in *l.* that man may naturally understand; 52: 16 he whose *l.* is meek and edifies is of God; 67: 5 saints seek knowledge beyond what imperfections of *l.* can express; 90: 11 every man shall hear gospel in own *l.*; 90: 15 saints to become acquainted with *l.*; OD–1 elders using *l.* encouraging polygamy have been reproved.

Moses 6: 5–6 book of remembrance kept in *l.* of Adam; 7: 13 God gives Enoch² great power of *l.*

LAST (*see also* End; First; Last Days)

D&C 29: 41 Adam's spiritual death was first death, same as *l.* death, which is spiritual; 76: 22 this is testimony, *l.* of all, which we give of him; 76: 85 telestial heirs will not be redeemed from devil until *l.* resurrection.

LAST DAYS (*see also* Day of the Lord; Destruction; End; Israel, Gathering of; Jesus Christ, Second Coming of; Judgment; Lift; Millennium; Restoration; TG Last Days)

D&C 1: 4 voice of warning by disciples whom the Lord has chosen in *l.* days; 4: 2 serve God with all heart, that ye may stand blameless at *l.* day; 18: 24 men will be called by name given of Father at *l.* day; 19: 3 Satan and his works to be destroyed at end of world and *l.* great day of judgment; 20: 1 (33: 4) rise of Church of Christ in these *l.* days; 27: 6 (109: 23) restoration of all things spoken by prophets concerning *l.* days; 39: 11 fulness of gospel sent forth in these *l.* days; 52: 1 elders called and chosen in these *l.* days; 61: 14 in *l.* days God cursed waters; 61: 17 in *l.* days God has blessed land for saints' use; 63: 58 the Lord is not to be mocked in *l.* days; 64: 30 agents set to provide for saints in *l.* days; 64: 34 the obedient shall eat good of land of Zion in *l.* days; 64: 37 in *l.* days church is made like judge; 66: 2 (128: 17) glories to be revealed in *l.* days; 77: 15 two prophets to be raised up to Jewish nation in *l.* days; 84: 2 church established in *l.* days for restoration of the Lord's people; 84: 117 desolation of abomination in *l.* days; 86: 4 in *l.* days the Lord is beginning to bring forth the word; 88: 102 many who remain until great and *l.* day shall be filthy still; 89: 2 Word of Wisdom shows order of God in temporal salvation in *l.* days; 89: 4 evils and designs in hearts of conspiring men in *l.* days; 109: 45 the Lord has spoken terrible things concerning the wicked in *l.* days; 112: 30 power of priesthood given for *l.* days and *l.* time; 113: 6, 8 priesthood and keys of kingdom for gathering of people in *l.* days; 115: 4 name of church in *l.* days; 132: 7 Joseph Smith appointed to hold power in *l.* days; 136: 22 God's arm is stretched out in *l.* days to save Israel.

Moses 7: 60, 65 the Lord will come in *l.* days; **JS-M** 1: 44 in *l.* days one shall be taken and the other left.

LATTER DAY (see Last Days)

LAUGH, LAUGHTER (see also Lightmindedness; Scorner; TG Laughter, Laugh)

D&C 45: 49 they who have *l.* shall see their folly; 59: 15 much *l.* is sin; 88: 69 cast away excess of *l.*; 88: 121 cease from all *l.*

Moses 7: 26 Satan looked up and *l.*

LAW (see also Agency; Commandments of God; Crime; Decree; Law, Civil; Law of Moses; Lawful; Lawgiver; Obedience; Ordinance; Punishment; Statute; Transgression; TG Law)

D&C 20: 20 by transgression of *l.*, man became sensual, devilish, fallen; 24: 17 whosoever goes to *l.* against the shall be cursed by *l.*; 29: 34 all *l.* are spiritual, the Lord has never given a *l.* which was temporal; 38: 22 saints to have no *l.* but the Lord's when he comes; 41: 3 (42: 59) *l.* teaches how to govern church; 41: 3 by prayer of faith men receive *l.*; 41: 4 (58: 19) see that the Lord's *l.* is kept; 41: 5 he who receives the Lord's *l.* and does it is his disciple; sec. 42 revelation on *l.* of the church; 42: 2 hear and obey the *l.*; 42: 28 *l.* given in scriptures; 42: 59 scriptures given for *l.* to govern church; 42: 66 observe the *l.*; 42: 81 deal with adulterers according to *l.* of God; 42: 87 those who do iniquity should be delivered to *l.* of God; 42: 91 offenders who confess not should be delivered to *l.* of God; 43: 2–7 church to receive commandments as *l.* only through one appointed to receive revelation; 43: 8–9 when assembled, saints to instruct each other how to act upon points of *l.*; 44: 6 all things to be done according to the Lord's *l.*; 45: 54 they who knew no *l.* will have part in first resurrection; 51: 2, 15 the Lord's people to be organized according to his *l.*; 58: 18 counselors to assist bishop according to *l.*

of church; 58: 21 he who keeps God's *l.* has no need to break *l.* of land; 58: 23 *l.* received from God are *l.* of church; 58: 36 (70: 10) *l.* of consecration binding on all; 59: 22 this according to the *l.* and the prophets; 64: 13 hold court to be justified in eyes of *l.*; 76: 72 terrestrial glory inherited by those who died without *l.*; 82: 4 justice and judgment are penalty affixed to *l.*; 82: 21 he who breaks covenant should be dealt with according to *l.* of church; 85: 11 names of apostates not in book of *l.*; 88: 13 light in all things is *l.* by which all things are governed; 88: 21–24 kingdom of glory man inherits will be determined by level of *l.* he abides; 88: 21 those not sanctified through *l.* of Christ inherit another kingdom; 88: 34 that which is governed by *l.* is preserved by *l.*; 88: 35 that which seeks to become a *l.* unto itself cannot be sanctified; 88: 36, 38 unto every kingdom is given a *l.*; 88: 42 the Lord has given a *l.* unto all things; 88: 84 (109: 46; 133: 72) bind up the *l.* and seal up the testimony; 93: 53 obtain a knowledge of *l.* of God and man; 98: 8 the *l.* makes you free; 98: 25–32 *l.* concerning vengeance upon enemies; 98: 33 *l.* concerning battle; 105: 4 union required by *l.* of celestial kingdom; 105: 5 Zion can be built only upon principle of *l.* of celestial kingdom; 105: 29 saints to possess lands according to *l.* of consecration; 105: 32 let us become subject unto *l.* of Zion; 105: 34 commandments concerning Zion and her *l.* should be executed; 107: 72 bishop to judge according to *l.*; 107: 84 none exempted from *l.* of God; 119: 1 tithing is standing *l.* forever; 128: 9 that which is done in authority in name of the Lord becomes *l.* on earth and in heaven; 130: 20–21 (132: 5, 21, 32) all blessings predicated upon obedience to *l.*; 132: 12 the Lord's word is his *l.*; 132: 21 except ye abide my *l.*, ye cannot attain celestial glory; 132: 32 those who enter into the Lord's *l.* shall be saved.

Moses 6: 56 the Lord has given another *l.* and commandment; **A of F** 3 mankind may be saved by obedience to *l.* and ordinances of gospel.

LAW, CIVIL (see also Crime; Government, Civil)

D&C 24: 17 whosoever goes to *l.* against thee shall be cursed by *l.*; 42: 79 deliver members who kill to *l.* of land; 42: 84–85 deliver robbers to *l.* of land; 42: 86 deliver liars to *l.* of land; 44: 4 church to be organized according to *l.* of man; 51: 5–6 all things under consecration to be made sure according to *l.* of land; 58: 21 he who keeps God's l. has no need to break l. of land; 93: 53 obtain knowledge of l. of God and man; 98: 4-7 people should observe l. of land; 98: 5-10 l. of land supporting principle of freedom is justifiable before God; 98: 6 saints to befriend constitutional l. of land; 101: 77 the Lord has suffered l. and constitution of nation to be established; sec. 134 statement of belief concerning governments and l. in general; OD-1 Congress has passed l. forbidding plural marriage; OD-1 saints to refrain from entering marriages forbidden by l. of land.

A of F 12 we believe in obeying, honoring, and sustaining l.

LAW OF MOSES (see also Carnal; Commandments of God; Jesus Christ, Types of; Law; Offering; Sacrifice)

D&C 22: 2 men cannot enter strait gate by l. of Moses; 74: 3 unbelieving husband wanted children circumcised and subject to l. of Moses; 84: 27 preparatory gospel is l. of carnal commandments.

LAW, WILLIAM

D&C 124: 82 to put stock in Nauvoo House; 124: 87-88, 107 to proclaim gospel; 124: 89-90 to support translation of scriptures 124: 91, 126 to be ordained counselor to Joseph Smith; 124: 97 to receive keys; 124: 98-101 signs shall follow.

LAWFUL (see also Right [adj.])

D&C 49: 16 l. to have one wife; 76: 115 not l. to utter mysteries shown in vision; 86: 8-9 those who receive priesthood through lineage of fathers are l. heirs.

LAWGIVER

D&C 38: 22 (45: 59) the Lord is l.; 64: 13 hold courts to avoid offending l.; 138: 41 Moses, the great l. of Israel.

LEAD, LED (see also Course; Direction; Guide; Inspire; Invite)

D&C 10: 22 Satan l. souls to destruction; 11: 12 trust in that Spirit which l. to do good; 21: 44, 49 apostles are to take l. of all meetings; 20: 45 elders to conduct meetings as l. by Holy Ghost; 38: 33 the Lord will l. his servants whithersoever he will; 78: 18 be of good cheer, for I will l. you along; 103: 16 the Lord will raise up a man to l. as Moses l. Israel; 105: 7 (124: 45) first elders appointed to l. people; 110: 11 Moses committed keys of the l. of ten tribes from north; 112: 10 the Lord shall l. thee

by hand; 136: 22 I am he who l. children of Israel out of Egypt.

Moses 4: 4 devil l. men captive at his will; **Abr.** 1: 18 I will l. thee by my hand.

LEAP (see Lame)

LEARN (see also Comprehend; Know; Learning; Study; Teach; Understand)

D&C 19: 23 (58: 1) l. of me, and you shall have peace in me; 88: 123 l. to impart one to another as the gospel requires; 90: 15 study, l., and become acquainted with good books, languages; 105: 6 the Lord's people must be chastened until they l. obedience; 107: 99 let every man l. his duty; 121: 35, 39 men's hearts are set so much on things of world that they do not l. this one lesson; 121: 39 we have l. by sad experience; 136: 32 let him who is ignorant l. wisdom.

LEARNING (see also Intelligence; Knowledge; Learn; Scriptures; Truth; Wisdom)

D&C 88: 118 (109: 7) seek l. by study and faith; 88: 119 establish house of l.

LEAST (see also Less)

D&C 1: 31 the Lord cannot look upon sin with l. degree of allowance; 42: 38 as ye do it unto the l., ye do it unto the Lord; 50: 26 he who is ordained of God is appointed to be greatest, notwithstanding he is l.; 67: 6 seek ye out of Book of Commandments, even the l. among them; 84: 98 all who remain shall know the Lord, from l. unto greatest; 88: 47 any man who has seen l. of these kingdoms has seen God.

LEAVE, LEFT (see also Depart; Left [adj.])

D&C 19: 36 l. thy house and home; 42: 75 members who have l. their companions for adultery shall be cast out; 45: 20 (Matt. 24: 2) not one stone of temple shall be l. upon another; 82: 23 l. judgment with the Lord; 121: 38 man who exercises unrighteous dominion will be l. unto himself; 123: 6 (124: 7) whole nation to be l. without excuse.

Moses 3: 24 (Abr. 5: 18) man shall l. father and mother.

LEAVES (see Fig)

LED (see Lead, Led)

LEE, ANN

D&C 49: Intro. Shaker belief concerning.

LEFT [adj.] (*see also* Leave, Left; Right Hand)

D&C 19: 5 weeping, wailing, gnashing of teeth of those on the Lord's *l.* hand; 29: 27 the Lord will be ashamed to own before the Father the wicked gathered on his *l.* hand.

LEHI—*Hebrew prophet who led his followers to promised land in western hemisphere* [c. 600 B.C.] (*see also* Lehi, Book of)

D&C 17: 1 directors were given to *L.* in wilderness.

LEHI, BOOK OF (*see* Book of Lehi)

D&C 3: Intro. lost 116 pages of manuscript from; 10: Intro. wicked men make alterations in.

LESS, LESSER (*see also* Least; Priesthood, Aaronic)

D&C 10: 68 whoso declares more or *l.* than this is not of the Lord; 68: 19 high priest has authority to officiate in all *l.* offices; 76: 81 glory of telestial is that of the *l.*; 88: 37 no space in which there is not either a greater or a *l.* kingdom.

Moses 2: 16 (Abr. 4: 16) *l.* light to rule night; Abr. 3: 5–6 *l.* light is greater than that upon which thou standest.

LESSON

D&C 121: 35 men set hearts so much on things of world that they do not learn this one *l.*; 138: 56 noble spirits learned first *l.* in spirit world.

LETTER (*see also* Epistle)

D&C 20: 84 members moving to new area should take *l.* of certification; 44: 1 elders to be called together by *l.*; 107: 20 Aaronic Priesthood is to administer in *l.* of gospel; 128: 7 revelation contained in the *l.* which Joseph Smith wrote.

LEVI—*son of Jacob* (*see also* Levitical; BD Levi)

D&C sec. 13 sons of *L.* to offer again an offering unto the Lord; 124: 39 memorials for your sacrifices by sons of *L.* are ordained by ordinance of the Lord's house; 128: 24 the Lord shall purify sons of *L.*

LEVITICAL

D&C 107: 1, 6, 10 Aaronic or *L.* Priesthood.

LIAHONA—*compass given to Lehi*

D&C 17: 1 Three Witnesses to see directors given to Lehi[1] in wilderness.

LIBERAL, LIBERALLY

D&C 42: 68 (46: 7) God gives *l.* to all who ask.

JS-H 1: 11–13 God giveth *l.* to all who ask.

LIBERTY (*see also* Agency; Bondage; Freedom; Government, Civil; Promised Land; Right [noun]; TG Liberty)

D&C 88: 86 (Gal. 5: 1) abide in the *l.* wherewith ye are made free; 134: 4 men's religious opinions should not infringe upon rights and *l.* of others; 138: 18, 31, 42 the Lord and his servants declare *l.* to captive spirits.

LIBERTY JAIL (in Liberty, Missouri— see D&C map, p. 297)

D&C secs. 121–123 revelations received at; sec. 121 prayer by Joseph Smith in.

LIBNAH (*see also* Idolatry)

Abr. 1: 6, 13, 17 heathen god of *L.*

LICENSE (*see also* Certificate)

D&C 20: 63 elders to receive their *l.*; 20: 64 who is entitled to *l.*; 57: 9 let Sidney Gilbert obtain a *l.*

LIE, LAY, LAIN (*see also* Lying)

D&C 5: 32–33 (10: 25) many *l.* in wait to destroy; 49: 20 (84: 49) world *l.* in sin.

LIFE (*see also* Death, Physical; Eternal Life; Immortality; Jesus Christ, Death of; Live; Resurrection; Tree of Life; TG Breath of Life; Life; Life, Sanctity of; Life after Death; Mortality)

D&C 10: 66 if house of Jacob come, they may partake of waters of *l.* freely; 10: 70 (11: 28; 12: 9; 34: 2; 39: 2; 45: 7; 50: 27) Christ is the *l.* and light of the world; 19: 25 thou shalt not seek thy neighbor's *l.*; 50: 5 those who endure, whether in *l.* or in death, inherit eternal *l.*; 76: 59 all things are theirs whether *l.* or death; 77: 8 four angels sent forth to save *l.* and to destroy; 78: 16 Holy One without end of *l.*; 86: 10 your *l.* and priesthood have remained; 88: 13 light which is in all things gives *l.* to all things; 89: 14 grain is ordained to be staff of *l.*; 93: 9 in Christ was the *l.* of men; 98: 13 (103: 28) whoso lays down his *l.* in the Lord's cause shall find eternal *l.*; 101: 15, 35 all who have given their *l.* for the Lord's name shall be crowned; 101: 30 infant's *l.* shall be as age of tree; 101: 35 they who lay down their *l.* for the Lord's sake partake of glory; 101: 37 care not for *l.* of body, but for soul; 103: 27–28 let no man be afraid to lay down his *l.* for the Lord's sake; 123: 13 saints to wear out *l.* in bringing to light hidden things of darkness; 128: 6–7 book of *l.* opened for judging of dead; 132: 22 strait is gate that leads unto continuation of the *l.*; 134: 10 no religious society has authority to try men on right of property or *l.*; 135: 3 Joseph and Hyrum Smith not divided in *l.*

Moses 3: 7 (Abr. 5: 7) God breathes into man the breath of *l.*

LIFT (*see also* Jesus Christ, Death of; Raise)

D&C 5: 35 (9: 14; 17: 8; 52: 43–44; 75: 16, 22) he who is faithful in keeping commandments will be *l.* up at last day; 9: 14 stand fast in work and you shall be *l.* up; 24: 1 I have *l.* thee out of thine afflictions; 25: 13 (27: 15; 31: 3; 35: 26) *l.* up thy heart and rejoice; 52: 44 Christ will *l.* up the faithful; 81: 5 *l.* up the hands that hang down; 98: 34 first *l.* standard of peace unto those who proclaim war; 104: 18 those who impart not to poor will *l.* up eyes in hell; 124: 9 Gentiles to come to exaltation or *l.* up of Zion.

Moses 7: 24 Enoch² is *l.* up in bosom of Father.

LIGHTLY (*see also* Light; Light-mindedness)

D&C 84: 54 (101: 8) saints' minds darkened because they have treated *l.* the things they have received.

LIGHT (*see also* Brightness; Darkness; Physical; Darkness, Spiritual; Day; Enlighten; Example; Glory [noun]; Holy Ghost; Intelligence; Jesus Christ; Knowledge; Lamp; Shine; Spirit; Holy/Spirit of the Lord; Truth; TG Light; Light of Christ; BD Light of Christ)

D&C 1: 33 those who repent not shall lose the *l.* received; 6: 21 (10: 58; 11: 11; 34: 2; 39: 2; 45: 7; 88: 49) Christ is *l.* which shines in darkness; 10: 70 (11: 28; 12: 9; 34: 2; 39: 2; 45: 7; 50: 27; 93: 9) Christ is the *l.* of the world; 14: 9 Christ is *l.* which cannot be hid in darkness; 45: 9 the Lord sent everlasting covenant to be *l.* to world; 45: 28, 36 *l.* to break forth among those sitting in darkness; 45: 29 those sitting in darkness will not perceive *l.*; 50: 24 he who receives *l.* and continues in God will receive more *l.*; 50: 24 *l.* grows brighter to perfect day; 50: 24 that which is of God is *l.*; 67: 9 righteousness comes from Father of *l.*; 77: 4 (Rev. 4: 6) eyes of beasts represent *l.* and knowledge; 82: 3 he who sins against greater *l.* receives greater condemnation; 84: 45 whatsoever is truth is

l., whatsoever is *l.* is Spirit; 84: 46 (93: 2) Spirit gives *l.* to every man; 85: 7 the Lord will send one mighty and strong clothed with *l.*; 86: 11 the Lord's servants to be *l.* unto Gentiles; 88: 7 Christ is *l.* of sun; 88: 40 *l.* cleaves unto *l.*; 88: 44 heavenly bodies give *l.* to each other; 88: 50 (93: 2) Christ is the true *l.* that is in man; 88: 67 he whose eye is single to God's glory shall be filled with *l.*; 88: 67 body filled with *l.* comprehends all things; 88: 87 in last days sun shall refuse to give *l.*; 93: 29, 36 intelligence, or the *l.* of truth, was not created; 93: 32 spirit that receives not *l.* is under condemnation; 93: 37 *l.* and truth forsake evil one; 93: 40 parents to bring up children in *l.* and truth; 103: 9 saints set to be *l.* unto world; 106: 8 Warren Cowdery to be *l.* unto church; 115: 5 *l.* of saints to be standard for nations; 124: 9 come to *l.* of truth; 128: 20 (129: 8) devil appeared as angel of *l.*; 133: 49 at the Lord's coming, moon shall withhold its *l.*; 138: 30 the Lord's messengers carry *l.* of gospel to spirits in darkness.

Moses 2: 3–5 (Abr. 4: 3–5, 16) creation of *l.*; **JS-M** 1: 26 (Matt. 24: 27) as *l.* of morning comes out of east and covers whole earth, so shall coming of Son be; 1: 33 (Matt. 24: 29) moon shall not give her *l.*; **JS-H** 1: 16, 25 pillar of *l.* descends upon Joseph Smith in grove.

LIGHT-MINDEDNESS (*see also* Laugh; Lightly; Merry; Soberness)

D&C 88: 121 cease from all your light speeches and *l.*

LIGHTNING (*see also* Destruction; Thunder)

D&C 20: 6 angel's countenance was as *l.*; 43: 22 *l.* shall streak forth from east to west saying, Repent; 43: 25 the Lord has called by voice of *l.*; 85: 8 man who steadies ark shall fall as a tree smitten by *l.*; 87: 6 earth shall feel God's wrath with vivid *l.*; 88: 90 testimony of voice of *l.*

LIKEN (*see also* Likeness; Parable; Teach)

D&C 88: 46–61 parable of kingdoms that are *l.* unto man having field; 101: 81, 85 children of Zion are *l.* unto parable of woman and unjust judge; 103: 21 Joseph Smith is *l.* unto servant in parable.

LIKENESS (*see also* Image; Similitude)

D&C 1: 16 every man walks after image of own God in *l.* of world; 20: 18 God created man in his own *l.*; 77: 2 that which is spiritual is in *l.* of that which is temporal; 107: 43 Seth's *l.* was express *l.* of his father; 128: 12 to be immersed in water is in *l.* of the dead.

Moses 2: 26 (6: 8; Abr. 4: 26) Gods make man in own *l.*; 6: 63 all things have their *l.*

LILIES

D&C 84: 82 consider *l.* of field.

LINE

D&C 98: 12 (128: 21) God gives unto the faithful *l.* upon *l.*, precept upon precept.

LINEAGE (see also Descendant; Father; Genealogy; Patriarch; Seed)

D&C 68: 21 descendants of Aaron may claim anointing to bishopric if they can prove *l.*; 86: 6–17 *l.* of priesthood from Adam to Moses; 86: 8–10 priesthood continues through *l.* of fathers; 113: 8 Zion has right to priesthood by *l.*

Abr. 1: 27 Pharaoh is of *l.* by which he could not have right of priesthood.

LINK

D&C 128: 18 earth to be smitten unless there is welding *l.* between fathers and children.

LION (see also Animal; Beast)

Moses 7: 13 roar of *l.* is heard out of wilderness.

LIPS (see also Mouth; Speak; Tongue; Word)

D&C 63: 6 let the unbelieving hold their *l.*; 63: 61 let all men beware how they take the Lord's name in their *l.*

JS-H 1: 19 professors of religion drew near the Lord with *l.*

LIST (see also Desire)

D&C 29: 45 men receive their wages of whom they *l.* to obey; 49: 6 men have done unto Son even as they *l.*; 98: 21 the Lord will chasten transgressors in church and whatsoever he *l.*

LISTEN (see also Hear; Hearken; Heed)

D&C 1: 1 (15: 1; 16: 1; 19: 23; 27: 1; 29: 1; 35: 1; 39: 1; 45: 3, 6; 63: 1; 72: 1; 78: 2; 81: 1; 100: 2; 133: 16; 136: 41) *l.* to the Lord; 88: 122 let all *l.* unto sayings of him who speaks.

LITTLE (see also Child; Season)

D&C 84: 119 a *l.* while and ye shall see the Lord exerting powers of heaven; 128: 21 angels give here a *l.*, there a *l.*

LIVE [verb] (see also Alive; Dwell; Eternal Life; Immortality; Life; Living)

D&C 42: 44 (124: 86) if those whom elders bless *l.*, they shall *l.* unto the Lord; 42: 45 *l.* together in love; 45: 1 the Lord made all things which *l.*; 45: 46 saints shall come unto the Lord, and their souls shall *l.*; 59: 2 they who enter Zion and *l.* shall inherit earth; 63: 50 the faithful who *l.* when the Lord comes will be blessed; 76: 22 testimony that Christ *l.*; 84: 22 without greater priesthood no man can see God and *l.*; 84: 44 (98: 11) *l.* by every word that proceeds from mouth of God; 95: 13 the Lord does not give unto saints to *l.* as the world; 110: 4 *l.* am he who *l.*; 135: 3 Joseph Smith *l.* great and died great; 138: 10, 34 (1 Pet. 4: 6) the dead hear gospel that they may *l.* according to God in spirit.

Moses 4: 28 if Adam had eaten of tree of life, he would have *l.* forever; 4: 30 as the Lord *l.* his words cannot return void; **Abr.** 2: 24–25 Abraham to say Sarai is his sister, that his soul shall *l.*

LIVING (see also Alive; Live; TG Living; Living Water)

D&C 14: 9 (20: 19, 32; 42: 1; 50: 1; 55: 2; 61: 28; 68: 6, 25; 70: 10; 76: 66; 77: 9; 82: 18; 138: 39) the *l.* God; 63: 23 (133: 29) *l.* water; 81: 3 proclaim gospel in land of the *l.*; 128: 11, 13, 15, 19 salvation for the *l.* and dead.

Moses 4: 26 Eve, the mother of all *l.*

LOINS (see also Descendant; Seed)

D&C 27: 15–16 (36: 8, 38: 9; 43: 19; 61: 38; 73: 6; 75: 22; 106: 5; 112: 7, 14) gird up your *l.*; 35: 14 the Lord will gird up *l.* of the weak; 132: 30 Abraham received promises concerning the fruit of his *l.*

Moses 8: 2 the Lord covenanted with Enoch[2] that Noah[1] would be fruit of his *l.*; 8: 3 from Methuselah's *l.* should spring kingdoms of earth; **Abr.** 1: 21 Pharaoh a descendant from *l.* of Ham.

LONG-SUFFERING (see also Patience)

D&C 107: 30 decisions of quorums are to be made in *l-s.*; 118: 3 preach in all lowliness and *l-s.*; 121: 41 power or influence maintained only by persuasion, *l-s.*; 138: 9, 28 *l-s.* of God waited in days of Noah[1].

LOOK (see also Behold; See)

D&C 1: 31 the Lord cannot *l.* upon sin with least degree of allowance; 6: 36 *l.* unto the Lord in every thought; 19: 27 Jews to believe gospel and *l.* not for

Messiah to come who has already come; 35: 15 (39: 23; 61: 38) l. forth for the Lord's coming; 38: 35 l. to the poor and needy; 42: 23 (63: 16) he who l. upon woman to lust shall deny the faith; 45: 43–44 remnant shall l. for the Lord; 45: 51 Jews shall l. upon Savior; 49: 23 l. forth for heavens to be shaken; 133: 15 not l. back lest sudden destruction come.

Moses 1: 14 Moses could not l. upon God except glory come upon him; 7: 62 the Lord's people to l. forth for his coming.

LOOSE (see also Bind; Deliver)

D&C 11: 21 (23: 3; 31: 3) tongue to be l.; 43: 31 (88: 110–111) Satan to be l. for little season at end of Millennium; 124: 93 (127: 7; 128: 8, 10) whatever elders l. on earth shall be l. in heaven.

LORD (see Jesus Christ—Lord)

LORD OF HOSTS (see Jesus Christ—Lord of Hosts)

LORD'S DAY (see Day of the Lord; Sabbath)

LORD'S HOUSE (see House; Temple)

LOSE, LOST (see also Astray; Fall of Man; Israel, Ten Lost Tribes of)

D&C 9: 14 hair shall not be l.; 10: 2 gift of translating is temporarily l.; 50: 42 none of those given to the Lord by Father will be l.; 58: 28 (84: 90; 127: 4) if men do good they shall not l. reward; 101: 40 (103: 10) if salt l. savor, good for nothing; 136: 26 if you find what neighbor has l., deliver it.

Moses 4: 1 Satan says no soul shall be l.

LOST TRIBES (see Israel, Ten Lost Tribes of)

LOT—Abraham's nephew

Abr. 2: 4, 6 son of Abraham's brother, travels to Canaan with Abraham.

LOT (see also BD Lots, Casting of)

D&C 85: 7 the Lord's servant will arrange inheritances of saints by l.; 102: 12, 34 twelve high councilors cast l. or ballot.

LOVE (see also Charity; Compassion; Esteem; God, Love of; TG Love)

D&C 4: 5 (12: 8; 50: 5) l. qualifies men for God's work; 20: 19 (42: 29; 59: 5) commandment to l. and serve God; 20: 31 sanctification comes to all those who l.

and serve God; 29: 45 men l. darkness rather than light; 42: 22 l. thy wife with all thy heart; 42: 29 if thou l. me, serve me and keep commandments; 42: 45 thou shalt live together in l.; 45: 27 l. of men shall wax cold in last days; 59: 5 thou shalt l. the Lord thy God with all thy heart; 59: 6 (88: 123; 112: 11) thou shalt l. thy neighbor as thyself; 63: 17 (76: 103) those who l. a lie will have part in lake of fire and brimstone; 76: 116 Holy Spirit bestowed on those who l. God and purify themselves; 88: 40 virtue l. virtue; 88: 123 l. one another; 112: 11 be not partial in l.; 121: 41 power of priesthood maintained by l.; 121: 43 show forth increase of l. after rebuke; 138: 52 blessings held in reserve for those who l. the Lord.

Moses 5: 13, 18, 28 men l. Satan more than God; 7: 33 commandment to l. one another; JS-M 1: 10, 30 because iniquity shall abound, l. of many shall wax cold.

LOVING KINDNESS (see Kindness)

LOW, LOWER (see also Humble; Lowliness)

D&C 49: 10 that which is now exalted of itself will be laid l. of power; 58: 47 call upon the high and the l. to repent; 104: 16 poor shall be exalted, in that the rich are made l.; 112: 8 by thy word many high ones shall be brought l.; 130: 9 all kingdoms of a l. order will be manifest.

LOWLINESS, LOWLY (see also Humble; Low; Meek; Poor)

D&C 32: 1 Parley P. Pratt is admonished to be meek and l. of heart; 42: 74 those who put away spouse for fornication should testify in l. of heart; 107: 30 decisions of quorums to be made in l. of heart; 118: 3 preach in l. of heart.

LUCIFER (see also Devil; BD Lucifer)

D&C 76: 26 Satan was L., son of morning.

LUST (see also Adultery; Carnal; Covet; Desire; Fornication; TG Lust; Sexual Immorality)

D&C 42: 23 (63: 16) he who looks upon woman to l. denies the faith; 46: 9 signs not given to gratify l.; 88: 121 cease from all l. desires; 101: 6 l. and covetous desires among saints.

LYING, LIE, LIAR (see also Beguile; Cunning; Deceit; Devil; False; Flatter; Fraud; Gossip; Guile; Honest; Hypocrisy; Slander)

D&C 10: 25 Satan says it is no sin to l.; 10: 28 l. not exempt from Justice; 20:

54 teachers see there is no *l.* in church; 42: 21 he who *l.* and repents shall be cast out; 42: 86 those who *l.* should be delivered to law of land; 62: 6 the Lord cannot *l.*; 63: 17 *l.* to have part in lake of fire and brimstone; 64: 39 *l.* to be proved by inhabitants of Zion; 76: 103 *l.* inherit telestial glory; 93: 25 wicked one was *l.* from beginning; 109: 30 there will be an end to *l.* against saints; 123: 7 fathers have inherited *l.*

Moses 4: 4 Satan the father of all *l.*; 5: 24 Cain shall be father of Satan's *l.*

LYMAN, AMASA

D&C 124: 136 counselor in high priests quorum presidency; 136: 14 to organize a company for journey west.

MACK, SOLOMON

JS-H 1: 4 Joseph Smith's maternal grandfather.

MAGGOTS (see also Curse; Plague)

D&C 29: 18 the Lord to send curse of m.

MAGISTRATE (see also Government, Civil)

D&C 134: 3 must enforce laws, protect the innocent.

A of F 12 we believe in being subject to m.

MAGNIFY (see also Enlarge; Office; Priesthood; TG Priesthood, Magnifying Callings within)

D&C 24: 3 (66: 11) m. thine office; 24: 9 attend to thy calling and thou shalt have wherewith to m. thy office; 84: 33 those who m. calling shall be sanctified; 88: 80 saints to teach each other, that they might be prepared to m. calling; 132: 64 the Lord will m. his name.

MAHALALEEL—*grandfather of Enoch²*

D&C 107: 46 ordained and blessed by Adam; 107: 53 called to gathering of Adam's posterity at Adam-ondi-Ahman.

Moses 6: 19 son of Cainan; 6: 20 father of Jared¹.

MAHAN

Moses 5: 30–31 Cain is M., master of great secret; 5: 49 Lamech¹ becomes Master M.

MAHIJAH—*man at time of Enoch²*

Moses 6: 40 questions Enoch².

MAHMACKRAH (see also Gods; Idolatry)

Abr. 1: 6, 13, 17 heathen god of M.

MAHUJAEL—*descendant of Cain*

Moses 5: 43 son of Irad, father of Methusael.

MAHUJAH

Moses 7: 2 Enoch² hears voice of heaven at M.

MAINTAIN, MAINTENANCE (see also Defence; Keep; Preserve; Provide; Retain; Support)

D&C 83: 2 women have claim on husbands for m.; 83: 4–5 children have claim on parents, then church, for m.; 98: 5 (101: 77) constitutional law that m rights and freedoms is justifiable before God; 121: 41 no power or influence can be m. by virtue of priesthood.

MAJESTY (see also Glory [noun])

D&C 20: 16 elders bear witness to words of the glorious M.; 88: 47 any man who has seen least of kingdoms has seen God moving in his m.; 109: 59 gathering to roll on in m.; 109: 77 God sits enthroned with m.; 128: 21 voices of angels declare their m.

MAJORITY

D&C 102: 22 m. of council has power to determine decision; 107: 28 m. may form quorum.

MAKE, MADE (see Creation; Formed [verb]; God—Creator; Jesus Christ—Creator; Organize; Straight)

MAKER (see God—Creator; Jesus Christ—Creator)

MALACHI—*Jewish prophet [c. late fifth century B.C.]* (see also BD Malachi)

D&C 110: 14 (133: 64; 138: 46; Mal. 4: 5–6) times spoken of in M. has fully come; 133: 64 (Mal. 4: 1) M. prophesied of day that would burn as oven.

JS-H 1: 36–39 Moroni² quoted words of M. to Joseph Smith.

MALE (see also Man)

D&C 20: 18 God created man, m. and female.

Moses 2: 27 (6: 9; Abr. 4: 27) m. and female created in image of Son.

MAMMON (see also Riches; BD Mammon)

D&C 82: 22 saints to make friends of m. of unrighteousness.

MAN, MEN (see also Agency; Body; Fall of Man; Flesh; Human; Jesus Christ—Son of Man; Male; Man of Counsel; Man of Holiness; Mankind; Nature, Natural; Soul; World; TG Man;

Man, a Spirit Child of Heavenly Father;
Man, Antemortal Existence of; Man,
Natural, Not Spiritually Reborn; Man,
New, Spiritually Reborn; Man,
Physical Creation of; Man, Potential to Become
like Heavenly Father; Man of God)

D&C 3: 3 works of m. are frustrated,
not works of God; 3: 6 how oft have you
gone on in persuasions of m.; 3: 7 (30: 11;
122: 9) should not fear m. more than God;
18: 34 these words are not of m.; 20: 18
God created m. after his own image; 20:
32 m. may fall from grace; 38: 2 every
m. should esteem his brother as himself;
45: 27 love of m. shall wax cold; 45: 29
those sitting in darkness turn hearts from
the Lord because of precepts of m.; 49:
17 m. created before world was; 49: 19
(89: 10) that which comes of earth is
ordained for use of m.; 49: 20 not given
that one m. should possess that which is
above another; 50: 12 when m. reasons,
he is understood of m.; 59: 18 all things
are made for benefit and use of m.; 63: 10
signs come by faith, not by will of m.;
67: 11 (84: 22) no m. has seen God except
quickened by Spirit; 67: 12 natural m.
cannot abide presence of God; 75: 28
every m. obliged to provide for own
family; 76: 61 let no m. glory in m.; 77:
12 (93: 10) God formed m. out of dust of
earth; 84: 16 father Adam was first m.;
93: 29 m. was in beginning with God; 93:
33 m. is spirit; 93: 35 m. is tabernacle of
God; 93: 38 every spirit of m. was innocent
in beginning; 101: 26 enmity of m.
and beasts to cease; 121: 35 few are
chosen, because their hearts aspire to
honors of m.; 121: 39 nature and disposition
of almost all m. to exercise unrighteous
dominion; 130: 1 we shall see
that Savior is a m. like ourselves.

Moses 1: 10 Moses sees that m. is
nothing; 1: 34 (Abr. 1: 3) the Lord calls first
m. Adam; 1: 39 the Lord's work and glory
is to bring to pass immortality and eternal
life of m.; 2: 26-27 (3: 7; 6: 8-10; Abr.
4: 26-27; 5: 7) creation of m.; 2: 28 m.
is given dominion over every living thing;
2: 28 m. is told to be fruitful, replenish
earth; 3: 5 (6: 51; Abr. 3: 23) God
created m. in heaven before placing them
on earth; 3: 18 (Abr. 5: 14) not good for
m. to be alone; 3: 24 m. is commanded to
cleave unto wife; 6: 48 m. are because
Adam fell; 6: 49 m. have become carnal,
sensual, devilish; 6: 65 Adam is born of
Spirit, quickened in the inner m.; 7: 48
earth is mother of m.; **JS-M** 1: 30 love of
m. shall wax cold; **A of F** 5 m. must be
called by prophecy.

MAN OF COUNSEL

Moses 7: 35 M. of C. is God's name.

MAN OF HOLINESS

Moses 6: 57 (7: 35) M. of H. is
God's name.

MANCHESTER, NEW YORK (see also
D&C map, p. 296)

D&C secs. 2, 19, 22-23 revelations
given at.

MANIFEST, MANIFESTATION (see also
God, Manifestations of; Jesus Christ,
Appearances of; Revelation; Show; Testify;
Unfold)

D&C 8: 1 scripture spoken by m. of
Spirit; 18: 2 the Lord has m. that the
things written are true; 18: 18 Holy
Ghost m. all things; 21: 9 Comforter m.
that Jesus was crucified; 70: 13 abundance
is multiplied through the m. of
Spirit; 84: 20 in ordinances of Melchizedek
Priesthood power of godliness in m.; 90:
14 revelations to be m. by Comforter;
91: 4 Spirit m. truth; 105: 36 those who
are chosen shall be m. by voice of Spirit;
130: 7 all things for angels' glory are m.,
past, present, and future.

MANIFESTO (see also Marriage)

D&C OD-1 official declaration on
practice of plural marriage.

MANKIND (see also Flesh; Human; Man)

D&C 98: 5 law supporting freedom
belongs to all m.

Moses 4: 1 Satan promised to
redeem all m.; 5: 9 all m. may be
redeemed, as many as will; **A of F** 3
through Atonement all m. may be saved.

MANNER

D&C 20: 37 m. of baptism; 95: 13
saints not to live after m. of world.

MANSION (see also Celestial Glory;
House)

D&C 59: 2 (106: 8) faithful shall
receive crown in m. of Father; 72: 4
(81: 6) he who is faithful in time is
worthy to inherit eternal life in m. of
Father; 76: 111 every man will receive
his own m. according to his works; 98: 18
(John 14: 2) in my Father's house are
many m.; 135: 5 (Ether 12: 37) he who
sees his weakness will be made strong to
sit in place prepared in m. of Father.

MANUSCRIPT, LOST (see also Book of
Mormon; Harris, Martin; Lehi, Book of)

D&C sec. 3 the Lord chastises Joseph
Smith for loss of translation; 10: 1-21
wicked men have altered words; 10: 12-
15, 20, 22-27, 29, 32-33 devil seeks to
destroy work; 10: 30 do not translate

again; 10: 38–42 account of lost pages is engraved upon other plates.

MARK (see also Curse; Skin)

Moses 5: 40 the Lord sets m. upon Cain.

MARKS, WILLIAM

D&C sec. 117 revelation concerning duties of; 117: 1 is called to settle business and journey from Kirtland; 117: 4 is called to repent of covetous desires; 117: 10 to preside in Far West; 124: 79 to ordain Isaac Galland.

MARRIAGE, MARRY (see also Covenant; Divorce; Father; Husband; Manifesto; Mother; Wife; TG Marriage; Marriage, Celestial; Marriage, Continuing Courtship in; Marriage, Fatherhood; Marriage, Husbands; Marriage, Interfaith; Marriage, Motherhood; Marriage, Plural; Marriage, Temporal; Marriage, Wives; BD Marriage)

D&C 25: 9 husband to support wife in church; 25: 14 wife's soul to delight in husband; 42: 22 thou shalt love thy wife with all thy heart; 42: 74 those who put away companions because of fornication should not be cast out; 42: 75 those who leave companions to commit adultery should be cast out; 49: 15 whoso forbids to m. is not ordained of God; 49: 15 m. is ordained of God; 49: 16 man to have one wife; 49: 16 twain shall be one flesh; 58: 11 the poor, the lame, the blind, and the deaf shall come into m. of Lamb; 74: 1 unbelieving husband is sanctified by wife; 75: 28 every man to provide for own family; 83: 2 women have claim on husbands for maintenance; 90: 18, 43 set house in order; 131: 2–4 new and everlasting covenant of m. required for highest degree of celestial kingdom; sec. 132 revelation concerning covenant of m.; 132: 15 if man and woman m. in world, it is of no force when they are out of world; 132: 16 those out of world neither m. nor are given in m.; 132: 19–20 m. by new and everlasting covenant leads to exaltation; 132: 61–62 order of plural m. not adultery; OD-1 announcement that plural m. has been discontinued; OD-1 saints to refrain from entering m. forbidden by law of land.

Moses 3: 18 (Abr. 5: 14) not good for man to be alone, God to make help meet for him; 3: 21–25 (Abr. 5: 15–19) God makes woman to be Adam's wife; 3: 24 (Abr. 5: 18) man shall cleave unto wife, and they shall be one flesh; 4: 22 woman's desires shall be to her husband, and he shall rule over her; 8: 21 men take

daughters of men in m.; JS-M 1: 42 (Matt. 24: 38) men were m. and giving in m. until day Noah¹ entered ark.

MARROW (see also Bone)

D&C 6: 2 (11: 2; 12: 2; 14: 2; 33: 1) the Lord's word is sharper than sword, to dividing of joints and m.; 89: 18 those who keep Word of Wisdom receive m. to bones.

MARSH, THOMAS B.

D&C secs. 31, 112 revelations to; 31: 2 has many afflictions because of family; 31: 3–5 is called on mission; 31: 5–8, 11 promises to; 31: 9, 12 advice to; 31: 10 a physician to church; 52: 22 to journey to Missouri; 56: 5 to travel; 75: 31 to preach with Ezra Thayre; 112: 16 holds keys pertaining to the Twelve; 118: 2 to remain in Zion to publish the Lord's word.

MARTYRDOM, MARTYR (see also Blood, Shedding of; Death; Physical; Kill; Murder; Persecution; TG Martyrdom; Prophets, Rejection of; BD Martyr)

D&C 93: 13 whoso lays down life in the Lord's cause shall find it again; 101: 15 they who give their lives for the Lord's name shall be crowned; 103: 27–28 let no man be afraid to lay down life for the Lord's sake; 109: 49 blood of saints to come up in testimony; sec. 135 announcement of m. of Joseph and Hyrum Smith; 136: 39 Joseph Smith sealed his testimony with his blood; 138: 40 Abel, the first m.

MARVEL (see also Marvelous; Wonder)

D&C 10: 35 (18: 8; 27: 5; 136: 37) m. not; 76: 13 vision causes Joseph Smith and Sidney Rigdon to m.

MARVELOUS (see also Marvel; Wonder)

D&C 4: 1 (6: 1; 11: 1; 12: 1; 14: 1) m. work is about to come forth; 6: 11 he who inquires shall know great and m. mysteries; 10: 60–61 the Lord will bring to light m. works of other sheep; 18: 44 by servant's hands the Lord will work a m. work; 76: 2, 114 (121: 12) great and m. are works of the Lord.

MASTER (see also Mahan)

D&C 87: 4 slaves shall rise up against m.; 104: 86 m. will not suffer his house to be broken up; 134: 12 elders should not preach to bondservants against will of their m.

MATERIALS (see also Element; Matter)

Abr. 3: 24 we will take of these m. and make an earth.

MATTER (see also Element; Materials)

D&C 131: 7 no such thing as immaterial m., all spirit is m.; 131: 8 when bodies are purified, it is all m.

McILLWAINE'S BEND, MISSOURI (see also D&C map, p. 297)

D&C sec. 61 revelation given at.

McLELLIN, WILLIAM E.

D&C secs. 66, 68 revelations received at request of; 66: 1 has received truth; 66: 2 has received everlasting covenant; 66: 3 needs to repent; 66: 5 (68: 7–8) is called to proclaim gospel; 66: 8 to accompany Samuel Smith; 66: 9 to administer to and heal sick; 66: 10 is warned against adultery; 75: 6–8 to travel south instead of east; 90: 35 the Lord is not well pleased with.

MEANING (see also Interpretation; Knowledge; Means)

JS-H 1: 74 true m. of mysterious passages of scriptures is revealed.

MEANS (see also Instrumentality; Meaning)

D&C 5: 34 the Lord will provide m. to accomplish what he commands; 10: 4 do not labor more than you have m.; 121: 46 dominion shall flow unto thee forever without compulsory m.

MEASURE (see also Mete)

D&C 1: 9 (101: 11; 103: 2) wrath poured out without m.; 1: 10 the Lord shall m. every man according to the m. which he has m.; 49: 17 earth to be filled with m. of man; 88: 19, 25 earth fills m. of its creation; 98: 24 persecution as a just m. to those who bear it not patiently.

Abr. 2: 9 Jehovah to bless Abraham without m.

MEAT (see also Flesh; Food)

D&C 19: 22 world cannot bear m. now, but must receive milk; 19: 15 he who forbids to abstain from m. is not of God; 51: 13 all things that are more than needful, both in money and m., should be kept in storehouse.

Moses 2: 29–30 (Abr. 4: 29–30) to man and beasts are given herbs and fruit for m.

MEDIATION, MEDIATOR (see Jesus Christ—Mediator)

MEDITATE (see also Ponder; Think)

D&C 76: 19 while Joseph Smith and Sidney Rigdon m., the Lord touches eyes of understanding.

MEEK, MEEKNESS (see also Contrite; Gentle; Humble; Lowliness; Poor)

D&C 19: 23 walk in m. of the Lord's Spirit; 25: 14 continue in spirit of m.; 31: 9 govern your house in m.; 35: 15 poor and the m. shall have gospel; 58: 41 William W. Phelps is not sufficiently m. before the Lord; 84: 106 the strong should edify the weak in all m.; 88: 17 the m. shall inherit the earth; 97: 2 the Lord shows mercy unto all the m.; 100: 7 declarations in name of the Lord to be made in spirit of m.; 121: 41 all power and influence to be maintained by gentleness and m.; 124: 4 proclamation to be written in spirit of m.

MEET [adj.] (see also Expedient; Meet, Meeting; Mete; BD Meet)

D&C 58: 26 not m. that the Lord should command in all things; 84: 58 (101: 100) bring forth fruit m. for Father's kingdom.

Moses 3: 18 (Abr. 5: 14) God will make an help m. for man.

MEET, MEETING (see also Assemble; Church of God; Conference; Congregation; Meet [adj.]; Mete; Worship)

D&C 6: 32 the Lord will be where two or three are gathered in his name; 20: 44–56 instructions for conducting m.; 20: 45 (46: 2) elders to conduct m. as led by Holy Ghost; 20: 55, 61, 75 church to meet together often; 42: 89 church courts to be held in private, not before world; 43: 8 when the saints assemble, they should instruct and edify each other; 45: 45 (88: 92, 96–98; 133: 10, 19) saints to be caught up to m. the Lord when he comes; 46: 3 no one to be cast out from public m. of church; 65: 5 Son to come down to m. kingdom of God on earth.

MELCHIZEDEK—King of Salem (see also Priesthood, Melchizedek; BD Melchizedek)

D&C 84: 14 gave priesthood to Abraham; 84: 14–15 received priesthood through lineage of fathers; 107: 2 priesthood so called because M. was great high priest.

MELCHIZEDEK PRIESTHOOD (see Priesthood, Melchizedek)

MELT

D&C 101: 25 elements to m. with fervent heat; 121: 11 prospects of the Lord's enemies melt m. away; 133: 41 presence of the Lord shall be as m. fire.

MEMBER (see also Believer; Church of God; Disciple; Saint; Sheep; TG Member)

D&C 20: 47, 51 priests to visit house of each m.; 20: 68 duty of m. after baptism; 20: 70 every m. of church should bring children to elders for blessing; 42: 78 m. to keep the commandments; 46: 4 m. not to be cast out of sacrament meetings; 46: 29 head is necessary so that every m. may be profited by spiritual gifts; 72: 24 m. appointed to go up unto Zion; 84: 110 body has need of every m.; 92: 2 Frederick G. Williams to be lively m. of united order; 107: 27 every m. in each quorum must be agreed to in its decisions; 134: 9–10 religious societies may deal with m. for fellowship, not right of life or property.

MEMORIAL (see also Remember)

D&C 112: 1 alms come up as m. before the Lord; 124: 39 m. for sacrifices by sons of Levi.

MEN (see also Man)

MEND (see also Change; Repentance)

D&C 75: 29 idler shall not have place in the church unless he m. his ways.

MERCY, MERCIFUL (see also Compassion; God, Love of; Grace; Jesus Christ, Atonement through; Justice; Love; Merit; Pity; Repentance; TG Mercy, Merciful)

D&C 1: 29 Joseph Smith given power to translate through m. of God; 29: 1 the Lord's arm of m. hath atoned for sins; 38: 14 (50: 16; 64: 4) I will be m. unto your weakness; 43: 25 how oft has the Lord called upon men by voice of m.; 46: 15 the Lord suits his m. to conditions of men; 54: 6 he who keeps covenant shall obtain m.; 61: 2 the Lord is m. unto those who confess their sins; 76: 5 the Lord is m. unto those who fear him; 88: 40 m. hath compassion on m.; 97: 2 the Lord shows m. unto all the meek; 99: 3 those who receive the Lord's servants shall obtain m.; 101: 9 in day of wrath the Lord will remember m.; 110: 7 the Lord will manifest himself to his people in m. in this house; 128: 19 gospel is voice of m. from heaven.

Moses 7: 31 m. shall go before my face.

MERIDIAN OF TIME (see also Jesus Christ, First Coming of; Time)

D&C 20: 26 (39: 3) the Lord came in m. of t. in flesh.

Moses 5: 57 (6: 57, 62; 7: 46) Christ to come in m. of t.

MERIT (see also Grace; Jesus Christ, Atonement through; Mercy; Virtue; Worth)

D&C 3: 20 rely upon m. of Christ.

MERRY (see also Glad; Happiness; Light-mindedness)

D&C 136: 28 if thou art m., praise the Lord with singing.

MESSAGE (see also Gospel; Messenger; Tidings)

D&C 129: 4, 7 when messenger says he has m. from God, offer him your hand as test; 138: 37 the dead hear m. of redemption.

MESSENGER (see also Angel; Jesus Christ; Message; Servant; TG Jesus Christ, Messenger of the Covenant)

D&C 45: 9 everlasting gospel sent to be m. to prepare the way; 93: 8 in beginning was the Word, the m. of salvation; 124: 25–26 send swift m., a chosen m., to call saints from afar; 129: 4–8 test to determine whether m. comes from God; 138: 30–31 the Lord appoints m. from among righteous spirits.

JS–H 1: 53–54 heavenly m. gives instructions to Joseph Smith; 1: 69 heavenly m. confers priesthood upon Joseph Smith and Oliver Cowdery.

MESSIAH (see also Jesus Christ—Messiah)

METE (see also Give; Measure)

D&C 84: 85 it shall be given that portion that shall be m. to every man; 98: 24 persecution m. out as a just measure to those who deal not patiently; 127: 3 God will m. out just recompense.

METHODIST

JS–H 1: 5 religious excitement begins with M.; 1: 8 Joseph Smith somewhat partial to M.; 1: 21 M. preacher condemns Joseph Smith's vision.

METHUSAEL—descendant of Cain

Moses 5: 43 son of Mahujael, father of Lamech[1].

METHUSELAH—son of Enoch[2]

D&C 107: 50 ordained by Adam; 107: 52 ordained Noah[1]; 107: 53 called to gathering of Adam's posterity at Adam-ondi-Ahman.

Moses 6: 25 (8: 2) son of Enoch[2]; 8: 2 not taken up with Enoch[2]; 8: 3 prophesies all kingdoms to spring from him; 8: 5 father of Lamech[2]; 8: 7 lived 969 years.

MICHAEL (see also Adam)

D&C 27: 11 (107: 54; 128: 21) is Adam; 29: 26 M., the Lord's archangel, shall sound trump; 78: 16 has been appointed prince; 88: 112–113, 115 will gather armies and fight Satan; 128: 20 voice of M. heard.

MIDST

D&C 1: 36 (45: 59; 49: 27) the Lord to reign in saints' m.; 6: 32 (29: 5; 32: 3; 50: 44) where two or three are gathered in the Lord's name, he will be in their m.; 38: 7 the Lord is in saints' m., but unseen; 84: 25 the Lord took Moses out of m. of Israel; 88: 13 God is in m. of all things.

Abr. 3: 21, 23 God stands in m. of spirits.

MIGHT (see also Arm; God, Power of; Mighty; Power; Strength)

D&C 4: 2 (59: 5) love the Lord thy God with all thy m.; 4: 4 (6: 3; 11: 3; 12: 3; 14: 3) he who thrusts in sickle with his m. brings salvation to soul; 20: 31 sanctification to those who love and serve God with all their m.; 45: 75 all nations will be afraid because of power of the Lord's m.; 75: 3 (124: 44) neither be idle, but labor with your m.; 76: 95 God makes those who dwell in his presence equal in m.; 76: 114 mysteries of God's kingdom surpass understanding in m.; 109: 77 God sits enthroned with m.

MIGHTY, MIGHTIER (see also God, Power of; Might; Strong)

D&C 1: 19 the m. to be broken by the weak; 3: 4 man may have power to do m. works, and yet fail; 85: 7 the Lord will send one m. and strong; 100: 10 the Lord will give power to be m. in testimony; 100: 11 the Lord will give power to be m. in expounding scriptures; 133: 47 the Lord is m. to save.

Moses 8: 21 our wives bear children who are m. men, like men of old.

MILCAH—Abraham's sister-in-law

Abr. 2: 2 Nehor, Abraham's brother, takes M. to wife.

MILD, MILDNESS

D&C 38: 41 preaching should be warning voice in m.; 42: 43 those without faith should be nourished with herbs and m. food; 89: 17 barley for m. drinks.

MILES, DANIEL

D&C 124: 138 one of seven presidents of seventies quorum.

MILK

D&C 19: 22 world must receive m. because they cannot bear meat; 38: 18 the Lord will give a land flowing with m. and honey.

MILL

JS-M 1: 45 (Matt. 24: 41) two grinding at m., one shall be taken.

MILLENNIUM (see also Day of the Lord; Jesus Christ, Second Coming of; Kingdom of God; Zion; TG Millennium; Millennium, Preparing a People for)

D&C 29: 11 the Lord to dwell with men on earth a thousand years; 29: 22 men will again deny Lord at end of M.; 43: 29 the Lord's people will reign with him; 43: 30 M. prophesied by the Lord's servants; 43: 31 (84: 100; 88: 110–111) Satan to be bound, then loosed for a season; 43: 32 righteous to be changed in twinkling of eye, and earth to pass away as by fire; 43: 33 wicked to go into unquenchable fire until judgment; 45: 58 children of those who abide the Lord's coming will grow up without sin; 63: 51 children to grow old during M.; 63: 51 old men will be changed in twinkling of an eye; 77: 12 in beginning of seventh thousand years the Lord will sanctify earth; 84: 98–102 new song describing M.; 88: 101 those under condemnation live not again until thousand years ended; 101: 23–24 description of M.; 101: 101 saints will build and another will not inherit; 133: 25 the Lord will reign over all flesh.

A of F 10 Christ will reign personally upon earth.

MILLER, GEORGE

D&C 124: 20 is without guile; 124: 20–21 office of a bishopric sealed upon head of; 124: 22–24, 60, 70 to help in building Nauvoo Temple.

MILLSTONE

D&C 121: 22 better that m. were hanged about necks of the wicked.

MIND, MINDED (see also Heart; Intelligence; Knowledge; Spirit)

D&C 4: 2 (20: 31) serve God with all m.; 6: 15 I did enlighten thy m.; 6: 23 did I not speak peace to your m.; 8: 2 I will tell you in your m.; 9: 8 study it out in your m.; 10: 2 (84: 54) m. became darkened; 11: 13 Spirit to enlighten m.; 11: 20 keep commandments with might, m.; 20: 31 sanctification to those who love and serve God with all m.; 43: 34

let solemnities of eternity rest upon m.; 45: 65 with one m., saints to gather riches to purchase land; 46: 10 retain in m. what gifts are given to church; 59: 5 love the Lord with all thy might, m.; 64: 34 the Lord requires the heart and a willing m.; 67: 10 man cannot see God with the carnal or natural m.; 68: 3–4 that which is spoken by Holy Ghost shall be the m. of the Lord; 84: 61 remain steadfast in your m.; 84: 80 he who preaches gospel faithfully shall not be weary in m.; 84: 85 treasure up in your m. continually the words of life; 88: 68 sanctify yourselves that your m. become single to God; 88: 124 retire and arise early that body and m. may be invigorated; 95: 13 (133: 61) here is wisdom and m. of the Lord; 102: 23 president may obtain m. of the Lord by revelation; 110: 1 veil was taken from m.; 112: 23 gross darkness covers m. of people; 121: 12 God blinds m. of his enemies; 133: 61 commandments given according to m. and will of the Lord.

Moses 4: 6 Satan knew not m. of God; 7: 18 people of Zion are of one m.; **JS-H** 1: 42 vision of place where plates are buried is opened to Joseph Smith's m.

MINGLE (see also Mix)

D&C 109: 79 saints to m. voices with seraphs; 134: 9 not just to m. religious influence with civil government.

MINISTER [noun] (see also Disciple; Minister [verb]; Ministry; Officer; Preacher; Priesthood; Servant)

D&C 84: 111 deacons and teachers appointed standing m.; 107: 39 the Twelve to ordain evangelical m.; 107: 97 seventy to be traveling m.; 124: 137 quorum of elders instituted for standing m.

MINISTER [verb], **MINISTRATION** (see also Administration; Angels; Ministering of; Ministry; Serve)

D&C 76: 86 telestial receive Holy Spirit through m. of the terrestrial; 76: 87 terrestrial receive Holy Spirit through m. of the celestial; 138: 37 the dead hear word through m. of the Lord's servants.

Abr. 2: 6 the Lord to make Abraham m. to bear his name.

MINISTRY (see also Calling; Minister [noun]; Minister [verb]; Office; Preach; Priesthood; Serve; TG Ministry; Ministry, Unpaid; BD Ministry)

D&C 6: 28 the Lord gives keys of gift, which shall bring to light this m.; 7: 7 (27: 12) keys of m. given to Peter, James, and John; 29: 12 Twelve who were with Christ in m. at Jerusalem will

judge Israel; 68: 22 bishop or high priests set apart for m. should be tried only before First Presidency; 77: 5 (Rev. 4: 4) four and twenty elders who had been faithful in work of m.; 84: 86 commandment to those called to m.; 88: 84 (90: 8; 97: 13) labor diligently, that you may be perfected in your m.; 88: 127 school of prophets established for those who are called to m.; 94: 3 house to be built for work of m. of presidency; 97: 13–14 house to be built for instruction of those called to work of m.; 107: 76 descendant of Aaron[1] has legal right to keys of m. of bishop; 115: 19 the Lord has given Joseph Smith keys of kingdom and m.; 124: 143 offices given for work of m.; 138: 25 the Lord spent three years in m. among Jews; 138: 27 Savior's m. among the dead limited to time between crucifixion and resurrection.

Abr. 1: 19 through m. of Noah[1], God's name to be known in earth forever; 2: 9 Abraham's seed to bear m.

MINUTES (see also Record)

D&C 128: 3 recorders appointed for taking accurate m.

MIRACLE, MIRACULOUS (see also Faith; God, Manifestations of; God, Power of; Marvel; Raise; Sign; Wonder; TG Miracle; BD Miracle)

D&C 17: 1 m. directors to be shown to Three Witnesses; 24: 13–14 require not m., except the Lord shall command you; 35: 8 the Lord will show m. unto those who believe; 45: 8 to those who received him, the Lord gave power to do m.; 46: 21 to some is given gift of working m.; 138: 26 notwithstanding Christ's mighty works and m., few Jews hearkened.

MISERY, MISERABLE (see also Anguish; Hell; Suffering; Torment; Tribulation)

D&C 19: 33 slighting the Lord's counsels causes m.; 76: 43 no man understands m. of sons of perdition; 87: 1 wars will eventually cause death and m. of many.

Moses 6: 48 because of Adam's fall, men are partakers of m.; 7: 37 m. shall be doom of the wicked; 7: 41 Enoch[2] weeps because of wickedness and m. of men.

MISSION (see also Abrahamic Covenant; Errand; Minister [noun]; Preach; Servant; Warn; TG Israel, Mission of; Jesus Christ, Mission of; Mission of Early Saints; Mission of Latter-day Saints; Missionary Work)

D&C 31: 3 hour of your m. is come;

58: 14, 16 m. appointed to Edward Partridge; 61: 7, 9 Sidney Gilbert and William W. Phelps to be in haste upon m.; 62: 2 your m. is not yet full; 68: 2 an ensample unto all ordained unto priesthood, whose m. is appointed to go forth; 71: 3 this is a m. for a season; 77: 14 (Rev. 10: 2, 9–10) John's little book is m. and ordinance to gather tribes of Israel; 88: 80 be prepared in all things when I send you again to magnify m. with which I have commissioned you; 90: 16 business and m. in all your lives to preside in council; 114: 1 David Patten to settle business that he may perform m.; 124: 102 m. in store for William Law and Hyrum Smith; 135: 3 Joseph Smith has sealed his m. with his blood.

MISSOURI (*see also* Jackson County; Missouri River; Zion; D&C maps, pp. 297, 298)

D&C 52: 2–3 next conference to be held in M.; 52: 42 (62: 6) saints to assemble themselves in M.; 54: 8 commandment to flee to M.; 57: 1 M. consecrated for gathering of saints; 57: 2 (84: 3) M. the place for city of Zion; 98: Intro. (101: Intro.) persecution of saints in M.; 124: 54 brethren slain in land of M.

MISSOURI RIVER (*see also* D&C map, p. 297)

D&C secs. 61–62 revelations given on banks of; 121: 33 as well might man stretch forth puny arm to stop M.R.

MIST (*see also* Cloud; Darkness, Physical; Darkness, Spiritual; Smoke; Vapor)

Moses 3: 6 (Abr. 5: 6) m. goes up from earth.

MITCHELL, DR.

JS-H 1: 65 sanctions authenticity of translation and characters from plates.

MIX, MIXTURE (*see also* Mingle)

D&C 115: 6 wrath to be poured out without m.

Moses 7: 22 residue of people are m. of all seed of Adam except Cain.

MOCK, MOCKER (*see also* Persecution; Revile; Scorner)

D&C 45: 50 calamity shall cover the m.; 63: 58 (104: 6; 124: 71) the Lord will not be m.

MOMENT

D&C 24: 6 (100: 6) it shall be given in very m. what to speak; 121: 7 (122: 4) afflictions shall be but small m.

MONEY (*see also* Debt; Mammon; Riches; Scrip; Tithing; Treasure; Wealth)

D&C 48: 4 save all the m. ye can; 51: 8 agent to be appointed to take m. for food and raiment; 51: 13 all things both in m. and meat should be kept by bishop; 58: 35 Martin Harris to be example to church in laying m. before bishop; 58: 51 (101: 72–73) churches to obtain m. to purchase lands; 69: 1 m. sent to Zion; 84: 89–90 he who gives m. to elders shall not lose reward; 84: 103–104 disposition of certain m.; 101: 56 (103: 22–23) vineyard has been bought with m.; 101: 70 purchase all lands that can be purchased with m.; 104: 26 Martin Harris to devote m. for proclaiming the Lord's words; 105: 30 armies of Israel to take possession of lands previously purchased with m.; 117: 16 saints to overthrow m-changers.

MONTH (*see also* Time)

D&C 88: 44 heavenly bodies give light to each other in their m.; 121: 31 all the appointed days, m., and years shall be revealed.

MOON (*see also* Astronomy)

D&C 5: 14 (109: 73) church to come forth out of wilderness, clear as m.; 29: 14 (34: 9; 45: 42; 88: 87) m. to turn to blood at the Lord's coming; 76: 71, 78, 81, 97 terrestrial glory compared with m.; 88: 8 Christ is in m. and is light of m.; 88: 45 m. gives her light by night; 105: 31 the Lord's army to be sanctified to become clear as m.; 121: 30 to be revealed whether there be bounds set to heavens, sun, m., or stars; 133: 49 so great shall be glory of the Lord's presence that m. shall withhold light.

Moses 2: 16–18 (Abr. 4: 14, 16) creation of m.; **Abr.** 3: 13 Olea, which is the m.

MORE

D&C 10: 68 whoso declares m. or less than the Lord's doctrine is not of God; 93: 25 whatsoever is m. or less than this is spirit of wicked one; 98: 7 (124: 120) that which is m. or less cometh of evil.

MOREH, PLAINS OF

Abr. 2: 18 Abraham offers sacrifice upon plains of M.

MORLEY, ISAAC

D&C 52: 23 to journey to Missouri, preaching word; 64: 15–16, 20 the Lord's anger toward.

MORNING (see also Time)

D&C 76: 26–27 Satan known as Lucifer, son of m.; 128: 23 let sun, moon, and m. stars sing together.

Moses 2: 5 (Abr. 4: 5) evening and m. were first day; JS-M 1: 26 as light of m. covers whole earth, so shall coming of Son be; JS-H 1: 14 Joseph Smith retires to woods on m. in spring.

MORONI[1] — righteous Nephite military commander

There are no references to Moroni[1] in the Doctrine and Covenants and Pearl of Great Price.

MORONI[2]—son of Mormon, last of Nephites [c. A.D. 421]

D&C sec. 2 extract from words of M.; 27: 5 (128: 20) is sent to reveal Book of Mormon; 27: 5 holds keys of record of stick of Ephraim; 138: 46 spoke to Joseph Smith of coming of Elijah.

JS-H 1: 30–42, 45 appears to Joseph Smith in room; 1: 34–35, 42 tells Joseph Smith about gold plates; 1: 41 appears to Joseph Smith in field; 1: 50 reveals where plates are deposited; 1: 53 forbids Joseph Smith to take plates; 1: 54 instructs Joseph Smith each year; 1: 59 delivers plates to Joseph Smith.

MORROW (see also Tomorrow)

D&C 84: 81, 84 (Matt. 6: 34) take no thought for the m.

MOSES—great Hebrew prophet [c. fifteenth century B.C.] (see also Law of Moses; TG Law of Moses; BD Moses)

D&C 8: 3 M. led Israel by revelation; 28: 2 Joseph Smith received commandments as did M.; 84: 6 M. received priesthood from Jethro; 84: 23–26 why M. was taken away from Israel; 84: 31–32 sons of M. and Aaron[1] shall offer acceptable offering, be filled with glory in the Lord's house; 84: 33–34 those who magnify priesthood calling become sons of M. and Aaron[1]; 103: 16–18 a man like M. promised; 107: 91 President of High Priesthood to be like M.; 110: 11 M. commits keys of gathering Israel; 124: 38 tabernacle built by M. for sacred ordinances; 132: 1, 38 the Lord gave M. many wives; 133: 53–54 the Lord redeemed and carried M. and other prophets; 133: 63 prediction of M. to be fulfilled; 138: 41 M. the great law-giver of Israel is seen among noble spirits; 138: 45 M. appeared with Elias on Mount of Transfiguration.

Moses 1: 1 M. is caught up into mountain; 1: 2, 31 sees God face to face;

1: 2, 31 can endure presence of God; 1: 2–3, 31 talks with God; 1: 2, 11, 31 glory of God is upon M.; 1: 4 is called son of God; 1: 6 God has a work for M.; 1: 6, 13 M. is in similitude of Only Begotten; 1: 8, 27–29 M. beholds the world and its inhabitants; 1: 9 presence of God is withdrawn from M.; 1: 10 M. knows that man is nothing; 1: 11 M. beholds God's face; 1: 11 M. is transfigured before God; 1: 12 Satan tempts M.; 1: 12, 19 Satan commands M. to worship him; 1: 13 M. defies Satan; 1: 13 M. affirms himself a son of God; 1: 14, 20–21 M. receives strength from God; 1: 15, 18 M. can judge between Satan and God; 1: 25 M. bears record of visitations of God and Satan; 1: 25 M. calls upon God after withstanding Satan; 1: 26 M. is to deliver Israel from bondage; 1: 30, 36 M. asks God about creation; 1: 40 M. is commanded to write the words of God; 2: 1 M. is to write things revealed to him concerning creation.

MOTE

D&C 29: 25 not one hair, neither m., shall be lost.

MOTHER (see also Child; Family; Father; Marriage; Parent; Wife; TG Marriage, Motherhood; Mother)

D&C 88: 94 that great church, the m. of abominations.

Moses 3: 24 (Abr. 5: 18) man shall leave father and m. and cleave to wife; 4: 26 Eve, the m. of all living; 7: 48 earth cries out as m. of men.

MOUNT [verb] (see also Rise)

D&C 124: 99 he shall m. up in imagination of thoughts.

MOUNT, MOUNTAIN (see also Hill; Olivet, Mount of; Simeon, Mount; Sinai, Mount; Zion, Mount)

D&C 17: 1 Urim and Thummim given to brother of Jared[2] on m.; 19: 29 publish glad tidings upon m.; 45: 48 the Lord shall set foot upon this m. and it shall cleave in twain; 49: 23 m. to be made low at the Lord's coming; 49: 25 Zion shall rejoice in the m.; 63: 21 saints have not yet received full account of things shown to apostles upon m.; 65: 2 (Dan. 2: 34–35, 44–45) stone cut out of m. without hands shall roll forth; 109: 61 children of Jacob are scattered upon m. for long time; 109: 74 (133: 40, 44) m. to flow down at the Lord's presence; 112: 7 thy path lies among the m.; 117: 8 the m. of Adam-ondi-Ahman; 124: 104 lift up voice on m.; 128: 19 how beautiful upon m. are feet of those who bring glad tidings; 128: 23 let the *m.* shout for joy; 133: 13 Judah to flee unto Jerusalem, unto the *m.* of the Lord's house; 133: 22 the Lord's voice shall break down *m.*

Moses 1: 1 Moses is caught up into *m.*; 1: 1–2, 42 God speaks to Moses on *m.*

MOURN, MOURNING (*see also* Comfort; Cry; Grieve; Groan; Lament; Suffering; Wailing; Weep)

D&C 45: 49 the Lord shall utter his voice, and nations shall *m.*; 87: 6 with sword and by bloodshed, inhabitants of earth shall *m.*; 95: 7 call solemn assembly that fastings and *m.* might come up to the Lord; 97: 21 Zion to rejoice, while all the wicked *m.*; 98: 9 when the wicked rule, the people *m.*; 101: 14 they who have *m.* shall be comforted; 112: 24 day of desolation, of weeping, of *m.*

Moses 7: 48–49 Enoch² hears earth *m.*; 7: 56 Enoch² hears all creations of God *m.*; **Abr.** 1: 20 great *m.* in Chaldea and court of Pharaoh.

MOUTH (*see also* Lips; Speak; Tongue; Word)

D&C 6: 28 (42: 81; 128: 3) in *m.* of two or three witnesses shall every word be established; 21: 5 saints to receive Joseph Smith's word as if from the Lord's *m.*; 28: 16 open thy *m.* at all times; 33: 8 (Ps. 81: 10) open your *m.*, and they shall be filled; 60: 2 elders will not open *m.*; 71: 1 open *m.* in proclaiming gospel.

Moses 4: 7 Satan speaks by *m.* of serpent; 5: 36 earth opened *m.* to receive Abel's blood; 6: 32 open thy *m.*, and it shall be filled.

MOVE (*see also* Remove)

D&C 45: 1 the Lord made all things which live and *m.*; 45: 32 (87: 8) disciples shall stand in holy places and shall not be *m.*; 68: 3 priesthood bearers shall speak as *m.* upon by Holy Ghost; 77: 4 (Rev. 4: 8) beasts' wings are representation of power to *m.*; 84: 40 Father cannot break oath and covenant, neither can it be *m.*; 88: 42 God has given law to all things, by which they *m.*; 97: 19 (101: 17) Zion cannot be *m.* out of her place; 121: 43 reprove with sharpness when *m.* upon by Holy Ghost.

Moses 2: 2 Spirit *m.* upon face of waters; 6: 8 Adam speaks prophecy as *m.* by Holy Ghost.

MUCH

D&C 82: 3 unto whom *m.* is given, *m.* is required.

MULTIPLY (*see also* Enlarge; Flourish; Grow; Increase)

D&C 45: 58 they who have received truth shall *m.* and wax strong; 132: 63 virgins are given unto man to *m.* and replenish earth.

Moses 2: 28 (Abr. 4: 28) man commanded to *m.* and replenish earth; 8: 14 men begin to *m.* upon face of earth.

MULTITUDE (*see also* Nation)

D&C 107: 55 *m.* of nations to come of Adam.

MURDER, MURDERER, MURDEROUS (*see also* Blood, Shedding of; Capital Punishment; Kill; Martyrdom; Secret Combination; Slay; Telestial Glory; BD Murder)

D&C 42: 18 he who kills shall not have forgiveness; 42: 79 any who kill shall be delivered up to laws of land; 59: 6 thou shalt not kill; 121: 23 wo unto those who *m.* the Lord's people; 132: 19, 26–27 commit no *m.* whereby to shed innocent blood.

Moses 5: 31 Cain is master of great secret, that he may *m.*; 5: 32 Cain slays Abel; 6: 28 in their own abominations men have devised *m.*

MURDOCK, JOHN

D&C 52: 8 to journey to Missouri by way of Detroit; sec. 99 revelation to; 99: 1 called to eastern countries.

MURMUR, MURMURING (*see also* Contention; Disobedience; Dissension; Hardheartedness; Rebel)

D&C 9: 6 do not *m.*; 25: 4 *m.* not because of things which thou hast not seen; 75: 7 the Lord chastens William McLellin for *m.* of heart.

MUSIC (*see also* Dance; Hymn; Sing; Song)

D&C 136: 28 praise the Lord with *m.*

MYSTERY (*see also* Godliness; Hide, Hidden; Knowledge; Secret; TG Mysteries of Godliness; BD Mystery)

D&C 6: 7 (11: 7) seek wisdom, then shall *m.* of God be unfolded; 6: 11 (8: 11; 42: 61) if thou inquire, thou shalt know the *m.* of God; 10: 64 (19: 8; 38: 13) the Lord explains *m.*; 19: 10 *m.* of godliness, how great it is; 28: 7 (35: 18; 64: 5) Joseph Smith given keys of *m.* and sealed revelations; 42: 61, 65 if thou ask, thou shalt receive revelations to know *m.* and peaceable things; 42: 65 world not to know *m.*; 43: 13 if *m.* are desired, provide support for Joseph Smith; 62: 23 he who keeps commandments will be given m. of kingdom; 63: 23 m. to be will of living water to everlasting life; 71: 1 expound m. out of scriptures; 76: 7 the Lord reveals m. of kingdom to those who serve him; 76: 10 the Lord reveals secrets of his will to those who serve him; 76: 114 m. of kingdom surpass all understanding; 77: 6 book which John saw contains m.; 84: 19 (107: 18–19) Melchizedek Priesthood holds keys of m. of knowledge of God; 97: 5 Parley P. Pratt is blessed in expounding all scriptures and m. to edification of school; 101: 33 at his coming the Lord will reveal hidden things which no man knew; 107: 19 Melchizedek Priesthood to have privilege of receiving m. of kingdom.

NAAMAH

   Moses 5: 46 sister of Tubal Cain.

NAIL

   D&C 6: 37 behold prints of n. in the Lord's hands.

NAKED (see also Charity; Clothing; Judgment; Needy; Poor)

   Moses 3: 25 (Abr. 5: 19) Adam and Eve are n. and are not ashamed; 4: 13 Adam and Eve know they are n. and make aprons.

NAME (see also Call; Name of the Lord)

   D&C 20: 82 representatives at conference to bring list of n. of those who have joined church; 20: 83 (85: 5) n. of those cast out of church should be blotted out; 76: 68 n. of those who come forth in resurrection of just are written in heaven; 78: Intro. explanation concerning code n.; 85: 3–5 n. of those who do not receive inheritance through consecration should not be enrolled with people of God; 88: 2 saints' alms are recorded in book of n. of the sanctified; 115: 3–4 (127: 12; 128: 21; 136: 2) ODI; OD-2) n. of the church; 117: 11 be bishop in deed and not in n. only; 122: 1 ends of the earth shall inquire after Joseph Smith's n.; 123: 3 keep history of n. of oppressors; 128: 3 recorders to take minutes of proceedings, giving dates and n.; 130: 11 white stone whereon a new n. is written, the key word.

   JS-H 1: 33 Joseph Smith's n. to be had for good and evil among all nations.

NAME OF THE LORD (see also Jesus Christ; Prayer; TG Name of the Lord; BD Christ, Names of)

   D&C 1: 20 every man to speak in n. of the Lord; 3: 20 Lamanites to be glorified through faith in the Lord's n.; 6: 32 where two or three gather in the Lord's n., he is in their midst; 11: 30 (49: 12; 76: 51) believe on the Lord's n.; 13: 1 Aaronic Priesthood conferred in n. of Messiah; 14: 8 (18: 18; 20: 77; 24: 5; 50: 29) pray to Father in the Lord's n.; 18: 21, 24 take upon you n. of Christ; 18: 23 Jesus Christ is only n. whereby men can be saved; 18: 25 they who know not the n. by which they are called cannot have place in Father's kingdom; 18: 27–28 the Twelve take the Lord's n. with full purpose of heart; 18: 29 the Twelve are ordained to baptize in the Lord's n.; 18: 40 worship Father in the Lord's n.; 19: 10 Endless is the Lord's n.; 20: 36 honor, power, and glory to be rendered to the Lord's holy n.; 20: 37 taking n. of Christ required for baptism; 20: 77 partakers of sacrament witness they are willing to take upon them n. of Son; 24: 10 Oliver Cowdery shall continue in bearing the Lord's n. before world; 35: 9 (84: 67) cast out devils in the Lord's n.; 41: 1 (50: 4; 112: 26) the Lord will curse those who have professed his name, but hear him not; 42: 4 first commandment, to go forth in the Lord's n.; 46: 31 all things done in Spirit must be done in the Lord's n.; 63: 61 (136: 21) let all men beware how they take the Lord's name on their lips; 63: 62 condemnation of those who use n. of the Lord in vain; 76: 51 celestial heirs received testimony of Jesus and believed on his n.; 84: 66 in the Lord's n. believers will do wonderful works; 88: 120 (109: 9) incomings, outgoings, salutations to be in n. of the Lord; 97: 15 (109: 2; 124: 22) build a house unto me in n. of the Lord; 104: 60 consecrate treasury unto the Lord's n.; 109: 22 we ask thee, Father, that thy n. may be upon thy servants; 112: 12 be faithful before the Lord unto his n.; 128: 23 let eternal creations declare the Lord's n.; 132: 64 the Lord will magnify his n. upon all who receive his law; 133: 18 Father's n. written on foreheads of 144,000; 138: 24 saints sing praises to the Lord's holy n.

   Moses 1: 15 blessed be n. of my God; 1: 17 (5: 8; 6: 52; 7: 50) call upon God in n. of Son; 1: 25 calling upon n. of God, Moses beholds his glory; 4: 1 Moses commands Satan in n. of Only Begotten; 5: 4 Adam and Eve call upon n. of the Lord; 5: 8 Adam is commanded to do all things in name of Son; 6: 52 (8: 24) be baptized in n. of Son; 6: 57 (7: 35) Man of Holiness is God's n. in Adam's language; 6: 57 n. of Only Begotten is Son of

Man, even Jesus Christ; 7: 11 Enoch² is commanded to baptize in n. of Father, Son, Holy Ghost; **Abr.** 1: 19 through ministry of Noah¹, God's n. to be known in earth forever; 2: 6 the Lord to make Abraham a minister to bear his n. in strange land; **JS-H** 1: 69 John the Baptist confers Aaronic Priesthood in n. of Messiah.

NATHAN—*Hebrew prophet during reign of David (see also* BD *Nathan)*

D&C 132: 39 David was given wives and concubines by N.

NATHANAEL—*one of Christ's disciples (see also* BD *Nathanael)*

D&C 41: 11 Edward Partridge is like N. of old, in whom there is no guile.

NATION *(see also* Country; Gentile; Government, Civil; Heathen; Land; Multitude)*

D&C 7: 3 John the Beloved to prophesy to every n., kindred; 10: 51 eternal life to be free unto all of whatsoever n., kindred; 34: 8 n. shall tremble at coming of the Lord; 35: 13 weak things of world to thrash n. by power of the Lord's Spirit; 42: 58 (133: 8) gospel to be preached to every n.; 43: 20 elders to call upon n. to repent; 45: 47 (84: 96; 101: 11) arm of the Lord to fall upon n.; 45: 49 n. shall mourn; 45: 69 (64: 42) people to be gathered unto Zion out of every n., kindred; 45: 75 n. afraid of terror of God; 49: 10 n. shall bow to everlasting covenant; 52: 14 Satan goes forth deceiving the n.; 56: 1 (101: 96) visitation and wrath to come upon n.; 58: 9 all n. shall be invited to supper of house of the Lord; 64: 37 church like a judge over n.; 64: 42 there shall come to Zion out of every n.; 64: 43 n. to fear and tremble because of Zion; 77: 8 angels have gospel to commit to every n., kindred; 77: 11 144,000 are high priests ordained out of every n., kindred; 87: 2 war will be poured out upon all n.; 87: 6 consumption decreed shall make a full end of all n.; 88: 79 saints to learn about wars and perplexities of n.; 88: 105 she is fallen who made n. drink of wrath of her fornication; 90: 10 the Lord's power shall convince heathen n.; 97: 19 n. shall honor Zion; 98: 33–36 the Lord's people should not go to battle against any n. except the commands; 101: 89 God's fury to vex n.; 107: 55 Adam to be prince of n.; 109: 54 have mercy, O Lord, upon all n.; 112: 21 the Twelve to open gospel door to n.;

115: 5 saints' light to be standard for n.; 133: 2 the Lord's judgment upon n. that forget God; 133: 14 go ye out from among n.; 133: 42 all n. shall tremble at the Lord's presence; 133: 58 little one shall become strong n.

Abr. 1: 2 Abraham desires to be father of many n.; 2: 9 God will make Abraham a great n.; **JS-H** 1: 33 Joseph Smith's name to be had for good and evil among all n., kindreds, tongues.

NATURE, NATURAL *(see also* Carnal; Earth; Fall of Man; Flesh; Temporal; World; **TG** Natural; Nature, Earth; Nature, Human)*

D&C 29: 35 commandments are no n. nor temporal; 29: 43 by n. death may be raised in immortality unto eternal life; 58: 3 ye cannot behold design of God with n. eyes; 67: 10 man cannot see God with carnal or n. mind; 67: 12 n. man cannot abide presence of God; 88: 28 celestial spirit shall receive same body which was a n. body; 121: 39 n. and disposition of almost all men to exercise unrighteous dominion.

Moses 1: 11 Moses could not behold God with n. eyes; 6: 36 Moses beholds things not visible to n. eye.

NAUGHT *(see also* Nothing; Vain)*

D&C 3: 4 men set at n. God's counsels; 19: 21 preach n. but repentance; 76: 9 understanding of the prudent shall come to n.

NAUVOO, ILLINOIS *(see also* D&C map, p. 297)*

D&C secs. 124–129, 132 revelations received at N.; 124: 27 build temple in N.; 125: 3 build Zarahemla opposite N.; 125: 4 saints to take inheritances in N.

NAUVOO HOUSE

D&C 124: 22–24 (124: 60–82) the Lord directs building of N.H.; 124: 119 only believers in Book of Mormon may put stock in N.H.; 124: 121–122 quorum responsible for building N.H. should receive recompense for labors.

NAVEL

D&C 89: 18 saints who obey Word of Wisdom will receive health to n.

NEAR *(see also* Nigh)*

D&C 88: 63 draw n. unto the Lord and he will draw n. unto you.

JS-H 1: 19 professors of religion draw n. the Lord with lips, but hearts are far from him.

NECESSITY (see also Need; Needful)

D&C 70: 7 if saints receive more than is needful for n., it should be given to storehouse; 101: 8 in day of trouble, of n. the saints feel after the Lord.

NECK (see also Pride; Stiffnecked)

D&C 113: 9–10 (Isa. 52: 2) Zion to loose herself from bands of n.; 121: 22 better that millstone were hanged about n.

Moses 7: 63 people of cities of Holiness and New Jerusalem shall fall upon each others' n.

NEED (see also Necessity; Needful; Needy; Want)

D&C 42: 33 every man who has n. will be amply supplied; 49: 21 wo unto man who wastes flesh and has no n.; 51: 3 bishop to appoint portions according to n. of every man; 84: 83 Father knows thy n.; 84: 110 body has n. of every member.

NEEDFUL (see also Necessity; Need)

D&C 51: 13 (70: 7) all things more than n. should be kept by bishop; 88: 119 (109: 8) prepare every n. thing; 88: 124 cease to sleep longer than is n.; 91: 3 not n. that Apocrypha be translated.

NEEDY (see also Alms; Charity; Hunger; Naked; Need; Orphan; Poor; Relief; Widow)

D&C 38: 35 look to the poor and n.; 42: 37 (51: 5; 72: 12) substance consecrated unto the poor and n. of church; 44: 6 visit the poor and n.; 52: 40 remember the poor and n.; 104: 18 those who do not impart to poor and n. will be in hell.

NEGLECT (see also Diligence; Slothful)

D&C 117: 8 warning against coveting the drop, and n. more weighty matters.

NEHOR (see also BD Nahor)

Abr. 2: 2 brother of Abraham.

NEIGHBOR (see also Brother; Charity; Love)

D&C 19: 25 thou shalt not covet thy n's wife nor seek thy n's life; 38: 41 let preaching be warning voice, every man to his n.; 42: 27 not speak evil of thy n.; 45: 68 every man who will not take sword against his n. must flee to Zion; 52: 19 every man to seek interest of his n.; 88: 81 every man who has been warned should warn his n.; 136: 25 restore that which is borrowed from n.

NEPHI—son of Lehi, great prophet, founder of Nephites [c. 600 B.C.] (see also Nephites; Plates of Nephi, Small)

D&C 98: 32 law of dealing with enemies given to N.

NEPHITES—descendants of Nephi and his followers

D&C 1: 29 Joseph Smith received record of N.; 3: 16–17 knowledge of Savior to come to N.; 3: 18 were destroyed because of iniquities; 38: 39 beware of pride lest ye become as N.

NEW (see also Covenant; Jerusalem, New; New Testament; New York; Renew)

D&C 29: 23 n. heaven and earth after Millennium; 29: 24 (63: 49; 101: 25) all things shall become n.; 130: 11 n. name.

NEW TESTAMENT (see also Bible; Scriptures; BD New Testament)

D&C 45: 60–61 to be translated.

NEW YORK (see also D&C maps, pp. 295, 296, 298)

D&C 84: 114 people of N.Y. to be warned.

JS–H 1: 3 Joseph Smith's family moves to Palmyra, N.Y., then to Manchester, N.Y.; 1: 51 Hill Cumorah near Manchester, N.Y.; 1: 56 Joseph Smith works in Chenango County, N.Y.

NICOLAITANE BAND (see also Secret Combination)

D&C 117: 11 Newel K. Whitney warned to be ashamed of N.b.

NIGH (see also Near)

D&C 1: 12 the Lord is n.; 29: 9–10 (35: 15; 45: 38; 84: 115; 133: 17) hour is n.; 35: 16 summer is now n. at hand; 43: 17 great day of the Lord is n.; 49: 6 (104: 59; 106: 4) time of Christ's coming is n. at hand.

Abr. 3: 9 Kolob is set n. unto throne of God.

NIGHT (see also Darkness, Physical; Darkness, Spiritual)

D&C 45: 19 (106: 4) day of the Lord to come as thief in n.; 133: 56 sing song of Lamb, day and n.

Moses 2: 4–5 (Abr. 4: 5) n. separated from day.

NOAH— patriarch at time of flood (see also BD Noah)

D&C 84: 14–15 priesthood passed through lineage of fathers from Melchizedek to N. to Enoch²; 107: 52 was ordained by Methuselah when ten years old; 133: 54 was among those redeemed; 138: 9, 28 (1 Pet. 3: 20) God's long-suffering waited in days of N.; 138: 41 among mighty ones in world of spirits.

Moses 7: 42 N. and posterity seen by Enoch[2]; 7: 43 builds ark; 7: 49–51 Enoch[2] prays the Lord to have mercy upon N. and his seed; 7: 52 remnant of N's seed always to be found among all nations; 8: 2 the Lord covenanted with Enoch[2] that N. would be fruit of his loins; 8: 3 all kingdoms of earth to come through N.; 8: 9 son of Lamech[2]; 8: 13 N. and sons hearken unto the Lord; 8: 16 prophesies and teaches things of God; 8: 19 is ordained after God's own order; 8: 20, 23–24 cries repentance; 8: 25 (Gen. 6: 6) it repented N. that the Lord had made man; 8: 27 finds grace in eyes of the Lord; 8: 27 a just man, and perfect; 8: 27 N. and three sons walk with God; **Abr.** 1: 19 as it was with N., so shall it be with Abraham; 1: 27 Pharaohs claim priesthood from N. through Ham; **JS–M** 1: 41–42 as it was in days of N., so shall it be at coming of Son.

NOBLE (see also Honorable; Nobleman; Valiant)

D&C 58: 9–10 the wise and n. to be invited to supper in house of the Lord; 122: 2 the wise and n. shall seek counsel from Joseph Smith; 138: 55 n. spirits chosen in beginning to be rulers in church.

Abr. 3: 22 wherein are many n. and great ones.

NOBLEMAN

D&C 101: 44–62 parable of n. and vineyard.

NOD, LAND OF

Moses 5: 41 Cain and family dwell in.

NOON-DAY (see also Light)

D&C 95: 6 those not chosen sinned grievous sin in walking in darkness at n.

NORTH, NORTHERN (see also Israel, Ten Lost Tribes of)

D&C 87: 3 n. states to be divided against southern states; 110: 11 (133: 26) ten tribes to come from n. country; 133: 23 great deep driven back to n. countries; 133: 26 those in n. are to be remembered.

Moses 7: 6 Enoch[2] looks to n. and beholds people of Canaan.

NOTHING (see also Humble; Naught)

D&C 6: 9 (11: 9) say n. but repent-ance to this generation; 8: 10 (18: 19) without faith you can do n.; 59: 21 in n. does man offend God except in failing to confess his hand in all things.

Moses 1: 10 Moses knows that man is n.; **Abr.** 3: 17 n. that the Lord shall take in his heart to do but what he will do it.

NOURISH (see also Feed; Food; Health; Strengthen)

D&C 42: 43 those who have not faith to be healed should be n. with all tenderness.

NUMBER (see also Innumerable)

D&C 132: 30 like sands on seashore, Abraham's seed could not be n.

Moses 1: 33 the Lord has created worlds without n.; 1: 35, 37 all things are n. unto the Lord; 1: 37 heavens cannot be n. unto man; 7: 30 if man could n. particles of earth, it would not be beginning of n. of the Lord's creations; **Abr.** 3: 14 n. of Abraham's seeds shall be as n. of sands.

OATH (see also Covenant; Priesthood; Promise; Secret Combination; Swear; Vow)

D&C 84: 33–41 o. and covenant of the priesthood; 124: 47 if saints do not do what the Lord says, he will not perform the o. which he makes; 132: 7 all o. not sealed by Holy Spirit of promise are of no force in and after resurrection.

Moses 5: 50 Lamech[3] slays Irad for o's sake; 6: 29 by their o. men have brought upon themselves death; 7: 51, 60 the Lord swears unto Enoch[2] with o. to stay the floods and call upon children of Noah[1].

OATS (see also Grain)

D&C 89: 17 for the horse.

OBEDIENCE, OBEDIENT, OBEY (see also Abide; Agency; Baptism; Blessing; Commandments of God; Diligence; Disobedience; Do; Duty; Endure; Faith; Faithful; Fear of God; Follow; Gospel; Hearken; Heed; Humble; Keep; Law; Observe; Steadfast; TG Obedience, Obedient, Obey)

D&C 28: 3 be o. to things revealed through prophet; 29: 45 men receive wages of whom they list to o.; 52: 15 he who o. ordinances is accepted; 56: 34 he who will not o. shall be cut off; 58: 2 blessed are the o.; 58: 6 saints sent to Missouri that they might be o.; 58: 30 the Lord will not hold him guiltless who does not o. commandments; 58: 32 the Lord commands, but men o. not; 59: 3 those in Zion who o. gospel will receive good things of earth; 59: 21 men offend God by not o. his commandments; 63: 5 the Lord utters his voice, and it shall be o.; 64: 5 Joseph Smith given keys of mysteries inasmuch as he o. ordinances; 64: 34 the o. shall eat good of land of Zion in last days; 84: 44 live by every word that proceeds from God; 89: 18 all saints who walk in o. to commandments will receive health; 93: 1 every soul who o. the Lord's voice shall see his face; 103: 4 parable showing necessity of o.; 105: 6 people must be chastened until they learn o.; 130: 19 knowledge and intelligence gained by o.; 130: 21 blessing obtained by o. to law upon which it is predicated; 133: 71 none to deliver those who o. not the Lord's voice when he called; 138: 4 mankind may be saved through atonement and o.; 138: 58 repentant dead redeemed through o. to ordinances of temple.

Moses 5: 11 eternal life given to the o.; **Abr.** 4: 10, 21 the Gods saw that they were o.; 4: 18 the Gods watched those things they had ordered until they o.; **A of F** 3 mankind may be saved by o. to laws and ordinances of gospel; 12 we believe in o., honoring, and sustaining the law.

OBLATION (see also Offering; Sacrifice)

D&C 59: 12 offer o. and sacraments on the Lord's day.

OBSCURITY (see also Darkness, Spiritual)

D&C 1: 30 church to be brought forth out of o.

OBSERVE (see also Obedience; Perform)

D&C 42: 13 o. the covenants and church articles to do them; 68: 33 he who o. not his prayers should be had in remembrance before judge; 97: 8 those who are willing to o. their covenants by sacrifice are accepted of the Lord; 98: 10 o. to uphold good men and wise men; 103: 7 by hearkening to o. all the Lord's words, saints will never cease to prevail; 119: 5 those who gather unto land of Zion shall o. law of tithing.

OBTAIN (see also Attain; Receive)

D&C 11: 21 o. word before declaring it; 78: 6 if saints not equal in earthly things, they cannot be equal in o. heavenly things; 84: 33 he who o. the two priesthoods enters oath and covenants of priesthood; 109: 15 those who worship in temple will be prepared to o. every needful thing.

OCCASION (see also Contention)

D&C 64: 8 disciples in days of old sought o. against one another and forgave not.

OFFEND, OFFENDER (see also Anger; Offense)

D&C 42: 88 if brother or sister o., reconcile privately; 42: 89 (64: 12) if person who o. confess not, deliver matter to church; 42: 90 those who o. many should be chastened before many; 42: 91 those who o. openly should be rebuked openly; 42: 92 those who o. in secret shall be rebuked in secret; 59: 21 man o. God by not confessing his hand in all things; 64: 13 elders should avoid o. lawgiver; 121: 19 those who o. the Lord's little ones shall be cut off from ordinances of his house; 134: 8 men should bring o. against good laws to punishment.

OFFENSE (see also Crime; Offend; Transgress; Trespass)

D&C 54: 5 wo to him by whom this o. comes; 134: 1 commission of crime should be punished according to nature of o.; 134: 8 crimes should be punished by government in which o. was committed.

OFFERING, OFFER (see also Altar; Broken Heart and Contrite Spirit; Give; Jesus Christ, Atonement through; Law of Moses; Oblation; Sacrifice)

D&C 13: 1 (128: 24) sons of Levi[1] shall offer unto the Lord an o. in righteousness; 59: 9 saints to o. sacraments in house of prayer; 84: 31 sons of Moses and Aaron shall offer acceptable o.; 95: 16 part of temple to be dedicated for sacrament o. and o. of holy desires; 97: 27 (105: 19) o. of Zion accepted; 101: 4 (132: 36) Abraham commanded to o. Isaac; 124: 49 the Lord will accept incomplete o. if saints be hindered by enemies; 132: 9 the Lord will not accept of o. not made in his name; 132: 51 the Lord requires o. by covenant and sacrifice.

Moses 5: 6 angel asks Adam why he o. sacrifices to the Lord; 5: 18 Satan commands Cain to make o. unto the Lord; 5: 19 Cain brings fruit of ground as o. to the Lord; 5: 20-21 the Lord respects Abel's o., but not Cain's; **Abr.** 1: 8-11 Pharaoh o. human sacrifice to strange gods; 1: 15 priests try to o. Abraham as sacrifice; 2: 17-18 Abraham makes o. to the Lord; **JS-H** 1: 15 Joseph Smith o. up desire of heart to God; 1: 69 priesthood never to be taken until sons of Levi[1] o. an o. unto the Lord.

OFFICE (see also Authority; Calling; Duty; Ministry; Officer; Ordain; Priesthood)

D&C 20: 65 no person is to be ordained to any o. without vote of church; 24: 3, 9 (66: 11) magnify thine o.; 24: 9 (66: 11) attend to thy calling and thou shalt have wherewith to magnify thine o.; 38: 23 teach one another according to appointed o.; 54: 2 (58: 40; 81: 5) stand fast in o. whereunto the Lord has appointed you; 68: 18 no man has legal right to o. of bishop except literal descendant and firstborn of Aaron¹; 68: 19 (107: 17) high priest has authority to officiate in all lesser o.; 78: 12 he who breaks covenant shall lose his o.; 84: 29–30 o. of elder, bishop, teacher, deacon necessary; 84: 109 let every man stand in own o.; 107: 5 other o. are appendages to priesthood; 107: 8 Melchizedek Priesthood has authority over all o. in church; 107: 9 Presidency has right to officiate in all o. in church; 107: 60–62, 85, 89 quorum president called to preside over o. of elder, priest, teacher, deacon; 107: 98 other officers do not travel, but they may hold as high and responsible o. in the church; 107: 99 let every man learn to act in o. in which he is appointed; 124: 143 why o. in the priesthood are given.

OFFICER (see also Authorities; Church of God; Government, Civil; Minister [noun]; Office; Priesthood)

D&C 88: 127 school of prophets established for all o. of church; 107: 21 there are presidents, or presiding o.; 107: 58 duty of the Twelve to ordain all other o.; 124: 123 the Lord gives keys to o. belonging to his priesthood; 134: 3 all governments require civil o.

OHIO (see also Kirtland, Ohio; D&C maps, pp. 296, 298)

D&C sec. 37 (38: 32) church to assemble at the O.; 48: Intro. saints to assemble in O.; 51: Intro. settlement of saints in O.; 58: 49 church agent in O.

OIL

D&C 33: 17 the wise have lamps trimmed and have o. with them.

OLAHA SHINEHAH, PLAINS OF

D&C 117: 8 plains of O.S., land where Adam dwelt.

OLD (see also Age; Ancient; Old Testament)

D&C 1: 16 men walk after own God, whose substance is that of idol which waxes o.; 29: 24 (63: 49) o. things to pass away; 43: 20 both o. and young should repent; 63: 51 (101: 30) during Millennium children will grow up until they become o.

OLD TESTAMENT (see also Bible; Scriptures; BD Old Testament)

JS-H 1: 36–41 O.T. prophecies quoted by Moroni² to Joseph Smith.

OLEA (see Moon)

OLIBLISH

Abr. Fac. 2, fig. 2 great governing creation next to Kolob.

OLIMLAH

Abr. Fac. 3, fig. 6 a slave belonging to the prince.

OLISHEM, PLAINS OF

Abr. 1: 10 sacrifices offered on altar standing by Potiphar's Hill, at head of plain of O.

OLIVE (see also Tree; BD Olive Tree)

D&C sec. 88 revelation designated as O. Leaf; 101: 44–62 parable of nobleman and o. trees.

OLIVET, MOUNT OF (see also BD Olives, Mount of, or Olivet)

D&C 133: 20 Bridegroom shall stand upon mount of O.

OMEGA (see Alpha)

OMNER, LAND OF

Moses 7: 9 Enoch² beholds land of O.

OMNIPOTENT (see God, Power of)

ONE (see also Unanimous; Unite, Unity)

D&C 18: 15 if you bring o. soul unto me, how great shall be your joy; 20: 28 (35: 2; 50: 43; 93: 3) Father, Son, and Holy Ghost are o. God; 27: 13 the Lord will gather in o. all things; 29: 13 the dead to be with the Lord, that they may be o.; 38: 27 if ye are not o., ye are not mine; 42: 9 saints to be gathered in o. in New Jerusalem; 51: 9 all men to receive alike, that they may be o.; 61: 18, 36 (93: 49) what I say unto o. I say unto all; 121: 28 whether there be o. God or many gods, they shall be manifest.

ONITAH

Abr. 1: 11 daughters of O. are sacrificed to idols.

ONLY BEGOTTEN (see Jesus Christ — Only Begotten Son)

OPEN (see also Answer; Openly)

D&C 4: 7 (66: 5; 11: 5; 12: 5; 14: 5; 88: 63) knock and it shall be o.; 28: 16 o. thy mouth at all times, declaring gospel; 29: 26 (88: 97; 133: 56) graves to be o.; 58: 52 the Lord wills that disciples and men should o. hearts; 60: 2 the Lord not pleased with elders who o. not their mouths; 76: 12 by power of Spirit our eyes were o.; 77: 13 sixth and seventh seals to be o.; 84: 69 those who believe shall o. eyes of blind in the Lord's name; 93: 15 heavens were o., and Holy Ghost descended upon Christ; 100: 3 (118: 3) an effectual door shall be o.; 101: 92 pray that ears of wicked may be o.; 107: 19 power of Melchizedek Priesthood is to have heavens o. unto them; 110: 11 (137: 1) heavens were o. unto us; 128: 6–7 that we the dead and books were o.; 138: 11, 29 eyes of understanding were o.

Moses 7: 3 heavens o., and Enoch² is clothed with glory; **JS-H** 1: 42 vision is o. to Joseph Smith showing where plates are deposited.

OPENLY (see also Open)

D&C 42: 91 if any one offend o., he or she shall be rebuked o.

OPERATION

D&C 46: 16 spiritual gift of knowing diversities of o.

OPINION (see also Belief)

D&C 134: 7 governments do not have a right to proscribe their citizens in their o.

OPPRESSION, OPPRESS (see also Affliction; Injustice; Oppressor; Persecution; Suffering; Tribulation; Trial, Try)

D&C 109: 48 saints have been greatly o. by wicked men; 109: 67 scattered remnants of Israel to be redeemed from o.; 121: 3 how long shall the Lord's people suffer unlawful o.; 123: 3 saints to gather names of those who have had hand in their o.; 124: 53 consolation of those who have been hindered by o.

OPPRESSOR (see also Oppression)

D&C 124: 8 portion of o. among hypocrites; 127: 3 just recompense to o.

ORACLE (see also Prophecy)

D&C 90: 4 through prophets the o. shall be given to church; 90: 5 all who receive o. of God must not account them a light thing; 124: 39 o. in most holy places wherein you receive conversations are ordained by ordinance; 124: 126 First Presidency to receive o. for whole church.

ORANGE, OHIO (see also D&C map, p. 296)

D&C sec. 66 revelation at.

ORDAIN, ORDINATION (see also Appoint; Authority; Confer; Decree; Hands, Laying on of; Office; Ordinance; Priesthood; TG Priesthood, Ordination)

D&C 5: 6 Joseph to be o. to preach; 5: 17 wait, for ye are not yet o.; 13: 1 (27: 8) o. of Joseph Smith and Oliver Cowdery to Aaronic Priesthood; 18: 29 the Twelve are o. to baptize; 18: 32 (20: 39; 107: 39, 58) the Twelve are o. to o. officers in church, 20. 2 (27: 12) Joseph Smith has been o. an apostle of Jesus Christ; 20: 60 priesthood bearers are o. according to gifts and callings of God; 20: 60 priesthood bearer to be o. by power of Holy Ghost, which is in the one who o. him; 20: 64–67 procedures for o. to priesthood offices; 20: 65 no person is to be o. without vote of church; 20: 60 those who have privilege of o. where there is no priesthood, bishop, high councilor, and high priest to be o. by direction of high council or general conference; 27: 12 Joseph Smith and Oliver Cowdery have been o. apostles by Peter, James, and John; 36: 5 men to be o. and sent forth to preach gospel; 36: 7 those who embrace gospel with singleness of heart should be o.; 42: 11 no one to preach or build church unless o. by one in authority; 43: 7 he who is o. of God should be o. as the Lord said; 49: 15 whoso forbids to marry is not o. of God; 49: 19 things of earth are o. for use of man for food and raiment; 50: 13–14 elders are o. to preach gospel by Spirit; 50: 26–27 all things subject to him who is o.; 53: 3 o. of elder to preach faith and repentance; 63: 45 agent to be o.; 63: 57 those who desire to warn sinner to repent are to be o.; 67: 10 those o. to ministry shall know God; 68: 2–4 those o. to priesthood shall speak as moved by Spirit; 68: 19 (107: 17) high priest may serve as bishop if he is called, set apart, and o. to this power; 68: 20 literal descendants of Aaron must be o. to be legally authorized; 70: 3 the Lord appoints and o. stewards of revelations; 76: 13 we saw things of God which were from beginning o. of Father through Son; 76: 48 no one understands the end of sons of perdition except those who are o. to this condemnation; 76: 52 those in celestial glory received Holy Spirit by laying on of hands of one who is o.; 77: 11 144,000 o. unto holy order of God to bring souls to church; 78: 2 Joseph Smith o. from on high; 84: 28 John was o. by angel when eight days old; 89: 10 God has o. wholesome herbs for use of man; 90: 11 every man to hear gospel through those who are o. unto this power; 95: 5 many among saints have been o. or called, but few are chosen; 107: 22 three Presiding High Priests o. to that office form quorum of Presidency of Church; 107: 29 quorums of three presidents o. after order of Melchizedek; 112: 1 brethren o. through instrumentality of the Lord's servants; 121: 32 that which was o. in premortal council; 124: 34 in the Lord's house are keys of holy priesthood o.; 124: 134–135 men are o. for standing presidents over stakes; 124: 137 elders are o. to be standing ministers.

Moses 8: 19 Noah¹ is o. by the Lord; **Abr.** 1: 2 Abraham seeks the right whereunto he should be o. to administer blessings of fathers; **JS-H** 1: 68–72 Joseph Smith and Oliver Cowdery o. each other to Aaronic Priesthood.

ORDER (see also Authority; Confusion; Consecration, Law of; Govern; Head; Law; Organize; Priesthood; Priesthood, Melchizedek; Regulate; Unite; United Order; TG Order)

D&C 20: 68 (28: 13; 58: 55; 107: 84) all things to be done in o. and by common consent; 76: 57 celestial heirs are priests after o. of Melchizedek; 77: 3 beasts necessary classes of beings in their destined o.; 78: 3–4 need for organization for o. unto church; 82: 20 the Lord appoints everlasting o.; 85: 7 set in o. the house of God; 88: 58–60 every servant receives light of his lord's countenance in his own o.; 88: 119 (109: 8; 132: 8) establish a house of o.; 90: 15–16 First Presidency to set in o. all affairs of church; 90: 18 (93: 43) set houses in o.; 93: 50 set family in o.; 94: 6 house to be dedicated to the Lord according to o. of priesthood; 107: 3–4 (124: 123) Melchizedek Priesthood called Holy Priesthood, after O. of Son of God; 107: 10 high priests after o. of Melchizedek Priesthood have right to officiate; 107: 40 o. of Melchizedek Priesthood confirmed to be handed down from father to son; 107: 41 this o. of priesthood was instituted in days of Adam; 107: 93 o. of the Seventy to have seven presidents; 127: 9 all the records to be had in o.; 129: 7 contrary to o. of heaven for just men to deceive; 130: 9 all things pertaining to kingdoms of lower o. will be manifest; 130: 10 things pertaining to higher o. of kingdoms will be made known by Urim and Thummim; 131: 2 man must enter in this o. of priesthood to obtain highest degree of celestial kingdom; 132: 8 the Lord's house is house of o.

Moses 6: 67 Adam is after o. of him who is without beginning of days or end of years; 8: 19 the Lord ordains Noah¹ after his own o.; **Abr.** 1: 26 Pharaoh seeks to imitate o. established by fathers.

ORDINANCE (see also Administration to the Sick; Anointing; Authority; Baptism; Blessing; Confer; Confirm; Covenant; Endow; Hands, Laying on of; Heal; Holy Ghost, Gift of; Law; Ordain; Priesthood; Priesthood, Melchizedek; Sacrament; Sacrifice; Statute; Temple; TG Ordinance)

D&C 1: 15 men have strayed from the Lord's o.; 52: 15–16 the Lord accepts those who obey his o.; 64: 5 Joseph Smith given keys of mysteries if he obeys o.; 77: 14 (Rev. 10: 2, 9–10) John's little book was a mission and an o. to gather Israel; 84: 20–21 in o. of Melchizedek Priesthood is power of godliness manifest; 88: 139–140 o. of washing of feet instituted to receive men into school of prophets; 107: 14, 20 Aaronic Priesthood to administer outward o.; 121: 19 persecutors of saints to be severed from o. of the Lord's house; 124: 33 build a house wherein o. of baptizing for the dead belongs; 124: 38–40 the Lord will reveal o. in his house; 128: 3 nature of o. of baptism for dead consists in binding power of priesthood; 136: 4 saints to covenant that they will walk in all the Lord's o.; 138: 54 great latter-day work to include temple o.; 138: 58 repentant dead redeemed through obedience to temple o.

Moses 5: 59 all things commanded by holy o.; **A of F** 3 all mankind may be saved by obedience to laws and o. of gospel; 4 first principles and o. of gospel; 5 man must be called of God to administer o. of gospel.

ORGANIZE, ORGANIZATION (see also Creation; Establish; Order; Regulate; TG Church Organization)

D&C 20: 1 church o. agreeable to laws of country; sec. 21 revelation at o. of church; 51: 2, 15 the Lord's people to be o. according to his laws; 78: 3 need for o. to regulate storehouse; 78: 11 saints to prepare and o. themselves by covenant; 88: 74, 119 (104: 11; 109: 8) o. yourselves; 102: 24 high priests, when abroad, have power to call and o. a council; 104: 1 the Lord commanded that United Order be o.; 136: 2 saints to o. into companies with covenant; 138: 30 the Lord o. his forces in spirit world.

Abr. 3: 22 the Lord shows Abraham intelligences that were o. before world was; 4: 1 the Gods o. and formed heavens and earth; 4: 27 the Gods o. man in their own image.

ORIGINAL (see Guilt)

ORPHAN (see also Needy)

D&C 83: 6 widows and o. shall be provided for; 123: 9 (136: 8) imperative duty owed to widows and fatherless.

OUTER (see Darkness, Spiritual; Outward)

OUTWARD (see also Temporal)

D&C 107: 14 lesser priesthood has power in administering o. ordinances.

OVEN (see also Heat)

D&C 133: 64 (Mal. 4: 1) day comes that shall burn as o.

JS-H 1: 37 day comes that shall burn as o.

OVERCOME (see also Conquer; Overpower; Prevail)

D&C 38: 9 enemy shall not o.; 50: 35 power to o. all things not ordained of God is given to those who obey; 50: 41 the Lord's servants shall o. world; 61: 9 through faith the Lord's servants shall o. all; 63: 20 he who endures to end shall o.; 63: 47 he who is faithful shall o. world; 64: 2 the Lord wills that elders should o. world; 76: 30 sufferings of those whom Satan o.; 76: 53, 60 those who o. by faith shall come forth in resurrection of just; 76: 107 (88: 106) the Lord has o. and has trodden wine-press alone.

JS-H 1: 15 power of darkness o. Joseph Smith.

OVERFLOWING (see Scourge)

OVERPOWER (see also Overcome; Overthrow)

D&C 10: 33 Satan thinks to o. your testimony.

OVERTAKE, OVERTAKEN

D&C 20: 80 members o. in a fault should be dealt with as scriptures direct; 45: 2 hearken unto the Lord's voice, lest death o. you; 106: 4 coming of the Lord will o. world as thief in night.

OVERTHROW (see also Conquer; Destruction; Overcome)

D&C 50: 3 Satan seeks to deceive men that he might o. them; 64: 21 the Lord will not o. the wicked for five years; 84: 28 John given power to o. kingdom of Jews; 117: 16 o. the moneychangers.

OWE (see also Debt; Duty)

D&C 134: 6 all men o. respect to law.

OX (see also Animal; Cattle)

D&C 89: 17 corn for o.

PACKARD, NOAH

D&C 124: 136 counselor in high priests quorum.

PAGE, HIRAM

D&C sec. 28 revelation concerning; 28: 11 things written by H.P. from stone are of Satan.

PAGE, JOHN E.

D&C 118: 6 (124: 129) is called to fill position among the Twelve.

PAID (see Pay, Paid)

PAIN (see also Affliction; Anguish; Grieve; Suffering; Torment)

D&C 18: 11 the Lord suffered the p. of all men; 19: 18 suffering caused God to tremble because of p. and to bleed at every pore; 38: 12 all eternity is p. because darkness reigns; 133: 35 after their p. the tribe of Judah shall be sanctified.

Moses 7: 48 earth is p. because of wickedness of children; 8: 25 heart of Noah¹ is p. because the Lord made man.

PALACE

D&C 124: 2 Zion shall be polished with refinement after similitude of p.

PALMS

D&C 109: 76 saints shall be clothed with p. in their hands.

PALMYRA, NEW YORK (see also D&C map, p. 296)

JS-H 1: 3 Joseph Smith's family moves to P.; 1: 61 Martin Harris is a resident of P.

PALSY (see also Shake)

D&C 123: 10 dark deeds make hands of devil p.

PARABLE (see also Liken; BD Parables)

D&C 35: 16 (45: 36-38) p. of fig-tree; 38: 26-27 the Lord gives p. to teach unity; 45: 56 (63: 54) p. of ten virgins to be fulfilled at the Lord's coming; 86: 1-7 (101: 65-67) the Lord explains p. of wheat and tares; 88: 51-61 the Lord likens kingdoms in heavens to p. of man who sends servants to dig in field; 101: 43-62 p. of nobleman and tower; 101: 81-91 the Lord likens children of Zion to p. of woman and unjust judge; 103: 21 Joseph Smith is servant referred to in p.

JS-M 1: 17 (Matt. 24: 28) p. of eagles gathering where carcase is; 1: 38 (Matt. 24: 32) p. of fig-tree putting forth leaves when summer is nigh.

PARADISE (see also Death, Physical; Eden, Garden of; Heaven; Prison; Rest; Resurrection; Spirit World; TG Paradise, Paradisiacal; BD Paradise)

D&C 77: 2 beasts are figurative expressions in describing heaven, the *p.* of God; 138: 12 spirits of the just are gathered in one place in spirit world.

PARDON (see also Excuse; Forgive; Remission)

D&C 56: 14 saints' sins are not *p.* because they seek to counsel in own ways.

PARENT (see also Child; Family; Father; Mother; TG Family, Children, Responsibilities toward; Honoring Father and Mother; Marriage, Fatherhood; Marriage, Motherhood)

D&C 68: 25–28 *p.* are responsible for teaching children the gospel; 83: 4–5 all children have claim upon their *p.* for maintenance; 138: 48 children to be sealed to *p.* during fulness of times.

Moses 6: 54 because of Christ's atonement, sins of *p.* cannot be answered upon heads of children.

PART (see also Partake; Portion)

D&C 29: 36 Satan turned away a third *p.* of host's of heaven; 45: 54 (63: 18; 76: 64) he who has *p.* in first resurrection; 49: 2 Shakers desire to know the truth in *p.*; 88: 99 some receive *p.* in prison prepared that they might receive gospel.

PARTAKE, PARTAKEN, PARTAKER (see also Drink; Eat; Inherit; Receive; Taste)

D&C 10: 66 *p.* of waters of life; 20: 75 saints to meet together often to *p.* of sacrament; 27: 2 it matters not what saints eat or drink when they *p.* of sacrament; 46: 4 trespasser should not *p.* of sacrament until he makes reconciliation; 66: 2 gospel sent forth that men might be *p.* of glories to be revealed; 93: 22 those begotten through Christ are *p.* of Father's glory; 101: 35 all who endure persecution for the Lord's name with *p.* of glory.

Moses 4: 28 Adam should not *p.* of tree of life; 6: 48 by Adam's fall are made *p.* of misery; Abr. 1: 21 Pharaoh a *p.* of blood of Canaanites by birth.

PARTICLES (see also Number)

PARTRIDGE, EDWARD

D&C secs. 36, 51 revelations to; 36: 1 sins are forgiven; 36: 1 is called to preach gospel; 36: 2 to receive Spirit from Sidney Rigdon; 41: 9 to be ordained bishop unto church; 41: 11 E.P.'s heart

is pure as Nathanael's; 42: 10 to stand in appointed office; 50: 39 (58: 14–15; 64: 17) warned to repent; 51: 1–18 is directed how to organize people; 51: 3 (57: 7) to appoint portions unto people; 52: 24 (58: 24) to journey to Missouri; 58: 62 to direct conference; 60: 10 to provide money for elders' return; sec. 115 revelation addressed to E.P. and counselors; 124: 19 is with the Lord.

PASS (see also Cease; End; Judgment; Past)

D&C 1: 38 (56: 11) the Lord's word shall not *p.* away; 29: 23, 26 (43: 32; 45: 22; 56: 11) heaven and earth shall *p.* away; 29: 24 (63: 49) all old things shall *p.* away; 38: 20 saints to possess earth in eternity, no more to *p.* away; 45: 21 this generation of Jews shall not *p.* away until desolation comes; 84: 5 this generation shall not all *p.* away until house shall be built unto the Lord; 89: 21 destroying angel shall *p.* by those who observe Word of Wisdom; 97: 23 the Lord's scourge shall *p.* over by night and by day; 122: 9 bounds of oppressors are set, they cannot *p.*; 132: 18–19 angels and gods are appointed by whom men must *p.*

PASSOVER (see TG Passover; BD Passover)

PAST (see also Pass; Present [adj.])

D&C 45: 2 when ye think not, summer shall be *p.* and your soul not saved; 56: 16 harvest is *p.* and soul is not saved; 130: 7 all things are manifest, *p.*, present, and future.

PASTOR (see also Bishop; TG Pastor)

A of F 6 organization of primitive church included *p.*

PATH (see also Course; Direction; Highway; Street; Walk; Way)

D&C 3: 2 God does not walk in crooked *p.*; 25: 2 walk in *p.* of virtue; 33: 10 (65: 1; 133: 11) make the Lord's *p.* straight; 112: 7 thy *p.* lieth among mountains, among many nations.

PATIENCE, PATIENT, PATIENTLY (see also Affliction; Experience; Humble; Long-suffering)

D&C 4: 6 remember faith, virtue, *p.*; 6: 19 (11: 19) be *p.*, sober; 21: 5 church to receive Joseph Smith's word in all *p.*; 24: 8 (31: 9; 54: 10; 66: 9; 98: 23–24) be *p.* in afflictions; 63: 66 these things remain to overcome through *p.*; 67: 13 continue in *p.* until ye are perfected; 98: 2 wait *p.* on the Lord; 98: 26 he who bears smitings *p.* shall receive double reward; 101: 38 in *p.* ye may possess your souls; 107: 30 decisions are to be made in p.; 127: 4 p. to be redoubled.

PATRIARCH, PATRIARCHAL (see also Father; Lineage; Priesthood; Priesthood, Melchizedek; BD Patriarch, Patriarchs)

D&C 107: 39 duty of the Twelve to ordain p.; 107: 40–52 succession in order of p.; 124: 91 (124: 124; 135: 1) Hyrum Smith to take office of p.

Abr. 1: 25 first government of Egypt was after order of Ham's government, which was p.; 1: 31 the Lord preserved records of p.

PATTEN, DAVID W.

D&C 114: 1 called to settle business and perform mission; 124: 19, 130 has been taken unto the Lord himself.

PATTERN (see also Example)

D&C 24: 19 those ordained shall do according to this p.; 52: 14 the Lord gives p. in all things; 52: 19 p. for knowing spirits; 88: 141 ordinance of washing of feet to follow p. given in John's testimony; 94: 2 city must be built according to p. given by the Lord; 97: 10 (115: 14) house should be built like unto p. given by the Lord; 102: 12 high council regularly organized according to the foregoing p.

Moses 6: 46 book of remembrance written according to p. given by God.

PAUL THE APOSTLE (see also Corinthians, First; BD Paul)

D&C 18: 9 Oliver Cowdery and David Whitmer are called with same calling as P.; 76: 99 these are they who are of P.; 128: 13–16 teachings of P. explained.

JS-H 1: 24 Joseph Smith feels much like P.; A of F 13 we follow the admonition of P.

PAVILION

D&C 121: 1, 4 where is p. that covers God's hiding place.

PAY, PAID (see also Debt; Recompense; Reward; Tithing; Wages)

D&C 42: 54 p. for what is received; 64: 28 the Lord should p. as seemeth him good.

PEACE (see also Calm; Peaceable; Rest; War; TG Peace of God)

D&C 1: 35 p. shall be taken from the earth; 6: 23 the Lord speaks p. to the mind; 10: 37 (11: 22) Joseph Smith is commanded to hold his p. until the Lord makes things known to world; 19: 23 he who walks in meekness of Spirit shall

have p. in the Lord; 27: 16 preparation of the gospel of p.; 45: 46 if ye have slept in p., blessed are you; 45: 66 New Jerusalem, a land of p.; 59: 23 he who does works of righteousness shall have p.; 84: 102 God is full of p.; 88: 125 charity is bond of perfectness and p.; 98: 16 renounce war and proclaim p.; 98: 34 (105: 39) lift standard of p.; 105: 38 sue for p.; 111: 8 place to tarry shall be p.; 121: 7 p. be unto thy soul; 134: 2 no government can exist in p. without laws securing rights; 134: 8 for the public p., men should bring offenders to punishment; 138: 22 among righteous spirits there is p.

Moses 7: 31 naught but p., justice, and truth is habitation of the Lord's throne; Abr. 1: 2 Abraham finds there is great p. for him.

PEACEABLE, PEACEABLY (see also Peace)

D&C 36: 2 Holy Ghost leadeth p. things of kingdom; 42: 61 thou shalt receive revelation to know mysteries and p. things of kingdom; 42: 61 p. things of kingdom bring joy and life eternal.

Moses 6: 61 p. things of immortal glory abide in you.

PEARL

D&C 41: 6 do not cast p. before swine.

PENALTY (see also Punishment)

D&C 82: 4 justice and judgment are p. affixed to the Lord's law; 138: 59 the dead receive reward after paying p. for transgression.

PENETRATE (see also Pierce)

D&C 1: 2 no heart that shall not be p.; 121: 2 how long shall thy ear be p. with saints' cries.

PENTECOST (see also BD Pentecost)

D&C 109: 36 let it be fulfilled upon the Lord's ministers as on day of p.

PEOPLE (see also Nation)

D&C 1: 4 (7: 3; 42: 58; 133: 37) warning and teaching to all p.; 42: 9 I will take you to me for a p.; 42: 58 (77: 8, 11; 88: 103; 90: 15; 98: 33, 36; 112: 1; 133: 37) all nations, kindreds, tongues, and p.; 43: 14 (100: 16) the Lord to reserve unto himself a pure p.; 45: 69 Zion shall be only p. not at war one with another; 84: 101 the Lord stands in midst of his p.; 98: 9 when the wicked rule, the p. mourn; 132: 34 from Hagar sprang many p.; 136: 31 the Lord's p. must be tried.

Moses 7: 18 the Lord calls his p. Zion.

PERCEIVE (see also Comprehend; Discern; Know; See; Understand)

D&C 45: 29 they who sit in darkness *p.* not the light; 133: 45 since beginning of world men have not *p.* how great things God has prepared.

PERDITION (see also Sons of Perdition)

D&C 76: 26 Satan is called *P.*
Moses 5: 24 Cain to be called *P.*

PERFECT, PERFECTED, PERFECTION (see also Godliness; Just; Righteous; Uprightness; TG Perfection)

D&C 50: 24 light grows brighter until *p.* day; 59: 13 food to be prepared with singleness of heart that thy fasting may be *p.*; 67: 13 continue in patience until ye are *p.*; 76: 69 (129: 3) celestial glory inherited by just men made *p.* through Jesus; 76: 106 fulness of times when Christ shall have *p.* his work; 84: 110 body has need of every member that system may be kept *p.*; 88: 34 that which is governed by law is *p.* by law; 88: 78 teach diligently, that you may be instructed more *p.*; 90: 8 those in school of prophets to be *p.* in ministry for salvation of Zion; 105: 10 the Lord's people to be taught more *p.*; 107: 43 Seth was a *p.* man; 124: 143 offices in church given for work of ministry and the *p.* of the saints; 128: 15, 18 the living are not *p.* without their dead; 138: 17 sleeping dust of dead to be restored to *p.* frame.

Moses 8: 27 Noah[1] was *p.* in his generation.

PERFORM, PERFORMANCE (see also Do; Duty; Fulfil; Observe; Undertake)

D&C 132: 7 all *p.* not sealed by Holy Spirit of promise are of no force in and after resurrection.

PERIL (see also Calamity; Danger)

D&C 29: 3 sin no more, lest *p.* shall come; 122: 5 if thou art in *p.* among false brethren, it shall be for thy good; 127: 2 *p.* seems but a small thing.

PERISH (see also Destruction; Die)

D&C 1: 16 men walk after own God, whose substance is that of an idol, which shall *p.*; 4: he who thrusts in sickle lays up in store that he *p.* not; 76: 9 wisdom of the wise shall *p.*

Moses 7: 1 many have believed not, and *p.* in sins; 7: 38 prison prepared for those who *p.* in flood; Abr. 2: 17 Abraham prays that famine be turned away, that father's house *p.* not.

PERMIT (see also Suffer)

D&C 101: 99 saints to hold claim upon land given them, though they should not be *p.* to dwell thereon; 109: 20 no unclean thing shall be *p.* to come into the Lord's house; 132: 4 no one can reject covenant and be *p.* to enter into the Lord's glory.

PERPLEXITIES (see also Calamity; War)

D&C 88: 78–79 saints to be instructed regarding wars and *p.* of nations.

PERRYSBURG, N.Y. (see also D&C map, p. 296)

D&C sec. 100 revelation given at.

PERSECUTION, PERSECUTE (see also Affliction; Chasten; Hate; Martyrdom; Mock; Oppression; Prejudice; Revile; Scourge; Smite; Tread; Tribulation; Trial, Try; Violence)

D&C 24: 16 those who *p.* violently will be smitten; 24: 17 whosoever shall go to law against the Lord's servants shall be cursed by law; 40: 2 fear of *p.* caused James Covill to reject the word; 45: 53 Jews shall lament because they *p.* their king; 88: 94 great church *p.* saints of God; 98: Intro. (101: Intro.) *p.* of saints in Missouri; 98: 23–27 elders will be rewarded if they bear *p.* patiently; 99: 1 proclaim gospel in midst of *p.*; 101: 1–2 brethren have been afflicted and be *p.* because of transgressions; 101: 35 they who endure *p.* shall partake of glory; 121: 38 he who exercises compulsion will be unto himself to *p.* the saints; 122: 7 *p.* gives experience; sec. 123 history of *p.* of church to be kept; 127: 4 they *p.* the prophets before you.

JS-H 1: 22–25, 27 *p.* of Joseph Smith after first vision; 1: 60 *p.* of Joseph Smith after receiving the ancient record.

PERSEVERANCE (see also Diligence; Endure; Faint; Steadfast)

D&C 127: 4 let your *p.* be redoubled.

PERSON (see Personage; Respect)

PERSONAGE

D&C 129: 1 angels are resurrected *p.*; 130: 22 Holy Ghost is *p.* of Spirit.

JS-H 1: 17 Father and Son appear to Joseph Smith; 1: 30 Moroni[2] appears to Joseph Smith in vision.

PERSUASION (see also Convince; Exhort; Plead)

D&C 3: 6 how oft you have gone

on in *p.* of men; 5: 21 Joseph Smith is warned to yield to *p.* of men no more; 121: 41 power or influence should be maintained only by *p.*

PERVERSE (*see also* Corrupt)

D&C 33: 2 (34: 6) elders are called to declare gospel unto *p.* generation.

PESTILENCE (*see also* Destruction; Plague)

D&C 43: 25 the Lord calls by voice of famines and *p.*; 63: 24 confusion brings *p.*; 97: 26 the Lord will visit Zion with *p.* according to her works.

PETER—*the apostle* (*see also* BD Peter)

D&C 7: 4–8 the Lord explains John's request to P.; 7: 7 keys of ministry given to P., James, and John; 27: 12 P., James, and John confer apostleship on Joseph Smith and Oliver Cowdery; 49: 11–14 preach as P. did; 128: 10 (Matt. 16: 18) thou art P., and upon this rock I will build my church; 128: 20 voice of P., James, and John heard; 131: 5 (2 Pet. 1: 19) more sure word of prophecy mentioned by P.

JS-H 1: 72 P., James, and John hold keys of Melchizedek Priesthood; 1: 72 John the Baptist acts under direction of P., James, and John.

PETERSON, ZIBA

D&C sec. 32 revelation to; 32: 3 is called on mission to Lamanites; 58: 60 is chastened for trying to hide sins.

PETITION (*see also* Plead)

D&C 90: 1 thy sins are forgiven, according to thy *p.*

PHARAOH—*ruler of ancient Egypt* (*see also* BD Pharaoh)

D&C 105: 27 the Lord will soften hearts as he did heart of P.

Abr. 1: 6, 17 Abraham's fathers had turned to god of P.; 1: 6 P., king of Egypt; 1: 7, 9, 13 priest makes offering to god of P.; 1: 20 P. signifies king of royal blood; 1: 21 descendant from loins of Ham; 1: 21 partaker of blood of Canaanites by birth; 1: 25 first government of Egypt established by P. after patriarchal manner of Ham; 1: 26 a righteous man, a wise and just ruler; 1: 27 does not have right of priesthood.

PHELPS, WILLIAM W.

D&C sec. 55 revelation to; 55: 4 to assist Oliver Cowdery in preparing books for schools; 57: 11–12 to be established as printer for church; 58: 40–41 warned to repent, not sufficiently meek; 61: Intro.

saw destroyer riding on waters; 67: Intro. to publish Book of Commandments; 70: 1 steward over revelations; 85: Intro. extract of letter to Joseph Smith.

PHYSICIAN

D&C 31: 10 Thomas Marsh a *p.* unto church.

PIERCE, PIERCING (*see also* Penetrate)

D&C 1: 3 the rebellious shall be *p.* with much sorrow; 6: 37 behold wounds which *p.* my side; 85: 6 still small voice *p.* all things.

Moses 6: 32 no man shall *p.* thee; 7: 36 God's eye can *p.* all creations.

PILGRIM

D&C 45: 13 people of Enoch[2] were strangers and *p.* on earth.

PILLAR

D&C 29: 12 the Lord to come in *p.* of fire; 88: 97 saints to be caught up to meet the Lord in *p.* of heaven.

JS-H 1: 16 *p.* of light descends upon Joseph Smith.

PIONEER

D&C 136: 7 companies to go as *p.* to prepare for putting in spring crops.

PISON (*see* River)

PIT (*see also* Persecution)

D&C 109: 25 he who digs *p.* shall fall into it himself; 122: 7 if thou shouldst be cast into *p.*, it shall be for thy good.

PITY (*see also* Compassion; Mercy)

D&C 133: 53–55 in his *p.* the Lord redeemed the prophets.

PLACE

D&C 18: 25 those who know not the name by which they are called cannot have *p.* in Father's kingdom; 24: 12 in all *p.*, open mouth and declare gospel; 29: 38 *p.* prepared for third of hosts of heaven who followed Satan is hell; 45: 32 (87: 8; 101: 22) the Lord's disciples shall stand in holy *p.*; 45: 55 Satan shall be bound, that he have no *p.* in men's hearts; 57: 2 Missouri is *p.* for city of Zion; 78: 7 if men will have *p.* in celestial world, they must prepare by obeying commandments; 84: 4 New Jerusalem to be built beginning at this *p.*; 87: 2 war will be poured out upon all nations, beginning at this *p.*; 90: 37 (97: 19; 101: 17) Zion shall not be removed out of her *p.*; 93: 49 pray always lest wicked one remove you out of your *p.*; 97: 13 house to be built as *p.* of thanksgiving, *p.* of instruction; 101: 18, 75 (103: 11) build up waste *p.* of Zion; 109: 13 the Lord's house, a *p.* of holiness; 109: 39 Zion and her stakes, the *p.* of appointment; 116: 1 Adam-ondi-Ahman, the *p.* where Adam shall come; 121: 1 where is pavilion that covers the Lord's hiding *p.*; 124: 39 oracles in most holy *p.*; 130: 8 *p.* where God resides is great Urim and Thummim; 138: 12 spirits of the just are gathered in one *p.*

Moses 2: 9 (Abr. 4: 9) waters are gathered in one *p.*

PLAGUE (see also Destruction; Pestilence)

D&C 84: 97 *p.* shall go forth; 87: 6 with famine and *p.* will inhabitants feel God's wrath; 97: 26 if Zion does not obey, the Lord will visit her with *p.*

PLAIN, PLAINLY, PLAINNESS (see also Clear; Simple)

D&C 42: 40 all garments should be *p.*; 84: 23 Moses *p.* taught this to children of Israel; 128: 18 Joseph Smith might have rendered a plainer translation, but it is sufficiently *p.*; 133: 57 the Lord sent forth his everlasting covenant, reasoning in *p.*

PLAN (see also Design; Gospel; Redemption; Salvation; TG Salvation, Plan of)

D&C 10: 12, 23 Satan has laid a cunning *p.*

Moses 6: 62 *p.* of salvation is unto all men through blood of Son; **Abr.** 4: 21 the Gods saw that their *p.* was good.

PLANET (see also Astronomy)

D&C 88: 43–44 course of *p.* fixed; 130: 4, 6 time reckoned according to *p.*; 130: 6–7 angels do not reside on *p.* like this earth.

Abr. 1: 31 Abraham keeps fathers' record of *p.*; 3: 5 *p.* which is lesser light is greater than that upon which thou standest; 3: 9 reckoning of time of one *p.* shall be above another; 3: 9 Kolob governs *p.*; 3: 17 *p.* or star may exist above any other.

PLANT (see also Grain; Grass; Herb; Seed; Sow; Till)

D&C 2: 2 Elijah shall *p.* in hearts of children promises made to fathers; 55: 5 saints to be *p.* in land of inheritance; 114: 2 others shall be *p.* in the stead of those who deny the Lord's name; 124: 61 receive counsel from those the Lord has set as *p.* of renown.

Moses 3: 5 (Abr. 5: 5) the Lord

created every *p.* before it was in earth; 3: 8 (Abr. 5: 8) the Lord *p.* garden eastward in Eden; 3: 9 the Lord *p.* tree of life and tree of knowledge of good and evil.

PLATES (see also Abridgment; Book; Book of Mormon; Characters; Engravings; Plates of Nephi, Small; Plates of Zeniff; Record; Scriptures)

D&C 3: 19–20 why preserved; 5: 1 witness of *p.* desired by Martin Harris; 5: 4 Joseph Smith given gift to translate *p.*; 17: 1 Three Witnesses to see *p.*

JS-H 1: 34 Moroni² tells Joseph Smith about book written on gold *p.*; 1: 52–53 Moroni² shows Joseph Smith gold *p.*; 1: 59 Joseph Smith obtains *p.*; 1: 62 Joseph Smith copies characters from *p.* and translates them.

PLATES OF NEPHI, SMALL—*spiritual history of Nephites, which constitutes the books of 1 Nephi, 2 Nephi, Jacob, Enos, Jarom, Omni*

D&C 10: 38–40 account of things in lost manuscript is contained in *p.* of Nephi; 10: 41 engravings on *p.* of Nephi to be translated; 10: 40, 45 things engraven on *p.* of Nephi throw greater views upon gospel.

PLEAD (see also Appeal; Cry; Exhort; Jesus Christ—Advocate; Persuasion; Petition)

D&C 38: 4 (45: 3) Christ *p.* before Father for those who believe in him; 90: 36 the Lord will *p.* with Zion's strong ones; 124: 75 *p.* the cause of the poor and needy.

PLEASE, PLEASED, PLEASING (see also Delight; Gladness; Pleasure)

D&C 1: 30 (38: 10) only church with which the Lord is well *p.*; 45: 4 Father well *p.* in Son; 59: 18 all things of earth are made to *p.* the eye; 60: 2 the Lord is not well *p.* with those who will not open mouths; 63: 10 signs come not by well of men as they *p.*; 63: 11 without faith no man *p.* God; 89: 13 *p.* unto the Lord that flesh not be eaten, only in times of winter or famine; 90: 35 (98: 19) the Lord is not well *p.* with many.

Moses 5: 21 Satan is *p.* that God respects not Cain's offering.

PLEASURE (see also Delight; Desire; Happiness; Joy; Will)

D&C 29: 48 given unto children according to the Lord's *p.*, that great things are required; 56: 15 the Lord's people have *p.* in unrighteousness; 63: 4 the Lord builds up at his own *p.*; 76: 7

the Lord will make known p. of his will concerning all things.

PLUCK (see also Destruction; Prune; Reap)

D&C 63: 54 the Lord to send his angels to p. out the wicked; 64: 36 the rebellious shall be p. out; 86: 6 the Lord commands angels not to p. up tares.

POINT (see also Direction; Doctrine)

D&C 121: 27 forefathers' minds are p. to gift of Holy Ghost by angels.

POISON, POISONOUS (see also Serpent)

D&C 124: 98 William Law to be delivered from those who would give him deadly p.

POLLUTE, POLLUTION (see also Corrupt; Defile; Filthiness; Sin)

D&C 84: 59 children of kingdom shall not p. holy land; 88: 134 (109: 20) the Lord will not suffer his house to be p.; 101: 97 let not that which the Lord has appointed be p.; 105: 15 enemies shall not be left to p. the Lord's heritage; 110: 8 I will appear unto my servants if my people do not p. this house; 124: 46 if the Lord's appointed p. his holy grounds, ordinances, they will not be blest.

POLYGAMY (see Marriage; Wife)

PONDER (see also Consider; Reasoning; Study; Think)

D&C 30: 3 p. upon things you have received; 88: 62 the Lord leaves his sayings to be p.; 88: 71 let those who have been warned p. warning in hearts.

POOL (see Water)

POOR, POOREST (see also Alms; Charity; Consecration, Law of; Humble; Lowliness; Meek; Naked; Needy; Poverty; Relief)

D&C 35: 15 the p. and meek shall hear gospel; 38: 16 the p. have complained before the Lord; 38: 35 administer to needs of the p.; 42: 30–31, 34, 39 (44: 6; 51: 5; 52: 40; 72: 12; 105: 3) saints should consecrate of properties to support the p.; 56: 16 wo unto the rich who will not give their substance to the p.; 56: 17 wo unto p. men whose hearts are not broken; 56: 18 blessed are the p. who are pure in heart; 58: 8–11 feast of fat things to be prepared for the p.; 58: 11 the p. to come in unto marriage of Lamb; 58: 47 call on the p. to repent; 78: 3 (82: 11–12; 83: 6) organization to manage the storehouse for the p.; 83: 6 the p. shall be pro-

vided for; 84: 105 if elders are given new coat, they should give old one to the p.; 84: 112 bishop to search for the p.; 88: 17 the p. and meek shall inherit earth; 104: 16 the p. shall be exalted in that the rich are made low; 104: 18 fate of him who imparts not unto the p.; 105: 3 some do not give to the p.; 124: 75 Vinson Knight to plead cause of the p.

Moses 7: 18 no p. among people of Zion; JS-H 1: 61 Joseph Smith was very p.

PORE

D&C 19: 18 suffering caused God to bleed at every p.

PORTION (see also Part)

D&C 19: 34 impart a p. of thy property; 51: 3 bishop to appoint p., every man equal according to his family; 78: 21 the Lord will appoint every man his p.; 84: 85 p. of word that shall be meted unto every man shall be given; 88: 29–31 quickened by p. of celestial, terrestrial, or telestial glory will receive that glory; 101: 90 (124: 8) the Lord will appoint to unjust stewards their p. among unbelievers; 104: 18 he who imparts not his p. shall lift up eyes in hell; 132: 39 David fell from exaltation and received his p.

POSSESS

D&C 10: 49 gospel to be made known to other nations that p. the land; 49: 20 one man should not p. that which is above another; 50: 27 he who is ordained and sent forth is p. of all things; 50: 28 no man is p. of all things unless he is purified; 69: 8 rising generations that grow up on land of Zion shall p. it; 88: 20 (103: 7) bodies who are of celestial kingdom may p. earth forever; 101: 38 in patience ye may p. your own souls; 101: 65 what may be secured to p. eternal life; 103: 20 ye shall p. the goodly land; 128: 20 Peter, James, and John p. keys of kingdom.

POSTERITY (see also Descendant; Seed)

D&C 107: 56 Adam predicted what should befall his p.; 121: 15 saints' enemies and their p. shall be swept from under heaven.

POTIPHAR'S HILL

Abr. 1: 10 place of human sacrifices to idols; 1: 20 in land of Ur, of Chaldea.

POUR

D&C 19: 38 (95: 4) the Lord will p. out Spirit; 87: 3 war shall be p. out upon all nations; 105: 12 great endowment and blessing to be p. out upon elders; 110: 9–10 blessing to be p. out upon the Lord's people; 115: 6 wrath to be p. out without mixture upon whole earth; 121: 33 man cannot hinder the Almighty from p. down knowledge upon saints.

POVERTY (see also Poor)

D&C 124: 30 baptisms for dead performed outside temple are acceptable only in days of p.

POWER (see also Authority; Dominion; Glory [noun]; Might; Priesthood; Strength; tg God, Power of; Jesus Christ, Power of; Power; Priesthood, Power of)

D&C 1: 8 they who preach gospel are given p. to seal on earth and in heaven; 1: 29 (10: 16) Joseph Smith is given p. to translate; 1: 30 Joseph Smith is given p. to lay foundations of church; 1: 35 the devil shall have p. over his dominions; 3: 4 though a man may have p. to do mighty works, God's vengeance on him if he follows own will; 11: 30 those who receive the Lord will be given p. to become sons of God; 18: 47 Jesus Christ speaks by p. of his Spirit; 20: 8 God gave Joseph Smith p. from on high; 21: 6 God will disperse p. of darkness from before saints; 29: 30–31 by p. of my Spirit created I all things; 29: 36 Satan asks God to give him honor, which is p.; 38: 11 p. of darkness prevail upon earth; 38: 32, 38 church to be endowed with p. from on high; 39: 12 p. shall rest upon thee; 42: 6 go forth in p. of Spirit, preaching gospel; 43: 16 elders to sanctify themselves and be endowed with p.; 45: 8 to as many as received him the Lord gave p. to do miracles; 50: 7 deception of hypocrites has given adversary p.; 50: 32 elders given p. over spirit that is not of God; 50: 35 elders given p. to overcome all things which are not ordained of God; 55: 3 elders have p. to give Holy Ghost; 58: 22 (134: 5) elders to be subject to p. that be; 58: 28 p. is in man to be agent unto himself; 68: 12 p. given to seal up unto eternal life; 71: 6 he who receives gospel shall be given p.; 76: 10 by his p. the Lord will make known secrets of his will; 76: 31–35 fate of those who defy the Lord's p.; 77: 11 144,000 elders to be given p. over nations; 84: 20 in ordinances of Melchizedek Priesthood the p. of godliness is manifest; 84: 119 the Lord has put forth his hand to exert the p. of heaven; 88: 114 devil and his armies shall not have p. over saints any more; 101: 28 at the Lord's coming Satan shall not have p. to tempt; 103: 15, 17 redemption of

Zion to be by p.; 107: 8 Melchizedek Priesthood has p. and authority over all offices in church; 112: 30 p. of priesthood is given to the Twelve; 113: 8 God will call men to hold p. of priesthood to bring again Zion; 121: 29 thrones and p. shall be revealed; 121: 33 what p. shall stay the heavens; 121: 36 rights of priesthood are inseparably connected with p. of heaven; 121: 41 no p. or influence can be maintained by virtue of priesthood; 128: 11 secret of whole matter consists in obtaining p. of Holy Priesthood; 128: 14 sealing and binding p. consists in key of knowledge; 128: 18 welding together of p. should take place; 132: 7 Joseph Smith is appointed to hold sealing p.; 132: 19 those sealed by Holy Spirit of promise will inherit p.; 132: 20 righteous to become gods because they have all p.; 138: 26 Christ proclaimed truth in great p.; 138: 30 the Lord clothed his messengers with p. and authority; 138: 51 the Lord gave spirits of just p. to enter Father's kingdom.

Moses 7: 13 the Lord gives Enoch² language of great p.; 7: 27 those upon whom Holy Ghost falls are caught up by p. of heaven into Zion; **JS-M** 1: 33, 36 p. of heaven shall be shaken.

PRAISE (see also Glorify; Honor; Praiseworthy; Rejoice; Shout; Thank; Vain; Worship)

D&C 52: 17 he who trembles under the Lord's power shall bring forth fruits of p.; 136: 28 p. the Lord with singing; 138: 24 saints sang p. to the Lord's holy name.

PRAISEWORTHY (see also Good)

A of F 13 if there is anything p., we seek after these things.

PRATT, ORSON

D&C sec. 34 revelation to; 34: 5 is called to preach gospel; 52: 26 to journey to Missouri, preaching along the way; 75: 14 to travel with Lyman Johnson; 124: 129 a member of the Twelve; 136: 13 to organize a company for journey west.

PRATT, PARLEY P.

D&C sec. 32, 49 revelations to; 32: 2 is called to declare gospel with Oliver Cowdery and Peter Whitmer; 49: 1 is called to preach gospel to Shakers; 50: 37 to strengthen the churches by exhortation; 52: 26 to journey to Missouri, preaching along the way; 97: 3–5 presides over school of prophets; sec. 103 revelation given after arrival of P.P. in Kirtland; 103: 30 to gather company to go up to Zion; 124: 129 member of the Twelve.

PRAYER, PRAY (see also Answer; Ask; Call; Cry; Faith; Fasting; Name of the Lord; Supplicate; TG Prayer; BD Prayer)

D&C 6: 22–24 p. answered by peace of mind; 10: 5 (19: 38; 20: 33; 31: 12; 32: 4; 33: 17; 61: 39; 75: 11; 81: 3; 88: 126; 90: 24; 93: 49) p. always; 14: 8 p. to Father in Christ's name; 19: 28 (23: 6; 81: 3) p. vocally as well as in heart; 20: 47, 51 priests to exhort members to p. vocally and in secret; 25: 12 song of righteous is p. unto the Lord; 28: 13 (93: 51; 104: 80) common consent by p. of faith; 29: 2 the Lord will gather those who call on God in mighty p.; 29: 6 ask in faith, being united in p.; 31: 12 p. that ye enter not into temptation; 41: 3 law given by p. of faith; 42: 14 Spirit shall be given by p. of faith; 42: 44 elders to p. for sick; 46: 7 do all things with p. and thanksgiving; 46: 30 he who asks in Spirit asks according to will of God; 52: 9 teach through p.; 52: 15 he who p. is accepted; 59: 9 go to house of p. and offer up sacraments; 59: 14 this is fasting and p., or rejoicing and p.; 65: Intro. revelation designated as a p.; 65: 4 p. unto the Lord, call upon his name; 65: 5 p. that kingdom may go forth; 68: 28 parents to teach children to p.; 68: 33 he who observes not p. shall be judged; 75: 11 (88: 126; 101: 81) p. that ye faint not; 84: 61 remain steadfast in your minds in spirit of p.; 88: 2 (98: 2) saints' alms of p. have come up into ears of the Lord; 88: 76 continue in p. and fasting; 88: 119 (109: 8) establish a house of p.; 93: 51–52 by your p. of faith with one consent I will uphold him; 98: 2 saints' p. have entered ears of the Lord and are recorded with seal and testament; 101: 7 the Lord is slow to hearken unto p. of those who are slow to hearken unto him; 103: 36 victory and glory brought by p.; 105: 19 I have heard their p.; 107: 22 First Presidency to be upheld by p. of church; 108: 7 strengthen your brethren in your p.; sec. 109 dedicatory p. of Kirtland Temple; 112: 10 be humble and the Lord will give thee answers to p.; 130: 13–14 Joseph Smith receives revelation on wars while p. to know time of Son's coming; 136: 28 praise the Lord with a p. of praise.

Abr. 2: 6 Abraham and Lot p. unto the Lord; 2: 17 Abraham p. that the Lord will turn famine away.

PREACH, PREACHING (see also Declare; Exhort; Gospel; Ministry; Mission;

Preacher; Proclamation; Prophecy; Publish; Teach; Testify; Warn; TG Preaching)

D&C 11: 15 do not suppose you are called to p. until you are called; 18: 28 Twelve called to p. gospel to every creature; 18: 41–42 (55: 2) p. repentance and baptism; 19: 21, 31 (44: 3) p. nothing but repentance; 19: 37 (36: 3; 60: 7) p., exhort, declare the truth; 20: 46 priest's duty is to p.; 36: 5 elders to be ordained and sent forth to p.; 38: 41 let your p. be warning voice; 42: 6 (60: 8) p. gospel, two by two, in the Lord's name; 42: 11 no one should go forth to p. unless he is ordained; 50: 13–14 elders are ordained to p. gospel by Spirit; 50: 17–21 p. by Spirit of truth; 50: 22 he who p. and he who receives understand one another; 52: 9, 36 elders to p. what prophets and apostles have written; 52: 10 elders to p. two by two, by the way; 53: 3 p. faith and repentance; 57: 10 gospel to be p. to those sitting in darkness; 58: 47 let elders p. by the way and bear testimony; 58: 64 (68: 8; 112: 28) gospel must be p. to every creature; 60: 13–16 instructions to those who p.; 63: 52 apostles p. resurrection of the dead; 76: 73 (138: 18–21, 28–37) Son p. gospel to spirits in prison; 84: 76 from you it must be p. unto them; 84: 78 p. without purse or scrip; 107: 25, 38 Seventy also called to p. the gospel; 112: 23 purify your hearts before me, and then go and p.; 133: 37 (134: 12) gospel shall be p. unto every nation, kindred, tongue, and people.

Moses 5: 58 gospel was p. from beginning; 7: 19 Enoch¹ continues to p. in righteousness unto people of God; 8: 23 Noah¹ continues p. to people; JS-M 1: 31 gospel of kingdom shall be p. in all the world; **A of F** 5 man must be called of God to p.

PREACHER (see also Elder; Minister [noun]; Preach)

D&C 21: 10–12 Oliver Cowdery, first p. of church.

Moses 6: 23 Adam's posterity are p. of righteousness.

PRECEPT (see also Commandments of God; Doctrine; Law; Persuasion; Principle)

D&C 45: 29 those in darkness turn their hearts from the Lord because of p. of men; 98: 12 (128: 21) the Lord gives unto the faithful line upon line, p. upon p.

PRECIOUS (see also Pearl; Worth)

D&C 97: 89 those whose hearts are honest and broken will bring forth p. fruit; 109: 43 souls are p. before the Lord.

PREDICATED

D&C 130: 20–21 all blessings are p. upon obedience to laws.

PREDICT (see also Prophecy)

D&C 107: 56 Adam p. what would befall his posterity unto last generation.

PREFACE

D&C 1: 6 p. to Doctrine and Covenants.

PREJUDICE (see also Hate; Persecution)

D&C 109: 55–56 remember kings, that p. may give way before truth; 109: 70 have mercy, that p. may be broken up.

JS-H 1: 22–25, 27 p. against Joseph Smith.

PREMORTAL EXISTENCE (see also Council; Estate; Foundation; Intelligence)

D&C 29: 36 devil rebelled against God, saying, Give me thine honor; 29: 36 Satan turned away a third of hosts of heaven; 38: 1 Christ looked upon expanse of eternity and hosts of heaven before world was; 49: 17 man was created before world was; 93: 29 man was in beginning with God; 138: 55 noble spirits chosen in beginning to be rulers in church; 138: 56 many received first lessons in world of spirits.

Moses 3: 5 all things were created spiritually before they were on earth; 4: 36 Enoch² beholds spirits God created; Abr. 3: 22 Abraham sees intelligences that were organized before the world was; 3: 23 Abraham was chosen before he was born.

PREPARE, PREPARATION, PREPARATORY (see also Establish; Probation; Read)

D&C 1: 12 p. for that which is to come; 19: 19 Christ finished his p. unto children of men; 27: 16 saints to stand with their feet shod with p. of gospel; 29: 8 saints to be gathered to p. for day of tribulation; 33: 10 (34: 6; 39: 20; 45: 9; 65: 1, 3; 77: 12; 88: 74; 133: 17) p. way of the Lord; 38: 9 gird up your loins and be p.; 38: 30 if ye are p., ye shall not fear; 38: 40 p. and accomplish the things which the Lord has commanded; 39: 20 go forth baptizing, the way; 42: 9 time to be revealed when New Jerusalem shall be p.; 43: 20–21 (133: 10) p. for great day of the Lord; 45: 61 translate New Testament, that saints may be p. for things to come; 58: 6 hearts to be p. to bear testimony of things to come; 59. 13 on

the Sabbath, food to be p. with singleness of heart; 71: 4 elders to p. way for commandments and revelations to come; 78: 7 if saints desire place in celestial kingdom, they must p.; 78: 11 saints to p. and organize themselves by covenant; 78: 20 Son p. all things; 84: 26 lesser priesthood holds keys of p. gospel; 85: 3 law of tithing to p. the Lord's people for day of burning; 88: 84 elders to p. saints for judgment; 88: 92 angels crying P. ye, p. ye; 88: 119 (109: 8) p. every needful thing; 101: 23 saints should p. for revelation to come; 101: 68, 72 (133: 15) gather not in haste, but be p.; 104: 59 the Lord's words should be printed to p. his people for time when he shall dwell with them; 105: 9–10 elders to wait and be p.; 109: 15 saints to be p. to obtain every needful thing; 109: 46 bind up testimony, that saints may be p. against day of burning; 132: 3 p. thy heart to receive and obey instructions; 133: 58 the Lord sent fulness of gospel to p. the weak for things to come; 138: 36 Christ p. faithful spirits to carry gospel to dead; 138: 55–56 noble spirits p. to labor in the Lord's vineyard in spirit world.

Moses 3: 9 all things which the Lord p. for use of man remain in sphere in which he created it; 5: 57 Son was p. from before foundation of world; 7: 62 the elect to be gathered unto Holy City which the Lord will p.; Abr. 4: 11 let us p. the earth to bring forth grass; 4: 20 let us p. the waters to bring forth creatures.

PRESBYTERIAN

JS-H 1: 5 involved in religious excitement; 1: 7 family of Joseph Smith's father is proselyted to P. faith; 1: 20 Joseph Smith learns that Presbyterianism is not true.

PRESENCE (see God, Presence of)

PRESENT [adj.]

D&C 38: 2 all things are p. before the Lord's eyes.

PRESENT [verb] (see also Give; Offering)

D&C 128: 24 saints to p. in temple a book containing records of the dead.

PRESERVE (see also Defence; Defend; Keep; Maintain; Protection; Safety; Spare; Support; Uphold)

D&C 42: 56 scriptures to be p. in safety; 62: 6 the Lord has brought saints together that the faithful should be p.; 88: 34 that which is governed by law is also p. by law.

Moses 7: 61 the Lord will p. his

people; **Abr.** 1: 22, 24 from Ham spring race that p. curse of land; 1: 31 the Lord p. fathers' records in Abraham's hands.

PRESIDENCY (*see also* First Presidency; President; Priesthood, Aaronic; Priesthood, Melchizedek)

D&C 68: 17 firstborn holds right of p. over Aaronic Priesthood; 81: 2 Joseph Smith holds keys of p. of High Priesthood; 88: 127–128 house prepared for p. of school of prophets; 107: 8 Melchizedek Priesthood holds the right of p.; 107: 15, 76 bishopric is p. of Aaronic Priesthood.

PRESIDENT (*see also* First Presidency; Government, Civil; Presidency; Priesthood, Aaronic; Priesthood, Melchizedek)

D&C 20: 67 P. of High Priesthood to be ordained by direction of high council or general conference; 21: 1 (107: 92; 124: 94, 125; 127: 12; 135: 3; O/D-2) p. of church is prophet, seer, revelator; 88: 128 man appointed p. of school shall be found standing in his place; 88: 140 washing of feet to be administered by p. of church; 102: 1 one or three p. of high council; 102: 8–9 p. of church is appointed by revelation; 102: 10–11 p. of church presides over council of church; 107: 21 necessity for p. or presiding officers; 107: 60–63, 85–89 presiding officers to preside over elders, priests, teachers, deacons; 107: 65–66 P. of High Priesthood is Presiding High Priest of High Priesthood; 107: 76, 82 trial of a P. of High Priesthood; 107: 85–95 duties of p. of quorums; 107: 87–88 p. of Aaronic Priesthood is to be bishop; 107: 88 p. of quorum of priests to be a bishop; 107: 91–92 (124: 125) functions of P. of High Priesthood; 107: 93–95 the Seventy to have seven p.; 124: 133–135 p. of stakes; 124: 134 high priest instituted to qualify stake p.; 124: 136–138, 142 the Lord gives p. of stake, high priests, seventies, priests, teachers, deacons.

A of F 12 we believe in being subject to p.

PREVAIL (*see also* Conquer; Overcome; Overpower; Overthrow; Prey)

D&C 6: 34 if ye are built upon rock, earth and hell cannot p.; 10: 69 (17: 8; 18: 5; 21: 6; 33: 13; 98: 22; 128: 10) gates of hell shall not p.; 32: 3 the Lord is elders' advocate with Father, and nothing shall p. against them; 38: 11 powers of darkness p. upon the earth; 103: 8 if

the Lord's people obey not, kingdoms of world shall p. against them.

Moses 5: 55 works of darkness begin to p.; **Abr.** 1: 30 famine p. throughout Chaldea.

PREY (*see also* Prevail; Subject)

D&C 133: 28 enemies shall become p. unto lost tribes.

PRICK (*see also* Stir)

D&C 121: 38 he who exercises compulsion will be left alone to kick against p.

PRIDE, PROUD (*see also* Boast; Envy; Hardheartedness; High; Rich; Stiff-necked; Vanity)

D&C 23: 1 (25: 14; 38: 39) beware of p.; 29: 9 (64: 24; 133: 64) the p. shall be as stubble; 42: 40 be not p. in heart; 49: 20 one man not to possess that which is above another; 56: 8 Ezra Thayre must repent of p.; 84: 112 bishop to administer to wants of poor by humbling the rich and p.; 88: 121 cease from all p. and light-mindedness; 90: 17 p. brings snare upon souls; 98: 20 many in church at Kirtland do not forsake p.; 101: 42 he who exalts himself shall be abased; 121: 37 Spirit is grieved when men undertake to gratify their p.

PRIEST (*see also* High Priest; Priests, False; Priestcraft; Priesthood; Priesthood, Aaronic; тG Priest, Aaronic Priesthood; Priest, False, Priest Melchizedek Priesthood; bd Priests)

D&C 18: 32 (20: 39) Twelve are ordained to ordain p.; 20: 46–52 (42: 12) p. to teach; 20: 46 to baptize; 20: 46 to administer sacrament; 20: 47 to visit homes; 20: 48 to ordain other priests, teachers, deacons; 20: 49–50 to take lead in meetings; 20: 52, 84 to assist elder; 20: 60 p. is ordained according to duties and callings of God to him; 20: 82 to serve as messengers; 42: 70 to have stewardship even as members; 76: 56–57 those in celestial glory are p. after order of Melchizedek; 84: 111 lesser p. should travel; 107: 10 high p. have right to officiate in office of p. of Levitical Order; 107: 61, 63 p. to preside over office of p.; 107: 87 president of Aaronic Priesthood presides over forty-eight p.

PRIESTCRAFT (*see also* Churches, False; Priests, False; Prophets, False; тG Priestcraft)

D&C 33: 4 men err in many instances because of p.

PRIESTHOOD (see also Authority; Bind; Calling; Confer; Covenant; Minister [verb]; Ministry; Office; Officer; Ordain; Order; Ordinance; Power; Priest; Priesthood, Aaronic; Priesthood, Melchizedek; TG Priesthood; Priesthood, Authority; Priesthood, History of; Priesthood, Keys of; Priesthood, Magnifying Callings within; Priesthood, Oath and Covenant; Priesthood, Qualifying for)

D&C 2 : 1 p. to be revealed by hand of Elijah; 20 : 60 p. bearers to be ordained by power of Holy Ghost; secs. 84, 107 revelations on p.; 84 : 17 p. continues in church in all generations; 84 : 17 p. is without beginning of days or end of years; 84 : 33–41 oath and covenant of p.; 84 : 44 wo unto those who come not unto this p.; 86 : 8 p. has continued through lineage of fathers; 86 : 10 p. must remain until restoration of all things; 86 : 11 elders are saviors unto Israel through p.; 107 : 1 there are two p. in church; 107 : 40–41 patriarchal order of p. was instituted in days of Adam; 112 : 30 power of p. given unto the Twelve; 113 : 6 root of Jesse is descendant of Jesse and Joseph¹ unto whom rightly belongs the p.; 113 : 8 Zion has right to p. by lineage; 121 : 21 saints' persecutors shall not have right to p.; 121 : 36 rights of p. are inseparably connected with powers of heaven; 121 : 37 amen to p. or authority of man who exercises compulsion; 121 : 41 no power or influence can be maintained by virtue of p.; 124 : 28 there is no place where the Lord can restore fulness of p.; 124 : 130 his p. no man takes from David Patten; 127 : 8 the Lord is about to restore many things pertaining to p.; 128 : 8 nature of ordinances of baptism for dead consists in binding power of p.; 128 : 17 (Mal. 4 : 5–6) Malachi saw restoration of p.; 128 : 21 angels declaring power of their p.; 132 : 45 I have conferred upon you the keys of the p.; OD-2 revelation extending p. to all worthy male members.

Moses 6 : 7 p. was in the beginning, shall be in the end of world; **Abr.** 1 : 2–4 Abraham seeks to be ordained to p.; 1 : 3 p. came down from fathers from before foundations of earth; 1 : 3 p. is right of firstborn; 1 : 18 Jehovah to put p. upon Abraham; 1 : 26 Ham was cursed as pertaining to the p.; 1 : 27 by lineage, Pharaoh could not have right of p., but claims it from Noah¹; 1 : 31 the Lord preserves record of patriarchs concerning right of p.; 2 : 9 Abraham's seed to bear p. unto all nations; 2 : 9, 11 promises of p. given to Abraham; **JS-H** 1 : 38 (Mal. 4 : 5) God will reveal p. by hand of Elijah.

PRIESTHOOD, AARONIC (see also Aaron; Bishop; Deacon; Presidency; President; Priest; Priesthood; Teacher; TG Priesthood, Aaronic; BD Aaronic Priesthood; Levites)

D&C 11 : Intro. revelation received after restoration of A.P.; 13 : 1 (27 : 8) A.P. conferred by John the Baptist; 13 : 1 (84 : 26; 107 : 20) holds keys of preparatory gospel and ministering of angels; 27 : 8 called the first p.; 68 : 17 (107 : 16, 76) right of presidency over A.P. belongs to firstborn sons of Aaron¹; 84 : 18 A.P. to abide forever with Melchizedek P.; 84 : 27 law of carnal commandments continued with house of Aaron¹; 84 : 30 offices of teacher and deacon are appendages to A.P.; 107 : 1 includes Levitical P.; 107 : 1, 6, 13 is one of two priesthoods in church; 107 : 13 so named because it was conferred upon Aaron¹ and his seed; 107 : 14 is called lesser p.; appendage to Melchizedek P.; 107 : 14, 20 has power to administer in outward ordinances; 107 : 15 bishopric is presidency of A.P.; 132 : 59 the Lord will justify acts of man who is called as was Aaron¹ and endowed with power of A.P.

JS-H 1 : 68–69 Joseph Smith and Oliver Cowdery ordained to A.P.; 1 : 69 A.P. holds keys of ministering of angels.

PRIESTHOOD, MELCHIZEDEK (see also Apostle; Elder; First Presidency; High Priest; Patriarch; Presidency; President; Priesthood; Seventy; TG Priesthood, Melchizedek; BD Melchizedek Priesthood)

D&C 27 : 12 (128 : 20) by Peter, James, and John, the Lord ordained and confirmed Joseph Smith and Oliver Cowdery to be apostles; 68 : 15, 19 (107 : 17, 69, 73) high priest of M.P. may be appointed bishop by First Presidency of M.P.; 76 : 57 celestial inhabitants are priests of the Most High, after order of Melchizedek; 76 : 57 order of M.P. is after order of Enoch¹, order of Son; 84 : 17 M.P. continues in church of God in all generations; 81 : 2 keys belong to presidency of High P.; 84 : 6–7 (107 : 40–41) lineage of Holy P. from Adam to Moses; 84 : 18 Aaronic P. abides forever with p. after holiest order of God; 84 : 19 greater P. administers gospel and holds keys of mysteries; 84 : 20–21 only in ordinances of M.P. is power of godliness manifest; 84 : 25 the Lord took Moses and the Holy P. out of midst of Israel; 84 : 29 offices of elder and bishop are necessary appendages to high p.; 84 : 33–41 oath and covenant of p.; 107 : 2–4 M.P. is named after great high priest;

107: 3 (124: 123) before Melchizedek it was called Holy *P.* after Order of Son of God; 107: 4 called M.P. to avoid too frequent repetition of name; 107: 5 all authorities and offices of church are appendages to this *p.*; 107: 8–10 M.P. holds keys of presidency, administers in spiritual things; 107: 18 M.P. holds keys of all spiritual blessings of church; 107: 64 High P. is greatest of all; 107: 65–66 one to be appointed as High P. to preside over *p.*; 124: 28 no place where the Lord can restore fulness of *p.*; 124: 123 officers of *p.* hold keys of M.P.; 128: 8 nature of baptisms for dead consists in binding power of *p.*; 131: 2 in order to enter highest degree of celestial kingdom, a man must enter into *p.* order of marriage; 132: 7 only one on earth at a time to whom sealing power and keys of *p.* are given; 132: 45 I have conferred upon you keys and power of *p.*

JS-H 1: 72 Peter, James, and John hold keys of M.P.

PRIESTS, FALSE (see also Idolatry; Priestcraft)

Abr. 1: 8–11 *p.* of Pharaoh offers human sacrifice; 1: 12–15 *p.* of Pharaoh try to sacrifice Abraham; 1: 20 (3: 20) the Lord smites *p.* that he dies.

PRIMITIVE (see also Ancient)

A of F 6 we believe in same organization that existed in *p.* church.

PRINCE (see also King)

D&C 27: 11 (78: 16; 107: 54) Michael, or Adam, the *p.* of all; 109: 55–56 prayer that hearts of *p.* of earth may be softened; 127: 11 *p.* of this world comes.

Abr. 1: 2 Abraham desires to be *p.* of peace.

PRINCIPALITY (see also Dominion; Kingdom)

D&C 121: 29 all *p.* and powers shall be revealed; 128: 23 voice heard from heaven proclaiming kingdoms, *p.*, powers; 132: 13 everything in world ordained by *p.* and not by the Lord shall be thrown down; 132: 19 those who marry by new and everlasting covenant shall inherit *p.*

PRINCIPLE (see also Doctrine; Point; Precept)

D&C 42: 12 priesthood bearers to teach *p.* of gospel found in Bible and Book of Mormon; 88: 78 (97: 14) saints to be instructed perfectly in theory, in *p.*; 89: 3 Word of Wisdom given for a *p.* with

promise; 98: 5 constitutional law supporting *p.* of freedom is justifiable before the Lord; 101: 78 constitution established that every man may act in doctrine and *p.* according to moral agency; 102: 23 in case of difficulty respecting doctrine or *p.* the president may obtain revelation; 105: 5 Zion to be built up by *p.* of law; 121: 36 power of heaven can be controlled or handled only upon the *p.* of righteousness; 130: 18 whatever *p.* of intelligence men attain unto in this life will rise with them in resurrection; 138: 34 those who died without gospel will be taught all necessary *p.*

PRINTER (see also Printing)

D&C 19: 35 Martin Harris commanded to pay debt to *p.*; 57: 11 William Phelps to be established as *p.* for church.

PRINTING (see also Publish)

D&C 58: 37 lands to be purchased in Independence for house for *p.*; 94: 10–12 house to be built in Kirtland for *p.* translation of scriptures; 104: 58–66 saints to organize for *p.* of sacred literature.

PRINTS (see Nail; Printing)

PRISON (see also Bondage; Hell; Prisoner; Spirit World)

D&C 76: 73 terrestrial glory inherited by men whose spirits were kept in *p.*; 76: 73 (138: 8–10, 18–21, 28–37) gospel preached to those in *p.*; 88: 99 those who received part in spirit *p.* will come forth at second trump; 122: 6 if thou be dragged to *p.*, it shall be for thy good; 128: 22 (138: 42) before world was, the Lord ordained that which enables spirits in *p.* to be redeemed.

Moses 7: 38 the Lord has prepared *p.* for those who perish in floods.

PRISONER (see also Prison)

D&C 128: 22 *p.* shall go free.

PRIVATE (see also Secret)

D&C 19: 28 (71: 7; 81: 3) pray in public as well as in *p.*; 134: 4 human law does not have right to dictate forms for public or *p.* devotion.

PRIVILEGE (see also Blessing; Right [noun])

D&C 20: 66 those who have *p.* of ordaining where there is no organized branch to vote; 51: 15 the Lord grants unto his people *p.* of organizing themselves; 76: 117 those who love the Lord and purify themselves are granted *p.* of seeing him; 88: 122 one shall speak at a time, that every man may have equal *p.*;

98: 5 law that supports freedom in maintaining rights and p. is justifiable; 102: 18 the accuser and the accused have p. of speaking in church court; 107: 19 Melchizedek Priesthood holds keys to have p. of receiving mysteries; 134: 9 not just to foster one religious society and proscribe another in spiritual p.

A of F 11 we allow all men same p. of worshipping God.

PRIZE (see also Reward)

Moses 6: 55 men must taste bitter so that they p. the good.

PROBATION (see also Endure; Prepare; Prove; Tempt; Trial; Try)

D&C 29: 43 the Lord appoints unto man days of his p.

PROCLAIM, PROCLAMATION (see also Declare; Decree; Preach; Publish)

D&C 1: 23 gospel to the p. by the weak and simple; 30: 9 (66: 5; 68: 1; 71: 1–2; 75: 2, 15, 24; 84: 86, 103; 99: 1; 124: 88) the gospel; 50: 32 p. against evil spirit; 75: 4 p. the truth according to the revelations; 93: 51 p. the acceptable year of the Lord; 98: 16 renounce war and p. peace; 105: 39 make p. of peace to ends of earth; 124: 2–3, 7, 107 p. of gospel to kings and rulers; 138: 31, 42 the Lord and his servants p. liberty to captive spirits.

PROFANITY (see Blasphemy; TG Profanity)

PROFESS (see also Claim)

D&C 46: 27 bishop to discern spiritual gifts lest some p. and yet be not of God; 50: 4 (41: 1; 112: 26) abominations in church that p. the Lord's name.

PROFIT (see also Advantage; Benefit; Gain; Prosper; Reward)

D&C 46: 16 manifestations of Spirit given to every man to p.; 46: 29 bishop to discern among spiritual gifts that every member may be p.; 84: 73 do not speak these things before world, for they are given for your p.; 88: 33 what does it p. a man if gift is bestowed but he does not receive it.

PROLONG (see also Increase)

D&C 5: 33 the Lord gives commandments that men's days may be p.

PROMISE (see also Covenant; Holy Spirit of Promise; Oath; Promised Land; Swear; Vow)

D&C 1: 37–38 p. in the commandments are true; 2: 2 (138: 47) Elijah to plant in children's hearts p. made to fathers; 3: 5 remember p. made to you if you did not transgress; 3: 13 Martin Harris broke most sacred p.; 3: 19 plates preserved so that the Lord's p. may be fulfilled; 3: 20 plates will teach Lamanites p. made to fathers; 27: 7 Elias p. Zacharias to have son; 27: 10 Abraham by whom p. remain; 45: 16 (49: 10; 58: 31) the Lord fulfills his p.; 45: 35 signs to show that p. have been fulfilled; 62: 6 the Lord has brought elders together to fulfill p.; 67: 10 the Lord gives p. unto those who have been ordained; 82: 10 (124: 47) when ye do not what I say, ye have no p.; 88: 75 the Lord will fulfill his great and last p.; 89: 3 Word of Wisdom given for principle with p.; 89: 21 the Lord gives p. that destroying angel will pass over those who keep Word of Wisdom; 100: 8 the Lord p. that Holy Ghost will bear record of what elders say; 107: 40 priesthood belongs to descendants of chosen seed, to whom p. were made; 118: 3 the Lord p. to provide for elders' families; 132: 30 (107: 40) Abraham received p. concerning his seed; OD-2 p. regarding priesthood made by prophets and presidents of church.

Abr. 2: 9–11 p. given to Abraham; **JS-H** 1: 39 (Mal. 4: 6) the Lord will plant in hearts of children p. made to the fathers.

PROMISED LAND (see also Covenant; Inherit; Land; Liberty; Zion; TG Promised Land)

D&C 10: 49–51 Nephite prophets leave blessing upon land, that those who possess it and believe gospel shall have eternal life, be free; 38: 18 the Lord gives saints land of p., flowing with milk and honey, with no curse; 38: 19–20 the Lord covenants to give saints land for inheritance; 52: 5 if saints are faithful, land of inheritance shall be made known; 57: 2 Jackson County is land of p., place for city of Zion; 58: 19 God's law to be kept upon this land; 77: 15 two prophets to be raised up after Jews shall return to land of p.; 103: 11 scattered brethren shall return to lands of inheritances and build waste places of Zion; 109: 64 prayer that Judah may begin to return to lands given to Abraham; 124: 38 Israel was commanded to build house for ordinances in land of p.

Moses 6: 17 Enos¹ and people of God dwell in land of p.; **Abr.** 2: 19 unto thy seed will I give this land.

PROPERTY (see also Consecration, Law of; Substance)

D&C 19: 26 Martin Harris is commanded to impart freely of p. to printing of Book of Mormon; 19: 34 Martin Harris is commanded to impart p., all save for support of family; 42: 30 consecrate of p. for support of poor; 42: 32–35 (119: 1) bishop to administer consecrated p.; 66: 6 think not of thy p.; 82: 17 all to have equal claims on p. to manage stewardships; 82: 18 common p. to be put in storehouse; 85: 1 record to be kept of those who consecrate p.; 104: 1–13, 55–56, 85 counsel concerning p.; 117: 4 what is p. unto me, saith the Lord; 117: 5 p. of Kirtland to be turned over for debts; 119: 1 surplus p. should be given to bishop; 119: 5 those who gather in Zion shall be tithed of their surplus p.; 134: 2 governments must frame laws to protect right and control of p.

PROPHECY, PROPHESY (see also Declare; Holy Ghost; Inspire; Oracle; Predict; Prophet; Revelation; TG Prophecy)

D&C 1: 18, 37–38 (52: 36) that p. will be fulfilled; 7: 3 John the Apostle to p. before nations; 11: 25 deny not spirit of p.; 20: 35 revelations neither add to nor diminish from p. of John; 34: 10 p., and it shall be given by the Holy Ghost; 35: 23 Joseph Smith to p.; 42: 16 as ye lift up voices by Comforter, ye shall p.; 45: 15 I will speak unto you and p.; 46: 22 spiritual gift to p.; 131: 5 (2 Pet. 1: 19) more sure word of p. explained.

Moses 5: 10 Adam p. concerning all families of earth; 6: 8 Adam speaks p. as moved upon by Holy Ghost; 6: 13 Seth¹ p. in all his days; 7: 2, 7 Enoch² p. as commanded by the Lord; 8: 3 Methuselah p. that from his loins shall spring all kingdoms of earth; 8: 16 Noah¹ p. and teaches things of God; JS-H 1: 36 Moroni² quotes p. of Old Testament to Joseph Smith; A of F 5 man must be called of God by p. to preach gospel; 7 we believe in the gift of p.

PROPHET (see also Apostle; Martyrdom; Oracle; Preach; Prophecy; Prophets, False; Revelation; Revelator; Servant; TG Prophets, Mission of; Prophets, Rejection of; BD Prophet)

D&C 1: 14 those who will not heed words of p. shall be cut off; 1: 18 (29: 10; 42: 39) words of p. to be fulfilled; 10: 46 p. desired the scriptures to come forth; 17: 2 faith of p. of old; 20: 26 p. spoke as inspired by Holy Ghost,

testified of Christ; 20: 26 those who believe words of p. have eternal life; 21: 1 (107: 92; 124: 94, 125; 127: 12; 135: 3) Joseph Smith, p., seer, and revelator; 35: 23 call on holy p. to prove Joseph Smith's words; 43: 3 only one p. is appointed to receive commandments; 52: 9 elders to preach only what p. and apostles have written; 58: 5 mouths of p. shall not fail; 58: 18 laws of kingdom are given by p.; 76: 101 telestial beings did not receive gospel or p.; 77: 15 two p. to be raised up to Jewish nation; 84: 2 church established as predicted by p.; 88: 127, 136–137 (95: 10) school of the p.; 98: 17 hearts of Jews to be turned to p.; 127: 4 (136: 36) they persecuted the p. before you; 133: 26 p. of lost tribes shall hear the Lord's voice; 138: 32 gospel taught to those who rejected the p.; 138: 36 spirits of p. are prepared to carry gospel to dead spirits; OD–2 Spencer W. Kimball recognized as p., seer, and revelator.

JS-M 1: 1 disciples understand that Christ is he of whom p. wrote; A of F 6 organization of primitive church included p.

PROPHETS, FALSE (see also Apostasy; Priestcraft)

D&C 64: 39 false p. to be known by inhabitants of Zion.

JS-M 1: 9 (Matt. 24: 11) many false p. shall arise.

PROSPER (see also Blessing; Gain; Profit; Reward; Rich; Riches; Righteousness)

D&C 9: 13 do what the Lord commands, and you shall p.; 71: 9 (109: 25) no weapon formed against the Lord's servants shall p.; 97: 18 if Zion does these things, she shall p.

PROTECTION, PROTECT (see also Preserve; Refuge; Safety; Security; Shield; Spare)

D&C 101: 77 laws should be maintained for rights and p. of all; 134: 2 governments must frame laws that will secure p. of life; 134: 5 men should uphold governments that p. their rights.

PROUD (see Pride, Proud)

PROVE (see also Probation; Reprove; Tempt; Testify; Trial; Try; Witness)

D&C 20: 11 Book of Mormon p. to world that holy scriptures are true; 35: 23 call on holy prophets to p. Joseph Smith's words; 68: 21 descendants of Aaron¹ can claim anointing if they can p. lineage; 84: 79 the Lord sends servants out to p. world; 98: 14 I will p. you, whether you will abide in my covenant; 121: 12 the Lord *p.* the saints' persecutors; 124: 55 saints to build the Lord's house that they may *p.* they are faithful; 132: 51 the Lord *p.* the saints as he did Abraham.

Abr. 3: 25 the Gods will *p.* man.

PROVIDE (see also Give; Maintain; Prepare)

D&C 5: 34 the Lord will *p.* means whereby his commands can be accomplished; 75: 28 every man is obliged to *p.* for own family; 104: 15 the Lord to *p.* for the saints.

PRUDENCE, PRUDENT (see also Wisdom)

D&C 76: 9 understanding of the *p.* shall come to naught; 89: 11 herbs and fruits to be used with *p.* and thanksgiving; 128: 18 those things which have been kept hidden from the wise and *p.* shall be revealed.

PRUNE (see also Cut; Pluck)

D&C 24: 19 (39: 17; 75: 2; 95: 4) the Lord's vineyard to be *p.*

PUBLIC (see also Open; Private)

D&C 19: 28 (81: 3) pray in *p.* as well as in private; 42: 35 lands to be purchased for *p.* benefit of church; 46: 3 no one should be cast out from *p.* meetings of the church; 71: 7 call upon enemies to meet you both in *p.* and in private; 134: 4 human law does not have right to dictate forms for *p.* or private devotion; 134: 5 governments should enact laws that will secure *p.* interest; 134: 8 for *p.* peace and tranquillity all men should bring offenders against good laws to punishment.

PUBLISH (see also Declare; Preach; Printing; Proclamation)

D&C 1: 6 book of commandments to be *p.*; 19: 29 *p.* glad tidings upon mountains; 112: 6 great work of *p.* the Lord's name among men; 123: 5–6 libelous histories that are *p.* should be presented to heads of government; 135: 3 Joseph Smith the means of *p.* Book of Mormon.

PULPIT

D&C 110: 2 the Lord stands upon breastwork of *p.* in temple.

PULSIPHER, ZERA

D&C 124: 138 one of seven presidents of seventies quorum.

PUNISHMENT, PUNISH (see also Buffeting; Chasten; Crime; Curse; Damnation; Hell; Indignation; Justice; Law; Penalty; Prison; Sin; Transgression;

Vengeance; Wrath; TG Punish, Punishment)

D&C 19: 6–10 the Lord gives endless *p.*; 19: 11 eternal *p.* is God's *p.*; 19: 12 endless *p.* is God's *p.*; 19: 20 those who do not repent will suffer *p.*; 76: 43–46 sons of perdition suffer everlasting *p.*; 134: 8 offenders against good laws merit *p.*

A of F 2 men will be *p.* for own sins.

PURCHASE (see also Buy)

D&C 27: 3 saints should not *p.* wine from enemies; 42: 35 surplus in storehouse to be used to *p.* land; 45: 65 saints to gather riches to *p.* inheritance; 48: 4 (57: 3–5; 58: 37, 49–52; 63: 27, 30; 101: 70–74; 103: 23; 105: 28–30) saints to *p.* land; 63: 29–31 Zion shall be obtained by *p.*

PURE (see also Blameless; Clean; Guiltless; Holiness; Innocent; Purify; Righteousness; Sanctification; Spotless; Undefiled; Unspotted; Virtue; White)

D&C 35: 21 the elect to abide the Lord's coming because they are *p.*; 41: 12 these words are *p.*; 43: 14 the Lord will reserve unto himself a *p.* people; 56: 18 blessed are the poor who are *p.* in heart; 97: 16 the *p.* shall see God; 97: 21 Zion is the *p.* in heart; 100: 16 the Lord will raise up unto himself a *p.* people; 101: 18 *p.* in heart shall return and come to their inheritance; 109: 76 garments to be *p.*; 121: 42 *p.* knowledge shall greatly enlarge soul; 124: 54 the Lord will save all those who have been *p.* in heart; 131: 7 spirit is matter but more fine or *p.*; 136: 11 blessed are those who render service with *p.* heart; 136: 37 marvel not at these things, for ye are not yet *p.*

PURGE (see also Purify; Refine)

D&C 43: 11 *p.* out iniquity which is among you; 128: 24 the Lord will *p.* sons of Levi[1] as silver and gold.

PURIFY (see also Cleanse; Fire; Pure; Purge; Refine; Sanctification; Wash)

D&C 38: 8 he who is not *p.* shall not abide the day; 50: 28 no man to possess all things unless *p.*; 50: 29 if ye are *p.*, ask whatsoever you will and it shall be done; 76: 116 Holy Spirit bestowed on those who *p.* themselves; 88: 74 (112: 28) *p.* your hearts; 128: 24 the Lord will *p.* sons of Levi[1] to offer an offering; 135: 6 fire to burn trees to *p.* vineyard of corruption.

PURPOSE (see also Desire; End; Intent; Will)

D&C 5: 9 (61: 35) the Lord has reserved sacred things for wise *p.*; 17: 1

(18: 27–28) rely upon the Lord's word with full p. of heart; 18: 27–28 the Twelve to take upon themselves the Lord's name with full p. of heart; 76: 3 the Lord's p. fail not; 101: 33 the Lord will reveal p. and end of earth.

Moses 1: 31 the Lord has made these things for his own p.

PURSE

D&C 24: 18 (84: 78, 86) elders should carry neither p. nor scrip.

PUSH (see also Gather)

D&C 58: 45 the Lord shall p. the people together; 66: 11 thou shalt p. many people to Zion.

QUAKE (see also Earthquake; Fear; Fear of God; Shake; Tremble)

D&C 29: 13 all the earth shall q.; 85: 6 still small voice makes bones q.

QUALIFY

D&C sec. 4 (12: 8) qualities needed to q. for ministry.

QUENCH (see also Satisfy)

D&C 27: 17 shield of faith enables saints to q. fiery darts of the wicked; 76: 44 fire of torment shall not be q. for sons of perdition.

QUESTION (see also Ask; Inquire)

D&C 50: 13, 16 ye shall answer this q. yourselves; 130: 13 war probably to arise through slave q.

QUICKEN (see also Alive; Enlighten; Living; Resurrection)

D&C 33: 16 power of Spirit q. all things; 67: 11 no man has seen God except he is q. by Spirit; 88: 11 light q. understandings; 88: 17 redemption comes through him who q. all things; 88: 26 earth shall die and be q. again; 88: 28–31 they who are q. by portion of celestial, terrestrial, or telestial glory shall receive fulness of that glory; 88: 32 they who remain shall also be q.; 88: 49 men shall understand God, being q. in him and by him 138: 7 (1 Pet. 3: 18) Christ put to death by flesh, but q. by Spirit; 138: 29 understanding was q.

Moses 6: 61 that which q. all things is given to abide in you.

QUICKLY (see also Fast; Haste; Quicken; Slow)

D&C 33: 18 (34: 12; 35: 27; 39: 24; 41: 4; 49: 28; 51: 20; 54: 10; 68: 35; 88:

126; 99: 5; 112: 34) the Lord comes q.; 87: 8 day of the Lord comes q.

QUORUM (see also Council; Priesthood)

D&C 102: 6–7 (107: 28) majority needed to form q.; 107: 22 (124: 126) q. of Presidency of Church; 107: 24 the Twelve form q. equal in authority and power to First Presidency; 107: 26 (124: 138–140) the Seventy form q. equal in authority to the Twelve; 107: 27 decisions of q. must be unanimous; 107: 30–32 decisions of q. to be made in all righteousness; 107: 32 general assembly of q.; 107: 36–37 standing high councils form q.; 107: 85–89 duties of presidents of priesthood q.; 124: 133–138 presidencies of high priests, elders, and seventies q. are called; 124: 137 q. of elders is instituted for standing ministers; 124: 140 difference between q. of seventies and q. of elders.

RACE

D&C OD-2 priesthood extended to all worthy male members without regard to r.

Abr. 1: 24 from Ham sprang r. that preserved curse of the land.

RAGE (see also Anger; Fury; Wrath)

D&C 122: 1 hell shall r.

Moses 6: 15 Satan shall r. in men's hearts.

RAHLEENOS (see Hieroglyphics)

RAILING (see also Revile)

D&C 50: 33 proclaim against evil spirit not with r. accusation.

RAIMENT (see also Apparel; Clothing; Garment)

D&C 49: 19 (59: 17, 19) things of earth prepared for use of man for food and r.; 51: 8 surplus money to be used for food and r.; 133: 51 the Lord has stained his r. with blood of people.

RAIN (see also Destruction; Famine; Flood; bd Rain)

Moses 3: 5 (Abr. 5: 5) things created spiritually before God caused it to r.; 7: 28 how is it that the heavens shed forth tears as r.; r. upon mountains.

RAISE (see also Death, Physical; Heal; Jesus Christ, Resurrection of; Miracle; Resurrection; Rise)

D&C 29: 43 by natural death man is r. in immortality unto eternal life; 88: 72 the Lord will r. elders; 100: 16 I will r. unto myself a pure people; 101: 80 the

Lord r. up wise men to establish Constitution; 124: 100 if the Lord will that William Laws r. the dead, let him not withhold his voice.

Moses 1: 41 the Lord will r. another like Moses.

RAMUS, ILLINOIS (see also D&C map, p. 297)

D&C secs. 130, 131 revelations given at.

RAPHAEL

D&C 128: 21 voice of Gabriel and R.

READ (see also Book; Language; Scriptures; Search; Study; Word; Writing)

D&C 18: 35 by the Lord's power men can r. his words to each other; 57: 9 (71: 5; 91: 4) whoso r., let him understand.

Moses 6: 6 children of Adam taught to r.; JS-H 1: 65 I cannot r. a sealed book.

READY (see also Prepare)

D&C 33: 17 (65: 3) saints to be r. at coming of Bridegroom; 35: 12 none do good except those who are r. to receive fulness of gospel; 50: 46 watch, that ye may be r.; 86: 5 angels are r. and waiting to be sent forth; 88: 94 mother of abominations is r. to be burned.

REAL (see also True)

JS-H 1: 6 good feelings of priests and converts are more pretended than r.

REAP (see also Harvest; Pluck; Receive; Reward; Sow; Thrash)

D&C 5: 3-4 (11: 3-4; 12: 3-4; 14: 3-4; 33: 7) whosoever thrusts in his sickle and r. is called of God; 6: 33 whatsoever a man sows he shall r.; 31: 4 r. in field which is white already to be burned; 38: 12 (86: 5) angels are waiting great command to r. down the earth; 109: 76 saints will r. eternal joy for sufferings.

REAR (see also Build)

D&C 84: 4 temple in New Jerusalem shall be r. in this generation.

REASONING, REASON (see also Consider; Ponder; Teach; Think)

D&C 45: 10, 15 the Lord will r. with men who come to his covenant; 50: 10-12 come let us r. together; 61: 13 the Lord to r. as with men of old; 66: 7 (68: 1) elders sent forth to r. with the people; 133: 57 r. in plainness and simplicity.

REASONS (see also Cause; Reasoning)

D&C 71: 8 saints' enemies to bring forth their strong r. against the Lord.

REBAPTISM (see also Baptism)

D&C sec. 22 revelation on.

REBEL, REBELLION, REBELLIOUS (see also Apostasy; Contention; Devil; Disobedience; Excommunication; Hardheartedness; Iniquity; Murmur; Reject; Resist; Stiffnecked; Trample; Transgression; Unbelief; TG Rebellion)

D&C 1: 3 the r. will be pierced with much sorrow; 1: 8 power given to seal the unbelieving and r.; 29: 36 (76: 25, 28) devil r. against God; 56: 1 (63: 2) the Lord's anger kindled against the r.; 56: 4-6 the Lord revokes commandments because of r.; 63: 6 let the r. fear and tremble; 64: 35 the r. to be cut off out of Zion; 64: 36 the r. are not of blood of Ephraim; 76: 25 angel of God r. against Son; 87: 1 wars to begin at r. of South Carolina; 112: 15 the Twelve are warned not to r. against Joseph Smith; 134: 5 sedition and r. are unbecoming every citizen; 138: 21, 37 Redeemer could not go among spirits of the r.

Moses 4: 3 Satan r. against God; 5: 53 wives of Lamech[1] r. against him; 6: 3 Seth[1] r. not.

REBUKE (see also Chasten; Confound; Reproachfully; Reprove; Warn)

D&C 42: 91 any who offend openly shall be r. openly; 42: 92 any who offend in secret shall be r. in secret; 93: 47 Joseph Smith must stand r. before the Lord for disobedience; 112: 9 thy voice shall be a r. unto the transgressor; 133: 68 at his r. the Lord dries up the sea.

RECEIVE (see also Accept; Answer; Obtain; Partake; Reap)

D&C 4: 7 (11: 5; 12: 5; 14: 5; 49: 26; 66: 9; 88: 63; 103: 31, 35) ask, and ye shall r.; 6: 21 (10: 57; 11: 29; 45: 8) mine own r. me not; 14: 8 ask Father and ye shall r. Holy Ghost; 20: 37 baptize those who manifest my works that have r. Spirit of Christ unto remission of sins; 25: 1 all who r. gospel are the Lord's sons and daughters; 39: 5 (112: 20) he who r. gospel r. the Lord; 39: 23 (76: 52; 84: 64) those baptized r. Holy Ghost by laying on of hands; 41: 5 he who r. law and does it is the Lord's disciple; 42: 14 if ye r. not Spirit ye shall not recei.; 42: 33 every man r. according to his wants; 46: 28 he who asks in Spirit shall r. in Spirit; 50: 24 he who r. light and continues in God,

r. more light; 50: 34 he who r. of God, let him account it of God; 50: 43 as ye have r. me, ye are in me and I in you; 56: 12–13 according to what they do will they r.; 62: 7 r. with thankful heart; 63: 64 ye r. Spirit through prayer; 71: 6 unto him who r. shall be given more abundantly; 76: 51 those who r. testimony of Jesus will inherit celestial glory; 76: 74 terrestrial glory includes those who r. not testimony of Jesus in flesh, but afterwards; 78: 19 he who r. with thankfulness will be made glorious; 84: 36, 88–89 he who r. the Lord's servants r. him; 84: 37 he who r. the Lord r. Father; 84: 40 all who r. priesthood, r. this oath and covenant; 84: 60 blessed if you r. these things; 93: 12–13 Christ r. not fulness at first; 93: 20 those who keep commandments shall r. of Father's fulness; 109: 15 those who worship in holy house may r. fulness of Holy Ghost; 130: 23 man may r. Holy Ghost without its tarrying with him; 132: 23 if ye r. me in world, ye shall know me and r. exaltation; 132: 29 Abraham r. all things; 137: 7–8 those who would have r. gospel may become heirs of celestial glory.

Moses 6: 52 (8: 24) those baptized shall r. gift of Holy Ghost; 7: 69 God r. Zion into his bosom.

RECKON, RECKONING (see also Count; Measure; Record; Time)

D&C 130: 4 r. of God's time and man's is according to planet on which they reside.

Abr. 3: 4–9 r. of the Lord's time is according to r. of Kolob.

RECLAIM (see also Deliver; Recover; Restoration; Save)

D&C 50: 7 those deceived by hypocrites shall be r.

RECOMMEND (see also Certificate; License)

D&C 52: 41 church leaders to take r. when they travel; 72: 19 elders who give account to bishop should be r. by church; 112: 21 those r. and authorized by Twelve shall have power.

RECOMPENSE (see also Pay; Remuneration; Repay; Revenge; Reward; Wages)

D&C 1: 10 (112: 34) the Lord shall come to r. unto every man according to his work; 56: 19 the Lord's r. shall be with him; 127: 3 God will mete out a just r.

RECONCILE, RECONCILIATION (see

also Forgive; Jesus Christ, Atonement through; Satisfy; Subject)

D&C 42: 88 if offender confesses to the offended, they should be r.; 46: 4 transgressor should not partake of sacrament until he makes r.

RECORD (see also Abridgment; Book; Book of Mormon; Engravings; History; Minutes; Plates; Recorder; Scriptures; Testify; Witness; Write)

D&C 1: 29 after receiving r. of Nephites, Joseph Smith is given power to translate; 1: 39 (59: 24) Spirit bears r. that the Lord is God; 6: 26 r. are kept because of people's wickedness; 8: 1, 11 old r. contain parts of scriptures; 9: 2 Oliver Cowdery to be given other r. to translate; 20: 9 Book of Mormon contains r. of fallen people; 20: 27 (42: 17) Holy Ghost bears r. of Father and Son; 20: 81–83 (21: 1; 47: 3; 85: 1) r. of church to be kept; 62: 3 elders' testimony is r. in heaven; 68: 6 (71: 4) elders shall bear r. of Christ; 68: 12 those of whom Father shall bear r. shall be sealed up unto eternal life; 72: 6 stewardship account to be had on r.; 76: 14 Joseph Smith and Sidney Rigdon bear r. of Son in vision; 76: 23 voice bearing r. of Only Begotten; 76: 40 voice our of heavens bears r. of gospel; 85: 1–2 clerk to keep general church r. of all things in Zion; 85: 4 genealogy of those who do not consecrate should not be on r.; 88: 2 saints' prayers are r. in book of names of the sanctified; 93: 6, 11 John bore r. of fulness of the Lord's glory; 93: 18 if you are faithful, you shall receive fulness of John's r.; 100: 8 Holy Ghost to bear r. of all that elders say; 112: 4 (124: 139) bear r. of the Lord's name to Jews and Gentiles; 127: 9 all r. should be in order, to be put in archives; 128: 2–8 r. to be kept of baptisms for the dead; 128: 7 the dead to be judged from books containing r. of their works; 128: 7 book of life is r. kept in heaven; 128: 8 whatsoever elders r. on earth shall be r. in heaven; 128: 9 faithful r. cannot be annulled; 128: 14 as are the r. on earth in relation to dead, so also we r. in heaven.

Moses 1: 23 r. of Moses lost because of men's wickedness; 1: 24 (5: 9; 7: 11) Holy Ghost bears r. of Father and Son; 6: 63 all things made to bear r. of God; **Abr.** 1: 28 r. come into Abraham's hands; 1: 31 r. preserved in Abraham's hands.

RECORDER (see also Clerk; Record)

D&C 85: 1–2 duty of r.; 127: 6 (128: 2–8) r. to be appointed to record baptisms for dead.

RECOVER (see also Gather; Heal; Reclaim; Restoration)

   D&C 39: 11 gospel is covenant sent forth to r. the Lord's people; 66: 9 elders to lay hands on the sick and they shall r.

RED (see also Red Sea)

   D&C 133: 48 the Lord shall be r. in his apparel.

RED SEA (see also BD Red Sea)

   D&C 8: 3 Moses brought Israel through R.S.; 17: 1 directors given to Lehi[1] on borders of R.S.

REDEEMER (see also Jesus Christ—Redeemer)

REDEMPTION, REDEEM (see also Death, Spiritual; Deliver; Eternal Life; Freedom; Immortality; Jesus Christ—Redeemer; Plan; Resurrection; Salvation; Save; TG Redeem, Redemption; BD Redemption)

   D&C 29: 1 angels declare to Adam repentance and r. through faith in Son; 29: 44 they who believe not cannot be r. from spiritual fall; 29: 46 little children are r. from foundation of world; 43: 29 the Lord's people shall be r. and shall reign with him; 45: 46 r. shall be perfected; 45: 54 heathen nations shall be r.; 49: 5 God sent Son for r. of world; 76: 38 sons of perdition are only ones not to be r. after suffering the Lord's wrath; 76: 85 telestial beings shall not be r. until last resurrection; 78: 12 (82: 21; 104: 9; 132: 26) transgressors are delivered to Satan until day of r.; 84: 99 the Lord hath r. his people; 88: 14, 16 through the r. the resurrection is brought to pass; 88: 17 r. of soul through Christ; 88: 99 (138: 36–37, 58) r. of those in prison; 93: 38 God r. man from fall; 100: 13 (101: 75; 136: 18) Zion shall be r.; 101: 80 the Lord r. the land by shedding of blood; 103: 13 after tribulation comes r.; 103: 15 r. of Zion must come with power; 105: 2, 9 r. delayed by disobedience; 105: 34 commandments concerning Zion to be executed after her r.; 124: 124 by Holy Spirit of promise men are sealed unto day of r.; 128: 22 plan of r. ordained before the world was; 133: 52 year of my r. is come; 133: 67 power to r. not shortened; sec. 138 Joseph F. Smith's vision of r. of the dead.

   Moses 4: 1 Satan promises to r. all mankind; 5: 9 all mankind to be r., as many as will; 5: 11 were it not for transgression, Adam and Eve never would have known joy of r.; 5: 67 Enoch[2] sees hour of r. of righteous.

REDRESS

   D&C 101: 76 (105: 25) saints to importune for r.; 134: 11 men should appeal to civil law for r. of wrongs.

REEL

   D&C 45: 48 (49: 23; 88: 87) earth shall r. to and fro like drunkard.

REFINE, REFINER (see also Chasten; Purge; Purify)

   D&C 128: 24 the Lord is like r's fire.

REFRAIN (see also Cease)

   D&C 82: 2 r. from sin, lest sore judgments fall; OD-1 saints are advised to r. from contracting marriages forbidden by law of land.

REFUGE (see also Escape; Protection; Safety)

   D&C 45: 66 New Jerusalem, a city of r.; 115: 6 (124: 36) gathering in Zion to be r. from storm; 124: 10 where shall be r. of remainder of the Lord's people; 124: 36 those places appointed for r.

REFUSE (see also Deny; Reject)

   D&C 34: 9 stars shall r. their shining; 88: 87 sun shall r. to give his light; 132: 36 Abraham did not r. to offer Isaac.

   Moses 7: 44 Enoch[2] r. to be comforted; **Abr.** 1: 5 fathers r. to hearken to my voice.

REGARD (see also Esteem; Heed; Respect)

   D&C 101: 82, 84 judge feared not God, nor r. man.

REGULATE (see also Govern; Government, Civil; Order; Organize)

   D&C 78: 3 organization needed in r. storehouse; 107: 33 the Twelve r. affairs of church in all nations; 134: 6 human laws are instituted to r. our interests as individuals.

REIGN (see also Authority; Dominion; King; Millennium; Power)

   D&C 1: 36 (76: 63; 84: 119; 133: 25) the Lord shall r. in saints' midst; 20: 24 Christ r. with almighty power according to will of Father; 29: 21 abominations shall not r.; 38: 12 powers of darkness cause silence to r.; 43: 29 the Lord's people shall r. with him on earth; 49: 6 Son to r. in heavens till he descends to earth; 58: 22 be subject to powers that be until he r. whose right it is to r.; 76: 44 sons of perdition to r. with devil and his angels in eternity; 76: 108 Christ shall sit on throne of his power to r. forever; 86: 3 Satan r. in hearts of the nations; 128: 3 behold, thy God r.

   Abr. 1: 26 Pharaoh imitates order established in first patriarchal r.; 4: 2

darkness r. upon face of the deep; **A of F** 10 Christ will r. personally upon the earth.

REJECT (see also Apostasy; Deny; Disobedience; Rebel; Refuse; Renounce; Resist; Unbelief; Withstand; TG Prophets, Rejection of)

D&C 6: 29–31 elders to be blessed whether people r. words or not; 6: 31 if people r. not the Lord's words, blessed are they; 39: 9 thou hast r. me many times because of pride; 84: 95 wo unto them who r. the Lord; 84: 114–115 desolation awaits those who r. these things; 99: 4 whoso r. elders shall be r. by Father; 124: 8 fate of wicked who r. testimony; 124: 32 if saints do not perform baptisms for dead, they shall be r. as a church; 132: 4 no one can r. covenant of marriage and be permitted to enter into the Lord's glory; 138: 21, 32 the rebellious r. prophets.

Moses 5: 16 the Lord may not r. his words; 5: 25 Cain r. greater counsel from God.

REJOICE, REJOICING (see also Delight; Glorify; Joy; Praise; Shout; Sing; Thank)

D&C 19: 39 canst thou read this without r.; 25: 13 lift up thy heart and r.; 28: 16 (29: 4) gospel to be declared with sound of r.; 35: 24 (49: 25) Zion shall r. upon hills; 50: 22 he who preaches and he who receives are both edified and r. together; 50: 33 warning against being overcome with boasting nor r.; 50: 34 let him who receives of God r. that he is accounted worthy to receive; 59: 14 fasting and prayer, or in other words, r. and prayer; 62: 3 angels r. over elders who have borne testimony; 88: 33 he who does not receive a gift r. not in that gift, nor r. in the giver; 97: 21 let Zion r.; 110: 5 your sins are forgiven, lift up your heads and r.; 132: 56 the Lord will make handmaid's heart to r.; 133: 44 the Lord will meet him who r. and works righteousness; 138: 15, 18, 23 spirits of just r. in their redemption.

Moses 7: 26 Satan laughs and his angels r.; 7: 47 Enoch² sees Son's coming and r.; **JS-H** 1: 73 after baptism, Joseph Smith and Oliver Cowdery r. in God of salvation.

RELEASE (see also Deliver; Escape; Loose)

D&C 19: 35 pay debt and r. thyself from bondage.

RELIEF (see also Alms; Charity; Help; Needy; Poor; Succor)

D&C 38: 35 appointed men shall administer to r. of poor.

RELIGION, RELIGIOUS (see also Belief; Church of God; Faith; Gospel; Worship)

D&C 134: 4 r. is instituted of God; 134: 7 governments should protect all citizens in free exercise of r. belief; 134: 9 r. influence should not be mingled with civil government; 134: 10 r. societies have right to deal with members according to own rules.

RELY (see also Trust)

D&C 3: 20 r. upon merits of Christ; 17: 1 r. upon the Lord's word; 18: 3 r. upon things which are written; 30: 1 warning against fearing men and not r. on the Lord for strength.

REMAIN (see also Abide; Sojourn; Tarry)

D&C 45: 25 remnant of Jews shall r. until times of Gentiles are fulfilled; 64: 24 the Lord will not spare any that r. in Babylon; 84: 98 all who r. after scourges will know the Lord; 88: 32 those who r. shall be quickened; 88: 35, 102 the wicked r. filthy still; 101: 18 they who r. and are pure will come to inheritances.

Moses 3: 9 all things r. in sphere in which God created them.

REMEMBER, REMEMBRANCE (see also Emblem; Forget; Forgive; Memorial; Type)

D&C 4: 6 r. faith, virtue; 20: 75, 77 (27: 2) partake of bread in r. of the Lord's body; 20: 75, 79 drink in r. of the Lord's blood; 20: 77, 79 during sacrament saints witness they will r. the Son; 42: 30 (52: 30) r. the poor; 46: 8 r. for what reason the best gifts are given; 46: 10 r. what the spiritual gifts given to church are; 58: 42 if man repents of sins, the Lord r. them no more; 84: 57 Zion to remain under condemnation until they r. covenant; 85: 9 they who are not found written in book of r. shall find no inheritance; 133: 26 those who are in north countries shall come in r. before the Lord.

Moses 6: 4, 46 book of r. kept in language of Adam.

REMISSION, REMIT (see also Baptism; Born of God; Faith; Fire; Forgive; Holy Ghost, Baptism of; Jesus Christ, Atonement through; Mercy; Pardon; Repentance)

D&C 13: 1 (49: 13; 55: 1–2; 68: 27; 84: 64, 74; 107: 20; 137: 6; 138: 33) baptism by immersion for r. of sins; 19: 31 (33: 11) r. of sins by baptism and by fire; 20: 5 (21: 8) manifested to first elder that he had received r. of sins; 20: 37 baptism candidates must manifest they have received of Spirit of Christ unto r. of sins; 21: 9 (27: 2) Christ was crucified for r. of sins; 53: 3 preach faith, repentance, r. of sin; 68: 27 children to be baptized for r. of sins when eight years old; 84: 27 gospel of repentance, baptism, and r. of sins; 132: 46 sins that elders r. on earth shall be r. in heaven.

JS-H 1: 68–69 (A of F 4) baptism by immersion for r. of sins.

REMNANT (*see also* Gather; Israel, Gathering of; Israel, Scattering of; Jacob, House of; Residue)

D&C 19: 27 Lamanites are r. of Jews; 45: 24 r. of Jews shall scatter among nations; 45: 43 r. shall be gathered; 52: 2 the Lord's people are r. of Jacob[1]; 87: 5 r. left in land shall vex Gentiles; 109: 65 r. of Jacob[1] who have been cursed because of transgression will be converted; 113: 10 scattered r. are exhorted to return.

Moses 7: 52 r. of Abraham's seed always to be found among nations of earth.

REMOVE (*see also* Move)

D&C 90: 37 Zion shall not be r. out of place; 93: 49 pray always lest the wicked one r. you out of place.

REMUNERATION (*see also* Recompense; Wager)

D&C 42: 72–73 bishop and counselor to receive just r. for services.

REND, RENT

D&C 38: 8 veil of darkness shall soon be r.; 67: 10 veil shall be r. and elders shall see the Lord; 84: 118 the Lord will r. kingdoms; 133: 40 the Lord to r. the heavens.

Moses 1: 19 Satan r. upon earth; 7: 56 rocks are r. at Crucifixion.

RENDER (*see also* Give)

D&C 63: 26 r. unto Caesar things which are Caesar's; 72: 3 every steward to r. account of stewardship.

RENEW (*see also* New; TG Earth, Renewal of)

D&C 84: 33 those who magnify callings are sanctified unto r. of bodies; 84: 48 Father has r. and confirmed covenant upon saints.

A of F 10 earth will be r.

RENOUNCE (*see also* Deny; Reject)

D&C 98: 16 r. war and proclaim peace.

RENT (*see* Rend, Rent)

REPAY (*see also* Pay; Recompense)

D&C 82: 23 judgment is the Lord's and he will r.

REPENTANCE, REPENT (*see also* Baptism; Change; Confession of Sins; Death, Spiritual; Excommunication; Faith; Forgive; Forsake; Gospel; Guilt; Mend; Mercy; Redemption; Remission; Salvation; Unrepentant; Work [noun]; Work [verb]; TG Repent, Repentance; BD Repentance)

D&C 1: 27 (98: 21) sinners chastened that they might r.; 1: 32–33 (58: 42) he who r. and does commandments shall be forgiven; 1: 33 (5: 21) those who r. not shall lose light received; 3: 10 r. and thou art still chosen; 3: 20 (18: 22) saved through r.; 5: 19 desolating scourge shall go forth if people r. not; 6: 9 (11: 9; 14: 8; 19: 21) say nothing but r. unto this generation; 10: 67 whosoever r. and come unto the Lord is his church; 13: 1 (84: 27) gospel of r. and of baptism; 15: 6 (16: 6) thing of most worth will be to declare r.; 18: 6 men must be stirred up unto r.; 18: 9, 22, 42 (19: 13, 15, 20; 20: 29; 49: 8, 26; 56: 14; 58: 48; 133: 16) the Lord commands all men to r.; 18: 11 the Lord died that men might r.; 18: 12 the Lord rose from the dead to bring men unto him on conditions of r.; 18: 13 how great is the Lord's joy in soul that r.; 18: 14 (33: 10; 34: 6; 36: 6; 43: 20–22; 44: 3; 55: 2) elders are called to cry r.; 18: 41–42 (33: 11; 42: 7; 44: 3; 49: 13; 53: 3) r. and be baptized; 18: 44 many to come unto r., that they may come into kingdom; 19: 15 r. lest the Lord strike you by rod of his mouth; 19: 17 if men do not r., they must suffer as God; 20: 37 r. required for baptism; 20: 71 age of accountability, capability of r., required for baptism; 29: 17 the Lord to take vengeance upon the wicked, for they will not r.; 29: 42 angels declare r. to Adam; 29: 44 men cannot be redeemed from spiritual fall because they r. not; 29: 49 whoso has knowledge is commanded to r.; 33: 11–12 (39: 6) r. is one of first principles of gospel; 35: 5 baptism by water unto r.; 39: 18 inasmuch as men r., the Lord will stay his hand; 42: 28 (104: 10) he who sins and r. not shall be cast out; 49: 8 all members must r., for all are under sin; 50: 39 r. and be forgiven; 54: 3 to escape enemies, r. of sins; 56: 8 r. of pride and foolishness; 58: 43 r. requires confessing and forsaking sins; 58: 47 call upon the rich, high, low, and poor to r.; 63: 63 let church r. of their sins; 64: 12 he who r. not of his sins shall be brought before the church; 68: 25

parents to teach children doctrine of r.; 84: 27 (107: 20) Aaronic Priesthood holds keys of preparatory gospel, gospel of r. and baptism; 84: 57 condemnation for failure to r.; 98: 27 testimonies against enemies unless they r.; 98: 39–40 forgive enemy if he r.; 98: 41–44 forgive enemy three times if he does not r.; 133: 62 unto him who r. and sanctifies himself shall eternal life be given; 138: 31 liberty proclaimed to captives who r.; 138: 33, 58 dead who r. will be redeemed; 138: 33 spirits who died without gospel are taught r. from sin; 138: 57 gospel of r. and redemption through Son's sacrifice.

Moses 5: 14–15 (6: 50, 57) all men are commanded to r.; 6: 53–62 r. and baptism explained to Adam; 7: 39 they who r. shall return unto God; 8: 24 people at time of Noah¹ were commanded to r.; 8: 26 it r. Noah¹ that God created man and beast; **Abr.** 1: 30 Abraham's father r. of evil he had determined against Abraham; **JS–H** 1: 69 Aaronic Priesthood holds keys of gospel of r. and baptism; **A of F** 4: one of first principles of gospel.

REPETITION

D&C 107: 4 priesthood called after Melchizedek to avoid too frequent r. of the Lord's name.

REPLENISH

D&C 132: 63 man is given wives to multiply and r. the earth.

Moses 2: 28 (5: 2; Abr. 4: 28) Adam and Eve commanded to r. earth.

REPORT (see also Slander)

D&C 97: 23 r. of the Lord's scourge shall vex all people; 109: 29 the Lord to bring shame to those who spread lying r. about saints.

REPRESENTATION (see also Emblem; Shadow; Type)

D&C 77: 4 beasts' eyes are r. of light and knowledge, beasts' wings are r. of power.

REPROACHFULLY (see also Rebuke; Reprove; Scorner; Shame; Upbraid)

D&C 42: 92 church not to speak r. of those who confess secret offenses.

REPROVE (see also Prove; Punishment; Rebuke; Upbraid; Warn)

D&C 84: 87 (84: 117) the Lord sends elders out to r. the world; 121: 43 r. with sharpness when moved upon by Holy Ghost.

REQUIRE (see also Command; Commandments of God)

D&C 10: 23 the Lord will r. this at hands of those who alter translation; 64: 10 of you it is r. to forgive all men; 64: 22, 34 the Lord r. the heart and a willing mind; 70: 4 the Lord r. an account of stewardships; 82: 3 of him to whom much is given much is r.; 88: 123 learn to impart one to another as gospel r.; 97: 12 the Lord r. tithing; 105: 4 union r. by law of celestial kingdom; 112: 33 cleanse garments lest blood of this generation be r. at your hands; 119: 1 the Lord r. surplus properties to be put in hands of bishop.

RESERVE (see also Keep; Withhold)

D&C 5: 9 the Lord r. those things entrusted to Joseph Smith for wise purpose; 43: 14 the Lord r. unto himself a pure people; 45: 12 Zion of Enoch², a city r. until day of righteousness; 49: 8 all are under sin except those whom the Lord has r. unto himself; 121: 24 the Lord has in r. swift judgment; 121: 32 things r. until end of world; 138: 52 blessing held in r. for those who love God; 138: 53 great spirits r. to lay foundation of work.

Moses 7: 57 remainder of spirits in prison are r. in chains of darkness.

RESIDE (see also Dwell)

D&C 20: 84 members removing from church where they r. should take letter certifying membership; 130: 4 time reckoned according to planet on which they r.; 130: 6–7 angels r. not on planet, but in presence of God; 130: 8 place where God r. is great Urim and Thummim; 134: 5 men are bound to uphold governments in which they r.

RESIDUE (see also Remnant)

D&C 38: 5 r. of wicked are kept in chains until day of judgment; 42: 33 r. of properties to be consecrated unto bishop.

Moses 6: 17 r. of people of God come out from the land; 7: 20 the Lord blesses Zion, curses r. of people; 7: 22 Enoch² beholds r. of people which were sons of Adam; 7: 43 floods come upon r. of the wicked.

RESIST (see also Deny; Hardheartedness; Rebel; Refuse; Reject; Renounce; Withstand)

D&C 108: 2 r. no more the Lord's voice.

RESPECT (see also Equal; Esteem; Honor; Regard; Respecter; Reverence; Worth)

D&C 107: 4 priesthood called after Melchizedek out of r. to the Lord's name; 134: 6 all men owe r. to laws.

Moses 5: 20 the Lord has r. unto Abel; 5: 21 the Lord has not r. unto Cain and his offering.

RESPECTER (see also Respect)

D&C 1: 35 (38: 16) the Lord is no r. of persons; 38: 26 what man who has twelve sons is no r. of them.

RESPONSIBILITY (see also Accountable; Duty)

D&C 107: 98 other officers under r. to travel; 124: 140 one of quorum has r. to preside.

REST (see also Abide; Comfort; Paradise; Peace; Sabbath)

D&C 15: 6 (16: 6) missionaries to r. with converted souls in kingdom of Father; 19: 9 the Lord explains mystery, that his chosen may enter into his r.; 39: 12 power shall r. upon thee; 43: 34 let solemnities of eternity r. upon your minds; 54: 10 they who have sought the Lord early shall find r.; 59: 2 those who die in Zion shall r. from labors; 59: 10 Sabbath appointed that men might r. from labors; 84: 24 the Lord sware Israel should not enter his r. while in wilderness; 84: 24 the Lord's r. is fulness of his glory; 101: 31 r. of those who die during Millennium shall be glorious; 121: 32 every man shall enter into God's immortal r.; 124: 86 (138: 57) those who die unto the Lord shall r. from labors and continue their works.

Moses 3: 2–3 (Abr. 5: 2–3) the Lord r. on seventh day; 7: 48 when shall earth r.; 7: 54, 61 when Son comes, earth shall r.; 7: 64 earth shall r. for thousand years.

RESTORATION, RESTORE (see also Church of God; Dispensation; Gather; Gospel; Israel, Gathering of; Judgment; Last Days; Reclaim; Recover; Redress; Resurrection; Return; TG Israel, Restoration of; Restoration of the Gospel; BD Restitution, Restoration)

D&C 27: 6 (77: 9, 14; 86: 10) Elias given keys of r. all things; 45: 17 the Lord to show disciples r. of scattered Israel; 77: 14 John the apostle is Elias who must come and r. all things; 84: 2 church was established for r. of the Lord's people; 86: 10 priesthood will remain until r. of all things; 98: 47 if children repent and r. all trespasses, indignation shall be turned away; 103: 13, 29 the Lord promises r. of Saints to land of Zion; 109: 21 when the Lord's people repent, blessings to be r.; 124: 28 no place on earth where the Lord can r. fulness of priesthood; 127: 8 the Lord is about to r. many

things to earth; 128: 17 Malachi had his eye fixed on r. of priesthood; 132: 40, 45 the Lord r. all things; 136: 25 r. that which is borrowed; 138: 17 sleeping dust of dead to be r. to perfect frame.

A of F 10 we believe in the r. of the Ten Tribes.

RESURRECTION (see also Body; Death; Physical; Eternal Life; Fall of Man; Grave; Immortality; Jesus Christ, Resurrection of; Life; Paradise; Quicken; Raise; Redemption; Restoration; Rise; Spirit World; TG Resurrection; BD Resurrection)

D&C 29: 13 (45: 45; 88: 97; 133: 56) at the Lord's coming saints will come forth; 29: 26 at Michael's trump, all the dead will awake; 29: 43 by natural death man might be raised in immortality unto eternal life; 42: 45 mourn especially for those who have no hope of glorious r.; 43: 18 the Lord shall say, Ye saints arise and live; 45: 54 they who knew no law shall have part in the first r.; 63: 18 those who have no part in the first r.; 63: 49 the dead who die in the Lord shall rise and not die after; 63: 52 apostles preached r.; 76: 15–17 r. of the just and that of the unjust; 76: 39 all the rest shall be brought forth by r. of the dead; 76: 39 r. through triumph and glory of Lamb; 76: 50–70 those to come forward in r. of the just; 76: 64–65 those who inherit celestial glory will have part in first r.; 76: 85 those who inherit telestial glory shall not be redeemed from devil until last r.; 88: 14 through the redemption is brought to pass the r. of the dead; 88: 16 the r. of the dead is the redemption of souls; 88: 27 those who die shall rise again, a spiritual body; 88: 28 spirit shall receive same body which was natural body; 88: 98 r. of those who are the first fruits; 88: 99 r. of those who are Christ's at his coming who have received their part in prison; 88: 101 rest of dead will not live again until thousand years are ended; 93: 33 spirit and element, inseparably connected, receive fulness of joy; 128: 12 baptism is likeness of r.; 129: 1 angels who are r. personages have bodies of flesh and bones; 130: 18 intelligence will rise with men in the r.; 132: 7, 19 only contracts authorized of God are valid after r.; 133: 55 prophets who were with Christ in his r. shall be in presence of Lamb; 138: 14 the just depart mortality with hope of r.; 138: 19 Son preached doctrine of r. to the dead.

Moses 7: 56 r. of saints foreseen by Enoch²; 7. 62 God will send forth truth out of earth to bear testimony of r. of Christ and all men.

RETAIN (see also Hold; Keep; Maintain)

D&C 46: 10 always r. in your minds what spiritual gifts are; 132: 46 sins r. by elders on earth shall be r. in heaven.

RETIRE

D&C 88: 124 r. to bed early.

RETURN (see also Gather; Israel, Gathering of; Recover; Restoration)

D&C 82: 7 former sins r. unto soul who sins again; 101: 18 they who remain and are pure in heart shall r.; 109: 64 children of Judah to r. to lands given to Abraham; 113: 10 scattered remnants are exhorted to r. to the Lord.

Moses 4: 25 by sweat of face shalt thou eat bread until thou r. unto ground; 7: 39 they who repent shall r. unto God.

REVELATION, REVEAL (see also Detect; God, Manifestations of; Guide; Holy Ghost; Inspire; Instruction; Knowledge; Manifest; Prophecy; Prophet; Revelation, Book of; Revelator; Scriptures; Spirit, Holy/Spirit of the Lord; Testimony; Vision; Visitation; Voice; TG Revelation; BD Revelation)

D&C 1: 3 (88: 108) secret acts shall be r.; 1: 34 the Lord is willing to make these things known to all flesh; 2: 1 the Lord will r. priesthood by hand of Elijah; 3: 4 although a man may have many r., if he follows his own will, he must fall; 11: 25 deny not the spirit of r.; 20: 35 (75: 1; 76: 116–118; 104: 36; 121: 26) r. come through power of Holy Ghost, voice of God, ministering of angels; 25: 9 (101: 32; 121: 31) all things shall be r.; 28: 2, 7 (43: 2–7) only one appointed to receive r.; 28: 7 (35: 18) Joseph Smith given keys to r. which are sealed; 29: 11 the Lord will r. himself from heaven with power and glory; 32: 4 give heed to that which is written and pretend to no other r.; 42: 61 he who asks shall receive r. upon r.; 59: 4 those who obey gospel shall be crowned with r.; 66: 2 gospel sent that men might be partakers of glories to be r.; 68: 21 lineage ascertained by r.; 70: 3–7 brethren appointed stewards over r.; 70: 6 r. not to be shown to church or world yet; 71: 4 (101: 23) elders to prepare way for r. to come; 72: 21 r. to be published; 75: 4 proclaim truth according to r.; 76: 5–8 many r. mysteries to those who serve him; 76: 10 the Lord r. secrets of his will to the righteous; 76: 46 end of sons of perdition was not r., will not be r.; 82: 4 call upon my name for r., and I give them unto you; 90: 14 Joseph Smith

to receive r. to unfold mysteries; 94: 3 (124: 40–41) house consecrated for receiving r.; 101: 32 when the Lord comes, he will r. all things; 102: 9 president of church is appointed by r.; 102: 23 in case of difficulty regarding doctrine, president may obtain mind of the Lord by r.; 107: 39 Twelve to ordain ministers as designated by r.; 124: 39 r. for foundation of Zion; 124: 40–41 house to be built, that the Lord may r. his ordinances; 128: 9 power given by r.; 128: 17 Malachi had eye fixed on glories to be r.; 128: 18 things never before r. are now r.; 132: 7 he who has sealing power is anointed by r. through the medium of the Lord's anointed; 132: 29 Abraham received all things by r.; OD-2 r. extending priesthood to all worthy male members.

Moses 2: 1 the Lord r. unto Moses concerning heaven and earth; 5: 49 Irad r. great secret unto sons of Adam; 6: 3 God r. himself unto Seth; **A of F** 7 we believe in gift of r.; 9 we believe all that God has r., that he will yet r. many great things.

REVELATION, BOOK OF (see also John the Beloved)

D&C sec. 77 interpretations of passages from.

REVELATOR (see also Prophet; Revelation)

D&C 43: Intro. persons making false claims as r.; 77: 2 John the R.; 10: 11 Joseph Smith to be r. unto Sidney Rigdon; 107: 92 (124: 125) president of the church a r.; 124: 94 Hyrum Smith a prophet, seer, and r.

REVENGE (see also Avenge; Recompense; Vengeance)

D&C 98: 23–26 if men smite you or your family, do not seek r.

REVERENCE (see also Fear of God; Honor; Respect; Worship; TG Reverence)

D&C 76: 93 all things bow in humble r. before God's throne; 84: 54 men's minds are darkened because they treated lightly things they have received; 107: 4 priesthood named for Melchizedek out of r. to the Lord's name; 109: 21 blessings to be poured out upon those who r. the Lord in his house.

REVILE (see also Hate; Mock; Persecution; Railing; Scorn)

D&C 19: 30 (31: 9) r. not against revilers; 98: 23 r. not against those who strike you or your families.

REVOKE (see also Deny; Renounce)

D&C 19: 5 the Lord r. not judgments he shall pass; 56: 4 the Lord commands and r.; 58: 32 the Lord r. blessings of the disobedient; 61: 19 the Lord r. not decree that destroyer shall ride.

REVOLUTION

D&C 121: 31 r. of heavenly bodies to be revealed.

Abr. 3: 4 Kolob is after manner of the Lord, according to times and seasons in r. thereof.

REWARD (see also Blessing; Crown; Increase; Judgment; Pay; Prize; Profit; Prosper; Reap; Recompense; Remuneration; Wages; Work [noun])

D&C 6: 33 they who sow good shall reap good for r.; 31: 12 pray always, lest you lose r.; 42: 65 great shall be r. of him who observes all things; 54: 10 (112: 34) the Lord comes quickly, and his r. is with him; 59: 19 (101: 65; 112: 34) the Lord shall come and r. every man; 58: 2 r. of him who is faithful in tribulation is greater in kingdom; 58: 28 if men do good, they shall not lose r.; 58: 33 r. of those who doubt the Lord's promises lurks beneath; 59: 3 those in Zion who obey gospel will receive r. of good things of earth; 59: 23 he who does works of righteousness shall receive r.; 63: 48 he who sends treasure unto Zion shall receive r. in world to come; 64: 11 let God judge and r.; 70: 15 the Lord gives r. for saints' diligence; 76: 6 (124: 16) great shall be r. of those who serve God; 84: 90 he who assists missionaries will lose r.; 98: 23 if men smite you, ye shall be r.; 98: 30 thou shalt be r. for righteousness; 98: 44 testimonies against trespasser shall not be blotted out until he repents and r. thee four-fold; 127: 3 God will mete out just recompense of r.; 135: 6 glory is eternal r. of Joseph and Hyrum Smith; 138: 59 transgressors who have paid penalty receive r. according to works.

RIB

Moses 3: 21–22 (Abr. 5: 15–16) God makes woman from Adam's r.

RICH (see also Pride; Prosper; Riches; Wealth)

D&C 6: 7 (11: 7) he who has eternal life is r.; 38: 16 the Lord has made the r.; 38: 17 the Lord made earth r.; 38: 39 seek true riches and ye shall be r.; 56: 16 wo unto r. men who will not give substance; 58: 10 the r. are invited to supper of the Lord; 58: 47 elders to call upon the r. to repent; poor shall be exalted in

that the r. are made low; 133: 30 ten tribes shall bring r. treasures unto children of Ephraim.

RICH, CHARLES C.

D&C 124: 132 member of high council.

RICHARDS, WILLARD

D&C 118: 6 (124: 129) called to fill position in Council of the Twelve; 135: 2 present at martyrdom of Joseph and Hyrum Smith.

RICHES (see also Gain; Greediness; Mammon; Money; Prosper; Rich; Treasure; Wealth)

D&C 6: 7 (11: 7) seek not for r., but for wisdom; 38: 18 the Lord to give greater r.; 38: 39 if ye seek the r. which it is will of Father to give, ye shall be richest of people; 38: 39 Father will give his people the r. of eternity; 38: 39 r. of earth are the Lord's to give; 42: 39 the Lord will consecrate of the r. of those who embrace gospel among Gentiles unto poor of Israel; 43: 25 the Lord calls nations by voice of glory, honor, r. of eternal life; 45: 65 saints should gather up their r. to purchase an inheritance; 56: 16 r. will canker souls; 67: 2 (78: 18) r. of eternity are the Lord's to give; 68: 31 inhabitants of Zion seek not earnestly the r. of eternity.

RID (see also Cleanse; Purify)

D&C 61: 34 they who declare the word shall r. garments.

RIDE

D&C 61: 19 destroyer r. upon face of waters.

RIGDON, SIDNEY

D&C secs. 35, 37, 40, 44, 49, 71, 73, 76, 100 revelations to; 35: Intro. called to serve as scribe on translation of Bible; 35: 3–4 has prepared for greater work; 35: 4 is sent forth like John and Elijah to prepare way; 35: 19–20 to watch over, write for Joseph Smith; 35: 23 to prove prophecies of Joseph Smith by scriptures; 36: 2 to bestow Spirit on Edward Partridge; 41: 8 to live as seemeth him good as long as he keeps commandments; 49: 1, 3 is called to preach gospel to Shakers; 52: 3, 41 to journey with Joseph Smith to Missouri; 58: 50 to write description of land of Zion; 58: 57 to consecrate spot for temple; 61: 23 not to travel upon waters; 61: 30 to preach next in Cincinnati; 63: Intro. arrives in Kirtland from Missouri; 63: 55–56 is warned about exalting himself; 70: 1 is appointed and ordained one of stewards over revelations and commandments; 71: 1 is commanded to proclaim gospel with Joseph Smith; 76: 11–12 sees heavenly vision with Joseph Smith; 76: 14, 19–23 sees and converses with Son; 90: 6 S.R. and Frederick G. Williams are equal with Joseph Smith in holding keys; 93: 44 is warned to set house in order; 93: 51 to journey and proclaim gospel as the Lord gives utterance; 100: 9–11 to be spokesman for Joseph Smith; 100: 10 is given power to be mighty in testimony; 100: 11 to be mighty in expounding scripture; 103: 29 (124: 106–107) to lift voice in preaching; 111: Intro. goes to Salem, Mass., with Joseph Smith; 115: 13 not to get in more debt to build the Lord's house; 124: 103, 126 to be retained as counselor to Joseph Smith if humble; 124: 104 to be healed.

RIGGS, BURR

D&C 75: 17 is called to journey into south.

RIGHT [adj.], **RIGHTLY** (see also Right [noun]; Right [adj.]; True)

D&C 9: 8 study it out in your mind, then ask the Lord if it be r.; 49: 2 Shakers are not r. before the Lord; 93: 43 set your house in order, for many things are not r. in your house; 101: 79 not r. that any man should be in bondage to another; 107: 40 priesthood r. belongs to literal descendants of chosen seed; 113: 5–6 priesthood r. belongs to root of Jesse.

RIGHT [noun] (see also Government, Civil; Liberty; Privilege; Right [adj.]; Right Hand)

D&C 51: 4 man to hold firm r. of inheritance until he transgresses; 58: 22 be subject to powers that be until he reigns whose r. it is to reign; 68: 17–18 (107: 76) firstborn among sons of Aaron holds r. of presiding over Aaronic Priesthood; 98: 5 law that maintains men's r. and privileges is justifiable before the Lord; 101: 77 law and constitution established for r. and protection; 107: 8 Melchizedek Priesthood holds r. of presidency; 107: 9 Presidency of High Priesthood have r. to officiate in all offices; 107: 10 high priests have r. to officiate in their own standing; 107: 11–12 elder has r. to officiate in high priest's stead when none is present; 113: 8 Zion has r. to priesthood by lineage; 121: 21 persecutors of saints shall not have r. to priesthood; 121: 36 r. of priesthood are inseparably connected with powers of heaven; 128: 21

voices of angels declare their r.; 134: 2 laws must secure r. and control of property; 134: 4 human law has no r. to prescribe rules of worship; 134: 5 all governments have r. to enact laws to secure public interest; 134: 9 not just for individual r. of members as citizens to be denied.

Moses 7: 59 thou hast given unto me a r. to thy throne; Abr. 1: 2 Abraham a high priest, holding r. belonging to fathers; 1: 3 r. of firstborn came down from before beginning of earth; 1: 31 the Lord preserves records concerning r. of priesthood; 2: 11 r. of priesthood to continue in Abraham and his seed.

RIGHT HAND (see also Left; Right [adj.]; Right [noun])

D&C 3: 2 God turns not to r.h. nor to left; 20: 24 (76: 20, 23) Christ sits on r.h. of God; 29: 12 Twelve to stand on r.h. at the Lord's coming; 29: 27 the righteous shall be gathered on the Lord's r.h.; 49: 6 Son of Man has taken power on r.h. of his glory; 66: 12 continue unto end and you shall have eternal life on Father's r.h.; 84: 88 the Lord will be on elders' r.h. and on their left; 124: 19 Joseph Smith, Sr., sits with Abraham at his r.h.; 133: 56 saints shall stand on r.h. of Lamb.

Moses 7: 56–57 saints and many spirits in prison are crowned at r.h. of Son.

RIGHTEOUSNESS, RIGHTEOUS, RIGHTEOUSLY (see also Faithful; Godliness; Holiness; Honest; Innocent; Integrity; Just; Obedience; Perfect; Prosper; Pure; Uprightness)

D&C 1: 16 they seek not the Lord to establish his r.; 10: 37 men cannot always tell the wicked from the r.; 11: 13–14 by Spirit saints know all things pertaining to r.; 13: 1 (128: 24) sons of Levi[1] to offer again an offering in r.; 20: 14 (25: 15) those who work r. shall receive crown; 25: 12 song of r. is a prayer; 27: 16 have on breastplate of r.; 29: 11 the Lord will dwell in r. with men on earth; 29: 12 Twelve to wear robes of r.; 29: 27 the r. shall be gathered on the Lord's right hand; 42: 46 death of the r. shall be sweet; 43: 32 he who lives in r. shall be changed in twinkling of eye; 45: 12 city of Enoch[2] reserved for day of r.; 45: 71 the r. shall be gathered from among all nations; 48: 4 obtain all ye can in r.; 52: 11 (84: 97; 109: 59) the Lord will cut his work short in r.; 58: 27 men should bring to pass much r.; 59: 8 thou shalt offer sacrifice unto the Lord in r.; 59: 23 he who does works of r. shall receive reward;

63: 37 man should take r. in his hands; 63: 54 separation of the r. and the wicked at the Lord's coming; 67: 9 that which is r. comes down from above; 76: 5 the Lord honors those who serve him in r.; 84: 53 (101: 95) way of knowing the r. from the wicked; 88: 17–26 the r. shall inherit the earth; 98: 30 thou shalt be rewarded for thy r.; 100: 16 the Lord will raise up a pure people, which will serve him in r.; 107: 29 quorum of three presidents anciently were r. and holy men; 107: 30 decisions of quorums are to be made in all r.; 107: 84 do all things in r.; 109: 76 saints to be clothed in robes of r.; 121: 36 powers of heaven can be controlled only upon principles of r.; 121: 46 thy scepter shall be unchanging scepter of r. and truth; 128: 24 church to offer an offering in r.; 132: 36 Abraham's willingness to offer Isaac was accounted for r.; 133: 44 when the Lord comes, he shall meet him when he works r.; 138: 22 among the r. spirits there was peace; 138: 30 the Lord appointed messengers from among r. spirits.

Moses 6: 23 sons of Adam were preachers of r.; 6: 41 land of Cainan a land of r.; 7: 18 people of Zion dwelt in r.; 7: 45 when shall blood of the R. be shed; 7: 47 the R. is lifted up; 7: 48 when shall r. abide for season upon earth; 7: 65 Son to dwell on earth in r. for thousand years; 7: 67 day of the r. foreseen by Enoch[2]; **Abr.** 1: 2 Abraham a follower of r.

RIPE, RIPEN

D&C 18: 6 world is r. in iniquity; 29: 9 day soon at hand when earth is r.; 61: 31 elders to preach among people who are well-nigh r. for destruction; 86: 7 wheat and tares to grow together until harvest is r.

RISE, ROSE, RISEN (see also Arise; Awake; Jesus Christ, Resurrection of; Raise; Resurrection)

D&C 18: 12 the Lord has r. again from the dead; 20: 1 r. of the church of Christ in these last days; 63: 49 those who die in the Lord shall r. from dead and not die after; 88: 27 the righteous shall r. again, a spiritual body; 128: 16 if the dead r. not, why are men baptized for the dead; 130: 18 intelligence will r. with men in resurrection.

RIVER (see also Fountain; Stream; Water)

Moses 3: 10–14 (Abr. 5: 10) r. running out of Eden waters garden, parts into four heads—Pison, Gihon, Hiddekel,

Euphrates; 6: 34 (7: 13) r. shall turn from their course.

ROAR

Moses 7: 13 r. of lions was heard out of wilderness.

ROB, ROBBERY (see also Steal; Thief)

D&C 42: 84 those who r. should be delivered unto law of land; 134: 8 r. should be punished.

ROBE (see also Apparel; Garment)

D&C 29: 12 the Twelve shall stand with the Lord, clothed with r. of righteousness; 38: 26 what father clothes one son in r. and another in rags; 109: 76 saints to be clothed with r. of righteousness.

JS–H 1: 31–32 Moroni[2] wears loose r. of exquisite whiteness.

ROCK (see also Cornerstone; Stone; TG Jesus Christ, Rock)

D&C 6: 34 if ye are built upon the Lord's r., earth and hell cannot prevail; 10: 69 (33: 13) whosoever is of the Lord's church he will establish upon his r.; 11: 16 wait until you have the Lord's word, his r., his church; 11: 24 build upon the Lord's r., which is his gospel; 18: 4, 17 you have the Lord's gospel and his r.; 18: 5 if saints build upon foundation of the Lord's gospel and his r., gates of hell shall not prevail; 33: 13 (Matt. 16: 18) upon this r. the Lord will build his church; 50: 44 he who builds upon the Lord's r. shall never fall; 133: 26 those in north countries shall smite r. and ice shall flow.

Moses 7: 53 Messiah the R. of Heaven; **Abr.** 2: 16 eternity was our r.

ROD

D&C 19: 15 repent, lest the Lord smite you by r. of his mouth; 113: 3 r. to come forth out of stem of Jesse.

ROLFE, SAMUEL

D&C 124: 142 S.R. and his counselors preside over priests.

ROLL, ROLLING

D&C 65: 2 (Dan. 2: 34–35, 44–45) stone cut out of mountain without hands shall r. forth; 88: 45 earth r. upon her wings; 88: 95 curtain of heaven to be unfolded as scroll is unfolded after it is r. up; 109: 59 gathering of the Lord's people to r. on; 121: 33 how long can r. waters remain impure.

ROOT (see also Branch; Tree)

D&C 97: 7 ax is laid at r. of trees; 109: 52 the Lord's anger to be kindled, that mob may be wasted away, both r. and branch; 113: 5–6 what is the r. of Jesse; 133: 64 day that burns shall leave the wicked neither r. nor branch.

ROSE

D&C 49: 24 Lamanites shall blossom as r.

ROUGH (see Smooth)

ROUND (see also God, Eternal Nature of)

D&C 3: 2 (35: 1) the Lord's course one eternal r.

ROUNDY, SHADRACH

D&C 124: 141 to preside over bishopric.

RULE (see also Authority; Dominion; Govern; Government, Civil; Kingdom; Kingdom of God; Millennium; Regulate; Reign; Ruler)

D&C 60: 4 the Lord r. in heavens and among armies of earth; 98: 9 when the wicked r., the people mourn; 133: 61 the Lord r. over all flesh; 134: 4 human law does not have right to prescribe r. of worship.

RULER (see also Government, Civil; King)

D&C 1: 23 gospel to be proclaimed before kings and r.; 38: 21 saints shall have no king nor r.; 41: 4 the Lord will be his people's r. when he comes; 52: 13 faithful shall be made r. over many things; 58: 20 let no man think he is r.; 78: 15 saints to be made r. over many kingdoms; 101: 76 saints to importune r. for redress; 101: 94 r. to hear and know that which they have never considered; 132: 53 the Lord appoints Joseph Smith r. over many things; 134: 6–7 r. to protect the innocent; 138: 55 noble and great spirits chosen in beginning to be r. in church.

Abr. 3: 23 r. chosen before world was; **JS-M** 1: 49–50 (Matt. 24: 45–46) lord makes faithful servant r. over house-hold; **A of F** 12 we believe in being subject to r.

RUMOR (see also Report; Slander)

D&C 45: 26 saints shall hear of wars and r. of wars.

RUN

D&C 10: 4 do not r. faster than you have strength; 89: 20 those who obey Word of Wisdom shall r. and not be weary.

RYDER, SIMONDS

D&C 52: 37 to receive that which Heman Basset had lost.

RYE (see also Grain)

D&C 89: 17 r. is for fowls.

SABAOTH (see also Jesus Christ—Lord; BD Sabaoth)

D&C 87: 7 (88: 2; 95: 7; 98: 2) Lord of S.

SABBATH (see also TG Sabbath; BD Sabbath)

D&C 59: 9–12 go to house of prayer and offer up sacraments upon the Lord's holy day; 59: 10 day set aside to rest from labors and pay devotions; 59: 13 on S. prepare food with singleness of heart, that thy fasting may be perfect; 68: 29 inhabitants of Zion to observe S. day to keep it holy; 77: 12 on seventh day God ended his work and sanctified it.

Moses 3: 2–3 (Abr. 5: 3) on seventh day God ended work, rested, sanctified it; **JS-M** 1: 17 (Matt. 24: 20) pray that flight be not on S. day.

SACKCLOTH (see also Darkness, Physical; Grieve; Humble)

D&C 133: 69 the Lord covers heavens with s.

SACRAMENT (see also Baptism; Blood; Bread; Covenant; Emblem; Flesh; Jesus Christ, Types of; Ordinance; Remember, Remembrance; Wine; TG Sacrament)

D&C 20: 40, 75–79 (27: 1–5) bread and wine are emblems of Christ's flesh and blood; 20: 46, 76 s. is administered by priest; 20: 58 teachers and deacons have no authority to administer s.; 20: 68 members to be taught before partaking of s.; 20: 75 partake of s. frequently; 20: 77 prayer on bread; 20: 79 prayer on wine; sec. 27 revelation on s.; 27: 2 matters not what you eat or drink; 27: 2 remember the Lord's body and blood; 46: 4 transgressors not to partake of s. until reconciliation is made; 46: 5 admission to s. meetings; 59: 9, 12 go to house of prayer and offer up s. upon the Lord's holy day; 62: 4 elders to offer s. unto Most High; 89: 5 saints should drink wine only when offering s. before the Lord; 95: 16 inner court of house to be dedicated unto the Lord for s. offering.

SACRED (see also Godliness, Godly; Holiness; Holy)

D&C 3: 12 Joseph Smith delivered up that which was s. to wicked man; 6: 10 gift is s. and comes from above; 6: 12 trifle not with s. things; 8: 11 ancient records which have been hid up are s.; 9: 9 cannot write that which is s. unless it is given from above is s.; 63: 64 that which comes from above is s. and must be spoken with care; 134: 5 governments must hold s. the freedom of conscience.

SACRIFICE (see also Altar; Blood; Blood, Shedding of; Broken Heart and Contrite Spirit; Idolatry; Jesus Christ, Atonement through; Jesus Christ, Types of; Justice; Law of Moses; Mercy; Oblation; Offering; Ordinance; TG Sacrifice; BD Sacrifices)

D&C 59: 8 offer s. of broken heart and contrite spirit; 64: 23 (97: 12) a day of s. and a day for tithing; 84: 31 sons of Aaron[1] shall offer an acceptable offering and s.; 97: 8 those willing to observe their covenants by s. are accepted of the Lord; 97: 12 tithing and s. required to build the Lord's house; 124: 39 s. by sons of Levi[1]; 132: 50 the Lord has seen saints in obedience and will forgive their sins; 138: 2, 35, 57 great atoning s. made by Son for redemption of world; 138: 13 the just offered s. in similitude of great s. of Son.

Moses 5: 5 Adam commanded to offer s.; 5: 7 Adam's s. is similitude of s. of Only Begotten; 6: 3 Seth offers s.; **Abr.** 1: 7–11 priests offer human s.; 1: 12–15 priests try to offer Abraham as s.; 2: 17–18 Abraham offers s. unto the Lord.

SAD (see also Experience)

D&C 121: 39 we have learned by s. experience.

SAFETY, SAFE (see also Defence; Preserve; Protection; Refuge; Security)

D&C 42: 56 scriptures shall be preserved in s.; 45: 66 New Jerusalem, a place of s. for saints; 45: 68 men will flee unto Zion for s.; 61: 15 no flesh shall be s. upon waters; 105: 25 the Lord will give his people favor in people's eyes that they may rest in peace and s.; 124: 10 where shall be s. of the Lord's people when he comes; 134: 1 governments were instituted of God for good and s. of society.

Moses 7: 20 Zion shall dwell in s. forever.

SAINT (see also Believer; Children of God; Church of God; Flock; Member; TG Saints; BD Saints)

D&C 1: 36 the Lord shall have power over his s.; 45: 45 (133: 56) s. who have slept shall come forth; 61: 17 land blessed for s.; 63: 34 s. also shall hardly escape wars to come; 76: 29 Satan makes war with s.; 84: 2 gathering of s. to stand upon Mount Zion; 87: 7 cry and blood of s. shall cease to come up to the Lord; 88: 84 elders to prepare s. for hour of judgment; 88: 94 mother of abominations persecutes s.; 88: 107 s. shall be filled with the Lord's glory; 88: 114 devil shall not have power over s.; 89: 3 Word of Wisdom adapted to capacity of weakest of all s. who are or can be called s.; 103: 7 earth is given unto s.; 104: 15 the Lord to provide for s.; 105: 3 it becomes s. to impart of substance; 121: 38 he who exercises unrighteous dominion shall be left unto himself to persecute s.; sec. 123 duty of s. as to persecutors; 124: 143 offices and keys of priesthood given for perfecting of s.

Moses 7: 56 Enoch[2] foresees resurrection of s.

SALEM, MASSACHUSETTS (see also **D&C** map, p. 295)

D&C sec. 111 revelation given at S.

SALT (see also Example)

D&C 101: 39–40 when men covenant with everlasting covenant, they are accounted as s. of earth; 103: 10 if saints are not saviors of men, they are as s. that has lost savor.

SALUTATION, SALUTE

D&C 88: 120 (109: 9) all s. to be in name of the Lord; 88: 132–133 teacher shall arise and s. his brother; 88: 133 I s. you in name of the Lord; 88: 133–134 he who is found unworthy of this s. shall not have place among saints; 88: 135 he who comes in shall s. the president with uplifted hands.

SALVATION (see also Baptism; Deliver; Escape; Eternal Life; Faith; Gospel; Grace; Jesus Christ, Atonement through; Jesus Christ—Savior; Obedience; Plan; Redemption; Repentance; Sanctification; Save; TG Salvation; Salvation, Plan of)

D&C 6: 3 (11: 3; 12: 3; 14: 3) treasure up everlasting s. in kingdom of God; 6: 13 no gift greater than gift of s.; 18: 17 saints have the Lord's gospel, his rock, and his s.; 38: 16 for your s. I give unto you a commandment; 43: 25 the Lord would have saved nations with s.; 45: 58 children shall grow up without sin unto s.; 46: 7 consider the end of your s.; 68: 4 whatever elders say when directed by Holy Ghost is power to s.; 76: 88 the telestial are heirs of s.; 78: 16 the Lord gave Michael keys of s.; 82: 9 commandments given as direction to s.; 84: 65–73 spiritual gifts bestowed for s.; 89: 2 Word of Wisdom given for temporal s.; 93: 8 Christ was messenger of s.; 109: 4 s. only in name of Jesus Christ; 123: 17 when saints do all in their power, they can stand assured of s.; 128: 11, 15 ordinance for s. of dead; 133: 3 ends of earth shall see s. of God; 138: 26 few among Jews received s. from Christ during his ministry; 138: 59 transgressors who have paid penalty are heirs of s.

Moses 6: 52 s. comes only through Jesus Christ; 6: 62 plan of s. through blood of Son; 7: 42 sons of Noah[1] to be saved with temporal s.; **Abr.** 2: 11 blessings of s. are blessings of gospel; 2: 16 eternity was our s.

SAME (*see also* Equal; Unchangeable)

D&C 1: 38 the Lord's voice and voice of his servants are s.; 20: 12 (35: 1; 76: 4) s. God yesterday, today, and forever.

SANCTIFICATION, SANCTIFY (*see also* Born of God; Cleanse; Consecrate; Dedicate; Exaltation; Faith; Glorify; Grace; Holiness; Holy; Holy Ghost; Baptism of; Jesus Christ, Atonement through; Justify; Purity; Righteousness; Salvation; TG Sanctification, Sanctify)

D&C 20: 31 s. through grace of the Lord is just and true; 20: 34 let those who are s. take heed; 20: 77 bless and s. this bread; 20: 79 bless and s. this wine; 39: 18 if they become s., the Lord will stay his hand; 43: 8–9 saints will be s. by commandments received; 43: 11 s. yourselves before the Lord; 43: 16 s. yourselves, and ye shall be endowed with power; 76: 21 those who are s. shall stand before God's throne and worship him forever; 76: 41 Christ came to s. the world; 77: 1 sea of glass is earth in its s. state; 77: 12 (88: 18, 26) at beginning of seventh thousand years God will s. the earth; 84: 23 Moses sought to s. his people that they might behold face of God; 84: 33 those who magnify priesthood calling will be s. by Spirit unto renewing of bodies; 88: 2 saints' prayers are recorded in book of names of the s.; 88: 21 they who are not s. through law of Christ shall inherit another kingdom; 88: 34 that which is governed by law is s. by law; 88: 68 s. yourselves that your minds become single to God; 88: 116 the s. shall not see death any more; 101: 5 those who will not endure chastening cannot be s.; 105: 31 the Lord's army to be s. before him; 105: 36 those that are chosen shall be s.; 119: 6 s. Zion by tithing; 130: 9 earth in s. state will be made

like crystal; 133: 62 eternal life shall be given unto him who repents and s. himself.

Moses 3: 3 (Abr. 5: 3) God s. the seventh day; 6: 59 men must be born again to be s. from all sin; 6: 60 by the blood ye are s.; 7: 45 all who mourn may be s. because of blood of the Righteous; 7: 48 when will Creator s. the earth.

SANCTUARY (*see also* Refuge; Synagogue)

D&C 88: 137 school of prophets to become s.

SAND

D&C 76: 109 inhabitants of telestial world shall be innumerable as s. upon seashore; 132: 30 Abraham's seed to be innumerable as s. of seashore.

Moses 1: 28 inhabitants of worlds are numberless as s. upon sea shore; **Abr.** 3: 14 number of Abraham's seeds to be as the s.

SARAH, SARAI—*wife of Abraham* [c. twentieth century B.C.] (*see also* BD Sarah)

D&C 132: 65 law of S. who administered to Abraham when God commanded him to take Hagar to wife.

Abr. 2: 2, 4 wife of Abraham; 2: 22–25 to be called Abraham's sister.

SATAN (*see also* Adversary; Devil; Evil; Lucifer; TG Satan; BD Satan)

D&C 10: 5 pray always, that you may conquer S.; 10: 14 the Lord will not suffer S. to accomplish evil design; 10: 20 has great hold on men's hearts and stirs them up to iniquity; 10: 22, 27 (64: 17) S. leads men's souls to destruction; 10: 23, 33 (132: 57) S. seeks to destroy work of God; 10: 25 S. leads men to lie; 10: 32 S. will harden people's hearts; 10: 33 S. thinks to overpower elders' testimony; 10: 63 S. stirs hearts to contention; 19: 3 Christ to destroy S. at end of world; 24: 1 Joseph Smith delivered from power of S.; 29: 47 S. has no power to tempt children; 35: 24 S. shall tremble; 43: 31 (45: 55; 84: 100; 88: 110) S. to be bound during Millennium, then loosed; 50: 3 (52: 14) S. seeks to deceive; 52: 12 S. desires to sift Lyman Wight as chaff; 52: 14 S. is abroad in the land; 61: 19 the destroyer rides upon face of waters; 63: 28 S. makes inhabitants' hearts angry against saints; 76: 25 angel who rebelled against Son was thrust down; 76: 26 Perdition, Lucifer, son of morning; 76: 28 old serpent sought to take kingdom of God; 78: 10 S. seeks to turn hearts away from truth; 78: 12 (82: 21; 104: 9–10; 132: 26) the wicked will be delivered over to the buffetings of S.; 86: 3 S. reigns in nations' hearts; 101: 28 S. shall lose power to tempt.

Moses 1: 12, 19 S. tempts Moses; 1: 12, 19 S. commands Moses to worship him; 1: 16, 18, 20–21 S. is commanded by Moses to depart; 1: 19 (5: 13) S. claims to be the Son; 1: 22 S. departs from Moses; 4: 1 S. was from the beginning; 4: 1 S. asks to be sent as God's son, will redeem all mankind; 4: 1 S. asks for God's honor; 4: 3 S. seeks to destroy agency of man; 4: 4 S. becomes the devil, father of all lies; 4: 6 S. speaks by mouth of serpent; 4: 7–11 S. tempts Eve to eat forbidden fruit; 5: 18, 28 Cain loves S. more than God; 5: 29–31 Cain enters secret oath with S.; 6: 15 S. has gained dominion among men; 6: 49 S. tempts men to worship him; 7: 37 father of the wicked.

SATISFY (see also Quench; Reconcile)

D&C 56: 15 hearts of the Lord's people are not s.; 56: 17 wo unto poor whose bellies are not s.

SAVE (see also Deliver; Reclaim; Redemption; Salvation)

D&C 3: 20 plates preserved that Lamanites might be s.; 18: 22 (20: 25, 29; 53: 7; 68: 9; 112: 29) those who believe, repent, are baptized, and endure shall be s.; 18: 23 (20: 29) Jesus Christ only name whereby man can be s.; 18: 46 (42: 60) those who keep not commandments cannot be s.; 33: 12 man cannot be s. without faith; 35: 25 Israel to be s.; 36: 5 elders to cry, S. yourselves from this generation; 38: 42 go out from among the wicked, s. yourselves; 42: 60 (100: 17) he who does commandments will be s.; 48: 4 saints to s. all the money that they can, to purchase lands; 49: 5 he who receives Son will be s.; 53: 7 he only is s. who endures to end; 68: 9 (112: 29) he who believes and is baptized shall be s.; 76: 42 through Jesus all may be s. whom Father puts into his power; 76: 43 Christ s. all except sons of perdition; 77: 8 angels sent forth from God to s. life; 100: 17 all who call on the Lord and keep his commandments shall be s.; 131: 6 impossible for man to be s. in ignorance; 132: 17 they who are not married by new and everlasting covenant remain without exaltation in their s. condition; 132: 32 enter ye into my law and ye shall be s.; 137: 10 children who die before age of accountability are s. in celestial kingdom; 138: 4 mankind may be s. through atonement and by obedience.

Moses 5: 15 believers in the Son will be s.; 7: 42 posterity of Noah[1] to be s. with temporal salvation; **Abr.** 2: 23 Egyptians will kill Abraham, but s. Sarai alive; **JS-M** 1: 11 (Matt. 24: 12) he who shall not be overcome shall be s.; 1: 20 (Matt. 24: 22) except those days be shortened, no flesh shall be s.; **A of F** 3 through Atonement all mankind may be s. by obedience.

SAVIOR (see also Jesus Christ—Savior)

D&C 103: 9–10 saints to be s. of men.

SAVOR

D&C 101: 39 those who covenant with everlasting covenant are accounted as salt of earth, s. of men; 103: 10 if saints are not saviors of men they are as salt that has lost s.

SAW (see See, Saw, Seen)

SAY (see also Sayings; Speak)

D&C 45: 26 men shall s. Christ delays his coming; 82: 5 (93: 49) what the Lord s. to one, he s. to all; 82: 10 the Lord is bound when men do what he s.; 84: 57 men must not only s. but do what the Lord has written; 84: 85 (100: 6; 124: 97) it shall be given him what he shall s.

SAYINGS (see also Commandments of God; Say; Teach; Word)

D&C 66: 11 keep these s., for they are true; 88: 62 I leave these s. with you to ponder; 89: 18 all saints who remember to keep and do these s. will receive health.

Moses 7: 69 s. went forth, Zion is fled.

SCATTER (see also Destruction; Disperse; Gather; Israel, Scattering of; Israel, Ten Lost Tribes of; Remnant)

D&C 101: 17 Zion not to be moved, though children are s.; 101: 57 (105: 16, 30) throw down enemies' towers and s. watchmen; 124: 35 baptisms for dead, by those s. abroad, not acceptable; 124: 134 standing presidents over stakes s. abroad.

SCEPTER (see also Authority; Dominion; Rule)

D&C 85: 7 the Lord will send one mighty and strong, holding s. of power; 121: 46 thy s. shall be unchanging s.

SCHOOL (see also Knowledge; Learn; Study; BD Schools of the Prophets)

D&C 55: 4 s. to be established for

children; 88: 127–141 (90: 7, 13; 95: 10; 97: 3) s. of the prophets; 95: 17 s. of apostles.

SCORNER (see also Laugh; Mock; Revile; Scoff)

D&C 45: 50 s. shall be consumed.

SCOTT, JACOB

D&C 52: 28 to journey to Missouri.

SCOURGE (see also Chasten; Destruction; Judgment; Persecution)

D&C 5: 19 desolating s. shall go forth; 45: 31 overflowing s. of sickness to cover land; 63: 31 if land of Zion is obtained by blood, enemies will s. saints; 84: 58 s. and judgment to be poured out upon children of Zion; 84: 96 the Almighty to s. nations; 97: 23 the Lord's s. shall pass over by night and by day; 124: 83 the Lord has s. prepared for inhabitants of Kirtland.

SCRIBE (see also Recorder)

D&C 25: 6 Emma Smith to be s. for husband; 90: 19 Frederick G. Williams, counselor and s. to Joseph Smith.

SCRIP (see also Money)

D&C 24: 18 (84: 78, 86) elders should not take purse or s.

SCRIPTURES (see also Bible; Book; Book of Commandments; Book of Mormon; Commandments of God; Doctrine and Covenants; Knowledge; Learn; New Testament; Old Testament; Plates; Prophecy; Read; Record; Revelation; Truth; Word of God/Word of the Lord; Write; Writing; TG Scriptures; Scriptures, Lost; Scriptures, Preservation of; Scriptures, Study of; Scriptures, Value of; Scriptures, Writing of; Scriptures to Come Forth; BD Scriptures)

D&C 8: 1 Oliver Cowdery to obtain knowledge of old records which contain s.; 10: 63 men err in wresting s. and do not understand them; 20: 10–11 the Lord's servants to prove to world that s. are true; 20: 35 neither add to nor diminish from s. to come; 20: 35 s. came through Holy Ghost, voice of God, angels; 20: 80 transgressing members to be dealt with as s. direct; 24: 9 expound the s.; 26: 1 devote time to studying s.; 33: 16 s. given for saints' instruction; 35: 20 s. given to salvation of elect; 42: 12 teach gospel from s.; 42: 15 elders to teach as the Lord has commanded until fulness of s. is given; 42: 28 laws given in s.; 42: 56 ask, and s. shall be given as the Lord has appointed; 42: 56 s. shall be preserved

in safety; 42: 57 do not teach s. until ye receive them in full; 42: 59 commandments given in s. to be law governing church; 68: 4 whatever is spoken under influence of Holy Ghost is s.; 71: 1 expound mysteries out of s.; 74: 7 s. tell that children are sanctified through atonement; 94: 10 house to be built for printing translation of s.; 104: 58 the Lord's commandment to print fulness of s.

JS-H 1: 36–41 Moroni² quotes s. to Joseph Smith.

SCROLL

D&C 88: 95 curtain of heaven to be unfolded as s.

SEA (see also Deep; Flood; Island; Red Sea; Water; Waves)

D&C 77: 1 (Rev. 4: 6) s. of glass is earth in sanctified state; 130: 7 angels reside on globe like s. of glass and fire; 133: 68 at his rebuke, the Lord dries up the s.

Moses 2: 10 the Lord calls gathering of waters s.; 7: 14 land comes up from depth of s.; 7: 66 Enoch² sees the s. troubled.

SEAL, SEALING (see also Bind; Elect; Hide; Marriage; Temple; Welding)

D&C 1: 8 (68: 12; 132: 46) power given to s. on earth and in heaven; 35: 18 the Lord gives Joseph Smith keys of mystery of things which have been s.; 76: 53 those in celestial glory are s. by Holy Spirit of promise; 76: 6–7 (Rev. 5: 1) seven s. on book represent seven thousand years; 77: 8 (Rev. 7: 1) four angels have power to s. up unto life; 98: 2 saints' prayers recorded with this s.; 124: 124 Hyrum Smith to hold the s. blessings; 128: 14 s. power consists in key of knowledge; 131: 5 more sure word of prophecy means knowing one is s. up unto eternal life; 132: 7 covenants not s. by Holy Spirit of promise end with death; 132: 7 (OD-1) keys of s. power held by one only on earth at a time; 135: 1, 3 martyrdom is s. on modern scriptures; 136: 39 prophet s. testimony with blood; 138: 48 latter-day temple work to include s. children to parents.

JS-H 1: 65 I cannot read a s. book.

SEARCH (see also Read; Seek; Study)

D&C 1: 37 s. these commandments; 63: 59 s. all things; 84: 94 (90: 24) s. diligently and spare not; 84: 112 bishop should s. after poor.

SEASON (see also Time)

D&C 29: 22 the Lord will spare earth for little s.; 51: 16 the Lord consecrates land to saints for little s.; 59: 18 all things of the earth, in the s. thereof, are made for man's benefit; 88: 42 law by which all things move in times and s.; 88: 44 planets give light to each other in their s.; 88: 111 Satan to be loosed for a s.; 89: 11 use every herb in its s.; 100: 13 (103: 14) Zion to be chastened for little s.; 105: 9 elders should wait for little s.; 121: 12 God has set his hand and seal to change times and s.

Moses 2: 14 (Abr. 4: 14) God sets lights in firmament for s., days, years.

SEAT (see also Judgment-seat)

D&C 69: 6 Zion shall be a s. to receive and do all these things.

SECHEM—*place situated in plains of Moreh*

Abr. 2: 18 Abraham travels to S.

SECOND (see also Death, Spiritual; Jesus Christ, Second Coming of)

D&C 77: 7 (88: 109) seal contains things of s. thousand years; 88: 99 another angel shall sound s. trump; 98: 25, 40 if enemy smite you s. time and you bear it, reward shall be hundredfold.

Abr. 3: 26 those who keep s. estate will have glory added upon their heads.
JS-H 1: 72 Oliver Cowdery to be s. elder of Church.

SECRET (see also Conspiracy; Hide; Private; Secret Combination)

D&C 1: 3 (88: 108–109) s. acts shall be revealed; 19: 28 (23: 6) pray before the world as well as in s.; 20: 47 pray vocally and in s.; 42: 92 he who offends in s. shall be rebuked in s.; 45: 72 the Lord commanded that s. things be kept from world; 60: 15 (99: 4) shake off dust, wash feet, in s.; 76: 10 the Lord makes known the s. of his will.

SECRET COMBINATION (see also Conspiracy; Murder; Oath; Plan; Sedition)

D&C 38: 28 enemy in s. chambers seeks your lives; 42: 64 converts to flee to west because of s.c.; 117: 11 the Nicolaitane band and all their s. abominations; 123: 13 s.c. bring to light hidden things of darkness.

Moses 5: 29–31, 49 Cain swears s. oath with Satan; 5: 51 from days of Cain there was a s.c.; 6: 15 death administered because of s. works.

SECT, SECTARIAN (see also Churches, False; Denominations)

D&C 123: 12 many among all s. are kept from truth only because they know not where to find it; 130: 3 that Father and Son dwell in man's heart is s. notion.

JS-H 1: 5–6, 8–9 contentions among s.; 1: 18 Joseph Smith desires to know which of s. is true; 1: 19 all s. are wrong.

SECURITY (see also Defence; Protection; Refuge; Safety)

D&C 70: 15 commandment given for s. of the Lord's servants.

SEDITION (see also Conspiracy; Rebel; Secret Combination)

D&C 134: 5, 7 s. is unbecoming every citizen.

SEDUCE (see also Tempt)

D&C 46: 7 be not s. by evil spirits.

SEE, SAW, SEEN (see also Behold; Eye; Look; Observe; Perceive; Sight; View; Vision; Watch)

D&C 1: 2 no eye that shall not s.; 17: 5 three witnesses to testify they have s. plates; 35: 21 (38: 8; 45: 44; 50: 45; 88: 68; 93: 1; 97: 16) the elect shall s. the Lord; 38: 7 The Lord is in saints' midst and they cannot s. him; 42: 49 he who has faith to s. shall s.; 67: 10 elders to s. God with spiritual mind; 67: 11 no man has s. God unless quickened by Spirit; 76: 10 the Lord will make known things that eye has not s.; 76: 23 we s. Christ on right hand of God; 76: 94 those in God's presence s. as they are s.; 84: 22 without priesthood no man can s. face of God and live; 84: 98 all shall be filled with knowledge of the Lord, s. eye to eye; 84: 119 ye cannot s. the Lord's workings now, yet a little while and ye shall s.; 88: 47 man who has s. least of kingdoms has s. God moving in majesty, power; 88: 93 all people wills. great sign in heaven; 93: 1 the obedient shall s. the Lord's face; 93: 1 he who forsakes sins shall s. the Lord's face; 97: 16 pure in heart who come into temple shall s. God; 101: 23 all flesh shall s. the Lord together; 107: 49 Enoch² s. the Lord; 110: 2 we s. the Lord standing upon breastwork of temple; 121: 24 the Lord's eyes s. and know all men's works; 130: 1 when the Savior shall appear we shall s. him as he is; 131: 8 we cannot s. spirit, but when bodies are purified we will s. it is matter.

Moses 5: 10 in the flesh I will s. God; Abr. 3: 12 God puts Abraham's eyes and he s. all God has made; JS-M 1: 36 (Matt. 24: 30) all shall s. Son coming with power; JS-H 1: 17, 25 Joseph Smith has s. two personages.

SEED (see also Children of God; Descendant; Heir; Lineage; Loins; Plant; Posterity; BD Seed of Abraham)

D&C 29: 42 the Lord gave unto

Adam and unto his s. that he would send angels; 84: 18 (107: 13) priesthood confirmed upon Aaron[1] and his s.; 84: 34 those who magnify priesthood callings become s. of Abraham; 103: 17 saints are children of Israel and of s. of Abraham; 104: 33 the Lord will multiply blessings upon the faithful and their s.; 110: 12 in our s. all generations are blessed; 124: 58 (132: 30) in Abraham's s. shall earth be blessed; 132: 19 the exalted shall have continuation of s. forever.

Moses 2: 11–12 (Abr. 4: 11–12) earth brings forth herb and tree yielding s. after its kind; 5: 11 were it not for transgression, Adam and Eve would never have had s.; 7: 52 s. of Noah[1] always to be found among all nations; **Abr.** 2: 11 in Abraham's s. shall all families of earth be blessed; 3: 14 the Lord to multiply Abraham's s.

SEEK (see also Ask; Desire; Inquire; Look; Prayer; Search; Watch)

D&C 1: 16 men s. not the Lord; 6: 6 (11: 6; 12: 6; 14: 6) s. to bring forth Zion; 6: 7 (11: 7) s. not for riches, but for wisdom; 11: 21 s. not to declare the word, but first s. to obtain it; 11: 23 s. kingdom of God first; 22: 4 s. not to counsel the Lord; 38: 19 the Lord will give land of inheritance if saints s. it with all their hearts; 38: 28 enemy in secret chambers s. your lives; 46: 5 those s. earnestly the kingdom should not be cast from meetings; 46: 8 s. earnestly the best gifts; 46: 9 gifts are given for the benefit of those who s. to keep commandments; 63: 7 he who s. signs shall see signs, but not unto salvation; 68: 31 inhabitants of Zion s. not earnestly the riches of eternity; 82: 19 every man s. interest of his neighbor; 88: 35 that which s. to become a law unto itself cannot be sanctified by law; 88: 63, 83 those who s. the Lord shall find him; 88: 118 (109: 7) s. diligently and teach one another; 101: 38 s. face of the Lord always; 106: 3 s. diligently the kingdom and its righteousness; 132: 57 Satan s. to destroy; 136: 20 s. and keep pledges.

SEEN (see See, Saw, Seen)

SEER (see also Prophet; Revelator; Translation; Urim and Thummim; BD Seer)

D&C 21: 1 (124: 125; 127: 12; 135: 3) Joseph Smith to be called a s.; 107: 91–92 President of church is a s.; 124: 94 Hyrum Smith appointed to be prophet and s.; OD-2 Spencer W. Kimball, a prophet, s., revelator.

Moses 6: 36 Enoch[2] to be called s.;

JS-H 1: 35 possession and use of Urim and Thummim constituted s. in former times.

SELFISHNESS (see also Covet; Greediness)

D&C 56: 8 repent of pride and s.

SELL, SOLD

Moses 8: 15 daughters of sons of Noah[1] have s. themselves.

SEND, SENT

D&C 27: 16 the Lord has s. angels to commit gospel; 43: 15 elders are not s. forth to be taught, but to teach; 84: 79 the Lord s. elders out to prove worlds; 84: 87 the Lord s. elders out to reprove world; 85: 7 the Lord will s. one mighty and strong; 107: 35 the Twelve are s. out to open door; 112: 4 s. forth the Lord's word unto ends of earth; 128: 17 I will s. you Elijah the prophet; 132: 24 life eternal is to know God and Jesus Christ, whom he has s.; 133: 8 s. forth the elders unto nations.

Moses 4: 1 (Abr. 3: 27) here am I, s. me.

SENECA COUNTY, NEW YORK (see also D&C map, p. 296)

D&C 128: 20–21 voice of God in Fayette, S. County.

SENSUAL (see also Carnal; Flesh; Lust; Nature, Natural)

D&C 20: 20 by transgression men became s., devilish, fallen; 29: 35 the Lord's commandments are not natural or s.

Moses 5: 13 (6: 49) men became carnal, s., devilish.

SENT (see Send, Sent)

SEPARATION, SEPARATE (see also Absence; TG Separation)

D&C 45: 12 Enoch[2] and his brethren were s. from earth and received unto the Lord; 63: 54 s. of righteous and wicked at the Lord's coming; 93: 34 when spirit and element are s., man cannot receive fulness of joy.

SERPENT (see also Devil; Jesus Christ, Types of; Viper; BD Fiery Serpents; Serpent, Brazen)

D&C 24: 13 require not miracles except against poisonous s.; 76: 28 (88: 110) Satan, that old s.; 84: 72 (124: 99) poison of s. shall not harm elders; 111: 11 be wise as s., yet without sin.

Moses 4: 6–7 Satan speaks by mouth of s. to tempt Eve; 4: 20–21 curse on s.

SERVANT (see also Angel; Angels of the Devil; Disciple; Follow; Follower; Messenger; Minister [noun]; Prophet; Serve; Service; Steward)

D&C 1 : 6 divine authority given to s.; 1: 38 whether by the Lord's voice or by voice of s., it is same; 10: 5 pray to escape s. of Satan; 13: 1 upon you, my fellow s., I confer Priesthood of Aaron; 43: 25 how oft have I called you by my s.; 50: 26 he who is ordained is appointed to be greatest s., even though he is least and s. of all; 58: 26 he who is commanded in all things is slothful and not wise s.; 76: 112 telestial inhabitants shall be s. of the Most High; 84: 36 he who receiveth my s. receiveth me; 93: 46 elders are world's s. for the Lord's sake; 101: 44–62 parable of nobleman and his s.; 112: 1 testimony sent abroad through instrumentality of the Lord's s.; 124: 45 if the Lord's people will hearken to voice of s., they will not be moved out of place; 132: 16 those who do not marry by new and everlasting covenant become ministering s.; 133: 30 children of Ephraim are the Lord's s.; 133: 38 s. of God to proclaim hour of judgment; 134: 12 elder not to interfere with bond-s.; 136: 37 the Lord called Joseph Smith by his angels, ministering s.; 138: 37 the Lord's s. take gospel to unrighteous spirits.

Moses 1: 36 be merciful unto thy s., O God; 6: 31 Enoch² asks why he is the Lord's s.; JS-M 1: 49–50 wise and faithful s. to be made ruler over goods; 1: 51–55 evil s. who smites fellow-s. shall be cut off.

SERVE, SERVICE (see also Duty; Help; Minister [verb]; Ministry; Obedience; Obey; Relief; Servant; Work [noun]; Worship)

D&C 4: 2 those who embark in s. of God must s. him with whole heart; 4: 3 those who desire to s. God are called; 20: 19 the Lord gave commandments that people should love and s. him; 20: 31 sanctification to all who love and s. God; 20: 37 determination to s. the Lord to end is required for baptism; 24: 7 devote all thy s. in Zion; 42: 29 (59: 5) if thou lovest me, thou shalt s. me; 42: 72 bishop's counselors to receive remuneration for s.; 59: 5 s. God in name of Jesus Christ; 76: 5 the Lord delights to honor those who s. him in righteousness.

Moses 1: 15 worship God, for him only shalt thou s.; 6: 33 choose ye this day to s. the God who made you.

SET (see Heart; Naught; Order; Set Apart; Time)

SET APART (see also Hands, Laying on of; Ordain)

D&C 30: 2 David Whitmer has not given heed to those s. over him; 42: 11 two elders or high priests to be s. apart as bishop's counselors; 68: 14 other bishops to be s. apart; 68: 19 (107: 17) high priest may officiate as bishop if he is called and s. apart; 107: 74 bishop shall be common judge where he is s. apart.

SETH—son of Adam (see also BD Seth)

D&C 107: 42 was ordained by Adam; 107: 43 (138: 40) was express likeness of father; 107: 53 was called to gathering of Adam's posterity at Adam-ondi-Ahman; 138: 40 among mighty ones in spirit world.

Moses 6: 2, 10 son of Adam; 6: 3 God reveals himself to s.; 6: 3 offers acceptable sacrifice; 6: 3 father of Enos¹; 6: 14 begets many sons and daughters; 6: 16 lives 912 years.

SEVEN, SEVENTH (see also Sabbath; Seventy)

D&C 77: 5–7 four and twenty elders who belonged to the s. churches; 77: 12 on s. day finished his work; 88: 106, 110, 112 s. angel shall sound his trump; 98: 40 forgive thine enemy until seventy times s.

Moses 3: 2–3 (Abr. 5: 3) God ends work on s. day, blesses it; 5: 40 vengeance to be taken on whoever slays Cain s-fold.

SEVENTY (see also Priesthood, Melchizedek; TG Seventy)

D&C 107: 25 are also called to preach; 107: 26 form a quorum equal in authority to the Twelve; 107: 34 are to act in name of the Lord; 107: 34, 38 (124: 139) traveling high council calls upon the s. when they need assistance; 107: 93–95 to have seven presidents; 107: 96 other s. to be called; 107: 97 s. are to be traveling ministers; 107: 93–97 (124: 138) men called to preside over quorum of s.

SEVERED (see also Cut)

D&C 121: 19 saints' persecutors shall be s. from ordinances of the Lord's house.

SHADOW (see also Foreshadow; Jesus Christ, Types of; Type)

D&C 57: 10 gospel to be preached to those who sit in s. of death.

SHAFT

D&C 85: 8 he who steadies ark shall fall by s. of death.

SHAGREEL (see Sun)

SHAKE, SHAKEN (*see also* Earthquake; Fear; Fear of God; Palsy; Quake; Tremble)

D&C 10: 56 the Lord will cause those who do wickedly to tremble and s.; 21: 6 (35: 24) heavens to s. for saints' good; 38: 30 wickedness may speak with voice louder than that which shall s. earth; 43: 18 (45: 48) heavens shall s.; 49: 23 continue looking forth for heavens to be s.; 60: 15 (75: 20) elders to s. off dust of feet against those who reject them; 84: 118 the Lord s. not the earth only; 129: 4, 7–8 ask messenger from God to s. hands; 132: 14 whatsoever things are not by the Lord shall be s.

Moses 7: 61 the heavens shall s.; JS-M 1: 33, 36 (Matt. 24: 29) powers of heaven shall be s.

SHAKERS (*see also* Sect)

D&C 49: Intro. Leman Copley held to teachings of S.; 49: 1 missionaries called to preach gospel to S.

SHAME (*see also* Ashamed; Guilt; Humble)

D&C 71: 7 s. of saints' enemies shall be made manifest; 76: 35 sons of perdition put Christ to open s.; 109: 29 the Lord will bring to s. all who spread lying reports; 133: 49 sun shall hide face in s.

SHARON, LAND OF

Moses 7: 9 Enoch² beholds land of S.

SHARP, SHARPLY, SHARPNESS

D&C 6: 2 (11: 2; 12: 2; 14: 2; 33: 1) the Lord's words are s. than two-edged sword; 15: 2 (16: 2) the Lord speaks with s.; 112: 12 admonish the Twelve s.; 121: 43 reprove with s. when moved upon by Holy Ghost.

SHEAVES

D&C 31: 5 (33: 9; 75: 5) you shall be laden with s.; 79: 3 faithful to be crowned with s.

SHED (*see also* Blood, Shedding of)

D&C 90: 11 administration of Comforter s. forth upon elders for revelation of Christ; 100: 8 Holy Ghost to be s. forth in bearing record.

Moses 7: 28 heavens weep and s. tears as rain.

SHEEP (*see also* Animal; Flock; Fold; Lamb; Saint; BD Sheep)

D&C 10: 59–60 other s. have I which are not of this fold; 112: 14 feed my s.

Moses 5: 17 Abel a keeper of s.

SHEM—*son of Noah*

D&C 138: 41 great high priest, seen among mighty ones in spirit world.

Moses 8: 12, 27 son of Noah¹.

SHEM, LAND OF—*land at time of Enoch²*

Moses 7: 9 Enoch² beholds land of S.

SHEPHERD (*see* Pastor; Sheep)

SHERMAN, LYMAN

D&C sec. 108 revelation at request of.

SHERWOOD, HENRY G.

D&C 124: 81 to put stock in Nauvoo House; 124: 132 member of high council.

SHIELD (*see also* Armor; Protection)

D&C 27: 17 take s. of faith to quench fiery darts of the wicked; 35: 14 the Lord will be s. of the weak.

SHINE, SHINING (*see also* Enlighten; Light)

D&C 6: 21 (10: 58; 34: 2; 45: 7; 88: 49) Christ is the light which s. in darkness; 34: 9 stars shall refuse their s.; 88: 7 truth s.; 88: 11 the light which s. is through him who enlightens eyes; 110: 3 the Lord's countenance s. above brightness of sun; 115: 5 s. forth, that thy light may be standard for nations.

SHINEHAH (*see* Sun)

SHIP

D&C 123: 16 large s. is benefited by small helm.

SHOD

D&C 27: 16 stand having feet s. with preparation of gospel of peace; 112: 7 let thy feet be s., for path lies among mountains.

SHORTEN, SHORT

D&C 35: 8 (133: 67) the Lord's arm is not s.; 52: 11 (84: 97; 109: 59) the Lord will cut his work s. in righteousness.

JS-M 1: 20 (Matt. 24: 22) except those days be s., no flesh to be saved.

SHOUT (*see also* Praise; Rejoice)

D&C 109: 80 saints s. aloud for joy; 128: 23 let mountains s. for joy.

SHOW, SHOWN (*see also* Appeal; God, Manifestations of; Jesus Christ, Appearances of; Manifest; Revelation; Sign; Unfold)

D&C 5: 3 (10: 34–35; 19: 21) plates not to be s. except to those persons whom the Lord chooses; 10: 34 I s. unto you wisdom; 39: 6 Holy Ghost s. all things; 45: 16 I will s. it plainly as I s. it unto my disciples; 63: 21 earth to be transfigured according to pattern s. to apostles; 107: 100 he who s. himself not approved shall not be counted worthy to stand; 121: 43 s. forth an increase of love after reproving.

Moses 1: 42 (4: 32) words given to Moses should not be s. to any except believers; 7: 4 the Lord s. Enoch² (See) world for many generations; 7: 21 the Lord s. Enoch² all inhabitants of earth; 7: 67 the Lord s. Enoch² all things; **Abr.** 3: 22 the Lord s. Abraham intelligences organized before world was.

SHRINK (see also Withdraw)

D&C 19: 18 Christ would that he might not drink bitter cup and s.

SHULON, LAND OF

Moses 6: 17 people of God come out from.

SHUM, PEOPLE OF

Moses 7: 5 Enoch² beholds valley of S., people of S.; 7: 7 people of Canaan to destroy people of S. in battle.

SHUT

D&C 77: 8 four angels have power to s. up heavens.

Moses 5: 4 Adam and Eve are s. out from God's presence; 5: 41 Cain is s. out from the Lord's presence; 6: 49 men have become carnal and are s. out from God's presence; 7: 38 the Lord will shut up in prison those who perish in floods.

SICK, SICKNESS (see also Administrations to the Sick; Heal; Health; Infirmity; Needy)

D&C 24: 13 (124: 98) require not miracles except healing of the s.; 35: 9 (84: 68) whoso asks in the Lord's name in faith shall heal the s.; 42: 43 whosoever are s. and have not faith to be healed, but believe, shall be nourished; 42: 44 (66: 9) elders to lay hands on s.; 45: 31 desolating s. shall cover land; 52: 40 remember the s. and the afflicted; 84: 68 (124: 98) he who believes shall heal the s.; 124: 87 s. of the land shall redound to your glory.

SICKLE (see also Reap)

D&C 4: 4 thrust in s. to lay up in store; 6: 3 (11: 3, 27; 12: 3; 14: 3; 33: 7) thrust in s. and reap; 6: 4 (11: 4; 12: 4; 14: 4) whosoever will thrust in s. is called

of God; 31: 5 thrust in s. and sins are forgiven.

SIDE

D&C 6: 37 behold the wounds which pierced my s.

SIFT

D&C 52: 12 Satan desires to s. Lyman Wight as chaff.

SIGHT (see also Eye; See)

D&C 3: 12 God gave Joseph Smith s. and power to translate record; 18: 10 worth of souls is great in s. of God; 35: 9 (84: 69) blind to receive their s.

Moses 3: 9 (Abr. 5: 9) the Lord makes trees grow that are pleasant to s.

SIGN (see also Faith; Jesus Christ, Second Coming of; Miracle; Prophecy; Token; Wonder; TG Sign Seekers; Signs)

D&C 24: 13 require not miracles except the Lord commands you; 29: 14 (45: 39; 88: 93) s. in heaven before day of the Lord; 35: 8 (58: 64; 68: 10; 84: 65) the Lord will show s. unto those who believe; 39: 23 (45: 16–33) s. of the Lord's coming; 45: 39–40 he who fears the Lord shall look for s. of coming; 46: 9 (63: 7–12) ask not for s. to consume it upon lusts; 63: 7 he who seeks s. shall see s., but not unto salvation; 63: 9–11 s. come by faith; 63: 10 s. come by will of God, not man; 63: 11 God will show no s. to those without faith; 68: 11 given to know s. of times and of coming of Son; 84: 65–72 (124: 98) s. follow him who believes.

Moses 2: 14 (Abr. 4: 14) let there be lights in firmament for s. and seasons; **JS-M** 1: 22 (Matt. 24: 24) false Christs and false prophets will show great s. and wonders.

SILENCE, SILENT

D&C 38: 12 powers of darkness cause s. to reign; 88: 95 s. in heaven for half an hour.

SILVER

D&C 128: 24 the Lord shall sit as refiner and purifier of s.

JS-H 1: 35 Urim and Thummim two stones in s. bow; 1: 56 Joseph Smith works in s. mine.

SIMEON, MOUNT

Moses 7: 2 God commands Enoch² to go upon mount S.

SIMILITUDE (see also Jesus Christ, Types of; Likeness; Shadow; Type)

D&C 124: 2 stake shall be polished after s. of palace; 128: 13 baptismal font was instituted as s. of grave; 138: 13 just spirits had offered sacrifice in s. of Son's great sacrifice.

Moses 1: 6, 13, 16 Moses is in s. of Only Begotten; 5: 7 sacrifice of Adam is s. of sacrifice of Only Begotten.

SIMPLE, SIMPLENESS (see also Plain)

D&C 1: 23 gospel to be proclaimed by the weak and the s.; 133: 57 the Lord reasons in plainness and s.

SIN (see also Abomination; Apostasy; Confession of Sins; Crime; Darkness, Spiritual; Death, Spiritual; Devil; Disobedience; Err; Evil; Fall of Man; Forgive; Guilt; Iniquity; Jesus Christ, Atonement through; Jesus Christ—Savior; Justice; Offense; Pollute; Punishment; Remission; Repentance; Sinner; Transgression; Trespass; Wicked; TG Sin)

D&C 1: 27 commandments given that the Lord's servants who s. might be chastened and repent; 1: 31 the Lord cannot look upon s. with allowance; 4: 35 (29: 3; 82: 2, 7) s. no more; 10: 25 Satan tells men it is no s. to lie; 18: 44 marvelous work without convincing of many of their s., that they might repent; 19: 2 (59: 12; 61: 2) confess your s.; 20: 37 those who confess they have repented of s. should be baptized; 29: 3 (64: 3) your s. are forgiven you; 29: 47 children cannot s. until they begin to become accountable; 42: 28 he who s. and repents not should be cast out; 42: 37 he who s. and repents not should have consecrated property; 45: 4 behold the sufferings and death of him who did not s.; 45: 58 in Millennium, children shall grow up without s.; 49: 20 (84: 49) world lies in s.; 50: 29 those who are purified and cleansed from all s. shall receive whatever they ask; 56: 14 saints' s. have come up unto the Lord; 59: 15 much laughter is s.; 64: 3 some among elders have s.; 64: 7 the Lord forgives s. unto those who have not s. unto death; 64: 9 greater s. remains in him who forgives not; 68: 25 s. is upon heads of neglectful parents; 82: 3 he who is against greater light receives greater condemnation; 82: 7 former s. return to souls who s. again; 84: 50–51 those who come not unto the Lord are under bondage of s.; 88: 35 he who abides in s. cannot be sanctified; 88: 82 men's s. are upon their own heads after being warned; 88: 86 entangle not yourselves in s.; 95: 6 walking in darkness is grievous s.; 98: 20 many members do not forsake their s.; 101: 9 notwithstanding saints' s., the Lord will remember mercy; 109: 34 as

all men s., forgive the transgressions of thy people; 111: 11 be wise as serpents, yet without s.; 121: 17 those who cry transgression do it because they are servants of s.; 121: 37 when men undertake to cover their s., Spirit withdraws; 132: 26 fate of those sealed in new and everlasting covenant who s.; 132: 39 David and Solomon did not s. save in wives not received from God; 138: 57 spirits in darkness are under bondage of s.

Moses 5: 23 if thou doest well, s. lieth at the door; 6: 55 inasmuch as children are conceived in s., when they begin to grow up, s. conceives in their hearts; A of F 2 all men will be punished for own s.

SINAI, MOUNT (see also Mount, Mountain)

D&C 29: 13 trump shall sound as upon M.S.

SINCERITY, SINCERE (see also Deceit; Honest; Hypocrisy; Integrity; Intent; Unfeigned)

D&C 5: 24 Martin Harris to humble himself in s. of heart; 20: 6 Joseph Smith humbled himself s.

SING, SINGING (see also Praise; Rejoice; Song)

D&C 45: 71 (66: 11; 101: 18; 109: 39; 133: 33) righteous shall come to Zion, s. songs of everlasting joy; 84: 98–102 those who remain will s. new song together; 128: 22 let the earth break forth into s.; 128: 23 morning stars s. together; 133: 56 resurrected saints shall s. the song of the Lamb; 136: 28 (138: 24) praise the Lord with s.

SINGLE, SINGLENESS (see also Diligence)

D&C 4: 5 eye s. to glory of God qualifies man for the work; 27: 2 partake of sacrament with eye s. to the Lord's glory; 36: 7 those who embrace gospel with s. of heart shall be ordained; 59: 1 blessed are they who come into land with eyes s. to the Lord's glory; 59: 13 on Sabbath prepare food with s. of heart; 82: 19 do all things with eye s. to glory of God; 88: 67 if your eye be s. to my glory, your whole bodies shall be filled with light; 88: 68 sanctify yourselves that your minds become s. to God.

SINNER (see also Sin)

D&C 43: 18 ye s. stay and sleep until the Lord calls again; 63: 57 those who desire to warn s. should be called.

SISTER (see also Family)

D&C 42: 88, 90 if brother or s. offends, be reconciled.

Abr. 2: 24–25 Abraham is instructed to tell Egyptians Sarai is his s.; JS-H 1: 4, 7 Joseph Smith's s., Sophronia, Catherine, Lucy.

SIX

D&C 77: 12 God made world in s. days.

SKILL

D&C 89: 8 tobacco to be used with judgment and s.

SKIN (see also Coat; Mark)

Moses 4: 27 the Lord makes coats of s. for Adam and Eve.

SLAIN (see Slay)

SLANDER, SLANDERER (see also Deceit; Gossip; Lying; Report)

D&C 109: 30 an end to lyings and s. against the Lord's people; 112: 9 let tongue of the s. cease its perverseness.

SLAUGHTER (see also Battle; Kill; Slay; War)

D&C 135: 4 I am going like lamb to s.

SLAVERY, SLAVE (see also Bondage; Freedom)

D&C 87: 4 s. shall rise up against masters; 130: 13 war will probably arise through s. question; 134: 12 dangerous to allow human beings to be held in servitude.

SLAY, SLEW, SLAIN (see also Death, Physical; Destruction; Jesus Christ; Death of; Jesus Christ—Lamb of God; Kill; Murder; Slaughter; Smite)

D&C 5: 22 he who keeps commandments shall be granted eternal life, even if he should be s.; 63: 33 wicked shall s. the wicked; 89: 21 destroying angel shall not s. those who keep Word of Wisdom.

Moses 5: 32 Cain s. Abel; 5: 39 Cain fears men will s. him; 5: 47–50 Lamech[1] s. Irad; 7: 7 people of Canaan to s. people of Shum in battle; Abr. 1: 12 priests try to s. Abraham.

SLEEP, SLEPT (see also Death, Physical; Death, Spiritual; Idleness; Retire; Slumber)

D&C 43: 18 sinners s. until the Lord shall call again; 45: 45 (88: 97) saints that have s. shall come forth; 63: 51 (101: 31)

children shall not s. but shall be changed in twinkling; 88: 97 they who have s. in graves shall come forth; 88: 124 cease to s. longer than is needful; 138: 17 sleeping dust of the dead to be restored to perfect frame.

Moses 3: 21 (Abr. 5: 15) God causes deep s. to fall upon Adam; JS-H 1: 46 vision of Moroni[2] causes s. to flee from eyes of Joseph Smith.

SLOTHFUL, SLOTHFULNESS (see also Diligence; Idle; Neglect)

D&C 58: 26 he who is compelled in all things is s. servant; 58: 29 he who keeps commandments with s. is damned; 90: 18 keep s. and uncleanness far from you; 101: 50 while servants of nobleman were at variance one with another, they became very s.; 107: 100 he who is s. shall not be counted worthy.

SLOW, SLOWLY (see also Quickly)

D&C 101: 7 God is s. to answer prayers of those who are s. to hearken to him.

Moses 6: 31 Enoch[1] s. of speech; Abr. 3: 5 lesser light moves more s.

SLUMBER (see also Sleep)

D&C 112: 5 let not inhabitants of earth s. because of thy speech.

SMALL (see also Little; Plates of Nephi; Small; Voice)

D&C 64: 33 out of s. things proceeds that which is great; 121: 7 (122: 4) afflictions shall be but a s. moment; 123: 15 much lieth in futurity, depending on s. things; 123: 16 large ship is benefited by very s. helm; 128: 6 I saw the dead, s. and great.

SMELL (see also Stink)

D&C 59: 19 things of earth given for taste and for s.

SMILE (see also Please)

D&C 84: 101 heavens have s. upon earth.

Moses 7: 43 the Lord s. upon ark of Noah[1].

SMITE, SMITTEN (see also Chasten; Destruction; Kill; Persecution; Slay)

D&C 19: 15 repent, lest I s. you by rod of my mouth; 27: 9 (110: 15; 128: 17; 138: 48) hearts of children to be turned to fathers lest earth be s. with a curse; 98: 23 if men s. elders or families, they should bear it patiently; 133: 26 those in north countries shall s. rocks and ice shall flow.

Abr. 1: 20, 29 God s. priest of Elkenah, that he dies.

SMITH, ALVIN

D&C 137: 5 Joseph Smith saw A.S. in vision.

JS-H 1: 4, 56 Joseph Smith's brother, dies.

SMITH, CATHERINE

JS-H 1: 4 sister of Joseph Smith.

SMITH, DON C.

D&C 124: 133 president of high priests quorum.

SMITH, EDEN

D&C 75: 36 to preach with Micah B. Welton; 80: 1–5 to preach gospel; 80: 2 to be companion of Stephen Burnett.

SMITH, EMMA HALE—*wife of Joseph Smith*

D&C sec. 25 revelation concerning will of the Lord to E.S.; 25: 2 the Lord promises to give E.S. inheritance in Zion if faithful; 25: 3 sins are forgiven; 25: 4 is warned against murmuring; 25: 5 is called to comfort husband; 25: 6 to serve as scribe; 25: 7–8 to be ordained by Joseph to expound scripture in church; 25: 10 to lay aside things of world; 25: 11 to make selection of hymns; 25: 14 is warned of pride; 132: 51–56 the Lord's counsel to E.S. regarding marriage.

JS-H 1: 57 marries Joseph Smith.

SMITH, GEORGE A.

D&C 124: 129 a member of the Twelve; 136: 14 to organize company for journey west.

SMITH, HYRUM—*older brother of Joseph Smith*

D&C secs. 11, 23 revelations to H.S.; 23: 3 calling is to exhortation; 52: 8 to journey to Missouri by way of Detroit; 75: 32 to preach with Reynolds Cahoon; 94: Intro. appointed to church building committee; 111: Intro. goes to Salem, Mass., with Joseph Smith; 115: 1, 5, 6 to labor for the gathering; 115: 13 not to get in debt any more for building the Lord's house; 124: 15 is loved by the Lord because of his integrity; 124: 91–96, 124 to take office of patriarch; 124: 95 receives blessings formerly put upon Oliver Cowdery; 135: 1, 6 martyrdom of H.S.; 138: 53 among mighty ones in spirit world.

JS-H 1: 4, 7 joins Presbyterians.

SMITH, JOHN

D&C 102: 3 member of high council.

SMITH, JOSEPH, JR. *(see also* Book of Mormon; *Joseph)*

D&C 1: 17 (19: 13) the Lord spoke to J.S. from heaven; 1: 29 (20: 8) translated Book of Mormon through power of God; 3: 9 (24: 1) is chosen to do work of the Lord; 5: 1 bore record of Book of Mormon plates; 5: 10 this generation will have the Lord's word through J.S.; 5: 21 (93: 47–48) is commanded to repent; 5: 22, 35 to be granted eternal life if obedient; 5: 30, 33–34 is directed to stop translating for a season; 9: 12 is given strength for his work; 10: 3 gift to translate restored; 13: 1 (27: 8) is ordained by John the Baptist; 17: 6 the Lord testifies that J.S. has translated book; 20: 2 (27: 12) is called of God, ordained apostle, first elder; 20: 5 is told that sins are remitted; 20: 5 is again entangled in vanities of world; 20: 6 is ministered to by angel; 21: 1 (124: 125) to be called seer, translator, prophet, apostle; 21: 2 is inspired by Holy Ghost to lay foundation of church; 21: 5 speaks for the Lord; 21: 10 is ordained by Oliver Cowdery; 24: 1 is delivered from powers of Satan and darkness; 24: 8 is told of many afflictions; 24: 9 is not called to temporal labors; 27: 13 (115: 19) keys of kingdom committed to J.S.; 28: 2 (132: 7) only J.S. to receive revelation for church; 28: 2 receives revelation as did Moses; 28: 7 (35: 18; 64: 5) is given keys of mysteries and sealed revelations; 28: 10 to preside over conferences; 35: 17 brought forth fulness of gospel; 35: 13 is blessed in weakness; 35: 18 another to be planted in J.S's stead if he abide not in the Lord; 37: 1 to discontinue translation until move to Ohio; 41: 7 to have house for translating; 52: 3 to journey to Missouri; 52: 41 should carry recommend from church; 58: 58 to return to Kirtland; 60: 6 to go to Cincinnati; 61: 23 not to travel on waters; 63: 41 is given power to discern who should go to land of Zion; 63: 41 keys not to be taken from J.S. if faithful; 73: 3 to translate again; 76: 14, 19–23 (110: 1–10) sees and converses with the Son; 81: 2 holds keys of presidency of High Priesthood; 84: 3 dedicates site of New Jerusalem; 90: 1–16 his duties and powers; 100: 9–11 Sidney Rigdon to be spokesman for J.S.; 102: 1 high council organized under direction of J.S.; sec. 109 dedicatory prayer for Kirtland Temple received by revelation and offered by J.S.; sec. 110 visions manifested to J.S. in Kirtland Temple; 112: 15 the Twelve not to rebel against J.S.; 115: 13 not to get in debt any more for building the Lord's house; sec. 122 word of the Lord to J.S. in Liberty Jail;

124: 1 was raised up so that the Lord might show his wisdom through the weak; 124: 42 temple service to be shown to J.S.; 124: 125 presiding elder over church; 130: 14–17 prays about time of Christ's coming; 132: 7 sealing power vested in J.S.; 132: 30 is from loins of Abraham; sec. 135 announcement of martyrdom of J.S. 135: 3 has done more for salvation of men than any other man except Christ; 136: 39 must seal testimony with blood; sec. 137 J.S.'s vision of celestial kingdom; 138: 53 among mighty ones in spirit world.

JS-H 1: 3 birth; 1: 4 family; 1: 8–9 is confused by contentions among religious sects; 1: 11 reads James 1: 5; 1: 13 decides to ask God; 1: 14 retires to woods to pray; 1: 15 is seized by power of darkness; 1: 16 pillar of light descends upon J.S.; 1: 17 sees two Personages; 1: 19–20 is forbidden to join religious sects; 1: 20 tells mother that Presbyterianism is not true; 1: 21 tells Methodist preacher of vision; 1: 22–25, 27 is persecuted because of vision; 1: 23 fourteen years of age at time of first vision; 1: 24 feels much like Paul before King Agrippa; 1: 28 temptations come to J.S.; 1: 28 guilty of levity; 1: 29–30 prays to God on September 21, 1823; 1: 30–42, 45–46 Moroni[2] appears to J.S. in bedroom; 1: 33 name to be had for good and evil; 1: 34–35, 42 is told of gold plates; 1: 42 sees in vision the hiding place of gold plates; 1: 46 is told Satan will tempt him; 1: 46 is forbidden to get plates for purpose of getting rich; 1: 49 Moroni[2] appears to J.S. in field; 1: 50 tells father of visions; 1: 52 sees plates deposited in hill; 1: 54 goes to hill each year as directed by Moroni[2]; 1: 56 works for Josiah Stoal in silver mine; 1: 57 marries Emma Hale; 1: 60 men try to get plates from J.S.; 1: 60 completes work, returns plates to Moroni[2]; 1: 60–61 is persecuted because of plates; 1: 68 prays concerning baptism; 1: 68–72 John the Baptist appears to J.S.; 1: 71–72 J.S. and Oliver Cowdery ordain each other to Aaronic Priesthood, baptize each other; 1: 72 to be called first elder of Church; 1: 73 is filled with Holy Ghost, has spirit of prophecy following baptism; 1: 74 scriptures are laid open to understanding of J.S.

SMITH, JOSEPH, SR.

D&C secs. 4, 23 revelations to J.S.; 23: 5 is called to exhort and strengthen church; 90: 20 God's aged servant; 102: 3 member of high council; 124: 19 is with the Lord.

JS-H 1: 3–4 father of Joseph Smith; 1: 50 tells son that messenger is from God.

SMITH, JOSEPH F.—sixth president of Church, son of Hyrum Smith

D&C sec. 138 J.F.S's vision of redemption of dead.

SMITH, LUCY

JS-H 1: 4 sister of Joseph Smith.

SMITH, LUCY MACK

JS-H 1: 4, 20 mother of Joseph Smith; 1: 7 joins Presbyterian faith; 1: 20 is told by son that Presbyterianism is not true.

SMITH, SAMUEL H.

D&C sec. 3 revelation to; 23: 4 is called to exhort; 52: 30 to journey to Missouri; 61: 35 to travel with Reynolds Cahoon; 66: 8 to travel with William McLellin; 75: 13 to travel with Orson Hyde; 102: 3 member of high council; 124: 141 to preside over a bishopric.

JS-H 1: 4 brother of Joseph Smith; 1: 7 joins Presbyterian faith.

SMITH, SOPHRONIA

JS-H 1: 4 sister of Joseph Smith; 1: 7 joins Presbyterian faith.

SMITH, SYLVESTER

D&C 75: 34 to preach with Gideon Carter; 102: 3 member of high council.

SMITH, WILLIAM

D&C 124: 129 member of the Twelve.

JS-H 1: 4 brother of Joseph Smith.

SMOKE (see also Cloud; Mist; Tobacco; Vapor)

D&C 45: 40–41 the Lord will show wonders in heavens and earth, vapors of s.

SMOOTH

D&C 49: 23 (109: 74) rough ways shall be made s.

SNARE (see also Guile; Pit)

D&C 10: 26 Satan causes men to catch themselves in own s.; 61: 18 warn brethren about waters, lest faith fail and they are caught in s.; 63: 15 adulterers and apostates must repent lest judgment come upon them as s.; 90: 17 pride brings s.

SNIDER, JOHN

D&C 124: 22–24, 60, 62, 70 to help in building Nauvoo House.

SNOW

D&C 110: 3 hair of the Lord's head was white like s.; 117: 1 saints to journey before the Lord sends again s. upon earth.

SNOW, ERASTUS

D&C 136: 12 to organize company to journey west.

SOAP

D&C 128: 24 the Lord is like refiner's fire, and fuller's s.

SOBERNESS, SOBER (see also Lightmindedness; Solemn)

D&C 6: 19 (43: 35; 61: 38; 73: 6) be s.; 6: 35 perform work with s.; 18: 21 speak truth in s.

SOCIETY (See Secret Combination)

SOFTEN (see also Hardheartedness)

D&C 105: 27 the Lord will s. hearts of people.

SOJOURN (see also Dwell; Journey)

Abr. 2: 21 Abraham decides to s. in Egypt.

SOLD (see Sell)

SOLEMN, SOLEMNITY (see also Soberness; Solemn Assembly)

D&C 20: 76 call upon Father in s. prayer; 43: 34 let s. of eternity rest upon your minds; 84: 61 remain steadfast in s.; 100: 7 declare all things in s. of heart; 107: 84 all things to be done in order and s.; 124: 2, 107 Joseph Smith and William Law called to make a s. proclamation of gospel.

SOLEMN ASSEMBLY (see also Conference; Meet, Meeting)

D&C 88: 70 (95: 7; 109: 6, 10; 133: 6) call a s.a.; 108: 4 wait patiently until a s.; 124: 39 s.a. are ordained by ordinance of the Lord's holy house.

SOLITARY (see also Waste)

D&C 117: 7 the Lord to make s. places to bud and blossom.

SOLOMON—king of Israel, son of David [c. 1000 B.C.] (see also BD Solomon)

D&C 132: 1, 38 was given many wives.

SON (see also Child; Children of God; Father; Jesus Christ—Only Begotten Son; Jesus Christ—Son of God; Jesus Christ—Son of Man; Mosiah, Sons of; Sons of Perdition)

D&C 11: 30 (34: 3; 35: 2; 39: 4; 42: 52; 45: 8) those who receive the Lord are given power to become s. of God; 13: 1 (124: 39; 128: 24; Mal. 3: 3) s. of Levi[1] shall offer again an offering in righteousness; 25: 1 all who receive gospel are s. and daughters in the Lord's kingdom; 27: 7 Elias promised Zacharias he would have a s.; 38: 26 what man having twelve s. is no respecter of them; 42: 52 those without faith to heal, but who believe in the Lord, will become s.; 68: 6 firstborn among s. of Aaron[1] have right to bishopric; 68: 21 (107: 40) right of priesthood descends from father to s.; 76: 24 inhabitants of worlds are begotten s. and daughters unto God; 76: 26–27 Lucifer, s. of morning; 76: 58 those in celestial glory are s. of God; 84: 30 priesthood was confirmed upon Aaron[1] and his s.; 84: 31–32 s. of Moses and of Aaron[1] will offer acceptable sacrifice; 84: 34 those who magnify priesthood become s. of Moses and of Aaron[1]; 101: 4 (132: 36, 50) Abraham was commanded to offer his only s.; 128: 23 all s. of God shouted for joy; 128: 24 Lord shall purify s. of Levi.[1]

Moses 1: 4, 40 God calls Moses his s.; 4: 1 (Abr. 3: 27–28) Satan offers to God's s.; 5: 2 s. and daughters are born to Adam and Eve; 5: 3 s. and daughters of Adam begin to divide two and two; 5: 13 Satan claims to be a s. of God; 5: 42–43 Cain and descendants beget many s. and daughters; 5: 42 Cain names city after his s., Enoch[1]; 6: 22 genealogy of s. of Adam, who was the s. of God; 6: 27, 68 God calls Enoch[2] his s.; 6: 68 all may become God's s.; 7: 1 many have believed and have become s. of God; 8: 13 Noah[1] and his s. are called s. of God; 8: 15 daughters of s. of Noah defile themselves; 8: 21 men claim to be s. of God and do not hearken to Noah[1]; Abr. 1: 17 God calls Abraham his s.; JS-H 1: 69 priesthood never to be taken until s. of Levi[1] offer offering.

SON OF GOD (see Jesus Christ—Only Begotten Son; Jesus Christ—Son of God)

SON OF MAN (see Jesus Christ—Son of Man)

SONG (see also Hymn; Sing)

D&C 25: 12 the Lord delights in s. of heart; 45: 71 (66: 11; 101: 18; 109: 39; 133: 33) sing s. of everlasting joy; 84: 98–102 all who remain will sing new s.; 133: 56 resurrected saints will sing s. of God.

Moses 7: 53 they shall come forth with s. of everlasting joy.

SONS OF PERDITION (see also Death, Spiritual; Perdition; TG Death, Spiritual, Second; Holy Ghost, Unpardonable Sin against; Sons of Perdition)

D&C 76: 31–32 s. of perdition deny

truth and defy the Lord's power; 76: 33, 36 will suffer with devil in eternity; 76: 34 (84: 41; 132: 27) to receive no forgiveness; 76: 35, 43 deny Holy Ghost after receiving it and deny Son; 76: 37–38, 43 only ones who will not be redeemed from second death; 76: 39 will not be brought back to presence of God in resurrection.

Moses 4: 3 because Satan rebelled against God, he was cast down; 5: 24 Cain to be called Perdition; **Abr.** 3: 28 second was angry, kept not first estate, many followed him.

SORCERER

D&C 63: 17 s. to have part in lake of fire and brimstone; 76: 103 s. inherit telestial glory.

SORE

D&C 19: 15 sufferings of those who do not repent will be s.

Abr. 2: 1 famine waxes s. in Ur.

SORROW, SORROWFUL, SORROWING

(see also Anguish; Grieve; Lament; Misery; Mourn; Pain; Sad; Suffering; Torment; Tribulation; Trouble; Weep)

D&C 1: 3 the rebellious shall be pierced with much s.; 101: 29 there shall be no s. because there is no death; 109: 48 hearts flow over with s. because of saints' grievous burdens; 123: 7 wives and children bow down with grief and s.; 133: 70 the wicked shall lie down in s.; 136: 29 he who is s. should call on the Lord; 136: 35 s. shall be great unless they speedily repent.

Moses 4: 22 I will greatly multiply thy s.; 4: 23 in s. shalt thou eat.

SOUL

(see also Body; Heart; Man; Mind; Spirit; TG Soul)

D&C 4: 4 (6: 3; 11: 3; 12: 3) service to God brings salvation to s.; 8: 4 enemies would destroy your s.; 10: 22, 27 Satan plans to destroy s.; 15: 6 (16: 6) declare repentance, that you may bring s. unto the Lord; 18: 10 worth of s. is great; 18: 15 if you bring one s., how great shall be joy; 18: 16 great joy if you should bring many s. unto the Lord; 25: 12 the Lord's s. delights in song of heart; 41: 12 words shall be answered upon saints' s. in the judgment; 45: 2 (56: 16) summer past and s. not saved; 45: 46 your s. shall live; 56: 16 riches canker s.; 59: 19 things which come of earth enliven s.; 63: 4 God is able to cast s. to hell; 84: 64 every s. who believes and is baptized will receive Holy Ghost; 88: 15 spirit and the body are s. of man; 88: 16 resurrection is redemption of s.; 101: 37 care not for body, but for s. and

for life of s.; 121: 42 pure knowledge shall greatly enlarge s.; 121: 45 doctrine of priesthood shall distil upon s.; 132: 63 wives given that they may bear s. of men; 134: 4 civil government should not suppress freedom of s.; 138: 43 spirits come forth in resurrection as living s.; 138: 56 spirits were prepared to labor for salvation of s.

Moses 1: 28 not a s. which Moses does not behold; 3: 7, 9 (6: 9; **Abr.** 5: 7) man became living s.; 4: 1 Satan promises that not one s. will be lost; 6: 59 through birth men become of dust a living s.; 7: 44 Enoch[2] has bitterness of s. because of men's wickedness; 7: 47 s. of Enoch[2] rejoices because of coming of Son; **Abr.** 2: 15 Abraham and Lot bring to Canaan the s. won in Haran; 2: 24–25 Abraham to say Sarai is his sister, that his s. may live; 3: 23 God saw s. in premortal world that they were good.

SOUND (see also Voice)

D&C 58: 64 s. must go forth from this place into all world; 77: 12 s. of trumpets explained; 110: 3 the Lord's voice was as s. of rushing of great waters; 124: 106 Joseph Smith to lift voice as with s. of trump.

JS-M 1: 37 (Matt. 24: 31) Son will send angels before him with great s. of trumpet.

SOUTH (see North; Southern States)

SOUTH CAROLINA

D&C 87: 1 (130: 12) rebellion to begin in S.C.

SOUTHERN STATES

D&C 87: 3 divided against the North.

SOW (see also Plant; Reap)

D&C 6: 33 whatsoever ye s. that shall ye reap; 86: 2 apostles were s. of seed.

SPACE (see also Time)

D&C 88: 12 light from God's presence fills immensity of s.; 88: 37 no s. in which there is no kingdom; 88: 95 silence in heaven about the s. of half hour.

Moses 1: 10 s. of many hours before Moses receives strength; 7: 64–65 earth to rest for s. of thousand years; **Abr.** 3: 24 there is s., and we will make an earth.

SPARE (see also Preserve; Protection; Salvation; Save; Sparingly; Withhold)

D&C 29: 22 the Lord will s. earth for little season; 33: 9 open your mouths and s. not; 34: 10 (43: 20) lift up your voice and s. not; 45: 5 s. these my brethren that believe on my name; 64: 24 the Lord will not s. any who remain in Babylon; 84: 94 search diligently and s. not; 104: 17 earth is full, there is enough and to s.

SPARINGLY (see also Spare)

D&C 89: 12 flesh should be used s.

SPEAK, SPAKE, SPOKEN (see also Language; Lips; Mouth; Say; Speech; Talk; Tongue; Utter; Voice; Whisper)

D&C 1: 3 iniquities shall be s. upon housetops; 1: 20 s. in name of God; 1: 24 (18: 35; 20: 36) God has s. it; 6: 23 did I not s. peace to your mind; 11: 10 believe in my power which s. unto thee; 19: 37 elders to s. freely to all; 20: 26 prophets as s. as they were inspired by gift of Holy Ghost; 20: 54 teachers should see that no evil is s.; 24: 6 it shall be given thee in the very moment what thou shalt s.; 28: 4 (68: 3) s. or teach as led by Comforter; 29: 33 the Lord s. that man may naturally understand; 42: 27 thou shalt not s. evil of thy neighbor; 52: 16 he who s. whose language is meek and edifies is of God; 63: 64 that which comes from above is sacred and must be s. with care; 84: 70 tongue of the dumb shall s.; 88: 122 one to s. at a time in church; 100: 5 s. the thoughts that I had put into your hearts.

SPEECH (see also Language; Speak; Tongue; Voice)

D&C 88: 121 cease from all light s.; 112: 5 let not the inhabitants of the earth slumber, because of thy s.; 124: 116 lay aside all hard s.

Moses 6: 31 Enoch[2] is slow of s.

SPHERE

D&C 77: 3 four beasts represent beings in their destined s. of creation; 93: 30 truth is dependent in that s. in which God has placed it.

Moses 3: 9 it remaineth in s. in which God created it.

SPIN

D&C 84: 82 lilies of field toil not, neither do they s.

SPIRIT (see also Broken Heart and Contrite Spirit; Mind; Soul; Spirit, Evil; Spirit, Holy/Spirit of the Lord; Spirit World; Spiritual; TG Spirit Body; Spirit Creation; Spirits, Disembodied; BD Spirit)

D&C 11: 25 deny not s. of revelation or of prophecy; 19: 18 Christ suffered both body and s.; 27: 7 John to be filled with s. of Elias; 45: 17 (138: 50) long

absence of s. from bodies looked upon as bondage; 46: 23 spiritual gift of discerning s.; 50: 30 as ye are appointed to the head, s. shall be subject to you; 50: 31 ask God whether s. is of him; 52: 15–16 he whose s. is contrite is accepted; 52: 19 pattern for knowing s.; 56: 17 wo unto the poor whose s. are not contrite; 76: 73 (138: 18–32) s. in prison hear gospel; 76: 73 Son visited s. of men in prison; 76: 88 angels appointed to be ministering s.; 77: 2 s. of man is in likeness of his person; 88: 15 s. and body are soul of man; 88: 28 celestial s. shall receive same body which was natural body; 88: 100 s. of men who are to be judged shall come forth; 93: 33 man is s.; 93: 33–34 (138: 17) s. and element inseparably connected receive fulness of joy; 93: 38 every s. of man was innocent in beginning; 97: 8 all whose s. are contrite are accepted of the Lord; sec. 129 keys by which to know s.; 129: 3 s. of just men made perfect; 130: 22 Holy Ghost is personage of s.; 131: 7 all s. is matter, more fine or pure; sec. 138 vision relating to s. world; 138: 53 choice s. reserved to take part in laying foundation of the Lord's work.

Moses 6: 5 given unto those who call upon God to write by s. of inspiration; 6: 36 Enoch[2] beholds s. that God created; 6: 59 men born into this world by water, blood, and s.; **Abr.** 3: 18 s. had no beginning, will have no end; 3: 22–23 Abraham sees s. that were organized before the world was; 5: 7–8 the Gods put man's s. into him.

SPIRIT, EVIL (see also Angels of the Devil; Devil; Devils; TG Spirits, Evil or Unclean)

D&C 46: 7 do all things with prayer and thanksgiving, that ye may not be seduced by evil s.; 50: 1–2 many false s. have gone forth in earth; 50: 15 then received ye s. which ye could not understand; 50: 31 if ye behold s. that you cannot understand, ask Father; 50: 32 power over that s. shall be given, proclaim against it; 93: 25 whatsoever is more or less than this is s. of wicked one; 129: 4–8 way of telling whether s. is of God or devil.

SPIRIT, GIFTS OF (see also Holy Ghost; Holy Ghost, Baptism of; Holy Ghost, Gift of; Interpretation; Sign; Spirit, Holy/Spirit of the Lord; Tongue; Translation; TG God, Gifts of; Holy Ghost, Gifts of)

D&C 6: 10 blessed art thou because of thy gift, for it is sacred and comes from above; 20: 26 prophets spoke as inspired by gift of Holy Ghost: 20: 35 revelations to come by gift and power of Holy Ghost; 46: 11–33 description of gifts of the S.; 46: 11 all have not every gift, for there are many gifts; 46: 11 to every man is given a gift by S.; 46: 26 all these gifts come from God for benefit of his children; 46: 29 to some it may be given to have all those gifts, that there may be a head; 107: 92 president of church has all gifts of God which he bestows on head of church; 121: 26 God shall give you knowledge by unspeakable gift of Holy Ghost.

Moses 5: 58 gospel preached from beginning by gift of Holy Ghost.

SPIRIT, HOLY/SPIRIT OF THE LORD
(see also Born of God; Holy Ghost; Holy Ghost, Baptism of; Holy Ghost—Comforter; Holy Spirit of Promise; Inspire; Light; Revelation; Spirit, Gifts of; Spiritual; Truth; TG God, Spirit of; Holy Ghost; Jesus Christ, Spirit of; Lord, Spirit of; BD Spirit, the Holy)

D&C 1: 33 the Lord's S. shall not always strive with man; 1: 39 (59: 24) S. bears record; 5: 16 manifestation of S. depends on faith; 5: 16 those who believe will be born of S.; 6: 14 those who inquire receive instruction of S.; 6: 15 thou hast been enlightened by S. of truth; 8: 3 this is the s. of revelation; 11: 12 put trust in that S. which leads to do good; 11: 13 (84: 46) S. shall enlighten mind, fill soul with joy; 11: 18 appeal unto my S.; 11: 21 after obtaining the word, elders shall have the Lord's S.; 18: 2 truth of things written manifested by S.; 18: 2–3, 35, 47 (75: 1; 97: 1) word of God given by S.; 19: 20 punishments tasted when S. is withdrawn; 19: 23 walk in meekness of S.; 19: 38 pray always, and I will pour out my S.; 20: 37 candidates for baptism must manifest they have received of S. of Christ; 20: 77, 79 those who partake of sacrament shall have S.; 27: 18 take the sword of my S.; 29: 30–31 the Lord created all things by power of his S.; 33: 16 power of S. quickens all things; 35: 13 the Lord to thrash nations by power of S.; 42: 6 go forth in power of S., preaching gospel; 42: 13 (43: 15) teach as directed by S.; 42: 14 (63: 64) S. given by prayer of faith; 42: 14 if ye receive not the S., ye shall not teach; 42: 23 (63: 16) he who looks upon woman to lust shall not have S.; 45: 57 the wise have taken H.S. for their guide; 46: 2 elders to conduct meetings as guided by H.S.; 46: 7 do that which S. testifies; 46: 28 he who asks in S. shall receive in S.; 46: 30 he who asks in S. asks according to will of God; 46: 31 all things done in S. must be

done in name of Christ; 50: 13–14 (124: 88) elders are ordained to preach gospel by S.; 50: 17 preach by S. of truth; 55: 1–3 (53: 3; 76: 52) reception of H.S. by laying on of hands; 61: 27–28 (62: 8) do as commanded by S.; 63: 32 (64: 16; 121: 37) the Lord holds his S. because of wickedness; 63: 41 Joseph Smith has power to discern by S. who should go to Zion; 63: 55 Sidney Rigdon grieves the S.; 63: 64 things to be spoken with constraint of S.; 70: 14 S. to be withheld if saints are not equal in temporal things; 72: 24 members are appointed by H.S. to go to Zion; 76: 12, 18 by power of S. our eyes were opened; 76: 35 sons of perdition deny H.S. after receiving it; 76: 52 those in celestial glory have received H.S. by laying on of hands; 76: 83 telestial inhabitants deny not H.S.; 76: 116 mysteries understood only through S.; 76: 116 S. bestowed on those who love God and purify themselves; 76: 118 man can bear God's presence only through manifestation of S.; 84: 33 those who magnify priesthood callings are sanctified by S.; 84: 45 whatsoever is light is S.; 84: 46 S. gives light to every man; 84: 47 everyone who hearkens to S. comes unto Father; 84: 88 my S. shall be in your hearts; 88: 66 my voice is S.; 88: 66 (91: 4; 93: 23–26) my S. is truth; 88: 137 pray as S. gives utterance; 93: 9, 11, 26 Christ is S. of truth; 95: 4 the Lord to pour out S. upon all flesh; 97: 1 the Lord speaks with voice of his S.; 99: 2 elders given power to declare word in demonstration of H.S.; 104: 81 write according to that which shall be dictated by S.; 105: 36 those who are chosen shall be manifest by voice of S.; 107: 71 high priest may serve as bishop, having knowledge of temporal things by S. of truth; 111: 8 place to tarry shall be signalized by peace and power of S.; 112: 22 hearken to voice of S.; 136: 33 S. is sent forth into world.

Moses 1: 15 God's S. has not altogether withdrawn from Moses; 1: 27–28 Moses discerns earth and its inhabitants by S. of God; 2: 2 (Abr. 4: 2) God's S. moves upon face of water; 6: 26 S. of God descends from heaven, abides upon Enoch²; 6: 60 by the S. ye are justified; 6: 65 S. of God descends upon Adam; 8: 17 S. will not always strive with man; **Abr.** 4: 2 S. of God broods upon the waters.

SPIRIT WORLD (see also Darkness, Spiritual; Death, Physical; Death, Spiritual; Hell; Paradise; Premortal Existence; Prison; Resurrection; Spirit)

D&C sec. 138 Joseph F. Smith's

vision of redemption of the dead in s. world.

Moses 6: 36 Enoch² beholds the s. God has created; **Abr.** 3: 22–23 Abraham sees s. that were organized before the world was.

SPIRITUAL, SPIRITUALLY (*see also* Darkness, Spiritual; Death, Spiritual; Holy Ghost; Spirit; Spirit, Holy/Spirit of the Lord)

D&C 14: 11 blessed both s. and temporally; 29: 31–32 the Lord created first s., secondly temporal; 29: 34 all things unto the Lord are s.; 29: 35 the Lord's commandments are s.; 50: Intro. revelation given in regard to s. phenomena; 67: 10–12 men can see God only with s., not natural eyes; 70: 12 he who administers s. things is worthy of hire; 72: 14 labors of the faithful who labor in s. things shall answer debt unto bishop; 77: 2 temporal things in likeness of s.; 88: 27 the righteous who die shall rise again, a s. body; 107: 8, 18 Melchizedek Priesthood administers in s. things; 107: 32 quorums constitute s. authorities of church; 128: 14 (1 Cor. 15: 46–48) s. was not first, but the natural, afterward the s.; 133: 14 go out from wickedness, which is s. Babylon.

Moses 1: 11 Moses beholds God by s. eyes; 3: 5, 7 God created all things s. before naturally.

SPOKESMAN (*see also* Speak)

D&C 88: 122 let not all be s. at once; 100: 9 (124: 104) Sidney Rigdon to be s. for Joseph Smith.

SPOT, SPOTTED (*see also* Filthiness; Guilt; Sin; Spot of Land; Spotless; Stain)

D&C 36: 6 hate garments s. with flesh; 38: 31 saints to be righteous people, without s.

SPOT OF LAND (*see also* Lot)

D&C 58: 57 dedicate land and s. for temple; 84: 31 house of the Lord to be built upon consecrated s.; 101: 44 nobleman had s. of land.

SPOTLESS (*see also* Blameless; Cleanse; Guiltless; Innocent; Pure; Spot, Spotted)

D&C 61: 34 rid garments and be s. before the Lord; 76: 107 Christ to deliver up kingdom unto Father s.

SPREAD (*see also* Enlarge; Flourish; Grow; Increase; Shed)

D&C 82: 5 the adversary s. his

dominions; 97: 18 Zion shall prosper and s.; 110: 10 fame of this house shall s. to foreign lands.

Moses 5: 52 abominations s. among men.

SPRING, SPRINGING (*see also* Fountain; Grow; Stream; Water)

D&C 63: 23 mysteries of kingdom shall be well of living water s. up unto everlasting life; 86: 4 blade is s. up and is yet tender; 132: 34 from Hagar s. many people.

Moses 8: 3 from Methuselah's loins shall s. all kingdoms of earth.

SPRING HILL, MISSOURI

D&C sec. 116 revelation given at S.H.

SPRINKLE

D&C 133: 51 the Lord has s. blood upon his garments.

STAFF (*see also* Stave)

D&C 89: 14 all grain is ordained to be s. of life.

STAIN (*see also* Filthiness; Guilt; Sin; Spot; Unclean)

D&C 133: 51 the Lord will s. his raiment with blood.

STAKE (*see also* Church of God; Zion)

D&C 68: 25–26 (82: 13; 94: 1; 96: 1; 104: 40) Kirtland consecrated for s. to Zion; 82: 14 (96: 1; 133: 9) Zion's s. must be strengthened; 101: 21 (115: 18) the Lord will appoint places to be called s. for curtains or strength of Zion; 107: 36 authority of high councils in the s.; 107: 74 bishop to be common judge in s. of Zion; 109: 39 converts to come forth unto Zion, or to her s.; 109: 59 (115: 18) the Lord will appoint unto Zion other s. in addition to Kirtland; 115: 6 gathering together upon Zion and her s. may be for a defense; 119: 7 this shall be ensample unto s. of Zion; 124: 2 s. planted in Nauvoo as cornerstone; 124: 133–134 presidency of high priests to qualify standing presidents over different s.; 136: 10 saints to remove to place where the Lord will locate s.

STAND (*see also* Ensign; Example; TG God, the Standard of Righteousness)

D&C 4: 2 serve God that ye may s. blameless before him; 27: 15 take up the Lord's whole armor, that ye may be able to s.; 29: 11 the wicked shall not s.; 38: 20 land of inheritance promised while earth shall s.; 42: 53 s. in the place of thy stewardship; 45: 32 (87: 8; 101: 22) s. in holy places; 78: 14 church to s. independent above all other creatures; 84: 101 (133: 25) the Lord s. in midst of his people; 84: 109 let every man s. in his own office; 88: 89 because of earthquakes men shall fall, not be able to s.; 107: 100 slothful shall not be counted worthy to s.; 110: 2 we saw the Lord s. upon breastwork.

Moses 1: 35 many worlds have passed away, many now s.; 6: 47 people cannot s. in God's presence; 7: 52 remnant of Abraham's seed always to be found while earth s.; JS-M 1: 12 when you see abomination of desolation, s. in the holy place.

STANDARD (see also Ensign; Example; Title of Liberty; τG God, the Standard of Righteousness)

D&C 45: 9 everlasting covenant to be s.; 98: 34 peace to be lifted as s.; 115: 5 shine forth, that thy light may be s. for nations; OD-2 candidates for priesthood ordination must meet s. of worthiness.

STANDING

D&C 20: 84 removing members should take letter certifying they are in good s.; 84: 111 deacons and teachers are s. ministers unto church; 107: 36 s. high councils at stakes; 119: 4 tithing shall be s. law; 124: 134 s. presidents over stakes shall be appointed; 124: 137 elders instituted as s. ministers.

STANTON, DANIEL

D&C 75: 33 to preach with Seymour Brunson.

STAR (see also Astronomy)

D&C 29: 14 (34: 9; 45: 42; 88: 87; 133: 49) s. to fall at the Lord's coming; 76: 81, 98 telestial glory compared with s.; 76: 109 inhabitants of telestial world innumerable as s.; 88: 9 the Lord is light of s. and power by which they were made; 128: 23 let sun, moon, morning s. sing together; 132: 30 Abraham's seed to continue as innumerable as s.

Moses 2: 16 (Abr. 4: 16) s. made according to God's word; **Abr.** 1: 31 fathers' record of knowledge of s. kept by Abraham; 3: 2 Abraham sees great s., one that is nearest throne of God; 3: 13 Kokob, which is s.; 3: 13 Kokaubeam signifies s., or all the great lights; 3: 17–18 planet or s. may exist above any other; JS-M 1: 33 (Matt. 24: 29) s. shall fall from heaven.

STATE (see also Condition)

D&C 77: 1 (130: 9) earth in its sanctified and immortal s.

STATUTE (see also Commandments of God; Law; Ordinance)

D&C 119: 6 (124: 39; 136: 2) saints must keep the Lord's s. and judgments in Zion.

STAVE (see also Staff)

D&C 24: 18 elders to take no purse nor scrip, neither s.

STAY (see also Cease; Hinder; Stop; Withhold)

D&C 1: 5 disciples shall go forth and none shall s. them; 29: 19 tongues of the wicked shall be s.; 38: 33 (76: 3) no power can s. the Lord's hand; 97: 23 scourge shall not be s. until the Lord come; 121: 33 what power shall s. the heavens; 133: 26 prophets shall no longer s. themselves.

STEADFAST, STEADFASTNESS (see also Diligence; Endure; Faithful; Firmness; Immovable; Obedience; Perseverance)

D&C 31: 9 govern your house in meekness, and be s.; 49: 23 be not deceived, but continue in s.; 82: 24 fall not from your s.; 84: 61 remain s. in your minds in solemnity and spirit of prayer.

STEADY

D&C 85: 8 man who puts forth hand to s. ark will fall by shaft of death.

STEAL (see also Fraud; Rob; Thief)

D&C 42: 20 (59: 6) thou shalt not s.; 42: 20 he who s. and will not repent shall be cast out; 42: 54 thou shalt not take brother's garment; 42: 84–85 members who shall s. shall be delivered unto law of land.

STEM OF JESSE

D&C 113: 1–4 explanation of S. of Jesse.

STEWARD, STEWARDSHIP (see also Servant)

D&C 42: 32 (104: 13) every man to be made s. over his own property; 42: 53 stand in place of thy s.; 42: 70 priests and teachers shall have their s.; 51: 19 wise s. shall enter into joy of his Lord; 52: 13 (78: 22) he who is faithful will be made ruler over many things; 64: 40 even bishopric shall be condemned if not faithful in s.; 69: 5 servants abroad shall send accounts of their s.; 70: 3–7 brethren appointed s. over revelations; 70: 9 what the Lord requires of every man in his s.; 72: 3-4 (70: 4; 104: 12-13; 124: 14) every s. to render account of s.; 72: 5, 16 elders to account for s. to bishop; 78: 22 faithful and wise s. shall inherit all things; 82: 17 all to have equal claims on property to manage s.; 101: 6 faithful is a ruler in the Lord's kingdom; 101: 90 the Lord will cut off wicked, unfaithful, and unjust s.; 104: 1 organize yourselves and appoint every man his s.; 104: 13 every man accountable as s. over earthly blessings; 104: 54-56 properties in s. belong to the Lord; 104: 74-77 treatment of unfaithful s.; 136: 27 be diligent that thou mayest be wise s.

STICK (see Ephraim)

STIFFNECKED, STIFFNECKEDNESS (see also Hardheartedness; Pride; Rebel; Unbelief)

D&C 5: 8 the Lord's anger is kindled against unbelieving, s. generation; 56: 6 the Lord revokes commandment because of s. of his people; 112: 13 if the Twelve stiffen not their necks against the Lord, they shall be converted.

STILL (see also Voice)

D&C 101: 16 be s. and know that I am God.

STINK (see also Smell)

D&C 133: 68 the Lord makes their fish to s.

STIR (see also Anger; Contention; Rebel)

D&C 10: 20-24, 63 Satan s. up hearts of people to contention; 18: 6 children of men must be s. up unto repentance.

STOAL, JOSIAH

JS-H 1: 56-57 Joseph Smith works for J.S.

STONE (see also Cornerstone; Foundation; Rock; Urim and Thummim)

D&C 28: 11 Hiram Page deceived by Satan by a s.; 45: 20 temple to be thrown down, that not one s. shall be left on another; 50: 44 Christ is s. of Israel; 65: 2 (Dan. 2: 34-35, 44-45) s. cut out of mountain without hands; 130: 10 white s. will become a Urim and Thummim; 130: 11 white s. to be given to each who comes into celestial kingdom.

Abr. 1: 11 virgins killed on altar because they would not worship gods of s.; **JS-H** 1: 35 Urim and Thummim, two s. in silver bows; 1: 51 plates lay in s. box under a s.

STOP (see also Hinder; Stay)

D&C 121: 33 as well might man stretch forth arm to s. the Missouri; 136: 17 enemies do not have power to s. the Lord's work.

STORE (see also Storehouse)

D&C 4: 4 he who thrusts in sickle lays up in s. that he perishes not; 57: 8 Sidney Gilbert to establish s.; 63: 42 Newel K. Whitney to retain s.; 64: 26 Newel K. Whitney and Sidney Gilbert not to sell s.; 90: 22 agent to be man with riches in s.

STOREHOUSE

D&C 42: 34, 55 (70: 7; 83: 6) surplus of consecrated property to be kept in s.; 42: 34 (51: 13; 72: 10) bishop to administer s.; 51: 13 let bishop appoint a s.; 58: 37 land to be purchased in Independence for s.; 70: 11 (90: 22-23) agent to keep the Lord's s.; 78: 3 need for organization to regulate s.; 82: 18 common property put in s.; 83: 5 children have claim upon the Lord's s.

STORM (see also Destruction; Tempest; Whirlwind; Wind)

D&C 90: 5 those who hold oracles as light thing shall fall when s. descend; 115: 6 gathering upon Zion shall be refuge from s.; 123: 16 large ship is benefited by small helm in time of s.

STRAIGHT, STRAIGHTNESS

D&C 3: 2 God's paths are s.; 33: 10 (65: 1; 133: 17) make the Lord's paths s.; 84: 28 make s. the way of the Lord.

STRAIT (see also Straight)

D&C 22: 2 you cannot enter in at s. gate by law of Moses; 132: 22 s. is gate that leads to exaltation.

STRANGE (see also Stranger)

D&C 95: 4 the Lord to bring to pass his s. act, pour out Spirit; 101: 95 the Lord to bring to pass his s. act, perform his s. work.

Moses 6: 38 s. thing in land, a wild man has come among us; **Abr.** 1: 8 women and children are offered to s. gods; 1: 16 (2: 6) Jehovah to lead Abraham into s. land.

STRANGER (see also BD Stranger)

D&C 45: 13 holy men confessed they were s. and pilgrims on earth; 124: 56 the Lord commands house to be built for boarding of s.

STREAM (see also River; Spring)

D&C 97: 9 fruitful tree planted in goodly land by pure s.; 121: 33 as well might man turn Missouri river up s.

STREET (see also Highway; Path; Way)

D&C 137: 4 Joseph Smith saw beautiful s. of celestial kingdom.

STRENGTH (see also Arm; Courage; Health; Might; Power; Strengthen; Strong; Virtue)

D&C 3: 4 if man boasts in own s., he must fall; 4: 2 (59: 5) love and serve God with all your heart, might, mind, and s.; 10: 4 do not turn faster or labor more than you have s.; 11: 20 keep commandments with all your s.; 59: 3 earth shall bring forth in its s.; 98: 47 turn to God with all your might, mind, and s.; 101: 21 stakes are for curtains or s. of Zion; 105: 16 s. of the Lord's house; 113: 8 Zion to put on her s.

Moses 1: 10 after many hours Moses receives natural s.; 1: 20 calling upon God, Moses receives s.; 5: 37 when thou tillest the ground, it shall not yield unto thee her s.; JS-H 1: 20 when light departs, Joseph Smith has no s.; 1: 48 Joseph Smith finds s. exhausted during labors.

STRENGTHEN (see also Nourish; Strength; Strong)

D&C 20: 53 teacher's duty is to watch over church and s. them; 31: 8 s. people and prepare them for gathering; 37: 2 s. up church; 50: 37 go forth among churches and s. them; 59: 19 things of earth given to s. body; 81: 5 s. feeble knees; 82: 14 (133: 9) Zion's stakes must be s.

Moses 1: 14 Moses could not look upon God except he were s. by God.

STRETCH

D&C 103: 17 saints must be led out of bondage with s-out arm; 104: 14 the Lord s. out heavens; 121: 33 as well might man s. forth puny arm to stop the Missouri.

Moses 7: 30 the Lord's curtains are s. out still; 7: 36 God can s. forth hands and hold all his creations; Abr. 2: 7 the Lord s. hand over sea and it obeys; 3: 12 the Lord's hand is out.

STRIFE (see also Contention; Dissension)

D&C 60: 14 proclaim the Lord's word among the wicked, not with s.; 101: 6 saints polluted inheritances by envyings and s.

STRIP

D&C 67: 10 s. yourselves from jealousies and fears.

STRIVE, STRIVING (see also Work [verb])

D&C 1: 33 Spirit shall not always s. with man.

Moses 8: 17 Spirit shall not always s. with man.

STRONG, STRONGER (see also Mighty; Power; Strength; Strengthen)

D&C 1: 19 the s. to be broken by the weak; 1: 28 the humble to be made s.; 27: 3 saints not to purchase wine or s. drink; 38: 15 be ye s. from henceforth; 50: 16 he who is weak shall be made s.; 52: 17 he who trembles under the Lord's power shall be made s.; 66: 8 the faithful shall be made s.; 84: 106 he who is s. in Spirit shall take him who is weak; 85: 7 the Lord will send one mighty and s.; 89: 7 s. drinks are not for belly; 121: 45 thy confidence shall wax s.; 133: 58 little one shall become s. nation.

STUBBLE (see also Destruction)

D&C 29: 9 (64: 24; 133: 64) all who do wickedly shall be s.

JS-H 1: 37 all who do wickedly shall burn as s.

STUDY, STUDYING (see also Knowledge; Learn; Ponder; Search)

D&C 9: 8 s. it out in your mind, then ask whether it is right; 11: 22 s. my words; 26: 1 let your time be devoted to s. scriptures; 88: 118 (109: 7, 14) seek learning by s. and by faith; 90: 15 s., learn, and become acquainted with all good books.

STUMBLE (see also Err)

D&C 90: 5 those who receive oracles should beware lest they s. and fall.

STUPOR

D&C 9: 9 if it is not right, you shall have s. of thought.

SUBDUE (see also Conquer; Overcome; Subject)

D&C 19: 2 the Lord to s. all things unto himself; 58: 22 (65: 6; 76: 61) the Lord to s. all enemies under feet; 96: 5 word should go forth to s. men's hearts; 103: 7 the Lord's people shall never cease to prevail until kingdoms of world are s.

Moses 2: 28 (Abr. 4: 28) replenish earth and s. it.

SUBJECT, SUBJECTION (see also Bondage; Conquer; Obedience; Prey; Reconcile; Subdue; Yield; Yoke)

D&C 29: 40 through transgression Adam became s. to will of devil; 50: 27 all things are s. unto him who is ordained of God; 50: 30 spirits s. to him who is appointed to head; 58: 22 be s. to powers that be until the Lord reigns; 63: 59 all things to be s. to the Lord at his coming; 105: 32 let us become s. unto Zion's laws; 121: 4 God controls and s. the devil; 132: 20 all things are s. unto them who are exalted.

A of F 12 we believe in being s. to kings, rulers.

SUSTANCE (see also Charity; Consecration, Law of; Property)

D&C 1: 16 men walk after their own God, whose s. is that of an idol; 42: 31 (105: 3) impart of your s. to the poor.

Abr. 2: 15 Abraham takes s. and comes in way to Canaan.

SUBTLETY, SUBTLE (see also Craftiness; Cunning; Guile)

D&C 123: 12 many in sects are blinded by s. craftiness of men.

Moses 4: 5 serpent was more s. than any beast.

SUCCOR (see also Help; Relief; Strengthen)

D&C 62: 1 the Lord knows men's weaknesses and how to s. them; 81: 5 s. the weak.

SUCK (see also Suckling)

JS-M 1: 16 (Matt. 24: 19) wo unto those who give s. in those days.

SUCKLING (see also Suck)

D&C 128: 18 things hid from wise and prudent shall be revealed unto babes and s.

SUFFER [= allow] (see also Long-suffering; Suffering)

D&C 10: 14 the Lord will not s. that Satan accomplish his evil design; 94: 8 the Lord's house will not s. any unclean thing to come into it; 104: 86 master will not s. his house to be broken up.

SUFFERING, SUFFER (see also Affliction; Anguish; Chasten; Infirmity; Misery; Mourn; Oppression; Pain; Sorrow; Tribulation; Trouble)

D&C 18: 11 the Lord s. pain of all men that they might repent; 19: 4, 15, 17 every man must repent or s.; 19: 16 (138: 7) God s. that men might not s.; 19: 17 if men do not repent, they must s. as

God; 19: 18 s. caused God to tremble and bleed, and to s. body and spirit; 45: 4 Father, behold the s. and death of him who did no sin; 76: 30–38 s. of those overcome by Satan; 76: 38 sons of perdition are only ones not redeemed after s. the Lord's wrath; 101: 35 they who s. persecution for the Lord's name shall partake of glory; 105: 6 saints to learn obedience by the things they s.; 109: 76 saints to reap eternal joy for all their s.; 121: 6 remember thy s. saints; 123: 1 record of saints' s. to be kept.

Moses 7: 39 God's chosen s. for men's sins.

SUFFICIENT (see also Enough)

D&C 68: 8 elders or priests are to have s. time to expound all things; 42: 32 each to receive by consecration as much as is s. for himself and family.

SUMMER

D&C 35: 16 (45: 37) s. is nigh; 45: 2 (56: 16) s. shall be past, but souls not saved; 135: 4 Joseph Smith is calm as s's morning.

JS-M 1: 38 (Matt. 24: 32) when fig tree puts forth leaves, s. is nigh.

SUN (see also Astronomy)

D&C 5: 14 (105: 31) church to come forth fair as s.; 29: 14 (34: 9; 45: 42) s. shall be darkened; 76: 70 celestial bodies have glory of s.; 76: 70 glory of s. is typical of glory of God; 88: 7 Christ is in s. and light of s.; 88: 45 s. gives his light by day; 88: 87 (133: 49) s. shall hide his face; 109: 73 church to come forth clear as s.; 110: 3 the Lord's countenance shone above brightness of s.

Moses 2: 16, 18 (Abr. 4: 16) God makes greater light, the s., to rule day; **Abr.** 1: 9 god of Shagreel was the s.; 3: 13 Shinehah, which is the s.; **JS-M** 1: 33 (Matt. 24: 29) s. shall be darkened; **JS-H** 1: 16 Joseph Smith sees pillar of light above brightness of s.

SUPPER (see also Sacrament)

D&C 58: 9 all nations shall be invited unto s. of house of the Lord; 58: 11 poor, lame, blind, deaf shall partake of s. of the Lord; 65: 3 prepare ye the s. of the Lamb.

SUPPLICATE, SUPPLICATION (see also Prayer)

D&C 136: 29 call on the Lord thy God with s.

JS-H 1: 29 Joseph Smith s. God for forgiveness.

SUPPLY (see also Provision)

SUPPORT (see also Help; Maintain; Preserve; Uphold)

D&C 3: 8 God would have s. you against fiery darts of adversary; 42: 30 consecrate of properties for s. of poor; 75: 24 duty of church to s. families of those sent unto world; 98: 5 law of land that s. principle of freedom is justifiable before the Lord.

SUPREME

D&C 107: 4 name of priesthood was changed out of reverence to name of S. Being.

SURE, SURETY

D&C 5: 12 witnesses shall know of s. these things are true; 11: 16 wait until you have my word, that you may know of s. my doctrine; 51: 6 all things shall be made s.; 64: 31 the Lord's words are s.; 131: 5 (2 Pet. 1: 19) explanation of more s. word of prophecy.

SURPLUS (see also Excess)

D&C 119: 1, 5 s. property to be put in bishop's hands.

SUSTAIN (see also Support; Uphold)

D&C 134: 5 men are bound to s. their governments.

SWALLOW (see also Destruction)

Moses 7: 43 floods s. the wicked.

SWEAR, SWORN (see also Oath; Promise)

D&C 63: 33 the Lord has s. in wrath and decreed wars; 88: 110 seventh angel to s. there shall be time no longer; 97: 20 God will be to s. of salvation of Zion; 121: 18 wo unto those who s. falsely against the Lord's servants.

Moses 5: 29–30 Satan tells Cain to s. unto him.

SWEAT (see also Labor)

Moses 4: 25 (5: 1) by s. of thy face shalt thou eat bread.

SWEEP, SWEPT (see also Destruction)

D&C 109: 30 enemies shall be s. away by hail and judgments; 109: 70 prejudices to be broken up and s. away; 121: 15 saints' enemies and their posterity shall be s. from under heaven.

Moses 7: 62 God will cause righteousness and truth to s. earth as with flood.

SWEET

D&C 29: 39 if men never knew bitter,

they could not know s.; 42: 46 those who die in the Lord will not taste of death, for it shall be s. unto them.

SWEET, NORTHROP

D&C sec. 33 revelation to; 33: 2 is called to declare gospel; 33: 10 to preach repentance.

SWELL (see also Grow; Increase)

Moses 7: 41 heart of Enoch[2] s. as wide as eternity.

SWINE

D&C 41: 6 pearls should not be cast before s.; 89: 17 rye for the fowls and for s.

SWORD (see also War; Weapon)

D&C 1: 13 the Lord's s. is bathed in heaven; 6: 2 (11: 2; 12: 2; 14: 2; 33: 1) the Lord's word is sharper than two-edged s.; 17: 1 three witnesses to see s. of Laban; 27: 18 take s. of my Spirit; 35: 14 the Lord will let fall s. in behalf of the weak; 45: 33, 68 in last days men will take up s. one against another; 87: 6 with the s., inhabitants of earth shall mourn; 97: 26 the Lord will visit Zion with s., according to works; 101: 10 the Lord would let fall s. of indignation; 121: 5 avenge us of our wrongs with thy s.

Moses 4: 31 God places flaming s. at east of Eden; JS–H 1: 45 great judgments coming with great desolation by s.

SYNAGOGUE (see also Building; Sanctuary)

D&C 63: 31 saints shall be scourged from s. to s.; 66: 7 bear testimony to every people and in s.; 68: 1 proclaim everlasting gospel in s.

TABERNACLE (see also Body; Building; BD Tabernacle)

D&C 88: 137 house of the Lord to become t. of Holy Spirit; 93: 4 Christ made flesh his t.; 93: 35 elements are t. of God; 101: 23 veil of covering of the Lord's temple in his t. to be taken off; 124: 38 Moses commanded to build t.

Moses 7: 62 the Lord's t. shall be in New Jerusalem.

TAKE, TAKEN (see also Deprive)

D&C 1: 33 from him who does not repent shall be t. light which he has; 13: 1 Aaronic Priesthood shall never be t. again from earth; 18: 21 (20: 77) t. upon you name of Christ; 38: 4 the Lord has t. Zion of Enoch[2]; 43: 10 (60: 3) if ye do it not, that which ye have received shall be t.; 84: 25 the Lord t. Moses and priesthood from Israel; 84: 106 he who is strong in Spirit should *t.* with him the weak; 93: 39 wicked one comes and *t.* away light; 110: 1 veil was *t.* from our minds; 136: 21 keep yourselves from evil to *t.* name of the Lord in vain.

Moses 7: 23, 31 Zion was *t.* up into heaven; **Abr.** 3: 17 nothing that the Lord in heart to do but he will do it.

TALENT (*see also* Steward; TG Talents)

D&C 60: 2 the Lord is not pleased with those who hide *t.*; 60: 13 thou shalt not bury thy *t.*; 82: 3 of him unto whom much is given, much is required; 82: 18 saints to be equal, that every man may improve his *t.* and gain other *t.*

TALK (*see also* Speak)

D&C 17: 1 brother of Jared² *t.* with the Lord; 105: 24 *t.* not of judgments.

Moses 1: 2, 31 Moses *t.* with God; 7: 4, 20 Enoch² *t.* with the Lord; **Abr.** 3: 11 Abraham¹ *t.* with the Lord face to face.

TANGIBLE (*see also* Touch)

D&C 130: 22 Father has body of flesh and bones as *t.* as man's.

TARBILL, SQUIRE

JS-H 1: 58 Joseph and Emma Smith are married at home of.

TARES (*see also* BD Tares)

D&C 38: 12 angels are waiting to gather *t.*; 86: 1–7 (101: 65) parable of wheat and *t.*; 86: 3 Satan sows *t.*; 86: 6–7 pluck not up *t.*; 88: 94 great church is *t.* of earth; 101: 66 *t.* shall be burned.

TARRY (*see also* Abide; Remain; Wait)

D&C 7: 3–4 John the apostle to *t.* until Christ comes; 63: 41, 45 Joseph Smith is given power to discern who shall *t.*; 105: 21 those who stay shall *t.* a little season.

TASTE (*see also* Bitter; Eat; Partake; Sweet)

D&C 42: 46 those who die in the Lord shall not *t.* of death; 59: 19 things of earth given for *t.* and for smell; 110: 13 Elijah was taken to heaven without *t.* death.

Moses 6: 55 men *t.* the bitter that they may know to prize the good.

TAYLOR, JOHN

D&C 118: 6 (124: 129) is called to fill position in Council of Twelve; 135: Intro. wrote about martyrdom; 135: 2 was wounded at martyrdom of Joseph

and Hyrum Smith; 138: 53 among mighty ones in spirit world.

TEACH, TAUGHT (*see also* Doctrine; Expound; Instruction; Learn; Liken; Preach; Reasoning; Sayings; Teacher; TG Jesus Christ, Teaching Mode of; Teachable; Teaching; Teach; Teaching with the Spirit)

D&C 11: 21 obtain the Lord's word before it; 20: 42 apostles to *t.* it; 20: 46, 50, 59 priest to *t.*; 28: 1, 4 (43: 15) *t.* by the Comforter; 36: 2 Comforter to *t.* peaceable things of kingdom; 38: 23 *t.* one another according to office appointed; 42: 12 elders, priests, teachers to *t.* gospel from scriptures; 42: 13 *t.* as directed by Spirit; 42: 14 if ye receive not the Spirit, ye shall not *t.*; 42: 57 do not *t.* scriptures until received in full; 42: 58 scriptures to be *t.* to all; 43: 15 elders sent forth to *t.*; 43: 16 elders to be *t.* from on high; 46: 18 to another is given word of knowledge that all may be *t.* to be wise; 50: 14 (52: 9; 75: 10) Comforter sent forth to *t.* truth; 52: 9 elders to preach only that which is *t.* them by Comforter; 63: 65 the Lord's servants to be *t.* through prayer by Spirit; 68: 25 parents' duty to *t.* children principles of gospel; 68: 28 parents to *t.* their children to pray and walk uprightly; 84: 48 Father *t.* covenant to him who hearkens; 88: 77 *t.* one another doctrine of kingdom; 88: 78 *t.* ye diligently; 88: 118 (109: 7) *t.* one another words of wisdom; 93: 42 you have not *t.* your children light and truth; 105: 10 elders to wait, that the Lord's people may be *t.* more perfectly; 107: 85–87, 89 duty of presidents over priesthood offices is to *t.* members their duties; 138: 25 Savior endeavored to *t.* Jews; 138: 51 the Lord *t.* righteous spirits.

Moses 6: 6 children are *t.* to read and write in pure language; 6: 23 faith is *t.* unto children of men; 6: 41 Mahijah is *t.* by father in all ways of God; 6: 57 *t.* your children that all men must repent; 6: 58 commandment to *t.* these things freely to children; 7: 1 father Adam *t.* these things; 8: 16 Noah¹ *t.* things of God; **JS-H** 1: 19 churches *t.* for doctrines commandments of men.

TEACHER (*see also* Teach; Teacher—Aaronic Priesthood; TG Teacher)

D&C 88: 122 saints to appoint among themselves a *t.*

A of F 6 *t.* are part of organization of primitive Church.

TEACHER—AARONIC PRIESTHOOD (*see also* Priesthood, Aaronic; TG Teacher, Aaronic Priesthood)

D&C 18: 32 (20: 39) to be ordained by Twelve; 20: 53–55, 59 (84: 111) duties of *t.*; 20: 56 to take lead in meetings in absence of elder or priest; 20: 58 have no authority to baptize, administer sacrament, lay on hands; 20: 59 (42: 12) have duty to warn and teach; 20: 60, 64 to be ordained according to gifts and callings of God; 38: 40 commanded to labor diligently; 42: 70 shall have their stewardships; 84: 30 office of *t.* an appendage to lesser priesthood; 107: 62–63, 86 president over office of *t.*

TEAR [verb] (*see also* Persecution; Rend)

D&C 122: 6 if enemies *t.* you from family, it shall be for your good.

TEARS (*see also* Joy; Sorrow; Weep)

Moses 7: 28 how is it heavens shed *t.* as rain.

TEETH (*see* Tooth)

TELESTIAL GLORY (*see also* Celestial Glory; Murder; Terrestrial Glory)

D&C 76: 81–90 vision of *t.*; 76: 81, 98, 109 glory compared to stars; 76: 82, 101 received not gospel; 76: 83 deny not Holy Ghost; 76: 84 thrust down to hell; 76: 85 not redeemed until last resurrection; 76: 86 receive of Holy Spirit through ministration of terrestrial; 76: 89 glory of *t.* surpasses understanding; 76: 98 degrees of glory in *t.* world; 76: 103 liars, sorcerers, adulterers, whoremongers in *t.g.*; 76: 104, 106 suffer wrath of God; 76: 105 suffer vengeance of eternal fire; 76: 109 inhabitants are innumerable as stars; 76: 110 to bow knees and confess; 76: 111 to be judged according to works; 76: 112 cannot dwell with God and Christ; 88: 24 he who cannot abide law of *t.* kingdom cannot abide *t.g.*; 88: 31 those who are quickened by a portion of *t.g.* receive fulness of it.

TELL, TOLD (*see also* Declare; Discern; Revelation; Teach)

D&C 6: 24 (15: 3) the Lord *t.* things which no man knows; 8: 2 the Lord will *t.* you in your mind and in your heart; 10: 25 Satan *t.* men it is no sin to lie; 10: 37 men cannot always *t.* the wicked from the righteous.

Moses 4: 17 who *t.* thee thou wast naked; 5: 29 if thou *t.* it, thou shalt die.

TEMPERANCE, TEMPERATE (*see also* Abstinence; TG Temperance)

D&C 4: 6 remember faith, virtue, knowledge, *t.*; 6: 19 be *t.*; 12: 8 those who

assist in the Lord's work must be *t.* in all things; 107: 30 decisions to be made in *t.*

TEMPEST (*see also* Destruction; Storm; Whirlwind; Wind)

D&C 43: 25 (88: 90) the Lord calls upon nations by voice of *t.*

TEMPLE (*see also* Baptism for the Dead; Body; Endow; House; Ordinance; Sanctuary; Seal; Tabernacle; TG Temple; Temple, House of the Lord; BD Temple)

D&C 36: 8 (42: 36; 133: 2) the Lord will come suddenly to his *t.*; 45: 18–20 *t.* at Jerusalem to be destroyed; 57: 3 spot for *t.* is west of Independence; 57: 3 spot for *t.* is west of Independence; 57: 3 spot for *t.* is to be consecrated by Sidney Rigdon; 59: Intro. *t.* to be built at Zion, Jackson County; 84: 3 *t.* lot dedicated by Joseph Smith; 84: 4 *t.* to be built in New Jerusalem; 84: 4–5, 31 *t.* to be built in this generation; 84: 5 glory of the Lord to rest on *t.*; 88: 119 (109: 8) establish a house of prayer, a house of God; 93: 35 man is tabernacle of God, even *t.*; 93: 35 God shall destroy whatever *t.* is defiled; 97: 15 (124: 24, 40) build house in name of the Lord; 97: 17 the Lord will not come into unholy *t.*; 101: 23 veil of covering of *t.* to be taken off; 105: 33 first elders to receive endowments in the Kirtland T.; sec. 109 prayer offered at dedication of Kirtland T.; 110: 7 the Lord will manifest himself to his people in his house; 124: 25–55 commandment to build *t.* at Nauvoo; 124: 39 the Lord's people are always commanded to build house unto his name; 124: 40 *t.* ordinances to be revealed; 128: 24 book containing records of the dead to be presented in *t.*; 138: 54 great latter-day work to include *t.* and performance of ordinances for the dead; OD–2 revelation extending priesthood and *t.* blessings to all worthy male members.

TEMPORAL, TEMPORALLY (*see also* Death, Physical; Flesh; Nature, Natural; Outward; Spiritual; World)

D&C 14: 11 (24: 3) ye shall be blessed both spiritually and *t.*; 29: 31–32 the Lord created all things both spiritual and *t.*; 29: 34–35 the Lord gives not *t.* laws or commandments; 63: 38 disciples in Kirtland to arrange *t.* concerns; 70: 14 be equal in *t.* things; 77: 2 the spiritual is in likeness of the *t.*, and the *t.* in likeness of the spiritual; 77: 6 seven thousand years of earth's *t.* existence; 89: 2 Word of Wisdom shows order and will of God in *t.* salvation; 107: 68, 71 bishop to administer all *t.* things.

Moses 6: 63 all things, both *t.* and spiritual, are made to bear record of God;

7: 42 posterity of sons of Noah¹ to be saved with *t.* salvation.

TEMPT, TEMPTATION (*see also* Agency; Devil; Probation; Prove; Seduce; TG Tempt, Temptation; BD Tempt)

D&C 9: 13 be faithful, and yield to no *t.*; 10: 15, 29 Satan leads men to *t.* God; 20: 22 the Son suffered *t.*, but gave no heed; 20: 33 (31: 12; 61: 39) pray always, lest ye enter into *t.*; 23: 1 beware of pride, lest you enter into *t.*; 29: 38 was *t.* of the devil; 29: 39 devil must *t.* men, or they could not be agents; 29: 47 power not given unto Satan to *t.* little children; 62: 1 Jesus knows how to succor those who are *t.*; 64: 20 the Lord does not allow men to be *t.* above what they can bear; 95: 1 with chastisement the Lord prepares way for deliverance out of *t.*; 101: 28 in that day Satan shall have power to *t.*; 112: 13 after their *t.*, the Lord will feel after the Twelve; 124: 124 sealed by Holy Spirit of promise, that ye fall not in hour of *t.*

Moses 1: 12 Satan to *t.* Moses; 5: 38 Cain says Satan *t.* him; 6: 49 Satan *t.* children of men to worship him; **JS-H** 1: 28 Joseph Smith is left to all kinds of *t.*

TEN (*see also* Israel, Ten Lost Tribes of; Tithing)

D&C 45: 56 (Matt. 25: 11-13) parable of *t.* virgins; 107: 52 Noah¹ was *t.* years old when he was ordained; 136: 3 captains of *t.* to be appointed.

TENDER, TENDERNESS (*see also* Gentle; Mercy)

D&C 42: 43 the sick to be nourished with all *t.*; 45: 37 leaves are yet *t.*, summer is nigh; 86: 4, 6 blade is springing up and is yet *t.*; **JS-M** 1: 38 (Matt. 24: 32) when branches are yet *t.*, summer is nigh.

TENET (*see also* Doctrine; Precept)

D&C 19: 31 talk not of *t.*; **JS-H** 1: 9 different denominations are equally zealous in endeavoring to establish *t.*

TENT

D&C 61: 25 like children of Israel, saints shall pitch their *t.*

Moses 5: 45 Jabal the father of such as dwell in *t.*; 7: 5-6 Enoch² beholds in valley of Shum a great people dwelling in *t.*; **Abr.** 2: 15 Abraham and followers dwell in *t.* along way to Canaan.

TENTH (*see* Tithing)

TERAH—*father of Abraham*

Abr. 1: 1 Abraham dwells at residence of father; 1: 27 Abraham's father is led away by Egyptians' idolatry; 1: 30 is sorely tormented because of famine; 2: 1 yet lives in Ur; 2: 4 follows Abraham into land of Haran; 2: 5 continues in Haran, returns to idolatry.

TERRESTRIAL (*see also* Celestial Glory; Telestial Glory)

D&C 76: 71-80 vision of *t.* world; 76: 71, 78, 91, 97 glory compared to moon; 76: 72 those who died without law; 76: 73 spirits of men in prison when Son preached gospel; 76: 74 received not gospel in flesh, but afterwards; 76: 75 honorable men of earth blinded by craftiness of men; 76: 76-77 receive of the Lord's glory, but not fulness of Father; 76: 79 those not valiant in testimony of Jesus; 76: 87 receive fulness through ministration of celestial; 88: 21 unsanctified to inherit *t.* or telestial kingdom; 88: 23 he who cannot abide law of *t.* kingdom cannot abide *t.* glory; 88: 30 they who are quickened by portion of *t.* glory shall receive fulness of the same.

TERROR, TERRIBLE (*see also* Fear)

D&C 5: 14 (105: 31; 109: 73) coming forth of church to be *t.* as army with banners; 45: 67, 75 *t.* of the Lord shall be in Zion; 45: 70 the wicked shall say inhabitants of Zion are *t.*; 64: 43 nations of the earth shall fear because of Zion's *t.* ones; 134: 6 without laws peace and harmony would be supplanted by anarchy and *t.*

TESTAMENT (*see also* New Testament; Old Testament; Testify; Testimony; Witness)

D&C 98: 2 saints' prayers recorded with this seal and *t.*; 135: 5 testators are now dead, and their *t.* is in force.

TESTIFY (*see also* Manifest; Preach; Prove; Record; Testament; Testimony; Verified; Witness)

D&C 17: 3 Three Witnesses to *t.*; 18: 34 elders to *t.* that words are of the Lord, not men; 18: 36 *t.* that you have heard my voice; 20: 26 (138: 36, 49) prophets of Christ in all things; 42: 74 those who put away companions because of fornication and *t.* before elders in lowliness of heart shall not be cast out; 46: 7 do that which Spirit is unto you; 88: 75 Christ to *t.* for the faithful; 88: 81 the Lord sends elders out to *t.* and warn; 107: 57 things written in the book of Enoch² are to be *t.*

of in due time; 110: 14 Malachi t. that Elijah should be sent.

TESTIMONY (see also Faith; Holy Ghost; Know; Knowledge; Revelation; Testament; Testify; Witness; TG Testimony)

D&C 3: 16 knowledge of Savior came through t. of Jews; 3: 1⁄–18 Lamanites to learn through their fathers' t.; 5: 11 t. of Three Witnesses to Book of Mormon shall go forth; 5: 18 t. shall go forth unto condemnation of this generation; 6: 31 the Lord's words shall be established by t.; 10: 33 Satan seeks to overpower elders' t.; 24: 15 (60: 15; 75: 20; 84: 92; 99: 4) elders to cast off dust, wash feet as t. against those who reject them; 58: 6 saints sent to Missouri that hearts might bear t. of things to come; 58: 13 saints sent to Missouri that t. might go out of Zion; 58: 47, 59, 63 (84: 61) elders to bear t. by the way; 62: 3 elders' t. recorded in heaven; 67: 4 t. of commandments in Book of Commandments; 76: 22 this is t. last of all, that he lives; 76: 50 this is t. of gospel of Christ; 76: 51 (138: 12) those who receive t. of Jesus inherit celestial glory; 76: 74 terrestrial glory inherited by those who accept t. of Jesus not in flesh, but afterwards; 76: 79, 82 terrestrial glory inherited by those not valiant in t. of Jesus; 84: 62 t. to go from saints into world; 88: 84 (109: 46; 133: 72) bind up law and seal up t.; 88: 88 after elders' t. comes wrath; 88: 89 t. of great calamities; 98: 27, 35, 44 three t. of persecution shall stand against enemies; 100: 10 Sidney Rigdon given power to be mighty in t.; 109: 38 put upon thy servants t. of covenant; 124: 7 elders to call upon kings and rulers with t.; 135: 1 Joseph Smith sealed t. with his blood; 138: 21 the rebellious reject t. of prophets.

Moses 7: 27 Enoch² beholds angels descending from heaven, bearing t. of Father, Son, Holy Ghost; 7: 62 God to send forth truth out of earth to bear t. of Only Begotten; JS-H 1: 26 Joseph Smith finds t. of James to be true.

THANK, THANKS (see also Blessing; Praise; Rejoice; Thankful; Thanksgiving)

D&C 46: 32 give t. unto God for blessings; 59: 7 (98: 1) t. the Lord in all things.

THANKFUL, THANKFULNESS (see also Thank; Thanksgiving)

D&C 62: 7 receive blessings from the Lord with t. heart; 78: 19 he who receives with t. shall be made glorious.

THANKSGIVING (see also Thank; Thankful)

D&C 46: 7 do all things with prayer and t.; 59: 15–16 remember Sabbath and fast with t.; 89: 11 herbs and fruits to be used with prudence and t.; 97: 13 house to be built for place of t.; 136: 28 praise the Lord with prayer of t.

THAYRE, EZRA

D&C sec. 33 revelation to; 33: 2 is called to declare gospel; 33: 10 to preach repentance; 52: 22 (56: 9) to journey to Missouri; 54: Intro. (56: Intro.) is involved in controversy; 56: 4–5 commandment is revoked because of rebelliousness; 56: 8 must repent of pride; 75: 31 to preach with Thomas B. Marsh.

THEORY (see also Doctrine)

D&C 88: 78 saints to be instructed more perfectly in t.; 97: 14 house to be perfected in t.

THIEF (see also Rob; Steal)

D&C 45: 19 desolation shall come as t. in night; 106: 4–5 (1 Thes. 5: 2) coming of the Lord to overtake world as t. in night.

JS-M 1: 47 (Matt. 24: 43) if man of house had known in which watch t. would come, he would have watched.

THING (see also God; Needful; Unclean)

Moses 1: 35 all t. are numbered unto God; 6: 63 all t. bear record of God.

THINK (see also Consider; Imagination; Intent; Ponder; Reasoning; Thoughts)

D&C 10: 23 Satan lays cunning plan, t. to destroy work of God; 45: 2 (51: 20; 61: 38; 124: 10) the Lord comes in hour when ye t. not.

JS-M 1: 48 (Matt. 24: 44) in such an hour as ye t. not, Satan cometh.

THIRD (see also Three)

D&C 20: 23 Christ rose from the dead the t. day; 29: 36–37 devil turned away t. part of hosts of heaven; 98: 28–30, 37, 46 (103: 26; 105: 30; 124: 50, 52) unto t. and fourth generation.

THIRST, THIRSTY (see also Athirst; Drink; Water)

D&C 133: 29 parched ground shall no longer be t. land; 133: 68 the Lord makes fish die for t.

THISTLE

Moses 4: 24 land shall bring forth thorns and t.

THOMPSON, OHIO (see also D&C map, p. 296)

D&C sec. 51 revelation given at; 54: Intro. (56: Intro.) controversy concerning members of branch at.

THOMPSON, ROBERT B.

D&C 124: 12–14 is promised blessings.

THORN

Moses 4: 24 ground shall bring forth *t.* and thistles.

THOUGHTS (see also Imagination; Think)

D&C 6: 16 (33: 1) God alone knows men's *t.*; 6: 36 look unto God in every *t.*; 9: 7 you took no *t.* save it was to ask; 9: 9 if it is not right, you shall have stupor of *t.*; 33: 1 the Lord is discerner of *t.*; 84: 81, 84 let the morrow take *t.* for the things of itself; 88: 69 cast away idle *t.*; 88: 109 secret *t.* to be revealed; 100: 5 speak *t.* that the Lord shall put into hearts; 121: 45 let virtue garnish thy *t.*

Moses 8: 22 every man lifted up in imagination of the *t.* of his heart.

THOUSAND (see also Millennium)

D&C 29: 11 the Lord will dwell with men on earth a *t.* years; 29: 22 (88: 101) when *t.* years are ended, the Lord will spare the earth; 77: 6 seven *t.* years of earth's temporal existence; 77: 7 each seal contains things of *t.* years; 77: 11 (133: 18) sealing of one hundred and forty and four *t.* out of tribes of Israel; 88: 108–109 angels shall sound trumps and reveal acts of *t.* year periods; 88: 110 devil shall not be loosed for *t.* years.

THRASH (see also Destruction; Harvest; Judgment; Reap)

D&C 35: 13 (133: 59) the Lord calls upon weak things of world to *t.* nations.

THREE (see also Third; Witnesses, Three)

D&C 6: 28 (128: 3) in mouth of two or *t.* witnesses shall every word be established; 6: 32 where two or *t.* are gathered in the Lord's name is there; 20: 61 elders to meet in conference once in *t.* months; 107: 22, 24, 29 Presiding High Priests form a quorum of the Presidency; 129: 9 *t.* grand keys; 131: 1 *t.* heavens in the celestial glory.

THRONE (see also Dominion; Exaltation; Judgment-seat; Kingdom of God)

D&C 76: 21 angels worship God before his *t.*; 76: 92 (88: 13, 40, 104, 110, 115; 124: 101; 132: 29) God reigns upon *t.* forever; 76: 108 Christ to sit on the *t.*

of his power; 121: 29 all *t.* and dominions shall be revealed; 132: 19 those married by new and everlasting covenant shall inherit *t.*, kingdoms; 132: 49 the Lord prepares *t.* for Joseph Smith; 137: 3 blazing *t.* of God whereon were seated Father and Son.

Abr. 3: 2 Abraham sees star nearest unto *t.* of God; 3: 9 Kolob is set nigh unto *t.* of God.

THROW, THROWN (see also Cast; Destruction)

D&C 45: 20 temple in Jerusalem to be *t.* down; 101: 57 (105: 16) *t.* down tower of the Lord's enemies; 103: 13 Zion to be established and no more to be *t.* down.

THRUST (see also Cast)

D&C 4: 4 (6: 3–4; 11: 3–4, 27; 12: 3–4; 14: 3–4; 31: 5; 33: 7) *t.* in sickle; 76: 25 Lucifer was *t.* down from presence of God; 76: 84 telestial inhabitants are *t.* down to hell.

THUMMIM (see Urim and Thummim)

THUNDER, THUNDERINGS (see also Lightning; Warn)

D&C 43: 21, 25 (133: 22) the Lord calls upon nations by voice of *t.*; 87: 6 with *t.* of heaven shall men feel God's wrath; 88: 90 after elders' testimony comes testimony of voice of *t.*

TIDINGS (see also Gospel; Message)

D&C 19: 29 declare glad *t.*; 76: 40 this is the gospel, the glad *t.* declared from heaven; 128: 19 glad *t.* for the dead.

TILL (see also Plant; Sow)

Moses 3: 5 (Abr. 5: 5) all things created spiritually before God created man to *t.* ground; 4: 29 God sends Adam from Eden to *t.* ground; 5: 1 Adam begins to *t.* earth.

TIME (see also Dispensation; Eternity; Full; Fulness; Generation; Hour; Meridian of Time; Month; Reckon; Season; Space; Today; Tomorrow; Week; Year; Yesterday; TG Time)

D&C 20: 26 (39: 3) Christ came in meridian of *t.*; 26: 1 let *t.* be devoted to studying of scriptures; 27: 13 keys of kingdom committed for last *t.*; 41: 9 bishop ordained to spend all his *t.* in labors of church; 45: 25, 28, 30 *t.* of Gentiles to be fulfilled; 60: 13 thou shalt not idle away thy *t.*; 64: 32 all things must come to pass in their *t.*; 68: 11 given unto elders to know signs of *t.*; 72: 3

stewards to render account of steward-ship both in *t.* and in eternity; 72: 4 he who is faithful in *t.* will inherit Father's mansions; 84: 100 Satan is bound and *t.* is no longer; 88: 42 law given by which all things move in their *t.* and seasons; 88: 73 the Lord will hasten his work in its *t.*; 88: 110 seventh angel to declare there shall be *t.* no more; 121: 12 God sets his hand to change *t.*; 121: 25 *t.* appointed for every man according to his works; 121: 31 *t.* of heavenly bodies to be revealed; 130: 4 God's *t.*, angel's *t.*, prophet's *t.*, and man's *t.* reckoned according to planet on which they reside; 132: 7 covenants sealed by him who is anointed for *t.* and eternity; 138: 27 ministry among dead limited to brief *t.* between crucifixion and resurrection.

Abr. 3: 4 Kolob is after manner of the Lord according to *t.* and seasons; 3: 4, 9 (5: 13) reckoning of the Lord's *t.* is according to reckoning of Kolob; 3: 4–10 *t.* reckoned according to heavenly bodies; 3: 10 Abraham to know set *t.* of all stars; 4: 8, 13, 19, 23, 31 (5: 2) periods of *t.* in creation are called night and day; 5: 13 in Eden the Gods had not yet appointed unto Adam his reckoning of *t.*

TITHING, TITHE (*see also* BD Tithe)

D&C 64: 23 he who is *t.* shall not be burned; 85: 3 the Lord *t.* his people to prepare them for day of burning; 97: 11–12 the Lord's house to be built by *t.* of his people; sec. 119 revelation on *t.*; 119: 4 those who have been *t.* shall pay one-tenth of interest annually; 119: 4 *t.* a standing law unto saints forever; sec. 120 revelation concerning disposition of property *t.*

TOBACCO (*see also* Word of Wisdom)

D&C 89: 8 *t.* is not good for man.

TODAY (*see also* Time)

D&C 20: 12 (35: 1) God is same yesterday, *t.*, and forever; 45: 6 hear the Lord's voice while it is called *t.*; 64: 23 it is called *t.* until coming of Son; 64: 24 after *t.* comes the burning; 64: 25 labor while it is called *t.*

TOIL (*see also* Spin)

TOKEN (*see also* Emblem; Sign; Type)

D&C 88: 131 offer prayer in *t.* of remembrance of everlasting covenant; 88: 133 salute in name of Jesus Christ, in *t.* or remembrance of everlasting covenant.

TOLD (*see also* Tell, Told)

TOLERABLE (*see also* Bear, Bore, Borne)

D&C 45: 54 it shall be *t.* for those who knew no law; 75: 22 more *t.* for heathen in judgment than for those who reject elders.

TOMORROW (*see also* Morrow; Time; Today)

D&C 64: 24 *t.* the proud shall be as stubble.

TONGUE (*see also* Gift; Holy Ghost; Interpretation; Language; Mouth; Nation; Speak; Speech; Spirit, Gifts of; Word; TG Tongue)

D&C 7: 3 (42: 58; 77: 8; 88: 103; 112: 1; 133: 37) unto every nation, kindred, *t.*, and people; 11: 21 (23: 3; 31: 3) obtain the Lord's word, and then shall *t.* be loosed; 29: 19 *t.* of the wicked shall be stayed; 46: 24 spiritual gift to speak with *t.*; 46: 25 spiritual gift of interpretation of *t.*; 76: 110 (88: 104) every *t.* shall confess to him who sits upon throne; 90: 11 every man shall hear the gospel in own *t.*; 90: 15 study and become acquainted with languages, *t.*, people; 109: 36 gift of *t.* to be poured out; 112: 9 let the *t.* of the slanderer cease.

A of F 7 we believe in gift of *t.*, interpretation of *t.*

TOOK (*see* Take, Taken)

TOOTH, TEETH

D&C 19: 5 (85: 9; 101: 91; 124: 8; 52; 133: 74) weeping and gnashing of *t.* **Moses** 1: 22 Satan gnashes at Moses with gnashing of *t.*; JS-M 1: 54 (Matt. 24: 51) wicked servant shall weep and gnash *t.* among hypocrites.

TORMENT (*see also* Anguish; Damnation; Gnashing; Guilt; Hell; Lake; Misery; Pain; Sorrow)

D&C 19: 6–12 explanation of endless *t.*; 76: 44 *t.* of devil is unquenchable fire; 76: 45 no man knows *t.* of sons of perdition; 104: 18 he who does not impart his portion dead in hell, in *t.* **Moses** 7: 1 those who die in sins look forward in *t.* to God's indignation; 7: 39 those who perish in floods will be in *t.*

TOUCH (*see also* Feel; Hand)

D&C 76: 19 the Lord *t.* eyes of understanding; 135: 7 martyrdom will *t.* hearts of honest men among all nations. **Moses** 4: 9 *t.* not fruit of tree.

TOWER (*see also* Protection)

D&C 97: 20 God has sworn to be Zion's salvation and her high *t.*; 101: 45

saints to build *t.*, that watchman may overlook land; 105: 16 strength of the Lord's house to throw down *t.* of his enemies.

TRADITION (see also Custom)

D&C 74: 4 children believed not gospel of Christ because of *t.* of fathers; 74: 6 *t.* to be done away which says little children are unholy; 93: 39 wicked one takes away light and truth because of *t.* of fathers; 123: 7 the fathers have inherited lies.

TRAITOR (see also Apostasy; Apostate)

D&C 122: 3 they people shall never be turned against thee by testimony of *t.*; 135: 7 Joseph Smith confined in jail by the conspiracy of *t.*

TRAMPLE (see also Disobedience; Rebel; Tread)

D&C 3: 15 Joseph Smith suffered counsel of his director to be *t.* upon; 133: 51 the Lord has *t.* the wicked in his fury.

TRANSFIGURE, TRANSFIGURE (see also Change; Translated Beings; TG Transfiguration, Transfigured; Translated Beings; BD Transfiguration, Mount of)

D&C 63: 20–21 day of *t.* to come was shown apostles on mount; 138: 45 Elias and Moses appeared on Mount of T.

Moses 1: 11 Moses is *t.* before God.

TRANSGRESSION, TRANSGRESS (see also Agency; Crime; Death, Spiritual; Disobedience; Err; Evil; Fall of Man; Fault; Guilt; Iniquity; Jesus Christ, Atonement through; Judgment; Knowledge; Law; Offense; Punishment; Rebel; Sin; Transgressor; Trespass; Wicked; TG Transgress)

D&C 3: 6 how oft Joseph Smith has *t.* the commandments; 3: 9 if not aware, thou wilt fall because of *t.*; 20: 20 by *t.* man became sensual, devilish, fallen; 20: 80 member who *t.* shall be dealt with as scriptures direct; 29: 40 Adam became subject to will of devil because of *t.*; 46: 4 those who have *t.* should not partake of sacrament until reconciliation is made; 51: 4–5 saints to hold inheritance until they *t.*; 51: 5 he who is not accounted worthy to belong to church; 82: 11 elders to be bound by covenant that cannot be broken by *t.*; 88: 25 earth *t.* not the law; 101: 2 some members are afflicted in consequence of *t.*; 104: 9 those cut off by *t.* cannot escape Satan; 104: 52 covenants are broken through *t.*; 105: 2, 9 church might have been redeemed were it not

for *t.* of people; 107: 82 if President of High Priesthood *t.*; 121: 17 those who cry *t.* are servants of sin; 132: 26 if those sealed by Holy Spirit of promise *t.*, they will be delivered to buffetings of Satan; 138: 32 gospel preached to those who died in *t.*; 138: 59 after paying penalty of *t.*, spirits shall receive reward.

Moses 5: 10 Adam's eyes are opened because of *t.*; 5: 11 except for *t.*, Adam would not have had seed; 5: 11 Adam and Eve never could end evil through *t.*; 6: 52–53 all men must repent of *t.* and be baptized; 6: 59 by reason of *t.* cometh the fall; A of F 2 all men will be punished for own sins, not for Adam's *t.*

TRANSGRESSOR (see also Transgression)

D&C 82: 4 those who keep not the Lord's sayings become *t.*; 101: 41 *t.* need chastening; 104: 8 *t.* cannot escape wrath; 107: 72 judge in Israel to sit in judgment upon *t.*

TRANSLATION, TRANSLATE, TRANSLATOR (see also Book of Mormon; Gift; Holy Ghost; Interpretation; Language; Seer; Tongue; Translated Beings)

D&C 1: 29 (20: 8; 135: 3) Joseph Smith *t.* through power of God; 3: 12 God gave Joseph Smith sight and power to *t.*; 5: 4 Joseph Smith given gift to *t.*; 6: 25, 28 Oliver Cowdery was given gift to *t.*; 8: 11 Oliver Cowdery to ask that he may *t.*; 9: 10 Oliver Cowdery could have *t.* if he had known the principle; 10: 1 *t.* by means of Urim and Thummim; 10: 30 lost pages not to be *t.* again; 10: 41 *t.* engravings on plates of Nephi; 17: 6 the Lord testifies that Joseph Smith has *t.* Book of Mormon; 17: 5 Three Witnesses to testify that Joseph Smith *t.* the book; 21: 1 (107: 92; 124: 125) Joseph Smith to be *t.*; 45: 60–61 Joseph Smith to *t.* New Testament; 73: 3 Joseph Smith and Sidney Rigdon instructed to resume *t.*; 76: 15–21 Joseph Smith and Sidney Rigdon receive vision of glories while *t.* Bible; 90: 13 Joseph Smith *t.* prophets; 91: 1 Apocrypha is mostly *t.* correctly; 93: 53 Joseph Smith should hasten to *t.* scriptures; 94: 10 house to be dedicated to printing *t.* of scriptures; 107: 91–92 President of High Priesthood to be a *t.*; 124: 89 William Law to publish *t.* of scriptures.

JS-H 1: 62 Joseph Smith begins to *t.* characters from plates; 1: 64 Martin Harris displays characters that Joseph Smith has *t.*; 1: 67 Joseph Smith commences to *t.* Book of Mormon; A of F 8 we believe Bible to be word of God as far as it is *t.* correctly.

TRANSLATED BEINGS (see also Change; Enoch²; John the Beloved; Transfiguration; Zion)

D&C 7: 3 John will tarry until the Lord comes; 38: 4 the Lord took Zion of Enoch² into his own bosom; 45: 12 Zion, a city reserved until day of righteousness; 107: 49 Enoch² walked with God and God took him; 110: 13 Elijah was taken to heaven without tasting death.

Moses 7: 21, 23, 31, 47 Zion is taken up into heaven, bosom of the Lord; 7: 69 Zion is fled.

TRAP (see Pit)

TRAVAIL (see also Labor)

D&C 84: 101 earth has t. and brought forth strength; 136: 35 days of sorrow come like woman taken in t.

TRAVEL (see also Depart; Flight; Journey)

D&C 20: 66 t. bishops to have privilege of ordaining; 49: 22 Son will come not in form of man t. on earth; 84: 111 (124: 135, 137) high priests, elders, priests should t.; 107: 33, 36 (124: 127) Twelve are t. Presiding High Council; 107: 97 (124: 139) seventy to be t. ministers; 107: 98 other officers not under responsibility to t.

TREAD, TRODDEN (see also Oppression; Persecution; Trample)

D&C 76: 107 (88: 106; 133: 50) the Lord has t. the wine-press alone; 101: 40 (103: 10) salt that has lost savor is good for nothing but to be t. under foot; 133: 48 the Lord's garments shall be like him who t. in wine-vat; 133: 51 the Lord t. upon the wicked in anger.

TREASURE (see also Money; Riches; Treasury)

D&C 6: 3 (11: 3; 12: 3; 14: 3) he who thrusts in sickle shall t. up everlasting salvation; 6: 20 (43: 34) t. up these words in thy heart; 19: 38 blessings of Spirit are greater than corruptible t. of earth; 38: 30 t. up wisdom; 63: 48 he who sends t. to Zion shall receive inheritance; 84: 85 t. up in your minds words of life; 89: 19 those who obey Word of Wisdom shall find great t. of knowledge, even hidden t.; 111: 2 the Lord has much t. in Salem for benefit of Zion; 133: 30 those in north countries shall bring rich t. unto children of Ephraim.

TREASURY (see also Agent; Financial)

D&C 104: 60–77 t. to be established.

TREE (see also Branch; Fig; Fruit; Fruit, Forbidden; Olive; Palms; Root; Tree of Life)

D&C 85: 8 man who steadies ark shall fall as t. smitten by lightning; 97: 7 t. that brings not forth good fruit will be hewn down; 97: 9 those accepted of the Lord will bring forth as fruitful t.; 101: 30 in Millennium, life shall be as age of t.; 128: 23 let woods and t. of field praise.

TREE OF LIFE (see also Eden, Garden of; Immortality)

Moses 3: 9 (Abr. 5: 9) the Lord plants t. of l. in midst of garden; 4: 28–29 God sends Adam from Eden lest he partake of t. of l. and live forever; 4: 31 God places cherubim and flaming sword to keep way of t. of l.

TREMBLE (see also Earthquake; Fear; Fear of God; Quake; Shake)

D&C 1: 7 fear and t., O ye people; 10: 56 the Lord will cause to t. those who build kingdom of devil; 19: 18 suffering caused even God to t.; 34: 8 (133: 42) all nations shall t. at the Lord's coming; 35: 24 Satan shall t.; 43: 18 (45: 48) when the Lord utters his voice, earth shall t.; 45: 74 when the Lord appears, enemies shall t.; 49: 23 (88: 87) look forth for earth to t.; 64: 43 nations of earth shall t. because of Zion; 84: 118 starry heavens shall t.; 123: 10 dark deeds make hands of very devil to t.; 133: 31 boundaries of everlasting hills shall t.

Moses 1: 21 Satan begins to t.; 6: 47 Enoch² speaks words of God, and people t.; 7: 13 Enoch² speaks word of the Lord, and earth t.

TRESPASS (see also Offense; Sin; Transgression)

D&C 46: 4 sacrament forbidden to those who have t.; 64: 9 he who forgives not his brother his t. stands condemned; 82: 1 if you have forgiven one another your t., the Lord forgives you; 98: 40 forgive enemy if he repents of t.; 98: 47 t. to be restored four-fold.

TRIAL, TRY (see also Chasten; Faith; Oppression; Persecution; Probation; Prove; Trial, Judicial; Tribulation; TG Test; Try, Prove)

D&C 98: 12 the Lord will t. you and prove you; 101: 4 saints must be chastened and t.; 105: 19 saints brought thus far for t. of faith; 136: 31 the Lord's people must be t. in all things.

TRIAL, JUDICIAL (see also Court; Government; Government, Civil; Judge [noun]; Law; Law, Civil; Transgression; Transgressor; Trial, Try)

D&C 42: 80–83 procedure for t. of

members before elders; 42: 80 he who commits adultery shall be *t.* before two elders; 68: 22 bishop to be *t.* only before First Presidency; 102: 12–33 procedures for *t.* before high council; 107: 72–76 bishop is common judge, to sit in judgment upon transgressors; 107: 78–81 *t.* before council of the church; 107: 82–83 *t.* of President of High Priesthood; 134: 10 religious societies have no right to *t.* men on right of property or life.

TRIBE (*see also* Israel; Israel, Ten Lost Tribes of; Jacob, House of; Judah)

JS–M 1: 36 (Matt. 24: 30) all *t.* of earth to mourn because of sign of Son's coming.

TRIBULATION (*see also* Affliction; Anguish; Calamity; Chasten; Destruction; Grieve; Misery; Oppression; Persecution; Sorrow; Suffering; Trial; Try; Trouble)

D&C 29: 8 *t.* to be sent upon the wicked; 54: 10 be patient in *t.* until the Lord come; 58: 2 he who is faithful in *t.* will receive greater reward in heaven; 58: 3 *t.* to be followed by glory; 58: 4 (103: 12; 112: 13) after much *t.* come blessings; 78: 14 *t.* to descend upon church; 112: 13 after much *t.* the Lord will feel after the Twelve; 122: 5–8 if thou art called to pass through *t.*, it shall be for thy good; 127: 2 like Paul, Joseph Smith delights in *t.*; 138: 13 the just suffered *t.* in Redeemer's name.

Moses 7: 61, 66 great *t.* to be among men at Christ's coming.

TRIFLE (*see also* Light-mindedness)

D&C 6: 12 (8: 10) *t.* not with sacred things; 32: 5 give heed unto these words, and *t.* not.

TRIM (*see* Lamp)

TRIUMPH (*see also* Victory)

D&C 76: 39 resurrection of the dead through *t.* and glory of Lamb; 121: 8 thou shalt *t.* over foes; 136: 42 keep commandments, lest enemies *t.* over you.

TRODDEN (*see* Tread, Trodden)

TROUBLE (*see also* Anxiety; Calamity; Care; Sorrow; Suffering; Tribulation; Vex)

D&C 3: 8 if faithful, God would have been with you in time of *t.*; 45: 35 be not *t.*; 98: 18 let not your hearts be *t.*; 101: 8 in day of their *t.*, saints feel after the Lord; 109: 38 prepare hearts of saints that faint not in day of *t.*

Moses 7: 66 in latter day, sea shall be *t.*; JS–M 1: 23 (Matt. 24: 6) see that ye be not *t.*

TRUE (*see also* Real; Right [adj.]; Truth)

D&C 1: 30 only *t.* and living church; 1: 37 search commandments, for they are *t.*; 10: 62 other sheep shall bring to light *t.* points of the Lord's doctrine; 20: 11 holy scriptures are *t.*; 20: 19 only living and *t.* God; 20: 30–31 justification through Jesus Christ is just and *t.*; 68: 34 these sayings are *t.* and faithful; 76: 53 Father sheds Holy Spirit of promise upon all who are just and *t.*; 88: 50 (93: 2) I am the *t.* light that is in you; 91: 1–2 in Apocrypha many things are *t.*, many not *t.*; 132: 24 eternal life, to know the only wise and *t.* God.

Moses 4: 32 the Lord's words are *t.* even as he will; JS–H 1: 26 Joseph Smith finds testimony of James to be *t.*

TRUMP, TRUMPET

D&C 24: 12 (33: 2; 36: 1; 42: 6; 75: 4) declare gospel as with voice of *t.*; 29: 13 (43: 18; 88: 94) *t.* shall sound at the Lord's coming; 29: 26 Michael shall sound *t.* when earth passes away; 43: 25 the Lord calls upon nations by sound of *t.*; 45: 45 before arm of the Lord shall fall, angel shall sound *t.*; 49: 23 signs to be given when angel sounds *t.*; 77: 12 sounding of *t.* in Revelation 8 explained; 88: 92, 98–110 angels shall fly through midst of heaven sounding *t.*; 109: 75 when *t.* shall sound for the dead, saints shall be caught up.

TRUST (*see also* Confidence; Faith; Hope; Rely; TG Trust; Trust in God; Trust Not in the Arm of Flesh; Trustworthiness)

D&C 1: 19 *t.* not in arm of flesh; 11: 12 put *t.* in Spirit which leads to do good; 19: 30 preach, in the Lord; 84: 116 let him *t.* in me, and he shall not be confounded.

TRUTH (*see also* Gospel; Intelligence; Knowledge; Learning; Light; Mystery; Scriptures; Spirit, Holy/Spirit of the Lord; True)

D&C 1: 39 (88: 66) *t.* abides forever; 6: 15 thou hast been enlightened by Spirit of *t.*; 18: 21 speak *t.* in soberness; 19: 26 Book of Mormon contains *t.*; 19: 37 declare *t.* with loud voice; 27: 16 loins girt about with *t.*; 45: 57 they who have received *t.* will abide the Lord's coming; 49: 2 Shakers desire to know *t.* in part, but not all; 50: 14 (79: 2; 124: 97) Comforter sent to teach *t.*; 50: 17 those sent forth to preach word of *t.* should preach by Spirit of *t.*; 50: 19 receive word of *t.* by Spirit of *t.*; 50: 25 know *t.* to chase darkness away; 50: 40 elders must grow in knowledge of *t.*; 58: 47 let elders bear testimony of *t.*; 66: 12 (84: 102) Father is full of grace and *t.*; 75: 4 proclaim *t.* according to revelations; 76: 5 God delights in those who serve him in *t.*; 76: 31 sufferings of those who deny *t.*; 78: 10 Satan seeks to turn hearts from *t.*; 84: 45 whatsoever is *t.* is light; 88: 6 Christ, the light of *t.*; 88: 7 *t.* is light of Christ; 88: 40 *t.* embraces *t.*; 91: 4 Spirit manifests *t.*; 93: 9, 23, 26 Christ is the Spirit of *t.*; 93: 11 Christ is full of grace and *t.*; 93: 24 *t.* is knowledge of things as they are, were, are to come; 93: 28 he who keeps commandments receives *t.*; 93: 29 intelligence, or light of *t.*; 93: 30 *t.* is independent in sphere in which God has placed it; 93: 36 glory of God is intelligence, or light and *t.*; 93: 39 wicked one takes away light and *t.*; 93: 40, 42 bring up children in light and *t.*; 97: 1 many in Zion seeking for find *t.*; 107: 84 things of God done according to *t.*; 109: 56 prejudices of great ones to give way before *t.*; 121: 46 thy scepter shall be one of *t.*; 123: 12 many among sects are kept from *t.* because they know not where to find it; 128: 19 voice of *t.* out of earth; 138: 26 Savior proclaimed in great power and authority; 138: 32 gospel preached to those who die without knowledge of *t.*

Moses 6: 61 given to abide in you *t.* of all things; 7: 31 naught but peace, justice, and *t.* is habitation of thy throne; 7: 62 God will send forth *t.* out of earth to bear testimony of Son.

TRY (*see also* Trial, Try)

TUBAL CAIN

Moses 5: 46 an instructor of every artificer in brass and iron.

TURN

D&C 10: 23 cunning plan of wicked men shall *t.* to their shame; 20: 15 hardening hearts in unbelief shall *t.* to own condemnation; 27: 9 (98: 16; 110: 15; 128: 17) hearts of fathers and children to be *t.* to each other; 29: 14 (34: 9; 45: 42) moon shall be *t.* into blood; 45: 29 those sitting in darkness *t.* hearts from the Lord because of precepts of men; 51: 17 saints to act upon the land as for years, and this shall *t.* unto them for good; 66: 1 you have *t.* from your iniquities; 78: 10 Satan seeks to *t.* hearts from *t.*; 84: 41 he who *t.* from covenant of priesthood shall not have forgiveness; 90: 9 elders shall go unto Gentiles first, then *t.* to

Jews; 98: 47 children shall repent and *t.* to the Lord; 121: 33 as well might man try to *t.* Missouri up stream; 133: 24 Jerusalem and Zion shall be *t.* back into own place.

Moses 4: 31 God places flaming sword which *t.* every way to keep way of tree of life; **Abr.** 1: 5–7 fathers' hearts *t.* from righteousness to idols.

TWAIN (*see also* Two)

D&C 45: 48 mount shall cleave in *t.*; 49: 16 they *t.* shall be one flesh.

TWELVE (*see also* Apostle; Disciple; Israel)

D&C 38: 26 parable of man with *t.* sons; 101: 44 nobleman tells servants to plant *t.* olive-trees; 102: 1 (107: 37) high council to consist of *t.* high priests; 107: 79 presidency of council has power to call *t.* high priests as counselors; 107: 82 *t.* counselors to assist council in trying President; 107: 85 president to preside over *t.* deacons.

TWINKLING

D&C 43: 32 (63: 51; 101: 31) the righteous to be changed in *t.* of eye.

TWO (*see also* Twain)

D&C 6: 2 (11: 2; 12: 2; 14: 2; 33: 1) the Lord's word is sharper than *t*-edged sword; 6: 28 in mouth of *t.* or three witnesses shall every word be established; 6: 32 where *t.* or three are gathered in the Lord's name, he is there; 42: 6 (52: 10; 60: 8) preach gospel *t.* by *t.*; 42: 44 *t.* or more elders to lay hands on sick; 42: 80 adulterer to be tried before *t.* elders; 42: 80–81 *t.* or more witnesses at trial of adulterer; 62: 5 bear record *t.* by *t.*; 77: 15 the *t.* witnesses are *t.* prophets to be raised up to Jewish nation; 84: 33 (107: 1, 6) *t.* priesthoods; 129: 1 *t.* kinds of beings in heaven.

Moses 2: 16 (**Abr.** 4: 16) God made *t.* great lights; **JS–H** 1: 17, 25 Joseph Smith sees *t.* personages.

TYPE, TYPIFY, TYPICAL (*see also* Remember, Remembrance; Representation; Shadow; Similitude; Token; TG Jesus Christ, Types of, in Anticipation; Jesus Christ, Types of, in Memory)

D&C 76: 70 glory of sun is *t.* of glory of God.

UNALTERABLE (*see also* Immutable; Unchangeable)

Moses 7: 52 God sends *u.* decree that seed of Enoch² should always be found.

UNANIMOUS (see also Common Consent; One; Unite; Unity)

D&C 102: 3 standing council for church chosen by u. voice; 107: 27 every decision made by Twelve or Seventy must be by u. voice.

UNBELIEF, UNBELIEVER (see also Apostasy; Belief; Believer; Dissension; Doubt; Hardheartedness; Rebel; Reject; TG Unbelief, Unbelievers)

D&C 3: 18 Lamanites dwindled in u. because of iniquity of fathers; 5: 8 the Lord's anger is kindled against unbelieving generation; 20: 15 hardening of hearts in u. shall turn to their condemnation; 58: 15 Edward Partridge's sins are u. and blindness; 63: 17 the unbelieving shall have part in lake of fire and brimstone; 74: 5 believer should not be united to u.; 84: 54 minds have been darkened because of u.; 84: 74 they who believe not shall be damned; 85: 9 (101: 90) those not recorded in book of remembrance shall receive portion among u.

UNCHANGEABLE, UNCHANGING (see also Change; God, Eternal Nature of; Immutable; Round; Same; Unalterable)

D&C 20: 17 God is u. from everlasting to everlasting; 88: 133 I receive you to fellowship in determination that is u.; 104: 2 u. promise that faithful should be blessed; 121: 46 thy scepter shall be u. scepter of righteousness.

UNCLEAN, UNCLEANNESS (see also Corrupt; Defile; Evil; Filthiness; Spirit, Evil; Spot; Stain; Unholy; Wicked; TG Uncleanness, Unclean)

D&C 88: 124 cease to be u.; 90: 18 keep slothfulness and u. far from you; 94: 8 (97: 15; 109: 20) no u. thing to come in unto the Lord's house.

Moses 6: 57 no u. thing can dwell in presence of God.

UNDEFILED

D&C 94: 12 house for printing to be consecrated to be holy, u.

Moses 6: 6 children of Adam have pure and u. language.

UNDERSTAND, UNDERSTOOD, UNDERSTANDING (see also Communication; Comprehend; Know; Knowledge; Learn; Perceive; Wisdom; TG Understand; Understanding)

D&C 1: 24 commandments given that the Lord's servants might come to u.; 9: 7 you have not u.; 10: 63 people wrest scriptures and do not u.; 20: 68

elders and priests to expound all things to their u.; 29: 33 The Lord speaks that man may u. naturally; 29: 50 he who has no u., it remains in me to do as it is written; 32: 4 unfold the same to their u.; 50: 12 the Lord reasons with men that they may u.; 50: 22 he who preaches and he who receives u. one another; 68: 25 parents' duty to teach children to u. principles; 71: 5 (91: 4) he who reads, let him u.; 76: 5 their u. shall reach to heaven; 76: 9 u. of prudent shall come to naught; 76: 12 our u. were enlightened; 76: 19 the Lord touched eyes of u., and they were opened; 76: 48 men u. not the end of sons of perdition; 76: 89 glory of telestial surpasses all u.; 76: 114 mysteries of kingdom surpass all u.; 76: 116 things that can be u. only by Holy Spirit; 78: 10 Satan turns hearts so men u. not things prepared for them; 88: 11 (138: 29) light of Christ quickens the u.; 88: 78 saints to be instructed more perfectly in things expedient for them to u.; 93: 19 I give these sayings that you may u.; 97: 14 saints to be perfected in u. of ministry.

UNDERTAKE, UNDERTAKEN (see also Do; Observe; Perform)

D&C 7: 6 John the apostle has u. a greater work; 121: 37 when men u. to cover their sins, Spirit withdraws.

UNFAITHFUL (see also Disobedience)

D&C 101: 90 u. stewards to be cut off; 104: 74, 77 u. and unwise steward.

UNFEIGNED (see also Sincerity)

D&C 121: 41 influence should be maintained by love u.

UNFOLD (see also Manifest; Revelation; Show)

D&C 6: 7 (11: 7) seek for wisdom, and mysteries of God shall be u.; 10: 64 (90: 14) the Lord will u. unto them great mystery; 88: 95 curtain of heaven shall be u.

UNFRUITFUL

D&C 107: 31 quorums shall not be u. in knowledge of the Lord.

Moses 7: 7 the land shall be barren and u.

UNGODLINESS, UNGODLY (see also Iniquity; Wicked)

D&C 76: 49 vision of sufferings of the u.; 84: 117 the Lord's servants should reprove world of all u. deeds; 97: 22 vengeance comes speedily upon the u.; 99: 5 the Lord comes to convince all of their u. deeds; 133: 2 curse of judgment upon all the *u.*; 136: 33 Spirit is sent to condemnation of the *u.*; 138: 20 Christ's voice was not raised among *u.* spirits.

UNHOLY (*see also* Unclean; Unworthiness)

D&C 74: 4 children became *u.* because they believed not gospel; 74: 6 tradition to be done away which says little children are *u.*; 97: 17 the Lord will not come into *u.* temples.

UNION (*see also* Unite, Unity)

D&C 105: 4 *u.* required by law of celestial kingdom; 128: 18 necessary that whole, complete, and perfect *u.* should take place.

UNITE, UNITY (*see also* Agree; Join; One; Order; Unanimous; Union; United Order)

D&C 20: 28 (35: 2; 50: 43) *u.* of Godhead; 23: 7 duty to *u.* with true church; 29: 6 ask, *u.* in prayer; 74: 5 believer should not be *u.* to unbeliever; 105: 4 saints are not *u.* in union required by law of celestial kingdom.

UNITED ORDER (*see also* Consecration, Law of)

D&C 51: 3, 9 (sec. 70; 78: 5; 82: 17) people of church to be equal; 82: 20 (104: 1) order to be an everlasting order; sec. 104 revelation concerning U.O.; 82: 5 result of breaking covenants of U.O.; 104: 47–48, 52–53 U.O. of Kirtland segregated temporarily from that of Zion; 104: 68 disposition of property of U.O.; 105: 34 law held in abeyance.

UNITED STATES (*see also* America)

D&C 101: 80 the Lord established Constitution of U.S. by men whom he raised.

UNJUST (*see also* Unlawful; Unrighteous; Unworthiness)

D&C 76: 17 evildoers to come forth in resurrection of the *u.*; 101: 81 parable of woman and *u.* judge; 101: 90 the Lord will cut off *u.* stewards; 104: 7 the innocent not to be condemned with the *u.*; 134: 12 interference with bond-servants is *u.*; 138: 7 Christ suffered for sins, the just for the *u.*

UNLAWFUL (*see also* Injustice)

D&C 121: 3 how long shall saints suffer *u.* oppressions; 134: 11 all men justified in defending themselves from *u.* assaults; 134: 12 interference with bond-servants is *u.*

UNLEARNED (*see also* Humble; Ignorance; Small; Weak)

D&C 35: 13 those who are *u.* shall thrash nations.

UNLOCK (*see also* Open)

D&C 112: 17 Thomas Marsh to *u.* door of kingdom in places where Joseph Smith cannot come.

UNNATURAL (*see* Nature, Natural)

UNQUENCHABLE (*see* Fire; Flame)

UNREPENTANT (*see also* Repentance)

D&C 64: 12 manner of dealing with the *u.*; 138: 20 Christ's voice not raised among the *u.*

UNRIGHTEOUS, UNRIGHTEOUSNESS (*see also* Iniquity; Unjust; Unworthiness; Wicked; TC Unrighteous Dominion)

D&C 42: 47 death of the *u.* is bitter; 66: 10 forsake all *u.*; 76: 41 Jesus to cleanse world from all *u.*; 82: 22 make friends of mammon of *u.*; 84: 87, 117 elders sent out to reprove world of *u.* deeds; 88: 18 earth must be sanctified from all *u.*; 107: 32 decision made in *u.* may be brought before quorums; 121: 37 when man exercises compulsion in *u.*, heavens withdraw themselves; 121: 39 nature of almost all men to exercise *u.* dominion; 138: 35 redemption made known among the *u.* as well as the faithful.

UNSPEAKABLE

D&C 121: 26 *u.* gift of Holy Ghost.

UNSPOTTED (*see also* Pure; Spotless)

D&C 59: 9 keep thyself *u.* from world.

UNVEIL (*see also* Revelation, Reveal)

D&C 88: 68, 95 the Lord will *u.* his face; 109: 74 the Lord shall *u.* the heavens; 124: 8 the Lord shall *u.* face of his covering.

UNWISE (*see also* Foolish; Wisdom)

D&C 104: 74, 77 unfaithful and *u.* steward.

UNWORTHINESS, UNWORTHY (*see also* Iniquity; Unholy; Unjust; Unrighteous; Wicked)

D&C 88: 88 he who is found *u.* shall not have place among saints.

UPBRAID (*see also* Reproach; Reprove)

D&C 42: 68 (James 1: 5) the Lord will give liberally and *u.* who is not; 84: 76 those

who have not received gospel should be *u.* for evil hearts of unbelief.
JS-H 1: 11, 13, 26 Joseph Smith reads promise of James that God gives liberally and not.

UPHOLD, UPHELD (*see also* Maintain; Preserve; Support; Sustain)

D&C 10: 5 servants of Satan *u.* his work; 43: 12 saints to *u.* Joseph Smith by prayer of faith; 98: 10 *u.* wise men; 107: 22 three Presiding High Priests to be *u.* by confidence, faith, prayer of church, 134: 3 voice of people should *u.* those who will administer law in justice; 134: 5 men are bound to sustain and *u.* governments.

UPRIGHTNESS, UPRIGHT, UP-RIGHTLY (*see also* Just; Righteousness)

D&C 5: 21 Joseph Smith to repent and walk more *u.* before the Lord; 18: 31 Twelve must walk *u.* before the Lord; 46: 7 all saints should walk *u.* before the Lord; 61: 16 only he who is *u.* shall go up to Zion; 68: 28 parents to teach children to walk *u.* before the Lord; 100: 15 all things shall work together for good to them that walk *u.*

UR, LAND OF

Abr. 1: 20 Potiphar's Hill in land of U. of Chaldea; 2: 1 famine in land of U.; 2: 15 Abraham took Sarai to wife in U.; 3: 1 the Lord gave Abraham the Urim and Thummim in U.

URIAH

D&C 132: 39 David sinned in case of U. and his wife.

URIM AND THUMMIM (*see also* Book of Mormon; Seer; Stone; BD Urim and Thummim)

D&C secs. 3, 6, 11, 14 revelations given through U. and T.; 10: 1 Joseph Smith given power to translate by means of U. and T.; 17: 1 Three Witnesses to see U. and T. given to brother of Jared⁴; 130: 8 God's residence is a great U. and T.; 130: 9 earth will be U. and T.; 130: 10 white stone given those who enter celestial kingdom will become U. and T.

Abr. 3: 1, 4 given to Abraham; JS-H 1: 35 deposited with ancient plates; 1: 35 possession and use of stones constituted seers in ancient times; 1: 42 Joseph Smith commanded not to show U. and T. to anyone; 1: 52 first seen by Joseph Smith; 1: 59 delivered into custody of Joseph Smith.

USE (*see also* Benefit; Profit)

D&C 49: 19 (59: 18) beasts, fowls, things of earth ordained for *u.* of man; 89: 10 wholesome herbs are for *u.* of man; 104: 63 make *u.* of stewardship the Lord has given.

Moses 3: 9 everything prepared by God for *u.* of man remains in sphere in which he created it.

UTTER, UTTERANCE (*see also* Speak; Word)

D&C 14: 8 (88: 137) Spirit gives *u.*; 29: 19 tongues of wicked are stayed that they shall not *u.* against the Lord; 43: 18 (45: 49) the Lord shall *u.* his voice out of heaven; 43: 21 thunders shall *u.* their voices; 76: 115 mysteries are not lawful for man to *u.*; 133: 21 the Lord shall *u.* his voice out of Zion.

VAGABOND

Moses 5: 37, 39 Cain to be fugitive and *v.*

VAIN (*see also* Naught; Vanity)

D&C 63: 62 (136: 21) condemnation of those who use name of the Lord in *v.*, not having authority; 121: 37 when men undertake to gratify *v.* ambition.

VALIANT, VALIANTLY (*see also* Courage; Diligence; Noble; Uprightness)

D&C 76: 79 they who are not *v.* in testimony of Jesus Christ inherit terrestrial glory; 121: 29 all powers to be set upon all who have endured *v.* for gospel.

VALID, VALIDITY (*see also* Effect; Void)

D&C 107: 27 all members must be agreed to make quorums' decisions same *v.*; 132: 18 marriages not sealed by Holy Spirit of promise are not *v.* when they are out of world.

VALLEY

D&C 49: 23 *v.* to be exalted at the Lord's coming; 107: 53 Adam called righteous posterity into *v.* of Adam-ondi-Ahman; 133: 22 *v.* shall not be found; 138: 43 (Ezek. 37: 1–14) Ezekiel saw *v.* of dry bones.

VANITY (*see also* Pride; Vain)

D&C 20: 5 Joseph Smith entangled in *v.* of world; 84: 55 *v.* and unbelief have brought church under condemnation.

VAPOR (*see also* Cloud; Mist; Smoke)

D&C 45: 41 *v.* of smoke, sign of the Lord's coming.

VARY (see also Change; God, Eternal Nature of; Unchangeable)

D&C 3: 2 God never v. from what he has said.

VEIL (see also Curtain; BD Veil)

D&C 38: 8 v. of darkness soon rent; 67: 10 v. shall be rent, elders shall see the Lord; 101: 23 v. of covering of temple shall be taken off; 110: 1 v. was taken from minds.

Moses 7: 26 chain in Satan's hand v. whole earth in darkness; 7: 56 heavens are v.; 7: 61 v. of darkness shall cover the earth.

VENGEANCE (see also Avenge; Destruction; Judgment; Justice; Punishment; Revenge)

D&C 3: 4 he who follows carnal desires incurs v. of God; 29: 17–20 (76: 105; 112: 24) the Lord to take v. upon the wicked; 85: 3 tithing to prepare saints against day of v.; 97: 22 (112: 24) v. comes speedily upon the ungodly; 97: 26 if Zion does not obey, the Lord will visit her with v.; 98: 23–48 the Lord's law of v.; 98: 47 repentance, a means of escaping v.; 112: 25 v. to begin at top and go forth from house of God; 133: 51 the Lord to tread upon the wicked in day of v.

Moses 5: 40 v. shall be taken sevenfold on him who slays Cain; 7: 45–46, 60 blood of the Righteous to be shed in days of wickedness and v.

VERIFIED (see also Testify; Witness)

D&C 5: 20 the Lord's word shall be v.

VERMONT (see also D&C map, p. 295)

JS–H 1: 3 Joseph Smith born in V.

VESSEL (see also Ship)

D&C 38: 42 (133: 5) be ye clean that bear v. of the Lord; 76: 33 sons of perdition are v. of wrath.

VEX, VEXATION (see also Trouble)

D&C 87: 5 remnants left in land shall v. Gentiles with a sore v.; 97: 23 the Lord's scourge shall v. all people; 101: 89 the Lord in his fury will v. the nation.

VICARIOUS (see Baptism for the Dead)

VICTORY (see also Triumph)

D&C 52: 11 the Lord will send forth judgment unto v.; 103: 36 all v. and glory brought to pass through diligence; 104: 82 as ye are humble, I will give you v.; 128: 22 courage, and on to v.

VIEW (see also Behold; See; Sight)

D&C 17: 1 (5: 13, 24, 28) Three Witnesses to v. plates; 10: 45 things on plates of Nephi throw greater v. upon gospel.

VINE (see also Grape; Vineyard; Wine; BD Vine)

D&C 27: 5 Christ will drink of fruit of v. with prophets; 89: 6 pure wine of grape of v. to be used for sacrament; 89: 16 fruit of v. is good for man.

VINEYARD (see also Grape; Olive; Spot of Land; Vine; TG Vineyard of the Lord)

D&C 21: 9 the Lord will bless all who labor in his v.; 24: 19 (33: 3; 39: 17; 43: 28; 71: 4; 75: 2; 95: 4) laborers called to prune v. for last time; 33: 4 v. has become corrupted; 39: 13 (50: 38) build church by laboring in v.; 101: 44–62 (103: 21) parable of nobleman and v.; 101: 101 saints shall plant v. and eat fruit thereof; 107: 96 when seventy to be called if labor in v. requires it; 135: 6 easy to burn dry trees to purify v.; 138: 56 choice spirits prepared to come forth to labor in v.

VIOLENCE (see also Persecution)

D&C 24: 16 elders to command that any who lay hands upon them by v. shall be smitten.

Moses 8: 28, 30 earth is corrupt and filled with v.; Abr. 1: 12 priests lay v. upon Abraham.

VIPER (see also Serpent)

D&C 121: 23 generation of v.

VIRGIN (see also Jesus Christ, First Coming of)

D&C 45: 56 when the Lord comes, parable of ten v. shall be fulfilled; 63: 54 until that hour there will be foolish v. among the wise; 132: 61–63 man desires to espouse more than one v.

Abr. 1: 11 v. are sacrificed to idols.

VIRTUE (see also Clean; Holiness; Merit; Pure; Strength; TG Virtue, Virtuous)

D&C 4: 6 remember faith, knowledge, v.; 25: 2 walk in paths of v. before the Lord; 38: 24 (46: 33) let every man practise v. and holiness; 88: 40 v. loves v.; 107: 30 decisions of quorums to be made in v.; 121: 41 no power ought to be maintained by v. of priesthood; 121: 45 let v. garnish thy thoughts unceasingly; 132: 7 performances not sealed by Holy Spirit of promise are of no v. after resurrection.

VISION (see also God, Manifestations of; Revelation; See)

D&C sec. 76 v. of the kingdom and glories; 76: 14 Joseph Smith and Sidney Rigdon converse with Son in v.; sec. 110 v. received at dedication of Kirtland Temple; sec. 137 Joseph Smith's v. of celestial kingdom; sec. 138 Joseph F. Smith's v. of redemption of dead.

Moses. ch. 1 v. of Moses; 6: 42 Enoch² beholds v. on journey from Cainan; 7: 21-67 v. of Enoch²; Abr. 1: 1s the Lord fills Abraham with v. of the Almighty; JS-H 1: 16-20 first v. of Joseph Smith; 1: 24-25 Joseph Smith feels like Paul when he related account of v. before Agrippa; 1: 42 hiding place² of plates is revealed in v.; A of F 7 we believe in gift of v.

VISIT (see also God, Manifestations of; Judgment; Visitation)

D&C 5: 16 the Lord will v. those who believe on his words; 20: 47, 51 priests are to v. house of each member; 27: 7 Elias v. Zacharias; 44: 6 v. the poor and the needy; 76: 73 (138: 8, 28) Son v. spirits in prison; 88: 53 the Lord v. servants with joy of his countenance; 97: 26 the Lord will v. Zion according to her works; 116: 1 Adam to v. his people at Adam-ondi-Ahman; 124: 8 the Lord will v. rulers in day of visitation; 124: 50 the Lord will v. iniquity upon those who hinder his work.

Abr. 1: 17 the Lord v. and destroys him who lifts hand against Abraham.

VISITATION (see also Judgment; Revelation; Visit)

D&C 56: 1 rebellious shall know the Lord's indignation in day of v.; 56: 16 the rich to lament in day of v.; 124: 8 the Lord to visit rulers in day of v.; 124: 10 v. comes speedily.

VOCALLY (see also Public; Voice)

D&C 19: 28 (81: 3) pray v. as well as in heart; 20: 47 priests to exhort members to pray v.; 23: 6 pray v. before the world.

JS-H 1: 14 Joseph Smith's first attempt to pray v.

VOICE (see also Common Consent; God, Manifestations of; Prayer; Preach; Revelation; Sound; Speech; Vocally; Warn)

D&C 1: 2, 11 (65: 1) v. of the Lord is unto all men; 1: 4 (63: 37; 112: 5) v. of warning unto all people; 1: 14 they who will not hear v. of the Lord or his servants shall be cut off; 1: 38 by the Lord's own v. or by v. of his servants, it is the same;

18: 35 the Lord's v. speaks words to the Twelve; 18: 36 Oliver Cowdery and David Whitmer testify they heard v.; 20: 35 scriptures and revelations to come by v. of God; 27: 1 (29: 1; 38: 22; 39: 1) listen to v. of Jesus Christ; 29: 4 declare gospel with sound of rejoicing, as with v. of trump; 29: 7 (35: 21) the elect may hear the Lord's v.; 34: 10 lift up your v. and spare not; 38: 34 men to be appointed by v. of church; 38: 41 (63: 37) let preaching be warning v.; 43: 18, 23 (45: 49; 133: 21) the Lord to utter v. out of heaven at his coming; 43: 25 (88: 90) how oft have I called upon you by mine own v., by v. of thunderings, lightnings, tempests, earthquakes; 50: 1 give ear to v. of the living God; 50: 45 day comes that saints shall hear the Lord's v.; 51: 4 man to hold inheritance until not accounted worthy by v. of church; 52: 1 elders called by v. of Spirit; 63: 5 the Lord utters his v., and it shall be obeyed; 65: 1 v. of God is mighty; 68: 4 whatsoever elders speak when moved upon by Holy Ghost shall be v. of the Lord; 71: 10 he who lifts v. against church shall be confounded; 75: 1 (97: 1) the Lord speaks by v. of his Spirit; 76: 23 Joseph Smith and Sidney Rigdon hear v. bearing record of Son; 76: 40 v. out of heavens bore record unto gospel; 84: 42 priesthood confirmed upon elders by the Lord's v.; 84: 52 whoso receiveth not the Lord's v. is not acquainted with his v.; 85: 6 still small v. which whispers; 88: 66 v. of one crying in wilderness; 88: 66 the Lord's v. is Spirit; 93: 1 those who obey the Lord's v. shall see his face; 104: 36 land to be sold as made known by v. of Spirit; 104: 71-72 dealings of united order to be by v. and common consent of the order; 107: 27 decision by quorums must be by unanimous v.; 108: 2 resist no more the Lord's v.; 110: 3 (133: 22) the Lord's v. is as sound of rushing of great waters; 128: 20 v. of the Lord in Fayette; 128: 21 v. of God heard at sundry times; 128: 23 v. from heaven is glorious; 130: 13 v. declares to Joseph Smith that war will arise through slave question; 133: 50 the Lord's v. shall be heard; 137: 7 v. of the Lord to Joseph Smith; 138: 20 the Lord's v. was not raised among the ungodly in spirit world.

Moses 1: 25-27 Moses hears v. of the Lord; 4: 4 Satan leads captive those who hearken not to God's v.; 4: 14, 16 (5: 4) Adam and Eve hear v. of God; 4: 23 ground cursed because Adam hearkened to v. of wife; 6: 27 Enoch² hears v. of the Lord; 6: 66 Adam hears v. out of heaven following baptism; 7: 48 Enoch² hears voice from bowels of earth; Abr. 1: 16

the Lord's *v.* comes unto Abraham; JS-H 1:49 Joseph Smith hears *v.* calling him by name.

VOID (*see also* Empty; Valid)

D&C 135:4 Joseph Smith's conscience *v.* of offense toward Lord.

VOTE (*see also* Common Consent)

D&C 20:63 elders to receive licenses by *v.* of church; 20:65 no person to be ordained without *v.* of church; 102:19 twelve councilors to sanction president's decision by *v.*

VOW (*see also* Covenant; Oath; Promise; Swear; BD Vows)

D&C 59:11 *v.* shall be offered up in righteousness; 108:3 be more careful in observing *v.*; 132:7 *v.* not sealed by Holy Spirit of promise will be of no force after resurrection.

WAGES (*see also* Hire; Labor; Pay; Recompense; Remuneration; Reward)

D&C 29:45 men receive *w.* from him whom they list to obey; 124:121 builders of Nauvoo House to have recompense of *w.* for labors.

WAGON

D&C 136:5 each company to provide all the necessary *w.*

WAILING (*see also* Cry; Lament; Mourn; Weep)

D&C 19:5 (85:9; 101:91; 133:73) *w.* and gnashing of teeth among the wicked; 29:15 weeping and *w.* among hosts of men.

Moses 1:22 Satan cries with loud voice, with weeping, *w.*

WAIT (*see also* Watch)

D&C 38:12 angels *w.* for command to reap; 98:2 *w.* patiently on the Lord; 133:45 God has prepared great things for those who *w.* for him.

WAKEFIELD, JOSEPH

D&C 50:37 to strengthen churches by exhortation; 52:35 to journey into eastern lands.

WALK (*see also* Act; Do; Live; Path; Way; TG Walking in Darkness; Walking with God)

D&C 1:16 every man *w.* in his own way; 3:2 God does not *w.* in crooked paths; 5:21 (18:31; 46:7; 68:28; 90:24)

w. more uprightly before the Lord; 19:23 *w.* in meekness of Spirit; 19:32 great and last commandment shall suffice for daily *w.*; 20:69 members to manifest by godly *w.* and conversation that they are worthy of sacrament; 25:2 *w.* in paths of virtue before the Lord; 35:9 whoso asks in faith shall cause the lame to *w.*; 68:28 parents must teach children to *w.* uprightly before the Lord; 88:133 *w.* in all commandments of God; 89:18 saints who *w.* in obedience to commandments receive health; 89:20 those who obey Word of Wisdom shall *w.* and not faint; 95:6 they who are not chosen have sinned in that they *w.* in darkness at midday; 95:12 he who keeps not commandments shall *w.* in darkness; 100:15 (109:1) all things shall work together for those who *w.* uprightly; 107:49 Adam *w.* with the Lord; 136:4 covenant to *w.* in all ordinances of the Lord.

Moses 6:34 *w.* in me.

WALL

D&C 101:57 break down *w.* of the Lord's enemies.

WANT (*see also* Need)

D&C 42:33 (51:3; 82:17) every man should receive portion equal to *w.* and needs; 70:7 that which exceeds *w.* should be given to storehouse; 72:11 bishop to administer to *w.* of elders; 84:112 bishop should administer to *w.* of the poor.

WAR (*see also* Army; Battle; Blood; Shedding of; Destruction; Fight; Government; Civil; Peace; Perplexities; Slaughter; Sword; TG War; BD War in Heaven)

D&C 38:29 (45:63) *w.* in far countries; 45:26 Christ prophesied of *w.* and rumors of *w.*; 45:63 *w.* in own lands are nigh; 45:69 Zion shall be only people not at *w.*; 63:33 the Lord has decreed *w.* in his wrath; 76:29 Satan makes *w.* with saints; sec. 87 revelation on *w.*; 87:1 *w.* will shortly come to pass; 88:79 saints to be instructed in *w.* and perplexities of nations; 98:16 renounce *w.* and proclaim peace; 98:34–36 if any nation proclaims *w.*, lift standard of peace.

Moses 6:15 from Satan come *w.* and bloodshed; 7:16 from that time there were *w.* among the people; JS-M 1:23, 28 (Matt. 24:6) you shall hear of *w.* and rumors of *w.*

WARD

D&C 128:3 recorder to be appointed in each *w.* of city.

WARN, WARNING (see also Chasten; Exhort; Forewarn; Mission; Preach; Rebuke; Reprove; Thunder; Voice; Watchmen)

D&C 1: 4 voice of w. shall be unto all people; 38: 41 let your preaching be the w. voice; 63: 37 every man to lift w. voice; 63: 57 those who desire to w. sinners to repent are to be ordained; 63: 58 a day of w., not a day of many words; 88: 71 those whom elders have w. should ponder in w. in hearts; 88: 81 it becometh every man who hath been w. to w. neighbor; 89: 4 the Lord w. saints by giving Word of Wisdom by revelation; 98: 28 w. enemy in the Lord's name; 109: 41 (134: 12) elders to w. people to save themselves from this untoward generation; 112: 5 let w. voice go forth; 124: 106 w. people to flee the wrath to come; 134: 12 w. the righteous to save themselves from corruption of world; 138: 21 the rebellious who reject w. of prophets do not behold the Lord's presence.

WASH (see also Baptism; Cleanse; Jesus Christ, Atonement through; Purify; Sanctification)

D&C 39: 10 be baptized, and w. away your sins; 60: 15 (84: 92; 99: 4) elders to w. feet as testimony against those who reject them; 76: 52 men are w. and cleansed by keeping commandments; 88: 139–141 ordinance of w. of feet; 89: 7 strong drinks are for w. of bodies; 124: 37–39 w. not acceptable unless performed in the Lord's house; 138: 59 transgressors who pay penalty and are w. clean receive reward.

Moses 6: 35 anoint thine eyes with clay, and w. them.

WASTE (see also Desolation; Destruction; Empty; Solitary; TG Waste)

D&C 2: 3 (138: 48) children's hearts to be turned to fathers lest earth be w. at the Lord's coming; 49: 21 wo unto man who w. flesh; 101: 18 (103: 11) children of Zion shall return to build up w. places of Zion; 105: 15 the Lord sends forth destroyer to lay w. his enemies; 123: 13 saints to w. and wear out lives bringing hidden things of darkness to light.

WATCH, WATCHFUL (see also Look; See; Seek; Wait; Watchmen)

D&C 20: 42 duty of apostles to w. over church; 20: 53 (84: 111) duty of teachers to w. over church; 45: 44 he who w. not for the Lord shall be cut off; 45: 50 they who have w. for iniquity shall be hewn down; 46: 27 bishop ordained to w. over church; 50: 46 w. that ye may be

ready; 52: 39 let elders w. over churches; 82: 5 w., for the adversary spreads his dominions; 133: 11 w., for you know neither day nor hour of the Lord's coming.

WATCHMEN (see also Warn)

D&C 101: 45–57 set w. to overlook the land; 105: 16 strength of the Lord's house shall scatter enemy's w.; 124: 61 receive counsel of those set as w. upon Zion's walls.

WATER (see also Baptism; Deep; Flood; Fountain; Immersion; Lake; Sea; Spring; Stream; Thirst; Waves)

D&C 5: 16 those who believe shall be born of w. and of Spirit; 10: 66 partake of w. of life; 61: 4–5 many dangers upon w.; 61: 6 faithful shall not perish by w.; 61: 14 in beginning the Lord blessed w.; 61: 14 the Lord cursed w. by mouth of John; 61: 15 no flesh to be safe upon w.; 61: 16 only the upright in heart shall go to Zion on w.; 61: 27 power given to command face of w.; 63: 23 mysteries of kingdom to be well of living w.; 84: 92 cleanse your feet with pure w.; 88: 94 mother of abominations sits upon many w.; 110: 3 (133: 22) the Lord's voice is sound of rushing of great w.; 118: 4 apostles sent over great w.; 121: 33 how long can rolling w. remain impure; 133: 29 pools of living w. in barren deserts; 133: 41 the Lord's presence is as fire that causes w. to boil.

Moses 2: 2 (Abr. 4: 2) God's Spirit moves upon face of w.; 2: 6–7 (Abr. 4: 6–7) dividing of w.; 2: 9 (Abr. 4: 9) let w. be gathered in one place; 6: 59 men are born into world by w., blood, spirit; 6: 59 men must be born again of w. and Spirit; 6: 60 by w. ye keep commandment; 6: 64 Adam is carried down into w. by Spirit; **Abr.** 1: 24 Egypt discovered under w. by daughter of Ham.

WAVES (see also Sea)

D&C 88: 90 voice of w. of sea comes as testimony.

WAX (see also Grow; Increase)

D&C 1: 16 substance of men's idols w. old; 45: 58 they who have received truth shall multiply and w. strong; 121: 45 confidence shall w. strong.

Moses 6: 27 people's hearts have w. hard; **Abr.** 2: 1 famine w. sore in Ur; **JS-M** 1: 10, 30 (Matt. 24: 12) because iniquity shall abound, the love of many shall w. cold.

WAY (see also Direction; Example; Gate; Highway; Means; Path; Street; Walk; Wayside)

D&C 1: 16 every man walks in his own w.; 24: 2 (6: 35; 82: 7) go thy w., and sin no more; 33: 10 (34: 6; 35: 4; 39: 20; 45: 9; 65: 1; 77: 12; 133: 17) prepare the w. of the Lord; 50: 18–20 word preached by some other w. is not of God; 52: 9 (58: 47, 63) elders to journey, preaching the word by the w.; 55: 2 preach repentance and remission of sins by w. of baptism; 61: 24 the Lord has appointed w. for journeyings of saints; 82: 6 all have gone out of the w.; 84: 28 John to make straight w. of the Lord; 88: 68 the Lord will unveil his face in his own w.; 104: 15–16 the Lord will provide for saints in his own w.; 132: 22 narrow is w. that leads to exaltation; 132: 25 wide is w. that leads to deaths; 132: 50 the Lord will make a w. for escape.

Moses 4: 31 flaming sword turned every w. to keep w. of tree of life; 6: 13, 21, 41 patriarchs teach sons in w. of the Lord.

WAYSIDE (see also Way)

D&C 24: 15 elders should cleanse feet by w. as testimony.

WEAK, WEAKNESS (see also Fault; Feeble; Humble; Infirmity; Strengthen)

D&C 1: 19 w. things of world shall break the strong; 1: 23 the w. to preach gospel to kings; 1: 24 commandments given to the Lord's servants in their w.; 35: 13 (133: 59) the w. to thrash nations by power of Spirit; 35: 17 Joseph Smith blessed in w.; 50: 16 the w. to be made strong; 62: 1 Christ knows w. of man and how to succor; 81: 5 succor the w.; 84: 106 he who is strong in Spirit shall take with him the w.; 86: 6 your faith is w.; 89: 3 Word of Wisdom adapted to capacity of the w. and weakest; 124: 1 the Lord to show forth wisdom through w. things of earth; 133: 58 the Lord sent gospel to prepare the w. for things which are coming; 135: 5 because thou hast seen thy w., thou shalt be made strong.

WEALTH (see also Gain; Money; Rich; Riches; TG Wealth)

D&C 111: 4 w. of city to be given to saints.

WEAPON (see also Bow [noun]; Dart; Sword)

D&C 71: 9 (109: 25) no w. formed against elders shall prosper; 109: 66 remnants of Jacob to lay down w.

WEAR (see also Apparel; Garment; Stiff-neckedness)

D&C 123: 13 saints to w. out lives bringing things of darkness to light.

WEARY

D&C 64: 33 be not w. in well-doing; 84: 80 he who preaches gospel shall not be w. in mind; 88: 124 retire to bed early, that you may not be w.; 89: 20 those who follow Word of Wisdom shall run and not be w.; 124: 23 good house to be built that w. traveler may find health, safety.

WEEK (see also Time)

D&C 88: 44 planets give light to each other in their days, w., months.

WEEP, WEPT, WEEPING (see also Cry; Lament; Mourn; Sorrow; Wailing)

D&C 19: 5 (29: 15; 101: 91; 133: 73) w. and wailing among the wicked; 21: 8 w. for Zion; 42: 45 w. for loss of those who die; 45: 53 Jews to w. because of iniquities; 76: 26 heavens w. over Lucifer; 112: 24 day of w. shall come upon earth; 128: 23 solid rocks w. for joy.

Moses 7: 28–29 God of heaven w.; 7: 41 Enoch² w. because of people's wickedness and misery; 7: 49, 59 when Enoch² hears earth mourn, he w.

WEIGHT (see also Weighty)

D&C 63: 66 those who overcome by patience receive more exceeding and eternal w. of glory; 123: 7 earth groans under w. of iniquity; 132: 16 ministering angels serve those worthy of far more, and an eternal w. of glory.

WEIGHTY (see also Weight)

D&C 117: 8 you covet the drop and neglect more w. matters.

WELDING (see also Seal)

D&C 128: 18 w. link between fathers and children is necessary.

WELL (see also Fountain)

D&C 63: 23 mysteries of the kingdom shall be w. of living water.

WELL-DOING (see also Righteousness)

D&C 64: 33 be not weary in w-doing.

WELTON, MICAH B.

D&C 75: 36 to preach with Eden Smith.

WEST, WESTERN (see also North)

D&C 42: 64 teach converts to flee to w.; 45: 64 elders called to assemble in w. countries; sec. 128 will of the Lord concerning saints' journey to w.

WHALE (see also Animal; BD Whale)

Moses 2: 21 (Abr. 4: 21) God created great w.

WHEAT (*see also* Grain)

D&C 86: 1 parable of *w*. and tares explained; 89: 17 *w*. for man; 101: 65 the Lord to gather his people according to parable of *w*. and tares.

WHERE

D&C 25: 15 keep commandments, or *w*. I am you cannot come; 27: 18 be faithful, and I am ye shall be; 29: 29 devil and his angels cannot come *w*. the Lord is; 105: 5 many will say, *w*. is that God; 132: 23 *w*. the Lord is, there shall be they who receive him in world.

WHIRLWIND (*see also* Destruction; Storm; Tempest; Wind)

D&C 6: day of wrath shall come upon the rebellious as *w*.; 97: 22 (112: 24) vengeance comes as a *w*.

Abr. 2: 7 the Lord tells mountains to depart, and they are taken away by *w*.

WHISPER (*see also* Speak)

D&C 85: 6 still small voice *w*. through and pierces all things.

WHITE, WHITER, WHITENESS (*see also* Brightness; Clean; Pure)

D&C 4: 4 (6: 3; 11: 3; 12: 3; 14: 3; 33: 3, 7) fields are *w*. already to harvest; 20: 6 angel's garments were *w*. above all other; 31: 4 reap in field which is *w*., already to be burned; 110: 3 hair of the Lord's head was *w*. like snow; 130: 10–11 *w*. stone given to each who enters celestial kingdom.

JS-H 1: 31–32 robe and whole person of Moroni[a] are exceedingly *w*.

WHITLOCK, HARVEY

D&C 52: 25 to journey, preaching by the way.

WHITMER, DAVID

D&C secs. 14, 17–18 revelations to; 14: Intro. one of Three Witnesses; 14: 8 to stand as witness, declare repentance; 18: 9 has been called as was Paul; 18: 37 is called to search out twelve apostles; 30: 1 fears man and does not rely on the Lord; 30: 2 mind is on things of earth; 52: 25 to journey to Missouri.

WHITMER, JOHN

D&C secs. 15, 26, 30 revelations to; 15: Intro. one of Eight Witnesses; 30: 9 is called to proclaim gospel; 30: 11 whole labor of J.W. to be in Zion; sec. 47 (69: 3–8) named as church historian and recorder; 69: 1–2 to accompany Oliver Cowdery in taking manuscript of revela-

tions to Independence; 70: 1 is steward over revelations and commandments.

WHITMER, PETER, JR.

D&C secs. 16, 30 revelations to; 16: Intro. one of Eight Witnesses; 30: 5 is called to journey with Oliver Cowdery; 30: 6 to share Oliver Cowdery's afflictions.

WHITMER, PETER, SR.

D&C 14: Intro. Joseph Smith lived at home of; secs. 21, 34 revelations given at home ot.

WHITNEY, NEWEL K.

D&C 63: 42–46 (64: 26) to retain store and act as agent; 72: 8 is called to be bishop; 84: 112 to travel and administer to the poor; 84: 114 to go to New York City, Albany, Boston; 93: 50 needs to be chastened and to set family in order; 96: 2 in charge of temple lot at Kirtland; 104: 39–42 stewardship of; sec. 117 revelation on duties of; 117: 1 to settle business and journey from Kirtland; 117: 4 to repent of covetous desires; 117: 11 is warned about secret abominations; 117: 11 to be bishop in Adam-ondi-Ahman.

WHOLESOME (*see also* Health)

D&C 89: 10 *w*. herbs for use of man.

WHORE (*see also* Adultery; Church, Great and Abominable; Fornication; Lust; Whoremonger; TG Sexual Immorality; Whore, Whoredom)

D&C 29: 21 *w*. of earth shall be cast down; 86: 3 the *w*. is Babylon.

WHOREMONGER (*see also* Whore)

D&C 63: 17 *w*. shall have part in burning lake; 76: 103 *w*. will inherit telestial glory.

WICKED, WICKEDNESS (*see also* Apostasy; Babylon; Carnal; Crooked; Deceit; Destruction; Devil; Disobedience; Evil; Filthiness; Hell; Hypocrisy; Iniquity; Injustice; Judgment; Lust; Lying; Rebel; Sin; Transgression; Unclean; Ungodliness; Unholy; Unjust; Unrighteous; Unworthiness; World; TG Wickedness, Wicked)

D&C 1: 9 wrath of God to be poured out upon the *w*.; 26 records kept back because of *w*.; 10: 8 *w*. men took translation; 10: 21 hearts are corrupt and full of *w*.; 10: 37 men cannot always tell the *w*. from the righteous; 29: 8, 18–20 tribulation to be sent upon the *w*.; 29: 9 (64: 24; 133: 64) the *w*. shall be as stubble; 29: 9 *w*. shall not be upon earth; 29: 17 venance on the *w.*, for they will not repent; 9: 27–28, 41 (63: 34, 54) the *w.* depart into everlasting fire; 29: 27 the *w.* on the Lord's left hand to be ashamed before Father; 34: 9 great destructions await the *w.*; 38: 5 the *w.* kept in chains of darkness until judgment; 38: 30 treasure up wisdom lest *w.* of men reveals things; 38: 42 go out from among the *w.*; 43: 33 (63: 54) the *w.* to go into unquenchable fire until judgment; 45: 32 *w.* men to curse God and die of scourge; 45: 67, 70 the *w.* will fear Zion; 60: 8, 13–14 (61: 33; 62: 5; 68: 1) preach among congregations of the *w.*; 61: 8 elders are chastened that they might not perish in *w.*; 63: 2, 32 the Lord's anger kindled against the *w.*; 63: 6 let the *w.* take heed; 63: 33 the *w.* shall slay the *w.*; 63: 37 (88: 85) desolation of abomination awaits the *w.*; 63: 54 separation of the righteous and the *w.* at the Lord's coming; 63: 54 angels to cast the *w.* into unquenchable fire; 68: 31 children of saints are growing up in *w.*; 84: 53 (101: 95) by this you may know the righteous from the *w.*; 93: 25 Satan, the *w.* one; 93: 39 the *w.* one takes away light and truth; 97: 21 let Zion rejoice while the *w.* mourn; 98: 9 when the *w.* rule, the people mourn; 101: 90 stewards will be cut off; 133: 14 *w.*, which is spiritual Babylon; 136: 39 the *w.* condemned by death of prophet; 138: 29 unto the *w.* the Lord did not go.

Moses 1: 23 account of Moses' meeting with Satan is not had among men because of *w.*; 5: 31 Cain glories in his *w.*; 7: 36 among all God's workmanship there has not been so great *w.* as among brethren of Enoch²; 7: 41 Enoch² looks upon *w.* of men and weeps; 7: 48 earth is weary because of *w.* of men; 7: 66 great tribulations to be among the *w.*; 8: 22 God sees that *w.* has become great in day of Noah¹.

WIDE (*see also* Broad)

D&C 38: 1 Christ looked upon *w.* expanse of eternity; 122: 7 if jaws of hell gape open *w.*, it shall be for thy good; 132: 25 *w.* is way that leads to the deaths.

Moses 7: 41 heart of Enoch² swells *w.* as eternity.

WIDOW (*see also* Needy; Orphan)

D&C 83: 6 *w.* and orphans shall be provided for; 123: 9 saints owe duty to *w.* of those murdered by persecutors; 136: 8 each company to bear equal proportion in taking the poor, the *w.*

WIFE, WIVES (*see also* Companion; Fam-

ily; Husband; Marriage; Mother; Woman; TG Marriage, Wives)

D&C 19: 25 thou shalt not covet neighbor's *w.*; 25: 5, 13–15 *w*'s calling to comfort husband; 42: 22 love *w.* with whole heart; 49: 16 have one *w.*; 74: 1 unbelieving husband is sanctified by *w.*; 83: 2 women have claim on husbands for maintenance; 132: 1, 37–39 ancient prophets were given many *w.*; 132: 19 if man marry *w.* by new and everlasting covenant, they shall come forth in first resurrection.

Moses 3: 24 (Abr. 5: 18) man shall cleave unto his *w.*; 4: 26 (5: 4) Adam calls his *w*'s name Eve; **Abr.** 2: 2 Abraham takes Sarai to *w.*

WIGHT, LYMAN

D&C 52: 7 to journey to Missouri; 52: 12 warned of Satan; 103: Intro. arrives in Kirtland; 103: 30 to gather company to go to Zion; 124: 18–19 to continue preaching in meekness; 124: 22–24, 60, 62, 70 to help in building Nauvoo House.

WIGHT'S FERRY

D&C sec. 116 revelation given near.

WILD (*see also* Beast; Wilderness)

D&C 109: 65 remnant of Jacob to be converted from *w.* and savage condition.

Moses 6: 38 a *w.* man hath come among us.

WILDERNESS (*see also* Darkness, Spiritual; Desolation)

D&C 5: 14 (33: 5; 109: 73) the Lord's church to come forth out of *w.*; 17: 1 miraculous directors given to Lehi in *w.*; 49: 24 Jacob shall flourish in *w.*; 84: 23 Moses taught children of Israel in *w.*; 86: 3 tares drive church into *w.*; 88: 66 voice crying in *w.*; 124: 38 Israel bore tabernacle in *w.*; 128: 20 voice of Peter, James, and John in *w.*; 133: 68 the Lord makes the rivers a *w.*

Moses 7: 3 roar of lions heard out of *w.*

WILL (*see also* Agency; Desire; Intent; Pleasure; Purpose; Willing; TG Will)

D&C 3: 4 one who follows his own *w.* must fall; 19: 2, 24 Christ accomplished *w.* of Father; 20: 24 Christ ascended to reign according to *w.* of Father; 29: 40 Adam became subject to *w.* of devil; 31: 13 these words are of Christ, by *w.* of Father; 46: 30 he who asks in Spirit asks according to *w.* of God; 58: 20 let God rule him who judges, according to counsel of his own *w.*; 58: 27 men should do many things of own free *w.*; 63: 20 he who does the Lord's *w.* shall overcome; 63: 22 the Lord will make known his *w.* not by commandment; 64: 29 whatever ye do according to the Lord's *w.* is the Lord's business; 68: 4 whatsoever elders speak shall be *w.* of the Lord; 76: 10 secrets of divine *w.* to be made known; 88: 1 elders assemble to receive the Lord's *w.*; 88: 35 that which *w.* to abide in sin cannot be sanctified; 89: 2 Word of Wisdom shows forth order and *w.* of God; 124: 5 Holy Ghost to know the Lord's *w.*; 124: 89 if he will do my *w.*, let him hearken to counsel; 133: 60–61 the Lord's *w.* that commandments go to all children.

WILLIAMS, FREDERICK G.

D&C 64: 21 not to sell farm; 81: Intro. (90: 19) is called to be high priest and counselor to Joseph Smith; 90: 6 is equal with Joseph Smith in holding keys; 90: 19 home to be provided for family of; sec. 92 revelation to; 92: 1 to be received into United Order; 93: 41-43 is condemned for failure to teach family; 93: 52–53 instructions given to; 102: 3 a president of the high council; 104: 27, 29 house given to.

WILLIAMS, SAMUEL.

D&C 124: 137 member of elders quorum presidency.

WILLING, WILLINGNESS (*see also* Desire; Will)

D&C 20: 37, 77 those who receive baptism and sacrament witness they are *w.* to take name of Son; 64: 34 the Lord requires heart and *w.* mind; 88: 32 they who remain shall enjoy that which they are *w.* to receive because they were not *w.* to enjoy that which they might have received; 97: 8 those who are *w.* to observe covenants by sacrifice; 101: 63 churches must be *w.* to be guided in right and proper way.

WILSON, CALVES

D&C 75: 15 is called to proclaim gospel in west.

WILSON, DUNBAR

D&C 124: 132 member of high council.

WIND (*see also* Storm; Tempest; Whirlwind)

D&C 90: 5 men to beware how they hold God's oracles, lest they fall when *w.* blow; 109: 37 let thy house be filled, as with rushing mighty *w.*; 133: 7 saints to gather out from four *w.*

Abr. 2: 7 the Lord causes *w.* and fire to be his chariot.

WINE (*see also* Drink; Drunken; Grape; Sacrament; Wine-press; Word of Wisdom)

D&C 20: 40 apostles to administer bread and *w.* of sacrament; 20: 75 church to partake of bread and *w.*; 20: 78 mode of administering sacramental *w.*; 27: 3–4 saints not to purchase *w.* from enemies; 35: 11 (88: 94, 105) Babylon makes nations drink of *w.* of wrath of her fornication; 89: 5 not good for any man to drink *w.*; 89: 6 pure *w.* of grape of vine should be used in sacrament.

WINE-PRESS (*see also* Wine)

D&C 76: 107 (88: 106; 133: 48, 50) Christ has trodden *w-p.* alone.

WING

D&C 10: 65 (29: 2; 43: 24) the Lord would gather his people as hen gathers chickens under her *w.*; 77: 4 beast's *w.* are representation of power; 88: 45 earth rolls upon her *w.*; 124: 18 the Lord will bear his servant as on eagles' *w.*; 124: 99 mount up in imagination as upon eagles' *w.*

WINTER

D&C 89: 13 flesh should not be used, only in times of *w.*
JS-M 1: 17 (Matt. 24: 20) pray that flight be not in *w.*

WINTER QUARTERS—*Omaha, Nebraska* (*see also* D&C map, p. 297)

D&C 136 revelation given at.

WISDOM, WISE, WISELY (*see also* God, Wisdom of; Knowledge; Learning; Prudence; Understand)

D&C 1: 26 those who seek *w.* shall be instructed; 5: 9 sacred things reserved for *w.* purpose; 6: 7 (11: 7) seek not for riches, but for *w.*; 9: 3, 6 be patient, for it is *w.* in me that I have dealt with you in this manner; 10: 34–37 (19: 21) *w.* not to show manuscript to world; 19: 41 conduct thyself *w.* before the Lord; 28: 5 Oliver Cowdery to write by way of *w.*, not commandment; 38: 30 treasure up *w.* in bosoms; 42: 68 (James 1: 5) he who lacks *w.*, let him ask of God; 45: 57 they who are *w.* shall abide the Lord's coming; 46: 17 spiritual gift of word of *w.*; 46: 18 word of knowledge given that all may be taught to be *w.*; 50: 1 hearken to words of *w.* to be given; 51: 19 *w.* steward shall enter joy of the Lord; 52: 17 bring forth fruits of praise and *w.*; 58: 26 he who is compelled in all things is not *w.* servant; 63: 54 foolish virgins among the *w.*; 72: 4 he who is *w.* in time is worthy to inherit Father's mansions; 76: 9 *w.* of those who serve the Lord shall be great; 76: 9 *w.* of the wise shall perish; 78: 2 he who has ordained you from on high shall speak words of *w.*; 82: 22 *w.* to make friends with mammon of unrighteousness; 88: 40 *w.* receives *w.*; 88: 118 (109: 7) teach one another words of *w.*; sec. 89 Word of W.; 97: 1 many are seeking diligently to learn *w.*; 98: 10 honest and *w.* men should be sought; 101: 61 blessing of being *w.* steward in the Lord's house; 101: 80 the Lord established Constitution by *w.* men; 105: 23 reveal not things the Lord has revealed until it is *w.* in him that they be revealed; 111: 11 be as *w.* as serpents; 124: 1 prophet raised to show *w.* through weak things; 128: 18 things kept hid from the *w.* shall be revealed; 133: 58 weak shall confound the *w.*; 136: 32 the ignorant to learn *w.* by humbling himself.

Abr. 1: 26 Pharaoh judges his people *w.*; 3: 21 God's *w.* excelleth them all; **JS-H** 1: 11–13, 26 (James 1: 5) if any of you lack *w.*, let him ask of God.

WITHDRAW, WITHDRAWN (*see also* Darkness, Spiritual; Excommunication; Shrink; Spirit, Holy)

D&C 121: 37 when man exercises unrighteous dominion, heavens *w.* themselves; 134: 10 religious societies can only *w.* fellowship from members.

Moses 1: 15 Spirit has not altogether *w.* from Moses; **Abr.** 2: 12 the Lord has *w.* from speaking to Abraham.

WITHER, WITHERED

Moses 1: 11 Moses would have been *w.* if natural eyes had seen God.

WITHHOLD, WITHHELD (*see also* Hinder; Hold; Keep; Reserve; Retain; Stay; Stop)

D&C 25: 4 things not seen are *w.* from world; 64: 16 Spirit is *w.* because elders sought evil; 70: 14 manifestations of Spirit will be *w.* if saints are not equal in temporal things; 121: 28 time to come in which nothing shall be *w.*; 133: 49 moon shall *w.* its light.

Moses 7: 51 the Lord could not *w.* from Enoch².

WITHSTAND, WITHSTOOD (*see also* Overcome; Reject; Resist)

D&C 27: 15 take the Lord's armor, that you may be able to *w.* evil day.

WITNESS (*see also* Apostle; Baptism; Convince; Prove; Record; Revelation; See; Testified; Witnesses; Three; TG Witness; Witness of the Father)

D&C 5: Intro. *w.* to Book of Mormon; 5: 2 (14: 8) Joseph Smith to stand as *w.* of plates; 6: 23 what greater *w.* can God give; 6: 28 (128: 3) every word to be established by two or three *w.*; 14: 8 Holy Ghost gives utterance, to stand as *w.*; 20: 13 world judged by *w.*; 20: 16 elders bear *w.* to Majesty on high; 20: 77, 79 partakers of sacrament *w.* they will take Christ's name, keep commandments, remember him; 27: 12 (107: 23, 26) apostles are especial *w.* of the Lord's name; 42: 80–81 at trial of adulterer, two or more *w.* required; 77: 15 two *w.* are two prophets raised to Jewish nation; 107: 25 seventies are special *w.*; 127: 6 (128: 2) recorder to be eye-*w.* to baptisms; 136: 40 the Lord has left a *w.* of his name.

WITNESSES, THREE (*see also* Book of Mormon; Cowdery, Oliver; Harris, Martin; Whitmer, David; Witness)

D&C 17: 7 T.W. receive same power and gift as Joseph Smith; 20: 10 ministering of angels to T.W.

WIVES (*see* Wife)

WOLF, WOLVES (*see also* Animal; Primal; Prophets, False)

D&C 122: 6 enemies prowl like *w.*

WOMAN, WOMEN (*see also* Creation; Daughter; Eve; Female; Mother; Wife; TG Woman)

D&C 18: 42 all men, *w.*, and children must repent and be baptized; 42: 73 (63: 16) to lust after *w.* is to deny faith; 42: 84 man or *w.* who robs should be delivered to civil law; 49: 22 Son of Man comes not in form of *w.*; 83: 2 *w.* have claim on husbands for maintenance; 101: 81 parable of *w.* and unjust judge; 136: 35 days of sorrow come like *w.* taken in travail.

Moses 3: 22 (Abr. 5: 16) God makes *w.* from Adam's rib; 3: 23 she shall be called W. because she was taken out of man; 4: 7–12 *w.* was beguiled by serpent in Garden of Eden; 4: 26 the Lord has called the first of all *w.* Eve, which are many; **Abr.** 1: 23–24 Egypt first discovered by *w.*

WOMB

D&C 84: 27 John the Baptist was filled with Holy Ghost from mother's *w.*

WONDER, WONDERFUL (*see also* Marvel; Miracle; Sign)

D&C 35: 8 the Lord shows *w.* to those who believe; 45: 40 those who fear the Lord will see *w.*; 65: 4 make known the Lord's *w.* works; 76: 5–8 *w.* of eternity to be shown to those who fear and serve the Lord; 84: 66 believers shall do many *w.* works; 128: 23 seas and lands tell the *w.* of Eternal King.

WOOD (*see also* Timber; Woods)

Abr. 1: 11 virgins are sacrificed because they will not worship gods of *w.*

WOODRUFF, WILFORD

D&C 118: 6 (124: 129) is called to fill position in Council of Twelve; 136: 13 to organize a company for journey west; 138: 53 among choice ones in spirit world; OD-1 issues manifesto against practicing plural marriage.

WOODS (*see also* Wilderness; Wood)

JS-H 1: 14, 68 Joseph Smith retires to *w.* to pray.

WORD (*see also* Language; Lips; Mouth; Read; Sayings; Tongue; Utter; Voice; Word of God/Word of the Lord; TG Word)

D&C 21: 4–5 receive prophets' *w.* as though from the Lord's own mouth; 42: 80 every *w.* against adulterer shall be established by two or three witnesses; 46: 17 to some is given *w.* of wisdom; 50: 17 he who preaches *w.* of truth preaches by Spirit of truth; 63: 58 day of warning, not of many *w.*; 84: 85 treasure up in minds the *w.* of life; 88: 118 (109: 14) teach one another *w.* of wisdom; sec. 89 the *W.* of Wisdom; 93: 8 in the beginning the *w.* was; 112: 8 the high shall be brought low by elders' *w.*; 130: 11 new name is key *w.*; 131: 5 (2 Pet. 1: 19) more sure *w.* of prophecy explained; 136: 24 let your *w.* tend to edifying one another.

Moses 6: 59 men must be born again and enjoy *w.* of eternal life; **Abr.** Fac. 2, figs. 3, 7 figure represents grand Key-*w.* of Holy Priesthood.

WORD OF GOD/WORD OF THE LORD (*see also* Gospel; Revelation; Word; TG Word of God; Word of the Lord)

D&C 1: 38 (56: 11) the Lord's *w.* shall not pass away; 3: 7 men despise God's *w.*; 5: 6 deliver the Lord's *w.* unto children of men; 5: 10 this generation shall have the Lord's *w.* through Joseph Smith; 5: 20 the Lord's *w.* shall be verified; 6: 2 (11: 2; 12: 2; 14: 2; 33: 1) the Lord's *w.* is sharper than two-edged sword; 11: 16 knowledge of doctrine through the Lord's *w.*; 11: 21–22 seek first to obtain my *w.*; 11: 22 study the Lord's *w.*; 18: 34 these *w.* are not of men, but of Christ; 18: 36 testify you know Christ's *w.*; 19: 23 listen to Christ's *w.*; 19: 26 *w.* of God in Book of Mormon; 29: 30 *w.* gone forth out of the Lord's mouth shall be fulfilled; 39: 16 the Lord cannot deny his *w.*; 41: 12 the Lord's *w.* to be answered upon souls in day of judgment; 42: 6 declare *w.* like angels; 60: 7–8, 13–14 (61: 33) declare *w.* among congregations of the wicked; 64: 31 the Lord's *w.* are sure and shall not fail; 68: 4 what elders speak when moved upon by Holy Ghost is *w.* of the Lord; 84: 44 (98: 11) live by every *w.* that proceeds from mouth of God; 84: 45 *w.* of the Lord is truth; 93: 8 in the beginning the *w.* was; 96: 5 the Lord's *w.* to go forth; 124: 128 Twelve to send the Lord's *w.* to every creature; 132: 12 no man shall come unto Father but by the Lord or his *w.*; 138: 37 spirits of transgressors also to hear the Lord's *w.*

Moses 1: 1, 3–7 the *w.* of God, which he spake unto Moses; 1: 4 *w.* of God never cease; 1: 32 (2: 5) God created worlds by *w.* in his power, which is his Son; 1: 38 no end to God's *w.*; 1: 41 when men take God's *w.* from book, he will raise up another like Moses, and he shall be read again; 4: 30 the Lord's *w.* cannot return void; 6: 47 as Enoch[2] speaks *w.* of God, the people tremble; 7: 13 Enoch[2] speaks *w.* of God, and earth trembles; **JS-M** 1: 35 heaven and earth shall pass away, yet the Lord's *w.* shall not pass away; 1: 37 whoso treasures up the Lord's *w.* shall not be deceived.

WORD OF WISDOM (*see also* Abstinence; Drunken; Food; Health; Meat; Temperance; Tobacco; Wine)

D&C sec. 89 a *W. of W.* showing order and will of God in temporal salvation of saints.

WORK, WORKS [noun] (*see also* Act; Creation; Deed; Faithful; Fruit; Grace; Judgment; Repentance; Serve; Working; Workings; Workmanship)

D&C 1: 10 (112: 34) the Lord to recompense unto every man according to his *w.*; 3: 1 *w.* of God cannot be frustrated; 3: 16 God's *w.* shall go forth; 4: 1 (6: 1; 11: 1; 12: 1; 14: 1) marvelous *w.* is about to come forth; 4: 3 if ye have desires to serve God, ye are called to the *w.*; 8: 8 doubt not, for it is the *w.* of God; 8: 8 (84: 66) you shall do marvelous *w.*; 9: 14 stand fast in the *w.* wherewith the Lord has called you; 10: 43 the Lord will not suffer that the wicked shall destroy his *w*.; 10: 61 the Lord will bring to light the *w*. of his other sheep; 11: 9 Hyrum Smith to assist in bringing forth the Lord's *w*.; 11: 20 this is your *w*., to keep my commandments; 17: 4 the Lord to bring about his righteous purposes in this *w*.; 18: 38 by their *w*. you shall know them; 19: 3 (76: 111; 112: 34) every man to be judged according to his *w*.; 20: 37 baptismal candidates must manifest by *w*. they have received Spirit; 29: 33 the Lord's *w*. have no end, neither beginning; 38: 33 the Lord have a great *w*. laid up in store; 42: 40 beauty of garments should be *w*. of your own hands; 52: 11 I will cut my *w*. short in righteousness; 59: 2 *w*. of those who die in Zion will follow them; 59: 23 he who does *w*. of righteousness shall receive reward; 63: 11 signs come by faith unto mighty *w*.; 64: 33 ye are laying foundation of a great *w*.; 65: 4 make known God's wonderful *w*.; 76: 114 how great and marvelous are *w*. of the Lord; 84: 66 in the Lord's name believers shall do wonderful *w*.; 88: 73 the Lord will hasten his *w*. in its time; 97: 6 *w*. of those to be chastened shall be made known; 101: 100 bring forth fruit and *w*. meet for my kingdom; 105: 24 boast not of mighty *w*.; 121: 24–25 time of judgment appointed for every man according to his *w*.; 124: 48 by your *w*. ye bring cursings; 132: 32 do the *w*. of Abraham; 138: 48 great *w*. to be done in temples; 138: 53 choice spirits reserved to take part in latter-day *w*.

Moses 1: 6 the Lord has a *w*. for Moses; 1: 39 this is my *w*. and my glory; 3: 2–3 (Abr. 5: 2) on seventh day God ended his *w*. and rested from all his *w*.

WORK [verb] (*see also* Labor; Perform; Strive; Work [noun]; Working, Workings; Workmanship; Wrought; tg Work, Value of)

D&C 90: 24 (98: 3; 100: 15; 105: 40) all things shall *w*. together for your good.

WORKING, WORKINGS (*see also* Work [noun]; Work [verb])

D&C 46: 21 to some is given the *w*. of miracles; 121: 12 the Lord blinds minds, that they understand not his marvelous *w*.

WORKMANSHIP (*see also* Creation; Work [noun])

D&C 29: 25 not one hair shall be lost, for it is *w*. of the Lord's hand; 109: 4 house of the Lord, the *w*. of saints' hands.

Moses 1: 4 God shows Moses all *w*. of his hands; 7: 32 men are *w*. of God's

hands; 7: 37, 40 all *w*. of God's hands weep over the wicked.

WORLD (*see also* Babylon; Creation; Earth; Flesh; Man; Nature, Natural; Spirit World; Temporal; Wicked; tg World; World, End of; Worldliness)

D&C 1: 16 image of men's God is in likeness of *w*.; 10: 70 (11: 38; 12: 9; 34: 2; 39: 2) the Lord is light and life of *w*.; 18: 6 *w*. is ripening in iniquity; 19: 1 Christ is Redeemer of *w*.; 19: 3 Satan and his works to be destroyed at end of *w*.; 21: 9 Christ crucified for sins of *w*.; 23: 2 make known thy calling before *w*.; 23: 6 pray vocally before *w*.; 24: 10 continue in bearing the Lord's name before *w*.; 25: 10 lay aside things of this *w*.; 29: 4 elders are chosen out of the *w*. to declare gospel; 34: 3 Christ so loved *w*. that he gave his life; 39: 7 James Covill has rejected the Lord because of cares of *w*.; 42: 89 trial of offenders not to be before *w*.; 45: 22 ye say ye know end of *w*. comes; 49: 17 man's creation before *w*. was made; 49: 20 (84: 49) *w*. lies in sin; 50: 8 those cut off by church are overcome by *w*.; 50: 41 the Lord has overcome *w*.; 53: 2 forsake the *w*.; 59: 9 keep thyself unspotted from *w*.; 59: 23 he who does works of righteousness will receive peace in this *w*.; 63: 47 he who is faithful and endures shall overcome *w*.; 64: 2 elders to overcome *w*.; 76: 12–13 vision of things which were before *w*. was; 76: 24 (93: 9–10) *w*. are made and created by Son; 76: 39 Lamb was in bosom of Father before *w*. were made; 76: 41 Christ came to bear sins of *w*.; 76: 112 *w*. without end; 84: 41 he who breaks covenant of priesthood will receive no forgiveness of sin in this *w*. nor in *w*. to come; 84: 53 *w*. groans under sin and darkness; 84: 62 ye out into *w*.; 84: 75 revelation is in force upon all *w*.; 84: 79 the Lord sends elders out to prove *w*.; 84: 87 the Lord sends elders out to reprove *w*.; 86: 9 lawful heirs been hid from *w*. with Christ; 95: 13 saints should not live after manner of *w*.; 101: 36 in this *w*. man's joy is not full; 121: 32 that which was ordained before this *w*.; 121: 35 men's hearts are set so much upon things of this *w*.; 127: 11 prince of *w*. comes; 132: 49 I will be with thee to end of *w*.; 138: 2 atoning sacrifice for redemption of *w*.

Moses 1: 7–8 God shows Moses this *w*. and then of thereof; 1: 33, 35 *w*. without number has God created; 1: 35 many *w*. have passed away; 1: 35 *w*. are numbered unto God; 4: 6 Satan seeks to destroy the *w*.; 5: 24 Cain was before in end of *w*.; 6: 7 same priesthood shall be in end of *w*.; 6:

51 I am God, I made the w.; 6: 59 men are born into w. by water, spirit, and blood; 7: 4 the Lord shows Enoch² the w. for many generations; 7: 67 the Lord shows Enoch² all things to end of w.; **Abr.** 3: 22 Abraham sees intelligences organized before w. was; **JS-M** 1: 4 (Matt. 24: 3) what is sign of end of w.; 1: 31 gospel of kingdom shall be preached in w.

WORM (see also Corrupt, Corruption)

D&C 76: 44 sons of perdition go where their w. dies not.

WORSHIP (see also Assemble; Bow [verb]; Fear of God; Idolatry; Meet, Meeting; Praise; Religion; Reverence; Serve; TG Worship)

D&C 18: 40 (20: 29) w. Father in name of Jesus Christ; 20: 19 God is only being whom men should w.; 42: 35 (115: 8) lands to be purchased for building houses of w.; 76: 21 those are sanctified who w. God and Lamb forever; 93: 19 sayings of John given, that saints may know how to w., what they w.; 133: 39 w. him who made heaven and earth, sea, and fountains of waters; 134: 4 human law has no right to prescribe rules of w.

Moses 1: 12 Satan tempts Moses to w. him; 1: 15 God commanded Moses to w. only him; 1: 20 Moses will w. only God; 5: 5 the Lord commands Adam and Eve to w. him; 6: 49 Satan tempts men to w. him; **Abr.** 1: 1 virgins are sacrificed because they will not w. idols; **A of F** 11 we claim privilege of w. God according to dictates of own conscience.

WORTH (see also Esteem; Merit; Precious; Respect; Worthy; TG Worth of Souls)

D&C 15: 6 (16: 6) thing of most w. is to declare repentance; 18: 10 w. of souls is great.

WORTHY, WORTHINESS (see also Clean; Faithful; Honorable; Noble; Righteousness; Uprightness)

D&C 31: 5 (70: 12; 84: 79; 106: 3) laborer is w. of his hire; 50: 34 let him rejoice who is accounted w. of God; 51: 4 he shall hold inheritance until he transgresses and is not accounted w.; 68: 15 bishops shall be high priests who are w.; 98: 14–15 saints must abide in covenant to be found w.; 105: 35 let those be chosen who are w.; 107: 100 slothful shall not be counted w. to stand; 119: 5 those who are not tithed shall not be found w. to abide among saints; 128: 24 saints to present book w. of all acceptation; 132: 16 ministering angels serve those w. of eternal weight of glory; 136: 31 he who

will not bear chastisement is not w. of the Lord's kingdom; OD-2 priesthood extended to all w. male members.

WOUND, WOUNDED (see also Bruise; Hurt; Jesus Christ, Death of)

D&C 6: 37 behold w. which pierced my side; 45: 51 Jews to see Savior's w.; 45: 52 these w. are w. with which I was w. in house of friends.

Moses 5: 47 Lamech¹ has slain a man to his own wounding.

WRATH (see also Anger; Destruction; Displeasure; Fury; Indignation; Judgment; Punishment; Rage)

D&C 1: 9 (63: 6; 103: 2) w. of God shall be poured out upon the wicked; 19: 15 repent lest I strike you by my w.; 35: 11 (88: 94, 105) Babylon has made nations drink of wine of w. of her fornication; 43: 26 cup of w. of the Lord's indignation is full; 56: 1 the rebellious shall know God's indignation in day of w.; 59: 21 against none is God's w. kindled except those who confess not his hand; 60: 1 proclaim the Lord's word not in w.; 63: 6 day of w. coming as whirlwind; 63: 11 signs given in w. to condemnation; 63: 33 the Lord has sworn in his w. and decreed wars; 76: 33 sons of perdition are vessels of w.; 76: 104 telestial beings suffer w. of God on earth; 84: 24 the Lord in his w. swore that Israelites should not enter his rest; 87: 6 inhabitants of the earth to feel w. of Almighty God; 88: 85 labor that saints' souls may escape w. of God; 88: 88 after elders' testimony comes w.; 98: 22 if saints do what the Lord commands, he will turn away all w.; 101: 9 in day of w. the Lord will remember mercy; 112: 24 day of w. comes speedily; 115: 6 gathering to be refuge from w.

Moses 7: 1 those who believed not look with fear for fiery indignation of w. of God to be poured out upon them.

WREST (see also Pervert; Scriptures)

D&C 10: 63 people w. scriptures and do not understand them.

WRITE, WRITTEN (see also Book; Engravings; Language; Plates; Record; Scriptures; Writing)

D&C 9: 4 Oliver Cowdery called to w. for Joseph Smith; 18: 3 rely upon things which are w.; 24: 1 Joseph Smith chosen to w. Book of Mormon; 24: 6 it shall be given thee what to w.; 28: 5 Oliver Cowdery not to w. by way of commandment; 47: 1 John Whitmer to w. church history; 52: 17 elders to teach only what prophets and apostles have w.; 55: 14

William W. Phelps to help Oliver Cowdery select and w. school books; 58: 50 Sidney Rigdon to w. description of land of Zion; 76: 68 names of the righteous are w. in heaven; 76: 80, 113 the Lord commanded that vision be w. while they were yet in Spirit; 85: 9 those not w. in book of remembrance shall find no inheritance; 90: 32 w. this commandment; 124: 4 proclamation to be w. by power of Holy Ghost; 128: 6 dead judged out of things w. in books; 130: 11 new name w. on white stone.

Moses 1: 40–41 Moses is commanded to w. words that God speaks; 2: 1 Moses is commanded to w. concerning creation; 6: 5 children of Adam are taught to w. and read; **Abr.** 1: 31 Abraham to w. upon record of fathers for benefit of posterity; **JS-H** 1: 1 Joseph Smith w. history to disabuse public mind.

WRITING, WRITINGS (see also Write)

D&C 10: 1, 8 w. delivered to wicked men have been lost; 63: 56 Sidney Rigdon's w. is not acceptable unto the Lord; 104: 68 holy w. reserved unto the Lord for holy purposes.

WRONG, WRONGFULLY (see also Evil; Injustice)

D&C 9: 9 stupor of thought shall cause you to forget thing that is w.; 64: 20 Isaac Morley not to counsel w.; 105: 25 (134: 11) redress us of our w.

WROUGHT (see also Do; Work [verb])

D&C 76: 69 Jesus w. out perfect atonement; 138: 35 redemption w. through sacrifice of Son.

YEAR (see also Accountability, Age of; Millennium; Time)

D&C 51: 17 saints should act upon land as for y.; 64: 21 the Lord to retain strong hold in Kirtland for five y.; 77: 6, 8–12 (88: 108–109) seven thousand y. of earth's temporal existence; 84: 17 priesthood is without beginning of days or end of y.; 88: 44 plants give light to each other in their times and y.; 93: 51 elders to proclaim acceptable y. of the Lord; 121: 31 appointed days, months, and y. of heavenly bodies will be revealed; 133: 52 y. of the redeemed will be come.

YESTERDAY (see also Time; Today)

D&C 61: 20 I was angry with you y.

YIELD (see also Subject, Subjection)

D&C 5: 21 Joseph Smith to y. to persuasions of men no more; 9: 13 y.

to no temptation; 29: 40 Adam became subject to will of devil because he y.; 89: 16 that which y. fruit is good for food of man; 97: 9 the broken-hearted to be made as tree that y. much precious fruit.

Moses 2: 11–12, 29 (Abr. 4: 11–12) earth to bring forth herb y. seed, fruit of tree y. fruit; 5: 37 ground shall not y. strength.

YOKE (see also Bondage; Subject, Subjection)

D&C 109: 32, 47 saints plead for complete deliverance from y.; 123: 8 duty is iron y.

YOUNG

D&C 43: 20 call upon nations to repent, both old and y.; 105: 16 strength of the Lord's house, his y. men.

YOUNG, BRIGHAM

D&C 124: 127 called to be president over the Twelve; sec. 126 revelation to; sec. 136 revelation to church through; 138: 53 among choice ones in spirit world.

YOUNG, JOSEPH

D&C 124: 138 one of seven presidents of seventies quorum.

ZACHARIAS—father of John the Baptist

D&C 27: 7 is visited by Elias with promise of son.

ZARAHEMLA, CITY OF

D&C 125: 3 saints to build city named Z.

ZILLAH

Moses 5: 44, 46–47 wife of Lamech[1], mother of Tubal Cain.

ZION (see also Consecration, Law of; Enoch[2]; Gather; Inherit; Jackson County; Jerusalem, New; Kingdom of God; Millennium; Promised Land; Stake; Translated Beings; Zion, Mount; TG Zion, Sion; BD Zion)

D&C 6: 6 (11: 6; 12: 6; 14: 6) seek to establish the cause of Z.; 21: 7 Joseph Smith inspired to move cause of Z.; 24: 7 devote all service to Z.; 28: 9 location of city of Z. to be revealed; 28: 9 Z. to be on borders to be Lamanites; 35: 24 (39: 13) Z. shall rejoice upon the hills; 38: 4 the Lord has taken them of Enoch[3] into his bosom; 45: 66–67 New Jerusalem to be called Z.; 45: 66–71 (62: 4; 63: 24, 36; 66: 11) righteous to be gathered to Z.; 45: 68 every man who will not take his sword must flee unto Z.; 45: 70 wicked will not go up to battle against Z.; 49: 25 Z. to assemble and flourish before the Lord's coming; secs. 57–60 revelations given at Z., Jackson County, Missouri; 57: 2–3 city of Z. to be in Missouri; 58: 7 saints sent to Missouri to lay foundation of Z.; 58: 13 testimony to go forth from Z.; 58: 49 agent to receive moneys to purchase lands in Z.; 58: 50, 57 Sidney Rigdon to write of Z., to dedicate land of Z.; 59: 1–2 those who come to Z. and live will inherit earth; 59: 2 those who come to Z. and die will receive crown in Father's mansions; 59: 3 those in Z. who obey gospel will receive reward; 63: 25 the Lord holds Z. in his hands; 63: 29–31 land of Z. to be obtained by purchase or blood; 63: 36 saints to assemble upon land of Z.; 64: 22 none to be held guilty who go to Z.; 64: 34 the willing and obedient shall eat good of land of Z.; 64: 35 the rebellious shall be cut out of Z.; 64: 38–39 inhabitants of Z. to judge all things pertaining to Z.; 64: 41 Z. shall flourish and have glory of the Lord; 68: 25–26 law that parents in Z. must teach children; 68: 31 the Lord is not pleased with inhabitants of Z.; 69: 6 Z. to be sent to receive accountings; 72: 15 he who comes to Z. should lay all things before bishop; 78: 15 the Lord God, the Holy One of Z.; 82: 14 Z. must increase in beauty and holiness; 84: 56 condemnation rests upon children of Z.; 84: 58 scourge and judgment upon Z.; 84: 99–100 the Lord to bring again Z.; 84: 104 money to be gathered for establishing Z.; 90: 36 the Lord will contend with Z.; 90: 37 (101: 17) Z. not to be moved out of her place; 93: 53 translate scriptures and obtain knowledge for salvation of Z.; 94: 1 Kirtland to be stake of Z.; sec. 96 order of Kirtland stake of Z.; sec. 97 revelation concerning saints in Z.; 97: 10 house to be built unto the Lord in land of Z.; 97: 18, 25 Z. to prosper if obedient; 97: 19 Z. is the city of God; 97: 21 Z. the pure in heart; 97: 25 Z. shall escape if she observe to do all that the Lord commands; 100: 13 Z. shall be redeemed, although she is chastened; 101: 18 pure in heart shall return to Z.; 101: 20 no other place for gathering except Z.; 101: 21 stakes are strength of Z.; 101: 43 parable concerning redemption of Z.; 101: 70 land of Z. for beginning of gathering; 101: 74 Z. to be established by gathering; 101: 81 children of Z. likened unto parable of woman and unjust judge; 101: 100 conditions upon which people shall dwell in Z.; 103: 15 redemption of Z. must come by power; 103: 18 as your fathers were led at first,

so shall redemption of Z. be; 105: 5, 32 Z. cannot be built up unless by principles of law of celestial kingdom; 105: 9, 13 delay in redemption of Z. because of transgression; 105: 14 the Lord to fight battles of Z.; 105: 32 kingdom of Z. subjects of God; 105: 34 law of Z. to be executed after redemption of Z.; 107: 36–37 high council in Z.; 107: 74 bishop to be common judge in Z.; 109: 39 the righteous to be gathered and come to Z.; 109: 51 the Lord did appoint a Z. unto his people; 109: 59 we ask thee to appoint unto Z. other stakes; 111: 6 the Lord will deal mercifully with Z.; 113: 8 power of priesthood to bring again Z.; 116: 6 (124: 36) the gathering together upon land of Z. to be a defense; 119: 2 surplus property to be given to bishop for laying of foundation of Z.; 119: 5–6 law of tithing to be observed in Z., and land of Z. to be sanctified thereby; 124: 6 time has come to favor Z.; 124: 118 authorities called to lay foundation of Z.; 124: 131 high council given for corner-stone of Z.; 133: 9 elders to cry, Go forth unto land of Z.; 133: 12 Gentiles shall flee unto Z.; 133: 21 the Lord shall utter his voice out of Z.; 133: 24 Jerusalem and land of Z. shall be turned back into own place; 133: 32 those from north shall be crowned with glory in Z.; 136: 10 every man to help remove to stake of Z.; 136: 18 Z. shall be redeemed in the Lord's due time; 136: 31 the Lord's people must be tried to receive glory of Z.

Moses 7: 18 the Lord calls his people Z.; 7: 19 Enoch[2] builds city of Holiness, even Z.; 7: 21, 23 Z. is taken up into heaven; 7: 31, 47, 69 Z. is in bosom of the Lord; 7: 62 the Lord to gather elect unto city to be called Z., a New Jerusalem; 7: 64 Z. is to be the Lord's abode; 7: 68 days of Z. in days of Enoch[2] were 365 years; 7: 69 Z. is fled; **A of F** 10 Z. (the New Jerusalem) shall be built upon the American continent.

ZION, MOUNT (see also Jesus Christ, Second Coming of; Zion)

D&C 76: 56 celestial heirs are they who come unto M.Z., city of living God; 84: 2 saints to stand upon M.Z.; 84: 32 sons of Moses and Aaron[1] shall be filled with glory of the Lord upon M.Z. in the Lord's house; 133: 18, 56 the Lamb shall stand upon M.Z.

ZORAMITES —descendants of Zoram

D&C 3: 17 knowledge of Savior to come to Z.